Fodor's

CITYGUIDE
NEW YORK

3RD EDITION

FODOR'S TRAVEL PUBLICATIONS

NEW YORK • TORONTO • LONDON • SYDNEY • AUCKLAND

WWW.FODORS.COM

STREETFINDER

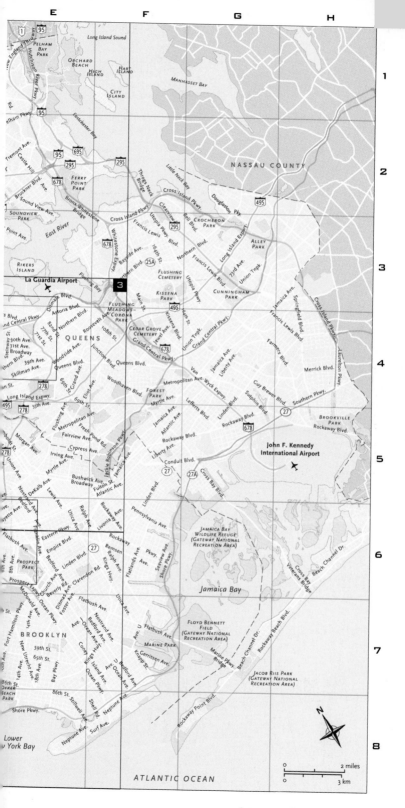

E **F** **G** **H**

Long Island Sound

1

New England Thruway
Hutchinson River Pkwy.
I-95
PELHAM BAY PARK
ORCHARD BEACH
HIGH ISLAND
HART ISLAND
CITY ISLAND
MANHASSET BAY

2

Pelham Pkwy.
I-95
Tremont Ave.
Castle Hill
I-95
I-695
I-295
I-678
I-295
FERRY POINT PARK
Throgs Neck Bridge
Cross Island Pkwy.
Little Neck Bay
Douglaston Pkwy.
I-495
NASSAU COUNTY
Bruckner Blvd.
Bronx-Whitestone Bridge
Sound View Ave.
SOUNDVIEW PARK
East River
Point Ave.

3

Whitestone Expwy.
Cross Island Pkwy.
Francis Lewis
Utopia Pkwy. Blvd.
Clearview Expwy.
Bell Blvd.
CROCHERON PARK
Northern Blvd.
Long Island Expwy.
Alley Ave.
ALLEY PARK
RIKERS ISLAND
I-678
La Guardia Airport
3
Flushing Bay
Bayside Ave.
Northern Blvd.
16th St.
25A
FLUSHING CEMETERY
Francis Lewis Blvd.
73rd Ave.
Union Tpk.
CUNNINGHAM PARK
Jamaica Ave.
Cross Island Pkwy.
Laurelton Pkwy.

4

Ditmars Blvd.
Astoria Blvd.
Northern Blvd.
and Central Pkwy.
Blvd.
30th Ave.
31st Ave.
Broadway
Steinway
77th St.
82nd St.
39th Ave.
thern Ave.
Skillman Ave.
QUEENS
Roosevelt Ave.
Woodside Ave.
108th St.
Junction Blvd.
Queens Blvd.
Main St.
KISSENA PARK
FLUSHING MEADOWS-CORONA PARK
CEDAR GROVE CEMETERY
Kissena Blvd.
I-678
Jewel Ave.
GRAND CENTRAL PKWY.
164th St.
Union Tpk.
Grand Central Pkwy.
Jamaica Ave.
Liberty Ave.
Van Wyck Expwy.
Farmers Blvd.
Springfield Blvd.
Francis Lewis Blvd.
MERRICK BLVD.
Merrick Blvd.
Guy Brewer Blvd.
Sutphin Blvd.
Southern Pkwy.

5

Long Island Expwy.
I-495
I-278
65th St.
Grand Ave.
Elliot Ave.
Woodhaven Blvd.
Metropolitan Ave.
FOREST PARK
Myrtle Ave.
Lefferts Blvd.
Linden Blvd.
Rockaway Blvd.
27
I-678
BROOKVILLE PARK
Rockaway Blvd.
55th Ave.
Flushing Ave.
Fresh Pond Rd.
Metropolitan Ave.
Fairview Ave.
Cypress Ave.
Jackie Robinson Pkwy.
Jamaica Ave.
Jamaica Ave.
Atlantic Ave.
Rockaway Blvd.
Liberty Ave.
Conduit Blvd.
27
John F. Kennedy International Airport
Morgan St.
Irving Ave.
Myrtle Ave.
I-278
BUSHWICK AVE.
Bushwick Ave.
Broadway
Fulton St.
Atlantic Ave.
Linden Blvd.
27A
Cross Bay Blvd.

6

Union Ave.
DeKalb Ave.
Lewis Ave.
Utica Ave.
Ralph Ave.
Livonia Ave.
Rockaway Ave.
Nostrand Ave.
Bedford Ave.
Eastern Pkwy.
Flatbush Ave.
PROSPECT PARK
Empire Blvd.
Bedford Ave.
Linden Blvd.
27
Remsen Ave.
Ralph Ave.
Kings Hwy.
Flatlands Ave.
Pennsylvania Ave.
Flatbush Ave.
Rockaway Pkwy.
Seaview Ave.
Shore Pkwy.
JAMAICA BAY WILDLIFE REFUGE (GATEWAY NATIONAL RECREATION AREA)
Jamaica Bay
Cross Bay Veterans Bridge
Beach Channel Dr.

7

8th Ave.
Prospect Expwy.
Ocean Pkwy.
McDonald Ave.
Church Ave.
Beverly Rd.
Ditmas Ave.
Clarendon Rd.
Foster Ave.
Flatbush Ave.
Ave.
Bedford Ave.
Ocean Ave.
Nostrand Ave.
Flatbush Ave.
Ave. U
MARINE PARK
Gerritsen Ave.
BROOKLYN
59th St.
65th St.
Fort Hamilton Pkwy.
New Utrecht Ave.
14th Ave.
18th Ave.
Bay Pkwy.
Coney Island Ave.
Ocean Pkwy.
King Hwy.
Ave. U
Ocean Ave.
Bedford Ave.
Knapp St.
FLOYD BENNETT FIELD (GATEWAY NATIONAL RECREATION AREA)
Marine Pkwy. Bridge
Beach Channel Dr.
Rockaway Beach Blvd.
JACOB RIIS PARK (GATEWAY NATIONAL RECREATION AREA)

8

St.
DYKER BEACH PARK
86th St.
Shore Pkwy.
86th St.
Stillwell Ave.
Shell Rd.
Neptune Ave.
Neptune Ave.
Surf Ave.
Rockaway Point Blvd.
Lower York Bay
ATLANTIC OCEAN
N
0   2 miles
0   3 km

NEW YORK OVERVIEW

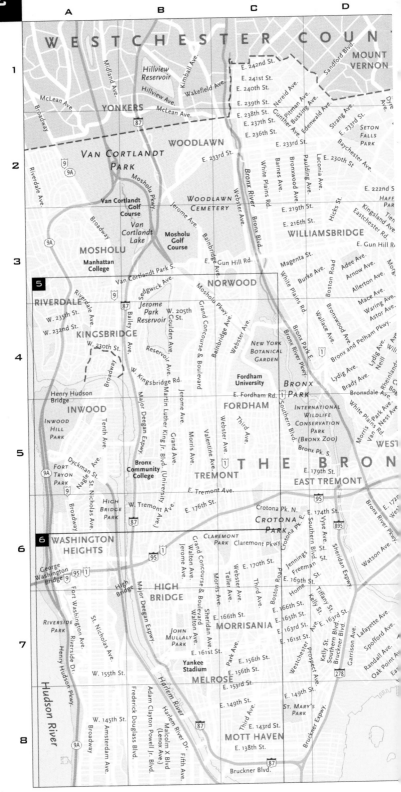

	A	B	C	D

WESTCHESTER COUN

MOUNT VERNON

1

Midland Ave.
Hillview Reservoir
Kimball Ave.
E. 242nd St.
Sandford Blvd.
McLean Ave.
Hillview Ave.
Wakefield Ave.
E. 241st St.
E. 240th St.
Broadway
YONKERS
McLean Ave.
E. 239th St.
Nereid Ave.
Pitman Ave.
Gunther Ave.
Bussing Ave.
Edenwald Ave.
Dyre
87
E. 238th St.
E. 237th St.
E. 236th St.
Strang Ave.
E. 233rd St.
SETON FALLS PARK
WOODLAWN
E. 233rd St.
Baychester Ave.

2

Riverdale Ave.
Van Cortlandt Park
9
9A
Mosholu Pkwy.
WOODLAWN CEMETERY
E. 233rd St.
Bronx River
White Plains Rd.
Barnes Ave.
Bronxwood Ave.
Paulding Ave.
Laconia Ave.
E. 230th St.
Hicks St.
E. 222nd S
HAFF PAR
Kingsland Ave.
Eastchester Rd.

Van Cortlandt Golf Course
Jerome Ave.
Webster Ave.
Bronx Blvd.
E. 219th St.
E. 216th St.
WILLIAMSBRIDGE
E. Gun Hill Rd.

3

9A
Broadway
Van Cortlandt Lake
MOSHOLU
Manhattan College
Bainbridge Ave.
Mosholu Golf Course
E. Gun Hill Rd.
Magenta St.
White Plains Rd.
Burke Ave.
Boston Road
Adee Ave.
Arnow Ave.
Allerton Ave.
Mace Ave.
Mor

Van Cortlandt Park S.
5
NORWOOD

4

RIVERDALE
Riverdale Ave.
9
87
Sedgwick Ave.
Jerome Park Reservoir
Bailey Ave.
Goulden Ave.
W. 205th St.
Mosholu Pkwy.
Grand Concourse & Boulevard
Webster Ave.
NEW YORK BOTANICAL GARDEN
Bronx Park E.
Wallace Ave.
Waring Ave.
Astor Ave.
Bronxwood Ave.
Bronx and Pelham Ave.
Lydig Ave.
Neill
Brady Ave.
W. 235th St.
W. 232nd St.
KINGSBRIDGE
W. 230th St.
Reservoir Ave.
W. Kingsbridge Rd.
Broadway
Jerome Ave.
Martin Luther King Jr. Blvd. (University)
Fordham University
E. Fordham Rd.
Bronx Park Pkwy.
Lydig Ave.
Bronxdale Ave.
Rheinland
White Plains Rd.

5

Henry Hudson Bridge
INWOOD
Tenth Ave.
Grand Ave.
Morris Ave.
Valentine Ave.
Webster Ave.
Third Ave.
FORDHAM
BRONX PARK
INTERNATIONAL WILDLIFE CONSERVATION PARK (BRONX ZOO)
Southern Blvd.
Bronx Pk. S.
Morris Park Ave.
Van Nest Ave.
WEST
INWOOD HILL PARK
Dyckman St.
Nagle St. Nicholas Ave.
9A
9
FORT TRYON PARK
Bronx Community College
TREMONT
E. 179th St.
EAST TREMONT

6

Broadway
HIGH BRIDGE PARK
87
Dyckman
W. Tremont Ave.
E. Tremont Ave.
W. 176th St.
E. 176th St.
Crotona Pk. N.
Crotona pk. E.
Southern Blvd.
E. 174th St.
95
Vyse Ave.
Sheridan Expwy.
895
Bronx River Pkwy.
E.
CROTONA PARK
Claremont Pkwy.
WASHINGTON HEIGHTS
George Washington Bridge
95
9
1
95
1
High Bridge
CLAREMONT PARK
Grand Concourse & Boulevard
Walton Ave.
Jerome Ave.
Morris Ave.
Teller Ave.
Webster Ave.
Third Ave.
E. 170th St.
Boston Road
Jennings
Freeman
E. 169th St.
Home
Watson Ave.

7

Riverside Park
Fort Washington Ave.
St. Nicholas Ave.
Riverside Ave.
Riverside Dr.
Henry Hudson Pkwy.
W. 155th St.
Major Deegan Expwy.
HIGH BRIDGE
John Mullaly Park
Sheridan Ave.
Walton Ave.
MORRISANIA
E. 166th St.
E. 165th St.
E. 163rd St.
E. 161st St.
Park Ave.
E. 161st St.
Yankee Stadium
E. 156th St.
Westchester
Prospect Ave.
Kelly St.
Tiffany St.
Kelly St.
Southern Blvd.
E. 163rd St.
Bruckner Blvd.
Garrison Ave.
Lafayette Ave.
Spofford Ave.
Randall Ave.
Oak Point Ave.
278

8

Hudson River
W. 145th St.
Amsterdam Ave.
Broadway
9A
Frederick Douglass Blvd.
Adam Clayton Powell Jr. Blvd.
Harlem River
Harlem River Dr.
Malcolm X Blvd. (Lenox Ave.)
Fifth Ave.
MELROSE
E. 156th St.
E. 153rd St.
E. 149th St.
MOTT HAVEN
E. 138th St.
Bruckner Blvd.
87
E. 149th St.
Third Ave.
E. 143rd St.
St. Mary's Park
Bruckner Expwy.
THE BRONX

STREETFINDER

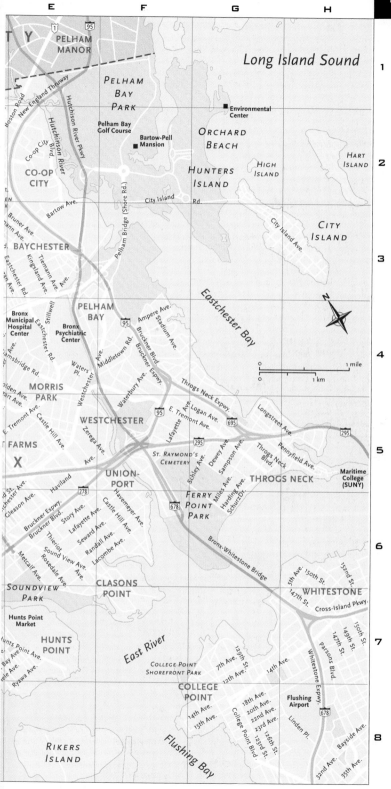

THE BRONX AND NORTHERN MANHATTAN

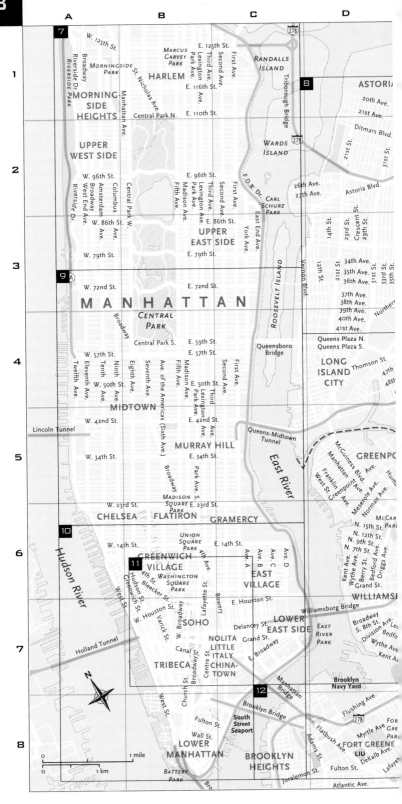

3

A   B   C   D

7

W. 125th St.   E. 125th St.

MARCUS GARVEY PARK

Broadway   Morningside Park

RIVERSIDE PARK   Riverside Dr.

St. Nicholas Ave.   HARLEM   Third Ave.   Lexington Park Ave.   Second Ave.   First Ave.

RANDALLS ISLAND

8

ASTORIA

MORNINGSIDE HEIGHTS   E. 116th St.

Manhattan Ave.   Central Park N.   E. 110th St.

20th Ave.

21st Ave.

Ditmars Blvd.

Triborough Bridge

278

UPPER WEST SIDE

WARDS ISLAND

21st St.   31st St.

W. 96th St.   E. 96th St.

Riverside Dr.   West End Ave.   Broadway   Amsterdam Ave.   Columbus Ave.   Central Park W.   Fifth Ave.   Madison Ave.   Lexington Ave.   Third Ave.   Second Ave.   First Ave.

F.D.R. Dr.   CARL SCHURZ PARK

26th Ave.

27th Ave.

Astoria Blvd.

278

14th St.   23rd St.   Crescent St.   29th St.

W. 86th St.   E. 86th St.

UPPER EAST SIDE

York Ave.   East End Ave.

W. 79th St.   E. 79th St.

12th St.   21st St.   31st St.   33rd St.   35th St.

34th Ave.

35th Ave.

36th Ave.

9 A

W. 72nd St.   E. 72nd St.

Roosevelt Island

Vernon Blvd.

37th Ave.

38th Ave.

39th Ave.

40th Ave.

41st Ave.

Northern

M A N H A T T A N

CENTRAL PARK

Central Park S.   E. 59th St.

Queensboro Bridge

Queens Plaza N.

Queens Plaza S.

W. 57th St.   E. 57th St.

LONG ISLAND CITY   Thomson St.

Twelfth Ave.   Eleventh Ave.   Tenth Ave.   Ninth Ave.   Eighth Ave.   Seventh Ave.   Ave. of the Americas (Sixth Ave.)   Fifth Ave.   Madison Ave.   Lexington Ave.   Third Ave.   Second Ave.   First Ave.

W. 50th St.   E. 50th St.

47th

48th

MIDTOWN

W. 42nd St.   E. 42nd St.

Lincoln Tunnel

Queens-Midtown Tunnel

MURRAY HILL

GREENPO

W. 34th St.   E. 34th St.

East River

McGuiness Blvd.   Manhattan Ave.   Franklin Ave.   West St.   Greenpoint Ave.   Meserole Ave.   Norman Ave.   Humb

Broadway   Park Ave. S

MADISON SQUARE PARK   E. 23rd St.

McCar

W. 23rd St.

CHELSEA   FLATIRON   GRAMERCY

N. 15th St.   PAR

N. 12th St.

N. 9th St.

N. 7th St.

10

UNION SQUARE PARK   E. 14th St.

Ave. D   Ave. C   Ave. B   Ave. A

Kent Ave.   Wythe Ave.   Berry St.   Bedford Ave.   Driggs Ave.

W. 14th St.

4th Ave.

11 GREENWICH VILLAGE

WASHINGTON SQUARE PARK

EAST VILLAGE

Grand St.

WILLIAMSI

Hudson River   West St.

Greenwich St.   4th St.   Bleecker St.   W. Houston St.   University Pl.

Bowery   Lafayette St.

E. Houston St.

Williamsburg Bridge

S. 8th St.   Leo

Broadway

Division Ave.   Bedfo

SOHO

Delancey St.

LOWER EAST SIDE

EAST RIVER PARK

Wythe Ave.

Varick St.   Broadway

Grand St.

Kent A

Holland Tunnel

NOLITA   LITTLE ITALY

Canal St.   Grand St.

Centre St.   E. Broadway

TRIBECA   CHINA-TOWN

N

Church St.   Broadway   Hudson St.

Manhattan Bridge

Brooklyn Navy Yard

Flushing Ave.

12

Fulton St.

Brooklyn Bridge

278

Myrtle Ave.   FOR GRE PAR

Wall St.

SOUTH STREET SEAPORT

Flatbush Ave.   FORT GREENE   LIU

Adams St.

0   1 mile

LOWER MANHATTAN

BROOKLYN HEIGHTS

Fulton St.   DeKalb Ave.   Lafaye

0   1 km

BATTERY PARK

Joralemon St.

Atlantic Ave.

STREETFINDER

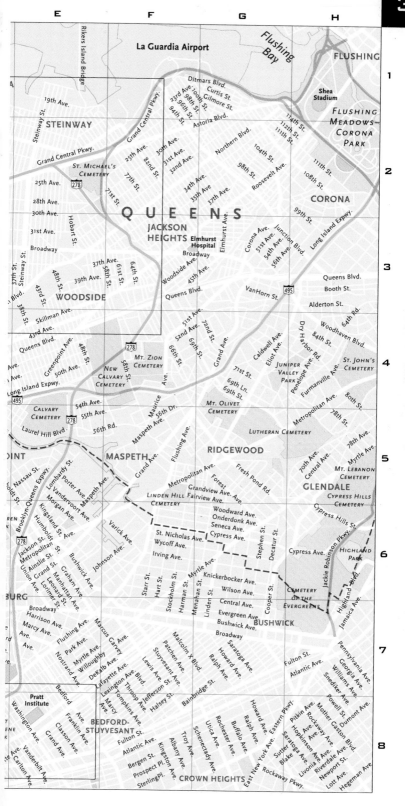

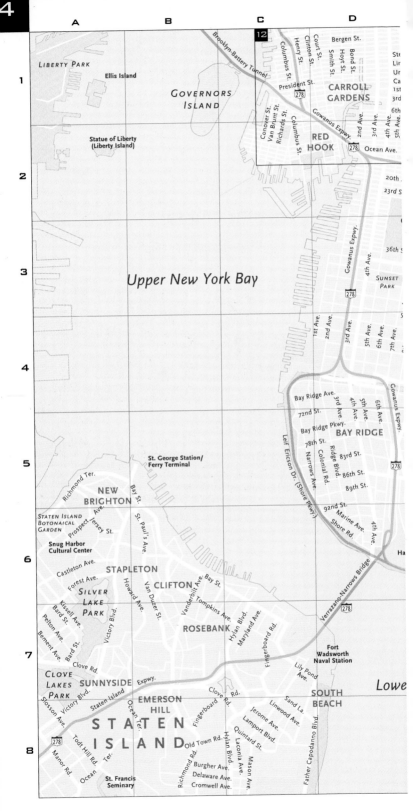

4

	A	B	C	D

12

LIBERTY PARK

Ellis Island

GOVERNORS ISLAND

Brooklyn-Battery Tunnel

President St.

Conover St.
Van Brunt St.
Richards St.
Columbus St.
Henry St.
Clinton St.
Court St.
Columbus St.
Hoyt St.
Smith St.
Bond St.
Bergen St.

CARROLL GARDENS

Ste
Lir
Ur
Ca
1st
3rd

Statue of Liberty (Liberty Island)

RED HOOK

Gowanus Expwy.

2nd Ave.
3rd Ave.
4th Ave.
5th Ave.
6th

Ocean Ave.

20th

23rd S

36th S

Upper New York Bay

Gowanus Expwy.

4th Ave.

SUNSET PARK

1st Ave.
2nd Ave.
3rd Ave.
5th Ave.
6th Ave.
7th Ave.

Gowanus Expwy.

Bay Ridge Ave.
3rd Ave.
4th Ave.
5th Ave.
6th Ave.

72nd St.
Bay Ridge Pkwy.

BAY RIDGE

78th St.
Ridge Blvd.
Colonial Rd.
Narrows Ave.
83rd St.
86th St.
89th St.

Leif Ericson Dr. (Shore Pkwy.)

St. George Station/ Ferry Terminal

92nd St.
Marine Ave.
Shore Rd.
4th Ave.

Ha

Richmond Ter.

NEW BRIGHTON

Bay St.

STATEN ISLAND BOTONAICAL GARDEN

Prospect

Jersey St.

St. Paul's Ave.

Snug Harbor Cultural Center

Castleton Ave.

STAPLETON

Forest Ave.

Howard Ave.

Van Duzer St.

CLIFTON

Vanderbilt Ave.
Bay St.

Tompkins Ave.

SILVER LAKE PARK

Kissell Ave.
Bard Ave.

Pelton Ave.

Bement Ave.
Bard St.

Clove Rd.

Victory Blvd.

ROSEBANK

Hylan Blvd.
Maryland Ave.

Fingerboard Rd.

Verrazano-Narrows Bridge

Fort Wadsworth Naval Station

CLOVE LAKES PARK

SUNNYSIDE

Slosson Ave.
Victory Blvd.

Staten Island Expwy.

EMERSON HILL

Ocean Ter.

Clove Rd.

Lily Pond Ave.

SOUTH BEACH

Lowe

STATEN ISLAND

Todt Hill Rd.

Manor Rd.

Ocean
Ter.

Fingerboard

Old Town Rd.

Richmond Rd.

Burgher Ave.
Delaware Ave.
Cromwell Ave.

Hylan Blvd.

Laconia Ave.

Quintard St.

Lamport Blvd.

Jerome Ave.

Linwood Ave.

Sand La.

Mason Ave.

Father Capodanno Blvd.

St. Francis Seminary

STREETFINDER

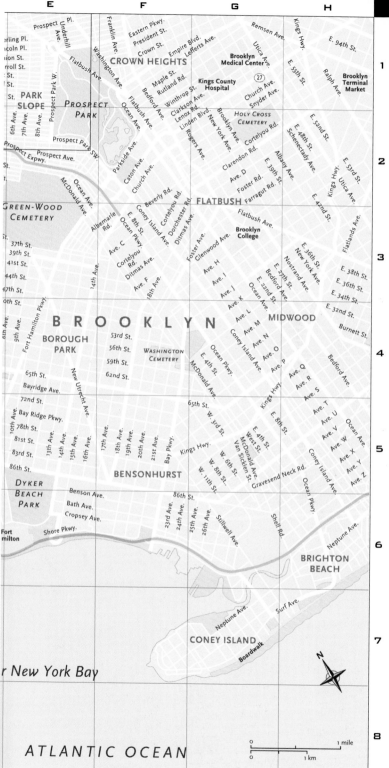

WESTERN BROOKLYN AND NORTHEASTERN STATEN ISLAND

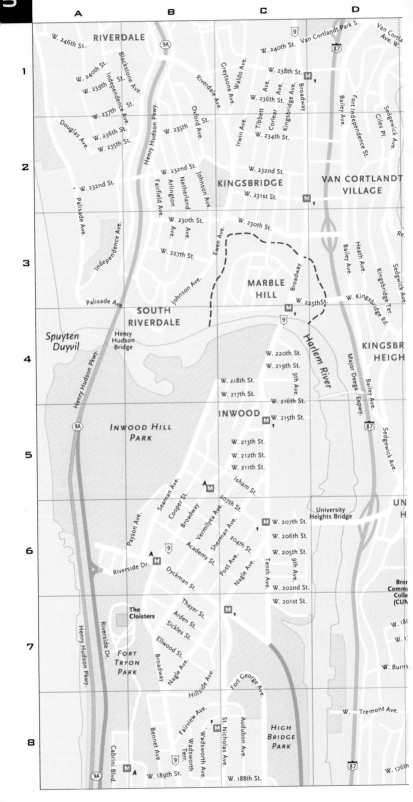

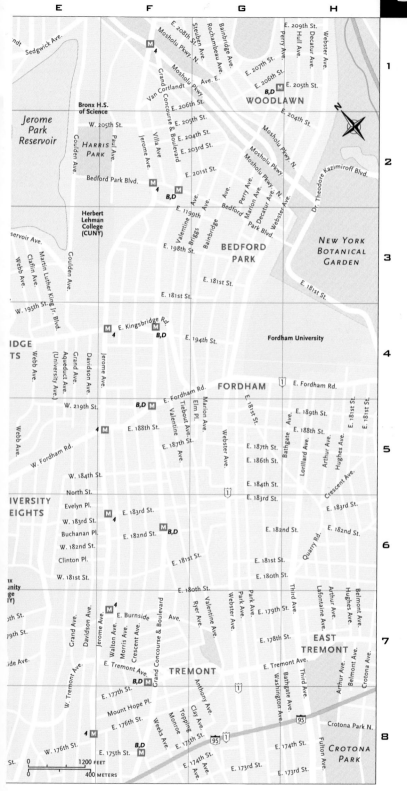

INWOOD AND THE WEST BRONX

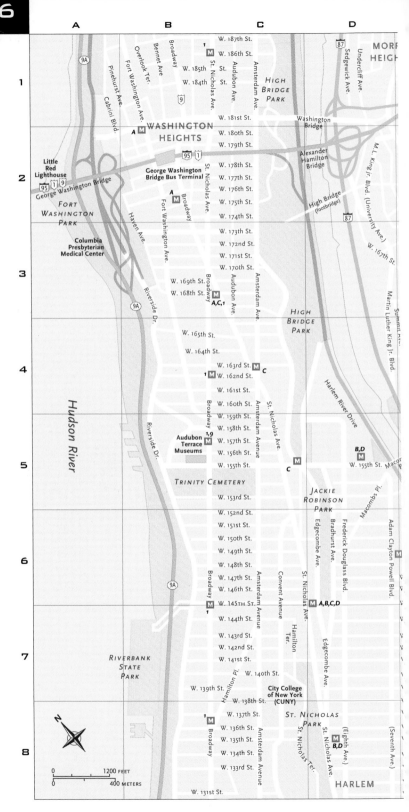

STREETFINDER

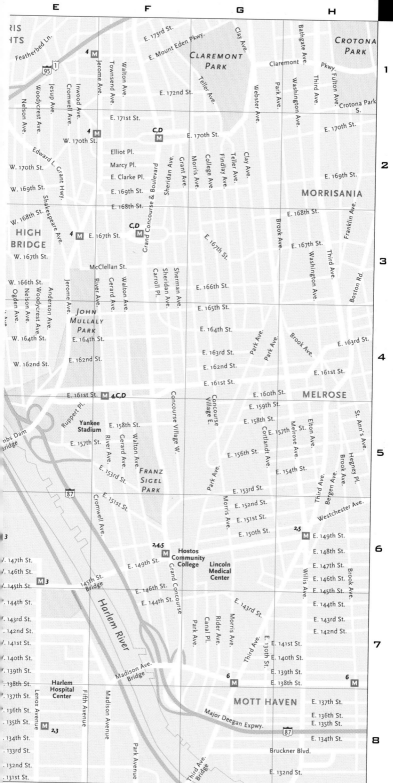

NORTHERN MANHATTAN AND THE SOUTH BRONX

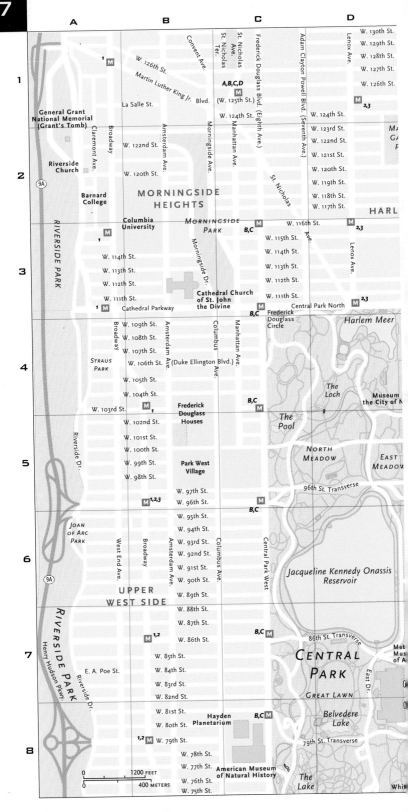

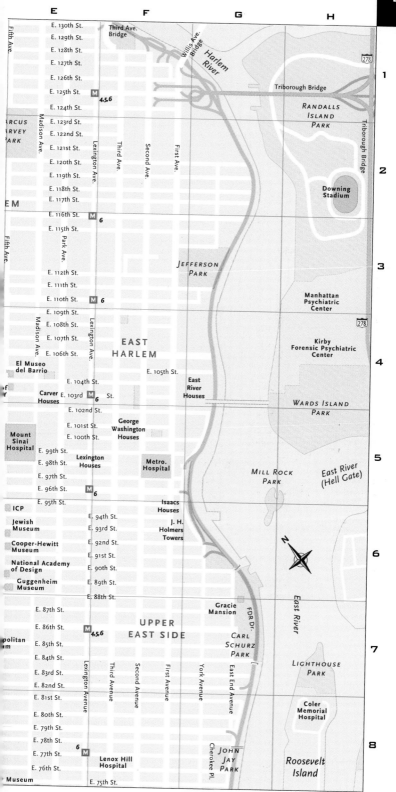

UPPER EAST AND UPPER WEST SIDES

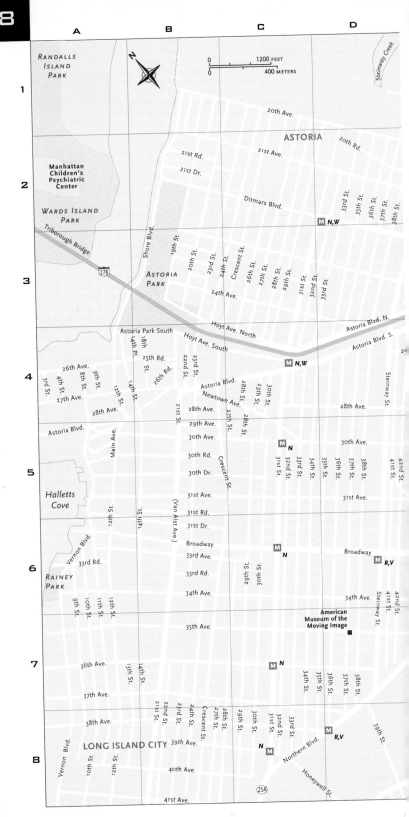

	A	B	C	D

RANDALLS ISLAND PARK

Steinway Creek

0 1200 FEET
0 400 METERS

20th Ave.

ASTORIA

20th Rd.

21st Rd.

21st Ave.

20th Rd.

Manhattan Children's Psychiatric Center

21st Dr.

Ditmars Blvd.

33rd St.
35th St.
36th St.
37th St.
38th St.

M N, W

WARDS ISLAND PARK

Shore Blvd.

19th St.

20th St.
23rd St.
24th St.
Crescent St.
27th St.
28th St.
29th St.
31st St.
32nd St.
33rd St.

Triborough Bridge

278

ASTORIA PARK

24th Ave.

Hoyt Ave. North

Astoria Blvd. N.

Astoria Park South

14th Pl.
18th St.
25th Rd.
22nd St.
33rd St.

Hoyt Ave. South

Astoria Blvd. S.

25

M N, W

26th Ave.

3rd St.
4th St.
8th St.
9th St.

26th Rd.

26th St.

Astoria Blvd.

28th St.
29th St.
30th St.

Steinway St.

27th Ave.

14th St.
12th St.

Newtown Ave.

27th St.

28th St.

28th Ave.

28th Ave.

21st St.

28th Ave.

Astoria Blvd.

Main Ave.

29th Ave.

30th Ave.

30th Ave.

M N

30th Ave.

Halletts Cove

12th St.

14th St.

(Van Alst Ave.)

Crescent St.

30th Rd.

30th Dr.

31st St.
32nd St.
33rd St.
34th St.
35th St.
36th St.
37th St.
38th St.
41st St.
42nd St.

31st Ave.

31st Ave.

31st Rd.

31st Dr.

Vernon Blvd.

Broadway

33rd Rd.

33rd Ave.

M N

Broadway

M R, V

RAINEY PARK

33rd Rd.

6th St.
9th St.
10th St.
11th St.
12th St.

29th St.
30th St.

34th Ave.

34th Ave.

41st St.
42nd St.
Steinway St.

13th St.

14th St.

35th Ave.

American Museum of the Moving Image

36th Ave.

M N

34th St.
35th St.
36th St.
37th St.
38th St.

37th Ave.

38th Ave.

21st St.
22nd St.
23rd St.
24th St.
27th St.
Crescent St.
28th St.
29th St.
30th St.
31st St.
32nd St.
33rd St.

M R, V

LONG ISLAND CITY

Vernon Blvd.

10th St.
12th St.

39th Ave.

N M

Northern Blvd.

39th St.

40th Ave.

Honeywell St.

25A

41st Ave.

STREETFINDER

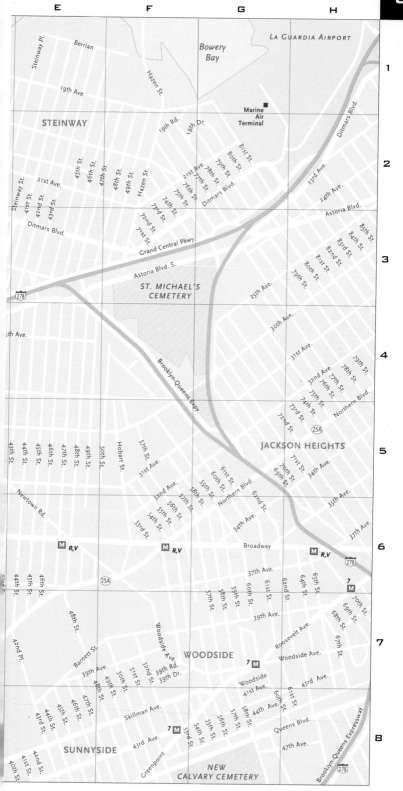

E   F   G   H

La Guardia Airport

Bowery Bay

Steinway Pl.
Berrian
19th Ave.

Hazen St.

Marine Air Terminal

Ditmars Blvd.

STEINWAY

19th Rd.
19th Dr.

45th St.
46th St.
47th St.
48th St.
49th St.
Hazen St.
21st Ave.
78th St.
80th St.
81st St.

23rd Ave.

Steinway St.
21st Ave.
41st St.
42nd St.
43rd St.
72nd St.
73rd St.
74th St.
75th St.
76th St.
77th St.
78th St.
71st St.

24th Ave.

Ditmars Blvd.

Ditmars Blvd.

Astoria Blvd.

85th St.
84th St.
83rd St.
82nd St.
81st St.
80th St.
79th St.

Grand Central Pkwy.

Astoria Blvd. S.

278

ST. MICHAEL'S CEMETERY

25th Ave.

30th Ave.

31st Ave.

79th St.
78th St.
77th St.
76th St.
75th St.
74th St.
73rd St.
72nd St.
32nd Ave.

Northern Blvd.

Brooklyn-Queens Expy.

25A

JACKSON HEIGHTS

5th Ave.

43rd St.
44th St.
45th St.
46th St.
47th St.
48th St.
49th St.
50th St.
Hobart St.
57th St.
31st Ave.

61st St.
60th St.
59th St.
58th St.
57th St.
56th St.
55th St.
54th St.
53rd St.
32nd Ave.

Northern Blvd.
34th Ave.
62nd St.

69th St.
71st St.

33rd Ave.

34th Ave.

37th Ave.

Newtown Rd.

M R,V

M R,V

Broadway

M R,V

278

7 M

43rd St.
44th St.
45th St.
46th St.

25A

37th Ave.

59th St.
60th St.
61st St.
62nd St.
64th St.
65th St.

70th St.
69th St.
68th St.
67th St.

48th St.
57th St.
58th St.
59th St.

39th Ave.

Roosevelt Ave.

Woodside Ave.

42nd Pl.

WOODSIDE

7 M

Woodside Ave.

Barnett St.

Woodside Ave.

39th Ave.
39th Rd.
39th Dr.
48th St.
49th St.
50th St.
51st St.
52nd St.

Woodside
41st Ave.

43rd Ave.

60th St.
61st St.

43rd St.
44th St.
45th St.
46th St.
47th St.

Skillman Ave.

7 M

53rd St.
54th St.
55th St.
56th St.
57th St.
58th St.

44th Ave.

60th St.
61st St.

Queens Blvd.

47th Ave.

Brooklyn-Queens Expressway

40th St.
41st St.
42nd St.
43rd St.

SUNNYSIDE

43rd Ave.

Greenpoint

NEW CALVARY CEMETERY

278

NORTHWESTERN QUEENS

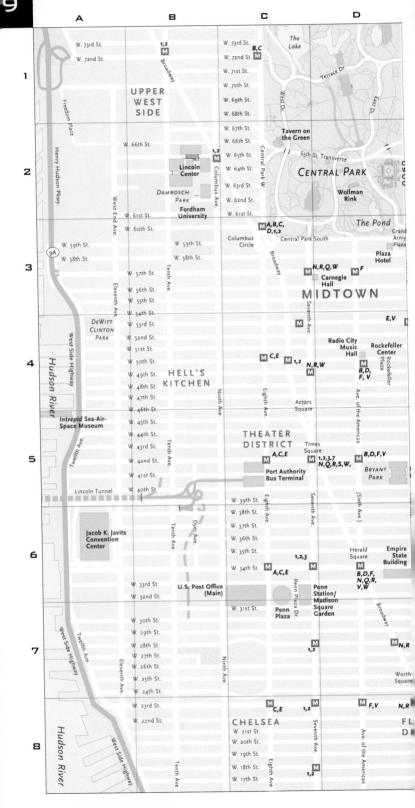

E | F | G | H

E. 73rd St.
E. 72nd St.
E. 71st St.
E. 70th St.
E. 69th St.
E. 68th St. **6** M

UPPER EAST SIDE

E. 67th St.
E. 66th St.
E. 65th St.
E. 64th St.
E. 63rd St. **F** M
E. 62nd St.
E. 61st St.
E. 60th St.
E. 59th St.
E. 58th St.
E. 57th St.
E. 56th St.
E. 55th St.
E. 54th St.
E. 53rd St.
E. 52nd St.
E. 51st St. **6** M
E. 50th St.
E. 49th St.
E. 48th St.
E. 47th St.
E. 46th St.
E. 45th St.
E. 44th St.
E. 43rd St.
E. 42nd St.
E. 41st St.
E. 40th St.
E. 39th St.
E. 38th St.
E. 37th St.
E. 36th St.
E. 35th St.
E. 34th St.
E. 33rd St.
E. 32nd St.
E. 31st St.
E. 30th St.
E. 29th St.
E. 28th St.
E. 27th St.
E. 26th St.
E. 25th St.
E. 24th St.
E. 23rd St.
E. 22nd St.
E. 21st St.
E. 20st St.
E. 19st St.
E. 18st St.

Lexington Ave.
Third Ave.
Second Ave.
First Ave.
York Ave.

NY Weill Cornell Medical Center

Rockefeller University

FDR Drive

West Channel

Roosevelt Island

East Channel

Central Park Zoo/ Wildlife Conservation Center

F M

M **N,R,W**
M **N,R,W**
4,5,6,

Fifth Ave.
Madison Ave.
Park Ave.

TRAMWAY TO ROOSEVELT ISLAND

Queensboro Bridge

Sutton Square

Sutton Place S.

Second Ave.
First Ave.

M
E,V M

St. Patrick's Cathedral
6 M

Waldorf-Astoria

TURTLE BAY

Mitchell Pl.

United Nations Plaza

United Nations Headquarters

Vanderbilt Ave.

Grand Central Terminal

Chrysler Building

E. 43rd St.

Queens-Midtown Tunnel

S M
M
4,5,6,7

N.Y. Public Library (Main)

Tudor City Pl.

Madison Ave.
Park Ave.

Pierpont Morgan Library

M **6**

Tunnel Exit
Third Ave.
Tunnel Entrance

FDR Drive

Kips Bay Plaza
First Ave.
NYU Medical Center

East River

Lexington Ave.

MURRAY HILL

M **6**

Bellevue Hospital

MADISON SQUARE PARK

Park Ave. South

M **6**

24TH ST. PARK

Flatiron Building
TIRON TRICT

GRAMERCY

GRAMERCY PARK

Broadway

Park Ave. South

Irving Pl.

Peter Cooper Village

Stuyvesant Town

0   1200 feet
0   400 meters

Union Square

Stuyvesant Square

N

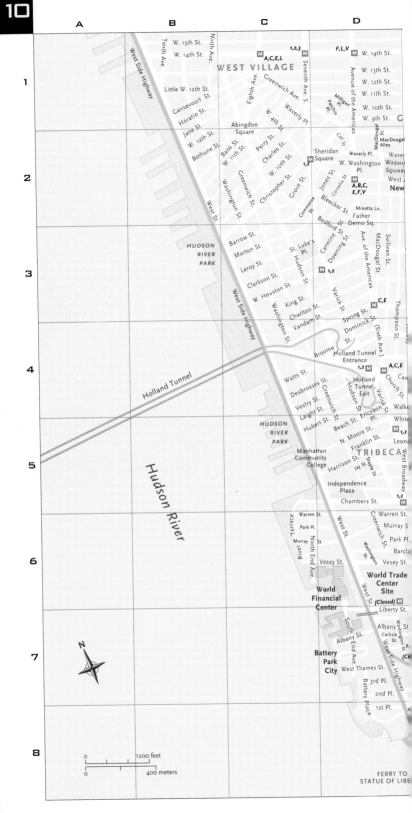

	A	B	C	D

Ninth Ave.
Tenth Ave.
W. 15th St.
W. 14th St.

West Side Highway

A,C,E,L **1,2,3** **F,L,V** W. 14th St.

WEST VILLAGE

Avenue of the Americas

W. 13th St.
W. 12th St.
W. 11th St.
W. 10th St.
W. 9th St.

Little W. 12th St.
Gansevoort St.
Horatio St.
Jane St.
W. 12th St.
Bethune St.

Eighth Ave.
Greenwich Ave.
Seventh Ave. S.
Waverly Pl.
W. 4th St.
Abingdon Square

Milligan Pl.
Patchin Pl.

Cay St.
MacDougal Alley

Bank St.
W. 11th St.
Perry St.
Charles St.
W. 10th St.
Christopher St.
Grove St.
Jones St.
Cornelia St.

Sheridan Square
1,2

Waverly Pl.
W. Washington Pl.

Waverly
WASHI
SQUAR

West

New

Washington St.
Greenwich St.

Commerce St.
Bleecker St.

A,B,C,
E,F,V

Minetta Ln.
Father Demo Sq.

HUDSON RIVER PARK

Barrow St.
Morton St.
Leroy St.
Clarkson St.
W. Houston St.
King St.
Charlton St.
Vandam St.

St. Luke's Pl.
Downing St.
Carmine St.

Bedford St.

Hudson St.
1,2

Varick St.

Sullivan St.
MacDougal St.

Ave. of the Americas

Thompson St.

West Side Highway

Washington St.

Spring St.
Dominick St.
St.

C,E

(Sixth Ave.)

Broome

Holland Tunnel Entrance
1,2

A,C,E

Watts St.
Desbrosses St.
Vestry St.
Laight St.
Hubert St.

Greenwich St.

Holland Tunnel Exit

Hudson St.

Varick St.
Church St.

Car

Walke

Beach St.
N. Moore St.
Franklin St.

Ericsson Pl.

White

1,2

Leona

Holland Tunnel

HUDSON RIVER PARK

Manhattan Community College

Harrison St.
Jay St.
Staple St.

TRIBECA

West Broadway

Independence Plaza

Chambers St.
1,2

Hudson River

Warren St.
Park Pl.
Murray St.

River Terrace
North End Ave.

West St.

Vesey St.

Greenwich St.
Washington St.

Warren St.
Murray S
Park Pl.
Barcla
Vesey St.

World Trade Center Site

World Financial Center

West St.

(Closed) **M**

Liberty St.

Battery Park City

South End Ave.

Albany St.
West Thames St.

Albany St
Carlisle St.

Washington St.
West Side Highway

C

3rd Pl.
2nd Pl.
Battery Place
1st Pl.

N

0   1200 feet
0   400 meters

FERRY TO
STATUE OF LIBE

STREETFINDER

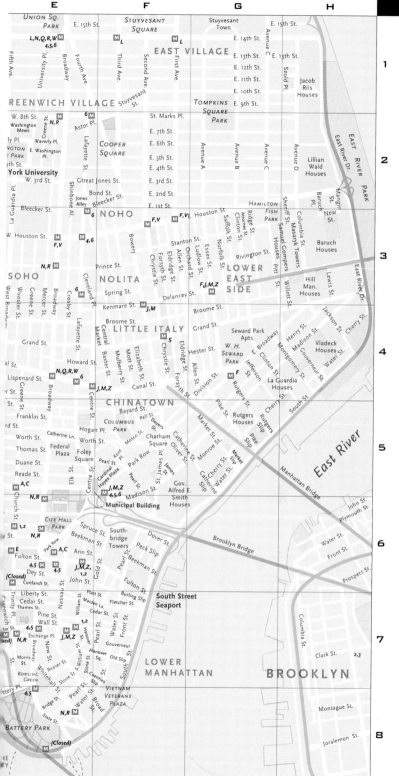

A   B   C   D

GREENWICH VILLAGE

W. 12th St.
Greenwich Ave.
Milligan Pl.
Avenue of the Americas
W. 11th St.
Fifth Ave.

1

Waverly Pl.
Patchin Pl.
W. 10th St.

Bank St.
Seventh Ave. S.
W. 9th St.

W. 11th St.
W. 4th St.
W. 8th St.

WEST VILLAGE

MacDougal Alley
Washington Mews

Perry St.
Gay St.
MacDougal St.

2

Charles St.
Sheridan Square
Waverly Pl.
Waverly Pl.

1,2 M

W. 10th St.
W. Washington Pl.
WASHINGTON SQUARE PARK
E.

M A,C,E,F,V
West 4th St.

New York University

Christopher St.
Jones St.
Cornelia St.
W. 3rd St.

3

Grove St.
Bleecker St.
MacDougal St.
Sullivan St.
Thompson St.
La Guardia Pl.

Greenwich St.
Commerce St.
Leroy St.
Minetta La.

Barrow St.
Bedford St.
Father Demo Sq.
Bleecker St.

Morton St.
St. Luke's Pl.
Carmine St.

4

Leroy St.
Hudson St.
Downing St.
Avenue of the Americas (Sixth Ave.)
W. Houston St.

Clarkson St.
M 1,2
Prince St.

W. Houston St.
Varick St.

5

King St.
M C,E
Spring St.

Charlton St.
Thompson St.
West Broadway
Wooster St.
Greene St.

Washington St.
Vandam St.
Spring St.
Dominick St.
Broome St.

Holland Tunnel Entrance

Holland Tunnel
Broome St.
Grand St.

6

West St.
West Side Highway

Watts St.
1,2 M
M A,C,E

Canal St.

Desbrosses St.
Hudson St.
Holland Tunnel Exit
Varick St.
Church St.
Lispenard St.

7

N
Vestry St.
Greenwich St.
Ericsson Pl.
Walker St.
Greene St.

Laight St.
Beach St.
White St.

Hubert St.
M 1,2
Franklin St.

Hudson River

0   600 feet
0   200 meters
N. Moore St.
Leonard St.

8

Franklin St.
West Broadway
Worth St.

Manhattan Community College
Harrison St.
TRIBECA

Jay St.
Staple St.
Thomas St.

E F G H

E. 11th St.

E. 10th St.

Stuyvesant St.

E. 9th St.

TOMPKINS SQUARE PARK

1

N,R

E. 8th St.

6

Cooper Union

St. Marks Pl.

Greene St.

Astor Pl.

COOPER SQUARE

E. 7th St.

E. 6th St.

Avenue A

Waverly Pl.

Broadway

Lafayette St.

Fourth Ave.

Third Ave.

Second Ave.

E. 5th St.

First Ave.

2

Washington Pl.

E. 4th St.

EAST VILLAGE

Great Jones St.

E. 3rd St.

Shinbone Al.

Bond St.

E. 2nd St.

Jones Al.

Bleecker St.

E. 1st St.

3

6 NOHO

F,V E. Houston St.

Norfolk St.

St.

F,V

6

F,V

Stanton St.

Allen St.

Orchard St.

Ludlow St.

Essex St.

NOLITA

Bowery

Chrystie St.

Forsyth St.

Eldridge St.

Rivington St.

4

N,R

Prince St.

Elizabeth St.

LOWER EAST SIDE

F,J,M,Z

Cleveland Pl.

Mulberry St.

Mott St.

6

Lafayette St.

Spring St.

Delancey St.

Mercer St.

Broadway

Crosby St.

Kenmare St.

J,M

Broome St.

5

Broome St.

Centre Market Pl.

LITTLE ITALY

Grand St.

6

S

Eldridge St.

Hester St.

Baxter St.

Mulberry St.

Mott St.

Elizabeth St.

Chrystie St.

Howard St.

Forsyth St.

Allen St.

7

N,R

6

J,M,Z

Canal St.

Division St.

Pike St.

Broadway

Lafayette St.

Centre St.

CHINATOWN

Manhattan Bridge

Bayard St.

Pell St.

Doyers St.

Market St.

Madison St.

8

COLUMBUS PARK

Mosco St.

Catherine La.

Hogan Pl.

Chatham Square

Catherine St.

Oliver St.

Monroe St.

Federal Plaza

Worth St.

Foley Square

Kent Pl.

Park Row

St. James Pl.

GREENWICH VILLAGE AND SOHO

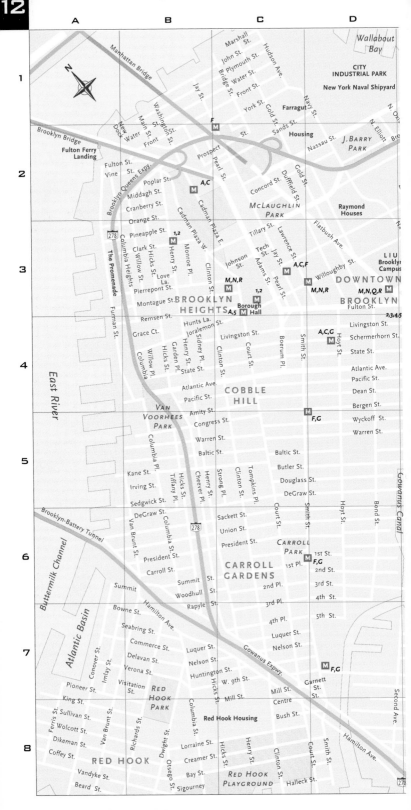

A   **B**   **C**   **D**

1

Manhattan Bridge

Marshall St.
John St.
Plymouth St.
Water St.
Front St.
Bridge St.
Jay St.
Hudson Ave.
York St.
Gold St.
Sands St.
Navy St.
Nassau St.

Wallabout Bay

CITY INDUSTRIAL PARK

New York Naval Shipyard

Farragut

Housing

N. Oxf

N. Elliott

J. Barry Park

Bro

Brooklyn Bridge

Fulton Ferry Landing

New Dock
Water St.
Front St.
Washington St.
Main St.

Prospect St.
Pearl St.

Concord St.
Duffield St.
Gold St.

McLaughlin Park

Raymond Houses

Ne

2

Fulton St.
Vine St.
Poplar St.
Middagh St.
Cranberry St.
Orange St.
Pineapple St.

Brooklyn-Queens Expwy.
Columbia Heights

A,C

Cadman Plaza W.
Cadman Plaza E.
Monroe Pl.
Clinton St.

Tillary St.
Tech Pl.
Lawrence St.
Jay St.
Adams St.
Pearl St.
Flatbush Ave.

LIU Brooklyn Campus

DOWNTOWN BROOKLYN

3

278

The Promenade

Clark St.
Hicks St.
Willow St.
Henry St.
Love La.
Pierrepont St.
Montague St.

1,2

Johnson St.

A,C,F

Willoughby St.

M,N,R

M,N,R

M,N,Q,R

BROOKLYN HEIGHTS

M,N,R

1,2

Borough Hall

A,5

Fulton St.

2,3,4,5

Remsen St.
Grace Ct.

Furman St.

Hunts La.
Joralemon St.
Sidney Pl.
Garden Pl.
Henry St.
Hicks St.
State St.
Columbia

Livingston St.
Court St.
Clinton St.
Boerum Pl.
Smith St.

A,C,G
Hoyt St.

Livingston St.
Schermerhorn St.
State St.
Atlantic Ave.
Pacific St.
Dean St.
Bergen St.
Wyckoff St.
Warren St.

East River

4

Columbia Pl.
Willow Pl.

VAN VOORHEES PARK

Atlantic Ave.
Pacific St.
Amity St.
Congress St.
Warren St.
Baltic St.

COBBLE HILL

Baltic St.
Butler St.
Douglass St.
DeGraw St.

F,G

5

Kane St.
Irving St.
Sedgwick St.

Columbia Pl.
Hicks St.
Tiffany Pl.
Henry St.
Cheever Pl.
Strong Pl.
Clinton St.
Tompkins Pl.
Court St.
Smith St.
Hoyt St.
Bond St.

Gowanus Canal

6

Brooklyn-Battery Tunnel

DeGraw St.
Van Brunt St.
Columbia St.
President St.
Carroll St.

278

Hamilton Ave.

Summit
Woodhull St.
Rapyle St.

Sackett St.
Union St.
President St.

CARROLL GARDENS

CARROLL PARK

2nd Pl.
3rd Pl.

1st St.
1st Pl.
2nd St.
3rd St.
4th St.
5th St.

F,G

Second Ave.

7

Atlantic Basin

Buttermilk Channel

Bowne St.
Seabring St.
Commerce St.
Delavan St.
Verona St.
Conover St.
Imlay St.

Luquer St.
Nelson St.
Huntington St.
Hicks St.
W. 9th St.
Mill St.

4th Pl.
Luquer St.
Nelson St.

Gowanus Expwy.

Garnett St.
St.

F,G

Hamilton Ave.

8

Pioneer St.
King St.
Ferris St.
Sullivan St.
Wolcott St.
Dikeman St.
Coffey St.
Vandyke St.
Beard St.

Van Brunt St.
Richards St.
Dwight St.
Otsego St.

RED HOOK PARK

Visitation St.

RED HOOK

Columbia St.
Lorraine St.
Creamer St.
Bay St.
Sigourney St.

Red Hook Housing

Hicks St.
Henry St.
Clinton St.

Bush St.

Centre

RED HOOK PLAYGROUND

Court St.
Smith St.
Halleck St.

278

E F G H

U.S. Naval Reserve

Clinton Ave.

Flushing Ave.

Park Ave.

278

Ryerson St.

Grand Ave.

Hall St.

Park Ave.

Steuben St.

Emerson St.

Myrtle Ave.

Taaffe St.

Kent Ave.

Classon St.

Franklin Ave.

Spencer St.

Bedford Ave.

Stillman St.

Walworth St.

Lafayette Ave.

M G

1

CLINTON HILL

Willoughby Ave.

Washington Ave.

Waverly Ave.

Clinton Ave.

Vanderbilt Ave.

Clermont Ave.

Adelphi Ave.

Carlton Ave.

Cumberland St.

Pratt Institute

De Kalb Ave.

Lafayette Gardens

The Quadrangles

Clifton Pl.

Greene Ave.

Grand Ave.

Classon St.

Lexington

M G

BEDFORD-STUYVESANT

Quincy St.

Gates Ave.

Monroe St.

Franklin Ave.

Madison St.

Bedford Ave.

2

Brooklyn-queens Expwy.

N. Portland

Auburn St.

Myrtle Ave.

Walt Whitman Houses

FT. GREENE PARK

Edwards St.

FORT GREENE

St. James Pl.

M G

Downing Ave.

Putnam Ave.

Fulton St.

3

Hudson Ave.

Rockwell Pl.

Ashland Pl.

Felix St.

Ft. Greene St.

S. Elliott St.

S. Portland St.

S. Oxford St.

DeKalb Ave.

Lafayette Ave.

M G

A,C

Greene Ave.

Fulton St.

Cumberland St.

Carlton Ave.

Adelphi Ave.

Clermont Ave.

Vanderbilt Ave.

Clinton Ave.

Waverly Ave.

A,C

M

Atlantic Ave.

M

Brooklyn Academy of Music

Flatbush Ave.

Atlantic Ave.

Pacific St.

Dean St.

Bergen St.

St. Mark's Pl.

Carlton Ave.

Vanderbilt Ave.

Underhill Ave.

Washington Ave.

Grand Ave.

PROSPECT HEIGHTS

4

M Q
1,2,4,5

M,N,R,W M

BOERUM HILL

St. Mark's Pl.

Nevins St.

Baltic St.

Butler St.

Douglass St.

DeGraw St.

Sackett St.

Third Ave.

Fourth Ave.

Prospect Pl.

Park Pl.

Sterling Pl.

St. John's Pl.

Lincoln Pl.

Berkeley Pl.

Flatbush Ave.

Q Park Pl.

M

Seventh Ave.

Eighth Ave.

Butler Pl.

Stirling Pl.

St. Johns Pl.

Lincoln Pl.

Montauk Club

1,2,4

M

GRAND ARMY PLAZA

Eastern Pkwy.

Brooklyn Public Library

Flatbush Ave.

1,2,4

M

5

Union St.

President St.

M,N,R

M

Fifth Ave.

Sixth Ave.

Carroll St.

Garfield Pl.

1st St.

2nd St.

Fiske Pl.

Polhemus Pl.

Montgomery Pl.

6

3rd St.

Denton Pl.

Whitwell Pl.

3rd St.

4th St.

5th St.

PARK SLOPE

PROSPECT PARK

Prospect Park W.

Litchfield Villa

GOWANUS

6th St.

7th St.

8th St.

Methodist Hospital

7

F M M,N,R

9th St.

10th St.

M F

Third Ave.

Fourth Ave.

Fifth Ave.

Sixth Ave.

Seventh Ave.

Eighth Ave.

11th St.

12th St.

13th St.

14th St.

15th St.

16th St.

8

0   1200 FEET
0   400 METERS

Prospect Expwy.

M,N,R

Bartel Pritchard Sq.

Prospect Park S.W.

M F

NORTHWESTERN BROOKLYN

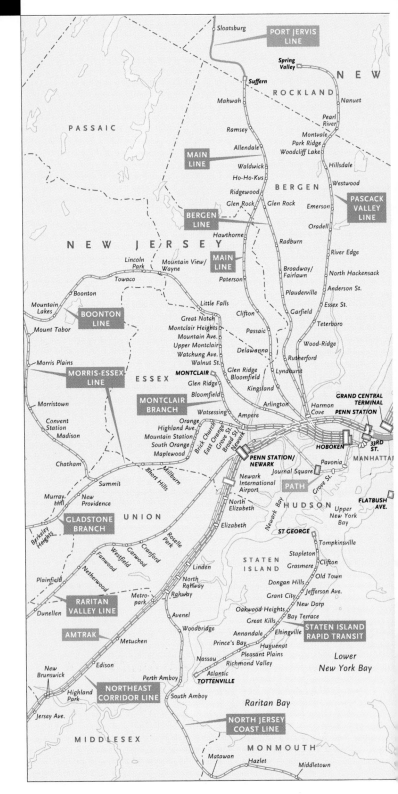

TRI-STATE COMMUTER RAIL

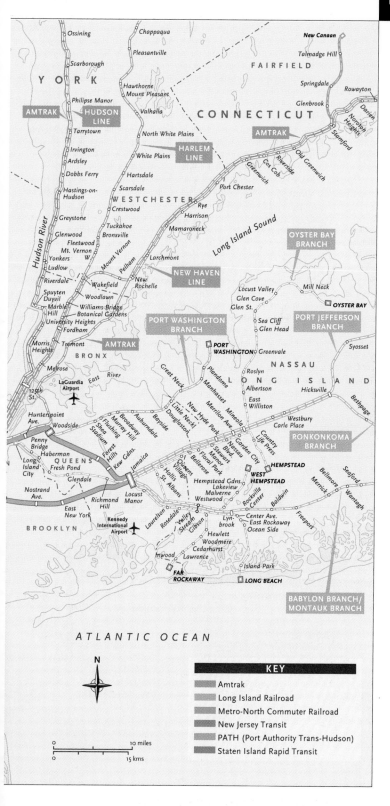

Ossining
Chappaqua
New Canaan
Pleasantville
Talmadge Hill
FAIRFIELD
Scarborough
Springdale
Y O R K
Hawthorne
Rowayton
Mount Pleasant
Philipse Manor
Glenbrook
Norroton
AMTRAK
HUDSON
C O N N E C T I C U T
Heights
LINE
Valhalla
Stamford
Darien
Tarrytown
North White Plains
AMTRAK
Old Greenwich
Irvington
HARLEM
Riverside
Ardsley
White Plains
LINE
Cos Cob
Dobbs Ferry
Hartsdale
Greenwich
Hastings-on-
Scarsdale
Port Chester
Hudson
W E S T C H E S T E R
Rye
Greystone
Crestwood
Harrison
Glenwood
Tuckahoe
Long Island Sound
Fleetwood
Bronxville
Mamaroneck
Mt. Vernon
OYSTER BAY
Yonkers
W.
Mount Vernon
Pelham
BRANCH
Ludlow
Larchmont
Riverdale
Wakefield
New
NEW HAVEN
Spuyten
Woodlawn
Rochelle
LINE
Locust Valley
Mill Neck
Duyvil
Glen Cove
Marble
Williams Bridge
Glen St.
OYSTER BAY
Hill
Botanical Gardens
PORT WASHINGTON
University Heights
Fordham
BRANCH
Sea Cliff
PORT JEFFERSON
Morris
Glen Head
BRANCH
Heights
Tremont
AMTRAK
PORT
Heights
B R O N X
WASHINGTON
Greenvale
Syosset
Melrose
Great Neck
Plandome
Roslyn
N A S S A U
LaGuardia
Manhasset
Mineola
Albertson
Hicksville
125th
Airport
L O N G   I S L A N D
St.
East
Huntspoint
Williston
Bethpage
Ave.
East
River
New Hyde Park
Westbury
Woodside
Little Neck
Merrillon Ave.
Carle Place
RONKONKOMA
Penny
Broadway
Auburndale
Garden City
Country
BRANCH
Bridge
Murray Hill
Bayside
Nassau
Life Press
Haberman
Shea
Flushing
Douglaston
Stewart
Long
Stadium
Forest
Manor
HEMPSTEAD
Island
Q U E E N S
Gdns.
Floral Park
WEST
City
Fresh Pond
Kew Gdns.
Bellerose
HEMPSTEAD
Glendale
Jamaica
Queens
Hempstead Gdns.
Rockville
Nostrand
Village
Hollis
Lakeview
Center
Baldwin
Ave.
Richmond
St. Albans
Malverne
Bellmore
Seaford
Hill
Locust
Westwood
Merrick
Wantagh
East
Manor
Lynbrook
Center Ave.
Freeport
New York
Laurelton
Rosedale
Gibson
East Rockaway
B R O O K L Y N
Kennedy
Valley
Ocean Side
International
Stream
Hewlett
Airport
Woodmere
Cedarhurst
Inwood
Lawrence
Island Park
FAR
ROCKAWAY
LONG BEACH
BABYLON BRANCH/
MONTAUK BRANCH

A T L A N T I C   O C E A N

N

KEY	
	Amtrak
	Long Island Railroad
	Metro-North Commuter Railroad
	New Jersey Transit
	PATH (Port Authority Trans-Hudson)
	Staten Island Rapid Transit

0   10 miles
0   15 kms

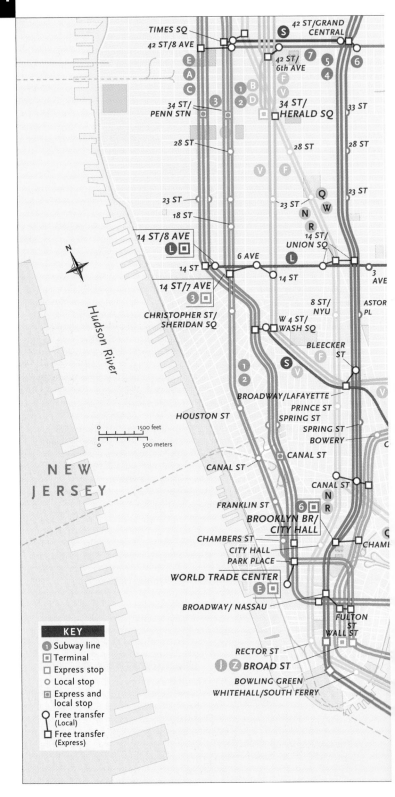

KEY
1 Subway line
◉ Terminal
□ Express stop
○ Local stop
◉ Express and local stop
○ Free transfer (Local)
□ Free transfer (Express)

SUBWAYS

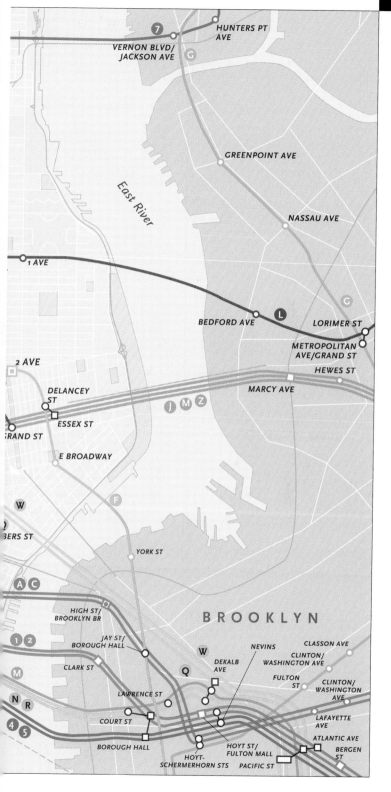

7 HUNTERS PT AVE

VERNON BLVD/
JACKSON AVE

G

GREENPOINT AVE

NASSAU AVE

1 AVE

L

BEDFORD AVE

G

LORIMER ST

METROPOLITAN
AVE/GRAND ST

HEWES ST

2 AVE

DELANCEY
ST

MARCY AVE

J M Z

ESSEX ST

GRAND ST

E BROADWAY

F

W

BERS ST

YORK ST

A C

HIGH ST/
BROOKLYN BR

BROOKLYN

1 2

JAY ST/
BOROUGH HALL

CLASSON AVE

CLARK ST

W

DEKALB
AVE

NEVINS

CLINTON/
WASHINGTON AVE

M

Q

FULTON
ST

CLINTON/
WASHINGTON
AVE

N R

LAWRENCE ST

4 5

COURT ST

LAFAYETTE
AVE

ATLANTIC AVE

BOROUGH HALL

HOYT ST/
FULTON MALL

HOYT-
SCHERMERHORN STS

PACIFIC ST

BERGEN
ST

East River

15

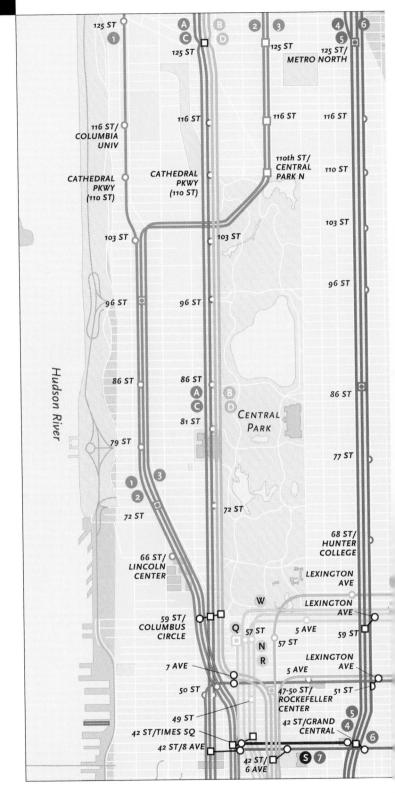

SUBWAYS

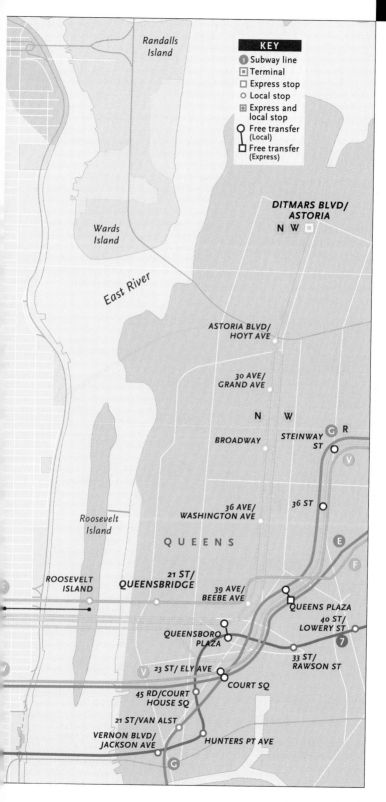

KEY
- Subway line
- Terminal
- Express stop
- Local stop
- Express and local stop
- Free transfer (Local)
- Free transfer (Express)

DITMARS BLVD/ ASTORIA
N W

East River

Randalls Island

Wards Island

ASTORIA BLVD/ HOYT AVE

30 AVE/ GRAND AVE

N W R G

BROADWAY STEINWAY ST

V

Roosevelt Island

36 AVE/ WASHINGTON AVE 36 ST

Q U E E N S

E

F

21 ST/ QUEENSBRIDGE

ROOSEVELT ISLAND

39 AVE/ BEEBE AVE

QUEENS PLAZA

40 ST/ LOWERY ST

QUEENSBORO PLAZA

7

33 ST/ RAWSON ST

V 23 ST/ ELY AVE

COURT SQ

45 RD/COURT HOUSE SQ

21 ST/VAN ALST

VERNON BLVD/ JACKSON AVE HUNTERS PT AVE

G

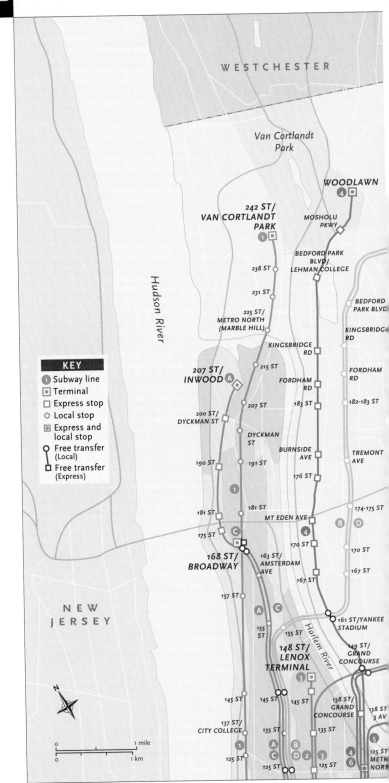

SUBWAYS

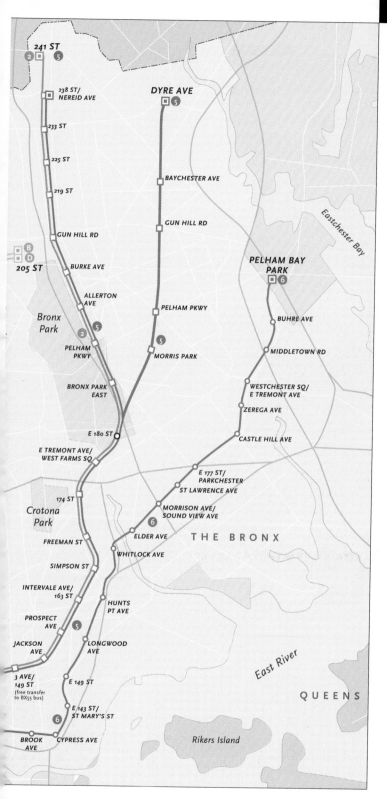

241 ST

238 ST/
NEREID AVE

DYRE AVE

233 ST

225 ST

219 ST

BAYCHESTER AVE

GUN HILL RD

GUN HILL RD

205 ST

BURKE AVE

PELHAM BAY
PARK

ALLERTON
AVE

Bronx
Park

PELHAM PKWY

BUHRE AVE

PELHAM
PKWY

MIDDLETOWN RD

MORRIS PARK

BRONX PARK
EAST

WESTCHESTER SQ/
E TREMONT AVE

ZEREGA AVE

E 180 ST

CASTLE HILL AVE

E TREMONT AVE/
WEST FARMS SQ

E 177 ST/
PARKCHESTER

174 ST

ST LAWRENCE AVE

Crotona
Park

MORRISON AVE/
SOUND VIEW AVE

FREEMAN ST

ELDER AVE

THE BRONX

WHITLOCK AVE

SIMPSON ST

INTERVALE AVE/
163 ST

HUNTS
PT AVE

PROSPECT
AVE

JACKSON
AVE

LONGWOOD
AVE

East River

3 AVE/
149 ST
(free transfer
to BX55 bus)

E 149 ST

QUEENS

E 143 ST/
ST MARY'S ST

BROOK
AVE

CYPRESS AVE

Rikers Island

Eastchester Bay

BRONX AND NORTHERN MANHATTAN

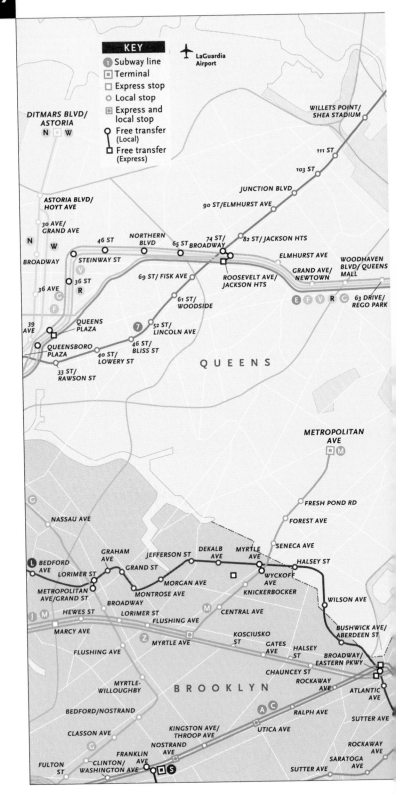

SUBWAYS

KEY
- ✈ LaGuardia Airport
- 1 Subway line
- ◼ Terminal
- ☐ Express stop
- ○ Local stop
- ⊞ Express and local stop
- Free transfer (Local)
- Free transfer (Express)

DITMARS BLVD/ ASTORIA
N W

WILLETS POINT/ SHEA STADIUM

111 ST

103 ST

JUNCTION BLVD

90 ST/ELMHURST AVE

ASTORIA BLVD/ HOYT AVE

30 AVE/ GRAND AVE

46 ST
NORTHERN BLVD
65 ST
74 ST/ BROADWAY
82 ST/ JACKSON HTS

N
W
BROADWAY
STEINWAY ST
ELMHURST AVE
WOODHAVEN BLVD/ QUEENS MALL

69 ST/ FISK AVE
ROOSEVELT AVE/ JACKSON HTS
GRAND AVE/ NEWTOWN

36 ST
R

36 AVE
G
F
61 ST/ WOODSIDE
E F V R G
63 DRIVE/ REGO PARK

39 AVE
QUEENS PLAZA
52 ST/ LINCOLN AVE
7

QUEENSBORO PLAZA
46 ST/ BLISS ST

40 ST/ LOWERY ST

33 ST/ RAWSON ST

QUEENS

METROPOLITAN AVE
M

G

FRESH POND RD

FOREST AVE

NASSAU AVE

SENECA AVE

L BEDFORD AVE
GRAHAM AVE
JEFFERSON ST
DEKALB AVE
MYRTLE AVE
HALSEY ST

LORIMER ST
GRAND ST
WYCKOFF AVE

METROPOLITAN AVE/GRAND ST
MONTROSE AVE
KNICKERBOCKER
WILSON AVE

MORGAN AVE

BROADWAY

J M
HEWES ST
LORIMER ST
FLUSHING AVE
M
CENTRAL AVE
BUSHWICK AVE/ ABERDEEN ST

MARCY AVE

Z
MYRTLE AVE
KOSCIUSKO ST
GATES AVE
HALSEY ST
BROADWAY/ EASTERN PKWY

FLUSHING AVE
CHAUNCEY ST
ROCKAWAY AVE
ATLANTIC AVE

MYRTLE-WILLOUGHBY
BROOKLYN

BEDFORD/NOSTRAND
A C
RALPH AVE
SUTTER AVE

CLASSON AVE
KINGSTON AVE/ THROOP AVE
UTICA AVE

G
NOSTRAND AVE
ROCKAWAY AVE

FULTON ST
CLINTON/ WASHINGTON AVE
FRANKLIN AVE
S
SARATOGA AVE

SUTTER AVE

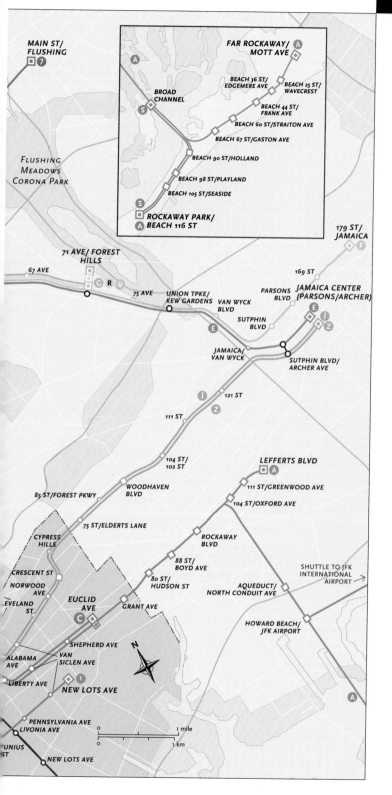

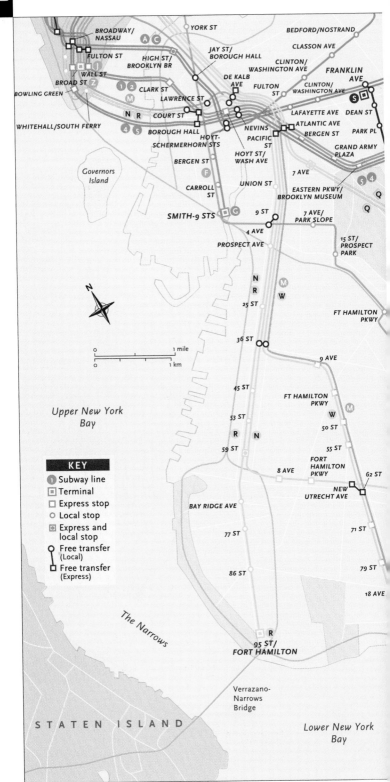

SUBWAYS

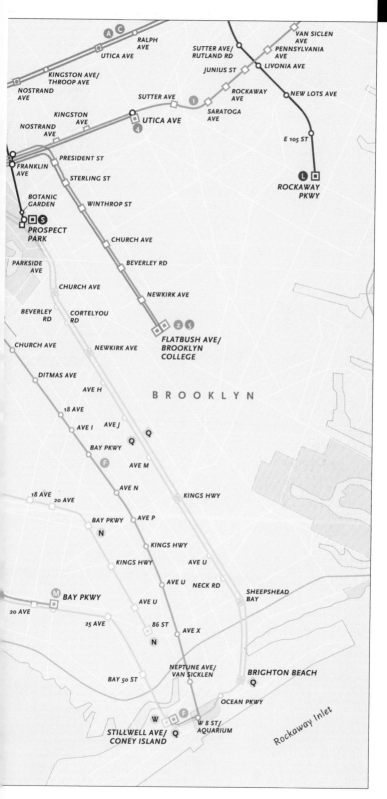

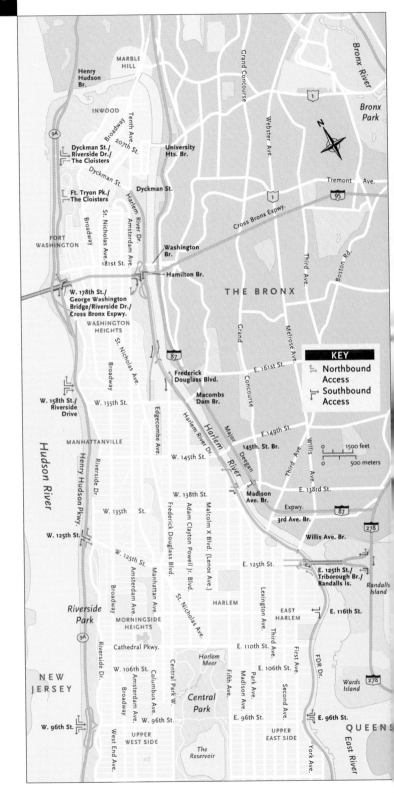

DRIVING UPTOWN: ENTRANCES & EXITS

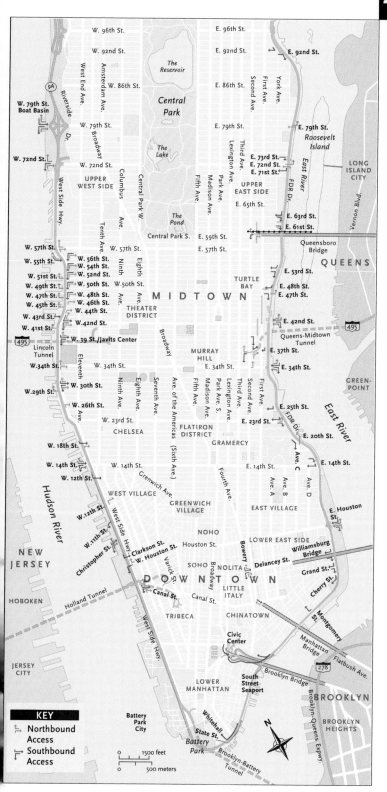

DRIVING DOWNTOWN: ENTRANCES & EXITS

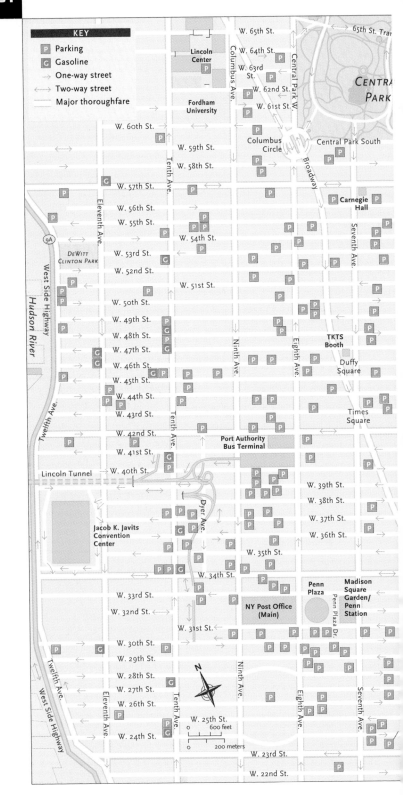

DRIVING

MIDTOWN MANHATTAN

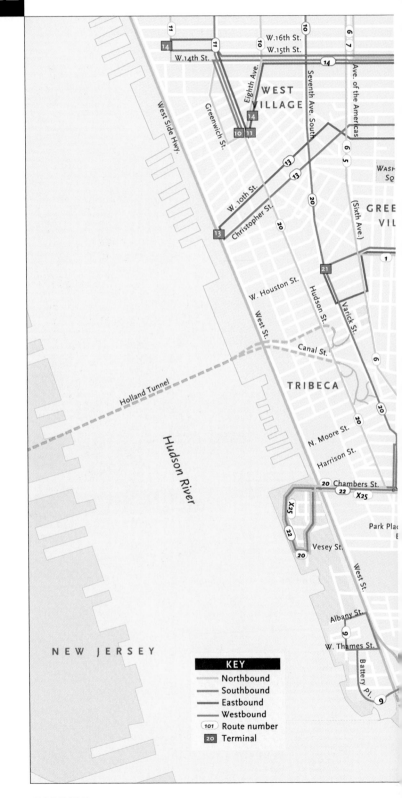

W.16th St.
W.15th St.
W.14th St.

WEST
VILLAGE

Eighth Ave.
Seventh Ave. South
Ave. of the Americas

West Side Hwy.
Greenwich St.

WASH
SQ

GREE
VIL
(Sixth Ave.)

W. 10th St.
Christopher St.
W. Houston St.
West St.
Hudson St.
Varick St.

Holland Tunnel

Canal St.

TRIBECA

N. Moore St.
Harrison St.
Chambers St.

Hudson River

Park Pla
E

Vesey St.

West St.

NEW JERSEY

Albany St.
W. Thames St.

Battery Pl.

KEY
— Northbound
— Southbound
— Eastbound
— Westbound
(101) Route number
20 Terminal

BUSES

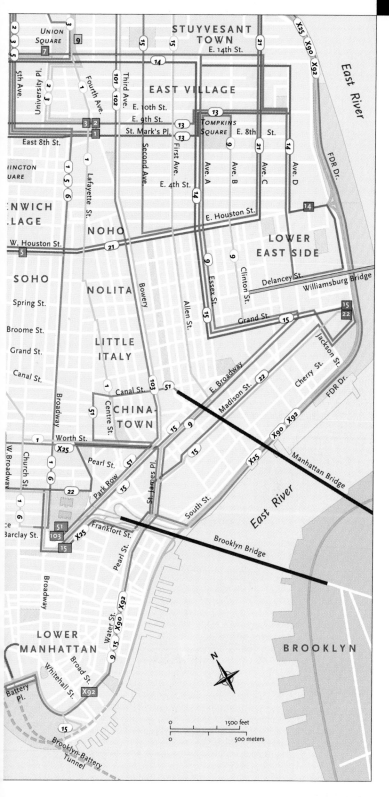

UNION
SQUARE

STUYVESANT
TOWN
E. 14th St.

EAST VILLAGE

E. 10th St.
E. 9th St.
St. Mark's Pl.
East 8th St.

TOMPKINS
SQUARE

E. 8th   St.

E. 4th St.

NOHO

E. Houston St.

LOWER
EAST SIDE

GREENWICH
VILLAGE

W. Houston St.

SOHO

Spring St.

Broome St.

Grand St.

Canal St.

NOLITA

LITTLE
ITALY

Delancey St.

Williamsburg Bridge

Grand St.

Jackson St.

Cherry St.

FDR Dr.

Canal St.

CHINA-
TOWN

Worth St.

Pearl St.

Park Row

Frankfort St.

E. Broadway

Madison St.

South St.

East River

Manhattan Bridge

Brooklyn Bridge

BROOKLYN

LOWER
MANHATTAN

Broadway

Whitehall St.

Broad St.

Battery
Pl.

Brooklyn-Battery
Tunnel

N

0   1500 feet

0   500 meters

BUSES

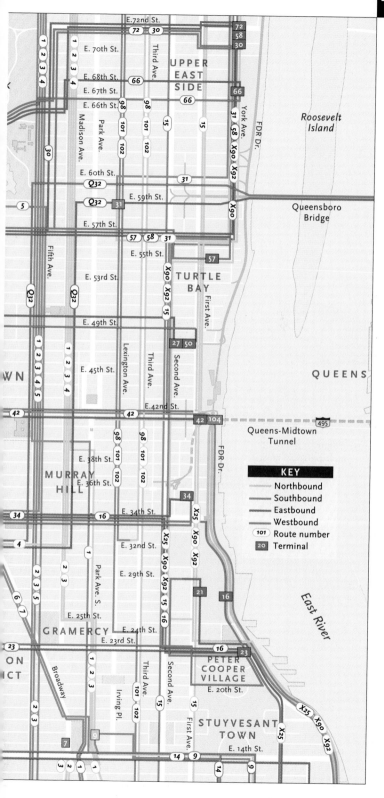

KEY
- Northbound
- Southbound
- Eastbound
- Westbound
- 101 Route number
- 20 Terminal

MIDTOWN

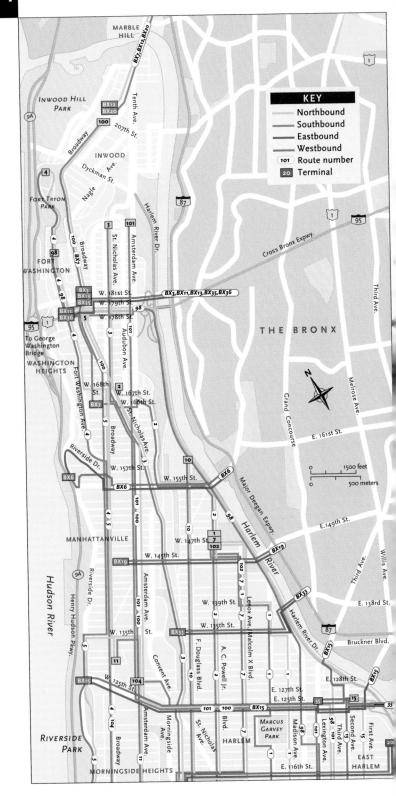

BUSES UPTOWN

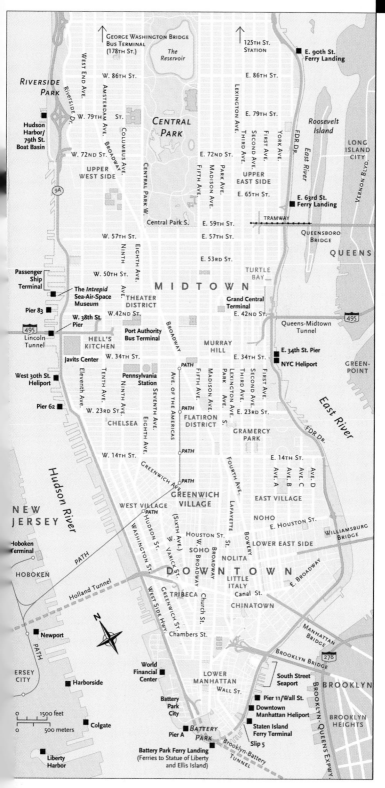

PIERS AND TERMINALS

The Sourcebook
for Your
Hometown

MANY MAPS • WHERE & HOW

FIND IT ALL • NIGHT & DAY

ANTIQUES TO ZIPPERS

BARGAINS & BAUBLES

ELEGANT EDIBLES • ETHNIC EATS

STEAK HOUSES • BISTROS

DELIS • TRATTORIAS

CLASSICAL • JAZZ • COMEDY

THEATER • DANCE • CLUBS

COCKTAIL LOUNGES

COUNTRY & WESTERN • ROCK

COOL TOURS & TRIPS

HOUSECLEANING • CATERING

GET A LAWYER • GET A DENTIST

GET A NEW PET • GET A VET

MUSEUMS • GALLERIES

PARKS • GARDENS • POOLS

BASEBALL TO ROCK CLIMBING

FESTIVALS • EVENTS

DAY SPAS • DAY TRIPS

HOTELS • HOT LINES

PASSPORT PIX • TRAVEL INFO

HELICOPTER TOURS

DINERS • DELIS • PIZZERIAS

BRASSERIES • TAQUERÍAS

BOOTS • BOOKS • BUTTONS

BICYCLES • SKATES

SUITS • SHOES • HATS

RENT A TUX • RENT A COSTUME

BAKERIES • SPICE SHOPS

SOUP TO NUTS

Fodor's

CITYGUIDE
NEW YORK

FODOR'S TRAVEL PUBLICATIONS

NEW YORK • TORONTO • LONDON • SYDNEY • AUCKLAND

WWW.FODORS.COM

FODOR'S CITYGUIDE NEW YORK

EDITOR
Constance Jones

EDITORIAL CONTRIBUTORS
Carissa Bluestone, Stephen Brewer, Daniella Brodsky, Mitchell Davis, John Donohue, Joshua Michael Greenwald, Elise Harris, Evelyn Kanter, Jennifer Kasoff,
Christina Knight, Jane Miller, Margaret Mittelbach, Tom Steele, William Travis, Carolyn Turgeon, Michael B. de Zayas

EDITORIAL PRODUCTION
Ira-Neil Dittersdorf

MAPS
David Lindroth Inc., cartographer; Bob Blake and Rebecca Baer, map editors

DESIGN
Fabrizio La Rocca, creative director; Allison Saltzman, text design; Tigist Getachew,
cover design; Jolie Novak, senior picture editor; Melanie Marin, photo editor

PRODUCTION/MANUFACTURING
Colleen Ziemba

COVER PHOTOGRAPH
James Lemass

COPYRIGHT

Third Edition

ISBN 0–676–90218–9

ISSN 1099–8527

SPECIAL SALES

Fodor's Travel Publications are available at special discounts for bulk purchases for
sales promotions or premiums. Special editions, including personalized covers,
excerpts of existing guides, and corporate imprints, can be created in large quanti-
ties for special needs. For more information, contact your local bookseller or write
to Special Markets, Fodor's Travel Publications, 280 Park Avenue, New York, NY
10017. Inquiries from Canada should be directed to your local Canadian bookseller
or sent to Random House of Canada, Ltd., Marketing Department, 2775 Matheson
Boulevard East, Mississauga, Ontario L4W 4P7. Inquiries from the United Kingdom
should be sent to Fodor's Travel Publications, 20 Vauxhall Bridge Road, London
SW1V 2SA, England.

PRINTED IN THE UNITED STATES OF AMERICA

10 9 8 7 6 5 4 3 2 1

CONTENTS

METROPOLITAN LIFE

O n a bad day in a big city, the little things that go with living shoulder-to-shoulder with a few million people wear us all down. But the special pleasures of urban life have a way of keeping us out of the suburbs—and thankful, even, for every second of stress. The field of daffodils in the park on a fine spring day. The perfect little black dress that you find for half price. The markets—so fabulously well stocked that you can cook any recipe without resorting to mail-order catalogs. The way you can sometimes turn a corner and discover a whole new world, so foreign you can hardly believe you're less than a mile from home. The never-ending wealth of possibilities and opportunities.

If you know where to find it all, the city can't defeat you. With knowledge comes power. That's why Fodor's has prepared this book. It'll put phone numbers at your fingertips. It'll take you to new places and remind you of those you've forgotten. It's the ultimate urban companion—and, we hope, your new best friend in the city.

It's the **citywise shopaholic,** who always knows where to find something, no matter how obscure. We've made a concerted effort to bring hundreds of great shops to your attention, so that you'll never be at a loss, whether you need a special birthday present for a great friend or some obscure craft items to make Halloween costumes for your kids.

It's the **restaurant know-it-all,** who's full of ideas for every occasion—you know, the one who would never send you to Café de la Snub, because he knows it's always overbooked, the food is boring, and the staff is rude. We'll steer you around the corner, to a perfect little place with five tables, a fireplace, and a chef on her way up.

It's a **hip barfly buddy,** who can give you advice when you need a charming nook, not too noisy, to take a friend after work. Among the dozens of bars and nightspots in this book, you're bound to find something that fits your mood.

It's the **sagest arts maven** you know, the one who always has the scoop on what's on that's worthwhile on any given night. In these pages, you'll find dozens of concert venues and arts organizations.

It's the **city whiz,** who knows how to get you where you're going, wherever you are.

It's the **best map guide** on the shelves, and it puts all the city in your briefcase or on your bookshelf.

Stick with us. We'll lay out all the options for your leisure time—and gently nudge you away from the duds—so that you can truly enjoy metropolitan living.

YOUR GUIDES

No one person can know it all. To help get you on track around the city, we've hand-picked a stellar group of local experts to share their wisdom.

From their vantage point at The James Beard Foundation, dining chapter writers **Mitchell Davis** and **Jane Miller**—two of our restaurant reviewers—keep their eyes (and palates) peeled on New York's ever-changing restaurant scene. They have worked together on numerous cookbooks and articles for magazines such as *Fine Cooking* and *Food & Wine*.

John J. Donohue is the nightlife editor of the "Goings On About Town" section at *The New Yorker*. His intimate knowledge of the city proved invaluable as he updated our nightlife coverage.

Food writer and former chef **Josh Greenwald** updated our City Sources chapter. He's cooked for top NYC restaurants such as Danube and Eleven Madison Park.

A native New Yorker and decade-long Brooklyn resident, **Elise Harris,** our Hotels updater, has never lived farther from the city than Princeton, NJ. She recently traded in her gig as an editor at *Out* magazine for a daily schlep to the New York Public Library, where she does freelance journalism.

Native New Yorker **Evelyn Kanter** loves the outdoors, so writing about parks, gardens, and recreation is a happy excuse to smell the flowers. She has reported on all aspects of her hometown for WABC TV, CBS radio, *New York* magazine, and national magazines and newspaper travel sections.

Jennifer Levitsky Kasoff, one of our parks, gardens, and sports updaters, is a former Fodor's staff editor. She has walked, bowled, and climbed her way around New York City since 1995.

Margaret Mittelbach, one of our places to explore updaters, has written about all aspects of the city: animal, vegetable, and mineral. She is coauthor of *Wild New York,* an acclaimed guide to the city's wildlife, wild places, and natural history.

One of our restaurant reviewers, **Tom Steele,** is currently food editor for *Our Town* and *Manhattan Spirit*. He recently wrote a cookbook for people with small kitchens, and he was the founding editor of *TheaterWeek, Opera Monthly,* and the *New York Native,* among other publications.

A corporate writer and aspiring novelist by day, shopping updater **Carolyn Turgeon** spends her weekends scouring the city's hippest clothing shops and glittering antiques scene. She has also covered parenting in New York for the guide *City Baby*.

Since earning a Master of Fine Arts degree from Sarah Lawrence College, **Michael de Zayas,** one of our places to explore updaters, has lived in the East Village, Midtown, and on the Upper West Side. He has worked at two of the city's more venerable institutions: the Metropolitan Museum of Art and the *New York Post*.

It goes without saying that our contributors have chosen all establishments strictly on their own merits—no establishment has paid to be included in this book.

HOW TO USE THIS BOOK

The first thing you need to know is that everything in this book is arranged by category and in alphabetical order within category.

Now, before you go any farther, check out the **city maps** at the front of the book. Each has a number, in a black box at the top of the page, and grid coordinates along the top and side margins. On the text pages, every listing in the book is keyed to one of these maps. Look for the map number in a small black box preceding each establishment name. The grid code follows in italics. For establishments with more than one location, additional map numbers and grid codes appear at the end of the listing. To locate a museum that's identified in the text as **7** *e-6*, turn to Map 7 and locate the address within the e-6 grid square. To locate restaurants nearby, simply skim the text in the restaurant chapter for listings identified as being on Map 7.

Where appropriate throughout the guide, we name the neighborhood in which each sight, restaurant, shop, or other destination is located. We also give you the nearest subway stop, plus complete opening hours and admission fees for sights; closing information for shops; credit-card, price, reservations, and closing information for restaurants; and credit-card information for nightspots.

At the end of the book, in addition to an alphabetical index, you'll find a directory of restaurants by neighborhood.

Chapter 7, City Sources, provides resources and essential information for residents and visitors alike—everything from vet and lawyer-referral services to entertainment hot lines.

We've worked hard to make sure that all of the information we give you is accurate at press time. Still, time brings changes, so always confirm information when it matters—especially if you're making a detour.

Feel free to drop us a line. Were the restaurants we recommended as described? Did you find a wonderful shop you'd like to share? If you have complaints, we'll look into them and revise our entries in the next edition when the facts warrant. So send us your feedback. Either e-mail us at editor@fodors.com (specifying Fodor's CITYGUIDE New York on the subject line), or write to the Fodor's CITYGUIDE New York editor at 280 Park Avenue, New York, New York 10017. We look forward to hearing from you.

Karen Cure
Editorial Director

chapter 1

RESTAURANTS

New York is the undisputed restaurant capital of the world. No other metropolis has New York's variety of cuisines, from haute French and pan-Asian to Nuevo Latino and New American. New restaurants appear with breathtaking swiftness, as old areas of the city are renovated and lofts are fancifully redesigned. Loft locus TriBeCa has seen a veritable avalanche of openings during the last decade. Art gallery-crowded Chelsea, the Flatiron District, and Gramercy Park have also become hot dining destinations. SoHo continues to add venues to its stylish roster; you can find somewhere to dine in this area virtually around the clock. New eateries have begun to populate the meatpacking district in southwest Chelsea as enterprising restaurateurs scramble to define the next dining trends.

general information

NO SMOKING

Smoking is not allowed in most restaurants, though you may be permitted to smoke at the bar or at a table outside, if alfresco dining is available. Some restaurants have smoking/dining areas near the bar. Restaurants with fewer than 35 seats often have smoking areas, but if a nearby table requests that you refrain, refrain you must.

CELL PHONES

Most restaurants frown upon the use of cellular phones—many don't permit it and often post signs or place a note on the menu stating their policy. Don't assume people around you won't mind overhearing your cellular conversations. Take it outside.

RESERVATIONS

It's not only common courtesy to make reservations at a restaurant—when you call you might discover that the restaurant is closed for a private party, or that the air-conditioning is on the blink, or some other important consideration. Likewise, if you can't make it at your reserved time (give or take 20 minutes), or if you can't make it at all, definitely call the restaurant. Believe it or not, cumulative no-shows can seriously hurt a restaurant.

TIPPING

The rule of thumb for wait-service tips is at least 15% of the total (exclusive of tax), a figure easily calculated by doubling the amount of the 8¼% city sales tax. It's safe to say that New Yorkers tend to leave closer to 20%. Most restaurants add a service charge for large parties, so if you are dining with a group of six or more, be sure to check the bill carefully before leaving a tip.

PRICE CATEGORIES

CATEGORY	COST*
$$$$	over $32
$$$	$25–$32
$$	$15–$24
$	under $15

*per person, for a main course at dinner

restaurants by cuisine

AFGHAN

9 *f-3*

PAMIR

A popular place for a quick, light dinner, Pamir serves dependable, budget-price Afghan fare in an exotic setting. Locals like the large portions of succulent shish kebabs and other grilled meats and stews. *1065 1st Ave. (at 58th St.), Upper East Side, 212/644–9258. AE, D, DC, MC, V. Closed Mon. Subway: 4, 5, 6, N, R, W to 59th St.–Lexington Ave. $–$$*

7 *f-8*

1437 2nd Ave. (at 75th St.), Upper East Side, 212/734–3791. Subway: 6 to 77th St.

678901234567890234567890

AFRICAN

10 2-g

LE SOUK

Serving inexpensive and delectable food under the stars or in a Bedouin-style tent, this restaurant attracts more diners than it can comfortably handle. If you dine early enough, you can enjoy steady service and such exotic North African fare as ruddy vegetable-strewn tagines with chicken, fish, lamb shank, or merguez (lamb sausage) with fluffy couscous; grilled whole fish; and citrus-sauced grilled octopus. *47 Avenue B (between 3rd and 4th Sts.), East Village, 212/777–5454. MC, V. No lunch. Subway: F, V to Second Ave. $–$$*

AMERICAN

4 7-c

AESOP'S TABLE

For Manhattanites phobic about crossing the water, this restaurant near the ferry is a good choice for a first excursion to Staten Island. The garden has an excellent view of the skyline and the New American food is always enticing. *1233 Bay St. (at Maryland Ave.), Rosebank, Staten Island, 718/720–2005. AE, D, MC, V. Closed Sun.–Mon. $–$$*

9 e-8

ALVA

Alva is the ultimate neighborhood restaurant, its cozy bar draped with regulars enjoying the perfect combination of intimacy and excitement. But past the bar lies a sophisticated dining room that pays visual homage to its namesake, Thomas Alva Edison, with dim, exposed bulbs and black-and-white photographs. The delicious American bistro fare is a bargain considering the location. For a great lunch: Dive inside for a toothsome burger or a fabulous "Reuben Cuban" sandwich at the bar. *36 E. 22nd St. (between Park Ave. S and Broadway), Flatiron District, 212/228–4399. AE, DC, MC, V. No lunch weekends. Subway: 6 to 23rd St. $$–$$$*

9 e-4

AN AMERICAN PLACE

Now luxuriously ensconced in the Benjamin Hotel, celebrated chef Larry Forgione wins unqualified raves for his artfully presented, regional American specialties. The wine selection (Ameri-can only) is not to be overlooked. Enjoy Maine crabmeat, Adirondack free-range duckling, chicken breast sautéed with apple-cider vinegar, three-smoked-fish terrine, or signature pot-roasted beef shortribs. *565 Lexington Ave. (between 50th and 51st Sts.), Midtown, 212/888–5650. Reservations essential. AE, DC, MC, V. Subway: 6 to 51st St./Lexington Ave.; E, V, to Lexington–3rd Aves./53rd St. $$$*

10 e-7

BAYARD'S

You'll feel as if you're dining at Monticello once you're nestled into this 1837 structure, which became the India House in 1914, a club for businessmen specializing in foreign trade. It turned restaurant in 1998, and the interior was painstakingly restored and many original details contribute to the beautiful setting. Raw silk swags frame the huge windows, and nautical oil paintings adorn the wainscotted walls. The menu, crafted by chef Eberhard Müller, lists such culinary creations as oysters warmed with champagne sauce and poached lobster with minced mangos. *One Hanover Sq. (between William and Pearl Sts., 3 blocks south of Wall St.), Lower Manhattan, 212/514–9454. AE, MC, V. Closed Sat. and Sun. No lunch. Subway: 1, 2 to Wall St. $$–$$$*

9 d-3

BEACON

Rainbow Room veteran Waldy Malouf delves deeply into grilling at this luxurious, complex space, filled with loopy balconies and egalitarian see-and-be-seen seating. House-baked breads are perfection, and the special cocktails will really clean your clock. Then tear into some wood-roasted Malpeque oysters that will flood you with sumptuous flavors. The main event is grilled meat, fish, or game. To get in touch with your inner Neanderthal, go for a 12- or 18-ounce hunk of Argentinean ranch-grazed rib-eye steak that gets precisely the kind of grill crusting that it begs for. Finish with one of the yowlingly tasty soufflés. *25 W. 56th St. (between 5th and 6th Aves.), Midtown West, 212/332–0500. AE, MC, V. Subway: N, R, W to 5th Ave. $$–$$$*

10 f-6

BRIDGE CAFE

Nestled beneath the Brooklyn Bridge in a wood-frame building from 1794, this

cozy and friendly former longshore-
men's café is now a favorite with Wall
Street suits. Try soft-shell crabs in season, grilled trout, red snapper with vegetable risotto, buffalo steak, and the
excellent pecan pie. *279 Water St. (at
Dover St.), Lower Manhattan, 212/227–
3344. AE, DC, MC, V. No lunch Sat.
Brunch Sun. Subway: 4, 5 to Fulton St.* $$

11 *d-7*
BUBBLE LOUNGE
And what a lounge it is! Quaff some
bubbly from the impressive champagne
list and find yourself flattered by the red
velvet curtains, brick walls, high ceilings,
comfortable couches, and other beauti-
ful people. The food is secondary; have
some caviar or pâté, then go some-
where else for dinner. Reserve ahead
with a party of six or more. *228 W.
Broadway (between Franklin and White
Sts.), TriBeCa, 212/421–3433. AE, DC, MC,
V. No lunch. Subway: 1, 2 to Franklin St.*
$–$$$$

9 *e-8*
CANDELA
This former brick warehouse near Union
Square has been transformed into a sort
of baronial hall, with wrought-iron rail-
ings, huge, dark mirrors, lighted tapers,
and wooden booths. The menu is
broad-ranging—spicy focaccia, a three-
tier seafood platter, hummus, fried cala-
mari, lamb shanks, and shortribs—the
bar is hopping, and the crowd is young.
*116 E. 16th St. (between Irving Pl. and
Park Ave. S), Gramercy, 212/254–1600.
AE, MC, V. Brunch Sun. Subway: L, N, Q,
R, W, 4, 5, 6 to 14th St./Union Sq.* $–$$

11 *5-e*
CANTEEN
A-list celebrities and hip downtowners
have discovered this basement space
decorated in the color scheme of a '70s
rec-room with a chic post-modern aesthetic: think vast white walls, Tang-
orange chairs in space-age shapes, and
brown circular booths that look like
modular sofas. By contrast, the food is
traditional down-home American—macaroni and cheese, pork chops with buttermilk smashed potatoes, and lobster
and cod pan roast. Though most who
dine here dress like they can afford to
pay top dollar, prices are surprisingly
reasonable. *421 Mercer St. (at Prince St.),
SoHo, 212/431–7676. AE, MC, V. Subway:
N, R to Prince St.* $$–$$$

10 *e-5*
CITY HALL
You can't help but chuckle at the
salad—an old-fashioned wedge of ice-
berg lettuce served with Russian dressing—but the real surprise will be how
much you like it. She-crab soup, chilled
seafood platters, Delmonico steak,
broiled salmon, and grilled calves' liver
are other well-executed dishes that hear-
ken back to our city's dining past. Cub
Room chef-owner Henry Meer has created a tasteful New York theme restaurant, complete with back-lit
black-and-white photographs of old New
York. Before you hit the dining room,
with its impressive raw bar, hit the
roomy and elegant bar area, where man-
size drinks and delicious homemade
potato chips will take the edge off even
the most wearying day. *131 Duane St.
(between Church St. and W. Broadway),
TriBeCa, 212/227–7777. Reservations essential. AE, MC, V. Closed Sun. Subway: A, C
to Chambers St.* $$–$$$

9 *e-8*
CRAFT
Having established himself at Gramercy
Tavern as one of the most gifted chefs in
the country, Tom Colicchio opened his
own place on the block behind, where
he and chef Marco Canora turn out
some of the most flavorful fare in town.
Here, à la carte dining is thoroughly par-
ticipatory. Diners choose main ingredients to entrées and side dishes, which
are grouped by cooking methods. Thus,
you could start with rabbit ballotine,
then have roasted hanger steak and
partner it with potato gratin or purée.
Hundreds of combinations are possible.
Portions are large enough to encourage
sharing "family-style." *43 E. 19th St.
(between Broadway and Park Ave. S),
Flatiron District, 212/780–0880. AE, D,
DC, MC, V Subway: N, R, 6 to 23rd St.*
$$–$$$$

11 *d-4*
CUB ROOM
A constant, lively bar scene keeps this
brick and wood restaurant packed. Make
your way to the dining room, in back, for
a quieter experience. The menu is far-
reaching (sometimes a bit too far) but
with some fine dishes, including tuna in
a sesame-seed crust on soy-flavored
Asian greens and pot roast with braised
red cabbage and spaetzle. *183 Prince St.
(at Sullivan St.), SoHo, 212/777–0030.*

AE, D, DC, MC, V. Brunch Sun. Subway: 6 to Spring St.; N, R to Prince St. $$$

10 *e-7*
DELMONICO'S
As the oldest restaurant in New York City, opened in 1827, Delmonico's is obviously steeped in history, both cultural, political, and culinary. Eggs Benedict, lobster Newburg, and baked Alaska were all invented here, and are still on the menu. Inside the stately yet informal mahogany-paneled dining room, tuck into a 20-ounce boneless rib-eye steak literally smothered with frizzled onions, dry-aged and spoon tender, and don't forget to order creamed spinach on the side. *56 Beaver St. (near S. William St.), Lower Manhattan, 212/509–1144. AE, DC, MC, V. Closed Sat. and Sun. Subway: 4, 5 to Bowling Green. $$–$$$$*

9 *d-5*
DISTRICT
Everything about this Times Square close-up is continually fine-tuned for a memorable and delicious meal. Owner–chef Sam DeMarco (who also owns First and Merge) matches an elegantly theatrical setting with an enthralling menu, including truffle butter melting in a warmer and three progressively sized portions of seared foie gras. The $38 three-course theater menu is quite a bargain, served 5:30–6:30 to get you to the show in plenty of time. *130 W. 46th St. (between Broadway and Sixth Ave.), Midtown West, 212/485–2999. AE, MC, V. No lunch Sat. or Sun. Subway: N, R, W to 49th St. $$–$$$$*

11 *d-8*
DUANE PARK CAFE
This sleek restaurant has a Japanese chef whose cooking synthesizes Italian, Japanese, Cajun, and Californian styles. Pasta is made on the premises. Try the grilled quail with homemade sausage, crab-crusted halibut, roast leg of lamb with polenta, and the excellent sorbets. *157 Duane St. (between Hudson St. and W. Broadway), TriBeCa, 212/732–5555. Reservations essential. AE, DC, MC, V. Closed Sun. No lunch Sat. Subway: 1, 2 to Chambers St. $$–$$$*

11 *h-1*
FIRST
With huge booths, low lights, professional service, and chef Sam DeMarco's (*see* District *and* Merge) internationally accented cuisine, First managed to transcend its own nascent attitudinal hipness with delightful aplomb. Open almost until dawn, it's truly a place to enjoy New York. Check out the creative martini selection, including one flavored with a rose-scent syrup and "tinis" (a little—or not so little—flask of top-shelf vodka tucked into an individual ice bucket and served with a miniature martini glass). Of course, you shouldn't neglect the food—try the Long Island duck marinated in soy honey; the Sunday-night "backyard barbecue," including roast suckling pig; and the deeply comforting warm chocolate pudding. *87 1st Ave. (between 5th and 6th Sts.), East Village, 212/674–3823. AE, MC, V. No lunch. Brunch Sun. Subway: F, V to Second Ave.; 6 to Astor Pl. $$–$$$*

11 *f-3*
FIVE POINTS
There is a sophisticatedly organic feel to the decor at Five Points, which employs running water, lots of blond wood, pots of grass on the tables, and soft lighting. The American–Mediterranean menu serves up hearty dishes like seafood stew with grilled octopus, pan-roasted herb-stuffed chicken, and casserole of wood-oven baked lamb. Of note is the small wine list that emphasizes moderately priced bottles. *31 Great Jones St. (between Lafayette St. and Bowery), East Village, 212/253–5700. AE, MC, V. Closed Sun. No lunch. Subway: 6 to Bleecker St.; F, V to Broadway–Lafayette St. $$*

9 *e-7*
GLOBE RESTAURANT
This spunky, futuristic American brasserie highlights chef Jeanne Courtenay-Price's reliable renditions of such regional classics as a grilled double-cut pork chop with fingerling potatoes and soft-shell crabs that lean together around a heap of Old Bay slaw. Don't overlook the well-stocked raw bar. Cocktails are ample, as is the supply of lusty singles. *373 Park Ave. S (between 26th and 27th St.), Gramercy, 212/545–8800. AE, MC, V Subway: 6 to 23rd St. $$–$$$*

10 *e-1*
GOTHAM BAR & GRILL
After 16-plus years, this remains one of city's best restaurants, a testament to chef and owner Alfred Portale's many talents. The dining room is a multilevel postmodern brasserie with 17-ft ceilings,

soft lighting, and cast-stone ledges that give the sense of a garden courtyard. Portale was the first to serve "architectural" (as in "stacked") food, and he still does it better (and higher) than anyone else. Try the chilled seafood salad, the rack of lamb, and any of the desserts. 12 E. 12th St. (between 5th Ave. and University Pl.), Greenwich Village, 212/620–4020. Reservations essential. AE, DC, MC, V. No lunch weekends. Subway: L, N, Q, R, W, 4, 5, 6 to 14th St./Union Sq. $$$–$$$$

9 e-8

GRAMERCY TAVERN

Most locals agree this is the best American restaurant in New York City. Gustatory pathfinder Tom Colicchio has his perfect match in pastry chef Claudia Fleming, and together they have attained a culinary stride that continually delights and captivates a vast and devoted audience. Add to that the award-winning amicably focused service, and a cozy city tavern atmosphere in which to enjoy it all, and it's easy to see why so many people swear by the place. Opened by Danny Meyer (see Union Square Café, 11 Madison Park, and Tabla), this large and handsome restaurant encompasses three suave dining areas and a tavern room, which features a less-expensive menu and a magnificent bar. Wooden beams, white walls, and country artifacts lend a rustic feel. The seasonal dishes are deeply flavored: exemplary tuna tartare with sea urchin and cucumber vinaigrette; lobster and artichoke salad; tender braised beef cheeks; roasted sea bass; a superlative cheese board. Desserts are imaginatively spectacular: unforgettable coconut tapioca with passion fruit sorbet, and the best chocolate cookies you've ever tasted. 42 E. 20th St. (between Broadway and Park Ave. S), Gramercy, 212/477–0777. Reservations essential for dining room, not accepted for the less formal "tavern." AE, DC, MC, V. No lunch weekends. Subway: 6, N, R to 23rd St. $$$$

11 b-3

THE GRANGE HALL

American farm cooking is served here in a mostly minimalist setting (introduced by an Art Deco bar) in a quiet section of the West Village. Highlights are the good, hearty breakfasts, organic sandwiches, pork chops with apples, and lamb steak with rosemary. Desserts include coconut cake, pies, and cobblers. 50 Commerce St. (at Barrow St.), West Village, 212/924–5246. AE. Brunch weekends. Subway: A, B, C, D, E, F, V to W. 4th St./Washington Sq.; 1, 2 to Christopher St.–Sheridan Sq. $–$$

11 c-2

HOME

This tiny restaurant's storefront consists of secondhand books in a bay window. Inside, there is always a crowd, with some enjoying the year-round (heated) garden. Chef David Page and his partner and wife Barbara Shinn make lovely, seasonal country food: blue-cheese fondue with caramelized shallots, roast chicken with onion rings, excellent fish, and a fine chocolate pudding. 10 Cornelia St. (between Bleecker and W. 4th Sts.), West Village, 212/243–9579. No credit cards. Subway: A, B, C, D, E, F, V to W. 4th St. $$

11 d-7

INDEPENDENT

Crowded and trendy, this bilevel bistro has a clubby, turn-of-the-20th-century feel. Downstairs there's a small bar and a row of candlelit tables (where you can smoke); upstairs, a larger dining room. The straightforward American menu includes fried calamari, pork ribs with applesauce, steak with fries, lamb stew with artichokes and thyme, and, for dessert, an excellent thin-crusted apple tart. 179 W. Broadway (between Worth and Leonard Sts.), SoHo, 212/219–2010. Reservations essential. AE, DC, MC, V. Subway: A, C, E to Canal St. $$$–$$$$

7 f-7

KINGS' CARRIAGE HOUSE

A perfect spot for a rainy night, this comfortable restaurant inhabits a beautifully restored brownstone on a quiet, tree-lined street. The two dining rooms are on separate floors and have different furnishings, both including hand-painted walls and antique tables and chairs. The food is as warm and comforting as the manor-house atmosphere: roasted venison is served with homemade fruit chutney, and wild Alaskan salmon comes perfumed with native herbs. 251 E. 82nd St. (between 2nd and 3rd Aves.), Upper East Side, 212/734–5490. AE, DC, MC, V. Closed Sun. Subway: 4, 5, 6 to 86th St. $$

10 *d-1*

MERGE

In a deep, silvery space that ends under a large skylight, Merge is another showcase for the culinary gifts of Sam DeMarco (*see* First *and* District). The menu continually evolves, with certain ingredients as steady staples. Miniature fish and plantain hard-shell tacos arrive on a quaint little rack. Rare "habañero tuna" is delightful, though not remotely spicy. Lamb in any form is worth trying, as are all the desserts. *142 W. 10th St. (between 6th and 7th Aves.), West Village, 212/691–7757. AE. Subway: 1, 2 to Christopher Street–Sheridan Sq. $$*

9 *d-8*

MESA GRILL

Terrific Southwestern in New York City? Superstar "grillin' and chillin'" chef Bobby Flay, at the peak of his form, serves up his highly stylized, delightfully spicy fare at this Flatiron District destination. The brash award-winning design provides an amusing counterpoint to the imaginative cooking. Try El Tesoro Reposado tequila in your margarita, then tuck into the intense chipotle- and hoisin-dappled duck confit blue-corn tortilla. Follow with pan-roasted rabbit loin medallions, enrobed in a pineapple–red chile vinaigrette. Wayne Harley Brachman's desserts—caramelized bananas Foster with butter-pecan ice cream is one option—are fanciful. Brunch is scrumptious. During peak hours, the restaurant can get quite loud. If you shun din, ask to be seated upstairs. *102 5th Ave. (between 15th and 16th Sts.), Flatiron District, 212/807–7400. Reservations essential. Brunch Sun. AE, MC, V. Subway: L, N, Q, R, W, 4, 5, 6 to 14th St./Union Sq. $$$–$$$$*

9 *c-2*

O'NEALS'

Featuring the most reasonably priced food near Lincoln Center, O'Neals' is also very child-friendly. The restaurant stays open every night until at least midnight (or "until the fat lady sings" at the Metropolitan Opera House just across Broadway). The menu offers something for pretty much everyone, from French onion soup or crab cakes to burgers or veal Milanese. A three-course pre-theater dinner (served from 4:30 to 8) is offered for $25.95. *49 W. 64th St. (near Broadway), Upper West Side, 212/787–*

4663. AE, MC, V. Subway: 1, 2 to 66th St.–Lincoln Center. $$

9 *e-4*

OSCAR'S

Poised on the northeast corner of the venerable Waldorf–Astoria, Oscar's has joined in the hotel's multi-million-dollar renovation. Named for New York's most legendary maître d', Oscar Tschirky (who invented lobster Newburg, veal Oscar, and Waldorf Salad), the gently priced menu was devised with his original cookbook as inspiration. Oscar salad is an enormous tower of stingingly fresh greens hugged by plentiful slender slices of pink grilled veal, lightly dressed with a fragrant tarragon cream. A few pudgy crab cakes and blanched asparagus ribbons complete the dish. Custardy chicken potpie is exemplary in its tawny, egg-brushed crust. Rice pudding is appropriately sumptuous. *E. 50th St. at Lexington Ave., Midtown, 212/879–4920. AE, MC, V. Subway: 6 to 51st St./Lexington Ave.; E, V, to Lexington–3rd Aves./53rd St. $$*

11 *a-1*

PARIS COMMUNE

Try to score a seat by the small fireplace to experience the full effect of this neighborhood spot. Even if you're not near the fireplace, the whole dining room is pleasant, with worn wood floors, ceiling fans, and gilt-framed mirrors. There is a selection of basic pasta dishes, appetizers, and comfort food such as meat loaf, as well several more creative dishes like skate with blood orange, ginger, and champagne reduction. *411 Bleecker St. (between Bank and W. 11th Sts.), West Village, 212/929–0509. AE, MC, V. No lunch weekdays. Subway: A, C, E to 14th St.; L to 8th Ave. $–$$*

9 *d-1*

PARK VIEW AT THE BOATHOUSE

On a wide boardwalk along the northeastern rim of the lake in Central Park, the Boathouse is a glorious and restful setting for dining in benevolent weather. (In cold weather, the restaurant is taken indoors, where the atmosphere is invitingly ski-lodge-ish.) Creative fare from the kitchen includes a hoisin-crusted pork tenderloin, perfectly roasted, partnered with a kafir lime and rice cake that's topped by a seared giant sea scallop. For dessert, try a pineapple "carpaccio" with guava sherbet. Try to time your evening meal so that you can catch the sunset. As the shadows lengthen, a limpid Maxfield Parrish radiance sets in. *Central Park (enter at E. 72nd St. and bear right on Park Dr. N), Upper East Side, 212/517–2233. Reservations essential. AE, MC, V. Subway: 6 to 68th St.–Hunter College. $$–$$$*

11 g-3
PRUNE

Downtown to its core, this diminutive spot serves up chef/owner Gabrielle Hamilton's sometimes peculiar but generally enjoyable interpretations of American fare (she considers Triscuits an ingredient). The menu is meat-oriented and the room can be smoky, but the very East Village staff and patrons always seem to be having a great time. *54 E. First St. (between 1st and 2nd Aves.), East Village, 212/677–6221. AE, MC, V. Brunch Sun. Subway: F, V to 2nd Ave. $$*

9 b-5
RACHEL'S
AMERICAN BISTRO

Theater-goers and locals alike are charmed by Rachel's soothing space, pressed-tin ceiling, and homey decor of the old-mirrors-and-dried-flowers variety. Quarters may be a bit cramped, but service is stellar—friendly and professional—and high-quality ingredients elevate a menu of simply prepared New American dishes. Best of all you'll find it very, very light on your wallet. *608 9th Ave. (between 43rd and 44th Sts.), Midtown West, 212/957–9050. AE, MC, V. Subway: A, C, E to 42nd St. $–$$*

9 c-3
REDEYE GRILL

If America is about size and crowds and money and choice and abundance, then the Redeye Grill is a quintessentially American restaurant. The place is always packed, and the menu has a little of everything, with an emphasis on seafood: lobster in salad, in potpie, and grilled; salmon cured like pastrami, smoked, and grilled; sturgeon, sable, pasta, steak, and burgers. It's no wonder the crowd is diverse. Desserts such as banana-cream pie and chocolate mousse are deliciously rendered classics. Nothing's really great, except

maybe the whole idea; but nothing really disappoints, either. *890 7th Ave. (at 56th St.), Midtown West, 212/541–9000. Reservations essential. AE, D, DC, MC, V. Subway: F, N, R, Q, W to 57th St. $$–$$$*

11 f-4
RIALTO

Rialto—with its shabby-chic dining room, pressed tin walls, simple wooden chairs, burgundy banquettes, and back garden— is almost the perfect neighborhood restaurant. The New American menu delivers interesting but not overly exotic offerings, such as grilled tuna with Asian spiced fries, roasted garlic soup, and a superlative hamburger. The main detracting feature is the difficulty involved in securing a table, but the wooden bar is a great place to hang out while waiting. *26 Elizabeth St. (between Houston and Prince Sts.), SoHo, 212/334–7900. AE, MC, V. Subway: 6 to Spring St. $$*

11 e-4
SAVOY

Peter Hoffman's cooking has come into its own. Here it's served on two floors of an 1830s redbrick building, with working fireplaces, exposed-brick walls, and a cozy upstairs room (with bar) where you can savor a prix-fixe meal cooked by Hoffman himself Tuesday–Saturday. Try the smoked skate with capers and fries, sea scallops in Riesling sauce, or venison with black beans and swiss chard. Deserts are particularly superb. *70 Prince St. (at Crosby St.), SoHo, 212/219– 8570. Reservations essential. AE, DC, MC, V. Closed Sun. No lunch Mon. Subway: N, R to Prince St.; 6 to Spring St.; F, V to Broadway–Lafayette St. $$–$$$*

10 d-4
SCREENING ROOM

A commercial movie theater is attached to this New American restaurant with a film theme, and the screening rooms are even available for rent. The idea was to create a multi-purpose space that would celebrate independent filmmaking and fine food at the same time. The movies and food are, for all intents and purposes, separate, except for the great dinner-and-a-movie bargain for $30, and the fact that lots of employees of nearby Miramax can often be found dining or having drinks at the long and elegant bar. *54 Varick St. (between Canal and Laight St.), TriBeCa, 212/334–2100. AE, D,*

DC, MC, V. Closed Sat. No lunch Mon. Subway: A, C, E to Canal St. $$

11 e-4
SOHO KITCHEN & BAR
This cavernous SoHo wine bar boasts a 60-ft-long bar and a long run of popularity, now drawing its share of tourists as well as locals. The city's largest Cruvinet dispenses over 120 choice wines by the glass, including champagnes. Nibbles include pizzas, pasta, salads, and burgers, all available at the bar or at tables. Along for the ride? Draft beer and ales are also available. 103 Greene St. (between Prince and Spring Sts.), SoHo, 212/925–1866. Reservations not accepted. AE, DC, MC, V. Subway: N, R to Prince St. $

11 h-4
TORCH
All the tables at this scaled down supper club overlook a stage where excellent singers and musicians perform jazz standards on a nightly basis. Selections from the tiny raw bar will always enhance the mood, and while the food is not exceptional it is good enough, especially when the scene is so electric. 137 Ludlow St. (between Rivington and Stanton Sts.), Lower East Side, 212/228–5151. AE, DC, MC, V. No lunch. Subway: F, J, M, Z to Delancey St. $$

11 c-7
TRIBECA GRILL
The flagship venture of the Robert DeNiro–Drew Nieporent partnership, this converted TriBeCa warehouse has a consistently charged atmosphere, both at the well-spaced tables and at the exquisite bar in the middle of the dining room. Chef Don Pintabona serves classic American grill food with creative international accents, such as lamb paillard with Israeli couscous or seared tuna with sesame noodles. The wonderful banana tart with chocolate-malt ice cream is a must. 375 Greenwich St. (at Franklin St.), TriBeCa, 212/941–3900. AE, DC, MC, V. No lunch weekends. Brunch Sun. Subway: 1, 2 to Franklin St. $–$$$

9 e-8
UNION SQUARE CAFE
One of the city's very favorite restaurants, this Flatiron District phenom has three dining areas and a long, lively bar where you can also dine. Michael Romano's cooking, with California–Italian overtones, is superb. Have the

black-bean soup with a shot of Austrian sherry; fried calamari with anchovy mayonnaise; marinated "filet mignon" of tuna; addictive hot garlic potato chips; smoked black Angus shell steak with mashed potatoes and frizzled leeks; and perhaps banana tart with caramel and macadamia nuts. The restaurant set a new standard for impeccable service. 21 E. 16th St. (off Union Sq. W), Flatiron District, 212/243–4020. Reservations essential. AE, DC, MC, V. No lunch Sun. Subway: L, N, Q, R, W, 4, 5, 6 to 14th St./Union Sq. $$–$$$

9 e-8
VERBENA
Refined and romantic, Verbena complements its large, enchanting garden with subtle and seasonal cooking by chef and owner Diane Forley. Try her foie gras with salsify, prunes, and pearl onions; homey roast chicken with celery root and wild rice; and crème brûlée scented with verbena. Desserts are especially wonderful, so save room. 54 Irving Pl. (at 17th St.), Gramercy, 212/260–5454. AE, DC, MC, V. Brunch weekends. Subway: L, N, Q, R, W, 4, 5, 6 to 14th St./Union Sq. $$–$$$

9 c-1
VINCE & EDDIE'S
Not many restaurants in Manhattan offer a country environment, but sitting among the gingham curtains, exposed brick, and plank floor of this quiet American bistro is truly transporting. Hearty fare such as roasted chicken, veal shank, and mashed potatoes is the perfect antidote to chilly New York winters. The whole package is terrific before or after a Lincoln Center event. 70 W. 68th St. (between Columbus Ave. and Central Park W), Upper West Side, 212/721–0068. Reservations essential. AE, DC, MC, V. Brunch Sun. Subway: 1, 2 to 66th St.–Lincoln Center. $$

10 e-7
WALL STREET KITCHEN & BAR
Want to hang out with investment bankers? Look no further. Although you'll find an excellent wines-by-the-glass list—many of which can be ordered by tasting "flights"—this place often feels more like a frat party than a destination for serious oenophiles. Although most don't go for dinner, its menu leans toward upscale bar food.

The soaring space, formerly a bank, is divided into several smaller areas. *70 Broad St. (at Beaver St.), Lower Manhattan, 212/797–7070. AE, D, DC, MC, V. Closed weekends. Subway: 4, 5 to Bowling Green. $–$$*

3 *c-5*

WATER'S EDGE

Who would ever guess that the barren, industrial stretch of waterfront in Long Island City is home to a restaurant as breathtakingly lovely as the Water's Edge? The view of the twinkling Manhattan skyline across the East River at night is one of the best in the world, and the well-executed, prix-fixe American menu does an admirable job of trying to compete with the scenery. Foie gras terrine is supple and succulent, rib-eye steak is state of the art, and "once-over-easy" cod is delightfully spongy and juicy. Service is attentive and caters to those visiting for a special occasion. A free water taxi at 34th Street transports guests between the restaurant and Manhattan. Try to time your visit to coincide with the sunset—an unforgettable experience. *44th Dr. between the East River and Vernon Blvd., Long Island City, Queens, 718/482–0033. Reservations essential. AE, DC, MC, V. Subway: E, V to 23rd St.–Ely Ave. $$$$*

10 *c-1*

YE WAVERLY INN

This 150-year-old Greenwich Village town house has been a restaurant since 1920, always retaining its Colonial-tavern feel. The food matches the ambience: simple and comfortable. Look for passable potpies, Southern fried chicken, and other traditional American dishes. In summer there's a pleasant back garden; in winter, two working fireplaces. *16 Bank St. (at Waverly Pl.), West Village, 212/929–4377. AE, DC, MC, V. Brunch weekends. Subway: 1, 2 to Christopher St.–Sheridan Sq. $$–$$$*

11 *e-4*

ZOË

Zoë is a big, very noisy, very SoHo restaurant with an open grill in the back and a long bar up front. Many dishes are wood-grilled or cooked on the rotisserie. Try the salmon tartare with mango-chile salsa, grilled tuna with wok-charred vegetables, grilled buffalo sirloin with garlic-potato cake. *90 Prince St. (between Mercer St. and Broadway), SoHo, 212/966–6722. AE, DC, MC, V. No lunch Mon. Brunch weekends. Subway: N, R to Prince St.; 6 to Spring St.; F, V to Broadway–Lafayette St. $$*

AMERICAN CASUAL

11 *f-2*

B-BAR

American food and lots of models are the story of the B Bar, in a former gas station with a velvet rope at the door. Opt for a simple burger or more complex fish and pasta dishes. The scene starts late. A particularly inviting, spacious, and popular outdoor dining area is available in gentle weather. *40 E. 4th St. (between Lafayette St. and Bowery), East Village, 212/475–2220. AE, MC, V. Brunch weekends. Subway: F, V to Broadway–Lafayette St.; 6 to Astor Pl. $–$$*

9 *f-3*

BILLY'S

In business since 1870, this East Side institution is cherished by the Sutton Place crowd, who enjoy it as a refuge from their more serious dining locales. The old tavern serves steaks and other pub fare from a blackboard menu, and beers and stout on tap. *948 1st Ave. (between 52nd and 53rd Sts.), Midtown East, 212/355–8920. Reservations not accepted. AE, DC, MC, V. Subway: 6 to 51st St./Lexington Ave.; E, V to Lexington–3rd Aves./53rd St. $–$$$*

9 *c-3*

BROOKLYN DINER USA

Though less authentic than the name would suggest—at what diner in Brooklyn would your eggs be served with crispy polenta fries instead of potatoes?—this quasi–theme restaurant delivers decent food and good value. Though the large portions of American standbys such as burgers and hot dogs make it difficult, try to save room for one of New York's best sundaes. *212 W. 57th St. (between Broadway and 7th Ave.), Midtown West, 212/581–8900. Reservations not accepted. AE, DC, MC, V. Subway: F, N, R, Q, W to 57th St.; 1, 2, A, B, C, D to 59th St.–Columbus Circle. $–$$*

`10` d-5

BUBBY'S

Always the most popular neighborhood brunch spot, these days crowds from all over the city line up on weekends, clamoring for coffee and fresh squeezed juice. Attractive furnishings and plate-glass windows make the dining room homey and comfortable. Brunch favorites include grits, homemade granola, or entrées such as sour cream pancakes and smoked trout with scrambled eggs. Eclectic comfort food such as macaroni and cheese, fusilli with wild mushrooms, or shepherd's pie make up the lunch and dinner menus. All of the homemade pies rock. But even though the restaurant expanded, you'll still usually suffer an interminable wait. *120 Hudson St. (at N. Moore St.), TriBeCa, 212/219–0666. AE, DC, MC, V. Brunch weekends. Subway: 1, 2 to Franklin St. $–$$*

`9` c-8

CAFETERIA

"Highly stylized" and "hopelessly hip" may well describe both the decor and clientele here; the food, however, is anything but. Stellar breakfasts—silver dollar pancakes with berries and whipped cream, ham steak with cheese grits and red-eye gravy—are served all day, and excellent lunch and dinner entrées tend toward the homey with such flourishes as rosemary-roasted apples served with the smoked pork chops and spicy fried oysters topping Caesar salad. Don't expect to find any ladies in hair nets at this cafeteria; service is of the restaurant variety, with just a touch more attitude than usual. *119 7th Ave. (at 17th St.), Chelsea, 212/414–1717. Reservations essential. AE, DC, MC, V. Subway: A, C, E to 14th St.; L to 8th Ave.; 1, 2 to 18th St. $–$$*

`10` c-1

CORNER BISTRO

You won't understand why you've come to eat at this dark, neighborhood bar until you taste a Bistro Burger. With or without bacon and cheese, the burger's juices drip down your chin and the flavor can't be beat. The thin-cut fries aren't bad, either. That everything is served on paper plates is almost endearing. Why it's called a bistro you'll probably never know. *331 W. 4th St. (at Jane St.), West Village, 212/242–9502. No credit cards. Subway: A, C, E to 14th St.; L to 8th Ave. $*

`12` g-7

DIZZY'S

The soi-disant "finer diner," Dizzy's is hands-down the top neighborhood joint for a casual meal in the Slope. The food is more than a step above diner grub—salads are generous; seasoned fries crispy; and sandwiches on delectable thick-sliced bread. If you're not up for a full prix-fixe brunch on weekend mornings (and you're ready to forego the pre-brunch muffin basket), grab a stool at the counter, where you can order off the well-priced breakfast and lunch menus. Whatever you do, come early. *511 9th St. (at 8th Ave.), Park Slope, Brooklyn, 718/499–1966. AE, MC, V. Brunch weekends. Subway: F to 7th Ave. $*

`7` b-7

EJ'S LUNCHEONETTE

The decor invokes the 1950s, when cherry pie and egg creams were the

---

BAR DINING

Dining at the bar of a restaurant has a strong appeal for many, particularly for people dining solo or for folks on–the–go. It's often less expensive and often times serves entirely different dishes specifically for those who enjoy dining on a stool.

Bistro Les Amis (French)
At the commodious bar in this cozy corner bistro you can order the full menu or a variety of bar snacks.

Chicama (Latin)
Circumvent the crowds at this tremendously popular ceviche destination by dining right at the ceviche bar itself.

Gramercy Tavern (American)
The tavern menu is completely different from the dining room's, benevolently priced and less formal.

Oyster Bar at Grand Central (Seafood)
The long and twisting bar is ideal for imbibing some of the best oysters on the Eastern seaboard.

Tabla (Indian)
The Indian/American "bread bar" menu is utterly delightful.

Union Square Cafe (American)
This highly beloved restaurant is famous in part for its superb bar menu.

thing, and it somehow persuades crowds to forget their current dietary habits and order enormous omelets or waffles slathered with butter and layered with pecans. The menu has a large selection of retro diner items, from root beer on tap to Salisbury steak and macaroni-and-cheese; but there are some concessions to post-1960 cuisine, such as the balsamic vinaigrette that dresses the Cobb salad or the grilled vegetable sandwich on seven-grain bread. Steer clear of weekend brunch hours unless you can get there by 10 AM or don't mind waiting at least 45 minutes. *447 Amsterdam Ave. (between 81st and 82nd Sts.), Upper West Side, 212/873–3444. Reservations not accepted. No credit cards. Breakfast daily. Subway: 1, 2 to 86th St.* $

9 e-1

1271 3rd Ave. (at 73rd St.), Upper East Side, 212/472–0600. Subway: 6 to 77th St.

11 d-1

432 6th Ave. (between 9th and 10th Sts.), Greenwich Village, 212/473–5555. Subway: A, B, C, D, E, F, V to W. 4th St.

9 b-8

EMPIRE DINER

This 24-hour Art Deco diner is a magnet for après-club late-night snacks. Ever stylish, it was here long before Chelsea became trendy. The menu is pricey for diner fare, but the food is generally good. There's live piano music all week, and you can sit outdoors in summer, albeit overlooking somewhat grubby 10th Avenue. *210 10th Ave. (at 22nd St.), Chelsea, 212/243–2736. Reservations not accepted. AE, MC, V. Subway: C, E to 23rd St.* $–$$

11 f-2

GREAT JONES CAFE

Pop into this crowded, down-home Bowery spot for flavorful burgers, chili, red- or bluefish fillets, and the house drink—a jalapeño martini, to go with your jalapeño corn bread, of course. To top it all off, the jukebox still works. The noise is deafening, but the crowd doesn't seem to mind. *54 Great Jones St. (between Bowery and Lafayette St.), East Village, 212/674–9304. No credit cards. Subway: N, R to 8th St.; 6 to Astor Pl.* $–$$

7 f-8

J. G. MELON

J. G. Melon's bar burger has long been called the best on the Upper East Side.

Locals love to hang out and sample the large beer selection while digging into a no-frills burger and a bowl of waffle-cut fries. Red-and-white check tablecloths and sports on the TV complete the aesthetic. *1291 3rd Ave. (at 74th St.), Upper East Side, 212/744–0585. Brunch Sun. Subway: 6 to 77th St. No credit cards.* $

12 d-3

JUNIOR'S

This famous restaurant is most known for its New York–style cheesecake, but the huge menu also has the Jewish specialties that originally made the restaurant famous—corned beef, pastrami, chopped liver, and other sandwiches served on fresh-baked club rye—as well as some soul food selections and complete dinners. The rugelach aren't bad either. Sure you can find better food and better service, but some kind of irreplaceable nostalgia makes a meal at Junior's a worthwhile experience. *386 Flatbush Ave. (at DeKalb Ave.), Downtown Brooklyn, 718/852–5257. AE, DC, MC, V. Subway: M, N, Q, R to DeKalb Ave.* $–$$$

10 d-6

KITCHENETTE

Small and comfortable, this popular downtown hangout serves comfort food to match the atmosphere. Weekend brunch is particularly popular, with oversize stacks of pancakes, French toast, good coffee, and other necessities. Don't miss the well-priced dinner specials, such as meat loaf and roasted chicken. Although the no-frills decor and slow service are too much for some diners to take, for others they just add to the experience. *80 W. Broadway (at Warren St.), TriBeCa, 212/267–6740. AE. Brunch weekends. Subway: 1, 2 to Chambers St.* $–$$

7 b-8

MISS ELLE'S HOMESICK BAR & GRILL

Even more comfortable than home, this tumbling space that ends in a huge greenhouse room serves up huge portions of comfort food that will indeed make you pleasantly homesick. Don't miss the spectacular pork chops and succulent chicken breast *Française*. And leave plenty of room for the supple banana cream pie. An especially luscious Sunday brunch is served here. *226 W. 79th St. (between Amsterdam Ave.*

and Broadway), Upper West Side, 212/595–4350. AE, MC, V. Subway: 1, 2 to 79th St. $–$$

9 *d-3*

OAK ROOM & BAR

This traditional wood-paneled restaurant and bar in the famed Plaza is still one of the classiest spots in town for a drink. Order light fare from the bar menu, or sit inside the restaurant for some heartier American food. If you aren't wearing a jacket and tie, you can order from the Oak Room menu and be served in the bar. *Plaza Hotel, 768 5th Ave. (at 59th St.), Midtown West, 212/546–5330. AE, DC, MC, V. Subway: N, R, W to 5th Ave.–60th St. $$$–$$$$*

9 *f-3*

P. J. CLARKE'S

P. J. Clarke's is the classic Old New York saloon. At lunch and happy hour, Midtown men pack the extremely popular front room for a beer, a burger, or both. If you're more interested in eating than socializing, elbow your way to the dark and atmospheric dining room in the back. Best bites include the burgers, home fries, chili, cold poached salmon, and spinach salad. *915 3rd Ave. (at 55th St.), Midtown East, 212/759–1650. AE, DC, MC, V. Open until 4 AM. Subway: N, R, W, 4, 5, 6 to 59th St.–Lexington Ave. $–$$*

9 *e-8*

PETE'S TAVERN

O. Henry, who lived across the street, penned "The Gift of the Magi" in this 1864 tavern. The original bar is quite popular, as is the sunny sidewalk café in summer. The menu mixes old-fashioned Italian food with hefty burgers and Reubens. *129 E. 18th St. (at Irving Pl.), Gramercy, 212/473–7676. AE, DC, MC, V. Subway: L, N, Q, R, W, 4, 5, 6 to 14th St./Union Sq. $–$$*

7 *b-7*

POPOVER CAFÉ

The weekend lines outside this Upper West Side brunch spot remind you that the local demand for comfort food far exceeds the supply. Wonderful omelets, cheese grits, creative pancakes, and, of course, warm popovers with strawberry butter attract families and friends toting the Sunday *Times*. More lunchlike options include sandwiches, hearty burgers, and tasty salads. *551 Amster-*

dam Ave. (at 87th St.), Upper West Side, 212/595–8555. Reservations not accepted. AE, MC, V. Subway: 1, 2 to 86th St. $–$$

9 *b-3*

ROUTE 66 CAFÉ

If you still think "glorified diner" is a pejorative, give Route 66 a try. True, the decor gives only a half-hearted nod to the restaurant's eponymous roadway, and service could be better, but with comfortable seating and reasonable prices the complaints are few. The real draw is a menu of huge and well-prepared salads, burgers, pastas, and sandwiches; the juice bar is a plus if you prefer a vitamin-induced boost to a caffeine buzz. Neighborhood residents find take-out a palatable option when waits (particularly at brunch) are long. *858 9th Ave. (between 55th and 56th Sts.), Midtown West, 212/977–7600. AE, D, DC, MC, V. Brunch weekends. Reservations not accepted. Subway: A, B, C, D, 1, 2 to 59th St.–Columbus Circle. $*

7 *e-6*

SARABETH'S

Sarabeth's is still considered *the* place for brunch on the East Side, so the wait can be torture. But if you get there early, you'll enjoy an elegant country breakfast à la Martha Stewart. Omelets, homemade muffins, potato and cheese blintzes, pancakes with fresh fruit, pumpkin waffles, and other tempting home-style entrées are served all day, every day. Wonderful marmalades, Linzer tortes, and shortbreads are available for takeout. *1295 Madison Ave. (between 92nd and 93rd Sts.), Upper East Side, 212/410–7335. AE, DC, MC, V. Breakfast daily. Subway: 6 to 96th St. $–$$*

7 *e-8*

Whitney Museum of American Art, 945 Madison Ave. (at 75th St.), Upper East Side, 212/570–3670. Closed Mon. Subway: 6 to 77th St.

7 *b-7*

423 Amsterdam Ave. (between 80th and 81st Sts.), Upper West Side, 212/496–6280. Subway: 1, 2 to 79th St.

9 *f-2*

SERENDIPITY 3

For over 35 years this combo ice cream parlor–gift shop has been an inviting spot for lunch, brunch, and late-night snacks. Standing favorites on the child-friendly menu include a wide range of burgers, foot-long hot dogs (with or without chili), French toast, omelets, ice cream, and Serendipity's signature dish, frozen hot chocolate. Lines can be long, but you can divert yourself during the wait by playing with the tchotchkes and novelties for sale. Decor falls into the "whimsical" category, with antiques, flashes of pink, Tiffany lamps, and a general sense of bells and whistles. *225 E. 60th St. (between 2nd and 3rd Aves.), 212/838–3531. AE, DC, MC, V. BYOB. Brunch Sun. Subway: N, R, W, 4, 5, 6 to 59th St.–Lexington Ave. $–$$*

11 *f-3*
TEMPLE BAR
One of downtown's coolest bars, Temple Bar has lost its trendiness but not its style—which means you can almost always find a seat, and you can hear yourself think. The vodka menu is unmatched; the martinis are gigantic and delicious; and the food is pretty good, too. Try the gourmet pizzas and oysters. *332 Lafayette St. (between Houston and Bleecker Sts.), Greenwich Village, 212/925–4242. AE, DC, MC, V. Subway: 6 to Bleecker St.; F, V to Broadway–Lafayette St. $–$$*

11 *d-4*
TENNESSEE MOUNTAIN
Feel like ditching the city? This popular SoHo spot, inside a 19th-century wooden building that looks more like a farmhouse-turned-diner than a restaurant, feels like anywhere U.S.A. Fill up on meaty beef and baby-back ribs; fried onion loaf; corn bread; and meat or vegetarian chili. If you still have room, chase it all with a piece of apple-walnut or pecan pie. *143 Spring St. (at Wooster St.), SoHo, 212/431–3993. AE, MC, V. Subway: 6 to Spring St. $–$$*

9 *e-2*
VIAND
This tiny New York coffee shop is famous for its turkey, roasted right before your eyes and carved steaming-hot to order. Have it in sandwiches, chef salads, or with gravy and cranberry sauce. The service is fast, but space is scarce, so expect a wait. Why not enjoy a bit of the killer rice pudding until a table is free? There's also a full diner menu. *673 Madison Ave. (at 61st St.), Upper East Side, 212/751–6622. Reservations not accepted. No credit cards. Subway: N, R, W, 4, 5, 6 to 59th St.–Lexington Ave. $–$$*

7 *f-7*
300 E. 86th St. (at Second Ave.), Upper East Side, 212/879–9425. Subway: 6 to 86th St.

7 *e-8*
1011 Madison Ave. (at 78th St.), Upper East Side, 212/249–8250. Subway: 6 to 77th St.

10 *d-5*
WALKER'S
When all you want is a great burger and a pint of cold beer but you crave atmosphere and service that is a notch above Corner Bistro, head to Walker's. The restaurant is down the block from a police precinct stable, where the NYPD's horses are housed, and the spot maintains an unconscious raffishness that suggests the city's colorful past. There are other choices for non burger-eating diners, and the occasional live jazz performance. *16 N. Moore St. (at Varick St.), TriBeCa, 212/941–0142. AE, DC, MC, V. Subway: A, C, E to Canal St. $*

11 *a-1*
WHITE HORSE TAVERN
Dylan Thomas drank himself to death here and many other literary figures managed to tie one on at the scarred wood bar. These days moms dine on hefty burgers with their little ones at the outdoor picnic tables by day and neighborhood dwellers interested in cold beer and mingling congregate by night. *567 Hudson St. (at W. 11th St.), West Village, 212/989–3956. No credit cards. Subway: A, C, E to 14th St.; L to 8th Ave. $*

7 *g-7*
YORK IMPERIAL
Precisely what this neighborhood craved: A comfortable, casual restaurant that serves state-of-the-art comfort food at friendly prices. Amid a 1950s Italianate lounge setting complete with a vintage cocktail shaker display and Sinatra, tuck into good old meat loaf, succulent pork chops, or grilled tuna smothered with frizzled potatoes and balsamic. Whatever you do, don't miss the grilled calamari appetizer—it's some of the best in town. *1573 York Ave. (between 83rd and 84th Sts.), Upper East Side, 212/535–2204. No credit cards. Closed Mon. Subway: 6 to 86th St. $–$$*

ARGENTINE

`9` *b-5*

CHIMICHURRI GRILL

Prepare for a panoply of lovingly prepared dishes, such as chorizo and morcilla sausages, flaky empanadas, and surprisingly good Italian-style pastas at this elegant little restaurant, a perfect spot to dine before or after theater. Argentine red wines—an exceptional value—are offered in addition to a full bar. *606 9th Ave. (between 43rd and 44th Sts.), Midtown West, 212/586–8655. Reservations essential. AE, DC, MC, V. Closed Mon. No lunch Sun. Subway: A, C, E to 42nd St. $$*

BARBECUE

`11` *b-3*

BROTHERS BBQ

Dig in to the hearty and satisfying food at this spacious downtown barbecue haven. Ribs, chicken, brisket, and Cajun shrimp come in giant portions, with such appropriate and delicious sides as greens, corn bread, coleslaw, and potato salad. Desserts are simple and rich. The decor is Midwestern kitsch; think traffic lights and memorabilia. *225 Varick St. (between Houston and Clarkson Sts.), SoHo, 212/727–2775. AE, DC, MC, V. Subway: 1, 2 to Houston St. $–$$*

`10` *b-1*

HOG PIT

At least you can say you went straight to the source. This meatpacking-district barbecue joint and restaurant serves large portions of American food—everything from barbecued ribs and chicken to good ol' home cookin', like meat loaf, mac and cheese, and collard greens. All of the traditional slaws and sides are there, too. Though there is better barbecue to be had, the Hog Pit saves you the trip to Kansas City or Memphis. *22 9th Ave. (at 13th St.), West Village, 212/604–0092. AE, MC, V. No lunch. Subway: A, C, E to 14th St.; L to 8th Ave. $*

`9` *d-5*

VIRGIL'S REAL BBQ

When you're stuck for a pre-theater meal, remember that there's almost always a free table at this immense barbecue joint—one of the best in the city—where the portions are large, the service is friendly, and the atmosphere

is noisy and fun (if a bit touristy). Highlights are the barbecued shrimp, chicken, beef, pork ribs, and pulled-pork sandwiches. Sides of corn bread, coleslaw, potato salad, baked beans, and other summertime favorites make dinner here feel like a country picnic. *152 W. 44th St. (between Broadway and 6th Ave.), Midtown West, 212/921–9494. AE, DC, MC, V. Subway: N, Q, R, S, W, 1, 2, 3, 7 to 42nd St./Times Sq. $–$$*

BELGIAN

`10` *c-1*

CAFÉ DE BRUXELLES

Bruxelles serves the hearty cuisine of Belgium in a handsome European setting. Classics such as mussels served about eight ways, waterzooi de poulet, *carbonnade flamanade* (classic Belgian beef stew with beer, onions, and bacon), and *boudin blanc* (sausage usually made with pork and chicken) are complemented by cones of addictive Belgian frites served with dipping mayonnaise and an extensive (and pricey) list of imported beers. *118 Greenwich Ave. (at 13th St.), West Village, 212/206–1830. AE, MC, V. Subway: A, C, E to 14th St.; L to 8th Ave. $$*

`10` *b-1*

MARKT

This huge Belgian restaurant, situated on the edge of the meatpacking district, feels like a typical European brasserie with its wood tables, globe light fixtures, and a long bar. As expected the kitchen turns out a variety of moules frites—mussels can be dry but the fries are right on—as well as more obscure Belgian dishes such as *stoemp* (mashed potatoes) and *carbonnade* (beef stew). A good selection of Belgian beers is available to wash it all down. *401 W. 14th St. (at 9th Ave.), West Village, 212/727–3314. AE, MC, V. Subway: A, C, E to 14th St., L to 8th Ave. $$*

`11` *b-3*

PETIT ABEILLE

It's hard to find home-style European food prepared this well, especially at these prices. In the space where Marnie's Noodle Shop used to be, this tiny Belgian café on Hudson Street serves delicious *soupe aux moules* (mussel soup); hearty entrées; and, of course, crisp and tasty French fries. The brunch, including omelets and fresh Belgian waffles, is also good. The original store, on 18th Street, serves lunch only—and how. *466 Hudson St. (between Barrow and Grove Sts.), West Village, 212/741–6479. AE, MC, V. Brunch weekends. Subway: 1, 2 to Christopher St.–Sheridan Sq. $–$$*

10 *c-1*

400 W. 14th St. (at 9th Ave.), West Village, 212/727–1505. No credit cards. Subway: A, C, E to 14th St.; L to 8th Ave.

9 *c-8*

107 W. 18th St. (between 6th and 7th Aves.), Chelsea, 212/604–9350. No dinner. Subway: 1, 2, 3 to 14th St.

10 *d-5*

134 W. Broadway (at Duane St., SoHo, 212/791–1360. No dinner. Subway: 1, 2, 3, 9 to Chambers St.

BRAZILIAN

9 *d-3*

CHURRASCARIA PLANTATION

In the luxurious ballroom of Hampshire House (a hotel so fancy that all three of the Three Tenors keep residences there), you can feast on 20 different meats, from beef shortribs to suckling pig, carved at your table from sword-like skewers. This, after imbibing from a 40-ft "salad buffet" with more than 50 choices, from traditional Brazilian dishes to all the old favorite salads, meats, and fish. A few caipirinhas, Brazil's national cocktail, made with crushed limes and a heady sugar cane liquor, will put you in just the right mood for all this indulgence. Be very hungry. *150 Central Park S. (between Sixth and Seventh Aves.), Midtown West, 212/489–7070. AE, MC, V. Subway: A, B, C, D, 1, 2 to Columbus Circle. $$$$*

9 *c-4*

CHURRASCARIA PLATAFORMA

This New York outpost of a São Paolo favorite so perfectly captures the feeling of a Brazilian barbecue restaurant that you'll be surprised to emerge back into Manhattan. While the jazz trio plays Jobim classics, an endless parade of waiters with giant skewers of grilled meats whizzes by. Chicken, turkey, salmon, lamb, prime rib, top sirloin, and other carnivore favorites, each mari-

nated in different seasonings, are deposited on your plate in succession until you say "when" by turning your green chip over to red. You're supposed to begin with the equally impressive salad bar, but be careful not to fill up. The restaurant can easily accommodate large groups. (Though it seems odd for such a good-time place, management claims that shorts, sandals, and tank tops are verboten after 5 PM.) *316 W. 49th St. (between 8th and 9th Aves.), Midtown West, 212/245–0505. AE, D, DC, MC, V. Subway: C, E to 50th St. $$$$*

9 *e-8*

COFFEE SHOP

True, this trendy Brazilian eatery has an unlikely name, but those velvet ropes are there to tell you that it attracts a mighty stylish crowd. One wonders how all those beautiful people can sit at the sidewalk tables all day long, and how any place can stay so busy until dawn. For all the attitude, the *feijoada* (a platter of thinly sliced meats accompanied by rice, black bean, vegetables) isn't bad, but don't expect any sparks from the kitchen. It's not about food. *29 Union Square W (at 16th St.), Flatiron District, 212/243–7969. AE, MC, V. Subway: L, N, Q, R, W, 4, 5, 6 to 14th St./Union Sq. $–$$*

3 *g-2*

GREEN FIELD CHURRASCARIA

This cavernous restaurant is one of your better bets if you want a traditional all-you-can-eat Brazilian churrascaria. The place bustles with energy as the large waitstaff marches around the restaurant, which is easily the size of an airline hangar, proudly bearing cuts of tender meat on skewers. Before the beef, however, the salad bar appears to go on forever. The place is a fantastic bargain for big eaters. *108–01 Northern Blvd. (at 108th St.), Corona, Queens, 718/672–5202. AE, MC, V. Subway: 7 to 103rd St.–Corona Plaza. $$*

9 *b-4*

RICE 'N' BEANS

"Sublime" is the only way to describe what the cooks at this Brazilian storefront do with the lowly legume. Order the eponymous dish by itself (you won't go hungry), or eat it with any of the excellent fish, chicken, or meat entrées. The restaurant's about as big as a pillbox, so consider take-out unless you want to jam yourself in and become buddies with folks at the next table. 744 9th Ave. (between 50th and 51st Sts.), Midtown West, 212/265–4444. Reservations not accepted. D, MC, V. Subway: C, E to 50th St. $–$$

11 c-3

120 W. 3rd St. (between MacDougal St. and 6th Ave.), Greenwich Village, 212/375–1800. Subway: A, B, C, D, E, F, V to W. 4th St.

11 f-1

RIODIZIO

The rodizio, an all-you-can-eat rotisserie meal for $35.95, is one reason why this place has been packed since it opened. The restaurant occupies a vast loft space a few doors down from the Public Theater and is huge and noisy, with an enormous bar flanked by an attractive display of seafood. Forget Brazilian samba: your meal is accompanied by thundering disco. Caipirinhas, made with lime, sugar, and cachaça (a Brazilian liquor made from sugar cane), are served by the pitcher. The grilled meats and fish are first-rate, and come with a huge house salad, black beans, collard greens, brown rice, polenta, and fried plantains. Be very hungry. 417 Lafayette St. (near Astor Pl.), Greenwich Village, 212/529–1313. AE, MC, V. Brunch weekends. Subway: 6 to Astor Pl. $$

CAFÉS

9 c-3

CAFE EUROPA

Whether you need a place to refuel after shopping or are meeting an old friend to catch up, this Midtown café is like an oasis in the rendezvous desert—and it has two locations to boot. Simple salads, good sandwiches, a large selection of desserts, and good coffee make it the perfect pit stop. 205 W. 57th St., Midtown West, 212/977–4030. Reservations not accepted. AE, D, DC, MC, V. Subway: F, N, R, Q, W to 57th St. $

9 d-4

1177 6th Ave. (at 46th St.), Midtown West, 212/575–7272. Subway: B, D, F, V to 47th–50th Sts.

11 d-3

CAFFÉ DANTE

Frothy cappuccino, bracing espresso, teas, pastries, salads, and little sand-

wiches make up one of the Village's more inviting Italian cafés. Dante is a throwback to a time before Starbucks, when Mediterranean cooking meant lying in the sun. 79 MacDougal St. (between Bleecker and Houston Sts.), Greenwich Village, 212/982–5275. No credit cards. Subway: 1, 2 to Houston St.; A, B, C, D, E, F, V to W. 4th St. $

11 b-2

CAFFE VIVALDI

Just off the chaotic runway that is Bleecker Street in these parts, Caffe Vivaldi quietly serves coffees, teas, biscotti, and desserts amid dark wood, old-fashioned sketches and prints, and often a good deal of smoke. In winter, wait for a table near the fireplace; it's worth it. 32 Jones St. (between Bleecker and W. 4th Sts.), 212/929–9384. Reservations not accepted. No credit cards. Subway: A, B, C, D, E, F, V to W. 4th St. $

7 c-7

COLUMBUS BAKERY

The open, self-service concept of these stylish bakeries adds to their pleasantly frenetic energy. Make your selection from a counter overflowing with baked goods—quiches, tarts, cakes, pastries, muffins—and very light lunch fare. Though a few things, the breads in particular, look better than they taste, the comfortable chairs, casual service, and neighborhood atmosphere make these places very popular for a quick bite. 474 Columbus Ave. (at 83rd St.), Upper West Side, 212/724–6880. Reservations not accepted. AE, D, MC, V. Subway: 1, 2 to 79th St. $

9 f-3

957 1st Ave. (between 52nd and 53rd Sts.), Midtown East, 212/421–0334. Subway: 6 to 51st St./Lexington Ave.; E, V, to Lexington–3rd Aves./53rd St.

7 b-7

EDGAR'S CAFÉ

The bright, almost surreal interior of this European-style café is a tribute to its namesake, Edgar Allan Poe. People talk for hours here over light salads, sandwiches, and most of all, appealing desserts. A full selection of coffees and teas and pleasant service make this the perfect place to grab a bite and some quality time after a movie—but everyone on the West Side knows it, so you may have to wait for a table. It's worth noting that the place is open 365 days a year.

255 W. 84th St. (between Broadway and West End Ave.), Upper West Side, 212/496–6126. Reservations not accepted. No credit cards. Subway: 1, 2 to 86th St. $

11 f-5

FERRARA

This famous, lively, very bright café claims to be America's oldest pasticceria, and the honor draws crowds (of tourists) that spill out onto Little Italy's streets in summer. If you can hold out for a seat, you'll enjoy espresso, cappuccino, pastry, and gelati the way they were meant to be. You can also take home boxes of Ferrara's delicious *torrone* candy. 195 Grand St. (between Mulberry and Mott Sts.), Little Italy, 212/226–6150. Reservations not accepted. No credit cards. Subway: 6 to Canal St. $

7 b-3

HUNGARIAN PASTRY SHOP

Cramped, cozy, and timeless, if tired, this Columbia University hangout serves good poppy-seed pastries, Linzer torte, and cappuccino. You can sit for hours with a newspaper or book and nobody will bother you. 1030 Amsterdam Ave. (between 110th and 111th Sts.), Morningside Heights, 212/866–4230. Reservations not accepted. No credit cards. Subway: 1 to 110th St.–Cathedral Pkwy. $

9 b-8

LE GAMIN

Scuffed wood floors, rickety tables, and indifferent service—just like Paris, but without as much cigarette smoke. Still, these cafés have charm to spare, and the huge bowls of steaming café au lait and selection of authentic crepes and baguette sandwiches make them perfect places in which to grab a quick morning bite or while away an afternoon. If you go for brunch, expect to wait for a table (and wait and wait). 183 9th Ave. (at 21st St.), Chelsea, 212/243–8864. Reservations not accepted. No credit cards. Subway: C, E to 23rd St. $

11 c-4

50 MacDougal St. (between Prince and Houston Sts.), Greenwich Village, 212/254–4678. Subway: C, E to Spring St.

11 a-1

MAGNOLIA BAKERY

If you grew up in a small town during the 1950s, Magnolia Bakery will feel like home. If you didn't, one bite of the golden cupcake with chocolate buttercream frosting and sprinkles will make you wish that you had. Although all of the homey baked goods in this small storefront are authentic—the banana pudding is made with Nilla wafers and the hummingbird cake is so dense one slice can feed two—they aren't all equally good. The golden cupcakes are wonderful (the chocolate ones are a little dry), as are most of the bundt and layer cakes, which are served in very generous portions. The apple pie filling tastes canned and the rice pudding has a slight fake flavor. But there's no denying the nostalgia everything in this place evokes. 401 Bleecker St. (at W. 11th St.), West Village, 212/462–2572. No credit cards. Subway: A, C, E to 14th St.; L to 8th Ave. $

11 d-6

PALACINKA

Palacinka is the word for crepe in Hungarian and this little café, decorated with a pleasing mix-and-match of vintage objects, tin ceilings, small metal tables, and folding chairs, delivers just that. On the savory side crepes are filled with ingredients such as roasted tarragon chicken, goat cheese, and roasted peppers, or ham, Gruyère, and egg, and each comes with a pile of lightly dressed greens. The sweet crepes range from the classic butter and sugar to a rich concoction of chestnut cream and crème fraîche. There are also a couple of sandwiches and salads. Throw in a huge cup of the frothy hot chocolate and Palacinka will surely become your new favorite SoHo café. 28 Grand St. (between 6th Ave. and Thompson St.), 212/625–0362. No credit cards. Subway: A, C, E to Canal St. $

10 f-1

VENIERO'S

A bakery and café since 1894, the venerable and obviously beloved Veniero's continues to pack 'em in, and with good reason. They come from all over town for espresso, cappuccino, and scrumptious traditional Italian pastry, as well as fresh fruit ices in summer. Hope that sfogliatelle is still warm when you arrive—it often is. 342 E. 11th St. (between 1st and 2nd Aves.), East Village, 212/674–4415. AE, DC, MC, V. Subway: N, Q, R, W, 4, 5, 6 to 14th St./Union Sq.; L to 1st Ave. $

CARIBBEAN

`10` f-1
BAMBOU

Noël Coward would be quite at home in this attractive and elegant restaurant, which rather resembles a grand old mansion in Jamaica. Thick curried eggplant soup makes a great beginning. Fairly searing "jerk" pork and chicken—marinated in chiles and spices and smoke-grilled over pimento (allspice) wood fires—are accompanied by bouillabaisse, braised oxtail, and coconut crème brûlée. *243 E. 14th St. (between 2nd and 3rd Aves.), East Village, 212/505–1180. Reservations essential. AE, MC, V. Closed Sun. No lunch. Subway: L, N, Q, R, W, 4, 5, 6 to 14th St./Union Sq. $$–$$$*

`10` d-1
NEGRIL

Spicy fare and cold drinks to wash it down are the hallmarks of Jamaican restaurants, and Negril happily excels at both. The jerked dishes (chicken, beef, pork, or fish) are excellent, as are the potent blender drinks (stick to a bottle of Red Stripe if you're a lightweight). Be sure to make reservations or expect a wait, particularly on weekends. *362 W. 23rd St. (between 8th and 9th Aves.), Chelsea, 212/807–6411. AE, DC, MC, V. Subway: C, E, 1, 2 to 23rd St. $–$$*

CHINESE

`9` f-3
BEIJING DUCK HOUSE

This is the place for those who can't anticipate a craving for Peking duck 24 hours in advance: 20 minutes after you order, a whole duck, perfectly crisp, is carved at your table and presented with all the trimmings (pancakes, scallions, cucumbers, and hoisin sauce). If you're really hungry, start with the duck soup. Don't let the uptown address fool you; the spirit is Chinatown-informal. *236 E. 53rd St. (between 2nd and 3rd Aves.), Midtown East, 212/759–8260. AE, DC, MC, V. Subway: 6 to 51st St./Lexington Ave.; E, V to Lexington–3rd Aves./53rd St. $$*

`9` f-4
CHIN CHIN

Jimmy Chin's large and casual but extremely stylish restaurant highlights imaginatively prepared nouvelle-Chinese offerings, including shredded duck salad, vegetable-duck pie, grilled baby quail, steamed or crispy whole bass, and veal medallions with spicy pepper sauce. The atmosphere, like the food, is swanky and contemporary. *216 E. 49th St. (between 2nd and 3rd Aves.), Midtown East, 212/888–4555. Reservations essential. AE, DC, MC, V. No lunch weekends. Subway: E, F, 6 to 51st St.–Lexington Ave. $$–$$$*

`9` f-2
CHINA FUN

All baking and barbecuing are done on the bright, clean premises with the very freshest ingredients at these popular restaurants. The highly reasonable menu is overflowing with Cantonese, Szechuan, and Hunan classics, but the elegant and resourceful Dorothea Wu and her chefs also have Chinese fun with a variety of special entrées. The ample and celebrated selection of dim sum is always made to order. *1221 2nd Ave. (at 64th St.), Upper East Side, 212/752–0810. MC, V. Subway: 6 to 68th St.–Hunter College. $*

`9` c-1
246 Columbus Ave. (at 72nd St.), Upper West Side, 212/580–1516. Subway: B, C to 72nd St.

`9` c-4
1653 Broadway (at 51st St.), Midtown West, 212/333–2622. Subway: N, R, W to 49th St.

`10` f-5
JING FONG

This glitzy, multi-level Chinese-food palace—known for its dim sum, the traditional meal served Sunday morning, comprised of an astonishing array of small dishes and dumplings—is the closest you'll come to Hong Kong in Chinatown. Go early to avoid interminable waits, and to get first dibs on such delicacies as fresh, sweetened bean curd served from a barrel; deep-fried shrimp with their heads and their shells; and fresh clams in black-bean sauce. Shrill-voiced servers push food trolleys around the dining room, calling out the name of each item in Cantonese. Whether or not you understand exactly what they're saying, you can count on finding delicious *har gow* (steamed shrimp dumplings), *shu mai* (steamed pork dumplings), *chow fun* (wide rice noodles with dried shrimp), turnip cake, sesame balls, and custard tarts among the offerings. Perhaps better places for dim sum exist in Chinatown, and certainly in Flushing, but none as lively and fun as Jing Fong. *20 Elizabeth St. (between Bayard and Canal Sts.), Chinatown, 212/964–5256. AE, MC, V. Subway: 6, N, R, Q, W, J, M, Z to Canal St. $–$$*

11 *g-7*
JOE'S SHANGHAI
This Chinatown outpost of the famous Flushing restaurant is every bit as good as the original and a little busier; be prepared to wait. Shanghai cuisine is richer than other Chinese food, so come hungry. For starters, don't miss the steamed soup dumplings (pork or pork with crab) or the turnip shortcakes. Traditional, delicious, and very rich main dishes include lion's head (actually pork meatballs), braised pork shoulder, and homemade Shanghai noodles. The braised bean curd on spinach and eggplant in garlic sauce is also superb. Most connoisseurs consider the *xiao lung bao*—Shanghai soup dumplings—the very best in town. *9 Pell St. (between Mott St. and Bowery), Chinatown, 212/223–8888. No credit cards. Reservations not accepted. Subway: 6, N, R, Q, J, M, Z to Canal St. $*

10 *f-5*
LIN'S DUMPLING HOUSE
If pork and leek, crabmeat, or scallop and pork dumplings sound good, head to Dumpling House. Most of the dumplings—about 10 varieties, not to be confused with the Shanghai soup dumplings popular all over Chinatown—are available fried, steamed, or boiled and all are equally delicious. There is also a full menu of tasty Chinese favorites and more exotic dishes such as pig's ears and cherry clam and ginger soup. *25 Pell St. (between Mott St. and Bowery), Chinatown, 212/577–2777. No credit cards. Subway: 6, N, R, Q, W, J, M, Z to Canal St. $*

11 *g-7*
MANDARIN COURT
Though not as impressive in setting or scope as Chinatown's huge dim sum emporia, this small restaurant has a terrific selection of dumplings and other dim sum favorites. Because the carts have less surface area to cover, the food is often fresher and hotter, too. *61 Mott St. (between Canal and Bayard Sts.), Chinatown, 212/608–3838. AE, MC, V. Subway: 6, N, R, Q, W, J, M, Z to Canal St. $*

9 *f-3*
MR. CHOW
As you pass through the Lalique doors, you realize that this restaurant is as much about sleek setting and hip crowd as it is about food—here, Chinese with a touch of French and California thrown into the wok. Overlook the frenetic ambience to enjoy the crispy spinach, gambler's duck, drunken fish, and Grand Marnier shrimp. *324 E. 57th St. (between 1st and 2nd Aves.), Midtown East, 212/751–9030. Reservations essential. AE, DC, MC, V. No lunch. Subway: N, R, W, 4, 5, 6 to 59th St.–Lexington Ave. $$–$$$*

11 *g-7*
NY NOODLE TOWN
Open until 3 AM, this humble restaurant has some of the best Chinese food in Chinatown. Order the shrimp-dumpling soup, barbecued duck with flowering chives, and salt-baked soft-shell crab (in season). Barbecued pork and the other items hanging in the window are also delicious. *28 Bowery (at Bayard St.), Chinatown, 212/349–0923. No credit cards. Subway: 6, N, R, Q, W, J, M, Z to Canal St. $–$$*

7 *f-8*
PIG HEAVEN
This delicious and authentic food is served in a handsome setting. Although pork is the menu's mainstay, plenty of other options will satisfy those who'd rather pass on porcine paradise, including superbly wrought Peking duck. Don't miss the dumplings—they're all winners, fried, steamed, or boiled. Prices are higher than in Chinatown, but still quite reasonable. *1540 2nd Ave. (at 80th St.), Upper East Side, 212/744–4333. AE, DC, V. Subway: 6 to 77th St. $–$$*

3 *g-3*
PINGS
Manhattan's upscale Chinese restaurants may look fancier than this Elmhurst, Queens, establishment, but none of them serves more sophisticated food. From extravagant Cantonese specialties such as shark-fin soup and braised, dried abalone, to more familiar dishes such as roasted duck and fried rice, the cooking of chef-owner Ping draws raves. Ping's other specialties include giant lobsters, served steamed

with braised noodles; stir-fried pea shoots; and sweet dim sum. To ensure an other-worldly experience, gather a large group, call ahead to set up a banquet and be prepared to spend a lot of money on the Chinese meal of your life. Otherwise, of course, you can always just order off the menu. *8302 Queens Blvd., Elmhurst, Queens, 718/396–1238. AE. Subway: R, V to Grand Ave. $–$$*

9 *e-3*

SHUN LEE PALACE

Shun Lee serves impeccably prepared Hunan and Szechuan dishes in two of the city's truly plush Chinese settings. There's a low-calorie menu for dieters, but the temptations of the regular menu are pretty irresistible—hot-and-sour cabbage, lobster Szechuan, beggar's chicken, crispy whole sea bass, shrimp puffs, spicy Hunan duckling with a smoky flavor. Occasional guest chefs from Hong Kong augment the regular menu. The less formal café at the Lincoln Center location is convenient for pre-concert meals, quicker, and more reasonably priced. But now there's also a $20.01 prix-fixe lunch at the Palace. *155 E. 55th St. (between Lexington and 3rd Aves.), Midtown East, 212/371–8844. Reservations essential. AE, DC, MC, V. Subway: N, R, W, 4, 5, 6 to 59th St.–Lexington Ave. $–$$$*

9 *c-2*

43 W. 65th St., Upper West Side, 212/595–8895. Subway: 1, 2 to 66th St.–Lincoln Center.

10 *f-4*

SWEET-N-TART

This tiny Chinatown "diner" is packed until the wee hours with a young, trendy Asian crowd. The food is inexpensive and superb. Highlights include fried rice with Chinese sausage in bamboo, yam noodle soup with assorted dumplings, and ginger and scallion lo mein. An array of special hot and cold drinks (called "teas") should not be missed. The mango shakes with tapioca pearls or black sago balls and the hot almond tea are among the best. *76 Mott St. (at Canal St.), Chinatown, 212/334–8008. No credit cards. Subway: 6, N, R, Q, W to Canal St. $*

11 *g-7*

TAI HONG LAU

First-rate seafood, dim sum, and Peking duck in an upmarket setting make Tai Hong Lau one of Chinatown's best restaurants. The flip side: it has some of Chinatown's rudest waiters. *70 Mott St. (between Bayard and Canal Sts.), Chinatown, 212/219–1431. AE. Subway: 6, N, R, Q, W to Canal St. $–$$*

10 *f-4*

YUMEE NOODLE

Situated off a hidden Chinatown alleyway, this excellent Cantonese noodle shop is worth hunting down. One of the restaurant's specialties—despite the place's name—is a rice casserole baked with any number of toppings, among which might be pork, chicken, and a variety of exotica. To eat it, you stir in some soy sauce and the crunchy crust that forms on the bottom incorporates into the dish giving it an interesting texture. Noodle dishes are also very good. The only disappointments are the barbecued items hanging in the window, which are better prepared elsewhere. *48 Bowery (between Canal and Bayard Sts.), Chinatown, 212/374–1327. No credit cards. Subway: 6, Q, N, R, Q, W to Canal St. $*

CONTEMPORARY

9 *e-8*

ALEUTIA

Named for the volcanic islands that connect America with Asia in the Bering Sea, this gorgeous bar (downstairs) and restaurant (upstairs) shamelessly flaunts its glamour and casually glamourous crowd through floor-to-ceiling windows on Park Avenue South. Nab one of the three booths upstairs if you can, to see and be seen. Service is remarkably focused, and Gavin Citron's up-to-the-minute culinary renditions have a lilting Asian accent. Minced wild mushroom and saffron dumplings redefine "earthy," skate fillet is cooked just to the sizzle, and red snapper is dressed to the nines with tequila-cured chorizo sausage and served on a bed of truffled whipped potatoes. Desserts are no less snazzy: blueberries adorn lavender crème brûlée, and molten chocolate cake arrives with stinging spearmint ice cream. *220 Park Ave. S (at 18th St.), Flatiron District, 212/529–3111. AE, MC, V. Subway: 6 to 23rd St. $$–$$$*

10 e-8
AMERICAN PARK AT THE BATTERY
This is waterside dining at its finest. In up-and-coming Battery Park, this airy dining room is distinguished by an incredible view of the Statue of Liberty and Ellis Island. True to the spirit of New York, the menu is more or less American with flavors borrowed from many far-flung cuisines. An outdoor café right on the water is set up as a casual grill in summer months. Also outside is an ingenious table (for groups of 10–12) with a hollowed out pool in the middle, where family-style dinner floats in wooden dishes. *Battery Park at State St., Lower Manhattan, 212/809–5508. AE, MC, V. Reservations essential. No lunch Sat. Subway: 4, 5 to Bowling Green. $$–$$$*

9 e-2
ARABELLE
In the luxurious space once occupied by Le Régence in the Hotel Plaza Athenée, chef Raymond Saja, who worked alongside Gotham Bar and Grill's Alfred Portale, exhibits his playful and inventive culinary prowess. Stacks are ubiquitous here, including stegosaurus-like back plates made of sliced almonds set on a slab of seared foie gras. Saja uncovers vanilla notes in lobster, which he doesn't so much cook as deconstruct, with quite marvelous results. All this luxury comes at a relatively high price, especially considering the fairly diminutive portions. But the general agreement is it's worth every penny. *37 E. 64th St. (between Madison and Park Aves.), Upper East Side, 212/606–4647. AE, MC, V. Subway: 6 to E. 68th St. $$$–$$$$*

9 e-2
AUREOLE
It's virtually unanimous: Some of the city's best food is served in the elegant, duplex dining room of this flower-bedecked town house. Founding chef Charles Palmer's hand-picked executive chef, Gerry Hayden, prepares an exquisite array of dishes with the freshest seasonal ingredients. If it's anywhere on the prix-fixe menu, lunge for grilled boneless quail—boneless except for the frenched leg bone that enables you to pick up the fat wad of juicy flesh and gnaw with abandon. Decorated with caramel curlicues and tuile triangles, the desserts are utterly otherworldly. *34 E. 61 St. (between Madison and Park Aves.), Upper East Side, 212/319–1660. Reservations essential. AE, MC, V. Closed Sun. Subway: N, R, W to 5th Ave. $$$$*

11 h-4
BABY JUPITER
For at least a decade, the once seedy Lower East Side has been on the brink of blossoming into a major food and drink destination; buds like Baby Jupiter have led the way. The menu brings together Cajun and Asian influences, with such results as honey-barbecued salmon with basil risotto and a nori salad. In the lounge you can often catch live music and comedy acts. *170 Orchard St. (at Stanton St.), Lower East Side, 212/982–2229. MC, V. No lunch. Subway: F, V to Second Ave. $*

9 d-5
BRYANT PARK GRILL
It's hard to believe that this immense and stylish restaurant looks out onto the same Bryant Park that used to shelter the city's drug dealers and homeless. But once the nearby fashion and publishing industries turned the park into a scoping ground, it seemed only fitting that a decent restaurant follow them. Both the food and the service are usually competent and portions tend to be large. The more relaxed outdoor café, on the restaurant's roof (open mid-April–mid-October), is idyllic on cool summer nights. *25 W. 40th St. (between 5th and 6th Aves.), Midtown West, 212/840–6500. Reservations essential for dining room. AE, D, DC, MC, V. Subway: B, D, F, V to 42nd St. $$*

9 d-3
CHINA GRILL
Although the atmosphere is corporate— suits and cell phones abound—the food at this noisy Midtown power-lunch spot is satisfying and delicious. Asian-inspired appetizers such as roasted beet dumplings, crunchy calamari salad, and cured salmon rolls are large enough to share, as are most of the entrées. Try the wasabi-crusted cod on mashed potatoes, the Szechuan spiced beef, or the black pasta with shrimp. Service is friendly, if reserved. *52 W. 53rd St. (between 5th and 6th Aves.), Midtown West, 212/333–7788. Reservations essential. AE, DC, MC, V. Subway: E, V to 5th Ave.–53rd St. $$–$$$*

`10` d-2

C3 RESTAURANT & LOUNGE

A few steps below street level, this smartly appointed space is surprisingly casual and cozy for a "hotel restaurant." Nice people come here, and even nicer people work here. Gorgeous glazed-tile Gustav Klimt reproductions (by Rita Paul) adorn the walls throughout the space. Sink into a booth and tuck into John McGrath's contempo spins on such fetching new classics as grilled octopus, pan-roasted duck breast, and a richly flavored grilled arctic char. Finish with a splendid cheese course or almond shortbread with fresh berries, but don't miss that muddy chocolate martini. A $28 prix-fixe three-course dinner is available. *Washington Square Hotel, 103 Waverly Place (at MacDougal St.), Greenwich Village, 212/254–1200. AE, MC, V. Subway: A, B, C, D, E, F, V to W. 4th St. $$*

`10` g-2

COUP

This sleek, beautifully lit, curvaceous, split-level space has two lovely outdoor deck areas. Journeyman chef Kevin Roth's seasonal menus nudge flavors together that inevitably fall in love. Steak and blue cheese quesadilla with a sour-cherry chutney will leave you panting. Daring hemp and poppy seed–crusted tuna loin takes you on a neo-Polynesian ride, with very deep, fruity flavors. Grilled filet mignon bestows considerable dignity upon its bed of summer beans and fingerling potatoes. The chef's sweet tooth, which bares itself often during the meal, comes into its own at dessert. Pineapple upside-down cake is a special labor of love. Small wonder this Coup is so popular. *509 E. 6th St. (between Aves. A and B), East Village, 212/979–2815. AE, MC, V. No lunch. Brunch Sun. Subway: 6 to Astor Pl.; F, V to 2nd Ave. $$*

`7` f-8

THE DINING ROOM

With a sophisticated yet laid-back setting and demeanor, this Upper East Side restaurant occupies the space that formerly housed Trois Jean. The owners imported Mark Spangenthal from their Screening Room downtown to showcase his startling and refreshing talents in their handsome new setting. The fat slab of sautéed foie gras, partnered with

diced pickled watermelon and spicy grilled peaches, is criminally delicious. Pan-fried crunchy slices of baby artichoke hearts are tossed with chicory and toasted coriander seeds and given a lemony cream dressing. Juicy slices of roasted rib-eye steak are plated with a tangled stack of deeply braised and boned short-rib meat resting on a disc of creamy potato gratin. Soft coconut bread pudding on pineapple chutney is a superb finish. *154 E. 79th St. (between Lexington and 3rd Aves.), Upper East Side, 212/327–2500. AE, MC, V. Subway: 6 to E. 77th St. $$–$$$*

`11` f-1

DANAL

Whether you're sitting on the sofa, at one of the country tables, or, in fine weather, in the rear garden, this popular, first-rate French bistro feels like an enchanted lakeside cottage. American brunch is lovely (and intensely popular) as well. *90 E. 10th St. (between 3rd and 4th Aves.), East Village, 212/982–6930. Reservations essential. AE, MC, V. Closed Mon. Subway: N, R to 8th St.; 6 to Astor Pl. $–$$*

`11` a-1

EQ

At half the price this would be a charming Greenwich Village establishment with very decent food. But at the going rate, diners are left to wonder what they are paying for. It certainly isn't the setting, which seems makeshift at best, or the size of the portions. The food is good, but not that good, and the service tends toward pretentious. Regardless, the restaurant fills each night with, as one might expect, people who look like they don't know what to do with their annual bonuses. *267 W. 4th St. (at Perry St.), West Village, 212/414–1961. AE, MC, V. Closed Sun. No lunch. Subway: 1, 2 to Christopher St.–Sheridan Sq. $$–$$$*

`7` f-7

ÉTATS-UNIS

As the name implies, this is American cooking from a French perspective, a refreshing twist from the New American trend of rushing toward foreign ingredients at the expense of our native bounty. The results are wonderful: Corn soufflé sits on wild greens dressed in a raspberry vinaigrette; Colorado beef is coated with peppercorns, simply seared, and served with a potato galette, or whatever potato the chef is in the mood to make that day. The small, cheerful room and exposed kitchen make you feel like you're in the chef's home, and the clientele is so regular that it sometimes seems as if only the restaurant's "family" is allowed in. If you're lucky enough to get a reservation, take it and run. *242 E. 81st St. (between 2nd and 3rd Aves.), Upper East Side, 212/517–8826. Reservations essential. AE, MC, V. Closed Sun. No lunch. Subway: 6 to 77th St. $$$–$$$$*

9 c-3

HUDSON CAFETERIA

The only aspects resembling a cafeteria here are the long tables in much of the indoor dining space and the comfort foods that comprise half the menu. Hudson's multi-faceted restaurant is delightfully affected, frisky, and luxurious. Especially inviting is the soaring bricked outdoor space between the Hudson hotel's towers, where 52 folks can dine and about twice that many can tipple and lounge. As the shadows lengthen, lit candles appear in all the right places, and a real magic descends. Openers include a sprightly julienne of jicama and red–yellow pepper accompanying crisp-tender duck-and-shiitake spring rolls. Comfort food spins contemporary with such classics as macaroni and cheese gratin (available with seared foie gras, if you like) and beef stew (rich short ribs). Cocktails (and, unfortunately, wine) are served in 12-ounce jelly glasses. This has rapidly become one of the great outdoor dining experiences in town, well worth the occasional wait. *256 W. 58th St. (between 8th and 9th Aves.), Midtown West, 212/554–6500. AE, MC, V. Subway: A, B, C, D, 1, 2 to Columbus Circle. $$–$$$*

9 d-3

JUDSON GRILL

With the soaring feel of the dining room on a luxury ocean liner, this Midtowner has really come into its own, taking a proud place among some of the city's finest restaurants. Chef Bill Telepan's menus plumb each season's produce to find and maximize flavors in often startling, delightful ways. All preparations bear his distinctive intonations and sensibilities—from delicate peekytoe crab in a martini glass graced with a dollop of sevruga caviar to duck breast with wild-rice bread pudding and cherry compote.

The impressive wine list includes some hard-to-find American labels and vintages. Deborah Snyder's great desserts include the restaurant's signature Jack Daniels chocolate ice cream soda and a reimagining of bread pudding with blood oranges and lemon sorbet. These perfectly partner Telepan's playfulness. All in all, the restaurant just feels mighty important, and so will you the entire time you're there. *152 W. 52nd St. (between 6th and 7th Aves.), Midtown West, 212/582–5252. Reservations essential. AE, DC, MC, V. Closed Sun. Subway: N, R, W to 49th St.; 1, 2 to 50th St. $$$–$$$$*

7 f-8

LENOX

This is where Upper East Siders come when they don't want the fuss and formality of Daniel or Le Cirque 2000. Dashing co-owner and host Tony Fortuna oversees the kitchen here, and Marc Van Steyn's resolutely contemporary American cooking is continually revelatory. Among the entrées, buttery lamb loin medallions turn sultry on their lentil bed, and a bourbon-rich short-rib roulade on a beefy spaetzle bed is better than it has any right to be. Try cool banana bombe jabbed with a coconut tuile and dribbled with a lush coconut sauce. The bar, with its comfortable seating and selection of $6 tasting plates, help make the restaurant a neighborhood hangout. *1278 3rd Ave. (between 73rd and 74th Sts.), Upper East Side, 212/772–0404. AE, D, DC, MC, V. Subway: 6 to 77th St. $$–$$$*

9 e-3

LITTLE DOVE

With a legacy of one of the most beloved restaurants in Manhattan's dining history—Sign of the Dove—this delightfully diminutive (seating just 50), almost erotic Little Dove has taken wing. The softly lit room really feels like a boudoir, complete with crushed Moroccan velvet curtains and slip covers. The menu fits the space: eight appetizers and seven entrées. A supple sea bass carpaccio shimmers with basil chiffonade in a gentle lime and olive oil broth. The ultimate comfort food: State-of-the-art risotto stirred with plenty of chopped chanterelle mushrooms and truffle shavings stays piping hot, thanks to a molten cheese fonduta at its center. End with a baby grilled pumpkin stuffed with a rich cheesecake filling and surrounded by a raisin and dried cherry compote. This is a very special, hopelessly romantic place. *200 E. 60th St. (at 3rd Ave.), 2nd floor, Upper East Side, 212/861–8080. AE, MC, V. Subway: N, R, W, 4, 5, 6 to 59th St.–Lexington Ave. $$–$$$*

`10` *b-1*
LOTUS

This swanky, up-to-the-minute glam lounge and restaurant requires a velvet rope to keep out the hoi polloi. Richard Farnabé (formerly at Mercer Kitchen) creates dishes that are served in rather a Japanese Bauhaus fashion. Foie gras four ways unveils flavors and textures that settle in together with a rare coziness. Sautéed sea scallops achieve an enviable balance of flavors, thanks to their unusual partners, roasted beets and clementine sauce. Desserts follow fancy suit, including a luscious crème brûlée ice cream cannelloni dribbled with caramel sauce. You're likely to be surrounded by young models, and quite a few movie stars have visited Lotus more than once. *409 W. 14th St. (between 9th and 10th Aves.), Chelsea, 212/243–4420. AE, DC, MC, V. Subway: A, C, E to 14th St. $$$$*

`10` *b-1*
MAN RAY

With such high-profile co-owners as Sean Penn, Johnny Depp, John Malkovich, Harvey Weinstein, and Simply Red lead singer Mick Hucknall, and a smashing predecessor in Paris, venerable record producer Thierry Klemeniuk has quite a hit on his hands. Two crimson mandalas of stained glass hang behind the bar; a kind of Tiki-hut lounge exotica prevails, with bamboo-framed walls and plenty of silly drinks on the menu. Chef Frédéric Kieffer has devised a contemporary menu with a decidedly French accent. Try the "Deep Red," a hand roll created from halved steamed lobster, avocado, and marinated white asparagus. Bottarga (dried mullet roe) gives brand new dimension to oysters, as does goat gouda crust to turbot. As for the *sopaipillas*—the thinking man's zeppole—anyone who can resist these pillows of bliss, fried and slathered with tangerine honey, ought to be checked for a pulse. *147 W. 15th St. (between 6th and 7th Aves.), Chelsea, 212/929–5000. Reservations essential. AE, DC, MC, V. Subway: A, C, E to 14th St. $$–$$$*

`9` *b-1*
MARIKA

Marika Somerstein (see Water's Edge) has crafted a marvelous new addition to the Upper West Side's dining scene. The restaurant is divided and sub-divided into highly linear, manageable areas; the cerise leather high-backed booths are among the most comfortable places to sit in the whole city. The most irresistible fresh warm chive biscuits are brought around, but not often enough to spoil your appetite. Among the chef Neil Annis's whimsical entrées, try a fat grilled sea scallop on a bed of spaghetti squash strands floating in lobster-carrot broth, or a tender John Dory fillet layered with fried slender discs of new potato. Marika joins the ranks of the most delicious and enchanting destinations in the city. *208 W. 70th St. (bet. Amsterdam and West End Aves.), Upper West Side, 212/875–8600. AE, MC, V. Subway: 1, 2, 3 to 72nd St. $$–$$$$*

`11` *e-5*
MERCER KITCHEN

The scene here, in the basement of the Mercer Hotel, may be hipper-than-thou, but diners looking for more than a scene are coming for the food. Jean-Georges Vongerichten has created a sleek, industrial space that's oddly comfortable, and interestingly organized his menu according to where in the kitchen each dish originates. Dinner selections might include black sea-bass carpaccio with lime juice, coriander, and mint (from the raw bar); figs with prosciutto, aged balsamic vinegar, and rosemary flatbread (from the pantry); Alsatian tarte flambé with fromage blanc, onions, and bacon (from the pizza oven); roasted lobster with tagliatelle and red-wine sauce (from the rotisserie); or lamb steak with tomato-orange marmalade (from the grill). *The Mercer Hotel, 99 Prince St. (at Mercer St.), SoHo, 212/966–5454. Reservations essential. AE, DC, MC, V. Brunch Sun. No dinner Sun. Subway: N, R to Prince St. $$–$$$$*

`10` *f-1*
NO. 9

In this dramatically transformed space that once housed the ramshackle Pageant Books resides one of downtown's most attractive dining room—lounge acts. A friendly staff, an unusually gifted chef in William Rodriguez, and reasonable prices add to its appealing attributes. For starters, try the perfectly seared foie gras with poached plums, then tuck into gorgeous venison tenderloin or gingersnap-crusted rack of lamb or sultry paella du jour. Pastry chef Fabianna Lima bakes a magical flourless chocolate cake—actually a warm soufflé cake with a molten center, sided by a chocolate crème. A four-course $35 prix-fixe dinner is available. *109 E. 9th St. (between Third and Fourth Aves.), East Village, 212/529–5333. AE, D, DC, MC, V. No lunch. Subway: 6 to Astor Pl. $$–$$$*

11 *f-6*

ONIEAL'S GRAND STREET

Supposedly, under this bar, a fragment remains of a tunnel that once allowed New York City police chief Theodore Roosevelt to sneak away from the police station across the street for a drink. The exquisitely paneled room, off the beaten path, is a calm oasis on the edge of Chinatown and far away from the commotion of SoHo. The dark, sexy lounge is a great place for a cocktail and a light nibble, or you can have a real meal of good

---

A BREATH OF FRESH AIR

New York may be an asphalt jungle, but there are eateries that provide a breath of real, unconditioned air on a hot summer night from a garden, terrace, or roof.

Aureole (Contemporary)
 Partake of one of the city's best tasting menus in an intimate flagstone patio and garden adjoining the back of the dining room.

Hudson Cafeteria (Contemporary)
 In a soaring brick-lined outdoor space between the Hudson Hotel towers atrium you can lounge and tipple under the vast atrium.

Tavern on the Green (Continental)
 More than 1,000 glimmering chintz-shaded lanterns festoon the canopy of trees over the flower dell at the city's largest outdoor bar (40 ft long).

Water's Edge (American)
 A long deck of thick pine planks runs along the entire 100-plus feet of this restaurant, with tables along shimmering water and stellar skyline views. Try to time your visit during sunset.

New American fare at one of the tables up front. *174 Grand St. (between Centre and Mulberry Sts.), SoHo, 212/941–9119. AE, DC, MC, V. Closed Sun. Subway: 6, N, R, Q, W to Canal St. $$*

9 *d-3*

OSTERIA DEL CIRCO

Opened by the three sons of Le Cirque owner Sirio Maccioni, this contemporary Italian eatery comes alive with circus-tent decorations and dancing sculptures. The line of celebrities waiting for tables creates a frenzied atmosphere. Traditional Tuscan specialties such as a 30-vegetable soup and salt cod *alla livornese* go up against contemporary favorites such as tuna carpaccio and lobster salad. Pizzas, pastas, and rotisserie items (particularly the duck) are excellent. Save room for dessert: the *bomboloncini*—little Italian donuts filled with chocolate, vanilla, and raspberry—have been voted the best in the city, and the other sweets are pretty spectacular, too. The reasonably priced list of Italian wines is also worth checking out. *120 W. 55th St. (between 6th and 7th Aves.), Midtown West, 212/265–3636. AE, DC, MC, V. Subway: F, N, R, Q, W to 57th St. $$–$$$*

7 *b-7*

OUEST

Upper West side foodies are hoping that the arrival of this seriously excellent dining room means that the restaurant scene in their neighborhood has finally graduated to the big leagues. An inviting bar, giant, round leather booths, and a view of the kitchen whet the appetite for the flavorful, solid creations—loin of pork, smoked duck breast, roasted salmon—of Tom Valenti. *2315 Broadway (at 84th St.), Upper West Side, 212/580–8700. AE, MC, V. Closed Mon. No lunch. Subway: 1, 9 to 86th St. $$$$*

10 *e-1*

POP

One of the few restaurants on 4th Avenue, Pop is the *very* last word in trendy overnight sensations that are clearly here to stay. The sleek, sexy decor immediately enrobes you and makes you feel comfortably puissant. Every aspect of your meal's presentation is carefully conceived, from the space-age flatware to the loose-leaf menu, which includes a bang-up wine list. And chef Kevin O'Connell's brilliant contemporary American is

always ready to tantalize. His lamb
chops are unusually juicy and tender,
and salmon au poivre is like being
invited to dine on a flank of heaven.
Desserts are resplendently delicious. The
later it gets, the more of a boisterous—
but always poised—party Pop becomes.
*127 4th Ave. (between 12th and 13th Sts.),
Greenwich Village, 212/767–1800. AE, MC,
V. No lunch. Subway: L, N, Q, R, W, 4, 5,
6 to 14th St./Union Sq. $$*

9 b-8
THE RED CAT
Fairly spacious quarters, a happening
bar scene (stop by for a bowl of fresh
radishes that you dip in sea salt), and
bright, original decor gave the Red Cat a
running start. But it's the seasonally
sensitive, carefully prepared menu that
has earned this restaurant its reputa-
tion. Offerings change regularly, but
recent standouts have included foie gras
with caramelized nectarines and an arc-
tic char with wild mushrooms and truf-
fle vinaigrette. *227 10th Ave. (between
23rd and 24th Sts.), Chelsea, 212/242–1122.
Reservations essential. AE, DC, MC, V. No
lunch. Subway: C, E to 23rd St. $$*

10 d-4
THOM
Arranged capaciously on the breezy
ground floor of the new 60 Thompson
Hotel, this swanky eatery shimmers with
several acres of beige and bamboo
accents. Chef Tim Byres delivers peeky-
toe crab won tons in the swim of a
dashing dashi consommé; perfectly
grilled and curried shrimp with tangy
fermented chile; a spoon-tender filet
mignon—a full three inches tall—
rubbed with satay marinade, grilled, and
topped with scallion shavings; and a
double-cut rack of lamb scattered with
fresh peppermint, all arranged on a
lightly dressed field salad. One bite of
the poppy seeded Meyer lemon curd
tart, and you're seriously hooked. Thom
has the chic location, the crowd to
match, but no attitude. *60 Thompson St.
(between Spring and Broome Sts.), SoHo,
212/219–2000. AE, MC, V. Subway: C, E
to Spring St. $$–$$$*

9 d-8
THE TONIC
The 19th-century mahogany bar alone
qualifies this restaurant as one of

Chelsea's classiest. On of the most talented chefs in town, Joe Fortunata plates
tuna, salmon, and red snapper tartars
with three matching roes and creamy
avocado purée; a toothsome lobster–
crayfish creamed stew escorts the
roasted monkfish. Cheeses are perfectly
ripe, and desserts are not to be missed.
*108–110 W. 18th St. (between 6th and 7th
Aves.), Chelsea, 212/929–9755. Reservations essential. AE, DC, MC, V. Brunch
weekends. Subway: 1, 2 to 18th St. $$–$$$*

9 d-3
TOWN
One of a handful of "downstairs" dining
rooms in town, Town unfolds in a beautiful, curvaceous space with three-story
ceilings and soaring walls. Chef–proprietor Geoffrey Zakarian, who has worked
with some of the greatest chefs in
France and America, creates such culinary works as a creamy, complex escargot risotto, damnably delicious and
redolent of black truffles, and three thick
slices of rib-eye steak, perched upon
short-rib meat braised to a fare-thee-
well, that triumphantly contrast flavors
and textures. Chocolate beignets are
absolutely extraordinary: miniature—the
size of puffy quarters—warm, and
swathed in a napkin. *15 W. 56th St.
(between 5th and 6th Aves.), Midtown
West, 212/582–4445. AE, MC, V. Subway:
S to 57th St. $$–$$$*

9 e-7
27 STANDARD
With its low lights and gloriously high
ceilings, 27 Standard brings terrific food
and live jazz together like nowhere else
on earth. Full performances are in the
jazz club downstairs; the restaurant
recently found its perfect new chef in
Matthew Lake, who composes flavor
upon flavor with results as intense and
memorable as great jazz itself. Buttery
seared foie gras is courted by a luscious
shallot-berry compote. Buttermilk-fried
oysters get a lime drizzle and a sultry
roasted corn-and-green-chile relish. Rare
tuna, so often bland, here receives a
complex studding of pine nuts, grilled
shiitake mushrooms, and ruddy peppers.
*116 E. 27th St. (between Lexington and
Park Aves.), Murray Hill, 212/576–2232. AE,
MC, V. Subway: 6 to 28th St. $$–$$$*

11 f-5

VELVET RESTAURANT & LOUNGE

The blood red walls may be oddly bordello-esque, but the well-made cocktails, lounge scene, and eclectic menu will bring you right back to a New York vibe. The food, which takes cues from all over the globe, is uniformly good—salmon tartare is fresh and zesty, the pork loin is spicy and exotic. After dinner you can relax to music (some nights live) in the upstairs lounge. *223 Mulberry St. (between Prince and Spring Sts.), SoHo, 212/965–0439. AE, D, MC, V. No lunch. Subway: 6 to Spring St.* $$

9 e-3

VONG

The second of Jean-Georges Vongerichten's four New York restaurants (*see* Jean-Georges *and* Mercer Kitchen; Jo Jo is temporarily closed), Vong is the chef's passion for Asian cuisine made manifest. Here he fuses French and Thai with tremendous success, bringing even peanut sauce to new heights. Presentation is emphasized: Spectacular food is showcased in dazzling dishes of varying size, color, and shape. The Thai decor is exotic and rich, with a thoroughly contemporary flair. While some complain about the prices, others say don't sweat it—this is Jean-Georges Vongerichten, and you're in for the meal of your life. *200 E. 54th St., Midtown East, 212/486–9592. AE, DC, MC, V. No lunch weekends. Subway: 6 to 51st St./Lexington Ave.; E, V, to Lexington–3rd Aves./53rd St.* $$–$$$$

9 e-1

WILLOW

The charm of this elegant turn-of-the-20th-century townhouse adds to the food's charisma, which is standard New American: goat cheese, wild greens, duck. The menu is not groundbreaking, but the chef executes it well, and if you factor in the soft lighting and view of the tree-lined street through the leaded-glass windows, you end up with a worthwhile experience. The downstairs room has a simpler menu of lighter meals, and on sunny days lunch is served on lovely sidewalk tables. *1022 Lexington Ave. (at 73rd St.), Upper East Side, 212/717–0703. Reservations essential for dinner. AE, DC, MC, V. Subway: 6 to 68th St.–Hunter College.* $$–$$$

CONTINENTAL

7 c-1

CAFÉ DES ARTISTES

The beautiful, nostalgic ambience; the imaginative kitchen that produces poised Continental specialties; and the famous, sweetly lascivious murals by Howard Chandler Christy—all fully restored after a fire in late 1997—make this West Side classic a favorite for romance. For intimacy in the evening, request one of the nooks surrounding the bar in the rear. Don't miss the foie gras floating on poached pears and peaches, and the steak tartare (which is lightly seared and cleverly studded with pine nuts) is justifiably famous. The parlor, adjacent to the main dining room, is easier on the wallet, just as charming, and far more accessible; reservations aren't even necessary. *1 W. 67th St. (on Central Park W), Upper West Side, 212/877–3500. Reservations essential. AE, DC, MC, V. Subway: 1, 2 to 66th St.–Lincoln Center.* $$–$$$$

9 e-7

ELEVEN MADISON PARK

New York's most beloved restaurateur, Danny Meyer, whose Union Square Café and Gramercy Tavern top many a favorite restaurant list, opened Eleven Madison Park and Tabla in a spectacular Art Deco space right on Madison Park. The menu is an homage to the Continental cuisine that was served in this once–highly fashionable neighborhood's restaurants around the turn of the 20th century. An appropriately French wine list has some great bottles and years. Kerry Heffernan's menu has a few historic startlers, such as beef shank–foie gras–veal feet terrine, but the seafood is exemplary. Whatever you do, don't miss the salmon and trout choucroute. And save room for a plate of special lemon desserts. *11 Madison Ave. (at 24th St.), Murray Hill, 212/889–0905. Reservations essential. No lunch Sun. AE, MC, V. Subway: 6 to 23rd St.* $$–$$$

9 e-3

FOUR SEASONS

Courtesy of Mies van der Rohe, this large, spectacularly beautiful, modern restaurant is one of the most famous dining destinations in New York, and the city's only restaurant with landmark status. The Grill Room has long been favored for power lunches by publishing, fashion, and financial movers and shakers. The more lavish and romantic Pool Room, centered around an illuminated marble pool, is popular for the prix-fixe pre-theater dinner, as well as post-theater meals. As the name implies, the menu changes with the seasons. *99 E. 52nd St. (between Lexington and Park Aves.), Midtown East, 212/754–9494. Reservations essential. AE, DC, MC, V. No lunch weekends. Subway: 6 to 51st St./Lexington Ave.; E, V to Lexington–3rd Aves./53rd St.* $$$$

11 b-2

ONE IF BY LAND, TWO IF BY SEA

The food is almost as appealing as the setting here, which is among the most romantic in town, including a roaring fire, fresh flowers, shimmering candlelight, and a live pianist, all in Aaron Burr's former carriage house. Although the menu still lists such traditionals as beef Wellington, it also includes an infusion of lighter, more up-to-date dishes, such as lobster salad, seared tuna, and roasted rack of lamb. *17 Barrow St. (between W. 4th St. and 7th Ave. S), West Village, 212/228–0822. AE, DC, MC, V. No lunch. Subway: 1, 2 to Christopher St.–Sheridan Sq.* $$–$$$$

9 e-7

SONIA ROSE

Many New Yorkers revere the cozy Sonia Rose as a romantic destination, and it's true that the restaurant's provincial atmosphere at its new location offers a change of pace. The three-course prix-fixe menu (with some supplements) changes daily and is quite reasonable, but something about the French-eclectic food falls a little short—perhaps it's the fact that the entrées seem virtually interchangeable, with similar sauces and the same side dishes. Still, you'll certainly have a quiet, pleasant evening. *150 E. 34th St. (between Lexington and 3rd Aves.), Murray Hill, 212/545–1777. Reservations essential. AE, MC, V. Subway: 6 to 28th St.* $$$$

9 c-1

TAVERN ON THE GREEN

This, one of the most profitable restaurants in the world, is the place New Yorkers pretend to shun—and can't wait for family or friends to visit so they can take them there. With 27,000 square ft, six dining rooms, and glorious Central Park

surrounding it, the restaurant serves a cavalcade of larger-than-life renditions of American Popular Standards, with a totally overwhelming wine list of over 800 selections. Perfect Caesar salad, user-friendly spice-rubbed barbecued ribs, and magnificent roast prime rib, dry-aged to collapsing tenderness, and served (if you like) on the bone for maximum flavor. Yorkshire pudding? Of course. Note that the Tavern no longer has a dress code. *Central Park W at 67th St., Upper West Side, 212/873–3200. AE, D, DC, MC, V. Subway: 1, 2 to 66th St.–Lincoln Center; B, C to 72nd St.* $$–$$$$

9 d-3

21 CLUB

Triple-parked limos mark this clubby establishment in a renewed but unchanged turn-of-the-20th-century setting. The noisy and celebrated downstairs bar is where the power folks lunch and sup; the upstairs is quieter, and less interesting. Accomplished chef Erik Blauberg has changed the menu substantially with his light touch and contemporary bent, but you can still order the famous oversize (and pricey) "21" burger or the steak tartare. The wine list is impressive, and if you're someone special (say, Gerald Ford) you can even lay away some special vintages for your next visit. Ask for a tour of the fascinating wine cellar in any case. For a rare treat, splurge on the private dining room near the wine cellar; this special enclave is one of the most beautiful in the city. *21 W. 52nd St. (between 5th and 6th Aves.), Midtown West, 212/582–7200. Reservations essential. AE, DC, MC, V. Closed weekends in summer. Subway: E, V to 5th Ave.–53rd St.* $$$–$$$$

CUBAN

11 b-3

LITTLE HAVANA

This tiny Cuban restaurant couldn't be any cuter. The kitchen, with its light touch and organic ingredients, makes a departure from most of New York's other Cuban eateries. The result is food that's bright and flavorful—from the standard *arroz con pollo* (rice and chicken) to the tamales with or without meat to the traditional *ropa vieja* (braised shredded beef). Prices are moderate and the restaurant is a perfect backup-plan when others on the block are packed. *30 Cornelia St. (between Bleecker and W. 4th*

29

Sts.), West Village, 212/255–2212. AE, DC, MC, V. Closed Mon. Subway: A, B, C, D, E, F, V to W. 4th St. $

9 *c-3*

VICTOR'S CAFE 52

Victor was the pioneer purveyor of upscale Cuban cuisine and atmosphere in his longtime café on Columbus Avenue. He's now been firmly ensconced in the Theater District for years, serving hearty paella, ropa vieja, grilled pork chops, black bean soup, fried bananas, and strong Cuban coffee, among other delicacies. Nightly entertainment adds to the fun. *236 W. 52nd St. (between Broadway and 8th Ave.), Midtown-West, 212/586–7714. AE, DC, MC, V. Closed Sun. Subway: C, E to 50th St. $–$$$*

DELICATESSENS

7 *b-7*

ARTIE'S NEW YORK DELICATESSEN

Spanning a glimmering 65 ft along Broadway, Artie's shamelessly reclaims an endangered tradition: post-Depression New York Jewish delicatessen fare in a setting that showcases this heritage with cinematic resonance. Portions are enormous: Matzo balls the size of cannonballs, the stuffed cabbage that ate Chicago, and a pastrami–corned beef open-faced Reuben steaming under about a half-pound of melted swiss and over homemade sauerkraut. Ardently devoted to its neighborhood, Artie's once provided free delivery of "emergency chicken soup" during a particularly brutal patch of winter. *2290 Broadway (at 83rd St.), Upper West Side, 212/579–5959. AE, MC, V. Subway: 1, 2 to 86th St. $–$$*

9 *c-3*

CARNEGIE DELICATESSEN

With ridiculously huge portions, this famous deli draws chaotic crowds of locals and tourists. The good, Jewish-style dishes are certainly not kosher, but they're about as authentic as New York Jewish cuisine gets. The deliciously fatty pastrami and succulent dry corned beef are made on the premises, and they're piled higher on rye than any sandwich you've ever seen. Don't miss the borscht with about a pint of sour cream in and on it, or the creamy cheesecake.

Be prepared to sit with strangers at the long tables, to get barked at by waiters, and to take home the leftovers. The deli serves until 4 AM. *854 7th Ave. (at 55th St.), Midtown West, 212/757–2245. No credit cards. Subway: B, D, C, E to 7th Ave.; N, R, Q, W to 57th St. $–$$*

10 *g-3*

KATZ'S DELICATESSEN

A Lower East Side institution, Katz's has terrific hot dogs, inexpensive pastrami, and the best hand-cut, corned-beef sandwiches in town (not kosher). On Sunday it's particularly unbeatable for local color and informality, especially on the part of the waiters; but if you're not in the mood, self-service is always an option. *205 E. Houston St. (at Ludlow St.), Lower East Side, 212/254–2246. No credit cards. Subway: F, V to 2nd Ave. $*

10 *f-1*

SECOND AVENUE KOSHER DELICATESSEN

Bar none, this is hands-down the best kosher deli in the city. Though some of the rough-and-tumble charm was renovated out of the hectic setting, delicious hot Jewish meals still vie aggressively with traditional deli delights for diners' affections (and arteries). A good lunch bet is matzo-ball soup and half a sandwich (the pastrami is to die for); for dinner on cold winter nights, try *cholent* (Jewish cassoulet) or chicken in the pot. You can always take the stuff out, or have your next event catered—think beautiful platters, and chopped liver in the shape of a heart. *156 2nd Ave. (at 10th St.), East Village, 212/677–0606. Reservations not accepted. AE, DC, MC, V. Subway: 6 to Astor Pl.; F, V to 2nd Ave. $–$$*

EASTERN EUROPEAN

7 *e-6*

ANDRUSHA

Among Andrusha's many charms is its owner, Liana Fingesten, who devises and daily prepares the "eclectic European cuisine"—meaning pretty much the best of high-end Czech and Russian cooking, prepared with conspicuously fresh ingredients. Share the assortment of appetizers, including salmon-roe-stuffed new potato, cognac-infused chicken liver pâté with madeira jelly, roasted beet salad, smoked salmon, and eggplant tartare. Follow with *pelmeni*—little dumpling pouches of savory ground beef, spiced to the nines. Duck is aggressively roasted to leave the skin crackling and the meat extremely rich. Finish with beautiful blueberry blinis. *1370 Lexington Ave. (between 90th and 91st Sts.), Upper East Side, 212/369–9374. AE, V. Subway: 4, 5, 6 to 86th St. $–$$*

7 *b-7*

BARNEY GREENGRASS

Self-proclaimed "sturgeon king" Barney Greengrass is tops for breakfast and brunch. If you don't like to wake up to orange juice, how about a cold glass of borscht? Order a large platter of smoked salmon and, of course, sturgeon; or try the scrambled eggs with onions and smoked sturgeon. Fresh bagels, bialys, and cream cheese round out the meal. If you still have room, try an individual chocolate babka for dessert. Only complete parties will be seated. *541 Amsterdam Ave. (between 86th and 87th Sts.), Upper West Side, 212/724–4707. Reservations not accepted. M, V; cash only on weekends. Subway: 1, 2 to 86th St. $–$$$$*

10 *f-3*

SAMMY'S ROUMANIAN

Eating at Sammy's is like attending a bar mitzvah in the Catskills. Rumored to be a favorite hangout of cardiologists, Sammy's serves up Romanian tenderloin steak "with or without garlic," potatoes with gribenes, veal chops, stuffed cabbage, egg creams, and other specialties, all clogging their way to your heart. The pitchers of *schmaltz* (chicken fat), bottles of seltzer, and bowls of pickles on the table add a certain charm. *157 Chrystie St. (between Delancey and Rivington Sts.), Lower East Side, 212/673–0330. AE, DC. Subway: S to Grand St. $–$$$*

11 *g-1*

VESELKA

A better bowl of borscht you will not find; it's served here with slices of delicious homemade egg bread. The pierogis—filled with cheese, mushroom and sauerkraut, or potato—and blintzes aren't bad, either. Renovated in 1996, this 24-hour, perpetually popular coffee shop may be the last place in New York where communist intellectuals congregate freely. *144 2nd Ave. (at 9th St.), East Village, 212/228–9682. Reservations not accepted. AE, MC, V. Subway: 6 to Astor Pl. $*

ECLECTIC

9 *d-3*

ATLAS

With a glorious view of Central Park right beyond the glass north wall of the restaurant, this prime location once was a showcase chef Paul Liebrandt's whimsical cuisine. In his stead is David Coleman, whose classic French training and respect for the freshest ingredients create a somewhat more soothing, but no less experimental, gustatory impression. Hibiscus syrup graces the foie gras ballotine with Asian pear and razor clam jelly, and wild striped bass is adorned with artichokes, radishes, mussels, and green licorice–infused velouté. Pastry chef Sam Mason is right in step, with a caramel tapioca tart with chocolate ice cream and vanilla roasted pineapple croustillant with tequila ice cream. If you're a truly adventurous diner, this is a place to check out. *40 Central Park S (between 5th and 6th Aves.), Midtown West, 212/759–9191, AE, MC, V. Subway: N, R, W to 5th Ave. $$$$*

10 *d-3*

BLUE RIBBON

The line spills onto the street outside this cheerful storefront, which serves until 4 AM. (Tip: It's a popular late-night haunt for chefs.) There's a raw bar; a pupu platter; a shrimp Provençal; and a heavenly, dark mousselike chocolate cake. The place is noisy, and waits can be long, but the food is worth it. *97 Sullivan St. (between Spring and Prince Sts.), SoHo, 212/274–0404. AE, D, DC, MC, V. Closed Mon. No lunch. Subway: 6 to Spring St.; N, R to Prince St. $–$$$*

9 *c-8*

BRIGHT FOOD SHOP

Asia and the American Southwest meet at this former coffee shop. The atmosphere is lunch counter, but the food is mega-fusion ("moo shu mex vegetable handrolls with chipotle-peanut sauce") and great. Flavors are bold and the portions are filling. Take-out is available next door at Kitchen Market. *216 8th Ave. (between 21st and 22nd Sts.), Chelsea, 212/243–4433. No credit cards. Subway: C, E to 23rd St. $–$$*

9 *f-4*

DELEGATES' DINING ROOM

Whether or not you're visiting the U.N., this is a fine place to lunch on Midtown's east end. The buffet food is good (representing the diverse origins of those who dine here), the setting civilized, and the view of the East River lovely. At neighboring tables are ambassadors and attachés. *United Nations, Conference Bldg., 1st Ave. at 46th St. (visitor entrance), 4th floor, Midtown East, 212/963–7625. Reservations essential. AE, DC, MC, V. Photo ID required. No dinner. Closed weekends. Subway: 4, 5, 6, 7, S to 42nd St.–Grand Central. $$*

9 b-8
LOT 61
This far-west Chelsea nightspot has about all you could want in a club—a dramatic space with some very interesting art, an exceptionally au courant crowd, and excellent (if pricey) drinks—and a dinner reservation is a tried-and-true way to avoid a wait behind velvet ropes. The eclectic menu is stronger on appetizers (baby lamb chops and the Asian-influenced crab salad are good choices) than it is on entrées, the latter being over-wrought and over-styled, so grazing is the way to go. *550 W. 21st St. (between 10th and 11th Aves.), Chelsea, 212/243–6555. Reservations essential. AE, D, MC, V. Closed Sun. No lunch. Subway: C, E to 23rd St. $–$$*

11 e-4
MATCH DOWNTOWN
A popular place for a drink both early and late at night, this lofty, bilevel restaurant is outfitted with booths, industrial beams, and wood paneling. The food is utterly multicultural—dim sum, sushi, Southwestern, and French—and there's an oyster bar for good measure. *60 Mercer St. (between Houston and Prince Sts.), SoHo, 212/343–0830. AE, DC, MC, V. Brunch weekends. Subway: 6 to Prince St.; F, V to Broadway–Lafayette St. $$–$$$*

7 b-7
MERCHANTS NY
This small chain of large "multi-area restaurants" features a thriving bar, various cozy candlelit dining areas, and a virtual living room that puts most "lounges" around town to shame. The attentive, carefully trained staff will bring you state-of-the-art renditions of beloved clichés such as tuna tartare or steak au poivre, or unusual creations such as masala-rubbed salmon fillet with cucumber-yogurt sauce or grilled

trout stuffed with leeks, tomato, garlicky asparagus, and pine-nut sofrito. The bar is extraordinarily well stocked, including 18 very different martinis. *521 Columbus Ave. (at 85th St.), Upper West Side, 212/721–3689. AE, MC, V. Subway: 1, 2 to 86th St. $$*

9 f-2
1125 1st Ave. (at 62nd St.), Upper East Side, 212/832–1551. Subway: N, R, W, 4, 5, 6 to 59th St.–Lexington Ave.

9 c-8
112 7th Ave. (at 17th St.), Chelsea, 212/366–7267. Subway: 1, 2 to 18th St.

9 b-5
REVOLUTION
This is one of the better meet-for-a-drink spots along the Ninth Avenue strip and, if drinks turn into dinner, the dining room in back serves some passable eclectic fare. Forgo the over-wrought and pretentious pastas such as farfalle with grilled chicken and caramelized cauliflower in Armagnac sauce in favor of such simpler dishes as the boneless roasted chicken with smashed sweet potatoes or the buffalo burger. *611 9th Ave. (between 43rd and 44th Sts.), Hell's Kitchen, 212/489–8451. AE, D, DC, MC, V. No lunch. Subway: A, C, E to 42nd St. $–$$*

11 f-5
RICE
First you'll choose from among different types of the signature grain—basmati, brown, Thai black, or Bhutanese red. Then you can add a savory topping such as Jamaican jerk chicken wings, warm lentil stew, or Indian chicken curry. Next thing you know you're eating a strangely exotic yet surprisingly comforting meal at this tiny dark storefront with a brick wall and tiny tables. Prices are gentle; the portions tend to be a little small but the rice is filling. *227 Mott St. (between Prince and Spring Sts.), SoHo, 212/226–5757. No credit cards. Subway: 6 to Spring St. $*

11 b-3
SHOPSIN'S GENERAL STORE
If owner Kenny Shopsin doesn't like your attitude, thinks you might be a corporate exec, or is just having a bad day, he will not hesitate to curse at you and throw you out onto the street. So watch your step or you'll miss an eclectic selection of more than 200 (really!)

soups and hundreds of entrées. The best meal, though, is breakfast, which is served only on weekdays because the weekends are too busy. (And during the week the place is open only 'til 7 PM.) The coffee is good, but you have to get it yourself (the milk is in the fridge). If you don't like it, you know what you can do. *63 Bedford St. (at Morton St.), West Village, 212/924–5160. DC, MC, V. Closed weekends. Subway: 1, 2 to Christopher St.–Sheridan Sq.* $$

9 *f-2*

TOMASHI

In line with the recent (and usually disastrous) trend that combines Chinese and Japanese cuisine under one roof, Tomashi surpasses them all by adding mainland Chinese cuisine to standard Szechuan and excitingly fresh Japanese. The prodigious sushi bar serves everything from sashimi to "tiger eye" (a sliced handroll of fluted squid, salmon, and seaweed). Don't miss the clam and bean-curd soup, the spicy sliced pork appetizer that brings back pork the way it used to taste, and the shockingly good sliced beef with peppercorns. *1367 1st Ave. (between 73rd and 74th Sts.), Upper East Side, 212/535–8726. AE, MC, V. Subway: 6 to 77th St.* $–$$

9 *e-7*

UNION PACIFIC

A waterfall at the entryway invites you into the soothing ambience of this stylish restaurant. Rocco DiSpirito's fusion cooking is feverishly delicious. Start with definitive, deep crimson bluefin tuna tartare and move on to blue crab with chanterelles and leeks, then try strawberry charlotte with pistachio ice cream. A superlative wine list aims to partner the extraordinary cuisine. *111 E. 22nd St. (between Lexington Ave. and Park Ave. S), Gramercy, 212/995–8500. Reservations essential. AE, MC, V. Subway: 4, 5, 6 to 23rd St.* $$–$$$

ETHIOPIAN

11 *f-4*

GHENET

African-inspired art adorns the walls at this welcoming Ethiopian restaurant where the food is authentic, spicy, and delicious. No utensils are offered and none are needed—a never-ending supply of spongy injera bread is used to scoop up the flavorful food. In addition to tasty poultry and meat dishes, there is a good selection of vegetarian dishes such as rich and fragrant collard greens with Ethiopian spices, and a dish of spicy potatoes with cabbage and carrots in an onion sauce. The menu suggests wine pairings for each dish. *284 Mulberry St. (between Houston and Prince Sts.), SoHo, 212/343–1888. AE, MC, V. Closed Mon. Subway: 6 to Spring St.* $

9 *b-4*

MESKEREM

Be prepared to eat with your hands at this authentic, no-frills Ethiopian joint. The best dishes come unceremoniously blobbed on huge pieces of injera, a soft, yeasty, lightly tangy flat bread traditionally used as both plate and utensil. Expect deeply spiced, currylike stews; the lamb selections are excellent, as is the vegetarian combination. *468 W. 47th St. (between 9th and 10th Aves.), Midtown West, 212/664–0520. D, MC, V. Subway: C, E to 50th St.* $

FRENCH

11 *c-5*

ALISON ON DOMINICK STREET

This understated restaurant is worth the trek; wonderful country-French food is served in a romantic, candlelit setting. Try the ragout of mussels, braised lamb shank, or sautéed sea bass in a tarragon-flavor broth; then go for the chocolate-hazelnut ice cream or crème brûlée. *38 Dominick St. (between Varick and Hudson Sts.), Soho, 212/727–1188. Reservations essential. AE, MC, V. Subway: 1, 2, A, C, E to Canal St.* $$$

11 *e-5*

BALTHAZAR

Balthazar is a serious scene and difficult to get into. (Just getting them on the phone becomes a crusade.) Keith McNally's recreation of a French brasserie with an adjacent bakery is a smash hit—crowded and noisy, but invigorating. The decor—fin-de-siècle mirrors, tile floor, banquettes—makes the place look a hundred years old. And lo, the food is good: try *plateau de fruits de mer* (raw-bar platter), creamy country rillettes of rabbit with marinated mushrooms, warm goat-cheese tart with caramelized onions, duck shepherd's pie, or seared salmon with porcini and polenta. For dessert, there is a wonderful lemon mille-feuille with sorbet and a fine crème brûlée. Avail yourself of the particularly fine wine list, with bottles in every price range. *80 Spring St. (between Broadway and Crosby St.), SoHo, 212/965–1414. Reservations essential. AE, MC, V. Subway: 6 to Spring St.; N, R to Prince St. $–$$$*

10 *d-1*
BAR SIX

The bar is always packed at this noisy hot spot, which comes complete with a chic and aloof waitstaff and matching clientele. Once you get past the bar, you'll find yourself in an attractively pared-down bistro with decent, inexpensive French-Moroccan dishes such as lamb couscous with preserved lemon. Be prepared for noise at night, when the music pounds and the crowd is in high spirits. *502 6th Ave. (between 12th and 13th Sts.), Greenwich Village, 212/691–1363. AE, MC, V. Subway: F, V to 14th St.; L to 6th Ave. $–$$*

10 *d-3*
BISTRO LES AMIS

At this enchanting bistro, perched on a quaint SoHo corner, you can dine alfresco in gentler weather—a surprising rarity in the neighborhood. The cozy space inside is set about with Brassai and Doisneau photographs; lighting is especially flattering, and the noise level is delightfully low. Feast on supple escargot ravioli, crab cakes with fragrant lobster sauce, monkfish medallions with green pepper mousse and wasabi, roasted duck with mango honey sauce, and especially good filet mignon béarnaise with caramelized onions. Finish with molten chocolate soufflé and a big smile. *180 Spring St. (at Thompson), SoHo, 212/226–8645. AE, MC, V. Subway: C, E to Spring St. $–$$*

11 *f-4*
BISTRO MARGOT

Inexpensive French home cooking is served here in rather cramped but friendly surroundings. The menu sticks to basic bistro fare—good pâté, steak frites, and the like. *26 Prince St. (between Elizabeth and Mott Sts.), SoHo, 212/274–1027. AE Subway: N, R to Prince St.; F, V to Broadway–Lafayette St. $–$$*

11 *c-4*
BLUE RIBBON BAKERY

Sometimes things unforetold change destiny, and such was the case with the Blue Ribbon Bakery. During its renovation in 1997, the Bromberg brothers, of Blue Ribbon (see Eclectic) and Blue Ribbon Sushi (see Japanese), came upon a century-old Italian-tile coal-burning oven. The pair were so enamored of their discovery that they let it dictate the destiny of the restaurant. The menu includes hefty sandwiches on homemade bread (from the oven of course), lots of baked goods, and entrées such as trout and Cornish game hen (also from the oven). There are also small plates of charcuterie, pâté, and tapas-style dishes. The basement dining room is dark and intimate, with a private area for parties of 8–10 that affords a view of the oven. Upstairs is a Parisian-style café, perfect for lingering over a glass of good wine and conversation. *33 Downing St. (at Bedford St.), West Village, 212/337–0404. Reservations not accepted. AE, DC, MC, V. Closed Mon. Subway: 1, 2 to Houston St. $–$$$*

11 *d-8*
BOULEY BAKERY

Who wouldn't want to try a sandwich by the chef once considered the best in this city of great chefs? Walk into the bakery side of this unusual "café" and order away. On the other side, you can sit at one of the 12 coveted elegant tables and enjoy the master in his true form. Tableside bread service—at least 12 varieties are always offered—starts the parade of interesting dishes, most good, some great. But despite the casual-sounding name, you'll pay formal prices in the dining room. *120 W. Broadway (between Duane and Reade Sts.), TriBeCa, 212/964–2525. Reservations essential. AE, MC, V. Subway: A, C to Chambers St. $$$*

9 *f-3*
BOUTERIN

The honeyed glow inside Bouterin spills across the fresh flowers and auberge bric-a-brac. Chef–owner Antoine Bouterin is obsessed with elongating the flavors of every ingredient in his Provençal cooking. A bay scallop gratin with elbow macaroni is deeply comforting, and the onion tart with anchovies and olives is moan-inducing. The seven-hour simmer given the luxurious lamb stew renders the meat spoon-tender.

And the "Floating Island" features twin meringues floating on a pond of perfectly smooth crème anglaise. *420 E. 59th St. (between 1st and York Aves.), Midtown East, 212/758–0323. Reservations essential. AE, MC, V. Subway: N, R, W, 4, 5, 6 to 59th St.–Lexington Ave. $$–$$$*

9 *f-4*
BOX TREE INN
This Art Nouveau town house not only serves classic French food, but has charming rooms upstairs for those interested in spending the night. If that's not romantic, what is? Attentive service and a fireplace help kindle those amorous sparks, and the caviar with blinis and chilled vodka catalyze matters even further. It's small and the five-course prix-fixe dinner is pricey, but no one ever said love was cheap. *242 E. 49th St. (between 2nd and 3rd Aves.), Midtown East, 212/758–8320. Reservations essential. AE, MC, V. No lunch weekends. Subway: 6 to 51st St./Lexington Ave.; E, V to Lexington–3rd Aves./53rd St. $$$$*

9 *d-3*
BRASSERIE 8½
At this swanky newcomer, Chef Julian Alonzo serves brasserie classics with a personal twist. He sides superbly wrought frisée aux lardons with brioche croutons, each bearing a fresh quail egg. And nowhere in town will you get a better, more generous prime rib-eye steak for under $30. Seafood is particularly fresh and fine, too, especially a fat fillet of striped bass with a horseradish crust. Such priceless artworks as Matisse lithographs and an imposing Legèr stained glass mural in the dining room adorn the interior. A highly inventive bartender (pink grapefruit margarita, anyone?) and a splendid, affordable wine list complete this marvelous picture. *9 W. 57th St. (near 5th Ave.), Midtown West, 212/829–0812. AE, MC, V. Subway: N, R, W to Fifth Ave. $$–$$$*

9 *b-1*
CAFÉ LUXEMBOURG
Reminiscent of 1930s Paris, the Art Deco Luxembourg continues to be one of the most popular late-night see-and-be-seen spots in town, with plenty of stargazing opportunities and highly flattering lighting. Best of all, you can also have a wonderful meal. The menu ranges from simple brasserie fare—

steak and pommes frites—to imaginative seasonal creations. Additional tables have been added, but the restaurant still gets so crowded that you'll have to wait a bit even if you have a reservation. *200 W. 70th St. (between Amsterdam and West End Aves.), Upper West Side, 212/873–7411. AE, MC, V. Subway: 1, 2, 3 to 72nd St. $$–$$$*

11 *b-2*
CAFÉ MILOU
The main draw at this clubby French bistro is its hours—the place stays open 24 hours a day. The basic French food is good and simple. The *croque monsieur* (a French-style grilled ham-and-cheese sandwich) is superlative, and the crispy frites will satisfy any late night hunger pang. Steamed mussels served in a cast-iron skillet are both novel and satisfying. *92 7th Ave. S (between Bleecker and Grove Sts.), West Village, 212/414–9824. AE, MC, V. Subway: 1, 2 to Christopher St.–Sheridan Sq. $–$$*

9 *d-5*
CAFÉ UN DEUX TROIS
This large, convivial Parisian brasserie-style eatery is perfect for pre-theater dinner. Leftover Corinthian columns, Crayolas for doodling on the paper tablecloths, and a menu of moderately priced basic-and-better French fare attract a diverse and noisy crowd. Service can be dicey (take this into account if you're trying to make curtain time), but you'll still leave happy. *123 W. 44th St. (between Broadway and 6th Ave.), Midtown West, 212/354–4148. AE, DC, MC, V. Subway: N, Q, R, S, W, 1, 2, 3, 7 to 42nd St./Times Sq. $–$$*

10 *c-4*
CAPSOUTO FRÈRES
It can be tricky to find the first time around, but once inside, the romantic rural French atmosphere will put you at ease. At least one of the three friendly Capsouto brothers will be on hand in the dining room. The inspired renditions of bistro classics are good, but sighs of ecstasy are to be reserved for one of the superb dessert soufflés at meals end. Brunch is one of the most revivifying experiences in town. *451 Washington St. (at Watts St.), TriBeCa, 212/966–4900. Reservations essential. AE, DC, MC, V. No lunch. Subway: 1, 2 to Canal St. $–$$$*

11 c-7
CHANTERELLE

In TriBeCa's historic Mercantile Exchange Building, chef David Waltuck serves sublime nouvelle French cuisine in a light, pretty dining room where the service, under the direction of Karen Waltuck, makes everyone feel like a privileged guest. Make tracks for chef Waltuck's signature seafood sausage, rack of lamb, Arctic char, and gorgeous desserts, and be sure to indulge in a cheese course. The prix-fixe menu, which changes weekly, is pricey, but worth every penny. *2 Harrison St. (at Hudson St.), TriBeCa, 212/966–6960. Reservations essential. AE, MC, V. Closed Sun.–Mon. Subway: 1, 2 to Franklin St. $$$$*

9 c-7
CHELSEA BISTRO & BAR

One of New York's best neighborhood restaurants, this comfortable bistro with booths and polished mirrors serves high-tone, well-seasoned French food, redolent of fresh herbs and country flavors. Don't miss the tangy chevre-slathered puff pastry with caramelized onions and potato galette. The fireplace roars in winter and the enclosed garden terrace, amply seating 30, is sheer April in Paris. *358 W. 23rd St. (between 8th and 9th Aves.), Chelsea, 212/727–2026. AE, MC, V. No lunch. Subway: C, E to 23rd St. $$–$$$*

7 e-2
DANIEL

The chef and owner of this four-star establishment, Daniel Boulud, first made a name for himself at Le Cirque. Now that he's in his own kitchen, critics and diners lunge en masse to his creations, and reservations can be very tough to obtain. The somewhat eccentric dining room is intended to resemble a Venetian palace. The entire staff is surprisingly attentive and friendly, the crowd is eclectic, and the food is some of the best in New York. Classic French dishes share the menu with updated versions of more rustic cuisine. Some of the more popular dishes include roasted squab with foie gras, lobster with wood sorrel in mushroom broth, an astonishing oxtail terrine, and black sea bass wrapped in crisp potatoes. *60 E. 65th St. (between Madison and Park Aves.), Upper East Side, 212/288–0033. Reservations essential. AE, D, MC, V. Subway: 6 to 68th St.–Hunter College. $$$$*

11 d-5
FÉLIX

A lively, neighborhood French bistro with doors that open onto the street in warm weather, this corner restaurant attracts spirited, young Europeans, shoppers, and gallery goers. The food is classic: onion tart, steak-frites, and seven-hour braised leg of lamb. *340 W. Broadway (at Grand St.), SoHo, 212/431–0021. AE. Subway: J, M, N, Q, R, W, Z, 6 to Canal St. $$*

10 b-1
FLORENT

This gritty storefront in the meatpacking district has become a wee-hours mecca for breakfast and for the crowd—a stylish but egalitarian mixture of up- and downtowners. The reasonably priced dishes include wonderful French onion soup, couscous, sweetbreads, mussels in white-wine broth, duck mousse, and *boudin noir* (blood sausage). Sit at the counter (think diner) or proper tables (think bistro). *69 Gansevoort St. (between Washington and Greenwich Sts.), West Village, 212/989–5779. No credit cards. Open 24 hours. Subway: A, C, E to 14th St.; L to 8th Ave. $–$$*

11 d-4
JEAN CLAUDE

This noisy, crowded, friendly bistro feels strikingly like Paris. The food is highly refined, and the menu changes daily. The fish, leg of lamb with roast-garlic mashed potatoes, and crème brûlée are all excellent. *137 Sullivan St. (between Houston and Prince Sts.), SoHo, 212/475–9232. No credit cards. No lunch. Subway: 6 to Spring St. $–$$*

9 c-2
JEAN GEORGES

Rarely can a restaurant live up to universally ecstatic acclaim. Jean-Georges Vongerichten is in his haute-French mode. Adam Tihany's decor is elegantly minimalist, allowing Central Park to encroach voluptuously. The food is formal French. Highlights on one seasonal spring menu include asparagus spears with morel sauce, skate with brown butter, and sweetbreads with demi-glace. Summer brings lemony young garlic soup with a floating stack of fresh herbs and user-friendly frogs' legs on the side. And pastry chef Eric Hubert practically reinvents dessert. A crème brûlée sampler—five varieties, including green tea and licorice—is other-worldly. The emphasis is on tableside service, not for show but for pampering. For a less expensive, less formal experience you can also try the Mistral Terrace (alfresco) or the Nougatine Room (open for breakfast), each with a different, lighter menu. *Trump International Hotel and Tower, 1 Central Park W (at 59th St.), Midtown West, 212/299–3900. Jacket and tie required. Reservations essential. AE, DC, MC, V. Subway: A, B, C, D, 1, 2 to 59th St.–Columbus Circle. $$$–$$$$*

9 *f-2*
L'ABSINTHE
If you're craving a true Paris fix, look no further. Highly stylized, the dining room is lined with giant gleaming mirrors and filled with a steady golden light. Chef and co-owner Jean-Michel Bergougnoux's dishes are as carefully composed as a classic elegy. Start with champagne and sautéed foie gras, or stay down to earth with snail fricassee with a Parmesan tuile and a deep-fried slice of prosciutto. Follow with mushroom-crusted lamb rack chop or "L'Absinthe surf and turf"—a perfectly roasted lobster tail and a rich slab of grilled hanger steak. Desserts are not to be missed: the ubiquitous "molten" chocolate cake gets its due here. *227 E. 67th St. (between 2nd and 3rd Aves.), Upper East Side, 212/794–4950. AE, MC, V. Subway: 6 to 68th St.–Hunter College. $$$–$$$$*

4 *b-12*
LA BOUILLABAISSE
Since the opening of this Brooklyn bistro more than a decade back, the subway is enough to transport New Yorkers to what feels like a restaurant on a quiet street in Paris. The menu is presented on a blackboard, brought to your table for inspection. The food is unpretentiously excellent. You'll always find satisfaction in the signature stew with lots of fish and a rich, flavorful broth. If you like sweetbreads, here's where to have them. A huge portion is crisply fried in butter and served with mashed potatoes and braised red cabbage. Other offerings change seasonally. The staff is always friendly, if sometimes so busy it's hard to get their attention. *145 Atlantic Ave. (between Clinton and Henry Sts.), Brooklyn Heights, 718/522–8275. No credit cards. No lunch weekends. Subway: M, N, R to Court St. $–$$*

9 *d-3*
LA CARAVELLE
La Caravelle has been one New York's most fashionable classic-French restaurants for over 30 years. The food has gone up and down during that time, but under chef Eric Di Domenico's utterly delicious tenure, the restaurant is now riding the crest of its wave. Nobody does the classics—quenelles, foie gras, terrines—better. Service is heavy on the tableside show, but the effect is charming in this amiable setting. *33 W. 55th St. (between 5th and 6th Aves.), Midtown West, 212/586–4252. Reservations essential. AE, DC, MC, V. Closed Sun. and holidays. Subway: E, V to 5th Ave.–53rd St. $$$$*

9 *e-3*
LA CÔTE BASQUE
Although this institution had to relocate down the street in 1995, not much has changed (least of all those spectacular murals), and in fact some feel that the move jogged the institution out of a long lull. Pushing 40, the restaurant still prepares classic French cuisine precisely as it was meant to be. Chef Jean-Jacques Rachou's oak-smoked salmon, cassoulet, and Dover sole are among the best choices, each skillfully plated tableside by dexterous waiters who have been known to toss attitude around with the entrées. Prices are high, but portions are large. *60 E. 55th St. (between 5th and 6th Aves.), Midtown East, 212/688–6525. Reservations essential. AE, DC, MC, V. Closed Sun. Subway: E, V to 5th Ave.–53rd St. $$$$*

9 *e-1*
LA GOULUE
This highly evocative, Art Nouveau Parisian restaurant serves traditional brasserie food and happens to be more comfortable than most of its Madison Avenue French neighbors—hence the usual presence of celebrities. True to the neighborhood (and to Paris itself), sidewalk seating is available for optimal people-watching. *28 E. 70th St. (off Madison Ave.), Upper East Side, 212/988–8169. AE, DC, MC, V. Closed Sun. Subway: 6 to 68th St.–Hunter College. $$$*

9 *e-3*
LA GRENOUILLE
La Grenouille is the grand dame of New York's haute-French cuisine, complete with lush floral arrangements, a deeply

romantic setting, and absolutely impeccable service. Enjoy beautifully prepared and perfectly served food (quenelles are particularly tender and fine) among New York's power elite and other crowned heads—if you can afford the prix fixe. *3 E. 52nd St. (between 5th and Madison Aves.), Midtown East, 212/752–1495. Reservations essential. AE, DC, MC, V. Closed Aug., and Sun.–Mon. Subway: E, V to 5th Ave.–53rd St. $$$$*

9 d-4
LE BERNARDIN
At this beautiful and spacious French restaurant, the emphasis is on seafood; and in chef Eric Ripert's hands, marine life becomes manna. Frothy "lobster cappuccino" bisque, Spanish mackerel tartare—anything is possible. The service is doting; the wine list extensive; and, for a new taste sensation, the sommelier will recommend some light-bodied reds that go well with creatures of the sea. The bill can be a shock, but what price the food of the gods? *Equitable Bldg., 155 W. 51st St. (between 6th and 7th Aves.), Midtown West, 212/489–1515. Reservations essential. AE, D, DC, MC, V. Closed Sun. No lunch weekends. Subway: N, R, W to 49th St.; B, D, F, V to 47th–50th Sts. $$$$*

9 e-2
LE BILBOQUET
A small, informal, yet fashionable destination, Le Bilboquet is a good place for an alfresco lunch in season, with sidewalk seating and wonderful salads. Evenings inside are filled with very attractive people and joie de vivre—i.e., a lot of ambient noise. *25 E. 63rd St. (between Madison and Park Aves.), Upper East Side, 212/751–3036. Reservations essential. AE. No dinner Sun. Subway: N, R, W, 4, 5, 6 to 59th St.–Lexington Ave. $$*

9 e-4
LE CIRQUE 2000
Gone are the low ceilings and monkey sconces: picture a spaceship landing in an Italian piazza. From the roller-coaster curves of the futuristic bar to the soaring, gilded, turn-of-the-20th-century ceilings, Adam Tihany's loopy design for Sirio Maccioni's new dining room of the rich and famous is certainly a study in contrasts. No surprises emerge from the multimillion-dollar kitchen; just straightforward, modern, state-of-the-art French cooking. Service can be doting or

nonexistent, depending on your stature. Love it or hate it, this is a restaurant that must be experienced to be believed. Order the crème brûlée for dessert and you'll leave happy. *New York Palace Hotel, 455 Madison Ave. (between 50th and 51st Sts.), Midtown East, 212/303–7788. Reservations essential. AE, DC, MC, V. Subway: E, V to 5th Ave.–53rd St. $$$–$$$$*

11 b-3
LE GIGOT
This adorable French bistro—on a block-long strip filled with great eateries—sets the mood with wood floors, mirror walls, dim sconces, and tables that are all but on top of one another. The menu sticks fairly close to bistro classics (bouillabaisse, steak frites, duck confit) and won't offer any culinary epiphanies. But the food is distinguished by the fact that it's lovingly prepared and always tasty. *18 Cornelia St. (between Bleecker and W. 4th Sts.), West Village, 212/627–3737. AE. No lunch. Subway: A, B, C, D, E, F, V to W. 4th St. $–$$*

11 f-5
LE JARDIN BISTRO
On a forgotten block just east of SoHo, Le Jardin Bistro feels like a country French restaurant that's been around forever. The food, too, is classic country French cooking—bouillabaisse, cassoulet, and the like—that speaks for itself without creative enhancements. The charming handwritten menu, bucolic back garden, pretty lace curtains, and the worn wood floors and tables create a cohesive and transporting dining environment. The service is warm and attentive, especially considering the reasonable menu and wine list. *25 Cleveland Pl. (between Kenmare and Spring Sts.), SoHo, 212/343–9599. Reservations essential. AE, DC, MC, V. Subway: 6 to Spring St. $–$$*

9 f-4
THE LEOPARD RESTAURANT
Inside an enchanting little townhouse built around a glassed-in garden, the Leopard's intimate main dining room purrs with a glittering crystal chandelier, no music, and a resulting restfulness. High-end brasserie fare is front and center including filet mignon bordelaise, superb boneless quail with minced duck and wild rice stuffing, and terrific profiteroles in a thick, fudgy

drizzle. When the menu does occasionally veer from Parisian, it's only in terms of ingredients. *253 E. 50th St. (between 2nd and 3rd Aves.), Midtown East, 212/759–3735. AE, MC, V. Subway: 6 to 51st St. $$$$*

9 *e-7*

LES HALLES

This trés Parisian butcher shop and bistro is casual and cacophonous, with a charming, fin-de-siècle decor. As the shadows lengthen, eager diners pack in like sardines—with very good reason— for the *frisée aux lardons* (frisée salad with bacon) with Roquefort; rich and ruddy rillettes; authentic cassoulet; boudin noir with apples; terrific steak frites (more than a few maintain that the fries are the best in town); supple steak tartare made tableside; and the interesting, affordable wine list. The restaurant serves a delightful brunch, and it's relatively quiet if you're there by noon. *411 Park Ave. S (between 28th and 29th St.), Murray Hill, 212/679–4111. Reservations essential. AE, DC, MC, V. Subway: 6 to 33rd St. $$–$$$*

9 *e-3*

LESPINASSE

When this over-the-top formal restaurant opened in the early 1990s, it helped revive fine dining in New York and hotel dining everywhere. Chef Christian Delouvrier creates food that wallops you with flavor, which interestingly contrasts with the soothing decor and quietly rich ambience. The impeccable waitstaff takes care of your every need while you concentrate on the chef's otherworldly creations. If you're lucky, these will include ragout of squab, braised salmon with crispy artichokes, or chocolate-banana soufflé. The large wine selection is made more approachable by an aim-to-please sommelier. *St. Regis Hotel, 2 E. 55th St. (between 5th and Madison Aves.), Midtown East, 212/339–6719. Reservations essential. Closed Sun. Breakfast daily. Subway: E, V to 5th Ave.–53rd St. $$$–$$$$*

9 *e-8*

L'EXPRESS

This wildly popular Flatiron District bistro is open 24 hours, and the later you visit, the better the experience you'll have. During peak hours, the place is often so mobbed that it doesn't exactly earn its name. The menu is more wide-ranging than that at most bistros in town, stretching to include such specialty items as blood sausage, roasted pig's foot, and pike quenelles. Seafood-of-the-day is usually splendid. *249 Park Ave. S (at 20th St.), Flatiron District, 212/ 254–5858. AE, MC, V. Subway: 6, N, R to 23rd St. $–$$*

10 *e-5*

LE ZINC

Karen and David Waltuck, hostess and chef and co-owners of the great Chanterelle, have finally unveiled this renovated and resurrected version of a late-night boîte of yore. Walls festooned with pop art, barrel-vaulted 15-ft ceilings, 10-ft beveled mirrors, and requisite bistro cacophony feel right in place here, especially during peak hours. Chef David Waltuck has devised a menu of such sophisticated comfort food as chicken liver pâté, which hoists that humble ingredient to brand new heights; crispy duck wings that achieve an ironic lightness; and a Meyer lemon tart that really sings—all at extremely reasonable prices. *139 Duane St. (between Church St. and West Broadway), TriBeCa, 212/513–0001 AE, MC, V. Subway: A, C to Franklin St. $$*

A NIGHT TO REMEMBER

When it comes to romance in New York, you've got to get it where you can. These places can help get things moving in the right direction.

Blue Ribbon (Eclectic)
Cuddling in the corner banquette at midnight, slurping briny oysters and sipping good white wine—of course it's worth the wait.

Firebird (Russian)
If caviar and champagne are your ultimate aphrodisiacs, this Tsarist Russian fantasy will work wonders.

The Four Seasons (Continental)
Soft light dapples the surface of the water in the remarkable pool, flanked by seasonal plants. Service is formal and many dishes are available for two.

Tanti Baci Caffé (Italian)
When you're forced to woo on a budget. The name means "lots of kisses," and there are lots of dark corner tables to steal a few.

10 c-1
LE ZOO

This somewhat cramped yet cozy bistro serves reasonably priced French items that often sound better than they taste. The seasonal, creamless turnip soup is smooth and satisfying, and the chicken breast with chanterelles is flavorful. The adorable French hosts are gracious and attentive, which can make up for the fact that you must climb over a radiator to get to your table. *114 W. 11th St. (at Greenwich St.), West Village, 212/620–0393. Reservations not accepted. AE, MC, V. No lunch. Subway: 1, 2 to Christopher St.–Sheridan Sq. $$*

10 f-3
LUCIEN

This first-class bistro, pulled together by a master restaurateur, in a neighborhood fairly wailing for one, serves state-of-the-art bistro fare, from exemplary, squeaky-clean mussels to plump, tender steak frites to a bulging wedge of tarte Tatin with cinnamon ice cream. Prices are low enough to keep the place perpetually jammed until 2 AM, but don't let that dissuade you: Sink in and you'll be grinning like a fool in no time. *14 1st Ave. (between 1st and 2nd Sts.), East Village, 212/260–6481. AE, MC, V. Subway: F, V to 2nd Ave. $–$$*

9 f-4
LUTÈCE

The fabled restaurant's newest chef, inspired young David Féau, is turning out some exciting, even daring new dishes, such as sautéed foie gras with dark chocolate sauce and orange marmalade, "black and white" sea scallops, sautéed with a white fish-based sauce and a dark-ink bordelaise sauce. Save room for the pistachio lime cake with rhubarb marmalade and basil and lime sorbet. *249 E. 50th St. (between 2nd and 3rd Aves.), Midtown East, 212/752–2225. Reservations essential. AE, DC, MC. Closed Sun. Subway: 6 to 51st St.–Lexington Ave./E, V to Lexington–3rd Aves./53rd St. $$$$*

11 d-7
MONTRACHET

One of the first restaurants to open in TriBeCa, Drew Nieporent's Montrachet remains a fine choice for imaginative French nouvelle cuisine in a spare, high-ceiling contemporary setting. The prix-fixe menu includes inventive fish choices, such as house lobster salad with asparagus and passion fruit vinaigrette, and truffle-crusted salmon, as well as elegant desserts. Spend some time perusing the award-winning wine list. *239 W. Broadway (between Walker and White Sts.), TriBeCa, 212/219–2777. AE. Reservations essential. No lunch Mon.–Thurs. and Sat. Closed Sun. Subway: A, C, E to Canal St. $$$*

11 d-8
ODEON

This large, 1930s-style cafeteria is one of TriBeCa's original late-night in spots. The French-bistro food is not terribly ambitious, but it always manages to please. The softly lit, low-frills ambience is timeless, as is the intriguing cast of characters, especially in the wee hours. *145 W. Broadway (at Thomas St.), TriBeCa, 212/233–0507. AE, DC, MC, V. No lunch weekends. Brunch Sun. Subway: A, C to Chambers St. $$*

7 e-8
ORSAY

The newest jewel in restaurateur Jean Denoyer's glittering crown (joining Le Colonial, La Goulue, and L'Absinthe), Orsay is a sassy brasserie that manages to completely eradicate the besmirched memory of the space's previous tenant, Mortimer's. After a costly renovation, Denoyer has given the Upper East Side a perfectly beautiful Art Nouveau space for 140 diners with glowing sconces and wraparound French doors. Start with the delectable rabbit terrine, then the spoon-tender Navarin lamb stew with three lamb rack chops riding on top, and finish with crêpes Suzette. *1057–58 Lexington Ave. (at E. 75th St.), Upper East Side, 212/517–6400. AE, D, DC, MC, V. Subway: 6 to 77th St. $$–$$$$*

10 b-1
PASTIS

A spinoff of Balthazar, Pastis has twice the ambience and half the hassle of the original. A no-reservations policy assures you'll get a seat, though you'll have to wait for it, and the menu lists the simple dishes that are best at Balthazar—steak frites, leeks vinaigrette, salmon in a herbal sauce, and of course the excellent crusty bread—at slightly lower prices. The casual atmosphere, with everything from French accordion music to the Rolling Stones emanating from the sound system, makes it perfect for any occasion. 9 9th Ave. (at Little W. 12th St.), Chelsea, 212/929–4844. Reservations not accepted. AE, DC, MC, V. Subway: A, C, E to 14th St.; L to 8th Ave. $$

12 c-5
PATOIS

Alan Harding's tiny bistro has become the perfect neighborhood spot, thanks to its cool, relaxed atmosphere and delicious, reasonably priced fare. Standouts are the goat cheese and roasted tomato charlotte, grilled salmon with red pepper sauce, and prime rib with fries and red-wine sauce. There's even a tented garden out back that has a cozy, cabin-like feel, and patrons must pass though the crowded kitchen to get to it. 255 Smith St. (between Douglass and Degraw Sts.), Carroll Gardens, Brooklyn, 718/855–1535. AE. No lunch. Subway: F to Carroll St. $–$$

9 d-3
PETROSSIAN

Amid lush Belle Epoque decor, deeply elegant caviar service awaits you at this posh Parisian palace. The $75 tasting of Beluga, Osetra, and Sevruga caviars arrives in a beautiful, three-side Christofle holder; the gold-plate paddle pushes the experience right over the top. An icy glass of champagne or premium vodka makes this the perfect pre-theater stop (or, more appropriately, pre-opera, with Lincoln Center so nearby). There are also bargain prix-fixe lunch and dinner menus available. 182 W. 58th St. (at 7th Ave.), Midtown West, 212/245–2214. AE, MC, V. No lunch Sun. Subway: F, N, R, Q, W to 57th St. $$$–$$$$

9 c-2
PICHOLINE

Picholine is the French countryside. Chef–owner Terrance Brennan's Mediterranean state of mind is announced with the bowl of olives (picholines) brought to your table with a basket of fresh-baked bread, and dominates the entire enticing menu. Delicate pastas, perfectly cooked whole fish, hearty game dishes . . . everything is delicious. Don't miss the cheese course; the restaurant actually has a cave in which they ripen the finest selection of cheeses in the city—some even say the best outside of France. The award-winning, friendly wine-and-cheese steward will guide you to the best choices. 35 W. 64th St. (between Broadway and Central

Park W), Upper West Side, 212/724–8585. Reservations essential. AE, D, DC, MC, V. Subway: 1, 2 to 66th St.–Lincoln Center. $$$–$$$$

11 d-4
PROVENCE

This rustic SoHo bistro wins high marks for its authentic Provençal food, moderate prices, and romantic little tented garden, complete with flower-encircled stone fountain. Try the bourride, a garlicky Mediterranean fish stew; steak frites; braised rabbit; and bouillabaisse. The Provençal wines are well-priced. 38 MacDougal St. (between Prince and Houston Sts.), SoHo, 212/475–7500. AE. Subway: C, E to Spring St. $$–$$$

7 f-8
QUATORZE BIS

Uptowners once trekked downtown for this off-the-beaten-track charmer. The downtown location is long closed, but its uptown outpost remains packed. The reasonably priced, reliable bourgeois-French fare; the compatible wine list; and the casual, authentic bistro setting combine to bring you pretty close to Paris. Have the steak frites. 323 E. 79th St. (between 1st and 2nd Aves.), Upper East Side, 212/535–1414. Reservations essential. AE, MC, V. Subway: 6 to 77th St. $$–$$$

11 d-4
RAOUL'S

Raoul's is a permanent fixture in an ever-changing neighborhood. Brave the dark, noisy, and smoky bar; the equally dark front room; and the bustle of the kitchen to get to the somewhat more serene dining room. Stick to the basics—veal chop, roasted chicken, seared tuna—and enjoy a fine meal. 180 Prince St. (near Sullivan St.), 212/966–3518. Reservations essential. AE, MC, V. No lunch. Subway: C, E to Spring St. $$–$$$

11 c-4
RESTAURANT BOUGHALEM

If only all the small French restaurants lining Greenwich Village streets had food as good as at this neighborhood destination. Ex-Bouley chef James Rafferty prepares a seasonal menu that might include appetizers of roasted cod cakes or potato and cheese dumplings with an herbed mayonnaise, and entrées of succulent sea bass accompanied by a sautée of broccoli rabe or an impressive grilled chicken. Tall and handsome, Monsieur Boughalem is a most gracious host and will probably greet you warmly at the door, a good thing because he will inevitably tell you to wait on the street for a table as the restaurant doesn't take reservations, and the bar is usually full. *14 Bedford St. (between Downing and Houston Sts.) West Village, 212/414–4764. No credit cards. No lunch. Subway: 1, 2 to Houston St. $$*

11 *d-5*
SOHO STEAK
The manly name belies the fact that SoHo Steak is really a French bistro that happens to serve wonderful food, mostly meat, at reasonable prices. Tables are close together—really close—but the fashionable crowd is usually happy, no doubt because of the excellent filet mignon, or the like, on the table in front of them. Other delicious dishes include braised oxtail ravioli and double-cut pork chops from the wood-burning oven. There are a couple of concessions for non-carnivores, as well as a pleasant Sunday brunch. *90 Thompson St. (between Prince and Spring Sts.), SoHo, 212/226–0602. No credit cards. No lunch. Brunch weekends. Subway: A, C, E to Canal St. $$*

11 *a-1*
TARTINE
Tartine is French for something, anything, spread on bread. (The verb *tartiner* is used for the act of spreading something on bread.) Language class aside, Tartine is also the name of this tiny restaurant in west Greenwich Village, where the neighborhood gathers at breakfast for café au lait and croissants, at lunch for things spread on baguettes, and at dinner for simple French food such as quiches and salads, at reasonable prices. Due to the diminutive size, there is often a wait. *253 W. 11th St. (at W. 4th St.), West Village, 212/229–2611. No credit cards. Brunch weekends. Subway: A, C, E to 14th St.; L to 8th Ave. $$*

9 *c-4*
THALIA
Thalia joins the growing roster of impressive new restaurants that have (finally) begun appearing in the Theater District. Inside the Gershwin building, the restaurant's soaring and labyrinthine interior is outfitted with gigantic vintage movie–entertainment posters. Chef Robert

Weiner's veal chasseur is stupendous enough—a big juicy chop smothered with mushrooms, shallots, and a thick tomato gravy, sided by remarkably tasty "steak fries." But one of the best potato preparations in town is his lobster mashed potatoes, wound through with nice chewy bits of lobster flesh and redolent of their roasted shells—just absurdly delicious. *828 Eighth Ave. (at 50th St.), Midtown West, 212/399–4444. AE, MC, V. Subway: C, E to 50th St. $$–$$$*

9 *d-5*
TRIOMPHE
With its diminutive jewel box size, glowing walnut floors underfoot, and succession of underlit recessed cornices overhead, Triomphe renders the pleasures of intimate dining with neoclassical flair. Though the restaurant happens to be in the lovely Iroquois Hotel, it could easily be up on chic East 78th Street near Fifth or in Paris near l'Opera. Try the lusty, thick oyster stew, which flaunts that bivalve flavor as few stews ever have. The rabbit "au vin" is a magnificent, rubicund folding of flavors—a classic rendition with distinct signature touches. Finish with the warm tarte tatin on a spill of crème anglaise dotted with raspberry coulis. *49 W. 44th St. (between 5th and 6th Aves), Midtown West, 212/840–3080. AE, MC, V. Subway: B, D, F, V to 47th–50th Sts. $$$*

GREEK

10 *f-1*
BRIAM
Authentic home-style Greek cooking, including inventive specialties that incorporate goat cheese and octopus, is served in a devoutly Mediterranean setting at friendly prices. The salads and whole grilled fish are tops; you'll be surprised not to find a beach out in back. You can choose from nine different ouzos—any one of them will really clean your clock. *322 E. 14th St. (between 1st and 2nd Aves.), East Village, 212/253–6360. AE, MC, V. No lunch. Closed Mon. Subway: N, Q, R, W, 4, 5, 6 to 14th St./Union Sq.; L to 1st Ave. $*

11 *d-5*
CHRISTO'S HASAPO-TAVERNA
Unlike most of the other tavernas that dot the streets of Astoria, the menu at

Christo's focuses as much on excellent steak as it does on more traditional Greek specialties. The atmosphere is congenial and fun and the staff is always welcoming. When you factor in the low prices for the high quality, you can't go wrong. *41–08 23rd Ave. (at 41st St.), Astoria, Queens, 718/726–5195. AE, MC, V. July–Aug. Subway: N, W to Astoria–Ditmars Blvd. $$–$$$*

3 *d-2*
ELIAS CORNER

Astoria is full of Greek restaurants, but this is the one with an hour wait to get in. The grilled fish has been touted by everyone from the former restaurant critic of the *New York Times* to the city's best French chefs. Whole fish are grilled over an open fire and drizzled with extra-virgin olive oil and fresh herbs. Unfortunately, nothing else on the menu—not the traditional Greek salads or side dishes—compares to the quality and freshness of the fish. But that doesn't make the wait for a table any shorter. *24–02 31st St. (at 24th Ave.), Astoria, Queens, 718/932–1510. No credit cards. No lunch. Subway: N, W to Astoria–Ditmars Blvd. $–$$*

9 *d-3*
ESTIATORIO MILOS

The soaring 26-ft ceilings; stretched white scrims; and stark, neoclassical decor of this Greek seafood restaurant at once evoke Santorini, the Acropolis, a Fellini movie, and a chic Manhattan club. The whole fish (on display on a mountain of crushed ice, near the open kitchen) are so fresh, you can almost smell the Mediterranean. The special appetizer of paper-thin slices of eggplant and zucchini, fried with saganaki cheese and served with a *tzatziki* (a yogurt and cucumber dip) dipping sauce, set the tone for the light, flavorful fare to come. An authentic Greek salad (no lettuce) comes garnished with creamy, goat's milk feta cheese and plump kalamata olives. Gently grilled fish with a light lick of olive oil and a squirt of lemon is the climax. And believe it or not, the thickened goat's milk yogurt drizzled with dark wild honey is one of the best desserts in town. *125 W. 55th St. (between 6th and 7th Aves.), Midtown West, 212/245–7400. AE, DC, MC, V. Subway: F, N, R, Q, W to 57th St. $$$$*

9 *c-1*
METSOVO

Though most Greek restaurants dish up the simple grilled seafood associated with islands and coastline, Metsovo serves the traditional foods of Greece's mountainous regions. Its menu leans toward hearty meat casseroles, lamb dishes, and Greek cheese. There's a good Greek wine list and a roaring fireplace set in a brick wall that makes this modest taverna one of the coziest restaurants on the Upper West Side. *65 W. 70th St. (between Columbus Ave. and Central Park W), Upper West Side, 212/873–2300. AE, DC, MC, V. Subway: 1, 2, 3 to 72nd St. $$–$$$*

9 *d-3*
MOLYVOS

It's almost impossible to find Greek food this good in Greece, let alone Manhattan. In this gorgeously appointed, spacious restaurant, executive chef Jim Botsacos starts you off with perfectly prepared *mezes* (little bites such as voluptuous caviar mousse, sweet roasted beets with marinated giant beans, stingingly delicious grilled marinated sardines). Follow with the best grilled baby octopus on the continent, and achingly delicious entrées such as flavorful rabbit stew with red wine and piquant pearl onions, and various daily whole fish (filleted, if you wish) simply grilled and dappled with a bit of olive oil and lemon. Desserts follow the straight-ahead luscious simplicity: honey-drenched buttermilk yogurt with crushed walnuts, and custard in phyllo will curl your toes. There are 10 ouzos to choose from, and a fascinating selection of Greek wines. *871 7th Ave. (between 55th and 56th Sts.), Midtown West, 212/582–7500. AE, D, DC, MC, V. Subway: F, N, R, Q, W to 57th St. $$–$$$*

9 *d-8*
PERIYALI

Just about the only thing unusual about the menu at this upscale Greek taverna is that everything tastes so good. Delicate and smoky grilled octopus, whole grilled fish, filet mignon on skewers, and other Greek specialties join more contemporary dishes such as salmon in phyllo on the menu. Don't leave without sampling the homemade baklava. *35 W. 20th St. (between 5th and 6th Aves.), Flatiron District, 212/463–7890. Reservations essential. AE, MC, V. No* lunch weekends. *Subway: F, N, R, V to 23rd St. $$–$$$*

3 *d-3*

UNCLE GEORGES

This giant 24-hour Greek restaurant would fit nicely into the commotion of Athens' plaka. The satisfying food—grilled meats and seafood, tangy tzatziki, smoky *taramasalata* (carp roe and olive oil spread), and stick-to-your-ribs moussaka—is served in large portions. Despite the 200-plus seats, there is almost always a wait, but the service is friendly and efficient. Strong coffee is a must. *33–19 Broadway (at 34th St.), Astoria, Queens, 718/626–0593. No credit cards. Subway: N, W to Broadway. $*

HUNGARIAN

7 *f-7*

MOCCA HUNGARIAN

Locals depend on this Old World outpost for extremely hearty and inexpensive Hungarian fare. The goulash and stuffed cabbage may not be gourmet, but they're comforting, filling, and reliably delicious. *1588 2nd Ave. (between 82nd and 83rd Sts.), Upper East Side, 212/734–6470. No credit cards. Subway: 4, 5, 6 to 86th St. $*

INDIAN

New York's best-known destination for Indian food is 6th Street between 1st and 2nd avenues (map 11/g-1). This short strip packs about 20 Indian restaurants, many with entrées under $10; Mitali and Passage to India are particularly good bets. Many feel the best of the lot is Haveli, just around the corner on 2nd Avenue, south of 6th Street. Further uptown, along an aromatic stretch of Lexington Avenue in the mid-20s (sometimes called "Curry Hill" instead of Murray Hill), may be found several adroit Indian restaurants.

BALUCHI'S

Lavishly decorated with Indian artifacts, these inexpensive restaurants all over town offer reliable tandoori food (curries and tasty breads), plenty of spiciness, and good service. *Numerous locations in Manhattan and Queens.*

9 *d-4*

BOMBAY PALACE

Some insist that this handsomely decorated Midtown restaurant serves some of the best Northern Indian cuisine in town. The tandoori dishes, curries, unusually delicious breads, and other traditional specialties are not cheap, but they are skillfully prepared. The reasonably priced and fabulously popular lunch buffet frequently attracts more than a few familiar faces from nearby network headquarters. *30 W. 52nd St. (between 5th and 6th Aves.), Midtown West, 212/541–7777. AE, DC, MC, V. Subway: E, V to 5th Ave.–53rd St. $$–$$$*

11 *e-1*

CAFE SPICE

It's not quite clear what kind of audience Cafe Spice is looking to attract. The food isn't good enough to attract Indian gourmets nor interesting enough to entice less adventurous eaters. Perhaps NYU students afraid to take their parents to 6th Street make up the bulk of the clientele. Still, if you order well, you can get a decent meal here. The appetizer assortment and the tandoori items are safe bets. *72 University Pl. (between 10th and 11th Sts.), Greenwich Village, 212/253–6999. AE, MC, V. Subway: L, N, Q, R, W, 4, 5, 6 to 14th St./Union Sq. $$–$$$*

9 *f-3*

DAWAT

When Dawat opened in 1986, the menu (overseen by actress–food writer Madhur Jaffrey) and the elegant setting made it New York's reigning *rani* of Indian eateries, and it's been justifiably popular ever since. While some claim the Indian restaurant scene has finally caught up with it, loyalists insist that Dawat still serves the most imaginative and best-executed Indian cuisine in town. Certainly, the marinated, tandoori-grilled-and-braised whole leg of lamb is extraordinarily tender and delicious. The usual roasted breads are unusually toothsome, too. The well-priced lunch makes it a terrific Midtown choice. *210 E. 58th St. (between 2nd and 3rd Aves.), Midtown East, 212/355–7555. Reservations essential. AE, MC, V. No lunch Sun. Subway: N, R, W, 4, 5, 6 to 59th St. $$–$$$*

3 *f-3*

JACKSON DINER

Neighborhood folk and Manhattanites flock to Jackson Diner. It recently relocated to a bigger space—complete with a spice-color design scheme—and continues to serve cheap, spicy, authentic Indian fare in huge portions. Despite its popularity, a vocal contingent will tell you the place is overrated. *37–47 74th St. (between Roosevelt and 37th Aves.), Jackson Heights, Queens, 718/672–1232. No credit cards. Subway: 7 to 74th St./Broadway; E, F, R, V to Jackson Heights–Roosevelt Ave. $*

9 *d-3*
NIRVANA
Nirvana's claim to fame is its extremely romantic setting, overlooking Central Park. The view and the setting (accented with billowing white cloth) are more memorable than the food—quite decent Indo-Bengali cuisine, and some spectacular *poori* (fluffy, delicately fried bread)—but the feeling of being in another world makes the experience heady and pleasant. *30 Central Park S (between 5th and 6th Aves.), penthouse, Midtown West, 212/486–5700. Reservations essential. AE, D, DC, MC, V. Subway: N, Q, R to 57th St. $$–$$$*

9 *e-7*
PONGAL
Don't let the fact that it's vegetarian and kosher distract you. From the papadams and green-mango relish that arrive when you sit down, to the spicy chopped *kachumber* salad (minced cucumbers, onions, and tomatoes), to the light and fragrant curries, giant paper-thin *dosai* (a crepe-like pancake made of rice flour and filled with potatoes, onions, and spices), and other specialties from southern India, the food at this quaint restaurant is nothing short of remarkable. Order the Mysore Special or the Gujarati Thali (on the back of the menu) to sample several dishes at one sitting. *110 Lexington Ave. (between 27th and 28th Sts.), Murray Hill, 212/696–9458. AE, MC, V. Subway: 6 to 28th St. $*

9 *e-7*
81 Lexington Ave. (at 26th St.), Murray Hill, 212/696–5130. Subway: 6 to 28th St.

9 *e-7*
TABLA
Floyd Cardoz's exciting and vivid cooking is best characterized as American ingredients with Indian spices and techniques. Thus, in a soaring mosaic-filled setting, you'll encounter such dishes as foie gras with black-pepper–anise–pear

compote, crab cakes jolted with Goan spices, and sweet-potato cheesecake with a cumin-cornmeal crust. For a more casual, less expensive experience you can dine at the downstairs "bread bar," where exotic naan is served with cumin-chili-cheddar fondue, among other condiments. This is the most exotic jewel in restaurateur Danny Meyer's well-deserved crown. *11 Madison Ave. (at 25th St.), Murray Hill, 212/889–0667. AE, MC, V. Subway: N, R, 6 to 23rd St. $$$*

9 *e-8*
TAMARIND
Raji Jallepalli, who has long attracted foodies to her Memphis fusion restaurant, has opened a decidedly new type of Indian eatery for New York. Absent are the dark tapestries, brass platters, and sitar music. Instead the dining room is sleek and modern with airy brown and beige decor, skylights, and private booths. The Franco-Indian menu reflects the regional cuisines of India interpreted by Jallepalli's contemporary sensibility. Shrimp bachlau is served in a pungent sauce, leg of lamb emerges from the tandoor oven crisp and fragrant, and fisherman's stew is a feast for seafood lovers. *43 E. 22nd St. (between Broadway and Park Ave.), Flatiron District, 212/674–7400. AE, DC, MC, V. Subway: N, R, 6 to 23rd St. $–$$*

9 *d-5*
UTSAV
Although the atmosphere and decor of this midtown Indian restaurant nearly resembles a hotel lobby in Bombay, the food is better than many of the other Indian restaurants in town. The long menu lists a mix of traditional dishes, meats and breads from the tandoor oven, and some more contemporary creations. Try a selection of appetizers to share and then dig into succulent lamb chops, spicy fish dishes, and other heavily seasoned entrées. *1185 6th Ave. (enter on 46th or 47th Sts.), Midtown West, 212/575–2525. AE, DC, MC, V. Subway: B, D, F, V to 47–50th St. $$*

IRISH

9 *c-6*
TIR NA NÓG
One of the best bets close to Madison Square Garden (it's directly across 8th

Avenue), this upscale pub-cum-restaurant with imported antiques, stained glass, and friendly service could make even Rangers fans behave. The chef puts out such decent Irish-accented contemporary dishes as duck confit and lentil salad, Irish oak-smoked salmon, and grilled beef sirloin with Bushmills roasted shallot sauce. Rest assured, the city's best shepherd's pie is still available. There's live music Friday and Saturday nights. *5 Penn Plaza (8th Ave. between 33rd and 34th Sts.), Midtown West, 212/630–0249. AE, D, DC, MC, V. Subway: A, C, E to 34th St.–Penn Station. $–$$$*

ITALIAN

12 *f-6*
AL DI LA TRATTORIA
The appealingly worn long wooden tables at this neighborhood trattoria make for an almost communal dining experience. The decor is homey and inviting, with lace curtains and rustic wood tables and chairs. There's always a mass of patient people milling on the sidewalk who know the wait will be rewarded with plates of homemade pasta and well-executed entrées such as steak tagliata. *248 Carroll St. (on 5th Ave.), Park Slope, Brooklyn, 718/783–4565. MC, V. Reservations not accepted. Closed Tues. No lunch. Subway: Q, 1, 2, 4, 5 to Atlantic Ave.; M, N, R, W to Pacific St. $–$$*

11 *C-2*
BABBO
This elegant Italian is the pride of TV personality Mario Batali and restaurateur Joseph Bastianich (the team behind Lupa and Esca). Since the day it opened, Babbo (a contraction of the owners' names and the Italian word for "daddy") has been one of the hottest tickets in town. This is Italian food as it was meant to be: The finest ingredients are combined with impeccable technique and a passion for adventure. A five-course pasta tasting menu is ethereal, as is the tender roast suckling pig. The place is particularly popular with fans of organ meats, who appreciate the delicious lamb's tongue salad, the calves' brain ravioli, and the warm head cheese (yes, really). The only challenge is getting a reservation. *110 Waverly Pl. (between MacDougal St. and 6th Ave.), Greenwich Village, 212/777–0303. Reservations essen-tial. AE, MC, V. No lunch. Subway: A, B, C, D, E, F, V to W. 4th St. $$–$$$*

11 *c-3*
BAR PITTI
Here's a friendly Tuscan restaurant with excellent, inexpensive food, an attractive clientele, and outdoor tables in summer. Try the bruschetta; the white-bean salad with tuna, red onions, and olive oil; the *panzanella* (bread salad with roast peppers); and the veal Milanese with mixed salad. Pastas change daily. *268 6th Ave. (between Bleecker and Houston Sts.), Greenwich Village, 212/982–3300. No credit cards. Subway: A, B, C, D, E, F, V to W. 4th St. $–$$*

9 *c-4*
BARBETTA
This century-old Italian serves traditional Piemontese specialties in four sumptuously appointed town houses. The innovative food is wedded to tradition, and is bound to please—rich *fonduta* (fondue) in a "bird's nest" with quail eggs or braised beef with polenta, and other regional classics. But in late spring and summer, the real draw is the luxurious outdoor garden, an oasis in the Theater District. In off months, when white Alba truffles are in season (mid-Oct.–Dec.), this is a particularly good place to splurge. Service is madness pre- and post-theater, but indulgent during the show. *321 W. 46th St. (between 8th and 9th Aves.), Midtown West, 212/246–9171. AE, DC, MC, V. Closed Sun. Subway: A, C, E to 42nd St. $$$*

9 *c-4*
BECCO
Though the name is Italian for "little beak," you'll need more than a bird's appetite to enjoy this busy trattoria. À la carte selections are available, but go for the prix-fixe menu. You'll be presented with an array of antipasti as soon as you sit down, including fried and/or grilled vegetables, white-bean spread, and fresh breads. Waiters roam the room with pans of pasta for you to sample, such as fresh pappardelle with duck ragu, orecchiette with broccoli rabe, fresh gnocchi with tomato sauce—the selection changes daily. If you still have room, you can upgrade to an entrée; osso buco, roasted lamb, suckling pig, and a selection of fish are usually on the list. Still hungry? The bread pudding is fantastic. Wines are all priced at $18 per

bottle. The experience is fast, friendly, fun, and delicious. 355 W. 46th St. (between 8th and 9th Aves.), Midtown West, 212/397–7597. Reservations essential. AE, D, DC, MC, V. Subway: A, C, E to 42nd St. $$–$$$

9 e-8
BEPPE
Inside Cesar Casella's Beppe, the bright room with comfortable, trattoria atmosphere puts diners in a good mood. The menu, a whimsical combination of traditional Italian dishes, such as pasta with "butcher's" sauce, and goofy hybrids, such as Tuscan fried chicken and lamb potpie, is enticing; deciding what to order isn't easy. But when the food arrives, it all seems a little different from what you were led to expect. Casella adds a subtle creative touch to just about everything he cooks, which means you may either be pleasantly surprised or disappointed. Don't miss the delicate homemade pastas or the roasted or braised meats. The service is friendly, professional, and extremely knowledgeable about the almost all-Italian wine list. 45 E. 22nd St.(between Broadway and Park Ave. S.), Flatiron District, 212/982–8422. AE, DC, MC, V. Subway: N, R, 6 to 23rd St. $$–$$$

9 e-3
BICE
This extremely successful Italian bistro was imported from Milan, where the original Bice was founded in 1926. Needless to say, the New York cousin attracts a Euro crowd—beautiful and fashion-forward. Regulars flock for the heavenly but high-priced Milanese pasta, risotto, grilled dishes, and game (in season). The service can be pretentious to the point of offense. 7 E. 54th St. (between 5th and Madison Aves.), Midtown East, 212/688–1999. Reservations essential. AE D, DC, MC, V. Subway: E, V to 5th Ave. $$$

9 c-7
BIRICCHINO
The location on a grimy street in the no-man's land between Madison Square Garden and Chelsea may seem less than auspicious, and the marble-and-vinyl decor is a bit tacky, but this is the place to go for fresh, homemade Italian sausage. Five varieties are served daily, the likes of which—chicken with mushroom, veal with sundried tomato, and

classic sweet pork—are guaranteed to warm the hearts of sausage fans. You'll also find a solid menu of Italian pastas and other classics. 260 W. 29th St. (at 8th Ave.), Midtown West, 212/695–6690. AE, D, DC, MC, V. Closed Sun. No lunch Sat. Subway: 1, 2 to 28th St. $–$$

9 b-7
BOTTINO
Despite some convincing evidence to the contrary, chic people dressed in black like good food, too. They get it *alla italiana* at this smartly designed west Chelsea restaurant, where a table can be as hard to come by as at Balthazar. The menu is straightforward—ripe Anjou pears with mountain Gorgonzola to start; pappardelle with rabbit, squab, olives and tomato, grilled salmon, roasted chicken, lamb, or steak to follow. In summer, a garagelike glass door opens to a secluded, covered garden. Service can be slow; those who prefer not to wait can try the take-out department. 246 10th Ave. (between 24th and 25th Sts.), Chelsea, 212/206–6766. Reservations essential. AE, MC, V. No lunch Sat.–Mon. Subway: C, E to 23rd St. $–$$$

7 g-8
BRUNELLI
Effulgent owner Russ Brunelli transmits the kind of delightful energy that perhaps only Italian-American restaurateurs can offer. The seven glittering chandeliers might make the place look unaffordable, but most entrées are under $20. If you're in no hurry, begin with an absolutely gigantic stuffed artichoke, with buttery breadcrumbed petals that will keep you and yours busy for about a half-hour. The *spiedino* is not to be missed: an egg-battered, fried mozzarella sandwich that's dappled with a lusty tomato–anchovy gravy. Then tuck into a huge veal chop, butterflied and pounded to 19-by-12 inches, then breaded and fried and covered with diced fresh tomatoes, basil, and red onions—a kind of veal bruschetta. 1409 York Ave. (at 75th St.), Upper East Side, 212/744–8899. AE, MC, V. Subway: 6 to 77th St. $–$$

7 b-6
CARMINE'S
The portions are huge and the wait is long at these family-style Italian trattorias. Everything, from the spaghetti with red sauce to the fancier veal dishes, sat-

isfies, and sharing huge, family-size portions is de rigeur. Chicken contadina (with sausage and peppers) is especially recommended. The kitchen has a heavy hand with garlic, so don't plan to kiss anyone after dinner. The atmosphere is bustling and loud. *2450 Broadway (between 90th and 91st Sts.), Upper West Side, 212/362–2200. Reservations not accepted. AE, MC, V. Subway: 1, 2, 3 to 96th St. $$*

200 W. 44th St. (between 7th and 8th Aves.), Theater District, 212/221–3800. Subway: N, Q, R, S, W, 1, 2, 3, 7 to 42nd St./Times Sq.

CENT'ANNI

This small, crowded, casual West Village trattoria serves simple and very good Florentine food. Try the wonderful shrimp and scallop sauté, grilled veal chop, or pasta, and finish with the zabaglione. *50 Carmine St. (between Bedford and Bleecker Sts.), West Village, 212/989–9494. AE, DC, MC, V. No lunch weekends. Subway: A, B, C, D, E, F, V to W. 4th St. $–$$$*

COCO PAZZO

Another hit from restaurateur Pino Luongo, this lively, unpretentious, East Side Italian place is a good stop for truly excellent, robust, regional-Italian specialties. The well-dressed local crowd (often joined by celebrities) enjoys a nightly array of hot and cold antipasti, as well as risotto, rigatoni with sausage and peas, and a wide array of game choices. The daily specials are always interesting. *23 E. 74th St. (between 5th and Madison Aves.), Upper East Side, 212/794–0205. Reservations essential. AE, MC, V. Subway: 6 to 77th St. $$$–$$$$*

CUCINA

This casual trattoria was among the first restaurants that heralded the Brooklyn dining revolution. Here, the portions are large, the flavors robust, and the prices right. Though the original chef has left, it's still hard to get a table in this giant space. Choose from the temptations on the antipasti table, ask for a half-order of pasta, and enjoy the generous entrées, such as succulent osso buco. *256 5th Ave. (between Carroll St. and Garfield Pl.), Park Slope, Brooklyn, 718/230–0711.*

Reservations essential. AE, MC, V. Subway: M, N, R to Union St. $$–$$$

CUCINA STAGIONALE

Despite the name, nothing changes with the seasons at this inexpensive and good Italian eatery. The menu includes myriad pastas and other starters— tortellini with prosciutto, mushrooms, peas, and cream sauce is among the best—and equally numerous entrées, including veal and salmon, each ample, tasty, and well prepared. The free antipasto is a welcome touch. *289 Bleecker St. (corner of 7th Ave.), West Village, 212/924–2707. Reservations not accepted. AE, MC, V. BYOB. Subway: A, B, C, D, E, F, V to W. 4th St. $–$$*

DA SILVANO

Even with a reservation you might find yourself waiting up to an hour for your table at this popular trattoria, which spills onto the Avenue of the Americas but still can't keep up with demand. A more thoroughly Italian experience would be hard to imagine, right down to the friendly if ineffective service and the hit-or-miss menu, which hits high notes on some dishes (the antipasti has the best odds for success) and falls flat on others (oddly, the pastas). Whole grilled fish and braised meats are usually well prepared. Lobster has a tendency to be overcooked. *260 6th Ave. (between Houston and Bleecker Sts.), Greenwich Village, 212/982–2343. Reservations essential. AE, MC, V. Subway: A, B, C, D, E, F, V to W. 4th St. $$–$$$*

DOMINICK'S

Arthur Avenue in the Bronx has long been considered a more authentic Little Italy than the touristy strip in Manhattan. One of the best and most popular restaurants on the avenue is this one, where tough waiters preside over communal tables in a room that is more or less devoid of ambience. The food is good Southern Italian, with lots of red sauce and mozzarella. *2335 Arthur Ave. (at 187th St.), Bronx, 718/733–2807. No credit cards. $–$$*

ELIO'S

Woody Allen had a window table here for years, and many less-famous locals have become regulars as well. The star-studded crowd and the chef's admirable Northern Italian fare have kept Elio's extremely popular. The handsome, wood-paneled setting is lively and noisy; expect a wait, even with a reservation. The veal Milanese and the basket of fried zucchini are menu favorites. *1621 2nd Ave. (between 84th and 85th Sts.), Upper East Side, 212/772–2242. AE, MC, V. No lunch. Subway: 4, 5, 6 to 86th St.* $$$$

7 *f-7*
ERMINIA
This family-run restaurant is one of the best-kept secrets on the Upper East Side. Candlelit, cozy (40 seats), and inviting, it's a great place for special occasions. Go for entrées grilled over a Tuscan-style wood fire, tasty pastas, or just go because it's one of those intimate, beautiful eateries that you normally find only on small, winding streets in the Village. *250 E. 83rd St., between 2nd and 3rd Aves., Upper East Side, 212/879–4284. Reservations essential. AE. Closed Sun. Subway: 4, 5, 6 to 86th St.* $$–$$$$

9 *b-5*
ESCA
From the team that brought us Babbo and Lupa comes this bright and bustling celebration of fish in the Theater District. Esca is Italian for fishing (a favorite pastime of chef David Pasternack), and the menu reflects both a love of the fruits of the sea and of contemporary Italian cooking. The most interesting part of the menu is Cruda (Italian for "raw"), and comprises a selection of seafood served raw and garnished with an impressive array or exotic ingredients, such as black lava salt and yuzu. The rest of the menu, with such simple dishes as linguine with clams and whole, salt-baked fish, is like the service: friendly, earnest, and unchallenging. *402 W. 43rd St. (at 9th Ave.), Midtown West, 212/564–7272. AE, DC, MC, V. Subway: A, C, E to 42nd St.* $$$

9 *f-3*
FELIDIA
New York's—and public television's—mother of Italian cuisine, Lidia Bastianich, creates a menu of wonderfully original Northern Italian creations for this handsome restaurant. Downstairs, where the exposed brick and wood cre-

ate a sophisticated warmth, is perfect for dinner, while the painted walls and skylight upstairs make for a cheerful lunch. Don't miss the tasty antipasti, homemade pastas with seasonal ingredients, and rustic regional specialties. An exceptional Italian-wine selection puts the finishing touch on a great meal. *243 E. 58th St. (between 2nd and 3rd Aves.), Upper East Side, 212/758–1479. Reservations essential. AE, DC, MC, V. Closed Sun. No lunch Sat. Subway: N, R, W, 4, 5, 6 to 59th St.–Lexington Ave.* $$–$$$$

7 *b-6*
GENNARO
The terrific Italian food at this tiny restaurant attracts crowds to an otherwise nearly cuisine-free neighborhood. Both the appetizers, such as *ribollita* (a hearty Tuscan soup) and beef carpaccio, and the classic homemade pastas, such as potato gnocchi with fresh tomato sauce and orecchiette with broccoli and provolone, have plenty of allure; and such entrées as tender osso buco and garlic-perfumed roasted Cornish hen add to the draw. Perhaps the best reason for the schlep, however, is the price. All of this means that lots of people wait endlessly for one of the 16 tables. Call before you go, not for a reservation, but to be sure they're open—otherwise, you might arrive to find a handwritten sign saying something like, "Sorry, Gennaro is tired and has stayed home today." *665 Amsterdam Ave. (between 92nd and 93rd Sts.), Upper West Side, 212/665–5348. Reservations not accepted. No credit cards. No lunch. Subway: 1, 2, 3 to 96th St.* $–$$

10 *d-1*
GRADISCA
Italian charm pervades this dimly lit, brick walled, basement storefront on a quiet West Village street. Once inside, the mood is festive and rakishly romantic with soft flickering candlelight that provides just enough illumination to see your dining companion, but not quite enough to read the menu. The food is quite satisfying, and some of it is even very good. Appetizers are fairly rote, but entrées, like pork chops with crispy leeks, and pastas, such as a spaghetti with an earthy, dark sauce of squid ink and bits of squid, are wonderfully enticing. Try to make friends with the owner and you'll be treated like a regular for life. *126 W. 13th St. (between 6th and 7th Aves.), West Village, 212/691–4886. No*

credit cards. No lunch. Subway: 1, 2, 3 to
14th St. $

11 d-3

GRAND TICINO

Fans of *Moonstruck* will recognize this
quaint restaurant from the film. A Village
institution, the place serves many delicious pastas and other simple Italian
favorites to the various artistic types that
populated the neighborhood in bygone
years. 228 Thompson St. (between W. 3rd
and Bleecker Sts.), Greenwich Village, 212/
777–5922. Reservations essential. AE, DC,
MC, V. Closed Sun. Subway: A, B, C, D, E,
F, V to W. 4th St. $$–$$$

9 e-3

HARRY CIPRIANI

An elegant, well-heeled, international
set, including some major celebrities,
veritably floats through the revolving
door, missing nary a beat before grasp-
ing a Bellini. As always, Cipriani serves
simple Italian food to a sophisticated
crowd in a faded setting. The atmosphere will make you homesick for
Venice, but the bill will make you think,
"Maybe next year." Hotel Sherry-Netherland, 781 5th Ave. (at 59th St.), Midtown
East, 212/753–5566. Reservations essential.
AE, D, DC, MC, V. Subway: N, R, W to
5th Ave. $$$–$$$$

10 g-2

IL BAGATTO

Order a tumbler of Chianti from the bar-
tender in the basement bar and settle in
for a long wait at this Alphabet City Ital-
ian. After looking expectantly at the host
for the hundredth time, your name will
be called and you too will be seated at
one of the cramped tables in the dimly lit
dining room upstairs. What keeps the
crowds patient? Simple, flavorful Italian
pastas and entrées—such as the entic-
ing, lemon scented chicken under a
brick—budget prices, and a casual vibe.
192 E. 2nd St. (between Aves. A and B),
East Village, 212/228–0977. No credit cards.
No Lunch. Subway: F, V to 2nd Ave. $

9 e-7

I TRULLI

One of the most authentic Italian dining
experiences in New York, this charming,
casual restaurant (with a beautiful gar-
den in season and a crackling fireplace
the rest of the year) is comfortable and
welcoming. The warm crusty bread is
served with a sinfully good ricotta-and-

roasted-garlic spread, and it's all uphill
from there. The pastas are all interest-
ing, the entrées flavorful, and the
desserts baked fresh each day. Even the
service is enchanting. 122 E. 27th St.
(between Lexington and Park Ave. S),
Murray Hill, 212/481–7372. Reservations
essential. AE, DC, MC, V. Subway: 6 to
28th St. $$–$$$

10 e-1

IL CANTINORI

Il Cantinori is a highly venerated Village
Italian restaurant known for lovely,
uncomplicated Tuscan specialties served
in two subtly charming, rustic dining
rooms. The front room spills out onto
the street in kind weather. The unusual
daily specials, cold antipasti, velvet
pasta, and grilled meats and vegetables
come with wonderfully high prices. 32 E.
10th St. (between Broadway and University
Pl.), Greenwich Village, 212/673–6044.
Reservations essential. AE, MC, V. Closed
Sun. in July and Aug. Subway: N, R to 8th
St.; 6 to Astor Pl. $$–$$$

11 d-2

IL MULINO

Some consider this the best Italian
restaurant in the city, but *cognoscenti* of
Italian food consider it the biggest farce.
Glorified Little Italy specialties com-
mand prices in the stratosphere—be
prepared to pay upwards of $50 for one
of the many enticing-sounding specials
recited tableside. Do yourself and your
wallet a favor, and skip that two-month
waiting list altogether. 86 W. 3rd St.
(near Sullivan St.), Greenwich Village,
212/673–3783. Reservations essential. AE,
MC, V. Subway: A, B, C, D, E, F, V to W.
4th St. $$$–$$$$

11 c-4

'INO

This 20-seat storefront wine-bar takes
its name from the Italian *panino* (a
sandwich pressed in a toaster), one of
three items on the menu. These aren't
just any sandwiches, though; they're on
homemade bread and filled with such
fresh ingredients as Portobello mush-
rooms, homemade mozzarella, pro-
sciutto, and the like. The other two
menu items are bread-related as well:
bruschetta and *tramezzini* (on thick
slices of crustless white bread). An
admirable and reasonable selection of
wines, mostly Italian, is served from the
six-stool bar by the glass, half-carafe,

and bottle. Keep this place in mind next time you catch a screening at Film Forum. *21 Bedford St. (at Downing St.), West Village, 212/989–5769. Reservations not accepted. No credit cards. Subway: A, B, C, D, E, F, V to W. 4th St.* $

9 b-4
LA LOCANDA

A thoroughly authentic Italian dining experience awaits at this casual trattoria, right down to the flabby white bread (an adjacent bakery bakes it on the premises) and the radio tuned to a faraway soccer game. The food is simple—fresh salads with tender arugula, generous portions of pasta with fragrant sauces, and simple entrées seasoned with olive oil and fresh herbs. The service is as authentic as the rest of the experience: very friendly, heavily accented, and not always paying attention. *737 9th Ave. (at 50th St.), Midtown West, 212/258–2900. AE, DC, MC, V. Subway: C, E to 50th St.* $–$$

10 d-1
LA NONNA

Old-style Italian food is served in a West Village brownstone with a garden. The large dining room has exposed-brick walls and—Eureka!—well-spaced tables. Try the linguine with lobster, roast pork loin in chianti-and-sage sauce, or veal Milanese topped with tomatoes and arugula. *133 W. 13th St. (between 6th and 7th Aves.), West Village, 212/741–3663. AE, DC, MC, V. No lunch weekends. Subway: 1, 2, 3 to 14th St.* $$

9 d-8
LE MADRI

This spacious, high-ceiling hot spot has died down somewhat since neighboring Barneys closed, but the menu still has consistently fine and imaginative Tuscan-style cooking. The great pizzas come from a central, wood-burning oven. Pan-roasted salmon rests comfortably on a bed of sweet corn and roasted beet succotash, and homemade swiss chard gnocchi is dressed with fresh tomatoes and Parmesan. Desserts include a nougat-flavored *panna cotta* ("cooked cream," an egg custard) with just the right silky texture. *168 W. 18th St. (at 7th Ave.), Chelsea, 212/727–8022. Reservations essential. AE, MC, V. Subway: F, V to 14th St.* $$–$$$$

11 d-4
LUPA

Mario Batali and Joseph Bastianich, the team behind the sensational Babbo and Esca, have produced this more casual, more moderately priced offspring just a couple of blocks away. Like the setting, the food is more casual than at their other restaurants, but fresh pasta dishes such as pappardelle with a rich meat ragù, and hearty entrées such as braised oxtail are every bit as satisfying, if on the small side. The front room of the restaurant is seated on a first-come, first-served basis, and reservations are taken for the back. *170 Thompson St. (between Bleecker and Houston Sts.), Greenwich Village, 212/982–5089. AE, DC, MC, V. Closed Sun. Subway: A, B, C, D, E, F, V to W. 4th St.* $$

10 c-2
MALATESTA TRATTORIA

Italian is the favored language at this small trattoria where the food is fresh and flavorful, the atmosphere congenial (even if you only speak English). A specialty is the *piadina*—an Italian tortilla—that comes with one of several fillings, among which might be mozzarella or sautéed spinach. Pastas are well cooked and seasoned with flair, and entrées, particularly the lamb chops, are satisfying. The portions are ample and an inexpensive wine complements the food. If uptown Italian eateries are too expensive, and Little Italy too red-saucy, Malatesta is a perfect middle ground. *649 Washington St. (at Christopher St.), West Village, 212/741–1207. No credit cards. No lunch weekdays. Subway: 1, 2 to Christopher St.–Sheridan Sq.* $$

3 d-4
MANDUCATI'S

A notch above the many casual, family-style spots in the city, Manducati's complements its red sauce with good homemade pasta and a well-chosen wine list. It may be off the beaten path, but regulars find the homey conviviality, especially among the New York–accented waitresses, appealing. On weekends two dining rooms and the bar area fill to the max. *13–27 Jackson Ave. (at 47th Ave.), Long Island City, Queens, 718/729–4602. AE, DC, MC, V. Closed Sun. in July and Aug. Subway: 7 to Vernon Blvd./Jackson Ave.* $–$$

7 f-8

MEZZALUNA

This bustling trattoria drew the in-crowd in the '80s. The crowd may be less chic today, but the food is just as good. As the name suggests, the decor is celestial, with a cloud-painted ceiling sprinkled with eponymous half-moons. Alas, the seating is not so airy; diners sit shoulder-to-shoulder and listen to ear-blasting music. The limited menu includes beef carpaccio with a choice of fixings, main pasta courses that change daily, vegetable-and-herb designer pizzas from wood-burning ovens, and fruit or sorbet for dessert. *1295 3rd Ave. (between 74th and 75th Sts.), Upper East Side, 212/535–9600. Reservations not accepted. AE, DC, MC, V. Subway: 6 to 68th St.* $$

11 d-5

MEZZOGIORNO

From the owners of the minuscule Mezzaluna comes another trendy, very Italian trattoria, this one with a bit more breathing room. Count on an excellent array of carpaccios, thin-crust brick-oven pizzas (at lunchtime and late at night), pastas, salads, and a great tiramisu for dessert. You can also dine at the long, marble-top bar. *195 Spring St. (at Sullivan St.), SoHo, 212/334–2112. AE. Subway: C, E to Spring St.* $$

12 b-2

NOODLE PUDDING

The name of this trattoria is a loose translation of the owner's last name, Migliaccio, which he shares with a Neapolitan dessert. Surprisingly, pasta is not the kitchen's strong point (save for the lasagna). Opt instead for fish, usually generously portioned, lightly grilled, and served with a dressing of extra-virgin olive oil and a bed of fresh steamed vegetables. Braised osso buco, roasted chicken, and baked rabbit are good alternatives to the fish, and to start, try an appetizer of carpaccio, fried calamari, or mussels in spicy tomato sauce. *38 Henry St. (between Cranberry and Middagh Sts.), Brooklyn Heights, 718/625–3737. Reservations not accepted. No credit cards. Closed Mon. No lunch. Subway: 1, 2 to Clark St.* $–$$

9 e-8

NOVITÁ

Innovative Italian cooking in a minimalist setting sums up this comfortable, largely yellow Flatiron District haunt, lit with Murano glass sconces. It's a favorite with Elite models, who can be seen tucking into red snapper, hand-made pasta, and roasted breast of duck with Barolo sauce, pine nuts, and pomegranate seeds. Have the warm chocolate tart for dessert. *102 E. 22nd St. (at Park Ave. S), Gramercy, 212/677–2222. AE, DC, MC, V. No lunch weekends. Subway: 6 to 23rd St.* $$

9 c-4

ORSO

This casual northern-Italian trattoria on Restaurant Row garners raves for pre- and post-theater pastas, thin-crust pizzas, and tasty grilled entrées. The open kitchen adds to the convivial atmosphere. After the curtain falls, Broadway's showbiz crowd fills the bar and the vaulted, whitewashed, skylit back room. *322 W. 46th St. (between 8th and 9th Aves.), Midtown West, 212/489–7212. Reservations essential. MC, V. Subway: A, C, E to 42nd St.* $$

9 d-4

PALIO

Wrapped by a striking four-wall mural of the Siena Palio by Sandro Chia, the circular bar at this posh Italian restaurant is an excellent stop for drinks, and you can grab a bite here if you wish. But if you must *dine*, take the elevator to the second-floor dining room, where worn leather banquettes and wood-grained walls make you feel like you're sitting in a boardroom. Though exorbitantly priced, the food is quite wonderful. Homemade pastas, perfect risottos, seafood, meat, and game dishes recall fine restaurants in northern Italy—and are priced to match. *Equitable Center, 151 W. 51st St. (between 6th and 7th Aves.), Midtown West, 212/245–4850. Jacket required (dining room only). Reservations essential. AE, D, DC, MC, V. Subway: N, R, W to 49th St.; B, D, F, V to 47th–50th Sts.* $$$–$$$$

9 c-3

PATSY'S

Founded in 1944, Patsy's has remained strictly in the Scognamillo family, employing only three chefs: grandfather "Patsy", then his son Joe, and, since 1986, his grandson Sal, whose ways with tried-and-true Neapolitan fare with complex flavors and uncompromisingly fresh ingredients are truly inspired.

Begin with superb *spiedino*—slabs of fresh mozzarella, breadcrumbed, deep fried, and sauced with anchovy butter—and you'll never want "fried mozzarella sticks" again. Linguine with fresh clams and just a touch of tomato is relentlessly delicious. Calamari are stuffed to bursting with chopped shrimp, crab, lobster, breadcrumbs, and toasted pine nuts. Don't confuse the numerous Patsy's pizza parlors around town with this Italian classic. It's West 56th Street, or bust. *236 W. 56th St. (between Broadway and 8th Ave.), Midtown West, 212/247–3491. D, DC, MC, V. Subway: A, B, C, D, 1, 2 to 59th St.–Columbus Circle. $$–$$$*

11 *f-5*
PEASANT
Fire is the theme of this simple Italian restaurant with an ironic name. In fact, just about everything is cooked in one of three wood-burning ovens at temperatures that reach up into the quadruple digits. The result is perfectly roasted fish, succulent and flavorful rabbit on a bed of fresh favas loaded with thick-cut bacon, and other fire-roasted goodies. Finish with an oversized lattice-topped peach pie with vanilla ice cream. Don't be put off by the Italian-only menu or the service that can throw some serious SoHo attitude. This is a place for peasants and sophisticates alike. *194 Elizabeth St. (between Prince and Spring Sts.), SoHo, 212/965–9511. AE, MC, V. No lunch. Subway: 6 to Spring St. $$*

10 *c-2*
PEPE VERDE
This West Village outpost of the tiny Pepe Rosso SoHo storefront serves a similar array of made-to-order pastas and simple Italian food. We're not talking spaghetti and meatballs, but authentic dishes including pesto, gnocchi, fresh tomato sauce, homemade focaccia, sandwiches, and salads. Though the kitchen here has less finesse than its downtown counterpart, this one still serves a satisfying meal at reasonable prices, and there are about three times as many seats. Also try Pepe Giallo in Chelsea, Pepe Rosso to Go in Soho, and Pepe Viola in Brooklyn. *59 Hudson St. (between Perry and W. 11th Sts.), West Village, 212/255–2211. No credit cards. Subway: A, C, E to 14th St.; L to 8th Ave. $*

11 *d-4*
149 Sullivan St. (between Houston and Prince Sts.), SoHo, 212/677–4555. Subway: 1, 2 to Houston St.

9 *b-7*
253 10th Ave. (at 25th St.), Chelsea, 212/242–6055. Subway: C, E to 23rd St.

12 *c-5*
200 Smith St. (at Baltic St.), Carroll Gardens, Brooklyn, 718/222–8279. Subway: F, G to Smith St.

11 *c-1*
PIADINA
A rustic wooden sign hangs outside this intimate, candlelit restaurant that attracts a regular following who love the simple food, gentle prices, and romantic atmosphere. The appealing, narrow space is bordered on one side by a brick wall and on the other by a stucco wall with wooden beams, both of which are adorned with Italian textile prints. The menu highlights *piadina*—a specialty from the Romagna region of northern Italy—which is unleavened bread baked in a coal oven coated with cheese and other toppings, as well as pasta and other entrées. *57 W. 10th St. (between 5th and 6th Aves.), Greenwich Village, 212/460–8017. No credit cards. No lunch. Subway: A, B, C, D, E, F, V to W. 4th St. $*

10 *c-1*
PICCOLO ANGOLO
Don't ask for directions to this popular Italian eatery; few people know that Hudson Street continues past 8th Avenue. Instead, just follow your nose—you'll smell the garlic sautéeing in olive oil a block away—and look for the hungry crowd milling about on the sidewalk while waiting for a table. Be prepared for the rapid-fire recitation of specials when you sit down. The pastas are all fresh, the classic Italian entrées are generous and well seasoned—the veal is particularly good—and the service is friendly, efficient, and very Italian. *621 Hudson St. (at Jane St.), West Village, 212/229–9177. D, MC, V. No lunch. Subway: A, C, E to 14th St., L to 8th Ave. $$*

11 *b-3*
PÒ
This tiny neighborhood restaurant is where the phenomenon of Mario Batali—chef–co-owner of Babbo, television star, and cookbook author—began.

(It's also what started the transformation of Cornelia Street into another Restaurant Row.) Though Batali is no longer involved with the restaurant, it remains a popular destination for an intimate meal of inventive and perfectly prepared Italian food. The white bean ravioli with brown butter is heavenly. *31 Cornelia St. (between Bleecker and W. 4th Sts.), West Village, 212/645-2189. AE, MC, V. Reservations essential. Closed Mon., no lunch Mon.-Tues. Subway: A, B, C, D, E, F, V to W. 4th St. $$*

11 *f-7*
PUGLIA
This festive Little Italy original (since 1919) now has an attached lounge, where a Sinatra-meets-Elvis cover act performs nightly. The room is set up cafeteria-style, with long communal tables, but the waitstaff is pleasant and efficient. There's lots to eat: steak contadina (grilled country-style), stuffed veal chop, tortellini Alfredo, and spaghetti bolognese, all best washed down with cheap red wine or a pitcher of beer. *189 Hester St. (between Mott and Mulberry Sts.), Little Italy, 212/966-6006. AE, DC, MC, V. Subway: 6 to Spring St. $*

12 *c-4*
QUEEN
Some people consider Queen one of the best Italian restaurants in New York City—not just Brooklyn. That's quite a lofty claim, but it is a good place to fill up on good Italian food. The antipasti change seasonally, the pastas are made to order, and the traditional entrées such as veal pizzaiola and shrimp fra diavolo are large enough to feed two (especially if you order a pasta to start). The restaurant is always packed with a neighborhood crowd. *84 Court St. (between Livingston and Schermerhorn Sts.), Brooklyn Heights, 718/596-5955. AE, DC, MC, V. No lunch weekends. Subway: 1, 2, 4, 5 to Borough Hall. $-$$$*

9 *d-4*
REMI
The elegant, two-story dining room, dominated by a spectacular mural of Venice and boldly striped banquettes, makes dining on tuna ravioli in ginger sauce, carpaccio, risottos, and wonderful vegetable antipasto even more pleasant. The bar serves far and away the best Bellini in town. Remi-to-Go, in a

glass-enclosed passageway next to the restaurant, serves breakfast and light lunch. *145 W. 53rd St. (between 6th and 7th Aves.), Midtown West, 212/581-4242. Reservations essential. AE, D, DC, MC, V. Subway: E, V to 5th Ave.-53rd St. $$-$$$*

9 *d-8*
RISTORANTE DA UMBERTO
The lacquered red exterior may seem a bit garish, but inside everything is calm and conservative—including the predominately older, uptown clientele. The draw is excellent Tuscan food and a terrific wine list heavy on high-end selections. Service is gracious and accommodating. *107 W. 17th St. (between 6th and 7th Aves.), Chelsea, 212/989-0303. Reservations essential. AE. Closed Sun. No lunch Sat. Subway: 1, 2 to 18th St. $$-$$$$*

9 *c-3*
SAN DOMENICO NY
Possibly New York's most ambitious Italian restaurant, San Domenico serves beautifully presented traditional and innovative Italian cuisine in uncompromisingly luxurious surroundings. Chef Odette Fada is known for her homemade pastas, and she has lightened the menu from days of yore, but the signature ravioli (with ricotta, soft egg yolk, butter, Parmesan, and white truffles) is still available. Game is also a specialty in season. *240 Central Park South (between Broadway and 7th Ave.), Midtown West, 212/265-5959. Reservations essential. AE, DC, MC, V. Subway: A, B, C, D, 1, 2 to 59th St.-Columbus Circle. $$$$*

9 *e-7*
SCOPA
If you've spent any time crawling around Italy in search of—and finding—great food, many of chef Vincent Scotto's preparations will be thrillingly familiar, but all bear his mark. The menu changes constantly, and Vincent is justifiably famous for his revelatory grilled pizzas, with their scorched grill marks and paper-thin, yet chewy crusts. Lunge if grilled sweet onion rings with parmigiano-reggiano are on the menu, and have them drizzled with Modena balsamic. Scotto's risottos and pasta preparations are almost as famous as his pizzas, and his seafood is always exemplary. In a neighborhood exploding with important new restaurants, Scopa places high among the best Italian

restaurants in New York. *26 E. 28th St. (near Madison Ave.), Murray Hill, 212/ 686–8787. AE, D, DC, MC, V. Subway: 6 to 28th St. $$*

9 *e-2*

SERAFINA FABULOUS GRILL

It's easy to see why this enormous place is consistently thronged, usually by the cellular phone crowd that works in the neighborhood: The vast wood-burning oven turns out consistently spectacular fare at reasonable prices. Service is extraordinarily focused; the wine list is exemplary. Not to be missed: lobster carpaccio, an occasional special risotto "Veuve Clicquot" with black truffles, filet mignon from corn-fed Colorado beef, and luscious salt-baked branzino. Desserts follow suit: grilled apple torte; supple panna cotta; and (for once) light, fluffy, dignified tiramisu. A sister pizza restaurant is a more casual but equally satisfying alternative (*see* Pizza). *29 E. 61st St. (between Park and Madison Aves.), Upper East Side, 212/734–2676. AE, MC, V. Subway: N, R, W, 4, 5, 6 to 59th St./Lexington Ave. $$*

10 *e-2*

393–399 Lafayette St. (at E. 4th St.), East Village, 212/995–9595. Subway: 6 to Bleecker St.; F, V to Broadway– Lafayette St.

11 *b-1*

TANTI BACI CAFFÉ

Of all the inexpensive Italian restaurants in and around Greenwich Village, this is the one that conjures warm feelings from just about everyone who's been there. Perhaps it's because of the rathskeller location that makes you feel like a real native for having found it (though the recent opening of Tanti Baci Flower Room on 7th Avenue South and an East Village branch now allows you a choice of atmosphere), or the friendly neighborhood crowd inside. It may even be the food, which although not out- standing, is fresh, well prepared, satisfy- ing, and inexpensive. You can mix and match pasta shapes and sauces, or opt for the classic Italian entrées, salads, and desserts. Service is friendly if a bit sporadic. *163 W. 10th St. (between 7th Ave. S and Waverly Pl.), West Village, 212/ 647–9651. MC, V. Subway: 1, 2 to Christo- pher St.–Sheridan Sq. $*

10 *g-2*

513 E. 6th St. (between Aves. A and B), East Village, 212/979–8184. Subway: 6 to Astor Pl.

9 *c-3*

TRATTORIA DELL'ARTE

The amusing decor—oversize pro- boscises and other body parts—and the lively, upbeat attitude of this casual and intensely popular trattoria make it a best bite pre– or post–Carnegie Hall. Por- tions, like the noses on the wall, are huge. Antipasto platters for two; thin- crust pizzas; pastas (available in half portions); grilled meats and fish; and other Italian fare are all well prepared. *900 7th Ave. (at 57th St.), Midtown West, 212/245–9800. AE, MC, V. Reservations essential. Subway: F, N, R, Q, W to 57th St. $$–$$$*

9 *e-1*

VIVOLO

This place serves simple, old-fashioned Italian food in a handsome, century-old brownstone with two working fireplaces. You have your choice of atmosphere— dark and clubby downstairs; high, fres- coed ceilings upstairs—but either scene is romantic. The friendly service and well-priced early bird dinner keep the locals coming. *140 E. 74th St. (between Lexington and Park Aves.), Upper East Side, 212/737–3533. AE, DC, MC, V. No lunch weekends Subway: 6 to 68th St.– Hunter College. $$*

JAPANESE

11 *d-5*

BLUE RIBBON SUSHI

Blue Ribbon Sushi serves excellent fresh sushi and sashimi—with creative twists such as filet-mignon sushi and a deli- cious lobster hand roll—as well as a decent selection of sake. The waitstaff is efficient, and the decor is stylish Japa- nese. Be prepared to wait for a table. *119 Sullivan St. (between Spring and Prince Sts.), SoHo, 212/343–0404. Reservations not accepted. AE, MC, V. Closed Mon. No lunch. Subway: C, E to Spring St.; N, R to Prince St. $$*

11 *e-3*

BOND ST

The ultra-stylish setting—sheer curtains, lots of black—complements the achingly trendy crowd that dines here. The food is very good, despite the fact that most of the clientele look like they never eat. If you go for the well-prepared sushi, you'll find rare treats such as four types of yellowtail, jumbo sweet shrimp, and unusual caviar. But the kitchen does an admirable job of preparing interesting alternatives to raw fish, too, such as broiled Chilean sea bass marinated in hearty red miso, rack of lamb with Asian pear and shiso sauce, or hot soba soup with duck and scallion. It will be hard to pick your server out from the beautiful masses, but they don't really seem like they want to be there anyway. *6 Bond St. (between Broadway and Lafayette St.), Greenwich Village, 212/777–2500. Reservations essential. AE, MC, V. No lunch. Subway: 6 to Bleecker St.; F, V to Broadway–Lafayette St. $$–$$$*

11 *f-1*

HASAKI
Wonderfully fresh and exquisitely presented sushi is your reward for waiting eons for a table. Don't be deterred by its diner appearance; the food is worth it, especially if you give the sushi chef the green light to surprise you. *210 E. 9th St. (between 2nd and 3rd Aves.), East Village, 212/473–3327. Reservations not accepted.*

STARGAZING

If you keep track of your run-ins, here are some places to up the ante:

Pastis (French)
You'll be in good company if you can get in, but try not to sprain your neck.

First (American)
Service in the wee hours means that you can watch the stars and see the sun come up.

Indochine (Vietnamese)
If you're a model—or just look like one—or will even settle for watching one, you'll find a glamorous backdrop here.

Nobu (Japanese)
Probably the most imaginative Japanese food in America—with a crowd to match.

Pravda (Russian)
Great appetizers, 65 kinds of vodkas, a fun scene—hey, maybe someone's watching you.

AE, MC, V. No lunch. Subway: 6 to Astor Pl. $$

9 *e-4*

HATSUHANA
While higher marks go to the original (48th St.) for atmosphere and consistency, true sushi connoisseurs know that both of these pricey bars are among the very best in town—that's why they wait so long. The teriyaki isn't bad, either, especially with one of the menu's several Japanese beers. *17 E. 48th St. (between 5th and Madison Aves.), Midtown East, 212/355–3345. Reservations recommended. AE, DC, MC, V. No lunch Sat., closed Sun. Subway: B, D, F, V to 47th–50th St./Rockefeller Center; E, V to 5th Ave. $$$*

9 *e-4*

237 Park Ave. (at 46th St.), Midtown East, 212/661–3400. Subway: 4, 5, 6, 7 to 42nd St.–Grand Central.

11 *e-4*

HONMURA AN
Honmura An is the best place in town for authentic Japanese noodle dishes (which, traditionally, must be slurped). The restaurant makes its own soba noodles daily; you can watch a chef at work in a glassed-in room at the back. Try the seasonal tasting menu and the giant prawn tempura. The dining room, on the second floor of a SoHo warehouse, is spacious and comfortable. *170 Mercer St. (between Prince and Houston Sts.), 212/334–5253. Reservations essential. AE, DC, MC, V. Closed Mon. No lunch Sun. or Tues. Subway: N, R to Prince St.; 6 to Spring St.; F, V to Broadway–Lafayette St. $–$$*

10 *e-1*

JAPONICA
This restaurant is always so busy that you can be sure the sushi is fresh. The sizable menu—which includes sushi, sashimi, tempura, and teriyaki—has something to delight every Japanese-food lover. If you can't decide, try one of the economical combo plates for a taste of several different dishes. Be prepared to wait during peak hours. *100 University Pl. (at 12th St.), Greenwich Village, 212/243–7752. Reservations not accepted. AE. Subway: L, N, Q, R, W, 4, 5, 6 to 14th St./Union Sq. $*

9 *e-4*

KATSUHAMA
Although the term "Japanese food" conjures images of austere sashimi and

other diet-friendly delights, this restaurant's specialty is serving some of the most popular everyday foods in Japan: *tonkatsu,* or fried pork cutlet. The pork is cut thick, breaded in panko (fluffy Japanese bread crumbs), fried crisp, and sliced and served with the requisite shredded cabbage, rice, miso, pickled vegetables, and a Worcestershire-based sauce. The utilitarian setting is fitting for the exemplary, but unadorned cutlet. *11 E. 47th St. (between 5th and Madison Aves.), Midtown East, 212/758-5909. AE, MC, V. Subway: B, D, F, V to 47th-50th Sts./Rockefeller Ctr. $$*

9 e-4
KURUMA SUSHI

If it is a truly Japanese sushi experience you are seeking, look no further than Kuruma Sushi, housed on the second floor of a nondescript Midtown office building (a common occurrence in Tokyo). Off the elevator guests are greeted by a rousing welcome from the sushi chefs (the owner, who has been in business in this space for over 20 years, being the most vocal). Though you can dine in the somewhat shabby dining room, the most rewarding experience is to sit at the sushi bar and order *omakase* ("chef's choice") from the effusive owner. The parade of dishes that appears will follow a strict order: impeccable sashimi then sushi, tartare made from live shrimp followed by the crunch of the broiled heads. This bounty doesn't come cheap, so try to remain calm when the bill arrives. *7 E. 47th St. (between 5th and Madison Aves.), Midtown East, 212/317-2802. AE, MC, V. Subway: B, D, F, V to 47th-50th Sts./Rockefeller Ctr. $$$$*

11 c-8
NEXT DOOR NOBU

Drew Nieporent, the owner of Nobu, has finally heeded the cries of distraught would-be customers who were perpetually unable to secure a reservation at his famed restaurant. Next Door Nobu is strictly first-come, first-served, which means painfully long waits, but non-VIPs are thrilled to have the opportunity to sample Nobu Matsuhisa's unique style of Japanese cooking. The menu focuses more on sushi and raw-bar selections, and is slightly less expensive than the one next door. The decor is fancifully Japanese and includes a wall papered with nori. *105 Hudson St. (between Franklin and N. Moore Sts.),* *TriBeCa, 212/334-4445. AE, DC, MC, V. Reservations not accepted. No lunch weekends. Subway: 1, 2 to Franklin St. $$*

11 c-8
NOBU

Nobu is one of New York's most exciting restaurants, and getting a reservation here can be a frustrating experience. But the food is sensational, reflecting chef Nobu Matsuhisa's time in Latin America—think "unusual use of chiles." Try the glazed black cod, the yellow-tail sashimi, squid ceviche, or the tartare of *toro* (tuna belly), and tuna salad with ponzu sauce. Best of all, put yourself in the hands of the chef—but be prepared to pay. If you can't get a reservation, go anyway and you will probably be seated at the sushi bar, which is a show in itself. You can also try Next Door Nobu, with its egalitarian no-reservations policy. *105 Hudson St. (at Franklin St.), TriBeCa, 212/219-0500. Reservations essential. AE, DC, MC, V. No lunch weekends. Subway: 1, 2 to Franklin St. $$$*

11 g-1
RAI RAI KEN

Diners have but five choices at this narrow storefront with 14 stools set along a wood counter behind which young hipster Japanese men take orders and prepare the food. Ramen—shoyu with a soy sauce broth, shio with a clear salt broth, and miso with a rich fermented soybean broth—all come with wheat noodles, greens, sliced roast pork, and various other toppings for a mere $6.50 each. If it's too hot for soup, a seasonal cold dish of broth and noodles or seafood fried rice promises to satisfy. Wash it all down with Sapporo beer or soda. *214 E. 10th St. (between 1st and 2nd Aves.), East Village, 212/477-7030. No credit cards. Subway: 6 to Astor Pl. $*

10 f-1
SHARAKU

The first (and certainly the largest) East Village Japanese restaurant to ride the 1980s sushi craze, Sharaku gets everything right, and at comparatively friendly prices. The place is therefore often very crowded, with a strong Japanese presence (always a good sign). The sushi bar is prodigious and its chefs are deeply focused; the *chirashi* is a favorite. *8 Stuyvesant Pl. (near 3rd Ave.), East Village, 212/598-0403. AE, MC, V. Subway: 6 to Astor Pl. $$*

11 *g-1*

SOBA-YA

This busy, casual noodle shop is one of the culinary highlights on the stretch of East 9th Street lined with Japanese eateries. On the limited but authentic menu, you can choose from a small selection of appetizers and a number of hot and cold soba dishes. Connoisseurs judge quality by the cold soba (buckwheat noodles), and here the chewy, subtle, refreshing noodles are served *comme il faut* with a flavorful dipping sauce and the requisite cooking-water chaser. The hot soba is equally delicious. Udon (thicker wheat noodles) and a few other non-noodle Japanese dishes are also available. *229 E. 9th St. (between 2nd and 3rd Aves.), East Village, 212/533–6966. AE, DC, MC, V. Subway: 6 to Astor Pl. $*

9 *c-3*

SUGIYAMA

The ancient Japanese tradition of *kaiseki* (tea ceremony cuisine) is celebrated at this diminutive restaurant on the fringes of the Theater District. In the open kitchen, chef Sugiyama prepares the ritualistic order of dishes himself. As is the custom, the meal starts with a selection of cold appetizers artfully arranged in a lacquered box. It then proceeds through sushi and sashimi, fried tidbits, soup, cooked meat and fish, and other treats, the selection and order of which depend on the season and the chef's reading of your culinary adventurousness and intent. An enthusiastic staff is eager to help you decipher what you are eating and instruct you on how to maximize the experience. *251 W. 55th St. (between Broadway and 8th Ave.), Midtown West, 212/956–0670. AE, DC, MC, V. Subway: B, D, E to Seventh Ave./53rd St.; N, R, Q, W to 57th St./Seventh Ave. $$$$*

9 *f-5*

SUSHI YASUDA

Although sushi restaurants of this quality and style are abundant in Tokyo, in New York they are few and far between. The stylish space is lined with a veneer of bamboo. Behind the sushi bar chef Yasuda busily works his magic, using only the freshest fish, much of it flown directly from Japan, some without English names. Exemplary appetizers, salads, and other dish emerge from a hidden kitchen. Freshly grated wasabi and homemade pickled ginger con-

tribute to the fine experience. The service is attentive and extremely friendly. *204 E. 43rd St. (between 2nd and 3rd Aves.), 212/972–1001. AE, DC, MC, V. Subway: 4, 5, 6, 7 to 42nd St.–Grand Central. $$$*

11 *b-2*

TAKA

Two things distinguish Taka from the many other small, cozy Japanese restaurants around the city: The sushi chef is a woman; and all of the beautiful ceramic dishes, in organic shapes and colors, are custom-made for the restaurant by her. Furthermore, the fish is always fresh and several creative rolls add flair to the meal. *61 Grove St. (between Bleecker St. and 7th Ave. S), West Village, 212/242–3699. AE, MC, V. Subway: 1, 2 to Christopher St.–Sheridan Sq. $$*

11 *h-2*

TAKAHACHI

The best sushi bargain in town, this no-frills East Villager is always packed with a young crowd, hungry for swimmingly fresh slabs of yellowtail, tuna, and salmon. Don't expect anything unusual, and don't demand too much of the frenzied waitstaff; just pray they're not out of sea urchin. Prepare for a wait. *85 Ave. A (between 5th and 6th Sts.), East Village, 212/505–6524. No lunch. AE, MC, V. Subway: 6 to Astor Pl. $*

11 *d-4*

TOMOE SUSHI

Few restaurants have as loyal a following as this small sushi place in the West Village. A line begins to form a full hour before the doors open at 5 in the evening and it doesn't subside until they close five or so hours later. What people wait upwards of an hour for is fresh, generously portioned sushi at reasonable prices, and other well-prepared Japanese food. There are no fireworks, but the food never disappoints. And many a new friendship has been made waiting on line or while sitting at the tightly packed tables. *172 Thompson St. (between Bleecker and Houston Sts.), West Village, 212/777–9346. AE. Reservations not accepted. Closed Tues. and Sun. Subway: 1, 2 to Houston St. $$*

9 *e-8*

YAMA

Yama is the place to take anyone who insists that sushi isn't filling. These huge slabs of sushi and sashimi literally fall off the plate. Moreover, the fish is always extremely fresh, tender, and delicious. The drawbacks are the inevitable wait outdoors and the nonexistent decor. The original store, on 17th Street, is the one to hit; the new Houston Street outpost doesn't measure up. *122 E. 17th St. (at Irving Pl.), Gramercy, 212/475-0969. Reservations not accepted. AE, MC, V. No lunch Sat. Subway: L, N, Q, R, W, 4, 5, 6 to 14th St./Union Sq.* $$

11 *d-4*
92 W. Houston St. (between LaGuardia Pl. and Thompson St.), Greenwich Village, 212/674-0935. Subway: 6 to Bleecker St.; F, V to Broadway–Lafayette St.

10 *d-2*
38-40 Carmine St. (between Bedford and Bleecker Sts.), West Village, 212/989-9330. Subway: 1, 2 to Christopher St.–Sheridan Sq.

10 *d-5*
ZUTTO
Long before Nobu arrived to define TriBeCa sushi, neighborhood residents were content to eat reasonably priced raw fish with minimal fanfare at Zutto. Dishes are always fresh, and seasonal delicacies often add to the menu. While the restaurant has never been destined to win any design awards the spare room is serene and pleasing. *77 Hudson St. (between Harrison and Jay Sts.), TriBeCa, 212/233-3287. Subway: 1, 2 to Franklin St.* $

KOREAN

11 *h-1*
DOK SUNI
This tiny storefront has a small, dark dining room with exposed bricks and just a dozen tables, piped-in rock music, and pleasant service. It serves homestyle Korean cooking—fresh, simple, and, of course, spicy, but never greasy or heavy. The kimchi and spicy broiled pork ribs are great. *119 1st Ave. (between 7th and 8th Sts.), East Village, 212/477-9506. Reservations not accepted. No credit cards. No lunch. Subway: 6 to Astor Pl.; F, V to 2nd Ave.* $–$$

9 *d-6*
GAM MEE OAK
Distressed brick walls, exposed beams, and an open industrial kitchen unfold in

this stylish restaurant, a popular spot for trendy Korean youth. Although the menu lists only eight choices, each is exemplary. The specialty of the house is a creamy white bone marrow and oxtail soup, served with rice noodles and slices of beef. Each table is set with a large bowl of chopped scallions and coarse sea salt. Though subtle on first taste, the soup develops a strong, almost haunting beef flavor that can become addictive. The freshly made mung bean pancakes with scallions are not to be missed. *43 W. 32nd St. (between 5th Ave. and Broadway), Midtown West, 212/695-4113. AE, MC, V. Subway: B, D, F, N, R, Q, V, W to 34th St.* $

9 *e-6*
HANGAWI
Everything but the kimchi is bound to baffle the uninitiated in this serene dining room, where you sit shoeless at a sunken table under dark-wood beams. Hangawi specializes in vegetarian Korean mountain cooking, whatever that is; the only way to start is to order a prix-fixe "Emperor's Meal," which translates loosely into a parade of exotic vegetable dishes that are at worst interesting and at best delicious. There are no fewer than 10 courses, several of which you may have to assemble yourself; and by the time you hit the last one your table will be covered with about 20 little bowls of unidentifiable but delicious things. If only the waitstaff could translate the names of the rare wild herbs into English . . . . Try one of the many teas—date and citrus are wonderful—and the milky-white Korean sake. *12 E. 32nd St. (between 5th and Madison Aves., Midtown East, 212/213-0077. AE, MC, V. Reservations essential. Subway: B, D, F, N, R, Q, V, W to 34th St.* $$

11 *b-4*
JUNNO'S
Master mixologist Junno Lee has created an innovative selection of specialty cocktails—the soju lemonade, made with Korean sweet-potato vodka, is exceptional—at his spare bar-restaurant. Food is sometimes an afterthought with such a lively bar scene, but a couple of dishes are worth sampling, such as the grilled squid with miso, beef short ribs, and wakame seaweed salad. *64 Downing St. (between Bedford and Varick Sts.), West Village, 212/627-7995. AE, MC, V. Subway: 1, 2 to Houston St.* $–$$

1 *f-3*

KUM GANG SAN

This 24-hour Korean eatery is almost the size of the Seoul airport and comes complete with a waterfall. There are tables as far as the eye can see, and as soon as you've grabbed one, one of the countless bowls of delicious kimchi (often spicy pickled vegetables and dried fish) will materialize. The highlight is excellent Korean barbecue, especially the beef short ribs, but you'll also have a full menu to choose from. *138–28 Northern Blvd. (at Union St.), Flushing, Queens, 718/461–0909. AE, MC, V. Subway: 7 to Main St.–Flushing. $*

9 *d-6*

NEW YORK KOM TANG SOOT BUL HOUSE

Korean "Seoul" food at its best is served at this lively restaurant on the 32nd Street strip. For the barbecue experience, cook thin slices of beef (*bul go gui*) or other marinated meats over red-hot coals, top with chiles and raw garlic, and wrap in lettuce. The large second-flour dining room is the more festive of the two, with communal tables situated around tabletop barbecues. The waitstaff speaks little English so be prepared for a lot of gesturing. *32 W. 32nd St. (between 5th and Broadway), Midtown West, 212/947–8482. AE, MC, V. Subway: B, D, F, N, Q, R, S, W to 34th St. $–$$*

11 *e-4*

WOO LAE OAK

SoHo style informs this chic Korean eatery, where guests dressed in their casual-chic best dine from tabletop barbecues set in huge marble tables. Black-clad waiters hauling plates of fiery kim chee and dishes, such as *jang au gui* (broiled eel served sizzling on a hot stone) and platters of raw *bul go gi* (short ribs) to be cooked at the table complete the picture. For a singularly satisfying meal try the sweet black cod simmered in a rich soy broth. *148 Mercer St. (between Houston and Prince Sts.), SoHo, 212/925–8200. AE, DC, MC, V. Subway: N, R to Prince St. $$*

9 *d-6*

YET JIP

This wood paneled restaurant is one of the hipper Korean spots in the Little Korea environs: wood-topped tables, plants, and youthful waiters in tea-dyed uniforms. The selection of kim chee is top notch, with seasonal variation such as young green onions in chili sauce. The menu centers around barbecue with excellent bul go gi and such other barbecued dishes as spicy pork and vegetables. Also try yam noodles sautéed with kim chee, mandoo (dumplings), and pajun (mung bean and scallion pancakes). *5 W. 36th St. (between 5th and 6th Aves.), Midtown West, 212/629–4466. AE, MC, V. Subway: B, D, F, N, R, S, W to 34th St. $–$$*

KOSHER

9 *d-6*

ABIGAEL'S

Chef Jeffrey Nathan, who is not Jewish, has developed quite a reputation for haute kosher cooking, both because of this contemporary American glatt kosher restaurant and his popular cooking show on PBS. The menu, which changes seasonally, includes appetizers and entrées you could find in many restaurants around town: a delicate salmon fillet that comes with olives and aioli, mahimahi served with Israeli couscous and apricot chutney. There isn't much ambience, but the staff is friendly and accommodating. *1407 Broadway (between 38th and 39th Sts.), Midtown West, 212/575–1407. AE, DC, MC, V. Closed Fri. dinner and Sat. Subway: N, Q, R, F, W, 1, 2, 3, 7 to 42nd St./Times Sq. $$–$$$*

9 *d-5*

LE MARAIS I

At this premier kosher French steak house, you certainly don't have to be Jewish to adore the supple, juicy steaks, lovely seafood, and toothsome fowl. The delicious kosher béarnaise sauce will have you wondering how it's created, and the crème brûlée is rendered virtually salubrious by the substitution of soy milk for cream. The street-level dining area in back is a bit less cramped and noisy than what's upstairs. Another quite different edition of Le Marais is in the Financial District. *150 W. 46th St. (between 6th and 7th Aves.), Midtown West, 212/869–0900. AE, MC, V. Subway: N, R, W to 49th St. $$–$$$*

10 *e-6*

LE MARAIS II

With a different menu and significantly jauntier space than its Theater District older sister, the Financial District edition of the kosher French steak house adds a light Moroccan accent to its menu. The cumin flatbread with curried lamb and liver notes is not to be missed. "Surprise Steak" is rare and deeply flavored, not unlike "butcher's tenderloin" (hanger steak). Vanilla roast pineapple makes a perfect ending, served with coconut sorbet, gently spiced shortbread, and a hale rum caramel sauce. *15 John St. (between Broadway and Nassau St.), Financial District, 212/285–8585. AE, MC, V. Subway: A, C, 4, 5 to Fulton St. $–$$$$*

9 e-3
SHALLOTS
Those who consider the height of kosher dining to be a bowl of matzoh ball soup and a pastrami sandwich should check out this posh kosher eatery in the Sony Building atrium. Not only is the vibe sophisticated and the decor tasteful and understated, but a romantic air fills the room, enhanced with mood lighting, backlit glass panels, and pretty flowers. The menu reads like a primer on contemporary American cuisine—though oenophiles beware, the wine list is all kosher—with dishes such as sweetbreads dusted with porcini flour, a salad of duck confit, and creamless soups. Everything is beautifully presented on colorful glass plates. *Sony Atrium, 550 Madison Ave. (between 55th and 56th Sts.), Midtown East, 212/833–7800. AE, MC, V. Closed Fri. dinner and Sat. Subway: E, V to 5th Ave./53rd St. $$–$$$*

LATIN

9 c-3
BISTRO LATINO
As you climb the narrow, worn staircase to this hidden, second-floor restaurant, you may wonder what you're getting yourself into; after all, you're not that far from Times Square. Rest assured: Behind the door is a fun-filled evening of cool rhythms and hot food. Enjoy succulent seafood, ceviche, and paella as you tango and samba the night away; the contemporary interpretations of South American classics will dance on your tongue. It's part kitsch, part Havana, and all very enjoyable. *1711 Broadway (at 54th St.), Midtown West, 212/956–1000. AE, D, DC, MC, V. Closed Sun. in Aug. Subway: F, N, R, Q to 57th St. $$*

11 f-4
CAFÉ HABANA
When the surrounding neighborhood was still bohemian and offbeat, this space was a fun local diner. The current owners, who also own Rialto down the block, wanting to preserve the feel of the place, opened this Cuban–Mexican-theme restaurant. Excellent Latin diner fare such as Cuban sandwiches, rice and beans, and *camarones al ajillo* (shrimp in garlic sauce) are all provided at budget prices. And, true to the owners' vision, the cheery space, with blue booths and pale green Formica tables, is usually filled with artist types eating late breakfasts and tapping their feet to festive Latin beats. *17 Prince St. (at Elizabeth St.), Lower East Side, 212/625–2001. AE, DC, MC, V. Subway: 6 to Spring St. $*

7 b-8
CALLE OCHO
This upscale Upper West Side Latino fiesta dishes up just what the neighborhood craves—cool cocktails, and good, zesty food in creative surroundings. Beyond the youthful bar scene, an upbeat cavernous dining room awaits with beaded curtains, colorful banquettes, and oversized lamp shades. Food is creative latin: the *chupe* (dense Peruvian shrimp chowder) is a meal in itself; ceviches, like lobster with passionfruit mojo, are refreshing and flavorful; and entrées such as beef tenderloin with a tomato-cabrales tart are attractively presented and satisfying. For dessert the *churros* (fried dough) with three dipping sauces rival those available in nearby subway stations. *446 Columbus Ave. (between 81st and 82nd Sts.), Upper West Side, 212/873–5025. AE, DC, MC, V. Subway: 1, 2 to 79th St. $$–$$$*

9 e-8
CHICAMA
A steady bar crowd that downs their share of pisco sours and other Latin cocktails fuels the energy at this lively Latin spot housed in a wood-beamed cantina within ABC Carpet & Home. *Nuevo latino* impresario Doug Rodriguez has created an appealing menu complete with a selection of ceviche, such as the spicy "Viagra," from a freestanding ceviche bar, and a wide array of tasty dishes, such as tender grilled octopus served on a bed of nutty quinoa. For dessert try the wonderful tapioca pudding served in a

whole coconut or the hot-out-of-the-oil churros. Wash it all down with a selection from the thoughtful Spanish and South American wine list. *ABC Carpet & Home, 35 E. 18th St. (between Broadway and Park Ave. S), Flatiron District, 212/505–2233. AE, MC, V. Subway: L, N, Q, R, W, 4, 5, 6 to 14th St./Union Sq. $$$*

9 *e-8*

PATRIA

This festive Flatiron District hot spot serves up creative and scrumptious *nuevo latino* fare to arouse even the most jaded palate. Sip a *mojito* while you play with a mortar of butter, cream cheese, and roasted garlic to spread on your warm olive bread. New chef Andrew DiCataldo has devised a most unusual menu. Tuna ceviche, limey and suffused with flavor, is served in a split coconut nested in crushed ice. A "suckling pig combo" changes regularly but might include two graceful bone-on rib chops that amount to luxury finger-food, and a leg that's been rubbed in deep, dark spices and watchfully braised. The desserts are as creative as the entrées, and include such highlights as rice pudding with apricot-mango salad and lemon grass ice cream, and an adorable white chocolate espresso cup served with a raspberry chocolate cigar. *250 Park Ave. S (at 20th St.), Gramercy, 212/777–6211. Reservations essential. AE, MC, V. Subway: N, R, 6 to 23rd St. $$–$$$$*

MALAYSIAN

11 *f-6*

NYONYA

Filled with Malaysians, which inspires confidence, this noisy and often hectic restaurant serves good food at very low prices. Try the Oriental sesame rolls or a whole deep-fried fish. *194 Grand St. (at Mott St.), Chinatown, 212/343–8899. No credit cards. Subway: S to Grand St.; 6 to Spring St.; J, M, Z to Bowery. $*

1 *f-3*

PENANG

You can now choose from three Manhattan outposts of this fabulous Flushing restaurant; but for an authentic Malaysian experience, make the trip to Queens. Don't miss the coconut shrimp, or the pull-apart roti appetizer with a fragrant chicken-curry dipping sauce. The whole fish and homemade

Malaysian noodles are also good. The Manhattan stores, alas, are merely cheap places to eat with 1960s Vistavision Tiki-Hut decor and merely okay food. *38-04 Prince St., Flushing, Queens, 718/321–2078. Reservations not accepted. AE, MC, V. Subway: 7 to Main St.–Flushing. $*

7 *f-7*

1596 2nd Ave. (at 83rd St.), Upper East Side, 212/585–3838. Subway: 4, 5, 6 to 86th St.

11 *e-5*

109 Spring St. (between Greene and Mercer Sts.), SoHo, 212/274–8883. Subway: 6 to Spring St.

9 *b-1*

240 Columbus Ave. (at 71st St.), Upper West Side, 212/769–3988. Subway: B, C to 72nd St.

MEDITERRANEAN

11 *h-1*

ALPHABET KITCHEN

An almost childlike mural of the alphabet dancing along the brick wall dominates one side of the long, narrow dining room of Alphabet Kitchen—so named for its location in Alphabet City, not for the simplicity of the menu, on which Portuguese and Spanish fare commingle. Most diners sample a selection of tapas like the fried chorizo, shrimp with garlic, or tortilla (a fluffy Spanish omelet served in bite-sized cubes) before moving on to more serious fare such as a rich braised lamb shank with polenta, seared tuna, and delicious sautéed chicken. The dining room can get quite busy, so service can be slow. *171 Ave. A (between 10th and 11th Sts.), East Village, 212/982–3838. AE, DC, MC, V. No lunch Mon. or Tues. Subway: 6 to Astor Pl. $$*

9 *f-2*

EAST RIVER CAFÉ

Gleaming French doors run along the front and north side of the restaurant; inside are vintage Hollywood studio portraits, Persian rugs, and gentle live light jazz piano. Sweet young clams are steamed with Venetian abandon in garlicky white wine. Desserts are scrumptious, especially the apple tart and white chocolate mousse cake. *1111 1st Ave. (at E. 61st St.), Upper East Side, 212/980–*

*3144. AE, MC, V. Subway: N, R, W, 4, 5, 6
to 59th St.–Lexington Ave. $$–$$$*

11 *f-3*
IL BUCO

Il Buco is an antiques shop by day, a
Mediterranean restaurant by night. The
dark, candlelit rooms look like the setting for a film scene of bohemian Village
life in the '50s. The menu consists of
tapas, including poached goose salad
with tarragon, chives, pine nuts, and
dried cherries; summery grilled baby
octopus with capers and olives; and
aged Serrano ham with melon. *47 Bond
St. (between Lafayette St. and Bowery),
East Village, 212/533–1932. Reservations
essential. AE. No lunch on weekends. Subway: 6 to Bleecker St.; F, V to Broadway–
Lafayette St. $$–$$$*

9 *e-8*
OLIVES

Chef Todd English took his neo-Mediter-
ranean concept from Boston around the
world before opening an outpost in New
York City. And since it opened in the W
Union Square hotel, the new Olives has
been packed. The David Rockwell–
designed room feels surprisingly like a
hotel lobby, but the food is far from
generic. English favors bold flavors and
rich ingredients, and he combines more
of them in a dish than you would think
possible and then serves them in huge
portions. Among his favorite foods is
foie gras and he uses it in everything
from a gargantuan stuffed chicken wing
to an ethereal custard. *W Union Square
Hotel, 201 Park Ave. S (at 17th St.), Flatiron District, 212/353–8345. AE, DC, MC,
V. Subway: L, N, Q, R, W, 4, 5, 6 to 14th
St./Union Sq. $$–$$$*

3 *d-6*
OZNOT'S DISH

One would never guess that this funky
Williamsburg eatery, with its quirky
decor of 50s era furniture and eclectic
artwork, has one of the deepest and
most interesting wine cellars in the borough of Brooklyn. The bigger neighborhood draw, however, seems to be the
creative Mediterranean fare, prepared
with a Middle Eastern accent like a
selection of mezze consisting of flavorful dips and crisp slices of pita, cold
cucumber and yogurt soup, and grilled
salmon on a bed of Israeli couscous. *79
Berry St. (at N. 9th St.), Williamsburg,*

*Brooklyn, 718/599–6596. MC, V. Subway:
L to Bedford Ave. $–$$*

9 *e-8*
PIPA

Nuevo latino maestro Douglas
Rodriguez has created another sensation with this deconstructed Spanish
tapas restaurant, just opposite his other
hit, Chicama, in the ABC Carpet &
Home store. Decorated like your Spanish grandmother's attic, only more styl-
ishly, the menu is similarly designed for
mixing and matching. Try one of the traditional plates of olives, artichokes, and
Serrano ham, or one of the more creative creations. The menu is so long and
the dishes so delicious sounding that
you will likely order too much food. But
this is food meant for sharing. *ABC Carpet & Home, 888 Broadway (entrance on
19th St. between Broadway and Park Ave.
S.), Flatiron District, 212/677–2233. AE,
MC, V. Subway: L, N, Q, R, W, 4, 5, 6 to
14th St./Union Sq. $$*

10 *f-1*
TAPPO

Huge wheels of Parmesan, wine bottles,
and toy trucks in the window are the
only signs that you've found Tappo, one
of the hippest new dining destinations
in the East Village. Inside the dimly lit
restaurant, divided into several small
rooms, communal farmhouse tables
rest underneath amusing artwork of
goats and other farm animals. The
menu has a large selection of tapas and
other small dishes, such as meaty
grilled sardines, *gambas a la mer*
(shrimp with sea salt), ravioli stuffed
with nettles, tastings of olives and
cheese, and inventive salads. For
entrées, you'll find a small list of good
dishes such as seasonally changing
pasta and gnocchi and steak tagliata.
The staff may not be the most efficient,
but what they lack in service skills they
make up for in charm. *403 E. 12th St. (at
1st Ave.), East Village, 212/505–0001. AE,
DC, MC, V. Closed lunch Mon., Tues.,
Wed. Subway: L to 1st Ave. $$–$$$*

MEXICAN

11 *h-4*
EL SOMBRERO

They'll even give you margaritas-to-go at
this almost-seedy diner-style Mexican
café, which is nicknamed "the hat" after

the huge neon sign out front. The food
is of the too-cheesy, taco-enchilada
brand of Mexican cuisine, but it is filling
enough to take the edge off the tequila
(margaritas come in pitchers, too).
Expect a fun, noisy crowd, loud Latin
music, and a potential hangover. *108
Stanton St. (at Ludlow St.), Lower East
Side, 212/254–4188. No credit cards. Subway: F, V to 2nd Ave. $*

10 *d-5*
EL TEDDY'S
A Statue of Liberty crown graces the roof
of this TriBeCa fixture, and the awning
resembles a faux Gaudì sculpture.
Inside, the funky decor includes
mosaics, lit dioramas, and lots of color.
The active bar provides potent margaritas, served on the rocks or straight up,
and a watchable crowd. Once you make
your way to one of the oversize booths,
should food happen to arrive—the service is maddeningly slow—you'll be
treated to upscale Mexican concoctions
made with the freshest ingredients. Skip
dessert and just order a cup of the
strong coffee: It comes with dishes of
natural sugar crystals and Mexican
chocolate shavings. *219 W. Broadway
(between Franklin and White Sts.),
TriBeCa, 212/941–7070. AE, MC, V. No
lunch weekends. Subway: 1, 2 to Franklin
St. $$*

7 *b-6*
GABRIELA'S
It's not the quietest place, and the ser-
vice isn't always speedy, but you proba-
bly won't find better value at any other
Mexican restaurant in Manhattan. The
flavors are authentic, the corn tacos are
fresh, and the *pozole* may be the most
satisfying soup you've ever tried. The
roasted chicken and pork are pretty
good, too. Expect an extended wait for a
table during peak hours; defuse the
waiting experience with a margarita or
sangria. *685 Amsterdam Ave. (at 93rd
St.), Upper West Side, 212/961–0574. AE,
MC, V. Subway: 1, 2, 3 to 96th St. $*

7 *b-8*
*315 Amsterdam Ave. (at 75th St.), Upper
West Side, 212/875–8532. Subway: 1, 2, 3
to 72nd St.*

11 *g-1*
LA PALAPA
Just east of the streetside T-shirt and
sunglass "mall" of St. Mark's Place,
you'll find this pleasant restaurant, with

seating that spills onto the street, sooth-
ing earth tones, and a funky back gar-
den. Specialty seasonal margaritas, like
blood orange and watermelon, are made
with real fruit, and the staff is helpful and
eager to offer suggestions. Try a selec-
tion of the delectable soft tacos or que-
sadillas filled with fresh ingredients or
venture toward more standard fare, such
as the *tamal de vagre* (a traditional pre-
Columbian combination of catfish and
cactus steamed in corn husks). Chicken
enchiladas come in a huge bowl covered
with rich, spicy mole, and *arrachera al
tequila con jalapeños* is a flavorful tequila-
marinated skirt steak doused with pun-
gent jalapeños. *77 St. Mark's Pl. (between
1st and 2nd Aves.), East Village, 212/777–
2537. AE, DC, MC, V. Subway: 6 to Astor
Pl. $–$$*

7 *a-5*
MAMA MEXICO
Two brothers, taught to cook by their
Mama in a small Mexican village, braved
the trip north and brought along a sunny
friendliness and some of the best authentic Mexican cooking around. Terrific guacamole, made tableside, can be nice and
spicy (for a change). Perfect grilled squid,
jumbo grilled lamb rack chops in a ruddy
gravy, zippy chicken mole, and *real* beef
tacos. Even the rice and beans are quite
thoughtfully prepared. Befriend brother
Juan (an easy task) and he'll let you sample house-infused pineapple tequila.
There's also terrific live mariachi music
on Friday night. *2672 Broadway (between
101st and 102nd Sts.), Upper West Side,
212/864–2323. AE, MC, V. Subway: 1 to
103rd St. $–$$*

9 *f-2*
MAYA
Executive chef Richard Sandoval has created spectacular and benevolently priced
dishes that are precisely the way you
always hoped Mexican food would taste.
Small wonder Maya is always jammed.
Margaritas are downright sinewy. Chiles
rellenos (stuffed with shrimp and
manchego cheese) are ridiculously delicious. Guacamole is spicy on request, so
request. Butterflied, lime-marinated, and
grilled beef tenderloin, plated with a
cheese enchilada dappled with mole
sauce, is remarkably flavorful. And buttery crepes folded into purses and
sauced with a warm goat milk reduction
on a plate studded with roasted pecans
may reduce you to tears. *1191 1st Ave.*

(between 64th and 65th Sts.), Upper East Side, 212/585–1818. Reservations essential. AE, MC, V. Subway: 6 to 68th St.–Hunter College. $$–$$$

7 b-5
MEXICANA MAMA
Bring your own six-pack of Dos Equis—a friendly waitress will bring the limes—to this adorable storefront where the food is cheap and traditional. Then get ready to chow down on four kinds of salsa, quesadillas, enchiladas, chicken mole, and the tour-de-force: chiles rellenos. *525 Hudson St. (between Charles and W. 10th Sts.), West Village, 212/924–4119. No credit cards. Closed Mon. Subway: A, C, E to 14th St.; L to 8th Ave. $*

10 c-1
MI COCINA
Authentic regional Mexican cooking (no spicy baby-food pap here) is served in newly renovated surroundings. A new menu was in the works at press time; but if it is anything like the old, you can bet it will be a delicious interpretation of traditional Mexican fare. *57 Jane St. (at Hudson St.), West Village, 212/627–8273. AE, DC, MC, V. No lunch. Brunch Sun. Subway: A, C, E to 14th St.; L to 8th Ave. $$–$$$*

9 c-8
ROCKING HORSE CAFÉ
Here you'll find good, fairly authentic Mexican fare that's a step above the usual south-of-the-border slop. Preparation can sometimes suffer under the weight of the crowds here—seafood can be overcooked, beans can be gluey, and anything can be over- or under-seasoned—but after a few of the justly celebrated margaritas it's unlikely you'll care. *182 8th Ave. (between 19th and 20th Sts.), Chelsea, 212/463–9511. AE, MC, V. Brunch weekends. Subway: 1, 2 to 18th St. $$*

9 f-3
ROSA MEXICANO
Many hold this festively elegant Mexican restaurant in high esteem, and not only for its wonderful guacamole (made to your specifications tableside) and signature pomegranate margaritas. The menu features mildly spiced regional dishes—not Tex- or Cal-Mex. Try the flaming fajitas, or the lamb shank steamed in a parchment pouch with three chilis, or beef tenderloin with a wild mushroom tequila sauce. The

Lincoln Center location has a whimsical decor and a similar menu. *1063 1st Ave. (at 58th St.), Upper East Side, 212/753–7407. AE, DC, MC, V. Closed lunch. Subway: N, R, W, 4, 5, 6 to 59th St.–Lexington Ave. $$–$$$*

9 b-2
61 Columbus Ave. (at 62nd St.), Lincoln Center, 212/977–7700. Subway: A, B, C, D, 1, 2 to 59th St.–Columbus Circle.

9 f-4
ZARELA
Zarela's is one of the more popular spots for "gourmet" Mexican. Renowned Mexican chef Zarela Martinez showcases her zesty, authentic home cooking in an even zestier environment. If you'd rather skip the fiesta atmosphere, opt for the somewhat quieter dining area upstairs, but anywhere you sit, it's a great party. But don't miss the poblano chile relleno, the roasted marinated pork tenderloin, and plenty of the loopiest margaritas in town. *953 2nd Ave. (between 50th and 51st Sts.), Midtown East, 212/644–6740. Reservations essential. AE, DC, MC, V. No lunch weekends. Subway: 6 to 51st St./Lexington Ave.; E, V to Lexington–3rd Aves./53rd St. $$*

MIDDLE EASTERN

9 b-4
AZURI CAFÉ
This tiny kosher storefront serves up the best falafel in the city—and, according to winsome ex-pats, the best outside Israel. Chicken and beef kebabs are also excellent and come with the same outstanding salads and condiments as the falafel. Service can cool, but compliment the food and it'll warm up. There's no decor but for three rickety tables, so consider take-out. *465 W. 51st St. (between 9th and 10th Aves.), Midtown West, 212/262–2920. Reservations not accepted. Breakfast daily. No credit cards. Closed Sat. Subway: C, E to 50th St. $*

11 d-8
LAYLA
Layla looks like a Middle East nightspot, with Moroccan tiles and dioramas of belly dancers and pashas (a real-life belly dancer appears once nightly). North African cooking is reinterpreted here, with great success. Try the *mezze* (appetizers), including feathery *burek* (phyllo dough filled with sharp feta cheese),

grilled octopus, and dips served with pita. For entrées try the braised lamb with dried plums and toasted almonds or the seafood couscous. *211 W. Broadway (at Franklin St.), TriBeCa, 212/431–0700. AE, DC, MC, V. No lunch. Subway: 1, 2 to Franklin St. $$–$$$*

10 g-2

MAMLOUK

At this prix-fixe Middle Eastern restaurant, diners sit on pillowed banquettes around low tables in the romantically lit dining room. There is no menu, so for $30 per person you'll receive a multicourse meal that includes fabulous dips and spreads, soup, salad, vegetable dishes, fish dishes, lamb or chicken dishes, and dessert. The selection changes daily, but the food is always delicious and there's almost always more of it than you can eat. The room is booked for an early and a late seating. If you come late you'll be able to order an after-dinner hookah and enjoy sweet apple tobacco while you listen to what can only be described as tribal Moroccan house music. *211 E. 4th St. (between Aves. A and B), East Village, 212/529–3477. AE, MC, V. Closed Mon. No lunch. Subway: F, V to 2nd Ave. $$$*

3 e-2

MOMBAR

Chef–owner–artist Moustafa El Sayed has created a personalized environment in this out-of-the-way Egyptian restaurant, where just about every inch of wall, floor, and table space contributes to a larger artistic installation. The tables are covered in mosaics, and murals adorn the walls. The food, an interpretation of southern Egyptian cuisine, is also one-of-a-kind. If you show an interest, Moustafa will likely come around from behind his open-kitchen counter and sit down with you to discuss the menu and life. Choose from a selection of dips and salads, the namesake sausage, chicken tagine, braised rabbit, or duck. It may not be the best food you've ever eaten, but in this caring environment it tastes just fine. *25-22 Steinway St. (at 25th Ave.), Astoria, Queens, 718/726–2356. No credit cards. Closed Mon. Subway: R, V to Steinway St. $$*

11 a-3

MOUSTACHE

You won't be able to contain yourself when you're presented with a pita—a piping hot pillow of dough straight from the oven—and a selection of delicious salads waiting to be scooped up. This is only part of the reason that crowds wait patiently outside Moustache for one of the 10 copper-top tables. The pitas are followed by delicious entrées, including leg of lamb or merguez sausage sandwiches or, if you're particularly hungry, the *ouzi*, a large phyllo package stuffed with chicken and fragrant rice. The falafel is bland and overcooked but nothing else on the menu disappoints. Although the service can be slow—it takes time to roll out those pita to order—it is always friendly. For quickest seating, plan to eat at off times. *90 Bedford St. (between Barrow and Grove Sts.), West Village, 212/229–2220. No credit cards. Subway: 1, 2 to Christopher St.–Sheridan Sq. $*

11 h-1

265 E. 10th St. (between 1st Ave. and Ave. A), East Village, 212/228–0022. No credit cards. Subway: 6 to Astor Pl.

PAN-ASIAN

9 d-8

AZ

Patricia Yeo's ambitious pan-Asian restaurant occupies an entire building in the Flatiron district. Professional types congregate in the bar and lounge on the first floor. Ride the glass elevator to the top floor and you'll step out into a striking glass atrium dining room (the roof retracts) lined with plants and other atypical New York design elements, like plenty of space. The prix-fixe menu offers many creative selections, such as duck schnitzel, ginger lacquered quail, and tea-smoked chicken, each skillfully prepared. The bread comes with a fantastic assortment of intensely flavored spreads—one of the highlights you won't even have to order. *21 W. 17th St. (between 5th and 6th Aves.), Flatiron District, 212/691–8888. AE, D, DC, MC, V. Subway: L, N, Q, R, W, 4, 5, 6 to 14th St./Union Sq.; F, V to 14th St. $$$$*

7 f-8

ORIENTA

It feels like a SoHo bistro, but this small crowd-pleaser is definitely Uptown, and definitely not a bistro. The kitchen turns out creative and well-presented French-Vietnamese cooking for a beautiful crowd that actually comes to eat. Amber lighting and large windows along the street soften the cramped quarters. *205 E. 75th St. (between 2nd and 3rd Aves.), Upper East Side, 212/517–7509. Reservations essential. AE, DC, MC, V. No lunch. Subway: 6 to 77th St. $$*

11 *h-2*

O.G. (ORIENTAL GRILL)

The decor is minimal: Japanese light fixtures on peach walls (so far as we could tell in the dim lighting), dark-blue banquettes, brown-paper tablecloths, and votive candles. The clever combinations of oriental techniques and ingredients—Japanese, Thai, Chinese, and Indonesian—mean that each dish is well conceived, not forced or bizarre (despite what you might think about banana won tons flambé). *507 E. 6th St. (between Aves. A and B), East Village, 212/477–4649. MC, V. No lunch. Subway: F, V to 2nd Ave. $–$$*

7 *b-7*

RAIN

Rain feels like a post-college party on weekend nights, but the food at this contemporary Pan-Asian restaurant is skillfully prepared and delicious. The menu reads like the greatest hits of Thai, Vietnamese, and Malaysian cooking. Appetizers of green-papaya salad and summer rolls wrapped in rice paper are cool and refreshing. The coconut chicken soup tastes like the real McCoy. For the main course, try the stir-fried beef in peanut sauce or the Chinese eggplant in bean sauce. Nothing disappoints, though some dishes are more authentic than others. Wash it all down with one of many Asian beers. *100 W. 82nd St. (between Amsterdam and Columbus Aves.), Upper West Side, 212/501–0776. AE, DC, MC, V. Subway: 1, 2 to 79th St. $–$$*

9 *e-8*

REPUBLIC

Republic is noisy, crowded, and doesn't take reservations unless you're having a good-size party. But it's fun, with a sleek, spare, neo-warehouse design and long, polished, blond-wood tables for communal seating. (Sit at the bar if you're shy.) This is essentially a sophisticated noodle house. Try curried chicken on skewers; spicy seafood salad; noodle dishes, including curried duck in chicken broth with taro chips; shrimp

won tons in chicken broth; and pad thai. For dessert, the coconut ice cream is conspicuously divine. *37 Union Sq. W (between 16th and 17th Sts.), Flatiron District, 212/627–7172. AE, DC, MC, V. Subway: L, N, Q, R, W, 4, 5, 6 to 14th St./Union Sq. $*

9 *e-3*

TAO ASIAN BISTRO

One can only guess at what the real Buddha would think of his likeness (in the form of a 30-ft-high gilt statue) presiding over this Midtown pan-Asian eatery. The dining room is a converted movie theater, and the soaring ceiling and clever design create an atrium-like effect that is enhanced by the pan-Asian decor. The menu attempts to cover the full Asian gamut, with a page devoted to sushi and assorted other dishes whose roots can be traced back to China, Thailand, or Vietnam. *42–44 E. 58th St. (between Madison and Park Aves.), Midtown East, 212/888–2288. AE, MC, V. Subway: N, R to 5th Ave. $–$$*

PERUVIAN

11 *h-2*

COCINA CUZCO

This brightly painted, noisy Avenue A storefront is a great stop for those who love the flavorful, sweetly spiced roast chicken for which Peru is known. Also on the menu are a selection of ceviches, appetizers such as grilled octopus or chicken hearts, and seafood and meat entrées—though none compare to the chicken. *55 Ave. A (at E. 4th St.), East Village, 212/529–3469. AE, D, DC, MC, V. Subway: F, V to 2nd Ave. $*

PIZZA

11 *d-4*

ARTURO'S PIZZERIA

Serving what many consider the best coal-oven pizza in town, Arturo's is a popular choice for those who can't get into Lombardi's. Live music starts nightly at 6 PM, and the setting is fun and timeless, if somewhat decrepit. *106 Houston St. (at Thompson St.), Greenwich Village, 212/677–3820. AE, MC, V. No lunch. Subway: 1, 2 to Houston St.; F, V to Broadway–Lafayette St. $*

12 *b-2*
GRIMALDI'S
Frank Sinatra made frequent pilgrimages to this red-check tableclothed classic (formerly known as Patsy's) where great (some say the best) New York–style pizza reigns supreme. The walls are covered with autographed black-and-white photos, and Frank Sinatra's silky voice emanates from the jukebox. Patsy usually sits at the table in the far right corner, making sure everyone is happy with the pies coming out of the coal-fired oven. Any combination of toppings is available, but be careful because the price adds up quickly. You can get salads and pastas with red sauce, but why bother when the pizza is so good. *19 Old Fulton St. (between Front and Water Sts.), Brooklyn Heights, 718/858–4300. Reservations not accepted. No credit cards. Subway: A, C to High St.–Brooklyn Bridge. $*

11 *c-3*
JOE'S PIZZA
If all you want is a slice of thin, crisp New York pizza at its best, drop into Joe's. A sprinkling of hot pepper flakes, garlic powder, oregano, and Parmesan cheese will make you think you've died and gone to heaven. Find a place to indulge; there's no seating here. *7 Carmine St. (at Bleecker St.), West Village, 212/255–3946. Reservations not accepted. No credit cards. Subway: A, B, C, D, E, F, V to W. 4th St. $*

11 *b-3*
JOHN'S PIZZERIA
As far as purists are concerned, this longtime Village pizzeria serves the city's only real pizza, baked in stone-floor ovens—thin-crusted, garlicky, and topped with fresh ingredients. Devour your pie (you can't order by the slice) on old-fashioned, red-check tablecloths, below celebrity photos, and painted murals of Italy. The Village original serves beer and wine, and some of the spin-off locations have full bars. The other branches are all splendid, but there's something about the original that keeps the lines long during peak hours. *278 Bleecker St. (between 6th and 7th Aves.), West Village, 212/243–1680. Reservations not accepted. No credit cards. Subway: A, B, C, D, E, F, V to W. 4th St. $*

9 *c-2*
48 W. 65th St. (between Central Park West and Columbus Ave.), Upper West Side, 212/721–7001. Subway: 1, 2 to 66th St.–Lincoln Center.

9 *c-5*
260 W. 44th St. (between Broadway and 8th Ave.), Midtown West, 212/391–7560. Subway: N, Q, R, S, W, 1, 2, 3, 7 to 42nd St./Times Sq.

9 *f-2*
408 E. 64th St. (between 1st and York Aves.), Upper East Side, 212/935–2895. Subway: 6 to 68th St.–Hunter College.

9 *e-8*
LA PIZZA FRESCA
Count on this find opposite the glitzy Gramercy Tavern for powerfully flavored pastas and risottos, huge arugula salads sparkling in a dressing of good olive oil and fresh lemon juice, and pizzas whose thin, crisp crusts are blistered and savory from the wood fire in the beehive brick oven at the back of the room. With the wood fire casting its glow on the rear tables and the sponged ochre walls, warm and mellow are the operative words here; La Pizza Fresca is particularly soothing at the end of a long day, or after a movie at the Loews 19th Street Theatre. Moreover, the prices are noticeably reasonable, even if the mostly young waitstaff often needs a gentle nudge. *31 E. 20th St. (between Broadway and Park Ave. S), Flatiron District, 212/598–0141. AE, DC, MC, V. No lunch weekends. Subway: 6, N, R to 23rd St. $–$$*

11 *f-5*
LOMBARDI'S
One of New York's original pizza-making families, the Lombardis have become synonymous with delicious coal-oven pizza. The secret is in the crust, which, according to finicky pizza lovers, has more flavor here than anywhere else. The best salad in any pizza joint and a comfortable, casual atmosphere make the experience a must. *32 Spring St. (between Mott and Mulberry Sts.), Little Italy, 212/941–7994. No reservations. No credit cards. Subway: 6 to Spring St.; F, V to Broadway–Lafayette St. $*

7 *f-2*
PATSY'S PIZZA
A contender for the best slice in the city, this no-frills pizza joint—the first to bear the Patsy's name—recently added a dining room so you can sit down. That's about all that has changed in almost a century, except for the neigh-

borhood around it. (You'll notice lots of other Patsy's locations around town, but this is by far the best.) 2287–91 1st Ave. (between 117th and 118th Sts.), Harlem, 212/534–9783. No credit cards. Subway: 6 to 116th St. $

7 e-8
SERAFINA FABULOUS PIZZA
There is a full menu at this sparkling Italian oasis, but the thin-crust, crispy, and intensely flavorful brick-oven pizza is simply not to be missed. The restaurant occupies the top two floors of a Madison Avenue building, but in summer the ceiling on the top floor retracts to form a lovely terrace, and downstairs, windows are flung open to what you'll swear are Mediterranean breezes. The hand-painted walls and terra-cotta floors add to the Italian look, as do the Italian accents, which start to fill the restaurant at about 9 PM. 1022 Madison Ave. (at 79th St.), Upper East Side, 212/734–2676. No reservations accepted. AE, DC, MC, V. Subway: 6 to 77th St. $–$$

POLISH

3 d-6
KASHA'S
From the street you might mistake this little, almost dingy restaurant for an ordinary diner. But the made-to-order Polish food sets Kasha's apart. Frequented by an arty Williamsburg crowd (often seen eating breakfast at 4 in the afternoon), the restaurant specializes in Eastern European brunch foods such as blintzes, apple pancakes, and latkes, each fried in butter to order. The cabbage rolls are of the salt-and-pepper variety (as opposed to the tomato-based sweet and sour kind), but they will satisfy your craving for any Polish home cooking. Even the coffee is delicious. 146 Bedford Ave. (at N. 9th St.), Williamsburg, Brooklyn, 718/387–8780. AE, MC, V. Subway: L to Bedford Ave. $

3 d-6
LOMZYNIANKA
Don't worry, few non-Poles have a clue as to how to pronounce the name of this Polish café, but luckily the menu is translated into English. Your order will depend on your taste for adventure—there's everything from rich borscht, flavorful kielbasa, and hearty goulash to earthy tripe and tongues in horseradish

sauce, and of course, pierogis. Prices are so low you will think they are written in zlote. 646 Manhattan Ave. (at Nassau St.), Greenpoint, Brooklyn, 718/389–9439. No credit cards. Subway: G to Greenpoint Ave. $

PORTUGUESE

10 c-2
ALFAMA
This breezy Portuguese restaurant, adorned with plenty of blue and white tile, serves authentic Portuguese with an impressive Portuguese wine list to match. Start with exemplary pulpo, tender slices of octopus doused with good olive oil, cod cakes, or assorted Portuguese cheeses. Entrées include such seafood dishes as baked cod with vegetables and potatoes and such other pleasing concoctions as chicken with a seductively sweet sauce. 551 Hudson St. (at Perry St.), 212/645–2500. AE, D, DC, MC, V. Subway: 1, 2 to Christopher St.– Sheridan Sq. $$

7 b-8
LUZIA'S
Though recently expanded, this neighborhood restaurant has maintained its mom-and-pop charm. Classic dishes such as caldo verde (potato and kale soup) and bacalhau (salt cod with potatoes and eggs) mingle well with Luzia's other home cooking, such as white-bean salad, paella, and peppery chicken legs. Don't miss the flan for dessert. 429 Amsterdam Ave. (between 80th and 81st Sts.), Upper West Side, 212/595–2000. AE, DC, MC, V. Subway: 1, 2 to 86th St. $–$$

10 d-5
PICO
Portuguese cooking has risen in popularity of late, and none is as sophisticated as the creative contemporary fare prepared by John Villa at this TriBeCa eatery. The dining room is a blend of modern New York and traditional Portuguese, with tiles, fringed chairs, and blown-glass chandeliers. The equally traditional fare includes chorizo, cockles, salt cod, and seafood and meat combinations. Don't miss the already-legendary suckling pig or anything that includes fresh sardines. 349 Greenwich St. (between Jay and Harrison Sts.), TriBeCa, 212/343–0700. AE, D, DC, MC, V. Subway: 1, 2 to Franklin. $$–$$$

RUSSIAN

9 e-3
CAVIAR RUSSE
This chandeliered Russian jewel box is tucked upstairs in a Midtown lair. Under a robin's-egg blue ceiling lurk opulent Georgian murals, green velvet banquettes, and wall-to-wall luxury. Splurge on the prix-fixe $115 seven-course tasting menu, and start with a tasting of the house caviars to appreciate fully the voluptuous fruits of the sturgeon's labors. Feast on tartare of sirloin served with your choice of sevruga, osetra, or beluga. Here's a special-occasion restaurant that will overjoy you. *538 Madison Ave. (between 54th and 55th Sts.), Midtown East, 212/980–5908. AE, MC, V. Subway: N, R, W, 4, 5, 6 to 59th St.–Lexington Ave. $$$$*

9 c-4
FIREBIRD
Prerevolutionary indulgence is the name of the game at this lush dining spot on Restaurant Row, where all of the classics—blini, smoked salmon, caviar, borscht, champagne, frozen vodka—are in fine form. Of the myriad *zakuski* (appetizers), the walnut and chicken *satsivi* (a shredded specialty of Georgia) is particularly good. Other appetizers include fruit with smoked salmon and marinated herring served over a potato blini. The entrées run the gamut from *karsky shashlik,* a marinated lamb loin, to salmon *kulebiaka,* which is served in pastry with mushroom, leeks, and lemon sauce. Desserts are something of a disappointment, and the service is spotty, but you can't help being pleased, as you sit among the ornate antiques, with the general authenticity. You'll find the same menu next door at the Firebird Café as well as nightly cabaret entertainment. *365 W. 46th St. (between 8th and 9th Aves.), Midtown West, 212/586–0244. AE, D, DC, MC, V. Subway: A, C, E to 42nd St. $$$–$$$$*

4 h-5
RASPUTIN
Visit this cavernous Russian nightclub–restaurant late on a weekend and you'll wake up the next morning transformed. This will be due partly to your throbbing headache (from copious vodka consumption) and partly to your hazy memory of the wild floorshow, one that rivals almost anything in Vegas. Food is pretty much beside the point, but keeps on coming throughout the evening—sample everything and maybe some of the traditional Russian dishes will surprise you. *2670 Coney Island Ave. (at Ave. X), Brighton Beach, Brooklyn, 718/332–8111. AE, MC, V. No lunch. Subway: F to Ave. X. $$$*

9 d-3
THE RUSSIAN TEA ROOM
In the annals of see-and-be-seen theatrical Power Dining, the RTR held a unique position from the moment it opened in 1927. But New Yorkers and veteran tourists were devastated when RTR was shuttered in 1995. The late impresario Warner LeRoy, who resuscitated Tavern on the Green, rebuilt RTR from the ground up, creating four all-new floors and adding 500 seats. That throbbing red ground floor is back, and so is a tunic-clad waitstaff, and the other three floors are absolutely breathtaking. Begin, of course, with vodka: There are dozens, more than a few house-infused. Next up: blini with caviar, anointed with melted butter and crème fraîche and rolled into flutes at your table. On a good night, chicken Kiev is the best you'll ever find, stuffed with herbed butter, breaded, and deep fried just until the tender juiciness peaks. Fromage *kissel* (a fluffy cheesecakelike tart) makes a delicious finale. *150 W. 57th St. (east of Carnegie Hall), Midtown West, 212/974–2111. AE, D, DC, MC, V. Subway: F, N, R, Q, W to 57th St. $$$–$$$$*

SCANDINAVIAN

9 e-6
AQ CAFÉ
Run by star-chef Marcus Samuelsson and his team at Aquavit and housed in the sleek Scandinavia house, AQ pays homage to all things Swedish, from design to cuisine. For a comprehensive taste try the smorgasbord plate, a selection of such traditional tidbits as herring and smoked salmon artfully presented on post-modern china. More traditional lunchtime fare includes a Swedish meatball sandwich, gravlax pizza, and a spicy chili chicken wrap. Diners that find themselves yearning to pare down their own surroundings can purchase most of the dining accouterment in the adjacent shop. *Scandinavia House, 58 Park Ave. (at 38th St.), Midtown East, 212/847–*

9745. AE, DC, MC, V. Lunch only. Subway: 6 to 33rd St. $

9 *d-3*

AQUAVIT

This handsome two-level townhouse (formerly owned by Nelson Rockefeller) is the perfect setting for the elegant food of wunderkind Swedish chef Marcus Samuelsson. The more formal dining room, downstairs, serves an array of Swedish specialties (including smoked fish and herring) and some innovative seafood and meat dishes. The soaring atrium and soothing waterfall make the evening relaxing and memorable. Upstairs, the more casual and less expensive bar and café delivers lighter fare: Danish open sandwiches, Swedish meatballs, smorgasbord plates, and a variety of aquavits. This restaurant has been called the finest Scandinavian restaurant in the country, though admittedly the competition is not stiff. *13 W. 54th St. (between 5th and 6th Aves.), Midtown West, 212/307–7311. Reservations essential. AE, MC, V. Subway: E, V to 5th Ave.–53rd St. $$$$*

9 *d-3*

CHRISTER'S

A native Swede, chef Christer Larsson has a flair for seafood, particularly the cold-water fish of his homeland. In the urban-lodge setting of his dining room—think Ralph Lauren meets Pee Wee's Playhouse—salmon cookery is elevated to an art form, and herring becomes a noble fish. Whether marinated with lime and ginger or simply cured with sugar and salt to make gravlax, the salmon never bores. Other fish are prepared with equal skill. Here, Swedish specialties such as *fricadelles* (veal meatballs served on mashed potatoes) have nothing in common with the sickeningly sweet hors d'oeuvres popular in the 1960s. For dessert, try the apple leaf (thinly sliced apples served with filo dough and caramel). *145 W. 55th St. (between 5th and 6th Aves.), Midtown West, 212/974–7224. AE, DC, MC, V. Closed Sun. Subway: F, N, R, Q, W to 57th St. $$–$$$*

SEAFOOD

11 *c-5*

AQUAGRILL

This cheerful, yellow-and-blue, candlelit fish restaurant is casual and laid-back. It has a first-rate oyster bar and terrific fish dishes, with interesting combinations such as grilled yellowfin tuna with crispy jasmine rice cakes and wok-seared vegetables in a ginger peanut sauce, or grilled salmon in a lovely falafel crust with lemon-coriander vinaigrette. *210 Spring St. (at 6th Ave.), SoHo, 212/274–0505. Reservations essential. AE, MC, V. Closed Mon. Subway: C, E to Spring St. $$–$$$*

9 *e-8*

BLUE WATER GRILL

Into a former bank with marble floors comes this bustling fish restaurant with a terrific oyster bar and first-rate seafood of all fins and stripes. Try the crab cakes, shrimp won ton, or blackened swordfish with salsa, and for dessert, the banana ice cream tower. Sunday brunch is accompanied by live jazz. *31 Union Sq. W (between 16th and 17th Sts.), Flatiron District, 212/675–9500. AE, MC, V. Subway: L, N, Q, R, W, 4, 5, 6 to 14th St./Union Sq. $$*

7 *b-6*

DOCK'S OYSTER BAR & SEAFOOD GRILL

Both of these friendly restaurants serve fresh, no-nonsense seafood in a casual, black-and-white setting. Best bites include fried oysters, fried clams, steamed lobsters, and crunchy coleslaw. Try to save room for the great desserts. *2427 Broadway (between 89th and 90th St.), Upper West Side, 212/724–5588. AE, D, DC, MC, V. Subway: B, C to 86th St. $$*

9 *f-5*

633 3rd Ave. (at 40th St.), Midtown, 212/986–8080. Subway: S, 4, 5, 6, 7 to 42nd St.–Grand Central.

7 *a-4*

FISH

Obviously, you'd come here for seafood; the proud menu lists only two non-seafood entrées. Deep-fried oysters with a ginger-wasabi mayonnaise give a good slug of briny flavor with an Asian kick. Searing calamari *fra diavolo* belongs on its red pepper linguine, and grilled honey-mustard salmon with arugula, endive, and raspberry vinaigrette is a fine tangle of flavors. The decor is nothing fancy, but the price is right for this Columbia University–area favorite. *2799 Broadway (at 108th St.), Upper West Side, 212/864–5000. AE, MC, V. Subway: 1 to Cathedral Parkway (110th St.). $–$$*

9 *d-4*

LE BERNARDIN
See French.

2 *h-3*

LOBSTER BOX
As you might expect, lobster is the specialty at this City Island mainstay. Try it steamed, with pasta, stuffed, or one of about a dozen other ways. You can also opt for other varieties of fresh seafood and fish. The restaurant overlooks a working harbor, with the lazy passage of boats as a pleasant backdrop. *34 City Island Ave. (between Rochelle and Belden Sts.), City Island, Bronx, 718/885–1952. AE, D, DC, MC, V. Closed Jan. and Feb. $$–$$$*

9 *d-3*

MANHATTAN OCEAN CLUB
Some of the finest seafood in town, and the friendly service and contemporary atmosphere, keep the lovely dining room filled. Among the myriad dishes, the simplest are best: crab cakes, red snapper, and striped bass, for instance. The wine list is substantial. Don't expect to be out quickly; although congenial, the staff will keep you waiting. *57 W. 58th St. (between 5th and 6th Aves.), Midtown West, 212/371–7777. AE, DC, MC, V. No lunch weekends. Subway: F, N, R, Q, W to 57th St. $$–$$$*

11 *a-1*

MARY'S FISH CAMP
This adorably distressed dining room is home to Mary Redding's vision of what a New England seafood restaurant should be. Absent are fusion preparations, a lengthy wine list, formal servers, and exotic, imported varieties of seafood. Instead, Redding prepares hit-the-spot shore food like rich New England clam chowder, a lobster roll on a hot dog bun served with shoestring fries, linguini with clam sauce, and an incomparable cod sandwich. Desserts are equally homey with such selections as strawberry shortcake. One drawback to the casual vibe is the waitstaff, who seem to take the relaxing atmosphere just a bit too seriously. *64 Charles St. (at W. 4th St.), West Village, 646/486–2185. AE, MC, V. Closed Sun. Subway: 1, 2 to Christopher St.–Sheridan Sq. $$*

9 *e-3*

OCEANA
Chef and sorcerer Rick Moonen has created the ultimate fish restaurant, right down to the decor, which virtually transports you to a luxury ocean liner. The service is smooth and doting, the wine list is superb (and 45 pages long!), and the 100% seafood menu is nothing short of spectacular, from magical crab cakes to *the* definitive bouillabaisse or "everything"-crusted tuna medallions or the monkfish of your dreams. Desserts—hardly an afterthought—are unusually whimsical and utterly delightful. With a prix-fixe $65 three-course dinner, it's pricey, but those who take the plunge come out knowing that it was worth every penny. *55 E. 54th St. (between Madison and Park Aves.), Midtown East, 212/759–5941. Reservations essential. AE, MC, V. Closed Sun. Subway: E, V to 5th Ave.–53rd St. $$$$*

9 *e-5*

OYSTER BAR & RESTAURANT
After a serious fire early in 1998, reconstruction, restoration, and a new chef have breathed considerable aquatic life into a spot frequented mainly by commuters and tourists. This Grand Central Station landmark, opened in 1915, claims it serves the most seafood in the world, and it probably does. Go for the wide selection of fresh oysters (flown in daily), six versions of clam chowder, oyster po'boys, and grilled fresh fish. Wines and desserts are equally various. You can sit at the old-fashioned lunch counter or in the dining room proper, although the beautiful tiled curvaceous ceiling of the latter results in a lot of clatter. *Grand Central Terminal, Lower level, 42nd St. at Park Ave., Midtown East, 212/490–6650. AE, D, DC, MC, V. Closed Sun. Subway: S, 4, 5, 6, 7 to 42nd St.–Grand Central. $$–$$$*

11 *b-3*

PEARL OYSTER BAR
This friendly New England oyster bar run by Rebecca Charles is one of the most enjoyable places to go for a casual meal. The dining room is really just a counter—so there's usually a wait for a stool. Your patience is rewarded with a Maine-style lobster roll, fried oyster po'boy, chowder, steamers in a bucket, and bouillabaisse. A nice selection of wines by the glass complements the

food, which might be served by one of the chefs if the waitress is too busy. *18 Cornelia St. (between Bleecker and W. 4th Sts.), West Village, 212/691–8211. MC, V. Closed Sun. Subway: A, B, C, D, E, F, V to W. 4th St. $–$$*

9 d-4

SEA GRILL

This elegant Rockefeller Center restaurant was designed to draw the sophisticated New Yorker as well as the tourist. The view of the skating rink ensures the happiness of the latter, and chef Ed Brown's cooking steadily enthralls the locals. Although many lay similar claims, Brown's Maryland crab cakes may well be the best in the city. The other seafood options, some classic, some contemporary, are pretty great as well. The wine list is excellent. Complimentary parking is available at the Rockefeller Center Garage from Monday to Saturday after 5:30 PM. *19 W. 49th St. (between 5th and 6th Aves.), Midtown West, 212/332–7610. Reservations essential. AE, DC, MC, V. Closed Sun. Subway: B, D, F, V to 47th–50th Sts.. $$$*

9 f-1

TRATA

Breezy as the northern Mediterranean, Trata has been jammed since the very moment it opened, so needful is this neighborhood of moderately priced, pristinely prepared Greco seafood. The casual dining room features a handsome spread of dozens of whole fish (including some rarities such as sargos and loup de mer) arranged on crushed ice, which are grilled to order. Startlingly delicious charcoal-grilled octopus makes the perfect opener, and honey-drizzled thickened goat's milk yogurt makes the perfect finish. *1331 2nd Ave. (between 70th and 71st Sts.), Upper East Side, 212/535–3800. AE, MC, V. Subway: 6 to 68th St.–Hunter College. $$–$$$*

SOUTHERN

11 e-3

ACME BAR & GRILL

This funky roadhouse setting is festooned with dozens of bottles of different hot sauces on ledges that run throughout the space. The home-style food is well priced and tasty, usually heavy and sometimes tongue-searing.

Southern specialties include fried oysters, fried shrimp, blackened trout, oyster po'boys, grilled pork chops, catfish sandwiches, and sides of corn fritters, hush puppies, and black-eyed peas. *9 Great Jones St. (between Broadway and Lafayette St.), East Village, 212/420–1934. D, DC, MC, V. Reservations not accepted. Subway: 6 to Astor Pl. $*

6 d-6

CHARLES' SOUTHERN STYLE KITCHEN

Charles serves some of the best soul food in Harlem. Ribs, oxtails, black-eyed peas, okra, macaroni and cheese, collard greens, and candied yams are all here. But the excellent fried chicken is the specialty, and if you stand by the takeout counter you can watch Charlie dip pieces of chicken in his peppery batter and fry it to a crispy golden brown in a giant cast-iron skillet. The only occasional disappointment comes when Charlie decides to take the day off and the kitchen is closed. *2841 Frederick Douglass Blvd. (between 151st and 152nd Sts.), Harlem, 212/926–4313. No credit cards. Closed Mon. Subway: B, D to 155th St. $*

6 c-6

COPELAND'S

Though Sylvia's gets all the publicity, many insider's believe this is the only place in Harlem for authentic soul food dinners (a cafeteria next door serves lunch). From fried chicken to smothered pork chops to ribs, Copeland's has everything your heart desires (especially cholesterol). Put on your best hat for the Sunday Gospel Brunch and dig in. *547 W. 145th St. (between Amsterdam Ave. and Broadway), Harlem, 212/234–2357. AE, MC, V. Closed Mon. Subway: A, B, C, D to 145th St. $–$$*

9 b-5

SOUL CAFÉ

This comfortable, spacious dining room—albeit with a sense of circa-1970 "luxe"—serves some of best and most upscale soul food in the city. Only in New York could sweet potato–crusted red snapper or Caribbean-influenced dishes such as coconut shrimp pass for soul food, but fans of traditional soul sides—candied yams, macaroni-and-cheese, collard greens—will be in heaven. Live jazz, funk, or R&B is featured most nights on a small stage near the hopping bar; check what's playing and request a quiet table if it's not your cup of tea. *444 W. 42nd St. (between 9th and 10th Aves.), Midtown West, 212/244-7685. Reservations essential. AE, D, MC, V. No lunch. Brunch Sun. Subway: A, C, E to 42nd St. $$–$$$*

7 *d-1*
SYLVIA'S
Sylvia Woods is known as the Queen of Soul Food, and her restaurant has been a Harlem institution for more than 30 years. Though there are probably better cooks, you shouldn't hesitate to head uptown for some of Sylvia's down-home Southern specialties, including her braised ribs, fried or smothered chicken with black-eyed peas, collard greens, yams, sweet-potato pie, and fresh-baked corn bread. Sunday brunch is served to the showiest ladies' hats in town, with the inspirational tunes of local gospel singers and two jukeboxes adding to the indelible '50s flavor. *328 Lenox Ave. (at 126th St.), Harlem, 212/996-0660. Reservations not accepted. AE, D, DC, MC, V. Subway: A, B, C, D to 125th St. $–$$*

SOUTHWESTERN

7 *b-8*
CITRUS BAR & GRILL
This big, loopy party of a place serves some of the best margaritas in town. Chile peppers—cascabel, ancho, pasilla, and poblano—are all over the menu,

---

FIRESIDE ROMANCE

The only thing harder to find in New York than romance itself is a working fireplace. If you've found the first, here's where they throw a log on:

Savoy (American)
This charming and elegant nook on the edge of SoHo keeps three fires burning for you.

Verbena (American)
The flickering light is the ornamentation for this zenlike room.

Vivolo (Italian)
In a late-1800s brownstone, fireplaces warm both the dimly lit downstairs and the frescoed upstairs.

Ye Waverly Inn (American)
Ye olde quaintest tavern in the city, in the West Village.

---

but the heat can be turned down to order. Coriander and three-pepper crusted yellowfin tuna delivers a whallop of flavor. So does marinated and grilled skirt steak in a sweet cascabel-coffee-nutmeg barbecue sauce with fried ribbon onion rings and cheddar mashed potatoes. Squeeze, the hopping downstairs lounge, completes the party. *320 Amsterdam Ave. (between 75th and 76th Sts.), Upper West Side, 212/595-0500. AE, MC, V. Subway: 1, 2, 3 to 72nd St. $–$$*

11 *g-2*
MIRACLE GRILL
For tasty Southwestern fare and deceptively potent margaritas you cannot beat Miracle Grill, the East Village mainstay with one of the best outdoor dining areas in all of New York City. There is always a wait for a garden table, but diners can sit on the porch with drinks, chips, and salsa to pass the time. The food may not seem like anything extraordinary, but after eating there it's easy to find oneself with a sudden hankering for the excellent catfish tacos in soft flour tortillas or a spicy pork chop. West Village denizens can enjoy a similar menu in the bistro setting of the Bleecker Street locale. *112 1st Ave. (between 6th and 7th Aves.), East Village, 212/254-2353. AE, MC, V. Subway: 6 to Astor Pl. $–$$*

11 *a-1*
415 Bleecker St. (between Bank and W. 11th Sts.), West Village, 212/924-1900. Subway: A, C, E to 14th St.

SPANISH

9 *e-8*
BOLO
The burgeoning fame of chef–co-owner Bobby Flay has drawn major attention to this popular Flatiron District restaurant with a palpable Spanish accent. The extremely vivid food—sea scallop and white anchovy ceviche, black squid ink risotto with grilled prawns and lobster, pork tenderloin filled with walnut romesco—is succulent. The menu is continually evolving, the decor is quirky and pretty, and the crowd is, well, there. Don't pass up the luscious sangria, then move on to one of the spicy, full-bodied Riojas. *23 E. 22nd St. (between Broadway and Park Ave. S), Flatiron District, 212/228-2200. AE, MC, V. Subway: 6, N, R to 23rd St. $$$–$$$$*

10 c-1

EL CID

An extensive list of standards—garlic shrimp, imported sausages and cheeses, marinated mussels—plus such seasonal specialties as baby eels or wild mushrooms, made El Cid popular long before tapas bars were trendy. It's pretty authentically Spanish in ways both good and bad: Cramped tables, minimal decor, and noise are the down side, while low prices, knowledgeable waiters, and simple, tasty food compensate. There's a wine list with some good Spanish vintages, but the potent house sangria is the drink of choice. *322 W. 15th St. (between 8th and 9th Aves.), Chelsea, 212/929–9332. Reservations essential. AE, DC. Closed Mon. No lunch. Subway: A, C, E to 14th St.; L to 8th Ave. $–$$*

10 c-1

EL FARO

Redolent with garlic, this small, extremely popular West Villager has been serving hearty portions of pungent Spanish food for more than 30 years. The decor is appealingly kitschy. *823 Greenwich St. (at Horatio St.), West Village, 212/929–8210. Reservations not accepted. AE, DC, MC, V. Subway: A, C, E to 14th St.; L to 8th Ave. $$–$$$*

9 d-8

FRANCISCO'S CENTRO VASCO

Crowds of eager diners (many of the bridge-and-tunnel variety) descend nightly on this noisy, dumpy Spanish old-timer in search of bargain-priced lobsters and paella. The sangria flows pretty freely, and only a cynic wouldn't get caught up in the convivial atmosphere. Reservations are accepted only for parties of six or more, but long waits are unusual. *159 W. 23rd St. (between 6th and 7th Aves.), Chelsea, 212/645–6224. AE, DC, MC, V. No lunch weekends. Subway: C, E, 1, 2 to 23rd St. $–$$*

9 f-4

MARICHU

Marichu's chef is a former diplomat who must have realized how parched the U.N. area is for interesting restaurants. This enchanting restaurant turns out delicious Basque cooking—particularly seafood—with a contemporary presentation. The satisfying combination has hooked those in the U.N. area, and the cheery atmosphere and back garden are

helping this relative newcomer gain a wider audience. *342 E. 46th St. (between 1st and 2nd Aves.), Midtown East, 212/370–1866. Reservations essential. AE, MC, V. Closed Sun. Subway: S, 4, 5, 6, 7 to 42nd St.–Grand Central. $$–$$$*

11 b-5

MEIGAS

Meigas is undoubtedly the most intriguing Spanish restaurant to hit New York City, and chef Luis Bollo's food reflects the exciting culinary revolution happening in Spain. Such dishes as deep black squid ink croquettes, a gazpacho deconstructed to its most basic elements, and deliciously sticky suckling pig are marvelous and light years beyond most other attempts at "contemporary" cooking. Unfortunately the dining room feels somehow bare and almost corporate, despite a colorful (and decidedly strange) mural of a magician on the back wall. But if you can forgive the barrenness of the room a truly exhilarating meal awaits. *350 Hudson St. (at King St.), SoHo, 212/627–5800. AE, DC, MC, V. Closed Sun.; no lunch. Subway: 1, 2 to Houston St. $$–$$$*

10 b-1

RIO MAR

It's doubtful a restaurant like this ever existed in Spain, but at one time this was all that Americans wanting Spanish food could hope for. The upstairs dining room is "Spanish" in an old-time sort of way, but the staff is genuinely glad to see you. The quasi-traditional food—garlicky tapas, paella, chicken and rice, seafood stews—is served in large portions, and low prices keep the place packed. *7 9th Ave. (at Little W. 12th St.), West Village, 212/242–1623. AE. Subway: A, C, E to 14th St.; L to 8th Ave. $–$$*

11 f-3

SALA

This intensely popular, idiomatic restaurant serves creative tapas in a festive atmosphere. The dining room is a highly theatrical indoor Spanish courtyard complete with faux backlit casement windows. The menu changes daily, but usually there are croquettes that redefine croquettes—more like deep-fried breaded pouches of thick savory pudding. The fried chunks of potato, rubbed with hot-and-sweet paprika and dribbled with thick béchamel sauce are the stuff of dreams. Steaks and chops are superbly turned out. Be prepared for quite a party. *344 Bowery (near Great Jones St.), East Village, 212/979–6606. AE, MC, V. Subway: 6 to Bleecker St.; F, V to Broadway–Lafayette St. Closed Sun. $–$$*

9 *f-4*
SOLERA

Authentic Spanish cooking from the Galicia region is presented with heart and soul in this delightful little Midtown eatery. The food is seriously good (some argue it's the best Spanish in town), and the following is accordingly fierce and loyal, despite the above-average prices for this light, Mediterranean fare. The service is unusually focused, too. *216 E. 53rd St. (between 2nd and 3rd Aves.), Midtown East, 212/644–1166. AE, D, DC, MC, V. No lunch weekends. Subway: 6 to 51st St./Lexington Ave.; E, V to Lexington–3rd Aves./53rd St. $$$–$$$$*

STEAK

9 *e-4*
BULL & BEAR

This is the place to feel utterly pampered by agreeably old-fashioned service, by luxurious comfort food prepared with confidence and flair, and by a sommelier totally adroit at matching food with wine from around the world. Ensconced in all the gleam and glitter of the restored Waldorf-Astoria, this deeply masculine, clubby, walnut-paneled room has never looked more impressive. Start with dense crab cakes stepped up with a cayenne-spiked corn relish and a bowl of B&B's famous black bean soup. Then tuck into a 2-inch-tall slab of dry-aged Black Angus prime rib partnered by (of course) crisp–tender Yorkshire pudding. A free-form key lime tart makes the perfect finish. You'll leave feeling very important, indeed. *570 Lexington Ave. (at 49th St.), Midtown East, 212/872–4900. AE, DC, MC, V. Subway: 6 to 51st St./Lexington Ave.; E, V to Lexington–3rd Aves./53rd St. $$$–$$$$*

7 *f-6*
DAN MAXWELL'S

If you're in the mood for a big New York steak but not big New York prices, this is the place for you. Rib, skirt, and strip steaks (or salmon and chicken, for the faint of heart) are served with your choice of potatoes and a salad for under $20 a person. Some say the fried onions

are "the best ever." As in every steak house, gooey desserts are in order; the triple chocolate-mousse cake is a favorite. The atmosphere is neighborhoody, the service friendly and efficient. *1708 2nd Ave. (between 88th and 89th Sts.), Upper East Side, 212/426–7688. AE, D, DC, MC, V. Subway: 4, 5, 6 to 86th St. No lunch. $–$$$*

10 *b-1*
FRANK'S

This old Italian steak house opened in 1912 in the Gansevoort meatpacking district. Despite having moved from its original store, a block north, in the mid-1990s due to fire, the place still has plenty of character. Count on good steaks, surf 'n' turf, double-thick lamb chops, and giant salads. The cheesecake is terrific. *85 10th Ave. (at 15th St.), Chelsea, 212/243–1349. Reservations essential. AE, DC, MC, V. Subway: A, C, E to 14th St.; L to 8th Ave. $$$*

9 *c-4*
GALLAGHER'S STEAK HOUSE

The most casual of the New York steak houses, with checkered tablecloths and photos of sports greats on the walls, Gallagher's has no pretensions—through the window from the street you can even peer into the dry-aging room where slabs of meat ripen to perfection. You won't be disappointed with the aged sirloin steaks, oversize lobsters, or any of the fabulous potato dishes. *228 W. 52nd (between Broadway and 8th Ave.), Midtown West, 212/245–5336. AE, D, DC, MC, V. Subway: C, E to 50th St. $$–$$$*

12 *f-6*
MIKE & TONY'S

This neighborhood steak house is no longer owned by Michael Ayoub, but his hand-blown glass fixtures remain. The steaks, made from prime aged beef, are properly cooked. The seafood is fresh, and the sides are all delicious. What more could you want? (Besides maybe an outpost in Manhattan.) *239 5th Ave. (at Carroll St.), Park Slope, Brooklyn, 718/857–2800. MC, V. No lunch. Subway: L, N, Q, R, W, 4, 5, 6 to 14th St./Union Sq. $$–$$$*

9 *c-7*
NICK & STEF'S STEAKHOUSE

Take a good old New York steak house and give the menu a French twist and you've got this Big Apple outpost of Joachim Splichal's Los Angeles original. The menu is steak house in style, with prime cuts and side dishes ordered à la carte. The difference lies in the array of choices from such sides as sweet potato fries with ginger chips and oven roasted tomatoes Provençal to entrées such as a venison chop or seared tuna to complement the beef. All is cooked to perfection, which makes this eatery one of the few worth a nod near Madison Square Garden. *9 Penn Plaza (between 7th and 8th Aves.), Midtown West, 212/563–4444. AE, DC, MC, V. Closed Sun. Subway: A, C, E to 34th St.–Penn Station. $$$–$$$$*

10 C-1
OLD HOMESTEAD RESTAURANT

Open since 1868—which may be when they last redecorated—this is New York's oldest steak house, appropriately in the meatpacking district. In addition to the steaks—including a Japanese Kobe steak at $125 a serving (reserve it a few days in advance)—the kitchen dishes up generous portions of shrimp, lobster, and prime rib. *56 9th Ave. (between 14th and 15th Sts.), Chelsea, 212/242–9040. AE, DC, MC, V. Subway: A, C, E to 14th St.; L to 8th Ave. $$–$$$$*

9 f-5
PALM RESTAURANT

Sawdusted floors and caricatures on the walls create the nostalgic backdrop for this very noisy, upbeat, and masculine steak and lobster house. Once considered the best by many, the Palm has paled some with time and the demands of managing its worldwide empire, but its history of famous and powerful clients (painted on the walls) still adds flavor to the high-quality steaks and enormous lobsters. Watch the bill add up—cottage fries, onion rings, and vegetables are all à la carte. If the restaurant is too crowded, go across the street to Palm Too. *837 2nd Ave. (between 44th and 45th Sts.), Midtown East, 212/687–2953. Reservations essential. AE, DC, MC, V. No lunch weekends. Subway: S, 4, 5, 6, 7 to 42nd St.–Grand Central. $$–$$$$*

3 d-6
PETER LUGER'S

No one really disputes the idea that this is the best steak you will ever eat. The setting is German beer hall—harsh lights, bare wood tables—rather than gentlemen's steak house, and you'll never see a menu; the friendly waiters know that all you want is shrimp cocktail, tomato-and-onion salad, home fries, creamed spinach, French fries, and a big, beautiful, dry-aged, perfectly cooked porterhouse steak big enough to feed everyone in your party. Save the steak sauce for the fresh onion rolls. If you have room left over, order the pecan pie or the cheesecake—both of which, in case you haven't had enough fat, come with a big bowl of *schlag* (whipped cream). If you arrive in a taxi, the restaurant's own car service will take you home. *178 Broadway (at Driggs Ave.), Williamsburg, Brooklyn, 718/387–7400. Reservations essential. No credit cards. Subway: J, M, Z to Marcy Ave. $$–$$$*

9 f-5
PIETRO'S

Regulars still flock to this 50-year-old Italian steakhouse, now in relatively new quarters. Pietro's serves Italian veal, chicken, and pasta dishes, as well as an exemplary Caesar salad, but it's basically known for its porterhouse, served with delicious shoestring, Lyonnaise, or au gratin potatoes, and pasta shells with bone marrow. The friendly staff is happy to modify almost anything on the menu to suit your tastes. *232 E. 43rd St. (between 2nd and 3rd Aves.), Midtown East, 212/682–9760. Reservations essential. AE, DC, MC, V. Closed Sun. Closed Sat. in summer. No lunch Sat. Subway: S, 4, 5, 6, 7 to 42nd St.–Grand Central. $$–$$$$*

9 f-4
SMITH & WOLLENSKY

Women beware: This is where Midtown business*men* enjoy steak. The clubby atmosphere and extensive wine list speak to a certain clientele that sometimes makes it difficult for women to get the best service. But the beautiful steak is well prepared, portions are generous, and the side dishes are good. Limited non–red-meat selections are available, but you're better off eating elsewhere if you're looking for a light meal. Next door to the dining room is Wollensky's Grill, a bit cheaper. *797 3rd Ave. (at 49th St.), Midtown East, 212/ 753–1530. Reservations essential. AE, D, DC, MC, V. No lunch weekends in dining room. Subway: 6 to 51st St./Lexington Ave.; E, V to Lexington–3rd Aves./53rd St. $$–$$$$*

9 *f-4*

SPARK'S STEAK HOUSE

If you're yearning for a macho atmosphere, head right over to this informal, clubby restaurant, well known for very fine steaks and lobsters that require a superhuman appetite. The double lamb chops also draw raves. An excellent wine list has earned the restaurant several awards. *210 E. 46th St. (between 2nd and 3rd Aves.), Midtown East, 212/687–4855. Reservations essential. AE, DC, MC, V. Closed Sun. No lunch Sat. Subway: S, 4, 5, 6, 7 to 42nd St.–Grand Central. $$–$$$$*

10 *e-1*

THE STRIP HOUSE

For almost 50 years this red-velvet–lined restaurant, dripping with historic photographs, was home to the operatic Italian restaurant Asti. In its new modern steakhouse incarnation, with an interior that resembles a 1920s brothel (the logo of a burlesque star helps inform that interpretation), top-quality and properly prepared dry-aged meats hold sway. Starters include ordinary salads and an exemplary torchon of foie gras. The large restaurant is sometimes depressingly empty, but that doesn't detract from the quality of the experience. *13 E. 12th St. (between 5th Ave. and University Pl.), Greenwich Village, 212/328–0000. AE, D, DC, MC, V. Subway: L, N, Q, R, W, 4, 5, 6 to 14th St./Union Sq. $$$–$$$$*

SWISS

11 *h-2*

ROETTELLE A. G.

Here's a charming find in (but not of) the East Village for a simple, inexpensive, satisfying Euromeal. German, Swiss, Italian, and French cooking are all represented nightly on the changing menu. Try the classic Swiss fondue; the smoked, mustard-infused pork chop with spaetzle and red cabbage; the sautéed chicken breast with sun-dried tomatoes and hazelnuts; or the veal in mushroom cream sauce with wonderful Swiss-style *rösti* (potato pancakes). Try to get a seat in the trellised garden. *126 E. 7th St. (between 1st Ave. and Ave. A), East Village, 212/674–4140. MC, V. Closed Mon. Subway: N, R to 8th St.; 6 to Astor Pl. $–$$*

TEA

9 *e-8*

LADY MENDL'S

Just as the Inn at Irving Place feels like a New York hotel from another era, Lady Mendl's tea salon, on the first floor of a Victorian townhouse, feels like an experience from a different time. The cozy room has a large fireplace and charming antique appointments, and sandwiches, sweets, and large scones are paraded by a friendly, but rushed staff. Fine tea is served in an impressive selection of English teapots. *The Inn at Irving Place, 56 Irving Pl. (between 17th and 18th Sts.), Gramercy Park, 212/533–4466. AE, MC, V. Closed Mon. and Tues. Subway: L, N, Q, R, W, 4, 5, 6 to 14th St./Union Sq. $$$–$$$$*

10 *c-1*

TEA & SYMPATHY

This authentic little English tearoom looks rather like your quirky old aunt's apartment. When it isn't teatime, the food is traditional, hearty British fare. No one argues with the tea, but the long wait, cramped space, and worn decor leave some wanting. *108 Greenwich Ave. (between 12th and 13th Sts.), West Village, 212/807–8329. Reservations not accepted. AE, MC, V. Subway: A, C, E to 14th St.; L to 8th Ave. $–$$*

9 *b-8*

WILD LILY TEA ROOM

A gem worthy of its place among the Chelsea galleries, this very special tearoom is a world away from the stresses of city life. The tiny goldfish pond, set into the floor and perfect in every detail, is guaranteed to cure whatever ails you. Food (finger sandwiches, scones, and delicate Asian specialties) is served on lovely china, and teas are described on the menu with such eloquence you might mistake the list for a book of poetry. *511 W. 22nd St. (between 10th and 11th Aves.), Chelsea, 212/691–2258. Reservations essential. AE, DC, MC, V. Closed Mon. Subway: C, E to 23rd St. $*

TEX/MEX

10 *c-1*

BENNY'S BURRITOS

For cheap and cheerful Tex/Mex on either end of the Village, head over to cramped and rowdy Benny's, ever popular with the budget crowd. Lava lights, Formica, and a jukebox with period tunes form a retro backdrop for the humongous, foot-long, overstuffed burritos and zippy margaritas. Beware: finish the whole thing and you'll suffer. *113 Greenwich Ave. (at Jane St.), West Village, 212/633–9210. No reservations. No credit cards. Subway: A, C, E to 14th St.; L to 8th Ave.* $

---

11 h-2

93 Ave. A (at 6th St.), East Village, 212/254–2054. Subway: F, V to 2nd Ave.

THAI

3 d-5

AMARIN CAFE

On the border of Greenpoint and Williamsburg in Brooklyn, this casual restaurant serves some of the freshest, most fragrant Thai food in town. Everything is spicy, not just the fiery red Penang curries. Lemon grass, coconut, and chicken soup; stir-fried chicken with basil and hot peppers; pad thai; and other traditional dishes are skillfully prepared. The service is extremely attentive and friendly. If one of your dishes is hotter than your palate can handle, the staff will gladly make it for you again with less spice. *617 Manhattan Ave. (between Driggs and Nassau Aves.), Greenpoint, Brooklyn, 718/349–2788. No credit cards. Subway: L to Lorimer St.* $

10 d-1

CAFE ASEAN

This charming little restaurant feels like a cross between an Italian trattoria and a Chinese restaurant. In truth, it's a creative southeast Asian restaurant with serious Thai and Malaysian influences. The flavors are tempered and the food is cheap. Try the rice-wrapped rolls with shrimp and shiitake, or the coconut curry with chicken and potatoes; pork and beef dishes are also available. The service is friendly, if on the slow side, and there's a funky garden out back. *117 W. 10th St. (between Greenwich and 6th Aves.), West Village, 212/633–0348. No credit cards. Subway: 1, 2 to Christopher St./Sheridan Sq.* $

11 g-1

HOLY BASIL

This brick-walled, second floor dining room adorned with gilt edged Thai

prints feels like an oasis of calm in the frenetic East Village. The menu consists of such Thai standards as pad thai, curries, and sautéed dishes, all of which are well seasoned, artfully presented, and less greasy than many of the other Thai places around town. *149 2nd Ave. (between 9th and 10th Sts.), East Village, 212/460–5557. AE, DC, MC, V. Subway: 6 to Astor Pl.* $–$$

3 f-3

JAI-YA THAI

There's not much in terms of decor to recommend Jai-Ya Thai. What there is, however, is boldly spiced, flavorful Thai food—such as curries, pad thai, and satays—that proves to be strangely addictive. There is a Manhattan branch, but true fans find the original Queens location more authentic. *81–11 Broadway (between 81st and 82nd Sts.), Elmhurst, Queens, 718/651–1330. AE, DC, MC, V. Subway: R, V to Elmhurst Ave.* $–$$

11 d-5

KIN KHAO

The inevitable wait for a table is made exponentially more exciting if you order a ginger kamikaze made with the restaurant's exceptional house-made ginger vodka. The slightly above-average food—the sticky rice and whole fish are delicious—doesn't suffice to explain the enormous popularity of this restaurant. It could be the chic decor, beautiful servers, or maybe just the liveliness of the very downtown scene. *171 Spring St. (between Thompson St. and W. Broadway), SoHo, 212/966–3939. AE, MC, V. No lunch. Subway: C, E to Spring St.* $–$$

3 d-6

PLANET THAILAND

This once tiny storefront restaurant in a Polish section of Williamsburg has tripled in size and added a sushi and sake bar. It still serves a delicious selection of Thai street food, somewhat toned down for the American audience. Still, the flavors are fresh and fragrant. Try the noodle dishes, the green-papaya salad, and the satay. And why not order a couple of sushi rolls while you're at it? *141 N. 7th St. (between Bedford Ave. and Berry St.), Williamsburg, Brooklyn, 718/599–5758. Reservations not accepted. No credit cards. Subway: L to Bedford Ave.* $

9 c-4

PONGSRI THAI

You'll dine well on spicy Thai specialties both uptown, in the spacious Theater District quarters, or downtown, in the more spartan Chinatown shop. The coconut chicken soup, rich duck curry, and sticky rice are among the highlights. Be prepared to pay more for the same dishes uptown. *244 W. 48th St. (between Broadway and 8th Ave.), Midtown West, 212/582–3392. AE, D, DC, MC, V. Subway: C, E to 50th St. $*

11 f-7

106 Bayard St. (at Baxter St.), Chinatown, 212/349–3132. Subway: 6 to Canal St.

9 c-8

ROYAL SIAM

Royal Siam is one of the best restaurants in trendy Chelsea, where the restaurant scene hasn't quite caught up to everything else. Classic Thai dishes, such as pad thai and shrimp in red curry, are well executed, and the service is friendly. The decor recalls suburban Chinese restaurants, complete with lacquered furniture and polyester tablecloths. *240 8th Ave. (between 22nd and 23rd Sts.), Chelsea, 212/741–1732. Reservations not accepted. AE, MC, V. Subway: C, E to 23rd St. $–$$*

TURKISH

9 f-7

TURKISH KITCHEN

The food at this comfortable restaurant is rather like Middle Eastern cooking, only more sophisticated. The traditional salads, such as hummus and babaghanoush, are good starters, as are the fried cheese and chicken livers with parsley and lemon. For dinner itself, try whatever lamb preparation is available or the dumplings in yogurt sauce. *386 3rd Ave. (between 27th and 28th Sts.), Murray Hill, 212/679–1810. AE, MC, V. Subway: 6 to 28th St. $–$$*

7 b-5

TURKUAZ

It's easy to imagine you are entering a Bedouin tent as you pass through the nondescript bar area into the dining room adorned with tapestries hung from the ceiling, gold threaded cushions, and various other Turkish exotica.

The authentic food, from the various kebabs to the heady spiced lamb dishes, will add to the illusion that you are somewhere farther away than the upper Upper West Side. *2637 Broadway (at 100th St.), Upper West Side, 212/665–9542. AE, D, MC, V. Subway: 1, 2 to 103rd St. $–$$*

VEGETARIAN & MACROBIOTIC

10 f-1

ANGELICA KITCHEN

From the scores of patient customers lining up to dine at this pleasant East Village spot, you'd think they were giving out the secret to eternal life. What you will find at Angelica Kitchen is vegan vegetarian food that is tasty enough, even if it's not worth the Svengali-esqe hype. The dragon bowl—steamed sea vegetables, beans, and tofu on a bed of rice (brown naturally)—is plentiful and good, and tofu pie in a spelt crust is worth going back for. *300 E. 12th St. (between 1st and 2nd Aves.), East Village, 212/228–2909. No credit cards. Subway: L to 1st Ave. $*

9 e-6

HANGAWI

See Korean, above.

7 b-8

JOSIE'S

Can you imagine a health-food theme restaurant? Josie's comes pretty close. The food is fresh, much of it is organically grown or raised, and the emphasis is on light, healthy fare. Many of the dishes are vegetarian, and all of them are dairy-free; not surprisingly, tofu, tempeh, fish, and seafood feature prominently. It's always busy, and the service is always friendly. *300 Amsterdam Ave. (at 74th St.), Upper West Side, 212/769–1212. AE, MC, V. Subway: 1, 2, 3 to 72nd St. $–$$*

9 f-3

565 3rd Ave. (at 37th St.), Murray Hill, 212/490–1558. Subway: S, 4, 5, 6 to 42nd St.–Grand Central.

11 h-1

QUINTESSENCE

At this diminutive East Village spot, with only eight tables in the mint green dining room, vegetarian dining takes one step further to what some people call "raw foodism." The totally uncooked menu is completely organic and vegan, which is designed to help diners attain "the mystical powers of our ancestors." Skeptics should keep an open mind as dishes such as black olive and cream dim sum, a hearty nut loaf, and faux pastas made with vegetable strands instead of wheat are surprisingly well seasoned and tasty. For dessert there is even a guilt-free version of pecan pie. *263 E. 10th St. (between 1st Ave. and Ave. A), East Village, 646/654–1823. AE, DC, MC, V. Closed Mon. Subway: 6 to Astor Pl. $*

11 f-5

SPRING STREET NATURAL RESTAURANT

This natural eatery spotlights fresh fish, fowl, and seafood while barring chemicals, preservatives, and red meat. Specialties include vegetarian lasagna, sautéed chicken breast with shiitake mushrooms, baked fillet of bluefish, and garlic chicken marinated in raspberry vinegar; but alas, most sound better than they taste. *62 Spring St. (at Lafayette St.), SoHo, 212/966–0290. Reservations not accepted. AE, DC, MC, V. Subway: 6 to Spring St.; F, V to Broadway–Lafayette St. $*

7 b-8

ZEN PALATE

Something like a cross between a Buddhist temple and a coffee bar, this Pan-Asian minichain with a takeout option serves a quick, healthy, vegetarian alternative to the ubiquitous salad bar. To a base of noodles or rice you can add toppings of vegetables, sauces, broths, and other condiments. Dumplings and stir-fries are also available. Though the flavors tend more toward Zen than toward other Asian palates, you always feel good about yourself when you finish a meal here. *2170 Broadway (between 76th and 77th Sts.), Upper West Side, 212/501–7768. AE, MC, V. Subway: 1, 2 to 79th St. $–$$*

9 b-4

663 9th Ave. (at 46th St.), Midtown West, 212/582–1669. Subway: A, C, E to 42nd St.

9 c-4

34 Union Sq. E (at 16th St.), Flatiron District, 212/614–9291. Subway: L, N, Q, R, W, 4, 5, 6 to 14th St./Union Sq.

VIETNAMESE

11 g-7

BO KY

Enjoy a terrific lunch for under $5 at this unpretentious (read: down-and-dirty) soup shop. The rich, spicy, chicken-coconut curry soup with eggplant, potatoes, and egg noodles is absolutely delicious, as is the unfortunately named beef-belly soup with noodles. The other soups are good, too, but you're best off staying away from the barbecued items. To cut the richness, order "vegetable," which inevitably turns out to be Chinese broccoli in oyster sauce. *80 Bayard St. (between Mott and Mulberry Sts.), Chinatown, 212/406–2292. Reservations not accepted. No credit cards. Subway: 6, N, Q, R, J, M, Z to Canal St. $*

11 f-2

INDOCHINE

Trendy French/Vietnamese cuisine is served in a clamorous, Hollywood-glam setting, where it seems as if you need a cell phone to get your waiter's attention. You can dine well just by sharing a bunch of appetizers and entrées, such as spicy shrimp with long beans, roast duck with ginger, and Vietnamese bouillabaisse. Watch out though—the tab can add up quickly. Sit up front if you want some peace and quiet—and if you want to keep tabs on who's coming and going. *430 Lafayette St. (between Astor Pl. and E. 4th St.), East Village, 212/505–5111. AE, DC, MC, V. Subway: 6 to Astor Pl. $$*

11 f-4

MEKONG

This dimly lighted Vietnamese place has paper tablecloths, candles, bamboo curtains, and pictures of a Mekong sunset. The cooking is light with clear flavors, and seasoned with fresh mint. Try the sizzling shrimp, barbecued beef in shiso leaves, summer rolls, and curries. *44 Prince St. (near Mulberry St.), SoHo, 212/343–8169. AE, MC, V. Subway: 6 to Bleecker St.; F, V to Broadway–Lafayette St.; N, R to Prince St. $–$$*

7 f-8

MISS SAIGON

Whatever it lacks in atmosphere, this small but popular restaurant makes up for in tasty Vietnamese cooking. Locals line up out the door to taste the grilled shrimp paste, green papaya and beef salad, and lemon grass pork with garlic and sesame seeds. The moderate prices contribute to the popularity; if you can, try the place at lunchtime, when it's less hectic and even cheaper. *1425 3rd Ave. (between 80th and 81st Sts.), Upper East Side, 212/988–8828. AE, DC, MC, V. Subway: 4, 5, 6 to 86th St.* $

7 *b-8*

MONSOON

Among the first restaurants to take authentic Vietnamese food outside Chinatown, Monsoon serves a fast, cheap alternative to Chinese food from its two Upper West Side locations. The menu hides no surprises. The classic rice-paper–wrapped summer rolls and shrimp-wrapped sugarcane are reliable starters; classic beef soups and noodle dishes satisfy; and a crispy, sweet version of Vietnamese barbecued pork chops, sliced extra thin, is delicious. Be prepared to wait. *435 Amsterdam Ave. (at 81st St.), Upper West Side, 212/580–8686. AE, DC, MC, V. Subway: 1, 2 to 79th St.* $

7 *b-3*

2850 Broadway (at 110th St.), Upper West Side, 212/655–2700. Subway: 1 to 110th St.–Cathedral Pkwy.

11 *f-7*

NHA TRANG

Negotiating a Vietnamese menu can be challenging for novices. At Nha Trang, one of Chinatown's most popular Vietnamese eateries, a good meal can be had by following these simple rules: Start with a large, steaming bowl of spicy sweet and sour seafood soup (a "small" will feed three or four) and an order of shrimp grilled on sugarcane; and follow up with the paper-thin pork chops grilled crispy and the deep-fried squid served on a bed of shredded lettuce with a tangy dipping sauce. If you decide to explore the menu on your own, ask the waiter for suggestions—the staff is glad to show you the ropes. *87 Baxter St. (between Bayard and Canal Sts.), Chinatown, 212/233–5948. No credit cards. Subway: J, M, N, Q, R, W, Z, 6 to Canal St.* $

11 *g-7*

VIET-NAM

It's hard to find, but this cheap, grungy Chinatown dive is the real thing, serving authentic and tasty Vietnamese dishes. Try anything in the pungent black-bean sauce; the green-papaya and beef-jerky salad; and the beef cubes with watercress, exceptional when dipped in tangy lemon-pepper sauce. Go with an adventurous palette, and don't be put off by the cafeteria atmosphere. *11–13 Doyers St. (between Bowery and Pell St.), Chinatown, 212/693–0725. Reservations not accepted. AE. Subway: J, M, N, Q, R, W, Z, 6 to Canal St.* $

chapter 2

SHOPPING

New York is a city whose merchants cater to a rather remarkable population that has discriminating and diverse tastes, along with easy access to nearly inexhaustible stocks of merchandise jockeying for space on the city's shelves. The abundance of styles and stores in New York does not necessarily make shopping here a breeze—just try, for example, to free a silk camisole from a tightly packed end-of-season rack at Macy's. And we've all experienced that pang of sympathy when some poor soul who's just bought a new TV steps onto a crowded subway. Apathetic service can also try our patience, but then again, New York is nothing if not inconsistent, so don't be surprised if you come upon the friendliest and most expert service you've ever encountered. And whatever happens during your shopping expedition, you'll probably have an experience that is, if nothing else, memorable.

shopping destinations

DEPARTMENT STORES

Most department stores and some designer boutiques offer the services of personal shoppers. You'll have to schedule an appointment a few days in advance, but for the price of spontaneity, you get a store-specific guru. The consultant will either walk with you through the store or, if you describe your size, budget, and taste, run off and make the appropriate selections so you can hit the dressing room ASAP. There is no obligation to buy, and the service is free.

9 *e-2*

BARNEYS NEW YORK
Having survived financial ups and downs that forced the closing of its landmark Chelsea store, Barneys manages to keep its cutting edge. The women's floors, especially, have an amazing range of high-end designers, from the minimalism of Jil Sander to the blue-blood class of Etro and Burberry to the extravagance of Christian Lacroix. The Chelsea Passage level has all of those *objets* that aren't exactly fashion but still look fabulous: Philippe Starck kitchenware, stationery, vases, crystal, china, beaded cocktail napkins. If the prices and the

---

ESSENTIAL WEB SITES

www.dailycandy.com Industry insiders and hipsters love dailycandy for sample sale listings, chic and often quirky product news, store openings and trend-spotting, and the slick format it's e-mailed to you in every day.

www.newyorkmag.com Home of the cult-followed Sales & Bargains and Best Bets page also provides a wide database of store descriptions and location information. And if you missed this week's glossy, you can check out the features and style page to find out what the hottest trends are and where to stock up on them.

www.newyork.citysearch.com Ultra-user-friendly, with thorough descriptions and contact information, this Web site categorizes shops by type and by neighborhood to make navigation simple. Daily features on the home page provide immediate gratification for those that want to stay in the loop.

www.nydailynews.com Click on Lifestyle, and then Cityscape. Under the Consumer section, you'll find sales and store info.

www.nypost.com Expert product reviews, features on current shopping events, and a Savvy Shopper section with sales and bargains for the week in the areas of apparel, home furnishings, and spas.

www.timeoutny.com Just like the magazine, TONY tells all—seasonal shopping, beauty booty, where to stock up on the hottest, newest, gotta-have-its, and a detailed categorized database to search.

attitude leave you winded, you can still find something that's affordable but nonetheless invokes extravagance: a pair of caviar spoons, for instance? Barneys turned its Chelsea warehouse (site of its famous fall and spring sales) into a single-level co-op housing such forward-looking labels as Marc by Marc Jacobs, Seven Jeans, and Earl Jeans. *660 Madison Ave. (at 61st St.), Upper East Side, 212/826–8900. Subway: N, R, W, 4, 5, 6 to 59th St./Lexington Ave.*

9 d-3
BERGDORF GOODMAN
With a men's and a women's store facing each other across 5th Avenue, Bergdorf Goodman dominates a solid block of good taste. But while the buildings themself whisper "old money," the selections are far from old-fashioned. Shoe mavens could be rendered delirious by the couture heels; upstairs, many designer labels hold court in separate boutiques: John Galliano, Yves St. Laurent, Celine, Christian Dior, Chanel, and their four-digit brethren. The John Barrett beauty salon and Susan Ciminelli Day Spa have managed to one-up their competitors by operating in the Goodman family's former penthouse apartment. The home department has roomfuls of especially wonderful linens, tableware, and gifts. *754 5th Ave. (at 57th St.), Midtown West, 212/753–7300. Subway: N, R, W to 5th Ave./59th St.*

9 d-3
754 5th Ave. (at 57th St.), Midtown East, 212/753–7300. Subway: N, R, W to 5th Ave./59th St.

9 e-3
BLOOMINGDALE'S
To tourists, Bloomie's is as New York as yellow cabs. To New Yorkers, Bloomie's is a good place to go for a sale on, say, hosiery or bedding. The ground floor includes the mazelike cosmetics area, whose mirrors and shiny black walls can be completely discombobulating. (Enter on 3rd Avenue instead of Lexington Avenue to avoid this experience.) Big-gun designers such as Calvin Klein, Donna Karan, and Ralph Lauren seem to be everywhere. Their names pop up on casual clothes, dressy suits, and underwear, not to mention in the home section. Buyers also reach out to the more avant-garde (Helmut Lang, Alexander McQueen). If you brave the clothing sales, prepare for a scrimmagelike experience amid messy piles and racks of

merch. *1000 3rd Ave. (at 59th St.), Midtown East, 212/705–2000. Subway: N, R, W, 4, 5, 6 to 59th St./Lexington Ave.*

9 e-5
LORD & TAYLOR
Once inside this 5th Avenue veteran, you might think the ground floor goes on forever. A trick of mirrors reflecting the arched white ceiling, this impression of cosmetic-department infinity is the store's most overwhelming aspect. (Make an immediate right from the entrance to get to the up escalator.) For the most part, L&T is a decidedly lady-like experience, with some floors decorated in powder-pink and white. Clothes lean heavily toward conservative American designers throughout; think St. John and Liz Claiborne for women, Nautica and Perry Ellis for men, and Ralph Lauren for all. *424 5th Ave. (at 38th St.), Murray Hill, 212/391–3344. Subway: B, D, F, N, Q, R, V, W to 34th St./Herald Sq.*

9 d-6
MACY'S
If you don't know the floor plan by heart (many do), Macy's requires the patience of a saint, or a stiff drink. With nine floors (not including the famous Cellar marketplace) and too few signs, you can easily find yourself among the baby booties when you're looking for luggage. Macy's has tons of almost everything, from sports gear to pianos. Major labels such as DKNY, Polo, Tommy Hilfiger, and Calvin Klein show up on floor after floor, from men's and women's jeans to suits. Dig a little deeper and you'll find some lesser-known streetwear labels such as Ecko and Diesel. What Macy's doesn't have is couture. Service can be amiably casual or surly, but is reliably slapdash. The list of amenities is impressive; there's even a post office. *155 W. 34th St. (Herald Sq.), Midtown West, 212/695–4400. Subway: B, D, F, N, Q, R, V, W to 34th St./Herald Sq.*

11 e-7
PEARL RIVER MART
From the street, you would never know that the shabby entrance leads to three floors packed with everything from tatami slippers and karate pants to bamboo steamers, parasols, lanterns, and porcelain teas sets—and it's wildly inexpensive. Rows of noodles, dried seaweed, and Asian sweets fill the food section. A second, smaller location smack

on the border of Little Italy and China-town carries the best of the larger branch. At press time, construction had begun on a store on Broadway between Broome and Grand streets. *277 Canal St. (at Broadway), Chinatown, 212/431–4770. Subway: Q, W to Canal St.*

11 *f-6*

200 Grand St. (between Mott and Mul-berry Sts.), Chinatown, 212/966–1010. Subway: Shuttle to Grand St.

9 *e-4*

SAKS FIFTH AVENUE

Saks soothes New Yorkers with two hard-to-find luxuries: superb service and a calm, non–nerve-fraying shopping experience. This fashion-only depart-ment store offers a full roster of conser-vative-to-hip clothing and accessories from international designers, as well as the city's largest selection of cosmetics and fragrances for men and women. *See also Clothing for Men/General and Clothing for Women/General below. Saks Fifth Ave., 611 5th Ave. (at 50th St.), Midtown East, 212/940–2243. Subway: B, D, F, V to 47th–50th Sts./Rockefeller Ctr.*

9 *e-2*

SHANGHAI TANG

Spoil yourself in luxurious garments in silk jacquard, brocade, velvet and lace (available for men, women and children), all designed for Shanghai Tang in China and custom-tailored. The four floors are also filled with ultra-elegant gifts and home decorative items. *714 Madison (at 63rd St.), Upper East Side, 212/888–0111. Subway: N, R, W to 5th Ave./59th St.*

9 *e-3*

TAKASHIMAYA

This Japanese retailer occupies a space of impeccable design and perpetual calm. The home collection is renowned, featuring delicate tablewares, lacquered chopsticks and silverware, and throw pil-lows covered in patchworks of patterned silks. Clothing for both men and women is limited to what Takashimaya calls "details." For men this means shirts, ties, watches, and the odd coat. For women, the "cause for indulgence" could be seed-pearl jewelry, hair ornaments, or silk scarves and purses. Head up to the 5th floor (loungewear, bedding, baby clothes) for silk robes, Japanese-style velvet thongs, and pale linens. The 6th-floor

cosmetics section has some rare product lines, including soaps and scents by Santa Maria Novella of Florence. The beautiful gardening section has glazed pots, gardening tools, and rather fasci-nating plants. Descend to the basement for beautiful teapots, loose teas, and per-haps a bento box lunch in the Tea Box café. *693 5th Ave. (between 54th and 55th Sts.), Midtown East, 212/350–0100. Sub-way: E, V to 5th Ave./53rd St.*

DISCOUNT STORES

Devastated by the World Trade Center disaster, Century 21, the crème de la crème of NYC discount stores, was forced to close. At this writing, however, it was planning to re-open in the same location, at 22 Cortlandt Street (between Broadway and Church Street). Ya gotta love bargain-loving New Yorkers.

11 *g-4*

DEMBITZER BROS.

Small and large appliances both sell for small prices here, but it's hectic, so you'd best know what you want. *5 Essex St. (at Canal St.), Lower East Side, 212/254–1310. Closed Sat. Subway: F, J, M, Z to Delancey St./Essex St.*

11 *e-3*

NATIONAL WHOLESALE LIQUIDATORS

You name it, it's here at a super-dis-counted price. These two floors are stuffed with home furnishings, electron-ics, clothing, cleaning supplies, storage bins and other plastic items, art sup-plies, and more. It's a bit of a mish-mash, but savvy downtowners swear by it. *632 Broadway (between Houston and Bleecker Sts.), East Village, 212/979–2400. Subway: 6 to Bleecker St.*

10 *e-6*

ODD JOB TRADING CORP.

Come here for closeouts of brand-name consumer goods. The best buys are in sports gear and small appliances. *390 5th Ave. (at 36th St.), Midtown West, 212/239–3336. Subway: B, D, F, N, Q, R, V, W to 34th St./Herald Sq.*

9 *d-6*

149 W. 32nd St. (between 6th and 7th Aves.), Midtown West, 212/564–7370. Sub-way: B, D, F, N, Q, R, V, W to 34th St./Herald Sq.; and other locations.

SHOPPING NEIGHBORHOODS

brooklyn

`12` *d-3*

DOWNTOWN BROOKLYN

With its 200 stores, downtown Brooklyn's Fulton Street Mall is usually abuzz with shoppers looking for cheap and fun outfits, hair extensions, discount shoes, and all kinds of other delights. Macy's anchors the pedestrian-only stretch, which is fairly packed on the weekends.

`12` *c-4*

COBBLE HILL

Smith Street burst into popularity at the turn of the new century, and the whole neighborhood has hipster written all over it with its funky coffeehouses, vintage furniture stores, swank restaurants, and girly, flirty shops (Crush, Flirt, Frida's Closet) filled with rock-star T's and lots of leopard print.

`12` *f-6*

PARK SLOPE

These days, it's hard to walk a block in this brownstone-lined neighborhood without running into half a dozen Peg Perego strollers. Kids stores (Fidgets, Jumpin' Julia's, Peek a Boo Kids) and family-friendly cafés and bookstores line 7th Avenue, making this a parent's haven. The colorful Boing Boing (294 6th Ave.) is probably the best maternity store in the city.

`3` *d-6*

WILLIAMSBURG

Still an eclectic mix of desolate industrial strips, large immigrant and ethnic populations, and paint-splattered young bohemians, Williamsburg is the stalwart of the newly hip Brooklyn neighborhoods. The hugely popular Bedford Avenue is the center of it all, with trendy, vintage-y shops like Beacon's, Chicabow, and Otte.

manhattan

`9` *a-6—e-6*

CHELSEA & THE FLATIRON DISTRICT

In the ultra-chic Chelsea (referred to more than once as the new SoHo), you'll find a mix of the hip, such as Emporio Armani, Intermix, and Paul

Smith, and the hard-core, such as the mega-discounter Loehmann's on 7th Avenue. Several blocks west, between 10th and 11th avenues, a few intrepid retailers, such as the edgy Comme des Garçons, have popped up amid the flourishing art galleries in what used to be Chelsea's desolate fringe. The Meatpacking District, farther south, has also become chic, thanks to high-fashion temple Jeffrey and a slew of restaurants-of-the-moment. Even the fabulous Sam (on *Sex and the City*) lives there now.

`3` *a-3—a-4*

COLUMBUS AVENUE

Between West 66th and West 86th streets, a former tenement district is home to a decent shopping strip. Stores are mostly modern in design, upscale but not top-of-the-line; many are branches of such familiar chains as Banana Republic. Still, you can find some not-too-common places, such as storefront Sean for quietly dapper menswear, Nautica for sport and prepster menswear, and the Maraolo factory store for discounted office-worthy shoes.

`9` *e-3—e-5*

5TH AVENUE

The avenue still wavers between the money-is-no-object crowd and an influx of shoppers in search of discount electronics and Gap-type offerings. It seems like the flag-bedecked Saks Fifth Avenue has always been there, and the always-packed Swedish sensation H&M has added affordable designer knock-offs to the mix. The perennial favorites will eat up a lot of shoe leather: Cartier jewelers, Takashimaya, Ferragamo and the other luxury stores in Trump Tower, Henri Bendel, Tiffany and Bulgari jewelers, F.A.O. Schwarz, and Bergdorf Goodman. Dizzyingly, Prada is a stone's throw from the über-chain The Gap, and a souped-up branch of good old Brooks Brothers is a few steps after that.

`9` *e-3—f-3*

57TH STREET

The postmodern, white glass Louis Vuitton Moet Hennesy headquarters, between Madison and 5th avenues, lends a light-hearted elegance to 57th Street and houses branches of Louis Vuitton and Christian Dior. These glamazons are surrounded by big-name art galleries and exclusive stores such as Burberry, Chanel, and Escada, but the block is no longer limited to top-echelon shopping. More affordable (and sizable) stores are an un-missable presence—monsters such as NikeTown and the Tourneau TimeMachine aren't just stores; they are high-tech marketing environments.

9 d-6
HERALD SQUARE

Reasonable prices on standard wares prevail at this intersection of West 34th Street, Broadway, and 6th Avenue. Giant Macy's is still the linchpin, while the latest H&M is right down the street. Also on 6th Avenue are the Manhattan Mall and Herald Center, both of them dwindling (Stern's went belly-up and Toys "R" Us left) but still good for bargain browsing, with branches of Daffy's, Payless Shoes, and Express.

10 f1–h-3
LOWER EAST SIDE & THE EAST VILLAGE

The spirit of "Have I got a bargain for you!" still fills Orchard Street, crammed with tiny, no-nonsense clothing and lingerie stores and open stalls. The area's gentrification has introduced groovy boutiques, and Ludlow Street especially has been buzzing lately with little storefronts selling hipster gear such as electric guitars, vintage '60s and '70s furniture, and clothing and accessories from local designers. Meanwhile, the East Village reliably continues to offer diverse, offbeat specialty stops, plenty of collectible kitsch, and some great vintage-clothing boutiques, especially along East 7th and East 9th streets.

9 e-1–e-3
MADISON AVENUE

Madison Avenue from East 57th to about East 79th streets can satisfy almost any fashion craving. Cerruti, Giorgio Armani, Dolce & Gabbana, Valentino, and Prada are the avenue's Italian compatriots, while hometown designer Donna Karan's first DKNY store still stands at the corner of East 60th Street, and, two blocks up, Hermès's skylit flagship—complete with top-floor art gallery and winding stone staircase—gleams expensively. British darling Nicole Farhi has also set up her fashion camp on East 60th Street, while Tod's, of driving-shoe fame, is a stone's throw away. The entire western side of Madison between East 69th and East 70th streets reinvented itself with the arrival of Chloe and branches of Cartier jewelers and menswear master Alfred Dunhill.

11 f-4–f-5
NOLITA

NoLita has taken over where SoHo left off. Tiny boutiques continue to sprout like mushrooms after rain. A cache of shops such as Calypso and Tracy Feith is rife with exotic glamour, and young, ultra-hip designers are featured at Hedra Prue, Eva, and Language. There are glamorous handbags at Jamin Peuch and Amy Chan, swank shoes at Sigerson Morrison, and chi-chi maternity clothes at Mommy Chic. Few stores have been around longer than a year or two, and international designers are heading into the area at a dizzying speed.

11 c-4–e-6
SOHO

The streets of SoHo have been packed with high-rent fashion boutiques and chain stores since the mid- to late 1990s. Big fashion guns—Vivienne Westwood, Louis Vuitton, Bottega Veneta, and Prada Sport—have footholds here, alongside secondary-line couture places, such as D&G and Miu Miu, and cutting-edge, multi-designer boutiques like the colorful Kirna Zabette. Much to the distress of locals, the mall element (Victoria's Secret, Old Navy, J. Crew, Banana Republic, French Connection, and many more) has firmly entrenched itself as well, and shows no signs of leaving. Traveling shoppers, especially Brazilians and Europeans, make the area their primary hunting ground.

queens

3 d-1–d-2
ASTORIA

Despite an influx of artists and young professionals, this predominantly Greek neighborhood clings to its working-class roots—Pakistani, Egyptian, Italian, Lebanese, Colombian, Eastern European, and Japanese restaurants vie with the bustling Greek restaurants, old-world cafés, live fish stores, butcher shops, and bakeries. On Steinway Street cheap little shops abound next to national chain stores like Express, Victoria's Secret, and the Gap.

3 *e-4, f-3*

QUEENS BOULEVARD
Best accessed by car, the mega-stores on this busy boulevard include well-known names like CompUSA, Toys "R" Us, Kinko's, and Bed Bath & Beyond, and are interspersed with a seemingly endless stream of malls, car lots, and strip-mall-like gatherings. Parking can be a pain, too, so come prepared to circle the block once or twice.

specialty shops

ANTIQUES

Nearly every neighborhood in New York has its own array of antiques stores, but there are some well-known pockets. These include SoHo (especially Lafayette Street, south of Houston Street); 9th–13th streets between Broadway and 2nd Avenue; and Madison and Lexington avenues from 72nd to 86th streets.

Call **Stella Management** (212/255–0020) for information on the Triple Pier Expo and Gramercy Park Antiques show; call **Sanford Smith Associates** (212/777–5218) for information on the Fall Antiques and the Modernism shows. **Anna and Brian Haughton Art and Antique Fairs** (212/642–8572) organizes the International Fine Art & Antique Dealers show; **Wendy Management** (914/698–3442) handles the New York Armory Antiques shows. **Metropolitan Art and Antiques** (212/463–0200) also produces several shows a year.

antiques centers & flea markets

9 *d-7*

ANNEX ANTIQUES FAIR & FLEA MARKET
A serious dealers' market with quality antiques and collectibles, the Annex is particularly strong on silver, jewelry, vintage clothing, glass, Americana, Victoriana, and ephemera, but there's much more. The stock varies from week to week, as most of the dealers are itinerant; they go where the action is. One block south of the Annex is a more chaotic lot with a preponderance of junk; it's also worth a look for good vintage clothing and the occasional quilt.

On Sunday, yet more dealers set up shop in a garage on 25th Street between 6th and 7th avenues. Parking for all Annex events is free. *6th Ave. and 26th St., Chelsea, 212/243–5343. Subway: F, V to 23rd St.*

9 *d-7*

CHELSEA ANTIQUES BUILDING
For antiques shopping in a conveniently mall-like setting, hit these three floors of antiques and collectibles any day of the week. The building's top nine floors have been converted into lofts, but there are still more than 100 dealers in this sprawling space. *110 W. 25th St. (between 6th and 7th Aves.), Chelsea, 212/929–0909. Subway: F, 1, 2 to 23rd St.*

7 *b-8*

GREENFLEA'S MARKET ON COLUMBUS
Greenflea's now rivals 26th Street as the Sunday flea market, though it's dark the rest of the week. Two hundred vendors offer antiques, collectibles, old clothes, jewelry, and new merchandise in both indoor and outdoor venues. Plus, there's a farmer's market. *Columbus Ave. and W. 76th St., Upper West Side, 212/721–0900. Subway: 1, 2 to 79th St.*

6 *d-8*

GREENFLEA'S UPTOWN MARKET
With both indoor and outdoor venues, this Saturday market is a friendly place to scout good-quality antiques and collectibles, including jewelry and linens. New goods round out the shopping experience. *W. 135th St. (between Lenox Ave. and Adam Clayton Powell Blvd.), Harlem, 212/721–0900. Subway: 2, 3 to 135th St.*

9 *f-3*

MANHATTAN ART & ANTIQUE CENTER
This is a class act. Under one roof, more than 100 shops and galleries sell a great selection of antiques and fine-art objects from around the world. Prices range impressively from $10 to $300,000. *1050 2nd Ave. (near 56th St.), Midtown East, 212/355–4400. Subway: N, R, W, 4, 5, 6 to 59th St./Lexington Ave.*

11 *e-2*

TOWER FLEA MARKET

These mainly young and earnest artisans and designers sell T-shirts, clothes, jewelry, hats, and other adornments every weekend. *Broadway and 4th St., East Village, no phone. Subway: N, R to 8th St.; 6 to Bleecker St.*

auction houses

9 *e-2*

CHRISTIE'S & CHRISTIE'S EAST

New York's branches of the famed London house hold auctions of fine art, furnishings, tapestries, books, and manuscripts and appraise art at no charge. "Low-end" antiques and collectibles are often up for grabs. *20 Rockefeller Plaza (49th St. between 5th and 6th Ave.), Midtown West, 212/636–2000. Subway: B, D, F, V to 47th–50th St./Rockefeller Ctr.*

9 *f-2*

219 E. 67th St. (between 3rd and 2nd Aves.), Upper East Side, 212/606–0400; 212/636–2000 information on current sales; 212/355–1501 information on lectures and courses. Subway: 6 to 68th St./Hunter College.

9 *d-3*

PHILLIPS AUCTIONEERS

Founded in London in 1796, Phillips still holds fine-art and estate sales. Items are displayed three or four days before the auction. Watch the paper for Phillips' ads. *3 W. 57th St. (between 5th and 6th Aves.), Midtown West, 212/570–4830. Subway: F, N, R, Q, W to 57th St.*

9 *g-1*

SOTHEBY'S

Appraiser and auctioneer since 1744, the world-famous Sotheby's sells paintings, jewelry, furniture, silver, books, porcelain, Orientalia, rugs, and more. The house is exciting to visit even if you won't be buying. Sotheby's Arcade, a sort of junior Sotheby's, sells more affordable pieces. *1334 York Ave. (at 72nd St.), Upper East Side, 212/606–7000 (call this number for the education department and Sotheby's Arcade) or 212/606–7909 (24-hr auction and exhibition line). Subway: 6 to 77th St.*

9 *e-7*

TEPPER GALLERIES

Large and lively, Tepper is popular with collectors for its fine furniture, paintings, rugs, accessories, and jewelry. Auctions are every other Saturday; viewing is on Friday. *110 E. 25th St. (between Park and Lexington Aves.), Murray Hill, 212/677–5300. Subway: 6 to 23rd St.*

7 *e-7*

WILLIAM DOYLE GALLERIES

Estates are the specialty here, particularly 18th- and 20th-century decorative and fine arts including furniture, paintings, rugs, and accessories. Auctions are usually held every other Wednesday, sometimes weekly; viewing runs from Saturday through Tuesday. *175 E. 87th St. (between Lexington and 3rd Aves.), Upper East Side, 212/427–2730. Subway: 4, 5, 6 to 86th St.*

collectibles

9 *e-2*

A LA VIEILLE RUSSIE

This exquisite collection includes European and American antique jewelry, Fabergé, gold snuffboxes, objets de vertu, and Russian decorative and fine arts. *781 5th Ave. (at 59th St.), Midtown East, 212/752–1727. Subway: N, R, W to 5th Ave./59th St.*

11 *e-4*

BACK PAGES

Back Pages is a center for antique amusement and slot machines, Wurlitzer jukeboxes, Coca-Cola vending machines, player pianos, and other large items. They also restore. Appointments are advised. *125 Greene St. (near Prince St.), SoHo, 212/460–5998. Subway: N, R to Prince St.*

11 *d-4*

BERTHA BLACK

A tiny SoHo shop with antique American painted furniture, folk art, and country dining accessories, Bertha Black also carries an extensive collection of Mexican retablos and santos, 1820–1900. *80 Thompson St. (near Spring St.), SoHo, 212/966–7116. Closed Mon.–Tues. Subway: C, E to Spring St.*

9 f-2
CHICK DARROW'S FUN ANTIQUES
For the Peter Pan in your family, hit the city's first antique toy shop, founded 40 years ago. Chick Darrow's is brimming with antique toys and gadgets of every description: dolls, radios, autographs, penny banks, toy soldiers, Star Trek, carousel animals, animation art, and memorabilia. Prices range widely, from $2 to $5,000, and you can buy, sell, trade, or rent. *1101 1st Ave. (between 60th and 61st Sts.), Upper East Side, 212/838–0730. Closed Sun.–Mon. except by appt. Subway: N, R, W, 4, 5, 6 to 59th St./Lexington Ave.*

11 d-5
ECLECTIQUES
This aptly named shop carries an interesting mix: art deco, art nouveau, 1920s Mica lamps, Mission furniture, 20th-century oils and illustrations, paisley shawls, and vintage Vuitton luggage. *55 Wooster St. (at Broome St.), SoHo, 212/966–0650. Subway: A, C, E to Canal St.*

9 f-2
ELIZABETH STREET CO.
Still named for the street in SoHo where its former owners, Urban Archaeology, had a location, this eclectic boutique of garden statuary, fireplace surrounds, and French and English decorative objects is now a little bit of SoHo on the Upper East Side. *1176 2nd Ave. (at 62nd St.), Upper East Side, 212/644–6969. Subway: N, R, W, 4, 5, 6 to 59th St./Lexington Ave.*

7 e-7
HUBERT DES FORGES
Hubert des Forges can be counted on for lovely French and English antiques and decorative accessories. The specialty here is lighting, and there's a huge variety, especially of table lamps. *1193 Lexington Ave. (near 81st St.), Upper East Side, 212/744–1857. Closed weekends. Subway: 6 to 77th St.*

9 f-8
IRVING BARBER SHOP ANTIQUES
These cramped quarters overflow with glassware, costume jewelry, beaded evening bags, prints, and sometimes antique linens, quilts, and vintage cloths. Browse—gingerly. *210 E. 21st St.*

(between 3rd and 2nd Aves.), Gramercy, no phone. Closed weekends. Subway: 6 to 23rd St.

7 f-8
JANA STARR ANTIQUES
Focusing on the years 1900–1979, Starr is jam-packed with wedding dresses from the turn of the 20th century to the 1970s, but also manages to stuff into its tight quarters beautiful embroidered table and bed linens, jewelry, hats, gloves, dressing-table items, bags, antique laces and textiles, and walking sticks, all obviously gathered with care. She also rents period props. *236 E. 80th St. (between 3rd and 2nd Aves.), Upper East Side, 212/861–8256. Closed Sun. Subway: 6 to 77th St.*

9 f-1
JEAN HOFFMAN ANTIQUES
Hoffman has an eye for wedding accessories, from the turn of the last century to the present: pick up pocketbooks, fans, gloves, linens, and gift items here. *207 E. 66th St. (between 3rd and 2nd Aves.), Upper East Side, 212/535–6930. Closed Sun.–Mon. Subway: 6 to 68th St./Hunter College.*

10 c-1
LE FANION
Feel like Provence? Peruse French country antiques, contemporary ceramics, and crystal chandeliers in a shop with a deliciously country atmosphere. *299 W. 4th St. (at Bank St.), Greenwich Village, 212/463–8760. Closed Sun. Subway: 1, 2 to Christopher St./Sheridan Sq.*

7 e-8
LEO KAPLAN LTD.
Leo Kaplan has an extensive selection of French and American antique and modern paperweights; 18th-century English pottery and porcelains; Russian enamels; English and French cameo glass of the art nouveau period; and contemporary studio glass. *967 Madison Ave. (near 75th St.), Upper East Side, 212/249–6766. Subway: 6 to 77th St.*

9 f-3
LILLIAN NASSAU LTD.
This is the place for art nouveau and art deco pieces, especially Tiffany glass and rare art glass as well as furniture, Tiffany lamps, and sculpture. *220 E. 57th St. (between 2nd and 3rd Aves.), Midtown*

East, 212/759–6062. Subway: N, R, W, 4, 5, 6 to 59th St./Lexington Ave.

7 e-8
LINDA HORN ANTIQUES
Linda has quite an eye for the unusual. Check out her opulent treasures from the 18th and 19th centuries in a setting to match. 1015 Madison Ave. (near 78th St.), Upper East Side, 212/772–1122. Subway: 6 to 77th St.

11 d-4
MOOD INDIGO
The 1930s and '40s get their due in this inviting shop full of Russell Wright, Fiesta, and Harlequin ware; art deco chrome accessories; and a wonderful selection of Bakelite jewelry. 181 Prince St. (between Thompson and Sullivan Sts.), SoHo, 212/254–1176. Closed Mon. N, R to Prince St.

7 b-8
MORE & MORE ANTIQUES
Steve Mohr has one of the best eyes in the business, and his wonderful shop is brimming over with late-19th- to early 20th-century French and English decorative antiques, with a bent toward the Victorian. Offerings include paisleys, wonderful hand-painted china, beadwork, bamboo furnishings, rugs, screens, and an eclectic selection of jewelry, from 1840 to 1940. 378 Amsterdam Ave. (at 78th St.), Upper West Side, 212/580–8404. Subway: 1, 2 to 79th St.

9 d-3
MORIAH GALLERIES
Antique Jewish ritual and ceremonial art, paintings and sculptures by early and modern artists, illustrated children's books, antique illustrated bibles, and curios make up this unique mix. 16 W. 56th St. (between 5th and 6th Aves.), Midtown West, 212/245–0101. Closed weekends. Subway: E, V to 5th Ave./53rd St.

9 f-2
OLD VERSAILLES, INC.
The specialty here is, bien sûr, French and Continental antique furniture and decorations. 315 E. 62nd St. (between 2nd and 1st Aves.), 3rd floor, Upper East Side, 212/421–3663. Closed weekends. Subway: N, R, W, 4, 5, 6 to 59th St./Lexington Ave.

7 e-8
PRICE GLOVER INC.
English pewter, pottery, and brass, circa 1690–1820, are joined by early 19th-century English brass light fixtures, and Chinese furniture, 1600–1700. 59 E. 79th St. (near Madison Ave.), 3rd floor, Upper East Side, 212/772–1740. Closed weekends. Subway: 6 to 77th St.

9 e-1
PRIMAVERA GALLERY
These decorative arts include paintings, furniture, glass, and jewelry from the turn of the 20th century to the 1950s. 808 Madison Ave. (near 68th St.), Upper East Side, 212/288–1569. Subway: 6 to 68th St./Hunter College.

11 e-4
SARAJO
Sarajo's large and impressive selection of textiles, antique furniture, and objects comes from Central Asia, Africa, the Far East, and Central and South America. 130 Greene St. (between Prince and Houston Sts.), SoHo, 212/966–6156. Subway: N, R to Prince St.

7 e-7
TROUVAILLE FRANÇAISE
Muriel Clark collects and purveys treasures from France and England with loving care: antique bed and table linens, laces, curtains, christening gowns, and much more. Upper East Side, 212/737–6015. Open by appt. only. Subway: 4, 5, 6 to 86th St.

9 c-7
WAVES
Vintage radios, microphones, wind-up phonographs, old telephones, and neon clocks are sold, repaired, and rented; other communications memorabilia include old advertisements and 78-rpm records. 251 W. 30th St. (between 7th and 8th Aves.), Midtown West, 212/273–9616. Subway: 1, 2 to 28th St.

furniture

11 c-4
CARPE DIEM ANTIQUES
This excellent cache of '50s and '60s furniture includes a particularly notable collection of lamps. 187 6th Ave. (between Spring and Prince Sts.), SoHo, 212/337–0018. Closed Mon. Subway: C, E to Spring St.

11 *f-2*

COBWEB

Cobweb has a good selection of antique furniture and accessories from Europe, the Middle East, and South America. *440 Lafayette St. (near Astor Pl.), East Village, 212/505–1558. Subway: 6 to Astor Pl.*

11 *d-4*

EILEEN LANE ANTIQUES

Spacious quarters show off a lovely and well-priced selection of Swedish and Viennese Biedermeier and art deco furniture, as well as period art glass and alabaster lighting. *150 Thompson St. (between Prince and Houston Sts.), SoHo, 212/475–2988. Subway: C, E to Spring St.*

9 *f-1*

EVERGREEN ANTIQUES

Some of this rustic, 19th-century Scandinavian and Northern European furniture has its original hand-painted finishing. Upstairs are neoclassical, Biedermeier, and Empire goods; downstairs is the painted furniture, along with accents like rag rugs, pottery, and wooden boxes. *1249 3rd Ave. (at 72nd St.), Upper East Side, 212/744–5664. Subway: 6 to 68th St./Hunter College.*

7 *e-8*

FLORIAN PAPP

Since 1900, Papp has been a source for antiques from the William and Mary, Sheraton, and other periods of fine English and European furniture, and the store carries Victorian items as well. *962 Madison Ave. (near 76th St.), Upper East Side, 212/288–6770. Subway: 6 to 77th St.*

11 *e-4*

GALLERY 532

Original furniture and ceramic pieces will delight the arts-and-crafts lover. *142 Duane St. (between Church St. and W. Broadway), TriBeCa, 212/219–1327. Subway: 1, 2 to Chambers St.*

11 *f-3*

GUÉRIDON

The name means "round end table" in French, and the store boasts a wide array of these and other funky modern pieces at a range of prices to suit almost any budget. The owners are highly knowledgeable and equally charming. *359 Lafayette St. (between Bond and Bleecker Sts.), East Village, 212/677–7740. Subway: 6 to Bleecker St.*

10 *e-1*

HOWARD KAPLAN ANTIQUES

An early purveyor of the Rustic French look, Howard Kaplan now carries a broader range of French (including country) and 19th-century English furnishings and a luscious group of decorative accessories, all in a beautiful shop. Upstairs, the bath shop is brimming with antique bathroom and reproduction bathroom furnishings and fixtures. *827 Broadway (between 12th and 13th Sts.), Greenwich Village, 212/674–1000. Closed weekends. Subway: L, N, Q, R, W, 4, 5, 6 to 14th St./Union Sq.*

11 *c-8*

INTÉRIEURS

Alas, truly choice vintage modern furniture, along with tabletop items, and other accessories from France, come with equally choice prices. Be prepared to drool, and bring the platinum card. *151 Franklin St. (between Varick and Hudson Sts.), TriBeCa, 212/343–0800. Subway: 1, 2 to Franklin St.*

9 *e-3*

ISRAEL SACK INC.

A patriarch of still-existing antique-furniture galleries, Israel Sack was begun almost 100 years ago, and the tradition of showing some of the finest 17th-, 18th-, and early 19th-century American furniture is continued by Sack's octogenarian sons Albert and Robert. Prices range from $3,000 to $3 million and beyond. *730 5th Ave. (between 56th and 57th Sts.), Suite 605, Midtown West, 212/399–6562. Subway: F, N, R, Q, W to 57th St.*

7 *e-8*

LEIGH KENO AMERICAN ANTIQUES

The patriarch of the "new generation," Keno is one half of the wunderkind twins who began collecting while still in short pants (brother Leslie is a specialist at Sotheby's). Included among the finds are an emphasis on 18th-century American furniture and paintings. *980 Madison Ave. (at 76th St.), Upper East Side, 212/734–2381. Subway: 6 to 77th St.*

11 *f-2*

LOST CITY ARTS

Come here for mid-20th-century modern furniture and fixtures, American and European. *18 Cooper Sq. (Bowery at 5th*

St.), East Village, 212/375–0500. Subway: 6 to Astor Pl.

9 *f-3*
NEWEL ART GALLERIES
It takes six stories to house this supreme collection of antique furnishings from the Renaissance to art deco, with an emphasis on the unusual and whimsical. The galleries cater to those in the trade, stylists scouting props, and those who know exactly what they want. *425 E. 53rd St. (near 1st Ave.), Midtown East, 212/758–1970. Closed weekends. Subway: 6 to 51st St./Lexington Ave.; E, V to Lexington–3rd Aves./53rd St.*

11 *a-1*
LES PIERRE ANTIQUES
Les Pierre Antiques specializes in exquisite 18th- and 19th-century French country furniture and accessories. *367 Bleecker St. (at Charles St.), Greenwich Village, 212/243–7740. Subway: 1, 2 to Christopher St./Sheridan Sq.*

10 *e-1*
RETRO MODERN STUDIO
The collection centers on avant-garde lighting of fine materials and unusual design. *58 E. 11th St. (between Broadway and University Pl.), 2nd floor, Greenwich Village, 212/674–0530. Closed Sun. Subway: N, R to 8th St.; 6 to Astor Pl.*

10 *c-2*
THE RURAL COLLECTION
You can go home again: finds from the farm, old cupboards, and weather-worn painted furniture from the Midwest are priced very reasonably here. *117 Perry St. (between Greenwich and Hudson Sts.), Greenwich Village, 212/645–4488. Subway: 1, 2 to Christopher St./Sheridan Sq.*

11 *e-3*
SECONDHAND ROSE
The focus here is 19th-century Moorish furniture, lamps, and accessories—the exotic Moroccan, Syrian, and Persian designs that made the late 19th-century English avant-garde set swoon. Think lush inlaid furniture and pierced, beaded lamps. *138 Duane St. (between Church and W. Broadway), TriBeCa, 212/393–9002. Subway: 1, 2 to Chambers St.*

7 *f-8*
TREILLAGE
Owned by Bunny Williams and John Rosselli, Treillage has made its name with furniture and accessories for the conservatory, garden, and home, but it now features an interesting selection of lighting, mirrors, and botanical prints as well. *418 E. 75th St. (between 1st and York Aves.), Upper East Side, 212/535–2288. Subway: 6 to 77th St.*

11 *b-5*
WYETH
Come here for steel furniture and other stylish Americana. *315 Spring St. (at Greenwich St.), SoHo, 212/925–5278. Subway: C, E to Spring St.*

quilts
Most antiques stores have a few quilts in stock, but the shops below have built collections of outstanding quality, originality, and quantity.

9 *f-2*
GAZEBO
A must for the hearth-and-home enthusiast, this Midtown shop features American quilts mainly from the 1920s and '30s, and new ones in traditional patterns. They're happy to take custom orders. Vintage wicker furnishings and accessories, old and new baskets, silk flowers, and other accessories round out the beautiful displays. *306 E. 61st St. (between 1st and 2nd Aves.), Upper East Side, 212/832–7077. Subway: N, R, W, 4, 5, 6 to 59th St./Lexington Ave.*

9 *f-3*
LAURA FISHER
Fisher has an exciting collection of pieced and appliquéd quilts, circa 1830–1930, including Amish and crib quilts. The wares extend to paisley shawls, woven coverlets, Marseilles bedspreads, hooked and Native American rugs, needlework, and decorative Victorian accessories. *Manhattan Art & Antiques Center, 1050 2nd Ave. (at 55th St.), Midtown East, 212/838–2596. Closed Sun. Subway: N, R, W, 4, 5, 6 to 59th St./Lexington Ave.*

11 *a-1*
SUSAN PARRISH ANTIQUES
Knowledgeable and caring, Susan Parrish has a lovely selection of pretty

quilts, original 19th-century painted American country furniture, and Native American weavings. *390 Bleecker St. (near Perry St.), Greenwich Village, 212/645–5020. Closed Sun. Subway: 1, 2 to Christopher St./Sheridan Sq.*

7 *g-8*

WOODARD & GREENSTEIN AMERICAN ANTIQUES
A known and respected source for American quilts from the 1850s on, Woodard & Greenstein also carries hooked rugs, samplers, game boards, baskets, and much more—mint Americana. *506 E. 74th St. (near York Ave.), 5th floor, Upper East Side, 212/988–2906. Subway: 6 to 77th St.*

ART SUPPLIES

9 *d-4*

ARTHUR BROWN & BRO., INC.
Long established, this superior art- and drafting-supply store has a fantastic pen department. *2 W. 46th St. (between 5th and 6th Aves.), Midtown West, 212/575–5555. Subway: B, D, F, V to 42nd St.*

9 *c-3*

LEE'S ART SHOP
Right across the street from the Art Students' League, Lee's caters to both professional and amateur artists. The large inventory includes stationery, pens, gifts, paint and brushes, and architectural and drafting supplies, and they're happy to frame your masterpiece once you're finished. *220 W. 57th St. (between 7th Ave. and Broadway), Midtown West, 212/247–0110. Subway: F, N, R, Q, W to 57th St.*

10 *e-1*

NEW YORK CENTRAL ART SUPPLY
Serving New York's artists for over 95 years, New York Central has the finest of everything: handmade papers, parchment, 3,000 different pastels, 200 different canvases, and much more, all for 20%–40% less than elsewhere. They specialize in finding the "impossible." *62 3rd Ave. (near 11th St.), East Village, 212/473–7705. Subway: 6 to Astor Pl.*

11 *e-6*

PEARL
With nine floors of art supplies, Pearl is the world's largest art, craft, and graph-

ics discount center—no mean feat. It's a wonderful source for this stuff, as well as house and industrial paints at 20%–50% off. *308 Canal St. (between Church St. and Broadway), TriBeCa, 212/431–7932. Subway: J, M, N, Q, R, W, Z, 6 to Canal St.*

9 *f-8*

207 E. 23rd St. (between 3rd and 2nd Aves.), Gramercy, 212/592–2179. Subway: 6 to 23rd St.

9 *d-8*

SAM FLAX, INC.
Sam Flax adds school and office supplies to its admirably complete selection of art materials. *12 W. 20th St. (between 5th and 6th Aves.), Chelsea, 212/620–3038. Subway: F, V to 23rd St.*

9 *e-3*

425 Park Ave. (at 55th St.), Midtown East, 212/935–5353. Subway: N, R, W, 4, 5, 6 to 59th St./Lexington Ave.

10 *e-1*

UTRECHT ART & DRAFTING SUPPLIES
Utrecht makes its own huge stock of paint, art, and drafting supplies right down the road in Brooklyn. Prices are reasonable, and quality is high. Other manufacturers' supplies are discounted as well. *111 4th Ave. (at 11th St.), East Village, 212/777–5353. Subway: 6 to Astor Pl.*

BEAUTY

fragrances & skin products
Be warned that counterfeit fragrances, packaged to look like the real thing, show up all over town; to avoid getting fooled, buy in reputable shops.

9 *c-8*

ALCONE
Although primarily a supplier of theatrical and professional makeup, Alcone has become popular with models, actresses, drag queens, and makeup artists who come for high-quality, dramatic brands not found in other stores—and then cover the walls with their signatures to let you know they've been there. *235 W. 19th St. (between 7th and 8th Aves.), Chelsea, 212/633–0551. Subway: C, E to 23rd St.*

11 c-4

AVEDA

Aveda offers European hair and skin-care products, makeup, bath preparations, and home fragrance, all made with natural ingredients. Tired of shopping? The Spring Street and West Broadway stores also offer massages and facials. *233 Spring St. (between 6th Ave. and Varick St.), Greenwich Village, 212/807–1492. Subway: C, E to Spring St.*

11 d-4

456 W. Broadway (between Prince and Houston Sts.), SoHo, 212/473–0280. Subway: F, V to Broadway–Lafayette St.

9 d-8

140 5th Ave. (at 19th St.), Flatiron District, 212/645–4797. Subway: N, R to 23rd St.

9 e-3

509 Madison Ave. (between 52nd and 53rd Sts.), Midtown East, 212/832–2416. Subway: E, V to 5th Ave./53rd St.

9 f-2

1122 3rd Ave. (between 65th and 66th Sts.), Upper East Side, 212/744–3113. Subway: 6 to 68th St./Hunter College.

11 e-1

THE BODY SHOP

This hugely successful toiletry chain has cheery shops citywide. The fragrant, all-natural products come in recyclable packaging, do not pollute the water, and have not been tested on animals—and in addition to saving the earth, they cleanse, polish, and protect the skin and hair. The various salves often come in good-to-go gift packages. For a full list of locations call 800/541–2535. *747 Broadway (near Astor Pl.), Greenwich Village, 212/979–2944. Subway: 6 to Astor Pl.*

9 d-6

Manhattan Mall, 901 6th Ave. (at 33rd St.), Midtown West, 212/268–7424. Subway: B, D, F, N, Q, R, V, W to 34th St./Herald Sq.

9 e-3

714 Lexington Ave. (between 57th and 58th Sts.), Upper East Side, 212/755–7851. Subway: N, R, W, 4, 5, 6 to 59th St./Lexington Ave.

7 b-8

2159 Broadway (at 76th St.), Upper West Side, 212/721–2947. Subway: 1, 2 to 79th St.

9 e-2

BOYD CHEMISTS

Boyd sells a dazzling array of European makeup and treatment products in addition to their own line, and now has a lingerie department and a huge selection of fine hair accessories. Experts-in-residence give beauty advice, makeup demonstrations, lessons, and encouragement to further ensure this is a mecca for beautiful people and wannabes alike. Oh, and they still fill prescriptions. *655 Madison Ave. (near 60th St.), Upper East Side, 212/838–6558. Subway: N, R, W, 4, 5, 6 to 59th St./Lexington Ave.*

9 e-2

CAMBRIDGE CHEMISTS

The fine British toiletries here include Original Yardley of London, Molton Brown (London), Cyclax, Innoxa, Sabona of London, and Simpson (shave brushes), and extend to French, Swiss, and German items. *21 E. 65th St. (near Madison Ave.), Upper East Side, 212/734–5678. Subway: 6 to 68th St./Hunter College.*

9 e-4

CASWELL-MASSEY CO.

In business since 1752, Caswell-Massey is the oldest apothecary in the United States, as well as the oldest retailer in New York City. (The original store was in Newport, Rhode Island; the New York City one opened in 1828.) The cologne specially blended for George and Martha Washington, the cold cream made for Sarah Bernhardt (Lafayette), and the world's largest collection of imported soaps—including pure Castile by the pound—are all for sale in this pretty and fragrant shop. *518 Lexington Ave. (at 48th St.), Midtown East, 212/755–2254. Subway: S, 4, 5, 6, 7 to 42nd St./Grand Central.*

10 d-1

C. O. BIGELOW CHEMISTS

A pharmacy the way pharmacies used to be, Bigelow has a huge selection of homeopathic remedies, cosmetics (especially European), a nice array of toiletries, and makeup accessories in addition to the usual stock. The dependable store has been in the same place since 1838. *414 6th Ave. (between 9th and 10th Sts.), Greenwich Village, 212/533–2700. Subway: A, B, C, D, E, F, V to W. 4th St./Washington Sq.*

9 e-4

COSMAIR BEAUTY RESPONSE CENTER

Anyone willing to test new fragrances and cosmetics from well-known manufacturers can get free products here. Make an appointment, fill out a profile, and, if accepted, go home to evaluate the products and come back to report the results. Guinea pigs receive a gift after each visit. *575 5th Ave. (at 47th St.), 8th floor, Midtown East, 212/984–4164. Subway: E, V to 5th Ave./53rd St.*

9 f-3

COSMETIC SHOW

This shop is a true find—save up to 60% discounts on name-brand makeup products and fragrances. *150 E. 55th St. (between Lexington and 3rd Aves.), Midtown East, 212/750–8418. Subway: N, R, W, 4, 5, 6 to 59th St./Lexington Ave.*

9 d-4

CRABTREE & EVELYN

England's famed all-natural toiletries and comestibles are beautifully packed and presented for a touch of luxury. Gift baskets can be made to order. *Rockefeller Center Promenade, 620 5th Ave. (between 49th and 50th Sts.), Midtown West, 212/581–5022. Subway: B, D, F, V to 47th–50th Sts./Rockefeller Ctr.*

9 e-3

520 Madison Ave. (at 53rd St.), Midtown East, 212/758–6419. Subway: E, V to 5th Ave./53rd St.

7 e-6

1310 Madison Ave. (at 93rd St.), Upper East Side, 212/289–3923. Subway: 6 to 96th St.

11 e-3

CREED

Now is your opportunity to live like royalty. Simply stop by this 240-year-old British import and purchase one of the custom fragrances the perfume house has created for nobles ranging from George III to Queen Victoria. In addition, there are literally hundreds of other scents to choose from. *9 Bond St. (between Broadway and Lafayette St.), East Village, 212/228–1940. Subway: 6 to Bleecker St.*

9 e-1

897 Madison Ave. (between 72nd and 73rd Sts.), Upper East Side, 212/794–4480. Subway: 6 to 68th St./Hunter College.

11 g-2

DEMETER

By now everybody knows the ubiquitous Demeter fragrances with terrifically playful scents like tomato and birthday cake. But this eponymous shop—the only outpost in the states—houses every single one of their scents (that's 150) in addition to another 135 special edition scents not found anywhere else. Also find super-smelling lotions, shower gels, oils, and bath salts. *83 2nd Ave. (between 4th and 5th Sts.), East Village, 212/505–1535 or 800/482–0422. Subway: F, V to 2nd Ave.; 6 to Astor Pl.*

9 c-1

FACE STOCKHOLM

A household name in Sweden, Face offers fabulous makeup in seasonally changing palettes. Trendy lipstick and nail-polish shades are especially popular. *226 Columbus Ave. (at 71st St.) Upper West Side, 212/769–1420. Subway: 1, 2, 3 to 72nd St.*

11 e-4

110 Prince St. (at Greene St.), SoHo, 212/996–9110. Subway: N, R to Prince St.

9 e-2

687 Madison Ave. (at 62nd St.), Upper East Side, 212/207–8833. Subway: N, R, W, 4, 5, 6 to 59th St./Lexington Ave.

7 e-8

FRESH

A buffet of quirky bath and body products, fresh has recipes for your face, from craveable chocolate-milk soap to a more diet-conscious sounding soy lotion. *1061 Madison Ave. (between 80th and 81st Sts.), Upper East Side, 212/396–0344. Subway: 4, 5, 6 to 86th St.*

11 d-5

57 Spring St. (between Lafayette and Mulberry Sts.), Little Italy, 212/925–0099. Subway: 6 to Spring St.

9 e-3

IL MAKIAGE

An Upper East Side trendsetter, Il Makiage has more than 200 eye and cheek colors and updates them seasonally. Makeover programs range from an elementary eye primer to a full makeup consultation and are really quite special. *107 E. 60th St. (at Park Ave.), Upper East Side, 212/371–3992. Closed Sat. Subway: N, R, W, 4, 5, 6 to 59th St./Lexington Ave.*

9 *e-8*

JAY'S PERFUME BAR

This stretch of 17th Street has several small, no-frills, down-and-dirty discount fragrance shops. Don't expect great service, but do expect great deals. *14 E. 17th St. (between 5th Ave. and Union Sq. W), Flatiron District, 212/243–7743. Subway: N, R to 23rd St.; F, V to 14th St.*

9 *e-8*

JO MALONE

This shop is the U.S. debut of London-based Jo Malone, known for her lush, flowery soaps, creams, and perfumes—with evocative names like Lime Basil & Mandarin, and Tuberose. *949 Broadway (at 23rd St.), Flatiron District, 212/673–2220. Subway: N, R to 23rd St.; F, V to 14th St.*

10 *f-1*

KIEHL'S PHARMACY

Since 1851 this fascinating pharmacy, now a New York institution, has carried a large selection of pure essences, perfumes, cosmetics, and homeopathic remedies to cure whatever ails you. The store makes its all-natural products on the premises, including the "Age Deterrent" cream. Alas, Kiehl's no longer carries leeches, but it does stock more than 300 different treatments for hair, body, skin, and nails. The staff is both knowledgeable and helpful and distributes handfuls of samples. *109 3rd Ave. (near 13th St.), East Village, 212/677–3171 or 212/475–3698. Subway: L to 3rd Ave.*

7 *e-8*

LAURA GELLER
MAKEUP STUDIOS

A former makeup artist on Broadway, Geller will make you up, give you an application lesson, sell you her own products, and bring out the best in your bridesmaids when the time comes. *1044 Lexington Ave. (at 74th St.), Upper East Side, 212/570–5477. Subway: 6 to 77th St.*

9 *e-4*

L'OCCITANE

Stepping into one of these boutiques is like crossing the threshold into Provence. Lovely soaps, shampoos, and body creams are scented with lavender, thyme, and a host of other herbs. Beautiful packaging make items from here especially well-received gifts. *510 Madison Ave. (at 48th St.), Midtown East, 212/826–5020. Subway: E, V to 5th Ave.*

11 *d-5*

146 Spring St. (at Wooster St.), SoHo, 212/343–0109. Subway: 6 to Spring St.

9 *b-2*

198 Columbus Ave. (near 69th St.), Upper West Side, 212/362–5146. Subway: 1, 2 to 66th St./Lincoln Ctr.

11 *c-1*

M.A.C

M.A.C., Make-Up Art Cosmetics, was created by makeup artist Frank Toskan in 1984. The popular products are vitamin-enriched, contain no mineral oil or fragrance, are not tested on animals, are extraordinarily long-lasting, and come in a variety of textures as well as tints. The store recycles the containers (six empties and you get a free lipstick). It's geared toward makeup professionals, but clients include Cher, Madonna, Gloria Estefan, and Paula Abdul. *14 Christopher St. (at Gay St.), Greenwich Village, 212/243–4150. Subway: 1, 2 to Christopher St./Sheridan Sq.*

11 *d-4*

113 Spring St. (near Wooster St.), SoHo, 212/334–4641. Closed Mon. Subway: C, E to Spring St.

9 *e-8*

1 E. 22nd St. (at 5th Ave.), Flatiron Bldg., Flatiron District, 212/677–6611. Subway: F, N, R, S to 23rd St.

11 *d-4*

MAKEUP FOREVER

A cult brand amongst cosmetics-lovers and professional makeup artists the world over, this hip and happening makeup keeps downtowners happy—even if they now live uptown—with its extensive color palettes, shimmery powders, and rich textures. *409 W. Broadway (between Spring and Prince Sts.), SoHo, 212/941–9337. Subway: C, E to Spring St.*

9 *d-8*

THE MAKEUP SHOP

Led by makeup artist Tobi Britton, The Makeup Shop offers makeovers, makeup lessons, eyebrow shaping, and a whole line of products, including Yonka, Japonesque, Kryolon, and Dinair airbrush systems. *131 W. 21st St. (between 6th and 7th Aves.), Chelsea, 212/807–0447. Subway: F, 1, 2 to 23rd St.*

9 *e-4*

MARY QUANT

A legend in London for her daring makeup colors made famous during the swinging '60s, the still funky, but somewhat subdued, queen of mod keeps a rainbow of colors for eyes, lips, cheeks, and nails in her U.S. shop: try a fuchsia eye shadow, one of 120 shades available. *520 Madison Ave. (between 53rd and 54th Sts.), Midtown East, 212/980–7577. Subway: N, R, W to 5th Ave./59th St.*

11 *d-4*

ORIGINS

This user-friendly SoHo store features exclusively Origins products: soaps, oils for massage and bath, lotions, aromatherapy, skin treatments, and related accessories. *402 W. Broadway (at Spring St.), SoHo, 212/219–9764. Subway: C, E to Spring St.*

11 *d-1*

PATRICIA FIELD

These are the raw materials for the downtown avant-garde look—nonsmudge matte liners, matte lipsticks and lip pencils, lip paint from Japan, and lots of glitter. Your most fabulous self will emerge during a full-service makeover—including eyebrow shaping, an eyelash application, and, if you dare, a visit to the one-of-a-kind custom wig salon. Even your mother won't recognize you. Note: the SoHo store is called Hotel Venus, but it's still the funky Pat Field that you know and crave. *10 E. 8th St. (near 5th Ave.), Greenwich Village, 212/254–1699. Subway: 6 to Astor Pl.*

11 *d-5*

382 W. Broadway (between Broome and Spring Sts.), SoHo, 212/966–4066. Subway: C, E to Spring St.

11 *e-1*

PERFUMANIA

The nationwide chain stocks hundreds of fragrances, from high-end designer scents to the more obscure. They promise an average discount of 70%. *755 Broadway (at 8th St.), Greenwich Village, 212/979–7674. Subway: N, R to 8th St.*

9 *d-6*

20 W. 34th St. (between 5th and 6th Aves.), Midtown West, 212/736–0414. Subway: B, D, F, N, Q, R, V, W to 34th St./Herald Sq.

9 *e-2*

782 Lexington Ave. (between 60th and 61st Sts.), Upper East Side, 212/750–2810. Subway: N, R, W, 4, 5, 6 to 59th St./Lexington Ave.

7 *b-7*

2321 Broadway (at 84th St.), Upper West Side, 212/595–8778, Subway: 1, 2 to 86th St.; other locations.

11 *e-2*

RICKY'S

A wall of brushes, stage makeup, rainbows of hair color, plastic containers from mini to maxi, a house makeup line—Mattesse—that bears a striking resemblance to M.A.C. and Bobbie Brown, and incredibly low prices make these stores a must stop for beauty mavens in the know. Plus, Halloween is so popular here they do it year-round. *718 Broadway (at Washington Pl.), Greenwich Village, 212/979–5232. Subway: N, R to 8th St.*

9 *c-3*

988 8th Ave. (at 58th St.), Midtown West, 212/957–8343. Subway: A, B, C, D, 1, 2 to 59th St./Columbus Circle.

11 *e-1*

44 E. 8th St. (at Greene St.), Greenwich Village, 212/254–5247. Subway: N, R to 8th St.

10 *d-1*

466 6th Ave. (between 11th and 12th Sts.), Greenwich Village, 212/924–3401. Subway: F, L, S to 14th St./6th Ave.

11 *e-5*

590 Broadway (between Houston and Prince Sts.), SoHo, 212/226–5552. Subway: N, R to Prince St.; and other locations.

11 *e-5*

SEPHORA

You'll feel like a kid in a candy store at this French import beauty emporium; the front has the dazzling jewel tone signature line of bath products, candles, and aromatherapy oils. In back, hip homespun makeup lines and scrumptious beauty imports from around the globe. Along the walls is an exhaustive collection of perfumes in alphabetical order. Dig in! *555 Broadway (between Prince and Spring Sts.), SoHo, 212/625–1309. Subway: N, R to Prince St.*

9 e-4

636 5th Ave. (between 50th and 51st Sts.), Midtown West, 212/245–1633. Subway: B, D, F, V to 47th–50th St./Rockefeller Ctr.; and other locations.

11 d-5

SHU UEMURA

One of the most popular Asian beauty lines, the store carries a nice selection of skin care products and makeup. Light simulators let you test how your color choices will look in office light or daylight. 121 Greene St. (between Prince and Houston Sts.), SoHo, 212/979–5500. Subway: N, R to Prince St.

9 e-2

TRISH MCEVOY

While you can buy the luxe makeup line bearing her name at top department stores, this is the only spot where intense one-on-one lessons with the master, or one of her personally trained staff, are available. Prices with McEvoy are incredibly steep, but the other makeup artists here are quite skilled as well. The price of a lesson ($200 and up) includes all makeup used on you; applications for special events are also available. 800A 5th Ave. (near 61st St.),

---

RUGGED GOOD LOOKS

Men are starting to get equal time at salons and spas throughout the city. Below are a few that go out of their way to make the boys feel at home.

Avon

Great massages and a men's locker room with super-intense multi-head showers.

Bliss

The macho locker rooms here come complete with beer and copies of Sports Illustrated and the Robb Report.

Origins

A full gym is adjacent to the Spa's locker room so you can combine a workout with some manly primping.

Peninsula Spa

Taking great pains to soothe their male clientele, the Spa introduced a men's facial which concentrates on such guy problems as razor burn and ingrown hairs.

Upper East Side, 212/758–7790. Subway: N, R, W to 5th Ave./59th St.

hair care & salons

Almost every high-end salon has a training night at least once a month, when haircuts and color are either greatly discounted or free. The catch is that a student cuts your hair, but the proceedings are highly supervised, and you never know who that student will be in three years.

Note that many salons are closed on Monday.

9 d-3

ANGELA COSMAI

Cosmai is the premier colorist in the city, dying the locks of socialites and starlets alike in her low-key salon in a Midtown brownstone. Using only plant-based dyes, Cosmai and her staff not only create completely natural and healthy looking color, but also fix a plethora of unfortunate coloring jobs. Other services available include precision haircuts and expert blowouts. All of this expertise does not come cheap, but training nights here are especially good. 16 W. 55th St. (between 5th and 6th Aves.), 2nd floor, Midtown West, 212/541–5820. Subway: F, N, R, Q, W to 57th St.

11 e-1

ASTOR PLACE BARBER STYLIST

Success story: a family-owned 1940s barbershop finds new life as the in place for the young and adventurous to have their tresses trimmed. Choose from the Guido, Detroit, Little Tony, Punk, Mohawk, James Dean, Fort Dix, Sparkle Cut, What-the-Hell, Spike, Spina di Pesce . . . . It's cheap and fun, but you may have to wait up to two hours on weekends. The street scene is interesting in itself. Astor Place still gives shaves, and now has an annex for perms, manicures, pedicures, facials, and all the rest. 2 Astor Pl. (near Broadway), East Village, 212/475–9854 or 212/475–9790. Subway: 6 to Astor Pl.

11 e-1

BUMBLE & BUMBLE

Beloved by stylists and stars alike, this hip, trend-setting salon has been creating new looks for more than 20 years. Cuts range from $75 to $150, and special deals abound: student cuts and coloring are offered on a regular basis, and dye jobs can go for as little as $20 on Mondays (call for times). *146 E. 56th St. (between Lexington and 3rd Aves.), Midtown East, 212/521–6500. Subway: N, R, W, 4, 5, 6 to 59th St./Lexington Ave.*

9 *e-3*

FREDERIC FEKKAI BEAUTÉ DE PROVENCE

A fashion-world darling, Fekkai now reigns in his own wonderful salon in the Chanel building, creating elegant, feminine looks in quiet private rooms. Clients include Cindy Crawford, Sigourney Weaver, and Kelly McGillis. *15 E. 57th St. (near Madison Ave.), Midtown East, 212/753–9500. Subway: N, R, W to 5th Ave./59th St.*

9 *d-3*

GARREN NEW YORK AT HENRI BENDEL

A fashion-world favorite—he made over Lisa Marie Presley for her Vogue cover shoot—Garren commands a huge celebrity clientele at his full-service salon (located at Henri Bendel). *712 5th Ave. (at 56th St.), Midtown West, 212/841–9400. Subway: N, R, W to 5th Ave./59th St.*

9 *b-1*

GEMAYEL SALON

Gemayel is the Upper West Side choice for fun, trendy cuts at reasonable prices, $75 for a wash, cut, and dry. *2030 Broadway (at 70th St.), Upper West Side, 212/787–5555. Subway: 1, 2, 3 to 72nd St.*

9 *b-1*

HAROLD MELVIN BEAUTY SALON

Specializing in African-American hair, Melvin has built quite a reputation among celebrities, and has done hair for magazine shoots and movie sets. *137 W. 72nd St. (between Broadway and Columbus Ave.), Upper West Side, 212/724–7700. Subway: 1, 2, 3 to 72nd St.*

9 *e-7*

JEAN LOUIS DAVID

Drop in here for the streamlined, quick-service approach. Designer cuts, styles, perms, and colors take less than an hour and are very reasonably priced, with a basic cut starting at $37. They don't make appointments, but you can wait for your favorite stylist if you want

an ongoing relationship. *303 Park Ave. S (at 23rd St.), Gramercy, 212/260–3920. Subway: 6 to 23rd St.*

9 *e-4*

367 Madison Ave. (at 46th St.), Midtown East, 212/808–9117. Subway: S, 4, 5, 6, 7 to 42nd St./Grand Central.

9 *d-4*

1180 6th Ave. (at 46th St.), Midtown West, 212/944–7389. Subway: B, D, F, V to 47th–50th Sts./Rockefeller Ctr.

9 *b-1*

2113 Broadway (at 73rd St.), Upper West Side, 212/873–1850. Subway: 1, 2, 3 to 72nd St.; other locations.

10 *e-7*

JOHN ALLAN'S

A respite for busy Wall Streeters, John Allan is a full-service salon for men only. Between haircuts and manicures, you can mess around with the pool table, drum set, and requisite humidor. *95 Trinity Pl. (at Thames St.), Lower Manhattan, 212/406–3000. Subway: 1, 2 to Wall St.*

9 *d-3*

JOHN BARRETT

Ensconced in the penthouse suite at Bergdorf Goodman, Barrett and his staff excel at precision cuts. Barrett makes a point of working on the floor, something other celebrity stylists do very little of—however, a meeting with the master needs to be booked at least a month in advance. *754 5th Ave. (at 58th St.), Midtown West, 212/872–2700. Subway: N, R, W to 5th Ave./59th St.*

11 *d-4*

JOHN DELARIA

This busy SoHo salon has three floors of stylists trained in every look from classic to au moment. Walk-ins are usually accommodated, and prices are reasonable. *433 W. Broadway (between Prince and Spring Sts.), SoHo, 212/925–4461. Subway: C, E to Spring St.*

11 *d-5*

JOHN MASTERS ORGANIC HAIRCARE

Masters and his colleagues specialize in color, using only plant- and vegetable-based dyes at this shoe-box downtown salon. *79 Sullivan St. (between Spring and Broome Sts.), SoHo, 212/343–9590. Subway: C, E to Spring St.*

9 *d-3*

LINDA TAM SALON

Once chosen for "Best Hair Coloring" by New York Press, Linda Tam is not cheap, but followers swear to a no-nonsense color job that won't fade after a few washes. *680 5th Ave. (between 53rd and 54th Sts.), Midtown West, 212/757–2555. Subway: E, V to 5th Ave./53rd St.*

9 *e-3*

LOUIS LICARI COLOR GROUP

For blended tone-on-tone coloring and a beautifully healthy, natural look, he's the tops—just ask Christie Brinkley, Ellen Barkin, or Jessica Lange. Ask also about training nights for huge discounts on cut or color. Come in for a free consultation weekdays 9–5. *693 5th Ave., 15–16th floors (between 54th and 55th Sts.), Midtown East, 212/758–2090. Subway: E, V to 5th Ave./53rd St.*

9 *c-8*

MARIO NICO

Velvet settees, marble floors, and gold mirrors help lend an air of elegance to this small salon in Chelsea. Nico himself is a lot like the clientele, fashionable and hip but without an attitude. Prices are quite reasonable—well, by New York standards, considering the surroundings and the level of expertise: Nico charges $125, and his stylists $80. *266 W. 22nd St. (between 8th and 9th Aves.), Chelsea, 212/727–8464. Subway: C, E to 23rd St.*

9 *e-2*

MARSHALL KIM

Kim is a favorite neighborhood barber with Upper East Siders. *788 Lexington Ave. (at 61st St.), Upper East Side, 212/486–2453. Subway: N, R, W, 4, 5, 6 to 59th St./Lexington Ave.*

9 *e-3*

ORIBE SALON LTD.

Now firmly ensconced behind Elizabeth Arden's red door, Oribe is booked months in advance. He's usually at photo shoots—you know, tending the models' tresses. This is the trendiest salon in town for individual, feminine-sexy looks like those of Kelly Klein, Darryl Hannah, and Linda Evangelista. *691 5th Ave. (at 54th St.), Midtown East, 212/319–3910. Subway: E, V to 5th Ave./53rd St.*

9 *e-3*

PIERRE MICHEL COIFFEUR

A longtime specialist in the treatment and styling of long hair, Pierre Michel is also a full-service beauty salon for both men and women. *131 E. 57th St. (between Park and Lexington Aves.), Upper East Side, 212/593–1460, 212/755–9500. Subway: N, R, W, 4, 5, 6 to 59th St./Lexington Ave.*

11 *a-1*

ROBERT KREE

This light, airy, open Greenwich Village salon gives great cuts that turn first-time clients into loyal devotees. It looks trendy, but there's no attitude. *375 Bleecker St. (between Charles and Perry Sts.), Greenwich Village, 212/989–9547. Subway: 1, 2 to Christopher St./Sheridan Sq.*

11 *c-4*

SPACE

The space makes the experience at this SoHo salon. The high ceilings and enormous windows fill the place with light, creating a serenity that's pervasive. Whether you've come for a simple cut, expert color, or a Brazilian bikini wax—for which beautician Ceia Creme is well known—you'll leave feeling pampered. *155 6th Ave. (at Spring St.), SoHo, 212/647–8588. Subway: C, E to Spring St.*

9 *c-8*

SUITE 303

Everything about this salon says cool—from its location in the notorious Chelsea Hotel, to its unmarked door, to its hip clientele of downtown rockers and models. Any of the stylists can give you a great cut, but only April can sculpt your eyebrows to perfection. *Chelsea Hotel, Room 303, 222 W. 23rd St. (between 7th and 8th Aves.), Chelsea, 212/633–1011. Subway: 1, 2, C, E to 23rd St.*

9 *e-3*

VIDAL SASSOON

The man who liberated hair now has 32 stylists and a helpful staff, providing cuts, color, and perms for both men and women. *730 5th Ave. (between 56th and 57th Sts.), Midtown West, 212/535–9200. Subway: N, R, W to 5th Ave./59th St.*

10 *d-1*

90 5th Ave. (at 15th St.), Flatiron District, 212/229–2200. Subway: L, N, Q, R, W, 4, 5, 6 to 14th St./Union Sq.

9 *d-3*

WARREN TRICOMI

Downtown style comes uptown in this fanciful full-service salon, with a regular clientele including many celebs who trust the flying blades of Edward "Scissorhands" Tricomi. *16 W. 57th St. (between 5th and 6th Aves.), Midtown West, 212/262–8899. Subway: N, R, W to 5th Ave./59th St.*

spas

9 *e-3*

AVON SALON & SPA

This is not your mother's Avon. Gone are the days of apricot lipstick and door-to-door sales. In their place is this slick spa that sports a waiting room as large as a hotel lobby and top-notch treatment rooms. Massages are delightful, facials are first class, and eyebrow guru Eliza is the best in the city—as you'll begin to discover when you try to get an appointment. Brad Johns, the king of blonde, oversees the hair salon. *Trump Tower, 725 5th Ave. (at 57th St.), 5th floor, Midtown East, 212/755–2866. Subway: N, R, W to 5th Ave./59th St.*

9 *e-4*

AWAY SPA

Your reward for traversing the frenetic lobby of the W Hotel is the quiet and elegant atmosphere of this New Age–style spa. Come with an open mind and try such unique treatments as the "yogassage" (45 minutes of yoga, 45 minutes of aromatherapy massage), a citrus-firming body polish (to get rid of cellulite using essential oils like lemon, juniper, and geranium), or the signature Javanese Lulur—a Far East treatment where you'll be massaged with rice, turmeric, and yogurt and leave feeling sensuously smooth. There's also a full menu of more traditional skin and body treatments. *W Hotel, 541 Lexington Ave. (at 49th St.), Midtown East, 212/407–2970. Subway: 6 to 51st St./Lexington Ave.; E, V to Lexington–3rd Aves./53rd St.*

11 *e-4*

BLISS SPA

Possibly the first spa that's as trendy as a nightclub—wasn't that Uma?—Bliss is so popular it can often take months to get an appointment here. What awaits when you finally make it in? Wine and cheese in the lounge area, oxygen facials,

dreamy pedicures, and first-rate massage. *568 Broadway (at Prince St.), SoHo, 212/219–8970. Subway: F, V to Broadway–Lafayette St.; N, R to Prince St.*

9 *e-3*

19 E. 57th St. (between 5th and Madison Aves.), 3rd floor, Midtown East, 212/219–8970. Subway: N, R, W to 5th Ave./59th St.

9 *e-3*

CHRISTINE VALMY

Renowned skin-care expert Christine Valmy helped American women discover skin care. Using Swiss fresh-cell therapy, she gives both men and women two-hour facials and offers post–plastic surgery care, makeup, and foot massage. A special pretheater package includes facial, manicure, shampoo, and blow-dry. Weekdays you can opt for a lower-price facial by a supervised student at the Valmy School for Aestheticians (212/581–1520 for appt.). *767 5th Ave. (at 58th St.), Midtown East, 212/752–0303. Subway: N, R, W to 5th Ave./59th St.*

9 *d-3*

101 W. 57th St. (between 6th and 7th Aves.), Midtown West, 212/581–9488. Subway: F, N, R, Q, W to 57th St.

9 *d-3*

DIANE YOUNG ANTI-AGING SALON

Come here for anti-aging skin care in a beautiful, serene setting. Young offers facial treatments, microdermabrasian, and waxing. To complete the assault against time, the salon also sells skin care and makeup products. *38 E. 57th St. (near Madison Ave.), Midtown East, 212/753–1200. Subway: N, R, W to 5th Ave./59th St.*

9 *d-3*

DORIT BAXTER

Facials, body scrubs and treatments, and a full-service salon are wrapped up in a convenient Midtown location. *47 W. 57th St. (between 5th and 6th Ave.), Midtown West, 212/371–4542. Subway: F, N, R, Q, W to 57th St.*

9 *e-2*

ELENA POCIU

Romanian-born Pociu runs a full-service skin-care salon, specializing in facials. Her masks are made on the premises. *815 5th Ave. (between 62nd and 63rd*

Sts.), Upper East Side, 212/754–9866. Subway: N, R, W to 5th Ave./59th St.

9 *e-3*
ELIZABETH ARDEN/ THE SALON

Just knock on the red door for head-to-toenail pampering in this Midtown mini-ispa. Expert facials and free makeup applications are among the many highlights. Treat yourself or a loved one to a Miracle Morning or a Main Chance Day: you get a spell in the sauna followed by massage, haircut and styling, facial, manicure and pedicure, eyebrow shaping, and makeup. *691 5th Ave. (near 54th St.) Midtown East, 212/546–0200. Subway: E, V to 5th Ave./53rd St.*

11 *d-4*
ERBE

A favorite with SoHo denizens, Erbe offers both facials and massages as well as an amazing line of Italian herb- and flower-based skin products. *196 Prince St. (near MacDougal St.), SoHo, 212/966–1445. Subway: N, R to Prince St.*

TWINKLE TOES

In a city where we often walk for miles on hard concrete just to get the subway, it's important to give your toes a little TLC. Treat your feet at one of the specialty pedicurists below (see Beauty, above, for addresses):

Avon
> *The peppermint massage cream here will make your toes tingle.*

Bliss
> *Your tootsies are soaked in hot paraffin wax for 90 minutes and come out feeling like a baby's bottom.*

Four Seasons
> *In a luxurious private room, an ace pedicurist massages and scrubs until feet are party perfect.*

J. Sisters
> *Brazilian style pedicures—a messy, slap-on polish job which is then meticulously cleaned up—can take as much as 1½ hours.*

Warren-Tricomi
> *A Moroccan souk acts as an oasis for your feet.*

---

9 *f-3*
ESTEE LAUDER

Reward yourself after a hard day of shopping at this spa nestled in the heart of Bloomingdale's. Facials are a specialty here, and are an exceptionally good value. Other top choices include a jet-lag treatment, sunless tanning, massage, and pedicure. *1000 3rd Ave. (at 59th St.), Midtown East, 212/705–2318. Subway: N, R, W, 4, 5, 6 to 59th St./Lexington Ave.*

9 *e-3*
FREDERIC FEKKAI BEAUTÉ DE PROVENCE

The top floors of celebrity stylist Fekkai's Provençal-style town house serve as a home to upscale services ranging from European facials to sunless tanning treatments. *15 E. 57th St. (near Madison Ave.), Midtown East, 212/753–9500. Subway: N, R, W to 5th Ave./59th St.*

9 *e-3*
GEORGETTE KLINGER SKIN CARE

Klinger's famously expert skin treatments include surface peeling, deep-pore cleansing, and scalp care for both women and men. Take advantage of the full-day, full-body "Full Day of Beauty," which includes a nine-step facial, therapeutic body massage, and spa lunch, among other delights. The only drawback is a hard sell of the product line. *501 Madison Ave. (near 52nd St.), Midtown East, 212/838–3200. Subway: E, V to 5th Ave./53rd St.*

7 *e-8*
978 Madison Ave. (near 77th St.), Upper East Side, 212/744–6900. Subway: 6 to 77th St.

9 *e-3*
JANET SARTIN

Come in for a consultation and get a product-and-treatment prescription from a world-famous skin expert—Sartin herself charges $400 for a two-hour pore-cleansing facial, though that's after a $1,000 first-time consultation and treatment. Services include crystal exfoliations, oxygen treatments, hair removal, massage, and facial toning. The staff is well trained and the clientele is high on the social registry. *500 Park Ave. (between 58th and 59th Sts.), Midtown East, 212/751–5858. Subway: N, R, W, 4, 5, 6 to 59th St./Lexington Ave.*

9 e-3

LIA SCHORR SKIN CARE

Every client's skin is analyzed prior to treatment, resulting in sensible care, especially for sensitive and acne-plagued skin. Services include seven types of facials, plus oxygen microdermabrasian, seaweed wraps and scrubs, and foot reflexology. Men are welcome, too. *686 Lexington Ave. (near 57th St.), Midtown East, 212/486–9670. Subway: N, R, W, 4, 5, 6 to 59th St./Lexington Ave.*

9 f-4

MARIO BADESCU SKIN CARE

Sadly, Mario is gone, but his expert analyses and natural-formula skin products for women and men still have a loyal following. Other options include manicures, pedicures, massage, waxing, and electrolysis. *320 E. 52nd St. (between 1st and 2nd Aves.), Midtown East, 212/758–1065. Subway: 6 to 51st St./Lexington Ave.; E, V to Lexington–3rd Aves./53rd St.*

11 c-8

MILLEFLEURS

Patterned after an Egyptian temple, Millefleurs offers herbal wraps, scrubs, massages, facials, reflexology, acupuncture, and even colonics in an incredible setting complete with incense and Middle Eastern music. *130 Franklin St. (at Varick St.), TriBeCa, 212/966–3656. Subway: 1, 2 to Franklin St.*

9 a-7

ORIGINS FEEL-GOOD SPA

Reward yourself after a hard Chelsea Piers workout at this somewhat cramped spa where massage, reflexology, facials, acupressure, and body treatments are administered using the popular line of Origins products. *The Sports Center, Pier 60, Chelsea Piers (12th Ave. and 23rd St.), Chelsea, 212/336–6780. Subway: C, E to 23rd St.*

9 d-3

PENINSULA SPA

Tucked in the Peninsula Hotel, this truly deluxe facility provides all the expected treatments plus a full gym, a salon, a pool, and an incredible sundeck with an equally incredible view. Facials here are some of the best in the city. *700 5th Ave. (at 55th St.), 21st floor, Midtown West,*

212/903–3910. Subway: N, R, W to 5th Ave./59th St.

9 e-2

PETER COPPOLA SALON

A solid hour of old-fashioned pampering, using hypo-allergenic Italian products, cleans your skin without the usual squeezing. *746 Madison Ave. (between 64th and 65th Sts.), Upper East Side, 212/988–9404. Subway: 6 to 68th St./Hunter College.*

11 e-5

SOHO SANCTUARY

An oasis of tranquillity in a hectic city, this women-only spa combines traditional facials and massages with soothing, Eastern-flavored music, meditation, and yoga to such a positive effect that you'll feel light-years away from the tension that sent you there. *119 Mercer St. (between Prince and Spring Sts.), SoHo, 212/334–5550. Subway: N, R to Prince St.*

11 c-7

ULA SKIN CARE SALON

In a discreet TriBeCa location, Ula offers nine different facials and seven different body treatments plus waxing, electrolysis, manicures, pedicures, and massages in a highly relaxing setting. *8 Harrison St. (between Hudson and Greenwich Sts.), TriBeCa, 212/343–2376. Subway: 1, 2 to Franklin St.*

11 c-3

YANA HERBAL BEAUTY SALON

Fans of Yana's have raved about her relaxing herbal facials for years. A little-known fact is that Yana also waxes, using the ancient Middle Eastern technique that involves sugar and honey instead of wax. *270 6th Ave. (between Houston and Bleecker Sts.), Greenwich Village, 212/254–6200. Subway: A, B, C, D, E, F, V to W. 4th St./Washington Sq.*

BOOKS

antiquarian

9 d-8

ACADEMY BOOK STORE

This shop specializes in art, literature, history, photography, the social sciences, and out-of-print books. *10 W. 18th St. (between 5th and 6th Aves.), Flatiron District, 212/242–4848. Subway: F, V to 14th St.*

7 b-7
GRYPHON BOOKSHOP
This general-interest used bookstore has a large selection of soft- and hard-cover titles on the arts and humanities, as well as a small but impressive cookbook collection. *2246 Broadway (between 80th and 81st Sts.), Upper West Side, 212/362–0706. Subway: 1, 2 to 79th St.*

9 d-3
J.N. BARTFIELD
Bartfield has one of the most impressive collections of leather-bound books, rare books, and first editions in the city, and will appraise collections. *30 W. 57th St. (between 5th and 6th Aves.), 3rd floor, Midtown West, 212/245–8890. Subway: F, N, R, Q, W to 57th St.; N, R, W to 5th Ave. Closed Sun.*

LARRY LAWRENCE RARE SPORTS
Larry specializes in rare sports books and ephemera. He no longer has an office but will make house calls to show you his wares. *212/362–8593. Open by appt. only.*

9 d-7
OLD PAPER ARCHIVE
It's as quaint as it sounds, and carries antique prints, children's books, movie posters, and antique prints on the performing arts. *122 W. 25th St. (between 6th and 7th Aves.), Chelsea, 212/645–3983. Subway: 1, 2, F, V to 23rd St.*

children

3 a-1
BANK STREET BOOKSTORE
Affiliated with Bank Street College, this cheerful store has two floors of children's books and fiction and nonfiction for every age. There are frequent store events geared towards both parents and children. *610 W. 112th St. (at Broadway), Morningside Heights, 212/678–1654. Subway: 1 to 110th St./Cathedral Pkwy.*

9 d-8
BOOKS OF WONDER
This is the largest collection of new, used, and out-of-print children's books in the city. The selection of 19th- and early 20th-century picture books and the knowledgeable staff are added draws. *16 W. 18th St. (between 5th and 6th Aves.), Flatiron District, 212/989–3270. Subway: F, V to 14th St.*

general

9 e-8
BARNES & NOBLE, INC.
Long a downtown institution, Barnes & Noble has stores all over the city. Some branches have specialties; the store that started it all, on lower 5th Avenue, has an excellent selection of textbooks, and the Lincoln Square branch keeps its eye on the performing arts. The Union Square branch is the grandest of them all. *33 E. 17th St. (between Broadway and Park Ave. So.), Flatiron District, 212/253–0810. Subway: 4, 5, 6, L, Q, W to 14th St./Union Sq. Multiple locations throughout the city.*

9 e-3
BORDERS BOOKS & MUSIC
What was once a cozy Ann Arbor independent is now very much a part of the New York landscape. The selections are vast and dense. As long as you've got stamina, it's hard to beat Borders for a healthy mixture of quantity and quality. *461 Park Ave. (at 57th St.), Midtown East, 212/980–6785. Subway: N, R, W, 4, 5, 6 to 59th St./Lexington Ave.*

9 f-6
550 2nd Ave. (at 32nd St.), Murray Hill, 212/685–3938. Subway: 6 to 33rd St.

7 e-6
THE CORNER BOOKSTORE
This welcoming Carnegie Hill shop specializes in literature, art, architecture, and children's books. They'll fill special orders in one day, search for out-of-print titles, and gift-wrap your choices for free. *1313 Madison Ave. (at 93rd St.), Upper East Side, 212/831–3554. Subway: 6 to 96th St.*

9 d-4

GOTHAM BOOK MART & GALLERY

This icon of the Gotham literary world is particularly strong in theater, general literature (especially fiction and classics), 20th-century first editions, film, and philosophy, and has the city's largest selection of poetry. The shop is planning to move to a new location soon. *41 W. 47th St. (between 5th and 6th Aves.), Midtown West, 212/719–4448. Subway: B, D, F, V to 47th–50th Sts./Rockefeller Ctr.*

9 e-1

LENOX HILL BOOKSTORE

Among the many strengths of this shop is the fabulous fiction section. They often have signed editions of hot new hardbacks, and book events are common. Entering this place feels like going into an old London bookstore. *1018 Lexington Ave. (between 72nd and 73rd Sts.), Upper East Side, 212/472–7170. Subway: 6 to 77th St.*

9 e-1

MADISON AVENUE BOOKSHOP

This bona fide neighborhood store bursts with books, which are stacked everywhere—even on the narrow winding staircase. You can find everything from coffee-table photo books to the latest biographies. *833 Madison Ave. (between 69th and 70th Sts.), Upper East Side, 212/535–6130. Subway: 6 to 68th St./Hunter College.*

9 e-5

POSMAN BOOKS

This independent brings quality fiction and non-fiction to midtown. The knowledgeable staff is always ready to recommend their favorites. *9 Grand Central Terminal (at Vanderbilt and 42nd Sts.), Midtown East, 212/983–1111, www.posmanbooks.com. Subway: 4, 5, 6, 7, S to 42nd St./Grand Central.*

9 d-3

RIZZOLI

Rizzoli is famously strong in art, architecture, photography, and university-press titles, but you can also pick up Italian books, translations, foreign magazines and newspapers, and classical recordings. *31 W. 57th St. (between 5th and 6th Aves.), Midtown West, 212/759–2424. Subway: F, N, R, Q, W to 57th St.*

10 f-1

ST. MARK'S BOOKSHOP

One of the hippest bookstores in the city, St. Mark's focuses on the humanities of the moment, including literature, poetry, drama, criticism, women's studies, contemporary theory, foreign titles, and small-press offerings. *31 3rd Ave. (at 9th St.), East Village, 212/260–7853. Subway: 6 to Astor Pl.*

11 e-1

SHAKESPEARE & COMPANY

Shakespeare has a good selection of fiction, poetry, philosophy, and general nonfiction titles. *716 Broadway (at Washington Pl.), Greenwich Village, 212/529–1330. Subway: N, R to 8th St.*

9 e-1

939 Lexington Ave. (between 68th and 69th Sts.), Upper East Side, 212/570–0201. Subway: 6 to 68th St./Hunter College.

9 f-8

137 E. 23rd St. (between Lexington and 3rd Aves.), Gramercy, 212/505–2021. Subway: 6 to 23rd St.

10 e-8

1 Whitehall St. (between Bridge and Stone Sts.), Lower Manhattan, 212/742–7025. Subway: 4, 5 to Bowling Green.

10 d-1

THREE LIVES & CO.

This lovely bookshop, named for the Gertrude Stein work and dedicated to literature, is a Village institution. Salon readings by noted authors are a special feature. *154 W. 10th St. (between 6th and 7th Aves.), Greenwich Village, 212/741–2069. Subway: 1, 2 to Christopher St./Sheridan Sq.*

second-hand

11 h-2

EAST VILLAGE BOOKS

A musty, crowded shop right in the heart of the East Village, this bookstore has mountains of yellowing paperbacks at good prices. *101 St. Mark's Pl. (between Ave. A and 1st Ave.), East Village, 212/477–8647. Subway: 6 to Astor Pl.*

11 *e-3*

MERCER STREET BOOKS & RECORDS

This bookstore has a high-quality selection of used contemporary fiction, classic literature, philosophy, and history, along with strong sections in math and science and a few tablefuls of old vinyl. *206 Mercer St. (between Houston and Bleecker Sts.), Greenwich Village, 212/505–8615. Subway: F, V to Broadway–Lafayette St.*

10 *e-1*

THE STRAND

America's largest secondhand bookstore has 8 mi of books (that's 2 million titles)—in appropriately dusty quarters in its main store on Broadway. Head downstairs for review copies of new books at 50% off. History, art, and Americana are particular strengths, both new and used. *828 Broadway (at 12th St.), Greenwich Village, 212/473–1452. Subway: L, N, Q, R, W, 4, 5, 6 to 14th St./Union Sq.*

10 *f-7*

95 Fulton St. (between William and Gold Sts.), Lower Manhattan, 212/732–6070. Subway: A, C, J, M, Z, 1, 2, 4, 5 to Fulton St./Broadway–Nassau.

special-interest

9 *b-1*

APPLAUSE THEATER & CINEMA BOOKS

This small, quaint store concentrates on theater and film books, with tons of scripts, history, and criticism. *211 W. 71st St. (between Broadway and West End Ave.), Upper West Side, 212/496–7511. Subway: 1, 2, 3 to 72nd St.*

10 *c-1*

BIOGRAPHY BOOKSHOP

True to its name, this appealing Greenwich Village shop specializes in biographies, diaries, and autobiographies as well as a good selection of fiction and children's books. *400 Bleecker St. (at 11th St.), Greenwich Village, 212/807–8655. Subway: 1, 2 to Christopher St./Sheridan Sq.*

10 *e-1*

CHESS BOOKSTORE

Yes, it's an entire store full of new and used books on chess, as well as chess-playing equipment. The store also offers weekly children's classes and lectures for adults. *80 E. 11th St. (at Broadway), Suite 334, Greenwich Village, 212/533–6381. Subway: 6 to Astor Pl. Closed Sun.*

9 *b-1*

CIVILIZED TRAVELLER

Everything you might need for a civilized trip, beginning with videos, maps, and guidebooks and moving on to irons, coffeemakers, security devices, converters, binoculars, games, and specialty luggage are sold here. *2003 Broadway (at 68th St.), Upper West Side, 212/875–0306. Subway: 1, 2 to 66th St./Lincoln Ctr.*

9 *e-2*

864 Lexington Ave. (at 65th St.), Upper East Side, 212/288–9190. Subway: 6 to 68th St./Hunter College; and other locations.

9 *e-6*

COMPLEAT STRATEGIST

The stock covers military and war games, science fiction, and fantasy. *11 E. 33rd St. (between 5th and Madison Aves.), Midtown East, 212/685–3880. Subway: 6 to 33rd St.*

9 *e-6*

THE COMPLETE TRAVELLER BOOKSTORE

Here, you can pick up guidebooks, maps, and dictionaries for the destination of your choice, or browse among the used and rare travel books, including yellowing travelogues and original WPA guides. It's worth a trip. *199 Madison Ave. (at 35th St.), Murray Hill, 212/685–9007. Subway: 6 to 33rd St.*

11 *a-2*

CREATIVE VISIONS

New York's first "out" erotic bookstore carries over 5,000 gay and lesbian titles, along with greetings cards and videos. *548 Hudson St. (between Perry and Charles Sts.), Greenwich Village, 212/645–7573. Subway: 1, 2 to Christopher St.*

9 *d-4*

DRAMA BOOK SHOP

The Drama Book Shop is well known for its extensive and well-organized selection of theater (especially criticism), film, and TV titles and published plays. You can also hunt down vocal scores and selections from Broadway musicals. *250 W. 40th St. (between Broadway and 8th Ave.), Midtown West, 212/944–0595. Subway: A, C, E to 42nd St./Port Authority.*

10 *d-1*

EAST-WEST BOOKS

True to its name, this spiritual book store carries titles on Buddhism, Christianity, and pretty much everything in between. *78 5th Ave. (between 13th and 14th Sts.), Flatiron District, 212/243–5994. Subway: F, V to 14th St.*

9 *c-7*

FASHION INSTITUTE OF TECHNOLOGY BOOKSTORE

The bookstore of the prestigious fashion college covers all aspects of the industry, including design and marketing. *227 W. 27th St., A-Building lobby (between 7th and 8th Aves.), Chelsea, 212/217–7717. Subway: 1, 2 to 28th St.*

9 *d-3*

HACKERS ART BOOKS

This large specialty shop has old, new, and rare titles on art, architecture, and crafts, and reprints of important art books. *45 W. 57th St. (between 5th and 6th Aves.), 5th floor, Midtown West, 212/688–7600. Subway: F, N, R, Q, W to 57th St.*

7 *e-6*

COOPER SHOP AT THE JEWISH MUSEUM

Selections cover all aspects of Jewish history and culture. *1109 5th Ave. (at 92nd St.), Upper East Side, 212/423–3211. Closed Sat. Subway: 6 to 96th St.*

9 *d-4*

KINOKUNIYA BOOKSTORE

Kinokuniya is one of the largest bookstore chains in Japan. These two floors of books in Japanese cover every topic imaginable; you'll also find books about Japan in English. *10 W. 49th St. (between 5th and 6th Aves.), Midtown West, 212/765–7766. Subway: B, D, F, V to 47th–50th Sts./Rockefeller Ctr.*

7 *e-6*

KITCHEN ARTS & LETTERS

For the cook in your life, Kitchen Arts & Letters has books from all over on food, cooking, and wine; food ephemera; original art and photography of food; and stationery items with a culinary theme. *1435 Lexington Ave. (near 93rd St.), Upper East Side, 212/876–5550. Closed Sun. Subway: 6 to 96th St.*

7 *b-3*

LABYRINTH BOOKS

This relative newcomer to New York's dwindling roster of independent bookshops (the store opened in 1997) carries academic titles, many from university presses, as well as scholarly remainders and fiction. *534 W. 112th St. (near Amsterdam Ave.), Morningside Heights, 212/865–1588. Subway: 1 to 110th St./Cathedral Pkwy.*

10 *d-1*

LECTORUM

This store specializes in Latin American fiction, nonfiction, and magazines, all in the original Spanish. *137 W. 14th St. (between 6th and 7th Aves.), Chelsea, 212/741–0220. Subway: 1, 2, 3 to 14th St.*

9 *d-4*

LIBRAIRIE DE FRANCE

An excellent source for French and Spanish books, this shop stocks new releases, dictionaries, cookbooks, mysteries, history, and social science titles, as well as literary fiction. *610 5th Ave. (in the Rockefeller Center Promenade), Midtown West, 212/581–8810. Subway: B, D, F, V to 47th–50th Sts./Rockefeller Ctr.*

9 *d-4*

MCGRAW-HILL BOOKSTORE

This shop specializes in business, engineering, and computer science titles from various publishers. It's located in the plaza of the McGraw-Hill Building in Rockefeller Center. *1221 6th Ave. (between 48th and 49th St., Ste. 383), Midtown West, 212/512–4100. Subway: B, D, F, V to 47th–50th Sts./Rockefeller Ctr.*

7 *e-6*

THE MILITARY BOOKMAN

Sure enough, the selection focuses on military, naval, and aviation history, including out-of-print and rare books. *29 E. 93rd St. (between 5th and Madison*

Aves.), Upper East Side, 212/348–1280.
Closed Sun.–Mon. Subway: 6 to 96th St.

9 d-7

MILLER'S

Miller's has been a leading source of equestrian books, riding apparel, and saddles for more than 100 years. *117 E. 24th St. (between Park and Lexington Aves.), Murray Hill, 212/673–1400. Subway: 6 to 23rd St. Closed Sun.*

9 f-2

MURDER INK

If you can't get enough of mystery and suspense novels, Murder Ink has them new, used, and out-of-print. *2486 Broadway (between 92nd and 93rd Sts.), Upper West Side, 212/362–8905. Subway: 1, 2, 3 to 96th St.*

9 d-3

MYSTERIOUS BOOKSHOP

New, used, and out-of-print murder, mystery, and mayhem are the selling points; the staff will also search for rare books. *129 W. 56th St. (between 6th and 7th Aves.), Midtown West, 212/765–0900. Closed Sun. Subway: F, N, R, Q, W to 57th St.*

9 e-5

NEW YORK ASTROLOGY CENTER

A complete line of astrology books is supplemented by titles on acupuncture and the healing arts. *370 Lexington Ave. (at 41st St.), Suite 416, Midtown East, 212/949–7211. Subway: S, 4, 5, 6, 7 to 42nd St./Grand Central. Closed Sat.–Sun.*

11 e-5

NEW YORK OPEN CENTER BOOKSHOP

The selection here includes holistic medicine, Eastern studies, health and nutrition, and meditation. *83 Spring St. (between Broadway and Crosby Sts.), SoHo, 212/219–2527. Subway: 6 to Spring St.*

11 a-2

OSCAR WILDE MEMORIAL BOOKSHOP

Specializing in gay and lesbian titles, this shop also sells stationery, cards, records, films, T-shirts, and jewelry. *15 Christopher St. (between 6th and 7th Aves.), Greenwich Village, 212/255–8097. Subway: 1, 2 to Christopher St./Sheridan Sq.*

10 d-1

PARTNERS & CRIME MYSTERY BOOKSELLERS

This downtown shop has new, used, and collectible books on crime, mystery, espionage, and the like, as well as frequent readings and signings. *44 Greenwich Ave. (between 6th and 7th Aves.), Greenwich Village, 212/243–0440. Subway: F, 1, 2, 3 to 14th St.*

10 e-3

PERIMETER BOOKS ON ARCHITECTURE

Perimeter's collection focuses on architecture and design. *21 Cleveland Pl. (near Spring St.), SoHo, 212/334–6559. Subway: 6 to Spring St.*

9 f-4

RAND MCNALLY: THE MAP & TRAVEL STORE

See Maps.

11 d-3

SCIENCE FICTION SHOP

This store carries science fiction, horror, and fantasy titles, including rare and used books. *214 Sullivan St. (between Bleecker and W. 3rd Sts.), Greenwich Village, 212/473–3010. Subway: A, B, C, D, E, F, V to W. 4th St./Washington Sq.*

11 g-2

SEE HEAR

This subterranean East Village shop carries tons of 'zines and hard-to-find magazines, along with books on anything from underground film to circus sideshows. *59 E. 7th St. (between 1st and 2nd Aves.), East Village, 212/505–9781. Subway: 6 to Astor Pl.*

9 e-4

URBAN CENTER BOOKS

Run by the Municipal Art Society, Urban Books specializes in architecture, urban design and planning, and historic preservation. It also has a top-notch section of books about New York. *457 Madison Ave. (near 51st St.), Midtown East, 212/935–3595. Closed Sun. Subway: 6 to 51st St.*

CHARITABLE CAUSES

There's a heavy concentration of thrift shops from 75th to 85th streets between 2nd and 3rd avenues; all offer secondhand and some new merchandise of varying quality. Patience can yield bargains, and the proceeds do go to charity. Caveat emptor: not all shops with "thrift" in their names are charity stores.

7 f-7
GODMOTHER'S LEAGUE THRIFT SHOP

It may be an old-fashioned thrift shop in an old tenement building, but the Upper East Side, thrift-shop-row location almost guarantees that you'll find treasures like a Gucci handbag for $45, a vintage Valentino coat for $250, or Manolo Blahnik shoes for $150, along with the usual thrift store bric-a-brac. The basement is full of furniture, the godmother's specialty. All profits go to the West End Children's Day Treatment Center and School. 1459 3rd Ave. (between 82nd and 83rd), Upper East Side, 212/988–2858. Subway: 4, 5, 6 to 86th St.

9 d-8
HOUSING WORKS THRIFT SHOP

The sleek Chelsea store seems more boutique than thrift shop, and donors like Todd Oldham, Isabella Rossellini, and Tommy Hilfiger keep it supplied in "gently worn" designer clothing and accessories as well as furniture and housewares. Proceeds of the sales go to homeless and at-risk men, women, and children living with HIV and AIDS in New York. Watch for the annual fall evening previews, when the new season's crop of clothing and furniture is put out on display. At the SoHo branch, snap up all the books you've been meaning to read—at ultra-cheap prices. 143 W. 17th St. (between 6th and 7th Aves.), Chelsea, 212/366–0820. Subway: 1, 2 to 18th St.

7 f-8
202 E. 77th St. (between 2nd and 3rd Aves.), Upper East Side, 212/772–8461. Subway: 6 to 77th St.

9 f-8
157 E. 23rd St. (between 3rd and Lexington Aves.), Murray Hill, 212/529–5955. Subway: 6 to 23rd St.

7 b-8
306 Columbus Ave. (between 74th and 75th), Upper West Side, 212/579–7566. Subway: 1, 2, 3 to 72nd St.

11 e-4
Used Book Cafe, 126 Crosby St. (between Houston and Prince Sts.), Soho, 212/334–3324. Subway: B, D, F, V Broadway/Lafayette, N, R to Prince St., 6 to Spring ST.

7 f-8
MEMORIAL SLOAN-KETTERING THRIFT SHOP

Known as the Tiffany's of thrift shops, this place has a decidedly boutique-y feel—and a whole room devoted to Armani, Hermès, Calvin Klein, Chanel, and other designers. All proceeds go to the hospital. 1440 3rd. Ave. (between 81st and 82nd Sts.), Upper East Side, 212/535–1250. Subway: 6 to 77th St.

7 f-8
OUT OF THE CLOSET: THE AIDS THRIFT SHOP

Stunning antiques, paintings, furniture, books, and designer clothing (Versace, Armani) fill this fundraising shop for AIDS groups, widely hailed as one of the best thrift shops in the city. 220 E. 81st St. (at 3rd Ave.), Upper East Side, 212/472–3573. Subway: 6 to 77th St.

9 b-5
SALVATION ARMY THRIFT STORE

The old standby of thrift shops has tons of junk, piles of Levi's, and the odd designer piece all crammed under one roof, along with books, furniture, plates, knick-knacks, and any other item that could be purged from a New York apartment. You know your dollars are going to good cause, though, no matter how hard you have to hunt to come up with a buried treasure. 536 W. 46 St. (between 10th and 11th Aves.), Midtown West, 212/664–8563. Subway: A, C, E to 42nd St./Port Authority.

9 f-8
220 E. 23rd St. (between 2nd and 3rd Aves.), Gramercy, 212/532–8115. Subway: 6 to 23rd St.

11 f-1
112 4th Ave. (between 11th and 12th Sts.), East Village, 212/873–2741. Subway: L, Q, R, W, 4, 5, 6 to 14th St./Union Sq.

9 c-8
208 8th Ave. (between 20th and 21st Sts.), Chelsea, 212/929–5214. Subway: E to 23rd St.; and other locations.

7 *f-7*

SPENCE-CHAPIN THRIFT SHOP

One of the big wigs of the Upper East Side thrift shop scene, Spence-Chapin has everything from a Chinese abacus to a plaster bust of Zeus—not to mention racks of Armani, Ungaro, and Bill Blass suits, wonderful Chanels and Versace couture, and deals like a Buggatelli ring for $400 instead of $1000, or a $600 Missoni sweater for $90. Donors have included a Colgate heir and Jackie O's press secretary, and the three dressing rooms count among the non-thrift-shop-like amenities. All profits go to Spence-Chapin Services to Families and Children. *1473 3rd Ave. (between 83rd and 84th Sts.), Upper East Side, 212/737–8448. Subway: 4, 5, 6 to 86th St.*

7 *f-5*

1850 2nd Ave. (between 95th and 96th Sts.), Upper East Side, 212/426–7643. Subway: 6 to 96th St.

9 *e-2*

THE WOMAN'S EXCHANGE

Sixty percent of the sale price of each hand-crafted item here goes to the con-signor, who is generally a craftsperson in need. Wares include hand-smocked clothing for children, furniture, sta-tionery, sweaters, toys, quilts, home-made jams, and chocolates. *149 E. 60th St. (between Lexington and 3rd Aves.), Upper East Side, 212/753–2330. Closed Sat. mid-June–Labor Day. Closed Sun. Subway: N, R, W, 4, 5, 6 to 59th St./Lex-ington Ave.*

CLOTHING & SHOES FOR CHILDREN

7 *e-7*

AU CHAT BOTTE

Besides little-princess party dresses, this store has delicate, snowy layettes, fine imported clothing from Europe (Majil, Simonetta, PNC), and an array of cra-dles, linens, highchairs, bassinets, and everything else a cosmopolitan baby could need. *1192 Madison Ave. (at E. 87th St.), Upper East Side, 212/722–6474. Subway: 4, 5, 6 to 86th St.*

9 *e-3*

BABY GAP

Granted, this is part of the leave-no-mall-untouched chain, but this branch lives up to its location with an exclusive, luxury line of cashmere, silk, leather, and velvet baby clothes. You can count on the other locations (over 20 and count-ing) for the regular cotton standards. *680 5th Ave. (at 54th St.), Midtown West, 212/977–7023. Subway: N, R, W to 5th Ave./59th St.*

7 *e-6*

BONPOINT

The sophistication in this Parisian label lies in the beautiful designs and impec-cable workmanship—jewel-tone cotton-velvet jumpers, linen shifts threaded with velvet ribbon, hand-embroidered sleepwear, and pristine layettes. *1269 Madison Ave. (at 91st St.), Upper East Side, 212/722–7720. Subway: 4, 5, 6 to 86th St.*

9 *e-1*

811 Madison Ave. (at E. 68th St.), Upper East Side, 212/879–0900. Subway: 6 to 68th St./Hunter College.

10 *d-5*

BU & THE DUCK

This is the place to find unique, vintage-inspired children's clothing like a 1930s-style overall, a Little Rascals–style roll-neck sweater, a Victorian-style cro-cheted cardigan, or 1920s- and 1930s-style cotton embroidery dresses—all designed by the owner, Susan Lane. Classic Italian leather school shoes, vin-tage furniture (cradles, bassinets), and handmade toys add to the old-fashioned feel. *106 Franklin St. (at Church St.), TriBeCa, 212/431–9226. Subway: 1, 2 to Franklin St.*

11 *e-6*

CALYPSO ENFANT & BEBE

You may find yourself dressing vicari-ously through your children at this off-shoot of Christiane Celle's hugely popular and island-y Calypso chain. Kids will look photo-ready in these colorful sailor-stripe tops, plaid schoolgirl jumpers, and sophisticated party dresses. *426 Broome St. (between Lafayette and Crosby Sts.), SoHo, 212/966–3234. Subway: 6 to Spring St.*

7 *e-6*

CATIMINI

These detailed, elaborate French clothes will lend your child a cosmopolitan air. Every collection has a theme, whether it's the kangaroo, rabbit, dog, or another animal popping up in the socks, cardigans, and mini-berets. *1284–86 Madison Ave. (between E. 91st and E. 92nd Sts.), Upper East Side, 212/987–0688. Subway: 6 to 96th St.*

11 g-3
CREMEBEBE
This tiny East Village shop is made up of cheerful popsicle colors, baby caps hanging in a line above the counter, racks of vintage denim, and sweet little decorated Ts. The bright yellow banner with the rounded pink baby on front makes it hard to miss. *168 2nd Ave. (between 3rd and 4th Sts.), East Village, 212/979–6848. Subway: 6 to Bleecker St.*

7 b-8
GREENSTONES
Catering to junior yuppies, these stores have a particularly good selection of sweaters and sportswear, plus some colorfully flowered jumpers and a huge selection of hats. Brands include Naf Naf, Catimini, IKKS, Jean Bourget, and Kenzo. *442 Columbus Ave. (between 81st and 82nd Sts.), Upper West Side, 212/979–6848. Subway: 1, 2 to 79th St.*

7 e-7
1184 Madison Ave. (between 86th and 87th Sts.), Upper East Side, 212/427–1665. Subway: 4, 5, 6 to 86th St.

11 e-1
IBIZA KIDZ
This children's boutique attracts the hippest celebrity parents with its range of European clothing—satiny, puffy Asian-theme Kenzo coats, luxurious Malina washable silk separates, funky Zutano leggings—and its collection of ethereal, multi-colored wings, wands, and tutus. Brands like IKKS, Portofino, and Petit Bateau round out the eclectic mix. Check out the shoes and toys at the store down the street (at 56 University Place). *42 University Pl. (between 9th and 10th Sts.), Greenwich Village, 212/533–4614. Subway: N, R to 8th St.*

7 e-7
INFINITY
Mothers gossip near the dressing rooms as their daughters try on slinky Les Tout Petits dresses, low-slung Juicy and Miss Sixty jeans, and Autumn Cashmere sweaters—and snap up the latest hair accessories at the counter. *1116*

Madison Ave. (at E. 83rd St.), Upper East Side, 212/517–4232. Subway: 4, 5, 6 to 86th St.

9 e-2
JACADI
The classic French clothes here, such as toggle coats and appliqued sweaters, evoke Madeline's "two straight lines." This is delicate, detailed clothing for gleaming boys and girls. *787 Madison Ave. (at E. 67th St.), Upper East Side, 212/535–3200. Subway: 6 to 68th St./Hunter College.*

7 e-6
1281 Madison Ave. (at E. 91st St.), Upper East Side, 212/369–1616. Subway: 4, 5, 6 to 86th St.

11 e-5
JULIAN & SARA
This small SoHo boutique specializes in imported French and Italian clothing for boys and girls. Pink and orange Indonesian-style Kenzo prints; black, red, and white checks from Mirtillo; pretty poppy-print dresses from Monalisa; matching sets from Jean Bourget—it's like an international fashion show for kids. *103 Mercer St. (between Spring and Prince Sts.), SoHo, 212/226–1989. Subway: N, R to Prince St.*

9 e-2
LA PETITE ETOILE
These European imports might cost as much as dinner at one of the neighboring French bistros, but they are unique and very well made. Brands include Sonia Rykiel, Cacharel, and Petit Bateau. *746 Madison Ave. (between 64th and 65th Sts.), Upper East Side, 212/744–0975. Subway: 6 to 68th St./Hunter College.*

11 e-5
LILLIPUT
You'll find retro items such as pint-size jeans with prints or dye on the bottom and Dick Tracy raincoats, as well as Curious George T-shirts and toys, leather motorcycle jackets ($250 and up), leather pants, bedding, accessories, and collectibles. Brands include Lili Gaufrette, Charabia, Diesel, and Paul Smith. Insect-, animal-, and fireman-covered raingear abounds. *240 Lafayette St. (between Prince and Spring Sts.), SoHo, 212/965–9201. Subway: N, R to Prince St.*

11 *e-5*

265 Lafayette St. (between Prince and Spring Sts.), SoHo, 212/965–9567. Subway: 6 to Spring St.

7 *e-7*

LITTLE ERIC

Hip adult styles—loafers with silver bits, velvet slippers, and brogues—inspire the children's shoes here. Prices can approach grown-up levels, too. 1118 Madison Ave. (at E. 83rd St.), Upper East Side, 212/717–1513. Subway: 4, 5, 6 to 86th St.

9 *d-6*

MACY'S

They do have the biggest children's floor in the world, so you're pretty much guaranteed to find something here if you don't mind maneuvering through the crowds. You'll find tons of shoes, christening gowns, layette items, and every other type of clothing, and most major brands. 155 W. 34th St. (Herald Sq.), Midtown West, 212/695–4400. Subway: B, D, F, S, W to 34th St./Herald Sq.

7 *b-7*

MORRIS BROS.

This gold mine of boys' and girls' active wear is brimming with Northface outerwear, mesh shorts, Quiksilver swim trunks, and stacks of Levi's. 2322 Broadway (at W. 84th St.), Upper West Side, 212/724–9000. Subway: 1, 2 to 86th St.

9 *e-1*

OILILY

Stylized flowers, stripes, animal shapes, and embroidered spells splash across the brightly colored play and school clothes sold at this Dutch shop, where a different theme and storyline livens up the designs every season. Most recently, you could find princes, princesses, wands, sorcerers, and frogs giving a magical bent to the little flared jeans and other pieces. 870 Madison Ave. (between 70th and 71st Sts.), Upper East Side, 212/628–0100. Subway: 6 to 68th St./Hunter College.

9 *e-1*

PRINCE & PRINCESS

Expect to pay in the $200 range for an Italian merino wool knit onesie or a silk, handsmocked dress at this very fancy uptown children's boutique. Everything is hand-picked by the owner, and often

is one-of-a-kind. 33 E. 68th St. (between Madison and Park Aves.), Upper East Side, 212/879–8989. Subway: 6 to 68th St./Hunter College.

7 *b-7*

SHOOFLY

Children's shoes and accessories range from Mary Janes and wing tips to hats, socks, tights, and jewelry. 465 Amsterdam Ave. (between W. 82nd and W. 83rd Sts.), Upper East Side, 212/580–4390. Subway: 1, 2 to 86th St.

10 *d-5*

42 Hudson St. (between Thomas and Duane Sts.), TriBeCa, 212/406–3270. Subway: 1, 2 to Franklin St.

9 *e-8*

SPACE KIDDETS

The funky (Elvis-print rompers) mixes with the tried-and-true (fringed cowboy and cowgirl outfits) at this casual, trend-setting store. Offerings include Wizard-of-Oz–type sequined shoes by Coastal Projections, plastic sushi-covered bibs, and collectible, kitschy kids toys from the '70s and '80s (think Japanese Astroboy). 46 E. 21st St. (between Broadway and Park Ave.), Gramercy, 212/420–9878. Subway: 6 to 23rd St.

9 *f-2*

SPRING FLOWERS

Fancy European clothing and shoes for uptown kids, from brands like Sonia Rykiel, Joan Calabrese, and Cacharel. The 3rd Avenue location has an extensive layette selection as well. 1050 3rd Ave. (at 62nd St.), Upper East Side, 212/758–2669. Subway: N, R, W, 4, 5, 6 to 59th St./Lexington Ave.

9 *e-1*

905 Madison Ave. (at 72nd St.), Upper East Side, 212/717–8182. Subway: 6 to 68th St./Hunter College.

11 *c-4*

STORK CLUB

This little store is geared for comfort, not sophistication—though a smattering of sequins here and there on the tiny T's steps up the kiddy glamour quotient. Chenille sweaters, painters' pants, and overalls share space with vintage toys and wagons. 142 Sullivan St. (between Prince and W. Houston Sts.), SoHo, 212/505–1927. Subway: N, R to Prince St.

11 g-2

TIGERS, TUTU'S & TOES

Stuffed and striped jungle animals, rows of sparkley tutus, and a wide variety of shoes (Aster, Elefanten, Keds) explain the name of this little downtown shop, while designs from Zutano and Petit Bateau and a selection of toys add more spice to the mix. *128 2nd Ave. (between St. Mark's and 7th St.), East Village, 212/228–7990. Subway: N, R to 8th St.; 6 to Astor Pl.*

9 b-1

Z'BABY COMPANY

Fun clothes such as Suss Design chenille sweaters are a specialty here. You can also find Charabia faux suede pants and tweed skirts, or, if you're early enough, a sweet Lili Gaufrette teddy bear turtleneck (this line sells out even before it hits the store). In 2001 the funky Z'Girl opened, too, at 976 Lexington (at 71st St.). *100 W. 72nd St. (at Columbus Ave.), Upper West Side, 212/579–2229. Subway: 1, 2, 3 to 72nd St.*

9 e-1

996 Lexington Ave. (at E. 72nd St.), Upper East Side, 212/472–2229. Subway: 6 to 68th St./Hunter College.

CLOTHING FOR MEN/GENERAL

classic & conservative

9 d-8

BANANA REPUBLIC

BR's come a long way since first opening as a dorky pseudo-safari outfitter in the mid-'80s. Since reinventing themselves as purveyors of casual urban chic, they've been on an unending quest to make cotton sexy. In that spirit, and one of remaining vaguely trendy, nearly everything these days is ribbed, fitted, and v-necked. They still retain a lovely selection of classic dress shirts, underwear, khakis, and semi-dressy shoes. *Menswear only: 655 5th Ave. (at 52nd St.), Midtown East, 212/974–2350. Subway: E, V to 5th Ave./53rd St.*

9 e-4

89 5th Ave. (at 18th St.), Flatiron District, 212/366–4630. Subway: F, V to 14th St.; Q, W to 23rd St.

7 e-7

1136 Madison Ave. (at 84th St.), Upper East Side, 212/570–2465. Subway: 4, 5, 6 to 86th St.; and other locations.

9 e-4

BRIONI

Elegant Italian men's clothing, featuring sumptuous fabrics and classic European styling and cut, sells for appropriately high prices at this luxurious, inviting boutique. Suits can be made to measure. *55 E. 52nd St. (between Madison and Park Aves.), Midtown East, 212/355–1940. Subway: E, V to 5th Ave./53rd St.*

9 e-3

57 E. 57th St. (between Madison and Park Aves.), Upper East Side, 212/376–5777. Subway: N, R, W, 4, 5, 6 to 59th St./Lexington Ave.

9 d-6

BROOKS BROTHERS

Since 1818 they've stood above and beyond fashion as the makers of the finest classic suit money can buy. But these days that isn't enough. With so many imitators nipping at their heels and their profits, Brooks Brothers sullied their dignified, discreet image in the early '90s by coming up with some bizarre Euro designs in an attempt to update and hold their market share. When it didn't work they scaled back to what they always did best, gray-wool sack suits, navy blazers, seersucker, repp ties, formal wear, and of course the original, glorious, 5-trillion thread count cotton dress shirt, tailored to perfection. The difference now is that they house it all in a huge, glitzy new storefront on 5th Avenue and have hired a new model (in his 20s) for their advertising: a kinder, gentler WASP. *666 5th Ave. (at 52nd St.), Midtown West, 212/261–9440. Subway: E, V to 5th Ave./53rd St.*

9 d-5

346 Madison Ave. (at 44th St.), Midtown East, 212/682–8800. Subway: S, 4, 5, 6, 7 to 42nd St./Grand Central.

9 b-8

CAMOUFLAGE

These Chelsea specialty shops feature classic, American-made menswear with an upbeat, imaginative feel, plus more-casual threads at No. 139. Don't miss the elaborate selection of ties. *139–141 8th Ave. (at 17th St.), Chelsea, 212/741–*

9118 or 212/691–1750. Subway: A, C, E, L to 14th St./8th Ave.

9 e-1

DAVID CENCI

This dignified shop is a handsome setting for an expensive but outstanding selection of impeccably tailored classics, showcasing wonderful fabrics in everything from suits and sportswear to coats and formal wear. 801 Madison Ave. (near 67th St.), Upper East Side, 212/628–5910. Closed Sun. Subway: 6 to 68th St./Hunter College.

9 e-3

FAÇONNABLE

A limber, sporty, Mediterranean mood dominates this unimposing two-story shop in the middle of Manhattan's poshest shopping strip. The clothes are simple, French interpretations of American classics: button-down check shirts, khakis, windbreakers, lightweight cotton sweaters, fun-in-the-sun accessories, colorful ties, and conservatively tailored suits and separates. Frenchmen can't get enough of this stuff; it combines the European flair for relaxed elegance with durable fabrics that can wear several hats. Perfect threads for a weekend jaunt to Sag Harbor, or a late weekday lunch at Balthazar. 689 5th Ave. (at 54th St.), Midtown East, 212/319–0111. Subway: E, V to 5th Ave./53rd St.

9 e-2

GIORGIO ARMANI

Armani's is filled with muted tones and inviting fabrics that make you want to whisper. The clothes are reverentially displayed, from the Black Label couture (up to five figures) to the shoes and sportswear. Who else could make a svelte ski jacket? It's funky, but certainly not excessive, and it's hard to beat for high-quality, supremely reserved, and ever-so-inhabitable styles for everyone from lawyers to Indian chiefs with a thing for beige. 760 Madison Ave. (between 65th and 66th Sts.), Upper East Side, 212/988–9191. Subway: 6 to 68th St./Hunter College.

9 e-2

HERMÈS

Madison Avenue is home to some of the most exclusive boutiques this side of the Rive Gauche, but the French import that has made the biggest splash is this longtime French saddle-maker and purveyor of ultrafine silk prints—a newcomer to the Avenue after leaving its 57th Street location. Any fashionable man will tell you that if you have $1,000 to spend on your whole ensemble, this is the place to buy that tie that you'll pass down to your grandson. The average price for a whimsical bridle-tack print? $120. Also on the block are Hermès suits, jackets, leather goods, and, of course, saddles. Don't forget to save the boxes! They're the best in retailing, and their signature color is now commonly known as "Hermès Orange." 691 Madison Ave. (at 62nd St.), Upper East Side, 212/751–3181. Subway: N, R, W, 4, 5, 6 to 59th St./Lexington Ave.

9 d-8

J. CREW

The best thing about the catalog was always the models, and they don't sell them at the store. Since its heyday 10 years ago, J. Crew has retrenched into the pale of modern preppiedom, not conservative enough to be fetishy, not flashy enough to be interesting. Go for the underwear, if it's on sale. The 5th Avenue store is one of the few retailers to feature the menswear front and center (the ladies have to climb those stairs to find what they're looking for). 91 5th Ave. (between 16th and 17th Sts.), Chelsea, 212/255–4848. Subway: F, V to 14th St.; Q, W to 23rd St.

10 f-7

99 Prince St. (between Mercer and Greene Sts.), SoHo, 212/966–2739. Subway: N, R to Prince St.

11 e-4

203 Front St. (South Street Seaport), Lower Manhattan, 212/385–3500. Subway: A, C, J, M, Z, 1, 2, 4, 5 to Fulton St./Broadway–Nassau; and other locations.

9 e-5

J. PRESS

It's been a hundred years since this store opened its doors in New Haven, Connecticut, ready to serve the basic sartorial needs of Yalies. In New York the stock has gone through precious few changes since the '60s—lapels and ties have gotten wider, maybe a few more belts have been added to the mix, but Press still delivers that natural-shoulder, hyperpreppy, button-down look for new generations determined to perpetuate Ivy League style (even if most people at the Ivies have moved on). If you've just gotten into Skull and Bones, this is where you go to buy your club tie. *7 E. 44th St. (near 5th Ave.), Midtown East, 212/687–7642. Closed Sun. Subway: S, 4, 5, 6, 7 to 42nd St./Grand Central.*

9 e-5
PAUL STUART

The mood here is natty, dashing, conservative but unstuffy, with an emphasis on variety where it counts; hence the tiny shoe section adjacent to the largest selection of good ties in the city (including more bows and knits than you've ever seen under a single glass display). Men who buy here spend huge amounts on a few choice items, don't noodle with the basics, and know that this is the place to come for, bar none, the best fedora in the Big Apple. Sales do happen, but they seem to be advertised by ESP; those who benefit are those who drop in often. *Madison Ave. (at 45th St.), Midtown East, 212/682–0320. Closed Sun. Subway: S, 4, 5, 6, 7 to 42nd St./Grand Central.*

9 e-1
POLO/RALPH LAUREN/
POLO SPORT

Ah, what a pompous paean to the vanished days of merrie olde England, all jammed, at the flagship store on Madison Avenue, into the Rhinelander Mansion amid more mahogany and green baize than anyone should ever see in one place. (The SoHo store achieves a certain *je ne sais quoi* country look.) Trimmings include dog prints, and plenty of them; images of bluebloods on horseback in red hunting jackets; weathered leather; and scads of clean-cut, impeccably bronze employees, buzzing around attending to every imaginable (or imagined) need. What Bronx-born Lauren has done is out-WASP those WASPs whose casual, hale-and-hearty, outdoorsman style inspired his designs. Frugality, however, is not one of the things he has borrowed from the Old Newport crowd: everything he sells is of obsessively high quality, maybe too high if you're not sure you need flannels designed for Arctic conditions or herringbone tweeds that weigh more than the average beagle. The khakis, signature polo shirts, shoes, sport coats, and other preppy staples are all here, but so is Lauren's Purple Label line of English suits. *867 Madison Ave. (at 72nd St.), Upper East Side, 212/606–2100. Closed Sun. Subway: 6 to 68th St./Hunter College.*

11 d-5
379 W. Broadway (between Spring and Broome Sts.), SoHo, 212/625–1660. Subway: E to Spring St.

9 e-1
888 Madison Ave. (at 72nd St.), Upper East Side, 212/434–8000. Subway: 6 to 68th St./Hunter College.

9 e-1
YVES SAINT LAURENT
RIVE GAUCHE FOR MEN

Saint Laurent's high-priced high fashion is worn by almost no one. Cowards. There are few other places in town to obtain a correctly cut, side-vented navy blazer, a Parisian standby. *859 Madison Ave. (between 70th and 71st Sts.), Upper East Side, 212/517–7400. Closed Sun. Subway: 6 to 68th St./Hunter College.*

contemporary & casual

10 f-7
ABERCROMBIE & FITCH

Wholesome and urbanely rugged (lots of plaid, woolly sweaters, flannel shirts), this chain tweaks its apple-pie image by finding excuses to show nude young men in its print ads. It also has the audacity to make a point of not producing any all-black clothes. *110 Water St. (at Fulton St.), Lower Manhattan, 212/809–9000. Subway: A, C, J, M, Z, 1, 2, 4, 5 to Fulton St./Broadway–Nassau.*

11 e-4
AGNÈS B. HOMME

Taking its cue from the early 1960s, this medium-size SoHo shop—bedecked with old French New Wave cinema posters and such baubles as postcards of *Psycho*'s Tony Perkins grinning in blue gingham and tweed—is perhaps the finest example anywhere of the Parisian take on American Rat Pack style. Suits, stacks of exquisite shirts, leather porkpie chapeaux (for that Dean Martin snap), dozens of ties no wider than 2 inches, leather car coats, striped boatsman T-shirts, and an assortment of witty accessories make Agnès B. Homme a must-stop for any cat infatuated with the Sands Hotel heyday of Old Blue Eyes or who simply wants to affect a chic Parisian style at its casual best. *79 Greene St. (at Spring St.), SoHo, 212/431–4339. Subway: 6 to Spring St.*

11 e-4
A.P.C.

This store resembles a cross between an American barn and a French farmhouse, yet the clothes are anything but country. Anything but cheap, either. The style tends to be nerdish urban slacker, drawing heavily on the aesthetic of thrift-store finds from the '70s: fuzzy wool sweaters, in colors such as aqua and avocado; narrow-wale corduroy jeans; velvet jackets with trousers to match, in chocolate; white shirts. All very Beck, circa 1996. It's not for everybody, but A.P.C. can generally be counted on for comfortable, unforced threads that mine current fringe trends in a high-quality manner (no one really wants to wear some moth-eaten mohair cardigan from Cheap Jack's, anyway). *131 Mercer St. (between Prince and Spring Sts.), SoHo, 212/966–9685. Subway: 6 to Spring St.; N, R to Prince St.*

11 e-4
A/X (ARMANI EXCHANGE)

Perhaps a bit more Euro than absolutely necessary, A/X is nevertheless a commendable distillation of the Milanese Master's easy, fluid, and in this case even colorful sportswear designs, meant to compete with The Gap and J. Crew. "A/X" is meant to recall the buy-everything U.S. Army "P/X" (Post Exchange) of the Gomer Pyle era; truth is, if you don't mind shelling out some heavy dollars for a shirt (say, $100), there's scant reason to shop anywhere else, so comprehensive is the A/X selection. The stuff—jeans, jackets, outerwear, T-shirts, and so on—is superbly made, beautifully textured and styled, and comfortable. Some of the sales are succulent. *568 Broadway (between Houston and Prince Sts.), SoHo, 212/431–6000. Subway: N, R to Prince St.; F, V to Broadway–Lafayette St.*

9 d-3
645 5th Avenue (at 57th St.), Midtown West, 212/980–3037. Subway: N, R to 59th St.

11 e-4
BEAU BRUMMEL

Here's where you can find the shiny silk ties Regis Philbin wears on "Who Wants to Be a Millionaire?" (they come in a huge array of shimmery colors), along with suits from Hugo Boss, Cerruti 1881, and Byblos. The whole vibe here is overly flashy, more discount than upscale—despite the steep prices. *421 W. Broadway (between Prince and Spring Sts.), SoHo, 212/219–2666. Subway: C, E to Spring St.*

9 e-2
CALVIN KLEIN

The boutique-as-art gallery metaphor flourishes at this multifloor architectural promo for America's prime minimalist. You name it, CK's got it: sportswear, the drapey suits, the textured, monochrome ties, socks, and, of course, scads of that underwear. Unadorned suits, overcoats, dresses, and blouses stream by in a wash of cream, beige, olive, and, of course, black. (For the color-starved, there are occasional punctuation pieces in, say, aqua or chartreuse.) Upstairs on the mezzanine are women's bathing suits, lingerie, and evening wear—though more than one customer has been overheard mistaking the long, thin-strap silk dresses for nightgowns. The neighboring evening accessories should have been a tip-off; the tiny, boxlike purses are hopelessly refined. The place is a real Madison Avenue scene on a Saturday afternoon in early spring or fall. *654 Madison Ave. (at 60th St.), Upper East Side, 212/292–9000. Subway: N, R, W, 4, 5, 6 to 59th St./Lexington Ave.*

9 e-8
CLUB MONACO

This mini-chain has caused a sensation with its sleek, trendy, reasonably priced sportswear. Known to some as the Gay Gap, it provides the same kind of no-brainer one stop shopping but in a sexier, more body-conscious, Prada knock-off way. Clingy sweaters, filmy shirts, bulky jeans, and skinny trousers are all the rage, if you've got the body for it. *160 5th Ave. (at 21st St.), 212/352–0936. Subway: L, N, Q, R, W, 4, 5, 6 to 14th St./Union Sq.*

7 b-7
2376 Broadway (at 87th St.), Upper West Side, 212/579–2587. Subway: 1, 2 to 86th St.

10 f-3
510 Broadway (at Spring St.), SoHo, 212/ 941–1511. Subway: F, V to Broadway–Lafayette St.; and other locations.

11 h-4
DDC LAB

High-tech futuristic fashions for downtown hipsters include Teflon-coated jackets, Rogan jeans, and stretch leather pants. Clothes are made from Tyvek, Lycra, Kevlar, Nomex, and other similarly named fabrics. *180 Orchard St. (between Houston and Stanton), Lower East Side, 212/375–1647. Subway: F, J, M, Z to Delancey St./Essex St.*

9 *e-8*
EMPORIO ARMANI
Against a mellow Milanese backdrop (blond wood, stainless steel, pale-cream lampshades), the oft-imitated but rarely equaled Italian master showcases his "mid" range: slightly less expensive, sportier, and more experimental than the Collezioni. If you're out to see what Gio has on his mind, this is the place to witness his ever-changing moods. They're generally arrayed around a basic theme—a concoction of Indian motifs, gray, corduroy, tweed, and red, each depending on the season—and take shape in classic separates, casual sweaters, trousers, ties, shoes, belts, accessories, and formal wear. This store is something of a touchstone; stroll by each season to take stock of menswear and to be entertained by the always-inventive and frequently modified window displays. *110 5th Ave. (at 16th St.), Chelsea, 212/727–3240. Subway: F, V to 14th St.*

9 *e-3*
601 Madison Ave. (between 57th and 58th Sts.), Midtown East, 212/317–0800. Subway: N, R, W, 4, 5, 6 to 59th St./Lexington Ave.

7 *a-7*
FRANK STELLA
Stella offers super men's fashions, including silk shirts in solids and stripes along with the more common, 100%-cotton variety; sweaters; hundreds of ties; and accessories. *440 Columbus Ave. (at 81st St.), Upper West Side, 212/877–5566. Subway: 1, 2 to 79th St.*

9 *c-3*
921 7th Ave. (at 58th St.), Midtown West, 212/957–1600. Subway: F, N, R, Q, W to 57th St.

9 *d-4*
FRENCH CONNECTION
Okay, okay; the colors and styles aren't for everybody, and unless you're in entertainment or advertising, it might be tough to get away with some of the four-button Euro-casual suits and separates in which this pseudo-Gallic,

slightly libertine version of Banana Republic specializes. They deliver big, though, on the inventory-clearing sales. *1270 6th Ave. (at 51st St.), Midtown West, 212/262–6623. Subway: B, D, F, V to 47th–50th Sts./Rockefeller Ctr.*

11 *e-4*
435 W. Broadway (at Prince St.), SoHo, 212/219–1197. Subway: N, R to Prince St.

GAP
Why, in New York City, shop at the Gap when you can go to a thousand other stores? Well, the clothes are comfortable, cheap, and no two items will ever clash. It's also convenient. They're probably building another one on your corner right now. *Locations throughout the city.*

9 *e-2*
GIORGIO ARMANI
Armani's is filled with muted tones and inviting fabrics that make you want to whisper. The clothes are reverentially displayed, from the Black Label couture (up to five figures) to the shoes and sportswear. Who else could make a svelte ski jacket? It's funky, but certainly not excessive, and it's hard to beat for high-quality, supremely reserved, and ever-so-inhabitable styles for everyone from lawyers to Indian chiefs with a thing for beige. *760 Madison Ave. (between 65th and 66th Sts.), Upper East Side, 212/988–9191. Subway: 6 to 68th St./Hunter College.*

11 *e-4*
LAUNDRY INDUSTRY
You have three color choices at this Amsterdam import: white, beige, and black—lots and lots of black. The clothes are nothing complicated, just reliable SoHo casual stuff with an eye toward body-consciousness that will carry the unflappable wearer from office to event to late-night bistro. *122 Spring St. (at Greene St.), SoHo, 212/343–2225. Subway: 6 to Spring St.*

9 *d-8*
OLD NAVY
From the people at the Gap, who brought you no-brainer clothing, comes this deeper discount emporium, specializing in almost disposable clothing. Not much sells for more than $20, and most of it has a short half-life. Secret bargains: belts, bathing suits. *610 6th Ave. (at 18th St.), Flatiron District, 212/645–0663. Subway: F, V to 14th St.*

10 *e-4*

503–511 Broadway (at Broome St.), SoHo, 212/226–0865. Subway: 6 to Spring St.

7

300 W. 125th St. (between 8th and St. Nicholas Aves.), Harlem, 212/531–1544. Subway: A, B, D to 125th St.

11 *e-8*

PAUL SMITH

Smith's ideas of menswear are a bit much for some. He adores pattern clash, is addicted to a slim, mod silhouette that hefty guys might not cotton to, and is excessively buffeted by the winds of change. Still, for top-flight duds, glibly designed accessories (the best watch, cufflink, and eyeglass styles going), supremely slick, wanna-be Italian suits, nifty ties, and shoes to die for—not to mention biannual seasonal sales (75% off during their final days)—Paul Smith continues to dazzle. Celebrity customers include David Hockney, which should reveal something about Smith's fearless attitude toward color. Not for the monochrome set. *108 5th Ave. (at 16th St.), Chelsea, 212/627–9770. Subway: F, V to 14th St.*

10 *e-3*

PHAT FARM

The boutique for hip-hop fashion, Phat Farm's house label offers baggy jeans, madras shirts, and colorful, sometimes bizarre T-shirts, in sizes ranging from large to XXL but meant to fit everyone. *129 Prince St. (between Wooster St. and West Broadway), SoHo, 212/533–7428. Subway: N, R to Prince St.*

9 *e-3*

PRADA

This very expensive, very Italian, very minimal boutique delivers the styles of the moment amid lime walls and chrome railings: slim, neo-mod suits in charcoal and black, chunky shoes, exquisite leathers, and no small measure of attitude. Absolutely the ever-It Store. *45 E. 57th St. (between Madison and Park Aves.), Midtown East, 212/308–2332. Closed Sun. Subway: E, V to 5th Ave./53rd St.*

9 *e-3*

724 5th Ave. (between 57th and 56th Sts.), Midtown West, 212/664–0010. Subway: Q, W to 5th Ave./60th St.

9 *e-1*

841 Madison Ave. (at 70th St.), Upper East Side, 212/327–4200. Subway: 6 to 68th St./Hunter College.

11 *e-5*

575 Broadway (at Prince St.), SoHo, 212/334–8888. Subway: N, R to Prince St.

10 *e-3*

PRADA SPORT

An odd mix of athletic, futuristic, and Euro-luxe characterizes Prada's Sport line. In the winter you'll find down parkas that look like space suits and hooded sweatshirts made of cashmere. Year-round finds more standard upscale warm-up clothes and possibly the ugliest selection of shoes ever created. What do you get when you cross mules with sneakers? Flats for nurses, but that doesn't mean no one's wearing them. *116 Wooster St. (between Prince and Spring), SoHo, 212/925–2221. Subway: N, R to Prince St.*

11 *d-4*

SEAN

Amid the black-and-white boxes that litter SoHo is this warm little boutique that quietly yet gleefully out-Euros them all. It's the only U.S. store to carry the understated, carefully crafted clothes of French designer Pierre Emile Lafaurie, and it quietly lays on its Continental hands with such gems as a corduroy "painter's jacket" (about $100) and multi-hued dress shirts. *132 Thompson St. (between Prince and Houston Sts.), SoHo, 212/598–5980. Subway: N, R to Prince St.*

10 *a-3*

224 Columbus Ave. (between 70th and 71st Sts.), Upper West Side, 212/769–1489. Subway: B, C to 72nd St.

11 *d-6*

TOMMY HILFIGER

When Tommy Hilfiger's specialty store in New York opened in late 2001, you can bet that red, white, and blue abounded—in preppy plaids, bold stripes, blocks of solid color, and that most American of staples, blue jeans. The ubiquitous designer is now making scents, home products, and clothes for young and old; the sweeping new store is a paean to the everything-Tommy lifestyle. *372 W. Broadway (at Broome St.), SoHo, 917/237–0983. Subway: N, R to Prince St.*

`10` e-2

TRANSIT

This boutique-size glorified sneaker store is cleverly designed to look like a subway station. Indeed it sells the sort of clothes that have the most street credibility. Designers such as Phat Farm, Triple Five Soul, Enyce, and Sean Jean can be found here along with the usual urban faddish duds by Guess and Ralph Lauren. *665 Broadway (at Bond St.), Greenwich Village, 212/358–8726. Subway: F, V to Broadway–Lafayette St.*

custom

`9` e-3

ALFRED DUNHILL TAILORS OF LONDON

Dunhill supplies old-school British tailoring perfection in the form of custom men's suits and shirts (remarkably, they'll come to you for a fitting) and off-the-peg imports. The facade is suitably imposing, as the wares are very luxurious and very expensive; secondary treats include sweaters, ties, scarves, leather goods, jewelry, writing instruments, fine gifts, and smokers' accessories. *450 Park Ave. (at 57th St.), Midtown East, 212/753–9292. Subway: N, R, W to 5th Ave./59th St.*

`9` e-4

CHIPP

Custom tailoring rules here. The high-quality, bespoke suits, plus ready-to-wear suits, jackets, and trousers, are very expensive. *11 E. 44th St. (between 5th and Madison Aves.), Suite 501, Midtown East, 212/687–0850. Closed Sun.; also closed Sat. in summer. Subway: S, 4, 5, 6, 7 to 42nd St./Grand Central.*

discount & off-price

`9` d-8

BURLINGTON COAT FACTORY

Don't let the fluorescent strip lights drive you away. Off-the-rack suits stretch for miles and are made by such dependable names as Perry Ellis and Ralph Lauren, and, of course, they're all amazingly cheap. The casual section is less impressive but will occasionally yield up something fabulous. *707 6th Ave. (at 23rd St.), Flatiron District, 212/229–1300. Subway: F, V to 23rd St.*

`10` e-4

45 Park Pl. (between Church St. and West Broadway), City Hall, 212/571–2630. Subway: 5, 6 to Brooklyn Bridge/City Hall.

`9` e-8

DAFFY'S

Daffy's is an endurance test, full of as much garbage as gold; it rewards the diligent shopper who visits often enough to recognize the dandy stuff. Don't miss the oceans of ties and socks, not to mention suits and formal wear from countries you didn't know were in the rag trade. *111 5th Ave. (at 18th St.), Chelsea, 212/529–4477. Subway: F, V to 14th St.; N, R to 23rd St.*

`9` e-5

335 Madison Ave. (at 44th St.), Midtown East, 212/557–4422. Subway: 4, 5, 6, 7, S to 42nd St./Grand Central.

`9` d-6

1311 Broadway (at 34th St.), Midtown West, 212/736–4477. Subway: B, D, F, N, Q, R, V, W to 34th St./Herald Sq.; and other locations.

`9` d-7

DAVE'S

The cheapest Levi's 501s in the city can be found here and every size is always in stock. There's also workwear and leather from Carhartt, Schott, and Dickies and an exhaustive selection of work boots by Red Wing, Caterpillar, and Carolina. *581 6th Ave. (between 16th and 17th Sts.), Flatiron District, 212/989–6444. Subway: 1, 2 to 18th St.*

`9` e-8

MOE GINSBURG

Need a suit? Why not get four? This is the place to go if you've just landed an entry-level job at Merrill Lynch and need something to wear for the first week. Slicker than Brooks Brothers, Moe provides a shot at some flash (read: designer) clothing for less than you would pay at a fine department store. The suits are many, and the salespeople are low-pressure, honest fellas who deliver competent advice on fit and alterations. *162 5th Ave. (at 21st St.), 2nd to 5th floors, Flatiron District, 212/242–3482. Subway: F, V to 23rd St.*

`9` e-8

ROTHMAN'S

Rothman's is a reliable source of quality men's clothing, though the overall sportswear look is stuck in the '80s, with lots of too-slick Italianate stuff upstairs. Belts and ties (some of the ugliest prints in town) are particularly lost in a vanished moment. A more businesslike demeanor reigns downstairs on the suit racks, which feature Hugo Boss and Calvin Klein as well as deep discounts on Hickey Freeman. *200 Park Ave. S (at 17th St.), Flatiron District, 212/777–7400. Closed Sun. Subway: L, N, Q, R, W, 4, 5, 6 to 14th St./Union Sq.*

9 e-4

SAINT LAURIE MERCHANT TAILORS

Founded in 1913, Saint Laurie is New York's oldest maker of men's clothing. Its specialty is well-tailored business suits made-to-measure in fine fabrics, supplemented by made-to-measure sport coats, shirts, overcoats, and slacks. The huge selection is discounted 30%. *350 Park Ave. (between 51st and 52nd Sts.), Midtown East, 212/317–8700. Closed Sun. Subway: 6 to 51st St./Lexington Ave.; E, V to Lexington–3rd Aves./53rd St.*

9 e-3

SYMS

This mondo-store offers three floors of off-price (30%–50%) men's apparel from shoes and socks to hats and coats to swimsuits and tuxes. Designers include Blass, Cerruti, Cardin, Hechter, and After Six. The specialty? Shirts, and they leave the original labels on, an uncommon practice at the city's other discount centers. Avoid lunch hour here; it's madness. *400 Park Ave. (at 54th St.), Midtown East, 212/317–8200. Subway: 6 to 51st St./Lexington Ave.; E, V to Lexington–3rd Aves./53rd St.*

10 e-7

42 Trinity Pl. (at Rector St.), Lower Manhattan, 212/797–1199. Subway: N, R to Rector St.

9 d-8

TODAY'S MAN

You'll have no trouble finding a suit here, even if the selection is sort of crummy. Today's Man is one of the superstores (along with Barnes & Noble and Bed Bath & Beyond) that led to the dazzling revival of a desolate stretch of 6th Avenue below 23rd Street, a turf once ruled by bike messengers. It aims to appeal to Everyman, a guy who might have any job or any budget, but who in any case dislikes shopping enough to

cleave to the promise that he can yank out his Visa once a year and stock up for the next 12 months. The stock includes the full upscale Monty: easy, Italian threads alongside more traditional button-down styles as well as accessories, shoes, and underwear. *625 6th Ave. (at 18th St.), Chelsea, 212/924–0200. Subway: F, V to 14th St.*

9 e-5

529 5th Ave. (at 44th St.), Midtown East, 212/557–3111. Subway: S, 4, 5, 6, 7 to 42nd St./Grand Central.

unusual sizes

9 d-3

ROCHESTER BIG & TALL

Yes, the large man can obtain a styling look in the Big Apple without having to slink into the tailoring nether-regions of the outer boroughs. This store, which stocks XL sizes from such formidable sources as Zegna, Canali, and Burberrys, plus shoes from Bally and Allen Edmonds, has branches in both Midtown and Wall Street, both territories where giants stride the earth. And giants need sharp clothes. *1301 6th Ave. (at 52nd St.), Midtown West, 212/247–7500. Subway: B, D, F, V to 47th–50th St./Rockefeller Ctr.*

10 f-6

67 Wall St. (at Pearl St.), Lower Manhattan, 212/952–8500. Subway: 1, 2 to Wall St.

vintage

10 e-6

CHURCH STREET SURPLUS

New and used government-issue, civilian surplus, and vintage clothing fill this store and the overflowing bins on the street, making for a candy store of dusty bargains. *327 Church St. (between Canal and Lispenard Sts.), Lower Manhattan, 212/226–5280. Closed Sun. Subway: 1, 2, A, C, E to Canal St.*

9 e-8

WEISS & MAHONEY

Here's an authentic army-navy surplus shop from the pre–cheap chic era (est. 1924). It bills itself as "peaceful" and delivers good buys on fatigues, pea coats, jumpsuits, sweaters, and leather flight jackets. *142 5th Ave. (at 19th St.), Chelsea, 212/675–1915. Subway: F, N, R to 23rd St.*

CLOTHING FOR MEN/SPECIALTY

coats & rainwear

9 e-3
BURBERRY
Maker of the original trench coat (in 1901 Burberry developed what would be a regulation raincoat during World War I), Burberry has enjoyed a resurgence in popularity. These are the coats Humphrey Bogart wore in Casablanca—though now they come in suede and other fabrics as well as the classic gabardine. Burberry recently bought the building next door to its 57th Street location—the expanded retail space is expected to open in late 2002. *9 E. 57th St. (between 5th and Madison Aves.), Midtown East, 212/371–5010. Subway: N, R, W to 5th Ave./59th St.*

formal wear

9 e-4
HARRISON FORMAL WEAR
Harrison can always be counted on for the latest styles, including After Six, Adolfo, Bill Blass, Yves Saint Laurent, and Lord West. The shop provides same-day service, along with free delivery and pickup. Hours on Sunday are by appointment only. *560 5th Ave. (at 46th St.), 2nd floor, Midtown West, 212/302–1742. Closed Sun. in summer. Subway: S, 4, 5, 6, 7 to 42nd St./Grand Central.*

9 f-3
ZELLER TUXEDO
The penguin suits range from traditional to trendy at these shops. Makers include Ungaro, Ferragamo, Valentino, Bally, and Canali, and the selection includes formal accessories. Alterations are free with a purchase. *1010 3rd Ave. (at 60th St.), Upper East Side, 212/688–0100. Subway: N, R, W, 4, 5, 6 to 59th St./Lexington Ave.*

9 e-5
459 Lexington Ave. (at 45th St.), Midtown East, 212/286–9786. Subway: S, 4, 5, 6, 7 to 42nd St./Grand Central.

9 c-6
421 7th Ave. (at 33rd St.), Midtown West, 212/290–0217. Subway: 1, 2, 3 to 34th St./Penn Station.

10 e-6
204 Broadway (at Fulton St.), Lower Manhattan, 212/571–0417. Subway: A, C, J, M, Z, 1, 2, 4, 5 to Fulton St./Broadway–Nassau.

leather

11 e-5
ROOTS
Canada's version of the Gap or Banana Republic (over 100 Roots stores have spread in Canada since 1973), these stores have only recently hit the U.S. The clothes are casual and collegiate, but it's hard to beat the handmade leather jackets, pants, and shoes. *270 Lafayette, #1410 (at Prince St.), SoHo, 212/324–3333. Subway: N, R to Prince St.*

10 2-f
TRASH & VAUDEVILLE
They've worked hard, here in the guts of Lou Reed and Ramones territory, to perfect the punk look in leather: jackets, boots, and accessories that will help you to pass as an East Village native. *4 St. Mark's Pl. (between 2nd and 3rd Aves.), East Village, 212/982–3590. Subway: 6 to Astor Pl.*

shirts

9 e-2
ADDISON ON MADISON
This small shop sells private-label, American-made cotton shirts and silk ties. *698 Madison Ave. (between 62nd and 63rd Sts.), Upper East Side, 212/308–2660. Closed Sun. Subway: N, R, W, 4, 5, 6 to 59th St./Lexington Ave.*

9 e-3
ASCOT CHANG
This prestigious address offers ready-to-wear and custom shirts from the renowned Hong Kong shirtmaker. The vast selection of glorious fabrics, along with 12 different collar styles, amounts to a guarantee that the shirt will, after multiple fittings, feel like you were born in it. Chang also sells made-to-measure suits, dressing gowns, PJs, and handcrafted umbrellas. *7 W. 57th St. (between 5th and 6th Aves.), Midtown West, 212/759–3333. Closed Sun. Subway: E, V to 5th Ave./53rd St.*

9 e-4

THOMAS PINK

London's Jermyn Street shirtmaker has hopped the pond with its traditional, impeccably tailored shirts in several styles. Besides the British-favored spread collars and French cuffs, there are button-down collars and buttoned cuffs. The eponymous color crops up often, sometimes in brighter shades than Americans are used to. Silk ties, cuff links, and two lines of women's shirts round out the selection at both locations. *520 Madison Ave. (at 53rd St.), Midtown East, 212/838–1928. Subway: N, R, W to 5th Ave./59th St.*

9 d-5

1155 6th Ave. (at 44th St.), Midtown West, 212/840–9663. Subway: B, D, F, V to 42nd St.

9 e-2

TURNBULL & ASSER

London's legendary haberdasher, T & A has supplied candy-stripe shirts to everyone from Dominick Dunne to media divas. *745 5th Ave. (at 58th St., in Bergdorf Goodman Men), Midtown East, 212/753–7300. Subway: N, R, W to 5th Ave./59th St.*

10 f-7

VICTORY, THE SHIRT EXPERTS

Victory sells its own 100% cotton shirts, comparable in quality to the clubwear uptown. Ready-to-wear shirts range from sizes 14/32 to 18½/36, but if nothing fits, they'll make to measure. Also on sale are silk ties, "braces," and other accessories. *125 Maiden La. (between Water and Pearl Sts.), Lower Manhattan, 212/480–1366. Closed Sun.; also closed Sat. from Jan. to Sept. Subway: 1, 2 to Wall St.*

ties

7 e-6

SEIGO

Atop the haughty shopper's miracle row that is Madison Avenue resides this small, exquisite shop, literally stuffed with neckwear style (and the biggest selection of bowties in the city). The only place with a more intriguing selection is Paul Stuart. The hook at Seigo is the marriage of East and West: the four-in-hands and bows are all classically English, the patterns borrow something from Italy, France, and the United States, but the printing process is the same one the Japanese use to create kimonos. The results, which begin around $60, are lovely. *1248 Madison Ave. (at 90th St.), Upper East Side, 212/987–0191. Closed Sun. Subway: 4, 5, 6 to 86th St.*

9 e-7

TIECRAFTERS

A sort of tie hospital, Tiecrafters will remove even the most difficult stains. For fussy stylists, they'll also narrow, widen, and shorten ties. *252 W. 29th St. (between 7th and 8th Aves.), Midtown West, 212/629–5800. Closed Sun. Subway: 1, 2 to 28th St.*

CLOTHING FOR WOMEN/GENERAL

classic & conservative

9 e-2

ANN TAYLOR

Like a good hardware store, Ann Taylor has nearly everything on hand for a quick fix-it. You can put together a very presentable boardroom outfit in no time, from crisp white blouse to hose. A tidy skirt suit runs about $400; put it together with an embroidered shell or merino wool sweater and you're set. Many items are dosed with rayon, but those that aren't are still reasonably priced, like the silk blouses for under $100. The Madison Avenue location is the biggest; four stories tall, it's got an entire floor for petites. The Loft store (150 E. 42 St. [at Lexington Ave.], Midtown East, 212/883–8766; 1492 3rd Ave. [at 84th St.], Upper East Side, 212/472–7281; 1155 3rd Ave. [at 68th St.], Upper East Side, 212/772–9952) carries only the more casual designs. *645 Madison Ave. (at 60th St.), Upper East Side, 212/832–2010. Subway: N, R, W, 4, 5, 6 to 59th St./Lexington Ave.*

9 b-1

2015–2017 Broadway (at 69th St.), Upper West Side, 212/873–7344. Subway: 1, 2, 3 to 72nd St.

9 e-4

850 3rd Ave. (at 52nd St.), Midtown East, 212/308–5333. Subway: 6 to 51st St./Lexington Ave.; E, V to Lexington–3rd Aves./53rd St.; and other locations.

9 e-5
BROOKS BROTHERS

The women's clothes in this menswear bastion are often variations on old-boy standards. Women can snag cotton polos (about $35), loafers, and men's-style, French-cuff dress shirts (about $60), plus such demure separates as pleated skirts and silk or merino wool twinsets. The Madison Avenue branch has a larger selection; the 5th Avenue store beckons the younger set with glass and chrome instead of dark wood and thick carpeting. *346 Madison Ave. (at 44th St.), Midtown East, 212/682–8800. Subway: S, 4, 5, 6, 7 to 42nd St./Grand Central.*

9 e-4
666 5th Ave. (at 53rd St.), Midtown West, 212/261–9440. Subway: E, V to 5th Ave./53rd St.

9 e-3
BURBERRY

With a sports-mad house designer, Burberry's functional aspects are still going strong—with a rising tempera-ture. Military influences speed up the jackets, pants, and mules (with camou-flage prints uncovered everywhere). Trench coats come in gunmetal gray. The trademark oversize plaid still comes in familiar forms, too, making up pleated kilts (about $200) and lining trench coats (over $1,000). *9 E. 57th St. (between 5th and Madison Aves.), Mid-town East, 212/371–5010. Subway: N, R, W to 5th Ave./59th St.*

9 e-3
ESCADA

Everything in this store appears to have a high-gloss polish, from the gold-tone railings to the buttons and sequins to the bright colors on the racks (royal pur-ple, taxicab yellow). Suits are nicely shaped, and skirts are normally just above the knee; even the few denim items look tailored. *717 5th Ave. (between 55th and 56th Sts.), Midtown East, 212/755–2200. Subway: N, R, W to 5th Ave./59th St.*

9 e-1
JAEGER

This staunch, century-old British label recently appointed Vivienne Westwood's quirky former assistant (and Sigmund's great-granddaughter) Bella Freud to revamp and rekindle the line's conserva-

tive designs. "Bella Freud for Jaeger" incorporates the designer's humor, trendiness, and distinctive tailoring with Jaeger's traditional looks—adding a touch of "fun and frippery" to the houndstooth and tweed. *818 Madison Ave. (between 68th and 69th Sts.), Upper East Side, 212/628–3350. Subway: 6 to 68th St./Hunter College*

7 c-8
LAURA ASHLEY

The Upper West Side shop is the last New York bastion of this squeaky-clean clothier. Downstairs are the mother-and-child lines and home furnishings; upstairs is a small selection of casual clothes, often in—yes—floral patterns. But this isn't a merciless flood of old-fashioned cabbage roses; there are pin-dot blouses, long madras or striped dresses, and versatile pastel separates. Still, a straw hat would go well with almost anything except the nightgowns. *398 Columbus Ave. (at 79th St.), Upper West Side, 212/496–5110. Subway: 1, 2 to 79th St.*

7 e-8
NORIKO MAEDA

This ultrafeminine store—perfumed air, silver tea service—is the designer's only post outside Japan. Some suits seem to be nodding to Audrey Hepburn, with their three-quarter-length sleeves and matching purses. Most start around $1,000 and can go up to more than double that. *985 Madison Ave. (between 76th and 77th Sts.), Upper East Side, 212/ 717–0330. Subway: 6 to 77th St.*

9 e-3
ST. JOHN

Owing more than a little to Chanel, this designer's suits are often two-tone with quarter-size gold buttons; others have a whiff of the nautical about them. Classic look notwithstanding, most fabrics have a certain percentage of rayon. *665 5th Ave. (at 53rd St.), Midtown East, 212/755–5252. Subway: E, V to 5th Ave./53rd St.*

contemporary & casual

11 f-4
A DÉTACHER

"To be detached," they call themselves, but it's easy to fall for these spare, knowing designs. Dresses, skirts, and tops are tweaked with off-kilter gathers, pleats, and seams; most cost the same as a good pair of shoes. *262 Mott St. (between Prince and Houston Sts.), NoLita, 212/625–3380. Subway: 6 to Bleecker St.*

11 *d-5*
AGNÈS B.
These stores feel more authentically French than a squashed beret. The French adoration for the "7th art," i.e., the movies, is indulged with posters (Godard, not Spielberg) and the occasional T-shirt proclaiming "j'aime le cinéma." The separates are low-key but flatteringly cut; seasonal staples are, naturally, in black and white. With its small but choice range of shoes, filmy scarves, and even makeup, this line could outfit you completely, without making you a cookie cutter. Just remember not to pronounce the "g" when you tell people where you got those trim pants. *103 Greene St. (between Prince and Spring Sts.), SoHo, 212/925–4649. Subway: N, R to Prince St.*

7 *e-7*
1063 Madison Ave. (between 80th and 81st Sts.), Upper East Side, 212/570–9333. Subway: 6 to 77th St.

9 *d-8*
13 E. 16th St. (between Union Sq. and 5th Ave.), Flatiron District, 212/741–2585. Subway: F, V to 14th St.

7 *e-8*
ALICIA MUGETTI
This store gives new meaning to the concept of the flowered silk dress. The softly hued silk, often crinkled, is embroidered or exquisitely hand-painted. Many of the gauzy items need to be layered. *999 Madison Ave. (between 77th and 78th Sts.), Upper East Side, 212/794–6186. Subway: 6 to 77th St.*

11 *e-4*
ANNA SUI
Anna Sui is not a designer opposed to rhinestones. Her purple-and-black SoHo boutique is bedecked with neon posters of alternative bands (Hole, the Beastie Boys) to match the rock-star clothes. Fringe, glitter, and suede make regular appearances; dresses, often with swirly takes on '70s themes, ring up to a couple hundred. If you're not up to this, try the tongue-in-cheek silk-screened T-shirts, like the popular "prom girl on a bike" design with its bit of real tulle jut-

ting from the whimsical, girly print. *113 Greene St. (between Spring and Prince Sts.), SoHo, 212/941–8406. Subway: N, R to Prince St.*

11 *d-5*
ANNE FONTAINE
A Parisian staple now making its way onto the East Coast, Anne Fontaine is the antidote to men's-style white shirts. Snowy rows play with the classic button-down, giving it laced cuffs, oversized mother-of-pearl buttons, white-on-white embroidery, or a gathered neckline. Most are in the $150–$200 range, and there are a few styles in black. *93 Greene St. (between Prince and Spring Sts.), SoHo, 212/343–3154. Subway: N, R to Prince St.*

9 *e-2*
791 Madison Ave. (at 67th St.), Upper East Side, 212/639–9651. Subway: 6 to 68th St./Hunter College.

11 *d-5*
ANTHROPOLOGIE
A corporate sibling of Urban Outfitters, older sis' anthropolgie lures those who have outgrown patchouli oil and butter-fly chairs with the same basic layout: not-too-serious housewares, not-too-fancy clothes. Trends are mellower here than at Urban; a crinkly silk or batik-print skirt could be paired with a crochet cardigan, for instance. Though most young working women can find something they'd like to play in here, many still find the goods overpriced and circle the store waiting for a great markdown. *375 W. Broadway (between Broome and Spring Sts.), SoHo, 212/343–7070. Subway: 6 to Spring St.*

10 *e-1*
85 5th Ave. (at 16th St.), Flatiron District, 212/627–5885. Subway: L, N, Q, R, W, 4, 5, 6 to 14th St./Union Sq.

11 *e-4*
A.P.C.
This place is for dressed-down starlets on a first-name basis with Sophia Coppola. Make your way across the rough-hewn, slightly warped floorboards to the hanging racks of ultracool French simplicity: straight-leg pants (starting around $110), cotton poplin shirts, indigo jeans, khakis, and the like. Most are in neutral, solid colors, but there are occasional outbursts—orange or egg-plant cotton velvet, for instance. *131*

Mercer St. (between Prince and Spring Sts.), SoHo, 212/966–0069. Subway: N, R to Prince St.

`11` *e-4*

ARMANI EXCHANGE

This "casual essentials" fiefdom of the Armani empire provides the requisite wooden-floor, high-ceiling environment. The beige, black, and denim staples are occasionally punctuated with an interesting green or blue. Those anxious to donate free chest advertising will find plenty of A/X-logo T-shirts and sweaters. 568 Broadway (at Prince St.), SoHo, 212/431–6000. Subway: N, R to Prince St.

`9` *e-4*

645 5th Ave. (at 51st St.), Midtown East, 212/980–3037. Subway: B, D, F, V to 47th–50th St./Rockefeller Ctr.

`11` *d-6*

BAGUTTA

The labels sound like Barneys: John Galliano, Alexander McQueen, Ann Demeulemeester, Chloé. But you won't have to rack-rake so strenuously in this SoHo space; they've winnowed out choice bits for you, like a mink-tipped Dolce & Gabbana jacket or svelte knits and suits by Narciso Rodriguez. 402 W. Broadway (at Broome St.), SoHo, 212/ 925–5216. Subway: 6 to Spring St.

`9` *e-4*

BANANA REPUBLIC

Banana Republic has fully embraced the Euro look for slim black suits, silk pullovers, merino wool sweaters, leather coats, and filmy neck scarves. As the most sophisticated sector of the Gap enterprise, Banana Republic gets to dabble in black-and-white photos and curvy cologne bottles. Technofibers may come and go, but you can depend on lightweight wool trousers (about $130), velvet tops (polyester), and little-boy tees for $20. The khaki selection is blessedly less complicated than the Gap's; the fabric has a tad more heft, as does the price tag. If this keeps up, the store may have to change its name to something in a romance language. 626 5th Ave. (at 50th St.), Midtown West, 212/974–2350. Subway: E, V to 5th Ave./53rd St.

`7` *e-7*

1136 Madison Ave. (between 84th and 85th Sts.), Upper East Side, 212/570–2465. Subway: 4, 5, 6 to 86th St.

`9` *e-3*

130 E. 59th St. (at Lexington Ave.), Midtown East, 212/751–5570. Subway: N, R, W, 4, 5, 6 to 59th St./Lexington Ave.

`11` *e-5*

Women's and Home only: 552 Broadway (between Prince and Spring Sts.), SoHo, 212/925–0308. Subway: F, V to Broadway–Lafayette St.; and other locations.

`11` *d-5*

BARBARA BUI

Thanks to this Parisian designer, we can inch closer to that mythically cool, aloof, City of Light elegance—at least from the outside. Long, lean silhouettes are achieved with stretchy wool pants and close-fitting jackets. Textures are also appealing; a jacket, for example, could be made of silk bonded with resin. For the ultimate hands-off trip, choose one of the shirts vacuum-packed in plastic. 115 Wooster St. (between Prince and Spring Sts.), SoHo, 212/625–1938. Subway: N, R to Prince St.

`9` *e-2*

BCBG MAX AZRIA

BCBG, a French acronym for "bon chic bon genre," encompasses designer Max Azria's global vision of "good style, good attitude." Although the Parisian slang translates into what Americans call "preppy," this American-based design house has nary an oxford shirt in sight. Besides carrying many stand-bys (black technofiber pants, cashmere sweaters, slip dresses, and lots of denim, all generally in the $150–$250 range), the higher-end Collection line throws in some ultra-feminine pieces like embroidered or beaded pants and skirts, specialty chiffon tops, and luxurious leather and suede silhouettes. The five-story Madison Avenue flagship has been revamped and showcases the entire line, including clothing, swimwear, intimates, handbags, footwear, eyewear, and fragrance products. For those who get nosebleeds, there's an outpost in SoHo. 770 Madison Ave. (at 66th St.), Upper East Side, 212/ 717–4225. Subway: 6 to 68th St./Hunter College.

`11` *d-5*

120 Wooster St. (at Prince St.), SoHo, 212/ 625–2723. Subway: N, R to Prince St.

11 *d-4*

BETSEY JOHNSON

Most branches have the signature hot-pink interiors, but the SoHo boutique is a sunny yellow splashed with crimson flowers, with a boudoir-y lounging room in back. Most designs get a sexy twist; schoolgirl plaid becomes a bustier, flowered dresses get lingerie straps and a clingy cut. If the thinner materials look loosely sewn at the seams, expect the worst. *138 Wooster St. (between Prince and Houston Sts.), SoHo, 212/995–5048. Subway: N, R to Prince St.*

9 *c-1*

248 Columbus Ave. (between 71st and 72nd Sts.), Upper West Side, 212/362–3364. Subway: 1, 2, 3 to 72nd St.

9 *f-2*

251 E. 60th St. (between 2nd and 3rd Aves.), Upper East Side, 212/319–7699. Subway: N, R, W, 4, 5, 6 to 59th St./Lexington Ave.

7 *e-7*

1060 Madison Ave. (between 80th and 81st Sts.), Upper East Side, 212/734–1257. Subway: 6 to 77th St.

11 *g-5*

BE YOU#(K)

This "techno-ethnic" London-based women's clothing line, already popular in France and England, made a splash when Meg Ryan sported their "punky skirt" in W magazine—a mix of light and dark denim with prints of Shiva and a Taxi-Driver-era Robert de Niro sewn in. The tiny store is known for its odd color combinations (like army green with baby blue), and its specialty pants (like the "shaker" pant made for belts to hook on the side). They also sell handmade plastic jewelry from France's Lolita Pompadour, handbags, and other accessories. *166 Elizabeth St., Store B (between Spring and Kenmore Sts.), NoLita, 212/226–4886. Subway: 6 to Spring St.*

7 *f-8*

BIG DROP

Women who don't go too much over a size 6 slink into this trendy store for tight, hip-hugging jeans, sexy tops, T-shirts, and fitted cardigans from brands like Vanessa Bruno, Rebecca Taylor, Ya-Ya, Mint, Earl, Seven, and Frankie B. *1321 3rd Ave. (between 75th and 76th Sts.), Upper East Side, 212/988–3344. Subway: 6 to 77th St.*

11 *d-5*

174 Spring St. (between W. Broadway and Thompson Sts.), SoHo, 212/966–4299. Subway: C, E to Spring St.

10 *g-2*

BLUE

Blue is a godsend for those whose budget doesn't quite equal their taste: it has simple and classy cocktail dresses, more-formal styles, and even bridal gowns. You can have anything made to order—all this without a stuffy attitude or a hefty price tag. *125 St. Mark's Pl. (between 1st Ave. and Ave. A), East Village, 212/228–7744. Subway: 6 to Astor Pl.*

11 *f-3*

BOND 07

The awesomely offbeat clothes—designs by Alice Roi and William Reid, Fake cashmere sweaters—or the blue-floored, sweeping space with dog paintings can make most people happy. But the cheerfully mod and kitschy store comes into its own with its tantalizing, out-of-the-ordinary accessories: purses by Exquisite J and Cyan, quirky hats, glamour sunglasses, playful shoes, and finely crafted, delicate antique beads. Stock is often limited, so don't hesitate over your purchases. *7 Bond St. (between Lafayette St. and Broadway), East Village, 212/677–8487. Subway: 6 to Astor Pl.*

11 *f-6*

BUILT BY WENDY

Wendy's kitschy custom guitar straps have earned her a loyal following from the likes of Sonic Youth and Hole (a strap might feature pinup girls, cowboys, or cherubs), while her playful belt buckles (big red lips, jagged declarations of ROCK or ICE CREAM) and feminine clothes (majorette blouses, angel-sleeve dresses and tops, low-rise fuschia jeans) evoke rock 'n' roll with equal panache. *7 Centre Market Pl. (between Broome and Grand Sts.), SoHo, 212/925–6538. Subway: 6 to Spring St.*

11 *f-4*

CALYPSO

Born on St. Barthélemy, Calypso has found cozy niches in NoLita, SoHo, and uptown. Snug cashmere sweaters; fringed, embroidered shawls; and long, full, raw silk skirts come in equatorial colors: orchid, deep pink, peacock blue.

Sequined bikinis and delicate slip dresses beg you to take them back to the Caribbean. *280 Mott St. (between Prince and Houston Sts.), NoLita, 212/965–0990. Subway: 6 to Bleecker St.*

11 *e-6*
424 Broome St. (between Crosby and Lafayette Sts.), SoHo, 212/274–0449. Subway: 6 to Spring St.

7 *e-8*
935 Madison Ave. (between 74th and 75th Sts.), Upper East Side, 212/535–4100. Subway: 6 to 77th St.

11 *e-5*
CANAL JEAN COMPANY
One of downtown's best pawing-around spots, this sprawling space caters to at least half-a-dozen clothing personalities. In 5 minutes, you can lay hands on rubber fetish wear, sarong skirts ($15–$20), vintage housedresses, punky plaid pants (about $75), and wildly printed Todd Oldham jeans (roughly half that). Climb to the mezzanine for underwear, including Calvin Klein and Ralph Lauren (damn, the bras are still $30). The third floor is loaded with Levi's. Down in the basement are more vintage racks with a huge coat selection and army–navy surplus, along with streetwear from Ecko, Dickies, and Carhartt. *504 Broadway (between Spring and Broome Sts.), SoHo, 212/226–1130. Subway: J, M, N, Q, R, W, Z, 6 to Canal St.*

11 *d-6*
CATHERINE MALANDRINO
Catherine Malandrino's first major mark was to magnify the cowboy hat trend—she suddenly had people wearing them in purple or dalmation. Now her American flag T-shirts have taken the fashion world by storm (Madonna wore one on her last tour), and the stars and stripes are cropping up in silk and hand-knit shirt dresses, handbags, sleeveless wool turtlenecks, cowl neck sweaters, body-hugging jackets, and even '80s-inspired neckties. Other designs, such as '70s-style starburst jeans, floaty silk slip dresses, and witty I Love NY T-shirts continue to dollop insouciance on the fashion landscape. *468 Broome St. (at Greene St.), SoHo, 212/925–6765. Subway: 6 to Spring St.*

9 *d-8*
CLUB MONACO
Club Monaco gear won't break your wallet or make your mother cringe. Clothes circle around neutrals with a few accent colors, making things easier for the matching-impaired. The styles pick up just enough trends to be interesting, and can still work for the office or dinner out. Weigh your choices, though: $50 for a straight twill skirt sounds good, but $40 for a rayon or tricot cotton tank is a bit much. *160 5th Ave. (between 20th and 21st Sts.), Flatiron District, 212/352–0936. Subway: F, V to 23rd St.*

9 *f-2*
1111 3rd Ave. (at 65th St.), Upper East Side, 212/355–2949. Subway: 6 to 68th St./Hunter College.

7 *b-7*
2376 Broadway (at 87th St.), Upper West Side, 212/579–2587. Subway: 1, 2 to 86th St.

11 *e-5*
520 Broadway (at Spring St.), SoHo, 212/941–1511. Subway: 6 to Spring St.; and other locations.

11 *e-4*
COSTUME NATIONAL
Two blue suede couches sit at an angle in the center of the store—rare bursts of color in an otherwise murky (black walls, black floor) store. Black rules the vampy night-crawler selection as well, with a few things such as a pea-green python jacket or electric blue bustier silk jumpsuit standing out against inky knit dresses, fur (rabbit and sheared lamb), and low-slung pants. *108 Wooster St. (between Spring and Prince Sts.), SoHo, 212/431–1530. Subway: C, E to Spring St.*

11 *d-5*
CP SHADES
This company projects a "natural fibers" image, and in a way it lives up to it—if you consider chemically processed wood pulp (a.k.a. rayon) natural. Linen and cotton crop up on the labels, too, though, and the stock turnover is brisk. Styles tend to be loose and drapey, colors subdued. *154 Spring St. (between Wooster St. and W. Broadway), SoHo, 212/226–4434. Subway: 6 to Spring St.*

9 *c-1*
300 Columbus Ave. (at 74th St.), Upper West Side, 212/724–9474. Subway: B, C to 72nd St.

11 d-4
CYNTHIA ROWLEY
Cynthia Rowley's shop is lined with simply cut dresses, both short and long, often in silk, eyelet lace, or mildly retro printed cotton. There are pants, too, but you're more likely to find cigarette or capri cuts than classic trousers. Colors are cheerful—buttercup yellow, bottle green, candy pink. Even the dressing rooms are upbeat; step inside, and the curtain is covered with "you're so pretty" exclamations. Prices generally fall in the $150–$250 range. *112 Wooster St. (between Prince and Spring Sts.), SoHo, 212/334–1144. Subway: N, R to Prince St.*

11 d-4
D&G
Glamourpusses Dolce & Gabbana spin ideas for their "Young Collection" off their couture lines. Leopard prints, lingerie straps, crochet, and black are as present here as at the designer store, but with less detail and a lower (if not exactly low) price tag. *434 W. Broadway (between Spring and Prince Sts.), SoHo, 212/965–8000. Subway: C, E to Spring St.*

9 e-3
DANA BUCHMAN
These dressy separates can often be worn for years without looking dated or staid. Try a ruby silk suit or a square-neck sweater and notice the thoughtful tailoring touches, such as a bra-strap securer in a tank-style shell. Stylized floral or batik designs show up often on long dresses or wrap skirts. A good stock of petites is in back. *65 E. 57th St. (between Park and Madison Aves.), Midtown East, 212/319–3257. Subway: N, R, W to 5th Ave./59th St.*

11 f-4
DEMOO PARKCHOON MOO
Popular in South Korea since the late 1980s, Demoo's avant-garde designs hit the NoLita scene in 1999. A long, steep staircase sweeps into the minimal space with rough wood floors and mile-high ceilings. The line of starkly colored clothes is simple and versatile, with a lot of structural details like patchwork, pleating, and hand-sewing. Prices start at $200. *262 Mott St. (between Houston and Prince Sts.), NoLita, 212/941–7117. Subway: 6 to Bleecker St.*

9 e-2
DIESEL
With the washing machine–like windows and an in-house DJ, the Lexington Avenue superstore pitches to the hip. At $100 or more, the jeans may give you pause, but at least they give you plenty of options, with men's, women's, and unisex fits of varying degrees of bagginess, flare, and denim "dirtiness." Look for the fabric mixes (denim and gabardine, cotton and corduroy, nylon and cotton), and jewel and embroidery embellishments. A second location snazzes up a corner of Union Square. *770 Lexington Ave. (at 60th St.), Upper East Side, 212/308–0055. Subway: N, R, W, 4, 5, 6 to 59th St./Lexington Ave.*

10 e-1
1 Union Sq. West (at 14th St. and University Pl.), SoHo, 646/336–8552. Subway: L, N, Q, R, W, 4, 5, 6 to 14th St./Union Sq.

11 d-5
DIESEL DENIM GALLERY
Here, they'll not only sell you all the denim you'll ever need; they will even launder your purchase for you. *68 Greene St. (between Spring and Broome Sts.), SoHo, 212/966–5593. Subway: C, E, 6 to Spring St.*

11 d-5
DIESEL STYLE LAB
It may be much smaller than the flagship, but this outpost of the Diesel empire carries a good cross-section of the company's secondary line. Styles have futuristic leanings in graphic prints and souped-up fabrics. *416 W. Broadway (between Prince and Spring Sts.), SoHo, 212/343–3863. Subway: C, E to Spring St.*

9 e-3
DKNY
Hometown girl Donna Karan's breathlessly hip lifestyle store has been likened to a three-ring circus. Indeed, what with all the shiny decor happening on the ground floor, it can be hard to concentrate; the eye skips from designer chairs to motorcycles to healing incense. Upstairs you can circulate among the various women's lines with fewer distractions. Sprinkled among the DKNY labels you'll find individual vintage pieces; for instance, a lace dress or 1930s sequined bolero jacket could hang

among the crisp white shirts or black cashmere sweaters. This approach hits the nail on the head—it answers the ultimate fashion-plate demand by providing both designer "essentials" and unique items that no one else has. The clothing and furniture/home accessories/whatever stock changes rapidly, catering to those who are constantly on the fashion make. *655 Madison Ave. (at 60th St.), Upper East Side, 212/223–3569. Subway: N, R, W, 4, 5, 6 to 59th St./Lexington Ave.*

11 d-5

420 W. Broadway (between Prince and Spring Sts.), SoHo, 646/613–1100. Subway: C, E to Spring St.

11 f-2

DOLLHOUSE

For trendy, low-priced sportswear, these are good pickings—especially if you've made stretch viscose your friend. Flood pants and capris for under $50, short dresses for under $75, sparkley tube tops, and little-girl blouses make for lighthearted impulse buys. *400 Lafayette St. (at E. 4th St.), East Village, 212/539–1800. Subway: 6 to Astor Pl.*

11 d-5

DOSA

This store's modest size actually works for it, and it's in keeping with the serene, Eastern-influenced designs. Flourishes are kept to a minimum, but not a bare minimum—a pair of silk pants could gather into a drawstring, or a silk blouse could be made up in iridescent green/gold. *107 Thompson St. (between Prince and Spring Sts.), SoHo, 212/431–1733. Subway: C, E to Spring St.*

11 d-5

EILEEN FISHER

Cinched waists will never happen at Eileen Fisher. Her comfortably fluid dresses and skirts are lifesavers during a New York summer, and her swinging jackets, loose wool pants, and stretchy sweaters make for easy layering in colder months. *395 W. Broadway (between Broome and Spring Sts.), SoHo, 212/431–4567. Subway: 6 to Spring St.*

9 e-3

521 Madison Ave. (at 53rd St.), Midtown East, 212/759–9888. Subway: E, V to 5th Ave./53rd St.

7 e-8

1039 Madison Ave. (at 79th St.), Upper East Side, 212/879–7799. Subway: 6 to 77th St.

7 c-8

341 Columbus Ave. (at 76th St.), Upper West Side, 212/362–3000. Subway: 1, 2, 3 to 72nd St.

9 e-8

103 5th Ave. (at 17th St.), Flatiron District, 212/924–4777. Subway: F, V to 14th St.; N, R to 23rd St.; and other locations.

9 e-2

EMILIO PUCCI

Yes, it's the original. Ring the bell, walk up the pink-carpet stairs, and you'll find yourself surrounded by the timelessly psychedelic swirls of Pucci's dresses, scarves, blouses, even bikinis. The color palette is often a late-'60s time capsule: pink-and-purple combinations, or yellow-and-almost-avocado. *24 E. 64th St. (between Madison and 5th Aves.), Upper East Side, 212/752–4777. Subway: 6 to 68th St./Hunter College.*

9 e-3

EMPORIO ARMANI

It's funny how after half an hour here, you start thinking of white as a dazzling color. Somber tones dominate just about every season's palette, but think of it this way: dark colors hide spots, so they'll make great traveling clothes. Armani's way with a suit jacket is still obvious in this midrange label; the soft shoulders and plush fabrics are hard to resist, though you'll pay for the privilege of giving in. Fittingly discreet handbags, shoes, and accessories are also available. *601 Madison Ave. (between 57th and 58th Sts.), Midtown East, 212/317–0800. Subway: N, R, W, 4, 5, 6 to 59th St./Lexington Ave.*

9 d-8

110 5th Ave. (at 16th St.), Flatiron District, 212/727–3240. Subway: F, V to 14th St.

7 e-8

EN SOIE

Come here when you need an immediate pick-me-up. The playfulness of the interior (colorful bibelots everywhere; small, fanciful antlered heads in the dressing rooms) belies a very serious raison d'être: exquisite silk. There are blouses, scarves, even bolts of it, all beautifully textured; this is, after all, the

Swiss house that once provided fabric to Dior and Balenciaga. A silk taffeta blouse can run about $240; a long, full, raw silk skirt about $340. *988 Madison Ave. (at 77th St.), Upper East Side, 212/717–7958. Subway: 6 to 77th St.*

9 e-2
ETRO

The sartorial Italians have scored another hit with these softly exotic designs. The trademark paisley curls around scarves, evening trousers, and swimsuits; blouses and dresses are soaked with rich colors (deep blue, plum, russet). Even traditional button-downs are tweaked—perhaps striped with vertical wavy lines or layered three-deep. *720 Madison Ave. (between 63rd and 64th Sts.), Upper East Side, 212/317–9096. Subway: 6 to 68th St./Hunter College.*

11 f-5
EVA

Opened in the spring of 2001, Eva features the work of young, new designers like Kitty Boots, Sean, People Used to Dream About the Future, and Morteza Saifi, whose clothing ranges from sleek and clean to more edgy and avant-garde. The store has recently begun to bring in higher-end couture collections from such designers as Olivier Theysken and Zambon. *227 Mulberry St. (between Prince and Spring Sts.), NoLita, 212/925–3208. Subway: 6 to Bleecker St.*

9 d-4
FRENCH CONNECTION

A mix of lightning-speed runway steals and wardrobe staples in vivid hues, the (British) French Connection is at best a quick fix. Most choices are reasonably priced, at about $50 for a boxy, wool V-neck sweater, roughly $100 for flat-front pants; a long linen sundress; or a beaded, fine-spun wool cardigan. However, something is generally left to be desired—a little too sheer here, a little too tight there. There are plenty of Ts, often with a dash of Lycra, though you'll have to put up with the many variants of their wink-wink "fcuk" logo (i.e., unfortunate slogans like "too busy to fcuk" abound). *1270 6th Ave. (at 51st St.), Midtown West, 212/262–6623. Subway: B, D, F, V to 47th–50th Sts./Rockefeller Ctr.*

11 e-2
700 Broadway (at E. 4th St.), East Village, 212/473–4486. Subway: N, R to 8th St.

11 d-4
435 W. Broadway (at Prince St.), SoHo, 212/219–1197. Subway: N, R to Prince St.

7 c-8
304 Columbus Ave. (between 74th and 75th Sts.), Upper West Side, 212/496–1470. Subway: 1, 2, 3 to 72nd St.

GAP

It's hard to go six blocks without running into one of these look-alike student-wardrobe chains. With stacks of chinos, cotton Ts and tanks plain and ribbed, button-downs, and straightforward sweaters, it's easy to outfit as Everykid. Finding the right pair of khakis (about $40) or jeans (boy fit to boot cut, sandblasted to indigo, roughly $30–$50) can translate into 45 minutes in the dressing room, but with patience you can emerge victorious. For extra gratification, look for the three magic numbers: the $9.99, $19.99, and $29.99 sale price tags. Larger stores have pajamas, underwear, sweats, toiletries, and perfume—bonus point for the cool cube bottle design. *Multiple locations throughout the city.*

11 f-3
GHOST

Models love Tanya Sarne's lovely, floaty dresses that drift from the racks in dreamy colors like spun-sugar pink, grass green, and daffodil yellow. Ghost has been huge in England for years; the Bond Street outpost opened in May 2000. *28 Bond St. (between Lafayette and Bowery Sts.), East Village, 646/602–2891. Subway: N, R to 8th St.*

11 e-5
GUESS?

Long after contributing to the early designer-jean deluge, Guess? continues to revel in ring-spun denim. Sort through everything from Daisy Duke short-shorts (about $40) and indigo narrow-legs to relaxed-fit jeans ($50–$110). There's plenty of cleavage-hugging Spandex (tanks, stretchy button-downs, bikinis), and its natural counterpart (white shirts, black leather jackets, shades). *537 Broadway (between Prince and Spring Sts.), SoHo, 212/226–9545. Subway: N, R to Prince St.*

10 f-6
2325 Fulton St. (between Water and South Sts.), Lower Manhattan, 212/385–0533.

Subway: A, C, J, M, Z, 1, 2, 4, 5 to Fulton St./Broadway–Nassau St.

11 f-5

HADU

Designer Amy McCracken offers vintage-inspired classic clothes with modern details (think colorful silk print skirts with vintage beaded buttons) in this cheerful shop, with its chocolate-y wood floors and brightly painted walls. McCracken's flirty clothes, now exclusive to her new store, have gathered a small cult following downtown. Items also include velvet T's, handbags, some vintage items, and Cosabella lingerie. 239 Mulberry St. (between Prince and Spring Sts.), NoLita, 212/966–4072. Subway: 6 to Bleecker St.

9 e-4

H & M

Established in Sweden in 1947, H&M hit New York in 2000 and caused a veritable feeding frenzy. Crowds of locals and tourists swarm over the racks in search of up-to-the-minute fashions at unbelievably low prices (as in skirts, tops, sweaters for under $20). Fitting room lines are impossibly long and the clothing is rather cheaply made (lots of shimmery polyester and rayon), but at these prices you can afford to indulge your wilder fashion fantasies. 640 5th Ave. (at 51st St.), Midtown West, 212/489–0390. Subway: B, D, F, V to 47th–50th Sts./Rockefeller Ctr.

9 d-6

1328 Broadway (at W. 34th St.), Midtown West, 212/564–9922. Subway: N, R to 34th St.

11 e-5

558 Broadway (between Prince and Spring Sts.), SoHo, 212/343–2722. Subway: N, R to Prince St.

11 f-4

HEDRA PRUE

This NoLita shop carries between 40 and 50 cutting-edge designers at any one time, from New York and everywhere else, including loads of young, up-and-coming designers like Magda Berliner, Preen Martin, Lauren Moffatt, Ulla Johnson, and m.r.s. 281 Mott St. (between Houston and Prince Sts.), NoLita, 212/343–9205. Subway: 6 to Bleecker St.

11 d-5

HELMUT LANG

A fashionista favorite, this Austrian designer's boutique embodies his detached aesthetic. Freestanding walls segment the stark space. On the racks, stern tailoring is sometimes relieved by soft fabrics (gauze, sheer silk, suede), utilitarian touches (holster bags), or unsettling details (pants with tufted silk at the waistband, extended sleeves). A few colors occasionally break the overriding cream-black-white scheme. But the coolness does not come cheap—trousers run about $300, denim around $200. 80 Greene St. (between Spring and Broome Sts.), SoHo, 212/925–7214. Subway: 6 to Spring St.

9 e-3

HENRI BENDEL

Lately, Bendel's has been straddling varied tastes. Younger, trendier lines such as Catherine Malandrino and Rebecca Danenberg migrate here from downtown, and there are plenty of fun-but-glam accessories to match. Bendel's own clothes are nicely understated, especially the sweaters. On the upper floors you'll find more established designers, such as Michael Kors, as well as vintage clothes and accessories from Resurrection and Vintage couture. The first-floor cosmetics selection eschews the familiar (no Lancôme, Chanel, or Clinique) for such edgier names as Laura Mercier, Trish McEvoy, Smashbox, and M.A.C. Alas, there's no shoe department, but there are departments for home and babies—and even gifts for pampered pooches. 712 5th Ave. (at 56th St.), Midtown West, 212/247–1100. Subway: E, V to 5th Ave./53rd St.

11 f-4

HENRY LEHR

After decamping from Madison, Henry Lehr settled his denim reputation downtown. Fine-wale corduroy jackets from Katayone Adeli, Fake brand cashmere sweaters, and embroidered jeans make good, if not inexpensive, casualwear. Another storefront up the street (268 Elizabeth St.) provides the necessary T-shirts—embellished novelty shirts by Riley, retro designs from Jet—plus an accessory or two, such as decorated clogs. 232 Elizabeth St. (between Houston and Prince Sts.), NoLita, 212/274–9921. Subway: 6 to Bleecker St.

11 f-5

HIPONICA

Jem Fillippi's sweet designs include T-shirts in camouflage print woven through with teddy bears; shimmery, patterned polo shorts in colors like pale green and lavender; white shirts splattered with colorful, vintage-y polka dots; plus accessories like shiny vinyl wallets and dog-shaped key chains covered over in fake fur. *238 Mott St. (between Prince and Spring Sts.), NoLita, 212/966–4388. Subway: 6 to Bleecker St.*

9 e-3

HUGO BOSS

While Hugo Boss is known for its menswear, women will have no trouble occupying themselves here. Choose a business-meeting wool suit, then cut a dash with something leather or a wild striped shirt. *717 5th Ave. (at East 57th St.), Midtown East, 212/688–2800. Subway: F to 57th St.; N, R, W to 5th Ave.*

11 e-6

IF BOUTIQUE

Specializing in avant-garde high-end fashion, IF carries European and Japanese designers like Commes des Garçons, Dries Van Noten, Martin Margiela, Junya Watanabe, and Vernique Branquinho. The artistes who shop here think nothing of paying $200 for a T-shirt, and $3,000 and up for a coat. *94 Grand St. (between Greene and Mercer Sts.), SoHo, 212/334–4964. Subway: 6 to Spring St.*

7 e-8

INTERMIX

The uptown store made quite an inroad on the Upper East Side: it imported a horde of young, downtown designers. It feels like half of SoHo and NoLita are here: Catherine Malandrino dresses and Sigerson Morrison shoes, Jill Stuart jeans, and bags by Kate Spade, Amy Chan, and Jamin Puech. *1003 Madison Ave. (between 77th and 78th Sts.), Upper East Side, 212/249–7858. Subway: 6 to 77th St.*

9 e-8

125 5th Ave. (between 19th and 20th Sts.), Flatiron District, 212/533–9720. Subway: N, R to 23rd St.

9 b-1

210 Columbus Ave. (between 69th and 70th Sts.), Upper West Side, 212/769–9116. Subway: 1 to 72nd St.

7 e-8

ISSEY MIYAKE

Miyake is to polyester what Fortuny was to silk. The bare bones of this shop focus all attention on the uncommon clothes, whose ultratight pleats either cling to the body or form geometric shapes. In October 2001, the designer opened Tribeca Issey Miyake—a new showcase for the men's and women's collections and some collections previously unavailable in the U.S., like Miyake's latest project, A-POC. *992 Madison Ave. (at 77th St.), Upper East Side, 212/439–7822. Subway: 6 to 77th St.*

11 c-8

119 Hudson St (at N. Moore St.), TriBeCa, 212/226–0100. Subway: 1, 2 to Franklin St.

9 e-8

J. CREW

Ever the purveyors of rugged East Coast chic, these stores sell everything from the ubiquitous roll-neck sweaters, car coats, and flannels to prettily embroidered sweaters, gabardine suits, and silk button-downs. While they don't carry everything that's in the catalogs you've been getting every three weeks, they do have sales quite often, and after all, there's nothing like instant gratification. *91 5th Ave. (at 17th St.), Flatiron District, 212/255–4848. . Subway: F, V to 14th St.; N, R to 23rd St.*

11 e-4

99 Prince St. (between Mercer and Greene Sts.), SoHo, 212/966–2739. Subway: N, R to Prince St.

9 d-4

30 Rockefeller Plaza, Midtown West, 212/765–4227. Subway: B, D, F, V to 47th–50th St./Rockefeller Ctr.

10 f-7

203 Front St. (South Street Seaport), Lower Manhattan, 212/385–3500. Subway: A, C, J, M, Z, 1, 2, 4, 5 to Fulton St./Broadway–Nassau; and other locations.

11 d-4

JEANETTE LANG

Elegant clothes in swoon-inducing European silks, charmeuse, georgette, organza, taffeta, and cashmere make up this new line. Pick through the huge box of fabric swatches for your own custom dream creation, or retreat to the boudoir-ish dressing room (complete with red suede couch) to drape yourself in the lovely pret-a-porter confections.

171 Sullivan St. (between Houston and Bleecker Sts.), Greenwich Village, 212/254–5676. Subway: A, B, C, D, E, F, V to W. 4th St./Washington Sq.

10 b-1
JEFFREY

On a trip to Jeffrey you could easily run into one of those particularly New York contrasts—in this case, a limo or two pulled up in front of hardbitten delivery trucks. Once inside and up a few stairs you'll be looking at the stuff of a shoe hound's dreams: displays of shoes march straight down the center of the store. They can slake virtually any shoe-thirst, whether it's for velvet slippers, woven slides, spindly heels by Louboutin and Blahnik, or understated flats by Ferragamo or Jil Sander. And, God bless them, they carry a wide range of sizes. The clothing selection is carefully pruned, with tight selections from big guns like Gucci, Helmut Lang, and Josephus Thimister. Keep looking and you'll find some interesting, less-exposed items, like Courrèges shifts. The cosmetics and handbags selections are limited but choice (think Nars and Celine, respectively). 449 W. 14th St. (between Washington St. and 10th Ave.), Greenwich Village, 212/206–1272. Subway: A, C, E, L to 14th St./8th Ave.

11 d-5
JILL STUART

Now safely ensconced as a young-fashionable favorite, Jill Stuart continues to turn out girlish frocks. Fresh, gauzy, flower-print shells and dresses appear each spring. Standards get the femme treatment, too; blouses could be double-dosed with ruffles, at both cuff and hem, while a beige skirt could have a shocking-pink panel at the bottom. The racks are organized by color, and most items come in a variety of colors, so if you don't like the green or blue, just head over to another section. Price-wise, these clothes are meant for ladies with high credit limits. 100 Greene St. (between Prince and Spring Sts.), SoHo, 212/343–2300. Subway: N, R to Prince St.

9 e-1
JOSEPH

Some people call this place "the pants store," and that's not far from the truth. Pants practically dominate the window displays and sprawl their skinny legs on the walls. Virtually everything, be it

denim, cotton, or linen, has a certain amount of stretch, and there are a few unconventional fabrics (such as the shiny, ultra-lightweight "mirror" fabric made of plastic with metal fibers). The 804 Madison Avenue store has tops, too—jackets and shirts with trim lines to match. 804 Madison Ave. (at 68th St.), Upper East Side, 212/570–0077. Subway: 6 to 68th St./Hunter College.

9 e-1

796 Madison Ave. (at 67th St.), Upper East Side, 212/327–1773. Subway: 6 to 68th St./Hunter College.

11 e-5

106 Greene St. (between Prince and Spring Sts.), SoHo, 212/343–7071. Subway: 6 to Spring St.

11 f-3
KATAYONE ADELI

Katayone set up her ultrasleek shop on the block that Daryl K made hip. Now you can see the full collection of subtly sexy basics, plus exclusive pieces that are only carried here. The more reasonably priced line, K2, is also available. Pants tend to run very small and the larger sizes sell out fast, so prepare for disappointment. 25 Bond St. (between Bowery and Lafayette Sts.), East Village, 212/260–3500. Subway: N, R to 8th St.

11 d-5
KENZO BOUTIQUE

After Kenzo himself retired from fashion in 1999, designer Gilles Rosier stepped in to keep the tradition alive—with unconventional detail, flowery designs, and intricate embroidery. The new flagship store opened in SoHo in late 2000, and carries the complete line of women's and men's clothing (previously unavailable in the U.S.), including Kenzo Paris, Jungle, Jeans, Homme, and the sportswear line Ki. The uptown store carries a more limited selection. 80 Wooster St. (between Spring and Broome Sts., SoHo, 212/966–4142. Subway: 6 to Spring St.

9 e-1

805 Madison Ave. (between 67th and 68th Sts.), Upper East Side, 212/717–0101. Subway: 6 to 68th St./Hunter College.

11 d-5
KIRNA ZABÊTE

Cheerfully dubbing itself "the shangri-la of shopping," Kirna Zabête proves you can grin and still be cutting-edge. While the overall feel is lighthearted (friendly salespeople, candy bins, a boyfriend area, and purple floors), the selection is seriously high-caliber. Scan the signs above the racks and you'll see a roster of hard-to-find designers: Clements Ribeiro, Martine Sitbon, Susan Cianciolo, AF Vandevorst, Olivier Theyskens, Paul Smith. Accessories can be cunning (Lulu Guinness and Anya Hindmarch handbags) or startling (horsehair earrings or horned headbands). Head downstairs and the fun continues with Wink corduroys, Passion Bait lingerie, and Burberry dog coats. You might even be tempted to show your true colors with an e.vil tee emblazoned "little miss golddigger." Big plus in the dressing rooms: three-way mirrors so you can see the back of that Balenciaga. *96 Greene St. (between Prince and Spring Sts.), SoHo, 212/941–9656. Subway: N, R to Prince St.*

11 f-4
LABEL
The clothes here have subversion in their seams—whether the designer's whipping up edgy Ts or street-smart tops, skirts, and dresses with drawstrings, zippers, or Velcro tabs. Riot grrrls will have a field day. *265 Lafayette St. (between Prince and Spring Sts.), East Village, 212/966–7736. Subway: N, R to Prince St.*

11 f-5
LANGUAGE
One of the groundbreaking lifestyle stores, Language will quickly convince you that outstanding design is a sort of universal tongue. The conversations around you may be in Japanese or Spanish, but everyone here seems to Get It. The clothing selection is supplemented with ultrastylish nonwearables: Campana chairs and Chinese antiques, native Amazonian masks, Torpedo mopeds, Comme des Garçons perfume and the latest edition of *Visionaire*. Yank your attention back to the racks for Chloé and Marc by Marc Jacobs separates, touch-me cashmeres by Lucien Pellat Finet and Language's own line, Earl Jeans leather, rhinestone-studded Rachel Robarts T's, and "wave" design silk shirts from Jerome L'Huillier. *238 Mulberry St. (between Prince and Spring Sts.), NoLita, 212/431–5566. Subway: 6 to Spring St.*

11 e-2
LE CHÂTEAU
An excellent place for an unabashed knockoff, or something to wear below 14th Street, Le Château cadges quite well and keeps an eye on trends—lots of kitschy poly prints, sparkley T's, Asian-theme skirts, and camouflage that pops up in tops and bottoms. It's hardly verisimilitude, and prices are low; as an extra nudge, there's some tulle and marabou around the edges. Also look for deals such as a pair of cotton tank tops for $12. *611 Broadway (between 4th and 5th Sts.), Greenwich Village, 212/260–0882. Subway: F, V to Broadway–Lafayette St.*

9 d-6
34 W. 34th St. (between 5th and 6th Aves.), Midtown West, 212/967–0025. Subway: B, D, F, N, Q, R, V, W to 34th St./Herald Sq.

9 e-1
LES COPAINS
The day and evening wear here is so high-quality it's practically Old World. Trouser pockets are perfectly placed, wool is blended with cashmere or silk so it's not itchy—the attentive details add up. (As will the bill; one outfit can break $1,000.) Bear in mind that the cuts run a bit small. For something more casual, seek out the Trend Les Copains line. *807 Madison Ave. (between 67th and 68th Sts.), Upper East Side, 212/327–3014. Subway: 6 to 68th St./Hunter College.*

9 e-3
LEVI'S
Custom tailoring's not just for suits anymore. At these two stores, you can actually have a pair of jeans tailored with just the right length, width, fly, and slouch; they cost only $15 more than a regular pair and take three weeks to produce. You can even have them shipped to your door. If you'd just like to grab a pair off the stacks, you can choose from flares, slim fit, relaxed fit, and of course, the classic, button-fly 501s (deep blue or broken in). *3 E. 57th St. (just off 5th Ave.), Midtown East, 212/838–2188. Subway: N, R, W to 5th Ave./59th St.*

9 e-3
750 Lexington Ave. (at 59th St.), Upper East Side, 212/826–5957. Subway: N, R, W, 4, 5, 6 to 59th St./Lexington Ave.

9 e-2

LUCA LUCA

A welcome relief from the black-and-beige blahs. Instead of serving as the be-all and end-all, black is used to offset appealing colors, from soft lavender to kelly green. *690 Madison Ave. (at 62nd St.), Upper East Side, 212/755–2444. Subway: N, R, W, 4, 5, 6 to 59th St./Lexington Ave.*

7 e-8

1011 Madison Ave. (at 78th St.), Upper East Side, 212/288–9285. Subway: 6 to 77th St.

9 e-1

MALO

The plush cashmere here often appears in an extra-comfortable guise: drawstring pants, tunic-style tops, roomy cardigans. The palette is generally soft: oatmeal, slate gray, dark marine blue. *814 Madison Ave. (at 68th St.), Upper East Side, 212/396–4721. Subway: 6 to 68th St./Hunter College.*

11 d-5

125 Wooster St. (between Prince and Spring Sts.), SoHo, 212/941–7444. Subway: N, R to Prince St.

11 e-4

MARC JACOBS

Ah, another bare-bones boutique, this one with men's and women's wear in two separate straight lines. It's hard not to warm to the fabrics, though: divine silk, cashmere, soft wool. Instead of fashion histrionics, you'll find a few quiet quirks, such as an oversized scallop or restrained ruching. To anyone plugged into fashion, the details are an instant ID. The Bleecker St. spaces carry more casual clothes with a stronger sense of humor, such as halter dresses with bodice detailing and striped bootleg jeans. Pop into the accessories boutique at 385 Bleecker for toothsome handbags and shoes. *163 Mercer St. (between Prince and Houston Sts.), SoHo, 212/343–1490. Subway: N, R to Prince St.*

11 a-1

403–405 Bleecker St. (at W. 11th St.), Greenwich Village, 212/924–0026. Subway: 3 to Christopher St./Sheridan Sq.

11 a-2

Accessories Boutique: 385 Bleecker St. (at Perry St.), Greenwich Village, 212/924–6126. Subway: 3 to Christopher St./Sheridan Sq.

11 e-5

MARY JAEGER

Mary uses distinctive fabrics, like intricately patched vintage Japanese kimono fabrics or hand-tucked textured wool, in her avant-garde collection of capes, shawls, jackets, skirts, and other clothing. Her dresses, meant to be a canvas for the extravagant shawls, are made up of layers of chiffon and charmeuse, with beaded details. *51 Spring St. (between Cleveland Pl. and Mulberry St.), SoHo, 212/941–5877. Subway: 6 to Spring St.*

9 e-1

MAXMARA

One of the best "bridge" designers, MaxMara tends to show monochromatic suits enlivened with texture, such as a nubbly tweed or draped wool crepe. Most pieces are in neutrals, but a flash of lipstick-red or primary yellow isn't out of the question. *813 Madison Ave. (at 68th St.), Upper East Side, 212/879–6100. Subway: 6 to 68th St./Hunter College.*

10 e-3

450 W. Broadway (between Prince and Houston Sts.), SoHo, 212/674–1817. Subway: C, E to Spring St.

11 f-4

MAYLE

Designer Jane Mayle, who is often found lounging in the store, designs close-fitting knit tops, ultrasuede bags, and retro-style dresses, which are displayed alongside vintage items she culls from flea markets around the world. Word has it she is the hottest young designer around. *252 Elizabeth St., NoLita (between Houston and Prince Sts.), 212/625–0406. Subway: 6 to Bleecker St.*

7 e-8

MISSONI

This boutique is almost entirely devoted to knits—the distinctive, multicolor stripes zigzag through mohair, rayon, and wool in scarves, sweaters, long sparkly dresses, even bikinis. The colors can be toned down (gold, beige, and bone) or eye-popping (sharp green, deep purple, and blue). There's a men's department upstairs, too. *1009 Madison Ave. (at 78th St.), Upper East Side, 212/517–9339. Subway: 6 to 77th St.*

11 e-4

MIU MIU

New Yorkers' insatiable hunger for Miuccia Prada's designs won the city the first Miu Miu boutique in North America. Prada trends, such as utility bags and streamlined sport shoes, are put through a funk filter. And corresponding to the shop's younger audience, the prices are relatively lower. The colors can be hard to wear, but there's always black—and a quick stock turnover. *100 Prince St. (between Mercer and Greene Sts.), SoHo, 212/334–5156. Subway: N, R to Prince St.*

9 *e-2*

MORGANE LE FAY

The strongest influences here are not from this century or even from the last: there are lacings, rows of small mother-of-pearl buttons, and layers of chiffon over silk or wool. Many pieces are in soft grays, ivory, or black, but you can also move into something like wine red or slate blue. The echoing Wooster Street space has a rich selection of the billowing bridal and ball gowns. *746 Madison Ave. (between 64th and 65th Sts.), Upper East Side, 212/879–9700. Subway: 6 to 68th St./Hunter College.*

11 *d-5*

67 Wooster St. (between Spring and Broome Sts.), SoHo, 212/219–7672. Subway: C, E to Spring St.

11 *f-3*

NAKED APE

These youthful, trendy designs are for rockers who have entered the millennium. Look for the signature "Lisa" shirts, perfect for New York winters—cozy fleece turtlenecks with outside stitching and holes to stick your thumbs through—and the sassy, glittery T-shirts that decorate the walls. Clothing ranges from $29–$150. *36 E. 4th St. (between Lafayette St. and Cooper Sq.), Greenwich Village, 212/254–9011. Subway: N, R to 8th St.*

9 *e-3*

NICOLE FARHI

British import Farhi often hits just the right balance of soft-spoken desirability. The store's cool demeanor doesn't slip into sterility; likewise, the sophisticated clothes are warmed up with an inviting texture or flattering cut. A basic jacket or skirt could be done in fuzzy black alpaca; a tweedy blue-black wool makes a fantastic three-quarter-length coat. There are some hard-to-wear colors (orange, a sallow yellow), but plenty of black and neutrals to fall back on. Downstairs are her "lifestyle" choices: glassware and dishes,

a few antiques. There's also a restaurant, should you feel peckish. *10 E. 60th St. (between Madison and 5th Aves.), Upper East Side, 212/223–8811. Subway: N, R, W to 5th Ave./59th St.*

11 *d-4*

NICOLE MILLER

Instant recognition of a Miller design is almost guaranteed. The designer made her name with funny, themed silk prints. On the flip side of the coin are some simple dresses in solids. *134 Prince St. (between Wooster St. and W. Broadway), SoHo, 212/343–1362. Subway: N, R to Prince St.*

9 *e-2*

780 Madison Ave. (between 66th and 67th Sts.), Upper East Side, 212/288–9779. Subway: 6 to 68th St./Hunter College.

9 *d-8*

OLD NAVY

Cotton is king here—and cheap. Judging from the big, black supermarket shopping carts, they assume you'll be buying in bulk. Old Navy's own fashion timeline puts them somewhere between the '40s and '50s, but there's scant evidence of this beyond the retro edge to the mannequins and advertising. Instead, clothes are functional, casual, and vaguely trendy—capri and cargo pants have rack space alongside the Ts. Here's a sampling of what $30 will get you: a fleece vest, a pair of jeans (some under $25!), a couple of thermal shirts or tanks, an Old Navy disco-mix CD, or half a dozen tubes of body glitter. Be sure to scope out the clearance racks—when was the last time you saw a $3.99 price tag in a clothing store? The shoes are generally unexciting. *610 6th Ave. (at 18th St.), Flatiron District, 212/645–0663. Subway: F, V to 14th St.*

11 *e-5*

503–511 Broadway (between Spring and Broome Sts.), SoHo, 212/226–0865. Subway: 6 to Spring St.

9 *d-6*

150 W. 34th St. (at Broadway), Midtown West, 212/594–0049. Subway: B, D, F, N, Q, R, V, W to 34th St./Herald Sq.

7 *c-1*

300 W. 125th St. (between 8th and St. Nicholas Aves.), Harlem, 212/531–1544. Subway: A, B, C, D to 125th St.

7 *e-8*

OLIVE & BETTE'S

Entering Olive & Bette's is like visiting a cozy walk-in closet jam-packed with

Michael Stars T's, cashmere by Autumn Cashmere and TSE, Diesel jeans, Theory separates, and other girly, downtown fashions. The store does a big celebrity business, but that doesn't detract from the slumber-party feel. Neither do the zebra carpets, festive blue stars, or pink chairs and curtains. *1070 Madison Ave. (at 81st St.), Upper East Side, 212/717–9655. Subway: 6 to 77th St.*

9 *b-1*
252 Columbus Ave. (at 72nd St.), Upper West Side, 212/579–2178. Subway: 1, 2, 3 to 72nd St.

11 *d-5*
158 Spring St. (between Wooster and W. Broadway), SoHo, 646/613–8772. Subway: N, R to Prince St.

11 *f-5*
ONLY HEARTS
The uptown store sells mostly lingerie; the downtown shop features the brand's line of romantic, flirty, feminine clothes. Think gauzy, slinky fabrics, embroidered lacy fabrics, and sweet candy colors. The prices are reasonable, too—especially considering the prime NoLita location. *230 Mott St. (between Prince and Spring Sts.), NoLita, 212/431–3694. N, R to Prince St.*

7 *b-8*
386 Columbus Ave. (between 78th and 79th Sts.), Upper West Side, 212/724–5608. Subway: 1, 2 to 79th St.

11 *d-1*
PATRICIA FIELD/
HOTEL VENUS
It's hard not to open a magazine and read something about Patricia Field these days. As the trend-setting stylist for *Sex and the City* (along with partner Rebecca Weinberg), she's making and breaking trends faster than a New York minute. Her two stores are indefatigable—Patty Field's on East 8th Street, Hotel Venus on West Broadway—and crammed with kitsch accessories, feather boas, rhinestones, drag-queen makeup, and skin-tight anything. The best or craziest stuff (fuschia and gold capris, disco mesh halters, polyurethane five-pocket pants) always seems to be way over $100. The store's bringing in more burgeoning designers now, like Heatherette and the popular Japanese import Hysteric Glamour (modern reinterpretations of rock-n'-roll classics in pillow-soft T's). The beauty salon (212/598–0395) turns

out some awesome dye jobs, and the custom wig salon is the best in the city. *10 E. 8th St. (between 5th Ave. and University Pl.), Greenwich Village, 212/254–1699. Subway: N, R to 8th St.*

11 *d-5*
382 W. Broadway (between Spring and Broome Sts.), SoHo, 212/966–4066. Subway: C, E to Spring St.

11 *d-4*
PHILOSOPHY DI
ALBERTA FERRETTI
The "you are you" philosophy espoused here happily leads to interesting contrasts: perfectly executed inverted pleats and rough, exposed seams; precise lines of caviar beads and free-form drizzles of rubber; unassuming earth tones and bright hibiscus pink. They normally put out just one example of each piece, so go ahead and ask for other sizes. *452 W. Broadway (between Prince and Houston Sts.), SoHo, 212/460–5500. Subway: F, V to Broadway–Lafayette St.*

11 *d-5*
PLEATS PLEASE
Even looking in the window of this shop is a high-tech tease—the glass becomes transparent or opaque depending on your angle. Here the house of Issey Miyake renders less cerebral variants on the tightly pleated polyester theme. Hues are punchier, with solid colors joined by speckles, color blocks, or graphics, and the designs generally stick to simple long skirts and dresses, tunics, and blouses. Sizing (3, 4, or 5) is based primarily on length, as the pleating will expand to fit your width. Price tags dangle at the several-hundred mark. *128 Wooster St. (at Prince St.), SoHo, 212/226–3600. Subway: N, R to Prince St.*

9 *e-1*
POLO/RALPH LAUREN
Lauren's flagship store, ensconced in a grand, beautifully renovated turn-of-the-20th-century town house, is one of New York's most distinctive shopping experiences. The atmosphere is scrupulously groomed; portraits are clustered over carpeted stairs, polished display cases gleam. The women's clothes run from casual madras shorts and cashmere cable-knits (perfect for the Easthampton bungalow) to glimmering, silk evening gowns (perfect for the Academy Awards). Across the street is another

Ralph Lauren boutique, this one modern and glossy, with chiseled, tough-jawed mannequins in the windows. It focuses on casual clothes, sports gear, and vintage pieces Europeans love to snatch up: old denim, motorcycle boots, worn college T-shirts. The SoHo branch has an outdoorsy feel (canoes on the ceiling, that sort of thing). The decor may be rough-hewn but the selection isn't— besides the Sport lines and casual clothes, you can weigh a suede skirt, ebony evening separates, or palazzo pants better suited for Bermuda than Maine. *867 Madison Ave. (at 72nd St.), Upper East Side, 212/606–2100; 888 Madison Ave. (at 72nd St.), Upper East Side, 212/434–8000. Subway: 6 to 68th St./Hunter College.*

11 *d-5*

379 W. Broadway (between Spring and Broome Sts.), SoHo, 212/625–1660. Subway: C, E to Spring St.

11 *e-5*

QUIKSILVER

The SoCal term "Roxy girls," a.k.a. surfer girls, comes from the women's line of this long-established surf outfitter. Boardshorts (quite a bit shorter than boys') and bikinis should get you thinking of sand between your toes. Sizing runs on odd numbers, and the cuts are often on the small side—for instance, if you're normally an 8, get a 9. Load up, then head to the dressing rooms, in the back past the giant hip-wiggling Hawaiian girls. You can also bag such gear as flip-flops, Hawaiian-print backpacks, and Sex Wax. *109–111 Spring St. (between Mercer and Greene Sts.), SoHo, 212/334–4500. Subway: N, R to Prince St.*

9 *e-1*

SCOOP

With its excellent sampling of young, pricey designers, this store injected a bit of SoHo into the Upper East Side. The labels are a strong cross-section of chipper haute funk, but racks are arranged by color rather than designer. Scoop up (sorry, couldn't help it) TSE and Cashmere Studio shells, skinny Chaiken & Capone or Theory pants, a Tocca dress or two, plus a few accessories, and you're ready to take on the weekly manicure set. The 3rd Avenue store has two annexes: "Street," with more casual threads, and "What's the Scoop?" for accessories. A beach-oriented branch cropped up in East Hampton. *1275 3rd Ave. (between 73rd and 74th Sts.), Upper East Side, 212/535–5577. Subway: 6 to 77th St.*

11 *e-5*

532 Broadway (between Prince and Spring Sts.), SoHo, 212/925–2886. Subway: N, R to Prince St.; 6 to Spring St.

9 *e-3*

SEARLE

Searle is an exclusively East Side phenomenon. The knits are covetable but most outstanding are the coats. Wool, leather, shearling, pea coats, reversible coats—go to a trunk show at 609 Madison Avenue. Summer brings tempting separates, including fitted T-shirts with necklines to flatter every *poitrine*. A new branch is due to open on 3rd Avenue between 74th and 75th streets. *609 Madison Ave. (at 58th St.), Midtown East, 212/753–9021. Subway: N, R, W, 4, 5, 6 to 59th St./Lexington Ave.*

9 *f-2*

1051 3rd Ave. (at 62nd St.), Upper East Side, 212/838–5990. Subway: N, R, W, 4, 5, 6 to 59th St./Lexington Ave.

7 *e-8*

1035 Madison Ave. (at 79th St.), Upper East Side, 212/717–4022. Subway: 6 to 77th St.

7 *e-8*

1124 Madison Ave. (at 84th St.), Upper East Side, 212/988–7318. Subway: 4, 5, 6 to 86th St.

9 *e-1, 2*

805 Madison Ave. (between 67th and 68th Sts.), Upper East Side, 212/628–6665. Subway: 6 to 68th St./Hunter College

11 *f-4*

SHOP NOIR

There's no such thing as too much sparkle at this NoLita shop, where a T-shirt, cellphone, or belt (or anything else) can be crystal-studded until it glitters like a chandelier. Air-brushing is another specialty (bring in a favorite photo to spread across a purse or a T), while non-custom offerings include big hoop earrings, graffiti-covered T-shirts, and metal-studded belts—all snatched up by the most sparkle-loving celebs like Madonna, Jennifer Lopez, and Britney Spears. *248 Mott St. (between Houston and Prince Sts.), NoLita, 212/966–6868. Subway: 6 to Bleecker St.*

11 *f-5*

SMAAK

Swedish-born Susannah Gaterud-Mack offers designs from Sweden (Filippa K, Anna Holtblad), Denmark (munthe plus simonsen), and Holland (Magriet Nannings) that are popular in Scandanavia but not available anywhere else in New York. *219 Mulberry St. (between Spring and Prince Sts.), Little Italy, 212/219–0504. Subway: 6 to Bleecker St.*

11 *f-3*

SPOOLY D'S

The common denominator among these new and vintage pieces is their downtown hipness. Straight-cut pants by Katayone Adeli, separates (such as oxford-cloth skirts) by Wink, and dark Earl jeans join vintage piqué shifts and cocktail dresses. It's just a skip away from the going-uptown Bleecker Street subway stop. *51 Bleecker St. (at Lafayette St.), East Village, 212/598–4415. Subway: 6 to Bleecker St.*

11 *d-5*

STEVEN ALAN

Clothes are often coy but not necessarily cheap in these cramped quarters. Short-in-the-tooth designers include Milk Fed, Vanessa Bruno, and Development; there are also more established (but still funky) secondary lines such as Martin Margiela's 6, and the legendarily low-waisted jeans of Frankie B. and Kateyone Adeli. The clothes on display tend to be in small sizes; you may have to ask them to bring out anything larger than a 6. *60 Wooster St. (at Broome St.), SoHo, 212/334–6354. Subway: 6 to Spring St.*

11 *h-4*

TG 170

This is one of the best boutiques on the Lower East Side. Flip through downtown separates such as wool tanks with leather edging or paisley silk skirts, then look above and below the racks for street-y additions such as Freitag messenger bags, which are made from tarps. *170 Ludlow St. (between Stanton and Houston Sts.), Lower East Side, 212/995–8660. Subway: F, V to 2nd Ave.*

11 *e-4*

TOCCA

Feeling girly? Float down to Tocca for a liberal helping of slip dresses, eyelet cotton, and embroidered flowers. The dressing rooms styled as peaked tents are cool, and the slightly retro aspect makes the merchandise hip—but the couple-hundred-dollar price tags require a grown-up budget. Tocca also carries a complete line of Italian-made handbags. *161 Mercer St. (between Houston and Prince Sts.), SoHo, 212/343–3912. Subway: N, R to Prince St.*

11 *f-5*

TRACY FEITH

The sexy, frilly dresses here make it hard to believe that Tracy is actually a tall, lanky, long-haired man who wears a cowboy hat. The clothes are incredibly expensive (blouses can be $350, dresses $500), but it's worth a trip just to swoon. Tissue-thin, intensely colored silk is whipped into curvy, spaghetti-strap dresses and wrap skirts. Fuschia, purple, apple green, cerulean blue in paisleys and florals—the clothes practically radiate "steamy tropical island." It all looks best with a tan and will pack to nothing in your suitcase. Sizing runs as petite, 1, 2, and 3, so you may have to try on a few things to find the right fit. *209 Mulberry St. (between Spring and Kenmare Sts.), Little Italy, 212/334–3097. Subway: 6 to Spring St.*

11 *g-1*

TRASH & VAUDEVILLE

True to its St. Mark's form, Trash and Vaudeville is a good source of club wear. The racks can outfit rockabillies, punks, and goths; Lou Reed reportedly trolls for tight jeans here. Slouch your way among black spiderweb dresses, python print pants, and shirts printed with drag queens. There's plenty under $100. *4 St. Mark's Pl. (near 2nd Ave.), East Village, 212/982–3590. Subway: 6 to Astor Pl.*

9 *e-1*

TSE

Good-girl cardigans aren't the only things on TSE's mind; recent collections have shown zip-front "sweatshirts" with fur-trim hoods, shift dresses with panels of silk satin, double face coats, and trousers, all in impossibly soft cashmere. There are also forays outside the realm of cashmere—stretch wool pants, silk separates, and superfine cotton essentials. But don't move too fast past the sweater basics (round neck, V-neck, turtleneck), whose soft colors and stitching make them endlessly desirable. There is also tseSAY, the lower-priced label that uses a bright, juiced-up color palette, as well as the luxe TSE Men's collection. *827 Madison Ave. (at 69th St.), Upper East Side, 212/472–7790. Subway: 6 to 68th St./Hunter College.*

9 *e-4*
UNITED COLORS OF BENETTON
For the most atmospheric Benetton experience, head to the flagship in the beaux-arts Scribner building at 5th Avenue and 48th Street. Despite the building's pedigree, the clothes aren't too serious: pastel tricot knits; candy-color, stretchy separates; some neutral-color base pieces. The newest location is under construction on 7th Avenue in Chelsea. *597 5th Ave. (between 48th and 49th Sts.), Midtown East, 212/593–0290. Subway: E, V to 5th Ave./53rd St.*

9 *f-2*
805 Lexington Ave. (at 62nd St.), Upper East Side, 212/752–5283. Subway: N, R, W, 4, 5, 6 to 59th St./Lexington Ave.

11 *e-1*
749 Broadway (at 8th St.), Greenwich Village, 212/533–0230. Subway: N, R to 8th St.; and other locations.

7 *f-8*
178 E. 78th St. (at 3rd Ave.), Upper East Side, 212/327–1039. Subway: 6 to 77th St.; and other locations.

11 *e-3*
URBAN OUTFITTERS
This chain rides trends hard and long, snatching up street fashions and throwing them into dozens of combinations, such as the drawstring/cargo and sari fabric/Indian gauze fads. These duds aren't meant to last forever, but then again you can put together an outfit for under $75. *628 Broadway (between Houston and Bleecker Sts.), Greenwich Village, 212/475–0009. Subway: 6 to Bleecker St.*

11 *g-1*
162 2nd Ave. (between 10th and 11th Sts.), East Village, 212/375–1277. Subway: 6 to Astor Pl.

11 *c-1*
374 6th Ave. (at Waverly Pl.), Greenwich Village, 212/677–9350. Subway: A, B, C, D, E, F, V to W. 4th St./Washington Sq.

9 *e-3*
127 E. 59th St. (between Lexington and Park Aves.), Midtown East, 212/688–1200.

Subway: N, R, W, 4, 5, 6 to 59th St./Lexington Ave.

11 *e-4*
VIVIENNE TAM
Though known for her signature East-meets-West style (embroidered flowers, koi fish), Tam has been cutting down on the Asian references. Her recent collections feature clingy techno fabrics softened by intricate embroidery, one-shoulder asymmetry, and tie-dying (in splashes of aqua or purple); leather cigarette pants and jodhpurs; and sheer fabrics, metallics, and edgy graphic prints. *99 Greene St. (between Prince and Spring Sts.), SoHo, 212/966–2398. Subway: N, R to Prince St.*

11 *f-5*
WANG
One of the rash of NoLita boutiques, Wang shows a keen eye for detail. Edged and contrast-stitched pockets show up in unexpected places, or a small line of ruffle suddenly flirts with your shoulder or skirt hem. Best of all, prices are relatively low—$170 for a nonubiquitous black dress. *166 Elizabeth St. (between Prince and Kenmare Sts.), NoLita, 212/941–6134. Subway: 6 to Spring St.*

11 *f-5*
X-LARGE
Despite the name, the clothes here won't swim on you—check the tags and you'll see that they're relatively "mini." Most items, from uniform-style shirts and hooded sweatshirts to stretch twill skirts or zip-front jackets, are under $100. At these prices, you'll still have some money left over for the CBGBs cover. *267 Lafayette St. (at Prince St.), SoHo, 212/334–4480. Subway: 6 to Bleecker St.*

11 *e-6*
YELLOW RAT BASTARD
If you need a dose of aggressive streetwear, you've arrived. Ultra-baggy jeans by Kik Wear, Ecko, and Diesel; tough-girl pants and shorts by Buggirl (about $60); smart-ass T-shirts by Porn Star and Pimp Gear (roughly $30)—just make sure you've got the right attitude to wear them. *478 Broadway (between Broome and Grand Sts.), SoHo, 212/219–8569. Subway: J, M, N, Q, R, W, Z, 6 to Canal St.*

11 e-4
ZARA

Emphasizing its international status, Zara lists over a dozen countries' currencies on each price tag. Like fellow newcomer Club Monaco, Zara specializes in cutting-edge Euro knockoffs with more of a dressy approach. But what this store boils down to is a stash of low-price, solid-color basics, from miniskirts to sweater sets. You can even get a pinstripe suit for under $200 if you don't mind 100% polyester. Modern but not too-too trendy suits, sweaters, and separates for men can be found along with a lot of big-buckle, square-toe shoes. The discount does, however, show in the fabric. Shirts are paper thin and blazers tend to have a few loose threads. Still, if you can't afford Gucci for the office, it's about your only alternative. *580 Broadway (between Houston and Prince Sts.), SoHo, 212/343–1725. Subway: F, V to Broadway–Lafayette St.*

9 e-3
750 Lexington Ave. (between 58th and 59th Sts.), Upper East Side, 212/754–1120. Subway: N, R, W, 4, 5, 6 to 59th St./Lexington Ave.

9 d-8
101 5th Ave. (between 17th and 18th Sts.), Flatiron District, 212/741–0555. Subway: N, R to 23rd St.

9 d-6
39 W. 34th St. (between 5th and 6th Aves.), Midtown West, 212/868–6551. Subway: B, D, F, N, Q, R, V, W to 34th St./Herald Sq.

11 f-5
ZERO

Designer Maria Cornejo's designs are known for their unique, simple cuts—like the matte jersey circle top made from a single piece of fabric with holes cut in for the head and arms—and their defining details, like a T-shirt's offcenter neckline or a pant's spiralling seam. The store itself is airy and gallery-like. *225 Mott St. (between Prince and Spring Sts.), NoLita, 212/925–3849. Subway: 6 to Bleecker St.*

designer

9 e-1
CAROLINA HERRERA

This is romantic, exquisitely refined clothing for shimmering brides, glitter-

ing socialites, and the Ivana trumps of the world. Fabrics like chinchilla, double-faced cashmere, indigo satin, and butter-soft leather fill the designer's first North American flagship store, located in the landmark Hubert de Givenchy building. *954 Madison Ave. (at 74th St.), Upper East Side, 212/249–6552. Subway: 6 to 77th St.*

9 e-2
CERRUTI

The precise tailoring that made Cerruti's name in men's suits is equally in evidence in the women's line—but that's not to say it runs to masculine styles. Besides pieces like classic, single-pleat trousers, look for softly structured knits and long, simply cut dresses. *789 Madison Ave. (at 67th St.), Upper East Side, 212/327–2222. Subway: 6 to 68th St./Hunter College.*

9 e-3
CHANEL

This slim, gray building is a true Chanel temple, where even the doorknobs (modeled after the bottle stoppers on No. 5 perfume) pay homage. The interior shines with black lacquer and mirrors, and a grand double staircase leads you upstairs. House designer Karl Lagerfeld concocts a successful mix of classic Chanel design elements and modern forms, including the new sportswear line (chi-chi winter ski wear). The cap-toe shoe, the exquisite tweed suits, the signature camellia and interlocking "C"s continue to be subtly reinvented; they're joined by such pieces as the ergonomic "millennium bag" and a variety of luggage. The second story is lent extra glitter with the fine jewelry boutique (which now carries watches); higher up roosts Frédéric Fekkai's five-story beauty salon. *15 E. 57th St. (between 5th and Madison Aves.), Midtown East, 212/355–5050. Subway: N, R, W to 5th Ave./59th St.*

11 d-5
139 Spring St. (at Wooster St.), SoHo, 212/334–0055. Subway: C, E to Spring St.

9 e-1
CHLOÉ

With Stella McCartney in the driver's seat, this redoubtable Parisian fashion house had quite a makeover—transforming from tired to white-hot in a flash. Stella left to launch her own line in 2001, and her former assistant Phoebe

Philo has taken over. Phoebe, in turn, has been sweetening the designs and conjuring up light, airy confections with delicate detailing, like embroidered panels cropping up in palazzo pants and curvy jackets, buttons racing up shirt and dress sleeves, and scalloped edges rounding off white knickerbocker suits. *850 Madison Ave. (at 70th St.), Upper East Side, 212/717–8220. Subway: 6 to 68th St./Hunter College.*

9 *e-3*

CHRISTIAN DIOR

Within the gorgeous LVMH building, Dior's classic dove gray interior has made way for pearly and chill-silver tones. Accessories (including the Lady Dior handbag with the signature over-sized beads on the handle), cosmetics, and shoes are on the ground floor; waft upstairs to reach the clothes. House designer John Galliano's wild streak makes itself known with exaggerated necklaces, deep shawl collars, and other flourishes. Whether the outfit is sedate or over-the-top, the tailoring is utterly perfect. *19 E. 57th St. (between 5th and Madison Aves.), Midtown East, 212/931–2950. Subway: E, V to 5th Ave./53rd St.*

9 *b-8*

COMME DES GARÇONS

This house is often years ahead of the others, both in terms of its clothes and its retail concept. After pioneering the minimalist store look in SoHo, it moved to its current space in far west Chelsea in 1999, where many cutting-edge galleries have gathered. The store itself is mesmerizing; you walk in through a steel tunnel, then land in a gleaming, white space carved up by curving walls strongly reminiscent of Richard Serra's Torqued Ellipses sculptures. Rei Kawakubo's astoundingly expensive avant-garde designs (multifabric jackets, innovative textures, tricks with linings, funky shoes, $60 socks) keep pace with this groundbreaking approach. Dresses are sculptural and complex—you may need to ask how they're meant to be put on. *520 W. 22nd St. (between 10th and 11th Aves.), Chelsea, 212/604–9200. Subway: C, E to 23rd St.*

10 *b-2*

DIANE VON FURSTENBERG

After this icon of '70s fashion relaunched her white-hot, signature wrap dresses in the late '90s, it was only a matter of time before this glamorous shop appeared. Needless to say, it's filled with flirty clothing that drapes the body, falls off the shoulders, and clings to the waist. The wrap dress appears regularly, along with flouncy shirts and sexy, straight-leg pants. *385 W. 12th St. (between Washington and West Sts.), West Village, 646/486–4800. Subway: A, C, E to 14th St.*

9 *e-1*

DOLCE & GABBANA

Somewhere among the buzzing synapses of Domenico Dolce and Stefano Gab-bana, Sicilian widows became founts of sex appeal—and the resulting combination of bosomy black and movie-star flair is intoxicating. Sweep into the ruby velvet dressing rooms to try on sheer leopard prints, corset-influenced slinky black dresses, bead-encrusted bustiers, and devastating mules. *825 Madison Ave. (between 68th and 69th Sts.), Upper East Side, 212/249–4100. Subway: 6 to 68th St./Hunter College.*

9 *e-1*

EMANUEL UNGARO

Since its gorgeous revamping in spring 2001, this shop has gotten much less serious: hot pink splashes the walls and a pink glass staircase sweeps danger-ously from one floor to the next. Granted, the heavily beaded evening jackets haven't changed too much, but the suits have wonderfully textured fabrics, rich colors, and the occasional surprise, such as color-tipped Mongolian lamb trim. The evening gowns are as sumptuous as ever. *792 Madison Ave. (at 67th St.), Upper East Side, 212/249–4090. Subway: 6 to 68th St./Hunter College.*

9 *e-2*

GEOFFREY BEENE

This small boutique, tucked near the entrance to the Sherry-Netherland hotel, may not pack the floor space of the Madison Avenue flagships, but it's got an enviable stable of curvaceous evening dresses. The day wear is no slouch, either. *783 5th Ave. (between 59th and 60th Sts.), Midtown East, 212/935–0470. Subway: N, R, W to 5th Ave./59th St.*

9 *e-1*

GIANFRANCO FERRE

A shiny, steely decor is Ferre's backdrop for extravagant women's pret-a-porter. There's a bit of old Hollywood in the giant collars, the dramatic satin and fur, and the sometimes revealing ensembles. *845 Madison Ave. (at 70th St.), Upper East Side, 212/717–5430. Subway: 6 to 68th St./Hunter College.*

9 *e-4*
GIANNI VERSACE
With his trademark blend of deference and rebelliousness, Versace restored this turn-of-the-20th-century 5th Avenue building, inlaid his Medusa-head logo on the sidewalk out front, and lined the interior with neon lights. The five floors encompass all of Versace's designs, from housewares to $150 jeans to couture. It's possible to find something relatively sedate, such as a mid-length black coat, but with Donatella at the helm there's always something daring with revealing slits, metal mesh, fur trim, or brash color. *647 5th Ave. (between 51st and 52nd Sts.), Midtown East, 212/317–0224. Subway: E, V to 5th Ave./53rd St.*

9 *e-1*
815 Madison Ave. (between 68th and 69th Sts.), Upper East Side, 212/744–6868. Subway: 6 to 68th St./Hunter College.

9 *e-2*
GIVENCHY
This venerable French fashion house—Audrey Hepburn's favorite—has become increasingly daring in recent years, first with the direction of Alexander McQueen and more recently with the appointment of Julien Macdonald. Whether Macdonald will keep up his barely-there celebrity fashions remains to be seen. You're guaranteed to find some beautiful purses and accessories, and stunning formal gowns. The new Madison Avenue shop is larger and more elaborate than the old location. *710 Madison Ave. (at 63rd St.), Upper East Side, 212/772–1040. Subway: N, R, W, 4, 5, 6 to 59th St./Lexington Ave.*

9 *e-3*
GUCCI
Tom Ford's design revamp made Gucci one of the most gawked-at stores in the city, and the white-hot label shows no signs of cooling off. The most recent collections have been more subdued than sexy, but the devastating low-heeled, pointy-toed boots, cashmere coats striped with leather, silk-square coats and dresses, and slightly sheer

baby doll dresses (in silk, crepe, and velvet) still keep fashionistas running uptown. *685 5th Ave. (at 54th St.), Midtown East, 212/826–2600. Subway: N, R, W to 5th Ave./59th St.*

9 *e-2*
HERMÈS
Hermès goes far beyond scarves and handbags. Upstairs are flawless, quietly tasteful clothes, from decoratively stitched gloves to single-pleat wool pants and silk blouses. Many pieces cost around $1,000, and the must-have Birkin bag can cost in the several thousands (though you'd have to fight tooth and claw to lay your hands on one, anyway). After those prices, the crimson riding jacket at about $850 may sound feasible. The new landmark building comes complete with winding stone staircase; an ethereal, light-filtering skylight; and L'Atellier, the heavenly top floor reserved for art exhibits and shows. *See also* Handbags, *below. 691 Madison Ave. (at 62nd St.), Upper East Side, 212/751–3181. Subway: N, R, W, 4, 5, 6 to 59th St./Lexington Ave.*

9 *e-2*
KRIZIA
Look through the pieces and you'll notice a certain animal figure cropping up—a jaguar, or perhaps an eagle. This is the "protector" of that particular collection, something that began as a whim and is now a Krizia signature. This is a good place to go suit shopping; the jackets are often more interesting than the standards. *769 Madison Ave. (at 66th St.), Upper East Side, 212/879–1211. Subway: 6 to 68th St./Hunter College.*

11 *d-5*
LOUIS VUITTON
As though designer Marc Jacobs didn't have his hands full with his own label, he's lavishing talent on the relatively new Vuitton clothing line. The signature check and monogram make just-enough appearances, such as on sling-back pumps or belted raincoats. Understated luxe infuses both the extravagant (buttery suede pants, double-faced cashmere) and the practical (rubberized cotton raincoats, with the signature lining). Of course, all this comes at prices that could choke a horse. *116 Greene St. (between Prince and Spring Sts.), SoHo, 212/274–9090. Subway: N, R to Prince St.*

HOPPING

9 *e-3*

703 5th Ave. (at 55th St.), Midtown East, 212/758–8877. Subway: N, R, W to 5th Ave./59th St.

9 *e-1*

MICHAEL KORS

Michael Kors's flagship store opened in fall 2000—to the delight of socialites and celebrities like Madonna and Gwyneth Paltrow. Luxurious, sensual clothes are set against a tasteful, camel-toned backdrop meant to evoke the feel of a neighborhood dress shop, albeit one where a slinky stretch T can cost $500. 974 Madison Ave. (between 76th and 77th Sts.), Upper East Side, 212/452–4685. Subway: 6 to 77th St.

9 *e-1*

MOSCHINO

Moschino's flagship is crazy, silly, and a helluva lot of fun. Once drawn in by the tongue-in-cheek window displays, you'll be adrift in smiley faces, bright mosaic floors, and murals trumpeting maxims such as "It's Better to Dress As You Wish Than As You Should!" The women's Cheap and Chic line is on the ground floor, while the women's signature collection is up the curving staircase, with its question-mark shaped bars. Don't worry: things don't get serious even when the price tags hit four figures—chairs in the signature collection area are upholstered with red-check tablecloth fabric, and there's a sculpted bowl of spaghetti on a table. Make sure you visit the "Toy-lette," which has walls of Lego and a Monopoly-board mirror. 803 Madison Ave. (between 67th and 68th Sts.), Upper East Side, 212/639–9600. Subway: 6 to 68th St./Hunter College.

9 *d-3*

OMO NORMA KAMALI

One thing this store doesn't have to worry about is being run-of-the-mill. The dun interior, with its blocky, disjointed stairways and mysterious corners, looks like a cross between an army bunker and a set from the Star Wars trilogy. Against this grim background, the gleaming satin of a skirt or the shirring of a white bathing suit may be something of a shock. Kamali is unfailingly creative, dreaming up everything from parachute-ready outfits to gathered velvet tops, puffy coats to fringe-covered pants. Downstairs are low-key casual clothes, often in fleece or cotton knits.

11 W. 56th St. (between 5th and 6th Aves.), Midtown West, 212/957–9797. Subway: E, V to 5th Ave./53rd St.

9 *e-1*

PRADA

It's a dream come true for the status-hawks: Prada is going like gangbusters, doing double time both uptown and down. Within the Madison Avenue store's pale-green walls is one of the biggest Prada selections outside Milan. The women's collections include pale gossamer dresses, occasional flashes of brightly colored trim, and stark black technofabric suits. Naturally, you'll also find plenty of the items that fueled the frenzy: sleek black nylon bags and thick-sole shoes. The small 57th Street boutique stocks only the coveted shoes. The SoHo stores also stock the sport lines—ski jackets, tennis whites (and blacks), sailing gear; the Broadway store shows this merchandise off in an especially dramatic, bleacher-lined setting. 841 Madison Ave. (at 70th St.), Upper East Side, 212/327–4200. Subway: 6 to 68th St./Hunter College.

9 *e-3*

724 5th Ave. (between 57th and 56th Sts.), Midtown West, 212/664–0010. Subway: N, R, W to 5th Ave./59th St.

11 *d-5*

116 Wooster St. (between Prince and Spring Sts.), SoHo, 212/925–2221. Subway: C, E to Spring St.

9 *e-3*

45 E. 57th St. (between Madison and Park Aves.), Midtown East, 212/308–2332. Subway: N, R, W to 5th Ave./59th St.

11 *e-5*

575 Broadway (at Prince St.), SoHo, 212/334–8888. Subway: N, R to Prince St.

9 *e-1*

SONIA RYKIEL BOUTIQUE

Malcolm McLaren once wrote a song called "Who the Hell Is Sonia Rykiel?" Now that Rykiel has a boutique on Madison, there's no excuse for asking the question. The grande dame of French knitwear creates lovely sweaters, sometimes sprinkled with rhinestones, sometimes sailor-striped. 849 Madison Ave. (between 70th and 71st Sts.), Upper East Side, 212/396–3060. Subway: 6 to 68th St./Hunter College.

9 *e-2*

VALENTINO

Fabric snobs will be in seventh heaven: you can drape yourself with camel hair, satin, suede, cashmere/silk, and cashmere/angora blends—and let's not forget the pure silk linings. The designs serenely possess true cinematic glamour, with elegant silhouettes and striking (but not overpowering) details. Coats often have fur collars or trim; dresses and suits are enhanced with just enough embroidery, cutwork, beading, or braid. The store is serene, with smooth marble, and the occasional well-placed orchid. *747 Madison Ave. (between 64th and 65th Sts.), Upper East Side, 212/772–6969. Subway: 6 to 68th St./Hunter College.*

7 *e-8*

VERA WANG

Justly famous for her bridal gowns, Wang also has a stunning selection of made-to-order evening wear. Choosing one of these gowns is an event in itself, and happens by appointment only, so call a few days in advance. Turn to the shimmering footwear collection once you've found your showstopper; the shoes are dyed to match. *991 Madison Ave. (at 77th St.), Upper East Side, 212/628–3400. Subway: 6 to 77th St.*

11 *d-5*

VIVIENNE WESTWOOD

A good shock goes a long way, as this British designer can attest. Long a bastion for outrageous design, Westwood gives us the bustiers and towering, fetishy platform shoes that rocked runways years ago. The audacious spirit is still fresh, running from trashed denim in the Anglomania line to giant buttons and vibrant colors for the suits. Cuts run small, so take the next size up to the fitting room—and even then you may find yourself holding your breath. *71 Greene St. (between Spring and Broome Sts.), SoHo, 212/334–5200. Subway: 6 to Spring St.*

11 *e-5*

YOHJI YAMAMOTO

Fabric is folded, pleated, gathered, and slashed; shapes are immaculately asymmetrical, architectural, and deconstructed; and Yohji has always been the master of the inkiest black. Still, these designs aren't always as severe as they seem—wool sweaters can be so fine they're almost translucent, and necklines, hems, and waists are tweaked imaginatively. There's even been room for a recent streak of athleticism: in 2001, Yohji's reinterpretations of the Adidas sneaker hit the fashion scene and had fashionistas in a frenzy. *103 Grand St. (at Mercer St.), SoHo, 212/966–9066. Subway: J, M, N, Q, R, W, Z, 6 to Canal St.*

9 *e-1*

YVES SAINT LAURENT

Since Gucci and Tom Ford came in to revamp the venerable French line, Yves has taken off tremendously. Then Ford went to work on the stores, with architect William Sofield; the sleek concrete and black-steel Madison Avenue boutique opened in fall 2001 and is now the template of everything Yves. Fashionhounds are snatching up the sexy leopard-spotted skirts and tops, the low-slung leather pants, and the hippie-inspired peasant blouses. *855 Madison Ave. (at 71st St.), Upper East Side, 212/988–3821. Subway: 6 to 68th St./Hunter College.*

discount & off-price

9 *d-6*

DAFFY'S

The Daffy's experience can fluctuate, from depressing racks of lurid polyester (Herald Center) to well-tended cruise wear (57th Street). You may have to wander through racks of undesirables to hit upon something, but you'll know it when you do: Cynthia Rowley dresses at one-third the list price or maybe a coup from a store closing. The lingerie department (better at Herald Center than at 5th Avenue) has Calvin Klein, Ralph Lauren, and DKNY underwear at half price. The European designers section has lots of mysterious "Made in Italy" labels, but you could turn up an Armani blazer for under $350. Be sure to inspect the more delicate items, as they can be manhandled beyond repair. The 5th Avenue store is the most crammed. *1311 Broadway (at 34th St.), Midtown West, 212/736–4477. Subway: B, D, F, N, Q, R, V, W to 34th St./Herald Sq.*

9 *e-8*

111 5th Ave. (at 18th St.), Flatiron District, 212/529–4477. Subway: F, V to 14th St.; N, R to 23rd St.

9 e-5

335 Madison Ave. (at 44th St.), Midtown East, 212/557–4422. Subway: S, 4, 5, 6, 7 to 42nd St./Grand Central.

9 e-3

135 E. 57th St. (between Lexington and Park Aves.), Midtown East, 212/376–4477. Subway: N, R, W, 4, 5, 6 to 59th St./Lexington Ave.; and other locations.

9 c-8

LOEHMANN'S

Loehmann's rep as one of the city's best designer discounters took a few knocks after it opened stores across the country. Happily, you can still dredge up a great bargain or two here in its hometown; stock quality varies, but it's replenished quickly. Expansive selections of sportswear, suits, and coats are diluted with racks of unrecognizable labels, but you can nab something such as a BCBG cardigan or Polo twill pants. The highest fashion concentration is in the upstairs Back Room, where the clothes are 30%–65% off. Three familiar names show up a lot: Donna Karan, Calvin Klein, and Ralph Lauren. Rake through the separates and you could find a stunning deal such as a Donna Karan lambskin jacket for $450, down from $1,795. 101 7th Ave. (at 16th St.), Chelsea, 212/352–0856. Subway: 1, 2, 3 to 14th St.

9 e-3

SYMS

Syms's educated consumers have enabled the store to snag a Park Avenue address. Skip the dubious racks of shorts sets and head to the humble, hand-lettered signs marked "couture," where the range of designers is far from shabby: Gianfranco Ferre, Krizia, Dolce & Gabbana, Gianni Versace. Granted, the wares may be a collection or two old, but if you pick classic styles, the look won't tell. Prices are normally slashed about 50%; gauge about $160 for Calvin Klein black wool trousers. More stunning deals are not uncommon, however, like a $920 Donna Karan winter-white wool/cashmere skirt for $119. The shoe selection may require a little more weeding, but finds such as moc-croc Ralph Lauren flats for under $100 are standard. 400 Park Ave. (at 54th St.), Midtown East, 212/317–8200. Subway: 6 to 51st St./Lexington Ave.; E, V to Lexington–3rd Aves./53rd St.

10 e-7

42 Trinity Pl. (at Rector St.), Lower Manhattan, 212/797–1199. Subway: N, R to Rector St.

resale

11 h-5

ED KLEIN'S OF MONTICELLO

One of Orchard Street's more genteel shopping experiences, Ed Klein's has become more high-end over the years and now stocks labels like Max Mara, Michael Kors, Bruno Magli, and Sonia Rykiel. 105 Orchard St. (at Delancey St.), Lower East Side, 212/966–1453. Subway: F, J, M, Z to Delancey St./Essex St.

7 e-7

ENCORE

It may not look like much from the outside, but once inside great finds will jump out at you. A 15-minute run-through could turn up a pair of Manolo Blahniks for under $200, a Gucci silk blouse or Bottega Veneta flats for under $150, or TSE and Malo cashmeres for under $300. The stock is always chock-full of Armani, Prada, Dolce & Gabbana, Hermès, and anything else you can think of—and, since the offerings reflect the original owners' closets, there are plenty of black dresses and suits. 1132 Madison Ave. (between 84th and 85th Sts.), 2nd floor, Upper East Side, 212/879–2850. Subway: 4, 5, 6 to 86th St.

11 f-4

INA

This pair of resale shops focuses on designer separates rather than full-blown, four-figure suits. This makes it easier to add an Alexander McQueen embroidered skirt (about $220) or Miu Miu pants (around $200) to your closet. Rifle through the choice shoes and you just may stumble upon Manolo Blahniks for under $300 or Stephane Kélian sandals. 21 Prince St. (between Mott and Elizabeth Sts.), NoLita, 212/334–9048. Subway: N, R to Prince St.

11 d-4

101 Thompson St. (between Prince and Spring Sts.), SoHo, 212/941–4757. Subway: C, E to Spring St.

7 e-8

MICHAEL'S

A small black sign at the cash register reminds you, "The treasure you see today may not be here tomorrow." The women who shop here take this to heart: there's an air of unusual seriousness to the browsing. There are special areas for Chanel/Hermès and Dolce & Gabbana (classic Chanel suits go for a cool $1,000), plus rich racks of separates. Brides can make an appointment to see the gown selection; all are no more than two years old. *1041 Madison Ave. (at 79th St.), Upper East Side, 212/737–7273. Subway: 6 to 77th St.*

9 d-8

OUT OF OUR CLOSET

Small and select, this store maintains a reliably chic stock, with finds like a $390 Prada shift dress previously owned by Cameron Diaz and a $375 Helmut Lang cadet suit with the tags still on. They're not total label snobs, though—you could find a particularly cool Banana Republic shirt within arm's reach of an Hermès or Armani blouse. *136 W. 18th St. (between 6th and 7th Aves.), Chelsea, 212/633–6965. Subway: 1, 2 to 18th St.*

unusual sizes

Among the department-store selections, Macy's has one of the most extensive large-size collections, called Macy Woman. Saks's Salon Z (now housed on its own floor) has some great designer lines, such as Dana Buchman, Ellen Tracy, and Marina Rinaldi, plus a special intimate-apparel area.

9 c-6

ASHANTI BAZAAR

These unique styles in large sizes (14–30) are often made of handwoven and hand-dyed fabrics. *307 W. 38th St., #1901 (between 8th and 9th Aves.), Midtown West, 212/239–1109. Subway: A, C, E to 34th St.*

7 b-7

DAPHNE

There's an ethnic twist to many of the clothes here—rich colors, batik-style prints, chunky jewelry—and often flattering cuts such as bias-cut skirts and tapered pants. Hand-painted silks and hand-woven fabrics round out this exuberant collection. *467 Amsterdam Ave. (between 82nd and 83rd Sts.), Upper West Side, 212/877–5073. Subway: 1, 2 to 79th St.*

7 c-1

LANE BRYANT

One of the spearheading mass-marketers for larger sizes (going back to 1916!), Lane Bryant carries both casual and moderately dressy lines in sizes 14–28. *222–224 W. 125th St. (between 7th and 8th Aves.), Harlem, 212/678–0546. Subway: 2, 3, A, B, C, D to 125th St.*

9 e-2

MARINA RINALDI

For stylish dressing, this place is a gold mine. Weekend wear, business suits, evening clothes, accessories—all pick the right current looks, from tunic cuts to tie-back dresses. Sizing is Italian (and corresponds to women's sizes 10–22); just ask the staff for a translation. *800 Madison Ave. (between 67th and 68th Sts.), Upper East Side, 212/734–4333. Subway: 6 to 68th St./Hunter College.*

vintage

Most vintage-clothing shops have a final-sale policy, so purchase carefully and wisely.

11 e-5

ALICE UNDERGROUND

While the thrift-store standards—letter jackets, leather coats (there's a huge selection of vintage leather, denim, and suede)—have a decent amount of rack space, they don't overwhelm the cashmere sweaters ($45–$85), filmy nightgowns, suede miniskirts ($40-ish), and well-preserved beaded tops. You might find a '70s Gucci briefcase for $350, or a stunning vintage wedding dress for anywhere between $100 and $8,000 (the wedding dresses are popular at Halloween as well). Linens and heaps of crocheted doilies are in the back room. There's a lot of one-of-a-kind stuff here; the shop provides inspiration for countless designers from the worlds of fashion, film, and Broadway. Some things are really used, not vintage (Ralph Lauren, Calvin Klein). Scout around for the store's own label on bowling shirts with atmospheric slogans such as "Laverne's Cocktail Lounge." *481 Broadway (between Broome and Grand Sts.), 212/431–9067. Subway: J, M, N, Q, R, W, Z, 6 to Canal St.*

7 b-8

ALLAN & SUZI
The proprietors, whom you'll no doubt find sitting behind the counter, are the godfather and -mother of fashion collectors. Their wacky shop preserves 1980s shoulderpads and 1940s gowns for posterity (or sale). *415 Amsterdam Ave. (between 79th and 80th Sts.), Upper West Side, 212/724–7445. Subway: 1, 2, 3 to 72nd St.*

11 e-1

ANTIQUE BOUTIQUE
This store recently returned to its roots (after flirting with modern and even futuristic duds), and now exclusively offers carefully chosen vintage pieces ranging from Lee western-style shirts to silver-spangled disco tops. Plus, they showcase collector-quality denim from Levi's to Sergio Valente (again, they're ahead of the curve). *712 Broadway (between Astor Pl. and E. 4th St.), Greenwich Village, 212/995–5577. Subway: 6 to Astor Pl.*

10 e-1

CHEAP JACK'S
The ordinary size of this store's entrance belies the huge amount of clothes-jammed space upstairs, downstairs, and in between. Push through the racks and you'll brush against everything from shagadelic blue velvet blazers to Chinese silk jackets, stiff lederhosen to slippery soccer shirts. However, Jack isn't as cheap as you'd like him to be—over $50 for corduroy bell-bottoms, more than a couple of hundred for most of the coats, be they faux leopard or military wool. *841 Broadway (between 13th and 14th Sts.), Flatiron District, 212/777–9564. Subway: L, N, Q, R, W, 4, 5, 6 to 14th St./Union Sq.*

10 f-1

COBBLESTONES
The best word for this stuff is stuff—a lot of fun old stuff. Racks of carefully chosen vintage clothing, cases of costume jewelry, piles of floaty scarves, lines of delicate shoes, and hats perched on stands—plus sunglasses, cigarette cases, umbrellas. You never know what you'll find here: *314 E. 9th St., East Village, 212/673–5372. Closed Mon. Subway: 6 to Astor Pl.*

11 e-3

EYE CANDY
This little store is literally brimming over with vintage handbags (Vuitton, Chanel, Whiting and Davis delicate metal mesh bags) tons of hats and sunglasses, and armfuls of collectible jewelry (Bakelite, Trifari, Weiss) that glitters from glass cases. Entering this shop is like opening your coolest grandmother's old jewelry box. *329 Lafayette St. (between Bleecker and Houston Sts.), Greenwich Village, 212/343–4275. Subway: 6 to Bleecker St.*

11 d-5

THE 1909 COMPANY
These classy two-piece suits and cashmere sweaters look like they once belonged to a dame d'un certain âge. The scarves, gloves, and crocheted or beaded bags are appropriately dainty. *63 Thompson St. (between Spring and Broome Sts.), SoHo, 212/343–1658. Subway: A, C, E to Canal St.*

11 h-1

RESURRECTION
A fabulous source for '60s fashion, these stores are regularly picked over by celebrities and the stylists who dress them. Check the windows for Jean Muir, swirls of Pucci (around $150 and up), and the strict lines of Courrèges (can be well over $400). There are also more humble choices, such as sport coats, jeans, and fatigues. The shoe selection is generally far superior to that in most vintage shops, ranging from blunt-nose pumps to knee-high boots. *123 E. 7th St. (between 1st Ave. and Ave. A), East Village, 212/228–0063. Subway: 6 to Astor Pl.*

11 f-5

217 Mott St. (between Prince and Spring Sts.), NoLita, 212/625–1374. Subway: Spring St.

10 e-2

SCREAMING MIMI'S
Vintage here doesn't go too far back—mostly to the '60s and '70s—but the finds (dashikis, 1960s sundresses in the $50 range, flares) repeatedly end up in fashion spreads. The stock is in consistently great condition, from the polyester shirts to the kooky shoes up front. Hike the stairs to the narrow loft and you might find some Playboy bunny picks or Mai Tai glasses among the housewares. Definitely worth repeat visits. *382 Lafayette St. (at E. 4th St.), East*

Village, 212/677–6464. Subway: F, V to Broadway–Lafayette St.

11 d-3

THE STELLA DALLAS LOOK

Barbara Stanwyck would be perfectly happy here. Specializing in '40s and '50s clothes, this Village boutique has some swell dresses, generally of high quality. *218 Thompson St. (between W. 3rd and Bleecker Sts.), Greenwich Village, 212/674–0447. Subway: A, B, C, D, E, F, V to W. 4th St./Washington Sq.*

11 g-1

TOKIO 7

Japanese Kewpie dolls beckon from the display windows; inside are crowded racks of clothes a few seasons old. Most choices are downtown get-around favorites (Tocca, agnès b., or A.P.C separates for under $100), with a few couture names mixed in. Scout around for the under-$10 bin. *64 E. 7th St. (between 1st and 2nd Aves.), East Village, 212/353–8443. Subway: 6 to Astor Pl.*

11 d-5

WHAT GOES AROUND COMES AROUND

This is no fly-by-night operation; What Goes Around Comes Around is known for its collectible denim and high-quality pickings. They're quick to jump on trends, such as Lily Pulitzer skirts (about $85) and Pucci shirts ($350–$375), and sometimes, as in the case of '70s concert T-shirts, they catch them good and early. There's also a good selection of vintage couture (Gucci dresses, wallets, purses), and a growing collection of vintage watches (Omega, Heuer), beaded jewelry, and belts. *351 W. Broadway (between Broome and Grand Sts.), SoHo, 212/343–9303. Subway: J, M, N, Q, R, W, Z, 6 to Canal St.*

CLOTHING FOR WOMEN/SPECIALTY

bridal shops

9 f-1

JEAN HOFFMAN ANTIQUES

This shop has a stunning array of antique or vintage wedding gowns—from all periods and in all styles. Go delicate, lacy and old-fashioned, don a flirty, girly number from the '50s—or find something a little funkier from the

'60s or '70s. Hoffman also has an eye for wedding accessories, from the turn of the last century to the present: pocketbooks, fans, gloves linens, and gift items. *207 E. 66th St. (between 3rd and 2nd Aves.), Upper East Side, 212/535–6930. Closed Sun.–Mon. Subway: 6 to 68th St./Hunter College.*

9 c-5

RK BRIDAL

Sprawling and loud with eager brides-to-be, this warehouse stocks a huge assortment of wedding gowns from a long list of labels like Jessica McClintock, Christin Wu, and Mon Cheri. They promise to beat prices from any other store, so bargain-hunters should check with them first. *318 W. 39th St. (between 8th and 9th Aves.), Midtown West, 212/947–1155. Subway: A, C, E to 42nd St.*

7 e-8

VERA WANG

Famous for her exquisite, luxurious bridal gowns, Wang revolutionized wedding gown design with her sumptuous couture styles. From the simple and elegant to the achingly ethereal or extravagant, these dresses are for all those girls who dreamed and dreamed of their wedding days. By appointment only. *991 Madison Ave. (at 77th St.), Upper East Side, 212/628–3400. Subway: 6 to 77th St.*

9 e-1

YUMI KATSURA

Yumi Katsura makes romantic, fantastical gowns that combine the traditionally Japanese (like kimono fabrics) with contemporary western design. Entering the store itself is like walking into a wedding cake. Gowns start at $2,400 and come in over 200 styles—serious shoppers should make an appointment. *907 Madison Ave. (between 72nd and 73rd Sts.), Upper East Side, 212/772–3760. Subway: 6 to 68th St./Hunter College.*

coats & rainwear

9 e-3

BURBERRY

Maker of the original trench coat, Burberry and its signature plaid have enjoyed a resurgence in popularity in recent years. These are the coats Humphrey Bogart wore in *Casablanca*—though now they come in suede and other fabrics as well as the classic gabardine. Burberry recently bought the building next door to its 57th Street location—the expanded retail space is expected to open in late 2002. 9 E. 57th St. (between 5th and Madison Aves.), Midtown East, 212/371–5010. Subway: N, R, W to 5th Ave./59th St.

furs & leather

9 e-3

FENDI

Animal products (fur and leather) being the Fendi backbone, you'll find extremely high quality, and prices, in their second-floor salon. Fendi specializes in furs other than the serviceable mink: sable, chinchilla, lynx. Styles are extravagant, even in mink; you'll find oversize collars, interesting piecing, and out-there styles like fox and goat tufts or dyed baby-blue and brown ponyskin. See also Handbags, below. 720 5th Ave. (at 56th St.), Midtown West, 212/767–0100. Subway: E, V to 5th Ave./53rd St.

9 d-7

FURS BY DIMITRIOS

The salespeople here are more than happy to help out a fur novice. Coat designs are straightforward, and the company believes staunchly in American mink. Dimitrios is one of the few storefronts in the 30th Street area that's open on weekends. 130 W. 30th St. (between 6th and 7th Aves.), Midtown West, 212/695–8469. Subway: 1, 2 to 28th St.

9 e-2

J. MENDEL

This Parisian firm has impeccable, weak-in-the-knees coats. They're often in mink, or in thick cashmere with fur trim, and you can easily find a slim style that's not overwhelming. Besides the beautiful, long, classic shapes, there are lighter takes like zip-front or poncho styles. 723 Madison Ave. (between 63rd and 64th Sts.), Upper East Side, 212/832–5830. Subway: N, R, W, 4, 5, 6 to 59th St./Lexington Ave.

9 d-7

150 WEST 30TH STREET

This towering building is heavy with furriers, including the traditional craftsman Ben Kahn (212/279–0633) and George Mamoukakis Furs (212/564–2976), which carries mainly mink. 150 W. 30th St. (between 6th and 7th Aves.), Midtown West. Subway: 1, 2 to 28th St.

9 e-3

REVILLON

Another Parisian firm, Revillon is luxurious without being old-fashioned. Besides the dignified minks and foxes, there are short, zippered jackets and brightly dyed fur accessories (scarves, purses in Mongolian lamb). For something less conspicuous, there are fur-lined coats in wool, silk, or water-resistant microfiber. 717 5th Ave. (at 56th St.), Midtown East, 212/317–0039. Subway: E, V to 5th Ave./53rd St.

9 d-3

RITZ FURS

This is an excellent place to try for a "gently worn" fur. You can get a basic mink starting at around $1,000, though prices go up to about $5,000 (with a few $10,000-plus sable beauties thrown in). Everything is cleaned and glazed, and your purchase comes with free alterations and free storage. 107 W. 57th St. (between 6th and 7th Aves.), Midtown West, 212/265–4559. Subway: F, N, R, Q, W to 57th St.

9 d-7

345 7TH AVENUE

With 25 floors filled predominantly with furriers, you can hardly go wrong. David and Daniel Antonovich are here (212/244–3161 or 212/244–0666), and there are plenty of other glamorous names, like Furs by Frederick Gelb (212/239–8787), which is a good place to go for sable. 345 7th Ave. (between 29th and 30th Sts.), Midtown West. Subway: 1, 2 to 28th St.; A, C, E, 1, 2, 3 to 34th St./Penn Station.

handbags

11 f-5

AMY CHAN

The signature tile bags (acetate chips over soft fabric) are constantly being updated—currently in vivid religious prints and florals—and the handbag line has expanded to include gorgeous patent and embossed leather designs. The stock has expanded as well—with a selection of clothing that ranges from the lowest Frankie B. jeans to deconstructed and Victorian-style T's from Alice Lawhorn and Alabama. 247 Mulberry St. (between Prince and Spring Sts.), NoLita, 212/966–3417. Subway: 6 to Spring St.

9 *e-3*

ANYA HINDMARCH

If you're ever to empty your wallet while buying a new one, this may be the place to do it. Your eye might catch one of the tiny coin purses or a satin bag with a funny silkscreened photo on the front. The next thing you know, you're reeled in by the beaded strap of an evening bag or a leather passport holder decorated to look like an envelope. *29 E. 60th St. (at Madison Ave.), Midtown East, 212/750–3974. Subway: N, R, W to 5th Ave./59th St.*

9 *e-2*

ARTBAG

Besides selling new bags, this store is essential for those who can't part with their old ones: they arrange expert, albeit expensive, handbag repairs, plus custom jobs, alterations, and reconditioning. While they inspect your scruffy tote, check out the gleaming wares, some in alligator or ostrich. At press time, the store was planning a move farther uptown. *735 Madison Ave. (at 64th St.), Upper East Side, 212/744–2720. Subway: 6 to 68th St./Hunter College.*

11 *f-4*

BLUE BAG

Like Calypso (*see Clothing, above*), this is a St. Barth's import, giving us parched New Yorkers another swig of color and fun. Bags run from plain-and-simple (woven straw) to medium-well (patterned silk, painted fabric) to Statement (dripping with fringe). *266 Elizabeth St. (between Prince and Houston Sts.), NoLita, 212/966–8566. Subway: 6 to Bleecker St.*

9 *e-3*

FENDI

The baguette bag put Fendi firmly back onto society ladies' must-have lists. Besides the traditional cocoa-color double-Fs, you'll find suede and beading, mother-of-pearl detailing, and sequins. *See also Furs, above. 720 5th Ave. (at 56th St.), Midtown West, 212/767–0100. Subway: E, V to 5th Ave./53rd St.*

11 *h-4*

FINE & KLEIN

One of the best Lower East Side discount anythings, Fine & Klein sells chichi day and evening bags at great discounts. If you have your heart set on

something in particular, come with a picture and style number; often they can track it down or order it. Sunday is a feeding frenzy, so try to come on a weekday. *119 Orchard St. (between Delancey and Rivington Sts.), Lower East Side, 212/674–6720. Closed Sat. Subway: F, J, M, Z to Delancey St./Essex St.*

9 *e-2*

FURLA

This Italian firm specializes in smooth, classic shapes—but not too classic. A rectangular bag could have an extended line; flower-shape cutouts could lighten a square purse. Accessories include some adorable coin purses shaped like fruit. *727 Madison Ave. (between 63rd and 64th Sts.), Upper East Side, 212/755–8986. Subway: N, R, W, 4, 5, 6 to 59th St./Lexington Ave.*

11 *d-5*

430 W. Broadway (between Prince and Spring Sts.), SoHo, 212/343–0048. Subway: C, E to Spring St.

9 *e-2*

HERMÈS

Once a saddler, always a saddler. After well over a century, Hermès still has beautiful saddles and bridles (upstairs), as well as the famous scarves (about $275), the coveted, ultra-pricey Birkin bag, and the trim "Kelly" bags originally designed for Grace herself. A leather craftsman is available for special orders, repairs, and advice on leather care. *691 Madison Ave. (at 62nd St.), Upper East Side, 212/751–3181. Subway: N, R, W, 4, 5, 6 to 59th St./Lexington Ave.*

11 *f-4*

JAMIN PUECH

With an amazing color sensibility and a fin-de-siècle taste for richesse, this design team pulls off luxury without stuffiness, hipness without trendiness. Small sequined rounds glow in plum or chartreuse, patchworks are pieced of ponyskin or tweed, and if you haven't had enough, you can wrap something feathery around your neck. *252 Mott St. (between Prince and Houston Sts.), NoLita, 212/334–9730. Subway: 6 to Spring St.*

7 *e-8*

JUDITH LEIBER

These small, sparkling cases are meant to be cradled in the palm rather than slung over the shoulder. The bejeweled shapes include fruit, animals, and even seashells—beautiful, certainly, but you may have to ask your escort to carry your wallet. *987 Madison Ave. (between 76th and 77th Sts.), Upper East Side, 212/327–4003. Subway: 6 to 77th St.*

11 *e-5*
KATE SPADE
The signature satin-finish nylon handbags and totes are all here—and are imitated everywhere else—and now the collection includes a large variety of leather (vachetta, boarskin, glazed caramel) and other fabrics (herringbone, pony, tweed, linen), in the same cleanly geometric shapes. A new signature pattern, the '60s op-art-inspired "noel weave," was introduced in fall 2001, and is being incorporated into the shoe, glasses, and paper product designs. As the line becomes more travel-oriented, watch for the tell-tale patterns and shapes to crop up on suitcases and duffel and garment bags. *454 Broome St. (at Mercer St.), SoHo, 212/274–1991. Subway: C, E to Spring St.*

11 *f-5*
KAZUYO NAKANO
Elegant hand-crafted bags displayed like pieces of art populate this Japanese designer's NoLita shop, a favorite of stars like Cameron Diaz. *223 Mott St. (between Prince and Spring Sts.), NoLita, 212/941–7093. Subway: N, R to Prince St.*

9 *e-2*
LONGCHAMP
Long a Parisian favorite, Longchamp introduced its own boutique here in fall 1999. Most bags are in leather, from high gloss to matte finishes. Styles are modern without being trendy; they range from slim shoulder bags to polished backpacks, plus accessories such as wallets, cellphone holders, and belts. *713 Madison Ave. (at 63rd St.), Upper East Side, 212/223–1500. Subway: N, R, W, 4, 5, 6 to 59th St./Lexington Ave.*

9 *e-3*
LOUIS VUITTON
Vuitton's famous monogram adorns everything from wallets and yen holders to backpacks and dog carriers, and in the past few collections there's been a new, quick-paced energy. Besides the brown-on-brown LVs, there's the Epi leather line, with a striated texture and

fun colors (lipstick-red, rain-slicker yellow), the reintroduced brown checkerboard "Damier" canvas and new "Damier" hair calf collection, the new "Mini-Monogram" canvas line, and the "Monogram Vernis," which plugs the magic letters into shiny dyed leather (bronze, red, silver). Shapes are racing ahead, too, from small-scale oblong clutches to square holdalls. *703 5th Ave. (at 55th St.), Midtown East, 212/758–8877. Subway: N, R, W to 5th Ave./59th St.*

11 *d-5*
116 Greene St. (between Prince and Spring Sts.), SoHo, 212/274–9090. Subway: N, R to Prince St.

11 *a-2*
LULU GUINESS
With its gleaming checkerboard floors, lilac-striped walls, and colorful Parisian flourishes, this recent Brit import seduces even before you catch sight of the marvelously whimsical bags, shaped like tiny pagodas and corner shops, red lips and Chinese fans, or featuring punk poodles, multi-colored butterflies, and New York City skylines. The bags manage to be both kitschy and delicately feminine at the same time. *394 Bleecker St. (near Perry St.), Greenwich Village, 212/367–2120. 1, 2 to Christopher St.*

9 *b-1*
ROBERTO VASCON
Play designer with Roberto Vascon by creating a one-of-a-kind handbag from his arsenal of patterns and 200 Italian leather hides. Expect about a 20-day turnaround time for your purse to be completed; a bit longer around the holidays. *140 W. 72nd St. (near Columbus Ave.), Upper West Side, 212/787–9050. Subway: B, C to 72nd St.*

hats & gloves

11 *d-4*
THE HAT SHOP
Hats climb the walls, inviting a try-on (with the help of the friendly salespeople). Traditional shapes are often tweaked; a brimmed straw hat, for instance, could be hooked with fishing flies or corset-laced with ribbon. The cocktail hats are tiny, Dr. Seuss–like things with a precarious plume or two. Everything can be made to order at no extra charge. *120 Thompson St. (between*

Prince and Spring Sts.), SoHo, 212/219–
1445. Subway: N, R to Prince St.

11 f-4
KELLY CHRISTY
Woven berets, sun hats with a rose hidden under the wide brim, fall felts, and
other confections can be made to order;
you can even custom-pick the colors.
Prices start around $200. The men's
hats are increasingly popular as well. 235
Elizabeth St. (between Houston and
Prince Sts.), NoLita, 212/965–0686. Subway: F, V to Broadway–Lafayette St.

9 e-6
LACRASIA
The practice of wearing gloves for fashion or propriety instead of just warmth
may be history, but LaCrasia is a wonderful holdout. Do your hands a favor
and have them fitted for a custom pair.
LaCrasia's work goes far beyond the
short, everyday variety—for a heady
draft of elegance, try the elbow-length or
long gloves. Diehards can make an
appointment to see the Glove Museum.
For a lighthearted pair, nip into the
Grand Central Station branch. 304 5th
Ave. (between 32nd and 31st Sts.), Midtown West, 212/594–2223. Subway: 6 to
33rd St.

9 e-5
Grand Central Station, Midtown East,
212/370–0310. Subway: S, 4, 5, 6, 7 to
42nd St./Grand Central.

11 f-5
LISA SHAUB
Lisa's hats are as simple and cozy as
your favorite pair of jeans, but always
come with an unexpected twist, like
leather trim on a straw hat, or details
like interestingly stitched bands, top-
stitching, or uniquely contrasting colors
(Lisa dyes all her own colors). Lisa sold
her hats wholesale to Barneys and Bendels before opening her own store in
1998; now she works with customers
one on one to get the perfect fit and
style. Hats come in all shapes and sizes,
for women, men, kids, and babies. For
the truly inspired, Lisa offers millinery
classes. 232 Mulberry St. (between Prince
and Spring Sts.), NoLita, 212/965–9176.
Subway: 6 to Bleecker St.

lingerie & nightwear

9 e-1
BRA SMYTH
This dedicated shop really knows its
inventory; it's even got a bra hot line
(800/BRA-9466). Lacy, expensive European imports predominate—Aubade,
Chantelle, even Lise Charmel's authentic Chantilly lace. Look for Hanro and
Donna Karan for plainer, cheaper goods.
They've also got a great selection of
minimizers, uplift bras, and seamless
underwear. And they'll do alterations not
only on their stock but on your own. 905
Madison Ave. (between 72nd and 73rd
Sts.), Upper East Side, 212/772–9400.
Subway: 6 to 77th St.

11 g-2
ENELRA LINGERIE
Frank Sinatra is likely to be crooning
from the speakers as you peruse this
East Village staple's silky offerings,
which range from low-end (Leg Avenue,
Hanky Panky) to mid-level (La Cosa, Le
Mystere, Cosabella) to fancy, high-end
designer lingerie (Chantel Thomas,
Leigh Bantivoglio), along with satin eye-
patches, Kama Sutra edible oils, and
sexy temporary tattoos. 48 E. 7th St.
(between 1st and 2nd Aves.), East Village,
212/473–2454. Subway: N, R to 8th St.

9 e-2
FOGAL
Fogal carries luxurious Swiss-made
pantyhose, stockings, and bodysuits in
more than 100 colors—perfect underpinnings for women who wear Chanel
and Valentino. 680 Madison Ave.
(between 61st and 62nd Sts.), Upper East
Side, 212/759–9782. Subway: N, R, W, 4,
5, 6 to 59th St./Lexington Ave.

9 e-3
510 Madison Ave. (at 53rd St.), Midtown
East, 212/355–3254. Subway: E, V to 5th
Ave./53rd St.

11 d-4
JOOVAY
This store is so petite that it literally has
underwear up to the ceiling. One wall
climbs with underpinnings: Rigby &
Peller, with Queen Elizabeth II's seal of
approval (and a royal price tag); La
Perla; Le Mystère; Cosa Bella (bras
about $40–$75); and Oroblu hosiery.
The other wall is hung with nightgowns,
PJs, and robes; look for the silk gowns

with a textured, almost seersucker finish or contrast-color lace. *436 W. Broadway (between Prince and Spring Sts.), SoHo, 212/431–6386. Subway: N, R to Prince St.*

9 e-1
LA PERLA
Unabashedly gorgeous underpinnings hit the seduction buttons with lashings of creamy lace, embroidery, and unadorned silk. The fabrics—stretch tulle, silk georgette, opaque silk crepe—are every bit as aristocratic as the prices. The Italian sizing is a bit easier to navigate, though, with cup sizes now included on the labels. (If you're still not sure, the staff will be happy to help fit you.) *777 Madison Ave. (between 66th and 67th Sts.), Upper East Side, 212/570–0050. Subway: 6 to 68th St./Hunter College.*

10 e-1
LA PETITE COQUETTE
The autographed photos on the walls have extra cachet here; one thank-you came from Frederique, longtime Victoria's Secret model. (If she's spent that much time in just her underwear, she must know whereof she speaks.) The silky stuff is on the ground level—some Aubade (about $150 for a stunning bustier), Le Mystère, and La Petite Coquette's own rainbow selection of silk slips, camisoles, and nightgowns (around $70 for a full slip). Downstairs are cotton nightgowns and a few children's items. *51 University Pl. (between 9th and 10th Sts.), Greenwich Village, 212/473–2478. Subway: N, R to 8th St.*

11 d-5
LE CORSET
Sashaying beyond the norm, this boutique is made for indulgences. You could find something such as handmade silk-and-lace bra and underwear sets, white cotton PJs stitched with pale green "zzz"s, even a few dusty-pink vintage girdles. And of course there's the store's namesake, from vampy black to lacy white. *80 Thompson St. (between Spring and Broome Sts.), SoHo, 212/334–4936. Subway: C, E to Spring St.*

9 e-3
WOLFORD
Hosiery here runs about $28 and up, but if you invest in "Individual 10," a sheer stocking with a high percentage of Lycra, you stand a good chance of wearing it several times. Short- and long-sleeved bodysuits start at $160; the bathing suits have the same seamless fit. And then there's Logic, Wolford's no-waistband line of hosiery, and Long Distance, the first knee-high made to help boost circulation. *619 Madison Ave. (between 58th and 59th Sts.), Midtown East, 212/688–4850. Subway: N, R, W, 4, 5, 6 to 59th St./Lexington Ave.*

7 e-8
996 Madison Ave. (between 78th and 77th Sts.), Upper East Side, 212/327–1000. Subway: 6 to 77th St.

maternity

9 e-1
LIZ LANGE
Ms. Lange is of the "don't lose your fashion edge just because you're expecting" school. The slim pants, twinsets, and strappy dresses are pared-down but high-quality, and they don't shy away from sex appeal. By using stretch fabrics (everything from cashmere to denim) and elastic waistbands, she's eliminated the need for maternity panels. Many of the separates can be mix-and-matched; the ability to make several outfits out of a few pieces is especially welcome, since the styles don't come cheap. *958 Madison Ave. (between 75th and 76th Sts.), Upper East Side, 212/879–2191 or 888/616–5777. Subway: 6 to 77th St.*

9 f-2
MIMI MATERNITÉ
The approach here is not just ribbons and bows—when leggings and an oversize oxford shirt won't pass muster, they come through with business suits and dress-up knits. Current trends find their way in, too, such as the capri pants with a stretchy front panel or a raw-silk evening suit. *1021 3rd Ave. (between 60th and 61st Sts.), Upper East Side, 212/832–2667. Subway: N, R, W, 4, 5, 6 to 59th St./Lexington Ave.*

9 b-1
2005 Broadway (at 69th St.), Upper West Side, 212/721–1999. Subway: 1, 2 to 66th St./Lincoln Ctr.

7 e-7
1125 Madison Ave. (at 84th St.), Upper East Side, 212/737–3784. Subway: 4, 5, 6 to 86th St.

`11` *f-5*

MOMMY CHIC

Highend maternity fashion finally hits the NoLita scene with this breezy store, filled with deliciously colored, slightly loose clothing that even nonpregnant women would be happy to wear. Beaded tie-back halter tops, microfiber pants, ruffle neck paisley chiffon dresses, hand-beaded lace cocktail dresses—all delicately swooping over a curved stomach, while letting a mom-to-be keep her edge. *235 Mulberry St. (between Prince and Spring Sts.), NoLita, 212/244–2666. Subway: 6 to Bleecker St.*

`9` *f-1*

MOM'S NIGHT OUT

This second-floor boutique fills a small but crucial niche: it specializes in maternity evening wear and cocktail-dress rentals. Renters can choose from over 300 styles and colors; a four-day rental can run anywhere from $165 to $250. If you're thinking of investing in four-months-at-a-time evening wear, you can browse through the styles, create a design, and have an outfit custom-made. There's also a small ready-to-wear selection. Call ahead; you may need to make an appointment. *147 E. 72nd St. (between Lexington and 3rd Aves.), Upper East Side, 212/744–6667. Subway: 6 to 68th St./Hunter College.*

`7` *e-7*

MOTHERHOOD MATERNITY

A less-expensive chain, these stores concentrate on casual items such as denim overalls or jumpers and T-shirts. *1449 3rd Ave. (at 82nd St.), Upper East Side, 212/734–5984. Subway: 4, 5, 6 to 86th St.*

`9` *d-8*

641 6th Ave. (at 20th St.), Chelsea, 212/741–3488. Subway: F, V to 23rd St.

`9` *d-6*

Manhattan Mall (see Malls, above), 212/564–8170. Subway: B, D, F, N, Q, R, V, W to 34th St./Herald Sq.

`9` *e-3*

A PEA IN THE POD

Though the name is lighthearted, the clothing is in all seriousness: comfortable and well-made casual and career clothes, even bathing suits. *625 Madison Ave. (between 58th and 59th Sts.), Mid-town East, 212/826–6468. Subway: N, R, W, 4, 5, 6 to 59th St./Lexington Ave.*

`11` *f-1*

PUMPKIN MATERNITY

The city's first downtown maternity shop—complete with sleek wooden floors and a jungle-theme mural decorating the otherwise spare walls—Pumpkin Maternity carries sexy, hip, form-fitting clothes, like fake leather pants, boot-cut jeans, and stretchy black dresses. *407 Broome St. (at Lafayette St.), SoHo, 212/334–1809. Subway: 6 to 68th St./Hunter College.*

COINS & STAMPS

`9` *b-3*

CHAMPION STAMP CO INC.

The most respected and well-known open-to-the-public stamp shop in New York City sells stamps from all over the world, covers, and supplies for every level of collector—from beginners to philatelic experts. *432 W. 54th St. (between 9th and 10th Aves.), Midtown West, 212/489–8130. Subway: C, E to 50th St.*

`9` *d-4*

COIN DEALER, INC.

This shop in the Diamond District buys, appraises, and sells rare coins both domestic and foreign, and specializes in gold coins and coin jewelry. *15 W. 47th St. (between 5th and 6th Aves.), Midtown West, 212/246–5025. Subway: B, D, F, V to 49th–50th St./Rockefeller Center.*

`9` *e-7*

HARMER

Harmer specializes in stamps: it auctions, appraises, and arranges private treaties. *3 E. 28th St. (between 5th and Madison Aves.), Murray Hill, 212/532–3700. Subway: 6 to 28th St.*

`9` *d-4*

NEW YORK STAMP COLLECTION

New York Stamp is a favorite of Asian tourists seeking missing parts of their collections. Dating back 150 years, the collection here focuses on stamps, coins, and paper money illustrating the rich history of Asian countries (in addition to a selection of worldwide pieces). *135 Division St. (at Canal St.), Chinatown, 212/264–7117. Subway: F to E. Broadway.*

9 *f-3*

PAUL J. BOSCO

Bosco has America's most comprehensive stock of worldwide coins dated 1500–1900, and a top-notch selection of medals—from the Renaissance to art deco periods. *1050 2nd Ave. (at 55th St.), Midtown West, 212/758–2646. Subway: N, R, W, 4, 5, 6 to 59th St./Lexington Ave.*

9 *e-2*

SPINK AMERICA

A member of the Christie's group, Spink America deals in and auctions rare coins, historical medals, and bank notes from antiquity to the present. *55 E. 59th St. (between Madison and Park Aves.), 15th floor, Midtown East, 212/486–3660. Subway: N, R, W, 4, 5, 6 to 59th St./Lexington Ave.*

9 *d-3*

STACK'S

America's oldest and largest coin dealer, Stack's deals in rare coins (U.S. and foreign) and sells ancient gold, silver, and copper coins as well. The house holds eight auctions a year. *123 W. 57th St. (between 6th and 7th Aves.), Midtown West, 212/582–2580. Closed weekends. Subway: F, N, R, Q, W to 57th St.*

COMPUTERS & SOFTWARE

9 *e-6*

COMPUSA

CompUSA caters to technophobes and techies alike with an expertly trained staff that can figure out what you need even if your technical vocabulary is limited to the redundant use of the word "thingy." This dual-level superstore is stocked with all of the computers and accessories you could ever want. Need some training? CompUSA offers a full range of courses for all skill levels. *420 5th Ave. (between 37th and 38th Sts.), Midtown West, 212/–782–7720. Subway: B, D, F, V, N, Q, R, W to Herald Sq.*

9 *c-3*

1775 Broadway (between between 57th and 58th Sts.), Midtown West, 212/262–9711. Subway: B, D, A, C, E, 1 to Columbus Circle.

9777 Queens Blvd. (at 64th Rd.), Rego Park, Queens, 718/793–8663. Subway: R, V to 63rd Dr./Rego Park.

9 *e-8*

GATEWAY COUNTRY

Gateway can help you put together the personal or business system that suits your individual needs and also stocks printers, scanners, and cameras from brands like Intel, Hewlett Packard, Epson, Visioneer, and Visors. Allow 5–10 business days for a system to arrive at your home or office. The Columbus Circle outpost does sales and is the service center for New York City. Shipping services are available for pickups and returns. *45 E. 17th St. (between Union Sq. E and Union Sq. W), Flatiron District, 212/982–4240. Subway: N, R, 4, 5, 6, L to Union Sq.*

7 *e-7*

242 E. 86th St. (at Lexington Ave.), Upper East Side, 212/988–4425. Subway: 4, 5, 6 to 86th St.

9 *c-3*

4 Columbus Circle (57th St. and 8th Ave.), Midtown West, 212/246–5575. Subway: A, B, C, D, 1, 2 to 59th St./Columbus Circle.

10 *e-6*

J&R MUSIC & COMPUTER WORLD

It's chaos in here, but J&R is staffed with savvy salespeople who are far more patient than you'd think, if you can only flag one down. You'll find all the major brands: Apple, AT&T, Brother, Compaq, Epson, HP, IBM, Intel, NEC, Panasonic, Sony, Texas Instruments, and more. *15 Park Row (between Ann and Beekman Sts.), Lower Manhattan, 212/238–9100. Subway: 4, 5, 6 to Brooklyn Bridge/City Hall.*

9 *d-7*

TEKSERVE

It's almost quaint, their nickname: "The Old Reliable Mac Service Shop." True, Mac sales are secondary to service and repair at this haven for Mac users, but these salespeople are some of the most knowledgeable in New York, and they're incredibly honest and friendly. Doubts? This writer once spilled a beer on her PowerBook, and Tekserve was entirely sympathetic—said a Diet Coke would have been worse. And check out the line in their hallway at 8:55 AM. Now that it's been anointed with a *Sex and the City* mention, those who bring in their candy colored computers for servicing will be taking a number and having a 10¢ Coke while they wait. *155 W. 23rd St. (between*

6th and 7th Aves.), 4th floor, Chelsea, 212/ 929–3645. Subway: 1, 2, F, V to 23rd St.

COSTUME RENTAL

9 *d-8*

ABRACADABRA

Here's a huge inventory of costumes, with masks, magic, and makeup to top them off. *19 W. 21st St. (between 5th and 6th Aves.), Flatiron District, 212/627–5194. Closed Sun. Subway: N, R to 23rd St.*

9 *c-6*

CREATIVE COSTUME COMPANY

Choose from over 10,000 costumes in stock from Broadway to period to holiday looks. If you can't find what you're looking for to buy or rent, the company will custom-design to suit your needs. "Nobody leaves without fitting perfectly into their costumes," according to the staff that alters, adds details, or changes colors to create the perfect costume. If you can't make it to the shop, Creative Costume Company can e-mail pictures of costumes. *242 W. 36th St. (between 7th and 8th Aves.), 8th floor, Midtown West, 212/564–5552. Closed weekends; extended hours in Oct. Subway: B, D, F, N, Q, R, S, W to 34th St.; A, C, E, 1, 2, 3 to 34th St./Penn Station.*

3 *c-4*

DODGER COSTUME CO.

Specializing in Broadway rentals, Dodger has thousands of costumes in very good condition and can also manufacture to your specifications. *21–07 41st Ave. (near 21st St.), Long Island City, Queens, 718/729–1010. Closed weekends. Subway: F, V to 21st St./Queensbridge.*

10 *d-5*

FRANKIE STEINZ COSTUMES

This by-appointment-only custom design shop services the media and individuals with a unique collection of 1,500 rental costumes such as tornados, picnics, and fruit plates, guaranteed to turn heads; indeed, headware is a specialty. Allow 4–6 weeks for a custom order. *24 Harrison St. (between Hudson and Greenwich Sts.), 2nd floor, TriBeCa, 212/925–1373. Subway: 1, 2 to Franklin St.*

10 *e-1*

HALLOWEEN ADVENTURE

Need some fake vomit or a farting machine? Halloween Adventure makes sure that everyday is as fun as Halloween. Whether you're preparing for Mardi Gras, need props for a film shoot, or got stuck playing Santa at the corporate Christmas party, you'll find everything you need. Renting is not an option, but prices are reasonable enough to warrant a purchase. *104 4th Ave. (between and 11th and 12th Sts.), East Village, 212/673–4546. Subway: N, R, 4, 5, 6 to Union Sq.; 6 to Astor Pl.*

9 *c-7*

ODD'S COSTUME RENTALS

This huge loft area is filled with costumes and associated props. *231 W. 29th St. (between 7th and 8th Aves.), Midtown West, 212/268–6227. Closed weekends. Subway: A, C, E, 1, 2, 3 to 34th St./Penn Station.*

10 *d-1*

PARTY CITY

Perfect for last-minute Halloween ideas, this store carries wigs, masks, costumes, and party supplies, plus they'll deliver. *38 W. 14th St. (between 5th and 6th Aves.), Greenwich Village, 212/271–7310. Subway: L, N, Q, R, W, 4, 5, 6 to 14th St./Union Sq.*

CRAFT & HOBBY SUPPLIES

ceramics

10 *f-1*

CLAYWORKS POTTERY

Clayworks is a retail shop by day, and a studio in the evening, with classes in stoneware and earthenware. *332 E. 9th St. (between 1st and 2nd Aves.), East Village, 212/677–8311. Hours vary; call first. Subway: 6 to Astor Pl.*

miniatures

7 *e-6*

DOLLHOUSE ANTICS, INC.

Head here for your next dollhouse and all of its miniature furnishings, including fine hand-painted pieces; accessories; and, of course, occupants. The store can provide electrification and interior decoration. *1343 Madison Ave.*

(at 94th St.), Upper East Side, 212/876–2288. Subway: 4, 5, 6 to 96th St.

7 *e-8*

TINY DOLL HOUSE

Tiny Doll House has everything conceivable, but in miniature. They can wire and wallpaper the house before you start tinkering—or after you're done. *1146 Lexington Ave. (between 79th and 80th Sts.), Upper East Side, 212/744–3719. Subway: 6 to 77th St.*

model-making

9 *c-7*

AMERICA'S HOBBY CENTER

The comprehensive collection of vehicular models here includes airplanes, trains, boats, and cars, from beginner level to master, as well as parts, glues, woods, and accessories. Experts will appreciate the complete line of Megatech radio-controlled equipment. *263 W. 30th St. (between 7th and 8th Aves.), Chelsea, 212/675–8922. Closed Sun. Subway: 1, 2 to 28th St.*

7 *g-7*

JAN'S HOBBY SHOP

In business for over 30 years, Jan's is chockablock with model boats, planes, vehicular sets, and all the makings for dioramas. Find custom-built boats for collectors and wooden boats for kids, along with snap-together vehicular sets, rockets, tanks, dicast planes, cars, and boats. History buffs will appreciate the models (many handmade) and accessories ranging from Egyptian times to modern wars. Check out the in-house model aircraft museum. *1557 York Ave. (between E. 82nd and E. 83rd Sts.), Upper East Side, 212/861–5075. Subway: 4, 5, 6 to 86th St.*

9 *d-5*

RED CABOOSE

Under a number of names and proprietors, this property has housed one of New York's only true hobby shops since 1942. While the shop has catered to experts alone for many years, the collection now features many starter kits, from well-known brands like Marklin. Red Caboose carries plastic model kits, with a heavy emphasis on trains and die-cast airplanes in a range of scales. Model aficionados will appreciate the specialty military pieces and raw materials available. Also on site: Ready-made NYC subway models and supplies for architectural models and dioramas in various sizes. The staff will custom order products and allows the media to snap Polaroids and rent pieces. *23 W. 45th St. (between 5th and 6th Aves.), Midtown West, 212/575–0155. Closed Sun. Subway: 7 to 5th Ave.; B, D, F, V to 42nd St.*

needlework & knitting

9 *e-2*

ERICA WILSON NEEDLEWORKS

This store is a real resource for needle arts and supplies, including gear for knitting, embroidery, needlepoint, and crewel, and custom canvases. *717 Madison Ave. (near 63rd St.), 2nd floor, Upper East Side, 212/832–7290. Subway: N, R, W, 4, 5, 6 to 59th St./Lexington Ave.*

9 *d-3*

SEW FAST, SEW EASY

This homey, second floor shop specializes in selling sewing machines and sewing supplies to beginners. They even offer classes on learning to use the various machines they stock, so you can try your hand at them before making a selection. Lots of other classes for different skill levels are also given. *147 W. 57th St. (between 6th and 7th Aves.), 2nd floor, Midtown West, 212/582–5889. Subway: F, N, R, Q, W to 57th St.*

7 *b-7*

THE YARN COMPANY

Somebody's knitting on the Upper West Side; this shop has yarn, needles, patterns, buttons, needlepoint canvases, and kits. *2274 Broadway (near 82nd St.), Upper West Side, 212/787–7878. Closed Sun.–Mon. Subway: 1, 2 to 79th St.*

ELECTRONICS & AUDIO

10 *g-4*

ABC TRADING COMPANY

They stock most major brands of both household appliances and hi-fi audio/visual electronics. They will order what they don't have. Discounts are deep. *31 Canal St. (between Essex and Ludlow Sts.), Lower East Side, 212/228–5080. Closed Sat. Subway: F to E. Broadway.*

10 g-4

BANG & OLUFSEN

This Danish company offers designer electronics in the most modern and minimalist designs around. Custom multi-room audio systems and plasma television systems can be created. *927 Broadway (between 21st and 22nd Sts.), Flatiron District, 212/388–9792. Subway: N, R to 23rd St.*

7 e-8

952 Madison Ave. (at 75th St.), Upper East Side, 212/879–6161. Subway: 6 to 77th St.

9 e-5

FORTY-SECOND STREET PHOTO

Despite the name, Forty-Second Street Photo has more electronic equipment than photography equipment: Their VCRs, computers, fax machines, phones, CD and cassette players, and so forth are offered at discount prices. *109 E. 42nd St. (between Park and Lexington Aves.), Midtown East, 212/490–1994. Subway: 4, 5, 6, 7, S to 42nd St./Grand Central.*

9 d-6

378 5th Ave. (at 35th St.), Midtown West, 212/594–6565. Subway: B, D, F, N, Q, R, V, W to 34th St./Herald Sq.

9 d-4

HARVEY

Harvey has sold and installed fine audio and video systems since 1927. Current stock includes home-theater and stereo components from Adcom, McIntosh, Krell, Sony, Sharpvision, Meridian, and other high-end brands. Harvey's second location is a boutique in the ABC home-furnishings megastore. *2 W. 45th St. (at 5th Ave.), Midtown West, 212/575–5000. Subway: 7 to 5th Ave.; B, D, F, V to 42nd St.*

9 e-8

ABC Carpet & Home, 888 Broadway (at 19th St.), Flatiron District, 212/473–3000. Subway: L, N, Q, R, W, 4, 5, 6 to 14th St./Union Sq.

10 e-6

J&R MUSIC & COMPUTER WORLD

J&R may well have the most complete selection of electronic products anywhere, which, happily, assures that all budgets can be accommodated. The sales staff is knowledgeable, prices are competitive, and crowds are here in force. Be patient; it's worth it in the end. *23 Park Row (between Ann and Beekman Sts.), Lower Manhattan, 212/238–9000 or 800/221–8180. Subway: 4, 5, 6 to Brooklyn Bridge/City Hall.*

9 d-8

RADIOSHACK

RadioShack carries mainly its own brand of consumer electronics, including stereos, telephones, and pagers, and has a handy stash of electrical converters for travel abroad. It's worth a look if you're not a label snob. *641A 6th Ave. (at 20th St.), Chelsea, 212/604–0695. Subway: F, V to 23rd St.*

9 e-5

287 Madison Ave. (at 41st St.), Midtown East, 212/682–9309. Subway: S, 4, 5, 6, 7 to 42nd St./Grand Central.

7 f-7

1477 3rd Ave. (at 84th St.), Upper East Side, 212/327–0979. Subway: 4, 5, 6 to 86th St.

7 b-4

2812 Broadway (at 108th St.), Upper West Side, 212/662–7332. Subway: 1 to 110th St./Cathedral Pkwy.

9 e-3

SONY PLAZA

Sony has cleverly designed a consumer-friendly atrium housing Sony Wonder Technology Lab (an interactive multimedia exhibit) and the Sony Style store, which offers only the latest Sony products. Staff take a "no-pressure" approach, so browsing is welcome and encouraged, but complimentary personal shopping is also available for those who wish to purchase but require expert advice. *550 Madison Ave. (between 55th and 56th Sts.), Midtown East, 212/833–8830. Subway: N, R, W to 5th Ave./59th St.*

9 e-8

SOUND BY SINGER

Singer's sales and service get consistently high reviews from serious audio/videophiles, but the great sales staff will also work with tight budgets. *18 E. 16th St. (between 5th Ave. and Union Square West), Flatiron District, 212/924–8600. Subway: L, N, Q, R, W, 4, 5, 6 to 14th St./Union Sq.*

9 *d-5*

SOUND CITY

Here you'll find all major brands of stereo, video, and photo equipment at very reasonable prices. The affable staff shares expert knowledge. Air-conditioners and space heaters also are sold seasonally. *58 W. 45th St. (between 5th and 6th Aves.), Midtown West, 212/575-0210. Subway: B, D, F, V to 42nd St.*

10 *e-4*

UNCLE STEVE ELECTRONICS

Head to Canal for these low prices on stereo equipment, TVs, and VCRs. You can try the stuff out in the sound room. For sound on the move, step across the street to Uncle Steve Car Stereo at 334 Canal. *343 Canal St. (near Church St.), Lower Manhattan, 212/226-4010. Subway: A, C, E to Canal St.*

10 *g-3*

VICMARR AUDIO

Vicmarr is one of very few electronics stores that will give prices over the phone, indicating its uncommonly low-pressure sales approach. The store's well-organized shelves are packed with well-priced merchandise from brands such as JVC, Alpine, and Panasonic. *88 Delancey St. (at Orchard St.), Lower East Side, 212/505-0380. Subway: F, J, M, Z to Delancey St./Essex St.*

EROTICA

11 *b-2*

LEATHER MAN

An emporium for custom-fit leather jackets, pants, vests, tees, and briefs, many of which lean toward the homoerotic, is perfectly understandable on this block, only a few doors from the site of the Stonewall Riot and the beginnings of Gay Lib. Prices are moderately high, the quality first-rate. *111 Christopher St. (between Bleecker and Hudson Sts.), Greenwich Village, 212/243-5339. Subway: 1, 2 to Christopher St./Sheridan Sq.*

10 *g-3*

TOYS IN BABELAND

A comfortable environment for a possibly uncomfortable shopping venture, Toys in Babeland has been dubbed as the "Williams-Sonoma of the well stocked boudoir," by the New York

Press. Vibrators (about 100 varieties), harnesses, feathers, whips, blindfolds, condoms, lubricants, and just about anything else that will make your bedroom (or any room) a very fun place indeed. *94 Rivington St. (between Orchard and Ludlow Sts.), Lower East Side, 212/375-1701. Subway: F, J, M, Z to Delancy St./Essex St.*

EYEWEAR

11 *d-5*

MORGENTHAL-FREDERICS EYEWEAR & ACCESSORIES

Designer and president Richard Morgenthal's creations have lured the likes of Puff Daddy, Jackie O, and Uma Thurman. In addition to Morgenthal's own line, which includes vintage-inspired frames in solid gold and platinum, precious stones, ebony, and teakwood (accessories range from men's nubuck wallets to a combination magnifier-letter opener to women's "boudoir pieces"), specs by Oliver Peoples, l.a. Eyeworks, and Yohji Yamamoto can be found here. *399 W. Broadway (at Spring St.), SoHo, 212/966-0099. Subway: C, E to Spring St.*

9 *e-1*

944 Madison Ave. (at 74th St.), Midtown East, 212/744-9444. Subway: 6 to 68th St./Hunter College.

9 *e-2*

699 Madison Ave. (at 62nd St.), Midtown East, 212/838-3090. Subway: N, R, W, 4, 5, 6 to 59th St./Lexington Ave.

9 *3-e*

754 5th Ave. (at 57th St. in Bergdorf Goodman), Midtown West, 212/753-7300. Subway: N, R, W, 4, 5, 6 to 59th St./Lexington Ave.

9 *e-3*

ROBERT MARC OPTICIANS

Robert Marc is the only place in New York to find the exclusive lines of Lunor, Frédéric Beausoleil, and Kirei Titan, as well as the vintage line Retrospecs. *575 Madison Ave. (at 56th St.), Midtown East, 212/319-2000. Subway: N, R, W, 4, 5, 6 to 59th St./Lexington Ave.*

9 *b-1*

190 Columbus Ave. (at 68th St.), Upper West Side, 212/799-4600. Subway: 1, 2 to 66th St./Lincoln Ctr.; and other locations.

10 *f-2*

SELIMA OPTIQUE

For the coolest mid-price frames around, Selima Salaun's store is the place to go. In addition to her own line, she scours France for vintage, never-worn frames. Special orders and replications welcome. *84 E. 7th St. (between 1st and 2nd Aves.), Greenwich Village, 212/260–2495. Subway: 6 to Astor Pl.*

10 *e-4*

159 Wooster St. (at Broome St.), SoHo, 212/343–9490. Subway: N, R to Prince St.

FABRICS & NOTIONS

Orchard Street south of Houston Street is New York's center for discounted fabric. Be prepared to pick through roll after roll; you'll find major manufacturers' overstock at about 40% off the retail price. Most button and notions shops are in the West 30s between 5th and 6th avenues, and on 6th Avenue between 34th and 39th streets. On West 38th Street alone there are 20 stores full of trimmings.

11 *h-6*

A. FEIBUSCH ZIPPERS

Feibusch has zippers in every length and every color, with thread to match. If they don't, they'll cut it to order. *27 Allen St. (between Hester and Canal Sts.), Lower East Side, 212/226–3964. Closed Sat. Subway: J, M, N, Q, R, W, Z, 6 to Canal St.*

9 *c-5*

ART MAX FABRICS

The fashion fabrics include full lines of linens, English wool suitings, domestic and imported wools, cotton prints and solids, cashmere coatings, and silks. Bridal fabrics are a particular specialty. *250 W. 40th St. (between 7th and 8th Aves.), Midtown West, 212/398–0755. Closed Sun. Subway: N, R, Q, S, W, 1, 2, 3 to 42nd St./Times Sq.*

9 *c-5*

B & J FABRICS

Family-owned since 1940, B & J is three floors of fashion fabrics, many imported. *263 W. 40th St. (between 7th and 8th Aves.), Midtown West, 212/354–8150. Closed Sun. Subway: N, R, Q, S, W, 1, 2, 3 to 42nd St./Times Sq.*

9 *f-2*

BARANZELLI HOME

Designer silk, velvet, and brocades for draperies, upholstery, and slipcovers join Scalamandre closeouts and seconds in a shop popular with the trade as well as retail customers. *1127 2nd Ave. (between 59th and 60th Sts.), Midtown East, 212/753–6511. Subway: N, R, W, 4, 5, 6 to 59th St./Lexington Ave.*

10 *g-3*

BECKENSTEIN HOME FABRICS

This store has a wide variety of well-priced fabrics. *4 W. 20th St. (near 5th Ave.), Flatiron District, 212/366–5142. Subway: 1, 2 to 18th St.*

10 *g-3*

BECKENSTEIN MEN'S FABRICS

Some say this is the finest men's-fabric store in the United States. The nation's custom tailors, top men's-clothing manufacturers, and a who's-who list of clients shop here for the finest quality in every type of men's fashion fabric. *133 Orchard St. (near Delancey St.), Lower East Side, 212/475–6666. Closed Sat. Subway: F, J, M, Z to Delancey St./Essex St.*

12 *f-5*

FABRIC ALTERNATIVE

Pick up high-quality home-decor fabrics at a discount, including Schumacher, Waverly, and Riverdale. They'll do the sewing, too. *78 7th Ave. (at Berkeley Pl.), Park Slope, Brooklyn, 718/857–5482. Subway: D, Q, F to 7th Ave.*

11 *h-5*

FABRIC WORLD

Fabric World offers a lovely line of fabrics at discount prices, with a bonus if you're renovating: they'll convert your chosen fabric into wallpaper. *283 Grand St. (near Eldridge St.), Lower East Side, 212/925–0412. Closed Sat. Subway: S to Grand St.*

9 *c-5*

GORDON BUTTON CO.

Think about it: Ten million buttons and buckles in 5,000 varieties, from classic to novelty, from 10¢ to $2 each—and lo, service with a smile. *222 W. 38th St. (between 7th and 8th Aves.), Midtown West, 212/921–1684. Closed weekends.*

Subway: B, D, F, N, Q, R, V, W to 34th
St./Herald Sq.

9 d-5
HYMAN HENDLER & SONS
It's filled to the brim with ribbons: satin, grosgrain, velvet, silk, you name it, in every color, size, and width. 67 W. 38th St., Midtown West, 212/840–8393. Closed Sun. Subway: B, D, F, N, Q, R, V, W to 34th St./Herald Sq.

7 b-8
LAURA ASHLEY
The finest purveyor of the English country-house look, Laura Ashley offers genteel prints on natural cotton fabrics, with wallpapers and furnishings to match. 398 Columbus Ave. (at 79th St.), Upper West Side, 212/496–5110. Subway: 1, 2 to 79th St.

11 e-6
LONG ISLAND FABRICS
Selections include designer, upholstery, and some imported fabrics as well as a good selection of notions, all at fantastic savings. 406 Broadway (near Canal St.), Lower Manhattan, 212/431–9510. Subway: J, M, N, Q, R, W, Z, 6 to Canal St.

9 d-5
M & J TRIMMING
All you need supply is the idea. M & J has the trimmings for any day's fashion accessories: rhinestones, studs, feathers, cords, buttons, bindings, satin ribbons, lace, eyelets, embroidered trim, silk ropes, even large feather boas. A few doors up 6th Avenue, at No. 1014, the same folks sell home-decorating accessories. 1008 6th Ave. (near 37th St.), Midtown West, 212/391–9072. Closed Sun. Subway: B, D, F, N, Q, R, V, W to 34th St./Herald Sq.

9 e-1
PIERRE DEUX
Pierre Deux is the exclusive American outlet for hand-screened Souleiado print fabric from Provence; the store also has reproduction furniture and beautiful accessories. They custom-design window and bed treatments. 870 Madison Ave. (at 71st St.), Upper East Side, 212/570–9343. Subway: 6 to 68th St./Hunter College.

9 e-2
TENDER BUTTONS
This special shop displays every kind of button imaginable, including sets of old and rare buttons and antique buckles and cufflinks. Prices range from 25¢ to $3,500. 143 E. 62nd St. (between Lexington and 3rd Aves.), Upper East Side, 212/758–7004. Closed Sun. Subway: N, R, W, 4, 5, 6 to 59th St./Lexington Ave.

9 d-5
TINSEL TRADING COMPANY
Bring a pair of shades: this place specializes in metallic yarns, threads, lamés, gauzes, tassels, fringe, rosettes, buttons, antique ribbons, embroideries, and fabrics. There's much from the '20s and '30s. 47 W. 38th St. (between 5th and 6th Aves.), Midtown West, 212/730–1030. Closed weekends. Subway: B, D, F, N, Q, R, V, W to 34th St./Herald Sq.

FLOWERS & PLANTS

For the freshest flowers, go to the wholesale flower market on and around 28th Street between 6th and 7th avenues, where New York's florists buy their flowers. Wholesalers will often sell at retail if you're willing to pay cash.

florists
9 d-8
BLOOM FLOWERS HOME GARDEN
Bloom Flowers does everything from weddings to private and corporate parties to individual arrangements and fresh cut flowers. There's also a small selection of home furnishings. 16 W. 21st St. (between 5th and 6th Aves.), Chelsea, 212/620–5666. Closed Sun. Subway: F, V to 23rd St.

9 e-1
LEXINGTON GARDENS
Shop here for exquisite floral designs and antique accessories. 1011 Lexington Ave. (at 73rd St.), Upper East Side, 212/861–4390. Closed Sun. Subway: 6 to 77th St.

11 b-1
LOTUS NYC FLOWERS
Proprietor Luis Collazo opts for a modern approach to flowers, using rare combinations of classic and rare looks like "Thistle and Roses," "Brunia and

Peonies." With an emphasis on customizing for the individual, Lotus offers a variety of potting options, like the "wheat grass meadow" planted in a terra-cotta pot, with a hollow middle for flowers. Depend on Lotus for personal, gift, wedding, event, and media needs. *161 7th Ave. S (between Perry and Waverly), Greenwich Village, 212/620–5666. Closed Sun. Subway: 1, 2 to Christopher St.*

9 b-7
PRESTON BAILEY INC. ENTERTAINMENT & SET DESIGN
Preston Bailey has 15 years' experience designing floral arrangements for big events. Corporate clients include Tiffany & Co., Christie's, and Disney; weddings and large parties are a specialty. *147 W. 25th St. (between 6th and 7th Aves.), Chelsea, 212/691–6777. Open by appt. only. Subway: 1, 2 to 23rd St.*

9 e-2
RENNY
This well-known floral designer doesn't kid around; clients include some serious society, and prices can reflect that. The handiwork is extraordinary. *505 Park Ave. (between 59th and 60th Sts.), Midtown East, 212/288–7000. Closed Sun. Sept.–May, weekends July–Aug. Subway: N, R, W, 4, 5, 6 to 59th St./Lexington Ave.*

7 e-8
Carlyle Hotel, 35 E. 76th St. (at Madison Ave.), Upper East Side, 212/988–5588. Closed Sun. Sept.–May, weekends July–Aug. Subway: 6 to 77th St.

10 b-1
ROBERT ISABELL
Isabell is famous for decorating over-the-top society parties on big budgets. *410 W. 13th St. (near Washington St.), Greenwich Village, 212/645–7767. Subway: A, C, E, L to 14th St./8th Ave.*

9 e-1
RONALDO MAIA LTD.
These expensive and inventive floral creations come in natural cachepots or baskets and make elegant, simple centerpieces. The potpourri and candles are wonderful. *27 E. 67th St. (between 5th and Madison Aves.), Upper East Side, 212/288–1049. Subway: 6 to 68th St./Hunter College.*

11 d-4
SPRING ST. GARDEN
Order personalized floral arrangements, wreaths, garlands, or whatever strikes you. The small retail area includes plants, fresh cut flowers, and gardening objets. *186½ Spring St. (near Thompson St.), SoHo, 212/966–2015. Closed Sun. Subway: C, E to Spring St.*

11 b-1
SPRUCE
Rustic, country looks like roses, hydrangea, and gardenias in wooden crates, steel pails, or terra-cotta pots make the perfect thank-you, love-you, miss-you tokens, to delight even the most exacting eye. Spruce also does weddings, and all small and large scale events. *75 Greenwich Ave. (at 7th Ave.), Greenwich Village, 212/414–0588. Subway: 1, 2, 3 to 14th St.*

7 b-8
SURROUNDINGS
These designers do arrangements for parties and events and also make up floral and gourmet food gift baskets. *224 W. 79th St. (between Broadway and Amsterdam Ave.), Upper West Side, 212/580–8982. Subway: 1, 2 to 79th St.*

9 e-8
VICTOR'S GARDEN DISTRICT
The attentive staff designs stunning arrangements for all budgets, and the Midtown location makes this a convenient after-work stop for last-minute flower emergencies. *260 Madison Ave. (near 38th St.), Midtown East, 212/532–9838. Subway: S, 4, 5, 6, 7 to 42nd St./Grand Central.*

10 c-1
VSF
A-list clients hire this designer for English country–style weddings, special events, holiday decorations, or just the perfect flower arrangement. *204 W. 10th St. (near Bleecker St.), Greenwich Village, 212/206–7236. Closed Sun.; closed weekends in summer. Subway: 1, 2 to Christopher St./Sheridan Sq.*

9 f-3
ZEZÉ
Known for its dramatic arrangements, Zezé specializes in exotic orchids. *398 E. 52nd St. (between 1st Ave. and the East*

River), Midtown East, 212/753–7767. Closed weekends except holiday weekends. Subway: 6 to 51st St./Lexington Ave.; E, V to Lexington–3rd Aves./53rd St.

nurseries & garden supplies

11 g-3

CHELSEA GARDEN CENTER

The Bowery location houses the outdoor nursery, selling a wide variety of outdoor plants and furnishings, as well as gardening supplies, fertilizer, and soil. Chelsea Garden Center also offers indoor and outdoor landscape services for home or business. The Greenwich Village branch specializes in indoor plants, flowers, and trees. *321 Bowery (at 2nd St.), East Village, 212/777–4500. Subway: 6 to Astor Pl.*

7 e-8

435 Hudson St. (at Morton St.), Greenwich Village, 212/727–7100. Subway: 1, 2 to Christopher St./Sheridan Sq.

11 d-5

SMITH & HAWKEN

The chain that made gardening chic sells tools made from the finest materials (like stainless steel and aluminum alloy), as well as trellises, garden ornaments, fencing, birdfeeders, and a barrage of books—all for the bank-rolled gardener. *394 W. Broadway (between Broome and Spring Sts.), SoHo, 212/925–1190. Subway: C, E to Spring St.*

7 f-8

TREILLAGE LTD.

This unusual and stylish mix of antique and reproduction garden furniture and accessories encompasses English terracotta pots and planters, gardening tools, watering cans, gloves, candles, home- and garden-design books, and interesting Christmas decorations in season. *418 E. 75th St. (between 1st and York Aves.), Upper East Side, 212/535–2288. Closed Sun.; closed Sat. in July and Aug. Subway: 6 to 77th St.*

FOLK ART & HANDICRAFTS

11 b-3

AN AMERICAN CRAFTSMAN

With exclusives from many artists, An American Craftsman's New York City galleries house one of the largest collections of one-of-a-kind and limited edition crafts in wood, metal, glass, and clay and jewelry pieces in all price ranges. Co-owner/artisan Richard Rothbard's boxology line (poetry, psychology, and philosophy in wood) makes up about 15% of the collection; the remainder of works are from American and Canadian craftsmen with inspiration spanning all time periods and styles. *317 Bleecker St. (at Grove St.), Greenwich Village, 212/727–0841. Subway: 1, 2 to Christopher St.*

9 c-4

790 7th Ave. (at 52nd St.), Midtown West, 212/399–2555. Subway: N, R to 49th St.; 1, 2 to 50th St.

9 f-2

1222 2nd Ave. (at 64th St.), Upper East Side, 212/794–3440 or 212/794–3474. Subway: 6 to 68th St.

11 c-1

478 6th Ave. (between 11th and 12th Sts.), Greenwich Village, 212/307–7161. Subway: F, L to 14th St.

9 d-4

60 W. 50th St. (at 6th Ave.), Midtown West, 212/307–7161. Subway: B, D, F, V to 47–50 Sts./Rockefeller Ctr.

9 e-7

BACK TO AFRICA

Stop in this retail/wholesale shop for hand-crafted African and Indian gifts like wooden masks, soapstone and ebony figurines, jewelry, instruments like drums and African thumb pianos, paintings, and Kwaanza sets. *1133 Broadway (entrance at 26th St.), Flatiron District, 212/462–4848. Closed Sat. and Jewish holidays. Subway: N, R to 23rd St.*

9 e-5

CELTIC CROSSROADS

Inside the lobby of the Lincoln Building across from Grand Central, this Irish shop stocks imported pottery (by artisans like Nicholas Mosse), china, gold and silver jewelry, traditional wedding giftware, baby gifts, wall hangings, sweaters, CDs, and golf items from the old country. The heritage savvy can have their coat of arms plastered on coffee mugs, flags, and wall displays. *60 E. 42nd St. (between Park and Madison Aves.), Midtown East, 212/490–0848. Closed weekends except in holiday season, or by appt. Subway: S, 4, 5, 6, 7 to 42nd St./Grand Central.*

7 *e-6*

COOPER SHOP AT
THE JEWISH MUSEUM

Finds here include decorative exhibition reproductions, ceremonial objects like seder plates and menorahs, Judaica giftware, jewelry, children's items, historical videos, and movies. *Ketuvahs* (Jewish marriage contracts) are hand made for various levels of observance, interfaith couples, and gay and lesbian couples. *1109 5th Ave. (at 92nd St.), Upper West Side, 212/966–2646. Closed Sat. Subway: 4, 5, 6 to 86th St.*

11 *g-3*

LA SIRENA

This vibrant Mexican handcraft showcase is filled floor-to-ceiling with hand-embroidered clothing, woven bags, tin ornaments, small wooden instruments, statuettes in clay and wood, and just about any artful piece you would find south of the border—at extremely affordable prices. *27 E. 3rd St. (between 2nd Ave. and The Bowery), East Village, 212/780–9113. Subway: 6 to Astor Pl.*

11 *d-5*

LEPAGE NEW YORK

Among owner Cec LePage's lucite home accessories collection are thoroughly modern menorahs (available in custom colors) and a veritable rainbow of shabbat candlesticks, designed in-house and guaranteed to enhance any Friday night. *72 Thompson St. (between Spring and Broome Sts.), SoHo, 212/966–2646. Closed Mon. Subway: C, E, 6 to Spring St.*

10 *b-1*

MOVE LAB

Browse the eclectic mix of limited-edition, unique urban crafts like furnishings, pillows, shirts, accessories and gift items. There's nothing ordinary about this collection—from chairs and bowls fashioned from roadsigns to shirts embellished with mahogany. *803 Washington St. (between Gansevoort and Horatio Sts.), Greenwich Village, 212/741–5520. Closed Mon. Subway: A, C, E, L to 14th St./8th Ave.*

9 *e-5*

SAKIA FINE NATIVE
AMERICAN ARTS

The hand-made Native American art here includes pottery by sought after artist Nancy Youngblood Lugo, along with an array of silver and stone jewelry and books. *120 Park Ave. (at 42nd St.), Midtown East, 212/867–7888. Closed weekends. Subway: S, 4, 5, 6, 7 to 42nd St./Grand Central.*

11 *d-4*

TIBET ARTS & CRAFTS

The clothing, jewelry, antique furniture, tapestries, hand-woven rugs, religious items, meditation objects, books, and CDs here all come from Nepal, India, and Tibet. *144 Sullivan St. (between Houston and Prince Sts.), SoHo, 212/529–4344. Subway: N, R to Prince St.*

11 *c-3*

197 Bleecker St. (between MacDougal St. and 6th Ave.), Greenwich Village, 212/260–5880. Subway: A, B, C, D, E, F, V to W. 4th St./Washington Sq.

FOOD & DRINK

bread & pastries

9 *b-4*

AMY'S BREAD

Choose from sourdough, semolina, rosemary, black olive, organic whole wheat, and rye breads, as well as specialty breads, sandwiches, and sweets. All breads are made with a natural starter, quality ingredients, and no preservatives; the most popular are sourdough and semolina with golden raisins and fennel. *672 9th Ave. (at 46th St.), Midtown West, 212/977–2670. Subway: A, C, E to 42nd St./Port Authority.*

10 *b-1*

75 9th Ave. (at 15th St.), Chelsea, 212/462–4338. Subway: A, C, E, L to 14th St./8th Ave.

11 *e-5*

BALTHAZAR BAKERY

Adjacent to the trendsetting restaurant of the same name, this is a Parisian-style patisserie with an amazing array of French-style breads. Try chocolate, rye, multigrain, olive, cranberry-raisin-pecan, potato-onion, and the signature *pain de seigle* of rye and wheat. You can also pick up tarts, sandwiches, salads, soups, and delicious coffee by the cup. *80 Spring St. (at Broadway), SoHo, 212/965–1785. Subway: 6 to Spring St.*

9 *f-4*

BUTTERCUP BAKE SHOP

Opened by one of the original owners of the much loved Magnolia Bakery, the butter-yellow walls here house some of the most delectable desserts in midtown: scrumptious layer cakes, lick-your-fork-clean pies, and delicately iced cupcakes. The buttercream on the cakes here is habit forming, but worth every calorie. 973 2nd Ave. (between 51st and 52nd Sts.), Midtown East, 212/350–4144. Subway: 6 to 51st St./Lexington Ave.; E, V to Lexington –3rd Aves./53rd St.

9 *e-8*

THE CITY BAKERY

Beautiful tarts; an exceptional selection of cookies, brownies, desserts, and breads; and a tasty selection of lunchtime fare keeps City Bakery hopping. 3 W. 18th St. (between 5th and 6th Aves.), Flatiron District, 212/366–1414. Subway: L, N, Q, R, W, 4, 5, 6 to 14th St./Union Sq.; F, V to 14th St.

7 *f-8*

CREATIVE CAKES

Here's the deal: you name a person, pet, building, car, or any other shape or design you fancy, and they create a "portrait-likeness" three-dimensional cake—buttercream outside, chocolate fudge inside. It's expensive, but delicious and most impressive. Order two weeks in advance. 400 E. 74th St. (between 1st and York Aves.), Upper East Side, 212/794–9811. Subway: 6 to 77th St.

9 *b-5*

CUPCAKE CAFÉ

This funky store offers daintily decorated cupcakes and tantalizing cakes covered in sinfully rich buttercream icing. There are also pies, doughnuts, and muffins, as well as soups and sandwiches. 522 9th Ave. (at 39th St.), Midtown West, 212/465–1530. Subway: A, C, E to 42nd St./Port Authority.

9 *e-2*

ECCE PANIS

The aroma makes it difficult to pass this place by; and why should you? Ecce Panis serves glorious bread—light and dark sourdough, double-walnut, plain or rosemary neo-Tuscan, chocolate—as well as various focaccias, biscotti, cookies, brioches, and breakfast treats. 1120 3rd Ave. (at 65th St.), Upper East Side,

212/535–2099. Subway: 6 to 68th St./Hunter College.

9 *b-1*

Columbus Ave. (at 73rd St.), Upper West Side, 212/362–7189. Subway: 1, 2, 3 to 72nd St.

10 *d-1*

6th Ave. (at 10th St.), Greenwich Village, 212/460–5616. Subway: A, B, C, D, E, F, V to W. 4th St./Washington Sq.

10 *e-1*

LA BAGUETTE SHOP

The aroma outside of this shop makes it nearly impossible to pass by without indulging in a buttery, chocolaty, fruity, or savory French treat. Six varieties of croissants, freshly baked breads, muffins, cakes and coffee, cappuccino, and espresso are made fresh all day. 106 University Pl. (between 12th and 13th Sts.), Greenwich Village, 212/229–6752. Subway: L, N, Q, R, W, 4, 5, 6 to 14th St./Union Sq.

9 *b-5*

LITTLE PIE COMPANY

This gourmet bakery specializes in delicious all-American pies—just like Grandma used to make, only better. The ever-popular Sour Cream Apple Walnut Pie is legendary. 424 W. 43rd St. (between 9th and 10th Aves.), Midtown West, 212/736–4780. Subway: A, C, E to 42nd St./Port Authority.

10 *b-1*

407 W. 14th St. (at 9th St.), Chelsea, 212/414–2324. Subway: A, C, E, L to 14th St./8th Ave.

11 *a-1*

MAGNOLIA BAKERY

Tucked away on a quiet Greenwich Village corner, Magnolia has a loyal following of sweet-tooth devotees who line up for the legendary layer cakes topped with delectable buttercream icing. There's also an array of cupcakes that will make you wax nostalgic for elementary school, plus pies, brownies, and cookies. 401 Bleecker St. (at W. 11th St.), Greenwich Village, 212/462–2572. Subway: 1, 2 to Christopher St./Sheridan Sq.

11 *b-1*

MOISHE'S HOMEMADE KOSHER BAKERY

Moishe's is one of New York's oldest and finest kosher Jewish bakeries, serving very special corn bread, egg challah, homemade bagels (some call them the only authentic bagels in the city), rugelach, and hamantaschen. *115 2nd Ave. (between 6th and 7th Sts.), East Village, 212/505–8555. Subway: F, V to 2nd Ave.*

11 *h-3*

181 E. Houston St. (near Orchard St.), Lower East Side, 212/472–9624. Subway: F, J, M, Z to Delancey St./Essex St.

11 *c-4*
ONCE UPON A TART
Ensconced in a century-old storefront with tin ceilings and exposed brick, the cleverly named bakery serves tantalizing muffins, scones, cookies, and gourmet sandwiches. But the tart's the thing—freshly baked in both sweet and savory varieties. Tuck into one in the quiet café section and escape from SoHo's shopping hordes. *135 Sullivan St. (between Prince and Houston Sts.), SoHo, 212/387–8869. Subway: N, R to Prince St.*

7 *f-8*
ORWASHER'S
Certified kosher, Orwasher offers 35 varieties of handmade breads and rolls containing no preservatives or additives and baked on the premises in hearth ovens. Specialties include Hungarian potato bread and Vienna twists; inventions include raisin pumpernickel and marble bread. Pick up cheeses, coffees, teas, and condiments while you're here. *308 E. 78th St. (between 2nd and 1st Aves.), Upper East Side, 212/288–6569. Subway: 6 to 77th St.*

10 *b-1*
PATISSERIE LANCIANI
These beautiful baked goods include a great Sacher torte, over which you can linger in the adjoining café. *414 W. 14th St. (between 9th and 10th Aves.), Greenwich Village, 212/989–1213. Subway: A, C, E, L to 14th St./8th Ave.*

9 *e-1*
PAYARD PATISSERIE
Chef François Payard creates some of the most exquisite French pastries in the city, turning out light-as-a-feather croissants as well as sinfully rich chocolate delights. Among the latter is the Louvre—hazelnut dacquoise and chocolate and hazelnut mousse encased in a dark

chocolate shell. There are also amazing baguettes and other French breads, fruit tarts, decadent cakes, and luscious truffles. Afternoon tea is a special treat. *1032 Lexington Ave. (between 73rd and 74th Sts.), Upper East Side, 212/717–5252. Subway: 6 to 77th St.*

9 *c-5*
POSEIDON CONFECTIONERY CO.
Serving the best in Greek pastries, Poseidon also offers spinach-and-cheese pies and stuffed vine leaves. *629 9th Ave. (at 44th St.), Midtown West, 212/757–6173. Subway: A, C, E to 42nd St./Port Authority.*

9 *b-1*
SOUTINE
A full-service neighborhood bakery, Soutine makes American and French-style bread, croissants, and brioche. Birthday cakes and holiday goodies are specialties, and the store will ship them anywhere. *104 W. 70th St. (between Broadway and Columbus Ave.), Upper West Side, 212/496–1450. Subway: 1, 2, 3 to 72nd St.*

11 *b-5*
SULLIVAN ST. BAKERY
The crusty, chewy bread here is the stuff of food fantasies, but don't let it blind you to one of the greatest taste treats in the city: true Roman pizza. The golden, rectangular dough is served at room temperature and topped with simple ingredients such as fresh artichokes (only in spring); a combination of sea salt, rosemary, and extra-virgin olive oil (a pizza *bianca*); or fresh tomatoes. One taste and you're sure to be addicted. *73 Sullivan St. (near Broome St.), SoHo, 212/334–9435. Subway: A, C, E to Canal St.*

9 *c-8*
TAYLOR'S
Taylor's accompanies its sandwiches and salads with old-fashioned comfort food—huge fudge brownies, oversize muffins, and homey pies. *228 W. 18th St. (between 7th and 8th Aves.), Chelsea, 212/366–9081. Subway: A, C, E, L to 14th St./8th Ave.*

10 *c-1*
523 Hudson St. (near W. 10th St.), Greenwich Village, 212/645–8200. Subway: 1, 2 to Christopher St./Sheridan Sq.

10 *f-1*

175 2nd Ave. (near 11th St.), East Village, 212/674–9501. Subway: 6 to Astor Pl.

12 *g-8*

TWO LITTLE RED HENS BAKERY

The muffins, cakes, and pastries at this cozy nook a block off Prospect Park have inspired many a picnic. Bestsellers include the chocolate "crinkle" cookies, elegant cupcakes (the palette changes with the season), and raspberry-chocolate mousse cake. 1112 8th Ave. (near 12th St.), Park Slope, Brooklyn, 718/499–8108. Subway: F to 7th Ave.

10 *f-1*

VENIERO'S PASTICCERIA

In business since 1894, Veniero's makes Italian sweets as tasty as they are beautiful, including cannoli, gelato, and marzipan. The café serves old-fashioned espresso and cappuccino. 342 E. 11th St. (between 1st and 2nd Aves.), East Village, 212/674–7264. Subway: L to 1st Ave.

11 *d-4*

VESUVIO

White, whole-wheat, and seeded Italian breads are baked in coal-fired ovens in the basement, without sugar, fat, or preservatives. Just follow your nose. 160 Prince St. (near W. Broadway), 212/925–8248. Subway: N, R to Prince St.

7 *e-7*

WILLIAM GREENBERG, JR., BAKERY

Greenberg is said to make the best brownies in the city, and whips up spectacular custom cakes. 1100 Madison Ave. (at 82nd St.), Upper East Side, 212/744–0304. Subway: 4, 5, 6 to 86th St.

7 *b-8*

2187 Broadway (at 77th St.), Upper West Side, 212/580–7300. Subway: 1, 2 to 79th St.

9 *e-6*

518 3rd Ave. (near 34th St.), Murray Hill, 212/686–3344. Subway: 6 to 33rd St.

11 *e-1*

60 E. 8th St. (near Broadway), East Village, 212/995–9184. Subway: N, R to 8th St.

11 *b-2*

ZITO & SONS

Zito's best seller is a delicious, crusty whole-wheat loaf, followed closely by a Sicilian loaf. Frank Sinatra used to have this stuff delivered fresh to the Waldorf. 259 Bleecker St. (near 7th Ave.), Greenwich Village, 212/929–6139. Subway: A, B, C, D, E, F, V to W. 4th St./Washington Sq.

coffee & tea

11 *a-1*

CARRY-ON TEA & SYMPATHY

The takeout and retail portion of the quaint Brit restaurant Tea & Sympathy sells ten loose and eight bagged teas both from England and the New World, in addition to the full menu of high-comfort, high-fat English mainstays. Find brands like Typhoo and PG Tips and flavors like Apple Mango and Kiwi Strawberry as well as all of the accessories a tea lover could ever want from strainers to cups and saucers. If you're feeling the Anglophilic spirit, splurge on Union Jack novelties, Eastender videos, and royal family kitsch (they even sell Walker's crisps!). Afternoon tea is served all day, and heart-warming, artery-clogging English breakfast is available from 10–2 on the weekends. 110 Greenwich Ave. (between 12th and 13th Sts.), Greenwich Village, 212/989–9735. Subway: A, C, E, 1, 2 to 14th St.

10 *e-1*

DANAL

In this charming café and gift shop are more than 32 teas (in bulk or gift-boxed): aromatics from France (try the four red-berries), classics from India and China, decaf varieties, herbal infusions, and more. Highlights include Taganda, an exclusive from Zimbabwe; packaged teas by G. Ford; and Barrow's unblended Darjeeling. The only coffee in stock is the high-quality Sumatra blend served in the café, also available in decaf. 90 E. 10th St. (between 3rd and 4th Aves.), East Village, 212/982–6930. Closed Mon. Subway: 6 to Astor Pl.

9 *b-5*

EMPIRE COFFEE & TEA CO.

Those who live and die for the bean will appreciate the trend-free retail and wholesale coffee and tea shop and coffee bar offering over 70 whole-bean coffees, roasted and ground on the premises, and over 50 loose and bagged teas. Find coffee from around the world, including controlled crops like Kona Hawaiian. Empire is also an authorized dealer of Bunn and La Pavoni pump and steam espresso machines. *568 9th Ave. (between 41st and 42nd Sts.), Greenwich Village, 212/586–1717 or 800/262–5908. Subway: A, C, E to Port Authority; N, R, S, 1, 2, 3, 7 to Times Sq.*

9 *d-3*
FELISSIMO
The Japanese-owned boutique has a top-floor tea room, where you can sip tea between shopping spells or choose from over 50 varieties of loose tea to take home. *10 W. 56th St. (between 5th and 6th Aves.), Midtown West, 212/247–5656. Closed Sun. Subway: N, R, W to 5th Ave./59th St.*

11 *b-2*
MCNULTY'S TEA & COFFEE COMPANY
Established in 1895, this well-known Village shop sells rare teas and more than 200 choice imported coffees, straight or custom-blended. Imported jams and jellies are tempting accompaniments. *109 Christopher St. (near Bleecker St.), Greenwich Village, 212/242–5351. Subway: 1, 2 to Christopher St./Sheridan Sq.*

11 *d-1*
OREN'S DAILY ROAST
The widespread Oren's serves and scoops a wide selection of coffee from around the world. *31 Waverly Pl. (near University Pl.), Greenwich Village, 212/420–5958. Subway: N, R to 8th St.*

9 *e-6*
434 3rd Ave. (near 31st St.), Murray Hill, 212/779–1241. Subway: 6 to 33rd St.

9 *e-3*
33 E. 58th St. (near Madison Ave.), Midtown East, 212/838–3345. Subway: N, R, W to 5th Ave./59th St.

7 *e-8*
1144 Lexington Ave. (near 79th St.), Upper East Side, 212/472–6830. Subway: 6 to 77th St.; and other locations.

11 *c-3*
PORTO RICO IMPORTING CO.
Porto Rico has sold high-grade teas and coffees since 1907, and now roasts 50 different coffees each week. Options include custom blends, Jamaican Blue Mountain, decaffeinated espresso, 120 kinds of tea, and every conceivable coffee and tea accessory at 30%–50% off the list price. *201 Bleecker St. (near 6th Ave.), Greenwich Village, 212/477–5421. Subway: A, B, C, D, E, F, V to W. 4th St./Washington Sq.*

11 *g-1*
40½ St. Mark's Pl. (between 1st and 2nd Aves.), East Village, 212/533–1982. Subway: 6 to Astor Pl.

9 *c-1*
SENSUOUS BEAN
The friendly folks who run this pretty shop will blend from a wide variety of coffees. *66 W. 70th St. (between Central Park West and Columbus Ave.), Upper West Side, 212/724–7725. Subway: 1, 2, 3 to 72nd St.*

11 *e-1*
STARBUCKS
You can hardly walk three blocks in this town without passing one, maybe two, of these chain outlets. But the coffee is good, and the now-classic café mix of coffee-based drinks, baked goods, and a small lunch menu is a reliable standby for many a city dweller. The Astor Place location is the liveliest in town, with performers on some nights and a hip village crowd that infuses the franchise with a bit of personality. There are, of course, countless other locations around town. *13–25 Astor Pl. (near 4th Ave.), East Village, 212/982–3563. Subway: 6 to Astor Pl.*

9 *e-3*
TAKASHIMAYA
Fifth Avenue has the flagship American store for this 160-year-old Japanese company. The Tea Box, downstairs, serves lunch and afternoon tea and sells about 40 varieties of loose tea by the ounce. You'll find excellent, domestically grown black and herbal teas as well as green teas from Japan and a beautiful variety of teacups, teapots, and accessories. *693 5th Ave. (between 54th and 55th Sts.), Midtown East, 212/350–0100. Closed Sun. Subway: E, V to 5th Ave./53rd St.*

9 *f-2*
TIMOTHY'S COFFEES OF THE WORLD
This local chain sells passable coffee, cappuccino, iced tea, lemonade, baked

goods, and fresh coffee by the pound. *1033 3rd Ave. (at 61st St.), Upper East Side, 212/755–6456. Subway: N, R, W, 4, 5, 6 to 59th St./Lexington Ave.*

9 *f-1*
1296 1st Ave. (near 69th St.), Upper East Side, 212/794–7059. Subway: 6 to 68th St./Hunter College.

7 *e-7*
1188 Lexington Ave. (at 81st St.), Upper East Side, 212/879–0384. Subway: 6 to 77th St.; and other locations.

cheese

7 *f-8*
AGATA & VALENTINA
This Italian gourmet shop has an outstanding international selection of cheeses plus extremely attentive and friendly service. *1505 1st Ave. (at 78th St.), Upper East Side, 212/452–0690. Subway: 6 to 77th St.*

10 *g-3*
BEN'S CHEESE SHOP
Ben is renowned for his homemade farmer cheese, baked with vegetables, scallions, raisins, blueberries, strawberries, or pineapple. The homemade cream cheese is enhanced by chives, caviar, lox, or herbs and garlic. *181 E. Houston St. (near Orchard St.), Lower East Side, 212/254–8290. Closed Sat. Subway: F, V to 2nd Ave.*

9 *b-7*
CHEESE UNLIMITED
The name's no exaggeration: you'll find 400 varieties of cheese from the world over. *240 9th Ave. (at 24th St.), Chelsea, 212/691–1512. Subway: C, E to 23rd St.*

11 *f-5*
DI PALO'S DAIRY STORE
In the heart of Little Italy, Di Palo's offers fresh-ground Parmesan cheese, smoked mozzarella, and homemade ricotta-filled ravioli. *206 Grand St. (at Mott St.), Chinatown, 212/226–1033. Subway: J, M, Z to Bowery.*

10 *f-1*
EAST VILLAGE CHEESE STORE
The prices in this neighborhood shop can't be beat (but beware of prices that seem too good to be true—they usually indicate an overripe product). People

file in for the weekly specials (with a half-pound minimum purchase). *34 3rd Ave. (at 9th St.), East Village, 212/477–2601. Subway: 6 to Astor Pl.*

9 *f-2*
IDEAL CHEESE
This top-rated cheese shop has more than 300 varieties of domestic and imported cheese, and adds pâtés to the mix. *1205 2nd Ave. (at 63rd St.), Upper East Side, 212/688–7579. Subway: N, R, W, 4, 5, 6 to 59th St./Lexington Ave.*

9 *e-8*
LA MARCA CHEESE SHOP
Choose from a wide variety of cheeses cut to order, plus fresh-baked farmer cheese with various fruit fillings, and good croissants. *161 E. 22nd St. (between Lexington and 3rd Aves.), Gramercy, 212/673–7920. Subway: 6 to 23rd St.*

9 *b-1*
MAYA SCHAPER CHEESE & ANTIQUES
Among the food-related antiques like platters, glasses, and silverware from the 18th, 19th, and 20th centuries, Schaper sells around 70 cheeses from France, England, and Italy. Cheese accoutrements and Amy's Bread and Metro Bread round out the stock. Gift baskets and party platters are available. *106 W. 69th St. (at Columbus Ave.), Upper West Side, 212/873–2100. Subway: 1, 2, 3 to 72nd St.*

11 *b-3*
MURRAY'S CHEESE SHOP
Cheese connoisseurs consider the selection at this village institution the best in the city. Expert help will assist you with the overwhelming task of selecting from the tantalizing display. *257 Bleecker St. (at Cornelia St.), Greenwich Village, 212/243–3289. Subway: A, B, C, D, E, F, V to W. 4th St./Washington Sq.*

chocolate & other candy

9 *f-3*
AU CHOCOLAT
Boxed, loose, solid, filled, domestic, European—it's all here, from such makers as Godiva, Perugina, Laderach, Lindt, Corne, Dalloyen, and Bloomie's own. Custom gift baskets are available. *Bloomingdale's, 1000 3rd Ave. (at 59th St.), balcony level, Midtown West, 212/*

705–2953. Subway: N, R, W, 4, 5, 6 to 59th St./Lexington Ave.

10 f-1
BLACKHOUND

Under the black and white awning bearing a picture of the shop's namesake, you'll find signature hand-rolled Belgian bittersweet chocolate truffles and cakes made with darling detail that would put even Ms. Martha Stewart to the test. For special occasions, the shop will inscribe and decorate cakes. 149 1st Ave. (at 9th St.), East Village, 212/979–9505 or 800/344–4417. Subway: 6 to Astor Pl.

7 f-7
ELK CANDY

Elk's specialty is delicious homemade marzipan, coated with chocolate or otherwise flavored. 240 E. 86th St. (between 2nd and 3rd Aves.), Upper East Side, 212/650–1177. Subway: 4, 5, 6 to 86th St.

10 e-6
GODIVA

Eighty years old and justly famous, these Belgians proffer elaborately boxed sweets for spontaneous consumption or carefully meditated gifts. 33 Maiden La. (near Nassau St.), Lower Manhattan, 212/809–8990. Subway: A, C, J, M, Z, 1, 2, 4, 5 to Fulton St./Broadway–Nassau.

9 e-3
701 5th Ave. (near 54th St.), Midtown East, 212/593–2845. Subway: E, V to 5th Ave./53rd St.

9 e-1
793 Madison Ave. (near 67th St.), Upper East Side, 212/249–9444. Subway: 6 to 68th St./Hunter College.

9 c-1
245 Columbus Ave. (near 71st St.), Upper West Side, 212/787–5804. Subway: 1, 2, 3 to 72nd St.; other locations.

9 e-1
LA MAISON DU CHOCOLAT

Parisian chocolatier Robert Linxe whips up expensive, exquisitely flavored chocolate morsels filled with cinnamon, honey, mint, lemon, marzipan, kirsch, and more. Snap them up by the piece or the pound. 25 E. 73rd St. (near Madison Ave.), Upper East Side, 212/744–7117. Subway: 6 to 77th St.

11 b-2
LI-LAC CHOCOLATES

These homemade chocolates include French mint patties, hazelnut truffles, almond bark, and highly edible, hand-molded milk, dark, and white Empire State Buildings and Statues of Liberty. The goods have been made on the premises since 1923. 120 Christopher St. (at Bleecker St.), Greenwich Village, 212/242–7374. Subway: 1, 2 to Christopher St./Sheridan Sq.

9 d-6
MACY'S MARKETPLACE

This place is a dream—or a nightmare, depending on how you look at it. You'll find every boxed chocolate on the market, plus loose samples from Michel Guerard, Godiva, Neuhaus, and Perugina. It all adds up to over 2,000 square ft of candy. Macy's, 155 W. 34th St. (Herald Sq.), The Cellar (lower level), Midtown West, 212/695–4400. Subway: B, D, F, N, Q, R, V, W to 34th St./Herald Sq.

9 d-3
MANON, LE CHOCOLATIER

Shopping on 5th tiring you out? Duck into Bergdorf and choose from over 30 varieties of high-quality chocolate to nibble on the spot or ship to a friend. Bergdorf Goodman, 754 5th Ave. (at 57th St.), 7th floor, Midtown West, 212/753–7300. Closed Sun. Subway: N, R, W to 5th Ave./59th St.

9 e-3
MARTINE'S CHOCOLATES AT BLOOMINGDALE'S

Bloomie's on-site chocolatier turns out fresh truffles and white, dark, and milk chocolates with all the goodies like caramel and hazelnut all day long, sold by the piece or pound. Also in stock: marzipan, sugar-free chocolates, novelty shapes, and bars. Bloomingdale's 1000 3rd Ave. (at 59th St.), 6th floor, Midtown East, 212/705–2347. Subway: N, R, W, 4, 5, 6 to 59th St./Lexington Ave.

7 b-3
MONDEL CHOCOLATES

This family business has produced an amazing array of naturally flavored chocolates with little fat for over 45 years—mint, orange, coffee, amaretto, and more. Beautiful boxes and baskets make presentation a snap. 2913 Broadway (at 114th St.), Morningside Heights,

212/864–2111. Subway: 1 to 116th St./Columbia University.

NEUCHATEL CHOCOLATES
9 d-3

In business for five generations, Neuchatel has more than 60 different Swiss-European chocolates, truffles, and treats, with a specialty in champagne truffles. Other truffle options include Grand Marnier, espresso, and white chocolate. *Plaza Hotel, 5th Ave. and 59th Sts., Midtown East, 212/751–7742. Subway: N, R, W to 5th Ave./59th St.*

PERUGINA
9 e-3

Pick up a box of chocolate Baci and lovely gift-packaged candies at the company's own store. *520 Madison Ave. (at 53rd St.), Midtown East, 212/688–2490. Subway: E, V to 5th Ave./53rd St.*

RICHART DESIGN ET CHOCOLAT
9 e-3

Resembling a gallery more than a chocolate shop, Richart presents edibles that are truly works of art. The signature Petits Richart Collection of miniature chocolates that resemble jewelry are embellished with modern abstract designs. All are made in France, flown in weekly, and made with the finest cocoa available. *7 E. 55th St. (near 5th Ave.), Midtown East, 212/371–9369. Closed Sun. Subway: E, V to 5th Ave./53rd St.*

TEUSCHER CHOCOLATES OF SWITZERLAND
9 e-2, d-4

The ultimate Swiss-chocolate treats are flown in weekly from Switzerland. Try the delectable champagne truffles— happily, you can buy just one. *25 E. 61st St. (between 5th and Madison Aves.), Upper East Side, 212/751–8482. Subway: N, R, W, 4, 5, 6 to 59th St./Lexington Ave.*

9 e-4

620 5th Ave. (at 50th St.), Midtown West, 212/246–4416. Subway: B, D, F, V to 47th–50th Sts./Rockefeller Ctr.

ethnic foods

ATLANTIC AVENUE (MIDDLE EASTERN)
12 b-4

Dodge the traffic for such Mediterranean delights as Turkish coffees, Lebanese pita breads, hummus, stuffed grape leaves, halvah, and baklava. *Atlantic Ave. from Henry to Court Sts., bordering Brooklyn Heights. Subway: A, C, F to Jay St./Borough Hall.*

BELMONT (ITALIAN)
5 h-5

Belmont is still good for homemade pasta, pepperoni, bread, pastries, and espresso cafés. *Arthur Ave. and E. 187th St., Bronx. Subway: B, D to 182nd–183rd Sts.*

BENSONHURST (ITALIAN)
4 f-5

The shops teem with salamis, sausages, cheeses, prosciutto, and pizza rustica. *18th Ave. from 61st to 86th St., Brooklyn. Subway: N to 18th Ave.*

CHINATOWN (ASIAN)
10 f-4

Chinatown's main artery is Mott Street, but it takes the whole neighborhood to produce such a wealth of Chinese, Vietnamese, and Thai restaurants, tea parlors, bakeries, and gift shops. *Bordered by Canal, Worth, and Mulberry Sts.; the Bowery; and Chatham Sq. Subway: J, M, N, Q, R, W, Z, 6 to Canal St.*

EAST VILLAGE (UKRAINIAN & POLISH)
10 f-1

Emerge from that dive bar and check out the East Village's first cultural legacy: wonderful pierogi, blintzes, kielbasa, headcheese, babka, and black bread. If you need an excuse, the Ukrainian Festival shows them all off every May (*see* Events *in* Chapter 4). *1st Ave. near 7th St. Subway: F, V to 2nd Ave.*

HELL'S KITCHEN (WORLD)
9 c-5

Once predominantly Italian and Greek, stores with sidewalk stands have replaced the pushcarts of yore, and Hell's Kitchen is now a United Nations of food, with everything from apple pie to Ethiopian *injera* bread available for consumption. The 9th Avenue International Food Festival celebrates this rather cool diversity in May (*see* Events *in* Chapter 4). *9th Ave. from 37th to 49th St., Midtown West. Subway: A, C, E to 42nd St./Port Authority.*

3 *f-3*

JACKSON HEIGHTS (INDIAN)

Shop for Indian spices, condiments, sweets, meal and saris and stop for a breathtaking meal at one of several unassuming Indian restaurants in this melting pot of a neighborhood. *74th St. from 37th to Roosevelt Aves., Queens. Subway: 7 to 74th St./Broadway; E, F, R, V to Jackson Heights–Roosevelt Ave.*

7 *e-3*

LA MARQUETA (LATIN)

East Harlem has its own *muy* aromatic Latin American market, with more than 250 stalls displaying exotic fruits and vegetables, grains, spices, hot sauces, smoked meats, and fish. *Park Ave. from 110th to 116th St., East Harlem. Subway: 6 to 116th St.*

8 *d-4*

LITTLE ATHENS (GREEK)

Astoria houses one of the largest Greek communities outside Greece, so this is the place to explore Greek tavernas, *raffenion* (coffeehouses), restaurants, and churches to the tunes of bouzouki music and while enjoying baklava, and thick, rich Greek coffee. *Ditmars Blvd. from 31st to 38th Sts., Astoria, Queens. Subway: N, W to Ditmars Blvd./Astoria.*

11 *f-5*

LITTLE ITALY (ITALIAN)

Little Italy has more or less dwindled away as an Italian residential neighborhood, but its restaurants, pastry and espresso cafés, and cheese and pasta shops live on. You won't find cannolis like these uptown. The Feast of San Gennaro packs the streets each fall (*see* Events *in* Chapter 4). *Mulberry St. between Houston and Canal Sts. Subway: J, M, N, Q, R, W, Z, 6 to Canal St.*

3 *c-7*

LOWER EAST SIDE (JEWISH)

Okay, so it's becoming an extension of the East Village, but the Lower East Side retains a few vestiges of its Jewish heritage. Knishes, barreled schmaltz herring, pastrami, corned beef, pickles, and bagels share this neighborhood with the discount shops. *Roughly Houston–Canal Sts. from Bowery to the East River. Subway: F, J, M, Z to Delancey St./Essex St.; S to Grand St.*

7 *f-7*

YORKVILLE (GERMAN)

The German area has nearly disappeared, but a few restaurants still serve hearty, home-style foods and bock beer; a few Konditoreien serve exquisite pastries; and a few shops sell specialty foods. There's still a small Hungarian enclave within this district. *Lexington Ave. to York Ave., mainly on 2nd Avenue just south of 86th Street. Subway: 4, 5, 6 to 86th St.*

fish & seafood

9 *c-5*

CENTRAL FISH COMPANY

True, it's not centrally located, but the selection of fresh fish is enormous and prices are extremely reasonable. *527 9th Ave. (at 39th St.), Midtown West, 212/279–2317. Subway: A, C, E to 42nd St./Port Authority.*

7 *f-8*

CITARELLA

Its original claim to fame was fish, but Citarella now offers much more. The butcher counter is exceptional, and you'll find baked goods and prepared foods as well. The West Side shop has long been cherished for its amazing window displays of fresh seafood sculptures. *2135 Broadway (at 75th St.), Upper West Side, 212/874–0383. Subway: 1, 2, 3 to 72nd St.*

7 *f-8*

1313 3rd Ave. (at 75th St.), Upper East Side, 212/452–2780. Subway: 6 to 77th St.

7 *b-6*

JAKE'S FISH MARKET

Everyone seems to love this shop for its fresh fish and savvy staff. Prices are high, but the quality and variety are beyond dispute. *2425 Broadway (at 89th St.), Upper West Side, 212/580–5253. Subway: 1, 2 to 86th St.*

9 *f-1*

LEONARD'S

The exquisite selection includes smoked or poached salmon, caviar, crabmeat, and boiled lobster. Delivery is free. *1241 3rd Ave. (between 71st and 72nd Sts.), Upper East Side, 212/744–2600. Subway: 6 to 68th St./Hunter College.*

9 *f-4*

PISACANE

Here in U.N. territory is a good general selection of high-quality fish. *940 1st Ave. (between 51st and 52nd Sts.), Midtown East, 212/355–1850. Subway: 6 to 51st St./Lexington Ave.; E, V to Lexington–3rd Aves./53rd St.*

7 *e-8*

ROSEDALE

You can't beat Rosedale for quality and selection, but you can definitely beat its prices. This shop is known for delicious soft-shell crabs and superior salmon. *1129 Lexington Ave. (at 78th St.), Upper East Side, 212/288–5013. Closed Sun. Subway: 6 to 77th St.*

gourmet foods

10 *d-1*

BALDUCCI'S

This New York institution is a foodie destination for natives and tourists alike. Inhale olives, vinegars, cheeses, pâtés, breads and pastries, chocolates, meats, desserts, and coffees. *424 6th Ave. (at 9th St.), Greenwich Village, 212/673–2600 or 800/BALDUCCI. Subway: A, B, C, D, E, F, V to W. 4th St./Washington Sq.*

9 *f-3*

CALL CUISINE

Don't feel like cooking? Choose from about 15 different gourmet dinners, each prepared daily. The retail shop clues you in to the ingredients. *1032 1st Ave. (between 56th and 57th Sts.), Midtown East, 212/752–7070. Subway: N, R, W, 4, 5, 6 to 59th St./Lexington Ave.*

9 *e-3*

CAVIARTERIA

Beluga, osetra, sevruga—Caviarteria claims to be the leading importer of Russian Caviar in the U.S. Choose from twelve fresh varieties, along with their sought after freshly made buckwheat and white blinis, smoked salmon, foie gras, and all the accoutrements, like mother of pearl spoons and caviar servers. Caviarteria will deliver right to your door, and you can dine on decadent goodies in the restaurant. *502 Park Ave. (entrance on 59th St.) (between Park and Madison Aves.), Upper East Side, 212/759–7410. Subway: N, R, W, 4, 5, 6 to 59th St./Lexington Ave.*

10 *c-1*

CHELSEA MARKET

This giant warehouse space on the edge of the meat-packing district is an exciting development for foodies in New York. More than a dozen independently operated shops coexist within the enormous space, selling everything from delicious baked goods at Amy's Bread to freshly squeezed Juice Company juices, to decadent desserts at Sarabeth's, to aged prime rib at Frank's, to gourmet wholesale priced Italian goodies at Buon Italia. *75 9th Ave. (between 15th and 16th Sts.), Chelsea. Subway: A, C, E, L to 14th St./8th Ave.*

11 *e-4*

DEAN & DELUCA

Who doesn't love this fabulous food emporium? A well-edited department in every food category means you'll find only the best of the best. The quality and beauty of the food are matched only by the quality and beauty of the clientele. To prepare your purchase in style, head to the back of the store, where great-looking kitchenware and cookbooks are temptingly displayed. *560 Broadway (at Prince St.), SoHo, 212/431–1691 or 800/221–7714. Subway: N, R to Prince St.*

7 *e-8*

E.A.T.

Ah, such lovely imports at such breathtaking prices! The handsome E.A.T. offers daily specials on its excellent assortment of pâtés, cheeses, coffees, and breads. *1064 Madison Ave. (at 80th St.), Upper East Side, 212/772–0022. Subway: 6 to 77th St.*

7 *f-8*

ELI'S

This two-floor extravaganza of upscale gourmet treats is from the same food guru who brought us Zabar's, the Vinegar Factory, and E.A.T. Prices are quite high, but the selection of delicious prepared foods, extraordinary cheeses, and interesting produce keeps customers coming back. There's also a beautiful flower selection and a small but well chosen array of cookbooks and kitchen implements. *1411 3rd Ave. (at 80th St.), Upper East Side, 212/717–8100. Subway: 6 to 77th St.*

7 b-8

FAIRWAY

Fairway has one of the best cheese selections in the city, assembled by one of the foremost experts in the field. The first floor of the Broadway store is an extravaganza of fresh, prepared, and packaged foods, and the second floor holds an impressive array of organic and health foods. *2127 Broadway (at 75th St.), Upper West Side, 212/595–1888. Subway: 1, 2, 3 to 72nd St.*

6 c-8

133rd St. (at West Side Hwy.), Harlem, 212/234–3883. Subway: 1 to 137th St./City College.

11 e-5

GOURMET GARAGE

Known for such staples as fresh produce, pastas, breads, oils, and vinegars, Gourmet Garage sells a fine selection of quality goods at reasonable prices. *453 Broome St. (near Mercer St.), SoHo, 212/941–5850. Subway: 6 to Spring St.*

7 b-5

2571 Broadway (at 96th St.), Upper West Side, 212/663–0656. Subway: 1, 2, 3 to 96th St.

9 f-2

301 E. 64th St. (at 2nd Ave.), Upper East Side, 212/535–6271. Subway: 6 to 68th St./Hunter College.

9 f-1

GRACE'S MARKETPLACE

This upscale store has a loyal neighborhood following and is always busy. Pick up fresh produce, pasta, oils and vinegars, fresh dairy products and cheeses, sliced meats, olives, baked goods, candy, desserts, fresh coffee, prepared foods, sandwiches, and more. *1237 3rd Ave. (at 71st St.), Upper East Side, 212/737–0600. Subway: 6 to 68th St./Hunter College.*

10 d-1

JEFFERSON MARKET

This neighborhood Greenwich Village shop has a good selection of fresh produce, meat, and fish. The cheese and prepared food sections are ample, too. The shop is particularly appreciated for its friendly staff and personal service. *450 6th Ave. (near W. 10th St.), Greenwich Village, 212/533–3377. Subway: F, V to 14th St.*

9 e-3

MAISON GLASS

Maison Glass is a good general store for smoked Scottish and Nova Scotia salmon, Smithfield ham, foie gras, cheese, and canned and packaged gourmet food. *111 E. 58th St. (between Park and Lexington Aves.), Midtown East, 212/755–3316. Subway: N, R, W, 4, 5, 6 to 59th St./Lexington Ave.*

10 c-1

MYERS OF KESWICK

It may be a stretch to call it "gourmet," but anglophiles will love this charming grocer. Knock yourself out with sausage rolls, kidney pies, pork pies, Scotch eggs, Stilton cheese, and Aberdeen kippers, along with packaged British cookies, candy, and other foods. Yes—they do have HobNobs! *634 Hudson St. (near Jane St.), Greenwich Village, 212/691–4194. Subway: A, C, E, L to 14th St./8th Ave.*

7 e-7

PARADISE MARKET

Indeed, it's Eden for fresh produce, with a wide selection of exotic yet (may we hope?) permissible fruits and vegetables. The prices, alas, are postlapsarian. *1614 2nd Ave. (at 84th St.), Upper East Side, 212/737–0049. Subway: 4, 5, 6 to 86th St.*

9 d-3

PETROSSIAN BOUTIQUE

Indulge in the world's finest caviar, and try the delicious buckwheat blinis, sturgeon, pâté, and prepared foods. Prices are, um, not low. *182 E. 58th St. (between Lexington and 3rd Aves.), Midtown East, 212/245–2217. Subway: F, N, R, Q, W to 57th St.*

7 f-6

THE VINEGAR FACTORY

Eli Zabar, the founder of both Zabar's and E.A.T., has another big, bustling shop in a converted turn-of-the-20th-century vinegar factory. The great selection of everything from prepared foods to produce means you'll find whatever you need. The Factory sells Eli's famous bread for less than you'd pay at E.A.T. Bonus: there's free parking nearby. *431 E. 91st St. (between 1st and York Aves.), Upper East Side, 212/987–0885. Subway: 4, 5, 6 to 86th St.*

7 *e-8*

WILLIAM POLL

This Upper East Side caterer and store has undoubtedly made many a society dinner party. They're known for delicious hors d'oeuvres, thin sandwiches, prepared foods, spreads, and specialty items. *1051 Lexington Ave. (between 74th and 75th Sts.), Upper East Side, 212/288–0501. Closed Sun. Subway: 6 to 77th St.*

7 *b-8*

ZABAR'S

From its humble beginnings as a deli and cheese shop, Zabar's has become the king of New York's gourmet stores. Its mind-boggling array of cheeses, meats, smoked fish, coffees, teas, and prepared entrées has won the city over. Kitchenwares are discounted 20%–40%. Go just for the sights, sounds, smells, and social life. *2245 Broadway (at 80th St.), Upper West Side, 212/787–2000. Subway: 1, 2 to 79th St.*

health food

11 *c-7*

COMMODITIES NATURAL

With over 5,000 square ft to play with in its TriBeCa store, this supermarket has 24 kinds of granola, 50 kinds of honey, 125 kinds of tea, 30 bins of grains, and tons of fresh organic produce. *117 Hudson St. (at N. Moore St.), TriBeCa, 212/334–8330. Subway: 1, 2 to Franklin St.*

10 *f-1*

165 1st Ave. (at 10th St.), East Village, 212/260–2600. Subway: 6 to Astor Pl.

7 *f-6*

FOODS FOR HEALTH

This large natural food store sells organic produce and dairy products, herbal and homeopathic remedies, vitamins, natural cosmetics, freshly whipped up juices and, of course, plenty of healthy foods. *1653 3rd Ave. (between 92nd and 93rd Sts.), Upper East Side, 212/369–9202. Subway: 6 to 96th St.*

9 *f-5*

HEALTH NUTS

Find produce, bulk items, household necessities, vitamins, body care products, and a juice bar and deli counter at all locations. The 99th Street shop houses a snack counter and offers nutritional consultations. *853 2nd Ave. (at*

45th St.), Midtown East, 212/369–9202. Subway: 6 to 96th St.*

9 *f-2*

1208 2nd Ave. (at 63rd St.), Upper East Side, 212/593–0116. Subway: N, R, W, 4, 5, 6 to 59th St./Lexington Ave.

7 *b-8*

2141 Broadway (at 75th St.), Upper West Side, 212/724–1972. Subway: 1, 2, 3 to 72nd St.

7 *b-5*

2611 Broadway (at 99th St.), Upper West Side, 212/678–0054. Subway: 1, 2, 3 to 96th St.

10 *e-1*

HEALTHY PLEASURES

The feature presentations are an organic salad bar and a selection of healthy prepared foods. Other health- and environment-conscious products include vitamins, personal-care items, and cleaning products. *93 University Pl. (near 11th St.), Greenwich Village, 212/353–3663. Subway: N, R to 8th St.*

11 *d-6*

489 Broome St. (between W. Broadway and Wooster), SoHo, 212/431–7434. Subway: A, C, E to Canal St.

10 *c-1*

INTEGRAL YOGA NATURAL FOODS

Health-food enthusiasts flock here for the wide selection, including freshly made prepared foods. *229 W. 13th St. (between 7th and 8th Aves.), Greenwich Village, 212/243–2642. Subway: A, C, E, L to 14th St./8th Ave.*

10 *d-1*

LIFETHYME NATURAL MARKET

Appetizing even to junk food fans, this market offers organic produce, a juice and salad bar, a vegan bakery, and a wide selection of packaged all-natural products from soy ice cream to gluten-free pasta. *410 6th Ave. (between 8th and 9th Sts.), Greenwich Village, 212/420–9099. Subway: A, B, C, D, E, F, V to W. 4th St./Washington Sq.*

7 *b-8*

2275 Broadway (between 81st and 82nd Sts.), Upper West Side, 212/721–9000. Subway: 1 to 79th St.

7 e-7

LOTUS HEALTH FOOD

Shoppers at this small store benefit from owner Narain Chandra's vast knowledge. Chandra selects all the produce and other goods with an eye to the highest quality and makes sure the staff is tiptop. Fresh produce is available only on Tuesdays and Fridays; dry goods, cosmetics, vitamins, pre-made sandwiches, fish, organic poultry, supplements, and freshly squeezed organic juices are always available. *1309 Lexington Ave. (between 87th and 88th Sts.), Upper East Side, 212/423–0244. Subway: 4, 5, 6 to 86th St.*

9 f-8

NATURAL GREEN MARKET

Formerly Natural Frontier, this market is known for its organic produce and poultry (free-range, of course) and fish; even the pet foods are organic. *162 3rd Ave. (at 16th St.), Gramercy, 212/780–0263. Subway: Subway: L, N, Q, R, W, 4, 5, 6 to 14th St./Union Sq.*

7 b-6

UPTOWN WHOLE FOODS

This shop (not affiliated with Whole Foods Market) is a complete natural-food market, with specialties in produce, chicken, and fish. There's a large bulk department, many fresh herbs, and a selection of gourmet takeout meals. Natural cosmetics and vitamins complete your personal package nicely. *2421 Broadway (at 89th St.), Upper West Side, 212/874–4000. Subway: 1, 2 to 86th St.*

9 c-7

WHOLE FOODS MARKET

Bringing much-needed quality produce and organic foods to Chelsea, this outpost of the national chain is a grocery shopper's dream. In addition to fresh vegetables you will find an excellent butcher counter, cheese department, and coffee and tea counter. Adjacent is Whole Body at Whole Foods Market for all your health an beauty needs. *250 7th Ave. (at 24th St.), Chelsea, 212/924–5969. Subway: 1 to 23rd St.*

herbs & spices

11 g-1

ANGELICA'S

At this corner store, stock up on Western dried herbs, books, essential oils, teas, coffees, and spices. *147 1st Ave. (at 9th St.), East Village, 212/677–1549. Subway: 6 to Astor Pl.*

11 c-2

APHRODISIA

This inviting Villager has an interesting selection of herbs at reasonable prices. *264 Bleecker St. (near 6th Ave.), Greenwich Village, 212/989–6440. Subway: A, B, C, D, E, F, V to W. 4th St./Washington Sq.*

12 c-4

SAHADI IMPORTING CO.

This exotic market is well worth the trip for its great selection of spices and Middle Eastern food at excellent prices. Bulk purchases offer even more savings. *187–89 Atlantic Ave. (near Court St.), Brooklyn Heights, Brooklyn, 718/624–4550. Closed Sun. Subway: A, C, F to Jay St./Borough Hall.*

9 e-7

SPICE CORNER

Stop in for loose and pre-packaged ayurvedic and traditional Indian herbs and spices and Indian and Middle-Eastern cookbooks and foods. *135 Lexington Ave. (at 29th St.), Midtown East, 212/689–5182. Subway: 6 to 28th St.*

meat & poultry

11 c-2

FAICCO'S PORK STORE

In business since the exact turn of the 20th century, Faicco's has become a New York institution, renowned for its delicious sausages. *260 Bleecker St. (near 6th Ave.), Greenwich Village, 212/243–1974. Subway: A, B, C, D, E, F, V to W. 4th St./Washington Sq.*

4 e-4

6511 11th Ave. (at 65th St.), Bay Ridge, Brooklyn, 718/236–0119. Closed Mon. Subway: N to Fort Hamilton Pkwy.

11 h-1

KUROWYCKY MEATS

This family-run shop has been in business for nearly 40 years, preparing and purveying some of the city's finest smoked (on the premises) and cured meats. Look for baked hams, unusual sausages (including sausage with caraway seeds, or the spicy Ukrainian kielbasa). Top off your purchase with dark Lithuanian bread, homemade Polish mustard, and sauerkraut. *124 1st Ave. (near 7th St.), East Village, 212/477–0344. Subway: 6 to Astor Pl.*

9 *e-7*

LES HALLES

The popular French bistro (see French in Chapter 1) also has a highly regarded butcher shop for French cuts of meat. *411 Park Ave. S (between 28th and 29th Sts.), Murray Hill, 212/679–4111. Subway: 6 to 28th St.*

7 *e-7*

LOBEL'S

Many New Yorkers consider this to be the prime outlet for meat in the city. Although prices can be astronomically high, you definitely get what you pay for, and the service is knowledgeable professional. *1096 Madison Ave. (between 82nd and 83rd Sts.), Upper East Side, 212/737–1373. Subway: 4, 5, 6 to 86th St.*

7 *b-5*

OPPENHEIMER PRIME MEATS

The butcher and owner of this old-fashioned shop carries a top selection of meats, game, and poultry. *2606 Broadway (at 99th St.), Upper West Side, 212/662–0246. Closed Sun. Subway: 1, 2, 3 to 96th St.*

7 *g-7*

OTTOMANELLI BROS.

Catch prime cuts and fresh game in season. They'll deliver to nearby addresses. *1549 York Ave. (at 82nd St.), Upper East Side, 212/772–7900. Subway: 4, 5, 6 to 86th St.*

7 *e-7*

SCHALLER & WEBBER

A holdout of the German Yorkville stores that used to line the streets here—the high-quality smoked meats, sausages, and hams will make you think you're back in the old country. *1654 2nd Ave. (between 85th and 86th Sts.), Upper East Side, 212/879–3047. Subway: 4, 5, 6 to 86th St.*

pasta & noodles

9 *c-4*

BRUNO RAVIOLI CO.

Pasta makers since 1905, Bruno supplies many restaurants and caterers with its fresh manicotti; tortellini; vegetable lasagna; egg fettuccine; and ravioli with sun-dried tomatoes, shiitake mushrooms, or pesto. Pick up a homemade sauce, too. *653 9th Ave. (near 45th St.), Midtown West, 212/246–8456. Subway: A, C, E to 42nd St./Port Authority.*

9 *c-8*

249 8th Ave. (near 22nd St.), Chelsea, 212/627–0767. Subway: C, E to 23rd St.

7 *b-8*

2204 Broadway (near 78th St.), Upper West Side, 212/580–8150. Subway: 1, 2 to 79th St.

11 *f-5*

PIEMONTE HOMEMADE RAVIOLI COMPANY

In the heart of Little Italy, Piemonte makes a variety of fresh pastas daily, including gluten-free macaroni for those with an allergy. *190 Grand St. (near Mulberry St.), 212/226–0475. Closed Mon. Subway: J, M, N, Q, R, W, Z, 6 to Canal St.*

11 *d-3*

RAFFETTO'S CORPORATION

This long-standing Village shop (est. 1906) cuts fresh pasta and egg or spinach noodles to your specifications as you watch. Every day brings new batches of ravioli stuffed with cheese or meat. Nobody does it better, or for less. *144 W. Houston St. (near Sullivan St.), Greenwich Village, 212/777–1261. Closed Sun.–Mon. Subway: 1, 2 to Houston St.*

11 *c-5*

THE RAVIOLI STORE INC.

Will you go for the all-out gourmet ravioli with wild mushrooms and white truffles in a saffron pasta, or traditional with fresh ricotta in a parsley flecked dough? You won't go wrong with either one, or with any of the dozens of other fresh gourmet pastas cranked-out on the premises. Oh, and ever wonder where Dean & Deluca gets their pricey pasta? Well look no farther (and pay a lot less). *75 Sullivan St. (between Spring and Broome Sts.), SoHo, 212/925–1737. Subway: A, C, E to Canal St.*

wines & spirits

9 b-1

ACKER MERRALL & CONDIT
A grande dame of New York wine stores, Acker Merrall carries all the heavy hitters and has one of the city's largest selection of Australian wines. *160 W. 72nd St. (between Broadway and Columbus Ave.), Upper West Side, 212/787–1700. Subway: 1, 2, 3 to 72nd St.*

11 f-1

ASTOR WINES & SPIRITS
The largest liquor store in New York State is a must for bargain-hunting oenophiles. The service needs some work. *12 Astor Pl. (at Lafayette St.), East Village, 212/674–7500. Subway: 6 to Astor Pl.*

7 e-7

BEST CELLARS
With an eclectic group of white, red, dessert, and sparkling wines priced around $10 and helpful service, this store offers a welcome antidote to stuffy, overpriced wine purveyors. Stock up here for your next party. *1291 Lexington Avenue (between 86th and 87th Sts.), Upper East Side, 212/426–4200. Subway: 4, 5, 6 to 86th St.*

10 d-1

CROSSROADS
It's cramped, and not always cheap, but they have wines you won't find anywhere else. *55 W. 14th St. (between 5th and 6th Aves.), Chelsea, 212/924–3060. Subway: F, V to 14th St.; L to 6th Ave.*

9 e-1

GARNET WINES & LIQUORS
For selection and price, this is the best all-around wine store in town. *929 Lexington Ave. (between 68th and 69th Sts.), Upper East Side, 212/772–3211. Subway: 6 to 68th St./Hunter College.*

9 e-5

GRANDE HARVEST WINES
Don't expect bargains at this über-convenient store in Grand Central Terminal, just a good selection focusing on Italian and Californian wines and single malts. *33 Grand Central Terminal, across from Track 17, Midtown East, 212/682–5855. Subway: 4, 5, 6, 7, S to 42nd St./Grand Central.*

9 e-8

ITALIAN WINE MERCHANTS
A self-proclaimed "studio del gusto," Italian Wine Merchants offers classes and provides tastings in addition to selling wines. The shop houses a temperature and humidity-controlled cellar, leaving only one sample of each bottle on the floor. Two experts are available to consult with even the most experienced connoisseurs. *108 E. 16th St. (between Irving Pl. and Union Sq. E), Gramercy, 212/473–2323. Subway: L, N, Q, R, W, 4, 5, 6 to 14th St./Union Sq.*

9 e-3

MORRELL & COMPANY
This beautiful, well-run wine shop offers the best in every price range and from every corner of the globe. If you're buying for a special occasion, this is the place to come. *1 Rockefeller Plaza (between 5th and 6th Aves.), Midtown West, 212/688–9370. Subway: B, D, F, V to 47–50 Sts./Rockefeller Ctr.*

9 e-6

PARK AVENUE LIQUORS
Overlook the disheveled appearance and incongruous name of this Madison Avenue shop, and you'll find savvy help and some good, lesser-known bottles. *292 Madison Ave. (between 40th and 41st Sts.), Midtown East, 212/685–2442. Subway: 4, 5, 6, 7, S to 42nd St./Grand Central.*

9 e-2

SHERRY LEHMANN WINES & SPIRITS
One of the best liquor stores around, this elegant shop has a comprehensive stock and knowledgeable staff. *679 Madison Ave. (near 61st St.), Upper East Side, 212/838–7500. Subway: N, R, W, 4, 5, 6 to 59th St./Lexington Ave.*

9 b-2

67 WINE & SPIRIT MERCHANTS
Two floors of wine and spirits, plus a kitchen for visiting chefs and wine and food events. Wine club members get special discounts. *179 Columbus Ave. (between 67th and 68th Sts.), Upper West Side, 212/724–6767. Subway: 1, 2 to 66th St./Lincoln Ctr.*

9 e-8

UNION SQUARE WINES & SPIRITS

Choose from more than 4,500 wines from around the world, with an emphasis on Californian, Italian, French, Spanish, and Australian vineyards. Not sure what you're looking for? Ask the extremely helpful in-house expert for some advice. Expand your knowledge with regularly scheduled tastings Wednesdays through Saturdays. *33 Union Sq. W (between 16th and 17th Sts.), Flatiron District, 212/675–8100. Subway: L, N, Q, R, W, 4, 5, 6 to 14th St./Union Sq.*

11 d-6

VINTAGE NEW YORK

In a New York State of Mind? Vintage New York sells roughly 175 wines solely from the Empire State, all of which are available to sample before purchasing. The shop offers a 10% discount on cases and 6% off on six bottles or more. Call about cooking classes and food seminars. *482 Broome St. (at Wooster St.), SoHo, 212/226–9463. Subway: J, M, N, Q, R, W, Z, 6 to Canal St.*

FRAMING

9 d-8

A. I. FRIEDMAN

More than 2,000 styles of ready-made wood, plexi, and metal frames go for 20% off the list price, and the staff will custom-frame as well. *44 W. 18th St. (between 5th and 6th Aves.), Chelsea, 212/243–9000. Subway: F, V to 14th St.*

7 e-8

A.P.F., INC.

This company's own factory makes a variety of custom frames, including museum-quality reproductions as well as contemporary styles. *172 E. 75th St. (between Lexington and 3rd Aves.), Upper East Side, 212/988–1090. Subway: 6 to 77th St.*

9 f-2

231 E. 60th St. (between 3rd and 2nd Aves.), Upper East Side, 212/223–0726. Subway: N, R, W, 4, 5, 6 to 59th St./Lexington Ave.

11 e-5

BARK FRAMEWORKS

Bark has specialized in archivally correct framing for over 20 years. The service doesn't come cheap, but it's worth it for fine works of art and photography that you want to last a lifetime. *270 Lafayette St. (at Prince St.), SoHo, 212/431–9080. Open by appt. only. Subway: 6 to Spring St.*

9 c-8

CHELSEA FRAMES

This shop concentrates on custom and archival framing of everything from posters to conservation pieces. The staff is helpful, turnaround is fast, and prices are reasonable. *207 8th Ave. (between 20th and 21st Sts.), Chelsea, 212/807–8957. Subway: C, E to 23rd St.*

9 e-8

FRAMEWORKS

Allow Frameworks' skilled staff to help guide you through their collection of approximately 4,000 framing options—from handcarved gold-leaf to poster frames, all custom-constructed to suit your style and needs. Prints, posters, photographs, and framed artwork are also available. *51 E. 19th St. (at Park Ave. S), Flatiron District, 212/982–2929. Subway: 6 to 23rd St.*

7 g-8

HOUSE OF HEYDENRYK

Heydenryk has sold, repaired, and restored antique frames since 1935; the company now also sells reproduction frames, made by a staff of craftsmen who work above the showroom. Repros take four weeks. *417 E. 76th St. (between 1st and York Aves.), Upper East Side, 212/249–4903. Subway: 6 to 77th St.*

9 e-2

J. POCKER & SON

Expert framers since 1926, J. Pocker & Son provide custom work, including conservation, in a wide range of styles, from ornate, hand-carved gilt to plexi. They'll even pick up and deliver your piece. Drop into the gallery to browse prints and posters, including a selection of views of New York and English sporting scenes. *135 E. 63rd St. (between Lexington and Park Aves.), Upper East Side, 212/838–5488 or 800/782–8434. Subway: N, R, W, 4, 5, 6 to 59th St./Lexington Ave.*

9 f-4

ONE HOUR FRAMING SHOP INC

This shop's two New York City outposts are fast and cheap—two words every

Gotham dweller can appreciate once in a while. Metal and ready-made framing jobs can be completed in just one hour; wooden frames take up to three. *210 E. 51st St. (between 2nd and 3rd Aves.), Midtown East, 212/888–9130. Subway: 6 to 51st St./Lexington Ave.; E, V to Lexington–3rd Aves.*

9 *d-5*

131 W. 45th St. (between 6th Ave. and Broadway), Midtown West, 212/869–5263. Subway: B, D, F, V to 42nd St.; N, R, Q, S, W, 1, 2, 3 to 42nd St./Times Sq.

4 *d-2*

YALE PICTURE FRAME & MOULDING CORP.
This estimable firm imports and manufactures picture frames; discounts over 400 moldings for custom-made frames by 25%; and offers more than 20,000 ready-made frames. *770 5th Ave. (at 28th St.), Sunset Park, Brooklyn, 718/788–6200. Closed Sat.; Sun. by appt. only. Subway: M, N, R to 25th St.*

GIFTS

10 *f-6*

BROOKSTONE
The famed New Hampshire purveyor of hard-to-find tools and gadgets displays a sample of every item it sells. Pick up a clipboard upon entering—it's your order form. *South Street Seaport, Schermerhorn Row, 18 Fulton St., Lower Manhattan, 212/344–8108. Subway: A, C, J, M, Z, 1, 2, 4, 5 to Fulton St./Broadway–Nassau.*

9 *d-4*

Rockefeller Center, 5th Ave. between 49th and 50th Sts., Midtown West, 212/262–3237. Subway: B, D, F, V to 47th–50th Sts./Rockefeller Ctr.

9 *d-3*

20 W. 57th St. (between 5th and 6th Aves.), Midtown West, 212/245–1405. Subway: F, N, R, Q, W to 57th St.

9 *d-3*

FELISSIMO
An oasis of quiet in mid-Midtown, the whole of Felissimo is configured according to feng shui, the Eastern art of placement, so you've got to feel harmonious. The first floor features gardening accessories; the second floor has clothing, accessories, and a beautiful bedroom area with fine linens and bath products;

the third floor covers the dining-room table; and once you've made it to the fourth floor, you can plop elegantly down in the Tea Room (*see* Food—Coffee & Tea, *above*). *10 W. 56th St. (between 5th and 6th Aves.), Midtown West, 212/247–5656. Subway: N, R, W to 5th Ave./59th St.*

9 *f-4*

GRAFTON GIFTS & BASKETS
Her shop designed like a quaint Irish cottage, Grafton specializes in custom gift baskets for all occasions. Also find stocked and bare picnic baskets. The shop works with about ten basket manufacturers, so the selection is bountiful—whether you're looking for a home accessory or gift basket. *830 3rd Ave. (at 51st St.), Midtown East, 212/759–2850. Subway: 6 to 51st St./Lexington Ave.; E, V to Lexington–3rd Aves./53rd St.*

9 *e-3*

HAMMACHER SCHLEMMER
Established on the Bowery in 1848, Hammacher Schlemmer has been on 57th Street since 1926, filling its six floors with unique gadgets, conveniences, and indulgences for every room in the home; the car; the sauna; the yacht; or the private airplane. *147 E. 57th St. (between Lexington and 3rd Aves.), Midtown East, 212/421–9000. Subway: N, R, W, 4, 5, 6 to 59th St./Lexington Ave.*

THE KINGSLEY GIRAFFE
Forgot your anniversary? Need a baby gift sent ASAP? The Kingsley Giraffe is not a shop (there is, however, a virtual showroom at www.thekingsleygiraffe.com), but yet is one of the best last-minute gift options in the city. Call for same-day delivery of special occasion gift baskets packed with products for the golfer, gourmet, wine connoisseur, or just about anyone else on your list. Corporate services also available. *212/533–7052.*

9 *d-3*

MOMA DESIGN STORE
The Museum of Modern Art's retail showroom sells modern furniture, home accessories, kitchenware, tools, desk accessories, jewelry, children's toys, and books, all with a nod toward good design. *44 W. 53rd St. (between 5th and 6th Aves.), Midtown West, 212/708–9800. Subway: E, V to 5th Ave./53rd St.*

10 c-1

MXYPLYZYK

Don't even try to pronounce the name; just try to stop by this beautiful Greenwich Village store. Mxy focuses on high-style, but not high-price, home furnishings and gifts, including books, jewelry, and pet accessories. *125 Greenwich Ave. (between Jane and Horatio Sts.), Greenwich Village, 212/989–4300. Subway: A, C, E, L to 14th St./8th Ave.*

9 d-3

THE SHARPER IMAGE

The gadget-filled catalog comes to life: Here are all those intriguing items you know you can live without but aren't sure you want to. Fall for a massage chair, a robot that serves hors d'oeuvres, a safari hat with a built-in fan, a talking scale.... *4 W. 57th St. (between 5th and 6th Aves.), Midtown West, 212/265–2550. Subway: E, V to 5th Ave./53rd St.*

10 f-7

South Street Seaport, Pier 17, Lower Manhattan, 212/693–0477. Subway: A, C, J, M, Z, 1, 2, 4, 5 to Fulton St./Broadway–Nassau.

HOME FURNISHINGS

9 e-8

ABC CARPET & HOME

Opened in 1897, this amazing emporium boasts two of the largest carpet showrooms anywhere, as well as a fine selection of imported and domestic bed and bath linens, antique and contemporary furniture, and accessories galore. The carpet holdings include Oriental, designer, area, scatter, rag rugs, and over 5,000 rolls of national brands. *881 and 888 Broadway (at 19th St.), Flatiron District, 212/473–3000. Subway: L, N, Q, R, W, 4, 5, 6 to 14th St./Union Sq.*

9 d-8

BED BATH & BEYOND

Find everything for kitchen, bath, bed, storage, and, of course, tons of accessories like picture frames and candles. *620 6th Ave. (between 17th and 18th Sts.), Chelsea, 212/255–3550. Subway: 1, 2 to 18th St.; F, L, V to 14th St.*

9 f-2

410 E. 61st St. (at 1st Ave.), Upper East Side, 646/215–4702. Subway: N, R, W, 4, 5, 6 to 59th St.

96-05 Queens Blvd., Rego Park, 718/459–0868. Subway: G, R, V to 63rd Dr.

IKEA

Okay, okay, so it's not in the city, but this outpost of the Swedish home furnishings empire might as well be. Join your fellow New Yorkers and cross the river for good-looking, inexpensive furniture, kitchen and home office fittings, tableware, lighting, window treatments and more. A free shuttle runs to the store from Port Authority Bus Terminal on Saturday and Sunday, every half-hour 10–2:30, and returns every 30 minutes noon–6. *1000 Center Dr., Elizabeth, NJ, 908/289–4488, 800/BUS–IKEA.*

architectural artifacts

11 g-3

IRREPLACEABLE ARTIFACTS

Head to the East Village for original, spectacular architectural ornamentation for interior and exterior use—stained glass, mantel pieces, fountains, wrought iron, paneling, and much, much more. *14 2nd Ave. (at Houston St.), East Village, 212/777–2900. Subway: F, V to 2nd Ave.*

11 f-4

URBAN ARCHAEOLOGY

The name is literal: all of these gargoyles and other grand bygone architectural embellishments were saved from the wrecking ball. With a focus on New York City, this shop carries Americana from the 1880s to 1925, antique slot and arcade machines, and a celebrated collection of art deco interiors and exteriors. Displays spill outdoors. *285 Lafayette St. (between Prince and Houston Sts.), SoHo, 212/431–6969. Subway: F, V to Broadway–Lafayette St.*

11 d-7

143 Franklin St. (between Varick and Hudson Sts.), TriBeCa, 212/431–4646. Subway: 1, 2 to Franklin St.

9 f-3

239 E. 58th St. (between 2nd and 3rd Aves.), Midtown East, 212/371–4646. Subway: N, R, W, 4, 5, 6 to 59th St./Lexington Ave.

bedding & bath linens & accessories

7 e-6

DOWN & QUILT SHOP

These folks will custom-design your bedroom. They've got plenty to work with: private-label down quilts and down pillows; downlike polyester fiber-fill quilts and pillows (for customers with allergies); antique iron beds; hundreds of sheets and duvet covers; patchwork quilts; floor coverings; and probably whatever else you've dreamed up. *1225 Madison Ave. (near 88th St.), Upper East Side, 212/423–9358. Subway: 4, 5, 6 to 86th St.*

7 *c-7*

518 Columbus Ave. (near 85th St.), Upper West Side, 212/496–8980. Subway: 4, 5, 6 to 86th St.

11 *h-3*

ECONOMY FOAM & FUTON CENTER

Foam is cut to size and shape while you wait, or shredded by the pound for "piller filler." Fiberfill is another option. The Center also sells ready-made decorative and bed pillows, foam mattresses, designer sheets and spreads, and futons, all closing out at 30%–50% off retail. Accompaniments include custom covers, wall coverings, and upholstery fabric and vinyl. *173 E. Houston St. (at 1st Ave.), East Village, 212/473–4462. Closed Sat. Subway: F, V to 2nd Ave.*

11 *h-5*

EZRA COHEN

Known far and wide for its splendid selection of discount merchandise, Cohen carries the latest in sheets from every brand plus famous-maker bedspreads. Down comforters come both ready- and custom-made. Cover your bed and soften your bathroom for 15%–30% off retail. *275 Grand St. (near Eldridge St.), Lower East Side, 212/431–9025. Closed Sat. Subway: S to Grand St.*

9 *e-1*

FRETTE

Frette makes Italian bed and table linens and lingerie of very fine quality. It's expensive, but still cheaper than Porthault (*see below*). *799 Madison Ave. (near 67th St.), Upper East Side, 212/988–5221. Closed Sun. Subway: 6 to 68th St./Hunter College.*

9 *e-1*

GRACIOUS HOME

Gracious Home has linens for every room in your house. The sizable stock of high-end bed linens includes makers such as Peter Reed, Designer's Guild, and Palais Royal; top them off with bed

blankets, decorative throws, and baby bedding. Designer table linens for both everyday use and special occasions come in every price range. The folks over in bathroom linens make a point of stocking towels to match any bathroom color. The staff is knowledgeable and helpful. *1220 3rd Ave. (near 70th St.), Upper East Side, 212/517–6300. Subway: 6 to 68th St./Hunter College.*

9 *b-2*

1992 Broadway (at 67th St.), Upper West Side, 212/231–7800. Subway: 1, 2 to 66th St./Lincoln Ctr.

11 *h-5*

HARRIS LEVY

It's hectic, but this Lower East Side experience is worth the trouble for 20%–40% discounts on name-brand bed linens, bathroom linens, and imported tablecloths. The second floor features custom- and ready-made curtains, bedspreads, dust ruffles, throw pillows, lamp shades, and draperies. *278 Grand St. (near Eldridge St.), Lower East Side, 212/226–3102. Closed Sat. Subway: S to Grand St.*

11 *h-3*

I. ITZKOWITZ

Itzkowitz is the best quilt man in America, and, alas, the last of a breed. You pick the filling and the covering, and he'll make you a new quilt or refurbish your old one. Go for a custom-made sleeping pillow, too. *174 Ludlow St. (near Houston St.), Lower East Side, 212/477–1788. Closed Sat. Subway: F, V to 2nd Ave.*

11 *e-8*

IZ DESIGN

These chenille and velvet throw pillows are designed by Elizabeth Tapper. *92 Reade St. (near Broadway), TriBeCa, 212/608–4223. Subway: 1, 2 to Chambers St.*

10 *g-3*

J. SCHACHTER

This longtime Lower East Side source has new digs from which to wow you with their custom- and ready-made comforters and quilts. Choose a new filling, design, and covering, or have your favorite old patchwork quilt made into a comforter. Schachter will also re-cover and sterilize your down comforters and pillows. Current domestic and imported linens are 25%–40% off. *85 Ludlow St. (near Delancey St.), Lower East Side, 212/533–1150 or 800/468–6233.*

Closed Sat. Subway: F, J, M, Z to
Delancey St./Essex St.

7 f-7
LAYTNER'S LINEN
Laytner's delivers high-quality designer
linens for the bed, bath, and table. 237 E.
86th St. (between 2nd and 3rd Aves.),
Upper East Side, 212/996–4439. Subway:
4, 5, 6 to 86th St.

7 b-7
2270 Broadway (near 81st St.), Upper
West Side, 212/724–0180. Subway: 1, 2 to
79th St.

11 5-e
512 Broadway (between Spring and
Broome Sts.), SoHo, 212/965–9382. Subway: N, R to Prince St.

9 e-2
LERON
Beautiful hand-sewn linens and lingerie
can be matched here with Old World
handmade lace and appliquées. Leron
will custom-embroider table linens and
towels to match any fabric. 750 Madison
Ave. (near 65th St.), Upper East Side, 212/
753–6300. Closed Sun. Sept.–May, closed
weekends July–Aug. Subway: 6 to 68th
St./Hunter College.

11 h-3
PILLOW TALK
Head over to Ludlow Street for custom-
made seat cushions, decorative pillows,
and sleeping pillows in every shape and
size; you pick the filling. 174 Ludlow St.
(near Houston St.), 212/477–1788. Closed
Sat. Subway: F, V to 2nd Ave.

9 e-1
POLO/RALPH LAUREN
Ascend to the fourth floor for a wide
selection of bedding, including sheets,
wool and cotton blankets, decorative
comforters, down pillows, and duvets.
The "White Label" bedding features an
astonishing thread count of 350. Ample
towels come in bath, hand, and beach
sizes; table linens come in popular patterns. They will match department-store
prices if you ask. 867 Madison Ave. (at
72nd St.), Upper East Side, 212/606–2100.
Closed Sun. Subway: 6 to 68th
St./Hunter College.

9 e-3
PORTANTINA
This small shop carries a beautiful line
of pillows in velvet, silk, and satin, all
designed by Susan Unger. 895 Madison
Ave. (at 55th St.), Upper East Side, 212/
472–0636. Subway: N, R, W, 4, 5, 6 to
59th St./Lexington Ave.

9 e-1
PORTHAULT
Porthault makes the Rolls-Royce of
sheets. The store's exclusive and extrav-
agantly expensive line of 100%-cotton
bed linens come in 600 prints in a variety of colors. You can also shop for table
and bath linens, exquisite children's
clothes, and gift items. 18 E. 69th St.
(between 5th and Madison Aves.), Upper
East Side, 212/688–1660. Subway: 6 to
68th St./Hunter College.

11 d-4
PORTICO BED & BATH
A discerning eye creates this special mix
of fine domestic and imported linens for
the bed and bath. Portico also has a
wide array of cast- and wrought-iron
beds. The abundance of bath and body
products makes shopping here a sensual experience. 139 Spring St. (at
Wooster St.), SoHo, 212/941–7722. Subway: 6 to Spring St.

9 e-8
903 Broadway (at 20th St.), Flatiron
District, 212/328–4343. Subway: N, R to
23rd St.

7 c-7
450 Columbus Ave. (near 81st St.), Upper
West Side, 212/579–9500. Subway: 1, 2 to
79th St.

9 e-1
PRATESI
Pratesi has been manufacturing fine bed,
bath, and table linens in Florence since
the turn of the 20th century, as well as
linens and clothing for infants. It's all
mighty expensive. 829 Madison Ave. (at
69th St.), Upper East Side, 212/288–2315.
Subway: 6 to 68th St./Hunter College.

7 e-7
SCHWEITZER LINEN
An established purveyor of fine
imported linens, Schweitzer also specializes in sleeping pillows, custom-
made to odd sizes in both down and

poly. *1132 Madison Ave. (near 84th St.), Upper East Side, 212/249–8361. Subway: 4, 5, 6 to 86th St.*

7 *b-8*

457 Columbus Ave. (between 81st and 82nd Sts.), Upper West Side, 212/799–9642. Subway: B, C to 81st St.

candles

11 *d-5*

ANGELIC

Votives in a rainbow of colors are arrayed like the offerings in a candy shop in this tiny SoHo storefront. *160 Spring St. (at W. Broadway), SoHo, 212/334–3039. Subway: C, E to Spring St.*

11 *b-2*

CANDLE SHOP

It's the best, with candles in every color, shape, and size for every occasion, and holders in which to plunk them. *118 Christopher St. (near Bleecker St.), Greenwich Village, 212/989–0148. Subway: 1, 2 to Christopher St./Sheridan Sq.*

9 *d-8*

CANDLESHTICK

If you can picture it, they carry it. Feast your nose on the scented candles, and your eyes on the candlesticks and decorative votives. *181 7th Ave. (between 20th and 21st Sts.), Chelsea, 212/924–5444. Subway: 1, 2 to 23rd St.*

7 *b-6*

2444 Broadway (between 90th and 91st Sts.), Upper West Side, 212/787–5444. Subway: 1, 2, 3 to 96th St.

10 *f-1*

ENCHANTMENTS, INC.

This is the best selection of specifically inexpensive candles downtown, from votives to tapers to columns to those already poured into a jar. *341 E. 9th St. (between 2nd and 1st Aves.), East Village, 212/228–4394. Subway: 6 to Astor Pl.*

9 *e-8*

ILLUMINATIONS

The extensive stock at this large shop covers all candle categories—from floating to tapered to aromatherapeutic to seasonal items. Accessories such as bowls and lanterns are also available. *873 Broadway (between 18th and 19th Sts.), Flatiron District, 212/777–1621. Subway: 6 to Astor Pl.*

9 *d-4*

45 W. 50th St. (between 5th and 6th Aves.), Midtown West, 212/582–8850. Subway: B, D, F, V to 47th–50 Sts./Rockefeller Ctr.

11 *f-5*

54 Spring St. (between Lafayette and Mulberry Sts.), SoHo, 212/226–8713. Subway: 6 to Spring St.

11 *d-6*

LEMON GRASS

In addition to delightfully scented candles in sizes from tiny votive to giant four-wick table centerpieces, the store also sells whimsical soaps. *367 W. Broadway (at Broome St.), SoHo, 212/343–0900. Subway: 6 to Spring St.*

carpets *&* rugs

New York's rug district spans 30th–33rd streets between 5th and Madison avenues, where you'll find a particular concentration of Orientals and Persians. Bloomingdale's and Macy's also carry Oriental rugs.

11 *e-3*

A. BESHAR & CO.

Beshar has been selling handsome Oriental rugs, as well as cleaning and repairing them, since 1898. *611 Broadway (near Bleecker St.), Room 405, Greenwich Village, 212/529–7300. Subway: 6 to Bleecker St.*

9 *d-8*

ARONSON'S

This floor-covering supermarket meets all your flooring needs with carpet remnants, closeouts, or custom cuts; tile; and linoleum. *135 W. 17th St. (between 6th and 7th Aves.), Chelsea, 212/243–4993. Subway: F, 1, 2, 3 to 14th St.*

7 *b-7*

CENTRAL CARPET

Come here first—Central Carpet is a great source for low-priced (they guarantee New York's lowest) antique, semi-antique, and new handmade Chinese, Persian, and Caucasian rugs. There's a large selection of Art Deco Chinese rugs and flat-weave Indian dhurries, as well as modern Belgian rugs—a total of more than 5,000 rugs on two floors. Prices range from $19 to $10,000. *426 Columbus Ave. (near 81st St.), Upper*

West Side, 212/787–8813. Subway: 1, 2 to 79th St.

10 c-1

81 8th Ave. (at 14th St.), Chelsea, 212/741–3700. Subway: A, C, E, L to 14th St./8th Ave.

9 e-3

EINSTEIN-MOOMJY

This oddly named carpet department store features new Orientals, broadlooms, and area rugs. 150 E. 58th St. (between Lexington and 3rd Aves.), Midtown East, 212/758–0900. Subway: N, R, W, 4, 5, 6 to 59th St./Lexington Ave.

11 b-7

REGENERATION

The contemporary hand-embroidered, hand-tufted, and hand-dyed rugs by designer Judy Ross come in a myriad of styles, colors, shapes, and luxe materials. Custom styles are also available, as is lighting and a large selection of vintage '50s and '60s furnishings. 38 Renwick St. (between Spring and Canal Sts.), SoHo, 212/741–2102. Subway: C, E to Spring St.; 1, 2 to Canal St.

7 b-8

RUG WAREHOUSE

For more than 50 years this store has maintained a best-price guarantee on its Caucasians, Persians, Art Deco Chinese, dhurries, and kilims, both antique and modern. 220 W. 80th St. (between Broadway and Amsterdam Ave.), Upper West Side, 212/787–6665. Subway: 1, 2 to 79th St.

9 e-8

SAFAVIEH CARPETS

A reputable source for new and antique Oriental rugs, Safavieh will also buy, wash, appraise, and restore old rugs. 902 Broadway (between 20th and 21st Sts.), Flatiron District, 212/477–1234. Subway: N, R to 23rd St.

9 e-6

153 Madison Ave. (at 32nd St.), Murray Hill, 212/683–8399. Subway: 6 to 33rd St.

9 f-2

238 E. 59th St. (at Lexington Ave.), Midtown East, 212/888–0626. Subway: N, R, W, 4, 5, 6 to 59th St./Lexington Ave.

china, glassware, porcelain, pottery, silver

You can also buy fine china at Tiffany's and Cartier (see Jewelry–Contemporary, below). See also Antiques and Jewelry–Antique & Collectible.

9 e-3

ASPREY & CO., LTD.

This prestigious London firm is known for its exclusive silver patterns, both antique and modern, as well as crystal and china. Consider one of the luxurious gift items, such as a hand-bound book, rare first edition, or 18-karat gold beard comb. Trump Tower, 725 5th Ave. (at 56th St.), Midtown East, 212/688–1811. Subway: N, R, W to 5th Ave./59th St.

7 b-7

AVVENTURA

This wide selection of glassware and tablesettings contains china, serving pieces, and flatware. The stock is heavy on Italian manufacturers and hard-to-find pieces and tends to be of extremely high quality and unique design. Some distinctive Venetian jewelry is also on hand. 463 Amsterdam Ave. (near 83rd St.), Upper West Side, 212/769–2510. Closed Sat. Subway: 1, 2 to 86th St.

9 e-3

BACCARAT, INC.

Baccarat sells its own famed and expensive French crystal plus china by Limoges, Ceralene, and Raynaud; pewter by Etains du Manoir; and silver by Christofle and Puiforcat. 625 Madison Ave. (near 58th St.), Midtown East, 212/826–4100. Subway: N, R, W, 4, 5, 6 to 59th St./Lexington Ave.

9 e-3

CARDEL

Cast your eye on all major brands of high-end china, crystal, and silver in one location. This stuff makes great wedding gifts. 621 Madison Ave. (near 58th St.), Midtown East, 212/753–8690. Closed Sun. Subway: N, R, W, 4, 5, 6 to 59th St./Lexington Ave.

11 d-4

CERAMICA

Hand-painted ceramics and reproduction majolica are imported straight from Italy to this cheerful, charming, chockfull-of-china shop. New shipments arrive every three months. 59 Thompson

St. (near Spring St.), SoHo, 212/941–1307.
Closed Mon. Subway: C, E to Spring St.

9 e-2
CHRISTOFLE
Here you'll find Christofle's full line of
elegant sterling, silver-plate, and stainless tableware and home accessories in
addition to crystal by Baccarat and St.
Louis, china by Haviland and Ceralene,
and private-label linens. 680 Madison
Ave. (near 62nd St.), Upper East Side,
212/308–9390. Closed Sun. Subway: N, R,
W, 4, 5, 6 to 59th St./Lexington Ave.

11 a-2
DETAILS
An eclectic array of bath and home furnishings to put a little zip into your
home decor. Highlights of the well-
edited selections include gorgeous
glassware, lovely bath products, Walker
totes and cosmetic bags, and trendy
tabletop settings. 347 Bleecker St. (at W.
10th St.), Greenwich Village, 212/414–
0039. Subway: 1, 2 to Christopher
St./Sheridan Sq.

9 b-1
188 Columbus Ave. (between 68th and
69th St.), Upper West Side, 212/362–7344.
Subway: 1, 2 to 66th St./Lincoln Ctr.

10 g-4
EASTERN SILVER CO.
Eastern carries a large general selection
of silver items and does repairs. 54
Canal St. (near Orchard St.), 2nd floor,
Lower East Side, 212/226–5708. Closed
Sat. Subway: F to E. Broadway.

9 e-8
FISHS EDDY
These highly whimsical shops sell 1930s
and '40s china and glassware that once
belonged to corporations, restaurants,
hotels, private clubs, and the government—making for some fascinating
logos. Sugar bowls, creamers, and other
vintage kitchen and dining accessories
join the tableware, along with some
modern kitchen overstocks and retro-
looking pieces created just for this store.
There are always some interesting collectibles here, and their prices are low;
the shop is highly browsable. 889 Broadway (near 19th St.), Flatiron District, 212/
420–9020. Subway: L, N, Q, R, W, 4, 5, 6
to 14th St./Union Sq.

7 b-8
2176 Broadway (at 76th St.), Upper
West Side, 212/873–8819. Subway: 1, 2 to
79th St.

9 e-3
FORTUNOFF
The impressive antique-silver department at the jewelry giant has American,
Georgian, Russian, and Chinese silverware; tea services and various objets;
and contemporary flatware in sterling,
plate, and stainless. 681 5th Ave. (near
54th St.), Midtown East, 212/758–6660.
Subway: E, V to 5th Ave./53rd St.

9 e-3
GALLERI ORREFORS
KOSTA BODA
Top-of-the-line Swedish crystal is on display here—Orrefors shows traditional
vases and plates while Kosta Boda incorporates vibrant colors and funky designs.
58 E. 57th St. (between Madison and Park
Aves.), Midtown East, 212/752–1095. Subway: N, R, W to 5th Ave./59th St.

9 e-2
HOYA CRYSTAL GALLERY
Here is the world's largest collection of
this respected Japanese firm's art and
functional pieces. Hoya is known for its
low iron content, which results in glass
with no discolorations or bubbles.
Prices range from $30 to $30,000. 689
Madison Ave. (at 62nd St.), Upper East
Side, 212/223–6335. Subway: N, R, W, 4, 5,
6 to 59th St./Lexington Ave.

9 e-3
JAMES ROBINSON
For more than 70 years Robinson has
purveyed fine 17th- to 19th-century
English hallmark silver, rare porcelain
dinner sets, and antique jewelry. The
store is also known for its own hand-
forged silver flatware. 480 Park Ave. (at
58th St.), Midtown East, 212/752–6166.
Closed Sun. Subway: N, R, W, 4, 5, 6 to
59th St./Lexington Ave.

9 d-4
JEAN'S SILVERSMITHS
Jean's has the city's largest selection of
discontinued silver patterns—over
900—plus new flat- and hollowware at
winning prices. 16 W. 45th St. (between
5th and 6th Aves.), Midtown West, 212/
575–0723. Closed weekends. Subway: B, D,
F, V to 42nd St.

11 e-4

THE L.S. COLLECTION

A large selection of unique and stylish tableware including china, handblown crystal, glasses, and sterling. *494 Broome St. (between Wooster St. and W. Broadway), SoHo, 212/334–1194. Subway: C, E to Spring St.; N, R to Prince St.*

9 e-2

LALIQUE

Lalique's posh shop sells its own rightly famous, incredibly beautiful French crystal. *680 Madison Ave. (between 61st and 62nd Sts.), Upper East Side, 212/355–6550. Subway: N, R, W, 4, 5, 6 to 59th St./Lexington Ave.*

9 e-1

LA TERRINE

Concoct wonderful house presents or special accent pieces from the hand-painted Portuguese, Italian, and French ceramics in this neighborhood shop. Complementary table linens from Provence and India complete the international look. *1024 Lexington Ave. (at 73rd St.), Upper East Side, 212/988–6550. Closed Sun. Subway: 6 to 77th St.*

9 e-1

MACKENZIE-CHILDS LTD.

This is the flagship New York store for MacKenzie-Childs's whimsical line of hand-painted ceramics, glassware, and furniture. It is, shall we say, not the place to bargain-hunt. *824 Madison Ave. (near 69th St.), Upper East Side, 212/570–6050. Closed Sun. Subway: 6 to 68th St./Hunter College.*

10 d-1

MAD MONK

This shop is a longtime Village source for interesting handmade pottery and mirrors. *500 6th Ave. (near 13th St.), Greenwich Village, 212/242–6678. Subway: F, V to 14th St.*

9 e-5

MICHAEL C. FINA

This well-known store, a popular bridal registry choice, features an extensive stock of jewelry, sterling silver flatware, tea sets, giftware, clocks, and more. *545 5th Ave. (at 45th St.), Midtown East, 212/557–2500. Subway: S, 4, 5, 6, 7 to 42nd St./Grand Central.*

9 e-2

ROYAL COPENHAGEN PORCELAIN

Danish china and Orrefors and Kosta Boda crystal join Georg Jensen silver flatware and jewelry. *683 Madison Ave. (near 61st St.), Upper East Side, 212/759–6457. Subway: N, R, W, 4, 5, 6 to 59th St./Lexington Ave.*

9 e-1

SARA

Sara focuses on imported Japanese ceramics of fine handcrafted quality. *953 Lexington Ave. (near 69th St.), Upper East Side, 212/772–3243. Closed Sun. Subway: 6 to 68th St./Hunter College.*

11 d-4

SIMON PEARCE

All of these simple and elegant hand-blown glasses, pitchers, candlesticks, and vases are made in Vermont. *120 Wooster St. (near Spring St.), SoHo, 212/334–2393. Subway: C, E to Spring St.*

9 e-2

500 Park Ave. (near 59th St.), Midtown East, 212/421–8801. Subway: N, R, W, 4, 5, 6 to 59th St./Lexington Ave.

9 e-3

SOLANÉE

French through and through, Solanée sells fine tableware and glassware from prestige imports like Quimper, Luneville, and Segries of Moustiers, in addition to classic French furniture. The shop will customize pieces with monograms and family crests. *654 Madison Ave. (at 60th St.), Upper East Side, 212/439–6109. Closed Sun. Subway: N, R, W to 5th Ave./59th St.*

9 e-3

S. J. SHRUBSOLE

A trove of antique English and early American silver and jewelry, this is the best selection of silver in New York. *104 E. 57th St. (between Park and Lexington Aves.), Midtown East, 212/753–8920. Subway: N, R, W, 4, 5, 6 to 59th St./Lexington Ave.*

9 e-3

STEUBEN GLASS

Steuben's showroom is like a museum, its pieces both beautiful and precious. Make time to browse both the unique glass sculptures and the functional pieces. 715 5th Ave. (at 56th St.), Midtown East, 212/752–1441. Subway: N, R, W to 5th Ave./59th St.

9 e-1

S. WYLER, INC.

Established in 1890, S. Wyler is the oldest silver dealer in the United States, with antique and modern silver, fine porcelain, and antiques. 941 Lexington Ave. (at 69th St.), Upper East Side, 212/ 879–9848. Closed Sun. Subway: 6 to 68th St./Hunter College.

9 e-3

TIFFANY & CO.

The jeweler of renown sells its own china, crystal, and sterling tableware on the third floor, at surprisingly reasonable prices. 727 5th Ave. (at 57th St.), Midtown East, 212/755–8000. Closed Sun. Subway: N, R, W to 5th Ave./59th St.

9 e-4

VERSACE

You know the name, you know the game: anything but boring, bold patterns in the most imperial styles around. 647 5th Ave. (at 52nd St.), Midtown East, 212/317–0224. Subway: N, R, W to 5th Ave./59th St.

9 e-8

VILLEROY & BOCH

This prestigious German/French home shop has been in business since 1748. They offer an extensive range of pricey porcelain, china, crystal, earthenware, and cutlery in delightful provincial styles. Descend the stairs to check out the bath and tile showroom. 901 Broadway (at 20th St.), Flatiron District, 212/ 535–2500. Subway: L, N, Q, R, W, 4, 5, 6 to 14th St./Union Sq.

clocks

9 d-8

AIR CLOCKS & WATCHES OF THE WORLD, LTD.

This Chelsea shop discounts clocks from massive companies like Movado, Seiko, Linden, Seth Thomas, and West. Similarly, household-name watches from Seiko, Pulsar, Spoon, Calypso, and Swiss Army are also for sale. 119 W. 17th St. (between 6th and 7th Aves.), Chelsea, 212/517–2300. Subway: F, V to 14th St.

9 e-1

FANELLI ANTIQUE TIMEPIECES

This large selection of antique timepieces includes wall clocks, shelf clocks, tall case clocks, and carriage clocks. The quality is high, and rare pieces abound. Expert appraisals and repairs are available. 790 Madison Ave. (between 66th and 67th Sts.), Upper East Side, 212/517–2300. Subway: 6 to 68th St./Hunter College.

flooring

9 e-8

ANN SACKS TILE & STONE

Ann Sacks will fit limestone, slate, terracotta, marble mosaics, handcrafted tile, and stone antiquities to your commercial or residential specifications. 5 E. 16th St. (near 5th Ave.), Gramercy, 212/ 463–8400. Subway: L, N, Q, R, W, 4, 5, 6 to 14th St./Union Sq.

10 e-1

ARTISAN WORKSHOP

Inside this lofty Moroccan design shop you'll find concrete, pigment-dyed floor and wall tiles in 50 solids and a variety of patterns. In fact, fashion designer Todd Oldham recently debuted his patterned cement tiles at Artisan Workshop. Also available are plenty of mosaic tables and hand-crafted new and antique furnishings and accessories from Morocco. 50 E. 13th St. (between Broadway and University Pl.), Union Sq., 212/260–6700. Closed Sun. Subway: L, N, Q, R, W, 4, 5, 6 to 14th St./Union Sq.

9 e-8

ARTISTIC TILE

A wide range of beautiful tile is available, including tumbled stone mosaics in basketweave and fan patterns. 79 5th Ave. (at 16th St.), Flatiron District, 212/ 727–9331. Subway: L, N, Q, R, W, 4, 5, 6 to 14th St./Union Sq.

9 f-8

COUNTRY FLOORS

This appealing shop specializes in fine hand-painted tiles, both antique and modern; most are imported from Italy, France, Holland, Peru, Finland, Spain, and Portugal. Sinks can be designed to match tiles. 315 E. 16th St. (between 1st and 2nd Aves.), Gramercy, 212/627–8300. Closed weekends. Subway: L, N, Q, R, W, 4, 5, 6 to 14th St./Union Sq.

7 *e-1*

EASTSIDE FLOOR SERVICE

This vast showroom sells all types of wood flooring, and fills custom orders for contractors and the general public. Eastside also rents and sells sanding machines, buffers, and installation tools. *124 E. 124th St. (between Lexington and Park Aves.), Harlem 212/426–8500. 4, 5, 6 to 125th St.*

9 *e-8*

HASTING TILE & IL BAGNO

The whole store is a knockout, with artful designer floor tiles and bold designs for bathrooms and all the fittings. They do kitchens, too. *230 Park Ave. S (at 19th St.), Gramercy, 212/674–9700. Subway: N, R, 6 to 23rd St.*

9 *f-4*

IDEAL TILE

These importers of Italian ceramic tiles will provide expert installation or a do-it-yourself guide. *405 E. 51st St. (between 1st and 2nd Aves.), Midtown East, 212/759–2339. Subway: 6 to 51st St./Lexington Ave.; E, V to Lexington–3rd Aves./53rd St.*

9 *d-8*

MOSAIC HOUSE

Practicing the age-old art of mosaic since his childhood in Morocco, the proprietor of this charming store offers custom and ready-made mosaic accessories (like vases and bowls). He also does custom home design and installs mosaic floors, countertops, and sinks. *62 W. 22nd St. (between 6th and Broadway), Flatiron District, 212/414–2525. Subway: F, V to 23rd St.*

9 *b-8*

NORWEGIAN WOOD

Norweigan Wood installs, repairs, and refinishes all types of wood floors, from pre-finish to exotic to hardwood, and offers detailing work like borders and inlays. *174 9th Ave. (between 21st and 22nd Sts.), Chelsea, 212/929–3853. Subway: E to 23rd St.; 1, 2 to 18th St.*

9 *e-6*

THE QUARRY

New York's largest stock of reasonably priced Spanish, Dutch, French, Portuguese, and Mexican tiles comes mainly in bright colors and patterns. The Quarry will install your choices or provide do-it-yourself guidance and supplies. *128 E. 32nd St. (between Park and Lexington Aves.), Murray Hill, 212/679–8889. Closed Sat. after 3 PM. Subway: 6 to 33rd St.*

SULLIVAN'S FLOOR SERVICE INC.

This 35-year-old flooring company supplies and installs wood flooring of all varieties in homes and institutions. Call to schedule an appointment. *212/353–3490.*

furniture & accessories

In addition to these specialist shops, Bloomingdale's and Macy's have extensive collections of home furnishings, mostly contemporary and traditional.

11 *d-5*

AD HOC

If you want to breathe some life into your dwelling space, take a look at Ad Hoc's accessories collection, which features the work of many Scandinavian and Asian designers. Find everything from design-savvy mousepads by New York Architect Karim Rashid to Aalvar Aalto's "Amoeba Vase." *136 Wooster St. (between Prince and Houston Sts.), SoHo, 212/982–7703. Subway: N, R to Prince St.*

11 *d-4*

AERO

Aero sells highly chic furniture of its own design as well as vintage pieces. *132 Spring St. (near Wooster St.), SoHo, 212/966–1500. Closed Sun. Subway: 6 to Spring St.*

11 *c-1*

AMALGAMATED HOME

Amalgamated comprises three small stores all devoted to chic and sleek home furnishings, with an emphasis on funky, ultramodern designs and unusual materials. Traditionalists may cringe, but others find the mix fresh and pleasingly cutting-edge. *13, 19 Christopher St. (between 6th Ave. and Gay St.), Greenwich Village, 212/255–4160, 212/691–8695. Subway: 1, 2 to Christopher St./Sheridan Sq.*

11 *d-5*

ANTHROPOLOGIE

Now a national chain, Anthropologie features an interesting mix of both new and antique home furnishings, including upholstered pieces, smaller decorative items, and bath and kitchen accessories. There's also a great clothing department (*see* Clothing for Women, *above*). Both the home and the fashion selections are basic, but they're very well edited, and prices are fairly reasonable for such a trendy shopping destination. *375 W. Broadway (at Broome St.), SoHo, 212/ 343–7070. Subway: A, C, E to Canal St.*

10 *e-1*
85 5th Ave. (at 16th St.), Flatiron District, 212/627–5885. Subway: L, N, Q, R, W, 4, 5, 6 to 14th St./Union Sq.

11 *e-5*
THE APARTMENT
Designed to look like an extremely well-decorated apartment, this shop stocks some of the most unique and design-savvy home accessories and furnishings in the city. *101 Crosby St. (at Prince St.), SoHo, 212/219–3066. Subway: N, R to Prince St.; F, V to Broadway–Lafayette St.*

9 *d-8*
APARTMENT 48
The genius of this store is that it really does look like an apartment, but almost everything in it is for sale. In the living room, you'll find furniture and books; in the kitchen, a variety of kitchen utensils; in the bath, everything from rubber duckies to soap; and so on. It's probably the most comfortable shopping experience in the city. *48 W. 17th St. (between 5th and 6th Aves.), Chelsea, 212/807–1391. Subway: F, V to 14th St.; L to 6th Ave.*

10 *c-1*
BASICS FURNITURE
The furniture collection here is modern and sleek. The lower level is a maze of slashed-price furnishings, where you can find great bargains—check it when you need a bureau, table, or filing cabinet. *92 7th Ave. (between 15th and 16th Sts.), Chelsea, 212/691–5595. Subway: 1, 2, 3 to 14th St.*

9 *e-8*
THE BOMBAY COMPANY
Butler's tray tables, Biedermeier consoles, tole lamps, Verona mirrors—the Bombay Company sells an heirloom look in home furnishings, accessories, and wall decor at good prices. Okay, so it isn't heirloom quality, but that's for your heirs to worry about. *900 Broadway (at 20th St.), Flatiron District, 212/420–1315. Subway: N, R to 23rd St.*

9 *e-2*
1062A 3rd Ave. (at 63rd St.), Upper East Side, 212/759–7217. Subway: N, R, W, 4, 5, 6 to 59th St./Lexington Ave.

9 *b-1*
2001 Broadway (at 68th St.), Upper West Side, 212/721–7701. Subway: 1, 2 to 66th St./Lincoln Ctr.; and other locations.

9 *f-4*
BRANCUSI
Choose from a large selection of modern tables in glass, chrome, brass, stainless steel, and forged iron. *938 1st Ave. (near 51st St.), Midtown East, 212/688–7980. Subway: 6 to 51st St./Lexington Ave.; E, V to Lexington–3rd Aves./53rd St.*

10 *b-1*
BREUKELEN
This contemporary home shop has everyone buzzing about its designs and artwork from a slew of local and international artisans. Among them are the Paola Lenti collection of furnishings and flooring, from Italy, Burning Relic's steel and leather furniture and lighting, and an ever-changing mix of rugs, jewelry, sculptures and paintings. *68 Gansevoort St. (near Washington St.), Greenwich Village, 212/645–2216. Subway: A, C, E, L to 14th St./8th Ave.*

9 *e-3*
CASSINA USA
Cassina is the licensed representative for classic modern furniture, including pieces by Frank Lloyd Wright, Le Corbusier, Charles Rennie Macintosh, and Gerrit Rietveld. *155 E. 56th St. (between Lexington and 3rd Aves.), Midtown East, 212/245–2121. Closed weekends. Subway: N, R, W, 4, 5, 6 to 59th St./Lexington Ave.*

9 *d-7*
CASTRO CONVERTIBLES
This chain has one of New York's largest selections of sofabeds, recliners, and wall units. *43 W. 23rd St. (between 5th and 6th Aves.), Chelsea, 212/255–7000. Subway: F, V to 23rd St.; and other locations.*

9 *d-7*
CLASSIC SOFA
You'll find both sofas and chairs here available in a variety of custom fabrics and ready for delivery in just a few short weeks. *5 W. 22nd St. (between 5th and 6th Aves.), Chelsea, 212/620–0485. Subway: F, V to 23rd St.*

9 *e-2*

CRATE & BARREL

Crate & Barrel has become an all-American favorite for first-time furniture buyers, with a variety of styles in both traditional and modern silhouettes. You get good quality at a reasonable price. Plus there's an entire floor of decorative accessories to complement your new furnishings. *650 Madison Ave. (at 59th St.), Midtown East, 212/308–0011. Subway: N, R, W, 4, 5, 6 to 59th St./Lexington Ave.*

9 *e-7*

DEVON SHOP

Formerly for decorators only, the Devon Shop now offers its beautiful custom-made, hand-carved traditional furniture, as well as all of its design services, to the public. *111 E. 27th St. (between Park and Lexington Aves.), Murray Hill, 212/686–1760. Subway: 6 to 28th St.*

11 *d-5*

DIALOGICA

This duo is known for brightly colored velvet upholstery pieces in bold designs. *484 Broome St. (near Wooster St.), SoHo, 212/966–1934. Subway: 6 to Spring St.*

7 *e-7*

1070 Madison Ave. (near 81st St.), Upper East Side, 212/737–7811. Subway: 6 to 77th St.

9 *f-1*

DOMAIN

Domain specializes in European-country oversize upholstery pieces, reproduction painted farm tables, and armoires. *1179 3rd Ave. (at 69th St.), Upper East Side, 212/639–1101. Subway: 6 to 68th St./Hunter College.*

9 *e-8*

938 Broadway (at 22nd St.), Flatiron District, 212/228–7450. Subway: N, R to 23rd St.

9 *d-8*

DOOR STORE

This local chain tends toward reasonably priced contemporary furniture, with some traditional looks mixed in. There's an extensive chair selection. It's a solid option for the first-time apartment-filler. *123 W. 17th St. (between 6th and 7th Aves.), Chelsea, 212/627–1515. Subway: F, 1, 2, 3 to 14th St.*

9 *e-6*

1 Park Ave. (at 33rd St.), Murray Hill, 212/679–9700. Subway: 6 to 33rd St.

9 *e-3*

599 Lexington Ave. (at 53rd St.), Midtown East, 212/832–7500. Subway: 6 to 51st St./Lexington Ave.; E, V to Lexington–3rd Aves./53rd St.

9 *f-1*

1201 3rd Ave. (at 70th St.), Upper East Side, 212/772–1110. Subway: 6 to 68th St./Hunter College.

10 *d-1*

GALILEO

This small but extremely stylish store is devoted to the home, packing its shelves with new and vintage ceramics, linens, lighting, and other trimmings, including furniture by Heywood Wakefield. *167½ 7th Ave. S (at 12th St.), Greenwich Village, 212/243–1629. Subway: 1, 2 to Christopher St./Sheridan Sq.*

9 *e-8*

GOTHIC CABINET CRAFT

Gothic shops are sprouting up all over the place—and a good thing, too. The store sells both unpainted stock and custom-built furniture; one handy option is to pick an unfinished piece and have it finished in your choice of hue. They're fast and reliable, and the prices are great. *909 Broadway (between 20th and 21st Sts.), Flatiron District, 212/673–2270. Subway: N, R to 23rd St.*

10 *f-1*

104 3rd Ave. (at 13th St.), East Village, 212/420–9556. Subway: L, N, Q, R, W, 4, 5, 6 to 14th St./Union Sq.

7 *f-7*

1655 2nd Ave. (at 86th St.), 212/288–2999. Subway: 4, 5, 6 to 86th St.; and other locations.

11 *d-5*

JAMSON WHYTE

Imported from Singapore, Whyte showcases antiques, artifacts, and home furnishings that either come from Asia or look like they might have. It's so well styled as to be slightly intimidating, but don't be; just look at the prices, which are extremely reasonable for SoHo. Whether you have $20 or $2,000 to spend, you'll find something here. *47 Wooster St. (at Broome St.), SoHo, 212/965–9405. Subway: A, C, E to Canal St.*

10 c-1
JENSEN-LEWIS

This low-key Chelsea store started out featuring the director's chair in every possible shape, height, and color—and personalized if desired. You'll now find a roomy display of contemporary furniture and accessories, and canvas by the yard, in 34 colors. *89 7th Ave. (at 15th St.), Chelsea, 212/929–4880. Subway: 1, 2, 3 to 14th St.*

11 c-8
KEVIN HART & COMPANY

Furnish your apartment with a global spirit at this 3,000 square ft shop, which sells everything from industrial pieces to custom-upholstered seating to antique furnishing and lighting. And a collection of eclectic accessories to help turn your apartment into your home. *31 N. Moore St. (between Varick and Hudson Sts.), TriBeCa, 212/929–4880. Subway: 1, 2 to Franklin St.; A, C to Chambers St.*

9 e-8
KLEINSLEEP

"Have more fun in bed" with Stearns and Foster, Sealy, Aireloom, Simmons, Kingsdown, and Serta mattresses. This national mattress giant also sells a selection of bed frames and headboards. The shops ship from their New York warehouse, so depending on availability and the time you buy, you can have your mattress at your door as quick as the same day. *874 Broadway (at 18th St.), Flatiron District, 212/995–0044. Subway: L, N, Q, R, W, 4, 5, 6 to 14th St./Union Sq.*

9 f-3
962 3rd Ave. (between 58th and 59th Sts.), Upper East Side, 212/755–8210. Subway: N, R, W, 4, 5, 6 to 59th St.

7 b-7
2330 Broadway (between 84th and 85th Sts.), 2nd floor, Upper West Side, 212/501–8077. Subway: 1, 2 to 86th St.

11 e-4
KNOLL

Modern office furniture is mixed with residential furniture and textiles. Construction is high-quality, and prices are stiff. *105 Wooster St. (near Prince St.), SoHo, 212/343–4000. Closed Sun. Subway: N, R to Prince St.*

9 e-2
LIGNE ROSET

Crafted in France, this modern furniture by top European designers is both understated and distinctive. *1090 3rd Ave. (near 64th St.), Upper East Side, 212/794–2903. Subway: 6 to 68th St./Hunter College.*

9 c-8
LOBEL

You'll want to buy everything at this "classical modern" collection of vintage furnishings, mostly from the '50s and '60s. The staff will help you choose from the pristine-condition furniture, and even hunt down special pieces if you desire. *207 W. 18th St. (at 7th Ave.), Chelsea, 212/242–9078. Subway: 1, 2 to 18th St.*

9 b-1
LONG'S BEDDING & INTERIORS INC.

Long's has been specializing in mattresses since 1911, and the fourth-generation proprietors are available to guide you through your selection, whether you are looking to save a buck (by purchasing their in-house line) or want to invest in name brands like Therapedic, Englander, Aireloom, and Serta. Custom sizes are available, as are all-natural cotton mattresses, mattress pads, pillows (from Dacron to 24-ounce European down), sofa-beds, headboards, footboards, storage and platform beds, and recliners. Note: Long's delivers to anywhere in the world, and New Yorkers can usually have their mattresses the way they like it—the same day. *121 W. 72nd St. (between Columbus Ave. and Broadway), Upper West Side, 212/873–1752. Subway: 1, 2, 3 to 72nd St.*

9 e-6
MAURICE VILLENCY

High-quality contemporary furniture fills model rooms in this commodious Murray Hill store. *200 Madison Ave. (at 35th St.), Murray Hill, 212/725–4840. Subway: 6 to 33rd St.*

11 e-4
MODERN AGE

Come here for contemporary European furniture. The store is also the only NYC outlet for Christine Van Der Hurd rugs. *102 Wooster St. (near Prince St.), SoHo,*

212/966–0669. Closed Sun. Subway: N, R to Prince St.

11 e-4
MOSS
Moss is heaven for anyone into very, very modern, European-designed furnishings and accessories. Think Alessi, Kartell, Starck . . . if it's new and cool, or not-so-new but classically modern, it's here. *146 Greene St. (between Prince and Houston Sts.), SoHo, 212/226–2190. Subway: N, R to Prince St.*

9 e-3
PALAZZETTI
Palazzetti has faithful reproductions of 20th-century classic furniture, including licensed copies of styles by Eames, Breuer, Le Corbusier, and Mies van der Rohe. *515 Madison Ave. (near 53rd St.), Midtown East, 212/832–1199. Subway: 6 to 51st St./Lexington Ave.; E, V to Lexington–3rd Aves./53rd St.*

11 e-4
152 Wooster St. (near Prince St.), SoHo, 212/260–8815. Subway: N, R to Prince St.

11 d-4
PORTICO HOME
Simple French-country furniture is mixed with a good number of Shaker-inspired and cherry pieces. Prices can be quite steep, which isn't a surprise considering the neighborhood. *379 W. Broadway (near Spring St.), SoHo, 212/941–7800. Subway: C, E to Spring St.*

10 e-3
POTTERY BARN
Once known for its large array of tableware, Pottery Barn has recreated itself into a home design store that pretty closely resembles Crate & Barrel. Wares now run the gamut from leather couches to armoires with a few lamps and picture frames thrown in for good measure. *600 Broadway (near Houston St.), SoHo, 212/505–6377. Subway: F, V to Broadway–Lafayette St.*

9 b-2
1965 Broadway (near 66th St.), Lincoln Center, 212/579–8477. Subway: 1, 2 to 66th St./Lincoln Ctr.

11 e-5
QUINTO SOL
The four Flores brothers bring Mexi-chic furniture and accessories design to New York. And their newest, loft-like downtown location means more room to stock their unique furnishings like leather and metal tables, and mahogany and leather seating, which combine traditional Mexican design with modern aesthetics at affordable prices. A wide variety of unique accessories, barware, and table-top pieces are also available. *250 Lafayette St. (between Prince and Spring Sts.), SoHo, 212/334–2255. Subway: 6 to Spring St.; N, R to Prince St.*

10 d-5
ROOM
This collection of super-trendy furnishings is the sort that will incite the urge to redecorate your entire place. Accessories of the awe-inspiring variety are also in the mix. *182 Duane St. (near Greenwich Ave.), TriBeCa, 212/226–1045. Subway: 1, 2 to Franklin St.*

11 f-4
SALON MODERNE
These styles are either contemporary or '40s- and '50s-inspired, with a certain flair; most are new, but a few antiques are mixed in. *281 Lafayette St. (near Prince St.), SoHo, 212/219–3439. Subway: N, R to Prince St.*

9 e-8
SEE LTD.
SEE, or Spatial Environmental Elements, sells the work of more than 70 avant-garde designers of European and contemporary furniture, lamps, lighting, and accessories. *920 Broadway (near 21st St.), Flatiron District, 212/228–3600. Subway: N, R to 23rd St.*

11 e-4
SHABBY CHIC
The name says it all: this custom-slip-covered furniture has a homey, lived-in look that fits in as well in a SoHo loft as it does in a country home. Interesting throw pillows, linens, and period accessories follow through on the lovably scruffy theme. *93 Greene St. (between Spring and Prince Sts.), SoHo, 212/274–9842. Subway: 6 to Spring St.*

9 e-1
SLATKIN & COMPANY
This jewel box of a shop is owned by a decorator and features private-label traditional English country–style accessories. *131 E. 70th St. (between Park and*

Lexington Aves.), Upper East Side, 212/
794–1661. Closed Sun. Sept.–May, closed
weekends July–Aug. Subway: 6 to 68th
St./Hunter College.

9 *f-3*

TERENCE CONRAN SHOP

European home fashions and furnishings in a wide variety of contemporary
styles—this shop carries over 10,000
products to furnish and enhance every
room in your home. They set up their
room displays so beautifully, you may
just copy the entire look, candlesticks,
bed linens, headboard, lighting, and all.
407 E. 59th St. (at 1st Ave.), Upper East
Side, 212/755–9079. Subway: N, R, W to
59th St./Lexington Ave.

9 *c-8*

THOMASVILLE

A super-spacious furniture store, with a
wide—if somewhat uninspired—selection of reasonably priced leather and
wood furniture created to look like it
was passed down for generations. 91 7th
Ave. (at 16th St.), Chelsea, 212/924–7862.
Subway: 1, 2 to 18th St.

10 *e-5*

TOTEM GALLERY

A home design shop that takes furnishings and accessories quite seriously,
offering wares from American and European designers alike. Find thoroughly
modern furnishings and accessories,
which nod to retro looks like the iconic
marshmallow sofa. 71 Franklin St. (near
Broadway), TriBeCa, 212/924–7862. Subway: 1, 2 to Franklin St.

10 *e-4*

83 Grand St. (near Wooster St.), SoHo,
212/924–7862. Subway: J, M, N, Q, R, W,
Z, 6 to Canal St.

11 *e-4*

TROY

Yes, there is a Troy, and he has great
taste. Expensive taste. This store is an
incredibly chic mixture of contemporary
home furnishings and accessories, both
new and antique, and the only retail
source in the city for ICF furniture.
You're bound to fall in love with something here, so come in a generous
mood. 138 Greene St. (between Prince
and Houston Sts.), 212/941–4777. Subway: N, R to Prince St.

9 *e-2*

WILLIAM WAYNE & COMPANY

With a pair of shops on Lexington and
an offshoot downtown, this store
divides its stock between gardening
wares and a traditional mix of home
accessories, including well-chosen
objéts, lamps, furniture, and gifts. Monkeys are a favored motif. 846 Lexington
Ave. (at 64th St.), Upper East Side, 212/
737–8934. Subway: 6 to 68th St./Hunter
College.

9 *e-2*

850 Lexington Ave. (at 64th St.), Upper
East Side, 212/288–9243. Subway: 6 to
68th St./Hunter College.

10 *e-1*

40 University Pl. (at 9th St.), Greenwich
Village, 212/533–4711. Subway: 6 to
Astor Pl.

9 *e-6*

WORKBENCH

This attractive American and European
contemporary furniture is reasonably
priced, and the sales are excellent. The
overall look is somewhat minimal. 470
Park Ave. S (near 32nd St.), Murray Hill,
212/481–5454. Subway: 6 to 33rd St.

11 *c-4*

161 6th Ave. (at Spring St.), SoHo, 212/
675–7775. Subway: C, E to Spring St.; and
other locations.

9 *e-8*

XYZ TOTAL HOME

A treasure box filled with beautiful
pieces chosen for their handsome elegance. Upscale home accessories
include Indonesian wood pieces,
antique reproductions, sterling silver
picture frames, and elegant throw pillows. XYZ also offers accessory
makeovers and personal styling for your
entire home. 15 E. 18th St. (between 5th
Ave. and Broadway), Flatiron District, 212/
388–1942. Subway: L, N, Q, R, W, 4, 5, 6
to 14th St./Union Sq.

11 *d-5*

ZONA

Best known for hip, handmade home
accessories, Zona branches out into furniture as well. 97 Greene St. (between
Prince and Spring Sts.), SoHo, 212/925–
6750. Subway: N, R to Prince St.

kitchen & bathroom design

9 f-2

NEMO TILE

Finish off your bath project with these medicine cabinets, bath fixtures, porcelain and glass tiles, mosaics, and accessories. Nemo is a full-line distributor and importer of ceramic tile. *48 E. 21st St. (between Broadway and Park Ave.), Gramercy, 212/505–0009. Subway: N, R, 6 to 23rd St.*

9 e-3

SHERLE WAGNER INTERNATIONAL

Here they are: the world's most elegant and expensive bathroom fixtures. *60 E. 57th St. (at Park Ave.), Midtown East, 212/758–3300. Closed weekends. Subway: E, V to 5th Ave./53rd St.*

9 f-3

WATERWORKS

This pair of shops carries classic, elegant, British-inspired bath fixtures plus a full line of tiles and stones. *237 E. 58th St., Midtown East, 212/371–9266. Subway: N, R, W, 4, 5, 6 to 59th St./Lexington Ave.*

10 e-4

469 Broome St. (at Greene St.), SoHo, 212/966–0605. Subway: 6 to Spring St.; J, M, N, Q, R, W, Z, 6 to Canal St.

9 e-8

VILLEROY & BOCH

The lower-level of this French/German home shop is the showroom for "sanitaryware"—that's toilets, sinks, and faucets, as well as bathroom cabinets in wood and glass. *901 Broadway (at 20th St.), Flatiron District, 212/677–1151. Subway: L, N, Q, R, W, 4, 5, 6 to 14th St./Union Sq.*

lamps & lighting

The Bowery from Delancey to Grand streets is the city's cash-and-carry district for discounted lamps and light fixtures; shop after shop offers what's new and modern or—in most cases—what's tacky and tasteless, all below list prices.

11 e-5

ARTEMIDE

Artemide's very modern line of Italian lighting—tabletop, floor, hanging, and wall-mounted—includes the now-classic Tizio desk lamp. *46 Greene St. (near Broome St.), SoHo, 212/925–1588. Subway: 6 to Spring St.; A, C, E to Canal St.*

9 c-8

BARRY OF CHELSEA

Here's an antique twist: Barry specializes in original American lighting from 1880 to 1940. *154 9th Ave. (near 19th St.), Chelsea, 212/242–2666. Closed Sun.– Mon. Subway: C, E to 23rd St.*

9 c-4

CITY KNICKERBOCKER

This is the place to find antiques and reproductions, as well as contemporary pieces. Rentals, repairs, and custom designs are also available. And if the name reminds you of the New York of yore, it's no coincidence—this shop has been around since 1906. *781 8th Ave. (near 47th St.), Midtown West, 212/586– 3939. Subway: C, E to 50th St.*

11 g-6

GRAND BRASS LAMP PARTS

Inside this old-fashioned shop, you'll find more lamp parts (brass, nickel-plated, crystal and steel canopies, chains, finials, harps and hickeys) than you ever knew existed. The shop does repairs and can also make lamps for clients from just about anything—a cookie tin, a piece of wood, or even a motorcycle gas tank. International shipping is available. *221 Grand St. (at Elizabeth St.), Little Italy, 212/226–2567. Subway: B, D, Q to Grand St.*

11 g-5

JUST SHADES

Look no further for that elusive dream shade: SoHo has New York's largest selection of lamp shades. Every size and material is discounted 20%–30%. If you're still attached to the old girl, Just Shades can help you re-cover her. *21 Spring St. (at Elizabeth St.), 212/966– 2757. Closed Wed. Subway: 6 to Spring St.*

9 c-3

LEE'S STUDIO

Lee specializes in designer lighting from such makers as Halo, Lightolier, Kovacs, Artemide, Flos, and from smaller firms. There's a good selection of bulbs, and the studio will install, rent, and repair your lighting after helpful consultations. *1755 Broadway (at 56th St.), Midtown West, 212/581–4400. Subway: A, B, C, D, 1, 2 to 59th St./Columbus Circle.*

`9` f-2

1069 3rd Ave. (at 63rd St.), Upper East Side, 212/371–1122. Subway: 4, 5, 6, N, R, W to 59th St./Lexington Ave.

`11` e-5

LET THERE BE NEON

As the name suggests, there will always be a place for neon. Here, you'll find ready-made and custom pieces for home and business needs. 38 White St. (at Church St.), TriBeCa, 212/226–4883. Subway: J, M, N, Q, R, W, Z, 6 to Canal St.

`9` c-8

LIGHTFORMS

The mostly modern, groovy lighting by a variety of U.S. and foreign designers is accompanied by a full line of bulbs, shades, and dimmers. Repairs are made on-site. 168 8th Ave. (between 18th and 19th Sts.), Chelsea, 212/255–4664. Subway: C, E to 23rd St.

`7` b-7

509 Amsterdam Ave. (between 84th and 85th Sts.), Upper West Side, 212/875–0407. Subway: 1, 2 to 86th St.

`11` g-5

LIGHTING BY GREGORY

An almost overwhelming shopping experience, this store carries everything a body needs in residential and stage lighting. Rentals are available. 158 Bowery (between Delancey and Broome Sts.), Lower East Side, 212/226–1276. Subway: S to Grand St.

`9` f-2

THE LIGHTING CENTER

The Lighting Center has a generous selection of domestic and imported lighting and a critical mass of bulbs. 111 2nd Ave. (at 59th St.), Midtown East, 212/888–8383. Subway: N, R, W, 4, 5, 6 to 59th St./Lexington Ave.

`9` f-2

ROSETTA LIGHTING & SUPPLY INC.

Rosetta has a large selection of hanging fixtures, table and floor lamps, ceiling fans, and outdoor and track lighting by brands like Artemide, Kovacs, Lightolier, Lite-source, Luxo, and Dazor. The shop also sell bulbs, wiring, dimmers, breakers, connectors, and everything do-it-yourselfers and contractors need, and does repairs as well. 49 W. 45th St.

(between 5th and 6th Aves.), 212/719–4381. Closed Sun. Subway: B, D, F, V to 47th–50th Sts./Rockefeller Ctr.

paint & wallpaper

`7` g-7

DELMO PAINTS

Delmo will custom blend to create any paint hue you'd like, using Benjamin Moore or Pratt & Lambert paints. While Delmo does have a limited selection of pre-pasted and un-pasted wallpaper (which can be ordered to arrive within a week), paints are truly their specialty— and they've got all the tools you'll need to get the job done. Free same or next day delivery is a big bonus. 1641 York Ave. (between 86th and 87th Sts.), Upper East Side, 212/722–7797. Subway: 4, 5, 6 to 86th St.

`11` c-6

ELIZABETH DOW LTD.

At her eponymous shop, Dow uses an array of techniques, from collage to plant and feather inclusions, to create papers so beautiful that 15 of her designs are part of the permanent collection at the Cooper-Hewitt Museum. The studio can customize paper colors to match any Benjamin Moore paint, and utilizes a number of different finishes, like high-gloss for kitchens, baths, and children's rooms or mattes, faux suede, or parchment. By appointment only. 155 6th Ave. (between Spring and Broome Sts.), 4th floor, SoHo, 212/219–8822. Closed weekends. Subway: C, E to Spring St.

`11` c-4

JANOVIC/PLAZA

This wholesale and retail paint-and-wallpaper center has 15,000 wallpaper patterns and will mix paint to match any one of them. Bath, fabric, and window departments keep your imagination whirring. The professional staff is expert, and delivery is free. 161 6th Ave. (near Spring St.), SoHo, 212/627–1100. Subway: C, E to Spring St.

`9` c-7

215 7th Ave. (near 23rd St.), Chelsea, 212/243–2186. Subway: 1, 2 to 23rd St.

`9` e-1

1150 3rd Ave. (at 67th St.), Upper East Side, 212/772–1400. Subway: 6 to 68th St./Hunter College.

9 *b-1*

159 W. 72nd St. (between Amsterdam and Columbus Aves.), Upper West Side, 212/595–2500. Subway: 1, 2, 3 to 72nd St.; and other locations.

10 *g-4*

SHEILA'S DECORATING

The stock here includes more than 10,000 rolls of wallpaper, along with custom paints and window treatments. 68 Orchard St. (at Grand St.), SoHo, 212/219–8822. Subway: C, E to Spring St.

rentals

9 *f-5*

CORT RENTALS

While Cort does stock the run-of-the-mill furnishings that come to mind with the words "rental furniture," they also have an extremely wide variety of styles, from traditional to contemporary. You can rent an individual piece or a room, as well as all the decorative and kitchen necessities you may need, from flatware to blenders to tabletop, as well as office furniture. Deliveries arrive within 48 hours of lease signing. 711 3rd Ave. (between 44th and 45th Sts.), Midtown East, 212/867–2800. Subway: S, 4, 5, 6, 7 to 42nd St./Grand Central.

9 *e-4*

INTERNATIONAL FURNITURE RENTALS

This rental company offers more than ten different furniture styles, from modern minimalist to country. 345 Park Ave. (at 51st St.), Midtown East, 212/421–0340. Subway: 6 to 51st St./Lexington Ave.; E, V to Lexington–3rd Aves./53rd St.

wicker

9 *f-7*

COCONUT COMPANY

High-style furniture and decorative objéts for the home come in wicker and rattan—not to mention wood. Many of the pieces are from Bali and Indonesia. 129 Greene St. (between Houston and Prince Sts.), SoHo, 212/539–1940. Subway: N, R to Prince St.

7 *e-6*

PAMELA SCURRY'S WICKER GARDEN

Pamela Scurry specializes in antique

wicker furniture for both adults' and children's rooms. 1318–27 Madison Ave. (between 93rd and 94th Sts.), Upper East Side, 212/348–1166. Open by appt. only. Subway: 4, 5, 6 to 96th St.

HOUSEWARES & HARDWARE

Restaurant suppliers are clustered on the Bowery, near Cooper Square, and below Grand Street; travel here for good buys on practical, no-frills, professional cooking implements. Hardware buffs should wander over to the stretch of Canal Street from Lafayette to West Broadway.

9 *f-3*

BRIDGE KITCHENWARE

No-nonsense Bridge has best-quality professional equipment for the home at great prices: copperware (and retinning), earthenware, woodware, French porcelain baking supplies, restaurant-size stockpots, and more. Know what you want before you go—they have more than 40,000 items—but do go. Julia Child does. 214 E. 52nd St. (between 2nd and 3rd Aves.), Midtown East, 212/688–4220. Subway: 6 to 51st St./Lexington Ave.; E, V to Lexington–3rd Aves./53rd St.

11 *e-5*

BROADWAY PANHANDLER

This roomy and attractive SoHo store carries an extensive collection of top-notch gourmet cookware, cutlery, and gadgets at low prices. Check out the huge stock of bakeware; cake molds and decorating implements are a specialty. 477 Broome St. (between Wooster and Greene Sts.), SoHo, 212/966–3434. Subway: 6 to Spring St.

9 *e-1*

GRACIOUS HOME

Anything and everything you can think of for the home: custom kitchens, appliances, wall coverings, bath accessories, brass hardware, lighting, tableware, paint, and all the rest. 1220 3rd Ave. (at 70th St.), Upper East Side, 212/517–6300. Subway: 6 to 68th St./Hunter College.

9 *b-2*

1992 Broadway (at 67th St.), Upper West Side, 212/231–7800. Subway: 1, 2 to 66th St./Lincoln Ctr.

`9` d-6

HENRY WESTPFAL & CO.

This legendary cutlery shop will also sharpen your tired knives. *105 W. 30th St. (between 6th and 7th Aves.), Midtown West, 212/563–5990. Subway: B, D, F, N, Q, R, V, W to 34th St./Herald Sq.*

`7` e-1

HOFFRITZ
INTERNATIONAL CUTLERY

The purveyor of some of the finest cutlery and gadgetry around sells lemon zesters, pastry wheels and brushes, cheese graters, hatchets and slicers, and just about any kitchen and barware gadget one could ever need. The selection of German-made knives, sharpeners, and European scissors and shears is especially impressive. *367 Madison Ave. (between 74th and 75th Sts.), Upper East Side, 212/924–7300. Subway: 6 to 77th St.*

`9` c-3

203 W. 57th St. (between 6th and 7th Aves.), Midtown West, 212/757–3431. Subway: F to 57th St.; A, B, C, D, 1, 2 to 59th St./Columbus Circle; and other locations.

`9` c-8

HOLD EVERYTHING

What a great idea! This division of Williams-Sonoma sells the means for you to store almost anything neatly and attractively. *104 7th Ave. (near 16th St.), Chelsea, 212/633–1674. Subway: 1, 2, 3 to 14th St.*

`9` c-3

250 W. 57th St. (at 8th Ave.), Midtown West, 212/957–9313. Subway: A, B, C, D, 1, 2 to 59th St./Columbus Circle.

`9` f-1

1311 2nd Ave. (at 69th St.), Upper East Side, 212/535–9446. Subway: 6 to 68th St./Hunter College.

`11` a-2

KITSCHEN

Here is the kitchenware our parents grew up with: Kitschen is chockablock with vintage (circa 1920–60) mixing bowls, cookie jars, pitchers, waffle irons, salt and pepper shakers, corn-on-the-cob plates, and other dedicated nostalgia, all displayed in color-coordinated tableaux. *380 Bleecker St. (at W. 10th St.), Greenwich Village, 212/727–0430. Subway: 1, 2 to Christopher St./Sheridan Sq.*

`9` f-2

KRAFT HARDWARE

With more than 12,000 square ft of basic hardware and bath fixtures, Kraft is the largest store of its kind in Manhattan (*see* Home Furnishings–Bedding & Bath Linens & Accessories, *above*). *306 E. 61st St. (between 2nd and 1st Aves.), Upper East Side, 212/838–2214. Closed weekends. Subway: N, R, W, 4, 5, 6 to 59th St./Lexington Ave.*

`9` d-7

LAMALLE KITCHENWARE

One of the city's best high-end kitchenware stores, LaMalle's got pots and pans by Sitram, Paderno, and Mauviel Copperware; knives by Wusthof and Dexter-Russell; baking supplies; and every imaginable gadget. *36 W. 25th St. (between 5th and 6th Aves.), 6th floor, Chelsea, 212/242–0750. Subway: F, N, R to 23rd St.*

`9` d-6

MACY'S—THE CELLAR

A Shangri-La for cooks, Macy's beautifully stocked series of "shops" is dedicated to housewares. Wander through mazes of utensils and equipment for creative cookery. This floor always has a festive atmosphere. *155 W. 34th St. (Herald Sq.), lower level, Midtown West, 212/695–4400. Subway: B, D, F, N, Q, R, V, W to 34th St./Herald Sq.*

`10` b-1

P. E. GUERIN

This importers and manufacturer of decorative hardware and bath accessories is actually the oldest American firm of its kind. *23 Jane St. (near Greenwich St.), Greenwich Village, 212/243–5270. Open by appt. only. Subway: 1, 2, 3 to 14th St.*

`9` e-8

RESTORATION HARDWARE

Everything at this store has a slick retro feel, from actual hardware—house numbers to shower heads—to leather couches, gardening supplies, and cool kitchen gadgetry. The best part? It's actually fun to shop here. There's tons of space and the funky array of wares won't break the bank. *935 Broadway (at 22nd St.), Flatiron District, 212/260–9479. Subway: N, R to 23rd St.*

9 d-4
RIO TRADING INTERNATIONAL
Rio Trading is an authorized dealer of Henckels, Swiss Army, Gerber, and Buck knives. *10 W. 46th St. (near 5th Ave.), Midtown West, 212/819–0304. Subway: B, D, F, V to 42nd St.*

9 e-7
SIMON'S HARDWARE & BATH
This busy, highly regarded shop has ample decorative hardware and bath fixtures plus tools and supplies. Trust them; they're problem-solvers. *421 3rd Ave. (near 30th St.), Murray Hill, 212/532–9220. Closed Sun. Subway: 6 to 28th St.*

9 c-8
WILLIAMS-SONOMA
The famed San Francisco kitchen-supply chain excels in providing attractive, sturdy wares, well-stocked stores, and a total understanding of the yuppie aesthetic. *110 7th Ave. (near 17th St.), Chelsea, 212/633–2203. Subway: 1, 2 to 18th St.*

9 e-2
20 E. 60th St. (near Madison Ave.), Upper East Side, 212/980–5155. Subway: N, R, W, 4, 5, 6 to 59th St./Lexington Ave.

9 f-1
1309 2nd Ave. (near 69th St.), Upper East Side, 212/288–8408. Subway: 6 to 68th St./Hunter College.

7 e-7
1175 Madison Ave. (near 86th St.), Upper East Side, 212/289–6832. Subway: 4, 5, 6 to 86th St.

7 b-8
ZABAR'S
The gourmet giant's housewares department on the mezzanine offers some of the lowest prices in town on top-of-the-line kitchen accessories and cookware. *2245 Broadway (near 80th St.), Upper West Side, 212/787–2000. Subway: 1, 2 to 79th St.*

JEWELRY & WATCHES

New York's wholesale and retail jewelry center, also known as the Diamond District, is West 47th Street between 5th and 6th avenues. Taken together, the stores offer a dazzling selection of gold, silver, and precious stones in antique, traditional, and modern designs.

antique & collectible items

9 e-2
A LA VIEILLE RUSSIE
Focuses here are authentic Fabergé jewelry and accessories and American and European period jewelry, especially Victorian pieces. *781 5th Ave. (at 59th St.), Midtown East, 212/752–1727. Subway: N, R, W to 5th Ave./59th St.*

9 e-3
ALICE KWARTLER
Kwartler has amassed one of the city's largest collections of cufflinks, supplemented by such Victorian items as lockets and cameos. Engraving is available. *123 E. 57th St. (between Lexington and Park Aves.), Midtown East, 212/752–3590. Subway: N, R, W, 4, 5, 6 to 59th St./Lexington Ave.*

9 e-3
ARES RARE
The time line here is very long: Ares has jewelry from antiquity through the 1940s, though the focus does fall in the 19th and early 20th centuries. The store will appraise any piece, and offers a selection of books on jewelry. *605 Madison Ave. (between 57th and 58th Sts.), 4th floor, Midtown East, 212/352–2344. Subway: N, R, W, 4, 5, 6 to 59th St./Lexington Ave.*

CAMILLA DIETZ BERGERON
Bergeron deals in period and estate jewelry from all over the world, including a good selection of cufflinks, from her Upper East Side apartment. *212/794–9100. Open by appt. only.*

9 e-1
DECO DELUXE
Specializing in jewelry from the Art Deco period, Deco Deluxe also has a good selection of Bakelite. *993 Lexington Ave. (between 71st and 72nd Sts.), Upper East Side, 212/472–7222. Subway: 6 to 68th St./Hunter College.*

10 e-1
DULLSVILLE
Bakelite, Bakelite, Bakelite, in all of its adornment forms. *143 E. 13th St. (between 3rd and 4th Aves.), East Village, 212/505–2505. Subway: L, N, Q, R, W, 4, 5, 6 to 14th St./Union Sq.*

7 *e-8*

EDITH WEBER & ASSOCIATES

Weber's eclectic collection of period jewelry includes pieces formerly owned by such luminaries as Andy Warhol, Queen Victoria, and even Napoléon. *994 Madison Ave. (at 77th St.), Upper East Side, 212/570–9668. Subway: 6 to 77th St.*

9 *e-1*

FANELLI ANTIQUE TIMEPIECES

This large selection of antique timepieces includes pocket- and wristwatches, in addition to a range of larger timepieces. *Also see* Home Furnishings–Clocks, *above.*

10 *e-1*

FICHERA & PERKINS

We can't resist calling this a gem of a place; it has a fine variety of vintage pieces at prices to suit almost anyone's budget. *50 University Pl. (between 9th and 10th Sts.), Greenwich Village, 212/533–1430. Subway: N, R to 8th St.*

9 *e-1*

FRED LEIGHTON, LTD.

Devoted exclusively to luxurious and rare antique and estate jewelry, Leighton emphasizes the 1920s, particularly extravagant Cartier pieces. Other chronological concentrations are the 1800s and the 1950s. *773 Madison Ave. (at 66th St.), Upper East Side, 212/288–1872. Subway: 6 to 68th St./Hunter College.*

ILENE CHAZENOF

The jewelry and objéts that cram this Flatiron loft near Union Square date from the late-19th to mid-20th centuries; range across the Victorian, art deco, art nouveau, retro moderne, and post–WWII styles; and are priced very reasonably. Add to this Arts-and-Crafts jewelry, metalwork, furniture, and 1950s Scandinavian and Italian glass. The proprietor is knowledgeable, and her services include research, shipping, appraisal, and rental. Prices range from $1 to $5,000. *212/254–5564. Open by appt. only. Closed Sun.*

9 *e-3*

JAMES II GALLERIES

The bright and personable staff at James II will tell you all about their fine collection of English and Scottish 19th- and 20th-century jewelry, particularly their fine selection of cufflinks and 19th-century glass intaglio seals. Prices range from the hundreds to the thousands of dollars. *11 E. 57th St. (between 5th and Madison Aves.), 4th floor, Midtown East, 212/355–7040. Subway: N, R, W to 5th Ave./59th St.*

7 *e-8*

J. MAVEC & CO.

Mavec carries a wonderful selection of stick pins and other unique pieces from the 19th century, and hosts occasional exhibits of unusual items with an animal or garden theme. *946 Madison Ave. (between 74th and 75th Sts.), Upper East Side, 212/517–7665. Subway: 6 to 77th St.*

9 *e-2*

MACKLOWE GALLERY

Impressive and expensive, this jewelry hails mainly from the Art Deco, Georgian, Victorian, and Art Nouveau periods. Cartier, David Webb, Fouquet, and Van Cleef are among the many illustrious designers featured here. *667 Madison (between 60th and 61st Sts.), Upper East Side, 212/644–6400. Subway: N, R, W, 4, 5, 6 to 59th St./Lexington Ave.*

10 *e-1*

MULLEN & STACY

Mullen & Stacy is for the serious Bakelite collector, ready to pay serious prices. *17 E. 16th St. (between 5th Ave. and Union Sq. W), Gramercy, 212/226–4240. Subway: L, N, Q, R, W, 4, 5, 6 to 14th St./Union Sq.*

9 *e-1*

PRIMAVERA GALLERY

Elegant Primavera has a stellar collection of unusual antique and period pieces. *808 Madison Ave. (near 68th St.), Upper East Side, 212/288–1569. Subway: 6 to 68th St./Hunter College.*

7 *e-8*

SYLVIA PINES UNIQUITIES

Sylvia Pines has a truly exquisite (and indeed unique) array of antique and estate jewelry—from Victorian to deco, with some Georgian pieces thrown in.

Deco marcasite is a particular strength, and the collection of beaded and jeweled bags, bronzes, picture frames, and enameled boxes is spectacular. *1102 Lexington Ave. (near 77th St.), Upper East Side, 212/744–5141. Subway: 6 to 77th St.*

7 *e-8*
TIME WILL TELL
This shop is full of beautiful, one-of-a-kind classic timepieces from the 1920s to the present. Brands include Audemars Piguet, Cartier, Hamilton, Bulova, Rolex, Tiffany, and Patek Philippe; bands are made of alligator, ostrich, and lizard. Pocket-watch lovers, you have some choices here, too. Prices range from $300 to $40,000. Repairs are available. *962 Madison Ave. (near 75th St.), Upper East Side, 212/861–2663. Subway: 6 to 77th St.*

contemporary pieces

9 *d-3*
AARON FABER
Imaginative contemporary designs in gold join a fine collection of vintage wristwatches. Every eight weeks the gallery showcases a particular artist. Custom work, repairs, and restoration are available. *666 5th Ave. (entrance is at 53rd St. between 5th and 6th Aves.), Midtown West, 212/586–8411. Subway: E, V to 5th Ave./53rd St.*

11 *e-1*
BIJOUX
French-born Sophie Pujebet will customize any of her lovely sculptural gold and silver pieces. Many also have engraved floral and geometric designs. Look into custom wedding rings. *127 E. 7th St. (between 1st and 2nd Aves.), East Village, 212/777–1669. Subway: 6 to Astor Pl.*

9 *e-3*
BUCCELLATI
Each piece from this renowned Milanese silver- and goldsmith is uniquely handcrafted, but Bucellati's golden weave designs are most extraordinary. Peruse finely created artisan pieces with precious stones and gold pieces, priced in the medium range (a relative term). *46 E. 57th St. (between 5th and Madison Aves.), Midtown East, 212/308–2900. Subway: N, R to 5th Ave.*

9 *e-2*
BULGARI
Bulgari's contemporary Italian designs are marked by their stunning color combinations of large stones in unusual settings of 18-karat gold. *730 5th Ave. (at 57th St.), Midtown West, 212/315–9000. Subway: N, R to 5th Ave.*

9 *e-2*
Pierre Hotel, 2 E. 61st St. (at 5th Ave.), Upper East Side, 212/486–0326. Subway: N, R to 5th Ave.

9 *e-3*
CARTIER
One of Cartier's main attractions is its shell: the store is in a beautiful former mansion traded to Cartier for two strands of Oriental pearls. Inside you'll find jewelry, silver, fine porcelain, picture frames, and all the other prestigious items that have become modern classics. *653 5th Ave. (at 52nd St.), Midtown East, 212/753–0111. Subway: E, V to 5th Ave./53rd St.*

9 *e-3*
Trump Tower, 725 5th Ave. (at 56th St.), Midtown East, 212/308–0840. Subway: E, V to 5th Ave./53rd St.

9 *e-3*
CELLINI
Known as one of the best high-end watch shops in town, Cellini carries such exclusive brands as Frank Mueller, Breguet, and Cartier. *509 Madison Ave. (between 52nd and 53rd Sts.), Midtown East, 212/888–0505. Subway: E, V to 5th Ave.*

9 *e-4*
Waldorf-Astoria Hotel (Park Ave. and 50th St.), Midtown East, 212/751–9824. Subway: 6 to 51st St./Lexington Ave.; E, V to Lexington–3rd Aves./53rd St.

4 *d-4*
CLAY POT
Clay Pot's unique assortment of jewelry comprises work exclusively by American artisans. Handcrafted wedding rings are the specialty, and there is a variety of styles to choose from—from Victorian reproductions to sleek contemporary designs—at prices to suit any pocketbook. *162 7th Ave. (between 1st St. and Garfield Pl.), Park Slope, Brooklyn, 718/788–6564. Subway: D, Q to 7th Ave.*

9 e-2

EXCLUSIVELY BREITLING

It's an exclusive address for an exclusive line of superb Swiss watches, which start at about $900 and top out over $100,000. *740 Madison Ave. (between 64th and 65th Sts.), Upper East Side, 212/628–5678. Subway: 6 to 68th St./Hunter College.*

9 e-3

FORTUNOFF

The self-appointed "Source" is four floors of contemporary and antique gold, silver, diamonds, watches, flatware, and pewter, all at very special prices. *681 5th Ave. (near 54th St.), Midtown East, 212/758–6660. Subway: E, V to 5th Ave./53rd St.*

9 e-3

GEORGE PAUL JEWELERS

George Paul sells not watches, but a large selection of fine leather watchbands, including alligator, lizard, crocodile, pig, buffalo, snake, and bird. If they don't stock it, they'll make it to order. *1023 3rd Ave. (between 60th and 61st Sts.), Upper East Side, 212/308–0077. Closed Sun. Subway: N, R, W, 4, 5, 6 to 59th St./Lexington Ave.*

9 d-3

HARRY WINSTON

Behind these lovely, locked doors are the largest, rarest, finest gems in the world. The wealthy don't just buy Harry Winston jewelry; they invest in it. Service is reputed to be the best in town. *718 5th Ave. (at 56th St.), Midtown West, 212/245–2000. Subway: E, V to 5th Ave./53rd St.*

9 d-5

JOSEPH EDWARDS

The new and used watches include Omegas, Tags, Citizen, and Hamiltons. Repairs are done on-site. *500 5th Ave. (between 42nd and 43rd Sts.), Midtown West, 800/833–1195. Subway: B, D, F, V to 42nd St.*

9 e-5

323 Madison Ave. (between 42nd and 43rd Sts.), Midtown East, 212/682–0383. Subway: S, 4, 5, 6, 7 to 42nd St./Grand Central.

9 e-2

JULIE ARTISANS' GALLERY

The owner of this Madison Avenue standby, Julie Schafler Dale, is the author of *Art to Wear*. Here in her gallery-store, she presents her artful collection of unique handmade jewelry by contemporary artisans, and also displays a fine collection of vintage pieces. *762 Madison Ave. (between 65th and 66th Sts.), Upper East Side, 212/717–5959. Subway: 6 to 68th St./Hunter College.*

9 e-2

MICHAEL DAWKINS

Dawkins specializes in sterling silver pieces, many of which have simple pearl and diamond accents. His line of men's jewelry is elegant, and women will also find many classically influenced contemporary items that suit any style. Plus, the merchandise tends to be well priced. *33 E. 65th St. (between 5th and Madison Aves.), Upper East Side, 212/639–9822. Subway: 6 to 68th St./Hunter College.*

9 d-3

MOSTLY WATCHES

The small storefront hides a good selection of Omega, Swiss Army, and other watches, including both new and collectible Swatches. Repairs are done on-site. *200 W. 57th St. (between 7th Ave. and Broadway), Midtown West, 212/265–7100. Subway: F, N, R, Q, W to 57th St.*

9 d-4

MOVADO

Movado is the home of the famous Museum Watch, as well as several other watch styles and a selection of jewelry. *610 5th Ave. (between 49th and 50th Sts.), Midtown West, 212/218–7555. Subway: E, V to 5th Ave./53rd St.*

9 e-1

REINSTEIN/ROSS

Much of this handmade jewelry designed by Susan Reinstein has a medieval feel. In all of her finely wrought pieces, she uses 18-, 20-, or 22-karat gold, often with cabochon stones. *29 E. 73rd St. (between 5th and Madison Aves.), Upper East Side, 212/772–1901. Subway: 6 to 77th St.*

11 e-4

122 Prince St. (between Greene and Wooster Sts.), SoHo, 212/226–4513. Subway: N, R to Prince St.

11 d-5

ROBERT LEE MORRIS

Each one made by Morris himself, these adornments—necklaces, bracelets, earrings, hair ornaments—are really works of art. He creates jewelry to suit almost any budget: you'll find pieces with precious gems, diamonds, and cultured pearls, as well as less expensive pieces with gold overlay. *400 W. Broadway (between Broome and Spring Sts.), 212/431–9405. Subway: C, E to Spring St.*

9 d-3
SWATCH STORE

Each Swatch store is independently owned and operated, so selections may vary, but prices should be consistent for these high-design but well-priced cult icons. *5 E. 57th St. (between 5th and Madison Aves.), Midtown East, 212/317–1100. Subway: E, V to 5th Ave./53rd St.*

9 b-1
100 W. 72nd St. (at Columbus Ave.), Upper West Side, 212/595–9640. Subway: 1, 2, 3 to 72nd St.

10 e-3
640 Broadway (at Bleecker St.), NoHo, 212/777–1002. Subway: 6 to Bleecker St.

11 e-5
TED MUEHLING

These special pieces are designed by Muehling and other artists, including Gabriella Kiss. Many of the ring designs will suit both men and women. Owning one is worth the investment. *47 Greene St. (between Grand and Broome Sts.), SoHo, 212/431–3825. Subway: A, C, E to Canal St.*

9 e-3
TIFFANY & CO.

Now over a century old, the beloved treasure house still makes an elegant headquarters for fine gold and silver jewelry, including the designs of Jean Schlumberger, Elsa Peretti, and Paloma Picasso; diamond engagement rings; famous-name watches; gems; crystal, china, and sterling; clocks; and stationery. The newest additions are Tiffany's own scarves and perfume. Don't be intimidated; there are some very reasonably priced items here. The windows are almost as famous as the interior. *727 5th Ave. (at 57th St.), Midtown East, 212/755–8000. Subway: N, R, W to 5th Ave.; F to 57th St.*

9 e-3
TOURNEAU

Tourneau specializes in handsome, elegant, and famous watches for the fash-ion-conscious. Choose from Rolex, Cartier, Piaget, Omega, Corum, Patek Philippe, Baume & Mercier, Vaucheron Constantin, and many more; they're expensive, but battery replacements are free for life. (Let's see, where's my calculator. . . .) There's also a fine selection of vintage watches. *500 Madison Ave. (at 52nd St.), Midtown East, 212/758–6098. Subway: 6 to 51st St./Lexington Ave.; E, V to Lexington–3rd Aves./53rd St.*

9 e-3
635 Madison Ave. (at 59th St.), Midtown East, 212/758–6688. Subway: N, R, W, 4, 5, 6 to 59th St./Lexington Ave.

9 c-6
200 W. 34th St. (near 7th Ave.), Midtown West, 212/563–6880. Subway: A, C, E, 1, 2, 3 to 34th St./Penn Station.

9 d-3
VAN CLEEF & ARPELS

The name is synonymous with price and perfection. The Bergdorf Goodman setting is tiny, but it easily packs a king's ransom of diamonds, rubies, emeralds, pearls, and platinum. *744 5th Ave. (at 57th St.), Midtown West, 212/644–9500. Subway: N, R, W to 5th Ave.; F to 57th St.*

10 f-6
VINCENT GERARD

Gerard carries a good selection of both low- and high-priced brands, such as Fossil, Tissot, Omega, and Longines. *Pier 17, South Street Seaport, Lower Manhattan, 212/732–6400. Subway: A, C, J, M, Z, 1, 2, 4, 5 to Fulton St./Broadway–Nassau.*

9 e-3
WATCH WORLD

As the name suggests, this shop carries a wide variety of watches for children and adults. Brands include Guess, Citizen, Timex, Boy London, and such designer brands as Skagen and M & Co. *Trump Tower, 725 5th Ave. (at 56th St.), Midtown East, 212/310–0115. Subway: E, V to 5th Ave./53rd St.*

11 e-3
649 Broadway (at Bleecker St.), Greenwich Village, 212/475–6090. Subway: 6 to Bleecker St.

9 e-4
YAEGER WATCH OUTLET

Yaeger will meet or beat any price for a variety of name-brand watches, including Movado, Omega, Gruen, and Swiss Army. *578 5th Ave. (at 47th St.), Midtown West, 212/819–0088. Subway: B, D, F, V to 47th–50th Sts./Rockefeller Ctr.*

costume jewelry

11 *d-4*

AGATHA

Agatha's fun French jewelry encompasses everything from classic to kitsch, at good prices. Colorful earrings, bracelets, watches, and necklaces suit both young and mature tastes. *158 Spring St. (at W. Broadway), SoHo, 212/ 925–7701. Subway: C, E to Spring St.*

9 *d-4*

Rockefeller Center (Promenade, 5th Ave. between 49th and 50th Sts.), Midtown West, 212/586–5890. Subway: E, V to 5th Ave./53rd St.

9 *e-1*

611 Madison Ave. (at 58th St.), Midtown East, 212/758–4301. Subway: N, R to 5th Ave.

10 *d-3*

ANDREA RENEE BOUTIQUE

Andrea Renee and her husband Vincent Pólino offer their own delicate, often whimsical adornments along with friendly service and gracious discounts at this cozy SoHo boutique. Designs run the gamut from retro to trendy. They have a loyal celebrity clientele, but that doesn't mean the prices are in the stars. *119 Sullivan St. (between Prince and Spring Sts.), SoHo, 212/343–2059. Subway: C, E to Spring St.; N, R to Prince St.*

9 *e-1*

DIAMOND ESSENCE

All of these fantastic faux diamonds are set in 14-karat gold, and the faux pearls are attractive as well. Only you will know they're not real. *784 Madison Ave. (between 66th and 67th Sts.), Upper East Side, 212/472–2690. Subway: 6 to 68th St./Hunter College.*

9 *e-3*

ERWIN PEARL

This store is by no means just pearls, but it must be said that the big draw is the replica of Jackie O's famous triple-strand pearl necklace. You'll pay somewhat less than that piece fetched at auction. *677 5th Ave. (between 53rd and*

54th Sts.), Midtown East, 212/207–3820. Subway: E, V to 5th Ave./53rd St.

9 *e-3*

697 Madison Ave. (at 62nd St.), Upper East Side, 212/753–3155. Subway: N, R, W, 4, 5, 6 to 59th St./Lexington Ave.

9 *e-4*

GALE GRANT

Grant specializes in reproductions of such high-priced originals as Chanel and Tiffany. *485 Madison Ave. (between 51st and 52nd Sts.), Midtown East, 212/ 752–3142. Subway: 6 to 51st St./Lexington Ave.; E, V to Lexington–3rd Aves./53rd St.*

LEATHER GOODS & LUGGAGE

11 *h-4*

ALTMAN LUGGAGE

Come down east for luggage, trunks, and other leather goods from American Tourister, Travelpro, Andiamo, Delsey, Kenneth Cole, Briggs & Riley, Samsonite, and Halliburton. *135 Orchard St. (near Rivington St.), Lower East Side, 212/ 254–7275. Closed Sat. Subway: F, J, M, Z to Delancey St./Essex St.*

10 *e-1*

THE BAG HOUSE

Well placed in a university neighborhood, The Bag House has a huge selection of backpacks and duffels from such brands as Jansport, Manhattan Portage, Tumi, Gregory, Club USA, Le Sportsac, Kipling, EastPak, and Temba. The service isn't always as sweet as the selection. *797 Broadway (between 10th and 11th Sts.), Greenwich Village, 212/260– 0940. Subway: 6 to Astor Pl.*

9 *e-3*

COACH

Coach legend holds that the founders were inspired by the sturdy yet supple leather of a baseball glove. Now handbags and accessories come in the classic glove-tanned leather plus some textured leathers, twill-and-leather, weather-resistant leather, and microfiber. You can go the classic route with the bucket bags, satchels, and clasped pocketbooks, or dabble in the more streamlined totes and zip purses. Each design series has a range of colors, some including the likes of cherry red or pale blue as well as warm browns and black. Over the past couple of years, they've increasingly expanded into accessories, shoes, travel bags, and even furniture. *595 Madison Ave. (at 57th St.), Midtown East, 212/754–0041. Subway: N, R, W, 4, 5, 6 to 59th St./Lexington Ave.*

9 *e-2*
710 Madison Ave. (at 63rd St.), Upper East Side, 212/319–1772. Subway: N, R, W, 4, 5, 6 to 59th St./Lexington Ave.

9 *e-5*
342 Madison Ave. (at 44th St.), Midtown East, 212/599–4777. Subway: S, 4, 5, 6, 7 to 42nd St./Grand Central.

10 *e-3*
143 Prince St. (at West Broadway), SoHo, 212/473–6925. Subway: N, R to Prince St.; and other locations.

11 *d-5*
HOGAN
This Italian sneaker company re-invented themselves as of late, and along with the new look came some outstanding leather bags, from purses to travel bags of the soon-to-be-classics type. *134 Spring St. (between Green and Wooster Sts.), SoHo, 212/343–3039. Subway: N, R to Prince St.*

9 *e-5*
INNOVATION LUGGAGE
This chain has everything from the hardy to the hip, at not-bad prices. The sales staff is not always savvy about the merchandise, but Innovation's best when you've got a flight the next morning and have just discovered a tear in your favorite garment bag. *10 E. 34th St. (between 5th and Madison Aves.), Murray Hill, 212/685–4611. Subway: 6 to 33rd St.*

9 *f-5*
300 E. 42nd St. (at 2nd Ave.), Midtown East, 212/599–2998. Subway: S, 4, 5, 6, 7 to 42nd St./Grand Central.

9 *c-3*
1755 Broadway (at 57th St.), Midtown West, 212/582–2044. Subway: A, B, C, D, 1, 2 to 59th St./Columbus Circle; and other locations.

7 *e-8*
LOUIS VUITTON
Vuitton's famous monogram adorns everything from wallets to steamer trunks. Besides the brown-on-brown LVs, there's the Epi leather line, with a stri-

ated texture and fun colors. *49 E. 57th St. (near Madison Ave.), Midtown East, 212/371–6111. Subway: E, V to 5th Ave./53rd St.*

7 *e-6*
MOORMENDS LUGGAGE & CAMERAS
A neighborhood shop with a loyal clientele, Moormends has been a reliable source for such quality luggage brands as Tumi, Swiss Army, Travelpro, Kipling, and Metro for more than 40 years. The store also sells small leather goods, travel accessories, and, of course, cameras. *1228 Madison Ave. (between 88th and 89th Sts.), Upper East Side, 212/289–3978. Subway: 4, 5, 6 to 86th St.*

11 *f-5*
SIGERSON MORRISON
This design duo has already garnered a cult-like following for their super-sexy footwear and has now launched its first handbag shop, with a complete line of debut purses, totes, small leather goods, and luggage. Unexpected color combinations and fine detail and design are the norm. *242 Mott St. (between Prince and Spring Sts.), NoLita, 212/941–5404. Subway: N, R to Prince St.*

MAPS

9 *e-2*
ARGOSY BOOK STORE
Aficionados of antique maps will find a haven at Argosy, which specializes in maps from the 17th to the 19th centuries. Framing is available. Also a vintage book store, Argosy holds a strong collection of map books as well. *116 E. 59th St. (between Park and Lexington Aves.), 2nd floor, Midtown East, 212/753–4455. Subway: N, R, W, 4, 5, 6 to 59th St./Lexington Ave.*

11 *f-5*
DOWN EAST ENTERPRISES
This store deals primarily with books on outdoor travel, so within its solid selection of maps are those of our national parks. *50 Spring St. (between Lafayette and Mulberry Sts.), Little Italy, 212/925–2632. Subway: 6 to Spring St.*

9 *d-5*
HAGSTROM MAP & TRAVEL CENTER
Makers of the familiar yellow-and-green city maps, Hagstrom specializes, of

course, in cartography, globes, and atlases. *57 W. 43rd St. (between 5th and 6th Aves.), Midtown West, 212/398–1222. Subway: B, D, F, V to 42nd St.*

10 *f-7*

125 Maiden La. (at Water St.), Lower Manhattan, 212/785–5343. Subway: 1, 2 to Wall St.

9 *d-3*

RAND MCNALLY—THE MAP & TRAVEL STORE
A household name in travel aids, Rand sells guidebooks, maps, travel literature, luggage, gifts, and accessories in its own, peaceful Midtown store. There's even a children's section. *150 E. 52nd St. (between Lexington and 3rd Aves.), Midtown East, 212/758–7488. Subway: 6 to 51st St./Lexington Ave.; E, V to Lexington–3rd Aves./53rd St.*

9 *c-5*

555 7th Ave. (between 39th and 40th Sts.), Midtown West, 212/944–4477. Subway: N, R, Q, S, W, 1, 2, 3 to 42nd St./Times Sq.

MEMORABILIA

9 *c-2*

BALLET COMPANY
Ballet memorabilia abounds here, including rare programs, signed books, autographs, and art. They also have a strong collection of out-of-print dance books. *1887 Broadway (near 63rd St.), Upper West Side, 212/246–6893. Subway: 1, 2 to 66th St./Lincoln Ctr.*

10 *c-1*

JERRY OHLINGER'S MOVIE MATERIAL STORE
Ohlinger's has a large stock of still photos from films and TV shows, as well as movie posters. *242 W. 14th St. (between 7th and 8th Aves.), Chelsea, 212/989–0869. Subway: 1, 2, 3 to 14th St.*

9 *d-8*

MOVIE STAR NEWS
Another New York superlative: this store claims to have the world's largest collections of movie-star photos, both originals and reissues. Check out the posters, too. *134 W. 18th St. (between 6th and 7th Aves.), Chelsea, 212/620–8160. Closed Sun. Subway: 1, 2, 3 to 14th St.*

11 *f-4*

NEW YORK FIREFIGHTER'S FRIEND
Clothing, accessories, and toys celebrate the fire-slayers of yore. *265 Lafayette St. (between Spring and Prince Sts.), SoHo, 212/226–3142. Subway: N, R to Prince St.; 6 to Spring St.*

9 *c-4*

ONE SHUBERT ALLEY
It's a tourist's dream, but natives may also find themselves charmed amid these posters, buttons, T-shirts, sweatshirts, theatrical-theme jewelry, duffel bags, and soundtracks to past and present Broadway and off-Broadway shows. *1 Shubert Alley (between 44th and 45th Sts., west of 7th Ave.), Midtown West, 212/944–4133. Subway: N, R, Q, S, W, 1, 2, 3 to 42nd St./Times Sq.*

9 *e-8*

RICHARD STODDARD PERFORMING ARTS BOOKS
Everything in this great selection of old, rare, and out-of-print books and ephemera relates to the performing arts. Vintage playbills, autographs, original costume and scene designs, photographs, and memorabilia keep the glamorous past alive. *18 E. 16th St. (between 5th and 6th Aves.), Room 305, Flatiron District, 212/645–9576. Closed Wed. and Sun. Subway: L, N, Q, R, W, 4, 5, 6 to 14th St./Union Sq.*

MUSIC & MUSICAL INSTRUMENTS

cds, tapes & vinyl

11 *d-2*

BLEECKER BOB'S GOLDEN OLDIES
Bleecker Bob specializes in New Wave music, independent labels, British imports, and rare and collectible vinyl. The hip staff knows what's up with today's music, and the hip opening hours last well beyond midnight. *118 W. 3rd St. (between 6th Ave. and MacDougal St.), Greenwich Village, 212/475–9677. Subway: A, B, C, D, E, F, V to W. 4th St./Washington Sq.*

11 c-2
BLEECKER STREET RECORDS

Billing itself as the world's largest oldies shop, this Village standby carries rock, blues, reggae, jazz, and soundtrack LPs, 45s, and CDs. *239 Bleecker St. (between 6th and 7th Aves.), Greenwich Village, 212/255–7899. Subway: A, B, C, D, E, F, V to W. 4th St./Washington Sq.*

7 e-3
CASA LATINA

This store carries CDs, records, and books on all varieties of Latin music, as well as instruments. *151 E. 116th St. (between Lexington and 3rd Aves.), Harlem, 212/427–6062. Subway: 6 to 116th St.*

9 c-4
COLONY RECORDS

A Broadway institution, Colony carries the latest releases but specializes in hard-to-find items: rare and out-of-print LPs, cassettes, and CDs, as well as sheet music and books. *1619 Broadway (at 49th St.), 212/265–2050. Subway: N, R to 49th St.*

11 c-2
DISCORAMA

Choose from a large selection of discounted CDs, 12-inch dance records, cassettes, and videos. *186 W. 4th St. (between 6th and 7th Aves.), Greenwich Village, 212/206–8417. Subway: 1, 2 to Christopher St./Sheridan Sq.*

11 c-2

Classical and clearance titles. *146 W. 4th St. (between 6th Ave. and MacDougal St.), Greenwich Village, 212/477–9410. Subway: A, B, C, D, E, F, V to W. 4th St./Washington Sq.*

9 e-8

Annex. *40 Union Sq. E (between 16th and 17th Sts.), Flatiron District, 212/260–8616. Subway: L, N, Q, R, W, 4, 5, 6 to 14th St./Union Sq.*

9 d-5
DOWNSTAIRS RECORDS

Downstairs specializes in the hard-to-find and stocks a robust, well-organized selection of oldies, including doo-wop, R&B, and soul. There's even a phonograph on which to give things a whirl. *1026 6th Ave. (near 38th St.), Midtown West, 212/354–4684. Subway: B, D, F, N, Q, R, V, W to 34th St./Herald Sq.*

11 f-1
FINYL VINYL

This amply stocked and well-organized shop features the sounds of the '40s to the '70s—everything from Robert Johnson to Bootsy Collins. True to its name, the store stocks records only. *204 E. 6th St. (just off Cooper Sq.), East Village, 212/533–8007. Subway: 6 to Astor Pl.*

10 e-1
FOOTLIGHT RECORDS

Footlight's an excellent East Village outpost for out-of-print and hard-to-find Broadway cast albums, movie soundtracks, big bands, jazz, and vocals from the 1940s–'60s. *113 E. 12th St. (between 3rd and 4th Aves.), East Village, 212/533–1572. Subway: L, N, Q, R, W, 4, 5, 6 to 14th St./Union Sq.*

11 d-3
GENERATION RECORDS

This Greenwich Village shop specializes in punk, and is also a great place to save money on vintage CDs and vinyl. *210 Thompson St. (between Bleecker and 3rd Sts.), Greenwich Village, 212/254–1100. Subway: A, B, C, D, E, F, V to W. 4th St./Washington Sq.*

9 b-1
GRYPHON RECORD SHOP

Within its book shop on Broadway, Gryphon has amassed scores of thousands of jazz, rock, folk, and spoken-word recordings. Down on 72nd Street, they're selling rare and out-of-print LPs, mainly classical with some soundtracks, vocals, and jazz thrown in. Prices are reasonable, and they welcome "want" lists. *233 W. 72nd St. (between Amsterdam and West End Aves.), Upper West Side, 212/874–1588. Subway: 1, 2, 3 to 72nd St.*

7 b-7

2246 Broadway (between 80th and 81st Sts.), Upper West Side, 212/362–0706. Subway: 1, 2 to 79th St.

9 e-4
HMV

With more than 300,000 recordings, this English chain is giving Tower a run for its money. It's well stocked in all areas. *565 5th Ave. (at 46th St.), Midtown*

East, 212/681–6700. Subway: B, D, F, V to 47th–50th Sts./Rockefeller Ctr.

7 *e-7*

1280 Lexington Ave. (at 86th St.), Upper East Side, 212/348–0800. Subway: 4, 5, 6 to 86th St.

7 *c-1*

308 W. 125th St. (between St. Nicholas Ave. and Frederick Douglass Blvd.), Harlem, 212/932–9619. Subway: A, B, C, D to 125th St.

10 *e-6*

J&R MUSIC WORLD

J&R inspires faith by dividing its stock among different storefronts: classical CDs are at No. 33, jazz is at No. 25, and the rest is at No. 23. Selections are comprehensive, and, of course, you can also walk out with new equipment to play yours on (*see Electronics, above*). *23, 25, 33 Park Row (between Ann and Beekman Sts.), Lower Manhattan, 212/732–8600 (212/349–8400 for jazz; 212/349–0062 for classical). Subway: 4, 5, 6 to Brooklyn Bridge/City Hall.*

9 *c-8*

JAZZ RECORD CENTER

Videos, books, and pretty much any jazz record you can think of draw hardcore aficionados. *236 W. 26th St. (between 7th and 8th Aves.), 8th floor, Chelsea, 212/675–4480. Subway: 1, 2 to 28th St.*

11 *d-3*

NOSTALGIA & ALL THAT JAZZ

Recordings of jazz, movie soundtracks, and early radio broadcasts are surrounded by posters and movie stills. *217 Thompson St. (near Bleecker St.), Greenwich Village, 212/420–1940. Subway: F, V to Broadway–Lafayette St.*

10 *e-2*

OTHER MUSIC

A stone's throw from Tower, this shop offers all the independent, eclectic, and arcane selections the chains don't bother with. *15 E. 4th St. (between Broadway and Lafayette St.), East Village, 212/477–8150. Subway: 6 to Astor Pl.*

11 *c-1*

SAM GOODY

Goody has a large and standard stock and offers excellent weekly sales on current recordings. Sales on specific labels

pop up as well; check "Arts and Leisure" in Sunday's *New York Times* for detailed advertisements. *390 6th Ave. (between 8th St. and Waverly Pl.), Greenwich Village, 212/674–7131. Subway: A, C, E, F, V to W. 4th St./Washington Sq.*

9 *f-5*

230 E. 42nd St. (between 2nd and 3rd Aves.), Midtown East, 212/490–0568. Subway: S, 4, 5, 6, 7 to 42nd St./Grand Central.

9 *f-2*

1011 3rd Ave. (at 60th St.), Upper East Side, 212/751–5809. Subway: N, R, W, 4, 5, 6 to 59th St./Lexington Ave.; and other locations.

11 *f-4*

SATELLITE RECORDS

In their new, bigger digs, Satellite, a long-time institution for Industrial DJ's and club kids, houses one of the largest collections of dance music in the city. In back find all sorts of club tunes, from drum and base to garage to tribal. In front are listening stations, and accessories like bags and needles, and even turntables to give the tunes a whirl on. *259 Bowery (between Houston and Prince Sts.), 212/995–1744. Subway: 6 to Astor Pl.*

9 *b-1*

TOWER RECORDS & VIDEO

Tower has more than 500,000 titles, but finding more obscure recordings can still be difficult. The selection includes the usual assortment of rock, R&B, jazz, world, show tunes, and so forth. The classical section uptown may be the best anywhere. Check out the downtown store's annex for bargains. *1961 Broadway (at 66th St.), Upper West Side, 212/799–2500. Subway: 1, 2 to 66th St./Lincoln Ctr.*

11 *e-2*

692 Broadway (at 4th St.), Greenwich Village, 212/505–1500. Subway: N, R to 8th St.

11 *c-3*

VINYLMANIA

This never-say-die shop has used records, collector's items, LPs, and 45s, with a specialty in the 12-inch dance record. CDs and cassettes are also available. *60 Carmine St. (between 6th and 7th Aves.), Greenwich Village, 212/924–7223. Subway: A, B, C, D, E, F, V to W. 4th St./Washington Sq.*

9 c-4

VIRGIN MEGASTORE

The largest retail music and entertainment center in the world, Virgin has 1 million CDs in stock, and the store includes a 12,000-square-ft classical section. You feel rather like Jonah in the whale's belly. *1540 Broadway (near 45th St.), Midtown West, 212/921–1020. Subway: N, R, Q, S, W, 1, 2, 3 to 42nd St./Times Sq.*

10 e-1

52 E. 14th St. (at Broadway), Union Square, 212/598–4666. Subway: L, N, Q, R, W, 4, 5, 6 to 14th St./Union Sq.

music boxes

9 c-2

RITA FORD MUSIC BOXES

Rita Ford's is the best collection of working antique music boxes (circa 1830–1910) in the world, and it includes contemporary specimens, too. Some of the handcrafted carousels and other unique items are made expressly for this shop. The price range is wide, and the store restores and repairs as well. *19 E. 65th St. (between 5th and Madison Aves.), Upper East Side, 212/535–6717. Subway: 6 to 68th St./Hunter College.*

musical instruments

9 d-3

HAVIVI VIOLINS

These folks sell and appraise violins, cellos, violas, bows, strings, and accessories as well as repair all of the above. *881 7th Ave. (at 56th St.), Midtown West, 212/265–5818. Closed weekends. Subway: F, N, R, Q, W to 57th St.*

11 b-2

MATT UMANOV GUITARS

Umanov has a fine selection of new and used guitars in a wide price range, and an excellent repair department. *273 Bleecker St. (near 7th Ave. S), Greenwich Village, 212/675–2157. Subway: A, B, C, D, E, F, V to W. 4th St./Washington Sq.*

11 c-2

MUSIC INN

Come here for less-classical instruments, such as banjos, mandolins, dobros, dulcimers, sitars, balalaikas, ethnic flutes, tabla drums, zithers, and more. Guitars are a specialty; they're sold new and used, and expertly repaired. Browse ethnic art on the side. *169 W. 4th St. (near 6th Ave.), 212/243–5715. Closed Sun.–Mon. Subway: A, B, C, D, E, F, V to W. 4th St./Washington Sq.*

9 d-4

SAM ASH

If you're coming here for the first time, prepare to be whisked back to your days with the high-school band. In business since 1924, Sam Ash is popular with professional musicians for its wide inventory, good prices, and savvy staff. The wares are divided between a cluster of shops and include wind instruments and supplies; electronic keyboards, guitars, and amplifiers; and drums. Some instruments can be rented. Sheet music, scores, and books on music give you something to play. *155, 160, 166 W. 48th St. (near Broadway), Midtown West, 212/719–2299, 212/719–2625, or 212/719–5109. Subway: B, D, F, V to 47th–50th Sts./Rockefeller Ctr.*

9 d-3

STEINWAY & SONS

Steinway's longtime home, this elegant piano showroom is appropriately within whistling distance of Carnegie Hall. *109 W. 57th St. (between 6th and 7th Aves.), Midtown West, 212/246–1100. Subway: F, N, R, Q, W to 57th St.*

sheet music

9 d-3

JOSEPH PATELSON'S MUSIC HOUSE

Patelson's is one of those rare stores whose bag you're proud to carry. This quiet, wood-floored shop near Carnegie Hall is a musician's haven for classical and Broadway sheet music and scores, with an exhaustive, meticulously organized stock (both new and used), knowledgeable staff, and serious atmosphere. Your purchase is slipped into a delightfully unnecessary gray envelope adorned with Patelson's name dancing across a lute, and off you go to finger your cargo fondly before attempting to play it. *160 W. 56th St. (between 6th and 7th Aves.), Midtown West, 212/582–5840. Subway: F, N, R, Q, W to 57th St.*

NEWSPAPERS & MAGAZINES

10 *f-1*

GALLAGHER'S

Feel free to ask the staff for a bit of help in navigating this crammed collection of vintage magazines; just don't let them catch you reading issues from cover-to-cover—as they will clearly let you know, Gallagher's is not a library. And the prices will support that statement; vintage finds like this do not come cheap. *126 E. 12th St. (between 3rd and 4th Aves.), East Village, 212/473–2404. Subway: L, N, Q, R, W, 4, 5, 6 to 14th St./Union Sq.*

9 *f-4*

HOTALINGS NEWS AGENCY

With more than 200 out-of-town newspapers and 35 foreign-language newspapers, Hotalings is like a down-market university library. The scale of the magazine selection isn't far behind, and they throw in state maps for good measure. *1516 Broadway (between 46th and 47th Sts., in the Times Square Visitors Center), Midtown West, 212/840–1868. Subway: N, R, Q, S, W, 1, 2, 3 to 42nd St./Times Sq.*

11 *e-1*

HUDSON NEWS COMPANY

Hudson News is all over town, but this branch has a gratifyingly huge selection of magazines, both domestic and foreign, inspiring uptowners to make special trips. The biggest bonus: There's room to turn around, making browsing extra-pleasant. *753 Broadway (at 8th St.), Greenwich Village, 212/674–6655. Subway: N, R to 8th St.*

9 *d-7*

JAY BEE MAGAZINES

Some of these back-dated magazines and periodicals go back as far as 1920—Jay Bee has more than 2 million lying around. (Isn't that a fire hazard?) The setting is cluttered, but the store is now fully computerized, making it a great source for research. *150 W. 28th St. (between 6th and 7th Aves.), 6th floor, Chelsea, 212/675–1600. Subway: 1, 2 to 28th St.*

9 *c-3*

UNIVERSAL NEWS & MAGAZINE

If they don't have it, it may not exist. Universal stocks more than 7,000 titles, including foreign newspapers and magazines. *977 8th Ave. (between 57th and 58th Sts.), Midtown West, 212/459–0932. Subway: F, N, R, Q, W to 57th St.*

PET SUPPLIES

There are a number of mass retailers in the city that sell supplies and food for all sorts of animals, like Petco (3 locations), and Petland Discounts (12 locations), and some smaller, but well-stocked shops like Pet Party (which offers free delivery seven days a week). Below, find the specialists, for specific pet needs.

birds

9 *e-6*

THIRTY-THIRD & BIRD

Perhaps you may want to bring earplugs, but you won't want to leave without buying something fun for your birdie, like compressed seed treats, swings, toys, and maybe even a new cage (they have tons to choose from, and can order anything you don't see). *40 E. 33rd St. (between Park and Madison Aves.), Murray Hill 212/447–0021. Subway: 6 to 33rd St.*

9 *f-3*

SUTTON AVIARY

Everything you need for your feathered friend is here: cages, food, treats, playpens, vitamins, minerals, seed pellets, and a selection of books. Sutton also boards birds. *311 E. 60th St. (between 1st and 2nd Aves.), Upper East Side, 212/791–3177. Subway: N, R, 4, 5, 6 to 59th St./Lexington Ave.*

dogs & cats

9 *b-3*

CANINE CASTLE LTD.

Despite the name, this carpeted, crystal chandelier–ed boutique offers the best organic foods and all the necessities (and frivolities—like clothing and rhinestone collars) for both felines and pooches. *410 W. 56th St. (between 9th and 10th Aves.), Midtown West, 212/245–1291. Subway: A, B, C, D, 1, 2 to 59th St./Columbus Circle.*

11 *c-8*

DUDLEY'S PAW

This neighborhood store stocks foods, handmade beds, leather collars and leashes, and vitamins for cats and dogs, as well as a small selection of food and bedding for smaller furry friends like guinea pigs and rabbits. *327 Greenwich St. (between Duane and Jay Sts.), TriBeCa, 212/966–5167. Subway: 1, 2 to Franklin St.*

11 *b-1*

FETCH

Pet supplies and pet kitsch (from greeting cards to gift books) for chic pets and their chicer owners. *43 Greenwich Ave. (between Perry and Charles Sts.), 212/352–8591. Subway: A, C, E, L to 14th St.*

fish

9 *f-6*

NEW WORLD AQUARIUM INC.

At the only full-line aquarium store for both fresh and salt-water fish in Manhattan, you'll find anything and everything a fish (or reptiles) could ever want or need. Maintenance services are also available. *204 E. 38th St. (between 2nd and 3rd Aves.), Midtown East, 646/865–9604. Subway: S, 4, 5, 6, 7 to 42nd St./Grand Central.*

PHOTO EQUIPMENT

9 *c-6*

B & H PHOTO & ELECTRONICS

You may want to read up before you come: B & H stocks more than 200 camera styles from top manufacturers, as well as professional photo and video equipment. *420 9th Ave. (near 33rd St.), Midtown West, 212/444–6600. Closed Sat. Subway: A, C, E, 1, 2, 3 to 34th St./Penn Station.*

10 *d-1*

CAMERA DISCOUNT CENTER

These folks will meet or beat any advertised price with discounts on name-brand cameras. They also repair. *45 7th Ave. (near 14th St.), Chelsea, 212/206–0077. Closed Sat. Subway: 1, 2, 3 to 14th St.*

10 *e-2*

TAMARKIN

They cater to serious amateurs and professionals and have vintage Leica, Contax, and Hasselblad cameras, among

others, for collectors. *670 Broadway (between 3rd and Bond Sts.), Greenwich Village, 212/677–8665. Subway: 1, 2 to Houston St.*

9 *d-6*

WILLOUGHBY'S

This longtime top shop for cameras and audio carries a complete range of cameras, lighting, and darkroom equipment. There's also a secondhand department. *136 W. 32nd St. (between 6th and 7th Aves.), Midtown West, 212/564–1600. Subway: A, C, E, 1, 2, 3 to 34th St./Penn Station.*

9 *e-6*

385 5th Ave. (at 36th St.), Midtown East, 212/213–1515. Subway: 6 to 33rd St.

9 *e-5*

50 E. 42nd St. (near Madison Ave.), Midtown East, 212/681–7844. Subway: S, 4, 5, 6, 7 to 42nd St./Grand Central.

POSTERS & PRINTS

9 *e-3*

MOTION PICTURE ARTS GALLERY

Original movie posters take you from the silent era to the present, with the emphasis on older material, both American and European. Prices range from $20 to $10,000. *133 E. 58th St. (between Park and Lexington Aves.), 10th floor, Midtown East, 212/223–1009. Closed Sat.–Mon. Subway: N, R, W, 4, 5, 6 to 59th St./Lexington Ave.*

9 *d-8*

POSTER AMERICA

These original American and European posters range from 1890 to 1960; you'll also find a few advertising graphics. The staff is friendly and knowledgeable, and will arrange custom framing. *138 W. 18th St. (between 6th and 7th Aves.), Chelsea, 212/206–0499. Closed Mon. Subway: F, 1, 2, 3 to 14th St.*

7 *e-8*

REINHOLD-BROWN GALLERY

Expect fine posters of works by Klimt, Lautrec, Lissitzky, and more. *1100 Madison Ave. (between 82nd and 83rd Sts.), Upper East Side, 212/734–7999. Closed Sun.–Mon. Subway: 6 to 77th St.*

9 c-4

TRITON GALLERY

Triton has a huge inventory of posters featuring Broadway, Off-Broadway, and Off-Off-Broadway shows; West End productions; and dance. In much smaller form, they make nice note cards, also on sale. Custom framing is available. *323 W. 45th St. (between 8th and 9th Aves.), Midtown West, 212/765–2472. Subway: A, E to 42nd St./Port Authority.*

SHOES & BOOTS

9 c-1

AEROSOLES

This comfy, cushiony shoemaker, beloved by hard-walking women everywhere, now makes sleek boots and elegant heels as well as the classic bendable-soled varieties. Most pairs are under $50, too. *310 Columbus Ave. (between 74th and 75th Sts.), Upper West Side, 212/579–8659. Subway: 1, 2, 3 to 72nd St.*

7 b-5

2649 Broadway (between 100th and 101st Sts.), Upper West Side, 212/865–4934. Subway: 1 to 103rd St.; and other locations.

9 e-3

BALLY

For men, this is the place to come for high-quality, stylish shoes, all imported from Switzerland. Meanwhile, the standard women's line of cap-toe pumps is branching out into such things as sport shoes and suede pumps with saucily curved heels. *628 Madison Ave. (at 59th St.), Midtown East, 212/751–9082. Subway: N, R, W, 4, 5, 6 to 59th St./Lexington Ave.*

9 e-3

BELGIAN SHOES

If you'd like a real touch of Henri Bendel, you'll visit this modest store instead of the namesake emporium on 5th Avenue. Bendel sold the big store decades ago, then kept his hand in with these soft-sole, loaferlike flats. (The tiny-bow-on-the-vamp style is originally his.) The premise might be casual, but the materials (raspberry velvet, black suede) and the price tag (a few hundred) certainly aren't. Don't wait too late in the day to visit; it closes a little earlier than most boutiques. *110 E. 55th St. (between Park and Lexington Aves.), Midtown East,*

212/755–7372. Subway: E, V to 5th Ave./53rd St.

9 e-2

BOTTEGA VENETA

Many of these shoes would look right on Rita Hayworth—satin shoes sprinkled with rock crystals or done in the company's signature weave. But there's an increasingly modern edge, with stiletto boots and wedges. If it's flats you need, slide into a pair of leopard loafers. The cost of such sophistication is in the multi-hundreds, but the twice-a-year sales are phenomenal. *635 Madison Ave. (between 59th and 60th Sts.), Upper East Side, 212/371–5511. Subway: N, R, W, 4, 5, 6 to 59th St./Lexington Ave.*

9 e-4

BOTTICELLI

This store's cachet has fallen somewhat since the return to tailoring and a trimmer cut and the general disdain for flash. But the shoes are as sleek and soft as ever. *522 5th Ave. (between 43rd and 44th Sts.), Midtown West, 212/221–9075. Subway: S, 4, 5, 6, 7 to 42nd St./Grand Central.*

11 d-5

CHARLES JOURDAN

Many of these pairs are distinctly flirty: suede and patent leather T-straps, faux-snakeskin, open-toe heels, a few rhinestones here and there. "Bis" on the label means more casual and funky—but not necessarily less pricey. At press time, they were moving into the SoHo digs, and getting ready to set up shop in the GM Plaza (612 Madison Ave. at 58th St.). There's also a small boutique on Macy's sprawling 5th floor. *155 Spring St. (between Broadway and Wooster), SoHo, 212/219–0490. Subway: N, R to Prince St.*

9 e-1

CHRISTIAN LOUBOUTIN

This French import could give Manolo a run for his money. If you find yourself among a flock of gilded ladies, look for the flash of a crimson sole—it's Louboutin's signature. The niches in his boutique hold everything from pointed silk mules to low-vamped, strappy, sky-high heels, all perfectly balanced. Look for whimsical fillips, like a mosaiced heel. Prices are mostly $400-ish. *941 Madison Ave. (between 75th and 74th Sts.), Upper East Side, 212/396–1884. Subway: 6 to 77th St.*

11 *d-4*

CHUCKIES

Don't let the name fool you; this is no kiddie outlet. Chuckies has a dashing selection of designer shoes—lots of Dolce & Gabbana (at the 3rd Avenue store), some Sonia Rykiel and Jimmy Choo, and Chuckies' own line of cool pumps and boots. *399 W. Broadway (between Spring and Broome Sts.), SoHo, 212/343–1717. Subway: N, R to Prince St.*

9 *f-2*

1073 3rd Ave. (between 63rd and 64th Sts.), Upper East Side, 212/593–9898. Subway: N, R, W, 4, 5, 6 to 59th St./Lexington Ave.

9 *e-2*

COLE-HAAN

Cole-Haan's woven, moccasin, and loafer styles go through endless permutations and combinations. The shelves are filled with versatile brown or black—not adventurous, but very well made. Moccasins average around $165. *667 Madison Ave. (at 61st St.), Upper East Side, 212/421–8440. Subway: N, R, W, 4, 5, 6 to 59th St./Lexington Ave.*

9 *e-4*

620 5th Ave. (at 50th St.), Midtown West, 212/765–9747. Subway: E, V to 5th Ave./53rd St.

9 *e-3*

GUCCI

It's not just for shoes anymore, though you can still get the classic horsebit loafer in brown or black, a true barefoot-preppie standard. Lately, with the appointment of designer Tom Ford to run the label, Gucci has mined its '70s heyday, pillaging styles from slick to slicker. You can still find those ubiquitous interlocking G's on everything from purses to shoes to accessories for your dog, and, of course, the sought-after fashions by design guru Tom Ford. Gucci's footwear runs the gamut from sexy teetering heels to sensible flats—in some of the most beautiful designs around. Also find eyewear, jewelry, fragrance and even fireplace accessories, surfboards, and fitness equipment, all bearing that enviable Gucci label. *10 W. 57th St. (between 5th and 6th Aves.), Midtown West, 212/826–2600. Subway: F, N, R, Q, W to 57th St.*

7 *b-8*

HARRY'S SHOES

At some point in the life of every Upper-West-sider comes a pilgrimage to Harry's Shoes, a shoe mecca for all ages. The shopping is full-contact, but the salespeople know their way around every style, from Merrell's Jungle Mocs to rugged Timberland boots. Harry's even prints a catalog. *2299 Broadway (at 83rd St.), Upper West Side, 212/874–2035. Subway: 1, 2 to 86th St.*

9 *e-1*

J. M. WESTON

Exclusive bootmakers in Paris since 1865, this establishment makes the best penny loafer known to man or beast. Weston is renowned for styling and fit; 80% of each shoe is made by hand, and you can choose from among 60 styles in 24 sizes and five widths. *812 Madison (at 68th St.), Upper East Side, 212/535–2100. Subway: 6 to 68th St./Hunter College.*

9 *e-4*

JIMMY CHOO

Starlet shoes from tip to heel, these resemble their patrons: they're slender and expensive. Styles range from pointy-toe stilettos to svelte slides, patent leather to denim. Prices start around $350. *645 5th Ave. (at 51st St.), Midtown East, 212/593–0800. Subway: B, D, F, V to 47th–50th Sts./Rockefeller Ctr.*

11 *e-4*

JOHN FLUEVOG SHOES

Inventor of the Angelic sole (protects against most earthly liquids "and Satan"), Fluevog carries big, thick shoes and boots. These are no Doc Martens knockoffs, though—the liberal use of platforms, curvaceous heels, and extremely pointy toes on the various styles ensures the difference from the yellow-stitched standard. There's a Cuisinartlike blend of influences, with geisha, wing tip, cowboy, Space Age, and roller derby ideas all jumping in. *250 Mulberry St. (at Prince St.), NoLita, 212/431–4484. Subway: N, R to Prince St.*

9 *e-8*

KENNETH COLE

Cole provides a steady supply of fresh, never over-the-top shoe styles to younger customers. Accoutrements include ties, leather goods, jackets, and socks. *95 5th Ave. (at 17th St.), Chelsea,*

212/675–2550. Subway: F, V to 14th St.; N, R to 23rd St.

9 *5-e*

107 E. 42nd St. (at Park Ave.), Midtown East, 212/949–8079. Subway: S, 4, 5, 6, 7 to 42nd St./Grand Central.

11 *e-4*

597 Broadway (between Houston and Prince Sts.), SoHo, 212/965–0283. Subway: 6 to Bleecker St.

7 *b-8*

353 Columbus Ave. (between 76th and 77th Sts.), Upper West Side, 212/873–2061. Subway: 1, 2 to 79th St.

11 *d-1*
KINWAY INDUSTRIES LTD.
Nothing dainty here (including the decor)—it's crammed with well-priced Converse, Airwalk, and Simple sneakers plus Sketchers, Doc Martens, and Frye boots. *5 W. 8th St. (between 5th and 6th Aves.), Greenwich Village, 212/777–3848. Subway: N, R to 8th St.; A, B, C, D, E, F, V to W. 4th St./Washington Sq.*

11 *d-1*
LUICHINY
This little store holds the title of Biggest Shoes on West 8th Street. With platforms and towering heels, most of the stock defies anything under 6 inches tall. Relatively sedate styles include stacked sandals or slides with inflatable uppers—and then there are the unmissable knee-high, platform, glitter boots. *21 W. 8th St. (between 5th and 6th Aves.), Greenwich Village, 212/477–3445. Subway: N, R to 8th St.; A, B, C, D, E, F, V to W. 4th St./Washington Sq.*

9 *d-4*
MANOLO BLAHNIK
Blahnik's spindly-heel, pointy-toe shoes are the last word in luxury. Society dames swear by them, Hollywood types teeter in them, and Tori Amos loves them—all with good reason. The vamps are the shoe equivalent of a well-cut low neckline, making the foot a sensual thing indeed. A simple satin evening pump is roughly $445 and prices can skyrocket to over $2,000. *31 W. 54th St. (between 5th and 6th Aves.), Midtown West, 212/582–3007. Subway: E, V to 5th Ave./53rd St.*

9 *e-2*
MARAOLO
Midtown Manhattan is crawling with Maraolo-shod cubicle farmers. This is the place to go for a shiny moc-croc or trim pump in the $100–$200 range. They've also got jackets, handbags, and eyewear. *782 Lexington Ave. (at 61st St.), Upper East Side, 212/832–8182. Subway: N, R, W, 4, 5, 6 to 59th St./Lexington Ave.*

9 *b-1*

131 W. 72nd St. (between Columbus Ave. and Broadway), Upper West Side, 212/787–6550. Subway: 1, 2, 3 to 72nd St.

9 *e-3*

551 Madison Ave. (at 55th St.), Midtown East, 212/308–8794. Subway: E, V to 5th Ave./53rd St.; and other locations.

9 *e-2*
MCCREEDY & SCHREIBER
This longtime emporium has one of New York's best selections of boots (including Lucchese) and shoes for both casual and dress wear. Pick up Frye, Timberland, Sperry, Rockport, Sebago, Alden, Dan Post, Justin, and Tony Lama at competitive prices. *213 E. 59th St. (between 2nd and 3rd Aves.), Midtown East, 212/759–9241. Subway: N, R, W, 4, 5, 6 to 59th St./Lexington Ave.*

10 *e-1*
99x
These Brits have an enviably encyclopedic selection of Doc Martens and creepers. *84 E. 10th St. (between 3rd and 4th Aves.), East Village, 212/460–8599. Subway: 6 to Astor Pl.*

9 *e-8*
OTTO TOOTSI PLOHOUND
An essential part of the wardrobes of many downtown women, these shoes are often chunky-soled and somewhat heftily priced. Most shoes, including the store's own label, are made in Italy—you'll regularly find Costume National, Miu Miu, Prada, and a few designer numbers by Anna Sui or Vivienne Westwood. During sales, you can get some good stompers for about $90. *137 5th Ave. (between 20th and 21st Sts.), Chelsea, 212/460–8650. Subway: F, V to 23rd St.*

9 *e-3*

38 E. 57th St. (between Park and Madison Aves.), Midtown East, 212/231–3199. Subway: N, R, W, 4, 5, 6 to 59th St./Lexington Ave.

11 *d-4*

413 W. Broadway (between Prince and Spring Sts.), SoHo, 212/925–8931. Subway: C, E to Spring St.

11 *d-5*

PETER FOX

It's hard to pin down the lavish, offbeat look of these shoes—retro lines such as Louis heels are mixed with modern round toes or low platforms. The vintage romanticism has led them onto Broadway and the silver screen; Kate Winslet wore a pair in *Titantic*. There's a particularly substantial selection of bridal shoes; prepare for lots of lustrous satin and bows. *105 Thompson St. (between Prince and Spring Sts.), SoHo, 212/431–7426. Subway: C, E to Spring St.*

11 *d-1*

PETIT PETON

You can turn up some funky finds here, even by West 8th Street's standards; the patriotic mule, for instance, comes festooned with stars, stripes, and a 5-inch silver square heel. *27 W. 8th St. (between 5th Ave. and University Pl.), Greenwich Village, 212/677–3730. Subway: N, R to 8th St.; A, B, C, D, E, F, V to W. 4th St./Washington Sq.*

9 *e-2*

ROBERT CLERGERIE

These classy French shoes make their own fun: a pair of flats could have turned-up toes, an oxford could have its lacings shifted to the side. The various styles of high-vamped, dark-fabric-covered shoes work well with pants suits. Most pairs, including the famous wedges, run in the hundreds of dollars. *681 Madison Ave. (between 61st and 62nd Sts.), Upper East Side, 212/207–8600. Subway: N, R, W, 4, 5, 6 to 59th St./Lexington Ave.*

9 *e-4*

SALVATORE FERRAGAMO

Giant photos of happy customer Audrey Hepburn beam down on the gorgeous goods. These shoes know how to flatter a woman's foot—molded insteps, heels just the right height. Traditional styles, such as the square bow on the vamp,

are still holding their own, though you can also find updated loafers and teasing sandals. *661 5th Ave. (between 52nd and 53rd Sts.), Midtown East, 212/759–3822. Subway: E, V to 5th Ave./53rd St.*

9 *e-5*

SELBY FIFTH AVENUE

You'll never have to worry about pinched toes with this selection for men and women—which includes Rockport, Sebago, SAS, Mephisto, and Clarks—and the store specializes in hard-to-fit sizes. Selby's own line went out of business in 2000, but now they offer men's shoes, too. *417 5th Ave. (at 38th St.), Midtown West, 212/328–1020. Subway: B, D, F, V to 42nd St.*

9 *e-2*

1055 3rd Ave. (between 62nd and 63rd Sts.), Upper East Side, 212/328–1001. Subway: N, R, W, 4, 5, 6 to 59th St./Lexington Ave.

9 *e-1*

SERGIO ROSSI

These beaded stilettos and thin patent leather straps are sure to draw attention to your pedicure. More substantial shoes could include pointy crocodile pumps or ponyskin loafers. *835 Madison Ave. (between 69th and 70th Sts.), Upper East Side, 212/396–4814. Subway: 6 to 77th St.*

11 *d-1*

SEVEN BOUTIQUE LTD.

Cowboy boots and (almost) nothing but—they come in ostrich, snakeskin, ponyskin, lizard, and over a dozen colors. *19 W. 8th St. (between 5th and 6th Aves.), Greenwich Village, 212/533–5909. Subway: N, R to 8th St.; A, B, C, D, E, F, V to W. 4th St./Washington Sq.*

11 *f-4*

SIGERSON MORRISON

Shoe boxes line the walls of this tiny boutique; peer down and you'll find delicate leather shoes at your feet. Pay close attention to the details, such as small buckles or interesting hues (pale dove gray, bronzey brown). While some styles are whittled into narrow toes, you can generally find rounded slippers as well. Prices generally hover around $250. *242 Mott St. (between Houston and Prince Sts.), NoLita, 212/219–3893. Subway: F, V to Broadway–Lafayette St.*

11 d-4
STEPHANE KÉLIAN
Kélian's woven beauties are a Euro-hound's favorite; they do wonders to an all-black outfit. Sometimes the woven or strappy leather uppers are laced with a hard-to-match but too-chic color, such as ochre or burnt orange. They've also dabbled in thick soles, wedges, and pencil-thin heels. For perfect coordination, peruse the handbag selection. *158 Mercer St. (between Houston and Prince Sts.), SoHo, 212/925–3077. Subway: F, V to Broadway–Lafayette.*

9 e-2
717 Madison Ave. (between 63rd and 64th Sts.), Upper East Side, 212/980–1919. Subway: 6 to 68th St./Hunter College.

9 e-3
STUART WEITZMAN
Never let it be said that these guys don't love their shoes—cards, napkins, and other shoe-oriented accessories peek from the corners. And the selection is happily wide-ranging, in terms of both style and size: rubber-sole loafers; knee-high nappa boots; peau de soie evening pumps; from C to AAA in width and sized from 4–12. *625 Madison Ave. (between 58th and 59th Sts.), Midtown East, 212/750–2555. Subway: N, R, W, 4, 5, 6 to 59th St./Lexington Ave.*

9 d-3
TO BOOT
The famed boot selection, including handmade exotic leathers, has been joined by men's casual, leisure, business, and formal footwear. *745 5th Ave. (at 58th St., in Bergdorf Goodman Men), Midtown East, 212/339–3335. Subway: N, R, W to 5th Ave./59th St.*

9 e-3
TOD'S
Audrey Hepburn wore 'em; so did Steve McQueen. And they are way expensive, averaging around $400 for the coveted butter-soft driving loafer that comes in sedate black and brown or something eye-catching such as red crocodile; if you can't find exactly what you want, head to the custom area in back. The workmanship is excellent, and these are absolutely fabulous shoes. *650 Madison Ave. (between 59th and 60th Sts.), Midtown East, 212/644–5945. Closed Sun. Subway: N, R, W to 5th Ave./59th St.*

9 e-1
VARDA
These handmade Italian shoes are worth every penny. The exclusive designs often have softly rounded or open toes, ankle straps, and not-too-spindly 2- or 3-inch heels. You can have most styles in any color you want—as long as it's black. *786 Madison Ave. (between 66th and 67th Sts.), Upper East Side, 212/472–7552. Subway: 6 to 68th St./Hunter College.*

11 d-4
149 Spring St. (between W. Broadway and Wooster St.), SoHo, 212/941–4990. Subway: 6 to Spring St.

9 e-2
VIA SPIGA
The first U.S. branch of this old-world Italian shoemaker has wooed the city with just what it likes—shoes and low boots in an array of colors (and a lot of black), many in buffed-to-a-shine calf-skin or soft-as-butter suede. The boutique houses the men's and women's collections as well as the designer handbags and accessories. *765 Madison Ave. (between 65th and 66th Sts.), Upper East Side, 212/988–4877. Subway: 6 to 68th St./Hunter College.*

9 e-3
WALTER STEIGER
Following trends from a discreet distance, Walter Steiger makes lovely pumps (about $300), some in textured leather or fabric—wool flannel, for instance. There's also quite a range of golf shoes—those white leathers and cleats come spiked in candy colors—as well as sleek, sexy boots. Harper's Bazaar named the Steiger's stiletto-heel, glove-leather zipper boot the best of the fall 2001 season. *417 Park Ave. (at 55th St.), Midtown East, 212/826–7171. Subway: 6 to 51st St./Lexington Ave.; E, V to Lexington–3rd Aves./53rd St.*

SOUVENIRS & POSTCARDS

9 e-7
MEMORIES OF NEW YORK
Thousands of ways to remember a trip to the big city—from the ever-popular I ♥ NY variety to postcards to just about any other incarnation you could imagine—are all for sale at this 6,000 square ft, dual-entrance (Broadway and

5th Ave.) shop. Also find a collection of historical New York City books and videos. *206 5th Ave. (between 25th and 26th Sts.), Flatiron District, 212/252–0030. Subway: N, R to 23rd St.*

9 c-5
TIMES SQUARE TRIX INC.
Everything a resident New Yorker would hate, and everything a tourist could possibly want. This shop is chockablock with T-shirts, mugs, miniatures of Ms. Liberty herself, hand-sized Empire State Buildings, Big Apple'd frames, keychains, and of course posters of our fabulous city—literally thousands of kitschy items to choose from. *724 8th Ave. (at 45th St.), Midtown West, 212/582–5336. Subway: A, C, E to 42nd St./Port Authority.*

SPORTING GOODS & CLOTHING

9 e-3
GYM SOURCE
The largest exercise-equipment dealer in the area, Gym Source has bikes, stair and weight machines, rowers, and treadmills for rent or sale. The helpful staff will assist you in designing a home or office gym. *40 E. 52nd St. (between Madison and Park Aves.), Midtown East, 212/688–4222. Closed Sun. Subway: 6 to 51st St./Lexington Ave.; E, V to Lexington–3rd Aves./53rd St.*

10 e-5
MODELL'S SPORTING GOODS
Family-run since 1889, Mo's has a variety of sporting goods and footwear, particularly team wear. *280 Broadway (near Chambers St.), Lower Manhattan, 212/962–6200. Subway: 1, 2 to Chambers St.*

10 e-6
200 Broadway (near Fulton St.), Lower Manhattan, 212/964–4007. Subway: A, C, J, M, Z, 1, 2, 4, 5 to Fulton St./Broadway–Nassau.

9 e-5
51 E. 42nd St. (near Madison Ave.), Midtown East, 212/661–4242. Subway: 4, 5, 6, 7, S to 42nd St./Grand Central.

6 h-6
2929 3rd Ave. (between 151st and 152nd Sts.), Bronx, 718/993–1844. Subway: 2, 5 to 3rd Ave.

9 e-3
NIKETOWN
In a high-tech setting inspired by sports arenas and old school gyms, this Midtown monster has five floors of footwear, accessories, and apparel for tennis, golf, basketball, football, baseball, team sports (pro and college), running, and cross-training for men, women, boys, and girls. *6 E. 57th St. (between 5th and Madison Aves.), Midtown East, 212/891–6453. Subway: E, V to 5th Ave./53rd St.*

9 e-8
PARAGON SPORTING GOODS
Almost 100 years old, Paragon has the city's most impressive collection of clothes and equipment for every imaginable sport. The deep stock contains down jackets, track shoes, and shorts; baseball, football, lacrosse, golf, and hockey equipment; skates, skis, and swimwear; and camping, fishing, and backpacking paraphernalia. Values can be excellent. *867 Broadway (at 18th St.), Flatiron District, 212/255–8036. Subway: L, N, Q, R, W, 4, 5, 6 to 14th St./Union Sq.*

9 e-8
PRINCETON SKI SHOP
Make tracks here for ski equipment and apparel and the ever-important custom boot-fitting. Other specialized departments cater to tennis, skateboarding, and in-line skating. *21 E. 22nd St. (near Broadway), Flatiron District, 212/228–4400. Subway: N, R to 23rd St.*

9 d-6
THE SPORTS AUTHORITY
Departments include tennis, golf, skiing, camping, footwear, apparel, and exercise and there's plenty of selection. If you're looking for advice, don't count on the staff, who aren't particularly athletic or outdoorsy. *401 7th Ave. (at 33rd St.), Midtown West, 212/563–7195. Subway: A, C, E, 1, 2, 3 to 34th St./Penn Station.*

9 f-4
845 3rd Ave. (at 51st St.), Midtown East, 212/355–9725. Subway: 6 to 51st St./Lexington Ave.; E, V to Lexington–3rd Aves./53rd St.

9 d-3
57 W. 57th St. (between Madison and Park Aves.), Midtown East, 212/355–6430. Subway: N, R, W to 5th Ave./59th St.

9 d-8

636 6th Ave. (at 19th St.), Flatiron District, 212/929–8971. Subway: 1, 2 to 18th St.

bicycles

9 c-7

DIFFERENT SPOKES

A fireman and a tie salesperson teamed up with one of New York's best bike mechanics to open this crackerjack shop. Ask any bike messenger about the quality of the repairs. You get all the best brands, great service, and generous opening hours. 240 7th Ave. (at 24th St.), Chelsea, 212/727–7278. Subway: 1, 2 to 23rd St.

10 h-4

FRANK'S BIKE SHOP

Frank sells and repairs. The stock includes Schwinn, GT, Giant, Ross, Bianchi, Mongoose, Raleigh, and Diamond. 533 Grand St. (near Lewis St.), Lower East Side, 212/533–6332. Subway: F, J, M, Z to Delancey St./Essex St.

10 f-1

METRO BICYCLE STORES

Metro sells a complete line of performance parts, accessories, and clothing for racing, touring, and road, mountain, and city biking. They also rent bikes and do expert repairs. 332 E. 14th St., East Village, 212/228–4344. Subway: L to 1st Ave.

9 c-4

360 W. 47th St. (between 8th and 9th Aves.), Midtown West, 212/581–4500. Subway: N, R to 49th St.

7 e-6

1311 Lexington Ave. (at 88th St.), Upper East Side, 212/427–4450. Subway: 4, 5, 6 to 86th St.

7 b-5

231 W. 96th St. (at Broadway), Upper West Side, 212/663–7531. Subway: 1, 2, 3 to 96th St.; and other locations.

boating

9 d-6

WEST MARINE

Head straight here for marine supplies at a discount; they've got all the necessities, from global positioning systems to foul-weather apparel. 12 W. 37th St. (between 5th and 6th Aves.), Midtown West, 212/594–6065. Subway: B, D, F, N, Q, R, V, W to 34th St./Herald Sq.

camping & climbing

11 e-3

EMS—THE OUTDOOR SPECIALISTS

This familiar, ruggedly spiffy chain specializes in backpacking and climbing, and is also well stocked for downhill and cross-country skiing, tennis, and running. 611 Broadway (between Houston and Bleecker Sts.), Greenwich Village, 212/505–9860. Subway: F, V to Broadway–Lafayette St.; 6 to Bleecker St.

9 c-2

20 W. 61st St. (between Broadway and West End Ave.), Upper West Side, 212/397–4860. Subway: A, B, C, D, 1, 2 to 59th St./Columbus Circle.

10 e-6

TENTS & TRAILS

Top-quality camping supplies are for sale or rent next to apparel and footwear for adults and children. Shipping is available. 21 Park Pl. (between Church St. and Broadway), Lower Manhattan, 212/227–1760. Subway: 1, 2 to Park Pl.

fishing tackle & supplies

9 c-7

CAPITOL FISHING TACKLE CO.

A fisherman's friend since 1897, Capitol Fishing Tackle can equip you for freshwater, saltwater, deep-sea, and big-game fishing, all at ample discounts. Fly-casting lessons are also available. 218 W. 23rd St. (between 7th and 8th Aves.), Chelsea, 212/929–6132. Closed Sun. Subway: 1, 2, C, E to 23rd St.

9 e-3

HUNTING WORLD/ ANGLER'S WORLD

The Angler's World department has a fine selection of fly-fishing equipment. 16 E. 53rd St. (between 5th and Madison Aves.), Midtown East, 212/755–3400. Subway: E, V to 5th Ave./53rd St.

9 e-4

ORVIS NEW YORK

Peruse a complete line of fly rods, reels, and accessories including vests, jackets, hip boots, and waders at the oldest rod-building company in the country. 522 5th Ave. (at 44th St.), Midtown West, 212/827–0698. Subway: S, 4, 5, 6 to 42nd St./Grand Central; 7 to 5th Ave.; B, D, F, V to 42nd St.

9 *e-7*

URBAN ANGLER

True to the charming name, this Gramercy shop features fly-fishing rods, reels, and the attention of a caring specialist. Fly-fishing is Urban Angler's specialty, but those interested in spinning equipment will find their selection one of the best around. *118 E. 25th St. (between Park and Lexington Aves.), 3rd floor, Gramercy, 212/979–7600. Closed Sun. Subway: 6 to 23rd St.*

golf

9 *e-4*

AL LIEBER'S WORLD OF GOLF

Lieber has the latest in well-priced golf equipment. *147 E. 47th St. (between Lexington and 3rd Aves.), 2nd floor, Midtown East, 212/755–9398. Subway: 6 to 51st St./Lexington Ave.; E, V to Lexington–3rd Aves./53rd St.*

9 *e-4*

RICHARD METZ GOLF STUDIO

Richard Metz sells the latest and best of golf equipment and supplies for both men and women. Expert instruction will help improve your stroke, which you can refine to precision in their special practice area. *425 Madison Ave. (near 49th St.), Midtown East, 212/759–6940. Subway: 6 to 51st St./Lexington Ave.; E, V to Lexington–3rd Aves./53rd St.*

kites

7 *e-7*

BIG CITY KITES

Your spirits will soar in this joyful venue, with 200 varieties of colorful kites for every level of expertise and aspiration. Accessories include kite-making supplies and air toys. Prices range from $2 to $200. *1210 Lexington Ave. (near 82nd St.), Upper East Side, 212/472–2623. Subway: 6 to 77th St.*

riding

9 *e-3*

HERMÈS

Though most New Yorkers associate Hermès with chic silk items (for the horsey set), the French firm has in fact made saddles and bridle equipment for more than 150 years. *11 E. 57th St.*

(between 5th and Madison Aves.), Midtown East, 212/751–3181. Subway: E, V to 5th Ave./53rd St.

9 *e-7*

MILLER HARNESS COMPANY

This informed source has everything for the horse and rider: equipment, clothing (including a large selection of Barber), and an extensive selection of boots. *117 E. 24th St. (between Park and Lexington Aves.), Gramercy, 212/673–1400. Closed Sun. Subway: 6 to 23rd St.*

running

11 *e-2*

ATHLETE'S FOOT

This national outfit offers an incredible selection of moderately priced athletic footwear—by Reebok, Nike, Adidas, New Balance, Avia, Converse, et al.—as well as related accessories and clothing. *2563 Broadway (at 96th St.), Upper West Side, 212/961–9556. Subway: 1, 2, 3 to 96th St.*

9 *e-5*

390 5th Ave. (at 36th St.), Midtown West, 212/947–6972. Subway: B, D, F, N, Q, R, V, W to 34th St./Herald Sq.

9 *e-4*

41 E. 42nd St. (near Madison Ave.), Midtown East, 212/867–4599. Subway: 4, 5, 6, 7, S to 42nd St./Grand Central.

9 *e-1*

SUPER RUNNER'S SHOP

A complete running store, this chain has shoes, gear, and accessories from all the big names. Helpful service will find the styles that suit your needs. *1246 3rd Ave. (at 72nd St.), Upper East Side, 212/249–2133. Subway: 6 to 6 to 68th St./Hunter College.*

7 *b-8*

360 Amsterdam Ave. (at 77th St.), Upper West Side, 212/787–7665. Subway: 1, 2 to 79th St.

7 *e-6*

1337 Lexington Ave. (at 89th St.), Upper East Side, 212/369–6010. Subway: 4, 5, 6 to 86th St.

skating

9 *a-7*

BLADES BOARD & SKATE

These folks sell, rent, and repair in-line, ice, and hockey skates; snowboards; and skateboards, and sell related clothing and accessories. They also arrange bus trips to Hunter Mountain every Thursday, Friday, and Sunday in ski season. For general information, call 888/55–BLADES. *Chelsea Piers (12th Ave. and 23rd St.), Chelsea, 212/336–6299. Subway: C, E to 23rd St.*

11 *e-3*

659 Broadway (near Bleecker St.), Greenwich Village, 212/477–7350. Subway: 6 to Bleecker St.

9 *b-1*

120 W. 72nd St. (between Broadway and Columbus Ave.), Upper West Side, 212/787–3911. Subway: 1, 2, 3 to 72nd St.

9 *f-1*

1414 2nd Ave. (near 73rd St.), Upper East Side, 212/249–3178. Subway: 6 to 77th St.; and other locations.

9 *c-3*

PECK & GOODIE SKATES

Some say Peck & Goodie is New York's finest skate shop. Family-owned since 1940, it's in any case the city's original in-line and roller skate dealer. In addition to an excellent selection of in-line skates, you'll find a complete line of figure, hockey, and speed skates and roller blades, as well as equipment. You also can bring your old stuff in for sharpening or repair. *917 8th Ave. (near 54th St.), Midtown West, 212/246–6123. Subway: C, E to 50th St.*

skiing

9 *e-1*

BOGNER

These are the people who revolutionized the ski slopes with stretch pants in the 1950s. Ski fashions and Bogner ready-to-wear are imported from Germany. *821 Madison Ave. (near 68th St.), Upper East Side, 212/472–0266. Subway: 6 to 68th St./Hunter College.*

9 *d-3*

SCANDINAVIAN SKI & SPORTS SHOP

This top city source for ski equipment fills three floors with it, and throws in brand-name ski wear to boot. They also sponsor a ski clinic known as "rep rap" in early November, and run one-day ski trips to Hunter Mountain December–March, for which they have rental

equipment available. *40 W. 57th St. (between 5th and 6th Aves.), Midtown West, 212/757–8524. Subway: F, N, R, Q, W to 57th St.*

tennis

9 *e-4*

MASON'S TENNIS MART

Shop for rackets, balls, bags, high-fashion European tennis wear, and, in season, ski wear. They'll restring your racket, as well. *56 E. 53rd St. (between Madison and Park Aves.), Midtown East, 212/757–5374. Subway: 6 to 51st St./Lexington Ave.; E, V to Lexington–3rd Aves./53rd St.*

STATIONERY & OFFICE SUPPLIES

office supplies

9 *e-5*

AIRLINE STATIONERY COMPANY, INC.

Long-established and reputable, Airline is bound to have what you need. *284 Madison Ave. (at 40th St.), Midtown East, 212/532–6525. Subway: S, 4, 5, 6, 7 to 42nd St./Grand Central.*

9 *e-5*

155 E. 44th St. (between Lexington and 3rd Aves.), Midtown East, 212/532–9410. Subway: S, 4, 5, 6, 7 to 42nd St./Grand Central.

9 *e-3*

KROLL STATIONERS, INC.

This fine stationery and office-supply store also sells computer supplies and office furniture and arranges fine printing and engraving. *145 E. 54th St. (between 3rd and Lexington Aves.), Midtown East, 212/750–5300. Subway: 6 to 51st St./Lexington Ave.; E, V to Lexington–3rd Aves./53rd St.*

9 *c-6*

STAPLES

The office-supply megastore carries everything from paper clips to paper to printers to furniture. For a full list of locations, call 800/237–0413. *250 W. 34th St. (between 7th and 8th Aves.), Midtown West, 212/629–3990. Subway: A, C, E, 1, 2, 3 to 34th St./Penn Station.*

`9` *e-6*

16 E. 34th St. (between 5th and Madison Aves.), Murray Hill, 212/683–8003. Subway: 6 to 33rd St.

`9` *d-5*

1075 6th Ave. (between 40th and 41st Sts.), Midtown West, 212/944–6791. Subway: B, D, F, V to 42nd St.

`7` *e-7*

1280 Lexington Ave. (between 86th and 87th Sts.), Upper East Side, 212/426–6190. Subway: 4, 5, 6 to 86th St.; and other locations.

pens & pencils

`9` *d-4*

ARTHUR BROWN & BROS., INC.

Arthur Brown has one of the world's largest pen selections. Every brand you can name is here—including Mont Blanc, Cartier, Cross, and Waterman—in a wide variety of styles. The store also arranges repairs. *2 W. 46th St. (near 5th Ave.), Midtown West, 212/575–5555. Subway: B, D, F, V to 42nd St.*

`9` *d-3*

AUTHORIZED SALES & SERVICE

This shop sells and repairs vintage and contemporary pens—along with electric shavers and cigarette lighters. *30 W. 57th St. (between 5th and 6th Aves.), 2nd floor, Midtown West, 212/586–0947. Closed Sun. Subway: F, N, R, Q, W to 57th St.*

`9` *e-8*

BERLINER PEN

Jeffrey Berliner is a true pen historian, and his shop reflects his taste in both the new and the old. Brands include Waterman, Mont Blanc, and Omas. *928 Broadway (near 22nd St.), Flatiron District, 212/614–3020. Closed weekends. Subway: N, R to 23rd St.*

`10` *e-5*

FOUNTAIN PEN HOSPITAL

Collectors swear by this out-of-the-way shop, to the extent that its clientele extends worldwide. Bill Cosby is a regular. You'll find all major brands, limited editions, and collectible pens, and, true to the name, they'll fix what you already own if it's ailing. *10 Warren St. (across from City Hall), Lower Manhattan, 212/*

964–0580. Closed weekends. Subway: 1, 2 to Chambers St.

`9` *e-3*

MONT BLANC BOUTIQUE

The famous pen maker has a whole store for its "snow-capped" creations. *595 Madison Ave. (between 57th and 58th Sts.), Midtown East, 212/223–8888. Subway: N, R to 5th Ave.*

`9` *e-3*

REBECCA MOSS

At this midtown shop, they know their high-end writing instruments. *510 Madison Ave. (at 53rd St.), Midtown East, 212/832–7671. Subway: 6 to 51st St./Lexington Ave.; E, V to Lexington–3rd Aves./53rd St.*

stationery

Tiffany, Cartier, and the major department stores sell fine stationery.

`9` *e-3*

DEMPSEY & CARROLL

These folks know their business, having been at it since 1878. They create fine, hand-engraved stationery from more than 200 monogram styles. *110 E. 57th St. (between Park and Lexington Aves.), Midtown East, 212/486–7508. Subway: N, R, W, 4, 5, 6 to 59th St./Lexington Ave.*

`10` *f-1*

HUDSON ENVELOPE JAM PAPER

This store is a terrific source for both basic and unusual-hue stationery; they have more than 150 colors in stock. Try the map stationery for overseas mail. *111 3rd Ave. (near 13th St.), East Village, 212/473–6666. Subway: L to 3rd Ave.*

`9` *d-8*

611 6th Ave. (near 17th St.), Chelsea, 212/255–4593. Subway: F, V to 14th St. Closed weekends.

`7` *e-8*

IL PAPIRO

Direct from Italy, this charmer carries delightful gifts and stationery, all made with hand-marbled Florentine papers: picture frames, desk accessories, decorative boxes, albums, and more. *1021 Lexington Ave. (between 73rd and 74th Sts.), Upper East Side, 212/288–9330. Subway: 6 to 77th St.*

9 d-8
IS
Super-sleek IS carries minimalist looking stationery—no superfluous design elements here—perfect for the hip modern letter writer. They also have pens, photo albums, and notebooks. *136 W. 17th St. (between 6th and 7th Aves.), Chelsea, 212/620–0300. Subway: 1, 2 to 18th St.*

9 e-1
JAMIE OSTROW
Ostrow creates custom invitations, holiday greeting cards, and personalized stationery with a contemporary edge. *876 Madison Ave. (near 71st St.), Upper East Side, 212/734–8890. Closed Sun. Subway: 6 to 68th St./Hunter College.*

11 d-6
KATE SPADE PAPER
The hip handbag queen has turned her sights to charming paper products—day planners, address books, and calendars in Kate's signature fabrics. Also available are wrapping paper, stationery, and a range of other paper products. *59 Thompson St. (between Spring and Broome Sts.), SoHo, 212/965–8654. Subway: A, C, E to Canal St.*

11 e-4
KATE'S PAPERIE
Kate's is beloved for its handmade fine-art papers for artists, photographers, and mere mortals who just can't walk past them. The wonderfully spacious store is worth the trip to SoHo, with exquisite paper in all of its varieties: for writing, wrapping, and making collages or matting pictures. The gorgeous desk accessories are just as compelling, as are the handmade greeting cards and the diaries, photo albums, storage boxes—we could go on and on. There are also creative invitations for everything from backyard barbecues to black-tie weddings, and the Christmas-card selection is one of the finest in town. *561 Broadway (at Prince St.), SoHo, 212/941–9816. Subway: N, R to Prince St.*

9 f-1
1282 3rd Ave. (between 73rd and 74th Sts.), Upper East Side, 212/396–3670. Subway: 6 to 77th St.

10 d-1
8 W. 13th St. (near 5th Ave.), Greenwich Village, 212/633–0570. Subway: F, V to 14th St.

9 e-2
MRS. JOHN L. STRONG
The original stationer to the Duke and Duchess of Windsor, Mrs. Strong provides hand-engraved invitations, announcements, and social stationery on the company's own, 100%-cotton paper. Motifs are whimsical and interesting, and the matching envelopes are hand-lined. The boxed cards are also sold at Barneys (*see* Department Stores, *above*). *699 Madison Ave. (near 62nd St.), Upper East Side, 212/838–3775. Open by appt. only. Subway: N, R, W, 4, 5, 6 to 59th St./Lexington Ave.*

10 c-2
PAPIVORE
This tiny but delightful paperie carries vibrantly colored paper from Marie Papier Paris, as well as a small, expertly chosen selection of notebooks, photo albums, and desk accessories. While their custom calling cards are all the rage, Papivore also hand-prints customized stationery on a range of papers, offering lots of specialty inks for unique effects. Papers are also sold in boxed sets and by the piece. Find lots of French desk accessories and decorative items like candles and Marie-Papier's hand-made line of calendars, binders, and pencil holders. *117 Perry St. (between Greenwich and Hudson Sts.), Greenwich Village, 212/627–6055. Subway: 1, 2 to Christopher St./Sheridan Sq.*

9 e-2
PAPYRUS
Contemplate personalized stationery, wrapping paper, photo albums, cards, stickers, frames, address books, and the like. *852 Lexington Ave. (at 65th St.), Upper East Side, 212/717–0002. Subway: 6 to 68th St./Hunter College.*

9 e-1
107 E. 42nd St. (between Lexington and Park Aves.), Midtown East, 212/490–9894. Subway: S, 4, 5, 6, 7 to 42nd St./Grand Central.

TOBACCONISTS

9 e-3
ALFRED DUNHILL OF LONDON
The esteemed tobacconist produces custom-blended tobaccos, pipes, humidors, cigars, and gifts, including, of course, their own renowned and pricey

lighters. *450 Park Ave. (near 57th St.), Midtown East, 212/753–9292. Subway: N, R, W, 4, 5, 6 to 59th St./Lexington Ave.*

9 e-4
Saks Fifth Ave., 611 5th Ave. (at 50th St.), Midtown East, 212/940–2243. Subway: E, V to 5th Ave./53rd St.

10 e-6
BARCLAY-REX
The self-proclaimed "Blockbuster Video" of cigar shops, Barclay-Rex is also the city's oldest tobacconist. Mail order is available for anything from their array of hand-made pipes, cigars and cigarettes, and accessories including humidors and lighters. Pipe broken? They also repair. *7 Maiden La. (near Broadway), Lower Manhattan, 212/962–3355. Subway: 4, 5, A, C to Broadway–Nassau.*

9 e-5
70 E. 42nd St. (between Park and Madison Aves.), Midtown East, 212/692–9680. Subway: S, 4, 5, 6, 7 to 42nd St./Grand Central Station.

9 d-4
CONNOISSEUR PIPE SHOP
Established in 1917, the Connoisseur offers unique custom- and handmade pipes—including one-of-a-kind unstained, unvarnished, natural-finish pipes—and skillful pipe repairs. Fill them with hand-blended tobacco mixtures and choose from a full range of tobacco pouches, humidors, racks, and accessories. Prices range from $27.50 to $4,200. *1285 6th Ave. (between 51st and 52nd Sts.), concourse level, Midtown West, 212/247–6054. Closed weekends. Subway: B, D, F, V to 47th–50th Sts./Rockefeller Ctr.*

9 e-3
DAVIDOFF OF GENEVA
Davidoff sells fine tobaccos and a variety of smoking accessories. *535 Madison Ave. (near 54th St.), Midtown East, 212/751–9060. Subway: 6 to 51st St./Lexington Ave.; E, V to Lexington–3rd Aves./53rd St.*

9 e-4
J & R TOBACCO CORPORATION
The world's largest cigar store stocks over 2,800 different sizes, shapes, and colors, from nickel cigars to the rare and expensive. *11 E. 45th St. (between 5th and Madison Aves.), Midtown East, 212/983–*

4160. Closed Sun. Subway: S, 4, 5, 6, 7 to 42nd St./Grand Central.

10 f-7
1 Wall St. Court (at the corner of Wall and Pearl Sts.), Lower Manhattan, 212/269–6000. Subway: 1, 2 to Wall St.

9 d-5
NAT SHERMAN CIGARS
Choose from pipe tobacco, an imported selection of cigars in a walk-in humidor, and 30 blends of cigarette tobacco—wrapped in your choice of colored paper, with your name or company's name imprinted if you wish. Pipes and cigarette lighters are also in good supply. *500 5th Ave. (at 42nd St.), Midtown West, 212/764–4175. Subway: B, D, F, V to 42nd St./6th Ave.; 7 to 5th Ave./42nd St.*

9 c-8
TOBACCO PRODUCTS
A long-standing family-run operation, Tobacco Products custom-blends cigars using tobaccos from Brazil, the Dominican Republic, Nicaragua, and Mexico and sells pipes and lighters. *133 8th Ave. (near 16th St.), Chelsea, 212/989–3900. Subway: A, C, E, L to 14th St./8th Ave.*

TOYS & GAMES

collectibles

11 c-3
ALPHAVILLE
Check out vintage toys, posters, magic, TV memorabilia, comics, and games from the American past. *226 W. Houston St. (between Varick St. and 6th Ave.), Greenwich Village, 212/675–6850. Subway: 1, 2 to Houston St.*

7 e-7
BURLINGTON ANTIQUE TOYS
These miniature fighter planes, wooden boats, racing cars, and die-cast model cars are both new and collectible. There's a fine selection of tin soldiers (circa 1900–1960). *Burlington Books, 1082 Madison Ave. (near 81st St.), downstairs, Upper East Side, 212/861–9708. Subway: 6 to 77th St.*

11 d-3
CLASSIC TOYS
The mix is both new and antique, including military miniatures; a wonder-

ful collection of old Matchbox and other collectible cars; and zoo, farm, and pre-historic animals. *218 Sullivan St. (between Bleecker and W. 3rd Sts.), Greenwich Village, 212/674–4434. Subway: A, C, E, F, V to W. 4th St./Washington Sq.*

9 *f-2*
DARROW'S FUN ANTIQUES
Founded in 1964 by Chick Darrow (*see Antiques—Collectibles, above*), this longtime mecca for nostalgia is now lovingly tended by Chick's son. The stock includes vintage windup toys, rare robots, tiny trucks and cars, vending machines, arcade games, carousel figures, character watches, and campaign buttons. *1101 1st Ave. (near 60th St.), Upper East Side, 212/838–0730. Closed Sun.–Mon. Subway: N, R, W, 4, 5, 6 to 59th St./Lexington Ave.*

new

11 *h-1*
ALPHABETS
These fun stores sell small toys and novelty items for both children and adults. There's a good selection of Hello Kitty items (remember them?), kitschy T-shirts, cards, games, books, and gag gifts. It's a great stop for affordable last-minute gifts. *115 Ave. A (between 7th and 8th Sts.), East Village, 212/475–7250. Subway: 6 to Astor Pl.*

11 *a-1*
47 Greenwich Ave. (between Perry and Charles Sts.), Greenwich Village, 212/229–2966. Subway: 1, 2 to Christopher St./Sheridan Sq.

7 *b-7*
2284 Broadway (between 82nd and 83rd Sts.), Upper West Side, 212/579–5702. Subway: 1, 2 to 86th St.

11 *d-3*
THE CHESS FORUM
This Greenwich Village haven for chess-lovers sells hundreds of themed sets, and even gets as specific as sets fashioned after specific historical battles. On the whimsical side, find fantasy, mythical, literary, and even Bar and Bat Mitzvah sets. Accessories, clocks, and backgammon and checkers sets are also in stock. *219 Thompson St. (between W. 3rd and Bleecker Sts.), Greenwich Village, 212/475–2369. Subway: 6 to Astor Pl.*

11 *d-3*
THE CHESS SHOP
This small shop is literally overflowing with chess boards and pieces in every material, shape, size, price range, and theme. You'll also find boxes, travel sets, checkers sets, and backgammon. *230 Thompson St. (between W. 3rd and Bleecker Sts.), East Village, 212/473–5850. Subway: N, R to 8th St.*

7 *b-6*
CHILDREN'S GENERAL STORE
Conveniently located at Playspace, this shop focuses on classic, wooden, and educational toys. *Playspace, 2473 Broadway (at 92nd St.), Upper West Side, 212/580–2723. Subway: 1, 2, 3 to 96th St.*

9 *e-5*
Grand Central Station (Lexington Passage), Midtown East, 212/682–0004. Subway: S, 4, 5, 6, 7 to 42nd St./Grand Central Station.

10 *f-1*
DINOSAUR HILL
Dinosaur Hill specializes in hand-made toys from around the world, plus clothing for children ages 6 months–6 years. *306 E. 9th St. (between 1st and 2nd Aves.), East Village, 212/473–5850. Subway: N, R to 8th St.; 6 to Astor Pl.*

11 *e-5*
ENCHANTED FOREST
This shop is SoHo's own wonderland, with an interior created by a professional set designer. It's a magical place, with books and toys that will appeal to adults as well as children. *85 Mercer St. (between Broome and Spring Sts.), SoHo, 212/925–6677. Subway: C, E to Spring St.*

9 *e-3*
F.A.O. SCHWARZ
It's a child's idea of heaven, a parent's idea of sensory overload. F.A.O. Schwarz has three floors absolutely packed with toys and tourists. The Madison Avenue entrance is the secret way to slip in during the busy holiday season, albeit through the Barbie Shop. Can't deal? Hire one of the store's personal shoppers. *767 5th Ave. (between 58th and 59th Sts.), Midtown East, 212/644–9400. Subway: N, R to 5th Ave.*

10 *d-1*

GEPPETTO'S TOY BOX

This Greenwich Villager has become very popular. In addition to puppets, stuffed animals, books, and jack-in-the-boxes, they carry one the city's largest selections of Steiff, a full-line of Tucher Walthers wind-up toys, Thomas the Tank Engine train sets, and they are downtown's only merchant of Madame Alexander dolls. *161 7th Ave. S (between Waverly Pl. and Perry St.), Greenwich Village, 212/620–7511. Subway: 1, 2 to Christopher St./Sheridan Sq.*

11 *d-8*

JUST JAKE

Voted the "Best Downtown Toy Store" in 1997 by *New York Press,* Just Jake's is full of such brainy toys as ant farms, books, and—well—small, quirky stuff. There's even a personal-shopping service. *40 Hudson St. (between Duane and Thomas Sts.), TriBeCa, 212/267–1716. Subway: 1, 2 to Chambers St.*

7 *e-8*

PENNY WHISTLE TOYS

This is the place to go for gifts to the artsy-craftsy child. In addition to such items as jewelry-making sets and model cars, Penny Whistle carries a large selection of jigsaw puzzles and dolls. *448 Madison Ave. (at 81st St.), Upper East Side, 212/873–9090. Subway: 6 to 77th St.*

9 *e-6*

1283 Madison Ave. (at 91st St.), Upper East Side, 212/369–3868. Subway: 4, 5, 6 to 86th St.

9 *e-8*

TOYS "R" US

The holiday crowds and lines can be rough, but for the latest kid-fads in toys, games, bikes, and crafts—at decent discounts—you can't beat the world's largest toy store. *24–30 Union Sq. E (between 14th and 15th Sts.), Flatiron District, 212/674–8697. Subway: L, N, Q, R, W, 4, 5, 6 to 14th St./Union Sq.*

9 *d-6*

1293 Broadway (at Herald Square, 34th St.), Midtown West, 212/594–8697. Subway: B, D, F, N, Q, R, V, W to 34th St./Herald Sq.

VIDEOS

BLOCKBUSTER VIDEO

The national video megachain has a store in virtually every neighborhood in Manhattan and many 'hoods in the neighboring boroughs. Most stores are open until midnight and handle both rentals and sales. Check the business listings in your White Pages for the location nearest you.

10 *f-2*

KIM'S VIDEO

Despite its reputation for crabby service, Kim's is staffed with movie buffs who are actually pretty helpful, and these two branches sell hard-to-find, out of print, cult, and foreign titles you probably won't see anywhere else. *6 St. Mark's Pl. (between 2nd and 3rd Aves.), 2nd floor, East Village, 212/505–0311. Subway: 6 to Astor Pl.*

10 *e-3*

144 Bleecker St. (at La Guardia Pl.), Greenwich Village, 212/260–1010. Subway: A, B, C, D, E, F, V to W. 4th St./Washington Sq.

11 *f-2*

TOWER VIDEO

Never to be outdone, Tower has thousands of music and film video titles for rent or sale, and the Village and Upper West Side stores are open until midnight. *383 Lafayette St. (at 4th St.), East Village, 212/505–1166. Subway: 6 to Astor Pl.*

9 *b-1*

1961 Broadway (at 66th St.), Upper West Side, 212/799–2500. Subway: 1, 2 to 66th St./Lincoln Ctr.

9 *e-3*

Trump Tower (sales only: 725 5th Ave., at 56th St.), Midtown East, 212/838–8110. Subway: E, V to 5th Ave./53rd St.

9 *f-7*

VIDEO STOP

A cut above the homogenized chains, this store has a knowledgeable staff and a good selection of videos for rent and for sale. *367 3rd Ave. (between 26th and 27th Sts.), 212/685–6199. Subway: 6 to 28th St.*

chapter 3

PARKS, GARDENS & SPORTS

*I*t may seem counterintuitive, but New York is and always has been a great place for outdoor sports. It all goes back to why the city sprang up here in the first place—lots of water, a strong rock foundation, forests, marshlands, and proximity to other areas of commercial interest. Over the years, New Yorkers have made the most of their natural environment as well as creating indoor exercise options. Pick any block (well, almost any block), and what do you see walking down the street but gorgeous bodies, young and old. Then look at the facilities—the city with the biggest and best of everything is never willing to be outdone. Lured by the vast market potential and capital resources, sports outfitters will launch just about anything here, hence the endless cycle of fitness trends—roller basketball, a new trendy workout every month, even such seemingly rural pastimes as rock climbing and kayaking. It's hard to find a better combination of natural and man-made facilities—and if anyone tries to argue about that, you can just remind them that another popular New York exercise is kvetching.

parks

It's easy to get frustrated in a city where signs that say PARK point you to a garage rather than a green space. But New York City has an abundance of green space—28,358 acres at last count—dotted throughout its concrete canyons and residential neighborhoods, ranging from large to small, teeming to tranquil. From the seemingly endless Pelham Bay Park, the Staten Island Greenbelt, and the new Hudson River Greenbelt to midtown's vest-pocket delights, parks have saved the soul of many a harried New Yorker. One recent survey found that almost two-thirds of all New Yorkers visit a park more than once a week.

When visiting a park, use common sense: After dark, you're safer with other people. During the day, try not to interfere with activities, whether it's a ball game or a skater whizzing by. Motor vehicles are allowed on some park roads, so watch out for those, too.

PARK INFORMATION

The City of New York/Parks and Recreation, also known as the Parks Department or the Department of Parks and Recreation, is responsible for the vast majority of parks, beaches, malls, playgrounds, and woodlands within city limits. The department offers a number of phone information lines, provides permits for games and events in parks, and staffs Urban Park Ranger programs. Much of their work is handled by individual borough offices. The general **parks hot line,** for information and emergencies, is 800/201–PARK. For recorded information pertaining to **special events** in the city's parks, call 212/360–3456 or 888/NY–PARKS. **Borough headquarters offices** have information about the parks in their respective boroughs and can help you locate sporting facilities near you (718/430–1868 Bronx; 718/965–8900 Brooklyn; 212/408–0100 Manhattan; 718/520–5900 Queens; and 718/390–8000 Staten Island).

The New York State Department of Parks, Recreation and Historic Preservation (518/474–0456) also manages some of the city's outdoor spaces.

Gateway National Recreation Area, formed as the first urban national recreation area in 1972, consists of National Park Service parklands spread out over waterfront districts in Queens, Brooklyn, Staten Island, and New Jersey. Together, these spits of land form a natural gateway (get it?) to New York's great harbor. Among its treasures are a wildlife refuge, historic forts and airfields, and beaches. Headquarters are at Brooklyn's Floyd Bennett Field (718/338–3338).

PERMITS

For details about and permits for use of city ball fields, call or stop by the **Parks Department permit office** (16 W. 61st St., 6th floor, Manhattan, 212/408–0226), or call your other borough office. There's nothing to stop you from using an open field, but if someone with a permit and field reservation shows up, you'll have to leave, and any group larger than 20 people automatically requires a permit.

URBAN PARK RANGERS

Trained in the history, landscape design, geology, wildlife, and botany of the city's parks, these uniformed officers staff Urban Park Ranger Nature Centers in many parks, guide tours, and lead workshops to help visitors better understand and appreciate the parks. Topics include everything from horseshoe-crab mating habits to the buildings surrounding Central Park; all are free and fascinating. For program information call the appropriate number (718/430–1832 Bronx; 718/438–0100 Brooklyn; 212/360–2774 Manhattan ; 718/699–4204 Queens; and 718/667–6042 Staten Island).

bronx

2 d-4
BRONX PARK
Laid out in the 1880s, this 718-acre park became the home of the city's major zoo and botanical garden in 1899 (see Botanical Gardens and Zoos, below). *Bronx Park E at Brady Ave., Bronxdale. www.wcs.org. Subway: 2, 5 to Bronx Park E.*

2 c-6
CROTONA PARK
Formerly the estate of the Bathgate family and known as Bathgate Woods, it was renamed after the ancient Greek city of Croton. Purchased by the city in 1888, the 128-acre park contains a bathhouse and pool dating back to the 1930s, plus five baseball diamonds, 12 playgrounds, and several basketball courts. The Crotona Park Nature Center, alongside the 3-acre Indian Lake, offers year-round programs. *Fulton Ave. at E. 175th St., Claremont Village, 718/378–2061. www.crotonapark.org. Subway: 2, 5 to E. 174th St.*

2 g-2
PELHAM BAY PARK
This 2,117-acre park is one of the city's most versatile. It was named after Englishman Thomas Pell, who bought land in the area in 1654. Fish, egrets, frogs, raccoons, owls, fox, ospreys, and even seals share the land with New Yorkers. Habitats of the last group include tennis courts, baseball diamonds, a track, a playground, golf courses, and a stable. Some relics of the past include the Bartow-Pell Mansion. Orchard Beach, a crescent-shape Robert Moses creation, is one highlight. Southeast of here, Rodman's Neck is a meadow-and-scrub area where the NYPD practices shooting. The Thomas Pell Wildlife Refuge and Sanctuary, established in 1967, contains wetlands and woodlands. Split Rock, a massive glacier-split boulder, is where poet Anne Hutchinson died in 1643 at the hands of the Siwanoy Indians. Hunter Island is a coastal area full of tidal wetlands and the park's largest continuous forest. The 6-mi Siwanoy Trail runs through the entire park. *Bruckner Blvd. and Middletown Rd., Pelham Bay, 718/430–1890. Subway: 6 to Pelham Bay Park.*

2 b-2
VAN CORTLANDT PARK
Despite the intrusion of various parkways, this park's 1,000-plus acres of wetlands and woodlands are home to a remarkable variety of critters. The Parade Ground is the most popular area for people, featuring several fields and the Van Cortlandt House, the oldest building in the Bronx. The Van Cortlandt family burial, Vault Hill, has fine views from its perch 169 ft above sea level. Tibbets Brook flows through marshy areas into the 13-acre Van Cortlandt Lake. Hikers have plenty of options: the 1.7-mi John Muir Nature Trail runs alongside the lake, the Aqueduct Trail follows the route of the Croton Aqueduct, and the Cass Gallagher Nature Trail winds its way

---

OUTDOORS ONLINE

Many of the organizations and parks listed here tell their stories on the Web. Here are some URLs for rainy-day exploration.

Brooklyn Botanic Garden
   www.bbg.org

Central Park Conservancy
   www.centralpark.org

City of New York Parks and Recreation
   www.nyc.gov/parks

Hudson River Park Trust
   www.hudsonriverpark.org

New York Botanical Garden
   www.nybg.org

New York Roadrunners Club
   www.nyrrc.org

New York Sports On Line
   www.nysol.com

Prospect Park Alliance
   www.prospectpark.org

Transportation Alternatives
   www.tires-up.org

Wildlife Conservation Society
   www.wcs.org

through the Northwest Forest. Summer brings New York Philharmonic concerts and many other events. *W. 242nd St. to city line, between Broadway and Jerome Ave., Riverdale, 718/430–1890. www. vancortlandt.org. Subway: 1 to 242nd St./Van Cortlandt Park.*

brooklyn

4 *d-6*

DYKER BEACH PARK

This 217-acre park, adjacent to the Fort Hamilton Military Reservation, is one of the oldest parks in Brooklyn, and has beautiful views of Gravesend Bay and the Verrazano Narrows Bridge. Fine expanses of lawn, sea breezes, and good fishing make it a relaxing place to spend a few hours. *Shore Pkwy., east of the Verrazano Narrows Bridge, Fort Hamilton. Subway: M, W to 18th Ave.*

12 *b-1*

EMPIRE FULTON FERRY STATE PARK

New York City needs more parks like this one—a grassy area right on the waterfront. The views of Manhattan from between the Manhattan and Brooklyn bridges are spectacular, especially at sunset, the breezes keep summer sunbathers cool, and the out-of-the-way location means it's terribly underappreciated. *Plymouth St. at Main St., Brooklyn Heights. Subway: F to York St.; A, C, E to High St./Brooklyn Bridge.*

12 *e-2*

FORT GREENE PARK

The site of Fort Putnam during the Revolutionary War and Fort Greene during the War of 1812, this 30-acre hill was turned into Brooklyn's first major park by Olmsted and Vaux in 1848. (Then called Washington Park, it was renamed in 1897.) Pretty paths meander up and down the park's hills, past tennis courts, playgrounds, and harbor views. In the center stands the Prison Ship Martyrs' Monument, designed in 1908 by architect Stanford White. *Myrtle to DeKalb Aves.; St. Edward to Washington Park Ave. Subway: 1, 2, 4, 5, Q to Atlantic Ave.*

1 *f-7*

MARINE PARK

This 1,024-acre expanse borders Gateway National Recreation Area and includes several scenic coves as well as trails, fields, a golf course, and the Salt Marsh Nature Center. *Inlet between Gerritsen and Flatbush Aves., inland to Fillmore Ave., between Burnet and E. 32nd Sts., 718/421–2021 nature center.*

1 *h-6*

PROSPECT PARK

Frederick Law Olmsted and Calvert Vaux's ode to Brooklyn covers 526 acres, and its designers liked it better than Central Park. Though Brooklynites first planned to have their park designed around Flatbush Avenue by Egbert Viele, chief engineer of Central Park, the Civil War gave them time to reconsider. In an act that would surely be criticized today as a bureaucratic delay tactic, the park commissioners had Vaux reexamine the proposal. He quickly realized that a highway bisecting a park would greatly detract from the greenery, and instead suggested a layout west of Flatbush Avenue. Starting in 1865, he and Olmsted designed the park's broad meadows, gardens, terraces, and landscaped walks.

Like many large city parks, this one has endless recreational possibilities. Joggers and people on wheels seem to circle the loop road endlessly, yet other paths through woods and fields are barely touched. Boats float around in summer near where skaters spin in winter. The playgrounds are alive with children's squeals, the fields with barbecues and ball games (including cricket matches). Prospect Park's roadways are closed to motor vehicles the same hours as Central Park's.

The main entrance to the park is Grand Army Plaza, planned in the spirit of Paris's L'Etoile (a.k.a. Place Charles-de-Gaulle, home of the Arc de Triomphe). The neo-Roman Soldiers and Sailors Memorial Arch is a memorial to the Union Army (open to climbers mid-May–early July weekends and holidays 1–5). This grandiose structure and most of the other entrance gates were added after Olmsted and Vaux had finished their work, much to their chagrin. Just inside the park, along the footpath to the east of the roadway, Endale Arch beautifully frames your view of Long Meadow, whose crescent shape makes its 90 acres seem even bigger. Frisbee, volleyball, soccer, and lounging are popular on this luxurious expanse; it's also the site of summer Philharmonic concerts. Other concert venues are the Bandshell at 9th Street, which hosts "Celebrate Brooklyn" festivities of all kinds, and the Music Pagoda, designed to resemble a traditional Chinese gateway (just north of Lullwater, a kind of feeder to Prospect Lake). Between Long Meadow and Flatbush Avenue toward the northern end of the park, the Vale of Cashmere is a natural amphitheater and a refuge for small birds. The Prospect Park Zoo, Lefferts Homestead Children's Museum, and the restored 1912 Carousel (weekends and holidays noon–5, additional hours and days in summer) comprise the most child-friendly section of the park, right off Flatbush Avenue. Prospect Park Alliance offices are in Litchfield Villa (95 Prospect Park W, near 3rd St.). Woods, rocky hills, and a small stream distinguish the Ravine, the rugged central area, which was restored in 1998 and 1999 to its entrancing rustic state. The 60-acre Prospect Lake is the main body of water in the park; its water is delivered through a complicated plumbing and water-recycling system. Vaux's Terrace Bridge, added in 1890, gives a good view of the lake and Lullwater. You can rent boats from Kate's Corner at the Wollman Ice Skating Rink, which is at the northern end of the lake, and cruise past the breathtaking Italian-style Boathouse on Lullwater (unfortunately now closed to the public because of water damage to its terra-cotta facade), which stands practically in the shadow of the wonderfully gnarled Camperdown Elm. *Bordered by Flatbush Ave., Ocean Ave., Parkside Ave., Prospect Park SW, and Prospect Park W, Prospect Heights, 718/965-8999. Subway: 1, 2 to Grand Army Plaza; Q local/express to Prospect Park; F to 15th St./Prospect Park.*

manhattan

10 *e-8*

BATTERY PARK

Jutting out as if it were Manhattan's green toe, this verdant landfill is loaded with monuments and sculpture. Because it's at the junction of the Hudson and East rivers, it has a great view of New York Harbor: Governors Island, Brooklyn, the Verrazano Narrows Bridge, Staten Island, the Statue of Liberty, Ellis Island, and New Jersey. The park's name refers to a line of cannons once mounted here to defend the shoreline, which ran along what is currently State Street. Castle Clinton, first known as the West Battery, was erected offshore on a pile of rock for the War of 1812 (nary a shot was ever fired). Landfill later joined

it to the mainland, and it has since served as an entertainment and concert facility (Castle Garden), a federal immigration center, and the New York City Aquarium. Robert Moses tried to knock it down after forcing the aquarium out in the early 1940s—claiming that its 8-ft-thick walls weren't stable—but he lost that battle. Now slated for yet another renovation, Castle Clinton sits squarely in Battery Park and is home to the ticket booth for the Statue of Liberty and Ellis Island ferries. Greenery, sea breezes, and great vistas draw mainly bankers and brokers at noon on sunny days, but tourists come to catch the ferries no matter what the weather. *State St. and Battery Pl., Lower Manhattan, 212/344-3491. Subway: 4, 5 to Bowling Green.*

10 *c-6*

BATTERY PARK ESPLANADE

This 1.2-mi linear park, running along the perimeter of Battery Park City, is one of the city's newest and best. Old-fashioned lampposts, shade trees, well-maintained lawns, and benches facing unimpeded Hudson River views make this an inviting spot. *Enter at Battery Pl., 212/267-9700 Battery Park City Parks Corporation. Subway: 1, 2, 4, 5 to Wall St.*

10 *e-8*

BOWLING GREEN

Rented out to local residents for the outrageous price of one peppercorn a year starting in 1733, this park was not fully available to everyone until 1850, but it's still the city's oldest extant public park. The British erected its simple iron fence in 1771 to protect a statue of George III, but on July 9, 1776 the statue was toppled. The fence still stands, dwarfed by surrounding office buildings. *Broadway and Battery Pl., Lower Manhattan. Subway: 4, 5 to Bowling Green.*

9 *d-5*

BRYANT PARK

In 1823, these nine acres were set aside as a potters' field, but they became a public park (called Reservoir Square, after the drinking-water reservoir that lay where the library is now) in 1847. New York's version of London's Crystal Palace was erected here in 1853, but it burned down five years later. The land was renamed for poet and editor William Cullen Bryant in 1884. It degenerated into a good place to buy and sell drugs in the 1970s, but, having been

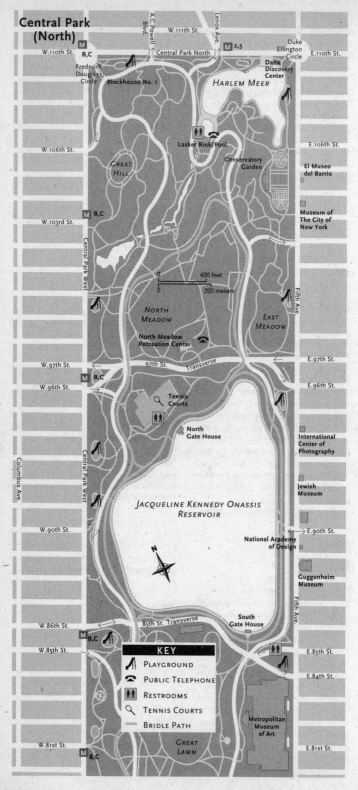

Central Park (North)

W.110th St.
B,C
W.111th St.
A.C. Powell Blvd.
Central Park North
Lenox Ave.
M 2,3
Duke Ellington Circle
E.110th St.

Frederick Douglass Circle
Blockhouse No. 1
Dana Discovery Center
HARLEM MEER

Lasker Rink/Pool

GREAT HILL

Conservatory Garden

El Museo del Barrio

W.106th St.
E.106th St.

Museum of The City of New York

W.103rd St.
B,C

0 600 feet
0 200 meters

NORTH MEADOW

EAST MEADOW

Fifth Ave.

North Meadow Recreation Center

97th St. Transverse
W.97th St.
E.97th St.

W.96th St.
B,C
E.96th St.

Tennis Courts

North Gate House

International Center of Photography

Jewish Museum

JACQUELINE KENNEDY ONASSIS RESERVOIR

W.90th St.
E.90th St.

National Academy of Design

N

Guggenheim Museum

Columbus Ave.
Central Park West
Fifth Ave.

85th St. Transverse
W.86th St.
B,C
South Gate House

W.85th St.
E.85th St.

E.84th St.

KEY
🧗 PLAYGROUND
☎ PUBLIC TELEPHONE
🚻 RESTROOMS
🔍 TENNIS COURTS
— BRIDLE PATH

Metropolitan Museum of Art

W.81st St.
B,C
GREAT LAWN
E.81st St.

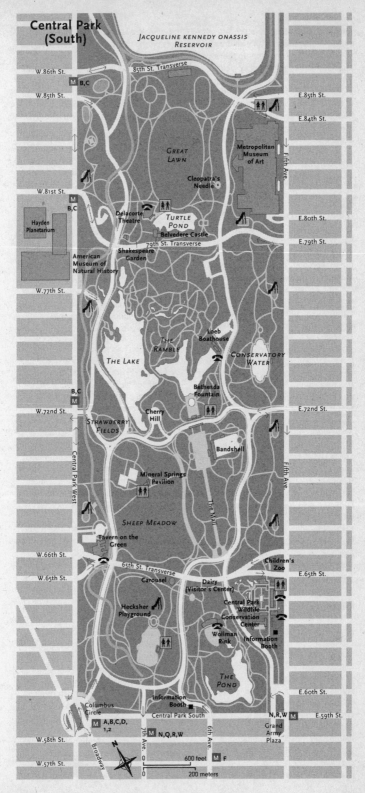

Central Park (South)

JACQUELINE KENNEDY ONASSIS RESERVOIR

W. 86th St.

Ⓜ B,C

85th St. Transverse

W. 85th St.

E. 85th St.

👫

E. 84th St.

GREAT LAWN

Metropolitan Museum of Art

Cleopatra's Needle

W. 81st St.

Ⓜ B,C

Fifth Ave.

Hayden Planetarium

Delacorte Theatre

👫

TURTLE POND

E. 80th St.

Belvedere Castle

E. 79th St.

79th St. Transverse

American Museum of Natural History

Shakespeare Garden

W. 77th St.

Loeb Boathouse

THE RAMBLE

CONSERVATORY WATER

THE LAKE

Bethesda Fountain

B,C

Ⓜ

W. 72nd St.

Cherry Hill

👫

E. 72nd St.

STRAWBERRY FIELDS

Bandshell

Mineral Springs Pavilion

👫

Fifth Ave.

Central Park West

SHEEP MEADOW

The Mall

Tavern on the Green

W. 66th St.

Children's Zoo

65th St. Transverse

E. 65th St.

W. 65th St.

Carousel

Dairy (Visitor's Center)

👫

Hecksher Playground

Central Park Wildlife Conservation Center

Wollman Rink

Information Booth

👫

THE POND

E. 60th St.

Information Booth

Columbus Circle

Central Park South

N,R,W

Ⓜ

E. 59th St.

Ⓜ A,B,C,D, 1,2

Grand Army Plaza

W. 58th St.

7th Ave.

Ⓜ N,Q,R,W

6th Ave.

N

0   600 feet

Ⓜ F

W. 57th St.

Broadway

0   200 meters

renovated and restored in the late 1980s, it now teems with well-dressed professionals who snatch up the lawn chairs for their brown-bag power lunches. Weekday and evening concerts, an outdoor movie festival (Monday night in summer), and daily chess and backgammon games help keep it hopping. *6th Ave. between 40th and 42nd Sts., behind New York Public Library Center for the Humanities, Midtown West, 212/768–4242. Subway: B, D, F, V to 42nd St.; 7 to 5th Ave.*

7 g-7

CARL SCHURZ PARK

During the American Revolution, a house on this promontory was used as a fortification by the Continental Army, then taken over as a British outpost. Later, in more peaceful times, the land became known as East End Park. It was renamed in 1911 to honor Carl Schurz, a prominent 19th-century German immigrant who had been a senator and secretary of the interior. A curved stone staircase leads up to John Finley Walk, lined with wrought-iron railings, which overlooks the East River. The view—of the Triborough, Hell's Gate, and Queensboro bridges; Wards, Randalls, and Roosevelt islands; and Astoria, Queens—is so tranquil that you'd never guess you're directly above the FDR Drive. Behind you, along the walk, are raised flower beds as well as some enclosed dog runs. Other popular hangouts are the hill at the north end (for sledding in winter and sunning in summer) and the playground. The city's first family—the mayor's—lives behind the high fence in Gracie Mansion, at the north end of the park. *East End Ave. to East River, between 84th and 90th Sts., Upper East Side. Subway: 4, 5, 6 to 86th St.*

1 d-4

CENTRAL PARK

America's premier urban park, this 843-acre oasis is 2½ mi long, ¾ mi wide, and smack in the middle of Manhattan. Every day, thousands of joggers, cyclists, skaters, and walkers make their daily jaunts about "the loop," the reservoir, and the rest of the park. Sunseekers crowd the grassy lawns in summer, and athletes of all stripes make use of the fields, trails, courts, and other facilities year-round. In fall, the foliage is magnificent and the air is crisp. Ice-skaters come out for the rinks and frozen lakes in win-

ter, while cross-country skiers and sledders hit the fields and trails. In spring, blooming flowers turn the park into a scented wonderland. Summer especially sees a crowded calendar of concerts, readings, and theater and opera performances. All told, some 20 million users take advantage of the park each year.

Although it appears to be nothing more than a swatch of rolling countryside excused from urban development, Central Park is an artificial landscape. Park superintendent Frederick Law Olmsted and landscape architect Calvert Vaux's "Greensward Plan"—part formal, part pastoral, part picturesque—skillfully blends man-made lakes and ponds, hills and dales, secluded glens, wide meadows, a bird sanctuary, bridle paths, and nature trails. Four transverse roads carry crosstown traffic beneath the park's hills and tunnels without disturbing those at play, and 40 bridges, each with a unique design and name, give people easy access to various areas.

Construction was a monumental task. Entire communities were displaced, swamps were drained, millions of cubic yards of soil were removed, walls of schist were blasted, and hundreds of thousands of trees and shrubs were planted. Almost a century and a half later, we can see ongoing construction, restoration, and maintenance. During the 1990s alone, the Turtle Pond was enlarged, the Great Lawn was completely reseeded and revamped, and entrance gates remodeled. The two-year restoration of the North Meadow's 28 acres was completed in the spring of 2000, providing 12 baseball and softball fields which host some 6,000 games each season. The landscape around the reservoir, including the jogging and bridle paths, and the 59th Street Pond will receive an 18-month, $4-million renovation beginning in the fall of 2001. (The area will remain open during the rehabilitation.)

Those who wish to stroll unharassed by traffic should bear in mind that the circular drive through the park is closed to auto traffic on weekdays 10 AM–3 PM (except the southeastern portion of the road, below 72nd Street, which remains open) and 7 PM–10 PM, and on weekends and holidays. Even without cars, traffic on the road is often heavy with joggers, cyclists, and roller bladers, and sometimes fast-moving, so always be careful when you're crossing the road, and stay toward the inside when you're walking. Tip: The first two digits of the number plate of each lamppost in the park indicate the nearest cross street.

For the classic old-fashioned indulgence, you can glide gently through the park on a horse-drawn carriage (operated by Chateau Stables, 212/246–0520, or Hansom Cabs). It's the perfect way to amuse visiting relatives from out of town. Just walk up to any carriage along Central Park South, especially near 5th Avenue; the rates, which are reasonable, should be posted on each one. Only on extremely hot or cold days do the horses take a break.

Whole volumes have been filled by writers extolling Central Park and its landmarks. In the southeast corner, the Pond, dominated by Overlook Rock, is home to swans and ducks. Picturesque Gapstow Bridge gives you a good view of midtown and leads to Wollman Rink, a popular ice- and roller-skating rink. The Dairy (mid-park at 64th St., 212/794–6564, closed Mon.) is to the north, with its pointed eaves, steeple, and high-pitched roof; once a working dairy, it's now one of four park information centers (the others are at Belvedere Castle, the Dana Discovery Center, and North Meadow Recreation Center). In what was planned as a Children's District is an antique-horse Carousel; the zoo is to the east. The expansive field in the southern section of the park is Sheep Meadow, once frequented by sheep but now a favorite of picnickers and sunbathers. The sheep who did graze here lived in what is now the lavishly decorated Tavern on the Green restaurant. East of Sheep Meadow is the Mall, a formal promenade lined by elms and statues of literary figures in a section called the Literary Walk. At the north end of the Mall, across the 72nd Street transverse, are Bethesda Terrace and Bethesda Fountain, the latter built in 1863. Willows, rhododendrons, and cherry trees surround the magnificent staircase. If you continue west on 72nd Street you'll come to Strawberry Fields, 2½ landscaped acres that form an "International Peace Garden" in memory of John Lennon. Follow the water northwest from Bethesda Terrace and you'll cross Bow Bridge into The Ramble, a heavily wooded, wild 37-acre area laced with twisting, climbing paths. This is prime bird-watching territory (remember, this is the largest patch of green in Manhattan, and along the Atlantic Fly-

way migration route). The neo-Victorian Loeb Boathouse, on the lake, has boats and bikes for rent and a chichi waterside café. On the east side of the park at 74th Street is Conservatory Water (commonly known as the Model Boat Pond), a symmetrical stone basin where model yachts race Saturday morning near statues of the fanciful Hans Christian Andersen and *Alice in Wonderland*. Midpark at 79th Street, Belvedere Castle towers above the Turtle Pond and the outdoor Delacorte Theater, where the Public Theater stages plays in the summer. On the castle's ground floor, the Henry Luce Nature Observatory (212/772–0210, closed Mon.) has nature exhibits, children's workshops, and educational programs. To its west is the dark-wood Swedish Chalet, a marionette theater. Behind all this are Turtle Pond and the Great Lawn, 13 acres of Kentucky bluegrass, ball fields, and courts. Between the Great Lawn and the Metropolitan Museum of Art, which encroaches on park territory, stands Cleopatra's Needle, an Egyptian obelisk given to the city in 1881. The Jacqueline Kennedy Onassis Reservoir (midpark, 85th–96th Sts.) is a 106-acre lake that is *not* used for drinking water—thus the ceaseless rumors that it might be drained. The path around it is usually overrun with joggers. Further north, at 105th Street, the formal Conservatory Garden presides over Fifth Avenue. Harlem Meer is another striking body of water—the adjacent Charles A. Dana Discovery Center (212/860–1370, closed Mon.) runs many family nature programs. *Bordered by Central Park W, 59th St., 5th Ave., and 110th St., Upper West Side/Upper East Side, 212/310–6600 general information. Subway: A, B, C, D, 1, 2 to 59th St./Columbus Circle; N, R to 5th Ave.; B, C to 72nd–110th Sts.*

10 *e-6*

CITY HALL PARK

Known in Colonial times as the Fields or the Common, this green spot has hosted hangings, riots, and demonstrations. Now as City Hall's front yard, it's full of concrete barricades and parked police cars. Restored lampposts and a fountain from 1871 give the site a 19th-century feel, though critics of these restorations have drawn attention to certain changes, like gate houses and high iron fences, that are designed to restrict access to City Hall, which overlooks the park. *Between Broadway, Park*

Row, and Chambers St., Lower Manhattan. Subway: 4, 5, 6 to Brooklyn Bridge/City Hall.

3 *c-1*

EAST RIVER ESPLANADE

You have to stretch your imagination to call this a park, but any long stretch of water with pedestrian access bears mentioning. This one starts near the heliport at East 59th Street—to reach the promenade, take the funky pedestrian suspension bridge at 60th Street. The paved strip, lined by benches, patches of grass, and the occasional small tree, continues to a staircase at 80th Street. Up the steps is the lovely Carl Schurz Park, and the esplanade continues past Gracie Mansion all the way to 125th Street. There's usually a crew of fishermen near 100th Street, but most other people on the path remain in motion. *East River from 59th St. to 125th St., Upper East Side/East Harlem. Subway: 4, 5, 6 to 59th St.–125th Sts.*

10 *h-2*

EAST RIVER PARK

This park is wider and greener than its newer cousin on the Hudson, but it doesn't draw half as many people. The facilities—tennis courts, a track, fields, a playground, basketball courts—aren't all in the best condition, but that's no reason to stay away. Plans have been laid to renovate the decrepit theater—the original home of the Public Theatre's "Shakespeare in the Park"—but so far nothing has happened. Keep your fingers crossed. *East River Dr. between 14th and Delancey Sts., East Village/Lower East Side. Subway: F to Delancey St.*

5 *b-7*

FORT TRYON PARK

Named after New York's last English governor, William Tryon, Fort Tryon Park occupies the site of Fort Washington, the last holdout against the British invasion of Manhattan (it fell November 16, 1776). Capping a hill 250 ft above the river, these 66 acres of densely wooded hills and dales overlooking the Hudson were a gift to the city from the Rockefeller family. The beautiful flower gardens and terracing, and the view of the Palisades across the Hudson to New Jersey, make you feel miles away from the city. The Cloisters museum is in the middle of the park and dominates the park's skyline. *Between Riverside Dr. and*

Broadway from 192nd to Dyckman Sts., Inwood, 212/795–1388. Subway: A to 190th or 200th/Dyckman St.

9 *e-8*

GRAMERCY PARK

This tiny patch of land, originally swamp, is New York's only surviving private square. It was bought and drained by early real-estate developer Samuel B. Ruggles, who then created a park (in 1831) for the exclusive use of those who would buy the surrounding lots. Sixty-six of the city's fashionable elite did just that, and no less than golden keys were provided for them to enter the park's 8-ft-high fence. Although no longer golden, keys are still given to residents only. The rest of us can only gaze through the Victorian wrought iron at the pristine park and the landmark 19th-century row houses that surround it; still, the pretty square is refreshing to look at. *Lexington Ave. between 20th and 21st Sts., Gramercy. Subway: 6, N, R to 23rd St.*

6 *d-3*

HIGH BRIDGE

The forested terraces and rocky ledges surround High Bridge, which was built as Aqueduct Bridge between 1837 and 1848 to carry upstate reservoir water to the city; the landmark Water Tower on the Manhattan side was also once in use. It is the oldest remaining bridge connecting Manhattan to the mainland and has good views across the Harlem River. *Between Harlem River Dr. and Edgecombe and Amsterdam Aves., from 155th to Dyckman Sts., Washington Heights/Inwood. Subway: B, C to 155th St. or 163rd St.*

1 *c-5*

HUDSON RIVER PARK

This stretch of waterfront property has been growing for a decade like a patchwork quilt, with pieces added and opened in no discernible pattern, until it emerged as a wondrous, linked corridor from 59th Street all the way down the West Side. A wide ribbon of concrete has marked lanes for walking, cycling, and blading; nine public piers offer everything from boating to volleyball. The park is popular with families, bladers, and Village people, convening at all hours to attest to how sorely New Yorkers need more waterfront space. The southern end of the park, now called Nelson A. Rockefeller Park, has

expansive green lawns and the lilliputian, cast-bronze "Real World" sculptures
by artist Tom Otterness. (Youngsters
love these; you can climb on them and
play in the water that surrounds some of
them.) Pier 25 at North Moore Street (a
few blocks north of Chambers Street)
has summertime activities for children,
including fishing, games, and environmental education, plus outdoor films,
live bands for swing and salsa dancing,
and a miniature golf course. One block
north, Pier 26 offers kayaking. Pier 34, at
Canal Street, houses the historic Holland Tunnel Vent shaft and, now, an art
installation. Pier 40, at Houston Street,
has soccer fields, batting cages, and a
climbing wall. Pier 62, at 23rd Street,
has roller rinks, gardens, and historic
vessels. Pier 84, at West 44th Street, is
mostly open space for picnics. Piers 45
(Christopher St.) and 54 (13th St.) also
allow public access. The Hudson River
Park Trust, the group working to realize
the park, sponsors activities such as
outdoor movies, regattas, and even
swims. *Battery Park to 59th St. along the
Hudson River, 212/533–PARK for event
information. Subway: 1, 2 to Canal–14th
Sts.; A, C, E to 14th St.; L to 8th Ave.*

5 *b-5*
INWOOD HILL PARK
The Hudson and Harlem rivers meet at
the tip of this unbelievably quiet, scenic
park. Its 196 acres of hill-climbing
woods are laced with hidden paths and
contain Manhattan's only remaining
natural forest. Its history is rich, too:
Algonquin Indians once dwelled in
caves on this site, and British and Hessian troops were quartered here during
the American Revolution, while their
officers were camped nearby in the
Dyckman family house, the last Dutch
farmhouse still standing in Manhattan.
A plaque at the northernmost tip of the
park commemorates the spot where
Peter Minuet is believed to have purchased the island for $24 in trinkets.
There is a new nature center operated
by the Urban Park Rangers and kayaking. *Dyckman St. to the Harlem River,
from Seaman to Payson Aves., Inwood,
212/304–2365. Subway: A to Dyckman
St./200th St. or 207th St./Inwood.*

7 *h-7*
LIGHTHOUSE PARK
This lovely green area has views you'd
otherwise need a boat to admire. Manhattan's Upper East Side and Ward's
Island, Queens's Long Island City and
Astoria, as well as a few bridges, are all
visible from water level. It's named for
the 50-ft stone lighthouse, vintage 1872,
that used to help sailors navigate the
East River. *Northern tip of Roosevelt
Island. Subway: F to Roosevelt Island.*

9 *e-7*
MADISON SQUARE PARK
At various times in its history this area
was a potter's field, the site of the city's
first baseball games (1845), a luxurious
residential area, and the location of the
original Madison Square Garden. Now
there are small flower plantings and
several splendid sculptures here,
including a statue of Alaska buyer
William H. Seward. The park is popular
nowadays with office workers and dog
owners. *23rd–26th Sts. between 5th and
Madison Aves., Murray Hill. Subway: 6,
N, R to 23rd St.*

7 *d-2*
MARCUS GARVEY PARK
As the city pushed northward, it didn't
want Harlem to be without a park, so it
built one around this 70-ft-high rocky
eminence in the middle of 5th Avenue.
From the street on the park's southern
side, you can see the three-tier, cast-iron
fire tower (1856), the only remaining
tower in a now-defunct citywide network. First called Mt. Morris Park, it was
renamed in 1973 after Marcus Garvey,
who led the back-to-Africa movement.
*120th–124th Sts. at 5th Ave., Harlem.
Subway: 2, 3 to 125th St.*

7 *b-2*
MORNINGSIDE PARK
This relatively small 1887 Olmsted and
Vaux gem in Morningside Heights follows the crest of the cliffs above Harlem,
pressing up to the gothic architecture of
the City University campus. *110th–123rd
Sts. from Morningside Dr. to Manhattan
and Morningside Aves., Morningside
Heights. Subway: B, C to 110th–125th Sts.*

9 *d-3*
PALEY PARK
A boon to midtown's weary, this memorial to former CBS executive William S.
Paley is remarkable not so much for its
features but for its historical status as
one of the first of New York's "vest-
pocket parks" to be inserted into the
concrete canyons. A recycling waterfall
blocks out traffic noise, and feathery

honey-locust trees provide shade. The snack bar opens in warm weather. *3 E. 53rd St. (between 5th and Madison Aves.), Midtown East. Subway: E, V to 5th Ave./53rd St.*

1 *d-3*

RANDALL'S & WARDS ISLAND PARKS

Formerly separate pieces of land, these East River islands have been joined by landfill and are undergoing a major renovation to turn the space into a state-of-the-art athletic and recreational destination. The decaying Downing Stadium, on Randall's Island, is being replaced with a complex of soccer fields, a new Olympic-size track and field center, and a family water park, the city's first. A new 19,500-seat amphitheater will be mainly for concerts and community events; all is scheduled to open in early 2003. Currently, both islands have parklands and playing fields used by many community groups; and quiet roads are great for running, skating, and biking. East Harlemites cross the footbridge at 104th Street; a new footbridge from the Bronx and ferry service from Manhattan are in the works. *Junction of East and Harlem rivers. Enter via Triborough Bridge or footbridge from East River Esplanade, 104th St. Subway: 6 to 103rd St.*

1 *c-3*

RIVERSIDE PARK

In the tradition of English landscaping, Frederick Law Olmsted met the challenge of this sloping terrain to provide a 300-acre playground for Upper West Siders along and above the Hudson River. Its various promenades make for usually uncrowded walking, especially beautiful in spring when crab apple and cherry trees are in bloom; there's a flower garden, planted and pruned by volunteers, at 90th Street. The 79th Street Boat Basin, home for those who live in its flotilla of houseboats, has a 110-slip public marina. The Rotunda, behind it, occupies a wonderful circular space punctuated by a fountain. The park holds several important monuments, including the Soldiers' and Sailors' Memorial and Grant's Tomb. The Eleanor Roosevelt statue, at the 72nd Street entrance, is a recent addition. A section officially called Riverside Park South extends from 72nd to 59th streets, where it marries up with Hudson River Park. This portion retains the industrial flavor of the railroad yard once

situated on its grounds, with paths that evoke the old tracks. There are handball and basketball courts, a soccer field, and quiet landscaped walkways. Most spectacular is the 715-ft-long pier at 64th Street with nothing on it but benches and views that, on a clear day, let you see forever, or at least as far south as the Statue of Liberty. *72nd–159th Sts. between Riverside Dr. and the Hudson River, Upper West Side. Subway: 1, 2 to 72nd St.–157th St.*

6 *b-7*

RIVERBANK STATE PARK

This unlikely 28-acre park opened in 1993 atop a sewage treatment plant. Elevated as high as 69 ft above the Hudson, it's not at all marred by its neighbor below, and its facilities—including indoor and outdoor pools, an outdoor track, a skating rink, numerous playing fields, and a playground—are state-of-the-art and popular with neighborhood residents. Just being cooled by the breeze and admiring the view is rewarding, too. *Entrances: Riverside Dr. at 138th and 145th Sts., Harlem, 212/694–3600. Subway: 1 to 137th St./City College or 145th St.*

7 *b-3*

ST. NICHOLAS PARK

Like Morningside Park, this thin green strip climbs a steep hill and backs up to a college—in this case, City College. Its designer, Frederick Law Olmsted, feared that its narrowness and difficult terrain would make it unsafe, and he was right. The playgrounds and courts that edge the park see a lot of use, but the interior is desolate and poorly maintained. If the National Park Service moves Hamilton Grange (*see* Chapter 4) here from its location just around the corner, per the rumors, the park might get some needed help. *128th–141st Sts. between St. Nicholas Ave. and St. Nicholas Terr., Harlem. Subway: B, C to 135th St.*

10 *f-1*

STUYVESANT SQUARE PARK

This historic square, now full of flower plantings, was once part of Peter Stuyvesant's farm but was ceded to the city in 1836 by his great-great-grandson. It comprised the core of fashionable New York in the late 19th century. *2nd Ave. from 15th St. to 17th St., Gramercy. Subway: 4, 5, 6 to 14th St./Union Sq.*

10 g-2

TOMPKINS SQUARE PARK

Named after one-time New York State Governor Daniel P. Tompkins, this 16-acre park is thriving again after years of decay. The oldest park on the Lower East Side, its post-1960s troubles have included violent clashes between city officials and the park's permanent residents, and its reputation as a drug center. The neighborhood has since been gentrified with art galleries and trendy shops, and none of those who now use it for basketball, dog walking, and relaxing seems to care or remember. *7th–10th Sts. between Aves. A and B, East Village. Subway: 6 to Astor Pl.; L to 1st Ave.*

10 e-1

UNION SQUARE PARK

Though its name comes from its function as a transportation nexus, the square has been the site of many union protests, and several radical groups once had their headquarters nearby. At the time—in the late 19th century—the surrounding neighborhood was a commercial area, with fine shops such as Tiffany's, but by World War I it had turned shabby. The park was refurbished in the 1980s and now has a colorful Greenmarket at its western and northern edges every Monday, Wednesday, Friday, and Saturday, not to mention manicured lawns, flower beds, and its own café. *14th–17th Sts. between Broadway and Park Ave. S, Flatiron District. Subway: 4, 5, 6, L, N, R to 14th St./Union Sq.*

9 g-5

UNITED NATIONS

Adjacent to the UN headquarters are lovely lawns and trees, full of energetic squirrels, and a small formal rose garden, all overlooking the East River. *Main public entrance: 1st Ave. at 46th St., Midtown East. Open weekdays 9 AM–4:45 PM, weekends 9:15–4:45. Subway: 4, 5, 6, 7 to 42nd St./Grand Central.*

11 g-8

WASHINGTON MARKET PARK

This former vacant lot has been turned into a delightful 1½-acre park with a Victorian gazebo and an adventure playground. *Greenwich St. between Chambers and Duane Sts., TriBeCa. Subway: 1; 2 to Chambers St.*

11 d-2

WASHINGTON SQUARE PARK

Once a marshy area favored by duck hunters, then a potters' field, then the site of hanging gallows, this square became a public park in 1828 and the centerpiece for a fashionable residential area shortly thereafter (Edith Wharton and Henry James lived in the row of Greek Revival houses on Washington Square North). At the park's center is its landmark arch, designed by Stanford White in 1892. Though it sometimes feels like NYU is trying to claim the park as its front yard, Washington Square is the emotional, if not geographical, heart of Greenwich Village. Park goers include playground-happy children, chess players, Frisbee throwers, skilled skaters, dog walkers, guitar strummers, folk singers, and magicians. *W. 4th St.–Waverly Pl. (at the foot of 5th Ave.) between MacDougal St. and University Pl., Greenwich Village. Subway: A, B, C, D, E, F, V to W. 4th St.*

queens

1 g-3

ALLEY POND PARK

Alley Pond was named after a row of 18th-century commercial buildings, including a gristmill and a general store. The buildings and the pond are long gone (the latter disappeared when the Long Island Expressway was built), but the parkland retains the name—and its 655 acres of highlands, ponds, marshes, creeks, trees, and an amazing array of wildlife, including rabbits, muskrats, and opossums. Bisected by the LIE, it has meadowlands to the north and woodlands to the south. Pitobik Trail is a 2-mi walk through a former Mattinecock Indian camp, and Turtle Pond Trail takes you through dense vegetation past glacial kettles. The Alley Pond Nature Center (228–06 Northern Blvd., 718/229–4000) has live animals, offers trail walks, and hosts lively children's programs on weekends (registration required). There are several tennis courts (permit required). *Grand Central Pkwy. at Winchester Blvd., Bayside.*

3 d-2

ASTORIA PARK

This waterfront park, opened in 1913, provides great vistas of several bridges and Manhattan. Facilities include tennis courts and a large outdoor pool. *Hoyt Ave.–Ditmars Blvd. between 19th St. and the East River. Subway: N, W to Ditmars Blvd./Astoria.*

1 *g-3*

CUNNINGHAM PARK

This large park, seemingly an endless array of fields, courts, and picnic grounds strung together, is all over the Queens outdoor-event calendar. In the summer it hosts the New York Philharmonic, the Metropolitan Opera, and the Big Apple Circus. *193rd–210th Sts. between Long Island Expressway and Grand Central Pkwy., Fresh Meadows. Subway: E, F to Union Tpke./Kew Gardens, then Q46 bus to 193rd St.*

3 *h-2*

FLUSHING MEADOWS–CORONA PARK

Queens's largest park (1,257 acres) has a Cinderella history: Originally a swamp, then a garbage dump, the area was the site of the 1939–40 World's Fair, the meeting ground of the nascent United Nations 1946–50, and the host of another World's Fair in 1964–65. Structures we now know as the Queens Museum of Art, Shea Stadium, the United States Tennis Association (U.S.T.A.) National Tennis Center, the New York Hall of Science, the boathouse, and the World's Fair marina are all remnants of the world's fairs, as is the steel Unisphere, the symbol of the later one. Smaller remnants from the fairs, such as salt shakers, ties, pins, programs, silverware, and general kitsch are on display in the Queens Museum along with a history of the land. The park's wide range of activities means you're bound to find something to do. Families enjoy the Queens Wildlife Center and the Playground for All Children (718/699–8283), which was first in the country to include facilities for both able and disabled children. Athletes have overwhelming options—tennis, golf, swimming, boating, bicycling, ice-skating, and lots of playing fields, plus a new facility housing a ten-lane Olympic-size pool and an ice hockey rink that meets NHL standards, scheduled to open early in 2003. The Theater-in-the-Park (718/760–0064) hosts performances with particular appeal to immigrants from the surrounding neighborhoods. *Union Tpke. from 111th St. and Grand Central Pkwy. to the Van Wyck Extension, Flushing, 718/760–*

6565. *Subway: 7 to 111th St. or Willets Point/Shea Stadium.*

1 *f-5*

FOREST PARK

This 538-acre park is another Olmsted treasure. Its roads, trails, and dense forests are well traveled by hikers, bikers, and bird-watchers; other draws are a golf course, tennis courts, fields, a carousel, a model-airplane field, and a bandshell. *Union Ave. and Union Tpke. to Park La. S, between Park La. and Cypress Hill Cemetery, 718/235–0684. Subway: J, Z to Woodhaven Blvd.; E, F to Union Tpke./Kew Gardens.*

1 *f-3*

KISSENA PARK

This 235-acre park has tennis courts and a golf course tucked among its hills. More unusual is a grove of exotic trees, many of them Asian imports, planted in the 19th century by Parsons Nursery. *Nature Center: Rose Ave. and Parsons Blvd., Kissena, 718/217–6034. Subway: 7 to Main St./Flushing.*

staten island

4 *a-7*

CLOVE LAKES PARK

Bucolic pleasures at this popular and picturesque park, created by the damming of an ancient glacial valley, include a brook, waterfalls, a quartet of lakes, forests of oaks and beeches, and picnic grounds. The more active might enjoy ice-skating, horseback riding, football, softball, jogging, and fishing. *Clove Rd. near Victory Blvd., Sunnyside, 718/390–8000.*

1 *b-3*

EVERGREEN PARK

Rare ferns and orchids grow in the 22½ acres of Staten Island's newest park. *Greaves St. between Dewey Ave. and Evergreen St., Great Kills.*

1 *d-8*

FORT WADSWORTH

First used during the Revolutionary War, this military installation was an active part of the harbor defense system up until the 1970s. Because of its location just off the Verrazano-Narrows Bridge, it's tromped on by thousands of runners (and becomes the site of the world's longest urinal) at the start of the New York City Marathon. Now part of Gateway National Recreation Area and newly open to the public, the place has a 1½-mi self-guided trail around its fortifications. Other ranger-led tours can be reserved in advance. *Bay St. at Wadsworth Ave., Shore Acres, 718/354–4500. Open Sun.*

1 *b-2*

GREENBELT

One of New York's newer large parks (land acquisition began in 1964), Greenbelt is also one of the best. Designed by the last of the great glaciers, its nearly 2,000 contiguous acres comprise linked woodlands, meadows, ponds, wetlands, golf courses, and cemeteries, all forming a green ring in the center of Staten Island. The rambling woods, teeming with plant and animal wildlife, are all the more remarkable given the developed lands—including the Fresh Kills landfill—that border them. The park protects five kinds of owls, shelters the most northerly example of the sweetbay magnolia tree, is home to more than 50 species of birds, and grows such rare wildflowers as blue cohosh and Virginia waterleaf. Hikers have 28 mi of trails to cover, so it's a good idea to carry a map (available at the main office). Urban Park Rangers lead hikes, bird walks, and other nature activities. *Office: 200 Nevada Ave., Egbertville, 718/667–2165. Office open weekdays 9–4.*

1 *b-2*

HIGH ROCK PARK
IN THE GREENBELT

Bird-watching is especially good in this 86-acre section of peaceful woods and ponds teeming with wildlife. A visit to the environmental education center is on many schools' calendars, but it offers walks, talks, and exhibits to all. *200 Nevada Ave., Egbertville, 718/667–2165. Center open weekdays 9–4.*

1 *b-2*

LA TOURETTE PARK
IN THE GREENBELT

This 511-acre park features a beautiful golf course and clubhouse—once the farmland and mansion of the La Tourette family—as well as wooded and uninterrupted wetland trails popular with cross-country skiers in winter. The best trail is Buck's Hollow. *Forest Hill and Richmond Hill Rds., Richmondtown.*

1 *c-2*

MILLER FIELD

Like Fort Wadsworth, this is a former military base (U.S. Army) that's now part of Gateway National Recreation Area, and tours sometimes focus on its military history (it has two post–World War I hangars). It is Staten Island's host for summer opera and Philharmonic concerts. *Between New Dorp and Elmtree Sts., New Dorp, 718/351–6970.*

1 *d-8*

VON BRIESEN PARK

A small but meticulously groomed city park, Von Briesen somehow doesn't attract many people. Its elevated, harbor-front location provides a stunning panorama of lower Manhattan, the Upper and Lower New York bays, and Brooklyn. *Bay St. and Wadsworth Ave., Shore Acres.*

1 *a-2*

WILLOWBROOK PARK
IN THE GREENBELT

American soldiers called it the Great Swamp when they hid here during the Revolutionary War, but Willowbrook is now one of Staten Island's more popular parks. Picnic tables, a fishing lake, athletic fields, an archery range, horseshoe pitches, a playground, and a kite-flying area are spread throughout 164 acres. *Victory Blvd. and Richmond Ave., New Springville, 718/698–2186.*

other outdoor attractions

AMUSEMENT PARKS

4 *g-7*

ASTROLAND
AMUSEMENT PARK

Gone are the days when this stretch of Brooklyn's oceanfront was a premier summer vacation destination for all New Yorkers. The garish hotels and summer bungalows have been replaced by decaying private homes and public housing; the world-famous Luna Park, Dreamland, and Steeplechase amusement parks have either burned down or been torn down, and the towering Parachute

Jump ride stands abandoned and forlorn. Ah, but all is not lost—many amusements remain and continue to draw crowds. In Astroland, the Cyclone, granddaddy of roller coasters, with a wooden track and monumental dips and curves, is a perennial favorite, as are the Bumper Cars. There's also a plethora of try-your-luck carnival games, stomach-turners for the adventurous, and gentler rides for the kids. The wide sandy beach and the saltwater waves of Coney Island are just across the boardwalk. *1000 Surf Ave., Coney Island, 718/372–0275. Subway: F, Q, W to Stillwell Ave.*

BEACHES

Manhattan lacks a sandswept beach, but that doesn't stop anyone from sun-bathing—on rooftops ("tar beaches"), river piers ("splinter beaches"), and in parks ("Manhattan Rivieras"). The other boroughs, however, are blessed with miles and miles of beaches, all easily accessible by bus, subway, or car. City beaches are officially open from Memorial Day weekend to Labor Day, sunrise to sunset, with swimming allowed when lifeguards are on duty (usually 10 AM–6 PM).

bronx

2 *g-2*

ORCHARD BEACH
For sun, sand, and salsa, this section of Pelham Bay Park is the place. A white-sand, crescent-shape beauty on the Long Island Sound, Orchard Beach was one of Robert Moses's pride and joys. It draws crowds, largely from the Bronx's Latino population. If you want to hear the surf and have enough room to spread out a blanket, avoid weekends and holidays. *Shore Rd. and City Island Rd., Eastchester, 718/885–2275. $14.99 daily for multiple rides; individually owned rides are pay-as-you-go. Drinking water, grills, picnic tables, phones, rest rooms, showers, snack bar. Subway: 6 to Pelham Bay Park.*

brooklyn

4 *h-6*

BRIGHTON BEACH
Brighton Beach is actually the "beginning" of the beach that becomes Coney Island farther west. At this end you'll find locals: mothers with children, older retired folks, and Russians who have emigrated to this shore, commonly called "Little Odessa." The boardwalk has little but benches, so bring your lunch or buy it on your way, and enjoy it on relatively uncrowded sand. *15th St. to Ocean Pkwy., Brighton. Drinking water, phones. Subway: Q to Brighton Beach or Ocean Pkwy.*

4 *g-7*

CONEY ISLAND BEACH
Named for the rabbits that were once its main inhabitants (from the Dutch *Konijn Eiland*), Coney Island began its resort days in the 1830s, when elegant hotels drew the elite. Railroads were eventually built to connect it with other parts of Brooklyn, carting in people attracted to its increasing array of entertainment: horse races, sporting events, amuse-ment parks, and, of course, sun, sand, and surf. The first roller coaster opened in 1884, and by 1904 there were three amusement parks. It's now a mere shadow of its early 20th-century self, but Coney Island still has a fine 2½-mi sandy beach and a 2-mi boardwalk with every-thing you'd expect to find at a beach resort (cotton candy, soft ice cream) plus a few unique extras. These include Nathan's Famous, famous for its hot dogs, Astroland Amusement Park, and Deno's Wonder Wheel Park. The not-for-profit group Coney Island USA operates the Coney Island Museum (1208 Surf Ave. at W. 12th St., 718/372–5159), home of the freak show Sideshows by the Seashore, and organizes the wacky annual Mermaid Day Parade on the first Saturday after the summer solstice. Hot summer days have brought as many as a million people to Coney Island at once, which at times makes it a bit diffi-cult to find a place in the sun without stepping on someone else's blanket. *Ocean Pkwy. to 37th St., 718/946–1350. Drinking water, phones. Subway: F, Q, W to Stillwell Ave./Coney Island.*

1 *f-8*

MANHATTAN BEACH
This small beach, in a reasonably well-to-do neighborhood of landscaped private homes, draws a young and energetic crowd for sunning and swimming. Adja-cent to the beach is a park with barbecue facilities as well as handball, tennis, and basketball. *Ocean Ave. between Oriental Blvd. and MacKenzie St., 718/946–1373. Drinking water, picnic tables, phones, rest rooms, showers, snack bar. Subway: Q express to Brighton Beach.*

queens

1 g-7
JACOB RIIS PARK
Just over the Marine Parkway Bridge from Brooklyn, this mile-long stretch of Rockaway Beach was named for the Depression-era reformer-photographer and is part of the Gateway National Recreation Area. There is a concrete "boardwalk" for strolling and a wide, sandy beach. Sports facilities include softball fields and paddle-tennis courts. Though it draws crowds, the less central areas are usually peaceful enough. *Beach 149th–Beach 169th Sts., 718/318–4300. Drinking water, grills, picnic tables, phones, rest rooms, snack bar. Access: Flatbush Ave. to Marine Pkwy./Gil Hodges Memorial Bridge.*

1 h-7
ROCKAWAY BEACH
Nearly 10 mi of glorious sandy beach and 7½ mi of boardwalk fronting the Atlantic form the core of this recreational area, with surfable waves and relatively clean water adding to its appeal. Best of all, the A train can get you—and everyone else—here. Due to lifeguard shortages, beach erosion, and plover nestings, parts of the strand have been closed in recent years; call ahead before reaching for your towel and Metrocard. *Beach 1st–Beach 149th Sts., 718/318–4000. Drinking water, picnic tables, phones, rest rooms, showers, snack bar. Subway: A, S to Rockaway Park/Beach 116 St.*

staten island

1 c-3
GREAT KILLS PARK
Built on landfill, with a major recent cleanup and renovations to the actual beach as well as public buildings, Great Kills offers surfable waves, a marina, fields, a public boat ramp, a model-airplane flying field, fishing, and trails. Migrating monarch butterflies stop here in late summer and fall. *Hylan Blvd. and Hopkins Ave., 718/987–6729. Drinking water, picnic tables, phones, rest rooms, showers, snack bar.*

4 d-8
MIDLAND & SOUTH BEACH
Connected by the Franklin D. Roosevelt Boardwalk, which starts at Miller Field and continues for 7,500 ft, these two beaches are sandy and attractive. Mid-

land is somewhat cleaner, though South Beach has been improved in recent years. You can fish off the boardwalk until 1 PM, except in summer. Even if you don't want to swim, you might enjoy the view of lower New York Bay. *From Miller Field to Fort Wadsworth, parallel to Father Capodanno Blvd., 718/987–0709 (Midland), 718/816–6804 (South). Drinking water, grills, picnic tables, phones, rest rooms, showers.*

1 b-4
WOLFE'S POND PARK
This 312-acre park has saltwater swimming and surfing, a large wooded area, a freshwater lake, and rustic picnic settings. *Holton–Cornelia Aves. on Raritan Bay, Prince's Bay, 718/984–8266. Changing rooms, drinking water, grills, picnic tables, phones, rest rooms, showers.*

long island
New York's Atlantic beaches don't stop at the city line, but extend east some 100 mi past Rockaway along Long Island all the way to Montauk. Several are popular among New York City daytrippers. **Long Beach**—a unique community in that its street plan discourages cars—has a mile-long boardwalk and is just two long blocks from the Long Island Railroad commuter train station. **Jones Beach,** built by Robert Moses, has some of the widest sand beaches, endless dunes, beautiful bathhouses, and teems with happy crowds, though it's big enough that if you're willing to walk, you can get away from the hubbub. **Robert Moses State Park,** on the westernmost tip of Fire Island, is also easy to reach from New York, but it draws more of a Long Island crowd. The Long Island Rail Road offers package day trips to all three beaches, and others, for under $15; call 718/217-LIRR.

BOTANICAL GARDENS

bronx

2 c-4
NEW YORK BOTANICAL GARDEN
This 250-acre garden, founded in 1891, was patterned after the Royal Botanical Gardens at Kew, England. Every season is spectacular. The Peggy Rockefeller Rose

Garden has 2,700 bushes of 230 different varieties; the Arlow B. Stout Daylily Garden glows in July; and there are also an herb garden, an azalea glen (spectacular in May), a pine grove, a rock garden full of Alpine plants (admission $1), trails through 40 acres of old-growth forest, and much more. The 11 interconnecting galleries of the Enid A. Haupt Conservatory (which closes an hour earlier than the garden grounds), including a striking Victorian glasshouse, showcase plant life around the world and seasonal flower shows. A restored 1840 Snuff Mill overlooking the Bronx River and a stone cottage from the same year are other man-made treasures. Narrated tram tours run every 30 minutes and can transport you across the immense grounds, while walks and self-guided tours focus on topics and areas of special interest. The 12-acre Everett Children's Adventure Garden has a hedge maze, hands-on gardening, and other discovery activities, indoors and out. *Bronx Park at 200th St. and Southern Blvd., Bronx Park, 718/817–8700, 718/817–8779 for directions. Admission: garden $3, conservatory $3.50, tram tour $1, Garden Passport (all admissions and tram tour) $10. Free Wed., Sat. 10–noon. Open year-round Tues.–Sun. and Mon. holidays, Apr.–Oct., 10–6, Nov.–Mar. 10–4. Subway: B, D to Bedford Park Blvd.*

2 *a-3*

WAVE HILL

A nonprofit environmental center, these 28 acres overlook the Hudson and the Palisades from their Riverdale location. The former estate of conservation-minded financier George Perkins, rented at various times to Theodore Roosevelt, Mark Twain, and Arturo Toscanini, Wave Hill was donated to the city in 1960. With 18 acres of gardens, it has greenhouses (open limited hours) and exquisite herb, wildflower, and aquatic gardens. Directors of other public gardens come from all over the country to admire the plants and their unusual juxtapositions, which change from year to year. Family art projects, guided garden walks, an art museum, and concerts round out the possibilities. *Main entrance: 249th St. and Independence Ave., Riverdale, 718/549–3200. Admission: $4; free Nov. 16–Mar. 14. Open Tues.–Sun. 9–4:30, and until dusk on Wed. during the summer. Metro-North: Harlem Line to Riverdale.*

brooklyn

4 *e-1*

BROOKLYN BOTANIC GARDEN

Founded in 1910 on the site of a city dump, Brooklyn's garden is just one-fifth the size of its Bronx cousin, but within its 52 acres are more than enough wonders to fill a day. Spring flowers include a spectacular display of the pink and white blossoms of Japanese cherry trees along the Cherry Esplanade, magnolias in Magnolia Plaza, lilacs in the Louisa Clark Spencer Lilac Collection, and daffodils on Daffodil Hill. More than 5,000 varieties of roses bloom through the summer in the Cranford Rose Garden. The Shakespeare Garden contains 80 plants mentioned by the playwright in his works. Lots of giant carp and turtles call the Japanese Hill-and-Pond Garden home, and the lily pools are another unusual delight. Other green attractions include the Fragrance Garden, designed for the blind but a pleasure for all; an herb garden; a rock garden; and a garden planted only with flora from the metropolitan region. While most of the Steinhardt Conservatory follows the "Trail of Evolution," one room has dozens of bonsai plants. Free guided tours leave from the conservatory at 1 PM on weekends. *1000 Washington Ave. (at Carroll St.), Park Slope, 718/623–7200. Admission: $3, free Tues. Open Apr.–Sept., Tues.–Fri. 8–5:30, weekends and Mon. holidays 10–5:30; Oct.–Mar., Tues.–Fri. 8–4, weekends and holidays 10–4. Subway: 1, 2 to Eastern Pkwy./Brooklyn Museum.*

manhattan

5 *a-7*

THE CLOISTERS GARDEN

Green-thumbed monks from the 15th century would be right at home with the 250 species of plants and flowers planted among the cloisters here. The Gothic Trie Cloister, a branch of the Metropolitan Museum of Art, houses the 50 species identified in the museum's *Unicorn Tapestries*. Flowering bulbs are displayed year-round in the skylighted St. Guilhem Cloister. *Fort Tryon Park, Inwood. Subway: A to 190th St. or 200th/Dyckman St.*

7 *d-4*

CONSERVATORY GARDEN

Established in 1937, this formal, 6-acre garden is almost secretly ensconced in a forgotten corner of Central Park. Named for the elegant old greenhouses that stood here before the Depression, the garden is a lavishly landscaped conglomerate: an ornate and manicured French garden, a classic Italian garden flanked by crab-apple allées, a densely planted perennial garden, and complicated patterns of trimmed box hedges. Opening onto the main lawn is the handsome wrought-iron Vanderbilt Gate, a popular spot for wedding portraits. *5th Ave. and 105th St., Central Park, 212/360–2766. Open daily 8 AM–dusk. Subway: 6 to 103rd St.*

11 *g-3*

LIZ CHRISTY MEMORIAL GARDEN

Planted in 1972 by the Green Guerrillas, this tiny but thriving garden is an unlikely rest stop. Since its creation, hundreds of other community gardens have sprung up in vacant lots around the city. *Northeast corner of Houston St. and Bowery, East Village. Open May–Sept., daily noon–4. Subway: F, V to 2nd Ave.*

7 *c-8*

SHAKESPEARE GARDEN

This garden grew from seeds and cuttings of the same mulberry and hawthorn trees Shakespeare himself once tended. The terraced hill provides a peaceful setting. *Central Park near W. 81st St., south of Delacorte Theater. Subway: B, C to 81st St.*

queens

1 *f-3*

QUEENS BOTANICAL GARDEN

Originally created for the 1939–40 World's Fair, held at Flushing Meadows, and later transplanted here, the garden is now 39 acres of specialized plantings. Stepping in here from Main Street feels like entering someone's backyard. Then, though, you see the bridal parties traipsing through to pose in the gazebo in the Wedding Garden. The best green attraction here is the rose garden, which has 1,440 bushes (as well as 13,000 tulips). Other treats include bird and bee gardens, a pine cove, and formal flower plantings along the center mall. *43–50 Main St., Flushing, 718/886–3800. Open Apr.–Oct., Tues.–Fri. 8–6, weekends 8–7; Nov.–Mar., Tues.–Sun. 8–4:30. Subway: 7 to Main St./Flushing.*

staten island

4 *a-6*

STATEN ISLAND BOTANICAL GARDEN

Visit the Snug Harbor Cultural Center and you can't help but stumble upon this garden, a newcomer to the outer-borough botanical-garden scene (established 1977) and a trove of English perennials. Other highlights are a Chinese garden, a pond garden, special plants meant to attract butterflies, and a greenhouse that houses the Neil Vanderbilt Orchid Collection. *Richmondtown Terr. from Tysen St. to Kissel Ave., Snug Harbor, 718/273–8200. Admission: $5 adults, $4 children and seniors. Staten Island Ferry; S40 bus to Snug Harbor. Open Tues.–Sun., dawn–dusk.*

NATURE PRESERVES

queens

1 *g-6*

JAMAICA BAY WILDLIFE REFUGE

Though departing planes from JFK command aural attention, it's the smaller aviators that are worth noting here. These 9,155 acres of salt marshes, fresh and brackish ponds, and open bay attract hundreds of species of shorebirds and constitute a major stop on the Atlantic Flyway. It's most exciting in spring, when hundreds of thousands of birds are nesting—including the great egret, snowy egret, and glossy ibis—and during the fall migratory season when kestrels, osprey, indigo buntings, and even the occasional peregrine falcon can be spotted. Now that Jamaica Bay is part of Gateway National Recreation Area, and cleaner thanks to pollution-control efforts, we can hope for even more avian action. There are over 5 mi of trails, and rangers guide tours regularly. *Broad Channel, 718/318–4340. Subway: A, S to Broad Channel.*

staten island

1 *a-4*

CLAY PIT PONDS STATE PARK PRESERVE

This 260-acre former clay mine is unique for its location at the terminal point for some northern and southern plant species, which live in its swamps,

bogs, spring-fed streams, sandy barrens, wetlands, and woodlands along
with numerous species of birds, reptiles, amphibians, and mammals. Birders, horseback riders, and hikers are
welcome on trails during daylight hours,
and the nature center leads weekend
programs (advance registration
required) year-round. An interesting
novelty is the composting toilet, which
you'll have to use if nature calls.
*Entrance off Carlin St., Charleston, 718/
967–1976. Nature center open Mon.–Sat.
9–5. S113 bus to Sharrotts Rd.*

1 *a-2*
**WILLIAM T. DAVIS
WILDLIFE REFUGE**
Named for noted Staten Island naturalist William Thompson Davis, these 802
acres of dry and wetland attract many
birds rarely seen in this area, and the
wide variety of habitats makes for an
ideal sanctuary. *Travis Ave. off Richmond
Ave., New Springville, 718/667–2165.*

ZOOS

After a decade of being called the politically correct term "wildlife conservation
centers," the city's zoos are back to
being called just that—zoos. All but the
Staten Island Zoo are run by the **Wildlife
Conservation Society** (212/439–6527),
headquartered in Central Park.

bronx

2 *b-3*
BRONX ZOO
Opened in Bronx Park in 1899, this 265-
acre behemoth is the world's largest
urban zoo. About 4,000 animals of 531
species live here, mainly in realistic
habitats and often separated from you
by no more than a moat—accommodations include Himalayan highlands
(snow leopards, red pandas, and
cranes), the rugged Patagonian coast
(penguins, terns, and cormorants), and
African plains (lions, gazelles, and
zebras, among others). The Beaux Arts
Keith W. Johnson Zoo Center's ele-
phants and tapirs; the World of Reptiles'
crocs, snakes, and turtles; and separate
giraffe, mouse, monkey, and aquatic
bird houses are among the popular
indoor exhibits. Bats, naked moles, rats,
and other nocturnal critters are fooled
into thinking it's night—which means
they're awake for you—in the World of

Darkness. The Congo Gorilla Forest
opened in 1999, and its 6-plus acres of
African rain forest are home to more
than 20 gorillas and 50 different species
of wildlife. (The exhibit's $3 admission
is donated to conservation efforts in
Africa.) In season, you can perambulate
via shuttle and skyfari through the entire
zoo, take the Bengali Express Monorail
through Wild Asia, or opt for a leisurely
camel ride. Children are encouraged to
act out their animal instincts, whether
it's sitting in a nest, wearing a turtle
shell, or outfoxing a fox at the Children's
Zoo (Apr.–Oct., $2 adults; $1.50 children 2–12); they can also pet and feed
domestic animals. *Fordham Rd. at Bronx
River Pkwy., Bronx Park, 718/367–1010.
Admission: Apr.–Oct. $9 adults, $5 children and seniors, Nov.–Dec. $7 adults, $4
children and seniors, Jan.–Mar. $5 adults,
$3 children and seniors; Children's Zoo
and tram rides $2 additional per person,
free Wed. year-round. Open Apr.–Oct.,
weekdays 10–5, weekends 10–5:30; Nov.–
Mar., daily 10–4:30. Subway: 2, 5 to Pelham Pkwy.*

brooklyn

4 *3-1*
PROSPECT PARK ZOO
This small zoo focuses on small animals, like prairie dogs, wallabies,
baboons, and capybaras. "The World of
Animals," "Animal Lifestyles," and "Animals in our Lives" exhibit areas help
children learn by observing, mimicking,
and touching. *450 Flatbush Ave., Prospect
Park, 718/399–7339. Admission: $2.50.
Open Apr.–Oct., weekdays 10–5, weekends
and holidays 10–5:30; Nov.–Mar., daily
10–4:30. Subway: 1, 2 to Grand Army
Plaza; Q to Prospect Park; F to 15th
St./Prospect Park.*

manhattan

9 *d-2*
CENTRAL PARK ZOO
Much of New York's oldest zoo has
been demolished (though several of the
WPA-era buildings have been restored),
and a more modern, more humane, 6.5-
acre habitat has taken its place. Clustered around the central Sea Lion Pool
are separate exhibits for each of the
earth's major environments: the Polar
Circle features a huge penguin tank and
polar-bear ice floe; the open-air Temper-
ate Territory is highlighted by an island

When you pack your MCI Calling Card, it's like packing your loved ones along too.

Your MCI Calling Card is the easy way to stay in touch when you travel. Use it to call to and from over 125 countries. Plus, every time you call, you can earn frequent flier miles. So wherever your travels take you, call home with your MCI Calling Card. It's even easy to get one. Just visit **www.mci.com/worldphone**.

EASY TO CALL WORLDWIDE

1 Just enter the WorldPhone® access number of the country you're calling from.

2 Enter or give the operator your MCI Calling Card number.

3 Enter or give the number you're calling.

Aruba ⁜	800-888-8
Bahamas ⁜	1-800-888-8000

Barbados ⁜	1-800-888-8000
Bermuda ⁜	1-800-888-8000
British Virgin Islands ⁜	1-800-888-8000
Canada	1-800-888-8000
Mexico	01-800-021-8000
Puerto Rico	1-800-888-8000
United States	1-800-888-8000
U.S. Virgin Islands	1-800-888-8000

⁜ Limited availability.

EARN FREQUENT FLIER MILES

SEE THE WORLD
IN FULL COLOR

Fodor's Exploring Guides bring all the great sights vividly to life with hundreds of photographs, fascinating historical background, and colorful anecdotes. Detailed maps and practical information keep you headed in the right direction.

Pair a **Fodor's** Exploring Guide with your trusted Gold Guide for a complete planning package.

of chattering monkeys; and the Rain Zone contains the flora and fauna of a miniature rain forest. The Tisch Children's Zoo on the north side of Denesmouth Arch has an Enchanted Forest, where small animals such as rabbits, frogs, and free-flying birds are all at home; children learn to relate to their fellow creatures by hopping on lily pads, peering underwater through a fish's-eye lens, and fidgeting with other interactive amusements. *Entrance: 5th Ave. and 64th St., Central Park, 212/861–6030. Admission: $3.50. Open Apr.–Oct., weekdays 10–5, weekends and holidays 10:30–5:30; Nov.–Mar., daily 10–4:30. Subway: N, R, W to 5th Ave.*

queens

3 *h-2*

QUEENS WILDLIFE CENTER

About 340 animals of just over 50 American species live in this lightly populated, 11-acre zoo. Strolling through treetops amid free-flying birds in the aviary is a highlight. Outside, elk are at home on the range, speckled bears play in their pseudo-Adirondack territory, and sea lions swim off a faux Pacific Coast. You can paw domesticated plants and animals in the petting zoo. *53–51 111th St., Flushing Meadows–Corona Park, 718/271–1500. Admission: $2.50. Open Apr.–Oct., weekdays 10–5, weekends and holidays 10–5:30; Nov.–Mar., daily 10–4:30. Subway: 7 to 111th St.*

staten island

1 *c-8*

STATEN ISLAND ZOO

Operated by its own Staten Island Zoological Society, this small zoo (established 1936) is known for its reptiles, especially rattlesnakes, who slither through the Serpentarium. Shrimp and sharks jockey for position in the aquarium, otters goof around in an outdoor pool, and endangered South American plants and animals live in an indoor re-creation of a tropical forest. Leopards and baboons lurk in the theatrical African Savannah at Twilight exhibit. The feeding schedule isn't for the faint of heart—mealtimes for reptiles, sharks, piranha, and bats are scheduled for your visiting pleasure. If you're weak-kneed, you might find the domesticated farm animals at the outdoor children's center more enjoyable. *614 Broadway, Barrett Park, 718/442–3100. Admission: $3, free Wed. after 2. Open daily 10–4:45. S48 bus to Forest Ave./Broadway.*

stadiums

1 *c-5*

CONTINENTAL AIRLINES ARENA

Formerly the Brendon Byrne Arena, this 20,000-seater has its hands full with the ferocious fans of the New Jersey Nets (basketball); New Jersey Devils (hockey); and, more recently, the Mad Dogs (arena football). NJ Transit runs buses to the complex, which leave from Port Authority. *Meadowlands Sports Complex, East Rutherford, NJ, 201/935–3900.*

1 *c-5*

GIANTS STADIUM

It's rumored that Jimmy Hoffa rests in peace under the Astroturf. It's much to the chagrin of New Yorkers that the Jets and the Giants hold their football games across the Hudson River, in a different state. The stadium also is home to the MetroStars (soccer) and—seating almost 78,000—hosts legions of concertgoers. NJ Transit runs buses to the stadium, which leave from Port Authority. *Meadowlands Sports Complex, East Rutherford, NJ, 201/935–3900.*

9 *c-6*

MADISON SQUARE GARDEN

There's never a dull moment in midtown's 20,000-seat showcase. The New York Knicks and the New York Liberty shoot hoops, and the New York Rangers slam pucks. Many up-and-coming college athletes, track stars, boxers, wrestlers, figure skaters, and the occasional rock star find themselves here at some point. *7th Ave. between 31st and 33rd Sts., Midtown West, 212/465–6741. Tours daily. Subway: 1, 2, 3, A, C, E to 34th St./Penn Station.*

NASSAU VETERANS MEMORIAL COLISEUM

Though the New York Islanders have rallied occasionally in the past decade, their 16,000-seat home, built in 1972, is showing its age. *1255 Hempstead Tpke., Uniondale, NY, 516/794–9300. LIRR to Hempstead, N70 or N71 to Hempstead Tpke.*

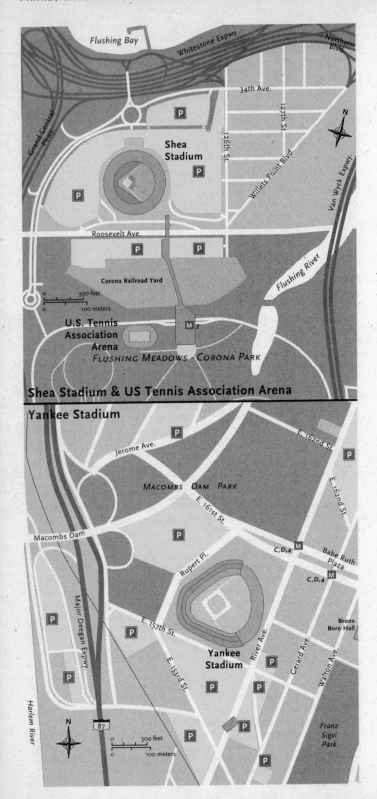

Flushing Bay

Whitestone Expwy.

Northern Blvd.

Grand Central Pkwy.

34th Ave.

127th St.

126th St.

P

Shea Stadium

P

P

Willets Point Blvd.

Van Wyck Expwy.

Roosevelt Ave.

P

P

Flushing River

Corona Railroad Yard

300 feet

100 meters

U.S. Tennis Association Arena

M 7

FLUSHING MEADOWS - CORONA PARK

Shea Stadium & US Tennis Association Arena

Yankee Stadium

P

Jerome Ave.

E. 162nd St.

P

MACOMBS DAM PARK

E. 162nd St.

E. 161st St.

Macombs Dam

P

C,D,4 **M**

Babe Ruth Plaza

Rupert Pl.

C,D,4 **M**

Major Deegan Expwy.

E. 157th St.

River Ave.

Gerard Ave.

Bronx Boro Hall

P

Yankee Stadium

P

Walton Ave.

E. 153rd St.

P

P

Harlem River

N

87

300 feet

100 meters

P

Franz Sigel Park

P

The Meadowlands

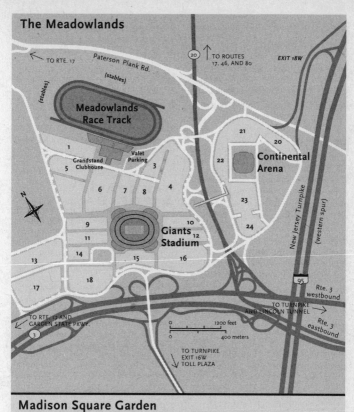

TO RTE. 17

Paterson Plank Rd.

(stables)

(stables)

20 → TO ROUTES 17, 46, AND 80

EXIT 18W

Meadowlands Race Track

Valet Parking

1

Grandstand Clubhouse

5

3

21

20

22

Continental Arena

N

6   7   8   4

23

9

10
12

24

Giants Stadium

11

13   14   15   16

New Jersey Turnpike (western spur)

17   18

95

Rte. 3 westbound

TO RTE. 17 AND GARDEN STATE PKWY.

3

TO TURNPIKE AND LINCOLN TUNNEL →

Rte. 3 eastbound

0   1200 feet
0   400 meters

TO TURNPIKE EXIT 16W TOLL PLAZA

Madison Square Garden

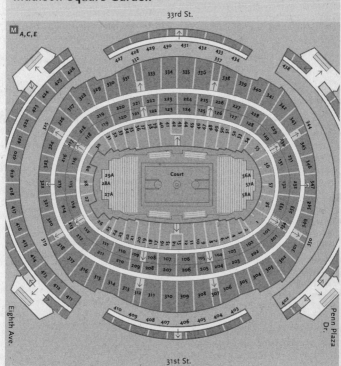

33rd St.

M A,C,E

Court

Eighth Ave.

Penn Plaza Dr.

31st St.

3 *h-1*
SHEA STADIUM
New York Mets ball games are always fun at this 55,777-seat stadium—and the fans drown out the noise from nearby La Guardia Airport. *126th St. and Roosevelt Ave., Flushing, Queens, 718/507–8499. Subway: 7 to Willets Pt./Shea Stadium.*

3 *h-1*
U.S.T.A. NATIONAL TENNIS CENTER
This is the largest public tennis facility in the world. It is open to the public daily, except for 60 days a year, when the USTA hosts its own events, including the U.S. Open, which is held in Arthur Ashe Stadium. There are 22 outdoor and nine indoor courts, available for play from 8 AM–midnight. *Flushing Meadows–Corona Park, Flushing, Queens, 718/760–6200, www.usta.com/ntc. Subway: 7 to Willets Pt./Shea Stadium.*

6 *f-5*
YANKEE STADIUM
The 57,545-seat 1923 "House That Ruth Built" has watched its boys win 26 World Championships, and lose a 27th by a hair. Steinbrenner makes noises regularly, but it doesn't look like the beloved Bronx Bombers are moving anywhere—Manhattan or New Jersey—any time soon. *161st St. and River Ave., Bronx, 718/293–6000. Subway: 4, B, D to 161st St./Yankee Stadium.*

sports & outdoor activities

ARCHERY

4 *e-5*
PRO STOP INDOOR ARCHERY
There are 25 target lanes here, with instruction but no rental; you can purchase your bows, quivers, and wrist guards in the attached shop. Open weekends until 11 PM. *7923 New Utrecht Ave., Bay Ridge, Brooklyn, 718/232–4040. Subway: W to 79th St.*

PROLINE ARCHERY RANGE
Open seven days and catering to families, this huge facility hosts leagues and

has an organized instruction program. *95–11 101st Ave., Jamaica, Queens, 718/845–9280. Subway: A to Rockaway Blvd.*

3 *h-1*
QUEENS ARCHERY
Twenty lanes, lessons, rentals, an adjoining pro shop, and a loud and friendly atmosphere. *170–29 39th Ave., Flushing, Queens, 718/461–1756. Subway: 7 to Flushing/Main St.*

BASEBALL & SOFTBALL
The professional baseball season runs from early April through September, a few weeks longer if your team is lucky. Tickets are usually available both in advance and at the stadium on game day.

New York has more than 600 baseball diamonds, heavily used by softball players. Many companies form softball teams and compete in leagues. If you're not part of a league, you'll need a permit; call your borough's parks office for fields near you.

teams to watch
NEW YORK YANKEES
Home games for this much beloved American League team are at Yankee Stadium. The Bronx Bombers' petulant owner, George Steinbrenner, has been threatening for a decade to pick up and move his boys to New Jersey—or, heaven forbid, into Manhattan—but ever since they won the World Series in '96, '98, '99, and again in 2000, and lost a seventh game cliff-hanger in 2001, bigger crowds have been returning to the South Bronx, and everybody is happy. *718/293–6000.*

NEW YORK METS
Even though they they beat the odds to win the National League pennant in 2000 (only to lose the World Series to their crosstown rivals), it's not always easy being a fan of the beleaguered team their fans call "The Amazins." Although they currently don't draw the same size crowds as the Yankees, the Mets do draw over 2 million fans each season. *718/507–8499.*

BROOKLYN CYCLONES
Professional baseball finally returned to Brooklyn after 44 years, with the arrival of this Class A minor league affiliate of

the New York Mets. But there's nothing minor about the welcome they received—baseball-famished fans have been gorging with delight and most home games sold out during its first season. The brand new 7,500-seat stadium, KeySpan Park, sits on the historic site of Coney Island's Steeplechase Park. Tickets are $5–$10. *Surf and Stillwell Aves., Brooklyn, 718/449–8497. Subway: F, Q local, W to Stillwell Ave.*

STATEN ISLAND YANKEES

Affectionately known as the Baby Bombers, this A-League affiliate is the feeder team for the venerable Bronx franchise. The Staten Island Yankees play in a new, 6,500-seat stadium steps from the Staten Island Ferry, with a panoramic view of the Manhattan skyline and the Statue of Liberty. *75 Richmond Terr., Staten Island, 718/720–9265.*

where to play

There are hundreds of municipal baseball facilities in the city, but many of them are reserved by softball and baseball leagues. For details on permits, *see* Permits *under* Parks, *above.*

BASKETBALL

The regular men's professional season (NBA) runs in the winter, from November to April. Women (WNBA) have been slotted into the traditionally slow summer season, mid-June–August. In addition to teams listed below, Madison Square Garden often hosts college games in winter.

teams to watch

NEW JERSEY NETS

The up-and-coming Nets can be seen at the Continental Airlines Arena. *Meadowlands Sports Complex, East Rutherford, NJ, 201/935–3900.*

NEW YORK KNICKS

Latrell Sprewell and Co. play to intense sell-out crowds at Madison Square Garden. *7th Ave. between 31st and 33rd Sts., Midtown, 212/465–JUMP. Subway: 1, 2, 3, A, C, E to 34th St./Penn Station.*

NEW YORK LIBERTY

They play halves instead of quarters and use a smaller ball than the men, but the Women's National Basketball Association (WNBA) is full of fierce competition as the NBA, and it's been gaining popularity and respect since its 1997 inaugural season. Olympic champ Rebecca Lobo is the center for New York's team, which plays at Madison Square Garden. *7th Ave. between 31st and 33rd Sts., Midtown West, 212/564–WNBA.*

where to play

Call the Parks Department for the basketball court nearest you—in some neighborhoods they're on almost every corner. Hoops on Manhattan's West 4th Street (at 6th Ave.) often have lively games with spectators. Other popular pickup locations in Manhattan are on West 76th Street (at Columbus Ave.), at **Asphalt Green** (90th St. at York Ave.), and at Riverbank State Park.

BICYCLING

With all of its long, flat, paved stretches, New York City should be a biker's dream. Unfortunately, motor vehicle traffic, potholes, and pollution make it one big obstacle course. Still, there are some good recreational routes, especially in parks and along the waterfront, and biking is often the fastest and most convenient way to get around town. The **Department of Transportation** (212/442–9890 Bicycle Program) and the **Department of City Planning** (212/442–4713 Bicycle Network Development Program) produce highly detailed bicycle maps for each borough; in addition to showing recommended routes (greenways and paths as well as street routes); these pinpoint bike shops and explain cycling regulations. They are free and can be found at the **Department of City Planning Bookstore** (22 Reade St., 212/720–3300) and at bike shops around town. Even if you read up, though, navigating roads and figuring out how to access bridges can be challenging, so ride with someone who's experienced before setting out on your own—the **Urban Park Rangers** (212/360–2774) lead guided bike tours in all five boroughs.

Bicycles are considered vehicles, which means they have to stop at red lights, obey speed limits, stay off sidewalks (if the rider's over 13 years old), and ride in the direction of traffic. In city parks, riding off trails is not allowed. Children under 14 must wear helmets. Bikes are permitted on the subway and the Staten Island ferry without a permit, and most other regional mass transports allow them with a free or inexpensive permit; Transportation Alternatives can provide details. The city's bike clubs send out calendars to their members, who generally pay a modest annual fee, but welcome everyone on rides.

clubs

CENTURY ROAD CLUB ASSOCIATION

The CRCA has been around for more than 100 years and is for *serious* racers. The club holds Saturday races in Central Park and offers coaching, clinics, and a monthly newsletter. 212/222–8062.

FAST & FABULOUS CYCLING CLUB

This lesbian and gay outfit was formed when a group of tri-athletes began training for the Gay Games in 1994. It holds weekly rides in and out of the city for every level of rider. 212/567–7160.

FIVE BOROUGH BICYCLE CLUB

The 5BBC has road and all-terrain bike (ATB) rides for all levels year-round, with many especially suited to cyclists not used to heavy mileage. Its parent organization, American Youth Hostels, is also the parent of Bike New York, which puts on an annual mass tour of the five boroughs in early May. 891 Amsterdam Ave. (at 103rd St.), 212/932–2300.

NEW YORK CYCLE CLUB

This club has something for everybody. Rides are classified by average speed, and the calendar has trips for all cyclists from beginners to pace-line racers. One member describes it as the "most aggressively enthusiastic club in the city." Its annual Escape from New York century ride (110 mi, usually in late Sept. or early Oct.) is a nice, early fall break. 212/828–5711.

STATEN ISLAND BICYCLING ASSOCIATION

Staten Island and New Jersey are the usual focus for this group's day rides. They're categorized by level and include mountain-biking outings and additional weekly on-island spins on Wednesday and Saturday. 718/605–2453.

TIME'S UP

Time's Up promotes environmental awareness through biking. Rides are generally just one or two hours, but offer unique glimpses of the city. The monthly Central Park Moonlight Ride, for example, travels the scenic paths. Other regular rides are the critical-mass attempt and historic tours. Though the club produces a free calendar every once in a while, you're better off calling for upcoming events. 212/802–8222.

TRANSPORTATION ALTERNATIVES

The city's bicycle-and-pedestrian advocacy group gets its members discounts at several bike stores and can help you decrease the amount of pollution in your life. Its bimonthly newsletter, "City Cyclist," available in bike stores throughout the city, lists rides and events of interest to cyclists. Every September, TA organizes the New York Century Bike Tour, a 100-mi ride within city boundaries. 115 W. 30th St., Suite 1207, 212/629–8080.

where to bike

BRONX

Mosholu Parkway and **Pelham Parkway** are paralleled by scenic bike routes for miles and they connect the borough's two premier greenspaces, Van Cortland Park and Pelham Bay Park, where you'll find Orchard Beach and routes to City Island, an area that feels like coastal New England set to a salsa beat. The **Bronx Chapter of Transportation Alternatives** (718/653–2203) leads tours throughout the borough.

BROOKLYN

The 3½-mi loop road in **Prospect Park** provides excellent cycling, especially when the park is closed to cars. Beware a short strip on the eastern side of the park near the boathouse and skating rink—cars can access the parking lot at all times. The **Ocean Parkway** bike path, which turned 100 in 1995, starts just outside the southwest exit of Prospect Park and ends about 6 mi later, near Coney Island, where the boardwalk is open to cyclists before 10 AM. Along the parkway, you ride on elevated medians in the shade of trees. The **Shore Parkway Path** goes from Owl's Head Park, in Bay Ridge, under the Verrazano Narrows Bridge to Bay 8th in Bensonhurst, and picks up again off Emmons Avenue in Sheepshead Bay. From here you can connect to a path that runs parallel to **Flatbush Avenue** and brings you to Rockaway, or continue to Jamaica Bay.

MANHATTAN

The 6-mi loop road in **Central Park** probably logs the most cycler miles in the city, but it's often crowded (sometimes with cars, when they're allowed in, forcing bikers, bladers, and joggers to share a narrow lane) and requires adept navigation skills. Always be aware of other park users. Bike rentals are available at the **boathouse** (212/861–4137). Central Park is getting competition from the new **Westside/Hudson Greenway**, a new, unbroken strip of pavement completed in 2001, running alongside the river for nearly the entire length of Manhattan island, from the Battery to the George Washington Bridge, passing skyscrapers, ocean liners, and riverside parks. The Greenway has marked lanes for bikers, bladers, and pedestrians. Cyclists can continue onto the "GW," where the pedestrian crossway offers spectacular views up and down the Hudson and easy access to Palisades Interstate Park (River Road, left off the bridge and then left again, is a hilly favorite) and Route 9W in New Jersey. There also are bike paths along the way. **Hudson River Park** from Battery Park to West 14th Street gets crowded with cruising bikers and skaters; the path along **East River Park** is much greener and less congested. Uptown, you can bike right along the water in the West Side's **Riverside Park** and from 61st Street up to 125th Street on the **East River Esplanade** between the F.D.R. Drive and the water's edge. From April to October a bridge at 103rd Street is open, leading to the calm expanse of Randall's Island.

The north outer roadway of the **Queensboro Bridge** is open to cyclists. The walkway on the **Williamsburg Bridge** has recently been renovated and cyclists and skaters split the spectacular elevated roadway–boardwalk on the **Brooklyn Bridge.** All of the Manhattan–Bronx bridges accommodate cyclists as well.

QUEENS

Rockaway Peninsula is a long, flat strip crying out for your cruiser on either the road or the boardwalk; take the Marine Parkway Bridge from Brooklyn's Flatbush Avenue bike path. In **Forest Park,** near the Brooklyn border, take the main road for a gorgeous ride through the woods. **Flushing Meadows–Corona Park** has lakeside routes as well as plenty of pavement separating playing fields and attractions. The lack of hills makes it popular with families, and rentals are available by the **tennis stadium** (718/699–9598). The few miles of bike path on the west edge of **Little Neck Bay, Fort Totten,** and **Little Bay Park** have great views of the Long Island Sound.

STATEN ISLAND

Staten Island's traffic often seems less threatening than that of other boroughs—which helps make up for the lack of separate bike paths on this park-filled island. For a relaxing and scenic ride, take the ferry and then follow Front and Edgewater streets to Fort Wadsworth, after which you can head down Father Capodanno Boulevard along several beaches on the eastern shore. The **Bayonne Bridge,** with its narrow pedestrian crossway separated from the main part of the bridge, makes for an exhilarating trip into New Jersey, where you'll find lovely Liberty State Park.

BILLIARDS

Tables usually cost $10–$15 per hour, many halls have lounges and/or snack bars attached, and most operate virtually around-the-clock.

bronx

5 *c-1*

FIELDSTON BILLIARDS
A huge friendly neighborhood hangout with 50 tables open until 3 AM. And right by a subway stop, too. *5905 Broadway (at 240th St.), Riverdale, 718/884–9800. Subway: 1 to 242nd St./Van Cortlandt Park.*

manhattan

7 *b-8*

AMSTERDAM BILLIARD CLUB
This upscale club, partly owned by comedian David Brenner, has 31 tables. *344 Amsterdam Ave. (at 77th St.), Upper West Side, 212/496–8180. Subway: 1, 2 to 79th St.*

7 *f-7*

The newer East Side location is equally well-equipped with 34 tables, including three for Ping-Pong. *210 E. 86th St. (at 3rd Ave.), Upper East Side, 212/570–4545. Subway: 4, 5, 6 to 86th St.*

9 *c-8*

THE BILLIARD CLUB

High ceilings, velvet curtains, and pseudo-Victorian decor give this place class. The 33 tables help, too. *220 W. 19th St. (between 7th and 8th Aves., Chelsea, 212/206–7665. Subway: 1, 2, C, E to 23rd St.*

10 *e-1*

CORNER BILLIARDS

East Village yuppies congregate around the 28 tables in this low-key yet noisy place. *85 4th Ave. (at 11th St.), Greenwich Village, 212/995–1314. Subway: 4, 5, 6, L, N, R to 14th St./Union Sq.*

9 *d-8*

SLATE

Crowds fill the two floors, looking to play pool or snooker—there are 50 pool tables and 8 snooker tables. You don't need to make separate dinner plans as Slate also serves full meals, not just snacks. *54 W. 21st St. (between 5th and 6th Aves.), 212/989–0096. Subway: F, N, R to 23rd St.*

11 *f-3*

SOHO BILLIARDS

These 28 tables have a choice NoHo location for after-hours action. *298 Mulberry St. (at Houston St.), Greenwich Village, 212/925–3753. Subway: 6 to Bleecker St.; F, V to Broadway–Lafayette St.*

9 *a-4*

WEST SIDE BILLIARD & TABLE TENNIS CLUB

Several Ping-Pong tables complement the pool offerings (12 tables) at this western outpost. *601 W. 50th St., Midtown West, 212/246–1060. Subway: C, E to 50th St.*

BIRD-WATCHING

Pigeons (rock pigeons, if you're in the know) may be the first species that comes to mind when you think about avian life in the city, but New York City's parks, marshes, and woodlands are home to thousands of species of birds, including Canada geese, Kentucky warblers, fork-tailed flycatchers, downy woodpeckers, barn owls, dark-eyed juncos, and glossy ibises, and some of the city's skyscrapers have become nesting areas for peregrine falcons and hawks. The city is also on the Atlantic Flyway, a major spring and fall migratory route; birds heading to or from as far away as the High Arctic pass through. May is the best season for bird-watching, since the songbirds are in their freshest colors; the fall migration is less concentrated and less colorful. As the local chapter of our nation's premier birding organization, the **New York City Audubon Society** (71 W. 23rd St., Room 606, 212/691–7483) can fill you in on area bird walks and help you with your watching. **Rare Bird Alert** (212/979–3070) has up-to-the-minute news on what's been seen where. In addition to the sources below, check with the Urban Park Rangers (*see* Parks, *above*) for information on walks.

bronx

2 *c-4*

NEW YORK BOTANICAL GARDEN

Many species of birds live on garden grounds year-round or stop by seasonally. Great horned owls are most likely found in the grove of evergreen trees, while ring-necked pheasants prefer the wetlands, daffodil hill, and the rose garden. There are bird walks every Saturday and Sunday at 12:30 and there's an annual bird count in late December. *Bronx Park at 200th St. and Southern Blvd., 718/817–8700, 718/817–8779 for directions. Admission: garden $3, conservatory $3.50, Garden Passport (all admissions and tram tour) $10; free Wed., Sat. 10–noon. Open Apr.–Oct., Tues.–Sun. and Mon. holidays 10–6; Nov.–Mar., Tues.–Sun. 10–4. Subway: D to Bedford Park Blvd.*

2 *g-2*

PELHAM BAY PARK

The saltwater marsh and lagoon have been known to attract bald eagles, ospreys, and great horned owls. *Bruckner Blvd. and Middletown Rd., 718/430–1890; 718/885–3466 Pelham Bay Park Environmental Center (near Orchard Beach). Subway: 6 to Pelham Bay Park.*

brooklyn

1 *f-7*

MARINE PARK

A springtime warbler watch is part of each year's birding highlights at the marsh. *Inlet between Gerritsen and Flatbush Aves., inland to Fillmore Ave., between Burnet and E. 32nd Sts.*

1 h-6

PROSPECT PARK

Birds similar to those in Central Park settle in Prospect Park's lakes and hills. The Rose Garden, Midwood, Prospect Lake, and Lookout Hill are good viewing spots. *Park bordered by Flatbush Ave., Ocean Ave., Parkside Ave., Prospect Park SW, and Prospect Park W, 718/965–8999. Subway: 2, 3 to Grand Army Plaza; Q to Prospect Park; F to 15th St./Prospect Park.*

manhattan

1 d-4

CENTRAL PARK

The Pond near East 59th Street, the Reservoir, the Ravine, and especially the Ramble are prime birding areas. Species that nest in the park include cardinals, gray catbirds, and mallard ducks; among those that pass through (typically March–mid-May) are blue-gray gnatcatchers, brown creepers, orioles, and warblers. The Henry Luce Nature Observatory, at Belvedere Castle (212/772–0210), loans out the *Discovery Kit* to help mainly (but not exclusively) children learn about park wildlife. The Dana Discovery Center (212/860–1370) invites families to learn birding basics while exploring northern sections of the park with the Family Bird Watching Club, a free program that meets Saturday at 11 AM in spring. *Park bordered by Central Park W, 59th St., 5th Ave., and 110th St. 212/360–3444 general information. Subway: 1, 2, A, B, C, D to 59th St./Columbus Circle; N, R to 5th Ave.; B, C to 72nd–110th Sts.; for Dana Discovery Center, 2, 3 to 110th St./Central Park North.*

queens

1 g-3

ALLEY POND PARK

Shorebirds and small birds live in abundance in Alley Pond's woodlands and wetlands. The active Queens County Bird Club (718/939–6224) meets at the environmental center on the third Wednesday of every month. The club welcomes new birders and arranges slide programs and weekly trips (though fewer in July and August). *Grand Central Pkwy. at Winchester Blvd., Bayside.*

1 g-6

JAMAICA BAY WILDLIFE REFUGE

Ten percent of the bird species known to live in the continental United States have been spotted here. It's a prime habitat for waterfowl and shelters migrating shorebirds and wading birds such as herons, plovers, and sandpipers. The visitor center has more details. *Broad Channel, 718/318–4340. Subway: A to Broad Channel.*

staten island

1 a-4

CLAY PIT PONDS STATE PARK PRESERVE

More than 40 species of birds breed in the preserve's fields, wetlands, barrens, and streams, and about 170 species live here. The visitor center has a checklist of birds you might see, and when you might see them. *Entrance off Carlin St., Charleston, 718/967–1976. Nature center open Mon.–Sat. 9–5.*

1 a-2

WILLIAM T. DAVIS WILDLIFE REFUGE

A variety of birds lives here due to the luxurious position between salt marshes and hardwood forests. It's an especially good place to sight hawks. *Travis Ave. off Richmond Ave., New Springville, 718/667–2165.*

1 b-4

WOLFE'S POND PARK

Duck, geese, herons, and cormorants are some of the waterbirds that like the mix of saltwater and freshwater here. *Holton to Cornelia Aves. on Raritan Bay, Prince's Bay, 718/984–8266.*

BOCCIE

New York has about 100 boccie courts; here are a few choice options.

7 f-1

CULLIVER PARK

There are eight courts near the East River at 125th St. *East Harlem. Subway: 4, 5, 6 to 125th St.*

9 g-5

EAST RIVER DRIVE AT 42ND STREET

There are two courts here, near the UN building. *Midtown East. Subway: 4, 5, 6 to 42nd St./Grand Central.*

10 h-2

EAST RIVER PARK

Like most facilities in this neglected park, the three boccie courts are under-utilized but perfectly good. *East River Dr. between 14th and Delancey Sts., East Village/Lower East Side. Subway: F to Delancey St.*

11 g-3

HOUSTON STREET & 1ST AVENUE

This playground has five courts. *East Village. Subway: F, V to 2nd Ave.*

BOWLING

bronx

2 f-4

FIESTA LANES

Open bowling times in these 28 lanes are mainly during the day. *2826 Westchester Ave. (near Middletown Rd.), Pelham Bay, 718/824–2600. Subway: 6 to Middletown Rd.*

brooklyn

4 d-3

MELODY LANES

Bumper bowling (with guard rails on the gutters) is usually available for children at this 28-lane facility. *461 37th St. (between 4th and 5th Aves.), Sunset Park, 718/499–3848. Subway: J, M, W to 36th St.*

manhattan

9 a-8

AMF CHELSEA PIERS BOWL

If it wasn't big (40 lanes) and new (Manhattan's first new lanes in decades) and state-of-the-art, it wouldn't be at Chelsea Piers. *Chelsea Piers (23rd St. and 12th Ave.), between Piers 59 and 60, 212/835–2695. Subway: C, E to 23rd St.*

10 e-1

BOWLMOR LANES

You won't find many middle-aged beer bellies at this lively, hip bowling center cum nightclub. (Pressure, a swanky, kitschy lounge, occupies the top floor.) There are 42 lanes on two floors, but you might have to wait up to two hours for a lane; luckily, there are several bars that serve decent (though pricey) pub grub and drinks. Monday night the lights go out and a DJ spins. But just about every day of the week Bowlmor stays busy with a downtown crowd until the wee hours. *110 University Pl. (between 12th and 13th Sts.), Greenwich Village, 212/255–8188. Subway: 4, 5, 6, N, R to 14th St./Union Sq.*

9 c-5

LEISURE TIME BOWLING & RECREATION

Bowling in a bus terminal? It makes sense when you think about it, given the central location and strangely festive surroundings. Complete with a bar and billiards, this modern center has 30 lanes. *Port Authority Bus Terminal, 2nd level, Midtown West, 212/268–6909. Subway: 1, 2, 3, 7, A, C, E to 42nd St./Port Authority.*

queens

3 h-1

AMF 34TH AVENUE LANES

One of the least expensive places in the city to bowl, AMF is popular with families. There are 35 lanes. *69–10 34th Ave., Flushing, 718/651–0440. Subway: 7 to Flushing/Main St.*

3 h-3

HOLLYWOOD LANES

Many consider this underground, 30-lane facility the finest in Queens. *99–23 Queens Blvd. (at 67th Ave.), Rego Park, 718/896–2121. Subway: R, V local to 67th Ave.*

2 h-8

WHITESTONE LANES

Can't sleep? These 48 lanes are open 24 hours a day, 7 days a week. *30–05 Whitestone Expressway (at Linden Pl.), Flushing, 718/353–6300. Subway: 7 to Flushing/Main St.*

BOXING

Major boxing events are held monthly at **Madison Square Garden.** Many health clubs offer "Boxercise," a noncontact exercise involving boxing drills, gloves, and punching bags—though you should be aware that these types of classes are a far cry from the real thing, so don't fall victim to a false sense of security: two boxercise classes do not a street fighter make. The gyms listed here have bona fide rings.

brooklyn

12 *b-1*

GLEASON'S GYM

Gleason's *is* boxing in New York. Since 1937 it's trained more than 100 world champions, including Muhammad Ali. You can spar (partners supplied, lessons available) or just watch, and women are welcome and encouraged. *75 Front St. (at Main St.), Brooklyn Heights, 718/797–2872. Subway: F to York St.; A, C to High St./Brooklyn Bridge.*

manhattan

9 *a-8*

CHELSEA PIERS

This waterside complex offers a boxing program that includes first-time training and an equipment circuit. There is a ring, but this program is closer to boxercise than competitive training (perhaps because of prohibitively high membership costs). Nonmembers have to pay the steep day-pass fee to access the ring, which is in the Sports Center. *Sports Center, Chelsea Piers (23rd St. and 12th Ave.), Pier 60, 212/336–6000. Subway: C, E to 23rd St.*

10 *6-e*

HEAVY HANDS CHURCH STREET BOXING GYM

Its lack of glitz allows it to focus on quality personalized training. *25 Park Pl., Lower Manhattan, 212/571–1333. Closed Sun. Subway: 1, 2 to Park Pl.*

CRICKET

Pitching wickets is especially popular among West Indian immigrants. The **World Cricket League** (914/827–3222) and the **Commonwealth Cricket League** (check www.usaca.org for info) have information on events.

bronx

2 *g-5*

FERRY POINT PARK

There are three pitches here, in the shadow of the Whitestone Bridge. *Schley Ave. at Emerson Ave.*

2 *b-2*

VAN CORTLANDT PARK

There are 10 pitches at the Parade Ground, at approximately 243rd Street. *Park: W. 242nd St. to city line, between Broadway and Jerome Ave., 718/430–1890. Subway: 1 to 242nd St./Van Cortlandt Park.*

brooklyn

1 *f-6*

CANARSIE BEACH PARK

There are four cricket pitches here; one pair at Seaview Avenue and 108th Street and another at Seaview Avenue and 88th Street. *Park: Seaview Ave., Paerdegat Basin. Subway: L to Canarsie/Rockaway Park.*

1 *f-7*

MARINE PARK

There are four cricket pitches at 33rd and Stuart streets. *Inlet between Gerritsen and Flatbush Aves., inland to Fillmore Ave., between Burnet and E. 32nd Sts.*

queens

3 *h-2*

FLUSHING MEADOWS–CORONA PARK

This park has six pitches. *Union Tpke. from 111th St. and Grand Central Pkwy. to the Van Wyck Extension, Flushing, 718/760–6565. Subway: 7 to 111th St.*

staten island

1 *b-1*

WALKER PARK

This park has one cricket pitch, the oldest in the city. *Delafield Pl. and Bard Ave., Livingston.*

CROQUET

You need a permit to play on the croquet grounds in Central Park; call 212/360–8133 for information. You can also show up at 6 PM on Tuesday in the summer for a free clinic for prospective members, hosted by **New York Croquet Club** (212/369–7949).

9 *d-1*

CENTRAL PARK

Just north of Sheep Meadow is the city's lovely croquet ground, where players in bright white and flat shoes wield mallets. The season runs from April to early November. *Enter park at Central Park W. and 72nd St., Upper West Side, 212/360–3444 general information. Subway: B, C to 72nd St.*

FENCING

9 *c-7*

BLADE FENCING

Private lessons are by appointment. *245 W. 29th St. (between 7th and 8th Aves.), Chelsea, 212/244–3090. Subway: C, E to 23rd St.*

9 *b-1*

FENCERS CLUB, INC.

Founded in 1883, this nonprofit organization is America's oldest fencing club—and the largest club in the area. Men and women of all levels and all ages (kids, too!) are invited to join. The pickup area is open nightly. *119 W. 25th St. (between 6th and 7th Aves.), Chelsea, 917/697–6673. Subway: C, E to 23rd St.*

9 *d-8*

METROPOLIS FENCING CENTER

Group lessons provide a supportive atmosphere for novices. *45 W. 21st St., between 5th and 6th Aves., Chelsea, 212/463–8044. Subway: F, V to 23rd St.*

FISHING

You need a New York State freshwater-fishing license (ages 16–70) to freshwater-fish in the city; get an application from tackle stores or the **Department of Environmental Conservation** (718/482–4999). Saltwater fishing requires only a rod, line, and reel, though if you drive to a spot in the **Gateway National Recreation Area,** you'll need a parking permit (718/318–4300 Breezy Point, Queens; 718/338–3799 Jamaica Bay, Brooklyn; 718/351–6970 Staten Island).

New York City Trout Unlimited (www.nyctu.org), dedicated to preserving cold-water fisheries, publishes a

bimonthly newsletter, available online, and sponsors events such as fly-casting in parks.

bronx

2 *h-3*

CITY ISLAND

Rent a skiff and head out into the sound for flounder and blackfish. Try Jack's Bait and Tackle (551 City Island Ave., 718/885–2042), Rosenberger's Boat Livery (663 City Island Ave., 718/885–1843), or any other outfitter that looks suitably salty. Fishing boats, including the *Riptide III* (718/885–0236) and *New Daybreak II* (718/409–9765), generally set out for day trips. *Subway: 6 to Pelham Bay Park, then BX29 bus to City Island Ave.*

2 *g-2*

PELHAM BAY PARK

Cast for black bass, flounder, catfish, bullheads, and fluke from Orchard Beach and Hunter's and Twins islands. *Park: Bruckner Blvd. and Middletown Rd., 718/430–1890. Subway: 6 to Pelham Bay Park.*

2 *b-2*

VAN CORTLANDT PARK

The catfish and bullheads are biting in the Bronx's largest freshwater lake. *W. 242 St., east of Broadway, 718/430–1890. Subway: 1 to 242nd St./Van Cortlandt Park.*

brooklyn

1 *h-6*

PROSPECT LAKE

Fish in designated areas—you might catch catfish and carp. *Prospect Park, bordered by Flatbush Ave., Ocean Ave., Parkside Ave., Prospect Park SW, and Prospect Park W, 718/965–8999. Subway: 2, 3 to Grand Army Plaza; Q to Prospect Park; F to 15th St./Prospect Park.*

1 *f-8*

SHEEPSHEAD BAY

Fishing boats line the piers along Emmons Avenue, crying out for you to join them in search of fluke, bluefish, striped bass, sea bass, and blackfish, among others. Many boats head to Mud-hole, a prime fishing ground, between 6 AM and 8 AM for all-day trips or at 8 AM and 1 PM for half-day outings. Options include the *Dorothy B. VIII* (Pier 6, 718/

646–4057). Check with Stella Maris Bait and Tackle (2702 Emmons Ave., 718/646–9754) for more information. *Subway: Q express to Sheepshead Bay.*

manhattan

7 *d-4*

CENTRAL PARK

The lake has carp, catfish, and bullheads. You can also use free bamboo poles and bait from the Dana Discovery Center to angle (catch and release) in the Harlem Meer, which is stocked with bluegills, bass, shiners, and catfish. No permit is required. This site is popular with families. *Dana Discovery Center, Harlem Meer (near 110th St. and 5th Ave.), 212/860–1370. Program runs July–Aug.; closed Mon. Subway: B, C to 110th St./Cathedral Pkwy.*

1 *c-5*

HUDSON RIVER PARK

Organizers supply bait and tackle for youngsters to catch and release in the Hudson. *Various piers; may include 25 (N. Moore St.), 62 (W. 23rd St.), and 84 (W. 44th St.), 212/533–7275.*

queens

1 *h-6*

ROCKAWAY

Catch bass, flounder, and porgies in the Atlantic saltwater off Breezy Point. There's freshwater fishing at Beach Channel Drive and Beach 32 Street. *Subway: A to Beach 36 St.*

staten island

1 *b-4*

WOLFE'S POND

There are freshwater fishing year-round and saltwater fishing October–May. *Wolfe's Pond Park: Holton to Cornelia Aves. on Raritan Bay, Prince's Bay, 718/984–8266.*

FOOTBALL

The pro-football season extends from early September through December. All local games take place at New Jersey's **Giants Stadium.** Tickets are extremely difficult, if not impossible, to come by, though you might luck out at the stadium just before a game if the visiting team hasn't used up its share. Arena

football, a chaotic game resembling a cross between indoor soccer and football, is played April–July.

teams to watch

NEW JERSEY GLADIATORS

New Jersey's arena football team got a new name and owner in 2000 (they used to be known as the Red Dogs). What the new name will mean for the team has yet to be seen. *Continental Airlines Arena, Meadowlands Sports Complex, East Rutherford, NJ, 888/733–3647.*

NEW YORK GIANTS

The Giants played at the New York Polo Grounds, Yankee Stadium, the Yale Bowl, and Shea Stadium before settling into their New Jersey home in 1976. Tickets are very hard to come by; all are sold through season subscriptions. *Meadowlands Sports Complex, East Rutherford, NJ, 201/935–8222.*

NEW YORK JETS

With a new head coach, Herman Edwards, and a new general manager, Terry Bradway, loyal Jets fans are hoping for a bright future—and a chance at Super Bowl glory. *Giants Stadium, Meadowlands Sports Complex, East Rutherford, NJ, 516/560–8200.*

where to play

There are about two dozen municipal football–soccer fields in New York City; call the Parks Department (*see* Parks Information, *above*) for a permit and a field near you.

GOLF

Manhattanites may find this hard to picture, but there are 13 public golf courses in the outer boroughs, and most are in good condition. Call the individual course to reserve your tee time. Fees are usually just under $20 for city residents (depending on tee time), slightly higher on weekends, and reservations and cart rentals cost about $2 extra. Golf season runs from mid-March through October or November.

bronx

2 *b-2*

MOSHOLU GOLF COURSE

The nine holes on this 3,119-yard course include many challenging shots. *Van*

Cortlandt Park, Jerome Ave. and 213th St., 718/655–9164. Subway: 1 to 242nd St./Van Cortlandt Park.

2 g-2

PELHAM GOLF COURSE

There are two scenic 18-hole courses here—the 6,281-yard Split Rock, one of the city's most challenging (USGA rating 70.3), and the 6,405-yard Pelham course. The former is hilly, with many trees, while the latter is flatter and open. *Pelham Bay Park, 870 Shore Rd., 718/885–1258. Subway: 6 to Pelham Bay Park.*

2 b-2

VAN CORTLANDT GOLF COURSE

Opened in 1895, this is the oldest public golf course in the country. Its 18 holes include two longer than 600 yards, for 6,102 yards total. *Van Cortlandt Park, Bailey Ave., 718/543–4595. Subway: 1 to 242nd St./Van Cortlandt Park.*

brooklyn

4 d-6

DYKER BEACH PARK

The wide fairways on this long (6,548 yards), busy course are tough but forgiving. *7th Ave. and 86th St., Bay Ridge, 718/836–9722. Subway: R to 86th St.*

1 f-7

MARINE PARK

Its 6,866 yards make this Robert Trent Jones–designed course the longest in the city, and its seaside location means it's flat and breezy. *2880 Flatbush Ave. (between Ave. U and Belt Pkwy.), Flatlands, 718/338–7113. Subway: 2 or 5 to Flatbush Ave., to Green Line bus.*

queens

1 g-3

CLEARVIEW

One of the most heavily trafficked courses in the country, if not the world, Clearview is straight, flat, and good for beginners. The championship course is 6,473 yards. *202–12 Willets Point Blvd., Bayside, 718/229–2570. Subway: 7 to Willets Pt./Shea Stadium, #16 bus.*

DOUGLASTON PARK

The 6,500-yard layout is rolling, with small greens and narrow fairways. *63–20 Marathon Pkwy. and Commonwealth*

Blvd., Douglaston, 718/224–6566. Long Island Rail Road: Port Washington line to Douglaston.

1 f-5

FOREST PARK

This course is 6,300 challenging yards in aptly named Woodhaven. *1 Forest Park Dr. S, Woodhaven, 718/296–0999. Subway: J, Z to Woodhaven Blvd.*

1 f-3

KISSENA PARK

The fairways are well-used and close together at this relatively short, hilly course. *164–15 Booth Memorial Ave., 718/939–4594. Subway: 7 to Main St./Flushing.*

staten island

1 b-2

LA TOURETTE GOLF COURSE

The fairways are long and varied at this scenic and challenging (par-72) course. *1001 Richmond Hill Rd., 718/351–1889.*

4 a-7

SILVER LAKE

At this pretty, 6,050-yard course, hills and tight fairways challenge golfers, of whom there are usually many. *915 Victory Blvd. (near Forest Ave.), 718/447–5686.*

1 a-3

SOUTH SHORE

Formerly part of a country club, this 6,366-yard course is still very well maintained, with lots of trees. *Huguenot Ave. and Rally St., 718/984–0101.*

HANDBALL

There are more than 2,000 municipal handball courts throughout the boroughs, many of them at playgrounds. Call your local Parks office for one near you.

HIKING

You don't have to leave the city to bushwhack, wade through marshes, or get lost on wooded paths. In addition to the trails described here, check out those at Jamaica Bay Wildlife Refuge, Pelham Park, and Van Cortlandt Park.

bronx

 a-1

WAVE HILL CENTER FOR ENVIRONMENTAL STUDIES

Known for its spectacular gardens, Wave Hill is one of NYC's prime get-away-from-it-all spots. For an easy hike, ramble along this 1½-mi marked trail. *675 W. 252nd St., 718/549–3200. MetroNorth to Riverdale.*

manhattan

 b-5

INWOOD HILL PARK

Short nature trails pass tree identifications and an Indian cave. *Urban Ecology Center, 218th St. and Indian Rd., 888/697–2757. Subway: A to 207th St.*

staten island

 b-2

GREENBELT

Trek through 28 mi of trails including a 13-mi loop and the 7-mi La Tourette Trail. *Greenbelt Conservancy, 200 Nevada Ave., 718/667–2165. Staten Island Ferry to Bus S74.*

HOCKEY

teams to watch

The professional hockey season runs from October through April.

NEW JERSEY DEVILS

After winning the Stanley Cup in 2000, the Devils' future continues to look bright, and the fans are loving every minute of it. *Continental Airlines Arena, Meadowlands Sports Complex, East Rutherford, NJ, 201/935–3900.*

NEW YORK RANGERS

Walk by the Garden on any game night, and you'll undoubtedly hear chants of "Here we go, Rangers, here we go" from this team's fans, who give new meaning to the word loyal. Rangers fans take their team—with past greats such as Mark Messier and Wayne Gretzky—very, very seriously. *Madison Square Garden, 212/465–6741. Subway: 1, 2, 3, A, C, E to 34th St./Penn Station.*

NEW YORK ISLANDERS

Of the three local teams, you'll have the easiest time getting tickets for this one—unless they ever again play half as well as they did in the 1980s. *Nassau Veterans Memorial Coliseum, 1255 Hempstead Tpke., Uniondale, NY, 800/882–4753.*

where to play

 d-4

LASKER RINK

You can drop in on games on weekends during the skating season; bring your own equipment. *Central Park at 106th St., 212/534–7639. Subway: B, C to 103rd St.*

HORSE RACING

 g-5

AQUEDUCT

Thoroughbreds have been racing at Aqueduct, the only racetrack in the city, since 1894. Its season runs from October to early May, Wednesday–Sunday. *Rockaway Blvd. and 110th St., Ozone Park, Queens, 718/641–4700. Subway: A to Aqueduct/North Conduit Ave.*

 g-3

BELMONT PARK

Thoroughbred races move here from Aqueduct in mid-May, continue through June, and then pick up again from early September through October (Wed.–Sun.). Belmont Stakes, held in June, is the third event in horse racing's Triple Crown. The so-called Breakfast at Belmont—trackside breakfast and then a tram tour—can be fun (weekends and holidays 7 AM–9:30 AM). *Hempstead Tpke. and Plainfield Ave., Elmont, NY, 516/488–6000 or 718/641–4700. LIRR: Hempstead Line to Belmont.*

MEADOWLANDS RACETRACK

Trotters and pacers race January through mid-August; the flat-track season is Labor Day through December. *Meadowlands Sports Complex, East Rutherford, NJ, 201/935–8500.*

YONKERS RACEWAY

There's harness racing every evening except Wednesday and Sunday year-round. *Yonkers Ave., Yonkers, NY, 718/562–9500 or 914/968–4200; 914/682–2020 for Westchester Bee Lines bus information.*

HORSEBACK RIDING

Manhattan's Central Park has 4½ mi of horse trails, including one around the reservoir (one level down from the jogging path). Though stables are usually busy, especially on weekends, the limited number of horses available means that your route won't be too congested.

bronx

2 a-3

RIVERDALE EQUESTRIAN CENTRE

This "centre" for learning and competing was created by two former Olympians, who renovated, expanded, and generally improved the Van Cortlandt Riding Academy. Facilities include an Olympic-size indoor arena (100 ft by 200 ft), outdoor rings, and the trails in Van Cortlandt Park. There are pony rides for children daily. *Broadway and W. 254th St., 718/548–4848. Subway: 1 to 242nd St./Van Cortlandt Park.*

brooklyn

4 e-2

KENSINGTON STABLES

These horses are good for easy rides through Prospect Park. *51 Caton Pl. (between E. State St. and Coney Island Ave.), Kensington, 718/972–4588. Subway: W to Fort Hamilton Pkwy.*

1 f-6

JAMAICA BAY RIDING ACADEMY

Choose between deserted wooded trails and sandy beaches as you explore the 300 acres open to you, or take a lesson on the indoor ring. *7000 Shore Pkwy., 718/531–8949. Subway: L to Rockaway Pkwy.*

manhattan

7 b-6

CLAREMONT RIDING ACADEMY

A National Historic Site, this academy has been in its Upper West Side location since it opened in 1892. Claremont has an indoor ring and prides itself on its teaching, but this is also the place to rent a horse for a ride through Central Park. *175 W. 89th St., Upper West Side, 212/724–5100. Subway: 1, 9 to 86th St.*

queens

1 f-4

LYNNE'S RIDING ACADEMY

This low-key place has an indoor ring, guided trail riding through Forest Park, and lessons. *88–03 70th Rd., Forest Hills, 718/261–7679. Subway: E, F, V, R to 71st–Continental Aves./Forest Hills.*

staten island

1 a-4

EQUUS STABLES

Children's lessons are the specialty, but adults are welcome, too. Everything is done in rings; there are no trail horses. *2498 Veterans Rd. W, 718/948–9515.*

ICE-SKATING

Skating is allowed on park lakes and ponds in all boroughs when there's a "hard freeze," which doesn't happen very often in the city. Call your local park to find out when pond skating is permitted. The Department of Parks and Recreation operates a number of rinks that get very crowded at predictable times; the season is November–April. Private rinks also fill up, but some have longer or year-round seasons. All rinks rent skates.

brooklyn

4 f-2

KATE WOLLMAN MEMORIAL RINK

This popular outdoor rink is surrounded by Prospect Park's trees and offers both open skating and closed figure-skating practice sessions. It's open daily in season. *East Dr. (near Lincoln Rd. and Parkside Ave.), Prospect Park, 718/287–6431. Subway: 2, 3 to Grand Army Plaza; Q to Prospect Park; F to 15th St./Prospect Park.*

manhattan

7 e-8

ICE STUDIO

Just 35 ft by 55 ft, this tiny indoor rink (open year-round) is fun for children. *1034 Lexington Ave. (at 74th St.), 2nd floor, Upper East Side, 212/535–0304. Closed Aug. Subway: 6 to 77th St.*

7 *d-4*

LASKER RINK

These large outdoor rinks are cheaper and less crowded than Wollman. Instead of skyscrapers, they have woodsy views. *Central Park at 106th St., 212/534–7639. Subway: B, C to 103rd St.*

6 *c-6*

RIVERBANK STATE PARK

This covered outdoor rink is popular with families. *Riverside Dr. at 145th St., Harlem, 212/694–3642. Subway: 1 to 145th St.*

9 *d-4*

ROCKEFELLER CENTER

This small, very busy, private outdoor rink is the classic place to skate in New York. Just watching from above is very entertaining—seasoned locals and giddy tourists scuttle around together. With late-night skating under the famous Christmas tree in December, it's festive and romantic. *Rockefeller Plaza (5th Ave. at 50th St.), Midtown, 212/332–7654. Open Oct.–Apr. Subway: B, D, F, V to 47th–50th Sts./Rockefeller Center; E, V to 5th Ave.*

9 *a-8*

SKY RINK

The entire Chelsea Piers Complex got started because its developer needed a place for his daughter to skate. Several years later, we have two private, Olympic-size indoor rinks—one for events and the other for general skating—with lessons, hockey leagues, and special events galore. The views from the top of the pier are amazing but sometimes disorienting—when the sun is beating down and sails are flapping on the Hudson, for example. *Chelsea Piers (23rd St. and 12th Ave.), Pier 61, 212/336–6100. Rink open 24 hrs year-round; call for open skating hours. Subway: C, E to 23rd St.*

9 *d-2*

WOLLMAN RINK

Nestled within trees nestled within skyscrapers, Wollman has a picture-perfect urban setting. Even when it's crowded, and it usually is, people are having the time of their lives. There's late-night skating to popular music on weekend evenings. *Central Park, East Dr. near 63rd St., 212/396–1010. Subway: N, R to 5th Ave.*

queens

1 *f-3*

WORLD'S FAIR ICE RINK

This indoor rink gets crowded; the critical mass can be intimidating. *Flushing Meadows–Corona Park, New York City Bldg., Long Island Expressway and Grand Central Pkwy., 718/271–1996. Closed Mon., Tues., Thurs. Subway: 7 to Willets Point/Shea Stadium.*

staten island

4 *a-7*

STATEN ISLAND WAR MEMORIAL RINK

These two enclosed outdoor rinks are the best places to skate on Staten Island. *Clove Lakes Park, Victory Blvd. at Clove Rd., 718/720–1010.*

IN-LINE SKATING & ROLLER SKATING

The in-line skating craze may have been eclipsed by scooters, but you'll still see plenty of New Yorkers whizzing by. All you need to join them are skates, a helmet, and wrist guards (other padding is recommended), which can fit in even the tiniest of apartments.

clubs & schools

EMPIRE SKATE CLUB

Founded in 1997 because New York skating needed at least some semblance of organization, Empire Skate runs recreational skating trips and skate-centric social events, including the Tuesday Night Skate, the leisurely Thursday Evening Roll through a car-free Central Park, and monthly midnight jaunts. *212/774–1774.*

LEZLY SKATE SCHOOL

A few skating lessons with Lezly's skating specialists (indoor and outdoor, traditional and in-line) will stop you from wobbling in no time. Roller-dancing is taught, too. This is also the home of the Central Park Dance Skaters Association, whose members you'll find disco dancing in a giant loop on the defunct park road south of 72nd Street on weekend afternoons. *212/777–3232.*

where to skate

For suggested routes beyond those listed here, see Bicycling, above.

Central Park—specifically the block-long stretch of Loop Road south of the West 67th Street entrance—is the heart of city skating. The less-traveled Cherry Hill, the Mall, and the "dead road" parallel to the Mall are good for practicing. The lower portion of the Loop Road is skate central, but only slightly more so than the rest of the park. **Wollman Rink** is good for tinier laps. Other popular skating grounds in Manhattan are the north section of **Union Square Park** (when it's not a Greenmarket), the waterfront esplanade from **Battery Park** to **Hudson River Park,** and **Riverside Park.** Aggressive skaters do tricks at what's known at the **Brooklyn Banks,** the sloped asphalt directly under the Manhattan side of the Brooklyn Bridge. Vert ramps, half pipes, quarter pipes, rails, and other amenities specifically for skating are at the skate parks at **Chelsea Piers** (23rd St. and 12th Ave., 212/336–6200) and **Riverside Park** (Riverside Dr. and 108th St., 212/408–0264). Both charge admission.

The **Central Park Skate Patrol** (212/439–1234) is the top source for all things skate-oriented in the park. The Patrol also offers in-depth classes on weekends.

9 b-8
ROXY

Manhattan's only indoor rink usually serves as a concert venue and dance club, but on Wednesday (when it opens to skaters) it becomes a roller disco, drawing a crowd that remembers when disco was the new thing. *515 W. 18th St., Chelsea, 212/645–5156. Subway: A, C, E to 14th St.*

9 d-2
WOLLMAN RINK

When the ice thaws, this wonderfully situated rink is turned over to the wheeled crowd. *Central Park, East Dr. near 63rd St., 212/396–1010. Subway: N, R to 5th Ave.*

LAWN BOWLING

Brought to us by the Dutch, lawn bowling was probably the first sport played in New York City, dating back to 1626—at Bowling Green. You'll need a seasonal permit to bowl on a municipal green; inquire with the Parks Department.

9 d-1
NEW YORK LAWN BOWLING CLUB

You must be a member to use the bowling green in Central Park, north of the Sheep Meadow (67th St. near West Dr.). Lawn bowlers and croquet players share the greens and clubhouse. Free lessons are given by appointment on Sunday mornings. *www.nybowls.com. Subway: B, C to 72nd St.*

MARTIAL ARTS

You can practice several varieties of martial arts in the city, including jiu-jitsu, judo, karate, aikido, tai chi chuan, and many others. Consult the Yellow Pages for an exhaustive listing of outlets.

brooklyn

4 d-1
BROOKLYN WOMEN'S MARTIAL ARTS

This all-women center has many loyal students and volunteers. Beginners' courses in self-defense, karate, and tai chi start at least once every three months. *421 5th Ave. (between 7th and 8th Sts.), 2nd floor, Park Slope, 718/788–1775. Subway: F, J, M to 4th Ave./9th St.*

manhattan

9 e-7
ULTIMATE GYM

This small, friendly, no-frills gym teaches Muay Thai, the physically demanding—the warm-up alone resembles boot camp—ancient fighting art of Thailand. Muay Thai combines boxing with kicking, kneeing, elbowing, and defensive techniques. All of the instructors have trained in Thailand, so the gym scores high on authenticity. Classes are coed and women encouraged; children are not allowed. This is not Tae Bo: don't come here if you don't want to sweat—a lot. *1 E. 28th St. (5th Ave.), Murray Hill, 212/725–4666. Subway: 6, N, R to 28th St.*

9 d-7
WORLD SEIDO KARATE ORGANIZATION

A traditional karate school, World Seido was founded by 9th-degree black belt Kaicho Tadashi Nakamura. Men, women, and children are welcome to observe or participate in classes, which run all day long and are excellent. The karate training can provide conditioning and teach skills useful for self-defense. *61 W. 23rd St., Chelsea, 212/924–0511. Subway: F, V to 23rd St.*

MINIATURE GOLF

brooklyn

1 *f-7*
GATEWAY SPORTS CENTER
Right on Rockaway Inlet, this 18-hole, rough-terrain course and 100-tee driving range offer peaceful putting. *3200 Flatbush Ave. (opposite Floyd Bennett Field), Flatlands, 718/253–6816, Subway: 2 to Flatbush Ave, Green Line bus Q35.*

manhattan

11 *a-8*
PIER 25
This outdoor course is open seasonally. The 18 holes are your typical miniature course, but the river breeze and views make it special. *Pier 25 (near Reade St.), TriBeCa, 212/732–7467. Subway: 1, 2 to Franklin St.*

7 *h-2*
RANDALL'S ISLAND GOLF & FAMILY ENTERTAINMENT CENTER
There are two 18-hole minigolf courses and a driving range at this off-the-beaten-track site—and they're worth the trip on a sunny day. You'll feel a million miles away from the bustle of Manhattan. A shuttle bus (times vary) will get you there. *Randall's Island Golf Center, 212/427–5689. Shuttle bus leaves from 3rd Ave. and 86th St., Upper East Side.*

queens

1 *g-3*
ALLEY POND GOLF CENTER
These two 18-hole courses are opposite the salt marshes of the Alley Pond Environmental Center. They have your basic greens, holes, and bumps, though the masters course is more challenging. *Alley Pond Park, Douglaston, 718/225–9187.*

PADDLEBALL, RAQUETBALL & SQUASH

There are more than 400 paddleball courts in the city—including **Coney Island**, Brooklyn; **Orchard Beach**, Bronx; and **Central Park**, Manhattan. Call the parks hotline in your borough for the nearest court. The National Paddleball Association organizes tournaments and instruction. Most clubs charge a guest fee in addition to an hourly court fee for nonmembers; many don't allow them at all.

brooklyn

12 *b-2*
EASTERN ATHLETIC CLUBS
The five racquetball courts and two squash courts host lessons and leagues in addition to regular games. Nonmembers pay a guest fee ($25), but the court fee during off-peak periods is only $6 per hour. It's $16 at peak times. *43 Clark St. (between Henry and Hicks Sts.), Brooklyn Heights, 718/625–0500. Subway: 1, 2 to Clark St.*

manhattan

9 *e-6*
ATHLETIC COMPLEX
Before this place became a complete fitness center it was strictly racquet sports; now there's just one squash court left. Nonmembers are permitted for a fee ($10 to enter, $20 to reserve the court). *3 Park Ave. (entrance on 34th St.), Murray Hill, 212/686–1085. Subway: 6 to 33rd St.*

10 *e-8*
NEW YORK HEALTH & RACQUET CLUB
This racquet-sports specialist club has squash and racquetball courts at two locations. Nonmembers pay an extremely steep visitor's fee. *39 Whitehall St. (Pearl St.), Lower Manhattan, 212/269–9800. Subway: 4, 5 to Bowling Green.*

9 *e-4*
20 E. 50th St. (5th Ave.), Midtown East, 212/593–1500. Subway: E, V to 5th Ave./53rd St.

9 *c-2*
NEW YORK SPORTS CLUB
Take your pick of locations; court availability and fees vary. *61 W. 62nd St.*

(between 5th and 6th Aves.), Upper West Side, 212/265–0995. Subway: 1, 2, A, B, C, D to 59th St./Columbus Circle.

7 e-7

You'll only find squash courts here; no racquetball. 151 E. 86th St. (between Lexington and 3rd Aves.), Upper East Side, 212/860–8630. Subway: 4, 5, 6 to 86th St.

12 c-4

110 Boerum Pl. (between Pacific and Dean Sts.), Cobble Hill, Brooklyn, 718/643–4400. Subway: F, G to Bergen St.

11 b-3

PRINTING HOUSE FITNESS & RACQUET CLUB

The racquetball court and six squash courts at this full-service fitness club are for members only. 421 Hudson St. (at Leroy St.), Greenwich Village, 212/243–7600. Subway: 1, 2 to Houston St.

queens

3 e-3

BQE RACQUETBALL CLUB

You'll pay a guest fee on top of the court fee to play here, but it's a very nice facility. There are seven courts. 26–50 Brooklyn–Queens Expressway W, Woodside, 718/726–4343. Subway: R, V to Northern Blvd.

PADDLING

Water, water, everywhere, and a lot more boating opportunities than you think, even if you don't own your own craft. Look for more operators as the city better utilizes its waterways. Most rental agents require identification and/or a deposit in addition to the hourly rental charge (usually $10–$20). The **Urban Park Rangers** offer free kayaking from mid-May through mid-November (weather permitting) at eight city parks, including three launch sites on the Hudson River.

bronx

2 h-3

CITY ISLAND

From here you can row to your heart's content in Pelham Bay and the Long Island Sound. Boat Livery, 663 City Island Ave., 718/885–1843. Subway: 6 to Pelham Bay Park, then BX29 bus to City Island Ave.

2 g-2

PELHAM BAY PARK

This is the only regatta course in the city for both canoeing and rowing, but you have to bring your own boat. Bruckner Blvd. and Middletown Rd., Hunter Island Lagoon, 718/430–1890. Subway: 6 to Pelham Bay Park.

brooklyn

1 h-6

PROSPECT PARK

You and up to three friends can rent a pedal boat to tool around Prospect Lake and Lullwater. Boat rentals: Kate's Corner (at the Wollman Center), off East Lake Dr. (near Flatbush Ave. and Empire Blvd.), 718/282–7789. Subway: 2, 3 to Grand Army Plaza; Q to Prospect Park; F to 15th St./Prospect Park.

manhattan

9 d-1

CENTRAL PARK

Row around the 18-acre lake under gorgeous arched bridges in fine view of some of Manhattan's most beautiful apartment buildings. Rentals are near the Loeb Boathouse. Enter park at 5th Ave. and 72nd St., Upper East Side, 212/517–2233. Subway: 6 to 77th St.

11 b-7

DOWNTOWN BOATHOUSE

Free kayaking lessons on summer weekends and some evenings from a friendly, informative, all-volunteer group, and a spectacular view of the city once you're in the water, makes for a memorable warm-weather outing, especially at sunset. Pier 26, N. Moore St., TriBeCa and Pier 64, Midtown West, 212/385–2790. Subway: 1, 2 to Franklin St. or A, C, E to Canal St. for Pier 26; and 1, 2, F, V to 23rd St. for Pier 64.

9 b-5

FLOATING THE APPLE

Comprised of maritime historians, boatbuilders, and the interested public, this group is dedicated to keeping New York's small-craft history alive. From their boathouses on Pier 84 (W. 44th St.), Pier 40 (W. Houston St.), in Red Hook, Brooklyn, and in Hunts Point, in the Bronx, they have weekly public rows and sails on boats made by community groups, and they also organize reenact-

ments of important boating events. *212/
564–5412.*

9 *a-8*

MANHATTAN KAYAK COMPANY

Kayak owners can keep their equipment here, and newbies can learn paddling basics. Statue of Liberty and nighttime tours depart regularly. *Pier 63 (23rd St. and 12th Ave.), 212/924–1788. Subway: C, E to 23rd St.*

queens

3 *h-2*

FLUSHING MEADOWS– CORONA PARK

You can rent rowboats on Meadow Lake. *Park: Union Tpke. from 111th St. and Grand Central Pkwy. to the Van Wyck Extension, Flushing, 718/699–9596. Subway: 7 to 111th St. or Willets Point/Shea Stadium.*

PAINTBALL

The sport requires acres to play on, so you won't find tons of options in the city proper. Safety is of the utmost importance, so be choosy about where you play.

staten island

1 *a-3*

SI PAINTBALL

Offering speedball, open sessions, and kids' days (10 and up), SI Paintball is your source in the city for splattery fun. Safety is emphasized at this spot that also holds tournaments for hardcore players. Session fees (including equipment) start at $50; the 1,200 or so paintballs you'll need cost from $60–$75. *2727 Arthur Kill Rd., 718/227–1400. SI Ferry to bus S74.*

ROCK CLIMBING

Walls require that you take a lesson or pass a belay test (in which you hold the rope while your partner climbs) before you can climb or spot. You can rent equipment if you don't have your own. Routes are changed regularly (by moving the holds around) to keep the climbing interesting.

9 *a-7*

CHELSEA PIERS

There are two walls here, one 30 ft high (primarily for children and nonmembers; in the field house) and the other 46 ft high (in the Sports Center). With 10,000 square ft total, the latter has endless challenging routes. There's a bouldering wall, too, for ropeless climbing. The only drawback to this beautiful space is that you either have to be a member of Chelsea Piers or pay exorbitant day pass fees. *Field House (between Piers 61 and 62), Chelsea Piers (23rd St. and 12th Ave.), 212/336–6500. Sports Center, Pier 60, Chelsea Piers, 212/336–6000. Subway: C, E to 23rd St.*

9 *c-2*

EXTRAVERTICAL CLIMBING CENTER

This wall ranges from 30 ft to 50 ft high, and since it's in the public, open-air Harmony Atrium, it's a fun place to watch. It's also a fun place to climb, especially in warmer months—if you conquer the toughest routes closest to the entrance, you'll feel like you're practically hanging over the traffic of Broadway. ExtraVertical offers membership packages, but its prices for day passes are reasonable; the belay test is free. *61 W. 62nd St., Upper West Side, 212/586–5718. Subway: 1, 9, A, B, C, D to 59th St./Columbus Circle.*

9 *b-5*

MANHATTAN PLAZA HEALTH CLUB

MPHC was one of the earliest climbing games in town, but the small wall was always a little, well, small. A brisk renovation and expansion has changed all that. Now, 20-ft squeeze-through chimneys and 160 ft of bouldering traverses will impress even the most jaded rock jock—and provide a good place to warm-up during nice weather between weekend trips to the Gunks. A day pass is $15.60, plus $8 for shoes and harness, and a one-time fee of $5 for a belay test. *482 W. 43rd St. (between 9th and 10th Aves.), Midtown West, 212/563–7001. Subway: A, C, E to 42nd St./Port Authority.*

RUGBY

The **New York Rugby Club** fields both men's and women's sides. In addition to training and games during the league seasons (spring and fall), the club schedules drinking practice around televised rugby events—or for no reason. New members are always welcome; call 212/988–9201 for more information.

3 *C-1*
RANDALL'S ISLAND
Playing fields are to the right of the ramp off the Triborough Bridge; there are games most Saturday mornings in spring and fall.

RUNNING & WALKING

clubs

NEW YORK CITY HASH HOUSE HARRIERS
They call themselves drinkers with a running problem, but they actually organize fun scavenger *runs* throughout New York. If you successfully follow the trail, you end up in a bar with a cold drink. *212/427–4692.*

NEW YORK ROAD RUNNERS CLUB
Best known for the New York City Marathon and the New Year's Eve fun run, this is the largest runner's club in the world. It offers a full range of classes, clinics, group runs, races, and even merchandise for everyone from beginning runners to elite champions. Members get substantial discounts and a subscription to *Running News*. The Achilles Track Club (42 W. 38th St., 4th floor, 212/354–0300) has programs for physically challenged runners. *9 E. 89th St. (between Madison and Park Aves.), Upper East Side, Manhattan, 212/860–4455. Subway: 4, 5, 6 to 86th St.*

where to run
The **Jacqueline Kennedy Onassis Reservoir** in Central Park is a beautiful, 1.6-mi gravel path that most Manhattan runners have circled more times than they'd care to count. Waterfront paths and trails through the larger parks in all five boroughs are all well traveled by runners. **Prospect Park** and **Central Park** both have popular running lanes around their loop roads. Manhattan's **East River Esplanade,** about 4 mi round-trip from Carl Schurz Park to 125th Street, is prettiest at sunrise, though you should probably run with someone at that hour. Watch the sunset from **Riverside Park** while running between 72nd and 116th streets, also about 4 mi round-trip. There are cross-country courses in the Bronx's **Van Cortlandt Park** (6 mi), Brooklyn's **Marine Park** (0.8 mi) and **Alley Pond Park** (1.5 mi), Queens's **Forest Park** (2.5 mi), and Staten Island's **Clove Lakes Park** (3.3 mi). The general rule for figuring mileage in Manhattan is 20 short blocks to a mile. Call the Parks office in your borough for the municipal running track nearest you, and for other distance-running ideas *see* Bicycling, *above.*

SAILING

New York City was the national center for sailing in the 19th century, and the New York Yacht Club is still very influential nationwide. On City Island, some people still make sails or boats for a living. Experienced sailors should be able to help crew a boat off the island during the summer-long Wednesday-night race series (**City Island Yacht Club,** 718/885–2487).

10 *d-7*
MANHATTAN SAILING SCHOOL
The Manhattan Sailing School teaches sailing at all skill levels on J-24 boats in New York Harbor; you can also rent or charter boats. The school was founded in 1991 by the Manhattan Yacht Club, which had just reintroduced recreational sailing to Manhattan in 1987 after the sport's absence for more than half a century. You can join the Yacht Club once you pass Basic Sailing. *393 South End Ave., Lower Manhattan, 212/786–0400. Subway: 4, 5 to Bowling Green.*

10 *d-7*
NORTH COVE SAILING SCHOOL
An affiliate of the American Sailing Association and a neighbor of the larger Manhattan Sailing School, North Cove also teaches you to sail on J-24s. Experienced sailors can skipper or crew on boats from the fleet. *393 South End Ave., Lower Manhattan, 800/532–5552. Subway: 4, 5 to Bowling Green.*

SCUBA DIVING

Most scuba certification is either through **NAUI** (National Association of Underwater Instructors, 800/553–6284) or **PADI** (Professional Association of Diving Instructors, 800/729–7234), and both organizations can direct you to local programs. Classes include pool instruction and an open dive, which most people choose to complete while on vacation. Fees start at about $250, and class sessions can last anywhere from intensive weekends to a few months.

manhattan

7 d-2

AQUA-LUNG SCHOOL OF NEW YORK

All levels of classes—from beginner to medic to specialties such as dry suit and wreck diving—are offered. Pool time is logged at a pool in Upper Manhattan. All equipment is provided. *Millbank Center, Children's Aid Society, 118th St. between 5th and Lenox Aves., 212/582–2800. Subway: 2, 3 to 125th St.*

9 b-5

PAN AQUA DIVING

Pan Aqua teaches certification courses at seven Manhattan locations, including the 92nd St. YM–YWHA, West Side YMCA, Vanderbilt YMCA, and Manhattan Plaza Health Club. Based at Manhattan Plaza, Pan Aqua also offers free scuba trials, dive vacations, rentals, and repairs. *460 W. 43rd St., Midtown West, 212/736–DIVE. Subway: A, C, E to 42nd St./Port Authority.*

queens

3 h-3

NEW YORK SCUBA

This center has everything—instruction, sales, rentals, and occasional weekend trips along the Eastern seaboard. In addition to a PADI certification program, you can take an evening-long refresher course. *95–58 Queens Blvd. (near 63rd Dr.), Rego Park, 718/897–2885. Subway: R, V local to 63rd Dr./Rego Park.*

SKIING

After a heavy snow, cross-country skiers emerge from their apartments and take to the streets in that brief period before the white fluff becomes trampled, slushy, and gray. Bridle paths and fields tend to remain fresh longer. The **Scandinavian Ski Shop** (40 W. 57th St.

[between 5th and 6th Aves.], Midtown West, Manhattan, 212/757–8524) rents equipment.

bronx

2 b-3

VAN CORTLANDT PARK

The vast terrain, when it's smooth, makes for lovely cross-country skiing. *W. 242nd St. to city line, between Broadway and Jerome Ave., 718/430–1890. Subway: 1 to 242nd St./Van Cortlandt Park.*

brooklyn

4 c-4

OWL'S HEAD PARK

The views of the harbor just after a snowfall are otherworldly. The skiing is good here if you're comfortable on rolling hills. *Colonial Rd. at 68th St., Bay Ridge. Subway: J to Bay Ridge Ave.*

1 h-6

PROSPECT PARK

Long Meadow and Nethermead are good for beginners, though most everyone will enjoy them. *Park bordered by Flatbush Ave., Ocean Ave., Parkside Ave., Prospect Park SW, and Prospect Park W, 718/965–8999. Subway: 1, 2 to Grand Army Plaza; Q to Prospect Park; F to 15th St./Prospect Park.*

manhattan

9 c-9

CENTRAL PARK

The Sheep Meadow, the Great Lawn, and North Meadow are big and relatively flat, but you'll need to get there early for the best conditions. The bridle paths and pedestrian walkways are also lovely trails. *Enter the park at Central Park W and 72nd St. or 85th St., 212/360–3444 general information. Subway: B, C to 72nd St. or 81st St.*

queens

1 g-3

ALLEY POND PARK

The old Vanderbilt Highway provides good, gladed skiing for miles. The wetlands trail is another option. *228-06 Northern Blvd., 718/229–4000 environmental center. Subway: 7 to Flushing/Main St., Q12 bus to Northern Blvd.*

3 *h-2*

**FLUSHING MEADOWS–
CORONA PARK**
The bike paths and walkways through-
out the park provide plenty of routes.
*Union Tpke. from 111th St. and Grand
Central Pkwy. to the Van Wyck Extension,
Flushing, 718/699–4209. Subway: 7 to
111th St. or Willets Point/Shea Stadium.*

staten island

1 *b-2*

HIGH ROCK PARK
The small hills and quick turns on the
nature trails are best for experienced
skiers. *Richmond Pkwy. and Moravian
Cemetery at Rockland Ave.*

SOCCER

teams to watch

METROSTARS
New York's local Major League soccer
team, born in 1996, hasn't realized its
potential yet. The season is late March–
September. *Giants Stadium, Meadowlands Sports Complex, East Rutherford,
NJ, 201/935–3900.*

where to play
You need a permit to reserve any of the
park soccer fields; call the appropriate
parks office for information and locations. At many fields you'll have to bring
your own net.

SWIMMING

More than 30 city-run outdoor pools
are open from the 4th of July weekend
through Labor Day, and they're free—
just bring a bathing suit, towel, and
lock. Hours are usually 11–7, with an
hour's break in mid-afternoon. The
**Aquatics Division of the Department of
Parks and Recreation** (718/699–4219)
has information about pools, lessons,
and lap swimming. They're generally a
safe (if crowded) diversion. Use common sense—city pools probably aren't
the best place to model your new
Brazilian bikini, for example, and even
with lifeguards on duty, you shouldn't
swim alone. Indoor pools are open
year-round, with the exception of those
at public-recreation centers that also
have outdoor pools. For more municipal pools, check the government listings pages of the phone book under
Parks and Recreation—Swimming
Pools.

bronx

5 *f-3*

APEX
The beautiful 50-meter, 8-lane indoor
pool at Lehman College's athletic center
allows anyone to be a member for a reasonable yearly fee. *Lehman College, 250
Bedford Park Blvd. W, Jerome Park, 718/
960–1117. Subway: 4 to Bedford Park
Blvd./Lehman College.*

5 *h-8*

CROTONA POOL
This outdoor pool is very large, but it
still gets crowded. *E. 175th St. and Fulton
Ave., Morrisania, 718/822–4440. Subway:
C, D to 174th–175th Sts.*

2 *c-8*

**ST. MARY'S
RECREATION CENTER**
The rec center has an indoor pool that
gets crowded. It's closed on Sundays. *St. Ann's Ave. and E. 145th St.,
718/402–5157. Subway: E. 143rd St./St.
Mary's St.*

2 *b-3*

VAN CORTLANDT POOL
Van Cortlandt's outdoor pool is bigger
than most. *W. 244th St. east of Broadway,
718/548–2415. Subway: 1 to 242nd St./Van
Cortlandt Park.*

brooklyn

1 *f-5*

**BROWNSVILLE PLAYGROUND
RECREATION CENTER**
For $10 a year you can swim as a mem-
ber in this 75-ft indoor pool. *1555 Linden
Blvd. (at Christopher Ave.), 718/345–2706.
Subway: L to New Lots Ave.*

1 *d-6*

RED HOOK POOL
This outdoor pool is Brooklyn's largest.
*Bay and Henry Sts., 718/722–3211. Sub-
way: F, G to Smith–9th Sts.*

4 *d-3*

SUNSET PARK POOL

This outdoor neighborhood pool is large and popular. *7th Ave. and 43rd St., 718/965–6578. Subway: J, M, W to 45th St.*

manhattan

7 *g-6*

ASPHALT GREEN AQUACENTER

This indoor sea—oops, pool—is state-of-the-art, with a movable bottom and bulkheads that can divide it into manageable subsections. It's Olympic-size—50 meters long—and nonmembers can swim at certain hours for a fee. *1750 York Ave. (at 91st St.), Upper East Side, 212/369–8890. Subway: 4, 5, 6 to 86th St.*

9 *g-8*

ASSER LEVY RECREATION CENTER

This public rec center used to be a bathhouse, and its indoor pool is small but beautiful—natural light, high ceiling. There's a larger outdoor pool, too; the indoor one closes when the other is open. *E. 23rd St. and Asser Levy Pl. (between 1st Ave. and FDR Dr.), Gramercy, 212/447–2020. Subway: 6 to 23rd St.*

11 *b-3*

CARMINE RECREATION CENTER

The indoor pool closes when the outdoor one opens. Both are no-frills but in good condition. *7th Ave. S at Clarkson St., West Village, 212/242–5228. Subway: 1, 2 to Houston St.*

9 *f-3*

EAST 54TH ST. RECREATION CENTER

There's a small indoor pool here. *348 E, 54th St., Midtown, 212/397–3154. Subway: 6 to 51st St.; E, V to Lexington–3rd Aves./53rd St.*

7 *g-8*

JOHN JAY PARK POOL

The park has a nice view from its perch above the East River. *E. 77th St. and Cherokee Pl. (near York Ave.), Upper East Side, 212/794–6566. Subway: 6 to 77th St.*

7 *c-4*

LASKER POOL

This is Manhattan's largest outdoor pool. *Central Park at 106th St., Morning-side Heights, 212/534–7639. Subway: B, C to 103rd St.*

9 *b-5*

MANHATTAN PLAZA HEALTH CLUB

The 75-ft lap pool at this private club is a big draw, especially on bright summer days when the atrium roof opens. Nonmembers are welcome, for a fee. *482 W. 43rd St. (between 9th and 10th Aves.), Midtown West, 212/563–7001. Subway: A, C, E, to 42nd St./Port Authority.*

6 *c-6*

RIVERBANK STATE PARK

This indoor lap pool is one of the cheapest nonmunicipal options ($3); there's also an outdoor pool in summer. *Riverside Dr. at 145th St., Harlem, 212/694–3600. Subway: 1 to 145th St.*

9 *f-4*

VANDERBILT YMCA

There are two pools here: a 75-ft shallow lap pool and a smaller pool with a deep end for lessons and classes. Nonmembers are welcome for a guest fee. *224 E. 47th St. (between 2nd and 3rd Aves.), Midtown East, 212/756–9600. Subway: 6 to 51st St.*

queens

8 *b-5*

ASTORIA PARK POOL

The 1936 Olympic trials were held in this large outdoor pool near the East River. *19th St. and 23rd Dr., Astoria, 718/626–8620. Subway: W to Ditmars Blvd./Astoria.*

1 *g-4*

ROY WILKINS RECREATION CENTER

There's an indoor pool at this St. Albans rec center. *177th St. and Baisley Blvd., 718/276–8686.*

staten island

1 *a-1*

FABER PARK POOL

This outdoor pool is a good size. *2175 Richmond Terr. at Faber St., Port Richmond, 718/816–5259.*

1 *a-4*
TOTTENVILLE POOL
This standard-size outdoor pool is on the country club–inspired south shore. *Hylan Blvd. and Joline Ave., Tottenville, 718/356–8242.*

TENNIS

Staten Islander Mary Outerbridge introduced Americans to tennis in the 19th century, and New Yorkers have loved the sport ever since. To play on a municipal court (Apr.–Nov.), you'll need a permit. In Manhattan they're available at the **Parks Department's headquarters** at the Arsenal (830 5th Ave., at 64th St.). Permits are $50 for the year; single-play passes are also available. Reservations, which are useful at some courts, cost extra, and many facilities have lockers for a charge as well. For complete information about permits, and for numbers to call in other boroughs, call 212/360–8131.

where to play
All of these courts are city-owned unless otherwise noted. For an exhaustive list, call your borough's Parks office.

bronx

2 *d-4*
BRONX PARK
There are six courts here. *Bronx Park E and Brady Ave., Bronxdale. Subway: 2, 5 to Bronx Park East.*

2 *c-6*
CROTONA PARK
These 20 hard courts are the among best in the Bronx. *E. 173rd St. and Crotona Ave., Morrisania. Subway: C, D to 174th–175th Sts.*

6 *f-4*
MULLALY PARK
There are 16 good courts here. *164th St. and Jerome Ave., Highbridge. Subway: 4, B, D to 161st St./Yankee Stadium.*

2 *g-2*
PELHAM BAY PARK
This park has 10 courts. *Bruckner Blvd. and Middletown Rd., Pelham Bay. Subway: 6 to Pelham Bay Park.*

2 *b-2*
VAN CORTLANDT PARK
There are eight clay courts here. *W. 241st St. and Broadway, Riverdale. Subway: 1 to 242nd St./Van Cortlandt Park.*

5 *g-1*
WILLIAMSBRIDGE OVAL
This area has eight hard courts. *E. 208th St. and Bainbridge Ave., Norwood. Subway: D to 205th St.*

brooklyn

4 *g-6*
BROOKLYN RACQUET CLUB
There are 11 clay courts under a bubble here. This private facility opens early and doesn't close until the wee hours; courts are available for an hourly fee. *2781 Shell Rd. (near Ave. Z and McDonald Ave.), Brighton Beach, 718/769–5167. Subway: F to Avenue X.*

12 *e-2*
FORT GREENE PARK
This park has six hard courts. *DeKalb and S. Portland Aves. Subway: 1, 2, 4, 5, Q local to Atlantic Ave.*

4 *g-7*
KAISER PLAYGROUND
There are 12 hard courts here. *Neptune Ave. and W. 25th St., Coney Island. Subway: F, M, Q express, W to Stillwell Ave./Coney Island.*

4 *d-4*
LEIF ERICSON PARK
There are nine hard courts here. *8th Ave. and 66th St., Bay Ridge. Subway: N to 8th Ave.*

1 *f-8*
MANHATTAN BEACH
This small beach has six hard courts that aren't too busy. *Oriental Blvd. and Mackenzie St. Subway: Q express to Brighton Beach.*

1 *f-7*
MARINE PARK
There are 15 hard courts here. *Inlet between Gerritsen and Flatbush Aves., inland to Fillmore Ave., between Burnet and E. 32nd Sts.*

4 *f-2*

**PROSPECT PARK
PARADE GROUND**

There are 10 clay courts here. *Coney Island Ave. and Parkside Ave., Prospect Park S. Subway: N to Fort Hamilton Pkwy.*

manhattan

7 *d-5*

**CENTRAL PARK
TENNIS CENTER**

Reservations are a good idea at these busy city courts. In addition to four hard courts and 26 Har-Tru courts, the center offers professional instruction, tournaments, and locker rooms. *Park bordered by Central Park W, 110th St., 5th Ave., and 59th St. Courts midpark (enter at W. 96th St.), 212/280–0205. Subway: B, C to 96th St.*

9 *d-6*

CROSSTOWN TENNIS

Take note: on hot summer days, these four indoor courts are air-conditioned. They're available for an hourly fee. *14 W. 31st St. (between 5th and 6th Aves.), Midtown West, 212/947–5780. Subway: B, D, F, N, Q, R, V to 34th St./Herald Sq.*

10 *h-2*

EAST RIVER PARK

These 12 courts are in good shape but are not busy—perhaps because they're a little too close to the cacophonous East River Drive. *East River Dr. between 14th and Delancey Sts., East Village/Lower East Side. Subway: F to Delancey St.*

6 *e-6*

**FRED JOHNSON
MEMORIAL PARK**

They turn the lights on at night for these eight hard courts. *Adam Clayton Powell, Jr., Blvd. at 151st St., Harlem. Subway: 3 to 148th St./Lenox Terminal.*

5 *b-5*

INWOOD HILL PARK

These nine courts are only busy on weekends. *W. 207th St. at Seaman Ave. Subway: A to 207th St./Inwood.*

9 *b-5*

**MANHATTAN PLAZA
RACQUET CLUB**

The five rooftop courts are covered by a bubble in the winter, open-air (with great views) in the summer, and lighted after dark. They're open to nonmembers by appointment; fees vary, so call ahead. *450 W. 43rd St. (between 9th and 10th Aves.), Midtown West, 212/594–0554. Subway: A, C, E to 42nd St./Port Authority.*

9 *c-7*

MIDTOWN TENNIS CLUB

The eight Har-Tru courts—all under a bubble in winter and half bubbled (and air-conditioned) in summer—charge an hourly fee for nonmembers. *341 8th Ave. (at 27th St.), Midtown West, 212/989–8572. Subway: C, E to 23rd St.*

1 *d-3*

RANDALL'S ISLAND

These 11 outdoor courts are covered by a bubble during the winter. *Randall's Island, 212/534–4845.*

7 *a-5*

RIVERSIDE PARK

There are 10 clay courts at 96th Street and 10 hard courts at 119th Street. *Enter park at Riverside Dr. and 96th St. or 115th St., Upper West Side. Subway: 1, 2, 3 to 96th St.; 1, 9 to 116th St./Columbia University.*

9 *g-2*

**SUTTON EAST
TENNIS CLUB**

From October to April there's a bubble under the Queensboro Bridge, with eight clay courts inside available for a steep fee. *488 E. 60th St., Upper East Side, 212/751–3452. Subway: 4, 5, 6, Q local, W to 59th St.*

9 *e-5*

**THE TENNIS CLUB
AT GRAND CENTRAL**

This very expensive club has the city's oldest and most uniquely located indoor courts. Enter Grand Central at 43rd and Vanderbilt. *15 Vanderbilt Ave., 3rd floor, Midtown East, 212/687–3841. Subway: 4, 5, 6 to 42nd St./Grand Central.*

queens

1 *g-3*

ALLEY POND PARK

In winter these 16 municipal courts are covered by a bubble to become the private Alley Pond Tennis Club. *Grand Central Pkwy. and Winchester Blvd., Bayside, 718/468–1239.*

3 *d-2*

ASTORIA PARK

There are 14 courts here under the Triborough Bridge. *21st St. and Hoyt Ave., Astoria. Subway: W to Astoria Blvd.*

1 *g-3*

CUNNINGHAM PARK

This park has 20 hard courts and indoor facilities for winter, too. *Union Tpke. and 196th St., Fresh Meadows.*

3 *c-4*

EAST RIVER TENNIS CLUB

You can take a shuttle bus from Manhattan to this large private tennis club. There are 20 courts outdoors in the summer, and 18 indoors in the winter. *44-02 Vernon Blvd. (at 44th Ave.), Long Island City, 718/784–0600. Shuttle from Sutton Theatre, 3rd Ave. and 57th St., Midtown East. Subway: F to 21st St./Queensbridge.*

3 *h-1*

FLUSHING FIELDS

In the shadow of the U.S.T.A. Center, these eight courts are kept in excellent shape and are accordingly busy. *Flushing Meadows–Corona Park, Flushing. Subway: 7 to Willets Point/Shea Stadium.*

1 *f-5*

FOREST PARK

This park has 14 courts—seven hard and seven clay. *Park La. S and 89th St., Woodhaven. Subway: J to 85th St./Forest Pkwy.*

1 *f-3*

KISSENA PARK

This quiet section of the park has four hard courts. *Rose Ave. and Parsons Blvd., Kissena. Subway: 7 to Main St./Flushing.*

3 *h-2*

U.S.T.A. NATIONAL TENNIS CENTER

Considering the great playing that takes place on these courts, the hourly fees are pretty reasonable, generally topping out at $25. There are 33 public courts, some of them indoors and lighted. *Flushing Meadows–Corona Park, 718/760–6200. Subway: 7 to Willets Point/Shea Stadium.*

staten island

1 *b-1*

SILVER LAKE PARK

These four courts have an idyllic locale, but they've seen better days. *Hart Blvd. and Revere St., Brighton Heights.*

1 *b-1*

WALKER PARK

There are six hard courts here. *Bard Ave. and Delafield Pl., Livingston.*

VOLLEYBALL

There are more than 300 volleyball courts in New York City; young 9-to-5ers spike hard after work. Call your borough's Parks office for the one nearest you.

clubs

BIG CITY VOLLEYBALL LEAGUE

Show up for the four-hour Friday Night Club to spike and socialize for a small fee. Call for locations, which depend on your level of play. *212/288–4240.*

NEW YORK URBAN PROFESSIONALS VOLLEYBALL LEAGUE

It sounds like a yuppie group, and it is, but they have teams to suit all skill levels. Locations vary depending on level and season. *212/877–3614.*

where to play

11 *b-7*

PIER 25

There's an outdoor sand volleyball court right on the Hudson, on so-called Manhattan Beach Inc. A group can rent the entire court for an hourly fee; individuals can play for a daily rate. *N. Moore St. and 12th Ave., TriBeCa, 212/732–7467. Subway: 1, 2 to Franklin St.*

WRESTLING

Madison Square Garden has championship, professional, and exhibition wrestling matches one weekend a month. For information, call 212/465–6741.

YOGA

Most gyms around town offer some kind of yoga program, but you usually have to be a member to take the classes.

brooklyn

12 *f-6*

PARK SLOPE YOGA CENTER

Hatha, Astanga, Vinyasa, and Jivamukti yoga are all offered at this laid-back center. *792 Union St. (between 6th and 7th Aves.), Park Slope, 718/789–2288. Subway: Q to 7th Ave.*

manhattan

9 *e-8*

DHARMA YOGA CENTER

This spare and peaceful space is run by Yogi Dharma Mittra and offers children's yoga, as well as more advanced classes. The drop in price is $15 ($12 for beginner classes) and there are discounts for monthly memberships. *297 3rd Ave. (between 22nd and 23rd Sts.), Flatiron District, 212/889–8160. Subway: N, R to 23rd St.*

10 *c-1*

INTEGRAL YOGA INSTITUTE

This is New York's best-known yoga institute, with Hatha classes, including partner classes and ones for prenatal needs, at all levels, for $10. *227 W. 13th St. (between 7th and 8th Aves.), West Village, 212/929–0586. Subway: A, C, E to 14th St.; L to 8th Ave.*

9 *b-1*

200 W. 72nd St. (7th Ave.), Upper West Side, 212/721–4000. Subway: 1, 2, 3 to 72nd St.

9 *d-7*

IYENGAR YOGA INSTITUTE

The Iyengar method is rooted in Hatha yoga and focuses heavily on postures and alignments. The postures are adapted to the needs of the students and while the classes are not overly athletic, they are not static either. This institute offers a free introductory class once a month and others at different levels for under $20 per class. *27 W. 24th St. (between 5th and 6th Aves.), Suite 800, Chelsea, 212/691–9642. Subway: F, N, R, V to 23rd St.*

9 *f-3*

JIVAMUKTI YOGA CENTER

The Taj Mahal of Manhattan yoga centers, this glamorous facility boasts meditation rooms, loads of classes, and the occasional celebrity client. Single classes cost $17 and are offered at all levels. *404 Lafayette St. (W. 4th St.), 3rd floor, Greenwich Village, 212/353–0214. Subway: 6 to Astor Pl.*

9 *c-7*

SIVANANDA YOGA VEDANTA CENTER

One of the oldest and busiest yoga centers in Manhattan, Sivananda teaches Hatha yoga and follows the practice of stilling the body to still the mind. It has classes for all ages and all levels. *243 W. 24th St. (between 7th and 8th Aves.), Chelsea, 212/255–4560. Subway: C, E to 23rd St.*

9 *e-3*

YOGA ZONE

The teaching method is called ISHTAR (Integral Science of Hatha and Tantra Arts), and the studios are elegant. Classes are $15. *160 E. 56th St. (between Lexington and 3rd Aves.), 12th Floor, Midtown East, 212/935–9642. Subway: 6, N, R, W to 59th St./Lexington Ave.*

9 *e-8*

138 5th Ave. (between 18th and 19th Sts.), 4th Floor, Flatiron District, 212/647–9642. Subway: N, R to 23rd St.

fitness centers, health clubs & spa services

MASSAGE & BODY WORK

In addition to the names listed below, almost all day spas in the city offer massage services. *See Beauty in Chapter 2, Shopping, for more information.*

9 *d-8*

CARAPAN

Decorated to look and feel like New Mexico, Carapan specializes in Swedish massage but offers seven other kinds, as well as facials, craniosacral therapy,

PARKS, GARDENS & SPORTS

and other healing measures. *5 W. 16th
St. (between 5th and 6th Aves.), Chelsea,
212/633–6220. Subway: F, V to 14th St.*

10 *d-1*

STONE SPA

Come here with an open mind, and
you'll leave with a relaxed body. At the
beginning of a massage, smooth stones
from the Salt River in Arizona are heated
through and placed at strategic points
on the body. The heat radiates from the
stones as skilled masseurs knead your
stress away. *104 W. 14th St. (at 6th Ave.),
2nd Floor, Chelsea, 212/741–8881. Subway: F, V to 14th St.*

9 *e-2*

THE STRESS LESS STEP

This no-nonsense massage center offers
Swedish, shiatsu, and reflexology.
Celebrities drop in from the Regency
Hotel, across the street. *48 E. 61st St.
(near Madison Ave.), Upper East Side,
212/826–6222. Subway: 4, 5, 6, Q local, W
to 59th St./Lexington Ave.*

PRIVATE
HEALTH CLUBS

Many of the more exclusive clubs are so
intent on keeping the riffraff out that
only members and prospective members are allowed past the front desk.
These institutions are designated
"Members Only" below. Those that
allow members to bring guests are designated "Member Guests Only." Others
charge visitors fees for classes or one-
day use of all facilities; often these fees
are discounted or waived if a member
brings you. Even the "members only"
clubs give potential members a few free
passes. Prices quoted below are subject
to change. Clubs without annual or
monthly fees listed run so many promotions that it's impossible to pin down a
price. Bargain hard.

7 *g-6*

ASPHALT GREEN

A unique public–private partnership
turned an old asphalt plant into this fitness and arts complex. The 50-meter
pool blows everything else in the city out
of the water, but don't underestimate
the rest of the place—weights and
weight training overlooking the East
River, aerobic and conditioning classes,
an eye-catching AstroTurf field, and

numerous community programs and
programs for people with disabilities.
Day passes are $25, and an annual
membership is $1,300. *555 E. 90th St.
(at East End Ave.), Upper East Side, 212/
369–8890. Subway: 4, 5, 6 to 86th St.*

9 *e-3*

BALLY TOTAL FITNESS

Inexpensive and convenient locations
(in the city and across the country) are
the pluses; waits for machines and limited class offerings and amenities are
the minuses. For a full list of locations,
call 800/846–0256. Day passes are $25.
The myriad specials and options make
membership fees hard to pin down.
Depending upon the deal you get,
expect to pay around $50–$75 per
month on average. *45 E. 55th St.
(between 5th and Madison Aves.), Midtown East, 212/688–6630. Subway: E, V
to 5th Ave./53rd St.*

7 *e-7*

*144–146 E. 86th St. (between Lexington
and 3rd Aves.), Upper East Side, 212/722–
7371. Subway: 4, 5, 6 to 86th St.*

10 *e-6*

*641 6th Ave. (between 19th and 20th
Sts.), Chelsea, 212/645–4565. Subway: F,
V to 23rd St.*

9 *f-3*

CRUNCH

A failed actor put his creative talents to
good use in building this empire of fitness clubs and associated paraphernalia. The classes are loud, in-your-face,
and sometimes ridiculous—Broadway
Dance, Disco Yoga, Karaoke Spin. The
machines are abundant, but locker-
room amenities are not. Expect to part
with about $1,000 per year to sweat
here. A $22 guest fee gets non-members
in the door for the day. There are eight
locations across Manhattan. *1109 2nd
Ave. (at 59th St.), Upper East Side, 212/
758–3434. Subway: 4, 5, 6, Q, W to 59th
St./Lexington Ave.*

11 *f-1*

*404 Lafayette St. (at Astor Pl.), Greenwich
Village, 212/614–0120. Subway: 6 to Astor
Pl.*

7 *e-7*

DAVID BARTON

Individual training, cardio equipment,
and cushy couches, rather than extensive classes, are what draw people to

this eponymous, bodybuilder-owned gym. You'll pay around $700 for an annual membership. *30 E. 85th St. (between 5th and Madison Aves.), Upper East Side, 212/517–7577. Members only. Subway: 4, 5, 6 to 86th St.*

10 *d-1*

522 6th Ave. (at 15th St.), Chelsea, 212/ 727–0004. Subway: F, V to 14th St.

12 *b-2*

EASTERN ATHLETIC CLUBS
These spacious Brooklyn centers have full programs of classes and numerous sports offerings, including swimming, martial arts, racquet sports, and dance. A day pass costs $20. After the $350 initiation fee (frequently lowered for special promotions), you'll pay $85 per month. *43 Clark St. (between Henry and Hicks Sts.), Brooklyn Heights, 718/625–0500. Subway: 2, 3 to Clark St.*

12 *g-5*

17 Eastern Pkwy. (between Plaza and Underhill Sts.), Park Slope, Brooklyn, 718/ 789–4600. Subway: 1, 2 to Grand Army Plaza.

7 *b-8*

EQUINOX FITNESS CLUB
All three of your selves—physical, mental, and spiritual—will be challenged here, with East-meets-West and martial arts–based classes taught by instructors who have become local celebrities. As you'd expect for the premium you pay to belong, equipment is up-to-date, plentiful, and in good working order. The steam room is a welcome bonus. A day pass costs $25. *344 Amsterdam Ave. (at 76th St.), Upper West Side, 212/721–4200. Subway: 1, 2 to 79th St..*

9 *b-5*

MANHATTAN PLAZA HEALTH CLUB
One of the few independent clubs in town, this Hell's Kitchen standout stays one step ahead of its bigger competitors without being outrageously expensive or intimidating. It has everything you expect in a complete health club—25-yard lap pool, quality equipment, and a full schedule of classes that includes the latest trends. Then there are the extras—the pool's retractable roof, the outdoor sundeck, the climbing wall that opened years before people had heard of such a thing, and the tennis club's

rooftop courts. A day pass goes for $25 here, but you can't use them during the summer months. *482 W. 43rd St. (between 9th and 10th Aves.), Midtown West, 212/563–7001. Members only. Subway: A, C, E to 42nd St./Port Authority.*

10 *e-8*

NEW YORK HEALTH & RACQUET CLUB
As the name suggests, this club is best for tennis and racquetball, but for people into those games it's a way of life— you get access to the club's party yacht, Westchester beach club, and special calendar. Its many locations offer plenty of courts, machines, and classes. Though visitors are allowed, the $50 fee is unwelcoming. The basic annual membership goes for $1,595. *20 E. 50th St. (5th Ave.), Midtown East, 212/593–1500. Subway: E, V to 5th Ave./53rd St.*

9 *c-2*

NEW YORK SPORTS CLUB
The omnipresence award goes to NYSC—chances are you're within a subway stop or two of one. They also win the high-strung–yuppie award: 9-to-5ers pack the clubs after work for reservations-only classes, willing to wait anxiously to burn their calories on equipment that's gathering dust the rest of the day. That said, the equipment is kept up-to-date, the classes incorporate the latest trends, and thousands of people swear by this gym. Day passes go for $25 here. *Multiple locations throughout the city.*

11 *b-3*

PRINTING HOUSE FITNESS & RACQUET CLUB
With great West Side views, plenty of space, and diverse offerings, this is another down-to-earth independent option, and it draws some West Village celebs. Racquetball and squash courts are available, as is a classes-only membership. After the $140 initiation fee, you'll pay about $100 per month here. *421 Hudson St. (at Leroy St.), West Village, 212/243–7600. Members only. Subway: 1, 2 to Houston St.*

9 *b-1*

REEBOK SPORTS CLUB NEW YORK
Here, the line between theme park and gym is a thin one. The facilities are awe-

some—25-yard lap pool, ⅛-mi track, full-size basketball courts with stands, 45-ft climbing wall, every machine you can think of. The classes, in 2,500-square-ft studios, also run the full range. The initiation fee is $1,200; after that, you'll pay $188 per month. *160 Columbus Ave. (at 67th St.), Upper West Side, 212/362–6800. Members only. Subway: 1, 2 to 66th St./Lincoln Center.*

9 a-7
SPORTS CENTER AT CHELSEA PIERS

Imagine passing endless rows of top-of-the-line weight machines, cardio equipment, and free weights; fitness studios with every imaginable class; a boxing ring; basketball–volleyball courts; and then a 46-ft climbing wall, and then seeing it all again on your way back to a six-lane, 25-yard pool, and you're probably out of breath already. Now imagine seeing all that as you run around an *indoor* ¼-mi track, and you have some idea of what the Sports Center is like. The pool is at the end of the pier above the Hudson and has deck-to-ceiling glass windows on three sides, just in case you didn't notice the view. Add a sundeck and appropriately luxurious locker rooms and you don't feel so bad about the $1,600 a year (or $36/day) it takes to be here. *Chelsea Piers (23rd St. and 12th Ave.), Pier 60, Chelsea, 212/336–6000. Subway: C, E to 23rd St.*

9 f-2
THE SPORTS CLUB/LA

The same folks who run the Reebok club bring a West Coast state of mind (and style) to the world of fitness for pay. The club measures 140,000 square ft and includes a rock-climbing wall, two NBA-size basketball courts, and a 4,000-square-ft rooftop where yoga classes are held in fair weather. The initiation fee at this exclusive club is a whopping $600. Monthly charges are $135. If you pay for 11 months upfront, you get the 12th free. *330 E. 61st St. (between 1st and 2nd Aves.), Upper East Side, 212/355–5100. Member guests only. Subway: 4, 5, 6 to 59th St./Lexington Ave.*

11 e-3
WORLD GYM

For pumping iron and an outrageous number of classes 24 hours a day, this is your place. A year-long membership

costs $900, and guest passes are $20. *232 Mercer St. (between Bleecker and W. 3rd Sts.), Greenwich Village, 212/780–7407. Subway: A, B, C, D, E, F, V to W. 4th St./Washington Sq.*

9 b-2
1926 Broadway (between 64th and 65th Sts.), Upper West Side, 212/874–0942. Subway: 1, 2 to 66th St./Lincoln Center.

PUBLIC HEALTH CLUBS

City-operated rec centers are unbelievable bargains. For just $10–$25 per year you have everything you'd expect from a health club—pools, basketball, weights, training equipment, machines, and even classes (usually for an extra fee). The schedules aren't as packed as those at private clubs, but neither are the locker rooms—nor are they as nice, but they do the job. Manhattan locations include the magnificent, former public-bath building **Asser Levy** (*see* Swimming, *above*), **Carmine Street** (*see* Swimming, *above*), and **West 59th Street** (10th Ave. and 59th St., 212/397–3159). All told, there are more than 30 centers throughout the five boroughs. For more information call the Parks Department.

THE Y

If you feel out-glitzed, out-priced, and old-fashioned at the city's other fitness emporiums, do yourself a favor and visit the Y. Built as veritable community centers, city Ys do a fine job of keeping you fit and making you feel good about the world. Check the phone book for the Ys other than those listed here.

9 f-4
VANDERBILT Y

Make no assumptions about the offerings here—equipment is in good shape, classes are challenging, locker rooms are clean, and the pool is excellent. You might not end up ahead of this week's fitness trend, but you'll stay in shape. *Vanderbilt Y, 224 E. 47th St., Midtown East, 212/756–9600. Subway: 6 to 51st St./Lexington Ave.*

7 e-6
92ND STREET YM–YWHA

Best known for its cultural programming, the 92nd Street Y deserves recognition for its fitness facilities, too. Classes here cover everything from yoga to spinning to line dancing, for all age groups; facilities include a 25-yard pool, racquetball courts, and a 5,000-square-ft, fully stocked "cardio court." You'll even find a spa for the total body pampering experience. Classes vary in price. *1395 Lexington Ave. (at 92nd St.), Upper East Side, 212/415–5500. Subway: 6 to 96th St.*

 e-3

YWCA

This predominantly female center is another down-to-earth deal. Enjoy the good array of machines and an unusually large selection of classes. *610 Lexington Ave. (at 53rd St.), Midtown East, 212/735–9753. Subway: 6 to 51st St./Lexington Ave.; E, V to Lexington–3rd Aves./53rd St.*

chapter 4

PLACES TO EXPLORE

galleries, gargoyles, museums, and more

N ew York is one of those cities that beguiles you into thinking you've seen it all, then reveals itself anew again and again. In fact, one of the greatest pleasures of exploring the city is to rediscover, its charms. Often, these discoveries are subtle. Walking through Grand Central Station for the hundredth time, for instance, you may suddenly be overwhelmed by the terminal's amazing ability to combine function and elegance. Or visiting a new neighborhood, you may be astonished to find yourself experiencing the thrill of culture shock in what appears to be a city unto itself. In truth, you can never really "know" New York—but you can try. As it's been said, there are 8 million stories in this crazy town—and about 8 zillion places to explore.

ESSENTIAL WEB SITES

www.papermag.com Click on "The Guide" at ultra-hip *Paper* magazine's Web site to unveil the editors' picks for the best literary events, club nights, and art openings of the week.

www.newyork.citysearch.com Citysearch has the most complete online listings and reviews for the performing arts, nightclubs, restaurants, and sporting events, with particularly good up-to-date listings for museums and galleries.

www.nytoday.com The *New York Times*'s "things-to-do" Web site connects you with articles about the arts and other happenings.

www.metronewyork.com Besides events listings, this regularly updated site from *New York* magazine features clever "best of" lists (Best Ice Cream, Best Places to Play Tennis, etc.) and first-rate shopping tips.

---

where to go

AQUARIUMS

4 h-7

AQUARIUM FOR WILDLIFE CONSERVATION

Inside this 14-acre complex you can hear beluga whales whistle and moan, look massive sharks in the eye, and drool over the walrus's 400-pound weekly ration of squid, smelt, and herring. All told, the aquarium has about 7,500 residents, including mammals (otters, dolphins, whales, seals), birds (penguins), reptiles (sea turtles), cartilaginous fish (sharks, rays, skate), bony fish (tarpon, eels, trout, cod, piranhas, puffers), and invertebrates (jellyfish, sea urchins, lobsters, mollusks), some of them lucky enough to live in beachside outdoor pools. Dolphins and sea lions perform in the 1,600-seat Aquatheater, and penguins, sharks, sea otters, seals, walruses, and other creatures don't mind if you watch them eat. Curious children can check out jellyfish, walk under a crashing wave, and touch crabs and sea urchins in the Discovery Cove. *W. 8th St. and Surf Ave., Coney Island, 718/265–FISH, www.wcs.org. $9.75 adults, $6 seniors and children under 12, free children under 2. Weekdays 10–6, weekends and holidays 10–7. Subway: F or Q to W. 8th St./Aquarium.*

4 h-7

THE ESTUARIUM

Run by the River Project, a nonprofit scientific organization, this small aquarium is connected to the Hudson River itself, with briny estuary water flowing through a 3,000-gallon tank system. Here, you can get to know your next-door neighbors: hundreds of fish and invertebrate species, including striped bass, blue crabs, flounder, and baby bluefish. *Pier 26 on the Hudson River, off the Westside Hwy. (between N. Moore and Hubert Sts.), 212/431–5787, www.riverproject.org. Free. Weekdays 11–5. Subway: 1 or 9 to Franklin.*

ARCHITECTURE

Nothing evokes New York City more dramatically than its skyline, an ever-evolving mountain range of steel, glass, and concrete. Here are the city's most significant achievements in urban architecture—the buildings that taken in sum constitute the world's most famous skyline but should be admired individually, too. Each site is introduced with the name of its architect and the year the project was completed. For more architecturally intriguing buildings and structures, *see* the Bridges, Churches & Synagogues, *and* Historic Structures & Streets sections of this chapter.

9 b-1
ANSONIA HOTEL

(Paul E. M. Duboy, 1904) An exuberant architectural masterpiece, complete with turrets, a mansard roof, and filigreed-iron balconies, the Upper West Side's Ansonia Hotel was inspired by turn-of-the-20th-century Beaux-Arts buildings in Paris. The luxury doesn't stop on the outside; the apartments inside are soundproof, and once attracted such musical stars as Enrico Caruso, Igor Stravinsky, Lily Pons, and Arturo Toscanini as longtime residents. *2109 Broadway (between 73rd and 74th Sts.), Upper West Side. Subway: 1, 2, 3 to 72nd St.*

10 d-7
BATTERY PARK CITY

(Master plan by Cooper, Eckstut Assoc., 1979; individual buildings by various architects) Not since Rockefeller Center has New York undertaken such an ambitious physical project. Battery Park City was a mere gleam in urban planners' eyes until the 1980s, and though it's largely complete, parts of it are still under construction, and now under reconstruction, as Battery Park City sustained substantial damage during the attack on the World Trade Center, which once towered above it. Built on a 92-acre stretch of landfill along the Hudson River at Manhattan's southern tip, this city within a city combines high-rise office and residential towers with open space, outdoor sculpture, and a delightful, riverside public esplanade. Its stone, ceramic, glass, and bronze buildings—in shapes recalling the '30s—are a spectacular addition to the downtown skyline. The most impressive of these, the four-tower World Financial Center (Cesar Pelli, 1988) has 6 million square ft of office space and 220,000 square ft of shops and restaurants. Its centerpiece is the Winter Garden, a towering glass pavilion beneath a 120-ft vaulted roof that overlooks a 3-acre river plaza and yacht marina; the garden was severely damaged in the attack. Nearby, a little commuter ferry shuttles workers to and from New Jersey. *Hudson River from Battery Pl. to Vesey St., Lower Manhattan. Subway: 1, 2 to Chambers St.*

9 d-4
CBS BUILDING

(Eero Saarinen & Associates, 1965) Best known for his sleek, minimalist designs, Saarinen applied Modernism only once to a skyscraper—and you can observe the results right here. Framed in concrete and covered with dark granite, the pet name of this 38-story high-rise is Black Rock. *51 W. 52nd St. (at 6th Ave.), Midtown West. Subway: B, D, F, V to 47th–50th Sts./Rockefeller Center; E, V to 5th Ave./53rd St.*

10 e-7
CHAMBER OF COMMERCE OF THE STATE OF NEW YORK

(James B. Baker, 1901) An ornate beaux-arts landmark deep in the heart of the financial district, this homage to trade features white-marble Ionic columns and a mansard roof. *65 Liberty St. (at Liberty Pl.), Lower Manhattan. Subway: 4, 5 to Wall St.*

9 e-5
CHANIN BUILDING

(Sloan & Robertson, 1929) Like the nearby Chrysler Building (*see below*), the Chanin Building is one of the masterpieces of Art Deco. Most notable are its stylized ornamentation and intricate detail, ranging from the terra-cotta bas-relief and bronze frieze on the lower facade to the bronze grills and "jeweled" clocks in the lobby. *122 E. 42nd St. (at Lexington Ave.), Midtown East. Subway: 42nd St./Grand Central.*

10 e-7
CHASE MANHATTAN BANK TOWER & PLAZA

(Skidmore, Owings & Merrill, 1960) In front of this 65-story tower, lower Manhattan's first boxy, aluminum-and-glass high-rise, is a plaza that contains a circular sculpture garden designed by famed sculptor Isamu Noguchi (*see Isamu Noguchi Garden Museum in Art Museums, below*) and a whimsical, 25-ton papier-mâché-like sculpture by Jean

Dubuffet, "Group of Four Trees." 1 *Chase Manhattan Plaza (between Nassau and William Sts., below Liberty St.), Lower Manhattan. Subway: 2, 4, 5 to Wall St.*

9 *e-5*

CHRYSLER BUILDING

(William Van Alen, 1930) Particularly at dusk, when the setting sun makes the building's gleaming Art Deco spire practically glow, the Chrysler Building is perhaps the most pleasing of New York's many skyscrapers. The Chrysler was one of the first skyscrapers to be faced with stainless steel—including the gargoyles, which were modeled after car-hood ornaments. At 1,048 ft, it was the tallest building in the world until the Empire State Building was completed only a few months later. *405 Lexington Ave. (at 42nd St.), Midtown East. Subway: 4, 5, 6, 7, S to 42nd St./Grand Central.*

9 *e-4*

CITICORP CENTER

(Hugh Stubbins & Associates, 1977) With its uniquely angled silhouette and greenish-silver satin veneer, the Citicorp Center is among the most eye-catching forms in the Midtown skyline. At street level it appears to stand on monster stilts, and its sunlit, three-level atrium—one of the city's most successful—is a modern agora of shops and pedestrian activity. The building's jauntily slanted top was meant to be practical: It was intended for a solar-energy collector that was never installed. *(See St. Peter's Church at the Citicorp Center in Churches & Synagogues, below.) Lexington Ave. (between 53rd and 54th Sts.), Midtown East. 6 to 51st St./Lexington Ave.; E, V to Lexington–3rd Aves./53rd St.*

9 *f-5*

DAILY NEWS BUILDING

(Howells & Hood, 1930) Although the *News* moved out in 1995, this building's inspiring Art Deco ornamentation, commissioned by Joseph Patterson, the founder of the nation's first tabloid newspaper, remains. After admiring the striped brickwork and the entrance relief depicting light dawning on the urban populace (an obvious reference to the enlightening power of the press), check out the lobby, which houses a huge, revolving globe (12 ft in diameter) and a floor that resembles a gigantic compass.

220 E. 42nd St. (between 2nd and 3rd Aves.), Midtown East. Subway: 4, 5, 6, 7, S to 42nd St./Grand Central.

9 *d-6*

EMPIRE STATE BUILDING

(Shreve, Lamb & Harmon, 1931) Although at 1,454 ft it's no longer the world's tallest building (it currently ranks sixth), the Empire State Building remains the world's most glamorous skyscraper—the defining and, with the destruction of the World Trade Center, tallest structure on the New York City skyline and the symbol of Manhattan. The skyscraper craze of the 1920s generated a slew of buildings in Manhattan, each outstretching the next in the quest to claim the title of world's tallest building. Developer John Jacob Raskob was no different, asking architect William Lamb, "Bill, how high can you make it so it won't fall down?" The Art Deco behemoth opened in April 1931 after a mere 13 months of construction; the framework rose at a rate of 4½ stories per week, making the Empire State Building the fastest-rising major skyscraper ever built. Its enormity (the steel frame alone weighs 60,000 tons) is belied by the delicacy and balance of its design; the needlelike spire and dramatic setbacks create a sense of height and majesty that when viewed for the first time (or even the thousandth) has sent many a heart aflutter with excitement. Illumination heightens the romance: blazing white light at nighttime and in holiday colors for special occasions: red and white for Valentine's Day, orange and yellow for Halloween, and blue and white when the Yankees win big. *350 5th Ave. (at 34th St.), Midtown East, 212/736–3100, www.esbnyc.com. Observation deck: $9 adults, $7 seniors, $4 children under 12, free children under 5. Daily 9 AM–midnight; last elevator up leaves at 11:30 PM. Subway: B, D, F, N, Q, R, V, W to 34th St./Herald Sq.*

10 *e-7*

EQUITABLE BUILDING

(Ernest R. Graham, 1915) An unrelenting mass, the 909-ft-high, 40-story Equitable Building swallowed up so much airspace from such a small plot of land (less than an acre) that it inspired the nation's first zoning laws in 1916. *120 Broadway (at Cedar St.), Lower Manhattan. Subway: 4, 5 to Wall St.*

9 e-8

FLATIRON BUILDING

(D. H. Burnham & Co., 1902) Thanks to its alluring triangular shape (conceived to fit its triangular plot between 5th Ave., Broadway, and 23rd St.), this 286-ft-tall example of early "modern" architecture was New York's first true skyscraper and most famous building in the early 1900s, the subject of as many picture postcards as the Empire State Building is today. The city's tallest building until 1908, the Flatiron was built with a revolutionary steel frame covered by a limestone and terra-cotta skin designed in the Italian Renaissance style. Due to blustery winds that kicked up at the building's busy front corner on the south side of Madison Square, policemen were assigned to chase away loafers who stopped to gaze at the upturned skirts of women, thus originating the phrase "23 skidoo." To see the Flatiron in all its splendor, take a walk down 5th Avenue from the north side of Madison Square. *175 5th Ave. (at 23rd St.), Flatiron District. Subway: N, Q, R, W to 23rd St.*

9 f-5

FORD FOUNDATION BUILDING

(Kevin Roche, John Dinkeloo & Associates, 1967) Home to one of the largest philanthropic organizations in the world, the Ford Foundation Building is best known for its glass-wall, 130-ft-high atrium. Filled with trees, shrubs, a still-water pool, and all manner of greenery, this enclosed garden is a real respite from the crush around Grand Central Terminal. *320 E. 43rd St. (between 1st and 2nd Aves.), Midtown East. Weekdays 9–5. Subway: 4, 5, 6, 7, S to 42nd St./Grand Central.*

9 d-5

GRACE BUILDING

(Skidmore, Owings & Merrill, 1974) This swooping glass behemoth across from Bryant Park has been derided as "flashy" and "flamboyant" yet is strangely appealing. The building's facade curves from a broad base to a slender top, accommodating public spaces on the lower floors and creating the overall effect of a ski jump. *41 W. 42nd St. (between 5th and 6th Aves.), Midtown West. Subway: B, D, F, V to 42nd St.*

9 e-5

GRAND CENTRAL TERMINAL

(Warren & Wetmore, Reed & Stem, 1913; Beyer Blinder Belle, restoration plan 1998) This massive beaux-arts pile boasts the grandest interior space anywhere in New York, and an incredible four-year renovation (completed 1998) has rendered it all the more appealing. Crossed by more than 500,000 commuters every weekday, its massive main concourse (200 ft long, 120 ft wide, and 12 stories high) maintains a humane scale. Its vaulted ceiling is an enchanting piece of theater that displays a restored map of the night sky with starry constellations shining with fiber-optic light. A new marble staircase (like its twin across the concourse), modeled after the Garnier stair at the Paris Opera and included in the original terminal plans but never before built, has been seamlessly installed onto the concourse's east end, while gold- and nickel-plated chandeliers gleam once more in the passageways. With the recent renovation's doubling the original shop space (much of which had been abandoned by merchants), Grand Central has once again become a place where you might go not just to catch the train but to have dinner or simply stroll. And the outside isn't bad, either; Grand Central's southern facade, with three 60-ft-high arched windows overlooking Park Avenue, is topped by a soaring statue of Mercury, Hercules, and Minerva and a giant clock. Although it's hard to imagine now, Grand Central was on the verge of destruction in the 1960s, when the station's owners planned to build an office tower there—despite its landmark status. In the ensuing fracas, the city's Landmarks Commission defended Grand Central all the way to the U.S. Supreme Court, and in 1978 they won, affirming the city's tough landmark laws and setting a precedent for preserving New York's thousands of other historic buildings. *Vanderbilt Ave. and 42nd St., Midtown East. Tours of Grand Central are given by the Municipal Art Society (212/935–3960) on Wed. at 12:30; meet at the information booth on the main concourse. 212/532–4900 (for train schedules and fares). Subway: 4, 5, 6, 7, S to 42nd St./Grand Central.*

7 e-6

GUGGENHEIM MUSEUM

(Frank Lloyd Wright, 1959) The Guggenheim is one of only two buildings in

Manhattan designed by Frank Lloyd Wright (the other is a Mercedes-Benz showroom at Park Avenue and 56th Street), and is often visited as much for its architecture as for the art inside. The white exterior resembles an inverted cone; the much-vaunted interior houses a six-story rotunda under a skylit glass dome and a ¼-mi-long spiraling ramp leads down past exhibitions of modern art. The 10-story tower annex, opened in 1992 to provide much-needed extra gallery space, was designed by Gwathmey, Siegel & Assoc. based on Wright's original conception for the museum (see Art Museums, below). 1071 5th Ave. (at 89th St.), Upper East Side, 212/423–3500, www.guggenheim.org. $12 adults, $8 students and seniors, free children under 12; pay what you wish Fri. 6–8. Sun.–Wed. 9–6, Fri. and Sat. 9–8. Subway: 4, 5, 6 to 86th St.

11 e-6
HAUGHWOUT BUILDING
(J. P. Gaynor, 1857) With each window framed by Corinthian columns and rounded arches, this five-story, Palladio-inspired building is considered one of the best examples of cast-iron architecture in the world. It was equipped with the world's first elevator, designed by Elisha Graves Otis, who went on to found an elevator empire and make high-rises (and the modern skyscraper) practical possibilities. (See SoHo Cast-Iron Historic District, below.) 488–492 Broadway (at Broome St.), SoHo. Subway: N, Q, R, W to Canal St.; 6 to Spring St.

9 e-3
IBM BUILDING
(Edward Larrabee Barnes, 1982) The 57th Street entrance to this sleek, green-granite-and-glass, prism-shape tower is set back under 40 cantilevered floors. Inside, a huge, glass atrium, filled with bamboo trees, is a tranquil public plaza for sitting. 590 Madison Ave. (at 57th St.), Midtown East. Subway: 4, 5, 6, N, R to 59th St./Lexington Ave.

9 a-6
JACOB K. JAVITS CONVENTION CENTER
(I. M. Pei & Partners, 1986) New York's mecca for conventions and trade shows occupies 1.8 million square ft of floor space on a 22-acre site and is built almost entirely of glass, drawing its inspiration from 19th-century "glass

houses" designed to showcase exotic botanical exhibits. Little wonder that, with a dark green, crystalline-glass exterior made up of 16,100 glass panes, the convention center is sometimes called the Crystal Palace. 11th and 12th Aves. from 34th to 39th Sts., Midtown West. Subway: A, C, E to 34th St./Penn Station.

9 f-4
LESCAZE HOUSE
(William Lescaze, 1934) Designed by pioneering architect William Lescaze as his home and office, this town house—with its glass-block and ribboned windows—is considered the first modern-style building in the city. 211 E. 48th St. (between 2nd and 3rd Aves.), Midtown East. Subway: 6 to 51st St./Lexington Ave.; E, V to Lexington–3rd Aves./53rd St..

9 e-4
LEVER HOUSE
(Gordon Bunschaft of Skidmore, Owings & Merrill, 1952) One of the first metal-and-glass skyscrapers, this slim, blue-green tower stands on a one-story horizontal slab supported by chrome columns. Made for the soap-and-detergent empire Lever Brothers, it was designed to exude an aura of cleanliness. Its completion was considered an architectural watershed, leaving older skyscraper designs behind in favor of the increasingly sleek and commercial international style. 390 Park Ave. (between 53rd and 54th Sts.), Midtown East. Subway: 6 to 51st St./Lexington Ave.; E, V to Lexington–3rd Aves./53rd St.

9 b-2
LINCOLN CENTER FOR THE PERFORMING ARTS
(Various architects, 1962–68) Although Lincoln Center is unsurpassed for artistic variety and integrity, its architectural whole is greater than the sum of its parts. The center's buildings, all classical imitations decked out in the same cream-color travertine, include Avery Fisher Hall (Max Abramovitz, 1962, redesign Johnson/Burgee 1976), the New York State Theater (Philip Johnson, 1964), the Metropolitan Opera House (Wallace Harrison, 1966), the Juilliard School of Music (Pietro Belluschi, 1968), and the Vivian Beaumont Theater (Eero Saarinen, 1965). Although the list of architects reads like a Who's Who of Modernism, none of the buildings is terribly impressive on its own. Still, there is something tremendously freeing about

the open spaces and plazas here at the foot of the Upper West Side. The public art is also notable: murals by Marc Chagall inside the Met, a Henry Moore sculpture in the reflecting pool, and two white marble sculptures by Elie Nadelman in the foyer of the New York State Theater. One-hour guided "Introduction to Lincoln Center" tours, given daily, cover the center's history and wealth of artwork. *Columbus and Amsterdam Aves. from 62nd to 66th Sts., Upper West Side, 212/546–2656 for general information, 212/ 875–5350 for tour schedule and reservations, www.lincolncenter.org. Tour $9.50. Subway: 1, 2 to 66th St./Lincoln Center.*

9 *f-4*

THE LIPSTICK BUILDING

(Philip Johnson for John Burgee Architects, 1986) Architecture buffs love this rose-color office tower, a truly unique design by Philip Johnson, the founder of American Modernism. Elliptical in shape, the smooth, 34-story exterior has no corners, making it a dramatic departure from the rectangular megaboxes that dominate the rest of Midtown. "Effect before everything" was Johnson's personal motto. The building's resemblance to a tube of lipstick is augmented by two setbacks in its midsection. *885 3rd Ave. (between 53rd and 54th Sts.), Midtown East. Subway: 6 to 51st St./Lexington Ave.; E, V to Lexington–3rd Aves./53rd St.*

9 *c-5*

MCGRAW-HILL BUILDING

(Raymond Hood, Godley & Fouilhoux, 1931) Sometimes said to look like a jukebox, this art moderne–cum–international style high-rise is considered a masterpiece of design. Covered in seagreen terra-cotta, it has art deco details at street level and Carrera glass in the lobby. *330 W. 42nd St. (between 8th and 9th Aves.), Midtown West. Subway: A, C, E to 42nd St.*

9 *e-1*

PAUL MELLON HOUSE

(Mazza & Seccia, 1965) Snug alongside Italianate brownstones and neo-Georgian mansions on one of the city's most beautiful residential blocks, this light-as-air postwar town house is characterized by the experts as "French provincial." *125 E. 70th St. (between Park and Lexington Aves.), Upper East Side. Subway: 6 to 68th St./Hunter College.*

9 *e-4*

METROPOLITAN LIFE BUILDING (FORMERLY PAN AM BUILDING)

(Emery Roth & Sons, Pietro Belluschi, and Walter Gropius, 1963) Plunked down in the middle of Park Avenue, hovering over Grand Central Station, the 808-ft-tall Pan Am Building was reviled as an outsize concrete-clad monstrosity when it was built in the 1960s. With 2.4 million square ft of office space, it was the largest office building in Manhattan, and it destroyed a cherished vista down Park Avenue. One architecture critic even called it "toxic." Since the 1960s, however, it's become such an integral part of the city's skyline that people were upset when the name on the top of the building was changed from Pan Am to MetLife in the early '90s. *200 Park Ave. (at 46th St.), Midtown East. Subway: 4, 5, 6, 7, S to 42nd St./Grand Central.*

9 *d-5*

NEW YORK PUBLIC LIBRARY (HUMANITIES & SOCIAL SCIENCES)

(Carrère & Hastings, 1911) Flanked by its two famous stone lions, the NYPL's Humanities and Social Sciences Library is considered, along with Grand Central Terminal, one of New York's most magnificent beaux-arts buildings. The beauty of its broad, plazalike stairway and columned exterior is matched by the interior, particularly the grand stairways of the lobby and the princely third-floor main reading room. Renovated in 1999, the reading room consists of two connected halls stretching for 297 ft and is lined with row after row of long wooden tables, brass reading lamps, and 15 massive arched windows. Its ceiling rises 52 ft above the floor and is painted with an ethereal sky-and-cloud mural: Completely lost before the renovation and recreated with the help of old lantern slides, it is said to be inspired by the Italian artists Tiepolo and Tintoretto. Even if you never crack a book, the library is, more than ever, worth a visit; it is one of New York City's most sumptuous public spaces. *(See Libraries, below.) 5th Ave. and 42nd St., Midtown West. 212/930–0830, www.nypl.org. Mon. and Thurs.–Sat. 10–6, Tues.–Wed. 11– 7:30; free tours of the library are offered Mon.–Sat. at 11 and 2. Subway: B, D, F, V to 42nd St.; 7 to 5th Ave.*

9 d-5

NEW YORK YACHT CLUB

(Warren & Wetmore; 1899) Built on land donated by yacht-club member J. P. Morgan, this beaux-arts structure is famous for its three decorative bay windows fashioned after the sterns of 18th-century sailing ships. The fanciful limestone facade is adorned with carvings of dolphins and waves. *37 W. 44th St. (between 5th and 6th Aves.), Midtown West. Subway: B, D, F, V to 42nd St.; 7 to 5th Ave.*

9 f-3

919 THIRD AVENUE

(Skidmore, Owings & Merrill, 1970) What's most interesting about this brown-glass office structure is the little, redbrick 1890 building that seems to stand as its sentry box—P. J. Clarke's Tavern, famed watering hole and hold-out against Tishman Realty. Have a peek at the mahogany and stained glass inside the bar—you might recognize it as the film set from the 1945 Best Picture–winner *The Lost Weekend*. (*See* American Casual *in* Chapter 1.) *919 3rd Ave. (between 55th and 56th Sts.), Midtown East. Subway: 4, 5, 6, N, R to 59th St./Lexington Ave.*

10 e-7

140 BROADWAY

(Skidmore, Owings & Merrill, 1967) A more successful version of Skidmore, Owings & Merrill's earlier Chase Manhattan Bank Tower & Plaza (*see above*), this sleek, elegant glass skyscraper rises 52 orderly stories above an attractive travertine plaza—home to Isamu Noguchi's delicately balanced red sculpture "Cube." When the building was completed, architecture critic Ada Louise Huxtable wrote, "Sometimes we do it right."*140 Broadway (at Cedar St.), Lower Manhattan. Subway: 4, 5 to Wall St.*

9 f-5

ONE & TWO UNITED NATIONS PLAZA

(Kevin Roche, John Dinkeloo & Associates; One: 1976; Two: 1984) This elegant pair of 500-ft-tall aquamarine, glass-and-aluminum towers holds offices and the U.N. Plaza Hotel (*see* Expensive Lodgings *in* Chapter 6). The attractive, reflective glass in which the buildings are clad reflects the surrounding buildings and passing clouds. Cool, green-and-white marble makes the towers' shared lobby one of the most attractive in the city. *1st Ave. and 44th St., Midtown East. Subway: 4, 5, 6, 7, S to 42nd St./Grand Central.*

9 g-4

RIVER HOUSE

(Bottomly, Wagner & White, 1931) Then and now, a classic residential building for the very rich, the 26-story River House boasts a gated entrance for cars and a cobbled circular driveway. When the house was first built, residents had their own private yacht mooring, but alas, it was displaced by the construction of the FDR Drive in the 1940s. *435 E. 52nd St. (at Sutton Pl.), Midtown East. Subway: 6 to 51st St./Lexington Ave.; E, V to Lexington–3rd Aves./53rd St.*

9 d-4

ROCKEFELLER CENTER

(Various architects, dir. by Raymond Hood, mostly 1931–40) A miniature art deco city in the heart of Manhattan, 22-acre Rockefeller Center encompasses 19 limestone buildings soaring above cleverly connected, people-friendly plazas. The Channel Gardens, with their rock pools, topiary, and colorful flower beds, lead from 5th Avenue between 49th and 50th streets past shops to the sunken Lower Plaza, which transforms itself into an open-air café in warmer months and an ice rink in winter. Towering above the plaza is the 850-ft G.E. Building (formerly the RCA Building), which in addition to being home to NBC Studios is famous for its sleek, black-granite deco lobby. In front of the G.E. Building is a gilt statue of Prometheus, which watches over the lighting of the Rockefeller Center Christmas tree every year in early December. A block farther north on 5th Avenue you'll find an enormous statue of Atlas supporting the world—ever a symbol of Manhattan's power and scale—before the International Building (*see* Atlas and Prometheus *in* Statues & Public Art, *below; and* Radio City Music Hall *in* Historic Structures & Streets, *below*). *5th and 6th Aves. from 48th to 51st Sts., Midtown West. Subway: B, D, F, V to 47th–50th Sts./Rockefeller Center.*

9 e-4

SEAGRAM BUILDING

(Ludwig Mies van der Rohe and Philip Johnson, Kahn & Jacobs, 1958) An austere tribute to modernity by Mies van der Rohe, this sleek, bronze-color skyscraper and its plaza and fountains—all highly innovative at the time of construction—create a pleasing geometry. Although this international-style skyscraper inspired many less-successful imitations, architecture critic Paul Goldberger still calls the Seagram "one of the great buildings of the [20th] century." The interior, much of which was designed by Philip Johnson, also features exquisite, minimalist detail. *375 Park Ave. (between 52nd and 53rd Sts.), Midtown East. Subway: 6 to 51st St./Lexington Ave.; E, V to Lexington–3rd Aves./53rd St.*

10 *e-8*
17 STATE STREET
(Emery Roth & Sons, 1988) A sleek, wedge-shape, reflective-glass tower following the arc of State Street, this late-model international-style building has a twist: a high-tech glass-enclosed lobby 25 ft up. *17 State St. (between Water St. and Broadway), Lower Manhattan. Subway: 4, 5 to Bowling Green.*

11 *e-5*
SINGER BUILDING
(Ernest Flagg, 1904) The SoHo Singer is sometimes known as the Little Singer Building to distinguish it from the beautiful Singer Tower, also designed by Ernest Flagg but demolished 30 years ago to make way for the hulking One Liberty Plaza in the financial district. The Little Singer is unique in its use of decorative terra-cotta paneling, recessed plate glass, and filigreed iron. Above 11 stories of balconies, the facade culminates in a graceful iron arch. *561 Broadway (between Spring and Prince Sts.), SoHo. Subway: N, Q, R, W to Prince St.; 6 to Spring St.*

9 *d-4*
666 5TH AVENUE
(Carson & Lundin, 1957) This embossed-aluminum skyscraper, just north of Rockefeller Center, is most notable for the Isamu Noguchi waterfall in its arcade and the sculpted Noguchi ceiling in its lobby. *666 5th Ave. (between 52nd and 53rd Sts.), Midtown East. Subway: E, V to 5th Ave./53rd St.*

10 *e-3*
SOHO CAST-IRON HISTORIC DISTRICT
One of the city's most vibrant areas, full of art galleries and upscale shops, SoHo is also home to the world's largest concentration of cast-iron architecture. In the mid-19th century, commercial builders successfully duplicated elaborate, carved masonry by buying prefabricated facades made from cast iron. Though made from molds, the results were anything but dull; SoHo is filled with five- and six-story commercial buildings that look like Italian palazzos, featuring Corinthian columns, multiple tiers of arched windows, and elaborate French Empire pediments. SoHo's Haughwout Building (*see above*) is generally considered the finest example of cast-iron architecture in the world. TriBeCa and the Village have some cast-iron gems as well. *Canal and Houston Sts. from W. Broadway to Crosby St. Subway: N, Q, R, W to Prince St.; 6 to Spring St.; A, C, E, N, Q, R, W to Canal St.*

9 *e-3*
SONY BUILDING
(Johnson & Burgee, 1984) Formerly the headquarters of AT&T, this monumental corporate statement is considered the first postmodern skyscraper. Its 36 stories of rose-color granite climb 660 ft (the equivalent of 60 stories) and are topped by a much-ballyhooed "Chippendale" pediment. Archways worthy of Imperial Rome lead to a six-story arcade with public seating and an elevator that whisks you to the Sony Wonder Technology Lab (*see Science Museums, below*). *550 Madison Ave. (at 56th St.), Midtown East. Subway: N, R, W to 5th Ave./59th St.; F, Q to 57th St./6th Ave.*

9 *d-4*
TIME-LIFE BUILDING
(Harrison & Abramovitz, 1960) The construction of the Time-Life Building, next to Rockefeller Center, led to a corporate building boom along Avenue of the Americas. The sleek but banal slab of limestone, aluminum, and glass is now but one of many such office high-rises along this stretch, including the Exxon (at 1251), McGraw-Hill (1221), and Celanese (1211) buildings. *1271 6th Ave. (at 50th St.), Midtown West. Subway: B, D, F, V to 47th–50th Sts./Rockefeller Center.*

9 *e-3*
TRUMP TOWER
(Swanke, Hayden, Connell & Partners, 1983) A 68-story, bronze-glass megastructure named for the headline-grabbing developer Donald Trump, Trump

Tower is most famed for the prices of its condos (90% cost over $1 million) and for its huge, glitzy atrium of peach-color marble—chosen because it flatters certain complexions. Manhattan's first vertical shopping mall, the public atrium comes complete with a five-story water-wall that, depending on your mood, is either glorious or just plain silly. *725 5th Ave. (at 56th St.), Midtown East. Subway: N, R, W to 5th Ave./59th St.; F, Q to 57th St./6th Ave.*

9 *f-5*
TUDOR CITY
(Fred F. French Co., 1925–28; head architect, H. Douglas Ives) Built in the 1920s to attract middle-income residents, this private "city" centers around 12 buildings containing 3,000 apartments. On a bluff above 1st Avenue, Tudor City now affords great views of the United Nations and the East River. Interestingly, some of the facades facing in this direction did not originally have windows at all—since they overlooked what were then riverside slaughterhouses and glue factories. *1st and 2nd Aves. from 40th to 43rd Sts., Midtown East. Subway: 4, 5, 6, 7, S to 42nd St./Grand Central.*

9 *f-4*
UNITED NATIONS HEADQUARTERS
(International Committee of Architects, Wallace K. Harrison, chairman, 1947–53) This complex became the U.N.'s permanent headquarters in 1952. The tall, slim, green-glass Secretariat Building; the much smaller, domed General Assembly Building; and the Dag Hammarskjold Library (Harrison, Abramovitz & Harris, 1963) form the current complex, before which the flags of its member nations fly in alphabetical order when the General Assembly is in session. Built on 17 acres, the U.N. was profoundly influenced in design by Le Corbusier's "towers in open space" philosophy. Although the buildings may look a bit dated today, their windswept park and plaza remain visionary: They are embellished with a beautiful riverside promenade, a garden with 1,400 rosebushes, views of open sky (rare in Manhattan), and sculptures donated by member nations. *1st Ave. from 42nd to 48th Sts. (enter at 46th St.), Midtown, 212/963–7713. Tours leave approximately every 30 min, daily 9:30–4:45. Tours: $7.50 adults, $6 senior citizens, $5 students, $4 children 6–13, children under 5 not permitted. Subway: 4, 5, 6, 7 to 42nd St./Grand Central.*

10 *e-6*
WOOLWORTH BUILDING
(Cass Gilbert, 1913) One of New York's most dramatic commercial buildings, this neo-Gothic tower rises 792 ft and, clad in terra-cotta, is the jewel of the downtown skyline. Fittingly dubbed a "cathedral of commerce," it was the world's tallest building until 1930. Don't miss the ornate lobby: Carved figures on the ceiling represent the architect holding a model of the building and F. W. Woolworth himself, counting nickels and dimes. (He paid $13 million in cash to have the place built.) *233 Broadway (between Park Pl. and Barclay St.), Lower Manhattan. Subway: 2, 3 to Park Pl.; N, Q, R, W to City Hall.*

10 *d-6*
WORLD FINANCIAL CENTER
See Battery Park City, *above.*

ART GALLERIES
As America's art capital, New York has hundreds of galleries and thousands of artists. The city's galleries are clustered into neighborhood enclaves—each with its own unique personality. To find out what's on view, consult the listings in *New York Magazine, The New Yorker, Time Out,* or the *Village Voice.*

A word of advice: if you make an art gallery trek during the summer, remember that many galleries keep limited summer hours and galleries that do stay open tend to present smaller-scale shows. It's a good idea to call for summer hours before you make the trip.

soho
Although some of the major neighborhood galleries have lately moved to cheaper, more expansive digs in West Chelsea, SoHo remains the place where art trends trace their roots.

11 *b-4*
A.C.E. GALLERY
This major-league space is more serious, perhaps, than some of the other players showing contemporary art, but not quite avant-garde—a superb example of the middle ground. *275 Hudson St. (at Spring St.), SoHo, 212/255–5599.*

Tues.–Sat. 10–6, Sun. 11–5; call for summer hrs. Subway: C, E to Spring St.; 1, 2 to Canal St.

AC PROJECT ROOM
11 b-5

It's just what it sounds like: an experimental space devoted to newer forms of expression (i.e., not painting)—video, performance, and installation. 15 Renwick St. (west of Hudson St., between Canal and Spring Sts.), SoHo, 212/219–8275. Call for hrs. Subway: C, E to Spring St.; 1, 2 to Canal St.

A.I.R. GALLERY
11 d-5

A.I.R. is a cooperative gallery for women artists. Special events include talks (say, women artists in history) and seminars on the biz of art. 40 Wooster St. (between Broome and Grand Sts.), SoHo, 212/966–0799, www.airnyc.org. Call for hrs. Subway: A, C, E, N, Q, R, W to Canal St.

AMERICAN FINE ARTS
11 d-5

Gallerist Colin de Land has an eye for the decadent and controversial. Work like Garry Gross's Brooke Shields kiddy porn photos sit alongside more conceptual, sometimes confusing, pieces for a thought-provoking mix. 22 Wooster St. (between Grand and Canal Sts.), SoHo, 212/941–0401. Tues.–Sat. 12–6. Subway: C, E to Spring St.

BRONWYN KEENAN
11 f-6

One of Manhattan's newer gallerists, Keenan features edgy, younger artists on their way up, working in a variety of mediums. The space is trendy, but intimate—a nice way of saying that it's very small. 3 Crosby St., 2nd floor (at Howard St.), SoHo, 212/431–5083. Tues.–Sat. 11–6; call for summer hrs. Subway: 6, N, Q, R, W to Canal St.

BROOKE ALEXANDER
11 d-5

Having weathered the art-market storms of the late 1980s and early '90s, Alexander continues to show the cream, if not the cutting edge, of the contemporary scene. Brooke Alexander Editions, in the same location, has contemporary prints, multiples, and illustrated books from such heavyweights as Richard Artschwager, Richard Bosman, Jasper Johns,

Claes Oldenburg, and Andy Warhol. 59 Wooster St. (at Broome St.), SoHo, 212/925–4338. Tues.–Sat. 10–6; call for summer hrs. Subway: A, C, E, N, Q, R, W to Canal St.

DAVID ZWIRNER
11 e-5

Zwirner is another far-SoHo gallery that's snatching the bright young things up. In this case, the star is installationist Jason Rhoades, whose postmodern gatherings of brightly colored junk and everyday objects are arranged into Rube Goldbergesque clusters that fill entire spaces. 43 Greene St. (between Grand and Broome Sts.), SoHo, 212/966–9074, www.zwirner.com. Tues.–Sat. 10–6 (during exhibitions). Subway: A, C, E, N, Q, R, W to Canal St.

DEITCH PROJECTS
11 e-5

This avant-garde, sometimes downright weird gallery shows a variety of work, from contemporary painting to installation to long-term performance pieces. 76 Grand St. (between Wooster and Greene Sts.), SoHo, 212/343–7300. Tues.–Sat. 12–6; call for summer hrs. Subway: N, Q, R, W to Canal St.

THE DRAWING CENTER
11 d-6

This far-SoHo stalwart refuses to bow to caprice, preferring instead to mount idiosyncratic shows—a group of artists with similar styles, say—or simply focus on the Center's ostensible purpose, drawing. Perhaps the most celebrated show of the past few years was one on the history of tattooing. Rising big-timers, such as Kara Walker, have exhibited large-scale works in the impressive quarters. Recently, the center has been focusing on historic works such as those of James Ensor. 35 Wooster St. (between Grand and Broome Sts.), SoHo, 212/219–2166. Tues.–Fri. 10–6, Sat. 11–6. Subway: A, C, E, N, Q, R, W to Canal St.

EXIT ART
11 e-4

This large SoHo space is atypical in that it encourages hanging out—in the gift shop or the café—rather than quick visits. The shows, mounted by freelance curators as well as staff, tend to focus on social concerns, so the place has a late '60s–early '90s feel that counters the cash chase currently raging elsewhere. Recent installations have included a clever show of artists invited to live and work in the space for a few weeks. *548 Broadway, 2nd floor (between Spring and Prince Sts.), SoHo, 212/966–7745, www.exitart.com. Tues.–Fri. 10–6, Sat. 11–6; call for summer hrs. Subway: N, Q, R, W to Prince St.*

JACK TILTON/ ANNA KUSTERA
11 d-6

Live nudes, even live pigs, might be found at Tilton's cutting-edge space, which favors off-the-wall performance and video installations. *49 Greene St. (at Broome St.), SoHo, 212/941–1775. Tues.–Sat. 10–6; call for summer hrs. Subway: F, V to Broadway–Lafayette St.*

JACQUES CARCANAGUES
11 e-4

Carcanagues specializes in ethno-graphic items—including ritual objects, furniture, and textiles—from India, Thailand, Tibet, Nepal, China, Japan, Korea, and the Philippines. *106 Spring St. (at Mercer St.), SoHo, 212/925–8110, www.jacquescarcanagues.com. Daily 11:30–7. Subway: N, Q, R, W to Prince St.; 6 to Spring St.*

JUNE KELLY
11 e-4

June Kelly's taste is solid, with a focus on a multicultural roster. *591 Broadway (between Prince and Houston Sts.), SoHo, 212/226–1660, www.junekellygallery.com. Mon.–Fri. 11–6; call for summer hrs. Subway: N, Q, R, W to Prince St.; F, V to Broadway–Lafayette St.*

KENT GALLERY
11 e-4

This tidy, two-level space is squeezed between SoHo and Little Italy, in a sliver of neighborhood just shy of the mythical NoHo in flavor. Kent shows mainly "smart" work, from such artists as Vivienne Koorland and Richard Artschwager. It's not a rock-the-world gallery, but it can be relied on show after show to mount lively, intelligent work that steers clear of obvious trends. *67 Prince St. (between Broadway and Lafayette Sts.), SoHo, 212/966–4500, www.kentgallery.com. Tues.–Sat. 12–6; call for summer hrs. Subway: N, Q, R, W to Prince St.; F, V to Broadway–Lafayette St.*

LOUIS K. MEISEL
11 d-5

Photorealist art by Audrey Flack, Charles Bell, Richard Estes, and the like covers the walls at this reliable space—alongside vintage pinup art. *141 Prince St. (between Wooster St. and W. Broadway), SoHo, 212/677–1340, www.meiselgallery.com. Tues.–Sat. 10–6; call for summer hrs. Subway: N, Q, R, W to Prince St.*

MULTIPLE IMPRESSIONS, LTD.
11 e-4

These contemporary American and European original graphics come from such artists as Kozo, Andre Masson, Johnny Friedlaender, Harold Altman, Elizabeth Schippert, and Mikio Watanabe. The gallery mounts several solo shows annually. *128 Spring St. (between Wooster and Greene Sts.), SoHo, 212/925–1313, www.multipleimpressions.com. Mon. 11–5:30, Tues.–Sat. 11–6:30, Sun. 12–6:30. Subway: C, E to Spring St.*

NANCY HOFFMAN
11 d-4

Hoffman shows good contemporary art, including works by Carolyn Brady, Don Eddy, Juan Gonzalez, Joseph Raffael, Rafael Ferrer, Howard Buchwald, John Okulick, and Alan Siegel. *429 W. Broadway (between Spring and Prince Sts.), SoHo, 212/966–6676, www.nancyhoffmangallery.com. Tues.–Sat. 10–6; call for summer hrs. Subway: C, E to Spring St.*

PETER BLUM
11 d-4

Blum's continues to indulge in its ongoing passion for intelligent contemporary painting. *99 Wooster St. (between Prince and Spring Sts.), SoHo, 212/343–0441. Tues.–Fri. 10–6, Sat. 11–6; call for summer hrs. Subway: N, Q, R, W to Prince St.*

PHYLLIS KIND GALLERY
11 e-4

Kind specializes in off-kilter contemporary American, Soviet, and European art, as well as 20th-century American and European art brut. *136 Greene St. (between Prince and Houston Sts.), SoHo, 212/925–1200, www.phylliskindgallery.com. Tues.–Sat. 10–6; call for summer hrs. Subway: N, Q, R, W to Prince St.; F, V to Broadway–Lafayette St.*

11 e-5
P.P.O.W.

Contemporary international artists have the spotlight here. *476 Broome St. (between Greene and Wooster Sts.), SoHo, 212/941–8642. Tues.–Sat. 10–6; call for summer hrs. Subway: A, C, E, N, Q, R, W to Canal St.*

11 e-6
RONALD FELDMAN FINE ARTS

Feldman has long been renowned as one of SoHo's prime tastemakers, not because he shows the big shots, but because he shows truly significant work by the likes of Ida Applebroog. As at Kent, scarcely a false note is struck here, so dive in if the rest of the long march through Art Land has been getting you down. *31 Mercer St. (between Grand and Canal Sts.), SoHo, 212/226–3232, www. feldmangallery.com. Tues.–Sat. 10:30–6; call for summer hrs. Subway: N, Q, R, W to Canal St.*

11 d-5
SPENCER BROWNSTONE

Another of those terribly contemporary spaces, Spencer Brownstone specializes in installation, which now rivals painting and sculpture as young artists' métier of choice. *39 Wooster St. (between Broome and Grand Sts.), SoHo, 212/334–3455. Tues.–Sat. 10–6; call for summer hrs. Subway: A, C, E, N, Q, R, W to Canal St.*

11 d-4
TONY SHAFRAZI GALLERY

This huge space was founded by an '80s style megadealer who, after he defaced Picasso's *Guernica* by spray-painting "Kill All Lies" on the canvas, went on to show artists such as Kenny Scharf, Keith Haring, and Jean-Michel Basquiat. *119 Wooster St. (between Spring and Prince Sts.), SoHo, 212/274–9300. Tues.–Sat. 10–6; call for summer hrs. Subway: N, Q, R, W to Prince St.; 6 to Spring St.*

11 d-4
VORPAL SOHO

Vorpal SoHo can claim the world's largest collection of M.C. Escher prints; other holdings include contemporary paintings, sculpture, and prints. *459 W. Broadway, 5th floor (between Prince and Houston Sts.), SoHo, 212/777–3939.*

Tues.–Sat. 11–6. Subway: N, Q, R, W to Prince St.; C, E to Spring St.

11 d-4
WARD–NASSE GALLERY

This cooperative gallery run by artists offers visual, spoken, and performing arts. *178 Prince St. (between Thompson and Sullivan Sts.), SoHo, 212/925–6951, www.wardnasse.org. Tues.–Sat. 11–6, Sun. 1–6. Subway: C, E to Spring St.*

uptown

These exclusive, white-glove spaces, catering largely to serious collectors and often emphasizing furniture and prints over paintings, are located primarily on and off Madison Avenue from 57th to 86th Street.

7 e-8
ACQUAVELLA GALLERIES, INC.

In a French, neoclassical town house, Acquavella specializes in impressionist and postimpressionist work by such heavyweights as Monet, Matisse, Picasso, Miró, and Pissarro. Downstairs you'll find post–World War II and contemporary paintings by such artists as Guston, Gottlieb, Lichtenstein, and Pollock. *18 E. 79th St. (between 5th and Madison Aves.), Upper East Side, 212/734–6300, www.acquavellagalleries.com. Mon.–Fri. 10–5; call for summer hrs. Subway: 6 to 77th St.*

7 e-6
ART OF THE PAST

The collection features art from Nepal, Tibet, Bhutan, and India—some of it dating back more than 2,000 years. *1242 Madison Ave. (at 89th St.), Upper East Side, 212/860–7070. Sept.–July, Mon.–Sat. 10–6; Aug., Mon.–Fri. 10–6. Subway: 4, 5, 6 to 86th St.*

9 d-3
BABCOCK GALLERIES

Established in 1852, this old-line gallery specializes in American art of the 19th and 20th centuries, but also has plenty of contemporary paintings, drawings, and sculpture. *724 5th Ave. (between 56th and 57th Sts.), Midtown East, 212/767–1852. Mon.–Fri. 10–5; call for summer hrs. Subway: N, R, W to 5th Ave./59th St.; F to 57th St./6th Ave.*

9 e-1
BERRY-HILL GALLERIES, INC.
American painting and sculpture from the 18th, 19th, and 20th centuries; contemporary art; and Old Masters are the order of the day in this posh town house gallery. *11 E. 70th St. (between 5th and Madison Aves.), Upper East Side, 212/744–2300, www.berry-hill.com. Mon.–Fri. 9:30–5, Sat. 10–5; call for summer hrs. Subway: 6 to 68th St./Hunter College.*

9 e-2
BRUTON GALLERY
Just the place to go if you have a spare pedestal: Bruton offers French and European sculpture of the 19th and 20th centuries by Joseph Bernard, Antoine Bourdekke, Stephen Buxin, Jean Carton, Paul Cornet, Aristide Maillol, Auguste Rodin, and others. *40 E. 61st St. (between Madison and Park Aves.), Upper East Side, 212/980–1640. By appointment only. Subway: 4, 5, 6, N, R, W to 59th St./Lexington Ave.*

7 e-8
CDS GALLERY
CDS is one of Manhattan's more formidable galleries for the lions of mid-20th-century abstraction. If Motherwell and de Kooning are your thing, put this space high on your list. *76 E. 79th St. (between Madison and Park Aves.), Upper East Side, 212/772–9555. Tues.–Sat. 10–5:30; call for summer hrs. Subway: 6 to 77th St.*

7 e-8
CLAUDE BERNARD GALLERY
Claude Bernard showcases 19th- and 20th-century South American, American, and European artists including Fernando Botero, Balthus, Jean Dubuffet, Fernand Léger, Miró, Picasso, and Toledo. *900 Park Ave. (at 79th St.), Upper East Side, 212/988–2050. By appointment only. Subway: 6 to 77th St.*

7 e-8
DAVID TUNICK, INC.
Tunick carries Old Master prints, modern prints, and drawings by such masters as Rembrandt, Dürer, Tiepolo, Brueghel, and Canaletto; 19th-century prints by Bonnard, Goya, Cézanne, Degas, Delacroix, Gericault, Manet, Toulouse-Lautrec, and Pissarro; and 20th-century works by Picasso, Matisse,

Braque, Whistler, Bellows, and Villon. *46 E. 65th St. (between Madison and Park Aves.), Upper East Side, 212/570–0090. Mon.–Fri. 9:30–5 (however, it's advisable to make an appointment). Subway: 6 to 68th St.*

9 e-2
DAVIS & LANGDALE CO.
Dignified 18th-, 19th-, and 20th-century American and English paintings, watercolors, and drawings hang at this town house gallery, which caters to the Ralph Lauren/Prince of Wales look. Contemporary means traditional here, with American work by such artists as Lennart Anderson, Aaron Shikler, Albert York, and Harry Roseman. *231 E. 60th St. (between 3rd and 2nd Aves.), Upper East Side, 212/838–0333. Tues.–Sat. 10–5. Subway: 4, 5, 6, N; R, W to 59th St./Lexington Ave.*

7 e-8
E & J FRANKEL LTD
E & J Frankel specializes in art from China (porcelain and jade from the Shang Dynasty through the 1840s) and Japan (screen paintings and furnishings from all periods). *1040 Madison Ave. (at 79th St.), Upper East Side, 212/879–5733, www.ejfrankel.com. Sept.–June, Mon.–Sat. 10:30–5:30; July–Aug., Mon.–Fri. 10:30–5:30. Subway: 6 to 77th St.*

7 e-8
THE ELKON GALLERY
Twentieth-century masters are the focus here: paintings, drawings, and sculpture from Balthus, Botero, Chagall, Dubuffet, Ernst, Magritte, Matisse, Miró, and Picasso. *18 E. 81st St. (between 5th and Madison Aves.), Upper East Side, 212/535–3940. Mon.–Fri. 9:30–5:30. Subway: 6 to 77th St.*

9 e-3
FITCH-FEBVREL GALLERY
Fitch-Febvrel specializes in fine prints and drawings from the 19th and 20th centuries. *5 E. 57th St. (between 5th and Madison Aves.), Midtown East, 212/688–8522, www.fitch-febvrel.com. Sept.–July, Tues.–Sat. 11–5:30; Aug. by appointment only. Subway: N, R, W to 5th Ave./59th St.*

9 e-3
FORUM GALLERY
Forum features contemporary American figurative paintings and sculpture. *745*

5th Ave., 5th floor (between 57th and 58th Sts.), Midtown East, 212/355–4545, www.forumgallery.com. Tues.–Sat. 10–5:30. Subway: N, R, W to 5th Ave./59th St.; F to 57th St./6th Ave.

7 e-8
GAGOSIAN

With a museum curator's flair, Larry Gagosian continues to show the heavyweights of the modern art world, including Francesco Clemente, Willem de Kooning, Francis Bacon, David Salle, and Andy Warhol, among a pantheon of others. 980 Madison Ave. (between 76th and 77th Sts.), Upper East Side, 212/744–2313, www.gagosian.com. Tues.–Sat. 10–6:30; call for summer hrs. Subway: 6 to 77th St.

9 d-3
GALERIE ST. ETIENNE

This private dealer specializes in 19th- and 20th-century Austrian and German expressionism, 19th- and 20th-century outsider art, folk art, and Grandma Moses. 24 W. 57th St., 8th floor (between 5th and 6th Aves.), Midtown West, 212/245–6734. Tues.–Sat. 11–5 (during exhibitions). Subway: N, R, W to 5th Ave./59th St.; F to 57th St./6th Ave.

9 d-3
GARTH CLARK

Clark's is a niche gallery specializing in high-quality sculpture and ceramics from around the world. The pieces are exquisite and the patrons armored with wealth. 24 W. 57th St. (between 5th and 6th Aves.), Midtown West, 212/246–2205, www.garthclark.com. Tues.–Sat. 10–5:30; call for summer hrs. Subway: N, R, W to 5th Ave./59th St.; F to 57th St./6th Ave.

9 d-3
HAMMER GALLERIES

Located in a multi-story town house, Hammer displays impressionists, postimpressionists, and European masters, as well as an impressive collection of ceramics by Picasso. It also produces a vast, ever-evolving selection of prints by sports artist LeRoy Neiman for its Graphics Gallery. 33 W. 57th St. (between 5th and 6th Aves.), Midtown West, 212/644–4400, www.hammergalleries.com. Mon.–Fri. 10–6, Sat. 10–5. Subway: N, R, W to 5th Ave./59th St.; F to 57th St./6th Ave.

7 e-1
HIRSCHL & ADLER GALLERIES

Top-quality 18th-, 19th-, and 20th-century American painting, sculpture, drawing, decorative art, and folk art rest here, and they're the kind of works that would send critic Robert Hughes scurrying for a thesaurus. Also on offer are European impressionist and modern painting and drawing, as well as the patron saint of bird painting, John J. Audubon. Mary Cassatt, Frederick Church, John Singleton Copley, Childe Hassam, Homer, Hopper, Matisse, O'Keeffe, Picasso, and Renoir flesh out the reserves. 21 E. 70th St. (at Madison Ave.), Upper East Side, 212/535–8810, www.hirschlandadler.com. Tues.–Fri. 9:30–5:30, Sat. 9:30–4:45. Subway: 6 to 68th St./Hunter College.

7 e-1
HIRSCHL & ADLER MODERN

Hirschl & Adler's 20th-century gallery shows both American and European art. 21 E. 70th St. (at Madison Ave.), Upper East Side, 212/535–8810, www.hirschlandadler.com. Tues.–Fri. 9:30–5:30, Sat. 9:30–4:45. Subway: 6 to 68th St./Hunter College.

9 e-3
JAMES GOODMAN GALLERY

A haven for 20th-century American and European paintings, drawings, watercolors, and sculpture, Goodman features work by Botero, de Kooning, Dubuffet, Léger, Lichtenstein, Matisse, Miró, Henry Moore, Rauschenberg, and Warhol. 41 E. 57th St. (at Madison Ave.), Midtown East, 212/593–3737, www.jamesgoodmangallery.com. Tues.–Sat. 10–6; call for summer hrs. Subway: N, R, W to 5th Ave./59th St.; F to 57th St./6th Ave.

9 e-1
JANE KAHAN

Kahan nearly always has a stunning roster of greats—everyone from Arp to Calder, from Delaunay to Miró. In addition to a large collection of prints, she specializes in Modern Art tapestries, fabric art created in collaboration with artists such as Chagall, Picasso, and Stella. 922 Madison Ave. (at 73rd St.), Upper East Side, 212/744–1490, www.janekahan.com. Tues.–Sat. 10–6; call for summer hrs. Subway: 6 to 77th St.

7 *e-7*

JAPAN GALLERY

Here the focus is Japanese woodblock prints from the 18th century to the present. *1210 Lexington Ave. (at 82nd St.), Upper East Side, 212/288–2241. Tues.–Fri. 11–6; call for Sat. appointments. Subway: 4, 5, 6 to 86th St.*

9 *e-3*

JOAN T. WASHBURN GALLERIES

American abstract art of the 1930s and '40s is mixed here with folk art and contemporary paintings, sculpture, and drawings. *20 W. 57th St. (between 5th and 6th Aves.), Midtown West, 212/397–6780. Tues.–Sat. 10–6; call for summer hrs. Subway: N, R, W to 5th Ave./59th St.; F to 57th St./6th Ave.*

7 *e-3*

KENNEDY GALLERIES

American paintings, sculpture, and graphics of the 18th, 19th, and 20th centuries share space with European fine prints. *730 5th Ave. (at 57th St.), Midtown West, 212/541–9600. Tues.–Sat. 9:30–5:30; call for summer hrs. Subway: N, R, W to 5th Ave./59th St.; F to 57th St./6th Ave.*

9 *e-1*

KNOEDLER & CO.

One of Manhattan's top-flight galleries, Knoedler is a must-stop for those in search of contemporary European and American paintings and sculpture. *19 E. 70th St. (between 5th and Madison Aves.), Upper East Side, 212/794–0550, www.knoedlergallery.com. Tues.–Fri. 9:30–5:30, Sat. 10–5:30; call for summer hrs. Subway: 6 to 68th St./Hunter College.*

9 *e-3*

KRAUSHAAR GALLERIES

The vibe here is distinctly unflamboyant: paintings, drawings, and sculpture by such 20th-century American artists as Peggy Bacon, William Glackens, Leon Goldin, Elsie Manville, Ben Frank Moss, and John Sloan. *724 5th Ave. (at 57th St.), Midtown East, 212/307–5730. Tues.–Fri. 9:30–5:30, Sat. 10–5; call for summer hrs. Subway: N, R, W to 5th Ave./59th St.; F to 57th St./6th Ave.*

7 *e-8*

LEO CASTELLI GALLERY

The grand old man of the sixties avant-garde passed away in the summer of 1999, but his gallery lives on through the continued representation of heavy hitters who include Rauschenberg, Johns, Nauman, and Lichtenstein. *59 E. 79th St. (between Madison and Park Aves.), Upper East Side, 212/249–4470, www.castelligallery.com. Tues.–Sat. 10–6; call for summer hrs. Subway: 6 to 77th St.*

7 *e-8*

LEONARD HUTTON GALLERIES

Here German Expressionists and Russian avant-garde art reign supreme. *41 E. 57th St. (at Madison Ave.), Midtown East, 212/751–7373. Tues.–Sat. 10–5:30; call for summer hrs. Subway: N, R, W to 5th Ave./59th St.; F to 57th St./6th Ave.*

9 *d-2*

MARGO FEIDEN GALLERIES

Feiden has a thorough collection of *New Yorker* cartoonist Al Hirschfield's drawings, watercolors, lithographs, and etchings. *699 Madison Ave. (between 62nd and 63rd Sts.), Upper East Side, 212/677–5330. Daily 10–6. Subway: 4, 5, 6, N, R, W to 59th St./Lexington Ave.*

7 *e-8*

MARIAN GOODMAN

Artists of proven reputation exhibit their excellent contemporary art here. You'll find Jeff Wall's staged photographs presented on light boxes and William Kentridge's video animations. *24 W. 57th St. (between 5th and 6th Aves.), Midtown West, 212/977–7160, www.mariangoodman.com. Mon.–Sat. 10–6. Subway: N, R, W to 5th Ave./59th St.; F to 57th St./6th Ave.*

9 *d-3*

MARLBOROUGH GALLERY

Along with Knoedler and Gagosian, Marlborough is one of the most important stops on any uptown gallery tour. The focus is on 20th-century and contemporary paintings, sculpture, photographs, and graphics; artists represented include Frank Auerbach, Francis Bacon, Fernando Botero, Red Grooms, Barbara Hepworth, Alex Katz, Antonio Lopez Garcia, Henry Moore, Larry Rivers, and Rufino Tamayo. *40 W. 57th St., 2nd floor (between 5th and 6th Aves.), Midtown West, 212/541–4900, www.marlboroughgallery.com. Mon.–Sat. 10–5:30; call for summer hrs. Subway: N, R, W to 5th Ave./59th St.; F to 57th St./6th Ave.*

9 e-3
MCKEE GALLERY
McKee exhibits contemporary paintings, drawings, sculpture, and prints. *745 5th Ave. (between 57th and 58th Sts.), Midtown East, 212/688–5951, www.mckeegallery.com. Tues.–Sat. 10–6; call for summer hrs. Subway: N, R, W to 5th Ave./59th St.; F to 57th St./6th Ave.*

7 e-7
MERTON SIMPSON GALLERY
Most of the art here is from Africa, but Oceanic and Native American works are mixed in. *1063 Madison Ave. (at 81st St.), Upper East Side, 212/988–6290. Tues.–Sat. 10:30–5:30; call for summer hrs. Subway: 6 to 77th St.*

9 e-3
NOHRA HAIME GALLERY
Contemporary Latin American, American, and European art are the main courses at this standby. *41 E. 57th St. (at Madison Ave.), Midtown East, 212/888–3550. Tues.–Sat. 10–6; call for summer hrs. Subway: N, R, W to 5th Ave./59th St.; F to 57th St./6th Ave.*

9 f-7
OLD PRINT SHOP
This is the place to retreat for original prints of Audubon, Currier & Ives, 18th-century maps, and nauticalia, as well as some American paintings. *150 Lexington Ave. (between 29th and 30th Sts.), Murray Hill, 212/683–3950, www.oldprintshop.com. Tues.–Fri. 9–5, Sat. 9–4; call for summer hrs. Subway: 6 to 28th St.*

9 e-3
PACE/WILDENSTEIN/MACGILL
The mighty Pace, a corporate art empire ruled by superdealer Arne Glimcher, is so big, so vast, and such a part of the art world that nothing as trivial as dips in the stock market can dent its business. After a merger with Wildenstein, one of New York's older and most venerable dealer clans, Glimcher's reach has extended even farther. Pace/Wildenstein, on the 2nd floor, exhibits paintings and sculpture; Pace/Wildenstein/MacGill, on the 9th floor, shows photography. Some of the heavyweights represented are Rothko, Nevelson, Mangold, and Steinberg. On the 10th floor, Pace Primitive features religious and ceremonial art, including antique African masks and sculpture, as well as Himalayan masks. On the same floor, Pace Prints' substantial collection includes 15th- to 20th-century master prints and drawings by Canaletto, Dürer, Goya, Kandinsky, Matisse, Miró, Picasso, Piranesi, Rembrandt, Tiepolo, Toulouse-Lautrec, and Whistler. It's probably the finest print annex (of a major gallery) in town. *32 E. 57th St. (between 5th and Madison Aves.), Midtown East, 212/421–3292. Tues.–Fri. 9:30–6, Sat. 10–6; call for summer hrs. Subway: N, R, W to 5th Ave./59th St.; F to 57th St./6th Ave.*

9 e-3
RALPH M. CHAIT GALLERIES, INC.
Chait shows top-quality Chinese art, including export silver; porcelain; and pottery from the Neolithic period to 1800. *12 E. 56th St. (between 5th and Madison Aves.), Midtown East, 212/758–0937, www.rmchait.com. Mon.–Sat. 10–5; call for summer hrs. Subway: N, R, W to 5th Ave./59th St.; F to 57th St./6th Ave.*

9 e-3
RONIN GALLERY
Ronin has a large selection of 17th- to 20th-century Japanese woodblock prints, as well as netsuke. *605 Madison Ave. (between 57th and 58th Sts.), Midtown East, 212/688–0188, www.japancollection.com. Call for hrs. Subway: 4, 5, 6, N, R, W to 59th St./Lexington Ave.*

7 e-8
SALANDER O'REILLY GALLERIES
One of uptown's more significant galleries, Salander O'Reilly represents 19th- to 20th-century American modernist paintings, primarily from the Ashcan, precisionist, and New York schools, as well as 19th-century British and French paintings. *20 E. 79th St. (between 5th and Madison Aves.), Upper East Side, 212/879–6606, www.salander-oreilly.com. Mon.–Sat. 9:30–5:30; call for summer hrs. Subway: 6 to 77th St.*

9 d-3
SCHMIDT BINGHAM GALLERY
The focus here is contemporary American realism. *41 E. 57th St. (at Madison Ave.), Midtown East, 212/888–1122, www.schmidtbingham.com. Tues.–Fri. 10–5; call for summer hrs. Subway: N, R, W to 5th Ave./59th St.; F to 57th St./6th Ave.*

7 e-8

SOLOMON & CO. FINE ART

Solomon's roster of 20th-century American and European painters and sculptors includes Avery, Calder, de Kooning, Dubuffet, Hoffman, Pollock, and Stella. *959 Madison Ave. (at 75th St.), Upper East Side, 212/737–8200. Mon.–Sat. 11–5; call for summer hrs. Subway: 6 to 77th St.*

7 e-8

SOUFER

Postimpressionist and European paintings of the 1920s–1940s are this gallery's forte, but there's also a cluster of German expressionist works. *1015 Madison Ave. (between 78th and 79th Sts.), Upper East Side, 212/628–3225. Tues.–Sat. 10–5; call for summer hrs. Subway: 6 to 77th St.*

9 d-3

TIBOR DE NAGY GALLERY

One of the city's prime purveyors of good taste with a forward eye, de Nagy eschews trends and high-concept, specializing instead in figurative masters of the 20th century. *724 5th Ave. (between 56th and 57th Sts.), Midtown East, 212/262–5050. Tues.–Sat. 10–5:30; call for summer hrs. Subway: N, R, W to 5th Ave./59th St.; F to 57th St./6th Ave.*

7 e-8

UBU GALLERY

This fresh space engages art that deviates from the tried-and-true. Shows focus on unusual practices—photomontage, for instance—as well as the funkier products of surrealist and Eastern European art. *16 E. 78th St. (between 5th and Madison Aves.), Upper East Side, 212/794–4444. Call for hrs. Subway: 6 to 77th St.*

9 e-3

WALLY FINDLAY

Findlay offers impressionist, postimpressionist, and contemporary art of the French school, all with mass appeal. *124 E. 57th St. (between Park and Lexington Aves.), Midtown East, 212/421–5390, www.wallyfindlaygalleries.com. Mon.–Sat. 10–6; call for summer hrs. Subway: 4, 5, 6, N, R, W to 59th St./Lexington Ave.*

9 e-3

ZABRISKIE GALLERY

Early 20th-century American painting, sculpture, and drawing, along with contemporary large-scale sculpture and photography, have built this gallery a loyal following. *41 E. 57th St. (at Madison Ave.), Midtown East, 212/752–1223, www.zabriskiegallery.com. Tues.–Sat. 10–5:30; call for summer hrs. Subway: N, R, W to 5th Ave./59th St.; F to 57th St./6th Ave.*

west chelsea

Never have so many traveled to so barren a landscape to make so few feel so hip so quickly. West Chelsea, a cluster of enormous galleries—many hewn from former taxi garages—west of 10th Avenue between 22nd and 26th Sts., has slowly but surely attracted many of SoHo's and even uptown's heaviest hitters. Slick, industrial-size spaces, primarily devoted to contemporary art, bring a stream of fashion-plate mobs to high-powered art openings and parties. Even if you're not an art aficionado, it's fun to check out the vibe.

9 b-8

ACA GALLERIES

Founded in 1932 and a recent defector to the West Chelsea scene from 57th Street, this socially conscious, standout gallery shows both contemporary art and 19th-century American works from its impressive collection. *529 W. 20th St. (between 10th Ave. and the West Side Hwy.), Chelsea, 212/206–8080. Tues.–Sat. 10:30–6; call for summer hrs. Subway: C, E to 23rd St.*

9 b-7

ANDREA ROSEN

Another SoHo migrator, Rosen has moved to wide open spaces up north, no doubt to have more room for her wacky installations, surveillance cameras, and Sean Landers comic strips. *525 W. 24th St. (between 10th and 11th Aves.), Chelsea, 212/627–6000. Tues.–Sat. 10–6; call for summer hrs. Subway: C, E to 23rd St.*

9 b-8

ANNINA NOSEI

Life springs eternal for the gallerist who gave the late Jean-Michel Basquiat a basement in which to crank out paintings, and signed on as his first dealer. Now in West Chelsea, Nosei continues to champion new painting. *530 W. 22nd St. (between 10th and 11th Aves.), Chelsea, 212/741–8695. Tues.–Sat. 10–6; call for summer hrs. Subway: C, E to 23rd St.*

9 *b-7*

BARBARA GLADSTONE GALLERY

Gladstone has on her commendable roster some of the most important artists currently working: Matthew Barney, Shirin Nashat, and Vito Acconci. *515 W. 24th St. (between 10th and 11th Aves.), Chelsea, 212/206–9300. Tues.– Sat. 10–6; call for summer hrs. Subway: C, E to 23rd St.*

9 *b-8*

BONAKDAR GALLERY

Yet another SoHoite to break camp and move up north, Bonakdar excels in group shows of sculpture, painting, photography, installation, and drawings. *521 W. 21st (between 10th and 11th Aves.), Chelsea, 212/414–4144. Tues.–Sat. 10–6; call for summer hrs. Subway: C, E to 23rd St.*

11 *e-4*

CHARLES COWLES

Cowles focuses on contemporary paintings, photography, and sculpture. *537 W. 24th St. (between 10th and 11th Aves.), Chelsea, 212/925–3500, www. cowlesgallery.com. Tues.–Sat. 10–6; call for summer hrs. Subway: C, E to 23rd St.*

9 *b-8*

CLEMENTINE

This small, smartly managed space has mounted a dozen fine exhibits of painting and photography since opening in late 1996. A gallery specialty is the two-person show, with each artist getting one side of the space. *526 W. 21st St. (between 10th and 11th Aves.), Chelsea, 212/243– 5937, www.clementine-gallery.com. Tues.– Sat. 10–6; call for summer hrs. Subway: C, E to 23rd St.*

9 *a-7*

EDWARD THORP

Contemporary American painting and sculpture get top billing here. *210 11th Ave. (at 26th St.), Chelsea, 212/691–6565. Tues.–Sat. 10–6; call for summer hrs. Subway: C, E to 23rd St.*

9 *a-7*

FISCHBACH GALLERY

Fischbach is a showcase for contemporary American realist paintings and drawings—very eclectic, very New York. *210 11th Ave., Suite 801 (at 26th St.),*

Chelsea, 212/759–2345. Tues.–Sat. 10– 5:30. Subway: C, E to 23rd St.

9 *b-8*

FRIEDRICH PETZEL

Petzel is a SoHo veteran (now located in Chelsea), considered by many to be in the same league with Gagosian and the other movers and shakers on the contemporary art scene. As we proceed into the new millennium, Petzel still has his ear to the ground with debut artists like Dana Hoey. *535 W. 22nd St. (between 10th and 11th Aves.), Chelsea, 212/680–9467, www.petzel.com. Tues.–Sat 10–6; call for summer hrs. Subway: C, E to 23rd St.*

9 *b-7*

GAGOSIAN

Well, what can you say? Twenty years ago the guy was selling posters on the beach in Venice, California. Now, with Arne Glimcher of Pace, he competes for the "Biggest Dealer" title on both coasts. Larry Gagosian's roster, featuring Schnabel, Salle, and Serra, might be starting to look a little too go-go art-star, but he continues to add new talent, including Ivory Coast painter Ouattara. Unlike his uptown temple, Gagosian's new Chelsea space is spare—actually it's more like an airplane hangar—which suits it to Serra's enormous iron curves and blocks, Damien Hirst's bisected livestock, and Annette Messager's creepy, gallery-filling installations of yarn, photos, and stuffed varmints. *555 W. 24th St. (between 10th and 11th Aves.), Chelsea, 212/741–1111, www.gagosian.com. Tues.–Sat. 10–6:30; call for summer hrs. Subway: C, E to 23rd St.*

9 *b-7*

GALERIE LELONG

At the American branch of this Paris-based gallery, the focus is on contemporary American, Latin American, and European sculpture, drawings, and paintings. *528 W. 26th St. (between 10th and 11th Aves.), Chelsea, 212/315–0470. Tues.–Fri. 10–5:30, Sat. 11–5:30. Subway: C, E to 23rd St.*

9 *b-8*

GAVIN BROWN'S ENTERPRISE

Brown's hipster meat-packing district gallery shows trendy British and American comers like elephant-dung artist Chris Ofili. An adjoining bar, the sceney Passerby, does nothing but add to the ultra-cool factor. *436 W. 15th St. (between 9th and 10th Aves.), Chelsea, 212/627–5258. Tues.–Sat. 10–6; call for summer hrs. Subway: A, C, E to 14th St.*

9 *b-7*
GORNEY, BRAVIN + LEE
Next door to the West Chelsea Arts Building, this hot new gallery represents some of the most intriguing young artists going: David Deutsch, Catherine Opie, and Alexis Rockman. *534 W. 26th St. (between 10th and 11th Aves.), Chelsea, 212/352–8372, www.gblgallery.com. Tues.–Sat. 10–6; call for summer hrs. Subway: C, E to 23rd St.*

9 *b-7*
GREENE NAFTALI
Of West Chelsea's smaller galleries, this one gets the most ink due to its zany contemporary-art installations. *526 W. 26th St. (between 10th and 11th Aves.), Chelsea, 212/463–7770. Tues.–Sat. 10–6; call for summer hrs. Subway: C, E to 23rd St.*

10 *b-1*
HELLER GALLERY
Contemporary glass sculpture gets its due in an absolutely enormous bilevel space in Chelsea. *420 W. 14th St. (between 9th and 10th Aves.), Chelsea, 212/414–4014, www.hellergallery.com. Tues.–Sat. 11–6, Sun. 12–5; call for summer hrs. Subway: 1, 2, 3 to 14th St.*

9 *b-8*
KIM FOSTER
Foster has relocated from the fringe of SoHo to the thick of Chelsea and still retains her edgy roster of twentysomething conceptualists. *529 W. 20th St. (between 10th and 11th Aves.), Chelsea, 212/966–9024. Tues.–Sat. 10–6; call for summer hrs. Subway: C, E to 23rd St.*

9 *b-7*
LUHRING AUGUSTINE GALLERY
Luhring takes advantage of a huge new space to stage elaborate group shows of contemporary art in every medium imaginable. *531 W. 24th St. (between 10th and 11th Aves.), Chelsea, 212/206–9100, www.luhringaugustine.com. Tues.–Sat. 10–6; call for summer hrs. Subway: C, E to 23rd St.*

9 *b-7*
MARY BOONE
Eighties art maven Mary Boone is still acting up. After she opened this new space in Chelsea, she was promptly arrested for giving out live ammo as party favors at an exhibition. Ross Bleckner, Eric Fischl, and Damian Loeb are among the artists she regularly exhibits. *541 W. 24th St. (between 10th and 11th Aves.), Chelsea, 212/752–2929. Tues.–Sat. 10–6; call for summer hrs. Subway: C, E to 23rd St.*

9 *b-7*
MATTHEW MARKS
Same telephone number, two vast and formidable spaces only two blocks apart. Marks was the first major gallerist to make the move west, and he can really be credited with setting the architectural tone for the area: big. His 24th Street space could shelter a blimp. He has cutting-edge taste, as well as the savvy to show older artists. The latter include arch-abstractionist Ellsworth Kelly, whose massive orange-and-blue curves and circles look right at home in Marks's white caverns. *523 W. 24th St. (between 10th and 11th Aves.), Chelsea, 212/243–0200. Tues.–Sat. 10–6; call for summer hrs. Subway: C, E to 23rd St.*

9 *b-8*
522 W. 22nd St. (between 10th and 11th Aves.), Chelsea.

9 *b-8*
MAX PROTECH
Like most Chelsea galleries, Protetch shows all things contemporary, including photo, sculpture, painting, and ceramics. An added specialty is a large collection of architectural drawings spanning the whole of the 20th century and including original drafting from the hands of Frank Lloyd Wright. *511 W. 22nd St. (between 10th and 11th Aves.), Chelsea, 212/633–6999. Tues.–Sat. 10–6; call for summer hrs. Subway: C, E to 23rd St.*

9 *b-7*
METRO PICTURES
Formerly on the northern edge of SoHo, Metro Pictures joined the exodus and opened a huge and spectacular space out west. Major artists represented include photographer Cindy Sherman and painter Carroll Dunham. *519 W. 24th St. (between 10th and 11th Aves.), Chelsea,*

212/206–7100. Tues.–Sat. 10–6; call for summer hrs. Subway: C, E to 23rd St.

9 b-7
PACE/WILDENSTEIN
Pace shows off oversized 20th-century artwork in an accommodating new gallery space designed by California light artist Robert Irwin. *534 W. 25th St. (between 10th and 11th Aves.), Chelsea, 212/431–9224. Tues.–Sat. 10–6; call for summer hrs. Subway: C, E to 23rd St.*

9 b-8
PAT HEARN
Hearn emerged from the style wars of the 1980s such a beloved figure that her bout with liver cancer galvanized the support of the entire art world, which established the Pat Hearn Fund so the gallerist could get a liver transplant (her insurance wouldn't pay) and continue to show incisive contemporary work. Hearn died in summer 2000, and since then the gallery has been exhibiting artists from American Fine Arts, the SoHo gallery owned by her husband, Colin de Land. *530 W. 22nd St. (between 10th and 11th Aves.), Chelsea, 212/727–7366. Tues.–Sat. 11–6. Subway: C, E to 23rd St.*

9 b-7
PAUL KASMIN
This lively, contemporary space keeps an eye on traditional mediums, mainly painting and drawing. *293 10th Ave. (at 27th St.), Chelsea, 212/563–4474. Tues.–Sat. 10–6; call for summer hrs. Subway: C, E to 23rd St.*

9 b-8
PAULA COOPER
One of the pioneers in Chelsea, Cooper is best known for conceptual art—which looks great in this luminous, lofty space. *534 W. 21st St. (between 10th and 11th Aves.), Chelsea, 212/255–1105. Tues.–Sat. 10–6; call for summer hrs. Subway: C, E to 23rd St.*

9 b-7
PLEIADES GALLERY
Figurative, abstract, and experimental art have their way here. *530 W. 25th St., 4th floor (between 10th and 11th Aves.), Chelsea, 646/230–0056. Tues.–Sat. 10–6; call for summer hrs. Subway: C, E to 23rd St.*

9 b-7
PRINCE ST. GALLERY
Despite a recent move to an airy Chelsea space, this gallery kept its SoHo street name (Prince St.). It shows contemporary expressionist and representational paintings, sculpture, and drawings; nothing anyone is going to be talking about in café society, but reliable. *530 W. 25th St., 4th floor (between 10th and 11th Aves.), Chelsea, 646/230–0246. Tues.–Sat. 11–6; call for summer hrs. Subway: C, E to 23rd St.*

9 b-7
ROBERT MILLER
A top gallery, Miller shows both contemporary American art and 19th- and 20th-century photography by such greats as Berenice Abbott, Diane Arbus, Jean-Michel Basquiat, Walker Evans, Man Ray, Robert Mapplethorpe, Herbert List, David McDermott, Peter McGough, Alice Neel, and Bruce Weber. *524 W. 26th St. (between 10th and 11th Aves.), Chelsea, 212/366–4774, www.robertmillergallery.com. Tues.–Sat. 10–6; call for summer hrs. Subway: C, E to 23rd St.*

9 b-7
SEAN KELLY
Relocated from SoHo to a spanking-new Chelsea loft, Sean Kelly's stable includes such luminaries as Julie Roberts, James Casebere, Lorna Simpson, and Ann Hamilton. *528 W. 29th St. (between 10th and 11th Aves.), Chelsea, 212/239–1181. Tues.–Sat 11–6; call for summer hrs. Subway: C, E to 23rd St.*

9 b-7
SONNABEND GALLERY
They needed a backhoe to pull the roots out of one of the most respected galleries in SoHo and transplant it to new digs. If anything signaled Chelsea's coming-of-age, it was the arrival of Illeana Sonnabend and her impeccable roster of contemporary photographers and established 1960s masters. *532–536 W. 22nd St. (between 10th and 11th Aves.), Chelsea, 212/627–1018. Tues.–Sat. 10–6; call for summer hrs. Subway: C, E to 23rd St.*

11 e-4
SPERONE WESTWATER
Westwater's bent is European and American contemporary art. *415 W. 13th St. (between 9th and 10th Aves.), Chelsea,*

212/431–3685, www.speronewestwater.com. Tues.–Sat. 10–6; call for summer hrs. Subway: A, C, E to 14th St.

303
9 b-8

This medium-size, street-level space has defined itself with medium-size shows by up-and-coming photographers and installationists. *525 W. 22nd St. (between 10th and 11th Aves.), Chelsea, 212/255–1121, www.303gallery.com. Tues.–Sat. 10–6; call for summer hrs. Subway: C, E to 23rd St.*

VIRIDIAN ARTISTS
9 b-7

A recent defector to Chelsea from 57th Street, Viridian specializes in contemporary art, painting, sculpture, and graphics. *530 W. 25th St. (between 10th and 11th Aves.), Chelsea, 212/245–2882, www.viridianartists.com. Tues.–Sat. 10:30–6; call for summer hrs. Subway: C, E to 23rd St.*

WESSEL & O'CONNOR
9 c-7

This interesting new space specializes in photography, sculpture, and installation. *242 W. 26th St. (between 7th and 8th Aves.), Chelsea, 212/242–8811. Tues.–Sat. 11–6, Sun. 11–5; call for summer hrs. Subway: C, E to 23rd St.*

williamsburg

In the late '80s, Williamsburg, Brooklyn, was already being touted as the new bohemia. Since then it has come into its own as a community where working artists, some established, some still up-and-coming, live and create. A handful of scrappy, tough galleries have sprouted up to show their work, and some have had astonishing success. Some gallery spaces are converted garages, some are lofts, some are people's living rooms. At times youthful enthusiasm overtakes good sense in regard to the quality of the work shown. But as the scene has been allowed to mature organically, it's become more and more interesting for the casual observer. The Williamsburg scene, though it's struggling, is definitely here to stay.

BINGO HALL (FARRELL/POLLOCK FINE ART)
3 d-6

Owner Dennis Farrell has used red and white paint to fashion a little jewel box of a gallery out of an old garage. Opened in March of 1999, this space focuses on paintings by local artists. *212 Berry St. (between Metropolitan Ave. and N. 3rd St.), 718/599–0844. Fri.–Mon. 1–5; call for summer hrs. Subway: L to Bedford Ave.*

FEED
3 d-6

One of the leading galleries in Williamsburg, Feed is famous for its down-and-dirty group shows and all-night, light-art exhibitions. *173A N. 3rd St. (between Bedford and Driggs Aves.), 718/486–8992. Weekends 12–6; call for summer hrs. Subway: L to Bedford Ave.*

MOMENTA ART
3 d-6

Dedicated to the exposure of emerging artists, Momenta is a non-profit gallery run by two working artists, Eric Heist and Laura Parnes. A big part of the mission here is to provide a venue for the sort of conceptual art passed over by other galleries due to lack of saleability. Happenings and large installations can be found along with almost any other form of artistic expression, including film screenings and readings. *72 Berry St. (between N. 10th and N. 11th Sts.), 718/218–8058. Call for hrs. Subway: L to Bedford Ave.*

PIEROGI 2000
3 d-6

Despite its goofy name, Pierogi is actually the longest-running (since September 1994) and most commercially viable of all the Williamsburg galleries. Founder and director Joe Amrhein credits his longevity to showing good work, and the space has an aura of businesslike credibility that makes it a cornerstone of the scene. A major innovation is the gallery's flat file, in which each artist gets a drawer space to fill with paintings, photos, lithographs, and whatever other work they have available for sale. *177 N. 9th St. (between Bedford and Driggs Aves.), 718/599–2144, www.pierogi2000.com. Fri.–Mon. 12–6; call for summer hrs. Subway: L to Bedford Ave.*

ROEBLING HALL
3 d-7

Founded in 1996, Roebling Hall is one of the first Williamsburg galleries to simultaneously represent emerging artists and put up commercially viable, Manhattan-style gallery shows. Despite the attention to business, curator Joel Beck keeps the focus on "adventurous" art. *390 Wyethe Ave. (at S. 6th St.), 718/599–5352, www.brooklynart.com. Fri.–Mon. 12–6; call for summer hrs. Subway: J to Marcy Ave.*

3 d-7
WILLIAMSBURG ART & HISTORICAL CENTER

Opened in November 1996 by painter, curator, and all-around neighborhood cheerleader Yuko Nii, the Art and Historical Center acts as a gallery, coffee shop, school, performance space, and community center for Williamsburg's ragged but up-and-coming south side. All of this is housed in the stunning former Kings County Savings Bank, a Victorian landmark erected in 1876 and one of the many architectural hints of the area's past glories. Nii's vision brings together local and international artists while building a sense of community—and publicity—that will keep Williamsburg connected to the larger artistic community and flourishing within it. *135 Broadway (at Bedford Ave.), 718/486–7372, www.wahcenter.org. Weekends 12–6; call for summer hrs. Subway: J to Marcy Ave.*

ART MUSEUMS

For lovers of art, New York City is a paradise. You could literally spend every day of the year at a different museum exhibition and never see the same thing twice. But with so many museums and so much art to choose from, it's easy to feel overwhelmed. The following listing should help you plan even the most elaborate art treks. Note: For even more ways to satisfy your appetite for art, some landmark buildings and mansions have their own collections and period furnishings; *see* Historic Structures & Streets, *below.*

bronx

6 f-4
BRONX MUSEUM OF THE ARTS

In a former synagogue on the Grand Concourse—a Bronx boulevard lined with art deco and art moderne apartment buildings—the permanent collection contains 20th-century works on paper by African, African-American, Latin, Latin American, South Asian, and Asian-American artists. Rotating exhibits in the museum's galleries feature contemporary works by international artists and often focus on the cultural and social history of the Bronx. *1040 Grand Concourse (at 165th St.), 718/681–6000. Suggested donation: $3 adults, $2 students and seniors, free children under 12; free Wed. Wed. noon–9, Thurs.–Sun. noon–6. Subway: 4 to 161st St.; D to 167th St.*

brooklyn

12 b-2
BROOKLYN BRIDGE ANCHORAGE

The two massive stone towers that support the Brooklyn Bridge are actually hollow, and inside the interior of the Brooklyn tower is a cool, cavernous gallery that hosts contemporary art, fashion, and design exhibits every summer. *Cadman Plaza W and Old Fulton St., 212/206–6674 (Manhattan office), www.creativetime.org. Call for hrs and exhibits. Subway: 2, 3 to Clark St.*

4 e-1
BROOKLYN MUSEUM OF ART

With approximately 1½ million pieces, the Brooklyn Museum is housed in a massive, regal building designed by McKim, Mead & White in 1893 and ranks as the second-largest art museum in New York City—and one that's hip quotient is on the rise. Its temporary exhibits are often among the city's best (and as "Sensation," a showing of work by young British artists, proved, most adventurous) and several of its permanent exhibits are world-renowned. Most notable are the Egyptian Art Collection, with its hieroglyphic-covered sarcophagi, and the American Painting and Sculpture Galleries, with works by Georgia O'Keeffe, Mark Rothko, Winslow Homer, Gilbert Stuart, and John Singer Sargent. *200 Eastern Pkwy. (at Washington Ave.), 718/638–5000, www.brooklynart.org. Suggested contribution: $6 adults, $3 students and seniors, free children under 12. Wed.–Fri. 10–5, weekends 11–6. On "First Saturdays" each month the museum is open until 11 PM with free admission from 5–11, gallery tours, popular films, and a dance band playing in the lobby. Subway: 2, 3 to Eastern Pkwy./Brooklyn Museum.*

manhattan

6 b-5

AMERICAN ACADEMY OF ARTS & LETTERS

Although the Academy is not usually open to the public, its doors are thrown open for two annual exhibitions featuring the work of American sculptors, painters, architects, composers, and authors. For more on the Academy's attractive Italian Renaissance surroundings, see Audubon Terrace Historic District in Historic Structures & Streets, below. 633 W. 155th St. (at Broadway, in the Audubon Terrace Museum Complex), Washington Heights, 212/368–5900. Call for exhibit schedules and hrs. Subway: 1 to 157th St.

9 d-4

AMERICAN CRAFT MUSEUM

Right across the street from the Museum of Modern Art, the American Craft Museum raises crafts—often taken for granted—to the level of high art. The museum's changing exhibits feature quilts, handblown glass, pottery, basketry, woodwork, and hand-woven textiles. Classes, workshops, and lectures bring expert craftspeople to New York and give novices a chance to weave, mold, carve, and create. 40 W. 53rd St. (between 5th and 6th Aves.), Midtown West, 212/956–3535, www.americancraftmuseum.org. $7.50, $4 students and seniors, free children under 12. Mon.–Wed. and Fri.–Sun. 10–6, Thurs. 10–8. Subway: E, V to 5th Ave./53rd St.

9 d-4

AMERICAN FOLK ART MUSEUM

If you ever watch the Antiques Roadshow on PBS, you already know that folk art is hotter than Georgia asphalt. This eight-floor museum, which opened in late 2001, is dedicated to meeting the needs of a public hungry for Americana. Folk paintings, folk sculpture, textiles, outsider art, dolls, trade signs, painted-wood carousel horses, weather vanes, and—of course—quilts are characteristic items on exhibition. 45 W. 53rd St. (between 5th and 6th Aves.), Midtown West, 212/977–7170, www.folkartmuseum.org. Call for admission fees. Call for hrs. Subway: E, V to 5th Ave./53rd St.

9 e-1

AMERICAS SOCIETY

In a 1911 mansion designed by the renowned architectural firm McKim, Mead & White that once housed the Soviet Union's mission to the U.N. (1948–1963), the Americas Society attempts to inform U.S. citizens about what's going on in the rest of the Western Hemisphere. To help fulfill this mission, their small art gallery mounts three to four exhibits a year from Latin America, the Caribbean, and Canada, covering everything from pre-Columbian art to contemporary painting, sculpture, photography, and the decorative arts. 680 Park Ave. (at 68th St.), Upper East Side, 212/249–8950, www.americas-society.org. Suggested contribution: $3. Tues.–Sun. noon–6. Subway: 6 to 68th St./Hunter College.

9 e-1

ASIA SOCIETY & MUSEUM

A nonprofit educational organization, the Asia Society regularly sponsors lectures, films, dance, and musical programs in addition to its art exhibits. The Asian art collection of Mr. and Mrs. John D. Rockefeller III forms the museum's major holdings, and a renovation completed in fall 2001 created a permanent space for exhibiting these works. The collection includes South Asian stone and bronze sculptures; art from India, Nepal, Pakistan, and Afghanistan; bronze vessels, ceramics, sculpture, and paintings from China; Korean ceramics; and paintings, wooden sculptures, and ceramics from Japan. A glassed-in atrium, sculpture garden, café, and visitor center on the first floor make the Asia Society one of the Upper East Side's most inviting stops. 725 Park Ave. (at 70th St.), Upper East Side, 212/288–6400, www.asiasociety.org. $7 adults, $5 students and seniors, free Fri. 6–9. Tues.–Thurs. and Sat.–Sun. 11–6, Fri. 11–9. Subway: 6 to 68th St./Hunter College.

9 c-4

THE AXA GALLERY

This free, eclectic museum in the lobby of the Equitable Building in Midtown has changing exhibits on everything from folk to fine art. Past exhibits have highlighted Colonial American furniture, Haitian sculpture and painting, and the stateside photography of Henri Cartier-Bresson. 787 7th Ave. (at 51st St.), Midtown West, 212/554–4818 (call for *information on current exhibitions). Free. Weekdays 11–6, Sat. noon–5. Subway: N, Q, R, W to 49th St.; 1, 2 to 50th St.*

9 *e-2*

CHINA INSTITUTE GALLERY

Housed in a redbrick mansion flanked by two stone lions, the China Institute's gallery features two exhibits of traditional and contemporary Chinese art each year, including painting, calligraphy, folk art, architecture, and textiles. *125 E. 65th St. (between Park and Lexington Aves.), Upper East Side, 212/744–8181, www.chinainstitute.org. $3 adults, $2 students and seniors; free Thurs. 6–8. Mon., Wed., Fri.–Sat. 10–5, Tues. and Thurs. 10–8, Sun. 1–5. Closed between exhibitions. Subway: 6 to 68th St./Hunter College.*

5 *b-7*

THE CLOISTERS

One of New York's artistic and spiritual treasures, the Cloisters is situated high on a hill in Upper Manhattan's wooded Ft. Tryon Park, overlooking the Hudson River. The castlelike structure, a branch of the Metropolitan Museum of Art, incorporates parts of five different cloisters from medieval monasteries, including a Romanesque chapel and a 12th-century Spanish apse; the collection of European medieval artwork includes the famed Unicorn Tapestries from the 15th and 16th centuries. Outside, three enchanting gardens shelter more than 250 species of plants similar to those grown during the Middle Ages, including herbs and medicinals. *Ft. Tryon Park (Riverside Dr. and Broadway from 192nd to Dyckman Sts.), Washington Heights, 212/923–3700. Suggested contribution: $10 adults, $5 students and seniors, children under 12 free. Mar.–Oct., Tues.–Sun. 9:30–5:15; Nov.–Feb., Tues.–Sun. 9:30–4:45. Subway: A to 190th St.*

7 *e-6*

COOPER-HEWITT NATIONAL DESIGN MUSEUM–SMITHSONIAN INSTITUTION

Beautifully restored, this 64-room Fifth Avenue mansion—built by industrialist Andrew Carnegie in 1901—is now home to the Smithsonian Institution's design and decorative arts collections. With more than 250,000 objects spanning 3,000 years of design history, the museum's holdings include ceramics, textiles, drawings, prints, glass, furniture, metalwork, book papers, woodwork, wall coverings, embroidery, and lace. The major exhibitions are typically both fun and creative, ranging from the history of water fountains to Walt Disney's impact on the American landscape. In summer, exhibitions often filter out into the Arthur Ross Terrace and Garden, a flower-filled, tree-shaded haven. *2 E. 91st St. (at 5th Ave.), Upper East Side, 212/849–8400, www.si.edu/ndm/. $3 adults, $1.50 students and seniors, free Tues. 5–9. Tues. 10–9, Wed.–Sat. 10–5, Sun. noon–5. Subway: 4, 5, 6 to 86th St.*

9 *e-4*

DAHESH MUSEUM

While the Whitney, MOMA, and Guggenheim vie for the latest contemporary artworks, the Dahesh revels in tradition. Opened in 1995 with the collection of late Lebanese art-collector Salim Moussa Achi (a.k.a. Dr. Dahesh), this free Midtown museum is devoted to 19th-century European "academic" art, most notably works by Bouguereau and Gérôme, who taught an entire generation of artists, including the impressionists. Shows are clever and highly informative, often reintroducing works by artists once famed, now forgotten. *601 5th Ave. (between 48th and 49th Sts.), Midtown East, 212/759–0606, www.daheshmuseum.org. Free. Tues.–Sat. 11–6. Subway: B, D, F, V to 47th–50th Sts./Rockefeller Ctr.*

9 *b-8*

DIA CENTER FOR THE ARTS

Surrounded by the ultra-trendy West Chelsea gallery scene, the Dia is a showplace and laboratory for contemporary artists, with three floors of galleries, a roof garden with permanent installations by Dan Graham, a bookstore, lectures, readings, and live performances. Occasional exhibits from the Dia's permanent collection include works by Joseph Beuys, Walter De Maria, Dan Flavin, Blinky Palermo, Cy Twombly, Richard Serra, and Andy Warhol. *548 W. 22nd St. (between 10th and 11th Aves.), Chelsea, 212/989–5566, www.diacenter.org. $6 adults, $3 students and seniors. Wed.–Sun. noon–6. Closed mid-June–early Sept. Subway: C, E to 23rd St.*

9 *b-2*

EVA & MORRIS FELD GALLERY OF AMERICAN FOLK ART

The collection of this intimate museum, a branch of the new American Folk Art

Museum on W. 53rd Street (*see above*), includes arts and decorative objects from the 18th century to the present day culled from all over the Americas. The gift shop has intriguing craft items, books, and great cards. Every other Sunday a workshop for children is held, usually based on the current exhibit. *2 Lincoln Sq. (Columbus Ave. between 65th and 66th Sts.), Upper West Side, 212/595–9533, www.folkartmuseum.org. Free (donations accepted). Tues.–Sun. 11:30–7:30. Subway: 1, 2 to 66th St./Lincoln Center.*

9 *e-1*

FRICK COLLECTION

Don't miss this tranquil jewel. Coke-and-steel baron Henry Clay Frick's former mansion (built in 1914) houses countless bona fide masterpieces of 14th- to 19th-century European painting, including pieces by Rembrandt, Vermeer, Gainsborough, Turner, Titian, Goya, and El Greco; exquisite 18th-century French and Italian Renaissance furniture; Oriental porcelain; and Limoges enamel. The intimate interior is wonderfully illuminated by overhead skylights, and there's a lovely garden court with a splashing fountain. *1 E. 70th St. (at 5th Ave.), Upper East Side, 212/288–0700, www.frick.org. $10 adults, $5 seniors and students. No children under 10. Tues.–Sat. 10–6, Sun. 1–6. Subway: 6 to 68th St./Hunter College.*

7 *e-7*

GOETHE INSTITUT

Smack in the middle of Museum Mile, in a 1907 beaux-arts town house, Goethe House showcases German art, film, and culture. The gallery features changing exhibits of contemporary German art. *1014 5th Ave. (between 82nd and 83rd Sts.), Upper East Side, 212/439–8700, www.goethe.de/newyork. Free. Mon., Wed., and Fri. 10–5, Tues. and Thurs. 10–7, Sat. noon–5. Subway: 4, 5, 6 to 86th St.*

10 *e-2*

GREY ART GALLERY

New York University's main building contains a welcoming street-level space with changing exhibitions, usually devoted to contemporary art. *100 Washington Sq. E (between Washington and Waverly Pls.), Greenwich Village, 212/998–6780, www.nyu.edu/greyart. Suggested donation $2.50. Tues. and Thurs.–Fri. 11–6, Wed. 11–8, Sat. 11–5; closed*

between exhibitions. Subway: N, Q, R, W to 8th St.

7 *e-6*

SOLOMON R. GUGGENHEIM MUSEUM

Frank Lloyd Wright's building (*see* Architecture, *above*) provides a unique setting for modern art and jam-packed openings for the Guggenheim's powerhouse exhibitions. Holdings of the Thannhauser Collection, a permanent display of 19th- and 20th-century impressionist, postimpressionist, and early modern masterpieces, include a renowned Kandinsky collection, Paul Klees, Picassos, Chagalls, and a newly acquired series of Mapplethorpes. Jazz performances are held on summer weekends in the Frank Lloyd Wright Rotunda. The warmer months are also a pleasant time to hang out on the LeFrak Sculpture Terrace, where you can examine the museum's oversize minimalist pieces and take in the view of Central Park. If you can't get enough of the Guggenheim franchise, *see* the Guggenheim Museum SoHo, *below,* and get ready for Guggenheim III (!!), a grand new Frank Gehry–designed building that will be erected on the East River piers below the South Street Seaport. *1071 5th Ave. (at 89th St.), Upper East Side, 212/423–3500, www.guggenheim.org. $12 adults, $8 students and seniors, free children under 12; pay what you wish Fri. 6–8. Sun.–Wed. 9–6, Fri.–Sat. 9–8. Subway: 4, 5, 6 to 86th St.*

11 *e-5*

GUGGENHEIM MUSEUM SOHO

Perhaps best known for its enormous museum shop, the Guggenheim's downtown space focuses primarily on multimedia installations, such as video art by Nam June Paik, work by Jenny Holzer, and Andy Warhol's *Last Supper*. The art is flattered by this landmark building, the lofty interiors of which were redesigned by architect Arata Isozaki. *575 Broadway (at Prince St.), SoHo, 212/423–3500, www.guggenheim.org. $5 adults, $3 students, free children under 12. Thurs.–Mon. 11–6. Subway: N, Q, R, W to Prince St.; F, V to Broadway–Lafayette St.*

6 *b-5*

HISPANIC SOCIETY OF AMERICA

Because it's off the beaten path, the Hispanic Society only draws about 20,000 visitors per year—but here's the secret:

it has what's considered the best collection of Spanish art outside of the Prado. And because its neighboring institutions in the Audubon Terrace district keep moving out (the Museum of the American Indian and the National Geographic Society are both former tenants), the Hispanic Society's been able to purchase extra gallery space. On display are paintings, sculptures, manuscripts, and decorative artworks from prehistoric times to the present (from Spain, Portugal, Latin America, and the Philippines), including pieces by Goya, El Greco, and Velazquez. For more on the handsome surroundings, *see* Audubon Terrace Historic District *in* Historic Structures & Streets, *below. Broadway and 155th St. (in the Audubon Terrace Museum Complex), Washington Heights, 212/926–2234, www.hispanicsociety.org. Free (donations accepted). Tues.–Sat. 10–4:30, Sun. 1–4. Subway: 1 to 157th St.*

9 *d-5*

INTERNATIONAL CENTER OF PHOTOGRAPHY (ICP)

Founded in 1974 by photojournalist Cornell Capa (photographer Robert Capa's brother), ICP is devoted exclusively to photography as a fine art and medium of communication. Exhibits often focus on a photographic genre (portraits, architecture, etc.) or the work of a single prominent artist. The permanent collection of 45,000 pictures contains works by important 20th-century photographers including Robert Capa, W. Eugene Smith, Henri Cartier-Bresson, Yousuf Karsh, Man Ray, Lee Miller, Gordon Parks, Roman Vishniac, and Ernst Haas. ICP's bookstore carries an impressive array of books, prints, and postcards. *1133 6th Ave. (at 43rd St.), Midtown West, 212/768–4682. $8 adults, $6 students and seniors; pay what you wish Fri. 5–8. Tues.–Thurs. 10–5, Fri. 10–8, weekends 10–6. Subway: B, D, F, V to 42nd St.*

9 *f-4*

JAPAN SOCIETY GALLERY

This spare and serene space—with interior bamboo gardens linked by a second-floor waterfall—displays ancient as well as contemporary Japanese art. The society also sponsors an eclectic program of films, performances, and lectures. *333 E. 47th St. (between 1st and 2nd Aves.), Midtown East, 212/832–1155, www.japansociety.org. Suggested contribution: $5 adults, $3 students and seniors. Tues.–Fri. 11–6, weekends 11–5. Subway: 6*

to 51st St./Lexington Ave.; E, V to Lexington–3rd Aves./53rd St.

7 *e-6*

THE JEWISH MUSEUM

Housed in a Gothic-style mansion (1908) facing Central Park, the Jewish Museum is one of the largest and most beautiful collections of Judaica in the country. Ceremonial objects, paintings, prints, drawings, sculpture, manuscripts, photographs, videos, and antiquities trace the development of Jewish culture over the past 4,000 years. Special exhibitions—on such subjects as German modernism and Sigmund Freud—are often among the city's most heavily attended. *1109 5th Ave. (at 92nd St.), Upper East Side, 212/423–3200, www.jewishmuseum.org. $8 adults, $5.50 students and seniors, free children under 12; pay what you wish Tues. 5–9. Mon. and Wed.–Thurs. 11–5:45, Tues. 11–9, Sun. 10–5:45. Subway: 4, 5, 6 to 96th St.*

7 *d-7*

METROPOLITAN MUSEUM OF ART

The Met is the largest museum in the Western Hemisphere, with 1.6 million square ft of gallery space and a permanent collection of more than 2 million works of art. Covering 5,000 years of cultural history, the Met is so enormous it's hard to know where to begin. You might want to start in the spectacularly renovated galleries for classical art, which contain Greek and Roman statuary, perfectly preserved Grecian urns, and rare Roman wall paintings excavated from the lava of Mt. Vesuvius. The renowned Egyptian collection centers around the Temple of Dendur, an entire Roman-period temple transported to the museum from Egypt and housed in its own, specially built atrium. A stunning collection of European paintings includes 30 by Monet, 17 by Cézanne, 7 by Vermeer (more than any other museum in the world), and works by Gauguin, Van Gogh, Degas, El Greco, Rembrandt, and Rubens. Monumental Chinese Buddhas, Ming Dynasty furniture, and the re-creation of a Ming scholar's garden are highlights of the Asian galleries. Three floors of 20th-century art, centering on Picasso's portrait of Gertrude Stein, make up the Lila Acheson Wallace Wing. The American Wing contains 25 period rooms, and paintings by Thomas Cole and Winslow Homer. The arms and armor collection holds more than 14,000 weapons and a cavernous hall of knights in helmets and chain mail, mounted on their steeds and ready for jousting. Moral of the story: don't try to pop in for a quick peek. *5th Ave. at 82nd St., Upper East Side, 212/535–7710, www.metmuseum.org. Suggested contribution: $10 adults, $5 students and seniors, free children under 12. Sun. and Tues.–Thurs. 9:30–5:30, Fri.– Sat. 9:30–9. (For sculpture garden, see Viewpoints, below.) Subway: 4, 5, 6 to 86th St.*

9 e-4
MUNICIPAL ART SOCIETY URBAN CENTER GALLERIES

The Municipal Art Society is dedicated to the idea of cities as aesthetic places and its free exhibits have focused on everything from 3-D re-creations of department-store window displays to architectural renderings of a better New York. *457 Madison Ave. (at 51st St.), Midtown East, 212/935–3960, www.mas.org. Mon.–Wed. and Fri.–Sat. 11–5. Subway: 6 to 51st St./Lexington Ave.; E, V to Lexington–3rd Aves./53rd St.*

7 e-4
EL MUSEO DEL BARRIO

The art and culture of Latin America and the Caribbean speak here through artifacts, photographs, sculpture, and paintings. The permanent collection of 8,000 objects contains numerous pre-Columbian artifacts and is particularly strong on Puerto Rican art, featuring numerous carved wooden folk-art figurines known as *santos*. Every year, the museum puts up a major exhibition of contemporary Latino artists. *1230 5th Ave. (at 104th St.), Harlem, 212/831–7272, www.elmuseo.org. Suggested contribution: $5 adults, $3 students and seniors, free children under 12. Wed.–Sun. 11–5. Subway: 6 to 103rd St.*

9 e-2
MUSEUM OF AMERICAN ILLUSTRATION

This specialized museum was founded in 1901 to "promote and stimulate interest in the art of illustration, past, present, and future." The Society of Illustrators assembles highly eclectic monthly exhibitions, focusing on everything from *New Yorker* cartoons to Norman Rockwell paintings to pictures from *Mad* magazine and children's books. *128 E. 63rd St. (between Park and Lexington Aves.), Upper East Side, 212/*838–2560. Tues. 10–8, Wed.–Fri. 10–5, Sat. noon–4. Subway: F to Lexington Ave/63rd St.; 4, 5, 6, N, R, W to 59th St./ Lexington Ave.*

11 e-4
MUSEUM FOR AFRICAN ART

Celebrating the art of an entire continent in one small space is a tall order, but the Museum for African Art manages to do it, and with panache. Exhibits range from ceremonial masks to contemporary painting. The unique interior, with galleries connected by a spiral staircase, was designed by Maya Lin, best known for her design of the Vietnam Veterans Memorial in Washington, D.C. *593 Broadway (between Houston and Prince Sts.), SoHo, 212/966–1313, www.africanart.org. $5 adults; $2.50 students, seniors, and children; free all day Sun. Tues.–Fri. 10:30–5:30, weekends noon–6. Subway: N, Q, R, W to Prince St.; F, V to Broadway–Lafayette St.*

9 d-4
MUSEUM OF MODERN ART (MOMA)

MOMA is the greatest repository of modern art in the world, its six stories brandishing such works as Van Gogh's *Starry Night*, Monet's *Water Lilies*, Matisse's *Dance*, Picasso's *Les Demoiselles d'Avignon*, and Warhol's *Marilyn Monroe*. Altogether, there are more than 100,000 works on display, including paintings and sculpture; architecture and design; drawings; prints and illustrated books; photography; and film and video. The first museum to recognize film as an art form, MOMA has documented the development of motion pictures for nearly 50 years and still screens six films daily in its two theaters. The museum's sculpture garden (designed by Philip Johnson), around which the galleries are built, remains one of New York's most treasured spaces and contains works by Rodin, Matisse, and Moore; in the summer it is the setting for a classical concert series. The museum shop has unusually fine art books, design objects, and gifts. What's more, MOMA is determined to remain modern and is starting the 21st century with a bang: A major expansion and redesign (slated for completion in 2004) will double the exhibition space, adding large skylit galleries, a new theater, and an education and research complex. Due to construction, MOMA will be closed from summer 2002 to late

2004, with exhibitions relocated to the P.S. 1 Contemporary Art Center (*see below*). *11 W. 53rd St. (between 5th and 6th Aves.), Midtown West, 212/708–9400, www.moma.org. $10 adults, $6.50 students and seniors, free children under 16; pay what you wish Fri. 4:30–8:15. Sat.–Tues. and Thurs. 10:30–5:45, Fri. 10:30–8:15. Subway: E, V to 5th Ave./53rd St.*

7 *e-6*

NATIONAL ACADEMY

Founded in 1825 as a drawing society and school, the academy is devoted to America's artistic and architectural heritage. The extensive collection of 19th- and 20th-century paintings, prints, drawings, photography, and sculpture includes works by Mary Cassatt, Winslow Homer, Frank Lloyd Wright, I.M. Pei, Jennifer Bartlett, Chuck Close, Red Grooms, and Robert Rauschenberg—all of whom were members of the academy. *1083 5th Ave. (at 89th St.), Upper East Side, 212/369–4880, www.nationalacademy.org. $8 adults, $4.50 students and seniors, free children under 12. Open Wed.–Thurs. and weekends noon–5, Fri. 10–6. Subway: 4, 5, 6 to 86th St.*

11 *e-4*

NEW MUSEUM OF CONTEMPORARY ART

Founded in 1977, this avant-garde center for art and ideas focuses exclusively on art by living artists, most of them emerging or experimental. A recently completed design spotlights international artists and includes a subterranean "project space"—free to the public—with a hip bookstore that hosts readings, performance art, and film and video screenings. *583 Broadway (between Prince and Houston Sts.), SoHo, 212/219–1222, www.newmuseum.org. $6 adults; $3 artists, students, and seniors; free under age 18; free Thurs. 6–8. Tues.–Wed. and Fri.–Sun. 12–6, Thurs. 12–8. Subway: N, Q, R, W to Prince St.; F, V to Broadway–Lafayette St.*

7 *a-4*

NICHOLAS ROERICH MUSEUM

In an Upper West Side 1898 town house, this eccentric little museum's permanent collection focuses exclusively on the work of the Russian artist Nicholas Roerich, who came to New York in the 1920s and quickly developed an ardent following. The museum centers on Roerich's vast paintings of the Himalayas. The museum also hosts a chamber-music series and poetry readings. *319 W. 107th St. (between Broadway and Riverside Dr.), Upper West Side, 212/864–7752, www.roerich.org. Free (donations accepted). Tues.–Sun. 2–5. Subway: 1 to 110th St./Cathedral Pkwy.*

7 *d-1*

STUDIO MUSEUM IN HARLEM

This distinguished museum is devoted to African-American, Caribbean, and African painting, sculpture, and photography. Major exhibits feature both established and emerging black artists. There are also frequent concerts and lectures, as well as a lovely sculpture garden and a hip museum shop. *144 W. 125th St. (between Lenox and 7th Aves.), Harlem, 212/864–4500, www.studiomuseuminharlem.org. $5 adults, $3 students and seniors, $1 children under 12. Wed.–Thurs. 12–6, Fri. 12–8, weekends 10–6. Subway: 2, 3 to 125th St.*

10 *f-1*

UKRAINIAN MUSEUM

This small East Village museum celebrates the culture and history of Ukrainian people, a small community of whom have settled in the neighborhood. Folk art and costumes, fine arts, documentary photography, letters and manuscripts, and hundreds of brilliantly colored Easter eggs are on display. A major expansion is in the works. *203 2nd Ave. (between 12th and 13th Sts.), East Village, 212/228–0110, www.ukrainianmuseum.org. $3 adults, $2 seniors and students; free children under 12. Wed.–Sun. 1–5. Subway: 6 to Astor Pl.; L to 3rd Ave.*

7 *e-8*

WHITNEY MUSEUM OF AMERICAN ART

Founded in 1930 in the studio of artist Gertrude Vanderbilt Whitney, who wanted to highlight the work of living American artists, the Whitney now occupies a striking modern building (it's an upside-down ziggurat) designed by the Bauhaus architect Marcel Breuer. Inside the cubist structure are five floors of modern works, including Georgia O'Keeffe's *White Calico Flower*, sculptor Alexander Calder's playful *Circus*, and Edward Hopper's haunting *Early Sunday Morning*. Special exhibits focus on major 20th-century artists, including photographers, filmmakers, and video artists;

and every even-numbered year the Whitney hosts its controversial Biennial, featuring the best (or the worst, depending on your point of view) new works of living American artists. *945 Madison Ave. (at 75th St.), Upper East Side, 212/570–3676, www.whitney.org. $10 adults, $8 students and seniors, free children under 12; pay what you wish Fri. 6–8. Tues.–Thurs. and Sat.–Sun. 11–6, Fri. 1–9. Subway: 6 to 77th St.*

9 e-5
WHITNEY MUSEUM OF AMERICAN ART AT PHILIP MORRIS

A wonderful retreat from Grand Central Terminal's maddening crowds, the Whitney's free Midtown branch in the Philip Morris building features a 42-ft-high sculpture court with outstanding examples of 20th-century sculpture—and an espresso bar. In the adjacent gallery, five shows annually cover all aspects of American art. *120 Park Ave. (at 42nd St.), Midtown East, 917/663–2453. Free. Sculpture court Mon.–Sat. 7:30–9:30, Sun. 11–7; gallery Mon.–Wed. and Fri. 11–6, Thurs. 11–7:30. Subway: 4, 5, 6, 7 to 42nd St./Grand Central.*

queens

8 a-6
ISAMU NOGUCHI GARDEN MUSEUM

In Long Island City, a large, open-air garden and two floors of gallery space hold over 250 pieces by the renowned Japanese-American sculptor Isamu Noguchi. Originally a photoengraving plant, the building was converted by Noguchi himself, and now houses his sculptures (in stone, bronze, wood, clay, and steel), models, drawings, and even stage sets for dances by Martha Graham. *Vernon Boulevard at 33rd Rd., 718/721–1932, www.noguchi.org. Suggested contribution: $4 adults, $2 students and seniors. Apr.–Oct., Wed.–Fri. 10–5, weekends 11–6. Weekend shuttle bus service leaves from the Museum of Modern Art in Manhattan 11:30–4:30 every hour on the half-hour. Subway: N to Broadway.*

3 d-4
P.S. 1 CONTEMPORARY ART CENTER

A former public school, this wonderful old Romanesque building in Long Island City has vast galleries (reopened with enormous hoopla after extensive renovations in 1997) and an enormous outdoor space for showing contemporary art. The emphasis at this seminal space is on an ever-changing cast of innovative new artists, plus old hands at the experimental game. There's also live music, films, performances, and sometimes even a D.J. with dancing. It's well worth the trip to Long Island City, a mere hop, skip, and a jump across the East River. P.S. 1 recently merged with the Museum of Modern Art (*see above*), giving P.S. 1—which has no permanent collection—access to MOMA's vast holdings. *22–25 Jackson Ave. (at 46th Ave.), 718/784–2084, www.ps1.org. Suggested admission: $4 adults, $2 students and seniors. Wed.–Sun. noon–6. Weekend shuttle bus service leaves from the Museum of Modern Art in Manhattan 11:30–4:30 every hour on the half-hour. Subway: E, V to 23rd St./Ely Ave.*

3 h-2
QUEENS MUSEUM OF ART

On the site of two famous World Fairs, the Queens Museum features painting and sculpture exhibitions from the classical to the avant-garde, often with an emphasis on New York City's own art history and ethnic heritage. On permanent view is Panorama, a detailed (9,000-square-ft) scale model of New York City's five boroughs that includes nearly every brownstone and skyscraper; it's fascinating and updated frequently. *New York City Building (opposite the Unisphere), Flushing Meadows–Corona Park, 718/592–9700, www.queensmuse.org. Suggested admission: $5 adults, $2.50 students and seniors, free children under 5. Tues.–Fri. 10–5, weekends noon–5. Subway: 7 to 111th St.*

staten island

1 b-2
JACQUES MARCHAIS MUSEUM OF TIBETAN ART

This replica of a Tibetan mountain temple houses a major collection of Tibetan and other Asian art, including bronzes, paintings, scrolls, and ritual objects. Surrounded by lovely gardens, it's the perfect spot for a day of contemplation. *338 Lighthouse Ave. (off Richmond Rd.), 718/987–3500. $3. Apr.–Nov., Wed.–Sun. 1–5; shorter hrs winter. Take S74 bus from Staten Island Ferry terminal to Lighthouse Ave. and walk ¼ mi up Lighthouse Hill.*

BRIDGES

New York has 65 bridges, connecting its boroughs and islands to each other and to the world beyond. Here are some of the most impressive.

10 g-6

BROOKLYN BRIDGE

(John A., Washington, and Emily Roebling, 1867–83) A triumph of Victorian engineering, this graceful 1,595-ft-long suspension bridge was the world's longest when it opened in 1883. Spanning the East River, it connected Manhattan island to the then-independent city of Brooklyn, and instantly became one of the city's most enduring symbols. Alas, the bridge's construction was fraught with peril. Designer John A. Roebling was killed in a construction accident while the bridge was being built; his son, Washington, took over the project and was himself permanently crippled in another accident. With the help of his wife, Emily, Washington nonetheless saw the bridge's construction through to completion. Today, a walkway across the bridge affords unparalleled views of the East River and the downtown skyline (*see* Viewpoints, *below*), as well as a unique look at the bridge's Gothic stone towers and arching steel cables. *City Hall Park, Manhattan, to Cadman Plaza, Brooklyn. Subway: 4, 5, 6 to Brooklyn Bridge/City Hall; A, C to High St./Brooklyn Bridge.*

6 a-2

GEORGE WASHINGTON BRIDGE

(O. H. Ammann, engineer, and Cass Gilbert, architect, 1931) New York City's only bridge to New Jersey, the GWB is one pure, 3,500-ft line across the Hudson River. A suspension bridge made entirely of exposed steel, the GWB was originally going to have its towers sheathed in concrete, but that plan was scrapped to save money. Most of the bridge's fans don't seem to mind its raw structure; according to architecture critic Paul Goldberger, the bridge "leaps over space in a way that still causes the heart to skip a beat." A walkway and bikeway on the upper deck provide stunning views of the Hudson and the New Jersey Palisades. *Hudson River and 178th St. to Fort Lee, N.J. (access to the Manhattan pedestrian ramp is at W. 178th St. and Cabrini Blvd.). Subway: A to 175th St. or 181st St.*

10 h-5

MANHATTAN BRIDGE

(O.F. Nichols and Gustav Lindenthal, 1905) A 1,470-ft-long suspension bridge of exposed steel, the Manhattan Bridge spans the East River just north of the Brooklyn Bridge and carries cars, trucks, and several subway lines between Manhattan and Brooklyn. Inspired by the Porte St. Denis in Paris and the Bernini Colonnade in Rome, its Manhattan entrance is adorned by a regal arch and colonnade by Carrère and Hastings (1905). A major rehabilitation project, to be completed in 2004, will add a bikeway next to the bridge's pedestrian walkway. *Canal St. and Bowery (Manhattan) to Flatbush Ave. Extension (Brooklyn). Subway: F to E. Broadway.*

9 g-3

QUEENSBORO BRIDGE

(Gustav Lindenthal, engineer; Palmer & Hornbostel, architects, 1909) An ornate, cantilevered mass of exposed steel, the 1,182-ft-long Queensboro Bridge spans the East River, connecting Queens to Manhattan and offering fantastic views of the Midtown skyline. In *The Great Gatsby*, F. Scott Fitzgerald writes, on driving into Manhattan: "The city seen from the Queensboro Bridge is always the city seen for the first time, in its wild promise of all the mystery and the beauty in the world"; his observation still holds true. *E. 59th St. (Manhattan) to Queens Plaza. Subway: 4, 5, 6, N, R, W to 59th St./Lexington Ave.; 7, N, W, to Queensboro Plaza; E, R, V to Queens Plaza*

7 g-1

TRIBOROUGH BRIDGE

(O. H. Ammann, engineer; Aymar Embury II, architect; 1936) The Triborough, one of the many bridge and highway projects with which state and municipal offical Robert Moses transformed the city and it's environs, was considered the ultimate congestion-buster when it opened to auto traffic in 1936. A series of four interconnecting bridges, it crosses the East River, Harlem River, and Bronx Kills, joining Manhattan, the Bronx, and Queens—with 1 million cars passing through every day. Lewis Mumford called the view from the Triborough's walkway "one of the most dazzling urban views in the world." *125th St. and FDR Dr. (Manhattan) to Bruckner and Deegan*

Expressways (Bronx) to Grand Central
Parkway and Brooklyn-Queens Expressway
(Queens). *Subway: 4, 5, 6 to 125th St.*

4 d-6

VERRAZANO-NARROWS
BRIDGE

(O. H. Ammann, 1964) At 4,260 ft
long, the beautiful Verrazano is the
world's second-longest suspension
bridge, surpassed only by the Humber
Bridge in England. Named for Giovanni
da Verrazano, the first European to sight
New York Harbor (in 1524), it spans the
mouth of the harbor to link Brooklyn
and Staten Island. The bridge inspired a
development boom on Staten Island;
before its construction, Staten Island
was accessible from the other boroughs
only by ferry. *Ft. Hamilton at 92nd St.,
Bay Ridge (Brooklyn) to Lily Pond Rd.,
Fort Wadsworth (Staten Island). Subway:
R to 95th St./Ft. Hamilton.*

3 d-7

WILLIAMSBURG BRIDGE

(Leffert L. Buck, 1903) When it was first
completed, this 1,600-ft steel suspension bridge snatched the title of
"World's Longest" from the Brooklyn
Bridge and had a profound effect on the
city's makeup, offering Lower East Side
immigrants easy access to a new
promised land: Brooklyn. But time and
tides have not been kind to this structure; in 1988 the bridge was found to be
deteriorating so seriously that it was
temporarily closed. An ongoing repair
project is bringing the bridge back up to
speed, and the plans include a new
walkway and bikeway, which should be
completed by the end of 2002. *Delancey
and Clinton Sts. (Manhattan) to Washington Plaza (Brooklyn). Subway: J to Essex
St. or Marcy Ave.*

CHILDREN'S
MUSEUMS

3 f-8

BROOKLYN
CHILDREN'S MUSEUM

The world's oldest museum specifically
for children was founded in 1899 and,
designed for children ages 2–14, is full
of tunnels to crawl through, animals to
pet, stories to read, and plants to
water. *145 Brooklyn Ave. (at St. Mark's
Ave.), Crown Heights, 718/735–4432,
www.bchildmus.org. Suggested contribution: $4. July–Aug., Mon., Wed., and*

Thurs. noon–5, Fri. noon–6:30, weekends
10–5; Sept.–June, Wed.–Fri. 2–5, weekends 10–5. Subway: A to Kingston–
Throop Aves.; 3 to Kingston Ave.; 2 to
President St.

7 b-7

CHILDREN'S MUSEUM
OF MANHATTAN

In this wonderful five-story building, children ages 1–10 can climb, crawl, paint,
make collages, try on costumes, test out
technology, and even film their own
newscasts. Outside, there's a brand-new
water garden for kids to explore. Every
day there are art workshops, storytelling
sessions, science programs, and drama
workshops. *212 W. 83rd St. (between
Broadway and Amsterdam Ave.), Upper
West Side, 212/721–1234, www.cmom.org.
$6 children and adults; $3 seniors; free children under 1. Mid-June–Aug., Tues.–Sun.
10–5; Sept.–mid-June, Wed.–Sun. 10–5.
Subway: 1, 2 to 86th St.*

10 e-4

CHILDREN'S MUSEUM
OF THE ARTS

For youngsters ages 10 months to 10
years, this bi-level art space has a "ball
pond," where children can play with
brightly colored physio-balls; an "actor's
studio" complete with costumes and
musical instruments where young divas
put on shows; and daily art activities
that get children painting, sculpting,
and making collages. *182 Lafayette St.
(between Broome and Grand Sts.), SoHo,
212/274–0986, www.cmany.org. $5 chil-
dren and adults. Wed.–Sun. noon–5. Subway: 6 to Spring St.*

4 a-6

STATEN ISLAND
CHILDREN'S MUSEUM

This award-winning museum assembles
changing exhibits that have focused on
bugs, international cooking, the mysteries of water, costuming for film and theater, and the five senses. There are also
special events and craft workshops on
weekends. *Snug Harbor Cultural Center,
1000 Richmond Terr., 718/273–2060. $4;
free for children under 2. Tues.–Sun.
noon–5. Call for directions to the museum.*

CHURCHES
& SYNAGOGUES

New York City has more than 2,250
churches and 600 synagogues. Here are

some of the most historic and architecturally interesting.

bronx

`2` *a-3*

CHRIST CHURCH
RIVERDALE (EPISCOPAL)

(R. M. Upjohn, 1866) This landmarked
19th-century stone church in Riverdale—
an affluent and disarmingly picturesque
community of hilly, winding streets in
the southwest Bronx—was designed to
look like a medieval English parish
church. Well-known members of its congregation have included baseball player
Lou Gehrig and Mayor Fiorello La
Guardia. *5030 Riverdale Ave. (at 252nd St.
and the Henry Hudson Parkway), 718/
543–1011, www.christchurchriverdale.org.
Sun. services: Sept.–June at 8:30 and 11
AM, July–Aug. 10 AM. Call for directions to
the church.*

`2` *a-3*

RIVERDALE PRESBYTERIAN
CHURCH & MANSE

(James Renwick, Jr., 1863) A Gothic
revival by master church-builder James
Renwick, this charming stone church in
Riverdale is very much in the style of the
English parish church, surrounded by
trees. *4765 Henry Hudson Pkwy. W (at
249th St.), 718/796–5560. Sun. services at
10:30 AM. Subway: 1 to 242nd St./Van
Cortlandt Park.*

`2` *c-8*

ST. ANN'S CHURCH
(EPISCOPAL)

Gouverneur Morris, Jr., built this fieldstone church on his estate for family
worship. Consecrated in 1841, it's the
earliest surviving church in the Bronx.
The cemetery and crypts contain many
members of the Morris family—after
which the Bronx neighborhood Morrisania was named. Among the family's
most prominent members was Gouverneur Morris, Sr., who helped draft the
U.S. Constitution. *295 St. Ann's Ave.
(between 139th and 141st Sts.), 718/585–
5632. Sun. services at 10 AM (English) and
11 AM (Spanish). Subway: 6 to Brook Ave.*

`2` *e-5*

ST. PETER'S CHURCH
(EPISCOPAL)

(Leopold Eidlitz, 1855) This picturesque
Gothic Revival church serves the community of Westchester Square. The

gravestones in the adjacent cemetery go
back to the 1700s. *2500 Westchester Ave.
(near St. Peter's Ave.), 718/931–9270. Call
for hrs of Sun. services. Subway: 6 to Westchester Sq./E. Tremont Ave.*

brooklyn

`4` *f-2*

FLATBUSH DUTCH
REFORMED CHURCH

Built 1793–98 with an elegant clock
tower and steeple, this Federal-style
church still has its original bell,
imported from Holland; it tolled the
death of President Washington in 1799
and still rings each year on the anniversary of his demise. Behind the church is
an old cemetery, with graves going back
to the 1600s. *890 Flatbush Ave. (at
Church Ave.), 718/284–5140. Call for hrs of
services. Subway: 2 to Church Ave.*

`4` *h-3*

FLATLANDS DUTCH
REFORMED CHURCH

This Georgian Federal church, with
white-clapboard siding and a tall
steeple, dates from 1848, and its congregation, which had several previous
church buildings on the same site,
dates from 1654, when this part of
Brooklyn was still farmland and many
of its residents still spoke Dutch. Many
graves in an adjacent cemetery are
from the 17th century. *3931 Kings Highway (between Flatbush Ave. and E. 40th
St.), 718/252–5540. Sun. services at 10:30
AM. Subway: 2, 5 to Flatbush Ave./Brook-
lyn College (from station, walk 1 mi down
Flatbush Ave.).*

`12` *b-4*

GRACE CHURCH, BROOKLYN
HEIGHTS (EPISCOPAL)

(Richard Upjohn, 1848) This neo-Gothic
brownstone church in the heart of historic Brooklyn Heights features three
stained-glass Tiffany windows. The
church is particularly popular for its outdoor entrance court, where benches are
shaded by an old elm. (See Grace Court
Alley in Historic Structures & Streets,
below.) *254 Hicks St. (at Grace Ct.), 718/
624–1850, www.gracebrooklynheights.org.
Sun. services at 8:30 and 10:30 AM. Subway: 2, 3, 4, 5 to Borough Hall; N, Q, R,
W to Court St.*

1 f-6

NEW LOTS REFORMED DUTCH CHURCH

Built in 1824, this one-story, white, wooden church with simple, Gothic-style windows and a short tower, stands virtually unaltered. Records show that the Dutch farmers of New Lots built it for $35. *630 New Lots Ave. (at Schenck Ave.), 718/257–3455. Call for hrs of Sun. services. Subway: 3 to Van Siclen Ave.*

4 f-5

NEW UTRECHT REFORMED CHURCH

The fieldstone for this 1828 Georgian Gothic edifice in Bensonhurst, Brooklyn, came from the original 1699 church that stood on the same site. The windows are made of Victorian milk glass. *18th Ave. (between 83rd and 84th Sts.), 718/232–9500. Subway: B to 18th Ave.*

12 b-3

OUR LADY OF LEBANON MARONITE CATHEDRAL (CATHOLIC)

(Richard Upjohn, 1846) A Romanesque revival by the architect of Manhattan's famous Trinity Church, this was the Congregational Church of the Pilgrims until 1934; it is said that a fragment of Plymouth Rock projects from one of its walls. Sadly, the church's original steeple has been removed, but two interesting post-Upjohn touches are the west and south doors, which were salvaged from the ocean liner *Normandie* after it was scuttled in the Hudson River in 1942. Look for the panel picturing an ocean liner. *113 Remsen St. (at Henry St.), 718/624–7228. Sun. services at 9 and 11 AM. Subway: 2, 3, 4, 5 to Borough Hall; N, Q, R, W to Court St.*

12 b-2

PLYMOUTH CHURCH OF THE PILGRIMS (CONGREGATIONAL)

(Joseph C. Wells, 1849) The abolitionist minister Henry Ward Beecher delivered fiery sermons in this simple Brooklyn Heights church from 1847 to 1887, preaching against slavery and for women's rights. Along with a fine statue of Beecher in the garden, the church's hall has stained-glass windows by Louis Comfort Tiffany. Inside, a plaque on Pew 89 points out that Abraham Lincoln once worshiped here. *75 Hicks St. (at Orange St.), 718/624–4743, www.*

plymouthchurch.org. Sun. services at 11 AM; tours Sun. 12:15 PM or by appointment. Subway: 2, 3 to Clark St.

12 b-3

ST. ANN & THE HOLY TRINITY (EPISCOPAL)

(Minard Lafever, 1847) The 60 stained-glass windows at this neo-Gothic brownstone church in Brooklyn Heights are the first ever made in the United States. Over the last 20 years, they have been painstakingly restored. *157 Montague St. (at Clinton St.), 718/875–6960. Open weekdays 10–1; Sun. services at 11 AM. Subway: 2, 3, 4, 5 to Borough Hall; N, Q, R, W to Court St.*

12 c-4

ST. ANN'S CHURCH (EPISCOPAL)

(James Renwick, Jr., 1869) Here, Renwick—of St. Patrick's Cathedral and Manhattan's Grace Church—gave Brooklyn its only example of the Venetian Gothic, characterized primarily by a facade of varying colors and textures of stone. *Clinton St. (at Livingston St.). Not currently open to the public. Subway: 2, 3, 4, 5 to Borough Hall; N, Q, R, W to Court St.*

12 f-5

ST. AUGUSTINE'S ROMAN CATHOLIC CHURCH

(Parfitt Brothers, 1897) Among the elegantly preserved brownstones on Park Slope's 6th Avenue is this monumental church, with its tall bell-tower, intricate sculptural detail (including carved owls on the exterior), and splendid stained-glass windows. Architects consider it one of Brooklyn's finest churches. *116 6th Ave. (between Park and Sterling Pls.), 718/783–3132, www.staugustineparkslope.org. Sun. services at 9 AM (English), 10:30 AM (Spanish), noon (English), 1:30 PM (Haitian Kreol). Subway: 2, 3 to Bergen St.*

12 g-5

ST. JOHN'S PROTESTANT EPISCOPAL CHURCH

(Edward T. Potter, 1869) This Park Slope intersection boasts a wonderful trio of Gothic revival churches. The oldest is St. John's, which resembles an English country church. Memorial Presbyterian (Pugin & Walter, 1883) is a brownstone church with a tall octagonal spire and stained-glass Tiffany windows. Grace United Methodist Church (Parfitt Brothers, 1882) completes the trio with varie-gated brownstone facade. Standing on this corner, you begin to understand why Brooklyn once was nicknamed "the city of churches." *St. John's Pl. and 7th Ave., 718/783–3928, www.stjohns1826.com. Sun. services at 10 AM. Subway: Q to 7th Ave.*

manhattan

6 e-8
ABYSSINIAN BAPTIST CHURCH

Abyssinian's congregation was originally founded in the early 1800s by African-Americans who were unwilling to accept segregation at the Baptist church they attended in downtown Manhattan. Under the direction of minister Adam Clayton Powell, Sr., this Gothic-style church was erected as the congrega-tion's permanent home in 1923. Pow-ell's son and successor, Adam Clayton Powell, Jr., went on to become the nation's first black congressman. Stop in on Sunday to hear a fiery sermon delivered by the present activist minister Calvin O. Butts and the church's gospel choir. *132 Odell Clark Pl. (formerly 138th St.), between Adam Clayton Powell and Malcolm X. Blvds., Harlem, 212/862–7474, www.adcorp.org/. Sun. services at 9 and 11 AM. Subway: 2 or 3 to 135th St.*

10 g-3
ANSCHE CHESED (OLD CONGREGATION)

(Alexander Saeltzer, 1849) Abandoned in the seventies, New York's oldest surviv-ing synagogue, and at one time its largest, had fallen into a state of woeful disrepair. The Lower East Side's well-remembered Jewish community had largely dispersed and the Ansche Chesed congregation had long since moved uptown. However, in the nineties, this venerable synagogue was revived by the Angel Orensanz Founda-tion Center for the Arts, which makes its residence in the synagogue and includes a performance space and gallery. Small services are even being held again. Brooding, Gothic-revival architecture gives this building's interior a magical air. *172–176 Norfolk St. (between Stanton and E. Houston Sts.), Lower East Side, 212/529–7194, www.orensanz.org. Sub-way: F, V to 2nd Ave.*

10 h-4
BIALYSTOKER SYNAGOGUE (ORTHODOX)

A federal-style stone building erected in 1826, this synagogue, like many others in the city, was originally a Protestant church. In 1908, reflecting the massive influx of Eastern European Jews into New York City, and into the Lower East Side in particular, it was turned into a synagogue and became the home of a congregation originally founded in Bialystok, Poland. Exquisitely restored, Bialystoker is one of the most active synagogues on the Lower East Side. *7–13 Bialystoker Pl. (at Grand St.), Lower East Side, 212/475–0165, www.bialystokersynagogue.org. Call for schedule of services. Subway: F to East Broadway.*

9 e-8
BROTHERHOOD SYNAGOGUE (FRIENDS' MEETING HOUSE)

Built in 1859 alongside Gramercy Park, this landmark house of worship was long the Friends' Meeting House, one of two original Quaker meeting houses in Manhattan. Simple in design and built from brownstone, it was lovingly reno-vated and turned into a synagogue in 1975. *28 Gramercy Park S (between Irving Pl. and 3rd Ave.), Gramercy, 212/674–5750, www.brotherhoodsynagogue.org. Shabbat services: Fri. 8 PM, Sat. 9:30 AM. Subway: 6, N, Q, R, W to 23rd St.*

7 b-3
CATHEDRAL CHURCH OF ST. JOHN THE DIVINE (EPISCOPAL)

Construction of the cathedral began on St. John's Day, December 27, 1892, and continued until 1941, when it was halted—still unfinished—by World War II. Work resumed in 1979 and is still going on sporadically in the medieval manner, each stone hand-cut. A fire in December 2001 destroyed some of the cathedral's interior, but repairs com-menced almost immediately. Two foot-ball fields (601 ft) long and 14 stories high, this massive, architecturally eclec-tic structure is already the world's largest Gothic cathedral. The church hosts several special events each year, including concerts and an enormous Halloween bash; the high point is the blessing of the animals, in honor of St. Francis (October), when the cathedral's bronze doors are opened to circus ele-phants and pet tarantulas. Special "vertical" tours, for which you must reserve in advance and cost $10, take visitors on a 12-story climb into the cathedral's neo-Gothic towers on the first and third Saturday of the month, at noon and 2 PM *Amsterdam Ave. at 112th St., Morningside Heights, 212/316–7540; 212/932–7347 for vertical tours, www.stjohnthedivine.org. Mon.–Sat. 8–6, Sun. 8–8 tours Tues.–Sat. at 11, Sun. at 1. Free; tours $3. Subway: 1 to 110th St./Cathedral Pkwy.*

9 *e-3*
CENTRAL SYNAGOGUE (REFORM)

(Henry Fernbach) Founded in 1872, this Moorish revival edifice—crowned by two fanciful onion-shaped domes and now surrounded by high-rises—was the oldest synagogue in the city in continuous use until a fire destroyed its sanctuary in 1998. Hundreds of workers helped to restore and re-dedicate the temple; it reopened in fall, 2001. *Lexington Ave. and 55th St., Midtown East, 212/838–5122, www.centralsynagogue.org. Shabbat services Fri. 5:45, Sat. 10:30; call for summer hrs. Subway: 6 to 51st St./Lexington Ave.; E, V to Lexington–3rd Aves./53rd St.*

10 *e-1*
CHURCH OF THE ASCENSION (EPISCOPAL)

(Richard Upjohn, 1841; interior remodeled by McKim, Mead & White, 1889) In the heart of Greenwich Village, New York's first Gothic revival church features a beautiful altar mural, *The Ascension,* and illuminated stained-glass windows, both by John La Farge, who was rivaled only by Louis Comfort Tiffany as the foremost stained-glass artist of the 19th-century. There's also a marble altar sculpture by Augustus Saint-Gaudens. *36–38 5th Ave. (at 10th St.), Greenwich Village, 212/254–8620, www.ascensionnyc.org. Usually open weekdays noon–2. Sun. services: Sept.–June at 9 and 11 AM; July–Aug. at 10 AM. Subway: N, Q, R, W to 8th St.*

6 *b-5*
CHURCH OF THE INTERCESSION COMPLEX (EPISCOPAL)

(Bertram Grosvenor Goodhue for Cram, Goodhue & Ferguson, 1914) Beautifully situated in rural Trinity Cemetery (*see* Graveyards, *below*), the local parish of this large, English Gothic–style country church was founded in 1846. Once the farm of famed artist and ornithologist John J. Audubon, the complex is also home to an impressive parish house, cloister, and vicarage. *Broadway at 155th St., Washington Heights, 212/283–6200. Call for hrs. Subway: 1 to 157th St.*

9 *e-7*
CHURCH OF OUR LADY OF THE SCAPULAR & ST. STEPHEN'S (ROMAN CATHOLIC)

(James Renwick, Jr., 1854) A brownstone Romanesque revival in Murray Hill, this church has a large cast-iron interior that features a mural by Constantino Brumidi. *149 E. 28th St. (between Lexington and 3rd Aves.), Murray Hill, 212/683–1675. Sun. services at 8, 10, 11 (Spanish), and 12:30. Subway: 6 to 28th St.*

7 *e-7*
CHURCH OF ST. IGNATIUS LOYOLA (ROMAN CATHOLIC)

(Ditmas & Schickel, 1898) This beaux-arts limestone landmark on Park Avenue was modeled on Jesuit churches in Rome. The main altar is dedicated to St. Ignatius Loyola, founder of the Jesuits, and the church is built upon an earlier house of worship (never completed) dedicated to St. Laurence O'Toole, a popular saint with the city's 19th-century Irish immigrants. *See also* Concerts in Churches *in* Chapter 5. *980 Park Ave. (at 84th St.), Upper East Side, 212/288–3588, www.saintignatiusloyola.org. Sun. services at 7:30 AM, 9:30 AM, 11 AM and 12:30 PM. Subway: 4, 5, 6 to 86th St.*

9 *d-4*
CHURCH OF ST. MARY THE VIRGIN (EPISCOPAL) COMPLEX

(Napolean LeBrun, 1895) Now surrounded by the theater district (TKTS is just around the corner), this 1895 French Gothic–style church is accompanied by a brick clergy house, a chapel, a rectory, and a mission house. The church is believed to be the first built on a steel frame à la the modern-day skyscraper. *145 W. 46th St. (between 6th and 7th Aves.), Midtown West, 212/869–5830, www.stmvirgin.org. Mon.–Fri. 7–9 and 11–7, Sat. 7–5:30, Sun. 8–6; Sun. services at 9, 10, and 11 AM. Subway: 1, 2, 3 to 42nd St./Times Sq.*

9 e-2

CHURCH OF ST. VINCENT FERRER (ROMAN CATHOLIC, DOMINICAN ORDER)

(Bertram Grosvenor Goodhue, 1918) Set inside a large Midtown church complex, Goodhue's Gothic-inspired church of granite with limestone carvings features a magnificent rose window and stunning interior. Nearby is the Victorian Gothic Old Priory of the Dominican Fathers (William Schickel, 1881), the Holy Name Society Building, and the St. Vincent Ferrer School. *869 Lexington Ave. (at 66th St.), Upper East Side, 212/744–2080. Sun. services at 8, 10, noon, and 5:30. Subway: 6 to 68th St./Hunter College.*

7 b-7

CONGREGATION B'NAI JESHURUN (CONSERVATIVE)

(Henry B. Herts & Walter Schneider, 1918) An exotic Byzantine edifice with a high, Romanesque entryway, this Upper West Side synagogue has an extremely active and socially progressive congregation. *257 W. 88th St. (between Broadway and West End Ave.), Upper West Side, 212/787–7600, www.bj.org. Call for hrs of services. Subway: 1, 2 to 86th St.*

9 c-1

CONGREGATION SHEARITH ISRAEL (ORTHODOX)

(Brunner & Tryon, 1897) The fifth home of North America's oldest Jewish congregation (founded in 1654), this Sephardic (of Spanish and Portuguese origin) synagogue contains religious articles from three centuries. Inside, a "Little Synagogue" is a Georgian-style replica of the congregation's first synagogue. For the synagogue's three associated burial grounds, *see Graveyards & Cemeteries, below. 8 W. 70th St. (at Central Park West), Upper West Side, 212/873–0300, shearith-israel.org. Morning services Sun.–Fri. 7:15 AM, Sat. 8:15 AM; evening services Sun.–Thurs. 6:30; call for hrs of Shabbat services. Subway: B, C to 72nd St.*

10 f-4

ELDRIDGE STREET SYNAGOGUE (ORTHODOX)

(Herter Brothers, 1887) The most luxurious of the hundreds of synagogues that once thrived on the Lower East Side, this Orthodox temple is lined with keyhole-shape arches and has an enormous Gothic-wheel window in its center. Although the main sanctuary was abandoned in the 1950s, it is currently being restored by the Eldridge Street Project, which also offers tours of the synagogue focusing on Jewish-American history and the history of the Lower East Side. Inside are an exceptional hand-carved ark of Italian walnut, a sculptured wooden balcony, and enormous brass chandeliers. *12 Eldridge St. (between Canal and Division Sts.), Lower East Side, 212/978–8800, www.eldridgestreet.org. Tours Tues. and Thurs. at 11:30 and 2:30, Sun. hourly 11–3. $4, $2.50 children, students, and seniors. Subway: F to E. Broadway.*

9 e-2

5TH AVENUE SYNAGOGUE (ORTHODOX)

(Percival Goodman, 1959) Opposite Central Park, this modern limestone temple is adorned with stained-glass windows that are best appreciated after dark, when the interior lights come on. *5 E. 62nd St. (at 5th Ave.), Upper East Side, 212/838–2122, www.fifthavenuesynagogue.org. Call for hrs of daily and Shabbat services. Subway: N, Q, R, W to 5th Ave.*

10 e-1

FIRST PRESBYTERIAN CHURCH

(Joseph C. Wells, 1846; south transept McKim, Mead & White, 1893) Near the Church of the Ascension (*see above*) and just a few years younger, this Gothic revival church features a square tower and elaborately carved turrets; its grounds are surrounded by a lovely fence of wood and cast iron. *48 5th Ave. (between 11th and 12th Sts.), Greenwich Village, 212/675–6150, www.firstpresnyc. org. Sun. services at 11 AM. Subway: N, Q, R, W to 8th St.*

10 f-1

FRIENDS' MEETING HOUSE & SEMINARY (QUAKER)

(Charles T. Bunting, 1860) These simple but elegant buildings of red brick and brownstone embody the no-frills Quaker style. *221 E. 15th St. (at Rutherford Pl.), Gramercy, 212/777–8866. Sun. meeting at 9:30 and 11 AM, Wed. meeting at 6:30 PM. Subway: L, N, Q, R, W, 4, 5, 6 to 14th St./Union Sq.*

`10` *e-1*

GRACE CHURCH & RECTORY (EPISCOPAL)

(James Renwick, Jr., 1846) One of the most magnificent examples of Gothic revival architecture in the nation, Grace Church was designed by James Renwick—later celebrated for his masterpiece, St. Patrick's Cathedral. The church's ornate marble tower, surmounted by a tall spire, is among Lower Manhattan's most picturesque sights. Countless society couples have wed here over the years, but one highly unusual union—that of P. T. Barnum's little trouper, Tom Thumb, in 1863—particularly scandalized the congregation. *800 Broadway (at E. 10th St.), Greenwich Village, 212/254–2000, www.gracenyc.org. Mon.–Thurs. 11–5:30, Sat. 12–4, Sun. 8:30–1; call for hrs of Sun. services. Subway: N, Q, R, W to 8th St.*

`10` *e-6*

JOHN STREET UNITED METHODIST CHURCH

(William Hurry) Now dwarfed by Wall Street high-rises, this Georgian-style brownstone is the home of America's oldest Methodist congregation. Built in 1841, it was already the third church on this site; the first was built in 1768. The church and a small museum are open Monday, Wednesday, and Friday noon–4. *44 John St. (between Nassau and William Sts.), Lower Manhattan, 212/269–0014. Sun. services at 11 AM. Subway: 2, 3, 4, 5 to Fulton St.*

`10` *d-2*

JUDSON MEMORIAL CHURCH (BAPTIST)

(McKim, Mead & White, 1892) Best known for its 10-story campanile, this church is considered one of architect Stanford White's most significant buildings. Designed in the Italian Renaissance style of yellow brick and limestone, it's adorned with 12 stained-glass windows by John LaFarge, intricate terra-cotta ornamentation, and a marble relief by Augustus Saint-Gaudens. Since the 1960s, the church has supported an avant-garde arts program, which showcases modern dance. *55 Washington Sq. S (between Thompson and Sullivan Sts.), Greenwich Village, 212/477–0351, www.judson.org. Weekdays 10–6; Sun. services at 11 AM. Subway: A, C, E, F, V to W. 4th St./Washington Sq.*

`9` *e-7*

THE LITTLE CHURCH AROUND THE CORNER (CHURCH OF THE TRANSFIGURATION, EPISCOPAL)

Founded in 1849, this Gothic revival complex is set back from the street in a well-landscaped garden. Here's how it got its nickname: In 1870, the minister at another local church refused to perform funeral services for the actor George Holland, and suggested that Holland's friends try "the little church around the corner." The name stuck, and the church's popularity with theater folks is now a tradition. The stained-glass windows by John LaFarge are dedicated to actors; one depicts the 19th-century superstar Edwin Booth in his most celebrated role, Hamlet. *1 E. 29th St. (at 5th Ave.), Murray Hill, 212/684–6770, www.littlechurch.org. Sun. services at 8:30 and 11 AM; free tours offered Sun. after the 11 AM service. Subway: N, Q, R, W, 6 to 28th St.*

`9` *e-7*

MARBLE COLLEGIATE CHURCH (DUTCH REFORMED)

(S. A. Warner, 1854) This Gothic revival church in Murray Hill gets its name from the Tuckahoe marble in which it is clad. Its congregation traces its roots back to the city's very first church, which was founded by the Reformed Protestant Dutch Congregation organized by the Dutch governor Peter Minuit, in 1628. Dr. Norman Vincent Peale (*The Power of Positive Thinking*) was the pastor here from 1932 to 1984, and his inspiring sermons were known for drawing thousands of listeners every Sunday. *1 W. 29th St. (at 5th Ave.), Murray Hill, 212/686–2770, www.marblechurch.org. Sun. services at 11:15 AM. Subway: 6, N, Q, R, W to 28th St.*

`10` *f-5*

MARINERS' TEMPLE (BAPTIST)

(Isaac Lucas, 1842) The AIA [American Institute of Architects] *Guide to New York City* refers to this building as a "temple to Athena"; indeed, the two Ionic columns at the church's entrance make this Greek Revival structure look like a shrine. The church was originally built to lift the spirits—and morals—of the many lonely sailors who passed through the city during the 19th century.

In later years, it served the needs of the neighborhood's immigrant community, with services given in multiple languages, including Spanish, Italian, Greek, and Chinese. *3 Henry St. (at Oliver St.), Chinatown, 212/233–0423. Sun. services at 11 AM. Subway: 4, 5, 6 to Brooklyn Bridge/City Hall.*

7 *f-5*

MOSQUE OF NEW YORK

(Main Building: Skidmore, Owings & Merrill; Minaret: Swanke, Hayden, Connell, Ltd, 1991) A focal point for New York's Muslims and a relatively new landmark on the uptown skyline, this granite-and-glass structure, topped with a copper dome and a thin gold crescent, is the first building in New York City to be built as a mosque. The cornerstone of the 130-ft minaret was laid by the Emir of Kuwait in 1988. *Islamic Cultural Center of New York, 1711 3rd Ave. (at 96th St.), Upper East Side, 212/722–5234. Friday prayers 12:30 PM (at 1 PM during daylight saving time). Subway: 6 to 96th St.*

11 *f-4*

OLD ST. PATRICK'S CATHEDRAL (ROMAN CATHOLIC)

(Joseph Mangin, 1815) New York's original Roman Catholic cathedral, Old St. Patrick's was replaced by the uptown St. Patrick's in 1879, after a disastrous fire in 1866. Although the building was restored in 1868, the cathedral was "demoted" to a parish church. Note the high walls surrounding the churchyard, designed to protect the cathedral from the anti-Catholic mobs who once threatened to burn the place down. (*See Graveyards, below.*) *260–264 Mulberry St. (between Prince and Houston Sts.), SoHo, 212/226–8075. Sun. mass at 9:30 AM (English), 10:45 AM (Spanish), and 12:30 PM (English). Subway: F, V to Broadway–Lafayette St.; N, Q, R, W to Prince St.*

7 *a-2*

RIVERSIDE CHURCH (INTERDENOMINATIONAL)

(Allen & Collens and Henry C. Pelton, 1930) Modeled after Chartres Cathedral, this impressive Gothic-style church is prominently sited above the Hudson River, right next to Riverside Park. Rising 21 stories (392 ft), the tower offers an astonishing view of the river (*see Viewpoints, below*) and houses a 74-bell carillon, the largest in the world. The church's interracial, interdenomina-

tional congregation sponsors numerous community, cultural, and political programs. *Riverside Dr. and 120th St., Morningside Heights, 212/870–6700, www.theriversidechurch.org. Admission to tower $2. Church open daily 9–6; tower open Tues.–Sat. 11–4, Sun. 12:15–4; Sun. services at 10:45 AM. Live carillon concerts can be heard throughout the immediate neighborhood on Sun. at 12:30 and 3 PM. Subway: 1 to 116 St./Columbia University or to 125th St.*

11 *g-8*

ROMAN CATHOLIC CHURCH OF THE TRANSFIGURATION

This unpretentious Gothic-Georgian blend, built from locally quarried Manhattan schist, was built in 1801 by English Lutherans. Sold to an Irish-Catholic congregation in the 1850s, it has served a succession of immigrants, first predominantly Irish, then Italian, and now Chinese. These days the church is distinguished by its trilingualism: Each Sunday mass is said in Cantonese, Mandarin, and English. *29 Mott St. (at Pell St.), Chinatown, 212/962–5157. Sun. services at 9 AM (Mandarin), 10:15 AM (English), 11:30 AM (Cantonese), and 12:45 PM (English). Subway: J, M, Z to Canal St.*

10 *h-4*

ST. AUGUSTINE'S CHAPEL (EPISCOPAL)

A landmark Georgian-Gothic building dating from 1810–1820, this Lower East Side fieldstone church was originally All Saints' Free Church—"free" meaning that you didn't have to pay to worship. However, it was not "free" to all. A separate gallery without pews was built for the slaves of congregants. Though slavery was abolished in New York in 1828, the gallery still stands, a testimony to past wrongs. *290 Henry St. (between Montgomery and Jackson Sts.), Lower East Side, 212/673–5300. Call for hrs of Sun. services. Subway: F to E. Broadway.*

9 *e-4*

ST. BARTHOLOMEW'S CHURCH (EPISCOPAL)

(Bertram Grosvenor Goodhue, 1919) Time and again, historic preservationists have saved this Byzantine-domed Park Avenue landmark from becoming one of the skyscrapers that surround it. The church's impressive triple-arch entry (McKim, Mead & White, 1902) was actually moved here from the congregation's former building on Madison Avenue. Classical concerts—choral music, early music, and organ recitals on the church's 12,422-pipe organ—are given throughout the year. And don't miss the church's café overlooking Park Avenue. *Park Ave. at 50th St., Midtown East, 212/378–0200; 212/378–0248 for concert information. www.stbarts.org. Open daily 8–6; Sun. services at 8, 9, and 11 AM and 7 PM. Subway: 6 to 51st St./Lexington Ave.; E, V to Lexington–3rd Aves./53rd St.*

9 b-4
ST. CLEMENT'S CHURCH (EPISCOPAL)

(Edward D. Lindsey, 1870) This picturesque parish church was originally known as Faith Chapel West Presbyterian. Perhaps reflecting its proximity to the theater district, the church regularly hosts performances in its sanctuary and parish house. *423 W. 46th St. (between 9th and 10th Aves.), Midtown West, 212/ 246–7277 (ext. 32 for information on upcoming performances). Sun. services at 8 and 11 AM (English) and 1:15 PM (Spanish). Subway: A, C, E to 42nd St.*

9 f-8
ST. GEORGE'S EPISCOPAL CHURCH

(Blesch & Eidlitz, 1856) A Romanesque brownstone known as "Morgan's church" after one of its most famous parishioners, financier J. P. Morgan, this beautiful complex features rounded exterior arches and, inside, lovely stained-glass windows. *Rutherford Pl. and 16th St. (off Stuyvesant Sq.), Gramercy, 212/475–0830. Sun. services at 8:30 and 10:30 AM. Subway: 4, 5, 6, L, N, Q, R, W to 14th St./Union Sq.*

11 g-2
ST. GEORGE'S UKRAINIAN CATHOLIC CHURCH

(Apollinaire Osadca, 1977) Topped by an impressive dome and graced with three brightly colored religious murals on its facade, this is the new religious centerpiece of an old Ukrainian neighborhood. It's also the focal point of the annual Ukrainian Festival (*see* Events, *below*). *30 E. 7th St. (between 2nd and 3rd Aves.), East Village, 212/674–1615. Sun. services at 9 and 10 AM, noon, and 7:30 PM. Subway: 6 to Astor Pl.*

10 f-5
ST. JAMES CHURCH (ROMAN CATHOLIC)

Founded by Irish immigrants in 1837, the city's second-oldest Roman Catholic Church is a stately building with a brownstone facade and two Doric columns. Al Smith, former governor of New York and renowned political reformer, was an altar boy here when this was still a predominantly Irish neighborhood. *32 James St. (between St. James Pl. and Madison St.), Chinatown, 212/233–0161. Sun. services at 8:30 AM (English), 10 AM (Spanish), and 11:30 AM (English). Subway: 4, 5, 6 to Brooklyn Bridge/City Hall.*

7 f-8
ST. JEAN BAPTISTE CHURCH (ROMAN CATHOLIC)

(Nicholas Serracino, 1913) A single patron, Thomas Fortune Ryan, paid for the construction of this two-tower, domed building after he could not find a seat one Sunday in the crowded little church that stood here earlier. The original congregation was French-Canadian. *184 E. 76th St. (between Lexington and 3rd Aves.), Upper East Side, 212/288– 5082, www.sjbrcc.org. Sun. services at 9 and 10:30 AM, noon, and 5:30 and 7:30 PM. Subway: 6 to 77th St.*

9 c-7
ST. JOHN THE BAPTIST ROMAN CATHOLIC CHURCH

(Napoleon Le Brun, 1872) A brownstone church with one spire, this exquisite building near Penn Station has a lovely, white-marble interior. *210 W. 31st St. (between 7th and 8th Aves.), Chelsea, 212/ 564–9070. Sun. services at 8:45 and 10:30 AM, noon, and 5:15 PM. Subway: 1, 2 to 28th St.*

11 c-2
ST. JOSEPH'S ROMAN CATHOLIC CHURCH

(John Doran, 1834) Just west of Washington Square Park on bustling 6th Avenue is Manhattan's oldest surviving Roman Catholic church, the exterior of which was renovated in 1998. In keeping with its Greek revival style it is topped with a simple triangular pediment, and its entryway is supported by two massive columns. *365 6th Ave. (at Washington Pl.), Greenwich Village, 212/741–1274. Sun. services at 9 and 11:30 AM. Subway: A, C, E, F, V to W. 4th St./Washington Sq.*

11 *a-3*

ST. LUKE-IN-THE-FIELDS CHURCH (EPISCOPAL)

(James N. Wells, 1822) To this church's early parishioners, today's West Village was the sticks; hence their name for what was then a charming country parish, an annex of Trinity Church, downtown. A fire devastated the building in 1981, but it was successfully restored in 1986. A peaceful little garden (open to the public) preserves some of the church's original country spirit. *487 Hudson St. (between Grove and Christopher Sts.), Greenwich Village, 212/924-0562, www.stlukeinthefields. org. Grounds open weekdays 7–7, Sat. 7–6, Sun. 7–3; Sun. services at 8, 9:15, and 11:15 AM and 5 PM. Subway: 1, 2 to Christopher St./Sheridan Sq.*

10 *f-1*

ST. MARK'S CHURCH IN-THE-BOWERY (EPISCOPAL)

Originally a stark Georgian structure (1799), St. Mark's served as the first parish in Manhattan that was independent of Trinity Church, farther downtown. The Greek revival steeple, an East Village landmark, was completed in 1828; the cast-iron Italianate portico was added in 1854. Beautifully restored following a devastating fire in 1978, St. Mark's stands on the site of Dutch governor Peter Stuyvesant's family chapel. Stuyvesant is buried in the churchyard (*see* Haunted Places, *below*). Even in its early days, St. Mark's was considered progressive, and historically it has been a haven for the arts as well as for the spirit. Ballerina Isadora Duncan once danced here, and poets Edna St. Vincent Millay and Robert Frost read their works; today, Danspace and the Poetry Project stage performances and readings. (*See* St. Mark's Historic District *in* Historic Structures & Streets, *below.*) *2nd Ave. and 10th St., East Village, 212/674-6377, www.stmarkschurch.org. Sun. services at 10:30 AM. Subway: 6 to Astor Pl.; L to 3rd Ave.*

9 *e-4*

ST. PATRICK'S CATHEDRAL (ROMAN CATHOLIC)

(James Renwick, Jr., 1858–79) The most famous church in New York City, St. Patrick's Cathedral is also one of the most architecturally significant churches in the nation. Designed by the famed 19th-century church architect James Renwick (and considered his masterpiece), the marble Gothic Revival edifice is based on Germany's Cologne Cathedral and took 21 years to build. The tallest structures in the area when first erected, the cathedral's two 330-ft-high towers are now dwarfed by Midtown's skyscrapers. St. Patrick's is the seat of the Archdiocese of New York. *5th Ave. and 50th St., Midtown East, 212/753-2261. Daily 7 AM–8:45 PM; Sun. mass at 7, 8, 9, and 10:15 AM; noon; 1, 4, and 5:30 PM. Subway: E, V to 5th Ave./53rd St.*

7 *b-2*

ST. PAUL'S CHAPEL (INTERDENOMINATIONAL)

(Howells & Stokes, 1907) Considered one of Columbia University's finest buildings, this wonderful brick, terra-cotta, and limestone chapel has 24 windows in its Byzantine-style dome, decorated with the coats-of-arms of old New York families associated with city and university history. *Columbia University, Amsterdam Ave. (between 116th and 117th Sts.), Morningside Heights, 212/854-6625. When classes are in session, the chapel is open daily from 10 AM–10 PM. Subway: 1 to 116th St./Columbia University.*

10 *e-6*

ST. PAUL'S CHAPEL (EPISCOPAL)

(Archibald Thomas McBean, 1764–66; tower, steeple, porch by James Crommelin Lawrence, 1794) This Georgian-style church, with its distinctive brownstone spire, is Manhattan's oldest surviving building. Early worshippers included George Washington (his pew can be found in the north aisle); New York's first governor, George Clinton; the Marquis de Lafayette; and General Cornwallis. The oak interior was designed primarily by architect Pierre L'Enfant, who later laid out the city plan for Washington, D.C. The chapel is fronted by a peaceful 18th-century cemetery, a unique bit of open space in the pit of Manhattan's bustling financial district (*see* Graveyards & Cemeteries, *below*). After the attack on the World Trade Center, the church served as an operations center and place of refuge for rescue workers. *Broadway and Fulton St., Lower Manhattan, 212/602-0800; 212/602-0747 for information on free lunchtime concerts, www.stpaulschapel.org. Subway: 2, 3, 4, 5 to Fulton St.*

9 c-8

ST. PETER'S CHURCH (EPISCOPAL)

(James W. Smith, 1836–38) Based on designs by Clement Clarke Moore, this fieldstone church in Chelsea was one of the first of the English-style Gothic revival churches that became so popular in New York in the years to follow. *346 W. 20th St. (between 8th and 9th Aves.), Chelsea, 212/929–2390. Sun. services at 10 AM. Subway: C, E to 23rd St.*

9 e-3

ST. PETER'S CHURCH (LUTHERAN)

(Hugh Stubbins & Associates, 1977) When the original St. Peter's Church was torn down to make way for Citicorp Center (*see Architecture, above*), this ultra-modern church—complete with a chapel by artist Louise Nevelson—went up on the same site, nesting in the skyscraper's shadow. In the modern spirit, "jazz vespers" are held at 5 every Sunday afternoon. *Lexington Ave. at 54th St., Midtown East, 212/935–2200. Sun. services at 8:45 and 11 AM (English) and 1:30 PM (Spanish). Subway: 6 to 51st St./Lexington Ave.; E, V to Lexington–3rd Aves./53rd St.*

10 e-6

ST. PETER'S CHURCH (ROMAN CATHOLIC)

(John R. Haggerty and Thomas Thomas, 1838) An impressive Greek revival building made of smooth blocks of granite, St. Peter's, like Trinity and St. Paul's, is a piece of early New York history that survives amid the glass-and-steel pillars of Wall Street. Its first incarnation, built on this site in 1786, was the city's second Catholic church. *22 Barclay St. (at Church St.), Lower Manhattan, 212/233–8355. Sun. services at 8, 9:30, and noon. Subway: 2, 3 to Park Pl.*

10 g-4

ST. TERESA'S ROMAN CATHOLIC CHURCH

Built in 1841 in the then-popular Gothic revival style, this was originally the First Presbyterian Church of New York. Converted into a Catholic church in 1863 to serve the Lower East Side's growing Irish population, today it conducts services in English, Spanish, and Chinese, reflecting the area's current ethnic makeup. *141 Henry St. (at Rutgers St.), Lower East Side, 212/233–0233. Sun. services at 8 AM (English), 9 AM (Spanish), 10 AM (English), and 11 AM (Chinese). Subway: F to East Broadway.*

9 d-4

ST. THOMAS CHURCH 5TH AVENUE (EPISCOPAL)

(Cram, Goodhue & Ferguson, 1914) Just two blocks north of St. Patrick's Cathedral, this richly detailed French Gothic church gives its more-famous 5th Avenue counterpart a run for its money in terms of aesthetics. Architects consider St. Thomas the more beautiful of the two; "St. Patrick's seems to want to be off in a tiny village somewhere," says *New York Times* architecture critic Paul Goldberger, while "St. Thomas was made to be on a Manhattan street and nowhere else." The elaborate interior is gloriously detailed, and the carvings on the "Bride's Door" include both a love knot and a dollar sign—the stonemason's comment on the institution of matrimony. St. Thomas's church music program is the best in the city, most notably because of its internationally renowned men's and boys' choir. *1 W. 53rd St. (at 5th Ave.), Midtown West, 212/757–7013, www.saintthomaschurch.org. Open 8–6:30; Sun. services at 8, 9, and 11 AM; guided tours follow the 11 AM service. Subway: E, V to 5th Ave./53rd St.*

10 g-5

SEA & LAND CHURCH (PRESBYTERIAN)

A Georgian federal church with Gothic windows—and one of four downtown churches of this period made from locally quarried Manhattan schist—this Lower East Side landmark was originally built in 1817 as the Northern Reformed Church. In 1865 it became the Sea and Land Church, dedicated to serving the city's seafaring population. It's now the First Chinese Presbyterian Church. *61 Henry St. (at Market St.), Lower East Side, 212/964–5488, www.fcpc.org. Sun. services at 11 AM (Cantonese and Mandarin) and 1 PM (English). Subway: F to East Broadway.*

9 d-7

SERBIAN ORTHODOX CATHEDRAL OF ST. SAVA

(Richard Upjohn, 1855) Originally Trinity Chapel, part of downtown's Trinity Parish, this brownstone church was transferred to the Serbian Orthodox Church in 1943. The neighboring parish house, designed by J. Wrey Mould in the

Victorian Gothic style in 1860, stands in contrast to the church's Gothic heaviness. *15 W. 25th St. (at Broadway), Chelsea, 212/242–9240, www.stsava.org. Sun. service at 10:30 AM. Subway: F, N, R, V to 23rd St.*

9 *e-2*

TEMPLE EMANUEL (REFORM)

(Robert D. Kohn, Charles Butler, and Clarence Stein, 1929) Built in the Byzantine-Romanesque style and covered with mosaics, this fashionable Upper East Side synagogue seats 2,500, making it the largest Reform temple in the nation. A free museum displays 250 artifacts from the congregation's history and Jewish life. *1 E. 65th St. (at 5th Ave.), Upper East Side, 212/744–1400, www.emanuelnyc.org. Temple and museum open Mon.–Thurs. 10–4:30, Fri. 10–4, Sat. 1–4:30; Sabbath services Fri. 5:15 PM and Sat. 10:30 AM. Subway: N, Q, R, W to 5th Ave.*

10 *e-7*

TRINITY CHURCH (EPISCOPAL)

(Richard Upjohn, 1846) Founded by royal charter during the reign of England's King William III in 1697, Trinity Church was the city's first Episcopal congregation. The first church built on this site was destroyed by fire during the Revolutionary War; Upjohn's Gothic revival edifice is the third, and remains one of New York's best-known landmarks. Its 280-ft spire made it New York's tallest building for the second half of the 19th century, and it is still sometimes credited as the city's first skyscraper—author Judith Dupré calls Trinity an "ecclesiastical exclamation point in Wall Street's sea of corporate towers." The adjacent 2½-acre cemetery is also a landmark, and a quiet green oasis in summertime (*see Graveyards & Cemeteries, below*). The church hosts a popular lunchtime concert series. *74 Trinity Pl. (at Broadway and Wall St.), Lower Manhattan, 212/602–0800, www.trinitywallstreet.org. Weekdays 7 AM–6 PM, weekends 7 AM–4 PM; daily tours at 2 PM; Sun. services at 9 and 11:15 AM. Subway: 4, 5 to Wall St.*

queens

2 *g-8*

FIRST REFORMED CHURCH OF COLLEGE POINT

This 1872 country church is a New York City rarity, built of wood and dressed with ornate details in the style of the well-known 19th-century architect Charles Eastlake. *14th Ave. (at 119th St.), 718/359–3956. Sun. services at 10 AM. Subway and bus: 7 to Flushing Main St., then Q65 bus to 119th St.*

1 *f-3*

FRIENDS' MEETING HOUSE (QUAKER)

This plain, wood-shingle building with cast-iron door hinges and latches is the oldest house of worship in New York City, and one of the oldest in the United States. It has been in continuous use since 1694, except for a period during the American Revolution when the occupying British used it successively as a prison, storehouse, and hospital. The two wooden doors in the rear were originally separate entrances for men and women. The Friends (popularly known as the Quakers) were pioneers in asserting the right of religious freedom; the meeting house was built following the trial and acquittal of John Bowne after he was arrested for "illegal worship and assembly." (*See Bowne House in Historic Structures & Streets, below.*) *137-16 Northern Blvd. (between Main and Union Sts.), 718/358–9636. Sun. meeting at 11 AM. Subway: 7 to Main St./Flushing.*

1 *g-4*

GRACE EPISCOPAL CHURCH

(Dudley Field, 1862) The third church to be built on this site in Jamaica, Queens, this rugged Gothic revival building serves a congregation that first assembled in 1702. Statesman and four-time U.S. senator Rufus King is buried in the charming churchyard, which dates from 1734. (*See King Manor Museum in Historic Structures & Streets, below.*) *155-03 Jamaica Ave. (at 155th St.), 718/291–4901. Sun. services at 8 and 10 AM. Subway: E, J, Z to Jamaica Center.*

3 *g-3*

REFORMED DUTCH CHURCH OF NEWTOWN

Topped with an elegant cupola, this white-clapboard church from 1831 is one of the oldest wooden churches in the

city. *85-15 Broadway (at Corona Ave.),
718/592–4466. Call for hrs of Sun. services. Subway: R to Grand Ave.*

staten island

1 *b-2*

CHURCH OF
ST. ANDREW (EPISCOPAL)

(William H. Mersereau, 1872) As if
transplanted from New England, or
even old England, this fieldstone parish
church and its ramshackle graveyard sit
on a picturesque green hillock in Staten
Island's Historic Richmondtown. Home
to Staten Island's oldest surviving congregation, the church was placed on the
National Register of Historic Places in
2000. *4 Arthur Kill Rd. (at Old Mill Rd.),
Richmondtown, 718/351–0900, www.
mindspring.com/~standrew/. Sun. services
at 8 and 10 AM. From Staten Island Ferry,
Bus S74 to Richmond Rd.*

4 *c-7*

ST. JOHN'S
EPISCOPAL CHURCH

(Arthur D. Gilman, 1871) Ferry magnate
Cornelius Vanderbilt was baptized in
this high-steeple Gothic revival church
of rose-color granite in Rosebank,
Staten Island. *1331 Bay St. (at New
Lane), 718/447–1605. Sun. services at 8
and 10 AM. Bus: From Staten Island Ferry,
Bus S51 to Highland Blvd.*

COLLEGES
& UNIVERSITIES

New York is a great college town. Even if
you're not a student, the ivied halls of
academia can be a welcome retreat from
the decidedly frenetic pace of the city at
large. And who knows? You might want
to sign up for a little continuing education. Here are just a few campuses
worth visiting.

bronx

2 *c-4*

FORDHAM UNIVERSITY

A small enclave of distinguished Collegiate Gothic architecture in the midst of
urban sprawl, this university opened in
1841 as a Jesuit college and was one of
the country's preeminent schools.
Although it's advisable to pre-arrange a
tour of the campus, you may be able to
(unofficially) enter the grounds via Bath-

gate Avenue to see Old Rose Hill Manor
Dig, the University Church, whose
stained glass was donated by King Louis
Philippe of France (1773–1850);
Edward's Parade quadrangle; and Keat-
ing Hall, sitting like a fortress in the center of it all. *441 E. Fordham Rd., 800/
367–3426, www.fordham.edu. Tours:
Weekdays at 12 and 2 (when classes are in
session), or by appointment. D to Fordham Rd., then walk downhill about 4
blocks to the campus.*

brooklyn

4 *g-3*

BROOKLYN COLLEGE

Founded in 1930, this surprisingly
bucolic campus sits on 26 tree-lined
acres in the heart of humming Brooklyn.
Its 13 Georgian-style buildings, surrounded by pleasant lawns, give this public university an Ivy League air. The
campus is frequently visited by bird
watchers eager to see a rambunctious
colony of escaped exotic green parrots
(that normally live in South America) that
have set up large nests in and around the
school. *2900 Bedford Ave. (at Ave. H),
718/951–5000, www.brooklyn.cuny.edu.
Call for information about campus tours.
Subway: 2, 5 to Flatbush Ave.*

12 *g-2*

PRATT INSTITUTE

Specializing in architecture, art, and
design, the Pratt campus in Brooklyn
covers 25 acres in the midst of the borough's "brownstone belt." Its parklike
quadrangle is the perfect spot to hit the
books. *200 Willoughby St. (between
Classon and Hall Sts.), 718/636–3600,
www.pratt.edu. Tours Mon.–Fri. at 11 and
2:30, leaving from the admissions office in
DeKalb Hall. G to Clinton Pl./Washing-
ton Ave.*

manhattan

7 *b-3*

BARNARD COLLEGE

Established in 1889 and one of the former Seven Sisters women's colleges,
Barnard has steadfastly remained sin-
gle-sex and independent from Columbia, although its students can take
classes there (and vice versa). Check out
the bear (the college's mascot) on the
shield above the main gates at 117th
Street and Broadway. Through the gates

is Barnard Hall, which houses class-rooms, offices, a pool, and dance studios. Its brick-and-limestone design echoes the design of Columbia University's buildings. To the right of Barnard Hall, a path leads through the narrow but neatly landscaped campus. *Broadway and 117th St., Morningside Heights, 212/854–2014, www.barnard.edu. Student-led tours Mon.–Fri. at 10:30 and 2:30 when classes are in session. Subway: 1 to 116th St.*

6 c-7
CITY COLLEGE
The beautiful neo-Gothic stone towers of City College (founded here in 1903) are the most striking landmarks in northern Manhattan's Hamilton Heights. The college's arched schist gates, green lawns, and white terra-cotta trim could easily be part of an Ivy League campus, but this has always been a public institution (tuition was free until the mid-1970s). *138th St. and Convent Ave., Harlem, 212/650–7000, 212/650–6448 for tours, www.ccny.cuny.edu. Tours by appointment when classes are in session. Subway: 1 to 137th St., then walk 3 blocks up 138th St.*

7 b-3
COLUMBIA UNIVERSITY
This wealthy, private, coed Ivy League school was New York's first college when it was founded in 1754. Back then, before American independence, it was called King's College. (Be sure to note the gilded crowns on the black wrought-iron gates at the Amsterdam Avenue entrance.) The brick paths of College Walk lead into the refreshingly open main quadrangle, dominated by neoclassical Butler Library to the south and the rotunda-topped Low Memorial Library to the north. The steps of Low Library, presided over by Daniel Chester French's statue *Alma Mater*, have been a focal point for campus life, not least during the student riots of 1968. Before Columbia moved here, this land was occupied by the Bloomingdale Insane Asylum; the sole survivor of those days is Buell Hall (1878), the gabled orange-red brick house, east of Low Library. *Broadway and 116th St., Morningside Heights, 212/854–4900, www.columbia.edu. Weekdays 9–5. Tours at 11 and 2 weekdays from Room 213, Low Library. Subway: 1 to 116th St./Columbia University.*

10 e-2
NEW YORK UNIVERSITY
Founded in 1831, NYU is spread out like the Sorbonne in Paris. You can't really say there is a "campus" as its 100-plus buildings dot the area around Washington Square Park and spread out into the Village and beyond. At La Guardia Place and Washington Square South, however, the new student center ties everything together. Interestingly, it stands on the site of a famous boarding house that had been nicknamed the House of Genius for the talented writers who lived there over the years: Theodore Dreiser, John Dos Passos, and Eugene O'Neill, among others. *100 Washington Sq. E (between Washington and Waverly Pls.), Greenwich Village, 212/998–1212, www.nyu.edu. Call for details about daily campus tours. Subway: N, Q, R, W to 8th St.; A, B, C, D, E, F, V to 4th St.*

GRAVEYARDS & CEMETERIES
Of some 90 known New York burial grounds from the 18th and early 19th centuries, only a few remain. A serious search for graveyards should take you off Manhattan Island—after 1830 one needed a special permit for burial south of Canal Street, and after 1852, burial in Manhattan was prohibited altogether.

bronx
2 d-5
OLD WEST FARMS SOLDIER CEMETERY
Forty veterans of the War of 1812, the Civil War, the Spanish-American War, and World War I are buried in this small land-marked cemetery built in 1815. *Bryant Ave. and 180th St. Subway: 2, 5 to E. 180th St.*

2 c-2
WOODLAWN CEMETERY
Along with Green-Wood Cemetery in Brooklyn, Woodlawn Cemetery in the northern Bronx is one of the most ornate and star-studded burial grounds in the world. First opened in 1863, it is filled with elaborate tombs, some of them replicas of European chapels and Egyptian burial sites. Among the resting luminaries are Mayor Fiorello La Guardia, F. W. Woolworth, R. H. Macy, J. C. Penney, Jay Gould, Henry H. Westinghouse, Joseph Pulitzer, Elizabeth Cady Stanton, Herman Melville, Duke Elling-

ton, and Miles Davis. Maps are available at the cemetery office, and guided tours are offered in spring and fall. *Entrances on Jerome Ave. north of Bainbridge Ave., 233rd St., and Webster Ave., 718/920–0500. Daily 9–4:30. Subway: 4 to Wood-lawn; 2 to 233rd St.*

brooklyn

4 *d-2*

GREEN-WOOD CEMETERY
(Grounds: Henry Pierrepont, 1840; Gates: Richard Upjohn, 1861–75) Break-ing with the traditional forms of inter-ment—churchyards, family plots, and compact enclosures—ingenious Brook-lyn planner Henry Pierrepont laid out Green-Wood's 478 rolling acres to cre-ate a cemetery full of hills, ponds, lakes, and meandering drives. Encompassing Brooklyn's highest point, 216 ft above sea level, the cemetery's natural setting is unsurpassed, and when it first opened in 1840 it was as much a public park as a burial ground. Magnificent Gothic revival mausoleums and monu-ments decorate many of the 500,000 graves, and the list of those interred reads like a Who's Who of the 19th cen-tury, including artists Nathaniel Currier, James Merrit Ives, and Louis Comfort Tiffany; Governor De Witt Clinton; William Marcy "Boss" Tweed; piano manufacturer Henry Engelhard Stein-way; newspaper king Horace Greeley; abolitionist minister Henry Ward Beecher; and inventors Samuel F. B. Morse (telegraph), Peter Cooper (steam locomotive), and Elias Howe (sewing machine). Green-Wood still operates as a full-service, nonsectarian, nonprofit cemetery; composer/conductor Leonard Bernstein was laid to rest here in 1990. For information on two-hour walking tours on Sunday in spring and fall, call the cemetery or visit its Web site. *Main Gate: 5th Ave. and 25th St., 718/768–7300, www.green-wood.com. Daily 8–4. Subway: J, M to 25th St.*

4 *g-5*

OLD GRAVESEND CEMETERY
Founded in 1643, this burial ground served the people of Gravesend, one of six original 17th-century towns in Brook-lyn. While the other towns were Dutch, Gravesend was founded by English Anabaptists fleeing religious persecu-tion in New England. Their leader was a woman, Lady Deborah Moody, and

though her grave is no longer marked, it lies here somewhere among the aging gravestones. *Gravesend Neck Rd., between McDonald Ave. and Van Siclen St. Subway: F, N to Ave. U.*

manhattan

10 *e-5*

AFRICAN BURIAL GROUND
In 1991, construction workers discov-ered that the area they were excavating, just two blocks north of City Hall, held the unmarked graves of thousands of 17th- and 18th-century African-Ameri-cans. Now designated a National His-toric Landmark, this long-forgotten burial ground honors some of the city's earliest residents and serves as a reminder that slavery was legal in New York City from 1626 to 1827. *Just off Duane St. near Federal Plaza, Lower Manhattan. Subway: 1, 2, 3 to Chambers St.; 4, 5, 6 to Brooklyn Bridge/City Hall.*

10 *f-5*

FIRST SHEARITH ISRAEL GRAVEYARD
Dating from its members' arrival from Brazil in 1654, the Congregation Beth Shearith is the oldest Jewish congrega-tion in America. Tucked into present-day Chinatown, this small graveyard is the earliest surviving burial ground of these Sephardic Jews. The graveyard was consecrated in 1656, and the oldest remaining gravestone is dated 1683; the newest dates from 1828. *St. James Pl. (between Oliver and James Sts.), Lower Manhattan. Subway: 4, 5, 6 to Brooklyn Bridge/City Hall.*

11 *g-3*

NEW YORK CITY MARBLE CEMETERY
The markers and headstones in this pri-vate East Village cemetery (opened in 1832) can be viewed from the sidewalk through a handsome iron fence. Ship-ping merchant Preserved Fish (his real name) and James Henry Roosevelt (the founder of Roosevelt Hospital) are among those buried here. *52–74 E. 2nd St. (between 1st and 2nd Aves.), East Village, www.nycmc.org. Subway: F, V to 2nd Ave.*

11 *g-3*

NEW YORK MARBLE CEMETERY
Opened in the East Village in 1830, this was Manhattan's first nonsectarian

graveyard and offered prominent New Yorkers an opportunity for burial in what was then a fashionable area. Among the 156 New Yorkers buried below ground in Tuckahoe marble vaults are members of the Scribner, Hoyt, Varick, and Beekman families. Instead of headstones, tablets on the brick wall serve as the only markers. The cemetery is closed to the public, but is visible from its gates. *Entrance on 2nd Ave. between 2nd and 3rd Sts., East Village, www.marblecemetery.org. Subway: F, V to 2nd Ave.*

11 *f-4*

OLD ST. PATRICK'S CEMETERY

On a quiet street in Little Italy next to Old St. Patrick's Cathedral, a 9-ft brick wall hides most of this churchyard from view. The crypt beneath the church holds the remains of two of New York's early bishops, as well as some of the country's first Irish-Catholic settlers. (The high wall and underground burials were a prudent response to anti-Catholic vandalism and, occasionally, violence.) The earliest graves date from 1804. The remains of Pierre Toussaint (1766–1863) were exhumed in the early 1990s and sent to the Vatican, a step toward the successful canonization of the former slave famous for his acts of charity. (*See* Old St. Patrick's Cathedral *in* Churches & Synagogues, *above.*) *Mulberry St. (between Prince and Houston Sts.), SoHo. Subway: N, Q, R, W to Prince St.*

10 *f-1*

ST. MARK'S IN-THE-BOWERY EAST & WEST YARDS

The former site of Peter Stuyvesant's country chapel, this peaceful graveyard has been covered over by cobblestones, but some memorial tablets and markers are still visible. Stuyvesant himself is buried in a crypt beneath the church. The East Yard is now a children's play area. (*See* St. Mark's Church in-the-Bowery *in* Churches & Synagogues, *above.*) *2nd Ave. and 10th St., East Village. Subway: 6 to Astor Pl.; L to 3rd Ave.*

10 *e-6*

ST. PAUL'S CHURCHYARD

Dating from the mid- to late 18th century, St. Paul's churchyard, with its tumble of blackened headstones, offers a pleasant, albeit somber, spot to reflect upon the city's past in the shadow of modern life: the the financial district towers above—and the contrast is pow-

erful. (*See* St. Paul's Chapel *in* Churches & Synagogues, *above.*) *Broadway and Fulton St., Lower Manhattan. Subway: 2, 3, 4, 5 to Fulton St.*

10 *d-1*

SECOND SHEARITH ISRAEL GRAVEYARD

Active from 1805 until 1829, the original burial ground was reduced and made triangular by the laying out of West 11th Street, making this the smallest surviving graveyard in Manhattan. The displaced graves were moved to the congregation's third cemetery, on West 21st Street. *72–76 W. 11th St. (between 5th and 6th Aves.), Greenwich Village. Subway: F, V to 14th St.*

9 *d-8*

THIRD SHEARITH ISRAEL GRAVEYARD

The northernmost burial ground of the Congregation Shearith Israel, this picturesque little graveyard, used 1829–51, is now surrounded by buildings. *W. 21st St. between 6th and 7th Aves., Chelsea. Subway: 1, 2, F, V to 23rd St.*

6 *c-5*

TRINITY CEMETERY

Once part of the farm belonging to artist and naturalist John James Audubon, who is buried here, Trinity Cemetery became the rural burial place for Wall Street's Trinity Church in 1842. In an uncrowded area of Upper Manhattan next to the Church of the Intercession, rural peace still prevails on these grounds, which climb from the Hudson River up to Amsterdam Avenue. Among those buried here are John Jacob Astor; Eliza Brown Jumel, once owner of the Morris Jumel Mansion; and Clement Clarke Moore, author of "A Visit from St. Nicholas." (*See* Church of the Intercession *in* Churches & Synagogues, *above.*) *153rd–155th Sts. (between Riverside Dr. and Amsterdam Ave.), Washington Heights, 212/368-1600. Daily 9–4:30. Subway: 1 to 157th St.*

10 *e-7*

TRINITY CHURCH GRAVEYARD

The oldest stone in this 2½-acre graveyard is dated 1681, predating the church and making it Manhattan's earliest burial ground. Here beneath the trees are Alexander Hamilton; Robert Fulton, the inventor of the steamboat; William Brad-

ford, the editor of New York City's first
newspaper; and Captain James Lawrence,
the War of 1812 hero who exhorted,
"Don't give up the ship!" Also of note is
the Martyr's Monument, honoring the
rebel soldiers who died imprisoned at the
old sugar house on nearby Liberty Street
during the American Revolution. At the
north end of the cemetery, a faded stone
reads "Hark from tombs a doleful sound
/ Mine ears attend the cry / Ye living men
come view the ground / Where you must
shortly lie." (*See* Trinity Church *in*
Churches & Synagogues, *above.*) *Broadway and Wall St., Lower Manhattan, 212/
602–0872. Weekdays 7–3:45, Sat. 8–4, Sun.
7–4. Subway: 4, 5 to Wall St.*

queens

8 *d-2*

LAWRENCE FAMILY GRAVEYARD
The distinguished Lawrence family, relatives of George Washington, first settled
in Queens in 1664. Their private burial
ground spans an incredible 272 years of
family history, with the earliest of 89
graves dated 1703 and the last dated
1975. *20th Rd. and 35th St. Subway: N to
Ditmars Blvd.*

1 *g-3*

LAWRENCE MEMORIAL PARK
A second Lawrence-family graveyard,
first used in 1832, contains the remains
of a New York City mayor, Cornelius W.
Lawrence, and a Native American
named Moccasin, who was given the
first name Lawrence and buried with the
family. *216th St. and 42nd Ave. Subway: F
to 179th St./Jamaica.*

staten island

1 *b-2*

MORAVIAN CEMETERY
Best known as the site of a million-dol-
lar mausoleum (1866) designed by
Richard Morris Hunt and landscaped by
Frederick Law Olmsted for railroad
tycoon Cornelius Vanderbilt and his
family, the Moravian Cemetery covers 80
green, terraced acres, with the earliest
grave dating back to 1740. *Richmond Rd.
at Otis Ave. (between Todt Hill Rd.
and Altamont), 718/351–0136, www.
moraviancemetery.com. Daily 8–4. From
Staten Island Ferry terminal, take the train
to the Grant City stop and walk north on
Lincoln Ave.*

1 *a-3*

SLEIGHT FAMILY GRAVEYARD
Also known as the Rossville or Blazing
Star Burial Ground, this was originally a
family plot and later served the entire
village of Rossville. The graveyard was in
use from 1750 to 1850; many of Staten
Island's early settlers are buried here.
*Arthur Kill Rd. at Rossville Ave. From
Staten Island Ferry, take Bus S74 to
Rossville.*

1 *b-2*

VAN PELT–REZEAU CEMETERY
A homestead burial plot containing five
generations of the Van Pelt–Rezeau families, this private cemetery (begun circa
1780) is on the grounds of Historic
Richmondtown. (*See* Historic Richmondtown *in* Historic Structures &
Streets, *below.*) *Tysen Court, Historic
Richmondtown (441 Clark Ave.), 718/351–
1611. From Staten Island Ferry, take Bus
S74 to Historic Richmondtown.*

HAUNTED PLACES
Some people just can't get enough of
New York. The spirits of former city
dwellers, from termagant tenants to
debauched bawds, are believed to
specter throughout Manhattan, rent-
free, harassing its current denizens.

9 *c-1*

THE DAKOTA
The Dakota luxury apartment building,
with the severe miasma of a mad French
marquis's torture castle, was the setting
for Roman Polanski's film *Rosemary's
Baby.* John Lennon was murdered just
outside the 72nd Street entrance in
1980. (*See* Historic Structures &
Streets.) *1 W. 72nd St., Upper West Side.
Subway: B, C to 72nd St.*

10 *b-1*

JANE STREET, GREENWICH VILLAGE
On this seemingly tranquil stretch of
posh, residential Greenwich Village wan-
ders the ghost of founding father
Alexander Hamilton, no doubt restless
after dying here following a duel with
Vice President Aaron Burr. Hamilton
most commonly makes his presence
known by flicking lights and flushing toilets; according to Jane Street residents,

he's fascinated by modern technology. Of course, Jane Street residents are known for tales—this street claims more writers than any other in New York City. *Jane St., between Hudson and Washington Sts., Greenwich Village. Subway: A, C, E, L to 14th St./8th Ave.*

11 *f-2*

OLD MERCHANT'S HOUSE

Once owned by the wealthy merchant Seabury Tredwell, this house is said to be haunted by a lovely young woman in 19th-century dress. She is assumed to be Tredwell's daughter, Gertrude, who became a solitary recluse following a romance thwarted by her father. She lived in the house 93 years, until 1933; the house became a museum in 1936, and shows off the family furnishings. *29 E. 4th St., East Village. Subway: N, Q, R, W to 8th St.; 6 to Astor Pl.*

11 *g-1*

ST. MARK'S CHURCH IN-THE-BOWERY

Seventeenth-century Dutch governor Peter Stuyvesant once owned this land, and he's buried under a bust in the church lawn. Worshippers have occasionally been disturbed by a strange tapping, which the psychically attuned have identified as the sound of the old governor angrily approaching on his peg leg. (*See* Churches & Synagogues, *above.*) *2nd Ave. and E. 10th St., East Village. Subway: 6 to Astor Pl.; L to 3rd Ave.*

11 *d-2*

WASHINGTON SQUARE

This former potter's field is estimated to have housed the graves of some 20,000 impoverished souls and executed convicts. An old elm tree that still stands in the park's northwest corner was once known as the "Hanging Elm"; public hangings took place here until 1819. *Between 4th St. and Waverly Pl. and University Pl. and MacDougal St., Greenwich Village. Subway: A, B, C, D, E, F, V to W. 4 St.; N, Q, R, W to 8th St.*

11 *a-1*

WHITEHORSE TAVERN

"Do not go gentle into that good night," wrote Dylan Thomas—and perhaps heeding his own verse, the Welsh poet died after downing close to 20 shots of scotch at this Greenwich Village hangout in 1953. Regulars say that his ghost still drops in late at night, when the cheerier patrons of this venerable watering hole have abandoned the table beneath his portrait. There he sits alone, drinking and scribbling away long past closing. *567 Hudson St. (at 11 St.), Greenwich Village. Subway: A, C, E, L to 14 St./8th Ave.*

HISTORIC STRUCTURES & STREETS

New York City's architecture and layout are deeply layered in history, ranging from the days of Dutch rule over Nieuw Amsterdam and the American Revolution to the gaslit era and the late 19th and early 20th centuries, when waves of European immigrants transformed the city's neighborhoods.

The **Metropolitan Historic Structures Association** is a coalition of 70 small history museums, including historic houses, religious sites, military sites, and historical societies. Call the association for information on historic sites throughout the five boroughs or for workshops on preserving historic buildings and their interiors. *212/685–9723.*

bronx

2 *f-2*

BARTOW-PELL MANSION

This mansion, built in 1841, was once owned by the Lords of the Manor of Pelham. A renovation enlarged and modified the house in a trim Federal style. The grounds feature attractive formal gardens, the Pell family plot, and a view of Long Island Sound. The interior rooms, a city landmark, are filled with rare period furnishings. *895 Shore Rd., Pelham Bay Park, 718/885–1461. $2.50 adults, $1.25 students and seniors. Sept.–July, Wed. and weekends noon–4. Call for directions.*

2 *h-3*

CITY ISLAND

A narrow, 230-acre island with a salty, New England flavor, City Island is just off the Bronx shore, attached to the mainland by a single narrow bridge. You'll find weathered bungalows, Victorian houses, boatyards, seafood restaurants, and sea breezes. *Subway: 6 to Pelham Bay Park, then BX29 bus to City Island Ave.*

2 c-4
LORILLARD SNUFF MILL
Built on the Bronx River in 1840 by the Lorillard tobacco family, this fieldstone building was originally a mill used to grind snuff. Today it's part of the New York Botanical Garden (see Botanical Gardens in Chapter 3), at the edge of a shady, green woodland. *New York Botanical Garden, Bronx Park, www.nybg.org. Subway: 4, D to Bedford Park Blvd.*

5 f-4
POE COTTAGE
Built in 1812, this little cottage was the home of Edgar Allan Poe and his consumptive young wife, Virginia, from 1846 to 1849. Here, Poe wrote such haunting works as "Annabelle Lee" and "The Bells." The site is administered by the Bronx Historical Society. *2640 Grand Concourse (at E. Kingsbridge Rd.), Fordham, 718/881–8900, www. bronxhistoricalsociety.org. $2. Mid-Jan.– mid-Dec., Sat. 10–4 and Sun. 1–5. Subway: 4, D to Kingsbridge Rd.*

5 g-1
VALENTINE-VARIAN HOUSE (BRONX COUNTY HISTORICAL SOCIETY MUSEUM)
Dating from 1758, this pre-Revolution fieldstone farmhouse now serves as a museum of local history. *3266 Bainbridge Ave. (between Van Cortlandt Ave. and 208th St.), Norwood, 718/881–8900, www.bronxhistoricalsociety.org. $2, free for children under 12. Sat. 10–4 and Sun. 1–5. Subway: D to 205th St.*

2 b-3
VAN CORTLANDT MANSION
Built in 1748, this Georgian-style, fieldstone manor house was Washington's headquarters at various times during the American Revolution. The interior houses a wealth of colonial artifacts and furnishings. *Van Cortlandt Park (Broadway north of 242nd St.), Riverdale, 718/ 543–3344, www.vancortlandthouse.org. $2, $1.50 seniors and students, free for children under 12. Tues.–Fri. 10–3, weekends 11–4. Subway: 1 to 242nd St./Van Cortlandt Park.*

brooklyn

4 f-2
ALBEMARLE-KENMORE TERRACES HISTORIC DISTRICT
In the heart of Flatbush, behind the Flatbush Dutch Reformed Church (see Churches & Synagogues, above), these two attractive dead-end streets are lined with landmark Georgian revival row houses and arts-and-crafts–revival cottages built 1916–20. *South of Church Ave. and east of 21st St. between Flatbush and Ocean Aves. Subway: 2, 5 to Church Ave.*

3 c-8
BROOKLYN HEIGHTS
Called Ihpetonga (high, sandy bank) by the Canarsie Indians, Brooklyn Heights sits high on a bluff above the East River. Its airy location attracted 19th-century financiers to build their mansions here—they could take the Fulton Ferry to their jobs on Wall Street—and today its 50 blocks of incredibly rich 19th-century architecture are among the best-preserved in the city. Almost every block has some kind of architectural gem; try wandering down Columbia Heights, Pierrepont Street, Joralemon Street, and Willow Place in particular. Save time at the end of your stroll for the Brooklyn Heights Promenade, with its breathtaking vista of the downtown-Manhattan skyline (see Viewpoints, below). *Bordered roughly by the East River (the Promenade), Atlantic Ave., Cadman Plaza W, and the Brooklyn Bridge. Subway: N, Q, R, W, 4 to Court St./Borough Hall; 2, 3 to Clark St.; A, C, F to Jay St./Borough Hall.*

12 f-3
FT. GREENE–CLINTON HILL HISTORIC DISTRICT
Small, quality restaurants, trendy but low-key bars, and shady avenues of remarkable residential architecture fill these pleasant neighborhoods. Ft. Greene, north of downtown Brooklyn, boasts impeccable mid-19th century brownstones and is home to Brooklyn Academy of Music, the country's oldest performing arts theater. North of Ft. Greene, little Clinton Hill is home to Pratt Institute, a prestigious art college, and is lined with well-maintained former mansions along Clinton and Washington Avenues. *Bordered roughly by Fulton St. to the south, Myrtle Ave. to the north, Ashland Pl. to the west, and Washington*

Ave. to the east. Subway: C to Lafayette
Ave.; G to Clinton-Washington.

12 b-4
GRACE COURT ALLEY
A charming mews, this was once the
stable alley for mansions on neighboring Remsen and Joralemon streets.
Today, those stables and brownstone
carriage houses are luxury homes. *East
of Hicks St. (between Joralemon and Remsen Sts.), Brooklyn Heights. Subway: 2, 3,
4, N, R to Court St./Borough Hall.*

12 h-5
GRAND ARMY PLAZA
(Frederick Law Olmsted and Calvert
Vaux, 1870) Grand is indeed the word for
this Park Slope plaza, designed in the
spirit of L'Etoile (a.k.a. Place Charles-de-
Gaulle) in Paris. At its center is the 80-ft-
tall Soldiers and Sailors Memorial Arch
(1892), reminiscent of the Arc de Triomphe, with enormous bronze sculptures
honoring the Union Army's efforts in the
Civil War. The Plaza is a fitting entry to
Brooklyn's beloved Prospect Park (*see
Parks in Chapter 3). Intersection of Flatbush Ave., Prospect Park W, Eastern Pkwy.,
and Vanderbilt Ave. Subway: 2, 3 to Grand
Army Plaza; D to 7th Ave.*

12 c-4
JENNIE JEROME HOUSE
Tucked away in Cobble Hill, this old
Greek revival was the birthplace of Jennie Jerome on January 9, 1854. While
Jerome Avenue in the Bronx is named
after her father, financier Leonard
Jerome, Jennie herself became better
known for marrying a British lord and
becoming the mother of Winston
Churchill. *197 Amity St. (between Clinton
and Court Sts.). Subway: F to Bergen St.*

4 f-1
LEFFERTS HOMESTEAD
A Dutch colonial farmhouse built in 1783
on Flatbush Avenue, the Lefferts Homestead was moved to its current Prospect
Park location in 1918. Today it's a historic museum geared toward children,
with reproductions of period furnishings. Next door is a painstakingly
restored 1912 carousel that operates on
weekends. *Prospect Park, Flatbush Ave.
at Empire Blvd., 718/789-2822,
www.prospectpark.org. Free. May–June,
Thurs.–Fri. 1–4 and weekends 1–5; July–
Aug., Wed.–Fri. 1–4, weekends 1–5. Subway: F to 15th St./Prospect Park.*

12 h-7
LITCHFIELD VILLA
(Alexander Jackson Davis, 1857) A
romantic Italianate pile built for railroad
baron Edwin C. Litchfield, the villa was
once the heart of a vast estate that took
in virtually all of present-day Park Slope.
It now serves as the Department of
Parks and Recreation's Brooklyn headquarters. *Prospect Park, Prospect Park W
between 4th and 5th Sts., Park Slope, 718/
789-2822, www.prospectpark.org. Subway:
2, 3 to Grand Army Plaza; D, Q to 7th
Ave.; F to 7th Ave.*

12 b-2
MIDDAGH STREET
One of the first streets laid out in Brooklyn Heights (circa 1817), Middagh Street
retains some of its oldest houses, many
made from wood. Take particular note of
No. 24 (1824), a gambrel-roof Federal
house—one of the finest in the city.
*Between northern ends of Willow and
Hicks Sts., Brooklyn Heights. Subway: 2, 3
to Clark St.; A, C to High St./Brooklyn
Bridge.*

12 b-3
MONTAGUE TERRACE
This delightful stretch of English-style
row houses was built in 1886 and has
been wonderfully preserved. In the 1930s,
novelist Thomas Wolfe lived at No. 5,
where he wrote *You Can't Go Home
Again. Montague Terr. (between Remsen
and Montague Sts.), Brooklyn Heights.
Subway: J, M, 2, 3, 4 to Court St./Borough
Hall; A, C, F to Jay St./Borough Hall.*

12 f-6
OLD STONE HOUSE
(VECHTE-CORTELYOU
HOUSE)
A 1935 reproduction of a house built in
1699 at this site, the Old Stone House is
a center for historic walks and activities
focusing on Brooklyn's role in the Revolutionary War. Some of the most heated
fighting of the Battle of Long Island in
1776 took place nearby. *3rd St. and 5th
Ave., Park Slope. Subway: F to 4th Ave.*

4 e-1
PARK SLOPE
HISTORIC DISTRICT
Covering more than 30 blocks, this
beautiful, tree-lined residential area contains 1,900 structures of architectural
interest, including some of the finest
Queen Anne and Romanesque revival

homes in the nation. Don't miss the dazzling 1880s and '90s gems on Montgomery Place and Carroll Street just below Prospect Park, or the palazzolike Montauk Club, at Lincoln Place and 8th Avenue, with its friezes depicting the history of the Montauk Indians. Prospect Park itself, designed by Frederick Law Olmsted and Calvert Vaux (the same pair who designed Central Park) is a triumph of landscape design; Olmsted and Vaux openly preferred it to Central Park. (See Parks in Chapter 3.) *Prospect Park W to as far as 6th Ave. from Grand Army Plaza to Bartel Pritchard Sq. (15th St.). Subway: 2, 3 to Grand Army Plaza; D, F, Q to 7th Ave.*

1 *f-7*
SHEEPSHEAD BAY
A small but active fishing port, Sheepshead Bay is best known for its fleet of "party boats," which whisk anglers to secret fishing holes out in the ocean. This salty old neighborhood is also known for its seafood restaurants, the preeminent of which—Lundy's—reopened a few years ago with much fanfare. *Emmons Ave. from Knapp St. to Shore Ave. Subway: D to Sheepshead Bay.*

4 *h-3*
VAN NUYSE HOUSE (COE HOUSE)
When the Dutch first settled New York, the southern part of Brooklyn was prime farmland. Sections of this landmark Dutch house date back to 1744, when it was part of Joost and Elizabeth Van Nuyse's 85-acre farm. *1128 E. 34th St. (between Flatbush Ave. and Ave. J). Subway: 2, 5 to Flatbush Ave.*

4 *g-3*
VAN NUYSE—MAGAW HOUSE
A Dutch colonial house from around 1800, this gambrel-roof structure was transported to its present site in 1916 to ensure permanent preservation. *1041 E. 22nd St. (between Aves. I and J), Midwood. Subway: D to Ave. J.*

4 *h-4*
WYCKOFF-BENNETT HOUSE
Built around 1766, complete with little dormers and a six-column porch, this house is considered Brooklyn's finest example of Dutch colonial architecture. Two glass windowpanes are etched with the name and rank of two Hessian soldiers quartered here during the Revolu-

tion. *1669 E. 22nd St. (at Kings Hwy.). Subway: D to Kings Hwy.*

manhattan

9 *d-2*
THE ARSENAL
(Martin E. Thompson, 1848) Predating the completion of Central Park itself by 10 years, this brick fortress was originally built to house the state's cache of artillery and ammunition. Troops were then quartered here during the Civil War. Over the years, the Arsenal has served variously as a police station and the original home of the American Museum of Natural History; today it houses the main offices of the city's Department of Parks and Recreation. *Central Park, 5th Ave. and 64th St., Upper East Side. Gallery open weekdays 9–4:30. Free. Subway: 6 to 68th St./Hunter College.*

6 *b-5*
AUDUBON TERRACE HISTORIC DISTRICT
Originally part of the estate belonging to artist and naturalist John James Audubon, Audubon Terrace was turned into a cultural center in 1908 by philanthropist Archer M. Huntington and his cousin, architect Charles Pratt Huntington. Several cultural institutions, all designed in the Italian Renaissance style, surround a small plaza; they include the American Numismatic Society, with a collection of coins dating from ancient times to the present; the Hispanic Society of America; and the American Academy of Arts & Letters. (See Art Museums, above.) *Broadway between 155th and 156th Sts., Washington Heights. Subway: 1 to 157th St.; A, C to 155th St.*

9 *g-4*
BEEKMAN PLACE
A retreat from Manhattan's chaos, this charming and exclusive two-block street on a bluff overlooking the East River is one of New York's almost-hidden treasures. Town-house residents have included Irving Berlin, Ethel Barrymore, and the Rockefellers. *East of (and parallel to) 1st Ave., from 49th to 51st Sts. Subway: 6 to 51st St./Lexington Ave.; E, V to Lexington–3rd Aves./53rd St.*

11 *f-3*
BOUWERIE LANE THEATRE
(Henry Englebert, 1874) Originally the Bond Street Savings Bank, and later the

German Exchange Bank (catering to the neighborhood's many German immigrants), this unusual cast-iron building is in the French Second Empire style, with paired Corinthian and Ionic columns running up the facade. It's currently an off-off-Broadway playhouse and the home of the well-respected Jean Cocteau Repertory Company. *330 Bowery (at 2nd St.—a.k.a. Bond St.), East Village, 212/677–0060, www.jeancocteaurep.org. Subway: 6 to Astor Pl.; F, V to 2nd Ave.*

9 d-3
CARNEGIE HALL
(William B. Tuthill, 1891) Built by steel magnate–cum–philanthropist Andrew Carnegie, this world-famous music hall opened in 1891 with a concert conducted by Tchaikovsky. Since then it has seen the likes of Leonard Bernstein, Isaac Stern, Yo-Yo Ma, the Beatles, and countless other stars. Hour-long tours are full of history and backstage anecdotes. And the free Rose Museum just around the corner (881 7th Ave.) holds memorabilia from Carnegie Hall's illustrious past, including photos of Maria Callas, Benny Goodman's clarinet, and a baton used by Arturo Toscanini. (*See Performance Venues in Chapter 5.*) *154 W. 57th St. (at 7th Ave.), Midtown West, 212/247–7800, www.carnegiehall.org. Tours mid-Sept.–June, Mon., Tues., Thurs., Fri. at 11:30, 2, and 3. Museum open mid-Sept.–mid-July, Thurs.–Tues. 11–4:30. Tours $6. Subway: N, Q, R, W to 57th St.; B, D, E to 7th Ave.*

10 e-8
CASTLE CLINTON NATIONAL MONUMENT
(John McComb, Jr., 1807–11) This circular brownstone fortress in Battery Park was first built as a defense for New York Harbor, in preparation for the War of 1812. Originally sited on an island 200 ft from shore, it was eventually connected to Lower Manhattan by landfill. The U.S. government gave the old fort to the city in 1823 and it successively became Castle Garden, an enormously popular concert hall where impresario P. T. Barnum presented "Swedish nightingale" Jenny Lind in 1850; the Emigrant Landing Depot, 1855–90, where 8 million of New York's immigrants were processed before the opening of Ellis Island; and then, until 1941, the city's first aquarium. Today Castle Clinton houses a small museum, as well as the ticket office for ferries to the Statue of Liberty

and Ellis Island. (*See Parks in Chapter 3.*) *Battery Park (State St. and Battery Pl.), Lower Manhattan, 212/344–7220, www.nps.gov/cacl. Daily 8–4:30. Free. Subway: 4, 5 to Bowling Green.*

11 c-5
CHARLTON-KING-VANDAM HISTORIC DISTRICT
Below Houston Street on the west side between MacDougal and Varick streets is the city's finest concentration of Federal-style row houses (characterized by red brick, high stoops, narrow dormers, and leaded-glass windows). Now surrounded by large commercial buildings, this area belonged originally to Aaron Burr and later to John Jacob Astor. Walking down these streets is like stumbling upon the turn of the 19th century. *9–43 and 20–42 Charlton St.; 1–49 and 16–54 King St.; 9–29 Vandam St.; 43–51 MacDougal St., Greenwich Village. Subway: 1, 2 to Houston St.*

9 b-8
CHELSEA HISTORIC DISTRICT
Composed mainly of land from the estate of Clement Clark Moore, an influential 19th-century clergyman and the author of "A Visit from St. Nicholas" (better known as " 'Twas the Night Before Christmas"), Chelsea was developed on Moore's plan between 1825 and 1860. Among the lovely buildings here are Greek revival row houses (the best of which are on West 20th Street's "Cushman Row," named for Moore's friend Don Alonzo Cushman, dry-goods merchant); 1890s apartment buildings; St. Peter's Episcopal Church (*see Churches & Synagogues, above*); and the block-long, high-fenced General Theological Seminary, which has a redbrick-and-brownstone campus accessible to the public from 175 9th Avenue. While not part of the historic district, Chelsea west of 10th Avenue, from about 20th to 28th streets, is considered the world art gallery headquarters. *8th–10th Aves. from 20th to 22th Sts. Subway: A, C, E to 23rd St.*

9 c-8
CHELSEA HOTEL
(Hubert, Pirsson & Co., 1884) Constructed of red brick with intricate wrought-iron balconies, this 12-story literary landmark began life as a cooperative apartment house in the late 19th century. In 1905 it became a hotel catering to long-term tenants and attracted

many famous authors, artists, and musicians, including Thomas Wolfe, Dylan Thomas, O. Henry, Mark Twain, Vladimir Nabokov, Tennessee Williams, Arthur Miller, and William S. Burroughs. The list even includes punk-rock star Sid Vicious, who allegedly stabbed his girlfriend Nancy Spungen to death here. (*See* Moderately Priced Lodgings *in* Chapter 6.) *222 W. 23rd St. (between 7th and 8th Aves.), Chelsea. Subway: 1, 2, A, C, E to 23rd St.*

10 *f-4*
CHINATOWN
Traditionally contained within Canal, Worth, and Mulberry streets; the Bowery; and Chatham Square, Chinatown has recently expanded on all sides due to an influx of new immigrants and capital, primarily from Hong Kong. A feast for the senses—full of tea and rice shops, Asian vegetable stands, and Chinese apothecaries—this bustling enclave has been the heart of New York's Chinese immigrant community since the mid-1800s. Chinatown's residents originally hailed mainly from the province of Canton but today are highly diverse, a fact reflected in the multiple dialects spoken, the seven different Chinese newspapers, and cuisine ranging from Hunan and Szechuan to Mandarin, Shanghai, and Southeast Asian. For restaurant selections, *see* Chinese *in* Chapter 1. *Subway: 6, J, M, N, Q, R, W, Z to Canal St.*

10 *e-6*
CITY HALL
(Mangin and McComb, 1802–1811) A surprisingly diminutive building, City Hall has been the seat of city government since 1811. Its architecture is Federal, enriched by French Renaissance detailing. The interior is striking: The main entrance opens into a dome rotunda with a graceful twin stairway that curves upward to second-floor rooms containing original 19th-century furnishings and portraits. Because security is tight, however, it is not always possible to get a peek inside. *City Hall Park, Broadway and Park Row. Subway: 4, 5, 6 to Brooklyn Bridge/City Hall.*

10 *g-5*
WILLIAM CLARK HOUSE
A superb, four-story Federal structure dating from 1824, this house was built for grocer William Clark and his wife,

Rosamond, and still has its original fan-lit entrance and window lintels. *51 Market St. (between Monroe and Madison Sts.), Lower East Side. Subway: F to E. Broadway.*

11 *f-2*
COLONNADE ROW (LA GRANGE TERRACE)
(Attributed to Alexander Jackson Davis, 1833) Across from Joseph Papp's Public Theater are four survivors of nine original Greek revival town houses that were the most coveted addresses in New York in their day. For a few years in the 1830s and '40s, these now-dilapidated marble buildings, lined by a patrician row of Corinthian columns, housed New York's elite—John Jacob Astor, Cornelius Vanderbilt, and Warren Delano (FDR's grandpa)—before the millionaires moved en masse to spanking-new 5th Avenue mansions. *428–434 Lafayette St. (between Astor Pl. and E. 4th St.), East Village. Subway: 6 to Astor Pl.; N, Q, R, W to 8th St.*

10 *f-2*
COOPER UNION
(Frederick A. Peterson, 1859) An enormous, Italianate brownstone with high-arch windows, this is the oldest building in America framed with steel beams. The beams—actually railroad rails—were provided by the college's benefactor, the 19th-century inventor and steel magnate Peter Cooper (whose statue dominates neighboring Cooper Square), who founded the school to provide free technical education to the working class. Cooper Union remains a tuition-free private college to this day—one of the city's best for architecture, design, and engineering. In 1860, Abraham Lincoln delivered his famous "Might Makes Right" speech here, which catapulted him into the White House. *7th St. between 4th Ave. and Bowery, East Village. Subway: 6 to Astor Pl.; N, Q, R, W to 8th St.*

9 *c-1*
THE DAKOTA
(Henry J. Hardenbergh, 1884) Built by Singer Sewing Machine heir Edward Clark amid rundown farms and shanties, New York's first luxury apartment house was initially criticized for being as remote as the "Dakotas in Indian territory." Though it's difficult to imagine now, the Dakota's severe trian-

gular turrets loomed alone, like a provincial castle, when it first went up on the edge of Central Park. In the end, of course, the Dakota became a prestigious address and served as a sort of grand cornerstone for the Upper West Side. Lauren Bacall, Boris Karloff, Rudolf Nureyev, Leonard Bernstein, Rosemary Clooney, and Gilda Radner all called the Dakota home, as did John Lennon, who was murdered outside by a "fan" on December 8, 1980. (See Haunted Places, above.) *1 W. 72 St., Upper West Side. Subway: B, C to 72nd St.*

9 d-4
DIAMOND & JEWELRY WAY

This is really the only street in America that comes close to being paved with gold. Eighty percent of all the diamonds in the country are bought and sold here, mainly by Hasidic Jews, who can sometimes be seen walking around with gem-packed briefcases handcuffed to their arms. Before World War II, the diamond district was on the Lower East Side, but, following the money, it eventually moved uptown. Lined with slightly retro jewelry stores, West 47th Street glimmers with activity on weekdays. *W. 47th St. between 5th and 6th Aves., Midtown West. Subway: B, D, F, V to 47th–50th Sts./Rockefeller Center; E, V to 5th Ave./53rd St.*

5 b-6
DYCKMAN FARMHOUSE MUSEUM

This gambrel-roof fieldstone building is the only 18th-century Dutch farmhouse still standing in Manhattan. Built in 1785, it was restored and furnished with Dutch and English colonial antiques and now serves as a museum of Dutch New York. *4881 Broadway (at W. 204th St.), Inwood, 212/304–9422. Tues.–Sun. 11–4. Subway: 1 to 207th St./Inwood.*

3 c-6
EAST VILLAGE

For a short time in the 1820s and 1830s, the East Village was aristocratic; later in the century, it housed a large German community; at the turn of the century, it was an extension of the Lower East Side, packed with Eastern Europeans; in the 1960s, hippies and flower children put the area on the wider cultural map; and in the 1970s and 1980s it was the capital of the punk rock music scene. Architecture and business reflecting all of these eras remain in this multi-ethnic neighborhood; in fact, it's the human fauna that give the neighborhood it's greatest appeal: fresh-faced NYU students with tattoos, gay lovers, aging Hells Angels, and former Mayor Ed Koch can often be found dining harmoniously at local restaurants that serve everything from kielbasa to lamb curry. *Houston–14th Sts., from Broadway to East River. Subway: 6 to Astor Pl.; 6 to Bleecker St.; L to 1st Ave. or 3rd Ave.; F, V to 2nd Ave.*

4 a-2
ELLIS ISLAND NATIONAL MONUMENT

(Boring & Tilton, 1898; restored 1990) Ellis Island was the first glimpse of America for more than 17 million European immigrants, from 1892 to 1954. Long abandoned, its buildings underwent an extraordinary restoration in the 1980s, and reopened in 1990 as the Ellis Island Immigration Museum—now one of the city's busiest tourist attractions. Through the magnificent Victorian Great Hall; the enormous Registry Hall; the Baggage Room; and the Ticket Office, visitors can retrace the steps of their immigrant forebears. The major exhibits—including historic photographs, documentary films, and audio tapes of immigrants' reminiscences—are poignant reminders of many Americans' roots. It's estimated that more than 40% of U.S. citizens have ancestors who passed through here. The island's Wall of Honor, overlooking the Statue of Liberty, is inscribed with the names of more than 400,000 immigrants. *Ferries to Ellis Island depart from Battery Park, Lower Manhattan, 212/269–5755 ferry information, www.statueoflibertyferry.com. $8 adults, $6 seniors, $3 children 3–17. Departures: Daily every 20 min 8:30–4:30. Subway: 4, 5 to Bowling Green.*

10 d-1
ENGLISH TERRACE ROW

(James Renwick, Jr., 1856–58) When the Dutch settled New Amsterdam, they brought their architectural styles with them, and one of the most enduring was the "stoop," a high stairway leading up to the front door. The stoop has become a fixture on New York brownstones and row houses, serving as a playground for children and a front porch for adults. These elegant homes on West 10th Street, however, were modeled on the English style—they were the first houses in the city without stoops, and their front doors are a mere two steps up from the sidewalk. *20–38 W. 10th St. (between 5th and 6th Aves.), Greenwich Village. Subway: N, Q, R, W to 8th St.; A, B, C, D, E, F, V to West 4th St./Washington Sq.*

10 *e-7*

FEDERAL HALL
NATIONAL MEMORIAL

(Town & Davis, 1842) Just up the street from the New York Stock Exchange, this imposing Greek revival building occupies one of the most historic sites in the city. Originally the site of New York's second city hall, Federal Hall later served as the nation's capital, in which the Bill of Rights was adopted and George Washington took his presidential oath in 1789. The present building served as a customs house from 1842 to 1862, and then as the U.S. subtreasury until 1920. Now a National Historic Site, with a statue of George Washington on the very spot where he took the oath of office, Federal Hall houses artifacts from colonial and early Federal New York, including Washington's inaugural suit. Free brochures outline self-guided walking tours through Lower Manhattan. *26 Wall St. (at Nassau St.), Lower Manhattan, 212/825–6888, www.nps.gov/feha. Free. Weekdays 9–5. Subway: 4 to Wall St.*

10 *e-7*

FEDERAL RESERVE BANK

A block-long, 14-story neo-Renaissance behemoth built of stone and iron in 1924, the Federal Reserve Bank in Lower Manhattan houses the largest stockpile of gold in the world—about $140 billion worth. One-hour tours of the Fed provide an overview of the bank's operations, an explanation of its role in the economy, a look at currency processing, and a visit to the gold vault, where you can salivate over bars of solid gold. Tour reservations must be made at least one week in advance. *33 Liberty St. (near William St.), Lower Manhattan, 212/720–6130, www.newyorkfed.org. Free. Tours depart weekdays at 9:30, 10:30, 11:30, 1:30, 2:30. Subway: A, C to Fulton St.; 2, 3, 4, 5 to Wall St.*

7 *e-2*

FIRE WATCHTOWER

Built in 1856 on the rocky high ground of what was once called Mt. Morris Park, this is the last remaining fire tower in the city. A landmark cast-iron structure with a spiral iron staircase and octagonal lookout, it became obsolete when fire-alarm boxes were invented in 1883. *Marcus Garvey Park, Madison Ave. and 121st St., Harlem. Subway: 4, 5, 6 to 125th St.*

7 *a-2*

GENERAL GRANT NATIONAL
MEMORIAL (GRANT'S TOMB)

(John H. Duncan, 1897) Civil War general and U.S. President Ulysses S. Grant and his wife, Julia Dent Grant, are entombed in this colossal white-granite mausoleum—made from 8,000 tons of stone. *Riverside Dr. and 122nd St., Morningside Heights, 212/666–1640, www.nps.gov/gegr. Open daily 9–5. Subway: 1 to 116th St./Columbia University or 125th St.*

9 *c-6*

GENERAL POST OFFICE

(McKim, Mead & White, 1913) Topping off an imposing row of enormous Corinthian columns and a two-block-long staircase, the letter carrier's famous motto is carved in stone: "Neither snow, nor rain, nor heat, nor gloom of night stays these couriers from the swift completion of their appointed rounds." This monumental post office is open 24 hours, 365 days a year, making it the site of an annual midnight frenzy on April 15th. Despite the sonorous credo, the building is slated to retire as a U.S. post office and become the new home of Amtrak's passenger trains, now harbored just across 8th Avenue in Penn Station. *8th Ave. from 31st to 33rd Sts., Midtown West. Subway: A, C, E to 34th St./Penn Station.*

1 *d-6*

GOVERNOR'S ISLAND

Sitting squarely at the mouth of the East River, this island was reputedly purchased by the Dutch governor of New Netherland from the Native Americans in 1637 for a bunch of trinkets. When the British arrived, they co-opted the island for the use of Colonial governors; their circa-1708 Governor's House is one of the city's only surviving Georgian buildings. From the 1790s on, the island was used mainly as a military fortification; the 1811 Castle William—a 40-ft-high circular fort with walls 8 ft thick—housed Rebel P.O.W.s during the Civil War. In 1966 the U.S. Coast Guard moved in, but in the late 1990s, they decided to give up the island. Now this former military base has become a political football, with community groups lobbying for it to become an offshore public park and developers hoping to turn it into a luxury housing development.

7 g-7
GRACIE MANSION

A Federal country villa built in 1799 by wealthy merchant Archibald Gracie, Gracie Mansion has served as the residence for New York's mayors since 1942. *East End Ave. and 88th St., Upper East Side, 212/570–4751 tour reservations. $4, $3 seniors. Tours of the public rooms, the garden, and the private quarters (except the mayor's bedroom) are given mid-Mar.–mid-Nov. Wed. at 10, 11, 1, and 2 and are arranged by appointment only. Subway: 4, 5, 6 to 86th St.*

3 b-6
GREENWICH VILLAGE

The largest designated historic district in New York City, Greenwich Village was a semirural retreat for the well-to-do during the early 19th century. It has since become a haven for students, artists, immigrants, and bohemians. Its winding streets (laid out before Manhattan adopted its orderly street grid pattern) offer a wealth of architectural treasures, charming bistros, coffee houses, and trendy boutiques. The best way to experience the Village is simply to meander. *Houston–14th Sts., from roughly Broadway to the Hudson River. Subway: A, B, C, D, E, F, V to W. 4th St./Washington Sq.; 1, 2 to Christopher St./Sheridan Sq.; N, Q, R, W to 8th St.*

11 a-3
GROVE COURT

Built in 1854 as laborers' quarters, this charming secluded mews in Greenwich Village was then known as Mixed Ale Alley for its residents' affinity for pooling beverages. The surrounding row houses on Grove Street—brick-and-clapboard Federal and Greek revival—date from the early 1800s. *10–12 Grove St. (between Bedford and Hudson Sts.), Greenwich Village. Subway: 1, 2 to Christopher St./Sheridan Sq.*

6 c-7
HAMILTON GRANGE
NATIONAL MONUMENT

Just north of City College, in Hamilton Heights, is founding father Alexander Hamilton's country retreat, designed by John McComb, Jr., and built in 1801. It's one of the few Federal frame houses still standing in Manhattan, and is now a National Historic Site administered by the National Park Service. *287 Convent Ave. (near W. 141st St.), 212/666–1640, www.nps.gov/hagr. Free. Fri.–Sun. 9–5. Subway: 1 to 137th St./City College.*

3 b-1
HARLEM

A thriving 17th- and 18th-century farming community, Harlem took off as a fashionable address in the 1880s, with brownstones, high-class apartments, and polo on horseback at the original Polo Grounds. In the decades that followed, Harlem housed succeeding waves of immigrants, first German and Irish, then Jewish and Italian; but by 1910, it was well on its way to becoming the largest black community in America. In the Roaring Twenties, nightclubs and dance halls like the Cotton Club and the Savoy Ballroom showcased Duke Ellington, Louis Armstrong, and Cab Calloway, and artists and writers, such as Langston Hughes, helped round out the fabulous Harlem Renaissance. The good times ended with the Depression, however, and by the 1960s most of the neighborhood's more affluent residents had moved away, and Harlem was deeply troubled by poverty. Today, as Harlem is being revitalized by black professionals and young families who are pumping new life into the community, there are still many burned-out buildings and vacant lots. But there are also vestiges of Harlem's proud past—elegant row houses, fine commercial structures, and historic churches. Be sure to visit the landmarked Apollo Theater which has showcased such singers as Billie Holiday, Ella Fitzgerald, and Aretha Franklin (*see* Performance Venues *in* Chapter 5) and features a "Wall of Fame" in the lobby. *Frederick Douglass Blvd. (8th Ave.) to the East River from 110th to 123rd Sts.; Hudson River to Harlem River from 124th to 148th Sts. Subway: A, B, C, D to 125th St., 145th St.; B, C to 116th St., 135th St.; 1, 9 to 125th St., 137th St., 145th St.; 2, 3 to Central Park North (110th St.), 116th St., 125th St., 135th St.; 3 to 145th St., 148th St. (The Apollo Theater: 253 W. 125th St. between 7th and 8th Aves., 212/531–5300. Tours are given daily; call for reservations and admission fees.)*

7 *e-2*

HARLEM COURTHOUSE

(Thom & Wilson, 1893) A richly decorated brick-and-stone courthouse with gables and a four-face clock, the Harlem Courthouse is now a landmark. *170 E. 121st St. (at Sylvan Pl.), Harlem. Subway: 4, 5, 6 to 125th St.*

11 *b-3*

ISAACS-HENDRICKS HOUSE

Built in 1799, Isaacs-Hendricks House is the oldest surviving house in Greenwich Village. Though some alterations have been made, the side and rear retain restored versions of the original Federal clapboard structure. The "Narrowest House" (*see below*) is next door. *77 Bedford St. (at Commerce St.), Greenwich Village. Subway: 1, 2 to Christopher St./Sheridan Sq.*

10 *d-1*

JEFFERSON MARKET LIBRARY

(Vaux & Withers, 1877; renovated interiors: Giorgio Cavaglieri, 1967) Originally a courthouse built on the site of an old market, this extraordinary building and its fanciful clock tower are a veritable celebration of the Victorian Gothic. Threatened with destruction in the 1960s, the building was saved by a determined band of Greenwich Village residents and is now a branch of the New York Public Library. *425 6th Ave. (at 10th St.), Greenwich Village, 212/243–4334, www.nypl.org. Subway: A, B, C, D, E, F, V to W. 4th St./Washington Sq. Mon. and Thurs. 10–6, Tues. and Fri. noon–6, Wed. noon–8, Sat. 10–5.*

9 *d-8*

LADIES' MILE HISTORIC DISTRICT

At the heart of the Gilded Age, the Ladies' Mile was the 5th Avenue of its day—a shopping district traversed by mostly female, mostly elegant, turn-of-the-20th-century shoppers. Once populated by well-known department stores, such as the original Macy's and Lord & Taylor, the Ladies' Mile was (and is) lined with imposing, block-long buildings—grandiose emporiums designed to impress shoppers both inside and out. A surprising number of these wonderful old buildings still have their original cast-iron and otherwise decorative facades; others have been restored as modern "superstores" such as Bed,

Bath, & Beyond, Today's Man, Barnes & Noble, and Old Navy. The retail recolonization of the late 1990s has re-established this area as one of the city's most popular shopping districts. *6th Ave. and Broadway from 14th to 23rd Sts., Chelsea. Subway: N, Q, R, W to 8th St., 14th St., 23rd St.*

11 *f-5*

LITTLE ITALY

First settled between 1880 and 1924, New York's old Italian community is shrinking as Chinatown expands, but visitors still clog the narrow streets in search of hearty Neapolitan fare, cappuccino, and cannoli at the area's many cafés. Mulberry Street remains the main drag, and becomes a proud, pedestrian-only fairground during the 10-day Feast of San Gennaro (*see September in Events, below*). *Canal–Houston Sts. from Lafayette St. to Bowery. Subway: 6 to Spring St.; J, M to Bowery.*

6 *a-2*

LITTLE RED LIGHTHOUSE (JEFFREY'S HOOK LIGHT)

Tucked under the George Washington Bridge is this 40-ft-tall namesake from the beloved children's story "The Little Red Lighthouse and the Great Gray Bridge." Originally constructed in 1880, and once a critical warning signal that kept Hudson River barges from dashing themselves against the rocky shore, the lighthouse is now a landmark, occasionally brought to life in tours given by the New York City Parks Department (800/201–7275). *Ft. Washington Park off 178th St., Washington Heights. Subway: A to 175th St.*

3 *c-7*

LOWER EAST SIDE

Historically the absorption center for New York's floods of Jewish immigrants in the 1880s and 1890s, the Lower East Side was at one time the world's largest Jewish community. Today the pushcarts are gone, and many of the synagogues stand abandoned. Lately, however, the neighborhood is being revitalized, and it's become the latest off-the-beaten-path Manhattan neighborhood to be trendified, with a slew of new low-key bars and clubs. For a closer look at the area's immigrant history, take one of the fascinating tours presented by the Lower East Side Tenement Museum (*see History Museums, below*). *Roughly Houston–*

Canal Sts. from Bowery to East River. Subway: F, J to Delancey St./Essex St.

11 d-2

MACDOUGAL ALLEY

A charming little dead-end street in Greenwich Village, MacDougal Alley is lined with tiny houses, originally built as stables in the 19th century. *Off MacDougal St. between Washington Sq. N and W. 8th St., Greenwich Village. Subway: A, B, C, D, E, F, V to West 4th St.; N, Q, R, W to 8th St.*

10 e-7

MERCHANTS' EXCHANGE

(Isaiah Rogers, 1836–42; remodeled by McKim, Mead & White, 1907) This massive building with two colonnades (one Ionic and the other Corinthian) originally had only one floor, serving first as a merchants' exchange and later as the U.S Customs House (1863–99). The second set of columns and the second story were added in 1907, when the building was turned into a bank. *55 Wall St. (between William and Hanover Sts.), Lower Manhattan. Subway: 4, 5 to Wall St.*

10 d-1

MILLIGAN PLACE/ PATCHIN PLACE

The houses on these two secluded Greenwich Village culs-de-sac were originally built in 1848–49 as boarding-houses for the Basque employees of a nearby hotel. Later many famous writers lived on Patchin Place, including Theodore Dreiser, Djuna Barnes, and e. e. cummings. *Off 6th Ave. (west side) between 10th and 11th Sts.; off W. 10th St. (north side) between Greenwich and 6th Aves. Subway: A, B, C, D, E, F, V to W. 4th St./Washington Sq.; F, V to 14th St.*

11 g-8

EDWARD MOONEY HOUSE

Chinatown's Georgian Mooney House is thought to be Manhattan's oldest surviving row house. Restored in 1971, it was built between the British evacuation (1785) and Washington's inauguration (1789) by merchant Edward Mooney, known in his day as a breeder of championship racehorses. *18 Bowery (at Pell St.), Chinatown. Subway: J, M, Z to Canal St.*

6 c-4

MORRIS-JUMEL MANSION

This pre-Revolution Georgian mansion, built in 1765 in the Palladian style (remodeled 1810), is the oldest surviving private dwelling on Manhattan. Originally the "summer villa" of British officer Roger Morris's family, it later served famously as General George Washington's headquarters in 1776. Bought in 1810 by the wealthy French merchant Stephen Jumel, it was occupied by his widow, Eliza Bowen (who married Aaron Burr in 1833) until 1865. (*See* Haunted Places, *above.*) The mansion contains nine rooms with magnificent Georgian, Federal, and French Empire furnishings, silver, and china; a colonial kitchen; and has a lovely herb and rose garden. While you're here, stop by Sylvan Terrace, a completely restored cobblestone street between Jumel Terrace and St. Nicholas Avenue which is lined with rare wooden row houses dating from 1882. *65 Jumel Terr. (near the intersection of Edgecombe Ave. and 160th St.), Washington Heights, 212/923–8008. $3 adults, $2 students and seniors, free children under 12. Wed.–Sun. 10–4. Subway: C to 163rd St./Amsterdam Ave.*

9 f-2

MT. VERNON HOTEL MUSEUM & GARDEN

Built in 1799, this elegant, Federal-style stone carriage house was converted into a country resort (the Mt. Vernon Hotel) in 1826 and a residence in 1833. Restored by the Colonial Dames of America, it is one of the few 18th-century historic structures left on Manhattan. Open to the public, its nine period rooms are decorated in the style of the old hotel, with Federal and Empire-style furniture. In June and July, and for special events throughout the year, period music is performed in a charming colonial-style garden adjoining the house. *421 E. 61st St. (between 1st and York Aves.), Upper East Side, 212/838–6878. Sept.–May, Tues.–Sun. 11–4; June and July, Tues. 11–4 and 6–9, Wed.–Sun. 11–4. $4 adults, $3 students and seniors, free children under 12; $6 events. Subway: 4, 5, 6, N, R to 59th St./Lexington Ave.*

10 e-5

MUNICIPAL BUILDING

(McKim, Mead & White, 1914) Straddling Chambers Street, the beaux-arts Municipal Building is an almost imperial civic skyscraper. The building looks like a wedding cake and is topped with a 10-story turreted central tower at whose pinnacle stands *Civic Fame*, a 25-ft-high gilt statue. Inside the building is a jumble of city offices; each year thousands of couples get married in a civil chapel on the second floor. *Centre St. at Chambers St. Subway: 1, 2, 3, A, C to Chambers St.*

11 *b-3*
"NARROWEST HOUSE"
Only 9½ ft wide, the "narrowest house" occupies what was once a carriageway. Built in 1873, it has the honor of snuggling up to the oldest residence in Greenwich Village, the Isaacs-Hendricks House next door. Poet Edna St. Vincent Millay lived here in 1923. *75½ Bedford St. (between Morton and Commerce Sts.), Greenwich Village. Subway: 1, 2 to Christopher St./Sheridan Sq.*

10 *e-7*
NEW YORK STOCK EXCHANGE
In front of what is now 60 Wall Street, 24 brokers met under a buttonwood tree in 1792 and agreed on some rules of business, thereby creating the New York Stock Exchange. The Exchange's current digs are in a neoclassical building with an august Corinthian entrance that dates from 1901. The largest securities exchange in the world, the "Big Board" can handle the transfer of a trillion shares of stock per day. The visitor center has a self-guided tour, interactive video displays, helpful docents, and a view of the chaotic 50-ft-high trading floor where brokers go about their frenetic business. *20 Broad St. (between Wall St. and Exchange Pl.), 212/656–5165. Free tickets distributed beginning at 8:45 AM; come before 11 AM to assure entrance. Open weekdays 9–4:30. Subway: 2, 3, 4, 5 to Wall St.*

11 *f-2*
OLD MERCHANT'S HOUSE
(Attributed to Minard Lafever, 1832) This completely intact, four-story Greek revival house became the property of Seabury Tredwell, a wealthy merchant and hardware importer, in 1835. It retains most of its original fittings and furniture, as well as clothing belonging to Tredwell's daughter Gertrude, who lived here until her death in 1933 at the age of 93. Restored and open to the public, the house is particularly appealing during the Christmas season, when it's decorated in the style of a 19th-century holiday party. *29 E. 4th St. (between Lafayette St. and the Bowery), East Village, 212/777–1089. $5 adults, $3 students and seniors, free children under 12. Thurs.–Mon. 1–5. Subway: 6 to Astor Pl. or Bleecker St.; B, D, F, V to Broadway–Lafayette St. N, Q, R, W to 8th St.*

10 *e-5*
OLD NEW YORK COUNTY COURTHOUSE
(John Kellum, 1872) This stately Italianate edifice is better known as the Tweed Courthouse. Built during political boss William Tweed's iron reign over city government, its construction dragged on for nine years at a then-unheard-of cost of $8–$12 million, most of which lined the pockets of Boss Tweed and his cronies. *52 Chambers St. (between Broadway and Centre St., behind City Hall), Lower Manhattan. Subway: A, C to Chambers St.*

10 *f-6*
PEARL STREET
Now in the financial district, this street formed the shoreline of the East River in Dutch colonial times, and was named for the mother-of-pearl oyster shells scattered along the beach. *Lower Manhattan. Subway: 2, 3, 4, 5 to Wall St.*

9 *e-8*
PLAYERS CLUB
Built in 1845, the Players Club was remodeled by Stanford White in 1888, when actor Edwin Booth turned it into a private club for members of the "theatrical profession." Peek through the bars of adjacent Gramercy Park to see a statue depicting Booth playing Hamlet (*see Statues & Public Art, below*). *16 Gramercy Park S (between Irving Pl. and Park Ave. S), Gramercy. Subway: 6 to 23rd St.*

9 *d-3*
THE PLAZA HOTEL
(Henry J. Hardenbergh, 1907) This 18-story French Renaissance building by the same architect who designed the Dakota is more than an architectural landmark. Its exuberant style; its fortuitous location on spacious Grand Army Plaza, across from Central Park; and its legendary past make it a sentimental favorite. Ernest Hemingway supposedly recommended to F. Scott Fitzgerald that when he died, he should leave his liver to Princeton but his heart to the Plaza.

(*See* Very Expensive Lodgings *in* Chapter 6.) *5th Ave. and Central Park S, Midtown East, 212/759–3000. Subway: N, Q, R, W to 5th Ave.*

11 *f-6*
POLICE HEADQUARTERS

(Hoppin & Koen, 1909) A baroque beauty with an impressive dome, this was the city's main police station when future President Teddy Roosevelt was New York City's police chief. The police moved out in 1973, and this lovely old building became a luxury co-op residence in the booming '80s. *240 Centre St. (between Broome and Grand Sts.), Little Italy. Subway: 6 to Spring St.; J, M, Z to Canal St.*

9 *g-8*
PUBLIC BATHS, CITY OF NEW YORK

(Arnold W. Brunner and William Martin Aiken, 1906) Public baths worthy of ancient Rome, these relics are now incorporated into the municipal swimming pool at the Asser Levy Recreation Center. *E. 23rd St. near FDR Dr., Gramercy. Subway: 6 to 23rd St.*

11 *f-2*
PUBLIC THEATER

(Alexander Saeltzer, 1849; additions by Griffith Thomas, 1859, and Thomas Sent, 1881; renovation by Giorgio Cavaglieri, 1967) Designed in the style of an Italian palazzo, the Public Theater was originally the Astor Library, New York's first free public library. Today, after a 1967 interior renovation, it houses the creative legacy of theater impresario Joseph Papp: the old reading rooms became auditoriums, which function as five different theaters. *Hair* and *A Chorus Line* both premiered here. *425 Lafayette St. (near Astor Pl.), East Village, 212/260–2400. Subway: 6 to Astor Pl.; N, Q, R, W to 8th St.*

11 *f-4*
PUCK BUILDING

(Albert Wagner, 1886–1993) This giant, redbrick Romanesque revival was home to the satirical weekly *Puck* from 1887 to 1916, and eventually housed the world's largest concentration of lithographers and printers. Today, it holds gallery and studio space and the Manhattan campus of the Pratt Institute. Two gold-leaf statues of Puck continue to gaze whimsically at passersby. *295–307 Lafayette St. (at*

Houston St.), SoHo. Subway: 6 to Bleecker St.; F, V to Broadway–Lafayette St.

9 *d-4*
RADIO CITY MUSIC HALL

(Edward Durrell Stone and Donald Deskey) The opulent interior of this 1932 art deco theater—seating 6,200—was designed on a grand scale. Two-ton chandeliers were hung from a 60-ft ceiling in the foyer, astonishing Depression-era patrons who came here to see movies accompanied by live acts, such as the famed Rockettes chorus line. One-hour tours of the theater are given daily. (*See* Performance Venues *in* Chapter 5.) *1260 6th Ave. (at 50th St.), Midtown West. 212/632–4041. Subway: B, D, F, V to 47th–50th Sts./Rockefeller Center.*

10 *f-1*
RENWICK TRIANGLE

Attributed to James Renwick, Jr., the architect of both St. Patrick's Cathedral and Grace Church (downtown), these 1861 brick row houses form a handsome historic enclave in the bustling East Village. *112–128 E. 10th St. (between 2nd and 3rd Aves.), and 2335 Stuyvesant St., East Village. Subway: 6 to Astor Pl.*

7 *a-4*
RIVERSIDE DRIVE—WEST 105TH STREET HISTORIC DISTRICT

Limestone beaux-arts houses built between 1899 and 1902 form a tiny enclave beside Riverside Park. *Riverside Dr. between 105th and 106th Sts., Upper West Side. Subway: 1 to 103rd St.*

9 *h-2*
ROOSEVELT ISLAND

Known as Blackwell's Island in the early 1700s when it was owned and farmed by Robert Blackwell and as Welfare Island in the mid-1800s when it came to house the city's poor and chronically ill, this 2-mi-long strip of land in the middle of the East River became a "self-sufficient" residential complex in the 1970s. Burnt-out traces of the old institutions peek out from the edges of this otherwise clean-lined environment, and north–south promenades offer impressive river views. Getting to Roosevelt Island is a delight: opened in 1976, the Roosevelt Island tramway is the only aerial commuter tram in the United States. From the tram plaza at 2nd Avenue and 60th Street, the 25-person cabin rises

250 ft in the air above the East River and glides to a stop on the island in four minutes. *East River, roughly parallel to 50th–86th Sts. 212/832–4543. Subway: F to Roosevelt Island.*

9 *e-2*

SARA DELANO ROOSEVELT MEMORIAL HOUSE

(Charles A. Platt, 1907–08) Mrs. Roosevelt commissioned Platt to build twin town houses, one for her son Franklin and his future wife, Eleanor, and one for herself. FDR lived here until he became governor of New York, in 1928; his mother lived at No. 47 until her death in 1941. *47–49 E. 65th St. (between Madison and Park Aves.), Upper East Side. Subway: 6 to 68th St./Hunter College; N, Q, R, W to 5th Ave.*

11 *b-4*

ST. LUKE'S PLACE

This handsome block of 1850s brick and brownstone row houses in Greenwich Village has billeted many famous residents. New York mayor Jimmy Walker (elected in 1926) lived in No. 6, poet Marianne Moore lived in No. 14, and novelist Theodore Dreiser wrote *An American Tragedy* in No. 16. *Between Hudson St. and 7th Ave. S. Subway: 1, 2 to Houston St.*

6 *d-7*

ST. NICHOLAS HISTORIC DISTRICT ("STRIVERS ROW")

In 1891, builder David H. King commissioned several leading architects of the day—James Brown Lord, Bruce Price, and Clarence S. Luce; and McKim, Mead & White—and the results were the King Model Houses, a harmonious grouping of row houses and apartments. Originally built for well-to-do white residents, they were purchased by aspiring African-American professionals in the '20s and '30s and acquired the collective nickname "Strivers Row" as Harlem evolved into a black community. *Adam Clayton Powell–Frederick Douglass Blvds. from 138th to 139th Sts., Harlem. Subway: C to 135th St.*

10 *f-1*

ST. MARK'S HISTORIC DISTRICT

This historic East Village oasis contains three of Manhattan's earliest Federal buildings: St. Mark's Church in-the-Bowery (1799), the Stuyvesant-Fish House

(1804), and 44 Stuyvesant Street (1795), all traceable back to Dutch governor Peter Stuyvesant, on whose farmland the district rests. Stuyvesant Street, the only true east–west street in Manhattan, was the driveway to the governor's mansion. *E. 10th and Stuyvesant Sts. between 2nd and 3rd Aves. Subway: 6 to Astor Pl.*

10 *f-2*

ST. MARK'S PLACE

In the 1960s, the 1830s Greek revival row houses lining these blocks went psychedelic and formed the main street of the hippie phenomenon. Later, St. Mark's became a haven for punk rockers, and though a few punks remain, the counterculture has largely given way to tourism. Jewelry stands, T-shirt stalls, ethnic restaurants, and body piercers now line the East Village's gritty main drag. *Between 3rd Ave. and Tompkins Sq. Park, East Village. Subway: 6 to Astor Pl.*

10 *f-7*

SCHERMERHORN ROW

Dating from the early 19th century, these 12 peak-roof Georgian Federal and Greek revival buildings were originally warehouses and countinghouses serving New York's then-bustling seaport. Now landmarks, they have been carefully restored as part of the South Street Seaport Museum's efforts to evoke the area's rich history (*see* History Museums, *below*). *2–18 Fulton St., 91–92 South St., 159–171 John St., and 189–195 Front St., Lower Manhattan. Subway: 2, 3, 4, A to Fulton St.*

9 *e-2*

SEVENTH REGIMENT ARMORY

(Charles W. Clinton, 1879) A Victorian incarnation of a medieval fortress, the vast armory houses a great drill hall (187 ft by 290 ft) and a Veterans' Room and library decorated under the direction of Louis Comfort Tiffany. Every January, this behemoth fills with the renowned Winter Antiques Show (*see* Events, *below*). *643 Park Ave. (between 66th and 67th Sts.), Upper East Side, 212/744–2968 (curator's office). Tours by appointment. Subway: 6 to 68th St./Hunter College.*

9 *c-5*

SHUBERT ALLEY

Now just a glitzy shortcut in the theater district, this private alley was the commercial domain of brothers J.J., Lee, and Sam Shubert, theater impresarios, in the early 1900s. Actors and chorus girls thronged to Shubert Alley whenever new shows were being cast. *Between 44th and 45th Sts., west of 7th Ave. Subway: 1, 2, 3, 7, N, Q, R, S, W to 42nd St./Times Sq.*

9 f-6
SNIFFEN COURT HISTORIC DISTRICT

In Murray Hill, New York's smallest designated historic district is a charming 19th-century mews of 10 Romanesque revival brick carriage houses. Built as stables in the 1860s, they were converted to residences in the 1920s. *150–158 E. 36th St. (between Lexington and 3rd Aves.), Murray Hill. Subway: 6 to 33rd St.*

11 f-1
STUYVESANT-FISH HOUSE

Dating from 1804, this brick Federal house in the East Village was built by the Dutch governor Peter Stuyvesant's great-grandson as a wedding gift for his daughter Elizabeth and her husband. *21 Stuyvesant St. (off 9th St., between 2nd and 3rd Aves.), East Village. Subway: 6 to Astor Pl.*

10 e-5
SURROGATE'S COURT/ HALL OF RECORDS

(John R. Thomas; Horgan & Slattery, 1899–1907) The Surrogate's Court forms a delightful and impressive civic monument opposite City Hall Park. With marble walls, a vaulted ceiling, and encircling corridors, its central hall is one of the finest beaux-arts rooms this side of the Paris Opera House. *31 Chambers St. (at Centre St.), Lower Manhattan. Subway: 1, 2, A, E to Chambers St.*

9 e-8
THEODORE ROOSEVELT BIRTHPLACE NATIONAL HISTORIC SITE

Theodore Roosevelt, the 26th President and the only U.S. president from New York City, was born on this site in 1858. The original 1848 brownstone was demolished in 1916, but this Gothic revival replica was constructed in 1923. Now administered by the National Park Service, Roosevelt's restored boyhood home has a fascinating collection of Teddyana in five Victorian period rooms.

28 E. 20th St. (between Broadway and Park Ave. S), Gramercy, 212/260–1616, www.nps.gov/thrb. $2. Wed.–Sun. 9–5. House tours on the hr. Subway: 6, N, Q, R, W to 23rd St.

9 c-5
TIMES SQUARE

Named for the Times Tower—which no longer houses the *New York Times,* but still "drops the ball" on hordes of revelers every New Year's Eve—Times Square has long been synonymous with Broadway shows, bright lights, and seedy doings. In a somewhat surprising recent turn, however, a redevelopment scheme has almost completely sanitized Times Square. The neon lights remain, but the porn businesses, which long occupied abandoned theaters on 42nd Street, have been booted out, and 42nd Street is filling with gleaming megastores, each visually louder than the last. Although tourists seem to like it, many New Yorkers smell Disneyland in this unlikely metamorphosis. Once just crass, Times Square is now crassly commercial. *42nd–47th Sts. at Broadway and 7th Ave. Subway: 1, 2, 3, N, Q, R, S, W to 42nd St./Times Sq.*

11 e-2
TRIANGLE FIRE SITE

Just east of Washington Square is a plaque commemorating a tragic fire in the building that once housed the Triangle Shirtwaist Company. On March 25, 1911, fire broke out on the upper floors of this sweatshop, and within a single hour 146 young women were killed, many of them leaping in flames to their deaths on the streets below. The building was equipped with fire escapes and was supposed to be fireproof, but supervisors had locked the workers into their workrooms. A state investigation following the fire led to new labor laws and improved safety conditions for factory workers. *Washington Pl. and Greene St., Greenwich Village. Subway: N, Q, R, W to 8th St.; 6 to Astor Pl.*

10 e-7
U.S. CUSTOMS HOUSE

(Cass Gilbert, 1907) A monumental beaux-arts building with 44 Corinthian columns, the Customs House is now home to the George Gustav Heye Center of the National Museum of the American Indian (*see* History Museums, below). Since the building was originally used to collect import taxes on foreign goods shipped into the Port of New York, its architectural theme is "world trade": Four massive limestone sculptures embedded in the facade represent Asia, the Americas, Europe, and Africa, while 12 smaller ones arrayed above represent the world's "greatest trading nations." The huge oval rotunda has 1937 WPA murals by Reginald Marsh. *1 Bowling Green (Broadway and Whitehall St.), Lower Manhattan. Subway: 4, 5 to Bowling Green.*

9 e-4

VILLARD HOUSES

(McKim, Mead & White, 1882–85) Surrounding a peaceful courtyard, this cluster of Italian Renaissance–style brownstones was modeled on Rome's Palazzo della Cancelleria. Built by newspaper owner and railroad entrepreneur Henry Villard, they have served variously as the home of the Catholic Archdiocese of New York and Random House Publishing Co. Today they comprise the landmark section of the New York Palace Hotel, containing its opulent public rooms and the hot Le Cirque 2000 (*see* French *in* Chapter 1). *451–457 Madison Ave. (between 50th and 51st Sts.), Midtown East. Subway: 6 to 51st St./Lexington Ave.; E, V to Lexington–3rd Aves./53rd St.*

10 e-7

WALL STREET

In 1653 this was the northern frontier of the city, fortified against attack by a Dutch wall of thick wooden planks. The wall was completely dismantled by the English in 1699, but the name stuck, and The Street is now synonymous with the downtown financial district and the world of high finance in general. *Broadway to William St., Lower Manhattan. Subway: 4, 5 to Wall St.*

11 d-2

WASHINGTON MEWS

Lined with converted stables, this 19th-century Greenwich Village mews once housed the carriage horses of fashionable Washington Square area residents. *University Pl. to 5th Ave. (between 8th St. and Washington Sq. N), Greenwich Village. Subway: N, Q, R, W to 8th St.*

11 d-2

WASHINGTON SQUARE NORTH

(Town & Davis, ca. 1831) Immortalized in Henry James's *Washington Square,* "the Row" housed New York's most prominent citizens when it was first built. No. 8 was the mayor's official residence. Lovingly preserved, these stylish Greek revival row houses are an affecting reminder of Old New York. *1–13 and 21–26 Washington Sq. N (between 5th Ave. and MacDougal St.), Greenwich Village. Subway: A, B, C, D, E, F, V to W. 4th St./Washington Sq.*

10 d-6

WORLD TRADE CENTER SITE

On September 11, 2001, terrorist hijackers steered two commercial jets into the World Trade Center towers, demolishing them and five outlying buildings, and killing nearly 3,000 people. Dubbed Ground Zero, the fenced-in 16-acre work site that emerged from the rubble has come to symbolize the personal and historical impact of the 9-11 attack. In an attempt to grasp the reality of the destruction, to pray, or simply to witness history, visitors now flock to the site for a glimpse of what is left, clustering at every viewpoint along the secured area's perimeter. People from around the nation and the globe leave notes, candles, photographs, baseball caps, and other mementos at impromptu memorial sites, evidence of the world's sympathy and support. The nexus of visitor activity is St. Paul's Chapel, where the church gates have been transformed into a constantly changing gallery of grief.

The World Trade Center (WTC) was a seven-building, 12-million-square-ft complex, home to more than 430 companies based in 28 countries. The daytime population of the WTC included 50,000 employees and 100,000 business and leisure visitors. Underground was a mall with nearly a hundred stores and restaurants and a network of subway and other train stations. The twin towers were New York's tallest buildings, the third tallest in the world after Kuala Lumpur's Petronas Towers and the Sears Tower in Chicago. Designed by Minoru Yamasaki and built in the early 1970s, the 1,350-ft, 110-story towers were synonymous with New York and emblematic of American ingenuity, success, and leadership in the world economy. All of this was left in ruins on September 11, and Manhattan was robbed of one of the most spectacular features of its skyline.

The best place to observe the WTC site is the viewing platform on Fulton Street, between Church Street and Broadway. (Three additional platforms are scheduled to be built.) The view is directly west to the World Financial Center. To access the platform you must have a ticket, which you can obtain at no charge from the ticket booth at the South Street Seaport Museum (at Fulton and South streets on Pier 16). From 11 AM to 6 PM daily, tickets are distributed on a first-come, first-served basis (limit two per person) and admit you to the platform for the next available, pre-assigned half-hour session. Half-hour blocks are assigned, earliest to latest, for the period between noon and 8 PM on the same day and, when those run out, for 9–11:30 AM the following day. To minimize crowding, once you have your ticket do not arrive at the platform entrance more than 15 minutes before your time slot. *Viewing platform: Fulton St. between Church St. and Broadway, Lower Manhattan, 212/732–7678 (ticket information), www.nycvisit.com. Free. Daily 9 am–8 pm. Subway: E to World Trade Center; 4, 5, to Fulton St.*

7 *f-7*
YORKVILLE
A remote hamlet known as Klein Deutschland (little Germany) in the 19th century, Yorkville has also been a haven for immigrants from Austria, Hungary, and Czechoslovakia. *Lexington–York Aves. from 75th to 88th Sts., Upper East Side. Subway: 6 to 77th St.; 4, 5, 6 to 86th St.*

queens

1 *f-3*
BOWNE HOUSE
The oldest building in Queens and the former home of Quaker John Bowne, this 1661 colonial residence was a clandestine meeting place for the then-forbidden Society of Friends (Quakers). Bowne's arrest and subsequent acquittal by Dutch authorities set a precedent for freedom of worship in the New World. *37–01 Bowne St. (between 37th and 38th Aves.), Flushing, 718/359–0528.*

Guided tours weekends at 2:15. $5 adults, $4 seniors, $3 children. Subway: 7 to Main St./Flushing.

3 *d-4*
HUNTER'S POINT HISTORIC DISTRICT
Dating from the 1870s, this block of middle-income row houses is excellently preserved. *45th Ave. (between 21st and 23rd Sts.), Long Island City. Subway: 7 to 45th Rd.*

1 *g-4*
KING MANOR MUSEUM
The home of Rufus King—member of the Continental Congress, the Constitutional Convention, U.S. senator, unsuccessful candidate for president, and outspoken opponent of slavery—this gambrel-roof farmhouse was built between 1750 and 1811. It's now a history museum with a nine-room interior restored and decorated in period furniture. *King Park, Jamaica Ave. between 150th and 153rd Sts., Jamaica, 718/206–0545. $2, $1 children. weekends noon–4. Subway: E, J, Z to Jamaica Center.*

3 *h-1*
KINGSLAND HOMESTEAD
Home to the Queens Historical Society, this farmhouse, built in 1774 by a wealthy Quaker farmer, is an interesting mix of Dutch and English architectural traditions. Moved from its original location on 155th Street, it now houses period rooms and changing exhibits. *Weeping Beech Park, 143–35 37th Ave. (at Parsons Blvd.), Flushing, 718/939–0647, www.preserve.org/queens. $3, $2 seniors and children. Tues., Sat., and Sun. 2:30–4:30. Subway: 7 to Main St./Flushing.*

8 *f-2*
LENT HOMESTEAD
Well preserved since its construction in 1729, this simple, Dutch colonial farmhouse retains its original stonework and overhanging, wood-shingle roof. *78-03 19th Rd. (at 78th St.), Astoria.*

staten island

4 *c-6*
ALICE AUSTEN HOUSE (CLEAR COMFORT)
Probably built between 1700 and 1750, this Dutch-style cottage was the home

of Alice Austen, a pioneering photographer, from 1866 to 1952. Austen's legacy: 3,000 glass-plate negatives of photos taken 1880–1930. View prints from those plates among Victorian furnishings at the house-cum-museum. The view of Upper New York Bay is breathtaking. *2 Hylan Blvd., Rosebank, 718/816–4506. $2, children under 6 free. Thurs.–Sun. noon–5. From Staten Island Ferry, take Bus S51.*

1 *a-4*

CONFERENCE HOUSE (BILLOPP HOUSE)

Built by British naval captain Christopher Billopp circa 1675, this manor house is renowned as the site of the only attempted peace conference during the American Revolution. On September 11, 1776, rebels Ben Franklin, John Adams, and Edward Rutledge met with British Admiral Lord Howe and refused to negotiate a cease-fire unless the Colonies were granted complete independence. *7455 Hylan Blvd., Tottenville, 718/984–2086. $2 adults, $1 seniors and children. Fri.–Sun. 1–4.*

4 *C-7*

GARIBALDI-MEUCCI MUSEUM

Housed in an old farmhouse, this quirky museum is full of letters and photographs from the life of Italian patriot Giuseppe Garibaldi, who lived in this house during a respite from his freedom fighting in 1850–51. The collection also documents Antonio Meucci's claim that he invented the telephone before Alexander Graham Bell did. *420 Tompkins Ave. (just north of Hylan Blvd.), Rosebank, 718/442–1608. Tues.–Sun. 1–5. From Staten Island Ferry, take Bus S78 or S52 to Chestnut and Tompkins Aves.*

1 *b-2*

HISTORIC RICHMONDTOWN

Known as Cocclestown when it was founded in 1685 by Dutch, French Walloon, and English settlers, present-day Richmondtown is a 25-acre site of major historical interest built between 1690–1890. About half of the 30 buildings have been restored and are open to the public. Highlights include the Voorlezer's House (1695), the oldest known elementary-school building in the United States, and the Stephens General Store & House, a reconstructed

19th-century store. In summer, costumed interpreters and craftspeople, such as a tinsmith, basketmaker, and shoemaker, recreate a 19th-century village; on Labor Day weekend the County Fair takes over; and in early December, folks convene for candlelight tours and holiday revels. From January to April, there are tavern concerts in a period tavern lit by candles and heated by a wood-burning stove. *441 Clarke Ave. (at Arthur Kill and Richmond Rds.), Richmondtown, 718/351–1611, www.historicrichmondtown.org. $4 adults, $2.50 seniors and children 6–18. Sept.–June, Wed.–Sun. 1–5; July–Aug., Wed.–Sat. 10–5, Sun. 1–5. From Staten Island Ferry, take Bus S74.*

4 *a-6*

SNUG HARBOR CULTURAL CENTER

Sailor's Snug Harbor originally consisted of five magnificent Greek revival buildings built in the 1830s and '40s as a home for "aged, decrepit and worn-out sailors." In all, there are now 28 buildings on 83 acres of park, and they serve as a performing- and visual-arts facility offering art exhibits, theater, recitals, concerts, and outdoor sculpture in a landmark maritime setting. Components include the Staten Island Botanical Garden (*see* Botanical Gardens *in* Chapter 3) and the Staten Island Children's Museum (*see* Children's Museums, *above*). *1000 Richmond Terr. (from Tysen St. to Kissel Ave.), Livingston, 718/448–2500. Grounds open daily 8 AM–dusk. In summer, tours depart from the main gate weekends at 2. From Staten Island Ferry Terminal take Bus S40.*

HISTORY MUSEUMS

Some landmark buildings and mansions have their own collections and period furnishings; *see* Historic Structures & Streets, *above, and* Libraries, *below.*

8 *d-7*

AMERICAN MUSEUM OF THE MOVING IMAGE

Adjacent to the Kaufman-Astoria Studios, this unique museum is devoted to the art, technology, and history of the film and television industries. It contains a state-of-the-art, 190-seat theater, a 60-seat screening room, and 25,000 square ft of exhibit space. In addition to the Zoetrope—a giant spinning disk on which the first primitive movies were shown—and costumes worn by Marilyn Monroe, Marlene Dietrich, Robin Williams, and Jerry Seinfeld, hundreds of classic films are "displayed" annually. Live demonstrations on computer animation and film editing are given every weekend. *35th Ave. (between 36th and 37th Sts.), Astoria, Queens, 718/784–0077, www.ammi.org. $8.50 adults, $5.50 seniors 65 and over and college students, $4.50 students 5–18, free children under 5 (screenings included in daytime admissions; $8 evenings, $4 seniors). Tues.–Fri. noon–5, weekends 11–6. Subway: R, V to Steinway St.*

6 *b-5*

AMERICAN NUMISMATIC SOCIETY

Founded in 1858 and devoted to the study of coins and currency, the Numismatic Society has two public galleries, displaying examples of "the root of all evil" from as far back as ancient Rome. *Broadway and 155th St., Washington Heights, 212/234–3130, www.amnumsoc.org. Tues.–Fri. 9–4:30. Subway: A, C to 155th St.; 1 to 157th St.*

12 *b-3*

BROOKLYN HISTORICAL SOCIETY

The gallery here, which typically features Brooklyn Dodgers baseball bats and trick mirrors from Coney Island alongside exhibits on the borough's history, is closed for a major renovation. It's scheduled to re-open in late 2001 with a larger space, re-vamped library, and Brooklyn-centric gift store. *128 Pierrepont St., Brooklyn Heights, 718/254–9830, www.brooklynhistory.org. Call for information on the gallery's new hours and fees. Subway: Borough Hall.*

4 *h-7*

CONEY ISLAND MUSEUM

In the same building as the Coney Island Sideshow, just a block away from the boardwalk, this museum documents the history of this beachside amusement park from the late 19th century to the present. On display are original horses from the old steeplechase, a wicker rolling chair in which older folks were pushed down the boardwalk for 75 cents an hour, and banners and photos from old sideshow acts. Lectures on the

history of Coney Island are staged Sunday nights in summer. *1208 Surf Ave. (at W. 12th St.), Brooklyn, 718/372–5159. 99¢. Year-round weekends noon–6. Subway: B, D, F, N to Coney Island/Stillwell Ave.*

10 *d-1*

FORBES MAGAZINE GALLERIES

This minimuseum in the Village displays the Forbes family's idiosyncratic collections, including 10,000 toy soldiers, more than 500 toy boats, jeweled Fabergé eggs made for the last two Russian czars, and a wealth of historic American manuscripts and presidential papers, including letters from Abraham Lincoln. Children tend to like the toy soldiers, while their parents may appreciate the adjacent picture gallery, with changing exhibitions. *62 5th Ave. (at 12th St.), 212/206–5548. Tues., Wed., Fri., and Sat. 10–4. Free. Subway: N, Q, R, W to 8th St.; F, V to 14th St.*

10 *e-7*

FRAUNCES TAVERN MUSEUM

This museum commemorates the site of the original tavern of Samuel Fraunces, where George Washington bade farewell to his officers in 1783 after having forced the redcoats from New York. Founded in 1907 in five reconstructed Federal buildings, the museum interprets the history and culture of Colonial America through Revolutionary War artifacts and colonial-period rooms, decorative arts, flags, prints, and paintings. Call for a current schedule of exhibits, lectures, performances, and workshops for children. *54 Pearl St. (at Broad St.), Lower Manhattan, 212/425–1778, www.frauncestavernmuseum.org. $2.50 adults, $1 students and seniors, free children under 6. Weekdays 10–4:45. Subway: J, M to Whitehall St.; 4, 5 to Bowling Green.*

10 *e-7*

GEORGE GUSTAV HEYE CENTER OF THE NATIONAL MUSEUM OF THE AMERICAN INDIAN

With access to more than 1 million artifacts, this is the world's largest and best collection of ethnology and archaeology on the Native Americans of North, South, and Central America and the West Indies. Run by the Smithsonian Institution, the museum is rich in sound and video recordings of Native Americans explaining the significance of exhibits, which range from Navajo weaving to pre-Columbian sculpture. Live dance performances and craft demonstrations by master craftspeople, such as totem-pole carvers, bring the exhibits to life. (*See* U.S. Customs House *in* Historic Structures & Streets, *above*.) *1 Bowling Green (at Broadway and Whitehall St., Battery Park), Lower Manhattan, 212/668–6624, www.si.edu/nmai. Free. Fri.–Wed. 10–5, Thurs. 10–8. Subway: 4, 5 to Bowling Green.*

1 *f-4*

LOUIS ARMSTRONG HOUSE & ARCHIVES

While Satchmo's former home at 34–56 107th Street in Corona, Queens, is being transformed into a museum (it's expected to open in 2003), his personal effects—including 5,000 photographs, 650 homemade audiotapes, and five gold-plate trumpets—are on display at the Louis Armstrong Archives at Queens College. *Rosenthal Library, Rm. 332, Queens College, 65–30 Kissena Blvd., Flushing, Queens, 718/997–3670, www. satchmo.net. Weekdays 10–5; hours, however, may vary, so call before visiting. Subway: 7 to Main St./Flushing.*

11 *h-5*

LOWER EAST SIDE TENEMENT MUSEUM

This restored 1863 tenement building is a poignant tribute to the immigrants who lived on New York's Lower East Side during the 19th and early 20th centuries. You'll be guided through apartments furnished as they were by those who actually lived here: the Gumpertzes, a German Jewish family from the 1870s; the Rogarshevskys, Eastern Europeans from the 1910s; the Confinos, Sephardic Jews from Turkey who lived here in the 1910s; and the Baldizzis, a Sicilian Catholic family from the 1930s. The museum also hosts walking tours and New York housing reform law tours. Reservations for all programs are best made in advance. *90 Orchard St. (at Broome St.), Lower East Side, 212/ 431–0233, www.tenement.org. $9, $7 students and seniors. Tues.–Fri. 1–4, weekends 11–4:30; June–Sept. additional evening tours Thurs. Subway: F, J to Delancey/Essex Sts.*

9 *c-7*

MUSEUM AT THE FASHION INSTITUTE OF TECHNOLOGY

Deep in the garment district, F.I.T. is home to a substantial museum space documenting the history of fashion both high and low. The textile collection holds more than 3 million indexed swatches, alongside ½ million costumes and accessories from the 18th century to the present. Past shows have addressed topics ranging from the history of automobile upholstery to haute couture of the past five decades. *7th Ave. and 27th St., Chelsea, 212/217–5800. Free. Tues.– Fri. noon–8, Sat. 10–5. Subway: 1, 2 to 28th St.*

10 *e-7*

MUSEUM OF AMERICAN FINANCIAL HISTORY

The nation's only public museum of finance tells the neighborhood story— the financial district of Wall Street brokers and famous tycoons. The museum building, ironically, was once headquarters of John D. Rockefeller's old Standard Oil Company, once the largest business in the world. Artifacts including a vintage ticker-tape machine. There are district walking tours Fridays all year. *28 Broadway (between Beaver St. and Exchange Pl.), Lower Manhattan, 212/ 908–4110, www.financialhistory.org. $2; walking tours $15 adults, $10 children. Tues.–Sat. 10–4. Subway: 1, 2 to Rector St.; 4, 5 to Wall St.*

11 *f-7*

MUSEUM OF CHINESE IN THE AMERICAS

In the heart of Manhattan's blossoming Chinatown, these exhibits document the vibrant history and culture of Chinese immigrants in New York, San Francisco, Canada, and Latin America. (*See* Walking Tours, *below*). *70 Mulberry St. (at Bayard St.), 2nd floor, Chinatown, 212/ 619–4785, www.moca-nyc.org. $3, $1 students and seniors, free children under 12. Tues.–Sat. noon–5. Subway: N, Q, R, W, 6, J, M, Z to Canal St.*

10 *d-8*

MUSEUM OF JEWISH HERITAGE

Opened in 1997 in a star-of-David-shape building designed by Kevin Roche, this three-floor museum is devoted to preserving the memory of the Holocaust and the history of Jewish culture through photographs, artifacts, and videotaped oral histories. Permanent exhibits include "The War Against the Jews" documenting the rise of Nazism, the Holocaust, and World War II; and "Jewish Life a Century Ago." *18 1st Pl. (at Battery Pl.), Battery Park City, Lower Manhattan, 212/968–1800, www.mjhnyc.org. $7 adults, $5 students and seniors, free children under 5. Sun.–Wed. 9–5, Thurs. 9–8, Fri. and eve of Jewish holidays 9–2. Subway: 4, 5 to Bowling Green.*

9 *d-4*
MUSEUM OF TELEVISION & RADIO

If you harbor secret addictions to reruns of "Mary Tyler Moore" and "I Dream of Jeannie," this is the place for you. With 75,000 radio and TV programs preserved forever in its permanent collection, the museum encourages visitors to select their favorite shows and watch them at one of the personal consoles. Try the Beatles on the "Ed Sullivan Show," the pilot episode of "Charlie's Angels," or the original radio broadcast of Orson Welles's "War of the Worlds." There are 96 television consoles, a 200-seat theater, a 96-seat theater, two 45-seat screening rooms, and a listening room for radio programs. Special screenings aired throughout the day in the various theaters bring rare programs—complete with vintage commercials—back to light. *25 W. 52nd St. (between 5th and 6th Aves.), Midtown West, 212/621–6800, www.mtr.org. Suggested admission $6, $4 seniors and students, $3 children under 13. Tues., Wed., and Fri.–Sun. noon–6, Thurs. noon–8. Subway: E, V to 5th Ave./53rd St.; B, D, F, V to 47th–50th Sts./Rockefeller Center.*

7 *e-4*
MUSEUM OF THE CITY OF NEW YORK

The amazing life and history of New York City—from the Native Americans and early Dutch settlers through the present day—is chronicled in this massive Georgian mansion via costumes, furniture, paintings, artifacts, oral histories, dollhouses, and toys. Special exhibits feature such topics as the Harlem Renaissance, the Astor Place Riot, and Tin Pan Alley. *(See* Walking Tours, *below.) 1220 5th Ave. (at 103rd St.), Upper East Side, 212/534–1672,*

www.mcny.org. Suggested admission $7; $4 students, seniors, and children; $12 families. Wed.–Sat. 10–5, Sun. noon–5. Subway: 6 to 103rd St.

9 *e-3*
NEWSEUM/NY

Opened in 1997, Newseum/NY, a branch of Newseum in Washington, D.C., presents changing exhibits on news and photojournalism, focusing on First Amendment issues and how news is made. Displays are accompanied by documentary films, lectures, and roundtable discussions with newsmakers and newsbreakers. *580 Madison Ave. (between 56th and 57th Sts.), Midtown East, 212/317–7596, www.newseum.org. Free. Mon.–Sat. 10–5:30. Subway: 4, 5, 6, N, R to 59th St./Lexington Ave.*

11 *b-5*
NEW YORK CITY FIRE MUSEUM

Examine hand-pulled and horse-drawn firefighting apparatus, uniforms, and sliding poles at this restored 1904 firehouse, which chronicles the efforts of New York's Bravest from the 18th century to the present. *278 Spring St. (between Hudson and Varick Sts.), Greenwich Village, 212/691–1303, www.nycfiremuseum.org. Suggested admission $4, $2 seniors, $1 children under 12. Tues.–Sun. 10–4. Subway: C, E to Spring St.*

10 *e-7*
NEW YORK CITY POLICE MUSEUM

In the Cunard Building on Bowling Green, this large collection features cop paraphernalia from the Dutch era to the present, including guns, ammo, handcuffs, billy clubs, and uniforms. *25 Broadway (at Morris St.), Lower Manhattan, 212/301–4440, www.nycpolicemuseum.org. Tues.–Sat. 10–6. Free. Subway: 4, 5 to Bowling Green.*

7 *c-8*
NEW-YORK HISTORICAL SOCIETY

Founded in 1804, this is the oldest museum in the city. Changing exhibits are culled from the society's elegant collection of paintings, prints, folk art, and vintage toys, and cover everything from the history of Central Park to the lights of Times Square. The society houses a major research library of 600,000 volumes; an impressive collection of 18th-century New York newspapers; and more than a million maps, prints, photos, lithographs, and architectural drawings—including the original watercolors for John James Audubon's *Birds of America*. One of the latest additions is the installation of 40,000 of the museum's most-treasured objects in the new Henry Luce III Center on the museum's fourth floor—including George Washington's inaugural chair, the largest U.S. collection of Tiffany lamps, and paintings by Hudson River School artists Thomas Cole and Frederic Church. Also on permanent display is "Kid City," a re-creation of a turn-of-the-20th-century New York City street corner. *2 W. 77th St. (at Central Park West), Upper West Side, 212/873–3400, www.nyhistory.org. Suggested admission $5, $3 students and seniors, free children under 12. Tues.–Sun. 11–5. Subway: B, C to 81st St.*

12 *c-4*

NEW YORK TRANSIT MUSEUM

Appropriately located underground, in a decommissioned 1938 subway station, the Transit Museum contains full-size classic subway cars dating back to 1903, including wooden cars with rattan seating. It's great for children, who can climb all over the seats and pretend they're driving without anyone looking askance. Volunteers dressed as subway conductors give impromptu tours. There are also vintage turnstiles, station signs, trolley models, and well-researched temporary exhibits on the history of the subway system. The museum is closed for renovation through early 2003. Its annex museum, which more closely resembles a gift shop, is open in Grand Central Station weekdays 8–8 and Saturdays 10–4. *Boerum Pl. and Schermerhorn St., Downtown Brooklyn, 718/243–3060, www. mta.nyc.ny.us/museum. $3, $1.50 seniors and children under 17. Tues.–Fri. 10–4, weekends noon–5. Subway: 2, 4, 5 to Borough Hall; A, C, F to Jay St.; A, C, G to Hoyt St.*

10 *e-7*

SKYSCRAPER MUSEUM

If you like big buildings, drop by this little museum to see exhibits on high-rises from around the world. The Skyscraper Museum is scheduled to moved to new digs in Battery Park City in 2002. Until then, the museum, near South Street Seaport, features an exhibition about the redevelopment of Times Square. *110 Maiden Lane (between Pearl and Water Sts.), Lower Manhattan, 212/968–1961. Free. Weekdays noon–6. Subway: A, C, 2, 3, 4 to Fulton St./Broadway Nassau.*

10 *f-7*

SOUTH STREET SEAPORT MUSEUM

Filling 11 square seaport blocks on the East River, this "museum without walls" features cobblestone streets, historic sailing ships, 18th- and 19th-century architecture, an old print shop, a boat-building center, and a children's crafts center with hands-on displays illuminating the history of seafaring. If you're feeling salty, book passage on the *Pioneer*, a 102-ft schooner built in 1885, and be sure to visit the other ships docked at Pier 16 as well, including the *Peking*, the second-largest sailing ship in the world; the lightship *Ambrose*; and the full-rigged *Wavertree*. Call for details on classes, special exhibitions, and events. *Visitor center: 12 Fulton St. (at South St.), Lower Manhattan, 212/748–8600, www.southstseaport.org. $7, $5 seniors and students, $3 children under 12. Open Apr. 1–Sept. 30, Fri.–Wed. 10–6, Thurs. 10–8; Oct. 1–Mar. 31, Wed.–Mon. 10–5. Subway: A, C, 2, 3, 4 to Fulton St./Broadway Nassau.*

4 *c-2*

WATERFRONT MUSEUM

In a historic wooden barge on the Brooklyn waterfront, this makeshift museum presents changing art exhibits and maritime artifacts from New York Harbor. The adjacent pier offers stunning harbor views stretching from the Verrazano Bridge to the Statue of Liberty. Call for information about museum tours, special events, circus performances, and concerts. *290 Conover St., Red Hook Garden Pier, Brooklyn, 718/624–4719, www.waterfrontmuseum.org. Free (donations accepted). Museum open for special events and by appointment only; pier open daily, 24 hrs. Subway: A, C, F, 2, 3, 4, 5 to Jay St./Borough Hall, then Bus B61 toward Red Hook.*

6 *C-1*

YESHIVA UNIVERSITY MUSEUM

Changing exhibits of paintings, photographs, ceremonial objects, and architectural models of synagogues around the world reflect the Jewish historical and cultural experience. The museum is housed within the Center for Jewish History. *15 W. 16 St. (between 5th and 6th Aves.), Chelsea, 212/294-8330, www.yu.edu/museum. $6 adults, $4 students and seniors, free children under 5. Sun., Tues., Wed. 11-5; Thurs. 11-8. Subway: F, V to 14th St.; L to 6th Ave.*

LIBRARIES

The five boroughs have close to 200 public libraries between them, which, in addition to loaning books, sponsor more than 500 free programs monthly, including film screenings, discussions with well-known and emerging authors, and storytelling hours for children. These are the city's most significant public and private collections; if you're conducting research in art, design, or history, tap the city's museums as well—many open their specialized collections to the public.

9 *C-2*

AMERICAN BIBLE SOCIETY ARCHIVES

This is the largest Bible collection in the world outside of the Vatican, with nearly 50,000 scriptural items in 2,000 languages and dialects. Appointments can be made to tour the library, which contains leaves of a first-edition Gutenberg Bible; Helen Keller's braille Bible; and a Kai Feng Fu Torah scroll from China. A public gallery holds exhibits on various forms of scriptural and sacred art. *1865 Broadway (at 61st St.), Upper West Side, 212/408-1200. Gallery: Mon.-Wed. and Fri. 10-6, Thurs. 10-7, Sat. 10-5. Library: by appointment. Subway: A, B, C, D, 1, 2 to 59th St./Columbus Circle.*

12 *g-5*

BROOKLYN PUBLIC LIBRARY (CENTRAL LIBRARY)

An art moderne building erected in 1941 next to the Grand Army Plaza entrance to Prospect Park, Brooklyn's central library is a grand affair. A recent renovation opened up the library's long, wonderfully curving interior spaces, and the exterior, with its golden doorways, gilt bas-reliefs, and uplifting carved maxims, is as glorious as ever. Brooklyn's independent, 58-branch library system, a holdover from the days when Brooklyn was a separate city, is headquartered here. In addition to the heavily trafficked circulating areas, periodical and microfilm rooms, and a Web-linked computer lab, the library's research facilities include the Brooklyn Collection, which contains tens of thousands of black-and-white historical photographs and the photo file from the *Brooklyn Eagle*, the newspaper for which poet and Brooklynite Walt Whitman wrote. *Grand Army Plaza, Park Slope, 718/230-2100, www.brooklynpubliclibrary.org. Mon.-Thurs. 9-8, Fri. and Sat. 9-6. Subway: 2, 3 to Grand Army Plaza.*

9 *e-6*

THE MORGAN LIBRARY

(McKim, Mead & White, 1906) Housed in an austere, Italian Renaissance–style palazzo, the library was originally built for the collections of Wall Street baron J. Pierpont (J. P.) Morgan (1837–1913). The opulent interior is rich not only in furnishings and paintings, but in medieval and Renaissance illuminated manuscripts, old-master drawings and prints, rare books, and autographed literary and musical manuscripts. Among countless historic documents in the collection are three Gutenberg bibles, the only known manuscript fragment of Milton's *Paradise Lost*, and letters penned by Jane Austen and Thomas Jefferson. Augmented in recent years by the acquisition of the adjacent 45-room brownstone mansion—once the residence of J. P. Morgan, Jr.—the library now includes a graceful, glass-enclosed garden court in which lunch and tea are served. Changing exhibits of works on paper bring visitors into intimate contact with great authors and artists. *29 E. 36th St. (at Madison Ave.), Murray Hill, 212/685-0008, www.morganlibrary.org. Suggested donation $8, $6 seniors and students, free children under 12. Tues.-Thurs. 10:30-5, Fri. 10:30-8, Sat. 10:30-6, Sun. noon-6. Subway: 6 to 33rd St.*

9 d-5

NEW YORK PUBLIC LIBRARY
(Humanities & Social Sciences)
A national historic landmark covering two city blocks, the New York Public Library first opened its doors—guarded always by the famous stone lions—on May 24, 1911 (*see* Architecture, *above*). Today the library is one of the greatest research institutions in the world, with 6 million books, 12 million manuscripts, and 2.8 million pictures. Among the more unusual items in the research collection are magician Harry Houdini's personal library and a selection of 19th- and 20th-century restaurant menus. The library's beautiful Main Reading Room (completely renovated in 1999) is now functional as well as inspiring: light flows in through new UV-light filtering panes (the original glass had been blacked out since World War II!) and the old hand-carved wooden tables have been wired to the Web and electrical outlets, making them Computer Age friendly. It's the perfect blend of old meets new. The library regularly mounts full-scale exhibits on such lettered topics as American novelists, early English Bibles, New York City history, and typography. *5th Ave. and 42nd St., Midtown East, 212/930–0830; 212/ 869–8089 current gallery exhibits, www.nypl.org. Mon. and Thurs.–Sat. 10–6, Tues.–Wed. 11–7:30; call for hrs for special collections. Tours Mon.–Sat. 11 and 2. Subway: B, D, F, V to 42nd St.*

9 b-2

NEW YORK PUBLIC LIBRARY FOR THE PERFORMING ARTS
While couch potatoes are gazing their way through the Museum of Television and Radio, the ear-trained should scrutinize this wonderful library's musical scores, videotapes of great ballets, and recordings of famous opera performances. Because the library's Lincoln Center facility is undergoing a two-year renovation (scheduled for completion in late 2001), circulating and research materials are being housed in temporary locations; call for hours and locations. *40 Lincoln Center Plaza (Broadway and 64th St., just north of the Metropolitan Opera), Upper West Side, 212/870–1600. Subway: 1, 2 to 66th St.*

9 e-6

NEW YORK PUBLIC LIBRARY SCIENCE, INDUSTRY, & BUSINESS LIBRARY
This state-of-the-art research facility, opened in 1996, houses the NYPL's science, technology, and business materials. A bank of TVs tuned to business news stations and an electronic ticker tape with the latest stock prices set the library's high-tech tone. But the real draw are the scientific, business, and government databases on the library's Web-linked computers. *188 Madison Ave. (at 34th St.), Murray Hill, 212/592–7000. Mon., Fri., and Sat. 10–6; Tues. and Thurs. 11–8; Wed. 11–7. Subway: 6 to 33rd St.*

6 e-8

SCHOMBURG CENTER FOR RESEARCH IN BLACK CULTURE
A branch of the New York Public Library, this internationally renowned cultural facility in the heart of Harlem began with Arthur Schomburg's personal collection of black literature and history. Now the largest collection of its kind in the world, the library has 20,000 microfilm reels of news clippings, over 1,000 rare books, 30,000 photographs, 15,000 hours of taped oral history, 10,000 records, and 3,000 videotapes and films. In addition to its research facilities, the library has exhibits on African and African-American art and history and hosts lectures and performances in the American Negro Theatre and Langston Hughes Auditorium. *515 Malcolm X Blvd. (at 135th St.), Harlem, 212/ 491–2200. Mon.–Wed. noon–8, Thurs.– Sat. 10–6; exhibit also open Sun. 1–5. Subway: 2, 3 to 135th St.*

9 d-8

YIVO INSTITUTE FOR JEWISH RESEARCH
Established in 1925 in Vilna, Lithuania, this academic-research center for Eastern European Jewry and Jewish culture contains more than 22 million archival documents, 100,000 photographs, and 300,000 books. *22 W. 17th St. (between 5th and 6th Aves.), Chelsea, 212/246– 6080, www.yivoinstitute.org. Mon.–Thurs. 9–5. Subway: N, R to 23rd St.*

SCIENCE MUSEUMS & OBSERVATORIES

7 *c-8*

AMERICAN MUSEUM OF NATURAL HISTORY

With 30 million artifacts and specimens, more than 800 staff members, and 42 exhibition halls, the largest museum of natural history in the world has slowly but surely been remaking itself. Alongside halls of Victorian-era dioramas depicting stuffed lions, gorillas, and zebras posed in front of hand-painted backgrounds, there are a dozen new, high-tech halls filled with the latest exhibits on everything from giant squid to dinosaurs—currently the museum's biggest draw. Three spectacular new dinosaur halls on the fourth floor—the Hall of Saurischian Dinosaurs, the Hall of Ornithischian Dinosaurs, and the Hall of Vertebrate Origins—use real fossils and dinosaur skeletons to explain the latest theories on how T. rex and velociraptors might have looked, lived, and behaved. But dinosaurs are just the beginning: Don't miss the Hall of Biodiversity and its life-size re-creation of the Dzanga-Sangha Rainforest; the Hall of Fossil Mammals, with interactive video monitors on virtually every exhibit; the Hall of Meteorites, featuring the 4-billion-year-old Ahnighito, the largest meteorite ever retrieved from the Earth's surface; the Hall of Human Biology and Evolution, with dioramas tracing human origins back to such early examples of the species as Lucy; or, the new Hall of Planet Earth, which explains the geological origins of Earth (with the help of 100 giant rocks) and links the museum to the spectacularly rebuilt Hayden Planetarium (*see below*). IMAX films exploring the natural world are shown daily on the museum's colossal screen, and there's even a "dinner theater" on Friday and Saturday nights that includes cocktails (beneath the museum's beloved 94-ft-long replica of a blue whale in the "Ocean Life Cafe") and an IMAX double-feature. *Central Park West and 79th St., Upper West Side, 212/769–5100, www. amnh.org. Suggested admission $10, $7.50 seniors and students, $6 children. IMAX $15, $13 students and seniors, $9 children (includes general admission). Sun.–Thurs. 10–5:45, Fri. and Sat. 10–8:45. Subway: C to 81st St.*

7 *c-8*

HAYDEN PLANETARIUM

Completely revamped and technologically updated by the progressive architectural firm James Stewart Polshek Partnership, the planetarium re-opened in early 2000. Now part of the American Museum of Natural History's new Rose Center for Earth and Space, the planetarium is housed inside a six-story-high, glass-walled sphere, with exhibits tracking 15 billion years of the universe's evolution. An ultra-modern Sky Theater transports visitors from galaxy to galaxy, showing scenes that otherwise can only be seen by traveling in outer space. *Central Park W and 81st. St., Upper West Side, 212/769–5100, www.amnh.org/rose. $19.50 adults, $11 children 3–12, free children under 3. Sun.–Thurs. 10–5:45, Fri. and Sat. 10–8:45. Subway: B, C to 81st St.*

9 *a-5*

INTREPID SEA-AIR-SPACE MUSEUM

Formerly the U.S.S. *Intrepid*, this 900-ft aircraft carrier docked in the Hudson River is now a floating museum dedicated to air, naval, and space technology—some of it formerly top secret. On deck is an envelope-pushing array of air- and spacecraft, including the A-12 Blackbird spy plane, lunar landing modules, helicopters, and seaplanes. Docked alongside, and ready for boarding, are the *Growler*, a strategic-missile submarine; the destroyer *Edson*; and other battle-scarred naval veterans. Children will enjoy exploring the *Intrepid*'s skinny hallways and winding staircases and (for an extra $5) flying a simulated F-18 fighter-jet mission off the flight deck. *Hudson River, Pier 86 (12th Ave. and 46th St.), Midtown West, 212/245–0072, www.intrepidmuseum.org. $12, $9 seniors, veterans, U.S. reservists, college students, and students 12–17; $6 children 6–11; $2 children 2–5; $1 teachers; and free active-duty U.S. military personnel. May–Sept., weekdays 10–5, weekends 10–7; Oct.–Apr., Wed.–Sun. 10–5. Subway: A, C, E to 42nd St.; M42 bus to pier*

1 *c-6*

LIBERTY SCIENCE CENTER

Just across the Hudson River in Liberty State Park, New Jersey, the high-tech Liberty Science Center is the New York area's largest science museum for children. Its three theme floors cover Environment, Health, and Invention. Highlights include the insect zoo, the 100-ft touch tunnel, the 700-pound geodesic globe, IMAX movies, and 3-D laser shows. Special exhibits well-staffed with volunteers get children involved with everything from robots to raptors. *Liberty State Park, 251 Philip St., Jersey City, NJ, 201/200–1000, www.lsc.org. Exhibits: $10, $8 seniors and children 2–18; $2 teachers with I.D.; free children under three. Laser show and IMAX extra. Apr.–Aug., daily 9:30–5:30; Sept.–Mar., Tues.–Sun. 9:30–5:30. Call for directions by ferry or train.*

3 *h-2*

NEW YORK HALL OF SCIENCE

An easy ride on the No. 7 train from Manhattan, the New York Hall of Science is ranked as one of the nation's top 10 science museums. Children and other budding researchers are invited to explore 160 hands-on exhibits on subjects ranging from lasers to microbes. Preschoolers can make crafts at the Discovery Center; older children will enjoy the museum's insanely popular outdoor science playground. *111th St. and 48th Ave., Flushing Meadows–Corona Park, Queens, 718/699–0005, www.nyhallsci.org. $7.50; $5 children and seniors; free children under 3; free to all Sept.–May, Thurs. and Fri. 2–5. Open Sept.–May, Mon.–Wed. 9:30–2, Thurs.–Sun. 9:30–5; Jun.–Aug., Mon. 9:30–2, Tues.–Sun. 9:30–5. Subway: 7 to 111th St.*

9 *e-3*

SONY WONDER TECHNOLOGY LAB

In the postmodern Sony Building (*see Architecture, above*), a free, four-floor science and technology exhibit (sponsored by guess who? Sony!) lets children log onto computers, play sound engineer, watch high-definition TV, and learn about video-game design. *550 Madison Ave. (at 56th St.), Midtown East, 212/833–8100, www.sonywondertechlab.com. Tues., Wed., Fri., and Sat. 10–6; Thurs. 10–8, Sun. noon–6. Free. Subway: 4, 5, 6, N, R to 59th St./Lexington Ave.; E, F, N, Q, R, W to 5th Ave.*

1 *b-1*

STATEN ISLAND INSTITUTE OF ART & SCIENCE

Founded in 1881 and just a block up the hill from the Staten Island Ferry terminal, the Staten Island Institute celebrates art, science, and history. The high point is the remarkable natural-history collection, with specimens covering anthropology to zoology. *75 Stuyvesant Pl., St. George, Staten Island, 718/727–1135. Mon.–Sat. 9–5, Sun. 1–5. Suggested contribution $2.50, $1.50 children.*

STATUES & MONUMENTS

From 19th-century memorials cast in bronze to 21st-century installations crafted from used hubcaps, outdoor artworks give the city's streets and parks some unexpected twists—and occasionally offer a history lesson. Many of these can be found in Central Park; to find out more, call 212/310–6600 or connect at www.centralparknyc.org.

10 *e-2*

ALAMO

(Bernard Rosenthal, 1967) One of the city's first abstract outdoor sculptures, this enormous black, all-steel cube—sited in the middle of an East Village traffic island—was originally intended to be a temporary installation. The cube's popularity proved overwhelming, however, and it's now a neighborhood fixture. Although *Alamo* doesn't look movable, the sculpture actually turns. You—and a couple of friends—can set the off-kilter cube in motion by leaning a shoulder against it and applying a little muscle. *Astor Pl. and Lafayette St., East Village. Subway: 6 to Astor Pl.*

7 *d-8*

ALICE IN WONDERLAND

(Jose de Creeft, 1959) One of Central Park's most beloved statues, bronze Alice—based on the popular drawings by Tenniel for the book *Alice in Wonderland*—is climbed and crawled upon by local youngsters. *Central Park, Sailboat Lake (near E. 74th St.), Upper East Side. Subway: 6 to 77th St.*

7 *b-3*

ALMA MATER

(Daniel Chester French, 1903) Atop the broad, sweeping staircase of Columbia's

Low Library and overlooking the university's main plaza, this 8-ft-tall seated lady in bronze has presided over hundreds of graduation ceremonies—and, in the 1960s, riots. On sunny days, it's nice to have a seat beside her, sip your coffee, and enjoy a bite—along with the view. *Low Library, Columbia University, east of Broadway and 116th St., Morningside Heights. Subway: 1 to 116th St./Columbia University.*

7 *d-8*

HANS CHRISTIAN ANDERSEN

(Georg John Lober, 1956) A gift to the city from Danish and American schoolchildren, bronze *Hans* provides the perfect setting for reading his fairy tales. (The Central Park Conservancy sponsors readings on weekends.) Sculptural sidekick the *Ugly Duckling* was stolen in 1974, but it was soon recovered and returned to its creator's side. *Central Park, Sailboat Lake (near E. 74th St.), Upper East Side. Subway: 6 to 77th St.*

9 *d-1*

ANGEL OF THE WATERS (BETHESDA FOUNTAIN)

(Emma Stebbins, 1868) Central Park's centerpiece and the focal point of one of the prettiest spots in the city, Bethesda Fountain was named for the biblical pool in Jerusalem, which was said to have been given healing powers by an angel. Fittingly, a bronze angel rises from the splashing fountain and is waited upon by cherubs representing Temperance, Purity, Health, and Peace. Behind them, rowboats and the occasional gondola drift by on the Lake. *Central Park, Bethesda Terr. (near 72nd St. Transverse). Subway: B, C to 72nd St.*

9 *d-4*

ATLAS

(Lee Lawrie, 1937) A 15-ft-tall bronze statue on a 9-ft-high granite pedestal, *Atlas*—terminally persistent in bearing the world on his shoulders—is the defining figure of Midtown's Rockefeller Center. Interestingly, the statue was picketed when originally installed because Atlas reputedly bore a resemblance to Benito Mussolini. *International Bldg., Rockefeller Center, 5th Ave. between 50th and 51st Sts., Midtown East. Subway: E, V to 5th Ave./53rd St.; B, D, F, V to 47th–50th Sts./Rockefeller Center.*

9 *d-2*

BALTO

(Frederick George Richard Roth, 1925) Adoring schoolchildren supposedly helped finance this bronze statue commemorating Balto, a real-life sled dog who led a team of huskies carrying medicine through a blizzard to Nome, Alaska, during a 1925 diphtheria epidemic. Note the shiny patches where children have petted his snout and sat on his back. *Central Park near E. 66th St., Upper East Side. Subway: N, Q, R, W to 5th Ave.; 6 to 68th St./Hunter College.*

12 *c-3*

HENRY WARD BEECHER

(John Quincy Adams Ward, 1891) This fine bronze of the abolitionist minister was cast by an abolitionist sculptor, one of the most prolific creators of public art in his day. A few blocks away is Beecher's former pulpit, Plymouth Church of the Pilgrims (*see* Churches & Synagogues, *above*), where his stirring oratory helped foster the anti-slavery movement in the years before the Civil War. *Fulton St. at Court St., Brooklyn Heights. Subway: A, C, F to Borough Hall.*

9 *d-3*

SIMON BOLIVAR

(Sally James Farnham, 1921) One of the many enormous bronze statues fronting Central Park to the south, this one has the South American liberator on horseback atop a polished-granite pedestal. *6th Ave. and Central Park S, Midtown West. Subway: F, V to 57th St./6th Ave.*

9 *e-8*

EDWIN BOOTH AS HAMLET

(Edmond T. Quinn, 1918) Booth was America's leading Shakespearean actor in his day. He lived at 16 Gramercy Park South from 1888 until his death in 1906. (*See* Players Club *in* Historic Structures & Streets, *above, and* Gramercy Park *in* Chapter 3.) *Gramercy Park, Gramercy. Subway: 6 to 23rd St.*

9 *d-5*

WILLIAM CULLEN BRYANT

(Herbert Adams, 1911) A bronze statue of the famed 19th-century poet and journalist sits fittingly in the now-hip Midtown park that bears his name. *Bryant Park, 6th Ave. and 42nd St., Midtown West. Subway: B, D, F, V to 42nd St.*

1 *f-4*

CIVIC VIRTUE
(Frederick William MacMonnies, 1922)
Once the most prominent sculpture in
City Hall Park, this nearly nude male figure carved from a single block of marble
appears to tred carelessly upon writhing
figures of women in similar dishabille.
It's not clear if citizens were more both-
ered by the nudity or by the idea that
virtue meant crushing women with bare
feet, but the muscular statue was
protested and banished to Queens in
1941. *Queens Blvd. and Union Tpke., Forest Hills, Queens. Subway: E, F to Union
Tpke./Kew Gardens.*

7 *d-8*

CLEOPATRA'S NEEDLE
Located behind the Metropolitan
Museum of Art, this hieroglyphic-covered obelisk was a gift from Egypt in
1880. It is believed to date from the year
1600 BC. *Central Park near E. 80th St.,
Upper East Side. Subway: 6 to 77th St.*

9 *c-4*

GEORGE M. COHAN
(Georg John Lober, 1959) Cast in bronze,
the famed song-and-dance man now
gives his regards to Broadway come rain
or shine. Pay him a visit next time you're
stuck in a queue at the TKTS booth.
*Broadway and 46th St., Midtown West.
Subway: 1, 2, 3, 7, N, Q, R, W to 42nd
St./Times Sq.; N, Q, R, W to 49th St.*

9 *c-3*

COLUMBUS MONUMENT
(Gaetano Russo, 1892) Now isolated in
a traffic island in busy Columbus Circle,
this white marble statue (perched on a
26-ft-high, 700-ton granite column) was
erected on the 400th anniversary of
Columbus's first voyage to the New
World. *Columbus Circle (Broadway and
59th St.), Upper West Side. Subway: A, B,
C, D, 1, 2 to 59th St./Columbus Circle.*

9 *d-2*

**DELACORTE
MUSICAL CLOCK**
(Andrea Spadini, 1965) Almost as popular as the zoo's live residents, these
bronze denizens do an hourly dance to
the tune of one of 32 nursery songs.
*Central Park Zoo, near 5th Ave. and 64th
St., Upper East Side. Subway: N, Q, R, W
to 5th Ave.; 6 to 68th St./Hunter College.*

10 *e-7*

ABRAHAM DE PEYSTER
(George Edwin Bissell, 1896) This
bronze statue of prosperous colonial
merchant Abraham de Peyster replaced
an ill-fated model of King George III.
George was pulled down by an angry
colonial mob following the signing of
the Declaration of Independence, and
was then melted down to make bullets.
*Bowling Green (Broadway at Whitehall
St.), Lower Manhattan. Subway: 4, 5 to
Bowling Green.*

9 *c-4*

FATHER DUFFY MEMORIAL
(Charles Keck, 1937) Cast in bronze atop
a polished granite base and cross, Father
Duffy was a figure straight out of Damon
Runyon. Duffy, whose parish was honky-
tonk Times Square in the 1920s, was
chaplain to the Fighting 69th in World
War I. *Duffy Sq. (Broadway between 46th
and 47th Sts.), Midtown West. Subway: 1,
2, 3, 7, N, Q, R, W to 42nd St./Times Sq.;
N, Q, R, W to 49th St.*

9 *c-1*

EAGLES & PREY
(Kristin Fratin, 1850) This is one of Central Park's earliest sculptures. *Central
Park northwest of the Mall. Subway: B, C
to 72nd St.*

9 *c-1*

THE FALCONER
(George B. Simonds, 1871) This bronze
statue rises a graceful 10 ft above Central Park. *72nd St. Transverse, Upper West
Side. Subway: B, C to 72nd St.*

7 *a-5*

FIREMEN'S MEMORIAL
(Attilio Piccirilli, 1912) The representa-
tions of Duty and Courage pay tribute
to New York's Bravest, and the bronze
plaque is a tribute to their horses,
which once pulled the apparatus for
the city's Fire Department. *Riverside Dr.
and 100th St., Upper West Side. Subway:
1 to 103rd St.*

10 *e-6*

BENJAMIN FRANKLIN
(Ernst Plassmann, 1872) Here the
founding father holds a copy of the
newspaper he edited, the *Pennsylvania
Gazette. Park Row at Nassau and Spruce
Sts., Lower Manhattan. Subway: 4, 5, 6 to
Brooklyn Bridge/City Hall.*

9 | d-3

DORIS C. FREEDMAN PLAZA

Old meets new. Not far from such New York landmarks as the Plaza Hotel, Saint-Gauden's monument to General Sherman, and the Pulitzer Fountain (*see below*), the southeast corner of Central Park has become a showcase for outdoor sculpture by contemporary artists. The Public Art Fund curates rotating exhibits here of oversize works by the likes of Keith Haring and Tom Otterness. *5th Ave. and 60th St., Midtown East, 212/ 980–4575. Subway: N, R to 5th Ave.*

9 | d-2

FRIEDSAM MEMORIAL CAROUSEL

You might not think that merry-go-rounds class as art or sculpture, but Central Park's carousel—originally built in 1903 and operated at a Coney Island amusement park (it was moved to the park in 1952)—is considered a fabulous example of turn-of-the-20th-century folk art. And, hey, it's interactive, too. While the organ plays, you can ride the colorful hand-carved wooden horsies for $1. *Central Park at Center Dr. and the 65th St. transverse, 212/879–0244. Apr.–Oct., weekdays 10–6, weekends 10–7; Nov.–Mar., weekends 10–4:30, weather permitting. Subway: 1, 2 to 66th Street/Lincoln Center.*

9 | f-4

GOOD DEFEATS EVIL

(Zurab Tsereteli, 1990) The dragon that St. George is spearing was made of slices of what were once Soviet SS-20 and American Pershing ballistic missiles, chopped up in accordance with the 1988 treaty eliminating intermediate-range missiles. The statue was a gift from the Soviet government. *United Nations (1st Ave. between 42nd and 48th Sts.), Midtown East. Subway: 4, 5, 6, 7 to 42nd St./Grand Central.*

10 | e-6

NATHAN HALE

(Frederick MacMonnies, 1890) This imagined bronze portrait of Hale depicts a very real hero, who was executed by the British as a spy in 1776. *City Hall Park (see above).*

7 | d-7

ALEXANDER HAMILTON

(Carl Conrads, 1880) This granite statue of the famed Federalist was presented to the city by Hamilton's son John C.

Hamilton. *Central Park, East Dr. near 83rd St. Subway: 4, 5, 6 to 86th St.*

11 | d-2

ALEXANDER LYMAN HOLLEY

(John Quincy Adams Ward, 1889) Holley was an American inventor; his bronze likeness is considered one of this prolific sculptor's best public works. *Washington Sq. Park (at foot of 5th Ave.), Greenwich Village. Subway: N, Q, R, W to 8th St.; A, B, C, D, E, F, V to W. 4th St./Washington Sq.*

5 | b-3

HUDSON MEMORIAL COLUMN

(Walter Cook, 1909) This 100-ft-high column was commissioned to commemorate the 300th anniversary of Hudson's discovery of the river down below. It's topped with a 16-ft-high bronze statue of Hudson himself (Karl Gruppe and Karl Bitter, 1938). *Henry Hudson Memorial Park at Kappock Ave. and Independence Pkwy., Bronx. Subway: 1 to 225th St.*

9 | c-1

INDIAN HUNTER

(John Quincy Adams Ward, 1866) Initially cast in plaster, this realistic bronze group grew out of sketches made during a visit to the American West. It was Central Park's first statue by an American sculptor, and it led to countless commissions for the prolific Ward. *Central Park northwest of the Mall. Subway: B, C to 72nd St.*

7 | a-6

JOAN OF ARC

(Anna Vaughn Hyatt Huntington, 1915) This bronze statue on a granite pedestal contains stone fragments from the tower where Joan was imprisoned in Rouen, and from Rheims Cathedral. It was the city's first public work to be erected to honor a woman and the first by a woman sculptor. *Riverside Dr. and 93rd St., Upper West Side. Subway: 1, 2, 3 to 96th St.*

10 | e-1

LAFAYETTE

(Frederic-Auguste Bartholdi, 1876) Quoting the Marquis de Lafayette, the inscription for the statue—by the same French sculptor who gave New York the Statue of Liberty (*see below*)—reads: "As soon as I heard of American independence my heart was enlisted." *Union Sq. (Broadway and 14th St.), Flatiron District. Subway: 4, 5, 6, L, N, Q, R, W to 14th St./Union Sq.*

4 f-2
ABRAHAM LINCOLN
(Henry Kirke Brown, 1869) Located in Brooklyn's Prospect Park, this statue is said to be the first of Lincoln cast after his assassination. Yet history has not been kind to it. Lincoln's right hand points to a manuscript that is now, alas, missing. And the nearby Kate Wollman Memorial Rink—a 20th-century addition to the park—has directed pedestrian and skating traffic toward Lincoln's back. For the sake of both art and history, Honest Abe deserves better treatment. *Concert Grove, Prospect Park, Brooklyn. Subway: D, Q to Prospect Park.*

9 d-5
LIONS
(Edward Clark Potter, 1911) The closest thing New York has to a mascot, these stone lions are a matched pair. Dubbed Patience and Fortitude by Mayor Fiorello La Guardia, they are dear to the hearts of New Yorkers and look especially smart at Christmastime, when they are bedecked with red-trimmed wreaths. *New York Public Library, 5th Ave. and 41st St., Midtown East. Subway: B, D, F, V to 42nd St.*

9 c-3
MAINE MONUMENT
(Attilio Piccirilli, 1913) A beaux-arts memorial of gleaming gilt-bronze equestrian figures atop an imposing limestone pedestal, this dramatic work—guarding the southwest entrance to Central Park—commemorates those who perished on the battleship *Maine* in 1898. *Columbus Circle (Broadway and 59th St.), Midtown West. Subway: A, B, C, D, 1, 2 to 59th St./Columbus Circle.*

4 e-1
MANHATTAN & BROOKLYN
(Daniel Chester French, 1916) This symbolic representation of the two boroughs originally stood at the Brooklyn end of the Manhattan Bridge. It now graces the entryway to a world-class museum. *Brooklyn Museum of Art, 200 Eastern Pkwy. (at Washington Ave.), Park Slope, Brooklyn. Subway: 2, 3 to Eastern Pkwy./Brooklyn Museum.*

9 d-1
MOTHER GOOSE
(Frederick G. R. Roth, 1938) This 8-ft granite embodiment of the feathered matriarch stands on the site of the old Central Park Casino. *Central Park, East Dr. near 72nd St. Subway: 6 to 68th St./Hunter College.*

10 f-8
NEW YORK VIETNAM VETERANS MEMORIAL
(Pete Wormser, William Fellows) Unveiled on May 6, 1985, 10 years after the war ended, New York's Vietnam Veterans Memorial is a translucent wall of glass blocks, 14 ft high and 70 ft long, inscribed with excerpts of letters to and from those who served. Only some of those commemorated here came home. Visitors leave candles, notes, and flowers on the granite shelves. *Vietnam Veterans Plaza, 55 Water St. (near Broad St.), Lower Manhattan. Subway: J, M to Whitehall St.*

9 e-2
107TH INFANTRY
(Karl M. Illava, 1927) An alumnus of the 107th in World War I, the sculptor includes himself in this bronze depiction of valiant doughboys. *5th Ave. and 67th St., Upper East Side. Subway: 6 to 68th St./Hunter College.*

9 f-4
PEACE
(Antun Augustincic, 1954) This heroic bronze statue was presented to the U.N. by the government of Yugoslavia. *United Nations Gardens, near 1st Ave. and 46th St., Midtown East. Subway: 4, 5, 6, 7 to 42nd St./Grand Central.*

12 e-2
PRISON SHIP MARTYRS' MONUMENT
(McKim, Mead & White, 1908) One of the world's tallest Doric columns—148 ft, 8 inches—is a memorial to the 11,500 American patriots who died on British prison ships anchored in New York Harbor during the Revolution. *Ft. Greene Park, Brooklyn. Subway: B, D, M, Q, J to DeKalb Ave.; C to Lafayette Ave.*

9 d-4
PROMETHEUS
(Paul Manship, 1934) Cast in bronze and finished in gold leaf, the fire thief is set

in a flashing fountain-pool overseeing ice-skaters in winter and alfresco diners in summer. *Lower Plaza, Rockefeller Center, 5th–6th Aves. between 50th and 51st Sts., Midtown West. Subway: B, D, F, V to 47th–50th Sts./Rockefeller Center.*

9 *d-3*

PULITZER FOUNTAIN

(Carrère & Hastings; sculptor: Karl Bitter, 1916) This fountain became a legendary icon of the Roaring Twenties once F. Scott and Zelda Fitzgerald went wading in it. Originally built of limestone, it eventually deteriorated to the point of crumbling, and was virtually rebuilt in more-durable granite. The goddess Pomona was given a new patina. *Grand Army Plaza (5th Ave. between 58th and 59th Sts.), Midtown East. Subway: N, Q, R, W to 5th Ave.*

10 *c-6*

THE REAL WORLD

(Tom Otterness, 1992) In this whimsical bronze sculpture garden in Hudson River Park, lilliputian bronze figures frolic along a trail of oversize pennies, playfully poking fun at the money-making activities in the nearby World Financial Center. *North end of Hudson River Park, near Chambers St., TriBeCa. Subway: 1, 2, 3 to Chambers St.*

9 *a-1*

ELEANOR ROOSEVELT

(Penelope Jencks, 1996) Unless you count fictional characters like Alice in Wonderland (*see above*), there aren't many statues commemorating women in the Big Apple. It's fitting, though, that the first monument commissioned to depict an American woman in a New York City park should be of former first lady Eleanor Roosevelt (1884–1962)— both a women's rights advocate and a longtime New Yorker. Mrs. Roosevelt gave many of her years to public service, most notably as U.N. Human Rights Commissioner during her tenure as U.S. delegate to the United Nations, and this statue is a suitable tribute. Gracing the southern entrance to Riverside Park, the 8-ft-high bronze is posed deep in thought. *Riverside Park (at W. 72nd St. and Riverside Dr.), Upper West Side. Subway: 1, 2, 3 to 72nd St.*

7 *c-8*

THEODORE ROOSEVELT MEMORIAL

(James Earle Fraser, 1940) Ride 'em, Teddy! At 16 ft tall, this bronze group— with president Theodore Roosevelt astride a sinewy steed—is one of the largest and best equestrian statues in the world. *American Museum of Natural History, Central Park West and 79th St., Upper West Side. Subway: B, C to 81st St.*

4 *e-1*

SCULPTURE GARDEN

The Brooklyn Museum's outdoor garden displays architectural sculpture and ornamentation salvaged from demolition sites around the city—most notably the original Penn Station. *Brooklyn Museum of Art, 200 Eastern Pkwy. (at Washington Ave.), Park Slope, Brooklyn. Subway: 2, 3 to Eastern Pkwy./Brooklyn Museum.*

9 *c-2*

SEVENTH REGIMENT MEMORIAL

(John Quincy Adams Ward, 1873) The 58 members of this New York State regiment who died in the Civil War are memorialized here. *Central Park, West Dr. near 67th St. Subway: B, C to 72nd St.*

9 *e-7*

WILLIAM H. SEWARD

(Randolph Rogers, 1876) Truth or fiction? Word on the street is that the sculptor set Secretary of State Seward's head on President Lincoln's body—for which he already had molds from another project in Philadelphia. *Madison Sq. Park (5th–Madison Aves., 23rd–26th Sts.), Murray Hill. Subway: 6, N, Q, R, W to 23rd St.*

9 *d-3*

SHERMAN MONUMENT

(Augustus Saint-Gaudens, 1903) A graceful equestrian group depicting William Tecumseh Sherman on horseback preceded by an all-powerful angel, this bronze tribute to the Civil War general is one of several monuments towering over the southern edge of Central Park. It was one of the last works created by Saint-Gaudens, who in the latter decades of the 1800s set the stage for works that blended sculpture and landscape architecture. *Grand Army Plaza, 5th Ave. and 59th St., Midtown East. Subway: N, Q, R, W to 5th Ave.*

3 *d-3*

SOCRATES SCULPTURE PARK

Once a local dump site, this 4.2-acre park was reclaimed by local artists in the 1980s as a venue for outdoor sculpture. Now officially a city park, it displays huge installation works, with the Manhattan skyline and East River as backdrops. *Vernon Blvd. at Broadway, Long Island City, Queens, 718/956–1819. Daily 10 AM–sunset. Subway: N to Broadway.*

7 *a-6*

SOLDIERS' & SAILORS' MEMORIAL

(Paul E. M. Duboy) Built in 1902 to commemorate the Civil War dead, this 96-ft white marble column along Riverside Park was fashioned after Athens's monument to Lysicrates. *Riverside Dr. and 89th St., Upper West Side. Subway: 1, 2 to 86th St.*

4 *e-1*

SOLDIERS' & SAILORS' MEMORIAL ARCH

(John H. Duncan, 1892) Designed after the Arc de Triomphe in Paris as a monument to Civil War veterans, this 80-ft-high, 80-ft-wide limestone arch dominates a busy traffic circle next to Brooklyn's Prospect Park, creating one of the city's grandest streetscapes. A fantastic bronze sculpture of a four-horse chariot (symbolizing victory) by Frederick MacMonnies adorns the top. Occasionally on weekends, Prospect Park's Urban Park Rangers open the interior stairways to the public, and the views from the roof are marvelous. *Grand Army Plaza at the intersection of Prospect Park W, Eastern Pkwy., and Flatbush and Vanderbilt Aves., Park Slope, Brooklyn, 718/965–8999. Subway: 2, 3 to Grand Army Plaza.*

1 *c-6*

STATUE OF LIBERTY NATIONAL MONUMENT

Probably the most famous statue in the world, *Liberty Enlightening the World* was sculpted by Frederic-Auguste Bartholdi and presented to the United States as a gift from France in 1886. Since then she has become a near-universal symbol of freedom, standing a proud 152 ft high on top of an 89-ft pedestal (executed by Richard Morris Hunt) on an island in New York Harbor. Gustav Eiffel designed the statue's iron skeleton, through which visitors can climb spiral stairs to reach the statue's crown (*see* Viewpoints, *below*). In anticipation of her centennial, Liberty underwent a long-overdue restoration in the mid-'80s and emerged with great fanfare on July 4, 1986, more beautiful and awe-inspiring than ever. *Liberty Island, New York Harbor, off Lower Manhattan. Ferry tickets: Castle Clinton, Battery Park, 212/269–5755; 212/363–3200 (National Parks Service) for statue information, www.statueoflibertyferry.com. $8 adults, $6 seniors, $3 children under 17; free children under 3. Boats leave for the island daily 8:30–4:30 every 20 minutes. Subway: 4, 5 to Bowling Green.*

7 *d-8*

STILL HUNT

(Edward Kemeys, 1883) Perched on one of the park's natural outcroppings, this crouched bronze panther is so realistic that you may feel the cat has snuck up on you. *Central Park, East Dr. near 76th St., Upper East Side. Subway: 6 to 77th St.*

7 *a-4*

STRAUS MEMORIAL

(Henry Augustus Lukeman, 1915) Although women were offered space in the *Titanic*'s lifeboats, Ida Straus chose to stay with her husband, Isador, and both perished on the doomed ocean liner's maiden voyage. The philanthropist couple had lived near this memorial. *Broadway and 106th St., Upper West Side. Subway: 1 to 103rd St.*

10 *f-1*

PETER STUYVESANT

(Gertrude Vanderbilt Whitney, 1941) This life-size bronze was cast by the founder of the Whitney Museum. Standing on what was once part of his farm, it depicts New York's last Dutch governor, the peg-legged Peter Stuyvesant, buried at nearby St. Mark's Church in-the-Bowery (*see* Churches & Synagogues *and* Haunted Places, *above*). *Stuyvesant Sq. (1st to 3rd Aves., between 15th and 17th Sts.), East Village. Subway: L to 1st Ave., 3rd Ave.*

SUBWAY STATION ART

As part of the ongoing capital improvement program for the subway system, historic subway mosaics and ceramics are being restored and many new works commissioned. One of the most nicely restored stations is the East Village's Astor Place, which is decorated with ceramic tiles of beavers (symbolizing how the wealthy Astor family made their fortune in the 19th-century fur trade). One of the most impressive new works, found in the Houston Street station on the "1" line, is a series of highly detailed, colorful glass mosaic "windows" (Deborah Brown, 1994). Featuring undersea creatures, such as sea turtles, the mosaics suggest what might be glimpsed if the subway traveled underwater instead of underground.

9 *g-4*

SWORDS INTO PLOWSHARES

(Evgeniy Vuchetich, 1958) This dramatic, 9-ft-tall bronze was a gift from the U.S.S.R. *United Nations Gardens, near 1st Ave. and 46th St., Midtown East. Subway: 4, 5, 6, 7 to 42nd St./Grand Central.*

7 *d-8*

TEMPEST

(Milton Hebald, 1966) Depicting Shakespeare's Prospero, the *Tempest* monument is dedicated to Joseph Papp, the theatrical guru who brought free Shakespeare to the park. This statue violated an 1876 law prohibiting commemorative statues until five years after the subject's death, but no one complained and Papp continued to work his magic on New York theater for 25 years after it was erected. *Central Park, near Delacorte Theater (enter at W. 81st St.). Subway: B, C to 72nd St. or 81st St.*

7 *d-5*

ALBERT BERTIL THORVALSDEN, SELF-PORTRAIT

(Donated by Denmark, 1894) Cast from the marble original, this self-portrait by the great neoclassical sculptor was donated by the Danish in recognition of Thorvalsden's influence on early American sculpture. *Central Park near E. 96th St. Subway: 6 to 96th St.*

3 *h-2*

UNISPHERE

(Peter Muller-Munk, 1964) Made for the 1964–1965 World's Fair in Flushing Meadows–Corona Park, the truly massive Unisphere is a 140-ft-high, 380-ton steel globe of the Earth. Its gleaming frame—famously adorning the back entrance to the U.S.T.A. Tennis Center and pictured in countless TV commercials—shows latitude and longitude

lines and the seven continents. *Flushing Meadows–Corona Park, Queens, near 54th Ave. Subway: 7 to Shea Stadium.*

7 *d-4*

UNTERMEYER FOUNTAIN (DANCING GIRLS)

(Walter Schott, 1947) These beautifully sculpted, spirited maidens from Untermeyer's Yonkers estate are among the showpieces of Central Park's only European-style garden. (*See* Botanical Gardens *in* Chapter 3.) *Central Park, Conservatory Gardens, 5th Ave. and 104th St., Upper East Side. Subway: 6 to 103rd St.*

9 *b-1*

GIUSEPPI VERDI

(Pasquale Civiletti, 1906) Made of Carrara marble, this statue in triangular Verdi Square commemorates the great 19th-century composer. It's flanked by figures from Verdi's operas *Aida, Otello,* and *Falstaff. Verdi Sq., Broadway and 73rd St., Upper West Side. Subway: 1, 2, 3 to 72nd St.*

10 *e-8*

GIOVANNI DA VERRAZANO

(Ettore Ximenes, 1909) Italian-Americans erected this monument to honor the captain of the ship that first sighted New York Harbor in 1524. *Battery Park, Battery Pl., and State St., Lower Manhattan. Subway: 4, 5 to Bowling Green.*

10 *e-1*

GEORGE WASHINGTON

(Henry Kirke Brown, with John Quincy Adams Ward, 1856) Washington on horseback marches beautifully into battle, in bronze. One of the oldest public sculptures surviving in the city, Washington and his horse were commissioned by Yankee merchants when the South first threatened to secede from the Union. *Union Sq. (Broadway and 14th St.), Flatiron District. Subway: 4, 5, 6, L, N, Q, R, W to 14th St./Union Sq.*

10 *e-7*

GEORGE WASHINGTON

(John Quincy Adams Ward, 1883) Occupying the site where Washington was inaugurated in 1789 as the first president of the United States, the statue is said to contain a stone (in its pedestal) from the spot where Washington stood. *Steps of Federal Hall, Wall and Broad Sts., Lower Manhattan. Subway: 4, 5 to Wall St.*

11 d-2

WASHINGTON ARCH

(McKim, Mead & White, 1892) First erected in wood in 1889 for the centennial of Washington's inauguration, this marble arch was designed by famed New York architect Stanford White. The statues, *Washington at War* (1916) and *Washington at Peace* (1917), were added later; bodybuilder Charles Atlas is said to have modeled for the civilian version of Washington. *Washington Sq. Park (at foot of 5th Ave.), Greenwich Village. Subway: N, Q, R, W to 8th St.; A, B, C, D, E, F, V to W. 4th St./Washington Sq.*

9 c-1

DANIEL WEBSTER

(Thomas Ball, 1876) The famed American statesman and orator is here adorned with his own memorable maxim "Liberty and union, now and forever, one and inseparable." *Central Park, West Dr. near 72nd St., Upper West Side. Subway: B, C to 72nd St.*

VIEWPOINTS

10 g-6

BROOKLYN BRIDGE

No bridge in the world had an elevated promenade when John Roebling conceived one for his bridge in 1869 (*see* Bridges, *above*). Dedicated exclusively to pedestrians (and now bicycles and Rollerbladers), the boardwalk was designed to allow uninterrupted views in every direction. When the Great East River Bridge (as it was then called) was opened, in 1883, 150,300 pedestrians paid a penny each to walk the mile across it. The walk is free now, and the view considerably different, but the experience is no less magnificent. Don't miss this trek, even if you only go to the first tower; if you do cross to Brooklyn, wander over to the Brooklyn Heights Promenade (*see below*) for another famous view. *City Hall Park, Manhattan, to Cadman Plaza W, Brooklyn. Subway: 4, 5, 6 to Brooklyn Bridge/City Hall; A, C to High St./Brooklyn Bridge.*

12 a-3

BROOKLYN HEIGHTS PROMENADE

Strolling, sitting on a classic park bench, and watching the sunset on this riverbank esplanade are divine, backed by an incomparable, bird's-eye view of the Manhattan skyline. (*See* Brooklyn Heights in Historic Structures & Streets, *above*.) *1 block west of Columbia Heights from Remsen to Orange Sts. Subway: 2, 3 to Clark St.*

9 d-6

EMPIRE STATE BUILDING

At 102 stories (1,250 ft), it's now only the sixth-tallest building in the world, but it's still the most elegant aerie. The observation deck—outdoors on the 86th floor—has 360° views, with 80-mi visibility on clear days. The views of the city's incomparable architecture, toy-size taxis jockeying on the streets below, and—at night—New York's twinkling lights never fail to take one's breath away. For a different kind of view, stop off on the second floor and take the New York Skyride, a big-screen "thrill ride" that simulates a flight over New York City. (*See* Architecture, *above*). *350 5th Ave. (at 34th St.), Midtown East, 212/736-3100. Observatory: $9, $7 seniors, $4 children under 12; free children under 5. Daily 9 AM–11 PM. New York Skyride, 212/279-9777. $13.50, $10.50 seniors, military, and children. 10 AM–10 PM. Subway: B, D, F, N, Q, R, V, W to 34th St./Herald Sq.*

7 e-7

METROPOLITAN MUSEUM OF ART ROOFTOP SCULPTURE GARDEN (THE IRIS & B. GERALD CANTOR ROOF GARDEN)

Topping off the Lila Acheson Wallace wing, the Met's rooftop sculpture garden overlooks Central Park, with Midtown and the Upper West Side as beautiful backdrops. Come at twilight and watch the city's lights slowly and glamorously emerge as the sky darkens. (*See* Art Museums, *above*.) *5th Ave. and 82nd St., Upper East Side. Sculpture Garden open May–Oct., weather permitting. Subway: 4, 5, 6 to 86th St.*

7 a-2

RIVERSIDE CHURCH

The church's observation platform affords a lovely, unobstructed view of the Hudson River, New Jersey Palisades, and George Washington Bridge from 392 ft. (*See* Churches & Synagogues, *above*.) *Riverside Dr. at 120th St., Morningside Heights, 212/870-6700. Free. Open Tues.–Sun 9–5. Subway: 1 to 116th St./Columbia University.*

10 f-7

SOUTH STREET SEAPORT, PIER 17

This shopping and dining pier juts 500 yards into the East River, offering superb views of the Brooklyn Bridge and the harbor. Sunset is the best time to visit; head to the far end of the pier, where you can sit right on the river on the upper or lower promenade. (*See* History Museums, *above, and* Malls *in* Chapter 2.) *Fulton St. and East River, Lower Manhattan. Subway: 2, 3 to Fulton St.; A, C, 2, 3, 4 to Fulton and Broadway/Nassau St.*

10 e-8

STATEN ISLAND FERRY

This 25-minute boat ride crosses Upper New York Bay and offers wonderfully panoramic views—and it's absolutely free. The ferry operates 24 hours a day all year. *Whitehall St. at State St., Lower Manhattan; foot of Bay St., St. George, Staten Island, 718/727–2508. Departures: usually every 30 mins, otherwise every 20 mins during rush hour and every hour after 12:30 AM and in the morning on weekends. Subway: 4, 5 to Bowling Green.*

1 c-6

STATUE OF LIBERTY NATIONAL MONUMENT

The 20-minute boat ride to resplendent Lady Liberty (*see* Statues & Monuments, *above*) provides lovely vistas of New York Harbor. Once you're there, the view from Liberty's crown (often available up to those on the 8:30 ferry) is unforgettable. *New York Harbor, off Lower Manhattan. Ferry tickets: Castle Clinton, Battery Park, 212/269–5755, www.statueoflibertyferry.com. $8 adults, $6 seniors, $3 children under 17; free children under 3. Boats leave for the island daily 8:30–4:30 every 20 mins. Subway: 4, 5 to Bowling Green.*

guided tours

BOAT TOURS

10 f-7

THE BEAST

Reaching speeds up to 45 mph, this speedboat takes you on a wild 30-minute ride around the harbor. *Pier 16*

(Fulton and South Sts.), South Street Seaport, 212/563–3200. May–Oct. Subway: Fulton St.

9 a-5

CIRCLE LINE CRUISES

Manhattan is an island, after all; and this 35-mi, 3-hour cruise circumnavigates it, offering odd views and a funny and informative commentary. The cruise also offers a much appreciated chance to put your feet up and relax while seeing the sights. For a more romantic ride, try the 2-hour, 7 PM "Harbor Lights" cruise from the same location. *Pier 83 (12th Ave. and 42nd St.), Midtown West, 212/563–3200, www.circleline.com. Subway: A, C, E to 42nd St.; take M42 bus to pier 83.*

9 a-5

NEW YORK WATERWAY

Like Circle Line, this large fleet offers numerous boat cruises around Manhattan. They also offer a wide range of interesting trips, including full-day Hudson Valley tours, with stops at major attractions; boat transport to and from Yankee and Mets baseball games and Army football games; and twilight and music cruises. You can hail one of the company's free shuttle buses to the waterfront; the buses pick up commuters for the line's heavily traveled ferry services to New Jersey. *Pier 78 (12th Ave. and 38th St.), Midtown West, 800/533–3779, www.nywaterway.com. Subway: A, C, E to 42nd St.; take M42 bus to pier 78.*

10 d-6

PETREL

Sail New York Harbor on the same spectacular 70-ft yawl that JFK sailed as President; just take care to reserve two days in advance. Cruises last 1–2 hours. *North Cove Yacht Harbor (in front of the World Financial Center, south of Vesey St.), Battery Park City, 212/825–1976. Subway: 4, 5 to Wall St.*

10 f-7

PIONEER

Take a 2-hour sail on a 102-ft twin-mast schooner built in 1885. *Pier 16, South Street Seaport (Fulton and South Sts.), Lower Manhattan, 212/748–8600, southstseaport.com. Sails May–Sept. Subway: A, C, 2, 3, 4 to Fulton St.*

`10` *f-7*

SEAPORT MUSIC CRUISES

When it's warm, 2-hour evening cruises feature live jazz, blues, and funk, as well as DJed dance parties. *Pier 16, South Street Seaport (Fulton and South Sts.), Lower Manhattan, 212/630–8888. Sails May–Sept. Subway: A, C, 2, 3, 4 to Fulton St.*

`9` *d-1*

VENETIAN GONDOLA

What to do with that breathless summer evening? Try gliding the waters of Central Park Lake in an authentic Venetian gondola—the 37½-ft *Daughter of Venice*—expertly navigated by a traditionally attired gondolier. It's expensive, but it's pure magic. The gondola can hold up to six people. *Loeb Boathouse, Central Park, near E. 74th St., 212/517–3623. Available May–Sept., nightly 5–10. Subway: 6 to 77th St.*

`9` *a-5*

WORLD YACHT CRUISES

These luxury restaurant yachts offer three-hour, four-course dinner and dancing cruises around the tip of Manhattan. You'll need to reserve in advance. *Pier 81 (12th Ave. and 41st St.), Midtown West, 212/630–8100. Dinner cruises nightly 7–10. Subway: A, C, E to 42nd St.*

BUS TOURS

`9` *c-5*

GRAY LINE NEW YORK

Great for tourists, Gray Line offers more than 20 bus tours of New York City, ranging from quick, 2-hour trips to all-day excursions. A popular option is the double-decker "Hop on, hop off" bus, which shuttles visitors to major sights around town and allows them to linger at each one as long as they like. *Port Authority Bus Terminal, North Wing, 8th Ave. and 42nd St., Midtown West, 212/397–2600, www.greylinenewyork.com. Subway: A, C, E to 42nd St.*

`9` *c-5*

HARLEM SPIRITUALS

This outfit offers 4-hour Sunday gospel trips to Harlem, as well as bus tours of Brooklyn and the Bronx. *690 8th Ave. (at 43rd St.), Midtown West, 212/757–0425. Subway: A, C, E to 42nd St.*

`9` *b-5*

KRAMER'S REALITY TOUR

Although "Seinfeld" addicts now can only get their fix from daily reruns, the real-life Kramer is still putting on a good show. The irascible Cosmo Kramer is based on real-life New Yorker Kenny Kramer, who, lacking no commercial spirit, started his own tour company to take visitors past the show's New York sites. You'll visit the real-life Soup Nazi, and, of course Tom's Restaurant, where Jerry, Elaine, and George vent their respective spleens. The 3-hour tours ($37) take place at noon on weekends. Reserve in advance. *Pulse Theater, 432 W. 42nd St. (between 9th and 10th Aves.), Midtown West, 212/268–5525, www.kennykramer.com. Subway: A, C, E to 42nd St.*

HELICOPTER TOURS

`9` *a-7*

LIBERTY HELICOPTER

Fasten your seat belt and choose from different flights overlooking sights from the Statue of Liberty and Brooklyn Bridge to Midtown's skyscrapers. These pilot-narrated tours range from the 4½-minute, $48 "Lady Liberty" to the 15-minute, $180 "Great Adventure," which includes views of all five boroughs. *Heliport: 12th Ave. and 30th St. on the Hudson River, Midtown West, 212/465–8905. Daily 9–9 (weather permitting). Subway: 1, 2, 3 to 34th St./Penn Station.*

SPECIALTY TOURS

`9` *b-2*

METROPOLITAN OPERA BACKSTAGE

Opera singers love this six-tier, 3,800-seat auditorium—and so does the Metropolitan Opera Guild. Their tours offer a fascinating backstage look at the often bustling scenery and costume shops, auditorium, stage area, and rehearsal facilities. They don't promise Pavarotti, but you never know. Reserve in advance; $10, $5 students. *Lincoln Center Plaza (Broadway at 64th St.), Upper West Side, 212/769–7020. Tours depart Oct.–June, weekdays 3:45, Sat. 10 AM. Subway: 1, 2 to 66th St./Lincoln Center.*

`9` d-4

NBC STUDIO TOUR

NBC has hung its hat in the GE Building for over 50 years. Daily hour-long $7 tours let visitors onto the sets of "Saturday Night Live," "The Today Show," "Late Night with Conan O'Brien," and "The Rosie O'Donnell Show." *30 Rockefeller Plaza (50th St. between 5th and 6th Aves.), Midtown West, 212/664–7174. Tours 9:30–4:30. Subway: B, D, F, V to 47th–50th Sts./Rockefeller Center.*

`10` g-3

SCHAPIRO'S WINERY

Napa Valley it's not, but Schapiro's, founded in 1899 as a maker of kosher wines, is Manhattan's only working winery. Its motto (no joke): "The wine you can cut with a knife." Tour the wine cellars, see the presses, and taste the wine; both are free. *126 Rivington St. (at Essex St.), Lower East Side, 212/674–4404 or 800/830–9108, www.schapiro-wine.com. Tours depart hourly Sun. 11–4. Subway: F, J to Essex St./Delancey St.*

WALKING TOURS

ADVENTURE ON A SHOESTRING

This group's motto is "Exploring the world within our reach, within our means." Rain-or-shine jaunts include historic walking tours of Chinatown, Hell's Kitchen, "elegant" Gramercy Park, "haunted" Greenwich Village; ethnic tours including Greek Astoria; and theme tours like "Marilyn Monroe's Manhattan." What makes this outfit really unique is the price: $5 per person, the same price they charged when they started up in 1963, and a fee they guarantee will never increase. *212/265–2663.*

BIG APPLE GREETER

Who says New York isn't welcoming? Friendly New Yorkers show the ins and out of their city on 2- to 4-hour jaunts on foot and via public transport through neighborhoods of your choice in all five boroughs. And it's free. *212/669–8159.*

BIG ONION WALKING TOURS

Focusing on urban history and the city's multiethnic neighborhoods, Big Onion—founded in 1990 by a group of Columbia University graduate students—leads 2-hour walking tours in Manhattan Thursday–Sunday. One of the most popular is "The Multiethnic Eating Tour," on which you can sample the Lower East Side's mozzarella, pickles, and dim sum. *212/439–1090, www.bigonion.com.*

BROOKLYN CENTER FOR THE URBAN ENVIRONMENT

These unique walking tours traverse Brooklyn's lesser-known neighborhoods and occasionally include boat rides on such unlikely waterways as the Gowanus Canal, focusing always on the borough's unique history, culture, and ecology. *718/788–8500.*

`9` e-5

GRAND TOUR

This free Grand Central neighborhood tour, sponsored by the Grand Central Partnership, focuses on the area's architecture and history. The walk includes Grand Central Terminal and its environs: the art deco interiors of the Chanin and Chrysler buildings, the Helmsley Building, and more. *212/883–2420, www. grandcentralpartnership.org.*

HERITAGE TRAILS

Explore 400 years of history from colonial New York to the present day. In addition to several guided tours of Lower Manhattan, heritage trails gives away free maps of downtown marked with self-guided trails. *212/269–1500.*

JOYCE GOLD HISTORY TOURS OF NEW YORK

Historian and author Joyce Gold's enthusiastic and highly informative tours cover over 20 different New York City neighborhoods, from the financial district to Harlem. *212/242–5762, www.nyctours.com.*

`9` d-6

MIRACLE TOUR OF 34TH STREET

The 34th Street Partnership offers free weekly walking tours of the architecture and history of this endlessly colorful street, the garment district, and its surroundings. *212/868–0521.*

MUNICIPAL ART SOCIETY

New York's premier preservationist group leads several walking tours each week, examining current happenings in city architecture and neighborhoods in light of their social history. *212/935–3960.*

MUSEUM OF THE CITY OF NEW YORK

For over 30 years the museum has sponsored leisurely explorations of New York neighborhoods, highlighting architectural and social history. 212/534–1672, www.mcny.org.

NEW YORK CITY CULTURAL WALKING TOURS

Longtime guide Alfred Pommer escorts folks around every Sunday at 2 to such theme 'hoods as Millionaire's Mile and Little Italy. He also organizes private tours for groups and individuals from a menu of over 25 different walks, ranging from "Gargoyles in Manhattan" to an Irish-heritage tour. 212/979–2388, www.nycwalk.com.

92ND STREET Y

The Y organizes fascinating treks through neighborhoods of historic, social, artistic, and architectural importance throughout the five boroughs. 212/996–1100, www.92ndsty.org.

RADICAL WALKING TOURS

If you're into movements and causes, revolutionary thinking, or the anarchic ideal, Radical Walking Tours are for you. They cast a different light on the history of New York and the figures who have tried to rouse its rabble, from Thomas Paine to Ethel and Julius Rosenberg. The 2- to 5-hour tours ($10) take place twice a month. 718/492–0069, www.he.net/~radtours.

STREET SMARTS NEW YORK

Street Smarts sponsors several excursions through downtown Manhattan each weekend, ranging from daytime tours of the Ladies' Mile Historic District to evening rambles through "Ghostly Greenwich Village." 212/969–8262.

URBAN PARK RANGERS, NEW YORK CITY DEPARTMENT OF PARKS

Park rangers conduct several free walking tours in parks throughout the city each weekend. Topics include bird-watching, tree identification, general ecology, history, and geology. 800/201–PARK, www.ci.nyc.ny.us/nyclink.

events

New Yorkers may be cynical, but they turn out for parties in droves. It's hard to imagine this town without, say, the Feast of San Gennaro, the New York City Marathon, or the Halloween Parade. **NYC & Company** (212/484–1222, weekdays 9–5, www.nycvisit.com) has exact dates and times for many of the annual events listed below. All of these events are free unless otherwise indicated.

JANUARY

LEGAL HOLIDAYS
New Year's Day Jan. 1.

Martin Luther King Day 3rd Mon.

10 f-1
POETRY PROJECT

Ring in the first day of the new year! Performances at the annual New Year's Benefit for the resident Poetry Project at this landmark church range from the traditionally modern to the East Village avant-garde. More than 100 poets, dancers, and musicians pop into the spotlight. *St. Mark's Church In-the-Bowery, 2nd Ave. at 10th St., East Village, 212/674–0910, www.poetryproject.com. Jan. 1, 2 PM–midnight.*

9 a-6
NATIONAL BOAT SHOW

New York's 10-day boat show is just the thing to float your spirits during a gray spell in early January. Check out the latest in pleasure craft (power boats and sailboats) and equipment, and dream of the Caribbean. *Jacob K. Javits Convention Center, 11th Ave. at 35th St., Midtown West, 212/216–2000. Early Jan.*

9 e-2
WINTER ANTIQUES SHOW

The grande dame of New York antiques shows has been around for more than 40 years. Dealers large and small converge from all over the country to show off their furniture, collectibles, clothing, and memorabilia at this 10-day extravaganza. *7th Regiment Armory, Park Ave. at 67th St., Upper East Side, 212/255–0020. Mid-Jan.–early Feb.*

10 f-5

CHINESE NEW YEAR

This two-week celebration is launched with a barrage of fireworks and a colorful paper-dragon dance through the narrow streets of Chinatown. Local restaurants put on extravagant banquets, making this a feast in more ways than one, and the price of flowering quince branches goes up all over the city. 212/484–1222. Mid-Jan.–late Feb.

11 f-4

OUTSIDER ART FAIR

This long weekend is a wild ride through the major artworks and practitioners of what's become known as outsider art, sometimes called naive art or art of the self-taught. If you like folk art, stop in and be amazed at this oft-misunderstood genre. Just vow beforehand not to blurt, "My three-year-old could do that!" It's not true. *Puck Bldg., 295 Lafayette St. (at Houston St.), SoHo, 212/777–5218. Late Jan.*

FEBRUARY

LEGAL HOLIDAYS

Lincoln's Birthday Feb. 12 (New York State holiday).

Presidents' Day 3rd Mon.

9 c-6

WESTMINSTER KENNEL CLUB DOG SHOW

For two days in early February, it's a dog's life at Madison Square Garden. This show of shows draws nearly 3,000 dogs and their humans from every state of the union to join paws and hands in competition. *Madison Sq. Garden, 4 Penn Plaza (7th Ave. between 31st and 33rd Sts.), Midtown West, 800/455–3647. Early Feb.*

9 d-6

EMPIRE STATE BUILDING RUN-UP

Forget cinder tracks: This course starts in the art deco lobby and ends on the 86th-floor observation deck. The Run-Up is a New York Road Runners Club invitational, so contact them in advance if you've decided that gravity is no object. *Empire State Bldg., 350 5th Ave. (at 34th St.), Midtown East, 212/860–4455 New York Road Runners Club. Late Feb.*

MARCH

3 b-3

MODEL YACHT RACES

Every Saturday in the milder months, beautifully crafted radio-controlled boats buzz around Central Park's Conservatory Water, also known as the Sailboat Lake. *Central Park, entrance at 5th Ave. at 74th St., Upper East Side. Mid-Mar.–mid-Nov., Sat. 10–2 (rain date Sun.).*

9 d-5

ST. PATRICK'S DAY PARADE

New York's first parade in honor of St. Patrick took place in 1762, and the tradition has yet to gather a speck of dust. It's a boisterous affair (a little too much so), with traditional music that sticks in your brain for days and a sea of "Kiss Me—I'm Irish" buttons. Don't stop at a measly button, though; 'tis a fine day for wearin' the green. Views are excellent all along the route. *5th Ave., from 44th St. to 86th St., 212/484–1222. Mar. 17 around 11:30.*

10 d-6

VERNAL EQUINOX

What are you doing for Vernal Equinox? Celebrate the very moment of spring's arrival by attempting to balance an egg on one end. The ritual is an ancient Chinese folk (yolk?) tradition, supposed to bring good luck for the coming year. Eggs are free. For details call performance artist Donna Henes, who initiated this annual event in 1976. *Call for location, 718/857–2247. Mar. 20 or 21.*

9 c-6

RINGLING BROS. & BARNUM & BAILEY CIRCUS

Forget Groundhog Day: You know winter has ended when this world-famous, three-ring circus arrives, filling the subways and sidewalks with giddy children and their parents, clutching cotton candy and spewing popcorn. Just before opening night the Animal Walk takes the show's four-legged stars along 34th Street from their train at Penn Station to the Garden; it happens around midnight and is well worth the sleep deprivation. *Madison Sq. Garden, 4 Penn Plaza (7th Ave. between 31st and 33rd Sts.), Midtown West, 212/465–6741, www.ringling.com. Late Mar.–early Apr.*

EASTER WEEKEND

3 b-3
EASTER EGG ROLL
Children ages 4–11 scramble to this traditional Central Park event. Don't worry; the eggs are wooden. Refreshments, prizes, and entertainment add activity to the charming sight of a sea of Easter bonnets. 212/360–3456. *Day before Easter 9–2.*

9 d-4
EASTER LILIES DISPLAY
Rockefeller Center's Easter feast of blooms is always dazzling. *Channel Gardens, Rockefeller Center, 5th Ave. between 49th and 50th Sts.*

9 d-5
EASTER PARADE
New York's traditional Easter procession is a showcase of springtime finery—especially millinery—rather than a real parade. The excitement centers around St. Patrick's Cathedral, at 51st Street. *5th Ave. from 44th to 57th Sts. 11–2:30 Easter Sun.*

9 d-6
EASTER SUNRISE SERVICE
Reverend Frank Rafter, who began this tradition in 1973, leads a special, high-rise, sunrise Easter service at 6. Most churches don't have these views—you're in the Empire State Building observatory, on the 86th floor. Reserve in advance; space is limited. *Empire State Bldg., 350 5th Ave. (at 34th St.), Midtown East, 718/849–3580. Easter Sun.*

9 d-6
MACY'S SPRING FLOWER SHOW
The week before Easter, Macy's sets its Broadway windows abloom, and arranges lush displays throughout the main floor. Step inside the emporium for a better whiff, and to hear talks by floral and interior designers. *Macy's Herald Sq., Broadway at 34th St., Flatiron District, www.macys.com. Palm Sun.–Easter Sun.*

10 f-1
UKRAINIAN EASTER EGG EXHIBIT
The Ukrainian Museum rolls out the heavy cultural artillery in mid-February and keeps it out until summer, with a display of more than 400 *pysanky*—colorful Ukrainian Easter eggs. Egg-decorating workshops run through Easter; call for details. *Ukrainian Museum, 203 2nd Ave. (between 12th and 13th Sts.), East Village, 212/228–0110. Admission: $3 adults, $2 seniors and students. Wed.–Sun. 1–5.*

APRIL

BIKE NEW YORK/FIVE BORO BIKE TOUR
More than 30,000 amateur cyclists hit the streets for America's largest bicycle ride and one of the greatest tours of New York. Starting in Battery Park in Lower Manhattan, the 42-mi route takes riders through all five boroughs, ending with a festival in Staten Island. The fun ride is meant to increase awareness of the benefits of biking in the city. *212/932–2453, www.bikenewyork.org. First Sunday in May.*

9 d-2
BROADWAY SHOW SOFTBALL LEAGUE
Is that Norma Desmond on the diamond? Two great American institutions merge when New York's theater people form a 20-team softball league. Generally, one Broadway show plays another—cast, crew, and all. *Heckscher Field, Central Park, near E. 62nd St. Mid-Apr.–July, Thurs. noon–5:30 (weather permitting).*

4 e-1
CHERRY BLOSSOM FESTIVAL
When the cherry trees blossom each spring, the Brooklyn Botanic Garden throws it *Sakura Matsuri*, or cherry blossom festival, to celebrate. The trees start to show their colors in mid-March, and the festival fills one weekend at the height of the bloom. The action includes Japanese flower arranging, Bonsai, music, calligraphy, tea ceremonies, dance, and more. *Brooklyn Botanic Garden, 1000 Washington Ave. (at Carroll St.), Park Slope, 718/623–7200, www.bbg.org. Late April.*

9 e-2
NEW YORK ANTIQUARIAN BOOK FAIR
First editions, manuscripts, autographs, atlases, drawings, prints, maps—it's book-lovers' heaven at the Armory. Wear

your tweed blazer and carry your leather checkbook: Prices range from $25 to more than $25,000. *7th Regiment Armory, Park Ave. at 67th St., Upper East Side, 212/944–8291. Mid-Apr.*

MAY

LEGAL HOLIDAY
Memorial Day Last Mon.

PARADES
Armed Forces Day Parade

Bronx Day Parade

Salute to Israel Parade

NYC & Company's Norwegian Constitution Day Parade

For exact dates and routes, call 212/484–1222 or visit www.nycvisit.com.

HISTORIC HOUSE TOURS
Private houses in several historic neighborhoods open their doors to the public in May. The Park Slope Civic Council sponsors an annual tour of 10 historic Brooklyn homes on the third Sunday (daytime 718/832–8227); the Brooklyn Heights Association offers a self-guided afternoon tour of five historic homes and private gardens, often including the sanctuary of the landmark Plymouth Church of the Pilgrims, usually on the second Saturday (718/858–9193). The Village Community School sponsors a tour of six Manhattan homes to benefit its school fund (212/691–5146).

STREET FAIRS
Street fairs and block parties have become traditional summer fare in New York, featuring music, games, food, and wares—often for the benefit of neighborhood and block beautification projects. Some street fairs have become epic events, but even the tiniest block parties make for fine people-watching and usually draw friendly folks. For each weekend's fairs and festivals, check the "Weekend" section of Friday's *New York Times* and watch for notices on billboards and lampposts.

12 g-5
WELCOME BACK TO BROOKLYN FESTIVAL
You can go home again, at least on the second Sunday in May. Street games, local-history exhibits, Junior's cheese-

cake, and Nathan's hot dogs educate tourists from Peoria, Pakistan, and Manhattan and confirm the locals' suspicions that they really do live in the coolest borough. *Eastern Pkwy., Grand Army Plaza (north end of Prospect Park) to Brooklyn Museum, Park Slope, 718/855–7882. 2nd Sun. in May noon–5.*

9 c-2
SEPHARDIC FAIR
Congregation Shearith Israel (The Spanish and Portuguese Synagogue) is the landmark home of America's oldest Orthodox Jewish congregation. Watch artists making prayer shawls and crafting jewelry, potters vending wine cups, and scribes penning marriage contracts, and nibble Sephardic delicacies. *Congregation Shearith Israel, Central Park West at 67th St., Upper West Side, 212/873–0300. One Sun. in mid-May, 10–5.*

9 b-5
9TH AVENUE INTERNATIONAL FOOD FESTIVAL
A mile-long annual gustatory celebration of New York's ethnic diversity greets wanderers in on the third weekend in May. Try kebabs and kimchi, chow mein and gazpacho, tempura and falafel, ravioli and bratwurst . . . it's all topped off with crafts and entertainment. *9th Ave., 37th–57th Sts., 212/581–7217. 3rd weekend in May, 11–7.*

10 f-2
UKRAINIAN FESTIVAL
Old-country music accompanies pierogi, polkas, *pysanky* (colored eggs), and dancing in the heart of the East Village Ukrainian community. *E. 7th St. between 2nd Ave. and Bowery. 3rd weekend in May.*

11 d-2
WASHINGTON SQUARE OUTDOOR ART EXHIBIT
For over half a century, Memorial Day has turned the Washington Square area into an open-air arts-and-crafts gallery, bringing some 600 exhibitors to lower Fifth Avenue, Washington Square Park, and the surrounding streets. The action continues for three weekends, from noon to sundown. *Greenwich Village, 212/982–6255. Late May–mid-June.*

3 *b-3*

STORYTELLING HOUR

If this town could talk, the stories it would tell—well, maybe not these stories. Come hear wonderful children's tales read aloud at the Hans Christian Andersen statue, near Central Park's Sailboat Lake—an appropriate and charming site for storytelling. Selections are geared toward ages 3–7. *Central Park, entrance at 5th Ave. and 74th St., 212/360-3456. Late May–Sept., Sat. 11–noon.*

YOU GOTTA HAVE PARK!

A variety of park-related festivities—races, concerts, games—celebrates our greenest patches and remind us why we've managed to live here for so many years. *212/360-3456.*

JUNE

PARADES

Puerto Rican Day Parade: Take a salsa lesson before joining New York's hottest parade. *212/484-1222.*

9 *d-1*

SUMMERSTAGE IN CENTRAL PARK

Talk about a crowd-pleaser: Summer-Stage offers free weekday-evening and weekend-afternoon blues, Latin, pop, African, and country music; dance; opera; and readings. You can often enjoy the sounds without stopping by in earnest. Recent performers have included Morrissey and the one and only James Brown. *Central Park (enter at 72nd St.), 212/360-2777, www.centralparknyc.org. June–Aug.*

10 *g-4*

LOWER EAST SIDE JEWISH FESTIVAL

Yiddish is now mixed with Spanish and Chinese in these parts, but once a year the neighborhood's Old World kicks up its heels. Baked goods, kosher food, books, and entertainment fill East Broadway from Rutgers to Montgomery Streets. So go—would it kill you to have a good time? *1 Sun. in late May or early June.*

1 *h-3*

BELMONT STAKES

This is New York's Thoroughbred of horse races, and the final jewel in the Triple Crown. *Belmont Park Racetrack,*

Hempstead Tpke. and Plainfield Ave., Belmont, Long Island, 718/641-4700. Early June.

11 *d-4*

FEAST OF ST. ANTHONY OF PADUA

The music, games of chance, and kids' rides at this classic street festival beg you to inhale and ingest the glorious Italian food. *Sullivan St. between W. Houston and Spring Sts., SoHo, 212/777-2755. Early June.*

3 *b-3*

MUSEUM MILE FESTIVAL

One evening in mid-June, 10 of New York's cultural treasure chests open their doors free of charge. Upper Fifth Avenue is closed to traffic, and musicians, clowns, and jugglers entertain strollers. *5th Ave. from 82nd to 104th Sts. 2nd or 3rd Tues. in June, 6–9.*

TEXACO NEW YORK JAZZ FESTIVAL

In 1997, Texaco climbed on board as primary sponsor of this decade-old festival, which began life as "What Is Jazz?", an alternative to the JVC Jazz Festival. If you need an excuse to give up your day job, the festival already sponsors 350 performances at clubs and public spaces around town. Exhaustion will most likely be the end of you, but it's not a bad closing riff. *The Knitting Factory (74 Leonard St., TriBeCa) is a main venue. 212/219-3006. 2 wks in mid-June.*

9 *b-2*

AMERICAN CRAFTS FESTIVAL

Some 400 skilled artisans display their crafts at Lincoln Center on June weekends. Support the arts and carry something home: leather, jewelry, blown and stained glass, quilts, baskets, furniture, and toys are all for sale. *Lincoln Center Plaza, Broadway at 64th St., Upper West Side, Mid- to late June, noon–9.*

9 *d-5*

BRYANT PARK SUMMER FILM FESTIVAL

Monday nights in summer are classic-movie nights in the nearly bucolic Bryant Park, behind the New York Public Library. This hugely popular (read: get there early) outdoor series runs throughout the summer and becomes more of a scene each year. Dash from work around 5 to claim a spot on the lawn, spread out your blanket and snacks, and get comfortable—films start at sundown. You can check the Web for the screening schedule— newyork.citysearch.com is a particularly good resource. *Bryant Park, 6th Ave. between 40th and 42nd Sts., Midtown West. Mid-June–late Aug.*

GAY & LESBIAN PRIDE WEEK

Hundreds of thousands of New Yorkers—gay, straight, and otherwise—attend a week of events that caps off Gay Pride month. A rally with speakers and entertainment kicks off the week, which culminates in a spectacular parade down 5th Avenue, followed by a festival and outdoor dance in the Village. *212/807–7433, www.nycpride.org. Last week in June.*

12 *h-7*

CELEBRATE BROOKLYN PERFORMING ARTS FESTIVAL

From mid-June to late August, a delectable potpourri of music—pop, jazz, rock, classical, klezmer, African, Latin, Caribbean—comes to Prospect Park, along with dance, film, and more. Take advantage! *Prospect Park Band Shell, Prospect Park W at 9th St., Park Slope, Brooklyn, 718/855–7882, ext. 52. Mid-June–late Aug.*

7 *d-8*

SHAKESPEARE IN THE PARK

Central Park's outdoor Delacorte Theater hosts one of New York's most blazingly popular summer traditions. Joseph Papp's Public Theater stages two major productions here each year, most featuring at least one star performer from the big or small screen. The program does depart from Shakespeare, but only to celebrate another masterpiece, such as Leonard Bernstein's *On the Town*. The whole affair is free, so while the play might later come indoors if it's a smash (as *The Tempest* did, with Patrick Stewart), you won't get the same bang for your buck. Tickets are distributed the day of the performance, two per person, at the Public Theater (425 Lafayette St., East Village, 1–3) and the Delacorte (beginning at 1)—line up early and bring some Mad Libs. (Call for information on ticket distribution in the outer boroughs on selected days.) *Central Park, Dela-*

corte Theater (enter at E. or W. 81st St.), 212/861–PAPP or 212/539–8750, www. publictheater.org. Mid-June–late Aug., Tues.–Sun. at 8.

THE MET IN THE PARKS

This summer, have some Puccini with your tortillas and Brie. Free outdoor performances by the Metropolitan Opera Company start at 8 PM in rotating city parks (*see below*). The acoustics are better elsewhere, and you might want to bring some bug spray, but the atmosphere and the price are unbeatable. *212/362–6000, www.metopera.org. Mid-June–July.*

Bronx Van Cortlandt Park

Brooklyn Prospect Park; Marine Park

Manhattan Central Park

Queens Cunningham Park

Staten Island Snug Harbor; Miller Field; Great Kills Park

JVC JAZZ FESTIVAL NEW YORK

This much-loved summer festival brings giants of jazz and new faces alike to Carnegie Hall, Lincoln Center, the Beacon Theater, Bryant Park, and other theaters and clubs about town. Check newspapers for performers and schedules. Tickets are available through TicketMaster. *212/501–1390, www.festivalproductions.net. Mid- to late June.*

4 *g-7*

MERMAID PARADE

The Mermaid Parade is a pagan tribute to Coney Island, once the parade capital of the world. This weird and wild affair begins at Brooklyn's Surf Avenue and West 10th Street, right in front of that proto–roller coaster, the Cyclone. Break out your sequins and blond wig, and become a mermaid for the day (you'll fit right in)—or dress as King Neptune. If you're weak on maritime history, build a float, don flippers and goggles, and be Liza Minnelli. Whatever. *718/372–5159. 1st Sat. after summer solstice at 2.*

9 *b-2*

MIDSUMMER NIGHT SWING

It's amazing to see: on balmy summer evenings, New York's highest-brow plaza becomes an enormous, old-fashioned dance hall. Top big bands provide swing, jump, salsa, merengue, mambo, Dixieland, R&B, calypso, and disco, and zillions of people of all ages fill both the checkerboard dance floor (for a fee) and the periphery (no charge). *Lincoln Center Plaza, Broadway at 64th St., Upper West Side, 212/875–5766, www. midsummerswing.org. Late June–late July, Tues.–Sat. at 8:15; dance lessons 6:30–7:30.*

INDEPENDENCE DAY WEEKEND

10 *e-8*

GREAT 4TH OF JULY FESTIVAL

Manhattan's oldest quarter celebrates the nation's birthday with arts, crafts, ethnic food, live entertainment, and a parade from Bowling Green to City Hall. *Water St. from Battery Park–John St., 212/484–1222. July 4, 11–7.*

9 *f-6*

MACY'S FIREWORKS DISPLAY

The nation's largest display of pyrotechnical wizardry is launched from barges in the East River. The best viewing points are FDR Drive from 14th to 41st Sts. (access via 23rd, 34th, and 48th Sts.) and the Brooklyn Heights Promenade. The FDR Drive is closed to traffic, but you'll want to get there early, as police sometimes restrict even pedestrian traffic. *July 4, 9:15. www.macys.com.*

10 *f-7*

SOUTH STREET SEAPORT INDEPENDENCE WEEKEND

The Seaport is awash in celebrations and jammed with visitors and residents alike for the entire weekend. Concerts, street performers, and other special events make for excellent people-watching. *South Street Seaport, Lower Manhattan.*

JULY

LEGAL HOLIDAY
Independence Day July 4.

9 *d-3*

SUMMERGARDEN

Enjoy 20th-century classical music in the Museum of Modern Art's popular sculpture garden. Performers are graduate students and alumni of the Juilliard School. *Museum of Modern Art, 11 W. 53rd St., Midtown East, 212/708–9400,*

www.moma.org. Early July–mid-Aug., Fri. at 6, Sat. at 8:30.

NEW YORK PHILHARMONIC PARK CONCERTS

Each summer the New York Philharmonic Orchestra performs a light program under the stars, and caps each concert with fireworks. Bring a picnic. *212/875–5709, www.newyorkphilharmonic.org. Mid-July–early Aug.*

Bronx Van Cortlandt Park

Brooklyn Prospect Park

Manhattan Central Park

Queens Cunningham Park

Staten Island Miller Field

11 *d-2*

WASHINGTON SQUARE MUSIC FESTIVAL

Washington Square Park gets even louder in midsummer, when one of the city's oldest open-air concert series kicks in. *Washington Sq. Park (5th Ave. at Waverly Pl.), Greenwich Village, 212/431–1088. Mid-July–mid-Aug., Tues. at 8.*

AUGUST

9 *b-2*

LINCOLN CENTER OUT-OF-DOORS

Lincoln Plaza devotes itself to a four-week open-air bonanza of music, dance, and theater. *Lincoln Center Plaza, Broadway at 64th St., Upper West Side, 212/875–5108, www.lincolncenter.org. Aug.*

9 *b-2*

MOSTLY MOZART FESTIVAL

This world-renowned August concert series is just what it sounds like: a generous helping of Mozart, with dashes of other masters for good measure. The Mostly Mozart Festival Orchestra holds forth, and various solo performers illuminate chamber works in recitals. Free outdoor afternoon concerts are followed by casual evening concerts at reasonable prices. *Avery Fisher Hall, 10 Lincoln Center Plaza (Broadway at 64th St.), Upper West Side, 212/875–5103. Aug.*

1 *d-3*

HARLEM WEEK

Fortunately for all, the largest black and Hispanic festival in the world actually runs for about two weeks. Indoor and outdoor activities for every age celebrate the community's past, present, and future. Try to catch a feature at the Black Film Festival, and don't rush through the Taste of Harlem Food Festival. *www. discoverharlem.com. Early to mid-Aug.*

3 c-7
NEW YORK INTERNATIONAL FRINGE FESTIVAL

In this event, modeled on the festival in Edinburgh, emerging theater companies and performing artists take over two dozen performance spaces on the Lower East Side for the last two weeks of August. Make the trip—summer's winding down, and this is what the Lower East Side does best. *212/420–8877, www.fringenyc.org. Last 2 wks of Aug.*

9 d-6
TAP-O-MANIA

Be a part of Broadway's—okay, 34th Street's—longest tapping chorus line, and try to outdo yourselves: The Guinness Book of World Records puts the biggest one at 6,676 dancers. *Macy's Herald Sq., Broadway at 34th St., Flatiron District. 3rd Sun. in Aug. Registration at 8 AM.*

4 e-1
U.S. OPEN TENNIS TOURNAMENT

The U.S.T.A. National Tennis Center hosts the nation's premier tennis event each summer. Celebrities always appear in the stands, and the boxes in Arthur Ashe Stadium are to die for, but the real excitement is the Grand Slam tennis. With a stadium ticket you can also catch matches in outlying courts and in the grandstand, where bleacher seating is first-come, first-served. *Flushing Meadows–Corona Park, 800/524–8440. Late Aug.–early Sept. Subway: 7 to Willets Point/Shea Stadium.*

SEPTEMBER

LEGAL HOLIDAY
Labor Day 1st Mon.

PARADES
Labor Day Parade 1st Mon.

Steuben Day (German) Parade.

For exact dates and routes, call 212/484–1222 or visit www.nycvisit.com.

11 d-2
WASHINGTON SQUARE OUTDOOR ART EXHIBIT

Like its Memorial Day cousin (*see above*), this fair turns Washington Square Park and its environs into an alfresco art gallery. *Greenwich Village, 212/982–6255. 1st weekend in early Sept., noon–6.*

4 e-1
WEST INDIAN AMERICAN DAY PARADE

Labor Day weekend brings out the largest parade in New York City—no mean distinction. Modeled after the harvest carnival of Trinidad and Tobago, this Caribbean revel has been observed in New York since the 1940s, when it sprang up in Harlem. The festivities begin with a Friday-evening salsa, reggae, and calypso extravaganza at the Brooklyn Museum (admission), and end on Monday afternoon with a gigantic, Mardi Gras–style parade of floats, elaborately costumed dancers, stilt-walkers, and West Indian food and music. *Eastern Pkwy. from Utica Ave. to Brooklyn Museum, Brooklyn, 212/484–1222. Labor Day weekend.*

9 b-2
AUTUMN CRAFTS FESTIVAL

More than 400 craftspeople show up and sell their unique and comforting wares to world-weary New Yorkers. Think you've seen it all? Drop by for the sheep-shearing demonstration. *Lincoln Center Plaza, Broadway at 64th St., Upper West Side. Two wks in early to mid-Sept.*

10 f-4
FEAST OF SAN GENNARO

The oldest, grandest, largest, and most crowded festa of them all, in honor of the patron saint of Naples, begins with the "Triumphal March" from Verdi's *Aida* and continues for 11 days of eating and shenanigans. *Mulberry St. from Canal to Houston Sts., Little Italy, 212/484–1222. Mid- to late Sept., 11 AM–11:30 PM.*

9 d-4
NEW YORK IS BOOK COUNTRY

This midtown stretch of Fifth Avenue contains—oops, used to contain—the country's largest concentration of bookstores, so on this Indian Summer day the street is filled with kiosks representing publishers of all stripes. Preview forthcoming books, meet authors, admire beautiful book jackets, chat with George Plimpton at the *Paris Review* booth, and enjoy live entertainment and bookbinding demonstrations. Bring the kids. *5th Ave. from 48th to 57th Sts., 212/207–7242. 3rd Sun. in Sept., 11–5.*

12 d-4
ATLANTIC ANTIC
This 12-block-long festival celebrates downtown Brooklyn, and there is much to celebrate. Food, entertainment, antiques, and a parade (at 11:30) beckon all toward the Williamsburg Clock Tower. *Atlantic Ave. from Flatbush to Furman St., Downtown Brooklyn, 212/484–1222. One Sun. in late Sept., 10–6.*

9 e-2
FALL ANTIQUES SHOW
Over 75 dealers converge from all over the U.S. for this relaxed yet refined affair, the foremost American-antiques show in the country and a bonanza for collectors of Americana. The Museum of American Folk Art benefits. *7th Regiment Armory, Park Ave. at 67th St., Upper East Side, 212/777–5218. 4 days in late Sept.*

7 e-7
FIFTH AVENUE MILE
The world's fastest runners crash New York's most exclusive strip, and thousands cheer them on—brief, but exhilarating. *5th Ave. from 62nd to 82nd Sts., Upper East Side, 212/860–4455. One Sat. in late Sept.*

9 b-2
NEW YORK FILM FESTIVAL
Founded in 1963, New York's exceptional international film festival is an autumn tradition for cinephiles. Afternoon and evening screenings provide plenty of temptations, and advance tickets make them real events. *Alice Tully Hall, Broadway at 65th St., Upper West Side, 212/875–5050, www.lincolncenter.org. 2 wks, late Sept.–early Oct.*

OCTOBER

LEGAL HOLIDAY
Columbus Day 2nd Mon.

PARADES
Columbus Day Parade

Hispanic Day Parade

Pulaski Day Parade

For exact dates and routes, call 212/484–1222 or visit www.nycvisit.com.

7 b-3
FEAST OF ST. FRANCIS
Obedience school too pricey? Ask for divine intervention at this wonderful service, otherwise known as the Blessing of the Animals. Most of the blessed are garden-variety cats and dogs, but you never know; often an elephant shows up. *Cathedral Church of St. John the Divine, 1047 Amsterdam Ave. (at 112th St.), Morningside Heights, 212/316–7540. 1st Sun. in Oct., mass at 11, blessings 1–5.*

9 b-2
BIG APPLE CIRCUS
No one is more than 50 ft from the action at this heated little big top in Lincoln Center's Damrosch Park. From late October through early January, this new New York tradition tips its hat to the classical American circus with simplicity, charm, and magic in one ring. Advance tickets are available. *Damrosch Park, Lincoln Center, Columbus Ave. at 63rd St., Upper West Side, 212/268–2500, www.bigapplecircus.org. Late Oct.–early Jan., generally Tues.–Sun., matinee and evening shows.*

7 b-3
HALLOWEEN EXTRAVAGANZA & PROCESSION OF GHOULS
The massive Cathedral Church of St. John the Divine lends gothic cachet to these creepy goings-on: a silent movie is accompanied by organ music, and a procession of giant puppets brings on spiders, skeletons, ghouls, and spooks. *Cathedral Church of St. John the Divine, 1047 Amsterdam Ave. (at 112th St.), Morningside Heights, 212/662–2133, www.stjohndivine.org. Oct. 31 at 7 and 10.*

3 b-6
VILLAGE HALLOWEEN PARADE
What started as a handful of weirdos in the streets now draws 50,000 yahoos of all ages and persuasions. This anything-goes annual procession features some bizarre but brilliant costumes and exu-

berant live music. Join the march or just watch the massive spectacle from the sidelines. *6th Ave. from Spring to 23rd Sts., SoHo/Greenwich Village/Chelsea, 914/758–5519. Oct. 31st, sundown (about 7)–about 10.*

NOVEMBER

LEGAL HOLIDAYS
Veteran's Day Nov. 11.

Thanksgiving Day 4th Thurs.

⑨ a-4
TRIPLE PIER EXPO
This semi-annual collectibles and antiques extravaganza (also held in March) is not for the faint of heart, even if the faint of heart love antiques. Wear comfortable shoes and be prepared for a feast of art deco furniture, 19th-century decorative arts, American quilts, memorabilia, silver, prints, jewelry, dolls, and much more. The price range is pleasingly broad. *Passenger Ship Terminals, Piers 88, 90, 92, 12th Ave. from 48th to 55th Sts., Midtown West, 212/255–0020. 1st two weekends in Nov.*

⑨ d-4
RADIO CITY CHRISTMAS SPECTACULAR
The famed Christmas Spectacular at the famed music hall features the famed Rockettes. A quieter tradition within the show is the Nativity Pageant, with live donkeys, camels, and sheep. Buy tickets in advance. *Radio City Music Hall, 1260 6th Ave. (at 50th St.), Midtown West, 212/247–4777, www.radiocity.com. Mid-Nov.–early Jan.*

⑨ d-5
LORD & TAYLOR'S CHRISTMAS WINDOWS
Early in the season the mannequins disappear, and lavish, animated holiday scenes fill this classic store's Fifth Avenue windows. The line moves quickly, but the best viewing is after 9 PM, when the shoppers have cleared out. *Lord & Taylor, 424 5th Ave. (at 39th St.), Midtown East, 212/391–3344. Tues. before Thanksgiving–Jan. 1.*

⑨ d-6
MACY'S THANKSGIVING DAY PARADE
You watched it on TV growing up; now break away from the set and watch the real thing. Macy's Thanksgiving Day parade moves south from Central Park West and 77th Street to Columbus Circle, then down Broadway to the float-reviewing stand at Macy's Herald Square (Broadway and 34th St.). The biggest stars are the gigantic balloons, which are inflated the night before the parade to antic effect (77th and 81st Sts. between Central Park West and Columbus Ave., 6–wee hours). Dress warmly, and take your position by 8. *212/695–4400, www.macyparade.com. Thanksgiving Day, 9–noon.*

⑨ d-6
MACY'S SANTA CLAUS ADVENTURE AT MACYLAND
St. Nick is in residence—and in demand—at Macy's from the day after Thanksgiving until Christmas Eve, greeting and posing with children of all ages. So who's stuck managing the elves? The Mrs.? There is a 20-minute holiday marionette show every hour 10:30–4:30. *Macy's Herald Sq., Broadway at 34th St., Midtown West, 212/695–4400, www.macys.com. Fri. after Thanksgiving–Dec. 24.*

⑨ b-2
THE NUTCRACKER
The Nutcracker is the most popular ballet in the world, and who better than the New York City Ballet to perform it? The company is ably assisted by children from the School of American Ballet. This magical show is very much a holiday tradition in New York, so buy tickets well in advance. *New York State Theater, Lincoln Center, Broadway and 64th St., Upper West Side, 212/870–5590, www.nycballet.com. Late Nov.–early Jan.*

NEW YORK CITY MARATHON
The world's largest marathon (30,000 runners) attracts the best runners from around the globe as well as thousands of dedicated amateurs. Starting on the Staten Island side of the Verrazano-Narrows Bridge, the race snakes through all five boroughs, past hordes of cheering onlookers, before finishing at Tavern on the Green in Central Park. *212/860–4455, www.nyrrc.org. First Sunday in November.*

DECEMBER

LEGAL HOLIDAY
Christmas Day Dec. 25.

9 *e-3*

CHANUKAH CELEBRATIONS

A 32-ft-tall menorah at Grand Army Plaza (5th Ave. and 59th St.) makes for a grand candle-lighting ceremony each night at sundown during the eight-day Festival of Lights. The 92nd St. Y (395 Lexington Ave., at 92nd St., 212/996–1100) holds a family celebration, geared toward ages 4–12, at which the gang can make holiday crafts, sing along to holiday music, hear an expert storyteller, and nibble refreshments (usually the Sun. before Chanukah).

7 *e-7*

METROPOLITAN MUSEUM OF ART CHRISTMAS TREE

Folks come from far and wide to see the Met's stunning tree in the solemn Medieval Sculpture Hall. The 30-ft Baroque wonder is decorated with 18th-century cherubs and angels and accompanied by an elaborate Neapolitan nativity scene. *Metropolitan Museum of Art, 5th Ave. at 82nd St., Upper East Side, 212/879–5500, www.metmuseum.org. Dec.–early Jan.*

9 *e-2*

MIRACLE ON MADISON AVENUE

Madison Avenue's slickest shopping stretch is closed to traffic on the first Sunday in December for an afternoon of (civilized?) holiday shopping, with participating stores donating 20 percent of every sale to children's charities. Festive heated tents keep the wee ones warm as they enjoy the strolling musicians and the hot cider and cookies. *Madison Ave. from 55th to 79th Sts., 212/988–4001. Noon–5. 1st Sun. in Dec.*

9 *e-3*

CAROUSEL & HOLIDAY DISPLAY

An animated carousel and colorful decorations will delight kids of all ages. Tantrum-prevention tip: Kids may look at, but may not ride, the carousel, so you may want to call a conference before taking Junior to see this gorgeous machine. *Lever House, 390 Park Ave. (at 53rd St.), lobby, Midtown East, 212/688–6000. Early Dec.–Jan. 2.*

9 *d-4*

TREE-LIGHTING CEREMONY

Perhaps New York's most famous holiday tradition, the Rockefeller Center tree-lighting began in 1933 and has only picked up steam since. All at once, on the first Tuesday in December, the 20,000 lights on Rockefeller Center's mammoth Christmas tree come into view, accompanied by cheers, carols, and, of course, figure skating down below. It's a magical sight—if you can see it, which is unlikely, as thundering hordes of people pack several of the plaza's surrounding blocks. *Rockefeller Plaza, 5th Ave. between 49th and 50th Sts., 212/632–3975. Early evening, 1st Tues. in Dec.*

1 *b-2*

CHRISTMAS IN RICHMONDTOWN

Restored buildings are decorated for Christmas in period (18th- and 19th-century) fashion and open to the public. Costumed guides explain local history, parlor games and popcorn stringing keep the kids occupied, and homemade food and gifts make a dent in your shopping list. *Historic Richmondtown, 441 Clarke Ave. (near Arthur Kill Rd.), Staten Island, 718/351–1611, www. historicrichmondtown.org. Admission to Historic Richmondtown. 1st or 2nd Sun. in Dec., 10–4.*

9 *b-2*

MESSIAH SING-IN

Led by 21 different conductors and punctuated by four soloists, the chorus for this *Messiah* consists of everyone else who shows up—a good 3,000. Handel never sounded so good. Make your big break from the shower to Lincoln Center; bring the score or buy one in the lobby from the National Choral Council. *Avery Fisher Hall, Lincoln Center, Broadway at 64th St., Upper West Side, 212/333–5333, www.lincolncenter.org. Admission. 1 evening several days before Christmas at 8.*

6 *c-5*

"'TWAS THE NIGHT BEFORE CHRISTMAS"

In a charmingly esoteric tradition that dates from 1911, a procession of carolers lays a wreath on Clement Clarke Moore's grave in Trinity Cemetery and reads his beloved poem "A Visit from St. Nicholas." *Church of the Intercession, Broadway at 155th St., Washington Heights, 212/283–6200. Sun. before Christmas at 4.*

7 *c-8*

KWANZAA AT THE AMERICAN MUSEUM OF NATURAL HISTORY

Music and dance help augment the re-creation of an African marketplace, complete with African-style gifts for sale. *American Museum of Natural History, Central Park West at 79th St., Upper West Side, 212/769–5000, www.amnh.org. Admission to museum. Late Dec.*

NEW YEAR'S EVE

FIREWORKS

Fireworks greet the New Year at midnight in Central Park. Catch the best views at Bethesda Fountain, 72nd St.; Tavern-on-the Green, Central Park West and 67th St.; Central Park West and 96th St.; and 5th Ave. at 90th St. Fireworks also light up Brooklyn's Prospect Park; in Park Slope's Grand Army Plaza, the show is tastefully accompanied by music, hot cider, and cookies; festivities begin at 11:30 PM. If it's just too cold to stand around until midnight, watch the 'works at South Street Seaport at 11:30 PM.

9 *e-5*

FIRST NIGHT

Sponsored by the Grand Central Partnership, New York's First Night is a wonderful new tradition, begun in 1991. It's a family-oriented alternative to high-priced, high-octane celebrations, though most revelers are in fact adults. Choose from more than 40 events—ice-skating, concerts, storytelling, circus arts, dance, and more—in places like the MetLife Building and Grand Central Terminal. A First Night button buys you admission to all events; children 3 and under get in free. *Grand Central Terminal and environs, Park Ave. and 42nd St., 212/883–2476, www.grandcentralpartnership.org. Dec. 31 noon–1 AM.*

9 *c-2*

MIDNIGHT RUN

Beginning and ending at Tavern-on-the-Green, some 3,000 men and women take a chilly but relatively short run around Central Park. Lose the sweats: many run in evening dress, others in costume. Prizes go to the fastest and best-dressed, and every runner gets champagne and a T-shirt. *Tavern-on-the-Green, Central Park West and 67th St., 212/860–4455. Registration fee. Jan. 1, midnight.*

7 *b-3*

NEW YEAR'S EVE CONCERT FOR PEACE

Leonard Bernstein used to conduct this stirring, 2-hour program at St. John the Divine. Like the cathedral itself, the music still soars. Doors open at 6 PM, a fact you should heed if you want a seat. *Cathedral Church of St. John the Divine, 1047 Amsterdam Ave. (at 112th St.), Morningside Heights, 212/662–2133, www.stjohndivine.org. Dec. 31 at 7:30; doors open at 6.*

9 *c-5*

TIMES SQUARE

There are people who spend every New Year's Eve in Times Square; this is not necessary. But there's nothing quite like Times Square on December 31. Ever since 1907 (well—minus a few electric-apple years in the '80s and the Waterford crystal ball for the new millennium), a 6-ft, illuminated, wrought-iron ball has welcomed the new year by moving slowly down a flagpole atop the Times Tower, now the One Times Square Building. The descent takes the last 59 seconds of the old year, and at midnight the ball is illuminated at the pole's base. Hardy revelers start to gather in the square in the afternoon; the rest of the country watches the event on TV. *Times Sq., Broadway and 42nd St., Midtown West, 212/484–1222.*

day trips out of town

Metro-North and the Long Island Rail Road (*see* Public Transportation *in* Chapter 7) offer package day trips to a variety of intriguing destinations, such as Long Island wineries and various historic homes. The tours are escorted and include all admission fees.

ATLANTIC CITY, NJ

If you're itchy for a little action, catch a bus down to Atlantic City, where casinos line the seaside boardwalk. Try your hand at craps, the slots, roulette, and table after table of blackjack. If your luck turns sour, there's still the saltwater taffy and ocean breezes. **Gray Line**'s (212/397–2600) one-day bus trips from Port Authority make transport a snap.

BAYARD CUTTING ARBORETUM

An easy jaunt from the city, this 690-acre arboretum is just a 10-minute walk from the train station. Spread out along the lazy Connetquot River, the arboretum is best known for its stands of pines, native woods and bogs, meandering paths, and carefully laid rows of rhododendrons and azaleas. *Oakdale, NY, 516/581–1002. Open Tues.–Sun. 10 AM–sunset. Long Island Rail Road: Montauk Line to Great River.*

BOSCOBEL RESTORATION

A grand Federal-style mansion surrounded by formal gardens and lawns and overlooking the Hudson River, Boscobel (from bosco bello, "beautiful woods") was built in 1808 by Morris Dyckman. You can tour both the grounds and the interior, with its canopy beds, elaborate woodwork, and wonderful collection of 19th-century furniture, including some pieces by the famous New York cabinetmaker Duncan Phyfe. Special events include nature walks, lectures on horticulture, concerts, and storytelling hours. *Rte. 9D (8 mi north of Bear Mtn. Bridge), Garrison-on-Hudson, NY, 914/265–3638. Open Apr.–Oct., Wed.–Mon. 9:30–5; Nov., Dec., and Mar., Wed.–Mon. 10–3:15. Metro-North: Hudson Line to Cold Spring.*

LYNDHURST

An 1838 Gothic revival mansion—perhaps America's finest— designed by Alexander Jackson Davis for Gen. William Paulding, an early New York City mayor, Lyndhurst was later purchased by railroad tycoon Jay Gould in 1870. Perched above the Hudson River and surrounded by 67 acres of lush grounds, the house itself—often referred to as "the castle"—is characterized by grandiose rooms and holds period furnishings and paintings. *635 S. Broadway, Tarrytown, NY, 914/631–4481, www.lyndhurst.org. Mid-Apr.–Oct., Tues.–Sun. 10–5; Nov.–mid-Apr., weekends 10–4. Metro-North: Hudson Line to Tarrytown.*

HISTORIC HUDSON VALLEY

These three Hudson River valley mansions, ranging in age from pre-Revolutionary to Federal, can be toured with guides dressed in period costumes. All three estates are designated as National Historic Landmarks; you're welcome to bring a picnic. For more information on these and other area landmarks, contact **Historic Hudson Valley,** 914/631–8200, www.hudsonvalley.org.

PHILIPSBURG MANOR

Once owned by Frederick Philips, a Dutch carpenter who rose to become the richest man in the colony, this working farm dates from the early 1700s, when it was run by African slaves. Now restored, Philipsburg features a stone manor house, a water-powered grist mill and mill pond, and a barn filled with farm animals. Guides in colonial dress demonstrate spinning and weaving. *Rte. 9, Sleepy Hollow, NY (2 mi north of Tappan Zee Bridge), 914/631–3992. Mar., weekends 10–4; Apr.–Dec., Wed.–Mon. 10–5; Nov.–Dec., Wed.–Mon. 10–4. $8, $7 seniors, $4 children ages 5–17, free children under 5. Metro-North: Hudson Line to Tarrytown.*

SUNNYSIDE

Covering 20 acres is the picturesque estate of Washington Irving, author of the classic American stories "The Legend of Sleepy Hollow" and "Rip Van Winkle." Purchased in 1835, Irving's charming cottage, topped by a Spanish-style tower, is filled with his furnishings and memorabilia, including more than 3,000 books. On the surrounding grounds, garden plantings and walkways follow a plan devised by Irving himself. *W. Sunnyside La. (off Rte. 9; 1 mi south of Tappan Zee Bridge), Tarrytown, NY, 914/591–8763. $8, $7 seniors, $4 children ages 5–17, free children under 5. Mar., weekends 10–4; Apr.–Oct., Wed.–Mon. 10–5; Nov.–Dec., Wed.–Mon. 10–4. Metro-North: Hudson Line to Tarrytown.*

VAN CORTLANDT MANOR

The centerpiece of this Revolutionary War estate is an 18th-century brick manor house filled with Georgian and Federal period furniture and paintings; also on the grounds is a restored 18th-century tavern. Frequent demonstrations of open-hearth cooking, brickmaking, and blacksmithing appeal to all five senses; and in summer, the staff cooks colonial-style dinners according to 18th-century recipe books. *S. Riverside Ave. (off Rte. 9, Croton Pt. Ave. exit), Croton-on-Hudson, NY, 914/271–8981. Apr.–Oct., Wed.–Mon.*

10–5; Nov.–Dec., weekends 10–4. $8, $7 seniors, $4 children ages 5–17, free children under 5. Metro-North: Hudson Line to Croton-Harmon.

OLD WESTBURY GARDENS

Several hundred acres of formal English gardens surround a beautifully furnished, Georgian-style country house, once the property of millionaire John S. Phipps. Each weekend brings concerts, hay rides, walking tours, art exhibits, and other activities. *71 Old Westbury Rd., Old Westbury, NY, 516/333–0048, www.oldwestburygardens.org. Late Apr.–Oct., Wed.–Mon. 10–5. Long Island Rail Road: Port Jefferson Line to Westbury.*

PLANTING FIELDS ARBORETUM STATE HISTORIC PARK

Between Oyster Bay and Locust Valley on Long Island's north shore, this 409-acre country estate comprises extensive European-style gardens, greenhouses, woodlands, and Coe Hall, a 65-room Tudor-style mansion. There is also a horticultural library and a herbarium with more than 10,000 mounted plant specimens. *Planting Fields Rd., Upper*

Brookville, Long Island, 516/922–9210, www.plantingfields.org. Gardens open daily 9–5. Free; parking $5. Long Island Rail Road: Oyster Bay Line to Locust Valley or Oyster Bay.

SAG HARBOR, LONG ISLAND

For a charming getaway, try this 19th-century whaling center on Long Island's South Fork. Along with historic houses and chic boutiques and cafés, there's an old cemetery, a Customs House dating from 1793, and a Whaling Museum (516/725–0770).

VANDERBILT MANSION

Designed by McKim, Mead & White, this sumptuous 1898 Italian Renaissance manor was the home of Frederick Vanderbilt, the commodore's son. The 54-room estate is perhaps the country's best example of 19th-century industrial wealth: Inside you'll find opulent furnishings and paintings from the 16th to 18th centuries; outside, magnificent views of the Hudson River. *Rte. 9, Hyde Park, NY, 914/229–9115, www.nps.gov/vama. Daily 9–5. Metro-North: Hudson Line to Poughkeepsie.*

chapter 5

ARTS, ENTERTAINMENT & NIGHTLIFE

New York has always been an epicenter for the arts, but today's scene is more dynamic and vigorous than ever. Purveyors and producers compete frantically for the patronage of increasingly savvy and voracious audiences. Who has not been chagrined about the long lines for The Producers or free Shakespeare in the Park tickets; the all-night queues of audience hopefuls for The Rosie O'Donnell Show; or the distraught crowds outside the Metropolitan Opera House moments before curtain time, offering incoming ticket holders a small fortune to see Tristan und Isolde?

These fans know precisely what they want, and pleasing them has become a real challenge—not least because of enormous production costs.

In each of the arts, there is a palpable sense of rising standards. As the Times Square renaissance continues with no end in sight, Broadway's theaters are booked solid with productions that seem more rewarding every season, both financially and (many agree) artistically. The Metropolitan Opera and its magnificent orchestra have not been this consistently exciting in decades. The art-gallery scene is flourishing in new Chelsea venues; and film lovers swarm to the Film Forum to catch movies they aren't likely to see on the big screen anywhere else in the world.

performing arts

PERFORMANCE VENUES

9 *b-2*
ALICE TULLY HALL
Many have declared the acoustics in this medium-size auditorium the fairest of them all, including a great many international soloists. The Chamber Music Society of Lincoln Center performs here, and the New York Film Festival takes over in late September. *1941 Broadway (at 65th St.), Upper West Side, 212/875–5050. Subway: 1, 2 to 66th St./Lincoln Center.*

10 *g-3*
ANGEL ORENSANZ FOUNDATION CENTER FOR THE ARTS
A former synagogue, this hip venue has the dramatic feel of a lost age. Everything from concerts by such indie rock darlings as Belle and Sebastian to premieres by Phillip Glass have filled its endearing, decrepit space. *172 Norfolk St. (between Houston and Stanton Sts.), Lower East Side, 212/780–0175. Subway: F, V to 2nd Ave.*

7 *b-1*

APOLLO THEATER

Ever since it opened in 1913, this legendary Harlem high point has been everything from a burlesque hall to a showcase for the ongoing Wednesday Amateur Nights. Ella Fitzgerald, Duke Ellington, Billie Holiday, Count Basie, Bill Cosby, and Aretha Franklin are only a few of those who have lit the place up. As of press time, the theater was scheduled for a multi-million dollar renovation. *253 W. 125th St. (between St. Nicholas and 8th Aves.), Harlem, 212/749–5838. Subway: A, B, C, D to 125th St.*

12 *b-3*

ARTS AT ST. ANN'S

This performing arts group moved out of its home in a Brooklyn Heights church in 2000. It hosts a wide variety of quality musical events, including jazz, blues, world music, experimental opera, and musical theater at venues around the city. Performances are held March–May and October–December. *70 Washington St. (between Front and York Sts.), DUMBO, Brooklyn, 718/858–2424. Subway: 1, 2, 4, 5 to Borough Hall.*

9 *b-2*

AVERY FISHER HALL

Well-worn as the home of the New York Philharmonic from September to June, this austere modern hall also hosts the beloved Mostly Mozart festival in summer and all sorts of other special events, from superstar recitals to the annual American Film Institute salutes. *Lincoln Center Plaza (Broadway at 64th St.), Upper West Side, 212/875–5030. Subway: 1, 2 to 66th St./Lincoln Center.*

12 *d-3*

BAM HARVEY THEATER

Named for Harvey Lichtenstein, the longtime director of the Brooklyn Academy of Music, this space was renovated by the architect Hugh Hardy to give the appearance of a building in decay. It looks great, but the seats are notoriously uncomfortable. *651 Fulton St. (two blocks west of the Brooklyn Academy of Music), Fort Greene, Brooklyn, 718/636–4100. Subway: 1, 2, 4, 5, Q to Atlantic Ave.; N, R, W to Pacific St.; BAM Bus to and from Manhattan.*

1 *a-1*

BARGEMUSIC LTD.

Bargemusic presents chamber music year-round on an enclosed former coffee barge. The attractive performance space is paneled in cherry and backed by a glass wall through which you get a view of the Brooklyn Bridge and Manhattan. *Fulton Ferry Landing, Brooklyn Heights, Brooklyn, 718/624–4061. Subway: A, C to High St. (Fulton exit); 1, 2 to Clark St.*

7 *b-8*

BEACON THEATER

This huge theater has a wildly diverse history, but it currently tends to present pop and rock concerts. *2124 Broadway (near 74th St.), Upper West Side, 212/496–7070. Subway: 1, 2, 3 to 72nd St.*

1 *e-3*

BROOKLYN ACADEMY OF MUSIC (BAM)

Home to the Brooklyn Philharmonic, BAM also presents important, often innovative operatic and theatrical performances, as well as experimental and established dance companies. *30 Lafayette Ave. (at Flatbush Ave.), Fort Greene, Brooklyn, 718/636–4100. Subway: 1, 2, 4, 5, Q to Atlantic Ave.; N, R, W to Pacific St.; BAM Bus to and from Manhattan.*

9 *c-3*

CARNEGIE HALL/ WEILL RECITAL HALL

Carnegie Hall's acoustics are as legendary as the musicians who have benefited from them over the last 100 years. Orchestras sound their very best here, but so do solo pianists; something about the place inspires all kinds of performers to outdo themselves. The hall still looks fresh from its total renovation in 1986. Intimate Weill Recital Hall is wonderfully unpretentious, with clean acoustics and a no-nonsense atmosphere. In December of 2002 a third, 650-seat concert hall is scheduled to open, beneath the Isaac Stern Auditorium, with an entrance on Seventh Avenue. A jazz, pop, and world music calendar are planned for this new venue. *154 W. 57th St. (between 6th and 7th Aves.), Midtown West, 212/247–7800. Subway: N, R, Q, W to 57th St./7th Ave.; F to 57th St./6th Ave.*

9 c-4

CIRCLE IN THE SQUARE

A small Broadway house with seating around the stage. *235 W. 50th St. (between Broadway and 8th Ave.), Midtown West, 212/239–6200. Subway: C, E to 50th St.*

9 d-3

CITY CENTER

This busy ballet and modern dance theater hosts the Paul Taylor Dance Company and the Alvin Ailey American Dance Theater on a regular basis. In addition to touring international dance companies it is also home to the "Encores!" series of staged Broadway musicals. *131 W. 55th St. (between 6th and 7th Aves.), Midtown West, 212/581–1212. Subway: N, R, Q, W to 57th St./7th Ave.; F, V to 57th St./6th Ave.*

7 d-7

DELACORTE THEATER

The alfresco Central Park home of the annual Public Theater's production of free Shakespeare. *Central Park at 81st St., Upper West Side, 212/539–8750. Subway: B, C to 86th St.*

9 e-3

FLORENCE GOULD HALL

The Alliance Francaise operates this four-hundred seat theater where the best of French culture is often on display. *55 E. 59th St. (between Madison and Park Aves.), Upper East Side, 212/355–6160. Subway: 4, 5, 6 to 59th St.*

7 e-7

GRACE RAINEY ROGERS AUDITORIUM

The Met presents classical music, mostly chamber, in the glorious surroundings of one of the world's greatest art museums. Concerts run from early October to late May, with a concurrent lecture series. *Metropolitan Museum of Art, 1000 5th Ave. (at 82nd St.), Upper East Side, 212/570–3949. Subway: 4, 5, 6 to 86th St.*

10 d-3

HERE

Three small theaters, an art gallery, and a café, where big imaginations and small budgets are the rule of the day. *145 6th Ave. (between Spring and Dominick Sts.), SoHo, 212/647–0202. Subway: C, E to Spring St.*

9 c-8

THE JOYCE THEATRE

A fine, highly eclectic modern-dance venue, the Joyce is the permanent home of the Feld Ballets/NY and features several other modern companies, including Pilobolus, Lar Lubovitch Dance Company, and Ballet Hispanico. It's medium-size and unusually comfortable. *175 8th Ave. (at 18th St.), Chelsea, 212/242–0800. Subway: A, C, E to 14th St.*

9 c-6

HAMMERSTEIN BALLROOM

This lovely concert hall was built in 1906 by the impresario Oscar Hammerstein, who insured great sight lines. Thanks to a 1997 renovation, it now has an impressive sound system and is a regular stop for touring rock acts. It is located inside the Manhattan Center recording studios. *311 W. 34th St. (between 8th and 9th Aves.), Midtown West, 212/564–4882. Subway: A, C, E to 34th St.*

9 b-8

THE KITCHEN

This diminutive space is currently the epicenter of performance art—but it highlights dance, video, and music as well. *512 W. 19th St. (at 10th Ave.), Chelsea, 212/255–5793. Subway: C, E to 23rd St.*

9 c-6

MADISON SQUARE GARDEN

Where else can 20,000 people see Barbra Streisand, Phish, or the New York Knicks? The Garden complex includes a 5,600-seat theater, where megamusical versions of *A Christmas Carol* and *The Wizard of Oz* make annual appearances. *7th Ave. at 31st–33rd Sts., Midtown West, 212/465–6741. Subway: 1, 2, 3, A, C, E to 34th St./Penn Station.*

9 b-1

MERKIN CONCERT HALL

This relative newcomer to the concert-hall pantheon gained rapid prestige with its ambitious programming: the smallish auditorium is almost entirely devoted to 20th-century chamber music. *Abraham Goodman House, 129 W. 67th St. (between Broadway and Amsterdam Ave.), Upper West Side, 212/501–3330. www.ekcc.org. Subway: 1, 2 to 66th St./Lincoln Center.*

9 *b-2*
METROPOLITAN OPERA HOUSE
This fabled structure is home to the Metropolitan Opera and the American Ballet Theater. At press time plans were being made to renovate the Lincoln Center complex. *Lincoln Center Plaza (Broadway at 64th St.), Upper West Side, 212/362–6000. Subway: 1, 2 to 66th St./Lincoln Center.*

7 *a-3*
MILLER THEATRE
Located on the campus of Columbia University, this stately and intimate venue is host to everything from poetry readings to classical music. *Broadway at 116th St., Morningside Heights, 212/854–7799. Subway: 1 to 116th St.*

9 *b-2*
NEW YORK STATE THEATER
The famed New York City Ballet holds court here April–June and November–February. It's also the home of the New York City Opera. *Lincoln Center Plaza (Broadway at 64th St.), Upper West Side, 212/870–5570. Subway: 1, 2 to 66th St./Lincoln Center.*

9 *e-1*
NEW VICTORY THEATER
This magnificently restored theater is host to a wide variety of children's programing. *209 W. 42nd St. (between 7th and 8th Aves.), Midtown West, 212/239–6200. Subway: 1, 2, 3, 7, N, Q, R, W to 42nd St./Times Sq.*

10 *f-1*
P.S. 122
Very obviously a tumble-down former public school, this fascinating and idiomatic experimental dance/performance space operates year-round. *150 1st Ave. (at 9th St.), East Village, 212/477–5288. Subway: 6 to Astor Pl.; F, V to 2nd Ave.*

9 *d-4*
RADIO CITY MUSIC HALL
Still breathtaking after all these years (thanks to a thoughtful renovation in 1999), Radio City's 6,000-seat auditorium features two-ton chandeliers, a 60-ft-high Art Deco lobby and foyer, and some of the glitziest acts ever concocted. The resident Rockettes still kick higher than any chorus line, and their Christmas and Easter performances will curl your toes. Pop stars from Bette Midler to k.d. lang to Tony Bennett also pack the house. *1260 6th Ave. (at 50th St.), Midtown West, 212/247–4777. Subway: B, D, F, V to 47th–50th Sts./Rockefeller Center.*

9 *e-1*
SYLVIA & DANNY KAYE PLAYHOUSE
A host to jazz concerts and such obscure international pop stars as the Italian singer Paolo Conte, this space is notable for its comfortable small-audience capacity, paired with a stage that accommodates good-size productions. *Hunter College, 68th St. between Park and Lexington Aves., Upper East Side, 212/772–4448. Subway: 6 to 68th St./Hunter College.*

7 *b-6*
SYMPHONY SPACE
Symphony Space boasts the most varied programs in town—all-day readings of *Ulysses*, zither recitals, gospel, Gershwin, exotic dancing—and the friendly flavor of its neighborhood. At press time it was undergoing renovations that will include the creation of a new version of the legendary revival movie house The Thalia. *2737 Broadway (at 95th St.), Upper West Side, 212/864–5400. Subway: 1, 2, 3 to 96th St.*

7 *e-6*
TISCH CENTER FOR THE ARTS
The Tisch Center at the 92nd Street Y offers an endless, fascinating, and fairly affordable array of readings, lectures, and concerts—classical, pop, and jazz. Most series take a breather in summer, but the jazz plays on. *92nd Street Y, 1395 Lexington Ave. (at 92nd St.), Upper East Side, 212/996–1100. Subway: 4, 5 to 86th St.; 6 to 96th St.*

9 *d-5*
TOWN HALL
This low-key historic beauty quietly hosts an eclectic mix of chamber music, staged readings, stand-up comedy, high-end cabaret acts, and pop. *123 W. 43rd St. (between 6th and 7th Aves.), Midtown West, 212/840–2824. Subway: 1, 2, 3, 7, N, Q, R, W to 42nd St./Times Sq.; B, D, F, V to 42nd St.*

11 c-8

TRIBECA PERFORMING ARTS CENTER

Catch fine international dance troupes at this versatile space with two theaters, one intimate, the other more substantial. Tickets are an encouraging $7–$20. *199 Chambers St. (between Greenwich Ave. and West Side Hwy.), TriBeCa, 212/346–8510. Subway: 1, 2 Chambers St.*

10 b-2

WESTBETH THEATER CENTER

A home to dance, comedy, and popular music. *151 Bank St. (between Washington St. and West Side Hwy.), West Village, 212/741–0391. Subway: A, C, E to 14th St.*

CONCERTS IN CHURCHES

Churches play a quiet but crucial role in New York's classical scene, allowing both amateur and professional performers to find their own audiences. See Friday's *New York Times* for additional venues and specific programs.

7 b-3

CATHEDRAL CHURCH OF ST. JOHN THE DIVINE

Huge, dark, and majestic, to say the least, St. John's has the acoustics and atmosphere to make any musical event a stirring experience. *1047 Amsterdam Ave. (at 112th St.), Morningside Heights, 212/662–2133. Subway: 1, B, C to 110th St./Cathedral Pkwy.*

7 e-7

CHURCH OF ST. IGNATIUS LOYOLA

The acclaimed "Sacred Music in a Sacred Space" concert series uses this lush Italianate setting to showcase the church's own professional choir and fabulous organ as well as to host visiting artists. Solemn mass, every Sunday at 11 AM, features Gregorian chant and a new musical program each week. *980 Park Ave. (at 84th St.), Upper East Side, 212/288–3588. Subway: 4, 5, 6 to 86th St.*

10 e-1

GRACE CHURCH

Further downtown, this magnificent church sponsors frequent concerts and recitals, usually in early evening. *802 Broadway (at 10th St.), Greenwich Vil-*lage, *212/254–2000. Subway: N, R to 8th St.; 6 to Astor Pl.*

9 e-4

ST. BARTHOLOMEW'S CHURCH

This Byzantine-style church has been making and sponsoring great music for more than 100 years. *109 E. 50th St. (between Lexington and Park Aves.), Midtown East, 212/378–0200. Subway: 6 to 51st St./Lexinton Ave.; E, V to Lexington–3rd Aves./53rd St.*

9 e-3

ST. PETER'S CHURCH AT CITICORP CENTER

Stop by on your lunch hour (or just peer through the street-level windows) for midday jazz or an organ recital on this innovative stage, or check out the unique Jazz Vespers on Sunday. Weekend evenings see choral action. *619 Lexington Ave. (at 54th St.), Midtown East, 212/935–2200. Subway: 6 to 51st St./Lexinton Ave.; E, V to Lexington–3rd Aves./53rd St.*

9 d-3

ST. THOMAS CHURCH

New York's most famous men-and-boys choir works magic in this soaring Episcopal space. *1 W. 53rd St. (at 5th Ave.), Midtown West, 212/757–7013. Subway: E, V to 5th Ave.*

9 e-2

TEMPLE EMANU-EL

The world's largest Reform synagogue offers regular recitals, organ and otherwise. *1 E. 65th St. (5th Ave.), Upper East Side, 212/744–1400. Subway: 6 to 68th St.*

DANCE

Ballet and modern dance flourish year-round in New York. Check the *New Yorker, New York* magazine, the *New York Times,* and *Time Out* for current programs. You have more than one performance option almost any night of the year.

companies

9 a-2

ALVIN AILEY AMERICAN DANCE THEATER

The quintessential modern dance company celebrated its fortieth anniversary in 2001 by announcing plans for a sparkling new studio made of glass and metal on Manhattan's west side. While construction is underway, expect the troupe to continue its always popular annual December run at City Center. *211 W. 61st St. (between Amsterdam and West End Aves.), Upper West Side, 212/767-0590. Subway: 1, 2 to 66th St./Lincoln Center.*

10 *f-1*

AMERICAN BALLET THEATRE

This renowned company presents a new season each year from April to June. *Lincoln Center Plaza (Broadway at 64th St.), Upper West Side, 212/362-6000. Subway: 1, 2 to 66th St./Lincoln Center.*

7 *b-6*

BALLET HISPANICO

For more than thirty years this troupe has been the leading interpreter of Hispanic dance culture. Elements of ballet, modern, and more ethnic dance forms are incorporated in their performances. *167 W. 89th St. (between Amsterdam and Columbus Aves.), Upper West Side, 212/362-6710. Subway: 1, 2, 3 to 96th St.*

6 *c-5*

DANCE THEATRE OF HARLEM

The country's first African-American ballet company, this neoclassical troupe was formed in 1968. Each fall they take up residency at City Center. *466 W. 152 St. (between Amsterdam and St. Nichols Aves.), Harlem, 212/690-2800. Subway: C to 155th St.*

10 *f-1*

DANSPACE PROJECT

DTW is one of the country's most ambitious and successful laboratories for modern dance and performance art. *Bessie Schoenberg Theater, 219 W. 19th St., 2nd floor (between 7th and 8th Aves.), Chelsea, 212/924-0077. Subway: C, E to 23rd St.*

9 *c-8*

ELIOT FELD BALLET TECH

This fine modern dance troupe makes its home at the Joyce Theatre. *175 8th Ave. (at 18th St.), Chelsea, 212/242-0800. Subway: A, C, E to 14th St.; 1, 9 to 18th St.*

1 *e-3*

MARK MORRIS DANCE GROUP

In 2001—twenty years after he founded his own company—the bad-boy of contemporary dance moved into a new home next to the Brooklyn Academy of Music. *3 Lafayette Ave. (at Flatbush Ave.), Fort Greene, Brooklyn, 718/624-8400. Subway: 1, 2, 4, 5, Q to Atlantic Ave.; N, R, W to Pacific St.; BAM Bus to and from Manhattan.*

9 *b-2*

NEW YORK CITY BALLET

The famed company holds court April–June and November–February at the New York State Theatre. From Thanksgiving through the New Year, the company stages its legendary production of George Balanchine's *Nutcracker*. *Lincoln Center Plaza (Broadway at 64th St.), Upper West Side, 212/870-5570. Subway: 1, 2 to 66th St./Lincoln Center.*

9 *d-7*

REPERTORIO ESPAÑOL

Located in the Gramercy Arts Theater, this company is best known as the frequent host of Spanish choreographer Pílar Rioja, who recently celebrated her 25th anniversary at this space. *138 E. 27th St. (between Lexington and 3rd Aves.), Gramercy, 212/889-2850. Subway: 6 to 28th St.*

festivals & special events

4 *e-2*

CELEBRATE BROOKLYN!

The performers move outdoors at this summertime festival in the "Borough of Kings." *Prospect Park Bandshell, Prospect Park West (at 9th St.), Prospect Heights, Brooklyn, 718/855-7882, ext. 45. Subway: F to 9th St.*

9 *d-1*

CENTRAL PARK SUMMERSTAGE

Manhattan's backyard is the place for mid-afternoon summertime performances by a wide variety of dancers. *Rumsey Playfield, mid-park at 72nd St., Upper East Side, 212/360-2777. Subway: B, C to 72nd St.*

FRINGE FESTIVAL

Each summer, the local offshoot of the fabled Edinburgh arts gathering brings a wide and fascinating variety of dancers to lower Manhattan venues. *212/505–8888.*

9 *b-2*

LINCOLN CENTER FESTIVAL

In summer this hopping festival features visiting national ballet companies, including the Royal Ballet. *Lincoln Center Plaza (Broadway at 64th St.), Upper West Side, 212/875–5456. Subway: 1, 2 to 66th St./Lincoln Center.*

1 *e-3*

NEXT WAVE FESTIVAL

Such dance visionaries as Pina Bausch join other experimental dance companies each fall at the Brooklyn Academy of Music. *30 Lafayette Ave. (at Flatbush Ave.), Fort Greene, Brooklyn, 718/636–4100. Subway: 1, 2, 4, 5, Q to Atlantic Ave.; N, R, W to Pacific St.; BAM Bus to and from Manhattan.*

FILM

Due mainly to the invention of the VCR, most of the fabled movie-repertory houses of the 1960s and '70s are gone now. Their absence makes the independent theaters listed here that much more valuable (and popular)—their programming supports not only the work of indie filmmakers but also keeps repertory fare alive, including films unavailable on video. For current listings, check any daily newspaper, the *New Yorker, New York* magazine, or *Time Out* (particularly good on art-house listings).

programs & theaters of note

8 *c-5*

AMERICAN MUSEUM OF THE MOVING IMAGE

This repository of cinematic history is located in what was once Paramount Studio's east coast production facility. Today it has several theaters, including one designed by the artist Red Grooms in homage to the movie palaces of the twenties, which regularly screen retrospectives and tributes to actors and directors. *36-01 35th Ave. (at 36th St.), Astoria, Queens, 718/784–0077. Subway: R, V to Steinway St.*

10 *e-3*

ANGELIKA FILM CENTER

This sixplex is a mecca for new foreign and independent films. On a Saturday night, the cavernous lobby is packed with crowds of cool-looking young people. The screening rooms, though, are small and some have poor sight lines. And the rumble of the subway too frequently adds an unexpected touch. *18 W. Houston St. (between Broadway and Mercer St.), Greenwich Village, 212/995–2570. Subway: 6 to Bleecker St.; F, V to Broadway/Lafayette.*

1 *e-3*

BAM ROSE CINEMAS

The four screens here show top-notch foreign and independent films, but the best thing about this attractively designed cinema is that there's hardly ever a crowd. Perhaps it's the trek to Brooklyn that scares them away, but Manhattanites don't know what they're missing. *30 Lafayette Ave. (at Flatbush Ave.), Fort Greene, Brooklyn, 718/623–2270. Subway: 1, 2, 4, 5, Q to Atlantic Ave.; N, R, W to Pacific St.; BAM Bus to and from Manhattan.*

10 *e-1*

CINEMA VILLAGE

This hip little cinema shows a wide variety of sometimes ridiculous, sometimes sublime art-house fare. *E. 12th St. (between 5th Ave. and University Pl.), Greenwich Village, 212/924–3363. Subway: 4, 5, 6, L, N, R to 14th St./Union Sq.*

10 *c-3*

FILM FORUM

The mother of all New York City art-houses, the Film Forum isn't actually a commercial theater. It's a non-profit, and as such offers different levels of membership that ease the crunch in trying to see their popular programming. *209 W. Houston St. (between 6th Ave. and Varick St.), West Village, 212/727–8110. Subway: 1, 2 to Houston St.*

9 *d-3*

MUSEUM OF MODERN ART

Among the 14,000 films in the museum's holdings are the original 1884 Kinetoscopes of Thomas Edison, so you can always expect highly authentic and compelling screenings here. The museum is also home to the New Directors/New Films series. *11 W. 53rd St. (5th*

Ave.), Midtown West, 212/708–9480. Subway: E, V to 5th Ave.

9 *d-3*

MUSEUM OF TELEVISION & RADIO

From reel after reel of "The Andy Griffith Show" to scenes from the short-lived 1983 sitcom "Zorro and Son," this is the place to catch up on television history. *25 W. 52nd St. (5th Ave.), Midtown West, 212/621–6600. Subway: E, V to 5th Ave.*

10 *e-1*

QUAD CINEMA

The Quad is small and cramped and its screens may have seen better days, but this is Manhattan's original multiplex (it opened in October of 1972), and it is often home to small, highly original films that you won't find anywhere else. *34 W. 13th St. (between 5th and 6th Aves.), Greenwich Village, 212/255–8800. Subway: 4, 5, 6, L, N, R to 14th St./Union Sq.*

9 *b-2*

WALTER READE THEATER/FILM SOCIETY OF LINCOLN CENTER

One big screen, lots of comfortable seats, and a wall-shaking sound system that would do a suburban multiplex proud makes this the best art house in the city. *165 W. 65th St. (at Broadway), Upper West Side, 212/875–5600. Subway: 1, 2 to 66th St./Lincoln Center.*

film festivals

DOCFEST

The New York International Documentary Festival takes place each spring. *212/668–1100.*

GENART FILM FESTIVAL

Each spring this event showcases the best of the many young and emerging filmmakers. *212/290–0312.*

9 *b-2*

NEW YORK FILM FESTIVAL

Run by the Film Society of Lincoln Center, this annual event rivals Cannes for the quality of its premieres. It takes place each fall and the screenings sell out immediately. Don't worry too much if you can't get in—the top films are sure to be re-released later in the year. *165 W. 65th St. (at Broadway), Upper West Side, 212/875–5600. Subway: 1, 2 to 66th St./Lincoln Center.*

NEW YORK INDEPENDENT FILM & VIDEO FESTIVAL

This annual fall round-up features edgier fare than its uptown counterpart, the New York Film Festival. *212/777–7100.*

OPERA

11 *f-2*

AMATO OPERA

Since 1947 this tiny theater has provided a unique showcase for some thrilling singing. Where else can you see and hear 50 (usually young) singers on a 20-ft stage, performing Verdi's *Falstaff* with real passion? Repertory standards are performed on varying weekends from September through June. *319 Bowery (at 2nd St.), East Village, 212/228–8200. Subway: 6 to Bleecker St.; F, V to 2nd Ave.*

1 *e-3*

BROOKLYN ACADEMY OF MUSIC (BAM)

BAM has hosted several of the most important operatic premieres of the last decade (including the brilliant *Nixon in China*), and several august companies, including the Welsh National Opera, have performed brilliantly here. *30 Lafayette Ave. (at Flatbush Ave.), Fort Greene, Brooklyn, 718/636–4100. Subway: 1, 2, 4, 5, Q to Atlantic Ave.; N, R, W to Pacific St.; BAM Bus to and from Manhattan.*

9 *b-2*

METROPOLITAN OPERA COMPANY

Tickets are pricey, to say the least, but most agree that the Met is the finest opera company in the country—the finest in the world, on some nights. The company's hefty season runs from September to April. *Metropolitan Opera House, Lincoln Center Plaza (Broadway and 64th St.), Upper West Side, 212/362–6000. Subway: 1, 2 to 66th St./Lincoln Center.*

9 *b-2*

NEW YORK CITY OPERA

This courageous and remarkable company performs standards (*Carmen, Traviata*); Broadway musicals with operatic aspirations (*Street Scene, A Little Night Music*); and, best of all, new works (*Malcolm X, The Times of Harvey Milk*) and unforgivably neglected masterpieces (*The Cunning Little Vixen, The Makropulos Case*). Ticket prices are decidedly more welcoming than those across the plaza. The season runs from September to November and from March to April. *New York State Theater, Lincoln Center Plaza (Broadway at 64th St.), Upper West Side, 212/870–5570. Subway: 1, 2 to 66th St./Lincoln Center.*

L'OPERA FRANCAIS DE NEW YORK

This intriguing company produces first-class performances of neglected operas from the French repertoire at a variety of venues around the city. *212/349–7009.*

9 *c-3*

OPERA ORCHESTRA OF NEW YORK

Under the intrepid guidance of Eve Queler, OONY performs concert versions of (usually) rarely performed works by major composers, often featuring star soloists and always furnishing libretti for the audience (the lights are kept up). *Carnegie Hall (see Concert Halls, above).*

ORCHESTRAS & ENSEMBLES

performing groups

9 *b-2*

AMERICAN SYMPHONY ORCHESTRA

This orchestra thrives under the direction of Leon Botstein, who also happens to be the president of Bard College. His brilliant programming ideas run from Soviet composers to such neglected masterpieces as Chausson's *King Arthur. Avery Fisher Hall, Lincoln Center Plaza (Broadway and 64th St.), Upper West Side, 212/581–1365. Subway: 1, 2 to 66th St./Lincoln Center.*

1 *e-3*

BROOKLYN PHILHARMONIC

Under the direction of the dynamic young American conductor Robert Spano, this orchestra is known for its daring modern repertoire. *30 Lafayette Ave. (at Flatbush Ave.), Fort Greene, Brooklyn, 718/636–4100. Subway: 1, 2, 4, 5, Q to Atlantic Ave.; N, R, W to Pacific St.*

9 *b-2*

THE CHAMBER MUSIC SOCIETY OF LINCOLN CENTER

The artistic director David Shifrin programs a wide variety of material, including many new commissions. *Alice Tully Hall, Lincoln Center Plaza (Broadway and 64th St.), Upper West Side, 212/875–5775. Subway: 1, 2 to 66th St./Lincoln Center.*

10 *d-3*

EOS ORCHESTRA

This impressive freelance orchestra reflects the tastes of its splashy young director Jonathan Sheffer. Its first concert, in 1995, for example, was a three-day celebration of the music of Paul Bowles. *161 6th Ave., Suite 902, SoHo, 212/691–6415.*

9 *b-2*

NEW YORK PHILHARMONIC

Often referred to as the world's greatest orchestra, the Philharmonic returned to form under the direction of Kurt Masur. In the fall of 2002 he is being replaced by the veteran American conductor Lorin Maazel. Expectations, and anxiety, are running high. *Avery Fisher Hall, Lincoln Center Plaza (Broadway and 64th St.), Upper West Side, 212/721–6500. Subway: 1, 2 to 66th St./Lincoln Center.*

7 *b-3*

NEW YORK'S ENSEMBLE FOR EARLY MUSIC

This remarkable group performs about 20 medieval and Renaissance music concerts in the Cathedral of St. John the Divine. *1047 Amsterdam Ave. (at 112th St.), Morningside Heights, 212/662–2133. Subway: 1, B, C to 110th St./Cathedral Pkwy.*

classical music festivals

9 *b-2*

LINCOLN CENTER FESTIVAL

Rarely heard operas and performances by the New York Philharmonic are often among the highlights of this summer festival. *Lincoln Center Plaza (Broadway at 64th St.), Upper West Side, 212/875–5456. Subway: 1, 2 to 66th St./Lincoln Center.*

9 *b-2*

MOSTLY MOZART FESTIVAL

Each August, Lincoln Center's longest running classical series featuring the music of Mozart and other classical favorites. *Lincoln Center (Broadway at*

64th St.), Upper West Side, 212/875–5399. Subway: 1, 2 to 66th St./Lincoln Center.

1 *e-3*

NEXT WAVE FESTIVAL

New works by international orchestras and local ensembles can be found each fall at the Brooklyn Academy of Music. *30 Lafayette Ave. (at Flatbush Ave.), Fort Greene, Brooklyn, 718/636–4100. Subway: 1, 2, 4, 5, Q to Atlantic Ave.; N, R, W to Pacific St.; BAM Bus to and from Manhattan.*

TELEVISION SHOWS

Getting free tickets to television tapings is a lot trickier than it used to be. Most shows require a postcard—with your name, address, phone number, and the number of tickets requested—at least a month in advance. But standby (same-day) tickets are usually available to those willing to spend several hours standing in line.

9 *d-4*

LATE NIGHT WITH CONAN O'BRIEN

Same-day standby tickets are available after 10 AM at the NBC Page Desk in the lobby of 30 Rockefeller Plaza—but you're better off writing well in advance. *NBC Tickets, Late Night with Conan O'Brien, 30 Rockefeller Plaza, New York, NY 10112. 212/664–3056 information. Subway: B, D, F, V to 47th–50th Sts./Rockefeller Center.*

9 *c-3*

THE LATE SHOW WITH DAVID LETTERMAN

Standby tickets are distributed by phone on the day of taping. To grab a pair, call 212/247–6497 at 11 AM. You're better off writing in advance. All audience members must be over 16. *Late Show Tickets, 1697 Broadway, New York, NY 10019. 212/975–1003 information. Subway: 1, 2, C, E to 50th St./8th Ave.; B, D, E to 7th Ave./53rd St.*

9 *c-1*

LIVE WITH REGIS & KELLY

You need to be over 18 to attend this one live. Standby tickets go on sale weekdays at 8 AM at the ABC headquarters; line up at the corner of 67th Street and Columbus Avenue. Otherwise, write a full year in advance. *Live Tickets, Anso-*

nia Station, Box 777, New York, NY 10023-0777. 212/456–3537 information. Subway: 1, 2 to 66th St./Lincoln Center.

9 *d-4*

THE ROSIE O'DONNELL SHOW

Highly coveted standby tickets (one per person) are distributed by lottery Monday–Thursday at 7:30 AM, at the 49th Street entrance to 30 Rockefeller Plaza. There is currently a 9- to 12-month wait for tickets requested by postcard; if you can plan ahead, write *during April, May, or June.* Only two tickets are allotted per postcard, and children under five are not permitted. Call 212/506–3288 for all sorts of information on Rosie's show, including recipes, internships, and how to apply for a guest appearance. *ABC Studios, Rosie O'Donnell Show, 30 Rockefeller Plaza, Suite 800E, New York, NY 10112. Subway: B, D, F, V to 47th–50th Sts./Rockefeller Center.*

9 *d-4*

SATURDAY NIGHT LIVE

Standby tickets go on sale at 9:15 AM, at the 49th Street entrance to 30 Rockefeller Plaza. Advance tickets for performances and dress rehearsals are available by lottery; postcards are accepted during August only. You must be over 16. *NBC Tickets, Saturday Night Live, 30 Rockefeller Plaza, New York, NY 10112. 212/664–4000 information. Subway: B, D, F, V to 47th–50th Sts./Rockefeller Center.*

9 *c-3*

WNET (CHANNEL 13)

There are no regular tapings with a live audience, but the network offers periodic tours. *356 W. 58th St. (between 8th and 9th Aves.), Midtown West, 212/560–2000. Subway: 1, 2, A, B, C, D to 59th St./Columbus Circle.*

THEATERS

Until fairly recently, "theater" in New York City meant "Broadway." Today, off-Broadway drama is just as vital and important as the blockbuster musicals. More than a few current Tony Award–winning megahits can claim to have originated off-Broadway, where ticket prices are usually about half of those on the well-traveled Great White Way. An off-off-Broadway experience may involve sitting on a folding chair in a church basement or at the back of a coffee-house, but many feel that the true pulse of American theater beats most steadily in these settings, where actors often work for free, runs are limited, and admission amounts to little more than a donation.

For current theater information, call New York City Onstage (see Tickets, below), or consult the New Yorker, New York magazine, the New York Times (especially Friday's "Weekend" and Sunday's "Arts and Leisure" sections), or Time Out. For off- and off-off-Broadway, Time Out is best.

Note that few Broadway box offices accept phone calls; Telecharge and TicketMaster field the thousands of calls for Broadway shows. The phone numbers below will lead you to the appropriate ticket vendor.

9 d-4

AMERICAN PLACE THEATER

Since its founding in 1964, this venerable institution has premiered works by Sam Shepard, Ed Bullins, Philip Hayes, and Robert Lowell. 111 W. 46th St. (between 6th and 7th Aves.), Midtown West, 212/840–3074. Subway: B, D, F, V to 42nd St.

9 d-8

ATLANTIC THEATER COMPANY

Founded by the playwright David Mamet and the actor William H. Macy (Fargo), this company is devoted to top-quality drama from all over the world. 33 W. 20th St. (between 5th and 6th Aves.), Chelsea, 212/645–1242. Subway: F, V to 23rd St.

10 d-4

BAT THEATRE COMPANY

Located in the tiny off-off-Broadway Flea Theatre, this company presents such eclectic fare as experimental drama and all-women circuses. 41 White St. (between Church St. and Broadway), TriBeCa, 212/226–0051. Subway: A, C, E to Canal St.

11 a-1

CHERRY LANE THEATER

Back in 1924, Edna St. Vincent Millay and a group of artist friends converted this former box factory into a theater. Ever since, it's been the site of quality off-Broadway productions. 38 Commerce St. (between Bedford and Barrow Sts.; off 7th Ave. S), Greenwich Village, 212/989–2020. Subway: 1, 2 to Christopher St./Sheridan Sq.

10 f-1

CLASSIC STAGE COMPANY

Known for reviving older works that still have relevance today, this East Village company recently put Uma Thurman on stage in an updating of Molière's 17th-century satire of French court life, The Misanthrope. 136 E. 13th St. (between 3rd and 4th Aves.), Greenwich Village, 212/ 677–4210. Subway: 4, 5, 6, L, N, R to Union Sq.

10 c-2

DRAMA DEPARTMENT

This remarkable off-Broadway company at the Greenwich House Theater is known for its productions of new plays by young writers. Recent seasons have seen works by David and Amy Sedaris, Douglas Carter Beane, and Paul Rudnick. 27 Barrow St. (at 7th Ave.), Greenwich Village, 212/633–9108. Subway: 1, 2 to Christopher St./Sheridan Sq.

9 a-3

ENSEMBLE STUDIO THEATER

A tried-and-true roster of players develops new American plays here. Each spring it presents a marathon of one-acts by prominent playwrights. 549 W. 52nd St. (between 10th and 11th Aves.), Midtown West, 212/247–3405. Subway: C, E to 50th St.

9 b-a

INTAR THEATER

A response to the lack of venues supporting Hispanic-American playwrights, Intar shows top quality productions in both Spanish and English. 508 W. 53rd St. (between 10th and 11th Aves.), Midtown West, 212/947–6542. Subway: C, E to 50th St.

9 a-3

IRISH ARTS CENTER

For more than 25 years this has been the place for drama, comedy, and song from the Emerald Isle. 553 W. 51st St. (between 10th and 11th Aves.), Midtown West, 212/ 757–3318. Subway: C, E to 50th St.

9 d-8
IRISH REPERTORY THEATER
Under the direction of Charlotte Moore, this company presents top-notch classic and contemporary Irish drama. *132 W. 22nd St. (between 6th and 7th Aves.), Chelsea, 212/727–2737. Subway: F, V to 23rd St.*

11 f-2
JEAN COCTEAU REPERTORY
With the help of its resident acting troupe, this East Village institution revives classics by playwrights such as Beckett and Brecht. *Bowerie Lane Theater, 330 Bowery (at 2nd St.), East Village, 212/677–0060. Subway: 6 to Bleecker St.; F, V to Broadway–Lafayette.*

9 c-5
JEWISH REPERTORY THEATER
Presenting plays about the Jewish American experience, this troupe moved from its home on the Upper East Side to a new theater on 42nd Street for its 2001 season. *229 W. 42nd St. (between Broadway and 8th Ave.), Midtown West, 645/223–3042, ext. 4251. Subway: 1, 2, 3, 7, N, Q, R, W to 42nd St./Times Sq.*

10 e-2
JOSEPH PAPP PUBLIC THEATER
Named in honor of its late founder and guiding light, this downtown institution continues to present new, innovative theater. This is the theater that first staged *Bring In 'Da Noise, Bring In 'Da Funk*, which went on to a successful Broadway run. In the summer the company heads uptown to central park for free productions of plays by Shakespeare. *425 Lafayette St. (between Church St. and Broadway), East Village, 212/260–2400. Subway: 6 to Astor Pl.; N, R to 8th St.*

11 g-2
LA MAMA E.T.C.
Ellen Stewart, also known—simply and elegantly—as La Mama, started the theater complex La MaMa E.T.C. in 1961. Over the past several decades, her East Village organization has branched out to import international innovators and has grown to include two theatres and a club. Productions include everything from African fables to new-wave opera to interpretations of the Greek classics. Past triumphs have included the original productions of *Godspell* and *Torch Song Trilogy*. *74A E. 4th St. (between Bowery and 2nd Ave.), East Village, 212/475–7710. Subway: F, V to 2nd Ave.; 6 to Bleecker St.*

9 d-4
LAMBS THEATER
Founded in 1979 with the help of a grant from Noel Paul Stookey (of Peter, Paul & Mary), this company is housed in the former headquarters of a theatrical fraternity known as the Lambs Club. *130 W. 44th St. (between 6th Ave. and Broadway), Midtown West, 212/997–1780. Subway: B, D, F, V to 42nd St.*

9 b-2
LINCOLN CENTER THEATER
Under the direction of Andre Bishop, the resident company here produces "good plays at good prices" in two theaters: the Vivian Beaumont, a 1,050-seat Broadway house, and the more intimate, 299-seat Mitzi E. Newhouse. *Lincoln Center, 150 W. 65th St., Upper West Side, 212/239–6200. Subway: 1, 2 to 66th St./Lincoln Center.*

9 c-5
MANHATTAN THEATER CLUB
This well-respected company, which makes its home at City Center, presents some of the most talked-about new plays and musicals in town. Always interesting and often controversial works by Terrence McNally, Athol Fugard, and August Wilson have all shown here. *131 W. 55th St. (between 6th and 7th Aves.), Midtown West, 212/399–3000. Subway: N, R, Q, W to 57th St./7th Ave.; F, V to 57th St./6th Ave.*

NATIONAL ACTORS THEATRE
This classic repertory theater was founded by the actor Tony Randall. *212/719–5331.*

9 b-3
NEGRO ENSEMBLE COMPANY
Founded in the mid-sixties after the playwright Douglas Turner Ward called for an autonomous black-oriented theater company, this troupe is a major producer of new plays about the black experience. They perform at a variety of theaters. *212/582–5860.*

10 *h-4*

NEW FEDERAL THEATER

Founded in 1970, this is one of the major black theater companies in the country. Ntozake Shange's *For Colored Girls Who Have Considered Suicide When the Rainbow Is Enuf* got its start here. *292 Henry St. (between Montgomery and Grand Sts.), Lower East Side, 212/353–1176. Subway: F, J, M to Delancey St.*

11 *g-2*

NEW YORK THEATER WORKSHOP

The NYTW produces new works by playwrights such as Tony Kushner and Claudia Shear's play about Mae West, *Dirty Blonde*, premiered here before heading to Broadway. *79 E. 4th St. (between Bowery and 2nd Ave.), East Village, 212/460–5475. Subway: F, V to 2nd Ave.; 6 to Bleecker St.*

9 *b-4*

PAN ASIAN REPERTORY THEATER

For more than 25 years this company has been producing comedy and drama that speaks to the Asian-American Experience. *47 Great Jones St. (between Lafayette St. and the Bowery), East Village, 212/505–5655. Subway: 6 to Bleecker St.*

11 *g-1*

PEARL THEATER COMPANY

This charming little company puts on about five classic plays each season. *80 St. Mark's Pl. (between 2nd and 3rd Aves.), East Village, 212/598–9802. Subway: 6 to Astor Pl.; N, R to 8th St.*

9 *b-5*

PLAYWRIGHTS HORIZONS

This company produces promising new works, and it has the Pulitzers to prove it—for the plays *Driving Miss Daisy* and *The Heidi Chronicles* and the musical *Sunday in the Park with George*. *416 W. 42nd St. (between 9th and 10th Aves.), Midtown West, 212/564–1235. Subway: 1, 2, 3, 7, N, Q, R, W to 42nd St./Times Sq.*

9 *c-4*

PRIMARY STAGES

New American plays by new American playwrights is the motto here. *345 W. 45th St. (between 8th and 9th Aves.), Midtown West, 212/333–4052. Subway: A, C, E to 42nd St./Port Authority.*

9 *b-4*

PUERTO RICAN TRAVELING THEATER

Formed in 1967, the Puerto Rican Traveling Theater presents shows in Spanish and in English. *304 W. 47th St. (between 8th and 9th Aves.), Midtown West, 212/239–6200. Subway: N, R, W to 49th St.; 1, 2 to 50th St.*

11 *c-1*

RATTLESTICK THEATER COMPANY

This troupe specializes in new plays by new writers. The authors are paired up with more established playwrights: past mentors have included Terrence McNally and Craig Lucas. *224 Waverly Pl. (between 11th and Perry Sts.; west of 7th Ave.), Greenwich Village, 212/627–2556. Subway: A, C, E to 14th St.*

9 *c-5*

ROUNDABOUT THEATRE COMPANY

A great non-profit company that's known for its revivals of classic plays and musicals has a Broadway home, the newly renovated Selwin Theater, now known as the American Airlines Theater. *227 W. 42nd St. (between 7th and 8th Aves.), Midtown West, 212/719–9393. Subway: 1, 2, 3, 7, N, Q, R, W to 42nd St./Times Sq.*

9 *c-5*

SECOND STAGE

This noted off-Broadway company moved into a stylish new theater in early 1999, a 299-seat space designed by the super-hip dutch architect Rem Koolhaus. *307 W. 43rd St. (at 8th Ave.), Midtown West, 212/246–4422. Subway: 1, 2, 3, 7, N, Q, R, W to 42nd St./Times Sq.*

9 *b-5*

SIGNATURE THEATRE COMPANY

Each season here is devoted to works by a single playwright, such as luminaries Edward Albee, Sam Shepard, and Maria Irene Fornes. *555 W. 42nd St. (between 10th and 11th Aves.), Midtown West, 212/244–7529. Subway: 1, 2, 3, 7, N, Q, R, W to 42nd St./Times Sq.*

10 *e-1*

VINEYARD THEATER

One of the best-regarded off-Broadway companies, the Vineyard knows how to pick a winner. Its productions of Paula Vogel's *How I Learned to Drive* and Edward Albee's *Three Tall Women* both won Pulitzers. *108 E. 15th St. (between Park Ave. S. and Irving Pl.), Gramercy, 212/353–3366. Subway: 4, 5, 6, L, N, R to 14th St./Union Sq.*

`9` *b-7*

WPA THEATER

American plays, both new ones and neglected classics, are the specialty of this theater company. *519 W. 23rd St. (between 10th and 11th Aves.), Chelsea, 212/206–0523. Subway: C, E to 23rd St.*

`9` *e-3*

YORK THEATER COMPANY

A very steady off-Broadway troupe. *St. Peter's Church at Citicorp Center, 619 Lexington Ave. (at 54th St.), Midtown East, 212/935–5820. Subway: 6 to 51st St./Lexinton Ave.; E, V to Lexington–3rd Aves./53rd St.*

TICKETS

You can buy advance tickets to most arts presentations at full price by mail, in person at the box office, or by phone (with a credit card). You can also buy tickets online; **Ticketweb** (www.ticketweb.com) and **Culturefinder** (www.culturefinder.com) are both good sites. Buying tickets directly from the theater by mail (using a certified check or money order) is the charmingly old-fashioned way, but you may end up in old-fashioned seats under the overhang in the side-rear orchestra—at $75 a pop: Your best bet for choice seats is to go to the box office well in advance of your preferred date; box-office personnel usually know the theater and its current production very well, and if they're in a good mood, they'll help you nab the best of what's available. Of course, this process can be inconvenient, so **Telecharge** (212/239–6200) and **TicketMaster** (212/307–7171) will describe seat locations upon request. Newspaper and magazine listings for each show will tell you which service to use. The catch is that you pay a surcharge of up to $7 when you order tickets by phone. If you call well in advance of the performance, your tickets can be mailed to you; otherwise they'll be held at the box office until just before curtain time. If you need to pick up held tickets to a very popular show, be sure to arrive at the theater in plenty of time and bring the credit card

you used to purchase the tickets. Less-expensive tickets to off- and off-off-Broadway shows (no less exciting than the biggies) may be similarly obtained through a joint box office called **Ticket Central** (416 W. 42nd St., 212/279–4200; open daily 1 PM to 8 PM).

TKTS sells half-price or ¾-price tickets (for cash or traveler's checks only) for same-day Broadway and off-Broadway shows, as well as some music and dance performances. Be prepared to stand in line after checking the board for available shows and performances, and be sure to have alternate selections; shows inevitably sell out as you wait your turn. Be prepared for the $2.50 service charge. TKTS makes a dizzying two transactions per minute, but you'll still have to queue outdoors here, so remember your umbrella if necessary. Tickets for Saturday matinees can be purchased on Friday at the downtown location in the Bowling Green Park Plaza; tickets for Sunday matinees can be bought only on Saturday; tickets for Wednesday matinees can be bought only on Tuesday.

If you can afford to lose, wait until just before curtain time (half an hour or less), when some shows release unclaimed or unsold tickets; lines are much shorter at that point.

Call 212/360–1333 daily for a list of the day's free events in city parks, and check Events (*see* Chapter 4) for special annual happenings, especially summer festivals.

`9` *c-4*

TDF TIMES SQUARE THEATER CENTER (TKTS)

Broadway at 47th St., Midtown West, 212/768–1818, ext. 8. Subway: 1, 2, 3, 7, N, Q, R, W to 42nd St./Times Sq. Open for same-day evening performances Mon.–Sat. 3–8 PM; for matinee performances Wed. and Sat. 10–2; for Sun. matinee and evening performances 11–7.

`10` *e-7*

Bowling Green Park Plaza, Battery Pl. at Broadway, Lower Manhattan Subway: 4, 5 to Bowling Green Open for next-day matinees and same-day evening performances weekdays 11–5:30, Sat. 11–3:30.

NEW YORK CITY ONSTAGE

Here's a phone number well worth memorizing: 212/768–1818. Courtesy of the Theater Development Fund (TDF), this touch-tone menu gives you an impressive and accurate array of recorded information, in English or Spanish, on theater, dance, and music events; performance cancellations; and arts events in all five boroughs, including subway directions.

STUBS & PLAYBILL ON-LINE

The glossy pamphlet *Stubs* gives detailed seating plans for all of New York's Broadway theaters and major off-Broadway theaters, stadiums, and concert halls. You can pick it up for $9.95 at many newsstands and bookstores. On-line, check out *Playbill*'s Web site at www.playbill.com, where you'll find a wealth of resources: links to seating charts for all Broadway theaters and quite a few others, including those on London's West End; access to Telecharge services; feature articles on Broadway and off-Broadway happenings; dozens of daily news items; listings for American regional theaters; and links to a dizzying 650 other theater-oriented sites.

nightlife

New York's nightlife has been shaken up in the past few years, thanks in part to former Mayor Rudy Guiliani's crackdown on "quality-of-life" issues, which included nightspots that disturbed their neighbors. The administration forced the world-famous superclub Twilo out of business. Drug raids, strict ID checks, and security guards have become as common as velvet ropes and disco balls, putting everyone on edge. Money woes did in another stalwart of the nightclub scene, the Tunnel, which closed as its owner, Peter Gatien, faced bankruptcy. Gatien's other dancehall, the Limelight, was sold and, at press time, was struggling to get the necessary licenses to return to form. The city also lost a beloved live-music venue, Wetlands, when the building it was in was slated to become a luxury apartment complex.

On the positive side, swing dancing, while not as popular as it was in the nineties, continues to draw couples to the dance floor nightly. There are also zydeco and country dances on a regular basis. More and more lounges and bars continue to open, especially down-

town—the Lower East Side has sprouted more watering holes in the last few years than in the preceding generation. The seamy, gritty meatpacking district, north of the West Village, has also become a hot new nightspot area. If you're looking for the velvet-rope crowd, SoHo continues to be a sure bet.

All nightspots stop serving alcohol at 4 AM, but diehards keep grooving in dance clubs until long after the sun rises.

BARS & LOUNGES

7 *e-8*

AMERICAN TRASH

Bikers, slackers, and yuppies mix well at this divey bar with a pool table and a good jukebox. *1471 1st Ave. (between 76th and 77th Sts.), Upper East Side, 212/988–9008. Subway: 6 to 77th St.*

11 *f-2*

B BAR

Although it's been replaced as *the* place to be seen, B Bar still has a cool vibe and a huge and wonderful outdoor patio. *40 E. 4th St. (at the Bowery), East Village, 212/475–2220. Subway: 6 to Astor Pl.*

10 *d-1*

BAR SIX

Beautiful people and not a lot of attitude distinguish this hip spot. During the summer they open the French doors and you can take in the breeze. *502 6th Ave. (between 12th and 13th Sts.), Greenwich Village, 212/691–1363. Subway: 4, 5, 6 to 14th St./Union Sq.; F, V to 14th St.; L to 6th Ave.*

10 *f-1*

BEAUTY BAR

Get a happy-hour manicure at this kitschy space with an old-time beauty-parlor vibe at an East Village clientele. *231 E. 14th St. (between 2nd and 3rd Aves.), East Village, 212/539–1389. Subway: 4, 5, 6, L, N, R to 14th St./Union Sq.*

12 *d-4*

BROOKLYN INN

You'll find a killer jukebox, a pool table, an elaborate mahogany bar, and great bartenders—but no television—at this stalwart pub. The crowd is a friendly lot in their mid-twenties to mid-thirties. *138 Bergen St. (at Hoyt St.), Boerum Hill,*

Brooklyn, no phone. Subway: F, G to Bergen St.

11 f-3
CHEZ ES SAADA
Follow the rose-petal strewn stairwell of this neo-Moroccan supper club to the catacomb-like lounge, recline on a hassock, and order a house cocktail. "Place of happiness" is the loose translation of the French-Arabic name, and it's hard not to be content in this setting that evokes the post-war Tangier of Paul Bowles. *42 E. 1st St. (between 1st and 2nd Aves.), East Village, 212/777–5617. Subway: F, V to 2nd Ave.*

9 c-8
CIEL ROUGE
The room is red and smoky, and the cocktails are creative. A chanteuse takes over the piano on Tuesday night and coos Piaf-like songs—you'll think you've touched down on the Left Bank. During the summer you can breathe easier in the garden. *176 7th Ave. (between 20th and 21st Sts.), Chelsea, 212/929–5542. Subway: 1, 2 to 23rd St.*

9 f-4
CONNOLLY'S
This midtown Irish tavern is the current home of Black 47. When the Celtic rockers aren't on tour, they're entertaining here on Saturday night. *14 E. 47th St. (near 5th Ave.), Midtown East, 212/867–3767. Subway: B, D, F, V to 42nd St.*

10 c-1
CORNER BISTRO
For more than 30 years this cozy, down-to-earth spot has been serving cold beer, mixed drinks, and the best hamburgers in town. Sometimes there's nothing better at 3 in the morning. Cash only. *331 W. 4th St. (at Jane St.), Greenwich Village, 212/242–9502. Subway: A, C, E to 14th St.; L to 8th Ave.*

11 g-1
DECIBEL SAKE BAR
The sign outside warns, "no sushi, no karaoke." The menu inside offers more than 40 kinds of sake. The crowd is young and hip and it's easy to loose the better part of the night here. *210 E. 9th St. (between 2nd and 3rd Aves.), East Village, 212/979–2733. Subway: 6 to Astor Pl.*

10 f-4
DOUBLE HAPPINESS
A subterranean lounge that opened in 1999, Double Happiness draws a hip crowd. Try the green tea martini and you won't regret it. If you arrive early enough you can secure the so-called kissing room, a small, out-of-the-way banquette-lined space that has glass in the ceiling leading to the sidewalk above. *173 Mott St. (at Broome St.), Chinatown, 212/941–1282. Subway: F to Delancey St.*

12 f-4
FREDDY'S
From the sidewalk it looks like a scary old-man's dive, but step in to this corner bar and you'll find a speakeasy-like back room with live music, film programs, and a hip, laid-back clientele. *485 Dean St. (at 6th Ave.), Prospect Heights, Brooklyn, 718/622–7035. Subway: 1, 2 to Bergen St.*

3 d-6
GALAPAGOS
Neighborhood hipsters flocked to this converted factory space when it opened in 1998. Since then the curious from across the East River have joined them, drawn by the reflecting pool, candlelight, experimental DJs, and by Ocularis, the popular Sunday night independent-film series. *70 N. 6th St. (between Wythe and Kent Aves.), Williamsburg, Brooklyn, 718/782–5188. Subway: L to Bedford Ave.*

10 g-3
GOOD WORLD BAR & GRILL
In a former Chinese barbershop, this stripped down way-out-of-the-way hangout with the Swedish menu has a happening late-night scene, and, on the weekends, a DJ who spins a wide variety of vaguely familiar beats. *3 Orchard St. (between Division and Canal Sts.), Lower East Side, 212/925–9975. Subway: F to East Broadway.*

12 f-6
GREAT LAKES
An outboard motor hangs from the ceiling and maps of Lake Michigan decorate the walls of this low-key lounge. It's frequented by Park Slope residents who prefer a night on a local barstool to one on the subway into Manhattan. Thursday nights feature live music. *284 5th Ave. (at 1st St.), Park Slope, Brooklyn, 718/499–3710. Subway: F, N, R to 4th Ave.*

10 b-1
HOGS & HEIFERS

Drew Barrymore and Julia Roberts have added their bras to the moose-head collection, and Harrison Ford once stopped in. Why? They needed a break from the slick-n-trendy spots where one is *expected* to hang out. This is a pseudo-redneck dive, plain and simple. Leave your politically correct friends at the door, order a domestic beer, and dance on the bar. But don't enter wearing a tie; they'll cut it off you. *859 Washington St. (at 13th St.), Greenwich Village, 212/929–0655. Subway: A, C, E to 14th St.; L to 8th Ave.*

11 g-2
K.G.B.

This second-story bar with red walls and Soviet-era posters isn't a fake theme bar. The room actually was once the Ukrainian Communist Party headquarters, and before that it was a speakeasy. Today the K.G.B. attracts a literary crowd. *85 E. 4th St. (between 2nd and 3rd Aves.), East Village, 212/505–3360. Subway: F, V to 2nd Ave.*

10 g-3
LANSKY LOUNGE

A former speakeasy and haunt of gangster Myer Lansky, this spot was such a hit when it opened a few years back that it recently expanded to take over what was once Ratner's. Girls in high heels and guys hoping to meet them love traipsing through an alley to down steeply priced cocktails. *104 Norfolk St. (between Delancey and Rivington Sts.), Lower East Side, 212/677–9489. Subway: F to Delancey St.*

12 c-4
LAST EXIT

In a neighborhood full of sports bars and divey holes-in-the-wall, this popular spot—a chic retro-lounge straight out of the East Village—stands alone. The crowd is mostly local, from Brooklyn Heights yuppies to Cobble Hill writers. *136 Atlantic Ave. (between Henry and Clinton Sts.), Cobble Hill, Brooklyn, 718/222–9198. Subway: 1, 2, 4, 5 to Borough Hall; F to Bergen St.*

11 f-6
MARECHIARO TAVERN

Also known as Tony's, this Little Italy watering hole is a real throwback, in manners as well as atmosphere. It draws a strange mix of locals, literary types, and Silicon Alley entrepreneurs. *176 Mulberry St. (between Broome and Grand Sts.), Little Italy, no phone. Subway: 6 to Spring St.*

11 f-3
MARION'S CONTINENTAL LOUNGE

The tiny bar at the front of this dimly lit restaurant serves up the best Martini in town, along with the occasional burlesque show. *354 Bowery (between Great Jones and W. 4th Sts.), East Village, 212/475–7621. Subway: 6 to Astor Pl.*

11 g-2
MCSORLEY'S OLD ALE HOUSE

Established in 1854, McSorley's is one of New York's oldest watering holes. The

---

HOTEL BARS

The city's hotel bars are among the most relaxing and refined places in town for a drink. And they can be a wonderfully deserted (and elegant) place to wind up a date.

Algonquin Hotel (59 W. 44th St.)
An old haunt of New Yorker writers, this gem lives on with a charmingly Victorian lobby.

King Cole Bar, St. Regis (2 E. 55th St.)
The cigar smoking can be overwhelming, but this spot with the famous Maxfield Parrish mural is where the Bloody Mary was invented.

The Mark (25 E. 77th St.)
Settle into one of the couches or arm chairs in this small salon and wait for the waiter to fill your request.

Oak Bar, Plaza Hotel (5th Ave. and 58th St.)
With dark wood walls and a convivial, monied atmosphere, this is a great place to warm up after a winter's afternoon in Central Park.

The Paramount (235 W. 46th St.)
Head upstairs upon entering and tell them you might order a snack so you can sit at one of the tables overlooking the Philippe Starck lobby.

Soho Grand (310 W. Broadway)
A casual yet refined resting stop during a day of gallery hopping.

epitome of a saloon, it's dark, cramped, and dusty. Too often its overrun with marauding suburbanites. Go in the afternoon to really enjoy the old Irish barkeeps and the excellent dark and pale brews that they serve. *15 E. 7th St. (between 2nd and 3rd Aves.), East Village, 212/473–9148. Subway: 6 to Astor Pl.*

9 *e-6*
MORGAN'S BAR
This dark subterranean space oozes coolness; it's popular with models, record-company executives, and those who just look like them. Thursday evenings during the summer, it fills up with young professionals bound for the Hamptons. Call ahead to reserve a table. *237 Madison Ave. (between 37th and 38th Sts.), Murray Hill, 212/726–7600. Subway: 4, 5, 6, 7, S to 42nd St./Grand Central.*

9 *e-8*
OLD TOWN BAR & RESTAURANT
The name is accurate: this classic, wood-paneled, New York bar has been around since 1892 and still serves a great burger. *45 E. 18th St. (between Broadway and Park Ave. S), Gramercy, 212/529–6732. Subway: 4, 5, 6, N, R to 14th St./Union Sq.*

9 *f-7*
PADDY REILLY'S MUSIC BAR
This Irish hole-in-the-wall launched the rocking roots band Black 47. Other up-and-coming Celtic rock outfits including The Prodigals (Fridays) and the McCabes (Saturdays) play on the weekends. Live music is frequent, including a regular Irish jam session on Thursday night. Grab a Guinness and pogo with the crowd. *519 2nd Ave. (between 28th and 29th Sts.), Gramercy, 212/686–1210. Subway: 6 to 28th St.*

11 *f-4*
PEN TOP BAR & TERRACE
Come summertime, if you're earning the big bucks, there's no better place for an after-work drink. This bar has outdoor seating 23 stories high; you'll have an eye-level view of the moon rising between the sky scrapers. *Peninsula Hotel, 700 5th Ave. (at 55th St.), Midtown East, 212/903–3097. Subway: E, V to 5th Ave.*

3 *e-6*
PETE'S CANDY STORE
This cozy out-of-the way Williamsburg watering spot is worth the trip from Manhattan and points further afield. The bar is cool, without being overly hip or trendy. A testament to its appeal: folks come from as far away as Westchester to play Bingo (on Tuesdays) and a trivia game called Quiz Off! (on Wednesdays). The minuscule back room regularly features some of the best jazz, country, and gospel bands you've never heard of. *709 Lorimer St. (between the BQE and McCarren Park), Williamsburg, Brooklyn, 718/302–3770. Subway: L to Lorimer St.*

11 *f-4*
PRAVDA
The martinis are divine at this trendy but friendly Russian-theme lounge with a tiny upstairs bar. If yours is an obscure brand of vodka, this is the place to track it down: there are more than 70 brands behind the bar. The street entrance is difficult to find; look for stairs going down. Tip: Brush up on your Russian before you venture into the loo. *281 Lafayette St. (between Prince and Houston Sts.), East Village, 212/334–5015. Subway: F, V to Broadway–Lafayette.*

9 *d-4*
THE ROYALTON
The lobby of this Philippe Starck–designed hotel is a cool place to keep an eye on the parade of celebrities and guests dining at 44. Everything, including the entrance to the hotel (look for the curved silver railings) is hidden. The intimate Round Bar is to your right as you enter from the street. Dress: sleek. *44 W. 44th St. (between 5th and 6th Aves.), Midtown West, 212/768–5000 or 212/869–4400. Subway: B, D, F, V to 42nd St.*

7 *b-8*
SHARK BAR
Anyone who wants to eat at this fantastic Southern restaurant has to make it through the slick but friendly yuppie crowd at the bar. *307 Amsterdam Ave. (between 73rd and 74th Sts.), Upper West Side, 212/874–8500. Subway: 1, 2, 3 to 72nd St.*

10 f-1

TELEPHONE BAR

Red English telephone booths decorate the entrance and a handsome, thirty-something crowd lines the bar at this publike restaurant. *149 2nd Ave. (between 10th and 11th Sts.), East Village, 212/529–5000. Subway: 6 to Astor Pl.*

10 f-1

TENTH STREET LOUNGE

Since this sleek lounge opened in 1992, its cavernous space (formerly an ambulance garage) has been packed with handsome patrons, who look even better in glow of the tapers on the cinder block walls. *212 E. 10th St. (between 1st and 2nd Aves.), East Village, 212/473–5252. Subway: 6 to Astor Pl.*

11 f-3

TEMPLE BAR

Look for the painted iguana skeleton (there's no sign) and walk past the slim bar to the back, where, in near-total darkness, you can lounge on a plush banquette surrounded by velvet drapes. *332 Lafayette St. (at Bleecker St.), East Village, 212/925–4242. Subway: 6 to Bleecker St.*

9 d-3

21 CLUB

Long a haunt for power suits toasting their latest M&A, the bar in this dark bastion is staid and discreet, and attracts more than its share of recognizable faces. *21 W. 52nd St. (between 5th and 6th Aves.), Midtown West, 212/582–7200. Subway: E, V to 5th Ave./53rd St.*

9 d-5

THE VIEW LOUNGE

This large, bilevel, slowly revolving lounge has a phenomenal view of the city. You might concede the prices are worth it when you sink into a banquette and notice how serene the city looks from the 48th floor. *Marriott Marquis, 1700 Broadway, 48th floor (at 44th St.), Midtown West, 212/398–1900. Subway: 1, 2, 3, 7, N, Q, R, W to 42nd St./Times Sq.*

9 g-7

WATER CLUB

You'll feel like you're in a private club in Darien, but you're actually on a docked barge on the East River. On one side is a polished wood bar accented by floral arrangements and framed prints; on the other is the lovely dining room, with New York's version of a water view. But if you hit the weather and the timing's right (call ahead), you can slouch in a director's chair at the open-deck bar upstairs. *500 E. 30th St., Murray Hill, 212/683–3333. Subway: 6 to 28th St.*

12 b-4

WATERFRONT ALE HOUSE

Come here for more beers-on-tap than you can taste in a single night, free popcorn, and decent grub from the kitchen. *155 Atlantic Ave. (between Henry and Clinton Sts.), Cobble Hill, Brooklyn, 718/522–3794. Subway: 1, 2, 4, 5 to Borough Hall; F to Bergen St.*

BLUES

9 c-5

B.B. KING BLUES CLUB & GRILL

This ain't no Mississippi juke joint. A lavish (read: expensive) Times Square club, B.B. King's is a vast and shiny venue for a wide range of musicians, from Bo Diddley to Peter Frampton. Every so often the relentlessly touring owner stops by as well. *243 W. 42nd St. (between 8th Ave. and Broadway), Midtown West, 212/997–4144. Subway: 1, 2, 3, 7, N, Q, R, W to 42nd St./Times Sq.*

10 f-6

SEAPORT MUSIC BOAT

Every Tuesday in the summer, these boats with live blues bands circle Manhattan. Thursdays there is a smooth-jazz cruise, and DJ's take over on the weekends. *Pier 16, South Street Seaport, Lower Manhattan, 212/630–8888. Subway: 1, 2, 4, 5 to Fulton St.*

11 c-2

TERRA BLUES

Smokin' local blues bands as well as traveling names take the stage here in New York's blues district. *149 Bleecker St. (between Thompson St. and La Guardia Pl.), Greenwich Village 212/777–7776. Subway: 6 to Bleecker St.*

CABARET

9 e-6
ARCI'S PLACE
Karen Mason, Marilyn Volpe, and Wesla Whitfield are a few of the singers who have taken the stage at the city's newest cabaret room since it opened at the end of 1999. *450 Park Ave. S (between 30th and 31st Sts.), Murray Hill, 212/532–4370. Subway: 6 to 28th St.*

9 c-4
DON'T TELL MAMA
Catch singers, comedians, and female impersonators in the long-running back-room cabaret. Extroverts will be tempted by the open mike at the piano bar up front. *343 W. 46th St. (between 8th and 9th Aves.), Midtown West, 212/757–0788. Subway: 1, 2, 3, 7, N, Q, R, W to 42nd St./Times Sq.*

9 b-5
LAURIE BEECHMAN THEATRE
Across from Theater Row, this basement space makes the most of its surroundings, serving up plays, cabaret, and musical revues. *407 W. 42nd St. (between 9th and 10th Aves.), Midtown West, 212/695–6909. Subway: 1, 2, 3, 7, N, Q, R, W to 42nd St./Times Sq.*

11 b-1
THE DUPLEX
Opened in 1951, this gay, campy cabaret claims to be New York's oldest. Upstairs you might find a singer, comedian, or rock band (or, on open-mike night, folks who fancy themselves any of the above); downstairs, a piano bar. *61 Christopher St. (at 7th Ave.), Greenwich Village, 212/255–5438. Subway: 1, 2 to Christopher St.*

9 e-2
FEINSTEIN'S AT THE REGENCY
Located in the 540 Park Restaurant, this is the stomping ground of the pianist Michael Feinstein, when it's not presenting some of the top names in the business. *540 Park Ave. (at 61st St.), Upper East Side, 212/339–4095. Subway: 4, 5, 6, N, R, W to 59th St.*

11 b-2
55 GROVE STREET
Above Rose's Turn, this landmark cabaret offers a piano bar, singers, celebrity impersonators, and sketch comedy. *55 Grove St. (between Bleecker St. and 7th Ave. S), Greenwich Village, 212/366–5438. Subway: 1, 2 to Christopher St.*

9 b-5
FIREBIRD CAFE
A mosaic of Klimt's *Kiss* on this intimate space's red walls is a good indication of the sophisticated music and cuisine on the bill; caviar and vodka are the choice accompaniment here. *356 W. 46th St. (between 8th and 9th Aves.), Midtown West, 212/586–0244. Subway: A, C, E to 42nd St./Port Authority.*

9 c-6
HIDEAWAY CABARET & SUPPER CLUB
Renovated for an opening in the fall of 2001, the performances here take place on the second floor, in the John Barrymore room, which takes its name from the Broadway actor who once lived in the building. *32 W. 37th St. (between 5th and 6th Aves.), Midtown West, 212/947–6428. Subway: B, D, F, V to 42nd St.*

11 h-3
JOE'S PUB
The Public Theatre's "pub" is the poshest one in town, with red-velvet walls chosen by legendary nightclub impresario Serge Becker. Among other sirens, the hybrid exclusive nightclub and cabaret space has hosted down-to-earth diva Ute Lemper. *425 Lafayette St. (between Astor Pl and W. 4th St.), East Village, 212/539–8770. Subway: 6 to Astor Pl.*

11 h-3
LUCKY CHENG'S
Lucky Cheng's is more a restaurant (serving mediocre Asian fare) than a cabaret, but you will see drag queens of all colors cavorting with Jersey brides-to-be on a stage near the bar. Costumed queens also strut their stuff to taped music in front of the cellar's goldfish pond. *24 1st Ave. (between 1st and 2nd Sts.), East Village, 212/473–0516. Subway: F, V to 2nd Ave.*

9 d-5
OAK ROOM
Gifted song stylists such as Andrea Marcovicci draw crowds at this sophisticated, long and narrow club–cum–watering hole. One of the great classic cabarets, the Oak Room is formal

(jacket and tie for men) and offers pre-theater dining; diners get better tables. *Algonquin Hotel, 59 W. 44th St. (between 5th and 6th Aves.), Midtown West, 212/840–6800. Subway: B, D, F, V to 42nd St.*

CAJUN & ZYDECO

ZYDECO EXPRESS

This isn't a club, but rather the name taken by the zydeco-music fan Laura Selikson, who regularly entices the top names in zydeco and cajun music to leave their Louisiana homes to play New York City clubs. *212/685–7597.*

COMEDY

10 *d-3*

BOSTON COMEDY CLUB

This club gets its name because of its owner's fondness for Beantown. It's often packed with NYU students. Be kind if you drop in on Monday, open-mike night. *82 W. 3rd St. (between Thompson and Sullivan Sts.), Greenwich Village, 212/477–1000. Subway: A, B, C, D, E, F, V, to W. 4th St.*

9 *c-4*

CAROLINE'S

This high-gloss stand-up club features established names as well as those on the brink; Joy Behar, Sandra Bernhard, and Gilbert Gottfried have appeared. Head downstairs when you arrive; the entrance to the show area is to the right of the bar. *1626 Broadway (between 49th and 50th Sts.), Midtown West, 212/757–4100. Subway: 1, 2 to 50th St.*

9 *f-2*

CHICAGO CITY LIMITS

This improv troupe has been doing what they describe as "comedy without a net" for almost 20 years. They're big on audience participation. *1105 1st Ave. (between 60th and 61st Sts.), Upper East Side, 212/888–5233. Subway: 4, 5, 6, N, R to 59th St.*

11 *c-3*

THE COMEDY CELLAR

Beneath the Olive Tree Café, this long-standing, tightly packed club has had consistently good bills for nearly 20 years and shows no sign of slowing down; it's open nightly until 2:30 AM. *117 MacDougal St. (between Bleecker and W.*

3rd Sts.), Greenwich Village, 212/254–3480. Subway: A, B, C, D, E, F, V to W. 4th St.*

7 *f-8*

COMIC STRIP

This classic comedy showcase is packed, yet it feels like a corner bar. Eddie Murphy got some of his first laughs here. *1568 2nd Ave. (between 81st and 82nd Sts.), Upper East Side, 212/861–9386. Subway: 4, 5, 6 to 86th St.*

9 *f-2*

DANGERFIELD'S

Comedian Rodney Dangerfield owns this club, an important stand-up showcase since 1969. *1118 1st Ave. (between 61st and 62nd Sts.), Upper East Side, 212/593–1650. Subway: 4, 5, 6, N, R to 59th St.*

9 *d-8*

GOTHAM COMEDY CLUB

This relative newcomer shoots for the upscale crowd. It's in a landmark building and is decorated with mahogany furnishings and a turn-of-the-century chandelier. Headliners have included Chris Rock and David Brenner. Once a month the club presents a Latino comedy show. *34 W. 22nd St. (between 5th and 6th Aves.), Chelsea, 212/367–9000. Subway: F, V to 23rd St.*

9 *c-6*

ORIGINAL IMPROV

Lots of now-famous comedians, including Richard Pryor and Bette Midler, got their first laughs with this troupe, which left its longtime home in the Garment District for these Restaurant Row digs in 1999. *Danny's Skylight Room, 346 W. 46th St. (between 8th and 9th Aves.), Midtown West, 212/475–6147. Subway: A, C, E to 34th St.*

7 *a-8*

STAND-UP NEW YORK

If you're on the West Side and need some comic relief, make tracks to this club—the stage gets some recognizable faces. *236 W. 78th St. (between Broadway and Amsterdam Ave.), Upper West Side, 212/595–0850. Subway: 1, 2 to 79th St.*

9 *c-8*

THE UPRIGHT CITIZENS BRIGADE THEATRE

Sketch comedy, improv, and even classes are available at this venue which was opened by the UCB—who had a show by the same name on Comedy Central—in 1999. *161 W. 22nd St. (between 6th and 7th Aves.), Chelsea, 212/366–9176. Subway: F, V to 23rd St.*

COUNTRY & WESTERN

The **New York Metropolitan Country Music Association** (718/763–4328) promotes country and western dancing in the city. Just about every Saturday night they host dances at the Glendale Memorial Building, in Glendale Queens. During the summer, they take their two-stepping out into the parks with live concerts.

3 *e-6*

GREG GARING & THE NEW ALPHABET CITY OPRY

Garing is one of reasons why it's great to live in New York City. He's a Pennsylvanian who, by way of Nashville, has become a local legend on the country music scene. Each Tuesday he leads an old-time country hootenanny at Pete's Candy Store. *Pete's Candy Store, 709 Lorimer St. (between the BQE and McCarren Park), Williamsburg, Brooklyn, 718/302–3770. Subway: L to Lorimer St.*

9 *d-7*

RODEO BAR

There's never a cover at this Texas-style roadhouse, complete with barn-wood siding, a barbecue, and Tex-Mex menu, and "music with American roots"— country, rock, rockabilly, swing, bluegrass, and blues. *375 3rd Ave. (at 27th St.), Murray Hill, 212/683–6500. Subway: 6 to 28th St.*

DANCE CLUBS

9 *f-2*

DECADE

This smart dance club draws a fortyish crowd—hence, perhaps, the tame music. There's a serious pick-up scene at the bar and, of course, a cigar lounge. The decor is spare and funky, and the food is passable. *1117 1st Ave. (between 58th and 59th Sts.), Midtown East, 212/835–5979. Subway: 4, 5, 6, N, R to 59th St.*

9 *d-8*

CENTRO-FLY

This ever-popular lounge and dance hall, which took over the much beloved

Tramps in 1999, is a geometric wonderland—black and white circles and other patterns cover its interior. You'll find friendly (for a nightclub) staff people, an enthusiastic crowd, and top-knotch DJs spinning house music on the weekends. *51 W. 21st St. (between 5th and 6th Aves.), Flatiron District, 212/627–7770. Subway: F, V to 23rd St.*

10 *c-1*

FILTER 14

Located in the former space of the famed Mother bar, Filter 14 has a refreshingly unpolished feel, thanks to a tenant-landlord dispute that brought a halt to renovations. Fortunately, the construction-site decor hasn't gotten in the way of a good party. The crowd during the week is young and passionate about the famously obscure DJs who work here. On Friday and Saturday nights, a slightly older crowd takes to the dance floor. *432 W. 14th St. (between 9th and 10th Aves.), Chelsea, 212/366–5680. Subway: A, C, E to 14th St.; L to 8th Ave.*

9 *b-3*

LE BAR BAT

Yes, there are fake bats and a Halloween feel at this flashy monster on Theme Restaurant Row, but don't expect to find Goths. There's no Bauhaus; just upbeat, danceable tunes to sing along to. *311 W. 57th St. (between 8th and 9th Aves.), Midtown West, 212/307–7228. Subway: 1, 2, A, B, C, D to 59th St.*

9 *d-8*

LIMELIGHT

After a law-enforcement-induced hiatus, this club, in a former church, reopened its doors in 1999. The ownership changed in 2001 from Peter Gatien to the up-and-coming local promoter John Blair, who at press time was trying to get a liquor license. Despite the changes you still never know what amusement you'll find in the dark corners of this labyrinthine space. *660 6th Ave. (between 20th and 21st Sts.), Chelsea, 212/807–7059. Subway: F, V to 23rd St.*

10 *c-1*

NELL'S

It's *in time* with all the trappings of a time past—overstuffed seating, subdued lighting, wood paneling, gilt mirrors, and quiet places to drink, dine, and talk. Downstairs you can dance to house, reggae, hip-hop, or whatever the

DJ decrees. *246 W. 14th St. (between 7th and 8th Aves.), Chelsea, 212/675–1567. Subway: A, C, E to 14th St.; L to 8th Ave.*

9 c-8
OHM

This sleek club draws hordes of twenty-something professionals who come to free themselves with house and techno music. *16 W. 22nd St. (between 5th and 6th Aves.), Chelsea, 212/229–2000. Subway: F, V to 23rd St.*

11 e-2
POLLY ESTHER'S

The walls of this club (really more like a bar) make it look like a suburban teenage bedroom, circa 1977: Posters and pinups of Charlie's Angels, Cheryl Tiegs, Leif Garrett, and Shaun Cassidy cover every inch. Young yups make new friends as they catch disco fever on the small dance floor. *186 W. 4th St. (between Jones and Barrow Sts.), Greenwich Village, 212/924–5707. Subway: A, B, C, D, E, F, V to W. 4th St.*

11 h-1
PYRAMID

This quintessential East Village club relives the '80s—in all of its New Wave glory—with "1984" on Friday. Other nights you'll find kitsch art shows, avant-garde theme parties, and a highly unpredictable assortment of live performances. *101 Ave. A (between 8th and 9th Sts.), East Village, 212/473–7184. Subway: 6 to Astor Pl.*

9 c-3
ROSELAND

They're serious about ballroom dancing here. It's no longer 10 cents a dance, but this enormous space still recalls another time. Dancing happens Thursday (with a DJ) and Sunday (with an orchestra *and* a DJ). The average age of the patrons nose-dives the rest of the week, when bands such as the Foo Fighters and GWAR fill the space with distinctly modern music. *239 W. 52nd St. (between Broadway and 8th Ave.), Midtown West, 212/247–0200. Subway: 1, 2 to 50th St.*

9 b-8
ROXY

Roxy's 5,000-square-ft dance floor turns into a chaotic, pulsating roller disco on Wednesday and a multiborough dance club Friday and Saturday. *515 W. 18th St. (at 10th Ave.), Chelsea, 212/645–5156. Subway: A, C, E to 14th St.*

10 d-4
SHINE

This Tribeca club is home to Giant Step parties (bringing top DJs to town weekly) as well as one-night stands by up-and-coming rock bands. *285 West Broadway (at Canal St.), TriBeCa, 212/241–0900. Subway: 1, 2 to Canal St.*

11 c-4
S.O.B.'S

The name stands for Sounds of Brazil. The decor is tropical, and a joyful carnival atmosphere prevails year-round. Regional Brazilian food is served, and there's live, spirited Brazilian, Caribbean, African, and Latin music and dancing on the small dance floor. *200 Varick St. (at W. Houston St.), Greenwich Village, 212/243–4940. Subway: 1, 2 to Houston St.*

10 d-1
SPA

Massage your psyche in the entrance lounge, where a waterfall cascades down behind the bar, before working out to the R&B and hip-hop beats on the dance floor. The super fit and attractive set can be found in the exclusive alabaster banquettes of the White Room. *76 E. 13th St. (between Broadway and 4th Ave.), East Village, 212/388–1060. Subway: 4, 5, 6, N, R to 14th St./Union Sq.*

10 d-4
VINYL

One of the high temples of dance, this intimate alcohol-free club regularly features top name international DJs, and hosts the popular Body & Soul party on Sunday afternoons. *6 Hubert St. (between Hudson and Greenwich Sts.), TriBeCa, 212/343–1379. Subway: 1, 2 to Canal St.*

10 e-1
WEBSTER HALL

A fave with NYU students and the bridge and tunnel crowd, Webster Hall has four floors, five eras of music, trapeze artists, and occasionally live bands. *125 E. 11th St. (between 3rd and 4th Aves.), East Village, 212/353–1600. Subway: 4, 5, 6, N, R to 14th St./Union Sq.; 6 to Astor Pl.*

DINING & DANCING

9 c-4
SUPPER CLUB

This is exactly what a supper club should look like: a true ballroom, two levels to explore, and plush banquettes to hide away in. A full orchestra plays big-band swing on Friday and Saturday nights. During the rest of the week, touring alternative and rock-and-roll bands take the stage. 240 W. 47th St. (between Broadway and 8th Ave.), Midtown West, 212/921–1940. Subway: 1, 2, 3, 7, N, Q, R, W to 42nd St./Times Sq.

GAY & LESBIAN BARS & CLUBS

11 g-2
BOILER ROOM

A relaxed, dark gay bar with cheap drinks and a pool table, this hot spot attracts Village dudes rather than Chelsea muscle boys. 86 E. 4th St. (at 2nd Ave.), East Village, 212/254–7536. Subway: 6 to Astor Pl.

10 f-1
G

This up-to-the-minute Chelsea favorite draws an upscale, mostly male crowd to its huge circular bar and two airy, relaxed rooms lined with leather settees. 223 W. 19th St. (between 7th and 8th Aves.), Chelsea, 212/929–1085. Subway: C, E to 23rd St.

11 b-3
HENRIETTA HUDSON

This pick-up joint with two huge rooms and a pool table attracts all types of women. Some nights feature live music. 438 Hudson St. (off Morton St.), Greenwich Village, 212/924–3347. Subway: 1, 2 to Houston St.

10 g-3
MEOW MIX

This East Village nightspot draws a funky lesbian crowd. The women are young, and they fill the leopard-skin chairs prepared to drink. 269 E. Houston St. (between Aves. A and B), East Village, 212/254–0688. Subway: F, V to 2nd Ave.

10 f-1
SPLASH

Most nights go-go dancers writhe in translucent shower cubicles at this large, perennially crowded Chelsea hangout. 50 W. 17th St. (between 5th and 6th Aves.), Chelsea, 212/691–0073. Subway: F, V to 14th St.

11 b-1
STONEWALL

This unpretentious gay bar, on the site of the eponymous 1969 riot, attracts a mix of tourists and neighborhood regulars. 53 Christopher St. (between 7th Ave. S and Waverly Pl.), Greenwich Village, 212/463–0950. Subway: 1, 2 to Christopher St.

10 g-3
WONDER BAR

Low sofas, an elevated DJ booth, and the hypnotic music on the speakers attract a hip, youngish, mixed crowd to this friendly, popular lounge. 505 E. 6th St. (between Aves. A and B), East Village, 212/777–9105. Subway: F, V to 2nd Ave.

JAZZ

10 c-2
ARTHUR'S TAVERN

Dixieland jazz is nearly always on tap at this ancient venue, which was once one of Charlie Parker's regular hangouts. There's rarely a cover charge. 57 Grove St. (at 7th Ave.), Greenwich Village, 212/675–6879. Subway: 1, 2 to Christopher St.

9 b-5
BIRDLAND

Originally Charlie Parker's place on 57th Street, this club was one of the centers of jazz's golden age, with everyone up to Miles Davis and the Bird himself taking the stage. From 5 PM to midnight you'll find up-and-coming groups and well-known performers, plus dinner. 315 W. 44th St. (between 8th and 9th Aves.), Midtown West, 212/581–3080. Subway: 1, 2, 3, 7, N, Q, R, W to 42nd St./Times Sq.

11 c-2
BLUE NOTE

This large jazz club presents respected jazz, Latin, and blues artists. Ticket prices dive on Monday, when record labels promote their artists' new releases. 131 W. 3rd St. (between 6th Ave.

and MacDougal St.), Greenwich Village, 212/475–8592. Subway: A, B, C, D, E, F, V to W. 4th St.

10 c-1
CAJUN

This landlocked Chelsea restaurant with a riverboat feel dishes New Orleans–style jazz alongside Cajun-Creole grub. Live music from the likes of former Louis Armstrong clarinetist Joe Muranyi makes you feel like you've ducked in off Bourbon Street. 129 8th Ave. (between 14th and 15th Sts.), Chelsea, 212/691–6174. Subway: A, C, E to 14th St.; L to 8th Ave.

9 c-4
IRIDIUM

This eight-year-old club, which moved into new digs in 2001, routinely features some of the top names in jazz. On Monday nights it is the home of the octogenarian innovator Les Paul, the inventor of the solid-body electric guitar. 1650 Broadway (at 51st St.), Midtown West, 212/582–2121. Subway: 1, 2 to 50th St.; N, R, W to 49th St.

9 e-7
JAZZ STANDARD

A relative newcomer to the jazz scene, this restaurant serves up top talent each week. As this writing, though, it was closed for renovations. The club was expected to reopen in 2002. 116 E. 27th St. (between Park Ave. S and Lexington Ave.), Flatiron District, 212/576–2232. Subway: 6 to 28th St.

11 d-7
KNITTING FACTORY

This downtown venue has become an institution. The bar is laid-back, and the three performance spaces often show-case avant-garde jazz artists, as well as rock acts and some electronica. 74 Leonard St. (between Broadway and Church Sts.), TriBeCa, 212/219–3055. Subway: 1, 2 to Franklin St.

7 d-1
LENOX LOUNGE

Uptown is the place for smoking jazz in an equally smoky ambience. This historic club was restored in 2000 and the back room with its zebra-skin motif now looks better than when the great jazz singer Billie Holliday and the writer James Baldwin were regulars. 288 Lenox Ave.

(between 124th and 125th Sts.), Harlem, 212/722–9566. Subway: 2, 3 to 125th St.

11 b-2
SMALL'S

If you're hankering for a jazz jam at 5 AM, head to this pocket-size club, where the nightly sessions run from 10 PM to 8 AM during the week and from 7:30 PM to 8 AM on Fridays and Saturdays. The look is exposed brick and low lighting. They don't serve liquor, but you can bring your own. The cover charge is only $10. 183 W. 10th St. (at 7th Ave.), Greenwich Village, 212/929–7565. Subway: 1, 2 to Christopher St.

6 c-5
ST. NICK'S PUB

A long narrow passage at this obscure Harlem nightspot leads to tables and a bandstand where there's live music just about nightly. The jazz great James Carter and the trumpeter Olu Dara are just two of the many musicians who have sat in unannounced. Monday nights it's home to the smoking Sugar Hill Jazz Quartet. 773 St. Nicholas Ave. (at 149th St.), Harlem, 212/283–9728. Subway: A, B, C, D to 145th St.

10 g-3
TONIC

Much in the way the Knitting Factory provided a home for experimental music in the eighties, this former kosher winery on the Lower East Side is now *the* place for avant-garde jazz and other unusual sounds. 107 Norfolk St. (between Delancey and Rivington Sts.), Lower East Side, 212/358–7503. Subway: F, J, M to Delancey St.

10 c-1
VILLAGE VANGUARD

Since 1935 this renowned New York jazz institution has featured all the greats—Monk, Coltrane, Charles Mingus, Gordon, Marsalis, and so on. It's a quintessential, noisy, smoky, no-frills, Greenwich Village basement club. Get there early if you want a good seat. 178 7th Ave. S (between 11th and Perry Sts.), West Village, 212/255–4037. Subway: A, C, E to 14th St.; L to 8th Ave.

10 d-3
ZINC BAR

This petite subterranean spot features Brazilian jazz on the weekends and the bebop guitarist Ron Affif most Monday nights. During the rest of the week you'll find a variety of swinging performers. *90 W. Houston St. (at La Guardia Pl.), Greenwich Village, 212/477–8337. Subway: 6 to Bleecker St.; F, V to Broadway–Lafayette St.*

LATIN

9 *b-5*
BABALU
Run by the legendary salsa impresario Ralph Mercado and the Cuban-born chef Alex Garcia (of the Food Network's "Melting Pot" show), this Midtown hotspot has drawn a star-studded crowd since it opened in 2000. They come for well-respected Latin cuisine and super-hot music. *327 W. 44th St. (between 8th and 9th Aves.), Midtown West, 212/262–1111. Subway: 1, 2, 3, 7, N, Q, R, W to 42nd St./Times Sq.*

9 *b-6*
COPACABANA NEW YORK
While it prepares new, grander digs on West 34th Street (scheduled to open in the summer of 2002), the granddaddy of Manhattan dance clubs (it has been open, almost continuously, since 1940) is holding its Tuesday and Saturday night parties at various metropolitan area nightclubs. Call for details. *212/239–2672.*

PIANO BARS

Of the cabarets listed above, Don't Tell Mama, Duplex, and the Oak Room have piano bars as well.

7 *e-7*
BRANDY'S PIANO BAR
This small, convivial neighborhood spot is packed with smiling people. There's piano entertainment nightly and sometimes other fare as well, such as folk or swing. It's also primarily a gay bar, though all are welcome. *235 E. 84th St. (between 2nd and 3rd Aves.), Upper East Side, 212/650–1944. Subway: 4, 5, 6 to 86th St.*

7 *d-8*
CAFÉ CARLYLE & BEMELMANS BAR
The unpretentious and elegant Café Carlyle is a must, especially when witty, urbane entertainer Bobby Short is in residence (September–December and April–June); he's as New York as Gershwin. The rest of the year you might find Barbara Cook or Eartha Kitt purring by the piano. The dining is intimate, especially if you're on a comfy banquette. You can dine at the bar for a fraction of the price. Next door, sophisticated Bemelmans Bar is perfect for a cocktail or cognac, with murals by the author of the *Madeline* books as a backdrop. *Carlyle Hotel, 35 E. 76th St. (enter through main hotel or at 981 Madison Ave.), Upper East Side, 212/744–1600. Subway: 6 to 77th St.*

9 *d-2*
CAFÉ PIERRE
The piano in this classy venue plays nightly to a dressy (jacket required), upscale international crowd. *2 E. 61st St. (at 5th Ave.), Upper East Side, 212/838–8000. Subway: 4, 5, 6, N, R to 59th St.*

9 *g-4*
TOP OF THE TOWER
This seductive, 26th-floor, penthouse cocktail lounge is filled with romantic duos gazing at one another and the twinkling city lights. The atmosphere is elegant and subdued. There's piano music every night save Monday. *Beekman Tower, 3 Mitchell Pl. (off 1st Ave./49th St.), Midtown East, 212/355–7300. Subway: 6 to 51st St./Lexinton Ave.; E, V to Lexington–3rd Aves./53rd St.*

POP/ROCK

Of the jazz clubs listed above, Knitting Factory and Tonic serve up rock and roll as well.

10 *g-3*
ARLENE GROCERY
Shane Doyle closed down his much-loved Sin-e Cafe in the East Village, and converted an old bodega into perhaps the best spot to catch an up-and-coming rock band. The grocery is small, friendly, and always free. *95 Stanton St. (between Ludlow and Orchard Sts.), Lower East Side, 212/358–1633. Subway: F, V to 2nd Ave.*

11 *c-2*
THE BITTER END
Once upon a time Bob Dylan, Lisa Loeb, and Warren Zevon played The Bitter

End, a Village standby for middle-of-the-road rock, fusion, folk, and blues. Moral: You never know which of this week's unknowns will be accepting a Grammy a few years hence. *147 Bleecker St. (between Thompson St. and La Guardia Pl.), Greenwich Village, 212/673–7030. Subway: A, B, C, D, E, F, V to W. 4th St.*

11 *e-2*
BOTTOM LINE
A warm and intimate space built mainly of wood, this grandaddy of clubs has showcased such budding talents as Stevie Wonder and Bruce Springsteen. David Johansen, a.k.a. Buster Poindexter, regularly tries out new projects here; other recent headliners include Mathew Sweet and Willie Nelson. When there's a crowd, patrons are packed like sardines at long, thin tables; but most don't mind, as there's not a bad seat in the house, and, remarkably, smoking is not allowed. *15 W. 4th St. (at Mercer), Greenwich Village, 212/228–7880. Subway: A, B, C, D, E, F, V to W. 4th St.; 6 to Bleecker St.*

10 *g-3*
BOWERY BALLROOM
The folks who own the Mercury Lounge opened this sparkling midsize venue a few years ago. It is one of the best places to see bands before they start selling out arenas. *6 Delancey St. (at the Bowery), Lower East Side, 212/533–2111. Subway: F, J, M to Delancey St.*

10 *g-1*
BROWNIES
This hole-in-the-wall has been a fixture on the guitar-rock circuit since it opened some 10 years ago. An upgraded sound system and a solid booking policy keeps Brownies among the best places to find the best new music. The cover is usually cheap and the music loud. *169 Ave. A (between 10th and 11th Sts.), East Village, 212/420–8392. Subway: F, V to 2nd Ave.*

11 *f-3*
CBGB & OMFUG/CB'S 313 GALLERY
Punk was born at CB's, a long, dark tunnel of a club featuring bands with inventive names like Shirley Temple of Doom and Reuben Kincaid (hey—who had heard of Blondie or the Ramones in 1976?). Next door, 313 attracts a quieter crowd with mostly acoustic music. *313–315 Bowery (between 1st and 2nd Sts.), East Village, 212/982–4052 to CBGB or 212/677–0455 to CB's 313 Gallery. Subway: 6 to Bleecker St.; F, V to Broadway–Lafayette St.*

10 *e-2*
FEZ
Below Time Cafe you'll find this swank neo-Moroccan hideaway. The music is eclectic, anything from folk to rock to the weekly Mingus Big Band, but it is uniformly good. *380 Lafayette St. (at Great Jones St.), East Village, 212/533–7000. Subway: 6 to Astor Pl.*

10 *e-1*
IRVING PLAZA
The perfect size for general-admission live music, Irving Plaza serves up everything from Macy Gray and Bob Mould to Southside Johnny and the Asbury Jukes. There's a small balcony with a bar and an even smaller lounge. *17 Irving Pl. (at E. 15th St.), Gramercy, 212/777–1224. Subway: 4, 5, 6, L, N, R to 14th St./Union Sq.*

10 *g-3*
MERCURY LOUNGE
A former tombstone display parlor hosts two to five bands a night, rocking away on an above-average sound system. There are only two rooms here, a bar in the front and the cozy space in the back where the bands perform. *217 E. Houston St. (between 1st and 2nd Aves.), East Village, 212/260–4700. Subway: F, V to 2nd Ave.*

11 *c-3*
ROCK 'N' ROLL CAFÉ
Nostalgic for the Doors, Led Zep, Hendrix, or Clapton? Choose a night and the appropriate sleeveless concert T, and rock out to a cover band. *149 Bleecker St. (between La Guardia Pl. and Thompson St.), Greenwich Village, 212/677–7630. Subway: A, B, C, D, E, F, V to W. 4th St.*

11 *c-2*
VILLAGE UNDERGROUND
A tiny subterranean space with a huge booking agent: Steve Weitzman draws the same type of top-notch blues, rock, country, and soul acts that he presented at the now defunct Tramps for some ten years. *130 W. 3rd St. (between 6th Ave. and MacDougal St.), Greenwich Village, 212/777–7745. Subway: A, B, C, D, E, F, V to W. 4th St.*

chapter 6

HOTELS

New Yorkers are surrounded by some of the finest hotels in the world. For residents of the city, these hostelries provide a hideaway for a romantic tryst, a crash pad during apartment renovations, a retreat from real life, or a welcome spot to stash visiting friends and relatives.

Unfortunately, whatever you seek from a hotel, the experience is likely to be expensive. It is truly difficult to find decent rooms for less than $200, most cost twice that, and better hotels often charge more than $550 for a standard room. Then add city and state taxes—another 13¼%. Luckily, there are usually corporate, seasonal, and group specials; plus there are a few tricks for getting the price down (see the "Working the System," box).

Unless otherwise noted, hotels in this book have air-conditioning and designated no-smoking rooms and/or floors. Our price categories reflect the cost of a standard double.

PRICE CATEGORIES

CATEGORY	COST*
Very Expensive	over $400
Expensive	$275–$400
Moderately Priced	$175–$275
Budget	under $175

*All prices are for a standard double room, excluding 13¼% city and state taxes plus an occupancy charge of $2 per room, per night.

VERY EXPENSIVE LODGINGS

9 d-5
THE BRYANT PARK HOTEL
This hotel has reanimated the American Radiator Building, a landmarked 26-story Gothic-inspired structure of black brick and gold terra-cotta that overlooks Bryant Park. Built in 1924 by Raymond Hood, and later immortalized by Georgia O'Keeffe in her painting "Radiator Building/Night, New York," the structure provides a perfect setting for a hotel that has style but doesn't constantly remind you that it does. The crisply modern

guest rooms are supplied with fresh flowers, Tibetan rugs, and cashmere blankets, and the travertine marble baths have separate tubs and showers and are well-stocked with Molton Brown bath products. The excellent service begins at check-in: guests aren't asked to stop at a desk, but instead are escorted directly to their rooms and registered as they unpack. A 24-hour butler mans a full pantry on each floor, chef Rick Laakkonen runs the hotel's well-reviewed restaurant, Ilo, and the subterranean Cellar Bar attracts the city's bright young things. 40 W. 40th St. (between 5th and 6th Aves.), 10018, Midtown West, 212/869–0100 or 212/642–2200, fax 212/869–4446, www.bryantparkhotel.com. 100 rooms, 29 suites. Restaurant, bar, spa, health club, parking (fee). AE, DC, MC, V. Subway: B, D, F, V to 42nd St.; 7 to 5th Ave.

7 e-8
THE CARLYLE
It's tough to decide where to spend your time in this extraordinary Madison Avenue landmark: Should you stay in your Mark Hampton–designed guest room, lolling in the whirlpool or admiring the fine antique furniture and artfully framed Audubons and botanicals? Or should you venture downstairs to the cozy little Bemelmans Bar, with murals by Ludwig Bemelmans, illustrator of the beloved Madeline books? Either way, you're sure to enjoy the glamorous yet refined ambience of this Manhattan classic, which is so desirable and discreet that about half of its rooms are occupied by permanent residents. The rooms in the tower have better views and light. 35 E. 76th St. (at Madison Ave.), 10021, Upper East Side, 212/744–1600 or 800/227–5737, fax 212/717–4682, www.dir-dd.com/the-carlyle.html. 145 rooms, 45 suites. Restaurant, bar, café, in-room data ports, in-room fax, kitchenettes (some), room service, health club, spa, parking (fee). AE, DC, MC, V. Subway: 6 to 77th St.

9 d-3
ESSEX HOUSE, A WESTIN HOTEL
The lobby here is an Art Deco masterpiece fit for Fred and Ginger, while guest rooms and suites, some with Louis XIV–style furnishings and others with English Chippendale, are comfortable and classic enough to make you want to move in. Many have dazzling views of Central Park, which is right across the street.

Some of the rooms are small and those facing the street are noisy, but service is uniformly excellent. Celebrity chef Alain Ducasse oversees his eponymous restaurant. *160 Central Park S. (between 6th and 7th Aves.), 10019, Midtown West, for reservations, 212/484–5100 or 800/937–8461 (WESTIN1); general inquiries, 212/247–0300, fax for reservations, 212/484–4602; for guests, 212/315–1839, www.essexhouse.com. 520 rooms, 77 suites. 2 restaurants, bar, in-room data ports, in-room fax, in-room VCRs, room service, spa, fitness center, baby-sitting, parking (fee). AE, D, DC, MC, V. Subway: S to 57th St.*

9 *e-3*

FOUR SEASONS

Everything about this I.M. Pei–designed hotel is epic: the spired, limestone-clad structure itself; the giant guest rooms (average size is 600 square ft, and all have 10-ft-high ceilings); and, of course, the prices. Even if you can't stay here, step inside just to see the marvelous Grand Foyer, with French-limestone pillars, marble, onyx, and acre upon acre of blond wood. Guest rooms are soundproof (a rarity in New York), and equipped with such amenities as Sealy PostureLux mattresses (if you decide you can never again sleep on anything less, you can purchase one, $799 for a queen) and walk-in closets paneled with English sycamore. Rooms on upper floors have fantastic views. The restaurant is popular with media moguls for power breakfasts. *57 E. 57th St., (between Madison and Park Aves.), 10022, Midtown East, 212/758–5700 or 800/332–3442, fax 212/758–5711, www.fourseasons.com. 310 rooms, 60 suites. Restaurant, bar, in-room data ports, room service, spa, health club, piano, baby-sitting, car rental, parking (fee). AE, DC, MC, V. Subway: 4, 5, 6, N, Q, R, W to 59th St./Lexington Ave.*

9 *b-1*

INN NEW YORK CITY

This private, romantic inn has just four suites, and while there's no common space, each unit provides fantastic decor and amenities. The Opera suite has a fireplace, a baby grand piano, a CD library, a Jacuzzi, an outdoor terrace, and a full kitchen. The Library has bookshelves that cover 14-ft-high walls, a fireplace, a large sofa, skylights, and a full kitchen with a dining table. The Vermont suite, rented out on a monthly basis, has a spiral staircase leading to a sub-

terranean bedroom with a quilt-topped bed. The Spa suite has a Jacuzzi, a glass-brick shower, sauna, and all the body-enriching products you need for a do-it-yourself treatment. The minimum stay is two nights, and no children under 12 are allowed. *W. 71st St. (between Broadway and West End Ave.), 10023, Upper West Side, 212/580–1900, fax 212/580–4437, www.innnewyorkcity.com. 4 suites. Breakfast room, in-room data ports, room service, indoor pool, spa, health club, baby-sitting, parking (fee). AE, MC, V. Subway: 1, 2, 3 to 72nd St.*

9 *d-3*

LE PARKER MERIDIEN

The atrium of this French-owned and -operated hotel strikes an exotic, eclectic note, with two-story arched mirrors, a mosaic ceiling, palm trees, artwork by Damien Hirst and Charles Long, and Doric columns. Equally dramatic are the glass-enclosed rooftop swimming pool (where it's fashionable to dine poolside), the rooftop outdoor track, and the enormous Club Raquette health club, with racquetball and squash courts. Rooms have an elegant neoclassical motif. The breakfasts at Norma's—smoothie shots, red-berry risotto oatmeal, and Hudson Valley duck-confit hash—have won awards. *118 W. 57th St. (between 6th and 7th Aves.), 10019, Midtown West, 212/245–5000 or 800/543–4300, fax 212/708–7471; for guests 212/307–1776, www.parkermeridien.com. 449 rooms, 249 suites. 3 restaurants, bar, in-room data ports, in-room fax, in-room safes, in-room VCR players, minibars, room service, indoor pool, spa, health club, jogging, racquetball, squash, nightclub, baby-sitting, parking (fee). AE, D, DC, MC, V. Subway: B, D, E, N, Q, R, W to 57th St.*

9 *e-2*

THE LOWELL

Like Noël Coward, you may be tempted to check in long-term at this pied-à-terre–style landmark on a tree-lined street between Madison and Park avenues. Guest rooms, most of which are suites, have all the comforts of home—kitchenettes (or minibars), stocked bookshelves, and even umbrellas; 33 of the suites have working fireplaces (wood included), and 10 have private terraces (the garden suite, in fact, has two, while the gym suite has its own fitness center). The Pembroke

Room serves a fine high tea, and the Post House is renowned for its steaks. *28 E. 63rd St. (between Madison and Park Aves.), 10021, Upper East Side, 212/838–1400 or 800/221–4444, fax for reservations 212/605–6808; for guests 212/319–4230, www.preferredhotels.com. 21 rooms, 46 suites. Restaurant, breakfast room, in-room fax, in-room data ports, in-room VCRs, kitchenettes, room service, massage, health club, baby-sitting, parking (fee). AE, D, DC, MC, V. Subway: 4, 5, 6, N, Q, R, W to 59th St./Lexington Ave.; F to 63rd St./Lexington Ave.*

7 e-8

THE MARK

The Mark is widely considered to be the classiest small hotel in New York. On a tree-lined street just steps from Central Park, and modern but romantic, the Mark is a bastion of serenity. The cool, Biedermeier-furnished, marble lobby is truly one of the New York's most charming small spaces and guest rooms are luxurious and soothing, with cream-color walls, museum-quality prints, plump armchairs, fresh flowers, and Frette bed linens. To offset any inconvenience posed by its Upper East Side location, the hotel offers a shuttle to Wall Street and the theater district at appropriate hours. *25 E. 77th St. (near Madison Ave.), 10021, Upper East Side, 212/744–4300 or 800/843–6275, fax for reservations 212/472–5714; for guests 212/744–2749, www.themarkhotel.com. 120 rooms, 60 suites. Restaurant, bar, in-room data ports, in-room fax, in-room VCRs, kitchenettes, room service, massage, health club, baby-sitting, parking (fee). AE, D, DC, MC, V. Subway: 6 to 77th St.*

11 e-5

MERCER HOTEL

The sprawling 100-seat lobby with its vintage book library and casual bar is so minimalist that you may not even realize you're in a hotel until you notice the unmarked reception desk toward the back wall. Guest rooms are enormous, with long entryways, high ceilings, and walk-in closets. No chintz or framed Monet prints here—instead, dark African woods and high-tech light fixtures make a subtle statement. But the bathrooms steal the show with showers that spray from all sides; some have decadent two-person tubs surrounded by mirrors. Bathroom products are from

FACE Stockholm, and guests receive passes to the nearby David Barton gym. The Mercer Kitchen restaurant is overseen by Jean Georges Vongerichten of the four-star Jean Georges restaurant uptown. Business amenities, however, are few and far between. *99 Prince St. (at Mercer St.), 10012, SoHo, 212/966–6060, fax 212/965–3838, www.themercer. com. 67 rooms, 8 suites. Restaurant, 2 bars, in-room data ports, in-room VCRs, room service. AE, D, DC, MC, V. Subway: N, Q, R, W to Prince St.*

9 e-4

NEW YORK PALACE

The New York Palace, recently bought and remodeled by the Sultan of Brunei, remains one of Manhattan's most inviting deluxe hotels and combines Old World flavor with modern pleasures. The guest rooms have an Empire flavor, with bold colors and dark woods, though some of the more luxurious rooms and suites in the Tower (Floors 41–55) have an art deco look, with oversize furniture and polished blond-wood headboards. The health club has top-of-the-line equipment and an awesome view of St. Patrick's Cathedral. Alongside the hotel are the landmark 1882 Villard Houses, a complex of Stanford White mansions known for Tiffany glasswork and frescoed murals. One now houses the ultrachic restaurant Le Cirque 2000, an outrageous, futuristic riot of color. For more modest meals, there's a lobby-lounge restaurant with an olive bar and an afternoon "tapas" tea service with a Mediterranean twist. Rock stars and royals regularly rent one of the four 4,000-square-ft penthouse triplexes for $10,000 a night. *455 Madison Ave. (between 50th and 51st Sts.), 10022, Midtown East, 212/888–7000 or 800/697–2522, fax 212/303–6000, www. newyorkpalace.com. 800 rooms, 100 suites. 2 restaurants, 2 bars, in-room data ports, in-room fax, room service, spa, health club, baby-sitting, parking (fee). AE, D, DC, MC, V. Subway: 6 to 51st St./Lexington Ave.; E, V to Lexington–3rd Aves./53rd St.*

9 e-3

THE PENINSULA

The marble, Art Nouveau lobby of this opulent landmark recalls a grander era, when bell captains wore sailor suits and afternoon tea was on everyone's schedule. Many of the rooms have sweeping views down Fifth Avenue, and the new sumptuous marble bathrooms feature separate shower stalls and, in some, a TV and radio built into the wall so you can be entertained while you bathe. The glass-enclosed, trilevel health club and spa has an indoor, rooftop swimming pool where you can gaze down at Midtown between laps. *700 5th Ave. (at 55th St.), 10019, Midtown East, 212/956–2888, 212/247–2200, or 800/262–9467, fax for reservations 212/903–3943; for guests 212/ 903–3949, www.peninsula.com. 200 rooms, 42 suites. 2 restaurants, bar, lounge, in-room data ports, in-room fax, room service, indoor pool, hair salon, spa, health club, baby-sitting, parking (fee). AE, D, DC, MC, V. Subway: E, V to 5th Ave.*

9 e-2
THE PIERRE
Since 1929, the Pierre has occupied its Fifth Avenue post with all the grandeur of a French château. The public areas drip with chandeliers, handmade carpets, and Corinthian columns. The king-size guest rooms are resplendent with traditional chintz fabrics and dark-wood furniture; spacious bathrooms have art nouveau fixtures. Service is predictably first-rate—the staff will scan an image for a business presentation or hand wash your delicates for a night out. After all, the Pierre is a Four Seasons hotel. *2 E. 61st St. (at 5th Ave.), 10021, Upper East Side, 212/838–8000 or 800/332–3442, fax 212/758–1615 for reservations; 212/940–8109 for guests, www. fourseasons.com/pierre. 149 rooms, 54 suites. Restaurant, bar, in-room data ports, in-room fax, room service, hair salon, massage, health club, baby-sitting, parking (fee). AE, D, DC, MC, V. Subway: N, R, W to 5th Ave.*

9 e-2
THE PLAZA
Ernest Hemingway is said to have advised F. Scott Fitzgerald to bequeath his liver to Princeton but his heart to the Plaza. Enjoy brunch at the fin-de-siècle Palm Court or a drink at the clubby Oak Bar, where horse-drawn carriages clip-clop past the windows. Though the guest rooms are small for such a luxury hotel, their high ceilings and lavish decor (including crystal chandeliers and marble fireplaces) lend a taste of old New York glamour. Most

of the design is of Edwardian vintage, but rooms were "updated" over the years, most ostentatiously during the Ivana Trump years. Service is fantastic, but public spaces do show the effects of high traffic. *5th Ave. at 59th St., 10019, Midtown East, 212/759–3000 or 800/ 759–3000, fax 212/546–5324 for reservations; 212/759–3167 for guests, www. fairmont.com. 670 rooms, 135 suites. 4 restaurants, 2 bars, in-room data ports, in-room fax, room service, massage, gym, baby-sitting, parking (fee). AE, D, DC, MC, V. Subway: N, R, W to 5th Ave.*

9 e-2
THE REGENCY, A LOEWS HOTEL
The Regency is a truly regal hotel, from the elegant lobby with its gilded antiques and massive chandelier to the posh Park Avenue location. The restaurant, 540 Park, has long been known as

---

OF BATHTUBS AND BIDETS

If you live in New York, chances are your bathroom has seen better days. This is where luxury hotels come in.

Four Seasons (Very Expensive)
The enormous tubs fill in 60 seconds.

The Mansfield (Moderately Priced)
High-style, black-marble bathrooms.

Morgans (Expensive)
Crystal shower doors and poured-granite floors.

Omni Berkshire Place (Expensive)
Loos in the suites have TVs and CD players.

The Paramount (Moderately Priced)
Conical steel sinks designed by Philippe Starck.

The Pierre (Very Expensive)
Gleaming white marble with red and black trim; luxurious lighted mirrors.

Roger Williams (Expensive)
Doorless, recessed showers with cedar-grill floors.

Trump International Hotel and Towers (Very Expensive)
Bath salts and loofahs are on the house.

the place for power breakfasts, but more inviting is the Library, a cozy, wood-paneled lounge full of bookcases and comfortable seating arrangements—here drinks and light meals are served all day long. The traditional guest rooms have celadon carpets and salmon-color silk bedspreads and exemplify the understated style of the traditional Upper East Side. *540 Park Ave. (at 61st St.), 10021, Upper East Side, 212/759–4100 or 800/235–6397, fax 212/688–2898 for reservations; 212/826–5674 for guests, www.loewshotels.com. 288 rooms, 74 suites. Restaurants, bar, lobby lounge, in-room data ports, in-room fax, room service, hair salon, massage, gym, baby-sitting, parking (fee). AE, D, DC, MC, V. Subway: 4, 5, 6, N, Q, R, W to 59th St./Lexington Ave.*

10 *e-7*
THE REGENT WALL STREET
The first five-star hotel in the Financial District opened in 2000. The building dates to 1842, when it was the Merchants' Exchange. Novelist Herman Melville worked here when it was the U.S. Customs House. (It still has basement cells once used to detain criminals.) The 12,000-square-ft ballroom, with 60-ft-high Corinthian columns, marble walls, and an elliptical Wedgewood dome, was once the NYSE trading floor. It is now a city landmark. Rooms are comfortable, offering great views, deep tubs for two, Bulgari toiletries, and every business amenity. The hotel's restaurant, 55 Wall Street, juts out onto a dramatic stone balcony where you can eat and drink among thrusting columns. *55 Wall St. (at William St.), 10005, Financial District, 212/845–8600 or 800/545–4000, fax 212/845–8601, www.regenthotels.com. 98 rooms, 46 suites. Restaurant, bar, in-room data ports, in-room fax, in-room safes, in-room VCRs, minibars, room service, gym, dry cleaning, laundry service, concierge, business services, meeting rooms, parking (fee). AE, D, DC, MC, V. Subway: 1, 2 to Wall St.*

9 *d-3*
RIHGA ROYAL
The Rihga Royal has 50 floors of contemporary suites. All have a living room, a bedroom, and a marble bath with separate shower and tub. Some have bay windows and French doors, and although decor in older rooms has a cherry red cast, refurbished suites have

a cleaner, more modern design. The location, privacy, and security suit many business travelers and celebrities, as do the fax machines in every room. The Pinnacle Suites (on the top floors) provide such added business amenities as cellular phones, voice mail with pager, business cards, and "miniature business center" machines that print and copy. *151 W. 54th St. (between 6th and 7th Aves.), 10019, Midtown West, 212/307–5000 or 800/937–5454, fax 212/765–6530, www.righa.com. 500 suites. Restaurant, bar, in-room data ports, in-room fax, in-room VCRs, room service, massage, gym, baby-sitting, parking (fee). AE, D, DC, MC, V. Subway: B, D, E to 7th Ave.; N, Q, R, W to 57th St.*

9 *d-5*
THE ROYALTON
Created by Ian Schrager and the late Steve Rubell and designed with minimalist elegance by Philippe Starck, this hotel can't help but attract those whose eyes like to flutter from beautiful person to more beautiful person. Fashion and media folk gather to drink martinis in the cooler-than-cool lobby. The showpiece of each spartan guest room is a low-lying, custom-made bed with a down comforter and Italian sheets; there are also window banquettes and fireplaces. The sensuality of the hotel extends to the rooms' minibars, which contain a disposable camera and an "Intimacy Kit" with condoms and lubricant. *44 W. 44th St. (between 5th and 6th Aves.), 10036, Midtown West, 212/869–4400 or 800/635–9013, fax 212/575–0012. 140 rooms, 28 suites. Restaurant, bar, in-room data ports, in-room VCRs, room service, massage, gym, baby-sitting, parking (fee). AE, DC, MC, V. Subway: B, D, F, V to 42nd St.*

10 *d-4*
SOHO GRAND
SoHo's first real hotel is a remarkable amalgam of the neighborhood's light-industrial past, its brief run as an art district in the 1970s and 80s, and its high-design, shopping-focused present. A translucent, bottle-glass staircase with cast-iron embellishments leads to the second-floor lobby, with its 24-ft ceilings, two-story windows, and oversize furniture. The rooms, designed by William Sofield, have an industrial look and display a clear emphasis on design:

custom-designed drafting tables serve as desks, nightstands mimic sculptors' desks, headboards are leather and saddle-stitched, and linens are by Frette. High floors on the northern side have sweeping nighttime views of the Midtown skyline. The Canal House restaurant serves remarkably creative renditions of American comfort food—macaroni-and-cheese is a trademark dish. The hotel is owned by Hartz Mountain, the pet-food company, so dogs get extra-special treatment and lone travelers are presented with goldfish. *310 W. Broadway (between Grand and Canal Sts.), 10013, SoHo, 212/965–3000 or 800/965–3000, fax 212/965–3244, www.sohogrand.com. 365 rooms, 4 suites. Restaurant, bar, in-room data ports, in-room VCRs, room service, massage, gym, baby-sitting, parking (fee). AE, D, DC, MC, V. Subway: 6, J, M, N, Q, R, W to Canal St.*

9 *e-3*

ST. REGIS

Built in 1904 by John Jacob Astor for those who could afford "the best of everything," this Fifth Avenue beaux-arts landmark was bought by Sheraton in the early 1990s and restored to its original splendor. Highlights are the Astor Court tea lounge, with its trompe-l'oeil cloud ceiling; the King Cole Bar, with its famous Maxfield Parrish mural; and the celebrated restaurant Lespinasse. The opulent guest rooms have crystal chandeliers, silk wall coverings, and Louis XV–style furnishings, while butlers are on hand to provide attentive service. *2 E. 55th St. (at 5th Ave.), 10022, Midtown East, 212/753–4500 or 800/759–7550, fax 212/350–6900 for reservations; 212/787–3447 for guests, www.luxurycollection.com. 221 rooms, 92 suites. Restaurant, bar, in-room data ports, in-room fax, room service, hair salon, massage, sauna, health club, baby-sitting, parking (fee). AE, D, DC, MC, V. Subway: 7 to 5th Ave.; B, D, F, V to 42nd St.*

10 *d-4*

TRIBECA GRAND

Some applaud the Tribeca Grand, the first major hotel in its stylish, eponymous downtown neighborhood, for its industrial-chic, while others see the three-sided building as nothing more than a dimly lit cell block. The Grand is built around an eight-story atrium that houses the fashionable Church Lounge,

a bar, café, and dining room, and from which twin glass-enclosed elevators rise toward a frosted glass skylight. While hallways on the guest floors overlook the buzzy atrium, rooms are well-appointed in calming hues of blue and white and have floor-to-ceiling windows that make average-size rooms feel larger; furnishings are sleek and modern and high-tech room amenities include Web TV, cordless phones, and high-speed Internet access. Pets are welcome. *2 Ave. of the Americas (between Walker and White Sts.), 10013, Tribeca, 212/519–6600, fax 212/519–6700, www.tribecagrand.com. 195 rooms, 8 suites. Bar, café, in-room data ports, in-room fax, in-room VCR, room service, gym, dry cleaning, laundry service, concierge, business services, meeting rooms, parking (fee). AE, D, DC, MC, V. Subway: A, E to Canal St.*

9 *c-2*

TRUMP INTERNATIONAL HOTEL & TOWERS

Donald Trump's namesake hotel caters to business travelers with money to burn. The rooms and suites, furnished in contemporary style, are equipped with such amenities as Sony sound systems, a selection of coffee-table books, and minitelescopes for discreet spying on the action in Central Park across the street (Lincoln Center is also nearby); depending on your circumstances, of course, one amenity that might make the hotel seem unlike home is the presence of a personal assistant for each guest. Italian marble bathrooms are equipped with Jacuzzis and Frette bathrobes, and slippers hang in the closets. The restaurant, Jean Georges, is one of the city's finest, and for a price a Jean Georges sous-chef will prepare a meal in your kitchenette. *1 Central Park West (at 59th St.), 10023, Midtown West, 212/299–1000, fax 212/299–1150, www.trumpintl.com. 86 rooms, 82 suites. Restaurant, bar, café, in-room data ports, in-room fax, in-room VCRs, kitchenettes, indoor pool, spa, baby-sitting, parking (fee). AE, D, DC, MC, V. Subway: 1, 2, A, B, D to 59th St./Columbus Circle.*

9 *e-4*

W NEW YORK

This boutique business hotel has made quite a splash, in part because members of the W group are stylish in the manner of Ian Schrager hotels but have less icy glamour and more warmth. The fuss here also has to do with the restaurant Heartbeat and bars Whiskey Blue and Oasis (for hobnobbing with the media elite, these are the places to be). Guest rooms are small but feature Internet TV, VCR, CD player, 250-thread-count sheets, complimentary Aveda products, and great views. An in-house spa and fitness center provide ample ways to unwind. *541 Lexington Ave. (at 50th St.), 10022, Midtown East, 212–755–1200, fax 212/319–8344, www.whotels.com. 722 rooms. Restaurant, 2 bars, in-room data ports, in-room fax, minibars, spa, health club. AE, D, DC, MC, V. Subway: 6 to 51st St./Lexington Ave.; E, V to Lexington–3rd Aves./53rd St.*

9 e-8
W NEW YORK— UNION SQUARE

The 1911 building, once home to Guardian Life Insurance, is a fine example of Renaissance Revival architecture. Even the interior is landmarked, from the mosaic-covered elevator banks to a gilded-ceilinged ballroom. When the W hotel chain bought the building, it added its trademark nature theme: A block of twisted medusa bamboo climbs by the front entrance, and the comfy lobby area has topiary for walls. W also added the Mediterranean restaurant Olives and Underbar, where you can drink apple martinis in curtained alcoves. Guest rooms have feather beds with goosedown comforters and pillows, high-speed data ports, and fantastic views, and a business center and fitness room are open 24 hours. *201 Park Avenue S (at 17th St.), 10016, Murray Hill, 212/253–9119 or 800/223–6725, fax 212/779–0148, www.whotels.com. 270 rooms, 16 suites. Restaurant, bar, café, room service, massage, spa, baby-sitting, parking (fee). AE, DC, MC, V. Subway: 4, 5, 6, L, N, Q, R, W to 14th St./Union Sq.*

9 e-4
WALDORF–ASTORIA

A New York institution, the Waldorf has catered to every U.S. President since Hoover and a handful of luminous long-time residents, including the late Frank Sinatra. The magnificent art deco lobby, with its original murals and mosaics, is a meeting place for the rich and powerful. Guest rooms, each individually decorated, are traditional and elegant. The premium "Astoria-level" rooms have the added advantages of great views, fax machines, and access to the Astoria

lounge, where Continental breakfast and a free afternoon tea are served. The even more premium Waldorf Towers have a separate entrance and the best amenities and views in the house. *301 Park Ave. (at 50th St.), 10022, Midtown East, 212/355–3000 or 800/925–3673, fax 212/872–7272, www.waldorf.com. 1,176 rooms, 276 suites. 4 restaurants, 2 bars, in-room data ports, room service, massage, health club, baby-sitting, parking (fee). AE, D, DC, MC, V. Subway; 6 to 51st St./Lexington Ave.; E, V to Lexington–3rd Aves./53rd St.*

EXPENSIVE LODGINGS

9 d-5
THE ALGONQUIN

Once the meeting place of the famed Round Table of wits and critics and the birthplace of *The New Yorker*, the Algonquin has attracted literary and theatrical types since it opened in 1902. In the clubby, oak-paneled lobby, overstuffed sofas and easy chairs encourage lolling over cocktails and conversation or afternoon tea. Victorian fixtures and furnishings give the small, comfortable guest rooms a traditional look; some are specialty suites dedicated to Dorothy Parker and her contemporaries. *59 W. 44th St. (between 5th and 6th Aves.), 10036, Midtown West, 212/840–6800 or 800/548–0345, fax 212/944–1618, www.camberleyhotels.com. 142 rooms, 23 suites. 2 restaurants, bar, in-room data ports, room service, cabaret, parking (fee). AE, D, DC, MC, V. Subway: B, D, F, V to 42nd St.*

9 e-4
THE BENJAMIN

The all-suites Hotel Benjamin is a true blend of Old World style and modern amenities. While the original pre-war design of famed architect Emery Roth remains much in evidence, state-of-the-art amenities in each suite provide business travelers with executive desks, ergonomic chairs, two-line phones with voice mail, data ports, and a separate line for a combination fax/printer/copier. Non-tech touches include a pillow menu that lists 11 choices, including one filled with buckwheat and a 5-ft body cushion for pregnant women. Noted chef Larry Forgione's restaurant, An American Place, is on the ground floor. *125 E. 50th St. (between Park and Lexington Aves.), 10022, Midtown East,*

212/753–2700 or 800/637–8483, fax 212/
715–2525, www.thebenjamin.com. 130
suites. Restaurant, bar, in-room data
ports, room service, spa, gym, parking
(fee). AE, DC, MC, V. Subway; 6 to 51st
St./Lexington Ave.; E, V to Lexington–3rd
Aves./53rd St.

9 e-5
THE DYLAN

The former Chemist Club is now a well-
designed Midtown retreat that manages
to make service a priority without
adding buzz and attitude. The beaux-
arts exterior and three-floor central staircase have been restored, but buffed
titanium walls and curved mirrors in the
elevators are decidedly modern touches.
Guest rooms have wall-mounted upholstered headboards and cantilevered
nightstands; the most spectacular
accommodation is the Alchemy Suite—
a medieval chamber with gothic floor-to-
ceiling stone columns and a
stained-glass window. In all rooms,
beaker-like drinking glasses and petri-
dish ashtrays reference the building's
history. Virot, the ground-floor restaurant run by Jean-Georges protégé Didiet
Virot, has a monumental 19th-century
fireplace from the original ballroom. 52
E. 41st St. (between Madison and Park
Aves.), 10017, Midtown East, 212/338–
0500 or 800/314–3101, fax 212/338–0569,
www.dylanhotel.com. 105 rooms, 2 suites.
Restaurant, gym, business services. AE, D,
DC, MC, V. Subway: 4, 5, 6, 7, S to 42nd
St./Grand Central.

9 f-6
THE ENVOY CLUB

One of the more appealing extended-
stay hotels in the city rents rooms only
for a month or more and provides many
homelike amenities in its small but
pleasant, earth-toned rooms: Frette bed
linens, Molton Brown bath products, a
daily New York Times, personalized business cards, fully stocked kitchens (and
housekeeper to wash the dishes). There
is a business center, a fitness center,
and laundry facilities. Many guests stay
here while receiving treatment at the
NYU Medical Center across the street
and others while relocating to New York.
The hotel also caters to recently separated guests with a Suddenly Single program, contacts for attorneys and
therapists, and a free copy of The New
Creative Divorce. 377 E. 33rd St. (at 1st
Ave.), 10016, Murray Hill, 212/481–4600,

fax 212/402–1070 for reservations; 212/
481–8600 for guests. 57 suites. In-room
data ports, in-room fax, in-room VCRs,
gym, dry cleaning, laundry service, concierge, business services. AE, D, DC, MC,
V. Subway: 6 to 33rd St.

9 e-8
THE INN AT IRVING PLACE

There are a dozen rooms in this 19th-
century townhouse in Gramercy Park.
The only public space is a parlor, where a
fire blazes in cooler months. Some
rooms are quite small, but all are
extremely comfortable and atmospheric,
with non-working fireplaces, Oriental
rugs, and four-poster beds. A full tea is
served, and room service comes from
the fantastic restaurant Verbena, which
is adjacent. The net effect is charm and
romance, and many of the guests are
return visitors who would not consider
staying elsewhere. 56 Irving Pl. (between
17th and 18th Sts.), 10003, Gramercy Park,
212/533–4600 or 800/685–1447, fax 212/
533–4611, www.innatirving.com. 12 rooms.
In-room data ports, in-room VCRs, minibars, dry cleaning, laundry service, business
services. AE, DC, MC, V. Subway: 4, 5, 6,
L, N, Q, R, W to 14th St./Union Sq.

9 d-3
INTER-CONTINENTAL
CENTRAL PARK SOUTH

The hotel is the ultimate in luxury, with
its prime Central Park South address,
polished service, and tasteful decor.
Fine art fills the public rooms, and guest
rooms are little masterpieces, with rich
brocades, polished woods, and marble
bathrooms. Some rooms have breathtaking views of the park. 112 Central Park
South (between 6th and 7th Aves.),
10019, Midtown West, 212/757–1900 or
800/937–8461, fax 212/757–9620, www.
new-york.interconti.com. 192 rooms, 16
suites. Restaurant, bar, in-room data
ports, room service, massage, health club,
baby-sitting, parking (fee). AE, D, DC,
MC, V. Subway: N, Q, R, W to 57th St.

9 e-5
THE LIBRARY

The Library, where rooms are themed
according to Dewey decimal system subjects (such as French literature or biogra-
phy), may have finally taken the theme
hotel concept too far. But to a true book-
worm for whom the nearby New York
Public Library is an exciting draw, this
may be a dreamscape. Public spaces

include the second-floor Reading Room (morning breakfast and evening wine and cheese are served), the 14th-floor Poetry Garden (a wicker greenhouse with a wraparound terrace), and the Writer's Den (with a fireplace and large-screen TV). Guest rooms are serene, with green and yellow decor, Japanese shadow-box windows in the bathrooms, jade bonsais on the desks, and Tibetan-pattern bedspreads. The service is top-notch. *299 Madison Ave. (at 41st Street), 10017, Midtown East, 212/983–4500, fax 212/449–9099, www.libraryhotel.com. 60 rooms. Restaurant, room service, baby-sitting, business services, parking (fee). AE, DC, MC, V. Subway: 4, 5, 6, 7, S to 42nd St./Grand Central.*

9 e-2

THE MELROSE HOTEL AT THE BARBIZON

A women's residence club from 1927 to 1981, the Melrose, formerly the Barbizon, was home at various times to Grace Kelly, Joan Crawford, and Liza Minelli; it is now owned by Ian Schrager, and while the premises do not reflect his usual standards of design, they are quite attractive. The lobby has a beautiful, marble-and-limestone floor and luxurious gilt chairs with mohair upholstery. Guest rooms, decorated in shades of shell-pink or celadon, are modest but pleasant, with eclectic accents such as zigzag wrought-iron floor lamps. The on-site health club has an Olympic-size pool. Since most rooms are minuscule, ask for one of the few larger ones when booking; if you want space at any cost, ask for the penthouse suite, which has a lovely view of Central Park. *140 E. 63rd St. (between Lexington and 3rd Aves.), 10021, Upper East Side, 212/838–5700 or 800/223–5652, fax 212/888–4271. 310 rooms, 13 suites. Breakfast room, in-room data ports, room service, indoor pool, spa, health club, baby-sitting, parking (fee). AE, D, DC, MC, V. Subway: 4, 5, 6, N, Q, R, W to 59th St./Lexington Ave.; F to 63rd St./ Lexington Ave.*

9 d-5

MILLENNIUM BROADWAY

The lobby is sleek and dramatic, with black marble floors; rich African-mahogany walls; enormous, outrageously stylized paintings of fleshy, classical figures; and striking flower

arrangements. Rooms, too, have a sleek, modern look: leather and suede are the materials of choice; appliances are high-tech chrome; and everything is black, brown, and gray. For $100 more than the standard rate, you can stay at the nearby Millennium Premier, which has a few more amenities, such as a room serving tea and coffee, fax machines and CD players in the rooms, separate tub and shower in the bathrooms, and a lounge serving complimentary breakfast and cocktails. *145 W. 44th St. (between 6th Ave. and Broadway), 10036, Midtown West, 212/768–4400 or 800/622–5569, fax 212/768–0847, www.millbdwy.com. 617 rooms, 10 suites. Restaurant, bar, in-room data ports, room service, massage, gym, baby-sitting, parking (fee). AE, D, DC, MC, V. Subway: 1, 2, 3, 7, N, Q, R, S, W to 42nd St./Times Sq.*

9 e-6

MORGANS

The first hotel created by Ian Schrager and the late Steve Rubell is also the quietest and most mature. It has aged surprisingly well for a hotspot—it's still a magnet for moguls and celebrities (there's no sign outside). A minimalist, high-tech look prevails in the stunning rooms, with low-lying, futonlike beds (to make the rooms seem bigger), 27-inch Sony TVs on wheels, and signed Mapplethorpe prints on the walls; the tiny bathrooms have crystal shower doors, steel surgical sinks, and poured-granite floors. Asia de Cuba, the scene-making restaurant, is booked solid by the young and the trendy—the same crowd that frequents the cavelike, candlelit Morgans Bar downstairs. *237 Madison Ave. (between 37th and 38th Sts.), 10016, Murray Hill, 212/686–0300 or 800/334–3408, fax 212/779–8352. 113 rooms, 26 suites. Restaurant, 2 bars, breakfast room, in-room data ports, room service, baby-sitting, parking (fee). AE, D, DC, MC, V. Subway: 4, 5, 6, 7, S to 42nd St./Grand Central.*

9 d-3

NEW YORK HILTON & TOWERS

New York City's largest hotel and the epicenter of the city's hotel-based conventions, the Hilton has myriad business facilities, eating establishments, and shops, all designed for convenience. The sprawling, brassy lobby is more businesslike than beautiful but always buzzing. Considering the size of this property, guest rooms are surprisingly well maintained, and all have coffeemakers, hair dryers, and ironing boards. The Towers section is a slightly higher-grade hotel within this complex and offers rooms with dazzling views. *1335 6th Ave. (at 54th St.), 10019, Midtown West, 212/586–7000 or 800/445–8667, fax 212/261–5902, www.newyorktowers.hilton.com. 2,041 rooms, 20 suites. 2 restaurants, café, sports bar, in-room data ports, room service, barbershop, hair salon, hot tub, massage, health club, baby-sitting, parking (fee). AE, D, DC, MC, V. Subway: B, D, F, V to 47th–50th Sts./Rockefeller Center.*

9 c-4
NEW YORK MARRIOTT MARQUIS

New Yorkers love to hate this theater-district behemoth, which has more than 2,000 rooms, plus a slew of restaurants (including a revolving restaurant and lounge on the 46th floor), shops, ballrooms, and even a Broadway theater. It's a favorite with tour groups and conventioneers (the Javits Center is nearby). Guest rooms are generic but clean and functional; some have nice city views. *1535 Broadway (at 45th St.), 10036, Midtown West, 212/398–1900 or 800/843–4898, fax 212/704–8966, www.marriott.com. 1,911 rooms, 95 suites. 3 restaurants, 3 bars, café, coffee shop, in-room data ports, room service, hair salon, massage, health club, theater, baby-sitting, parking (fee). AE, D, DC, MC, V. Subway: 1, 2, 3, 7, S, N, Q, R, W to 42nd St./Times Sq.*

9 e-3
OMNI BERKSHIRE PLACE

Watch Siamese fighting fish swim in little bowls as you relax in front of the fireplace in the two-story atrium lounge—or just retire to one of the 375-square-ft guest rooms. The bedside comfort controls and fax machines are nice additions to the contemporary, Asian-influenced decor. *21 E. 52nd St. (between Madison and 5th Aves.), 10022, Midtown East, 212/753–5800 or 800/843–6664, fax 212/754–5020 for reservations; 212/754–5018 for guests, www.omnihotels.com. 328 rooms, 68 suites. Restaurant, bar, in-room data ports, in-room fax, room service, massage, health club, parking (fee). AE, D, DC, MC, V. Subway: E, V to 5th Ave.*

9 f-5
REGAL U.N. PLAZA HOTEL

Beginning on the 28th floors of each of two sleek skyscraper towers, this dazzling hotel attracts an international, diplomatic set thanks to its location

---

WORKING THE SYSTEM

We New Yorkers are used to prices that often shock our visitors, and hotel tariffs are no exception. But there are numerous tricks you can use to get that room rate down.

You rarely have to pay the full "rack rate," or standard room cost that hotels print in their brochures and quote over the phone. Hotels almost always offer AAA, AARP, or corporate rates, seasonal specials, and weekend deals that typically include such extras as complimentary meals, drinks, or tickets to events. Ask about specials when booking; ask your travel agent for brochures; and look for advertisements on-line or in travel magazines or the Sunday travel section of *The New York Times*.

Room rates are particularly low in humid August, when beleaguered residents might well want deluxe, air-conditioned respite from their sweltering apartments, and in mid-January, when a hotel stay might provide a remedy for the post-holiday blahs. (By contrast, prices during high season—the last two weeks of November and the first two weeks of December—are correspondingly astronomical.)

If you're booking last-minute, consolidators like Quickbook (800/789–9887), the Hotel Reservation Network (800/964–6835), and Accommodations Express (800/906–4685) provide heavy discounts on remaindered rooms.

The city's tourist bureau, NYC&Company, publishes a comprehensive guide to 100 cheaper hotels (call 800/692–8474 for a free copy).

You can bargain the room price down, but don't skimp on tips. The hotel maid should receive 1% of your room rate (at least $1) for each night of your stay. The bellhop should get $2 per bag.

close to the United Nations. Guest rooms are simple but tasteful, with breathtaking river views; hallways and some rooms have tapestries, silks, brocades, and batiks that U.N. diplomats presented to the hotel. There's a pool on the 27th floor, also with superb views, and a health club with an indoor tennis court. *1 United Nations Plaza (44th St. between 1st and 2nd Aves.), 10017, Midtown East, 212/758–1234 or 800/223–1234, fax 212/702–5051, www. regal-hotels.com. 393 rooms, 33 suites. Restaurant, bar, in-room data ports, in-room fax, room service, indoor pool, massage, tennis court, health club, baby-sitting, parking (fee). AE, D, DC, MC, V. Subway: 4, 5, 6, 7, S to 42nd St./Grand Central.*

9 e-6
THE ROGER WILLIAMS
This circa-1920s building sits ideally between Midtown and Downtown. The minimalist rooms are extremely stylish, with custom-made blond-birch furnishings and dramatic downlighting, and each comes with a 27-inch Sony TV, VCR, and CD player (guests have access to complimentary VCR and CD libraries). The bathrooms are artworks unto themselves, with chrome surgical sinks and recessed showers with cedar-grill floors. Don't miss the complimentary Continental breakfast and nightly dessert buffets on the mezzanine. *131 Madison Ave. (at 31st St.), 10016, Murray Hill, 212/448–7000, fax 212/448–7007, www.uniquehotels.com. 183 rooms, 1 suite. Breakfast room, in-room data ports, in-room VCRs, free parking. Subway: 6 to 33rd St.*

9 e-2
SHERRY-NETHERLAND
This Fifth Avenue grande dame is actually a cooperative-apartment complex, with more permanent residents than guests. As a result, in-room amenities are somewhat hit-or-miss, depending on the whims of the individual owners; but all of the suites are utterly luxurious, with separate living and dining areas, pantries, decorative fireplaces, fine antiques, and marble baths. Many of the panels and friezes were taken from the razed Vanderbilt mansion. The dastardly expensive Harry Cipriani restaurant provides room service; a liter of water costs about $20, no joke. But you'll get it quickly—the staff-to-guest ratio is 2 to 1.

781 5th Ave. (at 59th St.), 10022, Midtown East, 212/355–2800 or 800/247–4377, fax 212/319–4306, www.sherrynetherland. com. 40 rooms, 35 suites. Restaurant, bar, in-room fax, in-room VCRs, room service, barbershop, hair salon, gym, parking (fee). AE, D, DC, MC, V. Subway: N, R, W to 5th Ave.

9 d-3
THE SHOREHAM
The rooms here have two decor motifs: One design emphasizes metal detailing and metallic colors—even the headboards behind the sleigh beds are made of perforated steel and lit from behind. Quieter, more calming rooms have fluffy bedding and Ultrasuede headboards. All rooms have cedar-lined closets, and in-room VCRs and CD players add to the high-tech amenities. There are plenty of freebies here, including Continental breakfast, a nightly dessert buffet, and 24-hour cappuccino and espresso that's good enough for coffee snobs. The bar has a trendy staff and fashionable music, and room-service dinner comes from the neighboring three-star restaurant La Caravelle. *33 W. 55th St. (between 5th and 6th Aves.), 10019, Midtown West, 212/247–6700, fax 212/765–9741, www. uniquehotels.com. 132 rooms, 42 suites. Breakfast room, in-room data ports, in-room VCRs, massage, baby-sitting, parking (fee). AE, DC, MC, V. Subway: E, V to 5th Ave.*

10 d-4
60 THOMPSON
This design-focused boutique hotel has a front courtyard filled with white birches, a staff in navy uniforms by Nino Cerutti, a lounge and bar with an asymmetrical marble fireplace, and design elements lifted from a Pompeii mosaic. The rooms are gorgeous, too: Beds have full-wall leather headboards, and Philosophy products complement the marble bathrooms. The coveted duplex penthouse loft has a four-poster king bed and two private garden decks. The house restaurant is Thom, serving Asian-American food by the people behind Indochine and Bond Street; the rooftop bar is a place to be seen. *60 Thompson St. (between Spring and Broome Sts.), 10012, SoHo, 212/431–0400 or 877/431–0400, fax 212/431–0200, www.60Thompson.com. 100 rooms. Restaurant, bar, in-room data ports, in-room fax, in-room VCRs, room service, concierge. AE, D, DC, MC, V. Subway: E to Spring St.*

9 e-3

SWISSÔTEL NEW YORK— THE DRAKE

This hotel is a model of Swiss-style efficiency; witness the extensive business center, where guests have access to work stations equipped with desks, telephones, and computers. The ultra-clean rooms have an art deco look, and all have oversize desks and overstuffed chairs and sofas. The Drake Bar is a convivial meeting place, with Swiss specialties and some good Swiss wines. *440 Park Ave. (between 56th and 57th Sts.), 10022, Midtown East, 212/421–0900 or 888/737–9477, fax 212/371–4190, www. swissotel.com. 385 rooms, 110 suites. Restaurant, bar, in-room data ports, in-room fax, room service, spa, baby-sitting, parking (fee). AE, D, DC, MC, V. Subway: 4, 5, 6, N, Q, R, W to 59th St./Lexington Ave.*

9 c-4

THE TIME

Like the Library, this hotel pushes the "theme trend" into the realm of the slightly goofy. You choose a primary color when you make your reservation, and the comfortable, charcoal grey guest rooms are detailed— from bedding and headboard to jelly beans to reading material to a color-inspired scent—to fit your preference. The rooms have Web TVs, fax machines, and electronic do-not-disturb signs that switch between green and red; mini-TVs outside each elevator ease the stress of waiting to get downstairs. There is a well-equipped fitness center with a giant flat-screen TV, and the hotel's Italian restaurant, Coco Pazzo Teatro, is the creation of well-known chef Joseph Drappalo. *224 W. 49th St. (between Broadway and 8th Ave.), 10019, Midtown West, 212/320–2900 or 877/846–3692, fax 212/245–2305, www.thetimeny.com. 193 rooms. Restaurant, in-room fax, in-room VCR players, gym, business services. AE, D, DC, MC, V. Subway: 1, 2, E to 50th St.; N, Q, R, W to 49th St.*

9 e-5

W NEW YORK–THE COURT

Like its sister hotel, the W Tuscany, the W Court is located in the peaceful residential neighborhood of Murray Hill, and offers spacious rooms decorated in soothing colors. Guest rooms feature oversize desks, down-and-feather uphol-

stered chaise longues, and pillow-top mattresses as well as the latest technology, including ultra-fast Internet access. The W Court offers more activity than the W Tuscany, but choose either one and enjoy the facilities of both, which include a state-of-the-art health club and spacious meeting room. Unlike the Tuscany, the Court has a restaurant (Icon New York) and bar (Wet Bar). *130 E. 39th St. (at Lexington Ave.), 10016, Murray Hill, 212/685–1100 or 800/223–6725, fax 212/779–0148, www.whotels.com. 199 rooms, 47 suites. Restaurant, bar, room service, massage, spa, baby-sitting, parking (fee). AE, DC, MC, V. Subway: 4, 5, 6, 7, S to 42nd St./Grand Central.*

9 e-5

W NEW YORK– THE TUSCANY

The W Tuscany is similar to its sister hotel, the W Court, but it offers a more private "club" atmosphere. Rooms are state-of-the-art, both in terms of comfort and technology. And when you stay at the W Tuscany, you can use the facilities of the W Court. *120 E. 39th St. (between Park and Lexington Aves.), 10016, Murray Hill, 212/686–1600 or 800/223–6725, fax 212/779–0148, www.whotels.com. 122 rooms, 11 suites. Café, bar, room service, massage, spa, baby-sitting, parking (fee). AE, DC, MC, V. Subway: 4, 5, 6, 7, S to 42nd St./Grand Central.*

10 e-7

THE WALL ST. INN

This modest boutique hotel, a rarity in an area dominated by chains, is in an old Lehman Brothers Bank building and provides every amenity a visitor might want, along with elegant design and a touch of luxury. Room colors are soothing, light shades of green or beige, and some of the marble bathrooms are equipped with Jacuzzis; Continental breakfast is included in the price. Since the Wall St. Inn is a hard-core business hotel, it loses money on weekends and locals should look out for the big discounts on Friday and Saturday nights. *9 South William St. (at Broad St.), 10005, Lower Manhattan, 212/747–1500, fax 212/ 747–1900, www.wallsinn.com. 36 rooms, 10 suites. In-room data ports, in-room fax, in-room VCRs, gym, dry cleaning, laundry, concierge, business services. AE, D, DC, MC, V. Subway: 1, 2 to Wall St.; 4, 5 to Bowling Green.*

9 *d-3*

THE WARWICK

The Warwick has a loyal following, thanks to its prime Midtown location and its sophisticated, but not stuffy, ambience. The elegant, marble-floor lobby is flanked by the convivial Warwick Bar and Ciao Europa Italian restaurant. Rooms are tastefully decorated, with soft pastel color schemes, mahogany armoires, and nice marble bathrooms. Ask for a view of Sixth Avenue, or a room with a balcony. *65 W. 54th St. (at 6th Ave.), 10019, Midtown West, 212/247–2700 or 800/223–4099, fax 212/957–8915, www.warwickhotels.com. 352 rooms, 75 suites. Restaurant, bar, room service, parking (fee). AE, DC, MC, V. Subway: E, V to 5th Ave.; N, Q, R, W to 57th St.*

MODERATELY PRICED LODGINGS

9 *c-3*

AMERITANIA

This busy crash pad just off Broadway has raised its standards (and its prices) and is now one of Midtown's trendiest hotels. Settle into one of the oversize chairs in the cavernous, terrazzo-floored lobby and size up the young, hip crowd, many of whom choose the Ameritania for its proximity to the Letterman Show's Ed Sullivan Theater. Black-metal furniture dominates the bedrooms, which have small, black-marble bathrooms. Bar 54 stays open until 2 AM. *1701 Broadway (at 54th St.), 10019, Midtown West, 212/247–5000 or 800/922–0330, fax 212/247–3316, www.nycityhotels.net. 195 rooms, 12 suites. Restaurant, bar, gym. AE, D, DC, MC, V. Subway: B, D, E to 7th Ave.*

9 *d-6*

BEST WESTERN MANHATTAN

Rooms come in three different styles— "Fifth Avenue" (ritzy), "Central Park" (lots of florals), and "SoHo" (bold colors)—and all have coffeemakers. Guests have access to a tiny exercise room. One of the biggest draws is the location: The heavily Korean neighborhood just south of the Empire State Building is lively, with lots of cheap shops and restaurants. *17 W. 32nd St. (between 5th and 6th Aves.), 10001, Midtown West, 212/736–1600 or 800/567–7720, fax 212/695–1813, www.applecorehotels.com. 136*

rooms, 40 suites. Restaurant, bar, gym, parking (fee). Subway: B, D, F, N, Q, R, V, W to 34th St./Herald Sq.

10 *f-6*

BEST WESTERN SEAPORT INN

This restored 19th-century building is one block from the waterfront, close to South Street Seaport and Wall Street. A cross between a Colonial sea captain's house and a chain hotel, this place is thoroughly inviting, with a cozy, librarylike lobby and a friendly staff. Rooms are standard chain-motel fare, and a few have whirlpool tubs and outdoor terraces with views of the Brooklyn Bridge. *33 Peck Slip (at Front St.), 10038, Lower Manhattan, 212/766–6600 or 800/468–3569, fax 212/766–6615, www.bestwestern.com/ seaportinn. 72 rooms. In-room VCRs. AE, D, DC, MC, V. Subway: A, E, J, M, 1, 2, 4, 5 to Fulton St./Broadway Nassau.*

9 *f-2*

BRISTOL PLAZA

This is an excellent one-month-minimum extended-stay hotel, at prices much lower than others with similar amenities. The apartments are fairly traditional but fit the bill for comfort and convenience; kitchens are fully equipped with refrigerator, range, microwave, dishwasher, coffeemaker, pots and pans, and utensils. There are coin-operated washer-dryers on each floor as well as business and exercise facilities. *210 E. 65th St. (at 3rd Ave.), 10021, Upper East Side, 212/753–7900, fax 212/753–7905 for reservations; 212/980–3457 for guests. 176 apartments. In-room data ports, in-room fax, in-room safes, in-room VCR players, indoor pool, health club, coin laundry, dry cleaning, concierge, business services. AE, D, DC, MC, V. Subway: 6 to 68th St./Hunter College.*

9 *d-6*

COMFORT INN MANHATTAN

Comfort is what you get here: all of the spacious rooms are equipped with big, comfy sofabeds for extra guests, and some have refrigerators and microwaves. On top of that, you get complimentary Continental breakfast and a quiet but convenient location. The lobby is surprisingly elegant, with atmospheric lighting, fresh flowers, and a classical motif set off by Corinthian columns and tall, Greek-style vases in mirrored recesses. *42 W. 35th St. (between 5th and 6th Aves.), 10001, Midtown West, 212/947–0200, fax 212/594–3047, www.comfortinnmanhattan.com. 131 rooms. AE, D, DC, MC, V. Subway: B, D, F, N, Q, R, V, W to 34th St./Herald Sq.*

9 *c-2*

EMPIRE HOTEL
This hotel, now part of the Ian Schrager empire, is one of the few lodging bargains near Lincoln Center, and it's thoroughly pleasant to boot. The lobby is modified English-country style, complete with warm wood furniture and a hanging tapestry. Rooms are small but perfectly adequate, with textured teal carpets and dark-wood furnishings. *44 W. 63rd St. (between Broadway and 9th Ave.), 10023, Upper West Side, 212/265–7400 or 800/333–3333, fax 212/244–3382, www.empirehotel.com. 355 rooms, 20 suites. Restaurant, bar, in-room data ports, in-room VCRs, minibars, parking (fee). AE, D, DC, MC, V. Subway: 1, 2 to 66th St.*

7 *b-7*

THE EXCELSIOR
Directly across from the American Museum of Natural History, on a block full of fine, prewar apartment buildings, the Excelsior is an old-time hotel with an old-time feel. The lobby's inlaid-gold ceiling recalls grander days, and the down-home coffee shop serves breakfast all day. An extensive refurbishing has given the rooms a much-needed pick-me-up; they now have warm, earth-tone color schemes and traditional furnishings. *45 W. 81st St. (between Central Park West and Columbus Ave.), 10024, Upper West Side, 212/362–9200 or 800/368–4575, fax 212/721–2994, www.excelsiorhotel.com. 130 rooms, 60 suites. Coffee shop. AE, MC, V. Subway: B to 81st St.*

9 *e-3*

THE FITZPATRICK MANHATTAN HOTEL
Just south of Bloomingdale's, the Irish-owned Fitzpatrick is one of the friendliest hotels around. The mostly Irish staff loves to chat with the guests—especially with celebrities. Rooms are spacious and cheerful, with emerald-green carpets and traditional furnishings. The publike bar at the heart of the hotel is as welcoming as any in Dublin. Guests have free access to the Excelsior

Athletic Club, next door. A sister property, the Fitzpatrick Grand Central Hotel at 141 E. 44th Street, has similar warmth but more amenities and polish. It's also much pricier. *687 Lexington Ave. (at 57th St.), 10022, Midtown East, 212/355–0100 or 800/367–7701, fax 212/355–1371, www.fitzpatrickhotels.com. 42 rooms, 50 suites. Restaurant, bar, in-room data ports, room service, massage, parking (fee). AE, D, DC, MC, V. Subway: 4, 5, 6, N, Q, R, W to 59th St./Lexington Ave.*

7 *e-7*

THE FRANKLIN
The Upper East Side's hippest, funkiest hotel has a pint-size lobby decorated with black granite, brushed steel, and cherry wood. The tiny rooms have custom-built steel furniture, gauzy white canopies over the beds, and cedar closets; bathrooms have steel-bowl sinks. Guests are invited to borrow CDs and videotapes for free (all rooms have CD players and VCRs). To add to the excellent value, there's a generous complimentary breakfast (including homemade granola) and a nightly dessert buffet, and—hold onto your seat—parking is free! What you sacrifice are hotel amenities—there is no fitness or business center, no concierge, and no restaurant. *164 E. 87th St. (between Lexington and 3rd Aves.), 10128, Upper East Side, 212/369–1000 or 877/847–4444, fax 212/369–8000, www.uniquehotels.com. 47 rooms. Breakfast room, in-room VCRs, free parking. AE, MC, V. Subway: 4, 5, 6 to 86th St.*

9 *e-8*

GRAMERCY PARK HOTEL
One of Manhattan's greenest, quietest, most delightful parks is locked to anyone who doesn't live right on its periphery—but you hold the key as long as you're a guest at this aged, Queen Anne–style hotel. Guest rooms are a little the worse for wear, with worn furniture and old-fashioned bathrooms; but the charming locale makes up for these flaws. Besides, renovations are continually underway, and you can ask for a newly refurbished room when you check in (but *not* when you reserve). *2 Lexington Ave. (at 21st St.), 10010, Gramercy, 212/475–4320 or 800/221–4083, fax 212/505–0535. 543 rooms, 157 suites. Restaurant, bar, hair salon. AE, D, DC, MC, V. Subway: 6 to 23rd St.*

9 *d-3*

HELMSLEY WINDSOR

The cozy, wood-paneled, red-carpeted lobby tells you that the Helmsley Windsor delivers comfort as well as value. Rooms are spacious and pleasant enough, with faux Old World decor that includes lots of red and gold, plush sofas in sitting areas, and dramatic Ming vases. The marble bathrooms, with mirrors on every conceivable surface, are fit for Louis XVI, or perhaps his mistress. Continental breakfast is complimentary. *100 W. 58th St. (at 6th Ave.), 10019, Midtown West, 212/265–2100 or 800/221–4982, fax 212/315–0371. 229 rooms, 15 suites. Breakfast room, parking (fee). AE, D, DC, MC, V. Subway: N, Q, R, W to 57th St.*

10 *e-4*

HOLIDAY INN DOWNTOWN

The excellent dim sum at Pacifica restaurant is reason enough to stay at this downtown hotel, a favorite with Chinese business travelers. Rooms and suites are sleek and modern, with pastel walls and carpets, black-frame furniture, and watercolors with an Asian motif. This is a great location for anyone who wants to be near Chinatown and Little Italy as well as SoHo and the Financial District. *138 Lafayette St. (between Canal and Howard Sts.), 10013, Chinatown, 212/966–8898 or 800/465–4329, fax 212/966–3933, www.holiday-inn.com/hotels/nycdt/welcome.html. 213 rooms, 12 suites. Restaurant, bar, room service, parking (fee). AE, D, DC, MC, V. Subway: 6, M, N, Q, R, W to Canal St.*

7 *b-8*

HOTEL BEACON

A true home away from home, the Beacon has a kitchenette in each room, and suites have full kitchens—and cost only $40 more than a standard room. All accommodations are large and comfortably outfitted with traditional-style furnishings, and many rooms enjoy airy views over the Upper West Side. What's more, the hotel is near Central Park and Lincoln Center, as well as scores of gourmet food stores such as Zabar's, so you can make good use of all those kitchen appliances. *2130 Broadway (at 75th St.), 10023, Upper West Side, 212/787–1100 or 800/572–4969, fax 212/724–0839, www.beaconhotel.com. 110 rooms, 100 suites. Kitchenettes, refrigerators, business*

services, meeting room, parking (fee). AE, D, DC, MC, V. Subway: 1, 2, 3 to 72nd St.

7 *e-6*

HOTEL WALES

The modestly priced Wales is a true find in the tony Carnegie Hill area. Built in 1901, it still has a turn-of-the-20th-century mood; there's even a "Pied Piper" parlor decorated with vintage children's illustrations (this is where the generous breakfast and nightly dessert buffets are served). Guest rooms are small and show signs of wear and tear, but they do have fine oak woodwork, and all are equipped with CD players. Most of the suites face Madison Avenue. *1295 Madison Ave. (between 92nd and 93rd Sts.), 10128, Upper East Side, 212/876–6000, 800/428–5252 or 877/847–4444, fax 212/860–7000, www.uniquehotels.com. 87 rooms, 30 suites. Breakfast room, in-room VCRs, parking (fee). AE, MC, V. Subway: 6 to 96th St.*

9 *e-5*

JOLLY MADISON TOWERS

Part of the Italian Jolly Hotel chain, this is a great little bargain in Murray Hill. Rooms are cheerful and well kept, and done in Italian-style traditional decor: green and brown fabrics, marble bathrooms (with separate glass shower stalls in the suites), and desks with leather chairs. The colorful restaurant, Cinque Terre, serves good Northern Italian cuisine. *22 E. 38th St. (at Madison Ave.), 10016, Murray Hill, 212/802–0600 or 800/225–4340, fax 212/447–0747. 245 rooms, 6 suites. Restaurant, bar, massage, sauna. AE, DC, MC, V. Subway: 6 to 33rd St.*

9 *d-5*

THE MANSFIELD

In a 1904 Stanford White building where well-heeled bachelors once lodged, this small hotel is Victorian and clublike. Guest rooms have stylish, black-marble bathrooms, ebony-stained floors and doors, dark-wood venetian blinds, and sleigh beds with Belgian linens. There are nightly piano and harp recitals in the intimate concert salon, where complimentary breakfast is served. *12 W. 44th St. (at Madison Ave.), 10036, Midtown East, 212/944–6050 or 800/255–5167, fax 212/764–4477, www.uniquehotels.com. 123 rooms, 25 suites. In-room safes, in-room VCRs, room service. AE, MC, V. Subway: 1, 2, 3, 7, N, Q, R, S, W to 42nd St./Times Sq.*

9 C-2

THE MAYFLOWER HOTEL ON THE PARK

You'll feel at home the moment you enter the wood-paneled lobby of this friendly hotel on Central Park West, where a basket of apples and complimentary coffee and cookies are offered all day long. Rooms are large and comfortable, with thick carpeting, fruit-and-flower–patterned drapes, dark-wood Colonial-style furniture, and walk-in closets. The furnishings may be beat-up and the window air conditioners ugly, but some rooms have park views, and most have walk-in pantries with refrigerators and sinks. *15 Central Park West (between 61st and 62nd Sts.), 10023, Upper West Side, 212/265–0060 or 800/223–4164, fax 212/265–2026, www.mayflowerhotel.com. 117 rooms, 160 suites. Restaurant, bar, in-room data ports, room service, gym, parking (fee). AE, DC, MC, V. Subway: 1, 2, A, B, D to 59th St./Columbus Circle.*

9 e-4

METROPOLITAN

This is a large, lively, reasonably priced hotel with an always-bustling lobby-lounge restaurant, a shopping arcade, and on-site parking. Rooms are decorated in what might be described as Miami coffee-shop style, though current renovations are adding a more contemporary look. Prices drop substantially during low-occupancy periods; even suites are under $250. *569 Lexington Ave. (at 51st St.), 10022, Midtown East, 212/752–7000 or 800/836–6471, fax 212/752–3817, www.metropolitanhotelnyc.com. 722 rooms, 40 suites. Restaurant, in-room data ports, room service, barbershop, hair salon, gym, parking. AE, D, DC, MC, V. Subway; 6 to 51st St./Lexington Ave.; E, V to Lexington–3rd Aves./53rd St.*

7 b-8

ON THE AVE

In the heart of the Upper West Side, this contemporary-style hotel in an old building offers state-of-the-art entertainment and communications. The beige-colored rooms have industrial sinks in the bathrooms and other high-tech touches, and guests are provided with passes to the nearby Equinox Fitness club and discount parking. All things considered, the hotel offers great value for the price; it's perfect place for West Siders to stash visiting relatives. *2178 Broadway (at 77th St.), 10024, Upper West Side, 212/362–1100 or 800/509–7598, fax 212/787–9521, www.ontheave-nyc.com or www.stayinny.com. 250 rooms. AE, D, DC, MC, V. Subway: 1, 2 to 79th St.*

9 C-4

THE PARAMOUNT

This hip hostelry with its dramatic, multilevel lobby is a creation of Ian Schrager and Philippe Starck, also responsible for Morgans and the Royalton. The young and the hip come here in droves to enjoy surroundings that are fashionable and fun for some, though way too attitudinal for others. The postage-stamp–size rooms have modern, angular furniture and beds with frame headboards, several of them bearing a print of Vermeer's *The Lacemaker*; bathrooms have bizarre conical sinks. There are several bars, a restaurant, a gourmet snack shop, and a playroom for young children. *235 W. 46th St. (between Broadway and 8th Aves.), 10036, Midtown West, 212/764–5500 or 800/225–7474, fax 212/575–4892. 590 rooms, 10 suites. 2 restaurants, bar, café, in-room data ports, in-room VCRs, room service, gym, nursery. AE, D, DC, MC, V. Subway: 1, 2, 3, 7, N, Q, R, S, W to 42nd St./Times Sq.*

9 e-4

THE ROGER SMITH

Here's a boutique hotel for art lovers, or for anyone who appreciates bold color schemes and unconventional combinations. Take the lobby, which might well be a very civilized nightclub—crimson carpet, splashy paintings, bronze busts here and there. All bedrooms are individually decorated, some with slightly outlandish touches such as ivy-trellis wallpaper. This is a very friendly and eccentric place. *501 Lexington Ave. (between 47th and 48th Sts.), 10017, Midtown East, 212/755–1400 or 800/445–0277, fax 212/758–4061, www.rogersmith.com. 134 rooms. Restaurant, bar, room service, parking (fee). AE, D, DC, MC, V. Subway; 6 to 51st St./Lexington Ave.; E, V to Lexington–3rd Aves./53rd St.; 4, 5, 6, 7, S to 42nd St./Grand Central.*

9 d-3

THE WELLINGTON

The Wellington's traditionally decorated rooms are surprisingly tasteful for such a well-priced hotel: dark-wood furniture, high-quality fabrics in soft color schemes,

3

and nicely framed prints. The lobby is constantly crammed with tourists and feels hectic, but that's part of this old-timer's charm. Carnegie Hall is a stone's throw away. *871 7th Ave. (at 55th St.), 10019, Midtown West, 212/247–3900 or 800/652–1212, fax 212/581–1719, www.wellingtonhotel.com. 550 rooms, 150 suites. Restaurant, bar, coffee shop, hair salon, parking (fee). AE, DC, MC, V. Subway: N, Q, R, W to 57th St.*

9 *d-3*
THE WYNDHAM
Anyone who appreciates fine art and whimsical colors will love the Wyndham, whose lobby is a cross between a museum gallery and the comfortable salon of an art collector. The spacious, individually decorated guest rooms all have the feel of a summer house with a breezy rococo motif: light powder-blue, peach, or yellow fabric wall-coverings; flowers everywhere; and, of course, fine art. Closets are enormous. It's hard to find a better deal anywhere in Manhattan, let alone in such a prime location, right across from Central Park. *42 W. 58th St. (between 5th and 6th Aves.), 10019, Midtown West, 212/753–3500 or 800/257–1111, fax 212/754–5638. 142 rooms, 70 suites. Restaurant, bar. AE, DC, MC, V. Subway: 1, 2, A, B, D to 59th St./Columbus Circle.*

BUDGET LODGINGS

9 *d-7*
ARLINGTON HOTEL
Signs are in both English and Chinese at this Chelsea hotel, a favorite of Chinese businesspeople on their way to import/export wholesale showrooms in the area. Rooms are spacious, with generic decor. There's a gift shop in the lobby, and American breakfast in the hotel's pleasant restaurant is included. The Flatiron District's Madison Park and trendy restaurants are just around the corner. *18 W. 25th St. (between Broadway and 6th Ave.), 10010, Flatiron, 212/645–3990, fax 212/633–8952, www.arlington.citysearch.com. 96 rooms. AE, D, MC, V. Subway: F, V to 23rd St.*

9 *f-3*
THE BRIDGE SUITE APARTMENTS
The cheapest of the city's one-month-minimum extended-stay hotels is a no-frills spot to seek out if you are suddenly booted from your apartment. The studio and one-bedroom apartments look like models in an ad for a low-end furniture store, but they are in a convenient residential part of the Upper East Side, have great views of the Queensboro Bridge (while being set far enough back to avoid traffic noise), and there is a coin-operated laundry on the ground floor and a courtyard with plants and flowers. New York Hospital/Cornell Medical Center, Rockefeller University, New York University Hospital, and Memorial Sloan Kettering are nearby. *315 E. 60th St. (at 1st Ave.), 10022, Upper East Side, 212/221–8300, fax 212/704–0915, www.bridgesuites.com. 100 apartments. Kitchenette, concierge. AE, D, DC, MC, V. Subway: 4, 5, 6, N, Q, R, W to 59th St./Lexington Ave.*

9 *c-4*
BROADWAY INN
Though it isn't the kind of bed-and-breakfast where you linger over omelets in the garden, the Broadway Inn is friendly and comfortable. Continental breakfast is served in the brick-walled lobby, where stocked bookshelves and photos of Old New York create a homey mood. Theater hounds can fall quickly into bed after their Broadway show. *264 W. 46th St. (between Broadway and 8th Ave.), 10036, Midtown West, 212/997–9200 or 800/826–6300, fax 212/768–2807, www.broadwayinn.com. 22 rooms, 11 suites. Breakfast room. AE, D, DC, MC, V. Subway: 1, 2, 3, 7, N, Q, R, S, W to 42nd St./Times Sq.*

9 *e-7*
CARLTON ARMS
Though the rooms here are phoneless, TV-less, lack air-conditioning, are almost free of furniture, and are sometimes bathless, they score a perfect 10 when it comes to character. Over the years the managers have commissioned artists to cover every wall, ceiling, and other surface with murals, some of them with outrageous themes. The Cow Spot Room (3C), for example, has a Holstein motif of cow-spotted rugs, bedspreads, and walls; the Versailles Room (5A) is a symphony of trompe l'oeil trellises and classical urns. Only in New York. Call to reserve at least two months in advance. *160 E. 25th St. (between Lexington and 3rd Aves.), 10010, Gramercy, 212/684–8337, www.carltonarms.com. 54 rooms, 20 with bath. MC, V. Subway: N, Q, R, W to 28th St.*

9 d-8

CHELSEA INN

Perhaps the best budget find in downtown Manhattan, this quaint old brownstone is just a few blocks from Union Square. The in-room cooking facilities (some have full kitchenettes; others have just a refrigerator and sink) make it a favorite of young travelers. Most rooms share a bath and are inviting, with dark-wood furniture, country-style quilts, and big TVs. *46 W. 17th St. (between 5th and 6th Aves.), 10011, Flatiron District, 212/645–8989, fax 212/645–1903, www.chelseainn.com. 27 rooms, 3 with bath. AE, D, MC, V. Subway: 4, 5, 6, L, N, Q, R, W to 14th St./Union Sq.; F, V to 14th St.*

9 d-7

GERSHWIN HOTEL

There's always a lot going on at this young, arty mecca for foreign budget travelers—summer rooftop barbecues, gallery openings, and socializing in the giant, art-filled lobby. Rooms are all painted in custard yellow and kelly green and are somewhat crumbly in places, and only some have air-conditioning. Dormitories have four or eight beds and a remarkable rate of $22 a person. The hotel occupies a 13-story Greek Revival building. *7 E. 27th St. (between 5th and Madison Aves.), 10016, Flatiron District, 212/545–8000, fax 212/684–5546, www.gershwinhotel.com. 120 rooms, 15 dorm rooms. Restaurant, bar. MC, V. Subway: 6, N, Q, R, W to 28th St.*

9 e-3

HABITAT HOTEL

Habitat has small yet comfortable and modern guest rooms with a distinct European feel. Formerly a run-down residence for women (a few tenants still legally remain), it now qualifies as a "sophisticated budget" hotel. Rooms have trundle beds, cable TV, and Internet hookup. Bathrooms are shared and showers are in a separate room. Bloomingdale's, Tiffany, Bergdorf Goodman, and Bendels are around the corner. *130 E. 57th St. (at Lexington Ave.), 10022, Midtown East, 212/753–8841 or 800/255–0482, fax 212/829–9605, www.stayinny.com. 350 rooms, 30 with bath. Restaurant, bar. AE, MC, V. Subway: 4, 5, 6, N, Q, R, W to 59th St./Lexington Ave.*

9 d-6

HERALD SQUARE HOTEL

Housed in the former headquarters of *Life* magazine, the Herald Square pays homage to its predecessor with framed vintage magazine covers in the hallways. The rooms are basic but equipped with TVs, phones with voice mail, and in-room safes; what really stands out here is the service, which is remarkably attentive for such an inexpensive hotel. Book far in advance. *19 W. 31st St. (at 6th Ave.), 10001, Midtown West, 212/279–4017 or 800/727–1888, fax 212/643–9208, www.heraldsquarehotel.com. 127 rooms. AE, D, MC, V. Subway: B, D, F, N, Q, R, V, W to 34th St./Herald Sq.*

9 c-4

HOTEL EDISON

Fans of Al Pacino may recall Sophia's, the Edison's restaurant, from the loan-shark murder scene in *The Godfather.* The hotel is a hit with tour groups, with its reasonable prices and on-site facilities. The pink-plaster coffee shop is a great place to spy on showbiz types. Rooms are no better than standard, but hey, the location is great and you get what you pay for. *228 W. 47th St. (between Broadway and 8th Ave.), 10036, Midtown West, 212/840–5000 or 800/637–7070, fax 212/596–6850, www.edisonhotelnyc.com. 1,000 rooms. Restaurant, bar, coffee shop, hair salon, airport shuttle. AE, D, DC, MC, V. Subway: 1, E to 50th St.*

9 c-1

HOTEL OLCOTT

This semiresidential hotel occupies a fine, prewar building, with easy access to Central Park and the Museum of Natural History. There are daily and weekly rates for both comfortable studios (each with cooking pantry) and suites (with kitchenette). The lobby is large and inviting, with ornate gilded elevators and Corinthian columns. The Olcott provides fantastic value in a beautiful neighborhood, and is a great choice for visitors who wish to see how New Yorkers actually live. *27 W. 72nd St. (between Central Park West and Columbus Ave.), 10023, Upper West Side, 212/877–4200, fax 212/580–0511. 150 rooms, 100 suites. Restaurant, bar, kitchenettes, parking (fee). MC, V. Subway: B to 72nd St.*

9 *f-8*

HOTEL 17

Madonna and David Bowie were among the first to frequent this trendy, dirt-cheap, Euro-style hotel, often used in the 1990s for heroin-chic magazine shoots. Guest rooms are small, grunged-out, standard-to-dumpy boxes, with beat-up dressers, 1950s striped wallpaper, and saggy mattresses, and most share a bath—in short, they offer ample ennui for the traveler keen to strike a bohemian posture. Besides, you come here for image, not luxury. The location, right off beautiful Stuyvesant Square, puts you within walking distance of the East Village and Park Avenue South's many restaurants. *225 E. 17th St. (between 2nd and 3rd Aves.), 10003, Gramercy, 212/475–2845, fax 212/ 677–8178, www.hotel17.citysearch.com. 200 rooms, 12 with bath. No credit cards. Subway: 4, 5, 6, L, N, Q, R, W to 14th St./Union Sq.*

10 *d-1*

LARCHMONT HOTEL

On this residential, West Village street, the Larchmont looks more like a charming brownstone home than a hotel. Compact rooms have a safari theme, with rattan furniture, ceiling fans, and framed animal or botanical prints. Bathrooms are shared, but kept clean, and every bedroom has a private sink; each floor has a shared kitchen. The staff is extra-friendly, and the rates include Continental breakfast. *27 W. 11th St. (between 5th and 6th Aves.), 10011, West Village, 212/989–9333, fax 212/989–9496, www.larchmonthotel.citysearch.com. 55 rooms. Breakfast room. AE, D, DC, MC, V. Subway: A, B, C, D, E, F, V to W. 4th St./Washington Sq.*

7 *b-5*

MALIBU STUDIOS HOTEL

Rock-bottom prices at the outer reaches of the Upper West Side seem to be especially appealing to European travelers and to family and friends who come to New York to visit students at nearby Columbia University. Plus, it's a 10-minute subway ride from Midtown, 20 from Greenwich Village. Breakfast is complimentary. The rooms are as basically furnished as those in a youth hostel and have no telephones, but there are pay phones in the lobby. *2699 Broadway (at W. 103rd St.), 10036, Upper West Side, 212/222–2954 or 800/647–2227, fax 212/678–6842, www.malibuhotelnyc.com. 150 rooms, 70 with bath. No credit cards. Subway: 1 to 103rd St.*

10 *f-3*

OFF SOHO SUITES HOTEL

In the trendy Lower East Side, with its chic boutiques and bars, this hotel is convenient to Chinatown, NoLita, and SoHo. The two- and four-person suites here have fully equipped kitchens and are clean and functional, if totally generic. *11 Rivington St. (between Chrystie St. and The Bowery), 10002, Lower East Side, 212/979–9808 or 800/633–7646, fax 212/979–9801, www.offsoho.com. 40 suites, 28 with bath. Kitchenettes. AE, MC, V. Subway: F, V to 2nd Ave.*

9 *f-4*

PICKWICK ARMS HOTEL

A convenient location, a rooftop garden, and views of the Manhattan skyline (from some rooms) are among the advantages at this bargain favorite. Drawbacks: the rooms are tiny, most have shared bathrooms, and the furniture is nothing special. Even so, the Pickwick tends to be busy, so book two to three weeks in advance. *230 E. 51st St. (between 2nd and 3rd Aves.), 10022, Midtown East, 212/355–0300 or 800/742–5945, fax 212/755–5029. 350 rooms, 175 with bath. Café, airport shuttle. AE, DC, MC, V. Subway: 6 to 51st St./Lexington Ave.; E, V to Lexington–3rd Aves./53rd St.*

9 *d-4*

PORTLAND SQUARE HOTEL

Built in 1904 as the Rio Hotel, this friendly little place was once the home of James Cagney and a few of his Radio City Rockette acquaintances. It's a good value as you get phones with voice mail, in-room safes, a laundry room, and even a small exercise room. Obviously, you shouldn't come here in search of luxury: The no-frills decor doesn't get fancier than floral drapes and bedspreads, but rooms in the east wing have bigger bathrooms. *132 W. 47th St. (between 6th and 7th Aves.), 10036, Midtown West, 212/382–0600 or 800/388–8988, fax 212/382–0684, www.portlandsquarehotel.com. 142 rooms, 112 with bath. Gym. AE, MC, V. Subway: N, Q, R, W to 49th St.*

7 *a-8*

RIVERSIDE TOWER

Rooms above the sixth floor have sweeping views of Riverside Park, the mighty Hudson River, and the New Jersey skyline. They're small, dark, and occasionally smoke-singed, but the location is good, and the price is right. European backpackers come in droves. *80 Riverside Dr. (at 80th St.), 10024, Upper West Side, 212/877–5200 or 800/724–3136, fax 212/873–1400, www.travelweb.com. 120 rooms, 116 with bath. AE, D, DC, MC, V. Subway: 1, 2 to 79th St.*

9 *d-6*

STANFORD HOTEL

Near Macy's and the Manhattan Mall, the Stanford attracts a Latin American and Japanese clientele. Rooms are tidy, and all are equipped with TVs and refrigerators. There's karaoke in the cocktail bar. *43 W. 32nd St. (between 5th Ave. and Broadway), 10001, Midtown West, 212/563–1500, fax 212/629–0043. 130 rooms. Bar. B, D, F, N, Q, R, S, W to 34th St./Herald Sq.*

9 *b-5*

TRAVEL INN

Though it's on a desolate block near the Port Authority Bus Terminal, the Travel Inn is worthwhile for its generous amenities and low price. The up-to-date rooms—all with reproduction colonial furniture, green carpets, and blue-tile bathrooms—occupy four wings that center around a lovely outdoor swimming pool surrounded by greenery and colorful plants. You also get free parking and a helpful travel-services desk. *515 W. 42nd St. (between 10th and 11th Aves.), 10036, Midtown West, 212/695–7171 or 800/869–4630, fax 212/967–5025, www.newyorkhotel.com. 160 rooms. Deli, room service, pool, travel services, free parking. AE, D, DC, MC, V. Subway: A, E to 42nd St./Port Authority.*

10 *d-2*

WASHINGTON SQUARE HOTEL

This is *the* place to stay in the Village: It's quaint and historic (built in 1902), with a European-style lobby full of wrought iron and gleaming brass; it's convenient, especially for night owls (the Blue Note jazz club is just around the corner); and, more to the point, it's one of the few hotels in the area. Free breakfast is served at the little restaurant, C3, on the premises. There's even a tiny exercise room. Rooms are simple but well maintained; a few don't have a window, so request one that does—better yet, request a room in front with a view over Washington Square. *103 Waverly Pl. (at MacDougal St.), 10011, West Village, 212/777–9515 or 800/222–0418, fax 212/979–8373, www.wshotel.com or www.washingtonsquarehotel.com. 165 rooms. Restaurant, bar, gym. AE, MC, V. Subway: A, B, C, D, E, F, V to W. 4th St./Washington Sq.*

9 *d-6*

THE WOLCOTT

Beyond the gilded lobby lie unremarkable but functional guest rooms. All have phones with voice mail, color TVs, and some have mini-refrigerators. You're just three blocks south of the Empire State Building, and have easy access to Macy's and Madison Square Garden. *4 W. 31st St. (at 5th Ave.), 10001, Midtown West, 212/268–2900, fax 212/563–0096, www.wolcott.com. 200 rooms, 190 with bath. AE, MC, V. Subway: B, D, F, N, Q, R, V, W to 34th St./Herald Sq.*

HOSTELS & THE Y

Hostels and Ys are useful if you are looking to put up a lot of people with not a lot of money—if you're convening 50 recent college grads for your low-budget wedding, for example. Independent hostels and those affiliated with Hostelling International (HI) are similar in price and style: they almost always have private rooms as well as dorms that sleep 4–12 people. The three private hostels in Harlem charge $14–$16 per dorm bed, while Midtown properties generally cost $20 or more. Very few hostels have air-conditioning. Many hostels have an unadvertised policy of accepting foreigners only; those listed below accept Americans but require identification for check-in. Hostelers would be wise to carry a passport.

Another budget option is to stay in one of Manhattan's several Ys, where double rooms generally range from about $60 to $90. Though most Ys have bare-bones rooms and offer few amenities, they compensate by offering guests free use of their extensive gym facilities.

9 d-4
BIG APPLE HOSTEL
In the heart of Times Square, the Big Apple has brisk service, bathrooms that sparkle, and a big outdoor patio where you can sip free coffee with an international crowd. There are four-person dorms and a handful of private doubles. *119 W. 45th St. (between 6th and 7th Aves.), 10036, Midtown West, 212/302–2603, fax 212/302–2605. 106 beds. Coin laundry. MC, V. Subway: 1, 2, 3, N, Q, R, S, W to 42nd St./Times Sq.*

6 d-6
BLUE RABBIT INTERNATIONAL HOUSE
In Harlem's affluent Sugar Hill, this hostel is just two blocks from St. Nick's Pub, one of Manhattan's best jazz clubs. Coed and women-only dorm-style rooms sleep four to eight, and there are also a few giant doubles. There's no air-conditioning, but fans are provided. You can survey the street scene from a rooftop terrace. Note: all guests, Americans included, must present a passport for check-in. *730 St. Nicholas Ave. (between 145th and 146th Sts.), 10031, Harlem, 212/491–3892 or 800/610–2030, fax 212/283–0108, www.hostelhandbook.com/bluerabbit. 25 beds. No credit cards. Subway: A, B, D to 145th St.*

9 c-8
CHELSEA INTERNATIONAL HOSTEL
The free pizza party every Wednesday night draws a boisterous young crowd. The four-person dorm rooms are somewhat cramped, and only some have air-conditioning, but they're half the price of the private doubles. A common room has a TV. A passport is required for check-in, even for Americans. *251 W. 20th St. (between 7th and 8th Aves.), 10011, Chelsea, 212/647–0010, fax 212/727–7289, www.chelseahostel.com. 310 beds. Kitchen, coin laundry. AE, MC, V. Subway: 1, 2, E to 23rd St.*

7 e-6
DE HIRSCH RESIDENCE AT THE 92ND STREET YM-YWHA
Right off Museum Mile in posh Carnegie Hill, the De Hirsch Residence is an excellent bargain: Every floor has its own kitchen, laundry, and shared bath, and you have free use of the excellent fitness facilities. The Y also sponsors many cultural and social events. There's a three-night minimum stay; reserve as far in advance as possible. *1395 Lexington Ave. (at 92nd St.), 10128, Upper East Side, 212/415–5650 or 800/858–4692, fax 212/415–5578, www.92ndsty.org. 350 beds. Health club, pool, coin laundry. Subway: 4, 5, 6 to 86th St.*

7 b-4
HOSTELLING INTERNATIONAL–NEW YORK
Nineteenth-century architect Richard Morris Hunt designed this building, now home to the largest youth hostel in North America. Besides its sheer size, the main draws here are a garden and outdoor terrace and an excellent neighborhood location. There are about 100 dorm rooms that sleep 4–12, as well as some private rooms (with bath) that accommodate up to four people; these cost $75. Those with a Hostelling International card get a $3 discount. *891 Amsterdam Ave. (at 103rd St.), 10025, Upper West Side, 212/932–2300, fax 212/932–2574, www.hinewyork.org. 540 beds. Kitchen, coin laundry. MC, V. Subway: 1 to 103rd St.*

6 c-6
SUGAR HILL INTERNATIONAL HOUSE
Like the Blue Rabbit International House (it has the same owners), this Harlem hostel is clean, comfortable, and friendly, with easy subway access and a sunny back garden. There are three four- to eight-bed dorms (some coed, some women-only) and one private double. Reserve in advance, check in before 9 PM, and remember your passport—it's required for check-in. *722 St. Nicholas Ave. (at 146th St.), 10031, Harlem, 212/926–7030, fax 212/283–0108, www.hostelhandbook.com/sugarhill. 20 beds. Kitchen. No credit cards. Subway: A, B, D to 145th St.*

7 *d-2*

UPTOWN HOSTEL

This beautiful Harlem brownstone is a real find thanks to Giselle, the hard-working Canadian owner who loves to debunk visitors' preconceptions about Harlem. (It's the friendliest neighborhood she's ever lived in, she says.) There are 30 coed dorms (four–six beds) and two private doubles. *239 Lenox Ave./Malcolm X Blvd. (at 122nd St.), 10027, Harlem, 212/666–0559. 30 beds. Kitchen. No credit cards. Subway: 2, 3 to 125th St.*

9 *c-7*

YMCA–MCBURNEY

Despite the uninviting entrance—with a security guard and a glassed-in reception window—the McBurney is a good deal. Rooms are small but decent, and guests have free use of the gym. Beware, though: there are only two large bathrooms for all 270 rooms. A $40 deposit is required to secure your reservation, unless you arrive before 6 PM. *206 W. 24th St. (between 7th and 8th Aves.), 10011, Chelsea, 212/741–9226, fax 212/741–8724, www.ymcanyc.org. 270 rooms, none with bath. Health club. Subway: 1, 2, E to 23rd St.*

9 *f-4*

YMCA–VANDERBILT

Tiny rooms with linoleum floors and shared bathrooms are a small sacrifice to make for such a prime location and great fitness perks: guests have free use of the pools, cardiovascular equipment, and Nautilus machines. *224 E. 47th St. (between 2nd and 3rd Aves.), 10017, Midtown East, 212/756–9600, fax 212/752–0210, www.ymcanyc.org. 377 rooms, none with bath. MC, V. 2 pools, health club, airport shuttle. Subway: 6 to 51st St./Lexington Ave.; E, V to Lexington–3rd Aves./53rd St.*

9 *c-2*

YMCA–WEST SIDE

A few blocks from Lincoln Center, this Y has extensive fitness facilities, including a pool, indoor track, and squash courts. Unlike those at hostels, the rooms here, even singles, are private, albeit modestly furnished. The bathrooms, however, are shared. You must be at least 18 years old to stay here; reservations (credit card required) are best made two weeks in advance. *5 W. 63rd St. (at Central Park West), 10023, Upper West Side, 212/875–*

4100, fax 212/875–1334, www.ymcanyc.org. 550 rooms, 100 with bath. Cafeteria, pool, sauna, health club, squash, coin laundry, airport shuttle. AE, MC, V. Subway: 1, 2, A, B, D to 59th St./Columbus Circle.

OUTER-BOROUGH HOTELS

Some of the best accommodation in the so-called "outer boroughs" are in bed-and-breakfast–type inns; in fact, look beyond Manhattan and you'll find some of the most romantic hideaways in the city.

1 *e-6*

AKWAABA MANSION BED & BREAKFAST

A hidden gem in an 1860s brownstone in Bedford–Stuyvesant, Akwaaba (the name means "welcome" in Twi, the language of the Ashanti of West Africa) is best known for its "Jumping the Broom" honeymoon suite, but all four rooms for rent in this 1860s Italianate villa (very Brooklyn) are distinctive and each have a theme. There's an opulent "royal" room, a white honeymoon suite, one themed for black history, and another with African textiles; two of the rooms have Jacuzzis. A full Southern breakfast is served in the morning, and tea at 4 PM. *347 MacDonough St. (between Stuyvesant and Lewis Aves.), Stuyvesant Heights, Brooklyn 11233, 718/455–5958, fax 718/774–1744, www.akwaaba.com. 4 rooms. AE, D, DC, MC, V. Subway: A, E to Utica Ave. Budget.*

12 *g-7*

BED & BREAKFAST ON THE PARK

With more florals than the Brooklyn Botanical Gardens, this family-owned 1895 building has been fully restored, filled with art and antiques and fitted with modem lines in the bedrooms. A lavish breakfast is included. This is a perfect place to install visiting parents or grandparents. *113 Prospect Park West (at 7th St.), Park Slope, Brooklyn 11215, 718/499–6115, please call only between 8 AM and 10 PM. 8 rooms. AE, D, DC, MC, V. Subway: Q to 7th Ave. Budget.*

2 *h-3*

LE REFUGE INN BED & BREAKFAST

This small inn is a perfect retreat for New Yorkers who wish to check out of city life for a night or two and enjoy the surroundings of a lovely old fishing area up by Pelham Bay Park in the Bronx. Le Refuge is warm, romantic, and, styled after a 19th-century French country inn, is replete with antiques, not technology. The two suites have private bathrooms and phones, but the six doubles have shared bathrooms and no phones. All rooms have cable television, and some have CD players; there are chamber music concerts on Sunday afternoons. *620 City Island Ave., City Island, The Bronx 10464, 718/885–2478, fax 718/885–1519, www.cityisland.com/lerefuge. 7 rooms, 2 suites. AE. Subway: 6 to Pelham Bay Park, bus #29 to City Island. Budget.*

12 *c-2*

NEW YORK MARRIOTT BROOKLYN

Built in 1998, this is the first full-service hotel to open in Brooklyn in 50 years. The surroundings are standard Marriott—pink and green carpets, fitness center, a small business center, rooms with two-line phones, data ports, and voicemail, and such amenities as complimentary breakfast on the concierge level. The location is excellent: the landmark Gage & Tollner restaurant and the Brooklyn Academy of Music are nearby, as are such pleasant residential enclaves as Brooklyn Heights, Cobble Hill, Carroll Gardens, and Boerum Hill. *333 Adams St. (between Tillary and Willoughby Sts., Brooklyn Heights, Brooklyn 11201, 718/246–7000 or 888/436–3759, fax 718/246–0563, www.marriotthotels.org. 355 rooms, 21 suites. AE, D, DC, MC, V. Subway: 1, 2, 4, 5 to Borough Hall. Moderately priced.*

HOTELS NEAR THE AIRPORTS

3 *f-1*

LA GUARDIA MARRIOTT AIRPORT HOTEL

A quarter-mile from the airport and—barring traffic—about 20 minutes from Manhattan, this hotel is out of the direct line of most flights. Aside from the typical Marriott ambience, there are business amenities and a free airport shuttle. *102–05 Ditmars Blvd., East Elmhurst, Queens 11369, 718/565–8900 or 800/882–1043, fax 718/899–0764, www.marriott.com. 432 rooms, 4 suites. Restaurant, sports bar, in-room data ports, room service, indoor pool, health club, airport*

shuttle, parking (fee). AE, D, DC, MC, V. Moderately priced.

1 *h-5*

HOLIDAY INN J.F.K. AIRPORT

While the decor is typical of a big chain, the atmosphere here is strangely serene. The sound-proofed rooms are indeed quiet, there's a Japanese garden, and the swimming pool is beneath a roof that retracts in warm weather. Room service will bring you ice cream while you enjoy an in-room movie. The free airport shuttle to JFK runs every half hour; three morning shuttles go to La Guardia. *144–02 135th Ave., Jamaica, Queens 11436, 718/659–0200 or 800/692–5350, fax 718/322–5769 or 718/322–2533, www.holidayinnjfk.com. 349 rooms, 11 suites. Restaurant, bar, in-room data ports, multi-line phones, room service, swimming pool, health club, sauna, business center, meeting room, laundry and dry cleaning, airport shuttle, parking (fee). AE, D, DC, MC, V. Moderately priced.*

1 *b-7*

NEWARK AIRPORT MARRIOTT

The Marriott is right on the airport premises and provides free 24-hour shuttle service to all terminals, as well as free parking. In light traffic the trip to Manhattan takes only 30 minutes. *Newark International Airport, Newark, NJ 07114, 201/623–0006 or 800/228–9290, fax 201/623–7618, www.marriotthotels.com/ewrap. 584 rooms, 6 suites. 2 restaurants, bar, room service, indoor-outdoor pool, health club, airport shuttle, free parking. AE, D, DC, MC, V. Moderately priced.*

B&B RESERVATION SERVICES

If you're looking to put someone up in your neighborhood at a reasonable cost, try one of the hundreds of bed-and-breakfasts that have opened throughout the city. A few of the higher-end B&Bs are independent and booked directly (they are listed above as regular hotels). You often pay less than $100 a night, the accommodations, amenities, service, and privacy may fall short of what you get in hotels, and, despite the B&B name, you often don't get breakfast. Even so, a clean room and bath at such a low price constitutes quite a bargain in New York. To make sure you'll be comfortable with your choice, ask your B&B reservation agency for the details on your property before checking in.

B&Bs booked through a service may be either hosted (you're the guest in someone's quarters) or unhosted (you have full use of someone's vacated apartment, including kitchen privileges). Most B&B services represent both kinds. Services charge no fees, but often require a 25 percent deposit. Make reservations as far in advance as possible; refunds (minus a $25 service charge) are possible up to 10 days before arrival.

A Hospitality Company *247 W. 35th St., New York, NY 10001, 800/987–1235 or 212/965–1102, fax 212/965–1149.*

All Around the Town *150 5th Ave., Suite 711, New York, NY 10011, 212/675–5600 or 800/443–3800, fax 212/675–6366.*

Bed-and-Breakfast (and Books) *35 W. 92nd St., Apt. 2C, New York, NY 10025, tel./fax 212/865–8740, please call only weekdays 10 AM–5 PM.*

Bed-and-Breakfast in Manhattan *Box 533, New York, NY 10150, 212/472–2528, fax 212/988–9818.*

Bed-and-Breakfast Network of New York *134 W. 32nd St., Suite 602, New York, NY 10001, 212/645–8134 or 800/ 900–8134.*

City Lights Bed-and-Breakfast *Box 20355, Cherokee Station, New York, NY 10021, 212/737–7049, fax 212/535–2755.*

Manhattan Home Stays *Box 20684, Cherokee Station, New York, NY 10021, 212/737–3868, fax 212/265–3561.*

New World Bed and Breakfast *150 5th Ave., Suite 711, New York, NY 10011, 212/ 675–5600; 800/443–3800 in the U.S., fax 212/675–6366.*

New York Habitat *307 7th Ave., Suite 306, New York, NY 10001, 212/647–9365, fax 212/627–1416.*

Urban Ventures *38 W. 32nd St., Suite 1412, New York, NY 10001, 212/594–5650, fax 212/947–9320.*

West Village Reservations *Village Station, Box 347, New York, NY 10014-0347, 212/614–3034, fax 425/920–2384.*

chapter 7

CITY SOURCES

getting a handle on the city

basics of city life

BANKS

Commercial banks are generally open weekdays from 9 AM to 3:30 PM and closed weekends and holidays. A few savings institutions are also open Friday evening and Saturday morning.

Amalgamated Bank of New York (212/255–6200).

Apple Savings Bank (800/722–6888; www.theapplebank.com).

Astoria Federal Savings & Loan (800/278–6742; www.astoriafederal.com).

Bank of New York (212/495–1784; www.bankofny.com).

Chase Manhattan (212/935–9935; www.chase.com).

Citibank (212/627–3999; www.citibank.com).

Dime Savings Bank (718/428–1803; www.dime.com).

EAB (212/557–3700; www.eab.com).

Greenpoint Savings Bank (212/935–9919; www.greenpoint.com).

HSBC (800/975–4722; www.us.hsbc.com).

DRIVING

Because owning, driving, and parking your own car is such a hassle here, most New Yorkers relish the role of perpetual passenger. In fact, only in New York City is it *not* a shameful thing to not know how to drive. (Just over 3 million New Yorkers have a license.) Go with the masses on this one—save your driver's license for weekend duty, and line up with fellow city dwellers at rental car agencies on Friday afternoon to escape the city. If you want to pony up the money and years off your life to own and drive a car here, you'll have little sympathy from others when complaining about the exorbitant cost of storage or dearth of streetside parking spots. Drivers in NYC are required to observe a 30 mph (48 kph) speed limit, and make no right turns at red lights unless a sign is posted permitting it.

licenses & registration

It turns out that the folks at the DMV don't want to see you any more than you want to see them. Clear and detailed instructions about how to get and renew a New York State license, the driver's test manual, and forms for car and plates registration hover in cyberspace on the DMV Web site (www.nydmv.state.ny.us), so you won't have to wait in line unnecessarily. And, if you have a New York State driver's license or ID, and your address hasn't changed, you can renew your vehicle registration online.

To register your car and get plates for the first time, you can download the MV-82: Vehicle Registration/Title Application forms in advance from the DMV Web site, but you must go in person with the following: proof of ownership; an original New York State Insurance Identification Card (FS-20), in the same name as the registration application; acceptable proof of identity and age; proof of sales tax payment or purchase price; and your checkbook. Registration is good for two years, and fees are determined by the weight of your vehicle ($29.50–$112), plus you'll pay a plate fee ($5.50), title fee ($5), and a passenger-vehicle-use tax ($30).

Residents who have kept the same address can renew their driver's license by mail. You will need to download and fill out a MV-44 License Application Form, and a Visual Acuity Report (MV-619). Furthermore, you will be required to pay a fee of $43 for a class D license (valid for eight years).

To get a new license or renew an old New York State license with changes, you'll have to pay a visit to one of the DMV offices. You'll need a valid license from another state (which you must surrender in exchange for your New York State one) or at least two pieces of valid ID, one specifying your date of birth, and another with your signature—assuming, that is, that you're at least 16 years old, with decent eyesight and a Social Security number. Some types of ID are not acceptable, so make sure your ID is one they'll recognize before you go. It's $44 for a new passenger-car license if you're exactly 16, and varying rates ($38.50–$44.50) if you aren't. (New licenses are valid for five years.)

DEPARTMENT OF MOTOR VEHICLES

Just like snowflakes, no two DMV offices are alike. Each has its own hours of operation, so do some research before setting out. Even the centralized phone number, the DMV Call Center, has its own hours of operation. If you want custom plates, you can call direct, seven days a week, and get a friendly, helpful person to take your order.

Custom Plates (Daily; 800/364–7528).

DMV Albany To renew or replace your license by mail (regular mail: License Production Bureau, Box 2688, ESP, Albany, NY 12220-0668; express-mail service: NYS DMV License Production Bureau, Room 223, 6 Empire State Plaza, Albany, NY 12228).

DMV Call Center Information about DMVs in the five boroughs (Open Mon.–Wed., Fri. 8–4:30; Thurs. 8–5:30; 212/645-5550 or 718/966–6155; www. nysdmv.com).

Harlem Office–NYSDMV (Mon.–Wed., Fri. 8:30–4; Thurs. 10–6; 2110 Adam Clayton Powell, Jr. Blvd., 10027).

Herald Square Office (Weekdays 8:30–4; 1293–1311 Broadway, 8th floor, 10001).

Manhattan License X-Press Office Only handles license and registration renewals and duplicates, and surrendered license plates (Mon.–Wed. 8–5:30, Thurs. 8–7; closed Fri.; 300 W. 34th St., 10001).

New York Office–NYSDMV (Weekdays 8:30–4; 11 Greenwich St., 10004).

TOLLS

Tolls are expensive in New York City, and it is impossible to cross the Hudson River from New Jersey without paying one. Getting across the East River from the Bronx and Manhattan to Queens and Brooklyn is a different story—the Queensboro Bridge, Williamsburg Bridge, Brooklyn Bridge, and Manhattan Bridge are all free—at least as of this writing.

E-ZPass One way to ease your bridge and tunnel woes is to register for this device, which automatically pays your toll as you breeze through the gate (you can pay in advance by credit card, or receive a monthly bill). It will undoubtedly save you time, and there is a small reduction in the fare. To order, call the 24-hour E-ZPass Service Center or check

the Web site (800/333–8655; www. e-zpassny.com).

The toll for cars is $3.50 each way for the Triborough Bridge, Verrazano-Narrows Bridge, Throgs Neck Bridge, Queens Midtown Tunnel, and Brooklyn-Battery Tunnel. That fare is reduced to $3 for E-ZPass holders.

For the George Washington Bridge, Lincoln Tunnel, and Holland Tunnel, the regular fare for cars is $6 (charged going from New Jersey to New York only). The fare is reduced to $4–$5 for E-ZPass holders.

TRAFFIC

It's always rush hour in New York. Just assume there's traffic wherever you're headed, particularly if it's over a bridge or through a tunnel into Manhattan in the morning or out of Manhattan in the afternoon. Leave it to the professionals with helicopters to tell you where there isn't any traffic and tune in to a radio station that has frequent traffic reports.

Following the World Trade Center disaster, access to lower Manhattan below Canal Street and east of Broadway is expected to be limited for the foreseeable future.

GAS STATIONS

Gas stations are most plentiful in west SoHo, on East Houston Street, and toward the island's outer rims, particularly in Hell's Kitchen and at various points on the West Side Highway. They're easy to stumble upon in the other four boroughs.

downtown

Amoco (Broadway at Houston St., Greenwich Village, 212/473–5924).

Gulf (FDR Dr. at 23rd St., Gramercy, 212/686–4546).

Mobil (E. Broadway at Pike St., Lower East Side, 212/966–0571; 6th Ave. at Spring St., SoHo, 212/925–6126).

uptown

Merit (7th Ave. at 145th St., Harlem, 212/283–9354).

Mobil (11th Ave. at 51st St., Midtown West, 212/582–9269).

Shell (Amsterdam Ave. at 181st St., Washington Heights, 212/928–3100).

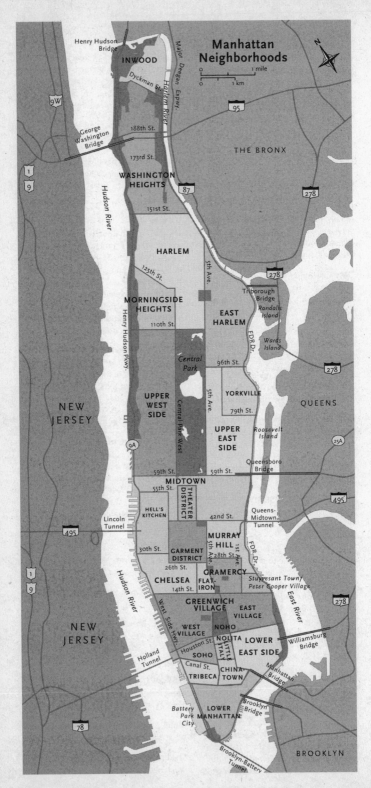

Manhattan
Neighborhoods

1 mile

1 km

Henry Hudson
Bridge

INWOOD

Dyckman St.

9W

George
Washington
Bridge

188th St.

173rd St.

WASHINGTON
HEIGHTS

151st St.

HARLEM

125th St.

MORNINGSIDE
HEIGHTS

110th St.

UPPER WEST
SIDE

Central
Park

Hudson River

Henry Hudson Pkwy.

NEW
JERSEY

9A

59th St.

MIDTOWN

55th St.

THEATER
DISTRICT

HELL'S
KITCHEN

Lincoln
Tunnel

495

30th St.

26th St.

GARMENT
DISTRICT

CHELSEA

14th St.

Hudson River

West Side Hwy.

GREENWICH
VILLAGE

WEST
VILLAGE

Holland
Tunnel

Houston St.

SOHO

Canal St.

TRIBECA

NEW
JERSEY

1
9

78

Battery
Park
City

Brooklyn-Battery
Tunnel

THE BRONX

Major Deegan Expwy.

Harlem River

95

87

278

Triborough
Bridge

Randalls
Island

EAST
HARLEM

5th Ave.

Wards
Island

FDR Dr.

96th St.

YORKVILLE

79th St.

UPPER
EAST
SIDE

5th Ave.

Roosevelt
Island

278

QUEENS

25A

Queensboro
Bridge

59th St.

42nd St.

Queens-
Midtown
Tunnel

495

MURRAY
HILL

28th St.

5th Ave.

1st Ave.

GRAMERCY

FLAT-
IRON

Stuyvesant Town
Peter Cooper Village

EAST
VILLAGE

NOHO

NOLITA

LOWER

LITTLE
ITALY

EAST SIDE

Williamsburg
Bridge

East River

278

CHINA
TOWN

Manhattan
Bridge

LOWER
MANHATTAN

Brooklyn
Bridge

BROOKLYN

GEOGRAPHY

New York City's five boroughs—the
Bronx, Brooklyn, Manhattan, Queens,
and Staten Island—are linked by a
series of bridges, tunnels, and ferries.
Most of Manhattan is laid out on a
grid, which makes getting around fairly
easy. Avenues run north and south,
with Fifth Avenue dividing the east and
west sides—the lower the house
address on a street, whether it's east or
west, the closer it is to Fifth Avenue.
Broadway, a former wagon trail, is the
grand exception to the rule—it cuts
diagonally through Manhattan from the
Upper West Side to Lower Manhattan
and the financial district. As it inter-
sects other avenues on its way, Broadway creates Columbus Circle (at 59th
St.), Times Square (at 42nd St.), Herald Square (at 34th St.), Madison
Square (at 23rd St.), and Union Square
(at 14th St.). Streets in Manhattan run
east and west and ascend in numerical
order going north. For the most part,
traffic is one-way going east on even-
number streets, one-way going west on
odd-number streets.

Most of Manhattan's downtown areas—
those below 14th Street on the west and
1st Street on the east—were settled
before the grid system and follow no
particular pattern. These are among the
city's oldest districts and include Greenwich Village, SoHo, TriBeCa, Chinatown,
and the financial district.

HOLIDAYS

New York's banks, post offices, schools,
offices, and most businesses close on
these days.

New Year's Day (January 1).

Martin Luther King Day (3rd Monday
in January).

Presidents' Day (3rd Monday in
February).

Memorial Day (last Monday in May).

Independence Day (July 4th).

Labor Day (1st Monday in September).

Columbus Day (2nd Monday in October).

Election Day (1st Tuesday in November).

Veterans' Day (November 11th).

Thanksgiving (4th Thursday in
November).

Christmas (December 25th).

ESSENTIAL NUMBERS

*These hot lines will help you make the
most of your free time.*

Central Park Information Line
*Recorded information covering all
park sites, as well as sports and
recreation programs and specials
events (212/360–3444, www.central-
parknyc.org).*

Citywide Special Events
*A recorded listing of upcoming events
on city properties (888/NY–PARKS).*

Department of Parks and Recreation
*There is a staffed hot line for infor-
mation and emergencies (800/201–
PARK). For details on specific parks
and for Parks Department headquarters in individual boroughs, see
Parks in Chapter 3.*

Film
212 or 718/777–FILM.

Greenmarket Information
*Market dates for the city's 26 loca-
tions (212/477–3220,
www.cenyc.org).*

Jazz
212/866–4900.

Library Branch Information
212/340–0849, www.nypl.org.

Sportsphone
*For scores and statistics (212/976–
1313 or 212/976–2525; charge
applies).*

Theater
*For details on this hot line—New
York City Onstage—see Tickets in
Chapter 5 (212/768–1818).*

Ticketron
*For schedules and ticket information
(212/307–7171).*

TKTS Booths Information
*For information on discount tickets
available for a number of Broadway
and Off-Broadway performances
(same-day purchases only) (212/
768–1818).*

Weather Channel Connection
*95¢ per minute from a touch-tone
phone (900/932–8437).*

Avenue Address Finder

Streets	West End Ave.	Broadway	Amsterdam Ave.	Columbus Ave.	Central Park West		
94–96	700-737	2520–2554	702–733	701–740	350–360		
92–94	660–699	2476–2519	656–701	661–700	322–336		
90–92	620–659	2440–2475	620–655	621–660	300–320		
88–90	578–619	2401–2439	580–619	581–620	279–295		
86–88	540–577	2361–2400	540–579	541–580	262–275		
84–86	500–539	2321–2360	500–539	501–540	241–257		
82–84	460–499	2281–2320	460–499	461–500	212–239		Central Park
80–82	420–459	2241–2280	420–459	421–460	211		
78–80	380–419	2201–2240	380–419	381–420	American Museum of Natural History		
76–78	340–379	2161–2200	340–379	341–380			
74–76	300–339	2121–2160	300–339	301–340	145–160		
72–74	262–299	2081–2114	261–299	261–300	121–135		
70–72	221–261	2040–2079	221–260	221–260	101–115		
68–70	176–220	1999–2030	181–220	181–220	80–99		
66–68	122–175	1961–1998	140–180	141–180	65–79		
64–66	74–121	1920–1960	100–139	101–140	50–55		
62–64	44–73	Lincoln Center	60–99	61–100	25–33		
60–62	20–43	1841–1880	20–59	21–60	15		
58–60	2–19	Columbus Circle	1–19	2–20	Columbus Circle		

	11th Ave.	Broadway	10th Ave.	9th Ave.	8th Ave.	7th Ave.	6th Ave.
56–58	823–854	1752–1791	852–889	864–907	946–992	888–921	1381–1419
54–56	775–822	1710–1751	812–851	824–863	908–945	842–887	1341–1377
52–54	741–774	1674–1709	772–811	782–823	870–907	798–841	1301–1330
50–52	701–740	1634–1673	737–770	742–781	830–869	761–797	1261–1297
48–50	665–700	1596–1633	686–735	702–741	791–829	720–760	1221–1260
46–48	625–664	1551–1595	654–685	662–701	735–790	701–719	1180–1217
44–46	589–624	1514–1550	614–653	622–661	701–734	Times Square	1141–1178
42–44	553–588	1472–1513	576–613	582–621	661–700		1100–1140
40–42	503–552	1440–1471	538–575	Port Authority	620–660	560–598	1061–1097
38–40	480–502	1400–1439	502–537		570–619	522–559	1020–1060
36–38	431–471	1352–1399	466–501	468–501	520–569	482–521	981–1019
34–36	405–430	Macy's	430–465	432–467	480–519	442–481	Herald Square
32–34	360–404	1260–1282	380–429	412–431	442–479	Penn Station	
30–32	319–359	1220–1279	341–379	Post Office	403–441	362–399	855–892
28–30	282–318	1178–1219	314–340	314–351	362–402	322–361	815–844
26–28	242–281	1135–1177	288–313	262–313	321–361	282–321	775–814
24–26	202–241	1100–1134	239–287	230–261	281–320	244–281	733–774
22–24	162–201	940–1099	210–238	198–229	236–280	210–243	696–732
20–22	120–161	902–939	162–209	167–197	198–235	170–209	656–695
18–20	82–119	873–901	130–161	128–166	162–197	134–169	613–655
16–18	54–81	860–872	92–129	92–127	126–161	100–133	574–612
14–16	26–53	Union Square	58–91	91–44	80–125	64–99	573–530

Crosstown Street Address Finder

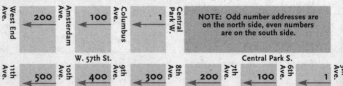

5th Ave.	Madison Ave.	Park Ave.	Lexington Ave.	3rd Ave.	2nd Ave.	1st Ave.	Streets
1130–1148	1340–1379	1199–1236	1449–1486	1678–1709	1817–1868	1817–1855	94–96
1109–1125	1295–1335	1160–1192	1400–1444	1644–1677	1766–1808	1780–1811	92–94
1090–1107	1254–1294	1120–1155	1361–1396	1601–1643	1736–1763	1740–1779	90–92
1070–1089	1220–1250	1080–1114	1311–1355	1568–1602	1700–1739	1701–1735	88–90
1050–1069	1178–1221	1044–1076	1280–1301	1530–1566	1660–1698	1652–1689	86–88
1030–1048	1130–1171	1000–1035	1248–1278	1490–1529	1624–1659	1618–1651	84–86
1010–1028	1090–1128	960–993	1210–1248	1450–1489	1584–1623	1578–1617	82–84
990–1009	1058–1088	916–959	1164–1209	1410–1449	1538–1583	1540–1577	80–82
970–989	1012–1046	878–911	1120–1161	1374–1409	1498–1537	1495–1539	78–80
950–969	974–1006	840–877	1080–1116	1330–1373	1456–1497	1462–1494	76–78
930–947	940–970	799–830	1036–1071	1290–1329	1420–1454	1429–1460	74–76
910–929	896–939	760–791	1004–1032	1250–1289	1389–1417	1344–1384	72–74
895–907	856–872	720–755	962–993	1210–1249	1328–1363	1306–1343	70–72
870–885	813–850	680–715	926–961	1166–1208	1296–1327	1266–1300	68–70
850–860	772–811	640–679	900–922	1130–1165	1260–1295	1222–1260	66–68
830–849	733–771	600–639	841–886	1084–1129	1222–1259	1168–1221	64–66
810–828	690–727	560–599	803–842	1050–1083	1180–1221	1130–1167	62–64
790–807	654–680	520–559	770–802	1010–1049	1140–1197	1102–1129	60–62
755–789	621–649	476–519	722–759	972–1009	Queensborough Bridge		58–60
720–754	572–611	434–475	677–721	942–968	1066–1101	1026–1063	56–58
680–719	532–568	408–430	636–665	894–933	1028–1062	985–1021	54–56
656–679	500–531	360–399	596–629	856–893	984–1027	945–984	52–54
626–655	452–488	320–350	556–593	818–855	944–983	889–944	50–52
600–625	412–444	280–300	518–555	776–817	902–943	860–888	48–50
562–599	377–400	240–277	476–515	741–775	862–891	827	46–48
530–561	346–375	Met Life (200)	441–475	702–735	824–860	785	44–46
500–529	316–345	Grand	395–435	660–701	793–823	United Nations	42–44
460–499	284–315	Central	354–394	622–659	746–773	Tudor City	40–42
424–459	250–283	68–99	314–353	578–621	707–747	666–701	38–40
392–423	218–249	40–67	284–311	542–577	666–700	Midtown Tunnel	36–38
352–391	188–217	5–35	240–283	508–541	622–659	599–626	34–36
320–351	152–184	1–4	196–239	470–507	585–621	556–598	32–34
284–319	118–150	444–470	160–195	432–469	543–581	Kips Bay	30–32
250–283	79–117	404–431	120–159	394–431	500–541	NYU Hosp.	28–30
213–249	50–78	364–403	81–119	358–393	462–499	446–478	26–28
201–212	11–37	323–361	40–77	321–355	422–461	411–445	24–26
172–200	1–7	286–322	9–39	282–318	382–421	390–410	22–24
154–170		251–285	1–8	244–281	344–381	315–389	20–22
109–153		221–250	70–78	206–243	310–343	310–314	18–20
85–127		184–220	40–69	166–205	301–309	280–309	16–18
69–108		Union Square	2–30	126–165	230–240	240–279	14–16

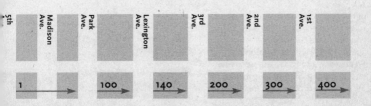

5th	Madison Ave.	Park Ave.	Lexington Ave.	3rd Ave.	2nd Ave.	1st Ave.
1		100	140	200	300	400

LIQUOR LAWS

You must be 21 years old to purchase alcohol in New York State. Your proof of age is a government-issued photo ID, such as a driver's license or a passport. Most restaurants have a liquor license, but smaller places—many of the Indian restaurants in the East Village, for example—allow diners to bring their own beer. Some BYOB restaurants charge a corkage fee when diners bring their own wine.

Wine and liquor stores cannot sell beer, and they are required to be closed on Sundays. Beer is regularly sold at bodegas, delis, specialty distributors, and supermarkets.

NO SMOKING

In 1988, New York City passed one of the toughest antismoking laws in the country: It is illegal to puff in hotel lobbies, banks, public rest rooms, and taxis and at playgrounds, sports stadiums, and race tracks. Smoking has also been restricted in restaurants seating more than 35 people, in retail stores, and in schools. There has even been talk of eliminating smoking in NYC restaurants altogether.

PARKING

rules & enforcement

Street parking in Manhattan, if you can find it, is subject to a variety of restrictions. Metered street parking lasts from 20 minutes to an hour. Be sure to read all of the signs carefully, since to understand New York's parking rules you have to be a genius; and once you do figure them out, you'll still have to move your car periodically to allow for street cleaning. There is no "grace period" for an expired or absent parking permit. And unless it's one of the city's 30 legal or religious holidays, strict alternate-side-of-the-street rules are probably in effect; call 718/ or 212/225–5368 or listen to a news radio station in the morning.

Simply put, alternate-side-of-the-street rules are in a class of their own. Signs typically read "No Parking 8 AM–11 AM Tuesday and Thursday or Monday, Wednesday, and Friday": these are for street cleaning. Signs that restrict parking for a longer period of time, for instance from 8 AM–6 PM, are to improve traffic flow and are still in effect when alternate-side-of-the-street rules are suspended. Got it?

If you stray from the rules, your car may be ticketed, vandalized with a fluorescent sticker that never entirely scrapes off, locked in place with a "boot," or towed away (if illegally parked); all can be expensive and a tremendous hassle.

Parking Violations Operations Pay your tickets by phone (credit card only) or mail; include your plate number, state of registration, and the ticket number(s) on the front of your payment. There is a $3 service charge for each violation paid by mail. (PVO, New York City Department of Finance, Box 2127, Peck Slip Station, New York, NY 10272-2127, 877/ 769–2729).

Towed Vehicle Information Want to know where your car is and how much money you'll have to shell out to get it back? (212/869–2929, 718/422–7800, or 212/971–0770).

parking lots

There are hundreds of private parking facilities in Manhattan, with costs varying by location, day, and time. Be sure to check the closing time, or you might lose your car for the night. Read the fine print on the price list, too; taxes and "special" conditions can make parking even more expensive than you expect. Even better, fix a price with the attendant before you park. These short-term parking facilities have long hours and reasonable prices:

DOWNTOWN
756 Parking Corp. (756 Washington St.).

MIDTOWN
Edison Park Fast (1120 Ave. of the Americas; entrances on 43rd and 44th Sts.).

Rapid 63 Street Corp. (411 W. 55th St.).

Real Pro Parking Corp. (330 E. 39th St.).

River Edge Sutton Garden Garage (425 E. 54th St.).

UPPER EAST SIDE
GMC (Garage Management Corporation) (177 E. 73rd St.).

Waterview (10 East End Ave.).

UPPER WEST SIDE
Central Parking System (50 W. 93rd St.).

Edison Park Fast (214 W. 80th St.).

PERSONAL SECURITY

In the wake of the World Trade Center disaster, New Yorkers have become more aware of their surroundings and the potential for terrorism within the city. With that in mind, be certain never to leave any of your bags unattended, and immediately report any suspicious packages or other items. Furthermore, expect to have your person and your possessions inspected much more thoroughly in places like government buildings, office buildings, airports, sports stadiums, museums, and tourist sites.

On a separate note, New York has enjoyed a reduction in violent crime of late, but of course it's always better to travel with a companion late at night, and to know where you are and where you're going. It may be even more important to *look* like you know where you are and where you're going. Secure your wallet or purse—wallets are better off in a front pocket than a back pocket. Don't flaunt cash or jewelry. On a crowded subway or bus and in restaurants, keep your bag zipped and in front of you, where you can see it.

PUBLIC TRANSPORTATION

New York's mass-transit system is extensive and efficient. Subways offer speed and economy, but minimal comfort and capricious schedules. Buses offer a view in exchange for a slower pace. Taxis can be expensive in rush-hour traffic jams and elusive during rainstorms, but a blessing when your feet hurt, or when you've got too many parcels. All cabs are required to have air-conditioning, and you have the right to ask the driver to turn it on (same thing goes with heat in the winter).

Information, including bus and train detours, and directions to any destination by subway or bus are available 24 hours daily from the **Travel Information Bureau** (718/330–1234), a courteous, knowledgeable bunch. The bureau staffs booths at Grand Central Terminal weekdays 8–8 and weekends 9–5, and at 370 Jay St. (downstairs lobby), Brooklyn Heights, weekdays 9–5.

metrocard

Though some nostalgia buffs lamented the demise of the token, the MetroCard has quickly become as ubiquitous to New York as the bagel. Available in stores, newsstands, and at in-station booths and vending machines, the MetroCard also answers a New York transit prayer with discounts for frequent riders. Regular riders are divided into two MetroCard camps: those who go with the unlimited ride card and those who choose pay-per-ride.

With the 7-day or 30-day unlimited-ride MetroCard, you get unlimited rides for a fixed price of $17 and $63, respectively. (A 30-day Express Bus Plus pass gives you unlimited rides on express buses, local buses, and subways for $120.) If you ride more than 12 times a week, but can't shell out the big bucks for the 30-day card (or fear you might lose it), the 7-day MetroCard is the one to get.

With pay-per-ride cards, you get 11 rides for the price of 10 if you put $15 on your MetroCard. Invest $30, and you'll get two free rides, and so on; and the system prorates cents toward your next free ride if you put an odd amount on your card—as long as the amount is over $15. If you have visitors, you might want to get them a Fun Pass ($4), good for unlimited travel from the day of purchase through 3 AM the following day—oddly, it's sold in stores, at newsstands, and underground vending machines, but not in station booths.

The MetroCard discounts and free bus-to-subway and subway-to-bus transfers (good for two hours) have caused the near extinction of the beloved token. In fact, many new MetroCard turnstiles at unstaffed station entrances no longer accept tokens, leaving would-be passengers in the lurch. The MTA's remedy has been to add MetroCard vending machines at most stations.

bus

Bus fare is $1.50. Reduced fare for senior citizens and travelers with disabilities is 75¢, except during rush hour, when the full fare applies. You need exact change, a subway token, or a MetroCard to ride the bus—no bills, pennies, or Susan B. Anthony or Sacagawea dollars. Bus stops are marked with signs showing the route numbers of buses that stop there, approximate schedules, and route maps. North–south (uptown–downtown) buses usually stop every two to three blocks; east–west (crosstown) buses usually stop on every block. Many bus stops have glass-enclosed shelters. Route maps for the bus system are available at most subway stations or (sometimes) from bus drivers.

Board and deposit your fare (or insert your card) in the machine at the front of the bus; exit in the rear. Smoking is not allowed, nor are animals, with the exception of pets in carrying cases and seeing-eye dogs. Most buses run 24 hours daily, though less frequently during off-peak hours and days.

If you don't have a MetroCard but want to transfer from an uptown or downtown bus to a crosstown bus, or vice versa, ask the driver for a transfer slip upon boarding; they're still free.

COMMUTER BUSES
MTA Long Island Bus (516/766–6722; www.mnr.org/libus).

George Washington Bridge Bus Terminal (Broadway at 178th St., Washington Heights, 212/564–1114).

LONG-DISTANCE BUSES
Adirondack, Pine Hill, and New York Trailways Service in New York State (800/858–8555).

Bonanza Bus Lines Service to Connecticut, Massachusetts, Rhode Island (800/556–3815).

Capital Trailways Service to Pennsylvania (800/333–8444).

Greyhound United States and Canada (800/229–9424, www.greyhound.com).

New Jersey Transit (NJTransit) (973/762–5100, www.njtransit.com).

Peter Pan Trailways Serving northeast United States (800/343–9999).

Port Authority Bus Terminal The NYC hub for long-distance bus travel (42nd St. and 8th Ave., Midtown West, 212/564–8484, www.panynj.gov).

car services
Outside of Manhattan, it can often be difficult to find a yellow cab. A popular alternative is a car service. It is not legal for car services to pick up riders on the street (although they sometimes will), and you can never be perfectly sure whose car you are getting into. To be on the safe side, call to order a car, either for immediate pick-up or to request a specific date and time. Prices vary depending on the length of the trip. *See* Car and Limousine Services *in* Vacation & Travel Information, *below.*

ferry
There is, in fact, such a thing as a free ride. The **Staten Island Ferry's** 50¢ fare was abolished in July 1997. The ride from South Street Seaport to Staten Island has wonderful views of the Statue of Liberty and Ellis Island, not to mention Manhattan. Did we mention it's free? Call 718/815–2628 for schedules.

NY Waterways provides ferry service from points in New Jersey, including Hoboken and Jersey City, to midtown and the financial district, and can be a pleasant alternative to rush-hour PATH trains. Call 800/53-FERRY for schedules or visit www.nywaterway.com.

subway
Subway fare is $1.50. Reduced fare for senior citizens and travelers with disabilities is 75¢, except during rush hour, when the full fare applies. (For a reduced-fare application, call 718/243–4999.) You need a MetroCard or token to access the subway platform. If you'll be riding the subway often, buy a MetroCard to save time and money. Free subway maps and information are available at every subway booth.

Smoking is not allowed in either stations or trains, and incorrigible smokers, like turnstile-hoppers, will most likely be fined by the sometimes plain-clothes transit police. Animals are not allowed on trains, with the exceptions of pets in carrying cases and seeing-eye dogs. The MTA's public service signs also ask riders to refrain from leaving newspapers behind, putting your bag on the seat beside you, and eating and drinking in stations and on trains.

The subways run 24 hours daily, though schedules are reduced during off-peak hours and days, and routes can be scrambled at night when maintenance and construction takes place. In the event of a stalled train or other unpleasant service interruption brought to your attention by an inco-herent MTA announcement, you should always be aware of alternate subway lines or bus routes that will get you to your destination. Or, you can call the **MTA Service Status Hotline** (718/243–7777) for information on subway lines that are slow or stopped due to an "incident" of some kind.

Following the World Trade Center disas-ter, service to the 1 and 9 subway lines at the Chambers Street, Cortlandt Street, Rector Street, and South Ferry stations was lost indefinitely—at this writing the MTA had awarded a contract for recon-struction of the 1 and 9 lines and was projecting completion of the project in late 2002. The 3 train makes its normal stops to 14th Street, where it terminates. The 1 train makes all normal stops to Chambers Street. Thereafter, it runs on the express track, taking the place of the 3 to New Lots Avenue in Brooklyn. The MTA's Web site (www.mta.nyc.ny.us) has constant updates on all service interrup-tions and changes.

To make things even more confusing, ongoing repairs to the Manhattan Bridge will impact the B, D, and Q lines well into 2004. In brief, the B and D trains run in two separate sections—between Brooklyn and Manhattan, and between the Bronx and Manhattan, with transfers available between the two sec-tions at 34th Street–Herald Square. And going from Manhattan to Brooklyn, the B is now the temporary W train, the D has become the Q Local (denoted by a Q in a circle), and the Q is now the Q Express (denoted by a Q in a diamond). Got all that?

taxi

Taxicabs are readily available in Manhat-tan except when it rains. Simply walk to the curb (ideally at a street corner) and extend your arm when you see a cab that's available. Licensed taxis are always yellow. You can tell if a cab is available by checking its rooftop light; if the center panel is lit and the side pan-els dark, the cab is available. It takes a trained eye to spot an available cab from a distance. That said, if others are wait-ing to hail a cab on your block, no mat-ter how incompetent they appear, it's polite to let them do so before you—going a smidgen upstream to get one is considered an unscrupulous tactic.

Base fare for a cab ride is $2, then 30¢ for each additional ⅕ of a mi and 20¢ for every 90 seconds in stopped or slow traffic. Pay only what's on the meter (there is a 50¢ surcharge from 8 PM to 6 AM), plus a 15%–20% gratuity. Make sure the driver remembers to start the meter. According to the rules, drivers must take you anywhere you want to go within the five boroughs, Nassau or Westchester counties, or Newark Inter-national Airport, though in practice you may find drivers who aren't interested in leaving Manhattan (or who need direc-tions when doing so).

If you have a preferred route to your destination, don't hesitate to tell your driver. They are required (but some-times reluctant) to follow your specified route. Taxi drivers must also travel in the most direct way possible, but some-times another route might be better if there are traffic or construction delays. Ask your driver if you are unsure.

For more information or to report a problem, call the **New York City Taxi and Limousine Commission** (212/221–8294, www.nyc.gov/taxi).

rail

Trains leave the city from **Grand Central Station** (Lexington Ave. at 42nd St.) and **Pennsylvania (Penn) Station** (33rd St. at 7th Ave.).

COMMUTER

Long Island Rail Road (LIRR) departs from Penn Station; Atlantic Avenue, Brooklyn; and Jamaica, Queens (718/217–5477, www.lirr.org).

Metro-North trains for service to lower New York State and Connecticut leave from Grand Central Station (212/532–4900; 800/638–7646 outside New York City, www.mnr.org).

New Jersey Transit (NJTransit), Penn Station (973/762–5100 or 800/626–7433, www.njtransit.com).

PATH serves New Jersey from various points in Manhattan, including 33rd, 23rd, 14th, and 9th streets at 6th Avenue. As a result of the World Trade Center dis-aster, there is currently no PATH train service to the WTC PATH station. Cus-tomers traveling to lower Manhattan from New Jersey are encouraged to take the PATH train to 33rd Street and switch to subway service traveling downtown.

There is also a ferry service available from Hoboken in New Jersey to Pier 11 near the South Street Seaport in Manhattan. (800/234–7284, www.pathrail.com.)

SEPTA picks up where NJTransit leaves off, in Trenton, to form the New Yorker's cheapest ride to Philadelphia (215/580–7800).

LONG-DISTANCE
Amtrak trains leave from Penn Station (800/USA–RAIL [800/872–7245]), www.amtrak.com).

PUBLICATIONS

New York is the publishing capital of the world, and many of its residents have a lot of commuting time to kill. Put the two together and you have an enormous reading public. All of these newspapers and magazines list goings-on, but each has a different angle. Pick them up at any newsstand and choose a favorite.

new york daily news

Subtitled "New York's Hometown Newspaper," the *Daily News* features hearty metro and entertainment coverage, with a broader editorial range than its tabloid rival the *Post*—though the cover photo is usually just as grisly. Gossip columnists Rush & Molloy have a faithful following.

new york magazine

New York made its name being ultracool and semi-elitist. Cover stories range from fashion to politics to food to (much on) social trends. It's especially strong on the arts. Weekly (Mon.).

new york observer

Easily spotted for its salmon-color paper, the *Observer* is New York's college newspaper for grown-ups. Gleefully trumpeting industry gossip on politics, publishing, and entertainment, it has many a closet addict. The focus shifts to the Hamptons in summer. Weekly (Wed.).

new york post

Owned by journalistic heavy hand Rupert Murdoch, the *Post* screams right-angle dish every day of the week, particularly on business and celebrity figures.

new york press

This downtown, Gen-X rag has aggressively targeted the *Village Voice*'s readership, but it tends to be more conservative in its views and skimpier in its content. Event listings, however, are solid. Weekly (Tues.).

new york times

The *Times* still leads the national pack, though recent innovations aimed at widening its audience have stirred predictable debate. The Friday edition is the city's best source for weekend highbrow arts events. Daily; expanded edition Sunday.

new yorker

New York's most literate and literary source is for culture vultures. Longtime readers love to complain that it's gone downhill in recent years, but they still can't live without it. The famous fact-checking department means that event listings are thorough and reliable, covering everything from classical recitals to nightly gigs at CBGB's. Weekly (Mon.).

paper

Paper will meet the needs of your inner club kid and reveal what the fashionistas are doing—oh, yes, and wearing. Listings for gay-friendly events, alternative music clubs, and new sites for shopping are particularly good, and columns favor the flavor of local scenesters such as Joey Arias. Monthly.

timeout new york

Modeled on its London predecessor, this magazine calls itself "The Obsessive Guide to Impulsive Entertainment" and lives up to the claim. The tone is young and cheeky, but fans of all ages appreciate the trendy restaurant reviews and virtually exhaustive event listings. Weekly (Wed.).

village voice

Culturally and politically lefty, the *Voice* is a great (and free in Manhattan) source for nightlife and music news and the last word on apartment listings—though the most eager apartment hunters visit www.villagevoice.com daily at 1 PM for the newest listings. Weekly (Wed.).

RADIO STATIONS

am

570 WMCA Religion

620 WSNR Sports

660 WFAN Sports

710 WOR Talk/news

740 WGSM News/talk/nostalgia

770 WABC Talk/news

820 WNYC News/talk

880 WCBS News

930 WPAT Adult contemporary

970 WWDJ Christian music

1010 WINS News

1050 WEVD Sports

1100 WHLI Easy listening

1130 WBBR News

1190 WLIB Talk/Caribbean

1230 WFAS Westchester news

1330 WWRV Ethnic

1370 WALK Adult contemporary

1380 WKDM Latin

1440 WNYG Music

1460 WVOX Talk/nostalgia

1480 WZRC Korean

1560 WQEW Children's programming

1580 WLIM Big band/talk

1600 WWRL Gospel/talk

fm

88.1 WCWP LIU/C. W. Post Campus

88.3 WBGO Varied, jazz

88.7 WRHU Hofstra University

89.1 WNYU New York University

89.5 WSOU Seton Hall University

89.9 WKCR Columbia University

90.1 WUSB SUNY/Stony Brook

90.3 WHCR C.C.N.Y.

90.7 WFUV Fordham University

91.1 WFMU Varied

91.5 WNYE Community services

92.3 WXRK Alternative/progressive rock

92.7 WLIR Modern rock

93.1 WPAT Latin

93.5 WRTN Big band/standards

93.9 WNYC Classical/NPR

94.3 WMJC Light contemporary

95.5 WPLJ Top 40

96.3 WQXR Classical

96.7 WKHL Oldies

97.1 WQHT Top 40/urban

97.5 WALK Adult contemporary

97.9 WSKQ Latin

98.3 WKJY Adult contemporary

98.7 WRKS Urban contemporary

99.5 WBAI Varied

100.3 WHTZ Top 40

100.7 WHUD Light contemporary

101.1 WCBS Oldies

101.7 WBAZ Light contemporary

101.9 WQCD Contemporary jazz

102.3 WBAB Rock

102.7 WNEW Rock/talk

103.5 WKTU Dance/freestyle

103.9 WFAS Adult contemporary

104.3 WAXQ Rock

105.1 WTJM R & B oldies

105.9 WNWK Latin

106.1 WBLI Adult contemporary

106.7 WLTW Light contemporary

107.1 WYNY Country

107.5 WBLS Urban contemporary

RECYCLING

Sanitation Action Center After a rough start, recycling is on the rise in New York City. Businesses, office buildings, and residences have started to comply with the laws in greater numbers. As a result, recycling bins for cans and bottles are available in most take-out restaurants, fast-food stores, and delis. Garbage cans specifically meant for newspapers, bottles, and cans can also be found on street corners and in most subway stations. The Department of Sanitation answers questions related to pick-up schedule, bulk disposal, leaf collection, etc. (Representatives available Mon.–Fri., 7 AM–4 PM; 212/219–8090, www.nyc.gov/sanitation).

REST ROOMS

Finding a rest room in New York City can be a difficult task indeed. The vast majority of restaurants, bars, and other businesses expect you to buy something before you use their facilities; that is, if they even have a bathroom. Large buildings such as department stores and hotels are a better bet, if you can find one. Fast-food restaurants usually have a bathroom, but you will likely need to ask for a key first. Barnes & Noble and other bookstores are also a good bet, as are museums. Starbucks' are also a good option, especially since there seems to be one (or two) every two blocks these days.

TAX & TIP

sales tax & beyond

You expect a lot from New York—and the city expects a lot from you in return in the form of sales tax and endless gratuities. Sales tax in the city is 8¼% and applies to all purchases not considered necessities. Guess what? That covers most store purchases and all restaurant meals. Clothing and shoes under $150 are no longer taxed, however. The parking garage tax is prohibitively high—18.25%—and the New York City rental car tax is a whopping 13.25%.

tipping

Of course, what you choose to tip service professionals is entirely your own business, but note that New Yorkers pride themselves on giving "New York tips" (i.e., generous). Bartenders are normally given $1 a drink, or 20% for bar tabs. Waiters also expect a 20% tip for good service, but you can get away with slightly less for taxi drivers (remember, though, they are putting their lives on the line for you, even if it feels at times that they are putting *your* life on the line as well). Coat check clerks expect to

receive $1 per coat. Some upscale restaurants also expect you to tip the wine steward $5 per bottle of wine ordered, and the captain 5%; but they will likely receive a cut from the waiters anyway, and their salary is usually pretty good (maybe even better than yours). Hair stylists, massage therapists, and the like should receive at least 15%.

Year-end gratuities for doormen vary based on neighborhood, but the proper amount can be anywhere from $25 to $50 per doorman, and somewhat more for supers. In a big building with lots of workers, your tab can get out of hand pretty quickly. As for tipping mail carriers, newspaper deliverymen, and the like, to each according to their needs and your means.

The total room tax at hotels is a hefty 13¼%, plus an occupancy charge of $2 per room per night. Those facts aside, you should leave the hotel maid about 1% of your room rate (at least $1) for each night of your stay; the bellhop should get about $2 per bag.

TELEVISION

major broadcasters
Channel 2—WCBS

Channel 4—WNBC

Channel 5—WNYW (Fox)

Channel 7—WABC

Channel 9—WWOR (UPN)

Channel 11—WPIX (WB)

Channel 13—WNET (PBS)

VOTER REGISTRATION

As long as you have been a resident of NYC for 30 days prior to an election in which you wish to vote, you can show up at the polls—that is, if you're a U.S. citizen over 18, not in jail or on parole for a felony, and not registered to vote elsewhere. First you'll have to **register** in one of three ways: call (212/VOTE–NYC) for a postage-paid registration form or to request a form by fax; visit the Web site (www.vote.ny.us) for a registration form (in .pdf format) or to request one be sent to you; or register in person 9–5 at one of the five borough offices.

Bronx (1780 Grand Concourse, Bronx, NY 10457, 718/299–9017).

Brooklyn (345 Adams St., Brooklyn, NY 11201, 718/330–2250).

Manhattan (200 Varick St., Greenwich Village, New York, NY 10014, 212/886–3800).

Queens (42–16 West St., Long Island City, NY 11101, 718/392–8989).

Staten Island (1 Edgewater Plaza, Staten Island, NY 10304, 718/876–0079).

WEATHER

New York has four distinct seasons, each lending the city its own character. Spring and fall bring moderate temperatures, although the occasional coastal hurricane can cause big problems in the fall, with deluges canceling flights and messing up transportation. The mercury in summer averages 75°F (23°C) with fairly high humidity; however, days of 90°F heat and stifling humidity are not uncommon. Winter temperatures often hover near 32°F (0°C), but it can go to as low as 0°F on rare occasions. However, indoor temperatures are often the opposite of those outside—chilly in summer from air-conditioning and toasty in winter due to central heating. Things are further complicated if you ride the subway: subterranean stations are tropical in summer. Dress for comfort, preferably in removable layers. In winter, snow and slush can turn sidewalks and corner crosswalks into treacherous courses and hazardous pools, so think seriously about sturdy boots. And remember to enjoy the view; the city is gorgeous under a blanket of snow, however fleeting.

resources for challenges & crises

APARTMENT LOCATOR SERVICES

If you want to live here, you'll have to pay the price. But while NYC rents remain prohibitively high, you can cir-

cumvent the web of real estate brokers by using an apartment locator service. For less than a broker's fee, they can help you find a home, a roommate, or both. Most companies issue you a password to browse their listings on the Web, although many will also send an e-mail or fax when apartments that meet your criteria become available.

Apartment Source Promises new daily listings; you can do your credit check online (fee). Open 9–7 daily; $120 for 2 months (212/343–8155; www.apartmentsource.com).

The Apartment Store If your definition of living in New York includes Brooklyn and Queens, this one's for you. The average client finds an apartment in just over a week. $89.99 for 30-day subscription, includes credit check (212/545–1996; www.apartmentstores.com).

Roommate Finders Drop in to the oldest New York City agency between noon and 7:30 PM weekdays or call their phone banks until 6 PM to find your match. They keep a turkey file on serious roommate rejects, so the seedy, thieving, and unreliable stay away. $300 for 1 year (250 W. 57th St., Suite 1629, Midtown West, 212/489–6862; www.roommatefinders.com).

BABY-SITTING SERVICES

See also Best Domestic *in* House Cleaning Agencies, *below.*

The Babysitters' Guild is a licensed and bonded organization. It has been in business for over 50 years and is recommended by major hotels. The staff, all 25 or older, speaks a total of 16 languages. Same-day service. Office open daily 9–9; sitters available 24 hours (60 E. 42nd St., Suite 912, New York NY 10165, 212/682–0227, www.babysittersguild.com).

CATERING

Gourmet food shops such as Zabar's, Balducci's, Dean & Deluca, and Gourmet Garage happily assemble all manner of prepared foods in small and large orders, for just about any event. City standbys such as Ess-a-Bagel and Katz's Deli also provide catering services. *See* Chapter 1 *and* Food & Drink *in* Chapter 2.

Some catering companies include:

Abigail Kirsch This big-name, full-service caterer specializes in weddings and other big events, either at one of its own locations or off-site (212/336–6060).

Cleaver Company They'll cater almost any kind of event—both large and small—with a focus on creative American cuisine (212/741–9174).

Glorious Food Plan on perfection from this veteran city caterer. Classic French and international cuisines (212/628–2320).

Newman & Leventhal In business for close to 100 years, this top kosher caterer focuses on big, fancy events (212/362–9400).

Simple Fare American regional cuisine. Prepares what the name suggests, with flair: breakfast pantry, salads, sandwiches, pasta, hors d'oeuvres, and desserts (212/691–4570).

Taste Caterers From corporate events to private parties. Versatile: American regional, Mediterranean, and Asian-influenced menus. Children's parties, too (212/255–8571).

CHILD CRISES

Child Abuse Hotline (800/422–4453).

New York State Child Abuse and Neglect Prevention Information Line (800/342–7472).

24-hour Child Abuse and Maltreatment Register (800/342–3720).

CITY GOVERNMENT

complaints
Civilian Complaint Review Board Handles complaints about police conduct (212/442–8833).

Department of Environmental Protection For complaints about water, air, noise, sewer, industrial wastes, hazardous materials, or water meter problems (718/337–4357).

Mayor's Action Center Handles complaints about city agencies; records your opinion for the Mayor; provides information on social service programs and housing; provides tax numbers; handles concerns related to parks, streets, and recycling; in English and Spanish; week-

days 9–5 (51 Chambers St., Lower Manhattan, 212/788–9600, www.nyc.gov).

New York City No To Bias Hotline Handles reports of racial, ethnic, religious, or sexual bias (212/662–2427).

COAST GUARD

General information (212/668–7000).

Emergency search and rescue (212/668–7936).

CONSUMER PROTECTION

Attorney General's Consumer Help Line (800/771–7755).

Better Business Bureau (212/533–6200).

Department of Consumer Affairs Hotline (212/487–4444).

COUNSELING & REFERRALS

aids advice & services
Advanced Counseling and Testing Service Board-certified counselors; FDA-approved test; results in 15 minutes (212/246–0800).

AIDS Hot Line New York City Department of Health; counseling and referrals, daily 9 AM–9 PM (800/825–5448 or 212/447–8200; 800/342–2437 national).

Gay Men's Health Crisis A leader in HIV/AIDS advocacy and education, providing a range of emotional support services, from crisis intervention and assigning a buddy to financial and nutritional information. The center is open weekdays 10 AM–9 PM, Saturday noon–3 PM (119 W. 24th St., Chelsea, 212/807–6655 or 800/AIDS–NYC [800/243–7692], www.gmhc.org).

alcohol treatment & support
Alcoholics Anonymous Hotline Support system for alcoholics who want to stop drinking; information and referrals to New York City area meetings; daily 9 AM–10 PM (212/647–1680; 212/870–3400 business office).

Alcoholism Council of New York A voluntary, non-profit organization that offers treatment services to individuals, families, and health care professionals (800/56–SOBER; 212/252–7022, www.alcoholism.org).

Bureau of Alcoholism and Substance Abuse Services This division of the New York City Department of Mental Health is responsible for planning and coordinating all alcoholism services in New York City (212/219–5380).

crime victims

Crime Victims Board of New York State Financial aid and reimbursement of out-of-pocket medical expenses for crime victims (55 Hanson Pl., 10th floor, Brooklyn, 718/923–4325. Weekdays 9–5, www.cvb.state.ny.us).

Crime Victims Hot Line 24-hour bilingual counseling and referral (212/577–7777).

domestic violence

Domestic Violence Hotline Shelter referrals available (800/942–6906 or 800/621–HOPE).

Violence Intervention Program Bilingual Hotline (212/360–5090).

drug abuse treatment

Daytop Village Rehabilitation facilities to help addicts with drug and drug-related problems. Weekdays 9–5 (54 W. 40th St., Midtown West, 212/354–6000; 800/232–9867 24-hour hot line, www.daytop.org).

Narcotics Anonymous Referral to meetings and drug-addiction related service organizations; crisis counseling (212/929–6262).

New York State Division of Substance Abuse Services 24-hour referral to treatment programs, clinics, and hospitals (800/522–5353).

Phoenix House Foundation The city's largest drug-free residential rehabilitation program for teens and adults, with five facilities. Encourages responsibility, self-reliance, and trust (164 W. 74th St., Upper West Side, 212/787–3000, www.phoenixhouse.org. Open 24 hrs).

families & housing

Citizens Advice Bureau Information, referral, and problem-solving center for housing, welfare, Medicaid, immigration, and social services; weekdays 9–3:30 (178 Bennett Ave., Inwood, 212/923–2599; 2070 Grand Concourse, Bronx, 718/731–3117).

Homeless Hotline Round-the-clock Department of Homeless Services emergency hot line provides shelter referral and Medicaid and food-stamps information for homeless residents of the New York area (including Long Island and Westchester counties) (800/994–6494).

Public Assistance/NYC Emergency Shelter (212/513–8849).

Salvation Army Social Services for Children Information and referral for family problems, foster homes, senior-citizen residence problems, adoption, and alcohol and drug rehabilitation. Two social workers on duty weekdays 8:30–4. Thirty-three centers throughout the city; summer camps; and a general hospital in Flushing, Queens (212/505–4327 emergency; 212/337–7200 business).

United Neighborhood Houses Information and referral for family and individual counseling; day care; nurseries; and senior-citizen programs; weekdays 8–5 (212/967–0322, www.unhny.org).

mental health information & referral

Lifenet The city's largest 24-hour crisis, information, and referral service for emotional and substance-abuse problems (800/LIFENET [800/543–3638]).

Mental Health Counseling Hot Line State-certified therapists available for information and referral. Don't be put off by the answering machine—someone always calls back (212/734–5876).

National Mental Health Association The New York chapter offers referrals and information (weekdays 9–5, 800/969–6642 or 212/254–0333, www.nmha.org).

new york city human resources administration

Provides public assistance in many areas; call for a referral to the appropriate division; weekdays 9–5 (718/291–1900; 877/472–8411).

Child Services Foster care, adoption, day care, Head Start.

Crisis Intervention Unit Emergency housing, food, and clothing.

Family and Adult Services Home care, foster care for adults, protective services.

General Social Services Referral, interceding unit, outreach center.

Medicaid/Medicare Medical-insurance benefits.

Office of Income Support Child support from absent parents.

psychotherapy
New York Psychotherapy Collective Staffed by psychotherapists (877/REFER–NY [877/733–3769]).

rape victim advocacy
New York Police Department Rape Hot Line Female detectives assist in filing a police report and can make counseling referral; 24 hours a day (212/267–7273).

Rape Crisis Program St. Vincent's 24-hour medical care and advocacy; counseling 9–5 (212/604–8068).

Rape Intervention Program St. Luke's–Roosevelt Hospital; crisis counseling for survivors of childhood or adult abuse and violence (411 W. 114th St., Room 2C, 212/523–4728).

Sexual Abuse Treatment and Training Institute Long-term support; services for adult survivors of childhood abuse (212/366–1490).

women's health
Women's Healthline Trained nurses available for reproductive information and referrals to low-cost or sliding-scale clinics; English and Spanish; weekdays 8 AM–6 PM (212/230–1111).

world trade center
The World Trade Center disaster on September 11, 2001, is having a lasting impact on thousands of New Yorkers, many of who require a variety of emergency services. Public agencies are stepping in to assist people in need of help, including those with financial difficulties. New York City is offering continuously updated information on services available to victims and families of victims via its official Web site (www.nyc.gov).

Federal Emergency Management Agency (FEMA) is providing crisis counseling to the survivors and families of victims of the attacks; disaster unemployment assistance; financial help for funerals; food stamps; unemployment benefits; low-interest housing loans or grants; business loans and legal counseling (800/462–9029, www.fema.gov).

The **Small Business Administration (SBA)** is offering business loans to those economically affected by the WTC disaster, as well as loans for homes and personal property (800/659–2955, www.sba.gov/disaster/).

Furthermore, the **New York State Bar Association** is working to provide lawyers free of charge for those victims and families of victims needing legal assistance (877/435–7321, www.nysba.org).

DOCTOR & DENTIST REFERRALS

Dental Referral Service National service based in Southern California (800/511–8663).

Mount Sinai Hospital Doctor Referral Service (800/637–4624).

Physician Referral Service of Beth Israel Medical Center (800/420–4004; 212/420–2000).

Saint Vincents Catholic Medical Centers Physician Referral Service (888/478–4362).

FAMILY PLANNING

Planned Parenthood (212/541–7800; 800/230–7526 24-hour clinic locator. Daily 8:30–5).

FIRE

Dial 911 for fire, police, or ambulance assistance in an emergency. Be prepared to give your location and the specific reason why you are calling.

GAY & LESBIAN CONCERNS

Anti-Violence Project A crime-victims agency for the gay, lesbian, and transgender community; counseling, hot line, and legal advocacy services; volunteer opportunities (240 W. 35th St., Suite 200, Midtown West, 212/807–6761).

Gay and Lesbian Anti-Violence Project 24-hour hot line arranges counseling, domestic-violence support groups, court and police accompaniment and monitoring, assistance in obtaining court-ordered protection, and legal services, all free (212/714–1141, www.avp.org).

Lesbian and Gay Community Services Center Counseling, therapy, education, library and museum, and resources for couples considering children (208 W. 13th St., between 7th and 8th Aves., Greenwich Village, 212/620–7310, www.gaycenter.org. Daily 9 AM–11 PM).

roommate referral services

Gay Roommate Information Network (212/627–4242).

Rainbow Roommates (212/627–8612).

HOMEWORK-HELP HOT LINE

Dial-A-Teacher The United Federation of Teachers staffs this service to help children answer difficult homework questions (212/777–3380. Mon.–Thurs. 4–7 during academic year).

HOUSECLEANING AGENCIES

Best Domestic In addition to general house cleaning, this citywide agency provides maid service, butlers, nannies, baby nurses, housekeepers, husband-and-wife teams, chefs and cooks, chauffeurs, majordomos, personal assistants, and office cleaners. Licensed, bonded, and insured, the company claims to reject about 85% of its candidates for employment (tougher than some Ivy League schools). Twenty-four hours' notice is preferred (212/685–0351).

Green Clean General housecleaning in Manhattan, Brooklyn, and parts of Queens using nontoxic and environmentally friendly products. Call a week in advance; 10 days in advance for large jobs (212/216–9109).

McMaid Daily, weekly, and monthly cleaning services available. Reservations must be made by phone (212/731–5555, www.mcmaid.com).

New York Maids Offers home cleaning services, either hourly or by the task. The company also provides after-party and unpacking services (866/NY–MAIDS [866/696–2437], www.nymaids.com).

LANDLORD/TENANT ASSISTANCE

Metropolitan Council on Housing This advocacy group advises tenants in rent-controlled and rent-stabilized apartments on their rights and helps organize tenants (212/979–0611; Mon., Wed. 1:30–5 PM. Walk-in location: 61 E. 4th St., Cooper Square Committee Office, East Village; 6:30 PM).

Rent InfoLine: Division of Housing and Community Renewal City offices assist both tenants and owners of rent-controlled and rent-stabilized apartments with legal advice on subletting, rent control, etc. (718/739–6400; 888/275–3427 information, weekdays 9–5; www.dhcr.state.ny.us. Walk-in offices: 25 Beaver St., Lower Manhattan, 212/480–6229).

Harlem Office (163 W. 125th St., 5th floor, Harlem, 212/961–8930).

Brooklyn Office (55 Hanson Pl., Room 702, Ft. Greene, Brooklyn, 718/722–4778).

Queens Office (92–31 Union Hall St., Jamaica, Queens, 718/739–6400).

Bronx Office (1 Fordham Plaza, 2nd Floor, Bronx, 718/563–5678. Walk-in hours: 9–4:45).

LEGAL SERVICES

Legal Aid Society (212/577–3300 general information, www.legal-aid.org).

Legal Referral Services Association of the Bar (212/626–7373 in English; 212/626–7374 in Spanish).

LOST & FOUND

airlines & airports

JFK International Airport Found property will be held by the airline on which you traveled. If loss occurred on airport grounds or at the International Arrivals Building, call 718/244–4225.

La Guardia Airport (718/533–3988 Port Authority Police). Also call the airline on which you traveled.

Newark International Airport (973/961–6000). Also call the airline on which you traveled.

other transportation
New York City Buses (212/424–4343;
212/712–4500).

New York City Subways (212/424–4343;
212/712–4500).

Port Authority Bus Terminal (212/435–
7000).

Railroads (212/424–4343 or 212/712–
4500 Penn Station; 212/340–2555 Grand
Central Terminal).

Taxicabs Items left in taxis should be
turned in to the police station closest to
your destination. To report a loss, call
the Taxi and Limousine Commission
(212/302–8294, www.nyc.gov/taxi).

animals
If your pet goes astray, post notices in
the area of the pet's home and most
recent whereabouts. Include a description and/or photo of your pet with your
phone number only. Call all local veteri-
narians to check if your pet has been
brought in, and inquire about posting
notices at their offices. Report the missing animal to the **ASPCA** (424 E. 92nd
St., 212/876–7700, www.aspca.org).

credit cards
American Express/Optima (800/528–
4800).

Chase (800/632–3300).

Citibank (800/843–0777).

Diners Club/Carte Blanche (800/234–
6377).

Discover (800/347–2683).

MasterCard (800/307–7309).

Visa (800/847–2911).

MEDICAL EMERGENCIES

ambulance
In an emergency, dial 911 and a city
ambulance will arrive. The patient will
be taken to one of the city's 13 municipal hospitals, based on location and
hospital specialty.

If the patient prefers a specific, nonpub-
lic hospital, **Rural Metro Ambulance** provides 24-hour ambulance service to all
five boroughs, for a fee (212/988–8800).

hospital emergency rooms
Beekman Downtown Hospital Mobile
intensive care, two paramedic units
(weekdays 9–5), Basic EMT unit (24
hours, 7 days), coronary intensive care
(170 William St., Lower Manhattan, 212/
312–5070).

Bellevue Hospital Center Intensive-care
units: coronary, surgical trauma, pediatric, psychiatric, neurosurgical, and
alcohol detoxification (462 1st Ave.,
Gramercy, 212/562–4347; 212/562–3025
pediatrics).

Beth Israel Medical Center Coronary
care, neonatal intensive care, alcohol
and drug detoxification (1st Ave. at 16th
St., Gramercy, 212/420–2840).

Cabrini Medical Center Coronary care,
trauma intensive care, alcohol detoxification and drug-overdose units, psychiatric facility (227 E. 19th St., Gramercy,
212/995–6000).

Columbia Presbyterian Medical Center
Intensive-care units: metabolic, neurosurgical, pediatric (622 W. 168th St.,
Washington Heights, 212/305–2500
main; 212/305–2255 emergency, adult;
212/305–6628 emergency, pediatric).

Harlem Hospital Coronary care; neonatal and respiratory critical care; alcohol
and drug detoxification. Crisis intervention center for rape victims and battered
wives and children (506 Lenox Ave.,
Harlem, 212/939–1000).

Lenox Hill Hospital Coronary and
neonatal intensive care (100 E. 77th St.,
Upper East Side, 212/434–3030).

Manhattan Eye, Ear and Throat Hospital
Ear, eye, nose, and throat emergencies
(210 E. 64th St., Upper East Side, 212/
838–9200).

Mount Sinai Hospital Coronary, trauma,
and medical intensive care; dental emergencies; emergency pharmacy until midnight (Madison Ave. at 100th St., East
Harlem, 212/241–7171).

New York Eye and Ear Infirmary 24-hour
emergency service for eye, ear, nose, or
throat problems (310 E. 14th St., East
Village, 212/979–4000).

**New York Hospital–Cornell Medical
Center** 24-hour paramedic unit; burn,
coronary, neurological, and neonatal
intensive care; high-risk infant-transport
unit and treatment (525 E. 68th St.,
Upper East Side, 212/746–5454).

New York University Medical Center
Coronary care (550 1st Ave., Murray Hill, 212/263–5550).

St. Clare's Hospital and Health Center
Coronary, medical, and surgical intensive care (415 W. 51st St., Midtown West, 212/586–1500).

St. Luke's Hospital Center Coronary, trauma, and neonatal intensive care; alcohol detoxification; rape-intervention team; 24-hour psychiatric emergency room (1111 Amsterdam Ave., Harlem, 212/523–3335).

St. Luke's–Roosevelt Hospital Coronary, surgical, and neonatal intensive-care units; alcohol detoxification (1000 10th Ave., Upper West Side, 212/523–6800).

St. Vincent's Hospital and Medical Center of New York Coronary, spinal-cord trauma, and psychiatric intensive care; alcohol detoxification; AIDS center; rape crisis program (153 W. 11th St., West Village, 212/604–7998).

poison control center
Poison Hot Line (212/340–4494 or 212/764–7667 [POISONS]).

suicide prevention
Help Line (212/532–2400).

The Samaritans (212/673–3000 24-hour hot line).

Suicide Prevention Hot Line (800/543–3638, 212/532–2400 24-hour hot line; 718/389–9608 7:30 PM–midnight).

ON-LINE INFORMATION
Citysearch (www.newyorkcitysearch.com) This free site is chock full of listings for all five boroughs, including restaurants, bars and nightlife, movies, and music.

Moviefone (777–FILM, www.moviefone.com). Online, you can get information on movie locations and times, watch previews, and buy tickets. The phone number works from any New York City area code.

New York Magazine (www.nymag.com) Check out the online version of this fashionable local magazine. There are articles on restaurants, movies, music, art, theater, and other cultural happenings.

NYC & Company (www.nycvisit.com) An invaluable directory of Web addresses for New York organizations of every stripe.

New York Public Library (www.nypl.org) Good for a variety of inquiries, this site has terrific New York City history information.

The New York Times (www.nytimes.com) This site provides news articles and events listings, though you'll have to pay to retrieve articles from the archives.

New York Today (www.nytoday.com) This site is the place to go for free *New York Times* reviews, listings, maps, and classified ads.

Time Out Magazine (www.timeoutny.com) The online version of the popular entertainment listings guide features articles, reviews, and local events.

The Village Voice (www.villagevoice.com) Get the best searchable housing listings, as well as comprehensive entertainment and events listings on this site.

PETS

adoptions
ASPCA The national headquarters of "America's first humane society" no longer euthanizes unwanted animals. For an adoption fee of about $50, your new companion will be spayed or neutered and given the proper shots (424 E. 92nd St., Upper East Side, 212/876–7700, www.aspca.org).

Bide-A-Wee Very sweet mutts for dog lovers; domestic shorthairs for the feline-inclined. Adoption fee: $30–$55 (410 E. 38th St., Murray Hill, 212/532–4455, www.bideawee.org).

Mighty Mutts Volunteer shelter works to rescue stray animals and place them for adoption. A fee of $75 includes a vaccinated and spayed or neutered animal (Box 140139, Brooklyn, 11214, 718/946–1074, members.tripod.com/~MightyMutts).

New Yorkers for Companion Animals Non-profit volunteer group works to offer up unwanted New York City pets for adoption. Fees range from $70–$100 for a dog or cat that has been vaccinated, as well as spayed or neutered (212/427–8273, www.geocities.com/~nyca).

North Shore Animal League Recommended by animal lovers region-wide. No adoption fee (25 Davis Ave., Fort Washington, NY, 516/883–7575, www.nsalamerica.org. Long Island Rail Road: Port Washington).

dog walking & pet-sitting services

New York Dog Spa & Hotel Offers boarding, day care, grooming, training, and veterinary services for dogs (145 W. 18th St., Chelsea, 212/243–1199, www.nydogspa.com).

Pet Mates Provides dog walking, as well as cat-sitting and puppy care in your home. Service is available primarily on the East Side of Manhattan. Fee is $21 per hour for dog walking, $19 per hour for cat sitting (322 E. 55th St., Suite D, 212/414–5158, www.petmates.com).

Puddles Pet Service Dog walking, pet-sitting, and animal training available throughout New York City. Cost is $30–$35 per hour for dog walking, $23 per half-hour visit for cat-sitting. Major credit cards accepted (212/410–7338, www.puddles.com).

grooming

Finishing Touches by Stephanie Dental care and therapeutic baths, in addition to basic grooming (414 E. 58th St., Upper East Side, 212/753–8234).

Furry Paws Professional grooming with natural products—no sedatives. Evening hours for the busy pooch. Three locations (120 E. 34th St., Murray Hill, 212/725–1970; 141 Amsterdam, Upper West Side, 212/724–9321; 1039 2nd Ave., Midtown East, 212/813–1388).

Private Grooming by Terrie Vitolo A veteran groomer who makes house calls (718/388–1442).

training

ASPCA Group training classes, two months long, range from Puppy Kindergarten to Therapy Training (212/876–7700).

Center for Applied Animal Behavior and Canine Training, Inc. Consulting and treatment of behavior, mainly for dogs. By appointment (212/544–8797).

Dr. Ellen Lindell Specializes in kittens and cats with behavioral problems, but will work with Fido, too. Phone consultations and house calls (845/473–7406).

veterinary care

Animal Emergency: Animal Medical Center 24 hours (Bobst Hospital, 510 E. 62nd St., Upper East Side, 212/838–8100).

Veterinary Clinics of America Prescription pet food and emergency service. Appointments available 8 AM–8:30 PM daily; emergency service open 24 hours daily (240 East 80th St., Upper East Side 212/988–1000).

Veterinary Medical Association of NYC (212/246–0057).

PHARMACIES OPEN 24 HOURS

CVS (342 E. 23rd St., Gramercy, 212/505–1555).

Duane Reade (224 W. 57th St., Midtown West, 212/541–9708; 2465 Broadway, Upper West Side, 212/799–3172; 1279 3rd Ave., Upper East Side, 212/744–2668).

Rite Aid (303 W. 50th St., at 8th Ave., Midtown West, 212/247–8384; 144 E. 86th St., Upper East Side, 212/876–0600).

POLICE

Emergency Dial 911.

Non-emergency Police services including reporting a burglary or auto theft, general information, and providing the location and phone number of the precinct nearest you (in all five boroughs), available 24 hours daily (212/374–5000).

POSTAL SERVICES

Post offices are open weekdays 8–5 or 8–6. Many branches are open for a few hours on Saturday as well.

J. A. Farley General Post Office The city's main post office is open 24 hours daily, as is their infoline for that zip code you need at 3 AM or for the address of the post office nearest you (8th Ave., at 33rd St., 800/725–2161, www.usps.com).

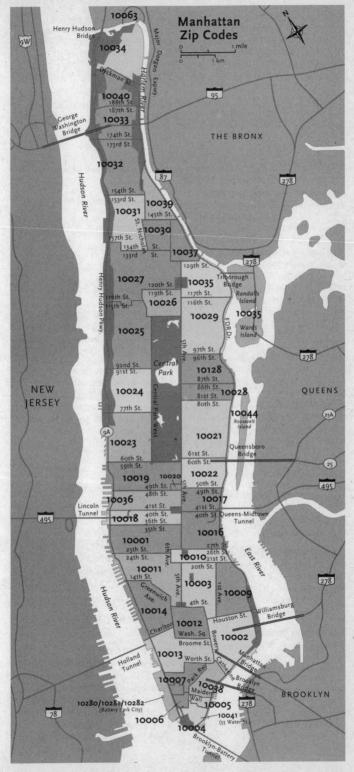

Manhattan Zip Codes

0 _____ 1 mile
0 _____ 1 km

N

10063

Henry Hudson
Bridge

9W

10034

Dyckman St.

Major Deegan Expwy.

Harlem River

THE BRONX

95

10040
188th St.
187th St.

10033
174th St.
173rd St.

George
Washington
Bridge

10032

87

278

Hudson River

154th St.
153rd St.

10039
145th St.

10031

St. Nicholas Ave.

10030

137th St.
134th
133rd St.   St.

10037

129th St.

278

Triborough
Bridge

10027

120th St.
119th St.
115th St.   116th St.

10035
117th St.
116th St.

Randalls
Island

10035

10026

10029

Wards
Island

10025

97th St.
96th St.

FDR Dr.

278

Henry Hudson Pkwy.

Central
Park

92nd St.
91st St.

Central Park West

10128
87th St.
86th St.
81st St.
80th St.

10028

QUEENS

25A

NEW
JERSEY

10024

77th St.

5th Ave.

10044
Roosevelt
Island

10023

9A

60th St.
59th St.

10021

61st St.
60th St.

Queensboro
Bridge

25

495

10019

49th St.
48th St.

10020

10022
50th St.
49th St.

10036

41st St.
40th St.
36th St.

Lincoln
Tunnel

10018

35th St.

10017
41st St.
40th St.   Queens-Midtown
             Tunnel

495

10001

25th St.
24th St.

6th Ave.

10016

10011

14th St.

Greenwich
Ave.

5th Ave.

27th St.
26th St.
21st St.

10010

20th St.

East River

278

10003

4th Ave.

1st Ave.

10009

Hudson River

10014

Charlton

Houston St.

Williamsburg
Bridge

10012
Wash. Sq.

Broome St.

Bowery

10002

Holland
Tunnel

10013

Worth St.

Manhattan
Bridge

78

10007

Park Row

Catherine St.

Brooklyn
Bridge

10038
Maiden
Wall Ln.

BROOKLYN

10280/10281/10282
(Battery Park City)

10005

278

10006

10041
(55 Water St.)

10004

Brooklyn-Battery
Tunnel

fedex

There are more than 50 FedEx staffed drop-off and pick-up centers in New York City, many of them located in Midtown Manhattan. You can also do your FedEx business at Mail Boxes Etc. and other authorized shipping centers located throughout the five boroughs. Call or check the Web site for further information on locations and pick-ups (800/463–3339, www.fedex.com).

mail boxes etc.

There are dozens of individually owned and operated Mail Boxes Etc. locations throughout New York City, with more than 30 available in Manhattan alone. All of them will send and receive your packages and letters as well as rent you a mailbox; however, their hours and prices may vary depending on the store location. Call the phone number listed below or visit the Web site for more information (212/642–5000 general info, www.mbe.com).

u.p.s.

You can register for pick-up or drop-off from your home or place of business. Alternatively, there are literally dozens of Mail Boxes Etc. outlets throughout the city that will process your UPS needs. Call or visit the UPS Web site for more information on pick-ups, drop-offs, rate information, and package tracking (800/742–5877, www.ups.com).

SENIOR CITIZEN SERVICES

Legal Aid Society (212/577–3300, www.legal-aid.org).

Legal Service for the Elderly Poor Part of the citywide agency Legal Services for New York City, LSEP provides free support for those elderly living below the poverty line (212/391–0120; 212/431–7200 for referral in all boroughs).

New York City Department for the Aging Extensive resources, including referrals to Meals on Wheels, at-home health care providers, etc. (212/442–1000).

Senior Action Line A part of the mayor's office, this information, referral, and advocacy program for senior citizens is staffed by volunteers (212/788–7504).

CABLE COMPANIES

Call yours for service, repairs, and general information.

Manhattan, Queens RCN (800/746–4726).

Manhattan Time Warner of New York (212/358–0900).

Bronx, Brooklyn Cablevision (718/617–3500).

Brooklyn Time Warner of New York (718/358–0900).

Queens Time Warner of New York (718/358–0900).

Staten Island Time Warner of New York (718/816–8686).

UTILITIES

gas & electric

Keyspan Energy Serves Queens (up to Jackson Heights), Staten Island, and Brooklyn (718/643–4050).

ConEdison Gas and electricity throughout the city, except Brooklyn, Staten Island, and part of Queens, where Keyspan provides gas service (800/752–6633; 212/683–8830 gas leaks or emergencies; 212/683–0862 electric and steam emergencies).

telephone

Verizon (212/890–1550 customer service; 800/698–3545 24-hr account information).

water

City of New York Dept. of Environmental Protection (718/595–7000 customer service; 718/337–4357 24-hr help).

VOLUNTEERING

organizations

Mayor's Voluntary Action Center Since 1967, this city agency has worked to encourage individuals and organizations (public, private, and nonprofit) to participate in a wide variety of volunteer opportunities (49–51 Chambers St., Suite 1231, 212/788–7550, nyc.gov/volunteer).

NYCares Matches you with New York City programs of all kinds, from one-time and seasonal opportunities to long-term placements that require training (116 E. 16th St., 6th floor, Gramercy, 212/228–5000, www.nycares.org).

ZONING & PLANNING

Department of City Planning The bookstore sells maps and publications; the office dispenses zoning information and schedules of upcoming meetings (22 Reade St., Lower Manhattan, 212/720–3300; 718/643–7550 Brooklyn; 718/392–0656 Queens).

New York City Landmarks Preservation Commission (100 Old Slip, Lower Manhattan, 212/487–6800, www.ci.nyc.ny.us/html/lpc).

learning

ACTING SCHOOLS

Actors Connection Audition Seminars attended by agents and casting directors; a popular vehicle for audition experience (630 9th Ave., Midtown West, 212/977–6666, www.actorsconnection.com).

The Actors Studio Inc. One of the most exclusive workshops for professional actors; over 50 years of experience (432 W. 44th St., Midtown West, 212/757–0870).

American Academy of Dramatic Arts Acting, speech, voice, movement, even mime (120 Madison Ave., Murray Hill, 212/686–9244, www.aada.org).

Atlantic Theater Company Acting School Teaches the practical aesthetic technique developed by David Mamet and William H. Macy, founding members who drop by to teach periodically. Full-time two-year conservatory program; part-time programs for beginners and pros. Intensive summer program in Vermont (453 W. 16th St., Chelsea, 212/691–5919, www.atlantictheater.com).

Creative Acting Company Beginner through pro. Scene study, monologue, commercials, sitcoms and more; some classes taught by casting directors. New

sketch-comedy and improv group. Thursday is agent night: all the biggies, from ICM to William Morris (122 W. 26th St., Chelsea, 212/352–2103, www.creativeacting.com).

Herbert Berghof Studio All subjects, all levels. Founded by Uta Hagen and Herbert Berghof (120 Bank St., West Village, 212/675–2370, www.hbstudio.org).

Lee Strasberg Theater Institute, Inc. Pacino and De Niro studied here. Founded by creative genius Lee Strasberg (115 E. 15th St., Gramercy, 212/533–5500, www.strasberg.com).

ART SCHOOLS

Art Students' League Founded in 1875. Drawing, painting, sculpture (215 W. 57th St., 2nd floor, Midtown West, 212/247–4510, www.artstudentsleague.com).

Greenwich House Pottery Wheel-throwing, hand-building, glazes, and more, including children's classes (16 Jones St., West Village, 212/242–4106).

International Center of Photography (ICP) Seminars, workshops, special lectures, and classes in black-and-white photography, color printing, and digital media (1130 5th Ave., Upper East Side, 212/860–1777, www.icp.org).

New York Studio School Full-time studio programs and weekly figure-drawing classes (8 W. 8th St., Greenwich Village, 212/673–6466, www.nyss.org).

Manhattan Graphics Center Not-for-profit printmaking workshop run by artists. Inexpensive courses in etching, lithography, silkscreen, and more. Fully equipped darkroom. $35 membership fee (481 Washington St., SoHo, 212/219–8783).

Parsons School of Design Printmaking, book design, sculpture, computer and digital design, interior design and architecture, fashion textile design, floral design, and more, at all levels (2 W. 13th St., Greenwich Village, 212/229–8900, www.parsons.edu).

School of Visual Arts (SVA) Drawing, painting, animation, computer art, graphic design, interior design, illustration, photography, film and video (209 E. 23rd St., Gramercy, 212/592–2000, www.schoolofvisualarts.edu).

COMPUTER TRAINING SCHOOLS

New York MacUsers' Group (NYMUG) A licensed training center for Adobe, Quark, and Claris applications, and Excel. Troubleshooting and other courses are offered as well. All are super-current (such as how to use new models and operating systems) and taught by professionals (1290 6th Ave., 39th floor, Midtown West, 212/906–1037, www.nymug.org).

Pratt Advanced computer applications programs, including Autodesk, Macromedia, Kinetix; electronic publishing, programming, software update training, computer competency, computer design (fashion, graphics, etc.), and myriad art classes (200 Willoughby Ave., Downtown Brooklyn, 718/636–3453, www.pratt.edu; 295 Lafayette St., Lower East Side, 212/461–6000).

CONTINUING EDUCATION

New York University NYU's School of Continuing Education offers more than 2,000 credit and non-credit courses around the city, for both business and pleasure, and a Virtual College of online courses (212/998–7080, www.spcs.nyu.edu).

The New School for Social Research Guitar study, foreign languages, business and career, film, music, writing, theater, dance, HTML, and culinary arts in a cool, sociable atmosphere or via distance learning ("attend" classes on your computer). Year-round (66 W. 12th St., Greenwich Village, 212/229–5620, www.newschool.edu).

92nd St. Y Language, literature, dance, music, arts, crafts, cooking, Jewish education (1395 Lexington Ave., Upper East Side, 212/996–1100, www.92ndsty.org).

COOKING & WINE PROGRAMS

Institute of Culinary Education Formerly known as Peter Kump's New York Cooking School, this is one of the city's most popular culinary-arts programs. Hundreds of courses, including kids in the kitchen, a well-attended knife-skills workshop, and wine workshops of all kinds. All levels (50 W. 23rd St., Flatiron District, 800/522–4610, www.pkcookschool.com).

The New School for Social Research Culinary arts classes, including pastry, wine, and global cuisine classes; culinary walking tours; and restaurant management courses. Year-round (66 W. 12th St., Greenwich Village, 212/229–5620, www.newschool.edu).

DANCE

Broadway Dance Center This high-energy, five-floor dance hub offers jazz, ballet, tap, modern, hip-hop, African, flamenco, aerobics, and more. All levels, including children's classes (221 W. 57th St., Midtown West, 212/582–9304, www.broadwaydancecenter.com).

Dance Space Inc. Most dancers come here for the Lynn Simonson jazz-technique and modern classes, but you can also study ballet, Capoeira, yoga, and more, at several levels, although the mood is quite studious (451 Broadway, 2nd floor, SoHo, 212/625–8369, www.dancespace.com).

DanceSport All levels of mambo, salsa, tango, swing, waltz, hustle, quickstep, and other Latin and ballroom classes in a bustling and sociable atmosphere, or in a private lesson (1845 Broadway, Upper West Side, 212/307–1111, www.dancesport.com).

Sandra Cameron Dance Center Affordable social ballroom, swing and lindy, and salsa and tango lessons; private or group lessons (20 Cooper Sq., Greenwich Village, 212/674–0505, www.sandracameron.com).

GENERAL INTEREST

The Learning Annex This group offers short-term education courses on a number of different topics including personal growth, business, and technology (16 E. 53rd St., 4th floor, Midtown East, 212/371–0280, www.thelearningannex.com).

LANGUAGE SCHOOLS

Berlitz Language Center Immersion courses for individuals and groups—in all spoken languages (40 W. 51st St., Midtown West, 212/765–1000, www.berlitz.com).

The New School for Social Research Six-teen levels, including Japanese, Greek (Classical and Modern), Brazilian Portuguese, Chinese (Mandarin), Sign Language, and Russian. Accredited classes, such as "Italian for Italian speakers" and business-language courses (66 W. 12th St., Greenwich Village, 212/229–5620, www.newschool.edu).

New York University NYU's School of Continuing Education offers a large variety (Arabic to Vietnamese) of credit and non-credit foreign-language, ESL, and translation classes, some of which are available through The Virtual College of online courses (212/998–7080, www.spcs.nyu.edu).

french
Alliance Française/French Institute French at all levels (22 E. 60th St., Upper East Side, 212/355–6100, www.fiaf.org).

german
The German House, New York University All levels plus business, conversation, and reading. "Meet the Authors" program: read them, meet them, discuss their work (42 Washington Mews, Greenwich Village, 212/998–8660, www.nyu.edu/deutscheshaus).

italian
Parliamo Italiano Language School Italian at all levels, in a lovely town house (132 E. 65th St., Upper East Side, 212/744–4793).

japanese
Toyota Language Center The Japan Society has 12 levels of Japanese classes, including English classes for Japanese speakers, and cultural and business-related courses (333 E. 47th St., Midtown East, 212/715–1256, www.japansociety.org/language.htm).

russian
Russian Institute for Language and Culture Russian at all levels (134 W. 32nd St., Midtown West, 212/244–5700).

spanish
Instituto Cervantes Spanish at all levels, and weekend immersion courses (122 E. 42nd St., Suite 807, Midtown West, 212/689–4232, ext. 6).

MUSIC SCHOOLS

Greenwich House Music School Instrumental and vocal classes and workshops; preschool program in music and art. Free concerts and recitals of students' work (46 Barrow St., West Village, 212/242–4770, www.gharts.org).

Juilliard School Evening Division Regular faculty teach music, dance, and drama. The most popular course seems to be piano lessons, but offerings extend to music criticism, studies of individual composers, and a wonderful class on overcoming performance anxiety (60 Lincoln Center Plaza, Upper West Side, 212/799–5040, www.juilliard.edu).

New York Singing Teachers Association Evaluation (all levels), referral, master classes (212/579–2461, www.nyst.org).

Third Street Music School Settlement Founded 1894. Private and group instruction for all ages (235 E. 11th St., East Village, 212/777–3240).

vacation & travel information

AIRLINES
The Central Airlines Ticket Office This satellite office handles ticketing for all major airlines (125 Park Ave., Midtown, 212/986–0888).

Aer Lingus (800/IRISHAIR [800/474–7424]).

AeroMexico (800/237–6639).

Air Canada (888/247–2262).

Air Europa (800/238–7672).

Air France (800/237–2747).

Air India (212/751–6200).

Air Jamaica (800/523–5585).

Alitalia Air Lines (800/223–5730).

America West Airlines (800/235–9292).

American Airlines (800/433–7300).

Austrian Airlines (800/843–0002).

Avianca Airlines (800/284–2622).

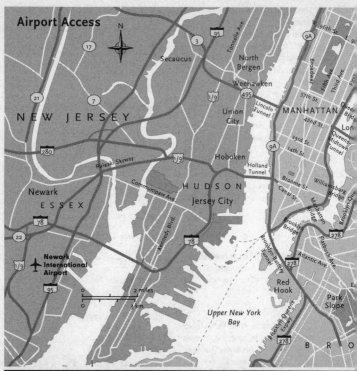

Airlines / Terminals

Airlines	JFK	LA GUARDIA	NEWARK
Aer Lingus ☎ 800/474–7424	4E		A, B
Aerolineas Argentinas ☎ 800/333–0276	4E		
AeroMexico ☎ 800/237–6639	2		B
Air Afrique ☎ 212/856–5908	4W		
Air Aruba ☎ 800/882–7822			B
Air Canada ☎ 888/247–2262			C
Air China ☎ 212/371–9898	3		
Air France ☎ 800/237–2747	4W		B
Air India ☎ 212/751–6200	4W		
Air Jamaica ☎ 800/523–5585	4W		B
Air Nova ☎ 888/247–2262			C
Alitalia ☎ 800/223–5730	4W		B, C
ALIA-Royal Jordanian ☎ 212/949–0050	4E		
Balkan Bulgarian ☎ 800/235–9262	3		
America West ☎ 800/235–9292	2	CTB-A	C
American ☎ 800/433–7300	8, 9	CTB-D	A
American Eagle ☎ 800/433–7300	9		
American Trans Air ☎ 800/435–9282	2		
Asiana Airlines ☎ 800/227–4262	4E		
Austrian Airlines ☎ 800/843–0002	3		
Avianca ☎ 800/284–2622	3		B
Balkan Bulgarian ☎ 800/796–5706	4E		
Biman Bangladesh ☎ 888/702–4626	4W		
British Airways ☎ 800/247–9297	7		B
BWIA ☎ 800/538–2942	8		
Canadian Airlines ☎ 888/247–2262	9	CTB-D	
Carnival ☎ 800/437–2110	4E	CTB-C	B
Cathay Pacific ☎ 800/233–2742	3		
China Airlines ☎ 800/227–5118	3		
Colgan Air ☎ 800/428–4322		CTB-B	A

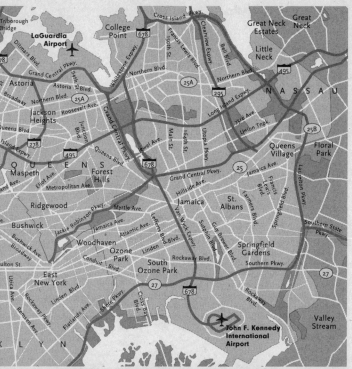

Airlines

Terminals (cont.)

Airlines	JFK	LA GUARDIA	NEWARK
Continental ☎ 800/525-0280		CTB-A	C
Continental Express ☎ 800/525-0280	2	CTB-A	C
Czech Airlines ☎ 212/765-6022			B
Delta International ☎ 800/325-1999	3	Delta	B
Delta Domestic ☎ 800/221-1212	3	Delta	B
Delta Express ☎ 800/325-1999		MAT	
Egypt Air ☎ 212/315-0900	4W		
El-Al ☎ 800/223-6700	4W		B
EVA Airways ☎ 800/695-1188	4E		B
Finnair ☎ 212/499-9026	2		
Ghana Airways ☎ 800/404-4262	4W		
Iberia ☎ 800/772-4642	4E		
Icelandair ☎ 800/223-5500	4E		
Japan Air Lines ☎ 800/525-3663	4E		
JetBlue ☎ 800/538-2583	6		
KIWI ☎ 800/538-5494			A
KLM ☎ 212/759-3600; 800/374-7747	4E		B
Korean ☎ 800/438-5000	4W		B
Kuwait ☎ 212/308-5454	4E		
Lacsa Airlines ☎ 800/225-2272	7		
Lan Chile ☎ 800/488-0070	8		
LOT Polish ☎ 800/223-0593	8		B
LTU ☎ 800/888-0200	4E		
Lufthansa ☎ 800/645-3880	4E		
Malev Hungarian ☎ 212/757-6446	3		B
Mexicana Airlines ☎ 800/531-7921	4W	CTB-D	
Midway Airlines ☎ 800/446-4392		CTB-C	A
Midwest Express ☎ 800/452-2022			B
North American ☎ 718/656-2650	5	Delta	
Northwest International ☎ 800/447-4747	4E	Delta	B
Northwest Domestic ☎ 800/225-2525	4E	Delta	B
Northwest Airlink ☎ 800/225-2525	4E		B

JFK International Airport

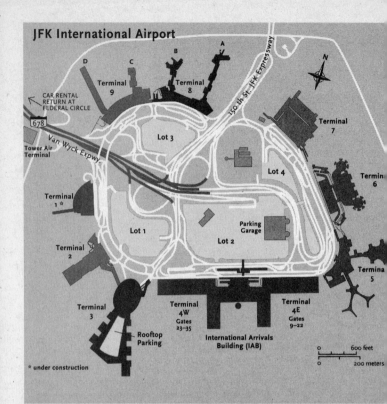

Terminal 9
Terminal 8
Terminal 7
Terminal 6
Terminal 5
Terminal 1 *
Terminal 2
Terminal 3
Terminal 4W Gates 23–35
Terminal 4E Gates 9–22
Tower Air Terminal
CAR RENTAL RETURN AT FEDERAL CIRCLE
678
Van Wyck Expwy
150 th St–JFK Expressway
Lot 1
Lot 2
Lot 3
Lot 4
Parking Garage
Rooftop Parking
International Arrivals Building (IAB)
N
0   600 feet
0   200 meters

* under construction

Airlines   Terminals (cont.)

Airlines	JFK	LA GUARDIA	NEWARK
Olympic ☎ 800/223–1226	4E		
Pakistan ☎ 212/370–9158	4W		
Pan Am ☎ 800/359–7262	4E		
Philippine Airlines ☎ 800/435–9725			B
Qantas ☎ 800/227–4500	4		
Royal Air Maroc ☎ 212/750–5115	4E		
SAS ☎ 800/221–2350	7		C
Sabena ☎ 800/955–2000	3		
Singapore Airlines ☎ 800/742–3333	3		
South African Airways ☎ 800/722–9675	8		
Sun Country ☎ 800/359–5786	6		
Sun Jet ☎ 800/359–5786			A
Swissair ☎ 800/221–4750	3		B
Tarom-Romanian ☎ 212/560–0840	3		
TACA International ☎ 800/535–8780	2		
TAP Air Portugal ☎ 800/221–7370	3		B
Tower Air ☎ 718/553-8500	Tower		
TransBrasil ☎ 800/872–3153	4W		
Turkish Airlines ☎ 212/339–9650			B
TW Express ☎ 800/221–2000	5		A
TWA ☎ 800/221–2000	5, 6	CTB-B	A
United ☎ 800/241–6522	7	CTB-C	A
United Express ☎ 800/241–6522	7	CTB-C	A
US Airways ☎ 800/428–4322	7	US Airways	A
US Airways Express ☎ 800/428–4322	7	US Airways	A
US Airways Shuttle ☎ 800/428–4322		US Airways Shuttle	
Uzbekistan Airways ☎ 212/489–3954	4W		
Varig ☎ 516/612–0200	2		
VASP ☎ 718/955–0540	4W		
Virgin Atlantic ☎ 800/862–8621	2		B

La Guardia Airport

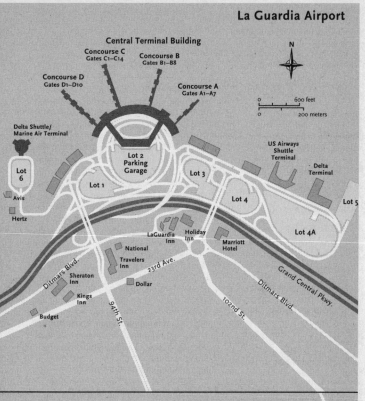

Central Terminal Building

Concourse C
Gates C1–C14

Concourse B
Gates B1–B8

Concourse D
Gates D1–D10

Concourse A
Gates A1–A7

N

0 ___ 600 feet
0 ___ 200 meters

Delta Shuttle/
Marine Air Terminal

US Airways
Shuttle
Terminal

Lot 2
Parking
Garage

Delta
Terminal

Lot 6

Lot 1

Lot 3

Lot 4

Lot 5

Avis

Hertz

Lot 4A

LaGuardia
Inn

Holiday
Inn

Marriott
Hotel

National
Travelers
Inn

Ditmars Blvd.

23rd Ave.

Sheraton
Inn

Dollar

Grand Central Pkwy.

Kings
Inn

Ditmars Blvd.

94th St.

102nd St.

Budget

Newark International Airport

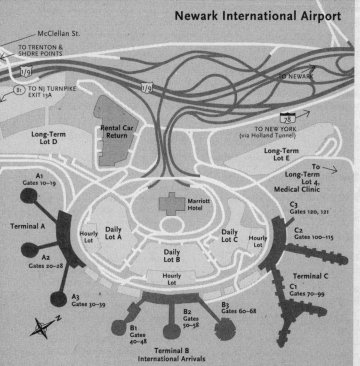

McClellan St.

TO TRENTON &
SHORE POINTS

1/9

TO NEWARK

81 TO NJ TURNPIKE
EXIT 13A

1/9

78

TO NEW YORK
(via Holland Tunnel)

Long-Term
Lot D

Rental Car
Return

Long-Term
Lot E

To
Long-Term
Lot 4,
Medical Clinic

A1
Gates 10–19

Marriott
Hotel

C3
Gates 120, 121

Terminal A

Hourly
Lot

Daily
Lot A

Daily
Lot C

Hourly
Lot

C2
Gates 100–115

A2
Gates 20–28

Daily
Lot B

Terminal C

Hourly
Lot

C1
Gates 70–99

A3
Gates 30–39

B3
Gates 60–68

N

B2
Gates
50–58

B1
Gates
40–48

Terminal B
International Arrivals

British Airways (800/247–9297).

British West Indian Airlines (800/538–2942).

China Airlines (800/227–5118).

Continental Airlines (800/525–0280; 800/231–0856 international flights).

Czech Airlines (212/765–6022).

Delta Airlines (800/221–1212; 800/241–4141 international flights).

Egyptair (212/315–0900).

El Al Israel Airlines (800/223–6700).

Finnair (800/950–5000).

Iberia Airlines (800/772–4642).

IcelandAir (800/223–5500).

Japan Airlines (800/525–3663).

JetBlue Airways (800/538–2583).

KLM/Northwest Airlines (800/225–2525 or 800/374–7747).

Lufthansa Airlines (800/645–3880).

Mexicana Airlines (800/531–7921).

Midway Airlines (800/446–4392).

Northwest/KLM Airlines (800/225–2525 or 800/447–4747).

Pan American World Airways (800/359–7262).

Qantas Airlines (800/227–4500).

Royal Air Maroc (212/750–5115 or 800/344–6726).

Sabena Belgian World Airlines (800/955–2000).

Scandinavian Airlines (800/221–2350).

Singapore Airlines (800/742–3333).

South African Airways (800/722–9675).

Swissair (800/221–4750).

TAP Air Portugal (800/221–7370).

Tower Air (800/34–TOWER [800/348–6937]).

Trans World Airlines (TWA) (800/221–2000).

United Airlines (800/241–6522).

USAir (800/428–4322).

Varig Brazilian Airlines (800/468–2744).

Virgin Atlantic (800/862–8621).

AIRPORTS

After the terrorist attacks of September 11, 2001, security has been dramatically increased in all of the area's airports. Specifically, all passengers are being asked by the airlines to arrive three hours before an international flight, and two hours before a domestic flight. Be sure to bring a government issued photo identification, such as a passport or driver's license. Furthermore, there are tight restrictions on what will be allowed in a customer's carry-on luggage; that means no potential weapons of any kind, including pocket knives, nail clippers, scissors, and razors.

John F. Kennedy (JFK) International Airport Driving directions, ground transportation information, airport conditions, parking information; staffed 7 AM–11 PM, plus 24-hour automated service (Howard Beach, Queens, 718/244–4444, www.kennedyairport.com).

La Guardia Airport (LGA) Driving directions, transportation information, airport conditions, baggage storage, foreign currency exchange information (Jackson Heights, Queens, 718/533–3400, www.laguardiaairport.com).

Newark International Airport (EWR) Driving directions and transportation information (Newark, NJ, 973/961–6000 or 888/EWR–INFO [888/397–4636], www.newarkairport.com).

getting there by public transportation

For general information on transportation to New York's three major airports—JFK, La Guardia, and Newark—call the Port Authority of New York and New Jersey weekdays 8–6 (800/247–7433, www.panynj.gov).

BY SUBWAY & BUS

The subway is the most economical way to reach the airports, but it can be slow given the length of the journey. That said, during rush hour the subway can beat cabs and car services by passing traffic altogether.

To reach JFK, take the Far Rockaway–bound A train (not the Lefferts Blvd.

train) to the Howard Beach–JFK Airport station, then board the free, 24-hour airport shuttle bus (every 10 minutes 5 AM–midnight, every 30 minutes other times).

To return from JFK, reverse the above directions or take the Q3 bus from JFK's Main Terminal to the 179th Street subway station in Queens, where you can pick up the F or R train to Manhattan and Brooklyn. Buses run every 15 minutes until midnight, then every 30 minutes until 1:30 AM.

To reach La Guardia from Manhattan or Brooklyn, take the E, F, G, R, or 7 train to the 74th Street/Roosevelt Avenue (or 82nd Street/Roosevelt Avenue) subway station in Jackson Heights, Queens, then the Triboro Coach Lines Q33 bus to La Guardia's Main Terminal. The bus shuttles between Roosevelt Avenue and the airport every 12 minutes during the day and evening, every 40 minutes after midnight. Alternatively, the Triboro Coach Q47 bus leaves La Guardia's Marine Terminal every 20 minutes between 5:20 AM and 12:45 AM for the Roosevelt Avenue station.

AIRPORT SHUTTLE
Gray Line Air Shuttle Operates door-to-door minibuses to all three airports from Manhattan hotels between 23rd and 63rd streets and Port Authority, 7 AM–11:30 PM. Fare to JFK or Newark is $19 to the airport, $14 from the airport, or $28 round-trip; to La Guardia $16, from La Guardia $13, or $26 round-trip (212/757-6840; www.graylinenewyork.com).

New York Airport Service Serves JFK ($13) and La Guardia ($10) from Grand Central, Port Authority, and Penn Station, every 30 minutes from 7 AM–10 PM and has transfers between the airports ($11)—call or visit the Web site for schedule information (718/875-8200, www.nyairportservice.com).

Olympia Trails Airport Express Serves Newark Airport from Penn Station, Port Authority Bus Terminal, Midtown hotels, and Grand Central Terminal. Buses depart every 15–30 minutes in both directions. Fare is $11 one way. Call for schedule (212/964-6233, www.olympiabus.com).

New Jersey Transit Airlink Leaves every 20 minutes from 6:15 AM to 2 AM for Penn Station in Newark, where you can catch the PATH Trains (800/234-7284).

Airlink bus fare is $4 and exact change is required (973/762-5100, www.njtransit.com).

CAR RENTAL

If possible, it is usually better to rent in Brooklyn, Queens, or New Jersey than in Manhattan: rates are often much more reasonable, and cars more available.

major agencies
Alamo (Reservations: 800/327-9633; 973/733-2723 Newark Airport, www.alamo.com).

Avis (Reservations: 800/831-2847 or 800/331-1212; 718/244-5400 JFK; 718/507-3600 La Guardia; 973/961-4300 Newark Airport, www.avis.com).

Budget (Reservations: 800/527-0700 or 212/807-8700; 718/565-6010 JFK; 718/639-6400 La Guardia, www.budget.com).

Enterprise (Reservations: 800/736-8222; 718/659-1200 JFK; 718/457-2900 La Guardia, www.avis.com).

Hertz (Reservations: 800/654-3131; 718/656-7600 JFK; 718/478-5300 La Guardia; 973/621-2000 Newark, www.hertz.com).

National (800/227-7368, www.nationalcar.com).

local agencies
AAMCAR (Manhattan and Bronx locations, 212/222-8500).

New York Rent-A-Car (Manhattan and Queens locations, 212/799-1100).

Speedy Rent-A-Car (Brooklyn, Queens, and Jersey City locations, 718/783-0800).

CAR & LIMOUSINE SERVICES

Car services and limousines are not allowed to pick up passengers who hail them, although they sometimes will. To be on the safe side, stick with yellow cabs or call a car or limousine service ahead of time. In the outer boroughs, check your neighborhood's yellow pages for local companies.

Carey Lincolns, Cadillacs, stretch limos, and chauffeurs available 24 hours. Hourly rates (212/599–1122; 800/336–0646 worldwide, www.careyint.com).

Carmel Car and Limousine Service Point-to-point service and hourly arrangements (212/666–6666, www.carmelcarservice.com).

Eastern Car Service Point-to-point service in the five boroughs and Long Island (718/499–6227).

Fugazy Limousine Ltd. Limousines and sedans with courteous, uniformed chauffeurs serving all five boroughs, Westchester, and parts of Pennsylvania 24 hours daily (212/661–0100).

Legends Car and Limousine Service For service to, from, and around Brooklyn. 24 hours daily (718/788–1234 or 718/788–2346).

Smith Limousine Located in Manhattan, Smith has Cadillacs and Lincoln limos, stretches, and sedans, plus vintage cars for special occasions. Big date? Ask for the 1948 Cadillac limousine in dark blue. Cars available 24 hours daily (212/247–0711).

Tel-Aviv Car and Limousine Service Point-to-point service in the five boroughs (212/777–7777).

CURRENCY EXCHANGE

If you're going abroad, you may want to buy some foreign currency here before you leave. You can buy and sell currency at the Manhattan branches of several national banks, or at the old standby Thomas Cook. **Chase** (800/287–4054) sells foreign currency at most of its Manhattan branches, and buys currency at all branches if the buyer has two forms of I.D. You can pay for foreign currency in cash, debit your Chase account, or use a Visa or MasterCard; if you charge it, the amount will be treated as a cash advance. Most exchanges are handled on the spot, but you may have to come back the next day for exotic currencies or very large amounts.

Most banks sell traveler's checks, which you can buy in U.S. dollars or in any of several foreign currencies. Traveler's checks are issued by American Express, MasterCard, or Visa and are accepted worldwide. Banks and nearly all stores in New York accept traveler's checks, though they may want to see a photo I.D. first.

american express travel services

American Express Travel Service Offices buy and sell foreign currency, buy and sell American Express traveler's checks (and buy other brands for a higher fee), issue refunds for lost checks, and provide all standard cardmember services. You can buy foreign currency with cash or, if you're a cardmember, with a personal check—just bring your AmEx card. If you lose your AmEx traveler's checks, there's someone to assist you 24 hours a day (800/221–7282, www.travel.americanexpress.com).

thomas cook currency services

Busy with other preparations? **Thomas Cook** can FedEx your foreign currency, traveler's checks, or foreign drafts right to your home. The JFK office is open daily. Call for general information and hours for all area branches (800/287–7362; 800/223–7373 for lost traveler's checks, www.us.thomascook.com).

EMBASSIES & CONSULATES

British Consulate General (845 3rd Ave., Midtown East, 212/745–0200).

Chinese Consulate of the People's Republic of China (520 12th Ave., Midtown West, 212/736–9301).

Dominican Republic's Consulate General (1 Times Sq. Plaza, Midtown West, 212/768–2480).

French Embassy (972 5th Ave., Upper East Side, 212/439–1400).

German Consulate General (460 Park Ave., Midtown East, 212/610–9700).

Irish Consulate General (345 Park Ave., 17th floor, Midtown East, 212/319–2555).

Italian Consulate General (54 E. 69th St., Upper East Side, 212/737–9100).

Japanese Consulate General (299 Park Ave., Midtown East, 212/371–8222).

Portuguese Consulate General (630 5th Ave., Midtown East, 212/765–2980).

Spanish Consulate General (150 E. 58th St., Midtown East, 212/355–4090).

INOCULATIONS, VACCINATIONS & TRAVEL HEALTH

Center for Disease Control's International Travel Line Knows which countries require which vaccines (877/FYI–TRIP [394–8747], www.cdc.gov).

International Health Care Service Staffed by specialists in infectious disease, the IHCS is devoted exclusively to the medical needs of international travelers, providing worldwide health information, immunizations, and post-travel tests and treatment. The fee varies, but it's always a worthwhile investment if you're traveling to a developing nation. Make an appointment four to five weeks before departure (New York Hospital–Cornell Medical Center, 440 E. 69th St., Upper East Side, 212/746–1601. Mon.–Thurs. 4–8 PM by appointment).

Kennedy International Medical Office Building Vaccinations and inoculations for a fee (198 S. Cargo Rd., Howard Beach, Queens, 718/656–5344. Daily 9 AM–9 PM; 24 hrs for emergencies. No personal checks).

U.S. Department of State Overseas Citizen Services Automated travel-warning and emergency information by country (202/647–5225, www.travel.state.gov).

PASSPORTS

You can apply for a passport at any of New York's Passport Acceptance Agencies: designated post offices, county clerks' offices, and, in a pinch, the New York Passport Agency. Call for the passport-accepting post office nearest you and for specific hours (800/225–8777, www.usps.gov).

During peak travel periods—spring and summer—apply for a first-time passport three months before your trip. All passport information, including printable applications and a locator of the passport agency nearest you, is handily available on the U.S. Postal Service Web site.

Passport *renewal* is handled most easily through the mail. Renewal forms are available at many post offices (or on the postal service Web site) and can be sub-mitted by mail or at any passport acceptance agency.

In a grave emergency after hours (such as the death of a relative abroad), call the passport duty officer at the U.S. State Department in Washington (202/647–4000).

A new U.S. passport costs $60 ($40 for those under 16); a renewal costs $40. If you need an emergency passport for travel within 10 days, you'll pay an additional $35 fee for "expedited processing"; bring your plane ticket with you to the office.

County Clerk's Office The secret is out: there are no lines here. Come on down, for passports at least three weeks before departure (New York County Courthouse, 60 Centre St., lower level, Lower Manhattan, weekdays 9–2 except holidays; 212/374–8361).

New York Passport Agency This office issues emergency passports for travel within two weeks. You must have an appointment, but you're still bound to spend most of the day waiting. First-timers must bring proof of U.S. citizenship, photo I.D. (or I.D. with description), and passport photos (376 Hudson St., West Village, 212/206–3500. Weekdays 7:30–3 except holidays).

Passport Plus This private document service is for travelers with more money than time. It can get you a passport in as little as one day and arrange visas to all countries, as well as snap your pictures on-site (20 E. 49th St., Midtown East, 212/759–5540).

TOURIST INFORMATION

nyc & company

The helpful, multilingual staff answers questions and provides printed guides and maps in six languages; tickets to TV shows; discount coupons for theater tickets; and a list of the city's current hotel rates, weekend packages, major attractions, and seasonal events (810 7th Ave., Midtown West, 212/484–1222 for general inquiries, 800/692–8474 for brochures, www.nycvisit.com).

new york state department of economic development/ division of tourism

There is no office in New York City, but the state office has information on city tour packages and on vacations and recreation statewide. This is the group behind the "I Love New York" campaign (800/225–5697, www.iloveny.state.ny.us).

tourist information carts & kiosks

The Grand Central Partnership (a sort of civic Good Samaritans' group) has installed a number unstaffed information kiosks near Grand Central Terminal, loaded with maps and helpful brochures on attractions throughout the city. There are also seasonal outdoor carts sprinkled throughout the area (there is one near Vanderbilt Ave. and 42nd St.), staffed by friendly, knowledgeable, multilingual New Yorkers. There's a kiosk in Grand Central Terminal's Main Concourse, and the 34th Street Partnership runs a kiosk on the concourse level at Penn Station (33rd St. and 7th Ave.); there's even a cart at the Empire State Building (5th Ave. at 34th St.).

TRAVELER'S AID

Crime Victims Hot Line 24-hour bilingual counseling and referral (212/577–7777).

Traveler's Aid Service Nationwide service helps crime victims, stranded travelers, and wayward children, and works closely with the police; staffed daily 9 AM to 8 PM (718/656–4870 International Arrivals Bldg., JFK Airport).

VISA INFORMATION & TRAVEL ADVISORIES

Call the embassy or consulate of the country you plan to visit for up-to-date information on visa requirements, travel advisories, and service strikes. For travel advisories on specific countries, call the **U.S. State Department** (202/647–5225).

Ask Immigration Answers questions on immigration—citizenship, visas, relatives abroad, and more (800/375–5283).

U.S. Customs Service Refers you to the appropriate authority on importation of goods (800/697–3662).

DIRECTORIES

restaurants by neighborhood

CITY NOTES

CITY NOTES

CITY NOTES

CITY NOTES